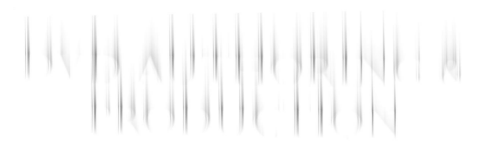

by Ralph LaBarge

CMP Books
Lawrence, Kansas 66046

CMP Books
CMP Media LCC
1601 W. 23rd Street, Suite 200
Lawrence, KS 66046
USA

Technical Editor: Kim Reed
Copyeditor: Liza Niav
Managing Editor: Michelle O'Neal
Cover design and art: Damien Casteneda and Audrey Welch

Distributed in the U.S. and Canada by:
Publishers Group West
1700 Fourth Street
Berkeley, CA 94710
1-800-788-3123

ISBN 1-57820-082-2

for others are the keys to success.

Acknowledgments

A book of this size and complexity can't be written in a vacuum. Dorothy Cox, Paul Temme, and David Tractenberg of CMP Media convinced me to write this book. Jerry McFaul, Dana Parker, and Jim Taylor volunteered their time to review drafts, and each contributed tremendously to the final version. During the editing process I worked closely with Kimberly Reed of *DV Magazine*, and her comments and suggestions were always invaluable. Michelle O'Neal of CMP Media and Liza Niav worked diligently to turn my scribbling into a finished book, ready for the printers. Jon Wenger of Zomax worked with me to replicate the *StarGaze* DVD in the back of the book. Hundreds of others who work in the DVD business also contributed to this book, either directly by providing me with information on their companies' products or services, or indirectly by talking with me about DVD over the past six years. I can't possibly mention them all, but this book could not have been written without their help. David Goodman of DVD International has taught me a lot about the business side of DVD, and was understanding when a few projects were delayed due to the amount of time I spent writing the book (and not working on his titles). Last, but not least, I would like to thank my wife Jan and our three daughters Kim, Jenny, and Cindy who put up with me working a bunch of extra hours in order to get this book, and all my other DVD projects, done.

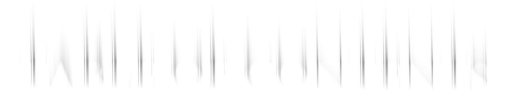

INTRODUCTION

DVD Authoring & Production is the result of more than six years of practical experience authoring and producing DVD-Video, DVD-ROM, and WebDVD titles. When I started developing DVD titles in early 1996 there was almost no documentation or literature available that described the process of producing a DVD title. In 1997 Jim Taylor's *DVD Demystified* was published and has since become the bible for everyone in the DVD business. *DVD Demystified* is a great book, and I strongly encourage anyone getting into DVD to buy a copy, but it is primarily a technical book. While both books cover some of the same material, *DVD Authoring & Production* provides an in-depth look at the process of authoring and producing DVD titles. Conversely, *DVD Demystified* provides an in-depth look at the technical details of the DVD specifications, the history of DVD and it's predecessors, as well as the future of the format. To sum it all up, *DVD Demystified* answers the question "Why DVD?", while *DVD Authoring & Production* answers the question "How do I make a DVD?". Although I am somewhat biased, I truly believe having both *DVD Demystified* and *DVD Production & Authoring* is worthwhile, particularly if you are directly involved with the authoring or production of DVD-Video, DVD-ROM, or WebDVD titles.

In writing *DVD Authoring & Production* I have drawn on my knowledge and experience gained in designing, authoring, and producing over 200 DVD titles. Developing a DVD title is still a fairly complicated process. A large number of issues can delay the completion of the project and result in a final product that does not meet all of your requirements. As you read *DVD Production & Authoring* you will see that there is more to producing a successful DVD title than just using a DVD authoring program to create a valid DVD disc image. In fact, the actual authoring of a DVD disc is just one of a dozen steps in the process, and is often the easiest part of the project.

During the year 2000, I completed over 25 new DVD-Video, DVD-ROM, and WebDVD titles. I am planning on releasing another 25 or so during 2001. Every time I complete a project, I feel that I have learned something new about the process of producing and authoring DVD titles. When I start a new project, I try to use a DVD feature in a new or different way, or some new combination of features that I have never used before. The DVD-Video format is an extremely rich multimedia-publishing medium. I am convinced that just about anything is possible in DVD as long as you have the desire, and patience, to make it happen.

As with skinning cats, there is more than one way to author and produce a DVD title. I will outline a process that has worked well for me over the past five years, and one that I believe will also work for you. However, as you become more proficient at developing DVD titles you'll find you need to use your own experience and knowledge to amend or modify the process I discuss in this book to suit your own specific business needs.

Who Should Read this Book?

Anyone who is involved in the production or authoring of DVD-Video, DVD-ROM, and WebDVD titles should read this book. The book covers every aspect of the DVD production and authoring process, so it may not be necessary for everyone to read every section of the book. For example, if you are only involved in the process of authoring DVD-Video titles, then you should definitely read Chapters 1–6, which discuss the process of producing DVD titles as well as the details of DVD authoring, and refer to Chapters 10 and 11, but you probably won't need to read Chapters 7–9, which cover Enhanced DVD, DVD-ROM, and the business aspects of producing DVD titles. Similarly, if your primary interest is in the production or sales of DVD titles, then you should read Chapters 1–3, covering the process of producing DVD titles, as well as Chapter 9, which covers the business of producing DVD titles.

Naturally, I would like everyone to read every chapter. Realistically, this is simply not practical in the fast-paced world of DVD title production. I have organized the book so that you can either read it from start to finish to fully understand the DVD production process, or read a chapter at a time to bone up on one specific DVD production issue. Finally, it is my hope that this book will become a useful tool for DVD producers and developers to improve their projects as they learn more about the process of developing DVD titles and bringing them to the market.

How Is this Book Organized?

DVD Authoring & Production includes eleven chapters and an index. Chapter 2 provides details on each of the DVD formats (DVD-ROM, DVD-Video, DVD-Audio, DVD-R, DVD-RAM, and DVD-RW). Chapter 2 also discusses the "unofficial" DVD formats (DVD+RW and SACD). Chapter 3 presents a step-by-step process for authoring and producing DVD titles. Chapter 4 covers entry level DVD authoring, concentrating on the use of low-end or consumer authoring tools. Chapter 5 covers mid-range DVD authoring, while Chapter 6 covers advanced DVD authoring. Chapter 7 covers enhanced DVD authoring, and Chapter 8 covers DVD-ROM authoring. Chapter 9 provides an in-depth look at the business aspects of DVD production and authoring. Chapter 10 reviews most of the major software and hardware tools required to develop DVD titles, as well as major DVD authoring service providers. Finally, Chapter 11 provides a detailed glossary of DVD terms and acronyms with definitions.

If you turn to the back of *DVD Production & Authoring* you will see that we have included a copy of *StarGaze*, one of my recent consumer DVD releases. I am a firm believer that a picture is worth a thousand words, so I wanted to include supplemental content to illustrate the DVD authoring and production processes discussed in the book. Rather than include a custom disc, which demonstrates specific features of the DVD specifications, I thought it would be better to include an example of a real world DVD title.

corporate, or educational market places. I think you will understand this process better with a thorough evaluation of a real world DVD project, such as *StarGaze*. If you would like to see a DVD title that demonstrates as many DVD-Video features as possible, I suggest you buy the second edition of *DVD Demystified*, which includes just such a demonstration and test disc.

Tips, Tricks & Techniques

Throughout *DVD Production & Authoring* you will also find *Tips, Tricks & Techniques* boxes, which offer some common sense advice on how to author and produce DVD titles.

A Brief History of DVD

DVD, also known as Digital Versatile Disc, was born in 1996 from a marriage of two competing optical disc technologies. DVD was developed by a group of ten consumer electronics companies, called the DVD Forum, who agreed on a set of technical specifications for each DVD format. Initially five specifications were published, including DVD-ROM, DVD-Video, DVD-Audio, DVD-R, and DVD-RAM. Recently a specification for DVD-RW has also been added to the list of "official" DVD formats. The DVD Forum has published "official" DVD formats, while "unofficial" DVD formats are those that are compatible with at least one official DVD format, but provide other features as well. DVD+RW is an example of an unofficial DVD format as it can read DVD-ROM discs, but can also read and write DVD+RW discs, which are not documented in any DVD Forum publications. The original members of the DVD Forum included Hitachi, Matsushita Electric Industrial Co. LTD (also known as Panasonic), Mitsubishi Electric Corporation, Philips Electronics, Pioneer Electronics, Sony Corporation, Thomson Multimedia, Time Warner, Toshiba Corporation, and Victor Company of Japan.

Prior to 1996 there were two competing groups of companies, one led by Sony, and the other by Toshiba. Each group was trying to develop proprietary high-density optical-disc formats to be used in the next generation of consumer electronics and personal computer products. Fortunately these two groups joined forces and agreed to form the DVD Forum. The DVD Forum actively encouraged participation from members of the entertainment and computer industries so that the DVD format had a broad base of support in both the consumer and computer electronics areas. The DVD Forum now has over 200 members representing a broad spectrum of companies offering a wide variety of DVD related products and services.

The early years of DVD were difficult and in many cases frustrating. DVD was viewed with some interest by many Hollywood studios looking to publish their content on a high quality medium, but they were concerned over copyright protection and conditional access issues. Several major motion picture studios such as Time Warner and Universal Pictures were committed to releasing their movies on DVD, while the rest of the studios remained uncommitted pending resolution of these copyright issues. The issue of how to protect content once it was distributed on a DVD-Video disc was the topic of a number of discussions between members of the DVD Forum and representatives from the motion picture and software industries. In late June of 1996 representatives from the computer, consumer-electronics and movie industries signed off on a technical working group recommendation for encrypting all data stored on DVD-Video discs and including decryption hardware in DVD Video players. During September and October of 1996 proposals from the computer industry recommending an alternative method of encrypting just the video content were considered and accepted by the Copyright Protection Technical Working Group. Finally in November 1996 all parties agreed to a specific set of analog and digital copy protection methods.

The first DVD-Video players were sold in Japan starting in November of 1996. The U.S. market for DVD-Video players and DVD-ROM drives was launched during early 1997. Initial projections for sales of DVD-Video players were quite optimistic, with many estimates as high as 2 million units or more sold during the first year. Actual sales fell far short of these initial projections due primarily to the high cost of consumer DVD-Video players as well as the limited number of DVD titles released by the major motion picture studios. When the DVD-Video format was officially launched in the U.S. on March 17, 1997 there were less than 200 titles available in only seven regional test markets. DVD went nationwide in the U.S. on August 22, 1997, although there were still several major motion picture studios not supporting the format, including Disney, Fox, and Paramount.

During 1997 a number of respected industry analysts expressed concerns over the viability of the DVD format. Some experts predicted that the DVD format would fail in its effort to become a viable home entertainment format, becoming a niche product only for high-end audio and videophiles. These predictions seemed justified by the failure of the Laser Disc format to break into the mainstream consumer market.

In September 1997 things started to look up for DVD as Disney announced that they would be releasing their non-animated movies on DVD, leaving only Fox and Paramount as major studios who were still not supporting DVD. Actual sales of DVD-Video players in the U.S. market during 1997 were only about 315,000 units, well below the industry predictions. While the future of DVD was looking brighter, total sales of DVD players and titles were below expectations, and it was not clear that DVD would become a success.

In April 1998 Paramount decided to release DVD versions of their movies, and Fox followed suit in August 1998. With all of the major motion picture studios now on board the future looked much brighter for DVD. Over 1,000,000 DVD-Video players were sold in the U.S. market during 1998, while at the same time the European DVD market was launched. Initial sales in Europe were slow due to a lack of Region 2 titles, as well as resistance by many consumers who did not want to purchase DVD players that due to region coding prevented them from watching movies released in the US. To this day most Europeans despise the use of Region Coding by the studios, while most American consumers don't even know that their players can only play Region 1 titles. By the end of 1998 with a worldwide installed base of over 2,000,000 players and more than 1,000 titles available, most of the critics of DVD had been silenced. All of the major motion picture studios had commitments to release their entire catalogs on DVD, as well as many independent distributors and smaller studios.

players registered to a specific household.

DVD solidified its claim to the most successful new consumer electronics format during 2000. In the U.S. market over 8,000,000 new DVD-Video players were sold and over 8,000 titles were available in the DVD format by the end of the year. The European market also grew significantly during 2000 with most major motion picture studios releasing specific versions of their movies for Europe, rather than simply repackaging the US versions of each release. The year 2000 was also a watershed year for DVD in several other areas. DVD branched out from the movie business to become a mainstream technology for corporate, educational, and government applications. DVD-ROM drives became common options for new consumer and corporate personal computers, and a large number of products and services were announced to help corporate, educational, and government clients move into the world of DVD. DVD-Video players were available in the U.S. for less than $100, and DVD-ROM drives became a no-cost option on many higher-end personal computers. The year 2000 ended in a bang for DVD with several recordable DVD products released worldwide, addressing the only major drawback to widespread adoption of the DVD format — the inability for the consumer to record their own content onto DVD discs.

While it is always difficult to predict how consumers will react to new technologies, it is clear that DVD will be successful for many years to come. DVD-Video is firmly entrenched as a mainstream high quality, low cost home entertainment format. Over the next few years DVD-ROM will replace CD-ROM as the standard optical disc format in all consumer and corporate personal computers. DVD-Audio products will come on the market during 2001, and it will compete directly with the new Super Audio CD format. It is too early to tell if DVD-Audio or Super Audio CD will be accepted as a mainstream replacement for CD-Audio technology, which is firmly entrenched worldwide. Finally the DVD-R, DVD-RAM, and DVD-RW formats will start to offer consumers the ability to create and record their own high quality content on recordable DVD discs. The future of DVD looks very bright; in fact, DVD is likely to be a dominant technology over the next decade.

Figure 1.1 shows the projected growth of DVD over the next ten years. (Source: DVD Intelligence, and independent market surveys.) It is easy to see from this graph that DVD has just begun its dominance as a critical component in consumer home entertainment products.

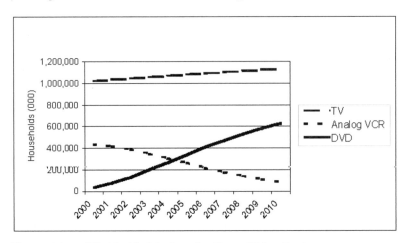

Figure 1.1   Worldwide Markets for Home Video Equipment

DVD FORMAT SPECIFICATIONS

The DVD Forum has released separate books to document each of the following DVD specifications (listed with the current version at the time of this writing).

- DVD-Video v1.11

- DVD-ROM v1.02

- DVD-Audio v1.2

- DVD-R v2.0

- DVD-RAM v2.1

- DVD-RW v1.1

- DVD-Video Recording v1.1

- DVD Stream Recording v1.0

Each of the listed formats are "official" DVD formats, which means they have gone through a formal submission and review procedure and they have been approved by a vote of DVD Forum member companies. The submission, review, and approval process can take up to two years for a new DVD format. The DVD Forum is currently developing specification for advanced interactive content, also know as WebDVD, which defines an optional mechanism to include links between content stored on DVD-Video titles and content available on the Web. The decision to develop a WebDVD specification was made in May 2001, so we may not see a formal specification approved by the DVD Forum until the end of 2002, if ever.

Sony and Philips have proposed an alternative to the recordable DVD specification called DVD+RW, which was published in 1999 and revised in 2000. Sony and Philips has also proposed an alternative to the DVD-Audio specification that is called Super Audio CD (SACD), which was published in 1999. As shown in Figure 2.1, all of the DVD format books include a physical layer section, which defines the physical properties of the

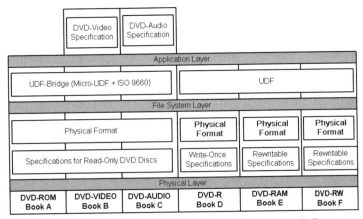

Figure 2.1   DVD Format Books Published by the DVD Forum

disc, and a file system layer section, which defines how data will be stored on the disc. The DVD-Video and DVD-Audio format books also include an application layer section, which defines how multimedia data will be formatted and stored on the disc and read back by DVD-Video and DVD-Audio players to create high quality home entertainment devices.

The physical layer section for the DVD-ROM, DVD-Video, and DVD-Audio formats are the same, and define the physical properties of a read-only DVD optical-disc. The physical layer section of the DVD-R write-once format and the DVD-RAM and DVD-RW read-write formats are different since these media types are physically different from the mass-produced DVD-ROM, DVD-Video, and DVD-Audio discs.

Each of the format books allows a micro-UDF file system to be used. Micro-UDF is a new optical disc file format specification developed by the Optical Disc Storage Association (OSTA) and is designed to allow optical discs to be compatible with all major operating system software (Windows, Mac OS, Unix, Linux, etc.). The DVD-ROM, DVD-Video, and DVD-Audio format books also allow for a standard ISO 9660 file system to be used in addition to UDF. The DVD-Video and DVD-Audio format books include an application layer section that defines how video, audio, graphic, and textual information will be digitized, compressed, and stored onto the DVD disc, and how the various interactive features of the DVD-Video and DVD-Audio formats will be implemented and used.

A copy of the DVD format books can be purchased for $5,000 from:

DVD Format/Logo Licensing Corporation
Shiba Shimizu Bldg. 5F
2-3-11 Shibadaimon, Minato-ku,
Tokyo, JAPAN, 105-0012
+81-3-5777-2883 (Voice)
+81-3-5777-2884 (Fax)
http://www.dvdfllc.co.jp (Web)

A signed confidentiality agreement and full payment must be received prior to shipment of the DVD format books. It is generally not necessary for DVD authoring or production companies to purchase a copy of the DVD format books. While the format books provide all of the low level details required to completely understand and implement the DVD-Video specification, they are typically only required for companies that are developing DVD-Video players, DVD-Video decoders, or DVD-Video authoring tools. Some advanced DVD-Video title developers may find access to these format books can be beneficial in understanding nuances of the DVD-Video format, but in general this is not required.

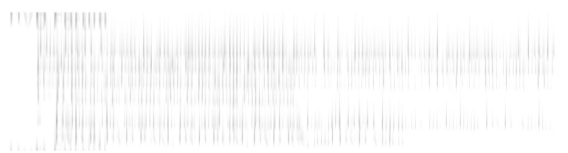

- Publishes the various DVD format books

- Licenses the DVD Format and DVD Logo, through the DVD FLLC organization

- Administers the DVD Verification Labs throughout the world

- Holds worldwide DVD conferences, promotes DVD through public relations activities, and maintains the DVD Forum web site (http://www.dvdforum.org)

The DVD Forum currently has 64 Principal Members and 235 Associate Members. Principal Members are allowed to participate in defining the DVD formats, and can vote at the DVD Forum general meetings. The annual fee to become a Principal Member of the DVD Forum is approximately $8,000 (1,000,000 Yen). Associate Members are provided access to the DVD Forum Technical Working Group reports. The annual fee to become an Associate Member of the DVD Forum is approximately $2,500 (300,000 Yen). Current members of the DVD Forum Steering Committee include Hitachi, IBM, Intel, ITRI, JVC, LG, Matsushita, Mitsubishi, NEC, Philips, Pioneer, Samsung, Sharp, Sony, Thomson, Time Warner, and Toshiba.

The DVD Forum currently has eight Technical Working Groups.

1. DVD-Video and Video Recording
2. DVD-ROM
3. File Format
4. DVD-Audio
5. Rewriteable (DVD-RAM)
6. Write-Once (DVD-R) and Re-Recordable (DVD-RW)
7. Copy Protection
8. Pro-Use Applications

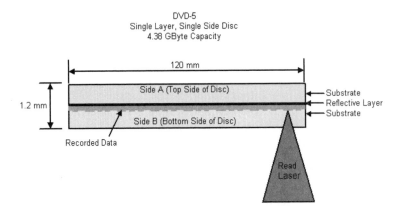

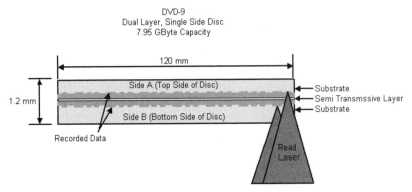

Figure 2.2   DVD Single Layer and Dual Layer Disc Construction Diagram

DVD Physical Specifications

Two of the primary technical goals of DVD are to provide both higher capacity and higher throughput than CD-ROM technology offers. All DVD formats and playback devices support a minimum throughput rate that is at least nine times faster than a conventional CD-ROM, and many DVD playback devices support even higher transfer rates. The DVD-ROM, DVD-Video, and DVD-Audio formats have storage capacities between 4.7 and 17.0 billion bytes. The variation in total storage capacity depends on the use of up to two data storage layers on each side of a DVD disc.

The DVD physical specification provides for up to four different data recording layers and two different sizes (12cm and 8cm in diameter). A single-layer, single-sided disc is referred to as a DVD-5; a dual-layer, single-sided disc is a DVD-9; a single-layer, dual-sided disc is a DVD-10; and a dual-layer, dual-sided disc is a DVD-18. It is technically possible to have a DVD disc that uses three recording layers, two on one side and one on the other. This is called a DVD-14, but is not very common.

Figure 2.2 shows how a single-layer and dual-layer DVD disc are constructed. Both single-layer and dual-layer discs are made from two distinct pieces of molded plastic that are bonded, or glued, together. For a DVD-5 disc only one recording layer is used so a reflective material is added to the middle of the disc. Then the laser can read the data stored just before the reflective material. For a dual-layer disc two data layers are recorded and separated by a semitransmissive layer. If the laser is focused on the data recorded on Layer 0, which is on the bottom of the disc, then it is reflected to the optical sensor. If the laser is focused in the data recorded on Layer 1, which in on the top part of the disc, then the semitransmissive material allows the laser to pass through and read the data on the top layer. The semitransmissive material used on most dual layer DVD discs is gold.

total storage capacity by over 700 percent compared to a traditional CD-ROM. Figure 2.3 shows the difference between the pits and track spacing on a CD-ROM and DVD-ROM, DVD-Video, DVD-Audio, DVD-R, and DVD-RW discs.

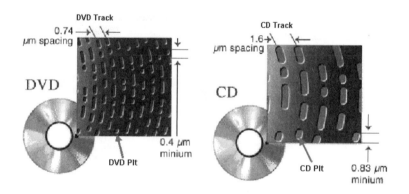

Figure 2.3   Comparison of DVD-ROM Vs CD-ROM Pit and Track Sizes

Using multiple layers and multiple sides for data storage has increased total capacity to a maximum of 15.9 Gb on a DVD optical disc compared to just 650 Mb on a standard CD-ROM — an increase of more than 25 times the capacity.

Table 2.1 provides the relevant physical properties and storage capacities for each type of DVD disc. The DVD format books refer to the storage capacity of each type of DVD disc as Gbytes, but this term has a different meaning than the classic definition for computer Gb. In the field of computer science a byte is defined as 8 bits of data, Kb as 1,024 bytes, Mb as 1,024 Kb, and Gb is 1,024 Mb. In the DVD format books a GByte is simply defined as 1 billion bytes. This is about 7.3 percent less than a computer Gb, which is actually 1,073,741,824 bytes. When working with DVD disc storage capacities it is important to keep this difference in mind.

It is also important to note that the capacity of a dual layer (DVD-9) disc is not simply double the capacity of a single layer (DVD-5) disc. Dual layer discs have a slightly larger mark pitch than single layer discs do, so a dual layer disc can only hold about 82 percent more than a single layer disc. Table 2.2 shows some of the common physical properties of DVD discs.

Table 2.1	DVD Storage Capacity Chart					
Parameters		DVD-5	DVD-9	DVD-10	DVD-14	DVD-18
User Data Capacity (Gb) *	12cm	4.37	7.95	8.75	12.3	15.9
	8cm	1.36	2.47	2.72	3.83	4.95

* Storage capacities are listed in computer Gb (2^{30})

Table 2.2	DVD Physical Parameter Chart					
Parameters		DVD-5	DVD-9	DVD-10	DVD-14	DVD-18
Laser Wavelength		650/635 nm				
Disc Diameter	12cm	120 mm				
	8cm	80 mm				
Disc Thickness		1.2 mm				
Disc Center Hole		15.0 mm				
Data Area Inner Radius		24.0 mm				
Data Area Outer Radius	12cm	58.0 mm maximum				
	8cm	38.0 mm maximum				
User Data Bit Rate		11.08 Mbps				

Disc Format) file formats for storing data on a DVD disc. The ISO-9660 format has been in use for a number of years, and most CD-ROM discs that are cross-platform compatible use this format. DVD currently implements a hybrid approach, called UDF-Bridge, that provides both the newer UDF system as well as the older ISO-9660 system used by the CD-ROM format. This allows DVD discs to be used with computer operating systems that do not have any provision for UDF support.

DVD-Video requires that data stored on the disc follow the volume structure shown in Figure 2.4. Lead-in and lead-out areas are provided at the start and end of the disc to facilitate synchronization of DVD players with the data stored on the disc. An ISO-9660 and Micro-UDF file format is used to store all data. Video, audio, subpicture, menu, and still image data elements are stored in the DVD-Video zone area of the disc. The data is logically organized into the Video Manager area, which acts as the table of contents for the disc, and up to 99 Video Title Set areas, which hold individual programs, or collections of multimedia content.

All DVD discs should be mastered to include all required data as specified by ISO 13346 and UDF. This allows the playback of DVD discs on standard computer systems that support either the ISO 13346 or UDF formats. The ISO is the International Standards Organization that sets worldwide standards for a wide variety of industries, including personal computers and consumer electronics devices. Examples of such required data include the time, date, permission bits, and a free space map (indicating no free space if ROM media). While DVD player implementations may ignore these fields, a UDF computer system implementation will not. The UDF format has many features and can be complicated, however much of the information can be ignored in a dedicated DVD player environment. Due to limited computing resources within a DVD consumer player, only a subset of the UDF format is used for storing data on the DVD disc. The following restrictions apply to using the UDF format for DVD-Video discs.

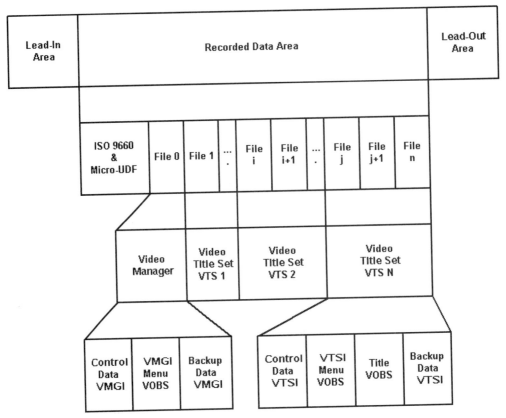

Figure 2.4   DVD-Video Volume Layout Hierarchy

- DVD-Video files should be stored in a subdirectory directly under the root directory. The directory name should be Video_TS.

- DVD-Video file names should consist of the characters A-Z (upper case), 0-9 (digits), _ (underscore), and . (period). Not more than one . should be used in a file name.

- Maximum compatibility will be ensured if the DVD-Video file names consist of no more than eight characters, optionally followed by a ., optionally followed by no more than three characters.

- There should not be any files in the DVD-Video directory that differ only by case (i.e., Movie and movie cannot coexist).

- DVD-Video authoring systems should constrain individual files to less than 1 Gb.

All these constraints apply only to the directory and files to which the DVD-Video player needs access. There may be other files and directories on the DVD disc that are not intended for the DVD-Video player and do not meet the listed constraints. Files outside the Video_TS directory, as well as files in the root directory, are ignored by the DVD player.

Copies of the UDF Specification can be obtained from:

Optical Storage Technology Association
311 East Carrillo Street
Santa Barbara, CA 93101
(805) 963-3853 Voice
(805) 962-1541 Fax
ray@osta.org (E-Mail)
http://www.osta.org (Web)

disc.

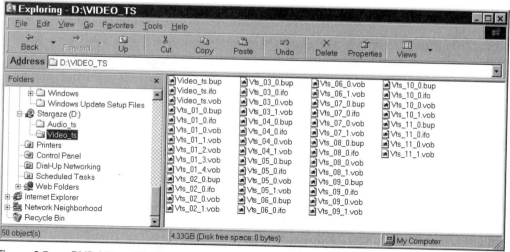

Figure 2.5   DVD-Video File Structure

Files that end with the .ifo extension are information files that describe the content stored in the DVD-Video zone of the disc and how that content can be accessed directly. Files that end with the .bup extension are backup copies of the .ifo files with the same name. Files that end in the .vob extension are Video Objects that contain all the still images, video streams, audio streams, subtitle streams, and menus that are included on the disc.

disc note:

Real World Example

StarGaze is a "hybrid" DVD title with features designed for both DVD-Video players as well as personal computers with DVD-ROM drives. Place the *StarGaze* disc into a DVD-ROM drive and look at the files and directories on the disc. You will notice that most of the capacity of the disc is used by files in the Video_TS directory. This is where the data is stored for the DVD-Video portion of the title. There are also ten files in the root-directory used to install a Windows screen saver program. DVD-Video players ignore these files.

DVD-Video

DVD-Video is a read-only optical-disc format that can be used for the interactive playback of high quality video, audio, and graphics content. The DVD-Video format allows consumers to playback full-length motion pictures as well as interactive games with higher quality than traditional VHS, SVHS, CD-i, and Laserdisc playback systems. The DVD-Video format can deliver full screen, full motion video at a resolution of 720×480 pixels per frame and a frame rate of 30 frames per second for NTSC countries, or 720×576 pixels per frame and a frame rate of 25 frames per second for PAL countries. Video quality delivered by a DVD-Video player has the potential to be as good as the original broadcast source tape.

The DVD-Video format supports extremely high quality audio using either Dolby Digital 5.1 channel surround-sound, linear PCM encoded audio, DTS surround sound audio, or Sony SDDS surround sound audio. Each of these digital audio formats provides significantly better quality than traditional Audio-CD devices. The DVD-Video format also provides the capability of storing up to eight different audio tracks that are all synchronized to the digital video stream.

The DVD-Video format supports up to 32 subpicture streams used for subtitles, closed captioning, graphical overlays, and even simple animations. Each subpicture stream is synchronized to the video and audio streams so that a wide variety of multimedia elements (video, audio, graphics, text, and animation) can be delivered to the user in a coherent fashion. The DVD-Video format can also deliver high quality still images that can be displayed for a fixed period of time, or until a user input is received.

The DVD-Video format supports a wide range of functions that enable the user to control and interact with the DVD-Video title. Simple functions such as start, stop, pause, fast forward, and reverse are provided so the user can control the playback of a title in a manner similar to a VHS, SVHS, or Laserdisc system. In addition to these simple interactive features, DVD-Video provides random access to all of the data on the disc, allowing the user to jump to any portion of the title in less than one second. Finally the DVD-Video format provides high-level interactive functions that allow the development of titles that ask the user to respond to questions, or to provide interactive menus to determine how the user wishes to view the title.

Video, audio, subpicture, still image, and control data are all multiplexed together within a DVD-Video title to form a single bit stream that can be decoded by a DVD-Video player in a manner that provides seamless transitions between different video scenes, language tracks, or subpicture streams. DVD-Video data has the following logical structure, as shown in Figure 2.6.

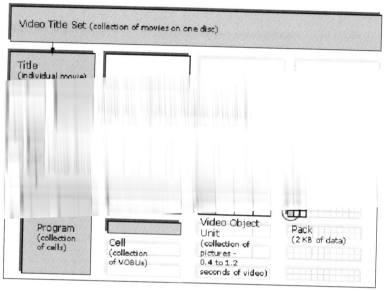

Figure 2.6   DVD-Video Logical Hierarchy

Title   The Title area provides the ability to have up to 99 titles or episodes on a single disc. Titles can consist of a single program chain or multiple program chains. A title is typically used to store an entire movie or any items of content that can stand on their own.

Program Chain   A collection of programs that are logically grouped together based on the content. Generally a movie is stored in a single program chain, while different episodes of a television series would be stored in separate program chains.

Part_of_Title   Links to one or more programs. Part_of_Title can be used to support different versions of the title. For example if you developed a DVD for a movie that had several different endings, you would create a Part_of_Title for each unique ending. The Part_of_Title would call out the specific programs used in each variation of playback.

Program   A collection of cells that are logically grouped together based on the content. Programs are usually used to identify different chapters within a movie.

Cell   A collection of video or audio data packets that are logically grouped together based on the content. Cells are usually used to identify different scenes within a chapter.

VOBU   Video Object Unit that is one or more MPEG Group of Pictures (GOP). A VOBU can be between 0.4 and 1.2 seconds long.

Group Of Pictures (GOP)   The smallest granularity of random access to video data on the disc. A GOP typically includes compressed video data from 15 sequential frames of NTSC video, or 12 frames of PAL video.

Packet   DVD-Video packets are 2048 bytes large and include only one type of data (video, audio, etc.). A packet is essentially equivalent to a single sector of data on the disc.

Navigation Packet (NAV)   Contains optional commands that define the playback behavior of a cell. Navigation packs are used to control playback of the content at a very detailed level, for example you could use a navigation pack to skip over a specific Cell if it had a parental rating level higher than the player was set up to play.

DVD-Video can achieve the lofty goal of providing significantly better quality and more features than conventional VHS, SVHS, or Laserdisc players because it utilizes the latest digital techniques for encoding video, audio, still images, sub-picture information, and animation data.

MPEG Video

The DVD-Video format requires that video data be compressed in either the MPEG-1 or MPEG-2 formats. A compressed format is used to reduce the total data storage requirements for the video elements to a manageable level. "Broadcast" or "CCIR-601" quality video requires approximately 21 Mbytes/second of storage space and throughput. This means that a DVD-5 disc (4.37 GBytes) could hold only about 3.7 minutes of uncompressed, or raw, video.

   MPEG-1 compressed video has a resolution of 352×240 pixels per frame and a frame rate of 30 non-interlaced frames per second (for NTSC countries). Most MPEG-1 files are compressed at a constant bit rate of approximately 1.4 Mbits/Second, which is consistent with the recommendations of the Video-CD standard. MPEG-1 compressed video provides quality roughly comparable to VHS tape, and if higher data rates are used the quality can approach SVHS tape. A standard DVD-5 (4.3 Gb) disc can hold approximately 7.5 hours of MPEG-1 video compressed at standard Video-CD rates. Video CD is an extremely popular format in Asia, but has never caught on in either the US or Europe since both areas had large installed bases of VHS players when Video CD first became available. Many DVD-Video players support the Video CD format, and some of the first titles released for DVD players were actually Video CD discs with MPEG-1 data. Despite Video CD's popularity in Asia, the vast majority of DVD-Video titles have been published using MPEG-2 compressed video in order to provide better overall video quality.

   MPEG-2 compressed video has a resolution of 720×480 pixels per frame and a frame rate of 30 frames per second for NTSC countries, or a resolution of 720×576 pixels per frame and a frame rate of 25 frames per second for PAL countries. MPEG-2 files can be created using a constant-bit-rate encoding process or a variable-bit-rate encoding process. If a constant-bit-rate encoding process is used a bit rate of approximately 6 Mbits/Sec or higher is required to provide compressed video that is as good as the original CCIR-601 source. If a variable-bit-rate encoding process is used, an average bit rate of less than 4.0 Mbits/Sec can be used to generate compressed video that looks nearly as good as the original CCIR-601 source.

Figure 2.7 shows the steps required to generate an MPEG-2 compressed digital video file. CCIR-601 component video is fed into a series of pre-filters and temporal and spatial scaling equipment to generate a high quality component digital video signal. The digital signal is then converted from RGB component format into the Y/Cr/Cb component format. Each frame of digital video is compressed using a Discrete Cosine Transform algorithm that removes redundant data (Intraframe Compression). Next each frame is compared to previous and future frames to eliminate redundant data between frames (Interframe Compression).

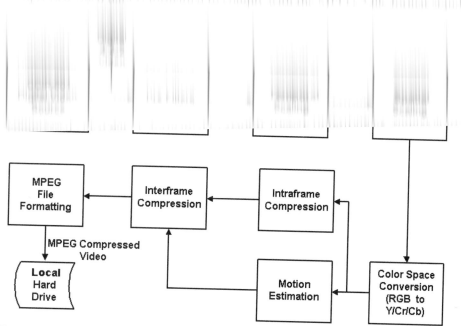

Figure 2.7   MPEG Video Compression Process Block Diagram

An MPEG-2 bit stream, as shown in Figure 2.8, is composed of a sequence of *Slices*, *Pictures*, and *Group Of Pictures*. An MPEG-2 *Picture* corresponds to a single full resolution frame, with two *Slices* that correspond to each field of the interlaced frame. There are three types of encoded frames in MPEG-2. An I frame includes all of the information required to fully reconstruct the source frame. Subsequent *Pictures* within the *Group Of Pictures* will be P or B frames. P and B frames are predictive frames, which means they only store the changes from the previous or next frame. A *Group Of Pictures* is a sequence of compressed frames that starts with a *Picture* that is an MPEG-2 I frame. The DVD-Video format book requires that the MPEG-2 compressed digital video stream include no more than 18 *Pictures* in each *Group Of Pictures*. The number of *Pictures* in a *Group Of Pictures* is also called the GOP size. The DVD-Video format book also requires that the MPEG-2 video data be multiplexed with any associated audio, sub-picture, still image, and control data.

When variable bit rate encoding is used, the actual number of bits dedicated to the MPEG encoding process is varied depending on the content of the video stream. If the video content is a scene of someone speaking, with a relatively static background, then fewer bits can be used to accurately describe the static scene. If the video content is a high action scene with both foreground and background motion, or a scene with a lot of fine detail, a higher bit rate must be used to avoid introducing digital artifacts into the compressed digital video file.

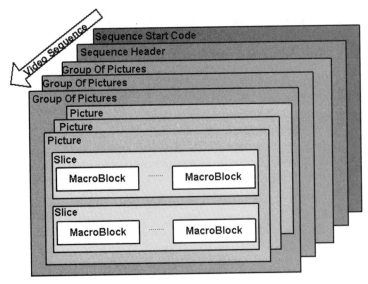

Figure 2.8   MPEG-2 Bit Stream Syntax

Lossy digital video compression techniques, including MPEG-1 and MPEG-2, can create digital artifacts during the compression process. Digital artifacts can include Color Distortion, Color Bleeding, Hue and Tint Degradation, Motion Degradation, Noise Pumping, Frame Duplication, Frame Drops, Aliasing, Blocking, Fringing, and Ringing. The most common digital artifacts generated in MPEG compressed video streams are Blocking, Color Bleeding, and Fringing. Blocking is the presence of 8×8 pixel pattern blocks in the compressed video stream that were not part of the original source. Blocking is caused by the use of the Discrete Cosine Transform algorithm, which operates on an 8×8 pixel block. Color Bleeding occurs when colors from one area of a frame migrate into neighboring areas of the same frame. Color Bleeding occurs more often with "hot" colors such as red, yellow or orange. Ringing is the presence of a blurring, or out of focus effect around the edges of an object that is moving from frame to frame. Ringing occurs more often when there is a large amount of motion between frames of the video.

Digital video artifacts can be eliminated using a variety of techniques. Most artifacts can be removed by increasing the average bit rate used to compress the content. Filtering the input video stream to eliminate high frequency noise is also a common technique for reducing artifacts. Artifacts that occur in only a single frame of the digital video can be removed by touching-up the pixels that have been distorted, although this is a very labor-intensive process.

Multiple Screen Aspect Ratios

In the early days of film all movies were shot in a 4:3 aspect ratio. As movie theatres got larger filmmakers started shooting in wide screen formats so that the movie would fill the

Tips, Tricks & Techniques

Use variable-bit-rate MPEG-2 to create broadcast quality DVD titles. For SVHS quality, use half-horizontal resolution (Half-D1) MPEG-2 compression. For VHS quality, use MPEG-1 compression at Video-CD data rates (1.4 Mbits/second).

available screen size on the stage. When television came along it was decided that all video displayed on a television would have a 4:3 aspect ratio. Today ~~...~~

~~...~~ on a wide-screen monitor. However, when a 4:3 formatted video is displayed on a 16:9 monitor, or a 16:9 formatted video is displayed on a 4:3 monitor, the original image will not be reproduced accurately. There are several techniques used to avoid this problem including Pan/Scan to convert a 16:9 image to a 4:3 resolution and letterboxing to display a 16:9 image on a 4:3 display in its entirety.

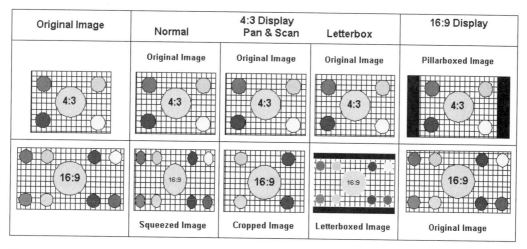

Figure 2.9   DVD-Video Multiple Aspect Ratio Comparison
(See color insert for color version of this figure.)

Multiple Camera Angles

Up to nine different camera angles are supported by the DVD-Video format. The viewer can seamlessly switch between viewing angles by using the "Angle" button on the DVD-Video player's remote control. There are some restrictions on the use of multiple video angles, such as the length and average bit rate of each unique video angle must be approximately the same. Multiple camera angles can be used to provide different perspectives, or to provide alternative content. For example multiple camera angles have been used to provide both a finished animated video sequence as well as the wire frame animation so the viewer can understand the process used to create the video sequence, or for a sporting event where one camera angle could provide a wide angle view of the entire playing field, another could have a close up view following the soccer ball, while a third angle could provide a close up of the goal keeper.

High Quality, Multiple Channel Audio

The DVD-Video Format provides for the incorporation of high-quality, multiple channel audio using one of the following formats: Dolby Digital Stereo, Dolby Digital 5.1 Channel Surround Sound, Linear PCM Stereo, MPEG-2 Stereo, MPEG-2 Surround Sound, DTS Surround Sound and Sony SDDS Surround Sound. The Dolby Digital and Linear PCM formats are required to be supported by DVD-Video players, with MPEG-2 (stereo and surround), DTS and SDDS audio optional. The vast majority of DVD-Video players throughout the world support Linear PCM and Dolby Digital audio. Many players support the DTS audio format as well. MPEG-2 audio is supported on some European model DVD-Video players, but in general it is not supported on US player models. Most of the DVD-Video players on the market today, and sold over the past five years will not support playback of DVD-Audio discs, which generally included linear PCM or Meridian Lossless Packing (MLP) data. Consumers will need to purchase a DVD-Audio player or upgrade their DVD-Video player to a Universal player in order to play back DVD-Audio titles.

DVD-Video supports up to eight simultaneous tracks for audio, in any of the formats listed above. Each audio track is multiplexed into the overall DVD-Video bit stream so that they are synchronized with the video stream. DVD-Video players are designed so that the user can switch between the available audio tracks at any time during playback of the title. Switching audio tracks is a seamless operation that requires less than a second to complete. Video playback will continue without interruption during an audio track change.

Most DVD-Video titles include Dolby Digital stereo, or Dolby Digital 5.1 Channel Surround Sound audio tracks. Dolby Digital is a perceptual digital audio coding technique that has been used in movie theaters since 1992. Dolby Digital divides the audio spectrum of each channel into narrow frequency bands of different sizes optimized with respect to the frequency selectivity of human hearing. This makes it possible to sharply filter coding noise so that it is forced to stay very close in frequency to the frequency components of the audio signal being coded. Reducing or eliminating coding noise wherever there are no audio signals to mask it can subjectively preserve the sound quality of the original signal.

In Dolby Digital, bits are distributed among the filter bands as needed by the particular frequency spectrum or dynamic nature of the program. A built-in model of auditory masking allows the coder to alter its frequency selectivity (as well as time resolution) to make sure that a sufficient number of bits are used to describe the audio signal in each band, thus ensuring noise is fully masked. Dolby Digital also decides how the bits are distributed among the various channels from a common bit pool. This technique allows channels with greater frequency content to demand more data than sparsely occupied channels, for example, or strong sounds in one channel to provide masking for noise in other channels.

Dolby Digital can process at least 20-bit dynamic range digital audio signals over a frequency range from 20 Hz to 20kHz x 0.5dB (-3dB at 3Hz and 20.3 kHz). The bass effects channel covers 20 to 120 Hz x0.5 dB (-3 dB at 3 and 121 Hz). For DVD-Video applications a sampling rate of 48 kHz is used. Data rates range from as low as 32 kb/s for a single mono channel to as high as 640 kb/s, thereby covering a wide range of requirements. Typical applications include 448 kb/s for 5.1-channel Dolby Digital consumer format, and 192 kb/s for two-channel audio distribution.

As shown in Figure 2.10, Dolby Digital 5.1

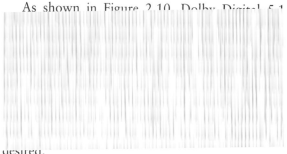

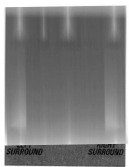

desired.

The sixth channel, called the Low Frequency Effects Channel, will, at times, contain additional bass information to maximize the impact of scenes such as explosions, crashes, etc. Because this channel has only a limited frequency response (3 Hz to 120 Hz), it is sometimes referred to as the ".1" channel. When added to the 5 full range channels, the Dolby Digital system is usually referred to as having "5.1" channels.

Figure 2.10   5.1 Channel Surround Sound Speaker Placement

For Linear PCM and DTS audio the sixth channel includes the same frequency response as the other five channels so it is capable of carrying sound other than low frequency effects. Very few DVD-Video titles have been developed using six channel Linear PCM audio as it uses over 60% of the available DVD-Video bit rate for just a single track of audio, leaving an inadequate amount of bandwidth for video, subpictures or additional audio tracks. DVD-Video titles with six channel DTS audio tracks are quite common, although in the vast majority of cases the sixth channel is used to carry low frequency effects sound.

Multiple Subpicture Streams

The DVD-Video format supports up to thirty-two (32) simultaneous subpicture streams for use as subtitles, closed captions, graphical overlays or simple animation. Each subpicture stream is multiplexed into the overall DVD-Video bit stream so that they are synchronized with the video and audio data. Subpicture streams are stored as Run Length Coded Bit Maps with 2 bits allocated per pixel of data. For countries that use the NTSC television standard Sub-Pictures have a resolution of 720×478 pixels, while in countries using the PAL standard have Sub-Pictures with a resolution of 720×573 pixels. A subpicture is created using only four colors from a 16-color palette, and four unique contrast levels. Special effects such as scroll up, scroll down, fade in, and fade out can be applied over a sequence of video frames. The sub-picture color palette can be changed for each program chain.

The use of subpicture streams on DVD-Video titles is quite common. Subpictures are routinely used for foreign language subtitles, closed caption, and captions for the hearing impaired. Innovative uses of subpictures have included an animated director commentary where the silhouette of the directors was displayed in the bottom corner of the video display while the director's commentary is played on a supplemental audio track. Subpicture streams have even been used to provide alien language translations in the Klingon language.

High Quality Still Images

The DVD-Video format supports the use of high quality still images that can be displayed for a fixed length of time, or until a defined user input is received. Still images are stored as either MPEG-1 or MPEG-2 I frames (full reference frames). When a still image is encountered in the DVD-Video bit stream the video and sub-picture streams are frozen, and the audio is muted. MPEG-1 still images have a resolution of 352×240 pixels for NTSC, and 352×288 for PAL. MPEG-2 still images have a resolution of 720×480 pixels for NTSC, and 720×576 for PAL. The size of each compressed still image is dependent on its content, and the degree of compression that can be applied without creating digital artifacts.

Navigation & Search Functions

DVD-Video supports a wide variety of navigation and search functions that allow users to control and interact with titles. User controlled search functions include:

Title Search   The user can select a specific title from the list of available titles on the DVD-Video disc.

Part_of_Title Search   The user can select a specific chapter available on the DVD-Video disk.

Program Search   The user can select a specific scene within a program chain.

Time Search   User can select a specific time code location within a program chain.

Scan   The user can scan either forward or backward in time through the current title.

GoUp   The user can jump to the start of the next program chain. Many DVD-Video players include this feature as the Return button on the remote control.

The DVD-Video title author can disable the Part_of_Title, Program, Time, Scan, and GoUp search functions.

Navigation commands allow the DVD-Video author to control the playback of the Title, Part_of_Title, or Program that has been selected by the user. Navigation commands can be used in four different command areas within a DVD-Video title. These are the Button, Cell, Pre, and Post command areas. Navigation commands are all eight bytes, and include Single Instruction Commands and Composite Instruction Commands. Single Instruction Commands include a single instruction while Composite Instruction Commands can include two or three instructions. There are six different types of Navigation Commands.

GoTo   Branch between commands

Link   Transfer between the same domain

Jump   Transfer between different domains

System Parameter Registers (SPRM)

There are 24 unique player SPRM, as shown in Table 2.3 (page 26). SPRMs store a fixed length, 16-bit numerical value, and are used to keep track of user preferences as well as player capabilities information. For example if the viewer prefers to see French language subtitles if they are available, then SPRM 17 and 18 will be set up to store that information. Some SPRM registers are set up by the player manufacturer and others are configured by the viewer when the use the DVD-Video players on-screen configuration menus. All SPRM registers can be read during playback of a DVD-Video title using standard navigation commands. DVD-Video titles can be designed to read the SPRM registers and take appropriate action based on the user preferences and player capabilities.

There are also 16 general parameter registers (GPRM) that can be used by the DVD-Video title author to control playback of the title. GPRMs can be used to stored fixed length, 16-bit numerical values, which are treated as unsigned integers. There are two modes of operation for GPRMs, register mode and counter mode. In counter mode the value of a GPRM is automatically increased by one every second. All GPRMs are set to zero and placed in register mode when a DVD-Video title is first started. Chapter 6 provides an in-depth discussion on how to use SPRM and GPRM registers to create highly complex or interactive DVD-Video titles.

Regional Coding

In order to gain the support of the major motion picture studios, the DVD Forum had to modify the original DVD-Video specification to include Region Coding. Region Coding is designed to allow the major motion picture studios to control the release of their titles throughout the world. The world was broken up into eight regions and if a studio only wanted to release a title in the United States, then they would create a DVD-Video title where only Region 1 (North America) playback was enabled. Consumers in other regions of the world would be unable to play back the title since their player's internal region code would not match the titles region code.

Table 2.3	DVD-Video SPRM Descriptions		
#	System Parameter Description	#	System Parameter Description
0	Menu Description Language Code	12	Country Code for Parental Management
1	Audio Stream Number	13	Parental Level
2	Sub-Picture Stream Number	14	Player Configuration for Video
3	Angle Number	15	Player Configuration for Audio
4	Title Number	16	Initial Language Code for Audio
5	VTS Title Number	17	Initial Language Extension for Sub-Pictures
6	Title PGC Number	18	Initial Language Extension for Audio
7	Part_of_Title Number for one sequential_PGC_Title	19	Initial Language Extension for Sub-Picture
8	Highlighted Button Number	20	Player Region Code Mask
9	Navigation Timer	21	Reserved
10	Title PGC Number for Navigation Timer	22	Reserved
11	Audio Mixing Mode for Karaoke	23	Reserved

When a DVD title is manufactured one or more regional codes can be stored on the disc. Similarly, when DVD players and DVD-ROM drives are manufactured, a regional code is stored within the player hardware. The DVD player performs a comparison of its own internal regional code with the code stored on a DVD disc loaded into the player. If the regional codes match, then the DVD player will display the menu of available titles, or will start playing the default title. If the regional codes do not match the DVD player will not provide the user with access to the titles stored on the disc. Regional coding methods have been used for many years by the movie industry to control distribution of their content throughout the world.

For DVD players and titles there are 7 regions that have been defined. A region number superimposed on a world globe is used to identify players and discs. If a disc plays in more than one region it will have more than one number on the globe. DVD-Video regional codes are defined as follows:

1. North America
2. Japan, Europe, Middle East, South Africa
3. Southeast Asia (including Hong Kong)
4. Australia, New Zealand, Central/South America
5. Northwest Asia (including Korea), North Africa

6. China

7. Reserved

8. Airplanes (In-Flight Entertainment)

The use of DVD regional coding is optional for content owners, but mandatory for DVD hardware manufacturers. Content owners can publish their titles using any combination of regional codes that they choose, or none at all. DVD hardware vendors must design their equipment to support the Region Coding system.

players in Europe have been modified to play titles from any region, so even if I wanted to limit playback of StarGaze to just North America most Europeans could play the title anyway.

Parental Lock Out

The DVD-Video format supports up to eight levels of parental management, also called parental lockout. Viewers can configure DVD-Video players to require a password when titles above a specific rating level (G, PG, PG-13, R, etc.) are inserted into the player. DVD-Video titles include the rating levels associated with each Title stored on the disc. The player performs a comparison of the rating levels of the content stored on the disc to the parental management level programmed into its memory by the user, and will only provide access to content that is rated equal to or lower than that value. Parental management levels vary depending on the country code of the DVD-Video player.

During the DVD-Video authoring process, only the differences between the various rating levels are encoded and stored on the disc. As an example take a title that has two different ratings, G and PG, based on the presence of a single scene that has some violence. The "G" version of the title substitutes a different, non-violent scene to preserve its G rating, while the PG version will include this scene. Both versions of the scene are encoded and stored on the DVD-Video disc. The DVD-Video author constructs two unique Program Chains, one for the "G" version and the other for the "PG" version. If the user has selected to view the "G" version, the DVD-Video control stream will play the substitute scene at the correct time. If the user has selected to view the "PG" version the original scene with some violence will be displayed.

Copy Protection

The issue of how to protect content once it is distributed on a DVD-Video disc was a major topic of discussion between members of the DVD Forum and representatives from the motion picture and software industries. The launch of the DVD-Video format in the United States was delayed almost a year in order to improve the copy protection features of DVD-Video so that it would satisfy the major motion picture studios. In late June of 1996 representatives from the computer, consumer-electronics and movie industries signed off on a technical working group report that recommended encrypting all data stored on DVD-Video discs and including decryption hardware in DVD Video players. Later that year proposals from the computer industry recommending an alternative method of encrypting portions of the video content were considered and accepted by the Technical Working Group. Finally in November of 1996 all parties agreed to a specific set of analog and digital copy protection methods.

There are currently three forms of copy protection used by the DVD-Video format, Analog Copy Protection (ACP), Copy Guard Management System (CGMS), and Content Scrambling System (CSS).

Analog Copy Protection

The analog copy protection feature of DVD-Video utilizes a proprietary copy protection process developed by Macrovision. Macrovision's DVD copy protection system utilizes two separate copy protection technologies: Automatic Gain Control (AGC) and Colorstripe. The AGC technology for DVD is virtually identical to the Macrovision protection system that has been used to protect prerecorded VHS titles against consumer copying since 1985. The AGC system adds bipolar pulse pairs to the output video signal causing a recording VCR to record a weak, noisy and unstable signal level. The AGC system takes advantage of the difference in the way television and VCR automatic gain circuits work.

The Colorstripe™ technology for DVD is similar to a protection method that Macrovision has implemented in digital set top boxes and digital video networks since 1994. This technology modulates the phase of the colorburst signal in a rapid, controlled manner, which causes annoying horizontal stripes on an unauthorized copy. The Colorstripe™ technology exploits the chroma processing necessary to record and replay the color signals within the limitations of the consumer videocassette formats.

The combination of the Macrovision AGC and Colorstripe™ copy protection technologies will degrade copies made on approximately 95% of consumer VCRs in the market. These copy protection technologies are designed to stop consumers, not professional pirates. Video engineers and others with access to sophisticated professional video equipment, such as time base correctors, can make unauthorized copies of Macrovision copy protected DVD titles.

Additional information on the Macrovision ACG and Colorstripe technologies can be obtained from:

Macrovision Corporation
1341 Orleans Drive
Sunnyvale, California 94089
408-743-8600 (Voice)
408-743-8610 (Fax)
http://www.macrovision.com (Web)

Copy Guard Management System (CGMS)

Digital copying is controlled by information on each disc specifying if the data can be copied. This is a "serial" CGMS designed to prevent copies, or copies from copies. Of course, the equipment making the copy has to abide by the rules. Each sector of data on a DVD-Video disc includes CGMS data that defines how many times the data can be copied. The possible values are zero copies, one copy or infinite copies. If CGMS is set to zero copies then recording devices or computer operating systems should prevent that data from being copied. If CGMS is set to one copy then recording devices or computer operating systems will allow the data to be copied, but the CGMS values of the copied data will be set to zero copies so that

ing it. DVD-ROM drives and MPEG-2 playback boards or software decoders that can be used to play DVD-Video titles exchange encryption keys so that the video is decrypted just before display by the encoder. During 1999 the Content Scrambling System was broken by a group of Linux programmers who wanted to watch DVD-Video titles on their personal computers. DeCSS, a simple hacking program to break CSS, has been published on the Internet, and several motion picture studios and the MPAA have sued these web sites in order to have these programs withdrawn. The MPAA has already been granted several preliminary injunctions directing various web sites to remove DeCSS from their servers. Unfortunately the MPAA and the courts can't possibly keep up with the speed of the Internet, so as soon as DeCSS is removed from one web site it then appears on several new sites. In this day an age of the Wild, Wild Web it will be virtually impossible to keep copies of DeCSS, or any other program that rips or hacks DVD-Video titles off the Internet.

The DVD Forum is currently developing more secure versions of CSS, dubbed CPPM and CPRM that will be used in DVD-Audio, Universal DVD players, and DVD recording devices. Figure 2.11 shows how the current DVD-Video Content Scrambling System works.

All three methods of copy protection are optional for the producer of a disc. These copy protection schemes are designed to guard against casual copying. Professional pirates who have access to high-end video and DVD disc replication equipment will be able to defeat each of these copy protection methods easily.

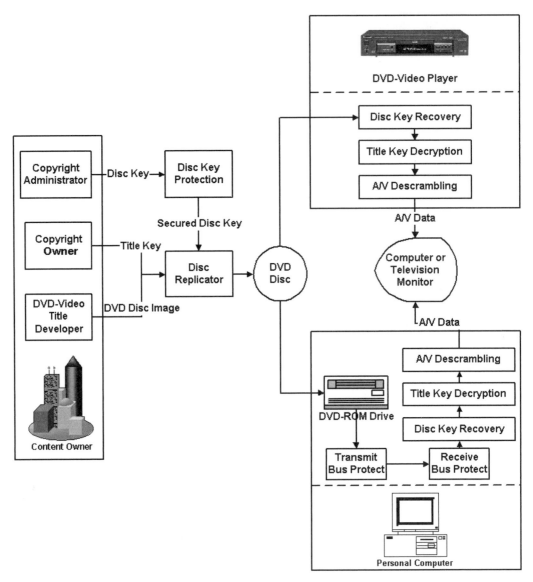

Figure 2.11   DVD-Video Content Scrambling System Block Diagram

DVD-Video Video Object Format

The DVD-Video Video Object (VOB) format is an extremely powerful publishing medium. The VOB format lets you use advanced multimedia features, such as multiple video angles, multiple audio streams, multiple subpicture streams, and seamless interactive branching. While the VOB format is an essential part of the DVD-Video specification, there is a significant potential for its use outside of DVD-Video players. A number of DVD-ROM title developers will store their multimedia content in the VOB format even though their titles will not be designed to work in DVD-Video players. In the past year a number of DVD authoring tool vendors have released DVD-on-CD products that allow data stored in the VOB format to be transferred to CD-ROM, and then played back on any personal computer, even if it does not have a DVD-ROM drive or DVD-Video decoding software. As more and more companies create development and authoring tools for the VOB format, I predict that it will become a popular publishing format in its own right, independent of DVD-Video playback.

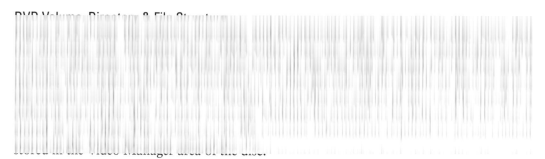

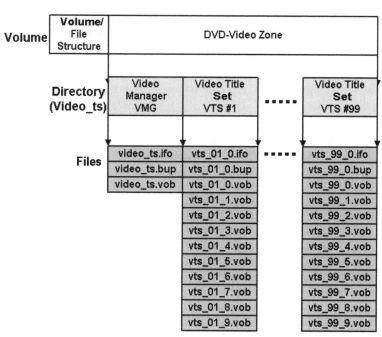

Figure 2.12   DVD-Video Volume, Directory and File Structure Hierarchy

The Video Manager area can include static menus or menus with video and audio content. This multimedia data is stored in the `video_ts.vob` file, which is accessed on a DVD-Video player through the TITLE MENU button on the remote control. A DVD-Video disc can hold up to 99 titles, each of which has its own information file. The information file for the first title on a DVD-Video disc is vts01_0.ifo, thus vts_99_0.ifo is the information file for the ninety-ninth title. Each title can include static menus or menus with video and/or audio content. This multimedia data is stored in the vts_xx_0.vob file, where xx is the title number. These title menus are usually accessed on a DVD-Video player through the MENU button on the remote control.

The main video, audio, and graphics used in a DVD-Video title are stored in the vts_xx_y.vob files, where xx is the title number and y is a number between one and nine. .vob files are limited to 1 Gb or less in size, so a title with a lot of video and audio content will require a number of .vob files. For example, a full-length movie published on a DVD-5 disc will typically have five .vob files within the main title — vts_01_1.vob, vts_01_2.vob, vts_01_3.vob, vts_01_4.vob, and vts_01_5.vob. The first four .vob files would each be 1Gb, while the last file would be less than 1GB. If the title developer includes additional content or trailers these are normally stored in a separate video title set and thus would have require a different set of .vob files.

DVD Video Manager

The Video Manager, shown in Figure 2.13, acts like a table of contents for all the data stored in the DVD-Video area of the disc. It includes up to eight different data tables stored in the video_ts.ifo file. Three of these tables are mandatory, two are optional, and three are required only if the Video Manager area includes a static or dynamic menu. The order of the data in the tables is typically as shown in Figure 2.13. Each table in the Video Manager file performs the following function.

1. The Video Manager Information Management Table (VMGI_MAT) provides information on the size of the video manager file, the start address of each table in the Video Manager file, and information about the DVD-Video title such as the number of titles, a volume set identifier, etc.

2. The Title Search Pointer Table (TT_SRPT) provides information on each title included on the DVD disc, such as the type of title (sequential or random), the number of video angles, the number of chapters, the parental ID code, and the start address of the video title set.

3. The Video Manager Menu Program Chain Information Unit Table (VMGM_PGCI_UT) provides information on the different menu languages used in the title menu (if it exists).

4. The Parental Management Information Table (PTL_MAIT) provides information on the parental levels defined for the Video Manager and each title (if parental levels are used).

5. The Video Title Set Attribute Table (VTS_ATRT) provides information on the attributes and start address of each video title set.

6. The Text Data Manager (TXTDT_MG) provides information such as volume name, title name, producer's name, and textual descriptions for each title.

7. The Video Manager Menu Cell Address Table (VMGM_C_ADT) provides the start and ending address of all cells used in the video manager .vob files, if they exist.

8. The Video Manager Menu Video Object Unit Address map (VMGM_VOBU_ADMAP) provides the start address of all video object units used in the video manager VOB files, if they exist.

Video Title Set Information

The Video Title Set Information (`vts_xx_y.ifo`) file contains information required to access and play each of the video titles stored on the disc. This file includes up to nine tables, as shown in Figure 2.14. The order of the data in the tables is typically as shown in Figure 2.14. Each table in the Video Title Set Information file performs the following function.

1. The Video Title Set Information Management Table (`VTSI_MAT`) provides the start address of

(`VTS_PTT_SRPT`) provides the start address of each chapter within the title.

3. The Video Title Set Program Chain Information Table (`VTS_PGCIT`) provides information for each of the program chains in the title.

4. The Video Title Set Menu Program Chain Information Unit Table (`VTSM_PGCI_UT`) provides information on the existence of Root, Subpicture, Audio, Video Angle, and Chapter menus, and the start addresses, if they exist, for each title.

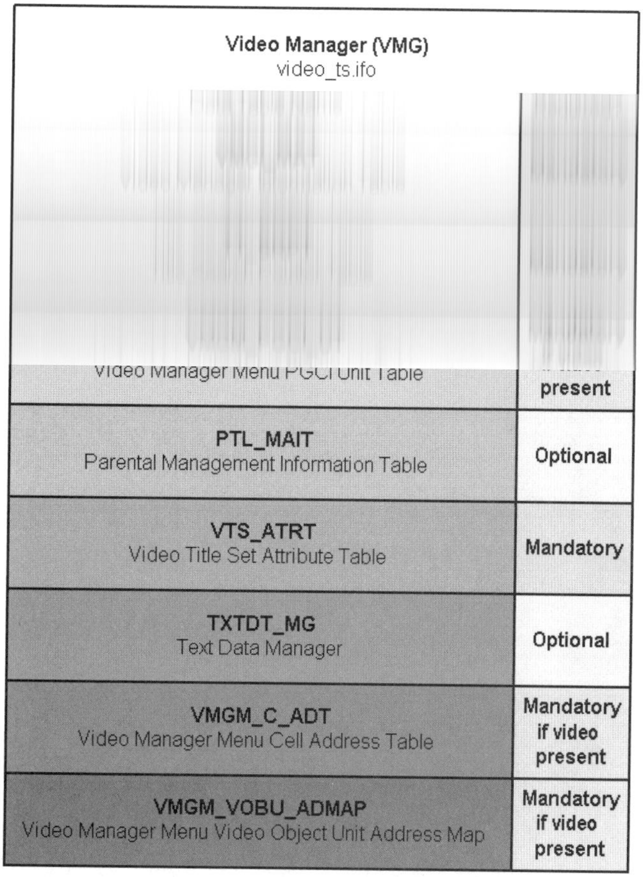

Video Manager (VMG) video_ts.ifo	
Video Manager Menu PGCI Unit Table	present
PTL_MAIT Parental Management Information Table	Optional
VTS_ATRT Video Title Set Attribute Table	Mandatory
TXTDT_MG Text Data Manager	Optional
VMGM_C_ADT Video Manager Menu Cell Address Table	Mandatory if video present
VMGM_VOBU_ADMAP Video Manager Menu Video Object Unit Address Map	Mandatory if video present

Figure 2.13 DVD Video Manager (VMG) Structure (See color insert for color version of this figure.)

5. The Video Title Set Time Map Table (`VTS_TMAFT`) provides the start address for each title's timetable, the units of measurement for the time map entries, and up to 2,048 time-map entries to allow searching through the title based on time.

6. The Video Title Set Menu Cell Address Table (`VTSM_C_ADT`) provides the start and end address of each cell in the `vts_xx_0.vob` file (if it exists).

7. The Video Title Set Menu Video Object Unit Address Map (`VTSM_VOBU_ADMAP`) provides the start address of each video object unit in the `vts_xx_0.vob` file (if it exists).

8. The Video Title Set Cell Address Table (VTS_VOBU_ADT) provides the start and end address of each cell in the vts_xx_y.vob file.

9. The video title set video object unit address map (VTS_VOBU_ADMAP) provides the start address for each video object unit in the vts_xx_y.vob file.

Video Object Set

Video Objects are the basic multimedia data type for the DVD format. A VOB includes one video stream, up to eight audio streams, up to 32 subpicture streams, and the navigation information required to connect video objects into program chains, titles, and title sets. Figure 2.15 shows the basic construction of a Video Object Set (VOBS). There are some restrictions on the data rate requirements of a Video Object Set and each of its component multimedia data types.

- The total data rate of a Video Object Set can't exceed 10.08Mbps.

- The maximum data rate of the video stream within a Video Object Set is 9.8Mbps.

- The maximum data rate for a single audio stream in a Video Object Set is 6.144Mbps.

- The maximum total data rate for all eight audio streams is 9.8Mbps.

- The maximum data rate for a single subpicture stream within a Video Object Set is 3.36Mbps

- The maximum total data rate for all subpicture streams is 9.8Mbps.

Video Title Set Information (VTSI) vts_xx_0.ifo	
Data Table Name	Required?
VTSI_MAT Video Title Set Information Management Table	Mandatory
VTS_PTT_SRPT Video Title Set Part_of_Title Search Pointer Table	Mandatory
VTS_PGCIT Video Title Set Program Chain Information Table	Mandatory
VTSM_PGCI_UT Video Title Set Menu PGCI Unit Table	Mandatory if video present
VTS_TMAPT Video Title Set Time Map Table	**Optional**
VTSM_C_ADT Video Title Set Menu Cell Address Table	Mandatory if video present
VTS_VOBU_ADMAP Video Title Set Menu Video Object Unit Address Map	Mandatory if video present
VTS_C_ADT Video Title Set Cell Address Table	Mandatory
VTS_VOBU_ADMAP Video Title Set Video Object Unit Address Map	Mandatory

Figure 2.14 DVD Video Title Set Information (VTSI) File Structure
(See color insert for color version of this figure.)

As discussed previously and shown in Figure 2.6, a Video Object Set is a collection of VOBs. Video Objects may be divided into cells, each of which is made up of a collection of Video Object units. A Video Object Unit (VOBU) is a sequence of packs, roughly equivalent to a sector on the DVD disc, and will include approximately 0.4 to 1.2 seconds of content. Video Object Units consist of a stream of navigation packs (NV PCK), video packs (V PCK), audio packs (A PCK), and subpicture packs (SP PCK). Video Object Units start with one navigation pack followed by a series of video, audio, and subpicture packs, if required. The Video Object Unit ends immediately before the next navigation pack, or at the end of the Video Object Set.

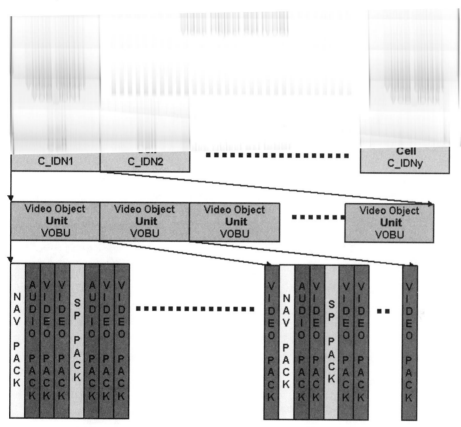

Figure 2.15   DVD Video Object Set Structure – The basic building block of DVD-Video

Why Is It So Complicated?

By now you're probably thinking that using the DVD Video Object format would be a big mistake. Why is it so complicated? Why are there so many different levels of structure, and why are there so many different terms? The DVD Video Object format is designed to deliver an unprecedented combination of video, audio, and graphics data types, at broadcast quality, with near-real-time switching between data streams. As you can see from Figure 2.15, the Video Object Unit, which is the basic building block of DVD-Video, is actually a multiplexed combination of video, audio, subpicture, and navigation data streams. The individual data packs are small enough so that a DVD-Video player, or a DVD-ROM computer system, can switch playback streams in real time, providing seamless playback from a multitude of video, audio, and subpicture streams.

The advantages of using the VOB format are tremendous: nine broadcast-quality video streams, eight theatre-quality audio streams, 32 high-resolution graphics overlay streams, and seamless branching between any of these streams. Perhaps the biggest advantage is that every DVD-ROM computer system available today has built-in software that handles the VOB format. The disadvantages of using the VOB format are not insignificant. You're required to use directory and file naming conventions of the DVD-Video specification, a complicated hierarchy that is not easy to understand, and it costs more to create your multimedia data files in the VOB format. These disadvantages will be minimized as new, low-cost tools come to market. Authoring tools will hide the complexities of the DVD-Video specification, and the tools you use to generate DVD-Video-compliant files can be expected to drop in price.

DVD-ROM

DVD-ROM is a high capacity, high throughput read-only optical-disc format that can be used as a general-purpose computer storage device. The DVD-ROM format book does not discuss the application programs or content that may be published in the DVD-ROM format. This means that the DVD-ROM format can be used for a wide variety of purposes within a personal computer environment.

The vast majority of DVD-ROM enabled personal computers sold today include hardware or software for playback of DVD-Video titles. In general a personal computer with a 400 MHz or faster CPU can play DVD-Video titles with a "software-only" DVD decoder, while slower systems will need an add-in card to help the CPU decode the MPEG-2 video and Dolby Digital audio streams in real time. Figure 2.16 illustrates the configuration of a DVD-ROM enabled PC with an add-in card for hardware DVD decoding. Personal computers that use software decoding will have the same basic configuration, except the add-in card will not be required to deliver acceptable playback performance.

Tips, Tricks & Techniques

DVD-Video title developers need to have several different DVD-ROM computers as part of their testing and quality assurance equipment. Many consumers play DVD-Video titles on DVD-ROM enabled personal computer systems, so these playback environments must be tested to insure title compatibility. DVD-ROM systems with hardware and software

Windows 98 PC with H/W decoder	Panasonic DVD-Video Player
Windows Me PC with S/W decoder	Pioneer DVD-Video Player
Windows NT4 PC with H/W decoder	Sony DVD-Video Player
Windows 2000 PC with S/W decoder	Toshiba DVD-Video Player
Mac OS 9 with software decoder	
Mac OS 9 with hardware decoder	

You're probably wondering why I listed an Oritron DVD-Video player in addition to the name brand players. The Oritron DVD-Video player is generally the cheapest player on the market, and has several known compatibility problems. If your title can work on the Oritron it will probably work on anything. I have not specified Mac OSX in the matrix since it does not currently support DVD-Video title playback.

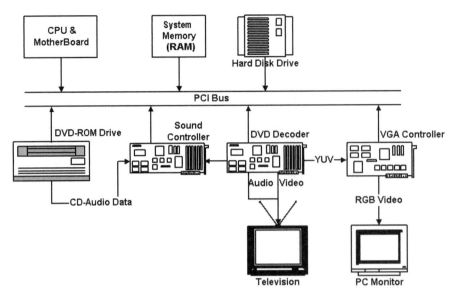

Figure 2.16   DVD-ROM Enabled Personal Computer Diagram

DVD-Audio

DVD-Audio is designed to replace CD-Audio as the primary prerecorded music format. Like DVD-Video, DVD-Audio is built on the foundation of DVD-ROM. So a DVD-Audio disc is actually a DVD-ROM that includes a zone of material supported by the DVD-Audio specification, and may or may not also contain a zone of DVD-Video material. These zones are held in the Audio_TS and Video_TS directories on the DVD disc.

DVD-Audio incorporates many DVD-Video navigational and architectural features, but it also includes several new interactive and playback features, such as still graphics slide shows. It also supports higher audio fidelity and more flexible multi-channel playback options than DVD-Video. Thus, while the two formats are closely related, DVD-Audio extends DVD-Video to create a truly distinct product tailored for audio-centric applications.

DVD-Audio Features

In developing the DVD-Audio format, the DVD Forum began with a specific set of desired features. The most important of these were:

- High Quality Audio — DVD-Audio is designed to support the very highest quality audio possible.

- Multi-Channel Audio — DVD-Audio is designed to permit extensive multi-channel capabilities, and recognizes that multi-channel programs might be played back in venues where only stereo monitoring is available.

- Additional data — DVD-Audio is designed to support synchronized text data, still images and video.

- Navigation — DVD-Audio is designed to support navigation similar to the DVD-Video format.

- Simple Interface — DVD-Audio is designed to support a simple CD player-like interface for playback settings.

- DVD-Video Compatibility — DVD-Audio is designed to be broadly compatible with DVD-Video and permits utilization of DVD-Video features, where appropriate.

one or more of several different players. The primary distinction between different players is the availability of a video display device. For a new audio format, it is essential to support playback without a video display, such as in a car, or with a portable player.

The DVD Forum defined five player types that might possibly be used to play back content from a disc in DVD-Audio format. These include:

- A "simple" Audio-only player that has no video output, and navigates the disc linearly using a list of tracks similar to the Table of Contents on a CD.

- A "smart" Audio-only player that gives the user more choices of how to navigate the material on the disc, and may include an LCD display to show song titles and other textual information such as lyrics, but does not include a video display.

- An "Audio-with-Video" player that supports navigational choice and includes video outputs to support multimedia, including visual menus, album artwork, "slide show" graphics and motion video.

- A "Universal" player that offers the same audio and multimedia support as the Audio-with-Video DVD-Audio player, but also plays DVD-Video discs.

- A DVD-Video player, which could be used to play optional video content that has been included on a DVD-Audio disc. Note that DVD-Video players will not be able to play the content stored in the DVD-Audio zone on the disc.

Figure 2.17 illustrates the type of DVD discs that most common DVD player types (DVD-Audio, Universal DVD, DVD-Video, and DVD-ROM) can accept. At the time this book was published most DVD-ROM enabled personal computers can't play DVD-Audio discs since neither Microsoft nor Apple has released DVD-Audio drivers for their consumer operating systems.

Most industry experts agree that the most common type of DVD-Audio players will be the "Audio-Only" and "Universal" player described above. A summary of the major features of DVD-Audio is shown in Table 2.4.

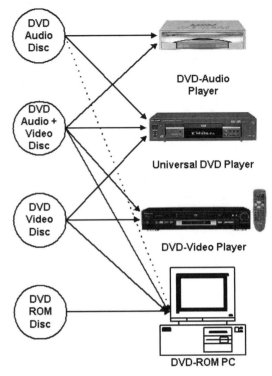

Figure 2.17   DVD-Audio Player and DVD Disc Type Matrix

Table 2.4	DVD-Audio Feature Chart	
DVD-Audio Parameter	Audio Objects	Video Objects
Coding Mode	LPCM or MLP	LPCM or Dolby Digital
Sampling frequency (kHz)	44.1/48/88.2/96/176.4/192	48/96
Bits per Sample	16/20/24	16/20/24
Maximum # of Channels	6 (up to 96 kHz) or 2 (176.4/192 kHz)	8
Maximum Bit Rate	9.6 Mbps	6.144 Mbps

DVD-Audio Formats

DVD-Audio's primary media content is audio so the specification attempts to deliver the highest possible audio fidelity, and thus focuses primarily on uncompressed PCM audio. PCM audio may be stored in either of two forms: linear (LPCM) or "packed" using MLP.

DVD-Audio Players are required to support both LPCM and MLP audio in either stereo, or multi-channel configurations. DVD-Audio Players may also, at the manufacturer's discretion, support optional audio formats such as Dolby Digital, or DTS. A DVD-Audio disc may offer up to two audio streams in any given program. The first stream is required to be PCM (stereo or multi-channel), while the second stream may be one of the optional audio types. It is likely that Universal players will support LPCM, MLP, Dolby Digital and DTS, as these will be commonly used for both DVD-Audio and DVD-Video titles.

DVD-Audio's PCM support covers two "families" of sample-rates. One family is based on the 44.1 kHz rate of CD-Audio, and also includes frequency multiples of 88.2 kHz and 176.4

DVD-Audio's maximum data-rate that can be used for audio is 9.6 Megabits per second. This places limits on the total data bandwidth available to spread among the channels. Six channels of 20-bit audio at either 88.2 kHz or 96 kHz, for instance, would substantially exceed the format's data-rate. The specification offers two strategies for dealing with this bandwidth limitation. One is MLP, and the other is called mixed resolutions.

Mixed resolutions allow the producer to prioritize the allocation of bits among channels in a given audio track. Each channel is assigned to one of two "Channel Groups," with the resolution of Group 1 always equal to or better than that of Group 2. Within a given track, the sample-rates used for all channels in both groups must be from the same family. Assignment of channels to groups, and selection of attributes within each group, may be changed on a track-by-track basis. To regularize the use of mixed resolutions among channels, most—but not all—of the reasonably foreseeable possibilities for varying the resolution of up to six channels are defined in the DVD-Audio format's 21 supported channel configurations.

As shown in Table 2.5, DVD-Audio is capable of delivering longer playing times than CD-Audio's 74 minutes. But even with DVD-Audio's greater data rate and data capacity, full support for high-fidelity surround sound (six channels of 24-bit/96 kHz audio, for instance) would exceed the format's maximum bit-rate and quickly use up the available storage. To address this issue, the DVD Forum adopted the MLP compression system. Because it is a completely Lossless system, a decoded MLP datastream is bit-for-bit identical to the pre-encoded PCM source stream. Table 2.5 assumes an average compression ratio from the MLP codec.

MLP permits substantial reduction in the bandwidth required to store high-quality multi-channel PCM audio. The efficiency of the algorithm varies with the program content, but in many cases MLP has reliably achieved a 45% reduction in bandwidth requirements. This allows a DVD-5 disc to be used for presentation of up to 74 minutes of audio content using six channels of 24-bit, 96 kHz audio. DVD-Audio discs are not required to use MLP, but decoding capability for MLP is mandated for all DVD-Audio players.

To ensure that a DVD-Audio disc will always play, regardless of the available monitoring configuration, the DVD Forum defined how a player should present multi-channel programs in situations where only stereo playback is available. Many programs mixed for surround presentation will not sound correctly balanced in stereo. Thus DVD-Audio allows both stereo and multi-channel mixes of the same music to be delivered on one disc. Additionally the DVD-Audio specification requires that all players support an approach called "SMART Content" (System Managed Audio Resource Technique).

Table 2.5	Sample Playback Times for Various DVD-Audio Configurations				
Audio Combination	Configuration	Single layer PCM	Dual layer PCM	Single layer MLP	Dual layer MLP
2 channels	48kHz, 24bits, 2ch	258 min	469 min	344 min	622 min
2 channels	192kHz, 24bits, 2ch	64 min	117 min	86 min	155 min
6 channels	96kHz, 24bits, 6ch	43 min	78 min	74 min	133 min
5 channels (2 groups)	96kHz, 24 bits, 3ch + 48kHz, 24 bits, 2ch	64 min	116 min	111 min	201 min

SMART uses a set of "coefficients" defining the relative level, panning and phase that will be applied to each channel of a multi-channel mix if it is combined into stereo. A SMART "downmix" will only be played if a discrete 2-channel mix of a given program has not been included on the disc. This provides a simple method to control the sound of the music in cases where the multi-channel mix is downmixed by the player.

While audio playback is at the heart of DVD-Audio, the format is also intended to offer a playback platform for the kinds of value-added multimedia features that have proven difficult to deliver to the mass market on formats such as CD-ROM and Enhanced CD. These features include graphical accompaniment for the music, textual information about the music and the artist, and motion video such as music videos or interviews. The DVD-Audio specification supports the display of still pictures during audio playback, and offers a wide range of options as to when and how the pictures are shown. Still images in DVD-Audio are encoded in MPEG-2. The basic graphical unit is an ASV (Audio Still Video), composed of an MPEG encoded still image; a subpicture overlay (SPU), and Highlight Information (HLI). The subpicture and highlight layers are optional.

ASVs are grouped into sets of graphics referred to as ASVUs (Audio Still Video Units), each of which may contain up to 99 ASVs (individual images). While the data size of an individual ASV may vary greatly, typical ASVs may be expected to average about 100 Kbytes. The total size of an ASVU may not exceed 2 Mbytes, which is the size of the buffer that player manufacturers are required to provide to allow ASVUs to be preloaded into player memory, so you should plan on having about 20 ASVs per ASVU. This preloading process ensures that players will not interrupt audio playback in order to read graphical data from the disc. This will allow the listener to browse a series of still graphics without affecting the currently playing song. For each ASVU, the producer defines a playback mode that determines the order and duration of graphical display. "Browseable" graphics have a defined minimum and maximum on-screen duration, but allow the user to skip forward through the set of images by using the remote control. "Slideshow" graphics, on the other hand, are displayed for a predetermined amount of time.

Within each of these modes the order in which the images is displayed is defined as "sequential", "random," or "shuffle". The DVD-Audio format supports a variety of start and end effects (wipes and dissolves) as transitions between images. The specification also allows the highlights within a given ASV to change over time. This is useful for content such as song lists, lyrics or libretto. Links allowing listeners to navigate to different parts of a song by clicking on lyrics are expected to be a common feature of DVD-Audio titles.

The DVD-Audio specification provides for storage of textual information on disc, though

name. It may also include optional information such as the name(s) of the artist and composer. Up to 64 Kb of data may be included for each language unit.

Real Time Text is stored on disc as part of the audio stream, and may be synchronized to audio playback. Ideal for lyrics and libretto, Real Time Text may also be used for context-dependent commentary such as running liner notes. The extent to which a given player supports Real Time Text or Audio Text Data is up to the hardware manufacturer.

Video on DVD-Audio

DVD-Audio's support for video is similar to that of DVD-Video, using VOBs comprised of MPEG-2 video plus audio and optional subtitles. However, some advanced features that are supported in DVD-Video, such as parental control and complex interactivity, are not supported in all DVD-Audio settings.

DVD-Audio includes a feature called the SAMG (Simple Audio Manager). Containing a list of up to 314 tracks, it serves the same function as the table of contents on a CD-Audio disc. Simple Audio-only players look at the SAMG to find the information they need for linear, track-based navigation of the disc. "Smart" Audio-only players, Audio-with-Video players and Universal players all support more sophisticated navigation than do simple Audio-only players. The directory information these players need is found in the AMG (Audio Manager). Smart Audio-only players use a section of AMG designated as AOTT, while Audio-with-Video players and Universal players use the AVTT section. Simple Audio-only players, meanwhile, ignore AMG completely.

DVD-Audio titles include two domains: AMG and Audio Title (ATT). The presentation data referenced from AMG is contained in a VOBS. The presentation data referenced from ATT is contained in one or more Audio Object Sets (AOBS). Each AOBS is comprised of some number of Audio Objects (AOBs). AOBs are made up of one or more tracks of audio, optionally accompanied by still images and/or Real Time Text.

DVD-Audio players that read AMG are able to take advantage of DVD-Audio's capacity to organize material hierarchically. This logical hierarchy exists in parallel to the format's data structure. It is based on five different levels: album, group, title, track and index. Each side of a DVD-Audio disc contains one album. Each album may contain up to nine groups, essentially a play list specifying the playback order of a number of titles. While any title may contain up to 99 tracks, there may be no more than 99 tracks total within a single group.

As on a CD, a track may be thought of as a single audio program. Audio attributes such as channel configuration, sample-rate, and word-length may be changed on track boundaries. An index is a reference point to a portion of an audio track, and there may be up to 99 indices within a single track. Because a group is simply a play list, more than one group may reference an individual track. On an album with twenty audio tracks, for instance, one group might be a sequence of all the songs, another could be a play list of just acoustic numbers, and a third might be a play list of just dance tracks. Groups thus allow up to nine different listening experiences drawn from one underlying set of material.

DVD-Audio discs are required to include three different content directories to facilitate navigation on different types of players. Simple Audio-only players use SAMG. SMART Audio-only players use AMG/AOTT. Players with a video output use AMG/AVTT. In players that use AVTT, navigation is supported via a visual menu like those used in DVD-Video. AOTT machines can't use visual menus, but the underlying method of enabling navigation is the same. As with DVD-Video players, navigation of the content referenced in both AVTT and AOTT is based on program-chains that are instructions to tell the player what to play and when to play it.

The DVD-Audio specification includes a set of Navigation Commands, as well as General and System parameters that are stored in player memory. As with DVD-Video, the commands are broken into various categories (Link, Jump, GoTo, SetSystem, Set and Compare), but the navigation commands supported in DVD-Audio are a subset of the DVD-Video set. The availability of nine groups allows navigation that is far more varied than that of CD-Audio, but the possibilities are more limited than in DVD-Video.

Among the most important navigational constraints in DVD-Audio are those relating to movement within a Group. A user may enter a Group at any point by selecting a specific track. But once playback has started within a given Group, that group will continue playing in order through to the end, unless the user exits playback by using the Menu or Group button on the remote to go to the album's main menu. The specification makes no provision for linking directly from a given Group to content outside that Group.

One important aspect of DVD-Audio Groups is that they may include audio tracks drawn from AOBS, as well as Video Title Sets (VTS) from a disc's optional Video zone. A VTS on a DVD-Audio disc is similar to a VTS on a DVD-Video disc, but there are a number of important distinctions in the video capabilities of the two formats. First, video title sets on a DVD-Audio disc do not include an individual menu (VTSM); the only menu in the Video zone on a DVD-Audio disc is the VMGM.

Second, the DVD-Audio specification requires that every audio program include a PCM stream, even content in the DVD-Video zone of the disc if they are to be played on Audio Only DVD-Audio Player (AOTT). If the DVD-Video soundtrack is not intended for playback on Audio-only players, a PCM stream is not required.

Like DVD-Video menus, DVD-Audio menus may use motion video backgrounds. The only domain on a DVD-Audio disc from which motion video is never referenced is ATT.

Therefore video may be used in the AMG menu (AMGM), the VMG menu, or a Video Title. The domain in which the DVD-Audio specification is most restrictive with video is VTS. Also, DVD-Audio does not support pre-commands or post-commands, as well as the use of dummy PGCs that are used to transition between domains in DVD-Video titles. Thus video title sets on DVD-Audio discs are less capable of complex interactivity than those on DVD-Video discs.

DVD-R

...substance is spin-coated onto a clear polycarbonate substrate that forms one side of the "body" of a complete DVD-R disc. The substrate is injection molded, and has a "pre-groove" spiral track formed onto its surface. This "pre-groove" is used by a DVD-R drive to guide the recording laser beam during the writing process, and also contains recorded information after writing is completed. A thin layer of metal is then sputtered onto the recording layer so that a reading laser can be reflected off the disc during playback. A protective layer is then applied to the metal surface, which prepares the side for bonding into a complete DVD-R disc.

These steps are done for each side of a disc that is required for recording. If only a single recording side is required, the opposite side can contain a label or some other visible information such as pit art. If both sides are needed for recording, then two recordable sides can be bonded together. In this case each side must be read directly (by flipping over the disc) as dual layer technology is currently not supported for DVD-R discs.

The recording action takes place by momentarily exposing the recording layer to a high power (approximately 10 milliwatt) laser beam that is tightly focused onto its surface. As the dye polymer is heated, it is permanently altered such that microscopic marks are formed in the pre-groove. These recorded marks differ in length depending on how long the write laser is turned on and off, which is how information is stored on the disc. The light sensitivity of the recording layer has been tuned to an appropriate wavelength of light so that exposure to ambient light or playback lasers will not damage the recorded information.

Using the first generation Pioneer drive (DVR-S101) a full capacity 3.68 GByte disc can be written in approximately 50 minutes in a disc-at-once recording, regardless of the data that will be contained. Using the second generation Pioneer drive (DVR-S201) a full capacity 4.37 GByte disc can be written in approximately one hour. Using the third generation Pioneer drive (DVR-A03) a full capacity 4.37 GByte disc can be written in approximately 30 minutes. Recorded DVD-R discs support "UDF Bridge" file system.

DVD-R discs can be played on almost all DVD-Video players, as well as the vast majority of personal computers equipped with a DVD-ROM drive. There are a number of older DVD-Video players that will not recognize a DVD-R disc when it is inserted into the player. Newer

DVD-Video players have better DVD-R compatibility, but there are still some players on the market today that can't reliably read DVD-R discs. There is no fundamental requirement for a DVD-Video player to support the playback of any discs other than those in the DVD-Video format. Recently the DVD Forum has undertaken a new initiative called DVD Multi-Read, which is designed to encourage player manufacturers to design their hardware so that it will read all CD and DVD optical disc formats. Player that comply with the DVD Multi-Read initiative will be able to display a logo which will help consumers to identify which players can read all DVD formats.

There are three fundamental applications for DVD-R: Testing and development, Distribution, and Storage and archival.

Testing and Development   Many DVD applications utilize replicated read-only discs that are mass-produced and distributed to a large number of users. Preparation of the content to be published can be a complex and time consuming process that must be completed accurately to avoid errors or functional defects. Mastering and set-up efforts required for replication of a DVD disc range from $1,000 for DVD-5 discs to $4,000 for DVD-9 discs. Thus DVD-R provides a more cost effective method of testing content prior to mass production. A single low cost disc can be quickly written and tested in a DVD-Video player or DVD-ROM enabled personal computer. While it is not possible to create a dual layer DVD-R at this time, many developers simply split their DVD titles into two sections in order to test the entire title on two DVD-R discs.

Tips, Tricks & Techniques
DVD-Video and DVD-ROM title developers own most of the DVD-R recorders sold to date. DVD-R offers a convenient, and inexpensive method of testing DVD titles prior to the disc replication process. Making a DVD-R "check-disc" will save you time and money, so make sure you have a DVD-R writer as part of your DVD development equipment. You will also need to make sure that you have at least one DVD-Video player that can correctly read both 3.68 and 4.37 GB DVD-R discs. I have found Pioneer DVD-Video players to offer the highest level of DVD-R playback compatibility, with Sony players running a close second.

Distribution   DVD-R's low-cost media and relatively portable recording equipment can aid small-scale distribution of DVD content. DVD mastering and replication expenses can be prohibitive when only a single disc or very small quantity is required. DVD-R allows discs to be recorded at the desktop level, which can result in very quick turnaround and significantly lower cost. Some users may not be comfortable with sending sensitive data files or other work in progress to an outside facility for replication, so the ability to maintain continuous in-house control of this information can be crucial. This is particularly true with classified data maintained by Government agencies. Complete confidentiality is afforded by DVD-R because it can be maintained as a completely in-house process.

Storage and Archival   DVD-R media provides archival lifetimes equal to or better than CD-R, which has been calculated to be 100 years. Thus, DVD-R is suitable for long-term archival of information that can be stored digitally. This includes image data, film and video archives, or any other media that need to be retrieved more easily by users. DVD-R's high capacity makes it especially suitable for storing large files that do not fit onto a single CD-R volume, thus creating new opportunities for inexpensive storage of these assets. Since DVD discs are dimensionally identical to the CD family of discs, they have the advantage of being compatible with existing CD-based jukebox and changer mechanisms. This allows automated retrieval of recorded DVD-R volumes in networked environments, with a seven-fold increase in storage

Don't use CD-ROM jewel cases as these have a slightly different spindle design that will not hold the DVD-R disc correctly. Store your jewel cases in a cool, dry environment if possible. Exposure to high temperature could warp the disc and make it unusable. If you follow these simple tips your DVD-R discs will last longer than your DVD-ROM reader.

In 1998 Pioneer released the DVR-S101 external SCSI-2 DVD-R device that is capable of storing up to 3.68 GBytes of data on a single layer, single sided DVD-R disc. The unit was available for a retail price of $17,000. Blank DVD-R discs were originally priced at $50 per disc. In 1999 Pioneer released the DVR-S201 external SCSI-2 DVD-R device that is capable of storing up to 4.37 GBytes of data on a single layer, single sided DVD-R disc. The unit was available for a retail price of $5,400. Blank DVD-R discs were then priced at $35 per disc. In early 2001 Pioneer released the DVR-A03 (an OEM product) and the DVR-103 (an after market product) internal IDE DVD-R and DVD-RW device that is capable of storing up to 4.37 GBytes of data on a single layer, single side DVD-R or DVD-RW disc. The unit is currently available for a retail price of less than $1,000 and blank discs are priced below $10 per disc.

DVD-R Media Types

In early 2001 a second type of DVD-R media was released, called DVD-R for General. The original DVD-R media was renamed DVD-R for Authoring. The two types of DVD-R media have the same storage capacities, and in general work in the same DVD-Video players and DVD-ROM PC drives.

The most significant technical difference between the two types of media is the wavelength of the laser used to record data on the disc. The main reason that the DVD-R for General format was introduced is for copy protection. DVD-R for General media is designed in a way that prevents a bit for bit copy of data from a CSS encrypted DVD-Video title onto a blank

DVD-R for General disc. Additionally the DVD-R for Authoring media has been enhanced through the addition of a new Cutting Master Format that will allow DVD-R for Authoring media to be used by DVD replication facilities for mastering. Thus DVD-R for Authoring media will become an acceptable alternative to DLT tape for delivering the master disc image to a DVD replication facility. A portion of the lead-in area of a DVD-R for Authoring disc is used to store the Disc Description Protocol (DDP) data required by disc replication facilities.

DVD-R for General discs are recorded using a 650 nm laser, while DVD-R for Authoring discs are recorded using a 635 nm laser. Essentially this means that only certain types of DVD-R drives can be used to record each DVD-R media type. The Pioneer DVR-S101 and DVR-S201 DVD-R drives must be used to record DVD-R for Authoring Media. The Pioneer DVR-A03, DVR-103 drives and the DVR-2000 set top recorder must be used to record DVD-R for General Media.

DVD-RAM

DVD-RAM is a high-capacity, high-performance optical disc that allows data to be read, written and erased. It is designed to work exactly like other writeable removable media such as floppy or Zip disks. DVD-RAM allows users to copy and delete files, and run programs. DVD-RAM offers all of the benefits of DVD, including high capacity, compatibility with CD formats, and enhanced rewriteability. Panasonic and Toshiba released the first DVD-RAM drive in 1998, and a number of additional companies have released both DVD-RAM computer and home entertainment products in the last several years. A sample DVD-RAM drive and media are shown in Figure 2.18.

With capacities of 2.40 GBytes to 8.75 GBytes per disk, DVD-RAM offers up to eight times the storage of a rewriteable CD. DVD-RAM is cheaper than a conventional magneto-optical disc drive; at less than one penny per megabyte it is the one of the most economical rewriteable mediums available today. DVD-RAM drives can read all of the CD and DVD formats including CD-ROM, CD-Audio, CD-R, CD-RW, DVD-ROM, DVD-R, and DVD-RW, making it an ideal choice for high-density data storage and exchange.

DVD-RAM drives use phase-change technology in which a laser heats the inner surface of the disc to magnetically charge it. This allows the data to be rewritten hundreds of thousands of times. A "wobble-land-groove" format, shown in Figure 2.19, provides clocking data, with marks written on both the grooves and the lands between grooves. The grooves and pre-embossed sector headers are molded into the disc during manufacturing. The DVD-RAM wobble-land-groove format or track structure makes DVD-RAM technology reliable, and the constant linear velocity format provides high access speed and capacity.

DVD-RAM discs consist of double layers of metallic film embedded in hard plastic. The drive motor constantly changes the disc's rotational speed to compensate for the location of data on the disc. A laser uses light of varying intensities to write and erase data. The metallic layers in the disc are made of a crystalline material that reflects light. To write data, the laser heats a metallic layer to 900 to 1,300 degrees

DVD-RAM Drive

DVD-RAM Media

drives. There are two types of cartridges: type 1 is sealed and type 2 allows the disc to be removed. The transfer rate for DVD-RAM is determined by the media specification. The 2.40 GBytes disc has a 1,385KB/sec. transfer rate, and the 4.37 GByte disc will have a 2,770KB/sec. transfer rate. Access times will also evolve with an increase in disc rotational speed, reducing drive latency. Further reductions in access time will come from mechanical improvements, a more robust servo technology and mass reductions in the optical pickup.

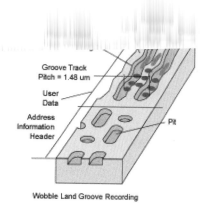

Figure 2.19   DVD-RAM Wobble Land Groove Format

DVD-RAM is designed to meet the requirements of mass commercial and consumer audiences, differing from the other writeable DVD standards in several ways. First, it provides random access rewriteability, like a floppy disc drive, making it suited for use and re-use by consumers. The low cost of both the drive and media make it a good choice for a wide audience of users, even those that are value-conscious. DVD-RAM drive shipments began in 1998, and more than 100,000 units were shipped that year.

DVD-RAM is designed to playback all DVD-ROM applications and is intended for use in desktop storage, data exchange, backup and archiving applications. Because of the wide variety of suitable applications, a DVD-RAM drive could be used as a viable replacement to do the job of several other devices, such as CD-ROM, CD-R, optical disc, tape, removable hard drive and floppy drive storage. DVD-RAM is an excellent choice for backup and archiving. At less than a penny per megabyte, cartridges are extremely inexpensive. Given the well-established durability of optical media, they are also far more reliable than tape, the only cost-competitive alternative. Since cartridges can be stored anywhere in a home or business environment, adding to archives or retrieving files from backup is infinitely easier than doing so from tape.

With their high capacity and rewriteability, DVD-RAM discs have excellent potential for many markets, such as education and entertainment. They also can be used for personal multimedia publishing, in applications such as presentations, sales tools, training and corporate communications. Future set-top box applications will give users the capacity and bandwidth to download or record their favorite movies. Research firm Disk/Trend expects traditional magneto-optical drives to be displaced by DVD-RAM drives after 1999, and DVD-RAM to begin its run as the dominant product in 1999. Disk/Trend predicts that DVD-RAM will remain the dominant DVD rewriteable format due to its current market predominance, with major growth beginning in 2000. It is difficult to say what the future holds for DVD-RAM. There are so many options for consumers who need recordable storage, including CD-R, CD-RW, Zip, Jazz, DVD-R, DVD-RAM, DVD-RW and DVD+RW to name a few. For the next few years DVD-RAM will compete directly with CD-R and CD-RW, which are extremely popular with consumers due to their low cost and almost universal playback compatibility.

DVD-RW

DVD-RW is a Rewriteable medium that allows users to record, erase and re-record their own DVD discs. The DVD-RW format was added to the original five DVD formats (DVD-ROM, DVD-Video, DVD-Audio, DVD-R and DVD-RAM) several years after their initial release. Despite DVD-RW's late arrival it has been designed to merge with the previous DVD formats. As with DVD-R, DVD-RW's primary goal is to provide a user-recordable medium that is physically compatible with existing DVD-Video players and DVD-ROM enabled personal computer systems. DVD-RW discs can hold up to 4.37 GBytes bytes of data per side, and can be used to store video, audio or any other type of data. Pioneer is the current leader in developing DVD-RW products although several other companies have announced their intent to release DVD-RW products during the second half of 2001.

DVD-RW uses a phase change technology for reading, writing and erasing information. Phase change technology takes advantage of materials that exhibit different reflectivity characteristics in the crystalline and non-crystalline (amorphous) states. A 650-nanometer wavelength laser beam heats a phase change material to change it between a crystalline (reflective) and amorphous (non-reflective) state. The resulting difference between the reflectivity of the two states of the phase change material is how a player or drive can read the stored information. There are two distinct power levels used for writing and erasing data on a DVD-RW disc. The highest power level causes the surface of the phase change material to become less reflective, while a lower, or intermediate, power level will cause the material to become more reflective. Since the intermediate power level must be reached before the writing power, direct overwriting of the phase change media can be achieved. This is a critical advantage of phase change technology.

Phase change technology can achieve a relatively high disc reflectivity ratio, making it suitable for use with traditional DVD players or DVD-ROM drives. The DVD-RW specification requires a reflectivity ratio of 18% to 30%, which is identical to the DVD-ROM, DVD-Video and DVD-Audio disc specifications. Thus DVD-RW discs can in theory be played back on all

DVD players and DVD-ROM enabled personal computers. However in the real world there are some exceptions to achieving full compatibility between existing DVD playback equipment and DVD-RW discs. Some DVD players incorrectly detect that a DVD-RW disc is actually a manufactured dual layer (DVD-9) disc, causing the player to try to locate a second data layer which does not exist on DVD-RW discs. Another potential compatibility problem is that some players detect the disc type by reading an identification code that is present on all DVD media types. Since DVD-RW is a new format, some older players or ROM drives will not recognize the new DVD-RW identification code, and thus reject the disc. In most cases these problems can be corrected by having the DVD-ROM drive or DVD-Video player firm-

g the DVD-Video disc. CPRM also provides a mechanism for copying and subsequently protecting "copy-once" content. The major features of CPRM include:

- Media type identification that allows a player or ROM drive to recognize that the disc is DVD-RW media. If copy protected data has been recorded onto DVD-RW media then the player or ROM drive should refuse to play back the disc.

- A pre-embossed area on the DVD-RW disc will prevent copying of the decryption key information stored in the disc's control data zone in the lead-in area. This is to prevent bit-for-bit copying of protected content to a DVD-RW disc.

- DVD-RW media will have a unique serial number written in the Narrow Burst Cutting Area (NBCA). An authorized DVD-RW media manufacturer places a unique serial number on each disc. This serial number can be used in conjunction with other protective measures to allow copy protected content to be stored on a DVD-RW disc.

- A media block key is used to allow a "copy-once" content to be stored on DVD-RW media. The media block key provides an encryption element that allows a CPRM compliant recorder to re-encrypt content that allows one legal copy to be made. A CPRM compliant player will be required to play back the newly encrypted data stored on the DVD-RW disc.

DVD+RW

DVD+RW, which is not an "official" DVD format, has been designed to be compatible with existing DVD-ROM and DVD-Video formats. The DVD+RW format allows both Constant Angular Velocity (CAV) and Constant Linear Velocity (CLV) recording. In CAV recording the disc is rotated at a constant speed. In CLV recording the rotation speed of the disc is varied based on the position of the laser relative to the inner data ring. As the laser moves away from the center of the disc the rotation speed is slowed to maintain a constant write throughput rate. Due to the constant rotation speed of the disc, CAV recording allows for fast random access. Two other benefits of the DVD+RW format are the incorporation of defect management, especially designed for reliability of the data, and quick formatting, enabling instant use of blank discs. DVD+RW includes the following features:

- Single-sided disc has 4.37 Gb capacity

- Double-sided disc has 8.75 Gb capacity

- Uses a bare disc - no cartridge required

- 650 nm laser

- CLV and CAV recording

- Write speeds from 1x to 2.4×

- Defect management handled by the drive

- Quick formatting

- Uses same 8-16 Modulation and Reed-Solomon Error Correction Code as DVD-ROM

The recording layer of a DVD+RW disc is polycrystalline. When the DVD is recorded, a laser beam selectively heats areas of the phase-change material above the melting temperature (500-700°C), so all the atoms in this area can move rapidly in the liquid state. Then, when cooled sufficiently quickly, the random liquid state is frozen-in and a so-called amorphous state is obtained. If the phase-change layer is heated below the melting temperature but above the crystallization temperature (200°C) for a sufficient time, the atoms revert back to an ordered state, i.e. the crystalline state. The amorphous and crystalline states have different refractive indexes, and can therefore be optically distinguished.

In the DVD+RW system, the amorphous state has a lower reflectance than the crystalline state and, during read out, this produces a signal identical to that of a dual layer DVD-ROM disc. An important feature of the DVD+RW disc is its compatibility with existing DVD-Video and DVD-ROM drives. All physical parameters fit within the DVD-ROM specification. The reflectivity is in the same range as the dual-layer reflectivity specification of a read-only disc and the density is the same as for the single layer specification.

In summary there are three official recordable DVD formats (DVD-R, DVD-RAM and DVD-RW) and one unofficial recordable format (DVD+RW). Each of these formats has their own particular strengths and weaknesses, as shown in Table 2.6.

Table 2.6	Comparison of Writeable DVD formats			
Format	DVD-RAM	DVD-R	DVD-RW	DVD+RW
Availability	Now	Now	Now	Mid 2001
Description	Random access storage similar to floppy disk or CD+RW.	Write-once. Provides sequential write, similar to CD-R. No overwrite capability.	Limited sequential rewriteability.	Random access storage similar to floppy disk or CD+RW. CLV and CAV recording.

Table 2.6	Comparison of Writeable DVD formats (Continued)			
Format	DVD-RAM	DVD-R	DVD-RW	DVD+RW
Capacity/Side	4.37 GB/side	4.37 GB/side	4.37 GB/side	4.37 GB/side
# Of Rewrites	100,000	0	1,000	1,000
Write method	Wobble land groove	N/A	Wobble groove	Spiral groove with
			Real time video recording.	Real time video recording.

Super Audio CD

Philips and Sony have developed an alternative to DVD-Audio, called Super Audio CD that uses a different audio coding method, Direct Stream Digital (DSD) and the use of a hybrid disc format. This hybrid format combines a traditional 650 MB CD-Audio data layer with a 4.37 GB DVD data layer onto a single disc. SACD offers high quality, multi-channel audio, CD compatibility, copy protection and added features. The main features of SACD are:

- Up to 100kHz bandwidth

- 120 dB dynamic range

- Full quality for all channels

- Hybrid disc (CD and DVD)

- Watermarking and copy protection

- Text, graphics and video

DSD was chosen as the encoding format because it avoids using PCM, which is a high quality, but uncompressed format. Sony and Philips believe that DSD offers high quality audio with lossless compression, and is more future proof than PCM. Watermarking for copy protection uses pit signal processing (PSP) which known piracy processes can't copy. SACD also includes a visible watermark. The SACD specification is contained in the Scarlet Book. SACD discs use the same sector size, error correction, modulation, and file system (UDF plus ISO 9660) as DVD discs.

The hybrid CD/DVD disc format allows the same disc to play on existing audio players as well as Super Audio CD players. This is possible by molding the CD-Audio pits on the outside of the otherwise blank DVD substrate and using a semi-reflective layer for the DVD, thus allowing the CD-Audio layer to be read by a conventional CD player.

This means that SACD discs can be played on existing CD players, easing consumer fears of obsolescence. However these DVD/CD hybrid discs are more difficult and therefore more expensive to manufacture than CDs. Since it's initial product launch in 2000 over 500 titles have been published in the SACD format. Suggested retail prices for most single album SACD titles are $19.98, making them about 33% more expensive than CD-Audio titles. SACD players were priced around $5,000 at product launch, but have come down to about $500 when this book was published, in 2001.

It remains to be seen if the SACD format can compete effectively with the DVD-Audio formats. Some manufacturers will include both SACD and DVD-Audio playback features on their new models, offering a Universal player that supports DVD-Video, DVD-Audio and SACD. It is also possible that consumers will prefer DVD-Audio to SACD, or SACD over DVD-Audio, and thus the less popular format will be relegated to the lengthy list of new consumer home entertainment formats that never achieved mass-market status.

DVD PRODUCTION PROCESS

Figure 3.1 shows a diagram of the DVD production process. This process has three major phases, with eleven unique steps. The three major phases of DVD Production are Planning, Development and Fulfillment. While all three phases are important, the Planning phase is crucial to insuring the successful completion of a DVD project. Let's take a quick look at the three phases of the DVD production process shown below, and then we can focus on each of the individual steps in more detail.

For many projects different organizations, or company divisions, are responsible for each phase of the DVD production process. A common scenario is to have the content owner perform the Planning phase, a DVD Authoring Service Company handle the Development phase, and a Distribution Company take charge of the Fulfillment phase. With this division of responsibility it is very important that each step of the production process be completed in sequence, which isn't as easy as it may seem.

Planning

The goal of the Planning phase is to clearly define the requirements and objectives of a DVD project. This phase consists of three steps, Project Definition, Content Acquisition and Flow-chart & Design. At the end of the Planning phase you should have the following items.

- Schedule
- Budget

- Media Assets

- Flowchart

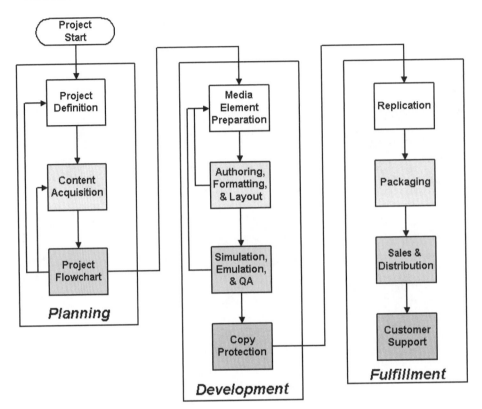

Figure 3.1   The DVD Production Process

One of the classic problems encountered by DVD title developers is to start the Development phase before completion of the Planning phase. This invariably leads to confusion and a great deal of wasted time, and money, on the project.

Tips, Tricks & Techniques
The old adage of "Don't put the cart before the horse" applies quite well to the DVD production process. On many projects I have been asked to start developing a title before the content owner signs off on the project flowchart. This is usually a prescription for disaster, as the content owner will change the project after I have finished authoring the title. The worst thing that can happen is for the content owner to add "just a few more minutes of video". Unless you have planned for this, adding another minute or two of video will mean going back to the start of the Development phase and re-encoding all the video to make room for the new content.

Development

Once the Planning phase has been completed the project can be moved into the Development phase. The goal of the Development phase is to generate a final version of the DVD title disc image. The steps in the development process are somewhat independent of the final delivery media, which can include recordable discs like CD-R and DVD-R, replicated discs like DVD-Video, and DVD-ROM, or even Internet delivery using a WebDVD. These steps include Media Element Preparation, Authoring, Formatting, Layout, Simulation, Emulation, and Copy Protection. At the end of the Development phase you should have the following items

Fulfillment

The final phase of DVD production is Fulfillment, which consists of Replication, Packaging, Sales & Distribution and Customer Support. The goal of the Fulfillment phase is to produce, sell and distribute the DVD title to the appropriate markets. For consumer titles this means getting the product onto the physical shelves of brick and mortar stores and the virtual shelves of on-line DVD retailers. For corporate, government or educational titles this means producing enough copies of the title to meet the client's requirements.

One of the most important steps in the Fulfillment phase is customer support. This ongoing support effort is required as long as the title is in use. Most DVD-Video titles require little or no customer support. However the addition of DVD-ROM or WebDVD content to a title requires a higher level of customer support than a traditional DVD-Video title. DVD-ROM and WebDVD content are designed for personal computers, which traditionally require more support than a set-top DVD player.

A Step-By-Step Guide to Producing a DVD

Now lets go into the details of the three phases and eleven steps of the DVD Production process. Throughout the following sections I will use *StarGaze* to illustrate various steps of the production process. *StarGaze* is not unique; it is a typical DVD-Video title with some DVD-ROM and WebDVD extras. However since I was responsible for all three phases of the production process it will serve as a good example.

Step 1: Project Definition

Long before I started developing DVD titles I worked as a system engineer on a variety of Department of Defense projects. These projects were usually quite complicated and involved the design and development of new signal processing equipment as well as custom application software. I learned several important lessons about project management during my years as a system engineer, and this experience has helped me in my more recent DVD production efforts. One of the most important lessons I learned was the need to have clear and concise goals before starting work on a new project.

The primary goal of the Project Definition step is to answer the following questions.

- What am I supposed to do?

- When am I supposed to be done?

- What resources can I use?

While these questions might seem somewhat simplistic, and at times the answers may be obvious, it is beneficial to write down the answers to each question at the start of a new DVD project.

What am I supposed to do?

Even the simplest DVD title has enough variables that it is necessary to write down some specific parameters about the project. At a minimum the information outlined in Table 3.1 needs to be defined for each DVD project.

Table 3.1	DVD Project Requirements List			
DVD Project Requirements Document				
Project Name:				
Client Name:		Client Phone:		
Client Fax:		Client E-Mail:		
Client Approval:		Approval Date:		
DVD Publishing Format(s)				
☐ DVD-Video	☐ DVD-ROM	☐ WebDVD	☐ DVD-Audio	☐ Other:
DVD Disc Type				
☐ DVD-5	☐ DVD-9	☐ DVD-10	☐ DVD-14	☐ DVD-18
☐ DVD-R	☐ DVD-RW	☐ CD-R	☐ DVD-RAM	☐ Other:
Copy Protection				
☐ CSS	☐ CGMS	☐ Macrovision ColorStripe	☐ Macrovision AGC	☐ Macrovision Both
Video Source				
☐ D1	☐ D2	☐ Digital Beta	☐ DVCPro	☐ BetaSP
☐ M2	☐ 1" Type C	☐ 3/4" Umatic	☐ SVHS	☐ Other:
Video Format				
☐ NTSC	☐ PAL	☐ Other:		
Video Aspect Ratio				
4:3	☐ Normal	☐ Pan & Scan	☐ Letterbox	

Table 3.1	DVD Project Requirements List (Continued)			
16:9	☐ Anamorphic	☐ Letterbox		
Other:	☐ Anamorphic	☐ Pan & Scan	☐ Letterbox	
Video Encoding				
☐ MPEG-2 CBR	☐ MPEG-2 VBR	☐ MPEG-2 HHR D1	☐ MPEG-1	
Track 2	☐ DD 2.0	☐ DD 5.1	☐ DTS	☐ Other
Track 3	☐ DD 2.0	☐ DD 5.1	☐ DTS	☐ Other
Track 4	☐ DD 2.0	☐ DD 5.1	☐ DTS	☐ Other
Track 5	☐ DD 2.0	☐ DD 5.1	☐ DTS	☐ Other
Track 6	☐ DD 2.0	☐ DD 5.1	☐ DTS	☐ Other
Track 7	☐ DD 2.0	☐ DD 5.1	☐ DTS	☐ Other
Track 8	☐ DD 2.0	☐ DD 5.1	☐ DTS	☐ Other

Audio Length (Minutes)

Track 1:	Track 2:	Track 3:	Track 4:	Track 5:
Track 6:	Track 7:	Track 8:		

Subpicture Streams (Language Code)

☐ 1	☐ 2	☐ 3	☐ 4	☐ 5	☐ 6	☐ 7	☐ 8	☐ 9	☐ 10
☐ 11	☐ 12	☐ 13	☐ 14	☐ 15	☐ 16	☐ 17	☐ 18	☐ 19	☐ 20
☐ 21	☐ 22	☐ 23	☐ 24	☐ 25	☐ 26	☐ 27	☐ 28	☐ 29	☐ 30
☐ 31	☐ 32								

Table 3.1		DVD Project Requirements List (Continued)							
Subpicture Streams Length (Minutes)									
1:	2:	3:	4:	5:	6:	7:	8:	9:	10:
11:	12:	13:	14:	15:	16:	17:	18:	19:	20:
21:	22:	23:	24:	25:	26:	27:	28:	29:	30:
31:	32:								
Menus									
☐ Title Menu		☐ Root Menu(s)		☐ Angle Menu		☐ Audio Menu		☐ Chapter Menu	
☐ Subpicture Menu		☐ Other Menu(s)							

Blank copies of the DVD Requirements List, along with all the other forms included in this book can be downloaded from http://www.dvdtoday.com.

Table 3.1 may be more complex than necessary for most DVD projects, but it does provide all of the critical information required in the development phase. One of the key items on Table 3.1 is the Client Approval line. I highly recommend you complete a form like this for every DVD project, and that you have your client sign it before you start the Development phase of the project. Even if your "client" is simply a different part of your organization you should still get the Approval block signed. Having a client approved DVD Project Requirements Document will help you negotiate cost or schedule impacts if, and when, there are changes to any of the design parameters. If you don't have your client approve this document you run the risk of having to accept changes to the design parameters without the benefit of additional time or funds to cover your increased efforts.

When am I supposed to be done?

Now that you and your client have agreed on what is to be done, the next step is to create a schedule for when the work will be completed. There are lots of great scheduling tools available for both the PC and the Mac. I have used both the Microsoft Project and Microsoft Visio programs to create detailed project schedules. DVD projects tend to be fairly complicated and usually involve more than one organization. To keep things on track it is a good idea to have a published schedule that each person working on the project has a copy of. Figure 3.2 shows a sample schedule for a typical DVD project.

This schedule is fairly typical for DVD-Video projects. As you can see from the schedule there is more time dedicated to the Planning and Fulfillment phases than to the Development phase. The actual development of a DVD-Video title does not take a long period of time if all the video, audio and subpicture elements already exist. Generally speaking it takes longer to design and create the various DVD menus and package artwork than it does to actually author the title. Naturally every DVD project is different, and in many cases the sample schedule shown in Figure 3.2 will be either too long or too short for a real world project.

As with the Project Requirements Document it is a good idea to have your client approve the Project Schedule once it has been created. This is particularly important if any of the tasks on the schedule are the responsibility of your client, such as Storyboard design. If for some reason one of these "client tasks" is not completed on time then you will be able to explain to your client that the entire project may be completed late since all these tasks are inter-related.

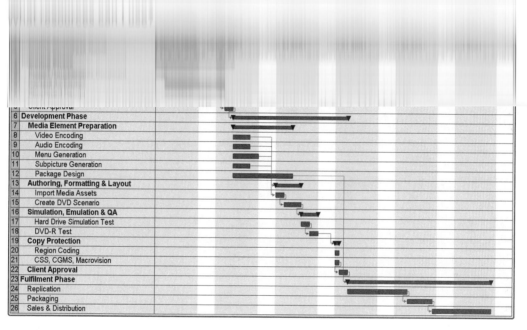

Figure 3.2   Sample DVD Project Schedule

The Project Requirements Document gives you a clear idea of what you are supposed to do, and the Project Schedule tells you when you have to be finished. The last, and sometimes most important question you need to address relates to the facilities, staff and funds you have available to complete the project. For many DVD production companies answering this question is a simple matter of scheduling internal resources so that the project can be completed on time. Thus a simple resource allocation step based on the Project Schedule may be all that is required.

Even in the largest DVD production facilities there can be contention for critical resources. Expensive items of equipment such as real-time MPEG-2 encoders, Dolby Digital or DTS workstations, DVD-R writers, and DVD-Video authoring workstations are often used around the clock, even if they are only used for short periods of time on any specific project. An effort must be made to ensure that the equipment and personnel will be available to complete the project on time. Many facilities develop a master schedule for all their major items of production equipment and assign specific dates and times for each production job that is "in-house". This can be done using a standard project scheduling tool, or even the old fashioned way with a whiteboard and colored markers. The techniques used to generate this master equipment schedule are not important. What is important is that equipment and personnel are assigned to complete the DVD project on time.

Some DVD production companies do not have everything they need in house to complete all aspects of developing a DVD title. It is fairly common to have third parties work on a DVD title in conjunction with a DVD production company. These third parties might perform specialty services such as Dolby Digital 5.1 or DTS encoding, subtitle and menu translations, or perhaps subpicture generation, which is the process of generating individual graphic elements from subtitle text. Regardless of the specific tasks assigned to third parties, an appropriate amount of time and money needs to be set aside to cover these outside services. It is a good idea to identify these outside services as separate tasks on the Project schedule so that they can be closely monitored. It is also a good idea to develop a budget for all outside services so you can track the actual expenditures against the plan for these out-of-pocket costs.

disc note:

Real World Example

StarGaze illustrates the various steps of the DVD Production process. Table 3.2 shows the Project Requirements for *StarGaze,* Figure 3.3 shows the Project Schedule and Table 3.3 shows the Project Budget. Keep in mind that each DVD project is different, thus the project requirements, schedule and budget will differ depending on the overall complexity of the project.

Table 3.2   StarGaze Project Requirements Document

DVD Project Requirements Document				
Project Name: StarGaze: Hubble's View of the Universe				
Client Name: Alpha DVD		Client Phone: 410-721-9460		
Client Fax: 410-721-9461		Client E-Mail: rlabarge@alphadvd.com		
Client Approval: Ralph LaBarge		Approval Date: April 1, 2000		
DVD Publishing Format(s)				
☑ DVD-Video	☑ DVD-ROM	☑ WebDVD	☐ DVD-Audio	☐ Other:
DVD Disc Type				
☑ DVD-5	☐ DVD-9	☐ DVD-10	☐ DVD-14	☐ DVD-18
☐ DVD-R	☐ DVD-RW	☐ CD-R	☐ DVD-14	☐ Other:
Copy Protection				
☐ CSS	☐ CGMS	☐ Macrovision ColorStripe	☐ Macrovision AGC	☐ Macrovision Both

Table 3.2	StarGaze Project Requirements Document (Continued)			
Video Source				
☐ D1	☐ D2	☐ Digital Beta	☐ DVCPro	☐ BetaSP
☐ M2	☐ 1" Type C	☐ 3/4" Umatic	☐ SVHS	☑ Other: Animation
Video Format				
☑ NTSC	☐ PAL	☐ Other:		
		D1		
Video Length (Minutes)				
Angle 1: 60 minutes	Angle 2:	Angle 3:	Angle 4:	Angle 5:
Angle 6:	Angle 7:	Angle 8:	Angle 9:	
Audio Source				
☐ DA-88	☐ DAT	☐ Video Source	☑ Other, 48 KHz, 24 bit LPCM Files	
Audio Track Format				
Track 1: Music	☐ DD 2.0	☑ DD 5.1	☐ DTS	☐ Other
Track 2: Music	☐ DD 2.0	☐ DD 5.1	☑ DTS	☐ Other
Track 3: Music	☑ DD 2.0	☐ DD 5.1	☐ DTS	☐ Other
Track 4: EN Narration	☑ DD 2.0	☐ DD 5.1	☐ DTS	☐ Other
Track 5: FR Narration	☑ DD 2.0	☐ DD 5.1	☐ DTS	☐ Other
Track 6: DE Narration	☑ DD 2.0	☐ DD 5.1	☐ DTS	☐ Other
Track 7: ES Narration	☑ DD 2.0	☐ DD 5.1	☐ DTS	☐ Other
Track 8	☐ DD 2.0	☐ DD 5.1	☐ DTS	☑ Other
Audio Length (Minutes)				
Track 1: 60 minutes	Track 2: 60 minutes	Track 3: 60 minutes	Track 4: 60 minutes	Track 5: 60 minutes
Track 6: 60 minutes	Track 7: 60 minutes	Track 8:		

Table 3.2 StarGaze Project Requirements Document (Continued)

Subpicture Streams (Language Code)

☑ 1: EN	☑ 2: FR	☑ 3: DE	☑ 4: ES	☑ 5: EN	☑ 6: FR	☑ 7: DE	☑ 8: ES	☐ 9	☐ 10
☐ 11	☐ 12	☐ 13	☐ 14	☐ 15	☐ 16	☐ 17	☐ 18	☐ 19	☐ 20
☐ 21	☐ 22	☐ 23	☐ 24	☐ 25	☐ 26	☐ 27	☐ 28	☐ 29	☐ 30
☐ 31	☐ 32								

Subpicture Streams Length (Minutes)

1: 60 min	2: 60 min	3: 60 min	4: 60 min	5: 60 min	6: 60 min	7: 60 min	8: 60 min	9:	10:
11:	12:	13:	14:	15:	16:	17:	18:	19:	20:
21:	22:	23:	24:	25:	26:	27:	28:	29:	30:
31:	32:								

Menus

☑ Title Menu (4)	☑ Root Menu(s) (4)	☐ Angle Menu	☑ Audio Menu (4)	☑ Chapter Menu (4)
☑ Subpicture Menu (4)	☑ Other Menu(s): Approximately 50 additional menus in four languages (EN, FR, DE, ES)			

Table 3.3 *StarGaze* Project Budget

Task Description	Man Hours	Hourly Rate	Equipment Hours	Equipment Amortization	Outside Service	Total
Project Planning Phase						
Project Requirements Document	8	$50				$400
Acquire Hubble Still Images	120	$50				$6,000
Acquire Music Rights	16	$50			$20,000	$20,800
Acquire Hubble Technical Data	80	$50				$4,000
Storyboard Design	40	$50				$2,000
Subtotal						$33,200
Development Phase						
Video Animation	40	$50	120	$240		$2,240
MPEG-2 Encoding	8	$50	120	$240		$640
Music Surround Mix					$3,000	$3,000
AC-3 Encode					$500	$500
DTS Encode					$500	$500

Table 3.3 *StarGaze* Project Budget (Continued)

Task Description	Man Hours	Hourly Rate	Equipment Hours	Equipment Amortization	Outside Service	Total
Script Generation	80	$50				$4,000
Script Translation					$4,500	$4,500
Narration Recording					$4,000	$4,000
Disc Label Design	8	$50				$400
Package Insert Design	8	$50				$400
Import Media Assets	8	$50	8	$80		$480
Create Scenario	40	$50	40	$400		$2,400
Hard Drive Simulation Test	24	$50	24	$240		$1,440
DVD-R Test	40	$50	8	$100		$2,100
Windows Screen Saver Program					$500	$500
Windows Install Program	20	$50				$1,000
Web Page Design	40	$50				$2,000
WebDVD Java Scripts	40	$50				$2,000
Subtotal						$47,020
Fulfillment Phase						
Check Disc Replication					$1,000	$1,000
Check Disc Approval	40	$50				$2,000
Package Art Printing (10,000)					$2,000	$2,000
Production Unit Replication					$15,000	$15,000
Production Unit Assembly					$5,000	$5,000
Subtotal						$25,000
Project Totals	956					$105,220

Note: Equipment amortization is based on a two year expected useful life for all hardware and software items.

Step 2: Content Acquisition

The purpose of the Content Acquisition step is self-evident. Before you can start working on a DVD project you need to get your hands on working copies of all the content. For most projects this step is fairly simple, your client gives you a professional video tape, such as Digital Beta or BetaSP with the video and audio content that will used on the title. For other projects this step may be more complex, particularly if a clean copy of the video and audio content does not exist. For all projects you need to make sure that the video and audio assets are delivered to you in a format that you can utilize. You will also need to make sure that all copyrights to the video and audio content have been cleared for use on your project.

Garbage-In, Garbage-Out

When developing DVD titles you should be mindful of the old adage, garbage-in, garbage-out. During the media acquisition phase you want to acquire the highest quality versions for each media element to be used in the DVD title. Since video elements can be stored on a variety of tape and computer formats it is sometimes difficult to know which format will provide the best quality version.

Some general guidelines for video element quality are:

- Digital tape is better than Analog tape. In general digital video tape formats such as D1, D5, Digital Betacam and DVCPro are better than analog video tape formats such as BetaSP, 1" Type C, or 3/4" Umatic.

- 1st Generation Analog is better than 2nd Generation Analog. If you only have analog tape formats available, then try to get your hands on tapes that are as close to the master tape as possible. Each time an analog tape is copied, there can be a slight degradation in the video quality, so the fewer "generations" your tape is away from the master the better.

- Computer generated video should stay in the computer. If any of your video elements have been generated by a computer, it is better to work with the uncompressed computer video files, such as AVI, MOV or OMF, than to output this video to digital or analog tape.

- Up-convert for convenience, not for quality. It is possible to convert a lower quality video format such as BetaSP to a higher quality format such as Digital Beta. Converting video from one format to another without any additional video post-production processes will not improve the quality, although it may make it easier to work with in your DVD production environment.

Audio elements come in a variety of formats; although the method of storing the data is less important than the sample frequency, sample depth, and the number of channels stored. Audio used on a DVD title in general must have a sample rate of 48,000 samples per second, with a sample depth of at least 16 bits. For DVD titles that will have stereo audio the most common method of storage is to include two synchronized audio tracks on the videotape. For DVD titles with surround sound audio the most common method of storage is on a digital multi-track audiotape format, such as a DA-88 with synchronous time code. Some general guidelines for audio element quality are:

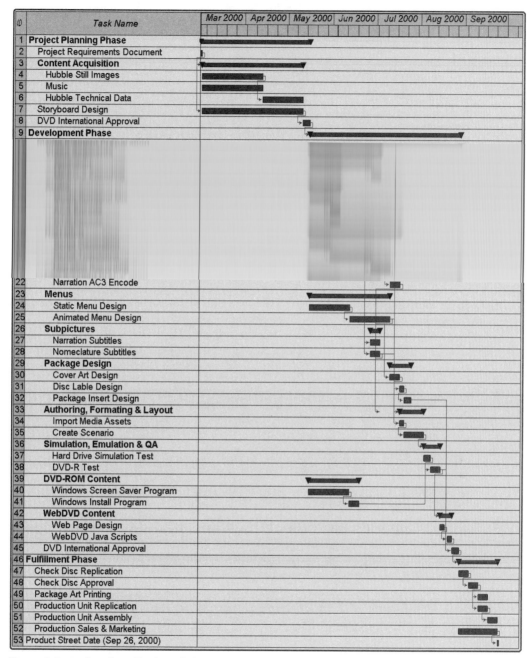

ID	Task Name	Mar 2000	Apr 2000	May 2000	Jun 2000	Jul 2000	Aug 2000	Sep 2000
1	**Project Planning Phase**							
2	Project Requirements Document							
3	**Content Acquisition**							
4	Hubble Still Images							
5	Music							
6	Hubble Technical Data							
7	Storyboard Design							
8	DVD International Approval							
9	**Development Phase**							
22	Narration AC3 Encode							
23	**Menus**							
24	Static Menu Design							
25	Animated Menu Design							
26	**Subpictures**							
27	Narration Subtitles							
28	Nomeclature Subtitles							
29	**Package Design**							
30	Cover Art Design							
31	Disc Lable Design							
32	Package Insert Design							
33	**Authoring, Formating & Layout**							
34	Import Media Assets							
35	Create Scenario							
36	**Simulation, Emulation & QA**							
37	Hard Drive Simulation Test							
38	DVD-R Test							
39	**DVD-ROM Content**							
40	Windows Screen Saver Program							
41	Windows Install Program							
42	**WebDVD Content**							
43	Web Page Design							
44	WebDVD Java Scripts							
45	DVD International Approval							
46	**Fulfillment Phase**							
47	Check Disc Replication							
48	Check Disc Approval							
49	Package Art Printing							
50	Production Unit Replication							
51	Production Unit Assembly							
52	Production Sales & Marketing							
53	Product Street Date (Sep 26, 2000)							

Figure 3.3   *StarGaze* Project Schedule

- Higher sample rates are better. Sample rates for audio can vary widely; from a 44.1 KHz rate used in Audio-CD productions to 192 KHz used for high end DVD-Audio production. In general the higher the sample rate, the better the audio quality will be.

- Higher bit depths are better. Typical bit depths used in DVD production are 16-bit, 20-bit and 24-bit. In general the higher the bit depth, the better the audio quality will be.

- Up-convert for convenience, not for quality. It is possible to take a lower quality audio format such as 16-bit, 44.1 KHz audio made for CD and convert it to a higher quality format such as 24-bit, 48 KHz audio. Converting audio from one format to another without any additional audio post-production processes will not improve the audio quality, however it may make it easier to work with in your DVD production environment.

Color Bars & Test Tones

Professional videotape formats are used to record high quality video and audio content. The start of professional videotapes typically includes a recording of video color bars and audio test tones, usually lasting for about 1 minute. Color bars and test tone data are used to calibrate the playback deck so that the video color, brightness, contrast and levels as well as the audio levels match the settings used on the recording deck. Video test equipment such as a Waveform Monitor and a Vectorscope are used to monitor the video output of the playback deck to insure that the various video signal parameters are set correctly. There are several important things to remember about color bars and test tones.

- If your source tapes do not include color bars and test tones you will not be able to set up the playback deck to the correct video and audio parameters. In this case the best you can do is to set up your deck to default parameters and hope that these settings are close to where they should be. Ideally all of your source tapes should include color bars and test tones to insure the highest quality throughout the production process.

- You need to "calibrate" the video playback deck using the color bars and test tones on each unique source tape. You can't assume different source tapes, even if they came from the same client or post-production facility will have the same video and audio characteristics. Calibrating your playback deck each time a new tape is inserted will insure the highest possible video and audio quality. To do this you need to use a Vectorscope and a Waveform Monitor, which are standard items of video calibration equipment. The Vectorscope allows you to correctly set up the playback decks color phase, and the Waveform Monitor lets you correctly configure the playback decks signal levels.

- Using color bars and test tones to calibrate your playback deck assumes the facility that created the source tape used the same color bars and test tones to calibrate their recording deck. In some cases post-production facilities will record video and audio content onto a tape that has no color bars or test tones, or even worse has color bars and test tones that don't match the recorded content. If you suspect that the color bars and test tones on the tape don't match the recorded content, you should request your client or post-production facility create a new tape.

Time Code

In addition to color bars and test tones all professional videotapes should include synchronous time code. Time code data is recorded on a separate time code track, an unused audio track, or in the vertical blanking area of the video signal. The vast majority of professional videotapes will have time code in the SMPTE (Society of Motion Picture & Television Engineers) format. There are two basic techniques used to record SMPTE time code onto professional videotape:

Linear Time Code (LTC) and Vertical Interval Time Code (VITC). LTC is recorded in an unused audio channel or a dedicated time code channel, while VITC is recorded in the vertical blanking area of the video signal. There are six different formats of SMPTE time code in use today including 30 FPS (also called 30 Non-Drop), 30 FPS Drop Frame, 29.97 FPS (also called 29.97 FPS Non-Drop), 29.97 FPS Drop Frame, 25 FPS (also called EBU) and 24 FPS.

- 29.97 Non-Drop Frame. This format is commonly used with NTSC color video. NTSC video has an actual frame rate of 29.97 frames per second. This means that an hour of video frames (108,000 frames) will take slightly longer than 1 hour of real time to play

frame has been skipped.

- 30 FPS Non-Drop Frame. The 30 FPS Non-Drop format is based on a frame rate of 30 frames/second, and is the original format developed by SMPTE for monochrome video. 30 FPS Non-Drop Frame is most commonly used in audio only applications.

- 30 FPS Drop Frame. The 30 FPS Drop Frame format is typically used for film content that is being converted for broadcast usage

- 25 FPS. This format is used with the European PAL video standard, which runs at 25 frames per second. This format is also called the EBU (European Broadcast Union) format because broadcast television stations throughout Europe use it.

- 24 FPS. This format is used exclusively for film applications. Film is typically photographed and projected at a frame rate of 24 frames per second, so this SMPTE time code format is useful when working with content that originated on film.

Typically professional video source tapes used in DVD production will have 29.97 non-drop frame time code, although occasionally they may contain 29.97 drop-frame time code. The specific time code format is less important than a consistent use of time code formats throughout a project. One common mistake in DVD production is trying to use video and audio content with different time code formats. For example if you tried to create a DVD title using video elements with 29.97 non-drop frame time code and audio elements with 29.97 drop frame time code, you will end up with the video and audio out of synchronization. If the content is fairly short in length you may never notice a problem. However you will experience a synchronization problem that is quite noticeable for content that is more than a few minutes in length.

Copyrights

An important issue during the media acquisition step is to make sure that you have properly cleared copyrights for all video, audio, graphics and textual content that will be used in the

DVD title. This is critically important if you will be developing a title that will eventually be sold, or even given away, to the public. The subject of copyright law and licensing is far too broad to be covered in this book, so refer to a book devoted to copyright issues, or discuss your project with a copyright attorney. However, there are some common sense guidelines that can be applied for DVD projects.

- Assume that a copyright exists. It is best to assume that someone holds a copyright for every item of content you plan on using on a DVD title. Having made this assumption it is much easier to start the process of getting approval to use each item from the copyright owner.

- It is a good idea to include a clause in your company's standard employment contract, or in your corporate policy manual, that conveys the copyright for all video, audio, graphics or textual materials created by an employee to the company.

- If you shoot video or record audio content for a DVD project make sure you get a signed release from each person appearing in the production. Signed releases should be obtained from actors and voice-over narrators as well as employees if they are used in the production.

- Content produced by the United States Government, or during the course of a contract paid for entirely by the United States Government is not copyrighted. Even though this material is not copyrighted you may still need to provide attribution to the specific government agency that produced the content.

- Each country has unique copyright laws. Do not assume that having clearance to use a specific item of content in the United States will convey clearance to use the same content in other countries. For example, under US copyright law music compositions become public domain 75 years after they were written, while in the United Kingdom the same composition does not become public domain until 75 years after the composer's death.

- If you are developing a DVD title for a customer, make sure that they assume responsibility for clearing all copyrighted material. You should include a clause discussing the client's responsibility for copyright clearance in your standard DVD services contract, as well as in the fine print of your proposal documents.

that were in the original storyboard, but were removed during the final production process to keep the movie at a certain MPAA rating level, or within a specific total running time length.

A flowchart is a hierarchical diagram that shows each media element used on a DVD title, and how they relate to each other. Flowcharts are generally created before the DVD production process begins, and are used to insure that the final DVD presents the media elements in a manner consistent with the original "story". Additionally flowcharts are used to ensure that extra media elements such as interactive menus and director's commentaries are integrated with the media elements from the story in a manner that is consistent with the content owner's vision of how the DVD version of their content is to be produced. Flowcharts can also be "living documents" that undergo changes as the DVD production process unfolds. For example if the content owner decides to include some behind the scenes footage after the project has been started, the project flowchart will need to be revised to include the new footage, as well as the menus that allow the user to access the new footage.

A well-designed project flowchart will be beneficial to every member of the DVD production team. The client will be able see how the DVD implementation of their content will compare with the original film, or video release. The project manager can see each video, audio, graphics and textual element required for the DVD title, and then insure that each element has been cleared of copyrights and that the highest quality version is on hand at the start of the project. The video and audio Compressionist will create digital versions of each media element called out by the project flowchart, and the graphic designer will use the flowchart when creating the DVD menus. Finally the DVD authoring system operator will use the flowchart to implement the DVD title and the Quality Assurance department will compare the final DVD disc image to the flowchart to make sure that the implementation is correct.

There are a number of excellent software tools that can be used to create, and maintain a DVD Project Flowchart. Many developers use off-the-shelf tools like Microsoft PowerPoint, or even Excel spreadsheets to create their flowcharts. I like to use Microsoft Visio which has a flowchart template built in. Some developers generate flow charts the old fashioned way, with pencil and paper, while others don't even bother to create a flowchart at all. The method you choose to use to develop a project flowchart is really not as important as your commitment to create and update a flowchart for each DVD project you work on. I strongly recommend that you ask your clients to approve the project flowchart before you move into the development phase of a DVD project. Having the client's signature on the project flow chart will make your life a lot easier when changes are made later on in the project that will have an impact on the cost or completion date of the project.

disc note:

> *Real World Example*
> Figure 3.4 shows the Project Flowchart for the DVD-Video zone of *StarGaze*. Since *Star-Gaze* was designed to have multilingual features, including menus in English, French, German and Spanish, the flowchart gets a bit complicated.

Step 4: Media Element Preparation

Now that you have completed the Project Planning phase you can start the Project Development Phase, which starts with Media Element Preparation. Simply put this step involves converting all of the video, audio, graphics and textual elements into the appropriate computer formats required for a DVD title. The process of preparing media elements for use in a DVD title is a trade-off between quality and storage space. Encoding the video into MPEG and the audio into Dolby Digital will result in lowering the amount of space required to store these media elements on a DVD disc. Since both MPEG and Dolby Digital are lossy compression techniques there will be some loss of quality when you convert the original video and audio assets into their compressed forms. The trick in developing a DVD title is to fit compressed versions of all of your media elements onto the disc at a quality level that is acceptable.

Bit Budgeting

Before you start encoding video or audio assets, you will need to have a clear idea of how much data storage space will be required for each media element, so that you can ensure everything will fit on your DVD disc. Bit budgeting is a simple mathematical process that calculates the amount of storage space required for each media element, and then determines if the total storage capacity required for all media elements is within the capacity of the desired DVD publishing media. The key to generating an accurate bit budget for a DVD project is having an accurate estimate of the type and length of each media element that will be included on the disc. The goal of bit budgeting to determine an optimal combination of compressed video and audio asset quality as well as total data storage capacity required.

There are many ways to generate a bit budget. Once you become familiar with the process of performing a bit budget calculation you may want to automate the process by creating a custom spreadsheet where you just need to enter a few video and audio parameters and the calculations are performed automatically. I have found it is easier to explain the bit budget process by calculating each item manually rather than using a pre-defined spreadsheet. Here are the steps you should go through to calculate the bit budget for your DVD title.

- Determine DVD Storage Capacity

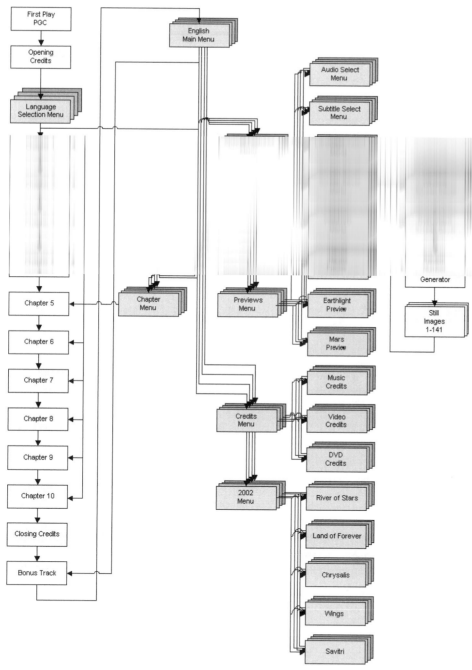

Figure 3.4   *StarGaze* Project Flowchart

- Reserve some bytes for overhead, as well as late changes. I typically set aside a reserve of 5% on my titles, but if you are new to the DVD production and authoring process you may want to have a reserve of 10%.

- Determine audio data storage requirements

- Determine subpicture data storage requirements

- Determine static menu data storage requirements

- Determine motion menu data storage requirements

- Reserve capacity for DVD-ROM requirements. The amount set aside will depend entirely on the size and complexity of the DVD-ROM application program and the amount of data associated with it.

- Determine capacity for "extra" content

- Use everything left over for video

DVD Storage Capacity

As discussed in Chapter 2 there are many different types of DVD discs, each with their own unique storage capacities. Table 3.4 provides a summary of data storage capacities of the most popular forms of DVD discs. Again, all of these capacities are listed in traditional computer bytes, not DVD-spec bytes.

Table 3.4	DVD Storage Capacities					
DVD Disc Type	DVD-R	DVD-5	DVD-9	DVD-10	DVD-14	DVD-18
Storage Capacity (GB)	4.37	4.37	7.95	8.75	12.3	15.9

The selection of the type of DVD disc used on a project should have been made during the Project Planning phase. It is possible that when you actually perform the bit budget process you will find that the chosen DVD disc format is inadequate to handle all of the media elements called out by the Project Requirements document and the Project Flow chart. If this happens you will need to go back to the planning phase to determine how to correct this problem. Possible solutions include changing the DVD disc type to one with a higher capacity, eliminating some content to reduce the total capacity requirements to within the amount provided by the specified DVD disc, or changing the format of some media elements to reduce the amount of data required for storage.

Reserve

While it is possible to use every byte on a DVD disc, it is not recommended that you develop your bit budget in this manner. There are three reasons why you should not try to allocate every byte on a DVD disc to a specific element of content. First, storing content in the DVD Video Object format requires some overhead, so that the number of bytes required for a VOB file is more than the number of bytes required for the individual video, audio, and graphics elements in their native MPEG, AC3 or TIF formats. The additional overhead required for the VOB format varies depending on the complexity of the title. Titles that include multi-angle video, multiple audio tracks and multiple subpicture streams will require more overhead than titles with one video stream, one audio track and no subtitles.

Secondly, content can be changed or added to a DVD project after the start of the DVD development phase. If you reserve some of the capacity of the disc for "future use" then you will be able to add a small amount of additional content to the title without having to go back an re-encode all of the media assets to make room for the new elements. Finally creating high quality MPEG encoded video files is not a simple process. After encoding you may find that a specific scene simply does not look good enough at the average bit rate calculated by the bit budgeting process. If you have reserved some of the storage capacity on the DVD disc

titles have higher overhead requirements as more sectors of the disc are used in support of interactive menus or advanced features such as multiple audio tracks, multi-angle video content or multiple subpicture streams.

Audio

Table 3.5 shows the most common data rates used for audio on DVD projects.

Table 3.5	Common DVD Encoded Audio Data Rates				
Audio Format	Dolby Digital Stereo	Dolby Digital Surround	DTS Surround (Half)	DTS Surround (Full)	PCM Stereo
Typical Encoded Data Rate (bps)	192,000	448,000	758,000	1,536,000	1,536,000

To calculate the total storage capacity required by an encoded audio stream use the following formula:

```
Audio Data (bytes) = Audio Minutes * 60 * Encoded Data Rate / 8
```

You will need to perform this calculation for each different type of encoded audio used on the disc, and then add all the results together to come up with the total number of bytes required for all the audio data on the project. A byte is simply 8 bits of data, in both standard computer and DVD-Video terminology.

Subpictures

Subpictures are stored as run-length-coded bit map images on a DVD disc. This is a lossless format, and typically requires so few bytes that it is insignificant compared to the storage required for the audio or video content on a DVD disc. The storage requirements of a run-length-coded bit map depend on the content of the image that is being encoded. In most cases subpicture streams of DVD titles are used to convey subtitle information, which is usually limited to text displayed in one specific area of the screen. Each unique subtitle will have an average size of approximately 5 Kb as a run-length-coded bit map. To calculate the total storage capacity required by an encoded subpicture stream use the following formula:

```
Subpicture Data (bytes) = # of Subpicture Graphics * 5,000
```

You will need to perform this calculation for each different subpicture stream used on the disc, and then add all the results together to come up with the total number of bytes required for all the subpicture data on the project.

Static Menus

Static Menus are stored as MPEG I-Frames on a DVD disc. This is a lossy format, and typically requires about 100 Kb for the background and highlight overlay images. To calculate the total storage capacity required by an encoded subpicture stream use the following formula:

```
Static Menu Data (bytes) = # of Static Menus * 100,000
```

Motion Menus

Motion Menus are stored as MPEG video and Dolby Digital on a DVD disc. Unfortunately it is often difficult to know how long a motion menu will be, or what bit rate it is compressed at during the bit budgeting phase since the menus generally don't exist at this stage of the project. The simplest way of dealing with this is to come up with the total number of minutes of motion menu content that will be included on the disc, and then use an average storage requirement of 40 MB per minute for motion menu content (video + audio). To calculate the total storage capacity required by motion menus, use the following formula:

```
Motion Menu Data (bytes) = Motion Menu Minutes * 40,000,000
```

DVD-ROM Requirements

If you are planning on including DVD-ROM content on your DVD-Video project then you need to reserve space on the disc for the required files. There is not much overhead required to store DVD-ROM files on a DVD-Video disc so you can just add up the storage requirements for all the files you need and set that amount aside. To calculate the total storage capacity required by DVD-ROM data use the following formula:

```
DVD-ROM Data (bytes) = the sum of the file sizes for all required files.
```

"Extra" Content

Many DVD-Video titles will include extra content such as an FBI warning, the production company logo, previews for coming attractions, etc. You will need to set aside space on the disc to hold this extra content. To calculate the total storage capacity required by extra content use the following formula:

```
Extra Data (bytes) = the sum of the file sizes for all requires files.
```

Video

After you have calculated the storage requirements for the audio, subpicture, static menu, motion menu and DVD-ROM elements of the disc you can finally figure out the bit budget for the video content. The first step is to calculate the amount of storage space left on the disc after allocating space for all the non-video elements. Use the following formula to do this:

```
Video Data (bytes) = (DVD Disc Capacity - Reserve - Audio Data - Subpic-
ture Data - Static Menu Data - Motion Menu Data - DVD-ROM Data - Extra
Data)
```

Tips, Tricks & Techniques

The bit budgeting process is designed to calculate the amount of storage required for all the non-video items of content on the disc, and then determine what the average compressed bit rate of the video content should be so that the final DVD disc is filled to capacity. You should always use as much of a DVD discs capacity as possible to maximize the overall quality of the video content.

disc note:

Real World Example

Here are the bit budget calculations for StarGaze. All of the data required to perform this bit budget calculation can be found in Table 3.2, the StarGaze Project Requirements Document.

StarGaze Data Item	Formula
DVD Disc Capacity = 4,700,000,000 bytes	DVD-5 Capacity
Reserve = 235,000,000 bytes	5% reserve
Audio Data = 1,312,650,000 bytes Audio Track 1 = 201,600,000 bytes Audio Track 2 = 679,050,000 bytes Audio Track 3 = 86,400,000 bytes Audio Track 4 = 86,400,000 bytes Audio Track 5 = 86,400,000 bytes Audio Track 6 = 86,400,000 bytes Audio Track 7 = 86,400,000 bytes	Audio Data (bytes) = Audio Minutes * 60 * Encoded Data Rate / 8

Subpicture Data = 19,000,000 bytes English Narration Track = 3,750,000 bytes French Narration Track = 3,750,000 bytes German Narration Track = 3,750,000 bytes Spanish Narration Track = 3,750,000 bytes English Nomenclature Track = 1,000,000 bytes French Nomenclature Track = 1,000,000 bytes German Nomenclature Track = 1,000,000 bytes Spanish Nomenclature Track = 1,000,000 bytes	Subpicture Data (bytes) = # of Subpicture Graphics * 5,000
Subpicture Data = 19,000,000 bytes English Narration Track = 3,750,000 bytes French Narration Track = 3,750,000 bytes German Narration Track = 3,750,000 bytes Spanish Narration Track = 3,750,000 bytes English Nomenclature Track = 1,000,000 bytes French Nomenclature Track = 1,000,000 bytes German Nomenclature Track = 1,000,000 bytes Spanish Nomenclature Track = 1,000,000 bytes	Subpicture Data (bytes) = # of Subpicture Graphics * 5,000
Static Menu Data = 18,400,000 bytes	Static Menu Data (bytes) = # of Static Menus * 200,000
Motion Menu Data = 40,000,000 bytes	Motion Menu Data (bytes) = Motion Menu Minutes * 40,000,000
DVD-ROM Data = 50,000,000 bytes	DVD-ROM Data (bytes) = the sum of the file sizes for all required files.
Extra Data = 400,000,000 bytes	Extra Data (bytes) = the sum of the file sizes for all requires files.
Video Data = 2,624,950,000 bytes	Video Data (bytes) = (DVD Disc Capacity – Reserve – Audio Data – Subpicture Data – Static Menu Data – Motion Menu Data – DVD-ROM Data – Extra Data)
Video Data Rate = 5.833 Mbps	Video Data Rate (bps) = Video Data / Video Minutes / 60 / 8

Data Rate Budgeting

Once you have completed the bit budgeting process you also need to make sure that the combined data rates of all your media elements do not exceed the maximum data rate called out by the DVD-Video specification, 9.8 Mbps in a single program chain. If you have more than one camera angle the total bit rate of all video angles + all audio tracks can exceed 9.8 Mbps, but the sum of the data rate for one video angle, plus all of the audio tracks can't exceed 8.0 Mbps.

To calculate the data rate budget you just need to add up the bit rates of the video and audio streams that will be combined into a single program chain to determine if they are below the maximum allowed data rate.

Video Encoding

The DVD-Video specification requires the use of either the MPEG-1 or MPEG-2 compression formats for storing video content on the disc. The MPEG specifications are fairly broad, and there are certain restrictions put in place on the type of MPEG files used for DVD titles. Table

disc note:

Real World Example

Here are the data rate budget calculations for StarGaze. All of the data required to perform this calculation can be found in Table 3.2, the StarGaze Project Requirements Document and the previous Real World Example box that covers the StarGaze Bit Budget.

Audio Track 1 = 448,000 bps
Audio Track 2 = 1,509,000 bps

Tips, Tricks & Techniques

While it is possible to have a combined data rate for video and audio in a program chain as high as 9,800,000 bits/second I recommend you keep your maximum data rate below 9,600,000 bits/second. There are a number of first generation DVD-Video players, as well as DVD-ROM systems with software-only decoders that have problems playing back DVD-Video titles encoded at the maximum allowed data rates.

3.6 shows the allowed MPEG-1 formats that can be used for DVD, while Table 3.7 shows the allowed MPEG-2 formats.

Table 3.6	Constraints on MPEG-1 video for DVD	
Parameter	NTSC TV Systems	PAL TV Systems
Source Picture Resolution	352×240	352×288
GOP Size	18 frames or less	15 frames or less
Frame Rate per second	29.97	25
Picture Aspect Ratio	4:3	4:3

Table 3.6	Constraints on MPEG-1 video for DVD (Continued)	
Parameter	NTSC TV Systems	PAL TV Systems
Compressed Video Data Rate	Constant or Variable bit rate with maximum of 1,856,000 bps.	Constant or Variable bit rate with maximum of 1,856,000 bps.

Other Restrictions:

The frame rate shall be identical for all video elements used within a DVD Volume

The picture resolution shall be identical for all video elements within a DVD domain (VMG or VTS).

Table 3.7	Constraints on MPEG-2 video for DVD	
Parameter	NTSC TV Systems	PAL TV Systems
Source Picture Resolution	720×480 704×480 352×480 352×240	720×576 704×576 352×576 352×288
GOP Size	18 frames or less	15 frames or less
Frame Rate per second	29.97	25
Picture Aspect Ratio	4:3 16:9	4:3 16:9
Compressed Video Data Rate	Constant or Variable bit rate with maximum of 9,800,000 bps.	Constant or Variable bit rate with maximum of 9,800,000 bps.

Other Restrictions:

Encoded MPEG-2 streams shall comply with the Main profile Main level (MP@ML) constraints as defined by the MPEG-2 specification.

The interlaced SIF (352×240) format is not allowed

The frame rate shall be identical for all video elements used within a DVD Volume

The picture resolution shall be identical for all video elements within a DVD domain (VMG or VTS).

Picture display extensions are allowed to support horizontal pan scan vectors

Most DVD title developers need not be concerned with the various restrictions placed on MPEG video data for DVD projects. As long as you use an MPEG encoder that has been designed to support DVD, these restrictions should be met. Many DVD development and authoring systems provide an integrated MPEG encoder, so these systems have been designed to generate MPEG streams that are fully compliant with the DVD-Video specification. If you are using a general purpose MPEG encoder, or your DVD development system does not include an integrated MPEG encoder, then you should be aware of the restrictions listed in Tables 3.6 and 3.7 so that your MPEG video data will comply with the DVD-Video specification.

Tips, Tricks & Techniques

If you decide to use an MPEG encoder that has not been specifically designed or tested to ensure its compliance with the DVD-Video specification you could be in for trouble. While most DVD authoring tools can accept MPEG files generated from a wide variety of MPEG encoders, you should verify that your authoring tool accepts files generated by your MPEG encoder. If a third party will be encoding your video have them send you a sample file encoded using your required encoding parameters. If the sample file can be

More sophisticated encoders will provide user controls for advanced encoding parameters such as motion vector search distance and technique, quantization levels and types, etc. A detailed discussion of how to use these compression parameters to create the highest quality, or lowest data rate MPEG stream is beyond the scope of this book, but I will review here some of the major MPEG compression parameters and describe how they can be adjusted to improve video quality.

Resolution

While the DVD-Video specification allows the use of several different resolutions of MPEG-2 encoded data, the vast majority of DVD titles use a resolution of 720×480 pixels per frame for NTSC video or 720×576 pixels per frame for PAL video. These resolutions deliver the highest possible quality video when played back by consumer DVD-Video players. Use of a lower resolution is appropriate under the following conditions:

- Low quality video source. If your video source resolution is less than broadcast quality (usually 720×480 pixels per frame or higher as defined by the CCIR-601 specification), you may want to decrease the resolution of the MPEG encoder to match the resolution of the video source material. A good rule of thumb is to use the highest resolution if your source tape is BetaSP or better. High-end DV cameras fall into this category if they record at CCIR-601 resolutions. For 1" Type C, 3/4" Umatic, Hi-8, SVHS or even VHS source tapes you should consider using the horizontal half resolution settings (352×480 for NTSC or 352×576 for PAL), or even the standard MPEG-1 resolution settings (352×240 for NTSC or 352×288 for PAL). Many inexpensive DV cameras fall into this category because they record at MPEG-1 resolutions.

- Quantity vs. Quality. If your project requirements emphasize the quantity of video stored on the disc over the quality of that video, then using a lower resolution will allow you to store more compressed video on the DVD disc. Horizontal half resolution MPEG requires approximately half the space required by full resolution MPEG-2, while the standard MPEG-1 resolutions only require about 25% of the storage space.

Tips, Tricks & Techniques

Many people believe that a DVD-5 holds 133 minutes of video. In reality there is no "maximum video capacity" of a DVD disc. Publishing a DVD-Video disc is a tradeoff between quantity and quality. With today's MPEG video encoders it is relatively easy to achieve acceptable quality at an average bit rate of 4.5 Mbps for MPEG-2, 2.5 Mbps for Half resolution MPEG-2, and 1.5 Mbps for MPEG-1. The following chart provides a summary of how much video can be stored on DVD discs using these three different encoding techniques. For calculation purposes I have assumed that a single Dolby Digital stereo audio track is included with the video

	MPEG-1 @ 1.5 Mbp	HHR MPEG-2 @ 2.5 Mbpss	MPEG-2 @ 4.5 Mbps
DVD-5	370 minutes	233 minutes	133 minutes
DVD-9	673 minutes	423 minutes	243 minutes
DVD-10	740 minutes	465 minutes	267 minutes
DVD-14	1,040 minutes	654 minutes	375 minutes
DVD-18	1,345 minutes	846 minutes	485 minutes

VBR or CBR

Most moderate to high end MPEG video encoders will allow you to create compressed video streams using either a CBR or VBR compression process. For constant bit rate encoders you only need to provide the desired video data rate and the encoder will attempt to generate an output stream where the actual data rate of the compressed video is close to the data rate you specified. Be aware that the actual data rate of the compressed video will vary somewhat over time, but it should stay within +/- 5% of the target data rate you specified.

VBR encoders can have as many as four different parameters that you will need to specify including the Maximum Data Rate, Average Data Rate, Minimum Data Rate, and number of encoding passes. The Maximum Data Rate is simply the highest data rate that you want the encoder to use. Typically the Maximum Data Rate will only be used by the encoder during scene changes in the video as well as when the video content is changing rapidly such as a fast pan or zoom, explosions, or other types of fast action. Many VBR encoders will not allow you to specify a Minimum Data Rate, but for those that do this parameter can be used to specify the lowest data rate used by the encoder. VBR encoders will attempt to generate an output stream where the actual average data rate of the compressed video is close to the average data rate you specified. The VBR encoder will attempt to optimize the overall quality of the output video stream by allocating more data bits to areas of content that are difficult to compress, and less data bits to content that is easy to compress.

Compressed Video Data Rate

Compressed Video Data Rate is one of the most critical parameters for MPEG compression. Using a data rate setting that is too low will result in poor quality video with visible digital artifacts such as blocking, fringing or ringing, as shown in Figure 3.5. Using a data rate that is too high will generate excellent quality video, but will also waste valuable space on the DVD disc. For many DVD projects the choice of the correct video data rate will flow directly from the bit budget calculation. You want to set the data rate of the encoder to the highest possible value that will still allow you to fit all of the video, audio, and menu content onto the disc.

Whenever possible you should use the data rate calculated in the bit budget process as the Average Data Rate setting for the encoder.

StarGaze Video Compressed in MPEG-2 @ 2.0 Mbps

Figure 3.5   Digital Video Compression Artifact Examples
(See color insert for color version of this figure.)

If you choose to use a VBR encoder then you will also need to specify the maximum data rate. The correct value for this parameter will flow from data rate budget process that was discussed earlier in this chapter. The correct setting for Minimum Data Rate will depend on your content, as well as the quality of your MPEG encoder. In general more sophisticated (and expensive) encoders will be able to generate acceptable quality compressed video at lower average data rates than less sophisticated (and less expensive) encoders. You may have to experiment with your encoder to determine where the video quality starts to break down as you reduce the minimum data rate. Once you have determined the point at which the encoder output quality starts to go below your acceptance criteria, you should use a slightly higher data rate as the Minimum Data Rate setting.

Tips, Tricks & Techniques

It is impossible to give specific guidelines on how to set the compressed video data rate for a DVD project. There are simply too many variables such as the quality of the source video, the make and model of the MPEG encoder, and the amount of space on the disc available for video data. In some respects video compression is more of an art than a science, and having an experienced "Video Compressionist" who understands how to use your video encoder is the best way to create high quality MPEG video streams.

GOP Size & Structure

Many encoders will allow you to change the size and structure of the Group of Pictures (GOP), the basic method of organizing video frames in MPEG. The DVD-Video specification requires a GOP size of no more than 18 for NTSC and no more than 15 for PAL video, however smaller GOP sizes are allowed.

The GOP size, also called N value, dictates how many frames are in each group, while the Reference Interval, also called M value, dictates the distance between reference frames (I-frames). I-frames are frames in which the complete image is stored. Each GOP begins with an I-frame, which is followed by P-frames and B-frames, which don't contain a complete image, but instead contain only the data that has changed relative to the I-frame. After the I-frame in that GOP, every third frame is a P-frame. These values have been shown to produce a good compromise between image quality and storage requirements. When changing these values, keep in mind that the M value has to be evenly divisible into the N value.

Finally GOP structures can be created as "open" or "closed". In general it is preferable to use "Closed GOP" structures for DVD projects, as this will allow you to define chapter points within 1/2 second of any frame in each video segment. To define chapter points using "Open GOP" structures you may have to re-encode the video segment with a forced I-frame near where you want the chapter in-point to be. Closed GOP structures are also preferable for DVD projects with multiple angle videos, as these will allow the DVD player to switch angles without introducing any blocking artifacts. A typical closed GOP used for a DVD-Video title would have the following display order:

B B I B B P B B P B B P B B P

Motion Vectors

MPEG encoders use a series of algorithms to analyze subsequent frames of video to determine if motion has occurred between the two frames. When motion between frames is detected a "motion vector" is generated to describe the motion between frames. A motion vector describing the frame-to-frame motion is stored in the compressed data stream, rather than the actual data from each frame, thus requiring significantly less data to represent the compressed video data. Some MPEG encoders have user selectable parameters related to motion vectors. These parameters control the technique for searching for motion between frames as well as the search distance. Search Distance dictates how far away from the current area the encoder looks in the next frame while it is searching for detail. Search Technique dictates how completely the encoder searches the surrounding area for signs of motion.

Real-time hardware MPEG encoders will generally not allow the author to control motion vector search techniques or distances, while non real-time software MPEG encoders may allow the user to control these parameters. In general the required storage space for an MPEG file will decrease as motion vector search techniques and distances are increased. For non real-time software MPEG encoders the processing time required to compress a video stream will increase as motion vector search techniques and distances are increased, so there is a tradeoff between the time required to compress the video and the efficiency of that compression process.

Filtering

Filters can be applied to the video stream prior to compression to minimize digital video artifacts in the output MPEG file. Most high-end hardware encoders include optional temporal or spatial filters designed to remove high frequency (noise) or low frequency (hum or DC Offset) signals from the input video data prior to the compression process. There are also devices called Digital Video Noise Reduction (DVNR) processors that can be used to clean up noisy or dirty video signals prior to the compression process. Most non real-time software MPEG encoders have filter options that can be applied to the input video signal prior to compression.

Used properly, filtering the input video signal to remove unwanted high frequency noise, hum, or DC offset signals will significantly improve the quality of the output MPEG streams, and will also allow lower compressed video data rates to be used. Used improperly filters applied to the input video signal can "soften" or "blur" the video data and result in a reduced level of quality. Filtering should be used only when needed to eliminate unwanted noise from the video signal or to reduce the high frequency components of the video so that a lower compression data rate can be used effectively.

Audio Encoding

There are a number of different audio formats supported for DVD-Video titles, including linear PCM, Dolby Digital, DTS, MPEG and SDDS. While there are other formats such as DVD-Audio, SACD, XCD, or MP3, these are not supported by the DVD-Video specification. There are some DVD-Video players that support more audio formats than required by the DVD-Video specification, but currently it is impossible to author or produce a DVD-Video title that includes these other audio formats. All DVD-Video titles are required to have either a PCM or Dolby Digital audio track, with DTS and SDDS as formats. The majority of DVD-Video titles released to date include at least one Dolby Digital audio track, although DTS audio tracks are becoming more common on releases from the major motion picture studios.

Since DVD titles can have up to eight audio tracks it is possible to create a single disc that includes Linear PCM, Dolby Digital, SDDS and DTS audio tracks.

> ### Tips, Tricks & Techniques
>
> A common consumer complaint is that audio levels on DVD-Video titles vary widely from title to title, as well as within individual titles. The best way to avoid this problem is to make sure your audio playback sources are properly calibrated. 1 KHz tones on an

Linear PCM is a lossless audio coding technique that provides the highest quality audio possible on a DVD-Video title. Table 3.8 shows the supported configurations of Linear PCM audio on a DVD-Video title. As you can see from Table 3.8 Linear PCM audio can have a sample rate of either 48 KHz or 96 KHz, with a sample size of 16, 20 or 24 bits. Up to 8 distinct audio channels can be included in a Linear PCM audio track, although the highest audio quality (96 KHz, 24 bit) is not supported for more than 2 channels of audio. The maximum data rate that can be used for Linear PCM audio is 6.144 Mbps, which is required for 4 channel, 96 KHz 16-bit audio as well as 8 channel, 48 KHz 16-bit audio.

In general Linear PCM audio requires 10 times more bandwidth and storage capacity than Dolby Digital audio, and 3 times more bandwidth and storage than DTS audio. This is due to the fact that Dolby Digital and DTS audio are compressed, while Linear PCM audio is uncompressed.

Table 3.8	Linear PCM Audio Modes		
# Of Audio Channels	Sample Frequency (kHz)	Quantization (Bits)	Data Rate (Kbps)
1 (Mono)	48	16	768
	48	20	960
	48	24	1,152
	96	16	1,536
	96	20	1,920
	96	24	2,304

Table 3.8   Linear PCM Audio Modes (Continued)

# Of Audio Channels	Sample Frequency (kHz)	Quantization (Bits)	Data Rate (Kbps)
2 (Stereo)	48	16	1,536
	48	20	1,920
	48	24	2,304
	96	16	3,072
	96	20	3,840
	96	24	4,608
3	48	16	2,304
	48	20	2,880
	48	24	3,456
	96	16	4,608
	96	20	5,760
4	48	16	3,072
	48	20	3,840
	48	24	4,608
	96	16	6,144
5	48	16	3,840
	48	20	4,800
	48	24	5,760
6	48	16	4,608
	48	20	5,760
7	48	16	5,376
8	48	16	6,144

Dolby Digital Audio

Dolby Digital, also known as Dolby AC-3, is a high quality, bandwidth-efficient perceptual audio coding algorithm originally developed for multi-channel digital sound in the cinema. It is a flexible coding system encompassing a wide range of data rates and audio coding modes. Dolby Digital uses masking and inter-channel redundancy to enable the efficient storage and transmission of multi-channel digital audio data streams. 16-bit, 20-bit or 24-bit data can be used to create a Dolby Digital audio track, but since the data is compressed using perceptual coding techniques the concept of input quantization levels, or bit depth, is not applicable to Dolby Digital audio. Perceptual coding is a compression technique whereby elements in the audio

3/1, 2/2 and 3/2 modes of Dolby Digital Audio can also include an optional Low Frequency Effects (LFE) audio channel. Since the data in the LFE channel is generally only audio in the 0-200 Hz range, it is not necessary to increase the compressed data bandwidth from the recommended levels when you have audio with an LFE channel. Table 3.9 shows the various configurations of Dolby Digital that are supported by DVD-Video players.

Table 3.9	Dolby Digital Audio Formats		
# Of Audio Channels	Sample Frequency (kHz)	Valid Data Rate Range (Bits/second)	Recommend Data Rate (Bits/second)
1/0 (Mono)	48	64,000 – 448,000	96,000
2/0 (Stereo)	48	96,000 – 448,000	192,000
3/0	48	128,000 – 448,000	288,000
2/1	48	128,000 – 448,000	288,000
3/1	48	192,000 – 448,000	384,000
2/2	48	192,000 – 448,000	384,000
3/2	48	224,000 – 448,000	448,000

Dolby Digital encoders have a number of compression and signal processing parameters that can affect the quality of the encoded signal. These parameters are set during the audio compression process, and include the following.

Audio Coding Mode   This parameter defines the number of full-bandwidth audio channels within the encoded bit stream and also indicates the channel format. The Audio coding mode is designated as two numbers, m/n, with m indicating the number of front channels, and n indicating the number of rear (surround) channels.

- 1/0   Center

- 2/0   Left, Right

- 3/0   Left, Center, Right

- 2/1   Left, Right, Surround

- 3/1   Left, Center, Right, Surround

- 2/2   Left, Right, Left Surround, Right Surround

- 3/2   Left, Center, Right, Left Surround, Right Surround

LFE Enable   This option enables or disables the encoding of the LFE or Low Frequency Effects channel. This channel is typically used as a sub-woofer channel.

Bit stream Mode   DVD can include multiple Dolby Digital bit streams, so this parameter can be used to specify the type of bit stream you are encoding. The default audio track should be set to Main Audio Service: Complete Main. Other possible settings are:

- Main Audio Service: Music and Effects

- Main Audio Service: Karaoke

- Associated Service: Visually Impaired

- Associated Service: Hearing Impaired

- Associated Service: Dialogue

- Associated Service: Commentary

- Associated Service: Emergency

Dialog Normalization Dialog normalization attempts to keep the dialog in the audio signal at a consistent level throughout the entire program. This parameter indicates how far, in decibels, the average dialog level of the encoded program is below digital 100%. The value of this parameter will directly affect the sound reproduction level when decoded. Possible values for dialog normalization are between –1 db and –31 db. The default value is typically –27 db. Setting this parameter too high or too low could result in a compressed audio signal where the spoken dialog is either too low or too high compared to the rest of the audio data.

Audio Bandwidth The Audio bandwidth field is an information-only parameter that d...

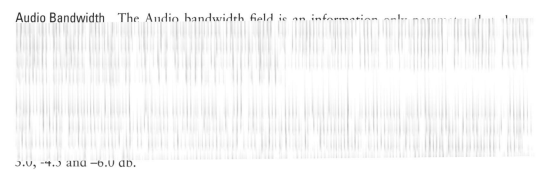

5.0, –4.5 and –6.0 db.

Surround Downmix Level Downmixing will occur on playback systems without surround capabilities. This parameter indicates the level of the surround channel(s) with respect to the left and right channels when and if they get downmixed on playback. Possible values for this parameter are –3.0, –6.0 db and none.

Dolby Surround Mode This parameter indicates whether or not the two-channel Dolby Digital encoded stream is conveying a Dolby Surround encoded program. This information is not used by the Dolby Digital decoding algorithm, but may be used by other portions of the audio reproduction equipment, such as a Dolby Pro Logic Surround decoder. This option is only available when encoding to the 2/0 mode.

Copyright Bit This parameter indicates whether or not the encoded Dolby Digital stream is copyright protected. In general if the audio data has a copyright associated with it, the copyright bit should be set to true.

Original Bit Stream This parameter indicates whether or not the bit stream is an original. If the audio data is an original recording then this bit should be set to true.

Info Exists This parameter indicates whether or not additional production information such as Mixing Level and Room Type are encoded in the Dolby Digital Stream. If this information is available it should be included so that audio receivers can attempt to recreate the original recording room if possible.

Mix Level This parameter indicates the acoustic sound pressure level (SPL) of the dialog level during the final audio mixing session. Setting this parameter to the appropriate value will make playback across multiple systems more consistent with the original mix. Possible values for this parameter are 80 db SPL through 111 db SPL.

Room Type This parameter indicates the type and calibration of the mixing room used for the final audio mixing session. The value of Room Type is not typically used within the Dolby Digital decoding algorithm, but may be used by other parts of the audio reproduction equipment. Possible values for this parameter are Not Indicated, Large Room X Curve Monitor, or Small Room Flat Monitor.

Digital Deemphasis This parameter will apply a deemphasis filter to the encoded stream when checked. This parameter should not be checked if a preemphasis filter was not applied to the source audio files.

DC High-Pass Filter This parameter will apply a DC High-pass filter to the encoded stream when checked. This filter is used to remove any DC offset that is present in the source audio files.

LFE Low-Pass Filter This parameter will apply a low-pass filter to the encoded LFE channel when checked. The low-pass cutoff frequency will be at 120 Hz. This is generally not necessary unless you are trying to create an LFE channel from a full bandwidth signal.

90-Degree Phase Shift This parameter will apply a 90-degree phase shift to the surround channels selected. A receiver uses this phase shift information when creating a stereo downmix signal from the surround sound audio.

3 dB Attenuation This parameter will apply 3 dB attenuation to the surround channels when selected. This may be necessary when creating Dolby Digital content that may be transferred onto a format for consumer home theater playback. Cinema soundtrack surround channels are mixed 3 dB "hot" relative to the front channels to compensate for cinema amplifier gains. Home theater surround channel gains are calibrated differently making 3 dB attenuation necessary in most cases.

Compression Characteristic This parameter determines the characteristic curve of the dynamic range compression algorithm. Dolby Digital decoders use this information to affect the output levels of the program. Selecting the appropriate Compression Characteristic for your content will ensure proper playback during the decoding process. Possible values for this parameter are:

- None
- Film: Standard (the most common setting for movie titles)
- Film: Light
- Music: Standard (the most common setting for music titles)
- Music: Light
- Speech (the most common setting for educational titles)

RF Overmodulation Protection   This parameter determines whether or not an RF preemphasis filter is used in the clip protection algorithm to prevent RF over-modulation in set-top-box decoders.

Time Code   The Dolby Digital encoding process provides an option to include time code stamps for each encoded Dolby Digital frame. These time stamps may later be used for synchronization of the playback to other devices. During the DVD-Video authoring process having Time Stamps in the Dolby Digital audio can be helpful in correctly synchronizing the video and audio streams.

MPEG Audio

In the preliminary version of the DVD-Video specification MPEG Audio was to be required for all PAL players, while Dolby Digital audio would be required for all NTSC players. In the final version of the DVD-Video specification MPEG audio became optional, while Dolby Digital was made mandatory for all DVD-Video players. The change in its status from mandatory for PAL players to optional for all players had the effect of severely limiting the use of MPEG audio on DVD titles. While some DVD-Video players support MPEG audio streams, most do not, thus MPEG audio can't be used as the main audio format for consumer DVD-Video titles. Other DVD-Video players provide support for the MP3 audio format, although it is not possible to create a DVD-Video title using MP3 audio. These players are used to play CD-R discs with MP3 audio tracks recorded on them.

For mono and stereo audio MPEG-1 Layer 2 audio coding is used. For audio with more than two channels MPEG-2 audio is used. The use of the MPEG audio 7.1 channel augmentation format is optional. Table 3.10 shows the supported modes of MPEG audio for DVD-Video titles.

Table 3.10 MPEG Audio Formats		
# Of Audio Channels	Sample Frequency (kHz)	Valid Data Rate Range (Bits/second)
1/0 (Mono)	48	64,000 – 192,000
2/0 (Stereo)	48	96,000 – 384,000
3/0, 2/1, 3/1, 2/2, 3/2	48	Main: 64,000 – 384,000 Extension - <= 528,000

It is unlikely that the MPEG Audio format will ever become very popular for DVD-Video titles. Since the DVD-Video specification requires all DVD-Video titles to include at least one Linear PCM or Dolby Digital audio track (if audio is available at all), the addition of MPEG audio data would be redundant, and a waste of bandwidth and storage capacity that could be used to improve the video quality.

DTS Audio

The DTS Coherent Acoustics audio compression algorithm was designed to significantly improve the quality of audio reproduction in the home. Coherent Acoustics uses perceptual coding techniques to compress the audio signal so that it requires less storage space, without negatively impacting the quality of the audio. Figure 3.6 shows a block diagram of the DTS Coherent Acoustics encoder. DTS Coherent Acoustics is an asymmetric compression algorithm, which means it takes more processing power to encode a signal than to decode the signal.

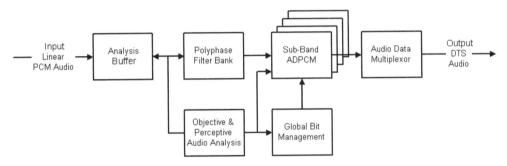

Figure 3.6   DTS Coherent Acoustics Encoder Block Diagram

At the first stage of the encoding process, a polyphase filter bank splits each single channel, full-band 24-bit linear PCM source signal into a number of sub-bands. Each sub-band signal still contains linear PCM audio data, but has a restricted bandwidth. The bandwidth and number of the subbands created is dependent on the bandwidth of the source signal, but in general the audio spectrum is divided into 32 uniform sub-bands. Within each sub-band, differential coding occurs, which removes redundancies from the signal. At the same time psychoacoustic and transient analyses are performed on the original linear PCM signal to determine perceptually irrelevant information. Global bit management is responsible for allocating, or distributing, the coding bits over all the coded sub-bands across all the audio channels. Adaptation occurs over time and frequency to optimize the audio quality. The final stage of the encoder is the data multiplexer which receives encoded audio data from each ADPCM process. The multiplexer packs the audio data from all the sub-bands from all the audio channels, into the specified data syntax of the output audio bit stream. Synchronization information is added at this stage to allow the decoder to reliably recognize this bit stream. There are two different DTS audio file formats. The "compacted" format stores only the encoded audio data, while the "padded" format stores the encoded audio data plus some padding to make data packets that are the correct size for DVD-Video sectors. The audio data contained in these two different file formats is identical, and most DVD-Video authoring systems that support DTS can accept either format.

There are relatively few encoding options for DTS compared to the fairly complex set of parameters for Dolby Digital. Essentially for DVD-Video titles you have three sets of parameters that need to be set in a DTS encoder, input sample rate, output data rate, and rear channel attenuation. DTS encoders support two different input audio frequencies, 44.1 KHz and 48 KHz. For DVD-Video titles only the 48 KHz sample rate is allowed. DTS encoders support only two output data rates for DVD-Video titles, a high bit rate of 1,536,000 bits per second and a lower bit rate of 768,000 bits per second. All DTS audio streams used for DVD titles include 6 audio channels (left, center, right, left surround, right surround and LFE). Finally the DTS encoder gives you the option of attenuating the surround channels by 3 db

sound systems. In my experience, high-end consumers can hear the difference between a Dolby Digital and a DTS encoded audio track, and many prefer to listen to a DTS encoded track. If you want to attract the high-end of the DVD-Video consumer market, add an optional DTS audio track to your DVD title.

Still Image Generation

Still images can be used in a DVD-Video title in a variety of ways. Still images can be displayed for a fixed amount of time from as little as 0.4 seconds to as much as 254 seconds, or indefinitely waiting for some user input. Still images can have audio tracks associated with them or they can be silent. Regardless of how you intend to use still images in your DVD-Video title they need to be created correctly so that they will look the way you intend them to when displayed by a DVD-Video player.

There are two basic methods that can be used to create still images for a DVD-Video title. The first is to use a computer graphics program, such as Adobe Photoshop to create a custom graphic, and then save it off in an appropriate file format that can be read by a DVD-Video authoring system. The second method is to grab a single frame from a video source and store it off in an appropriate file format. The most important issues concerning the creation of still images for DVD-Video titles are related to their resolution, and the manner in which they get displayed on televisions and computer monitors.

Resolution Issues

Some DVD-Video authoring tools are designed to perform the 16:9 to 4:3 conversions, as well as the square to non-square pixel adjustment process for you automatically. You should refer to the users guide of your DVD-Video authoring tool to see if your authoring software performs these conversions.

Different still image resolutions are required for different display aspect ratios, as well as different encoding techniques. The most common problem encountered when creating still images for DVD-Video titles is the failure to account for the difference between square pixels used on most personal computer systems and rectangular pixels used on television displays. Individual pixels on television displays are rectangular, not square. A graphic created on a computer with a square pixel display and then displayed on a television with a rectangular pixel display will not look correct. While the differences will be small, they are still visible to most consumers, particularly if circular objects are part of the still image. If you don't take the difference between computer pixels and television pixels into account circles that look round on your computer will look like ovals on your television.

There are two methods used to correct for the difference between square pixels and rectangular pixels. The first is to set up the graphics program on your PC to use rectangular pixels. Thus the final output files will already be adjusted for the non-square pixel aspect ratio of a television. If you use this method you will probably want to connect a television monitor to the PC you use to create the still images so that you can see the image on a monitor with rectangular pixels. If you look at a rectangular pixel image on a PC monitor it will look distorted.

The second method is to create the image on a standard computer at a resolution that has been adjusted to accommodate the square pixel format of a PC monitor. For example, as shown in Table 3.11, still images created on a computer for a 4:3 NTSC DVD-Video title should be created at a resolution of 720×540 pixels. Once the still image has been completed it needs to be resized to a resolution of 720×480 and output in a file format that is compatible with your DVD-Video authoring software. In general most DVD-Video authoring tools can accept a variety of graphic file formats, but the industry standard is the TIF format.

Table 3.11 Recommended DVD-Video Still Image Resolutions		
Aspect Ratio & Video Format	Computer Display (Square Pixels)	DVD-Video (MPEG-2)
4:3 NTSC	720×540	720×480
4:3 PAL	768×576	720×576
16:9 NTSC	960×540	720×480 (*)
16:9 PAL	1024×576	720×576 (*)

(*) Still Images for 16:9 DVD-Video titles should be resized, and the 16:9 flag must be set when the images are converted to MPEG I frames.

When you are creating still images for widescreen, or 16:9 aspect ratio content, you need to perform two sets of adjustments. First the original image created on the computer must be at a widescreen resolution (16:9) and it also must be adjusted to take into account the difference between square pixels and rectangular pixels. Referring to Table 3.11 again you can see that you want to create a 16:9 image for an NTSC title on your PC at a resolution of 960×540 pixels. Once the graphic has been finished you will squeeze it down to a 720×540 resolution and then resize the image to 720×480 for use in your DVD-Video authoring tool.

Figure 3.7 illustrates the process of creating a 16:9 still image for an NTSC DVD-Video title on a PC, and then converting it to the correct format for use by a DVD-Video authoring tool.

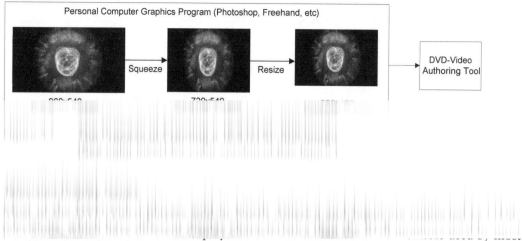

graphic artists when they are creating DVD still images. A still image or graphic that looks good on a computer display may look quite a bit different on an NTSC monitor. Some issues that negatively affect the display quality of still images on an NTSC monitor are Interlace, Contrast, Colors, Small Type, Small Patterns, and Safe Areas.

Interlace NTSC and PAL are interlaced technologies. NTSC is often described as displaying "30 frames per second," but it actually displays 60 fields per second by alternately displaying odd and even lines (fields). Similarly PAL televisions will display 50 fields per second, rather than 25 frames per second. Thus a single-pixel horizontal line routed to TV will appear to turn off and on, or flicker, 30 times per second for NTSC and 25 times per second for PAL, because its constrained to a single field. To avoid flicker caused by interlace don't use single-pixel lines. Use anti-aliasing on all thin horizontal lines so that they appear to be very thin, but span more than one scan line.

Contrast Sharp contrast, or color differences, between adjacent pixels in a horizontal direction can also cause problems because of the way NTSC encodes and displays images. NTSC displays color information as YCC (Luminance, Red Chrominance, Blue Chrominance), with each pixel sharing its luminance with an adjacent pixel. As a result of this sharing, flicker will be generated between sharply contrasting screen areas that are adjacent in a horizontal direction. To avoid this problem use blending to minimize the color or contrast difference between adjacent pixels in the horizontal direction.

Color NTSC has a color temperature of 9300 degrees Kelvin as its standard. Computer monitors generally have color temperatures between 11,000 and 12,000 degrees Kelvin. Due to this basic difference in color temperature between computer and NTSC monitors, it's easy to create colors on the computer that can't be displayed on NTSC. When computer graphics with bright colors are displayed on a TV, the guns may be overdriven, causing colors to bloom or bleed over into adjacent pixels. To avoid this problem make sure that all the colors used in your graphics are "NTSC Safe". Most computer graphics programs, such as Adobe

Photoshop include filters that allow you to adjust colors so they fall into the NTSC Color Safe range. Some guidelines for colors used for DVD graphics are to use maximum RGB values of 234 or less. In other words, consider an RGB value of 234,0,0 as pure red for NTSC. Pure NTSC blue by this measure would be 0,0,234, and pure NTSC green would be 0,234,0. Pure NTSC white (all guns on) has an RGB value of 234,234,234.

Small Type   Type designed for a computer display is typically too small for use on a television (NTSC or PAL). Type that is 12 point or less (in a standard font likes Times or Helvetica) is essentially unreadable because of the low resolution of a television screen. To avoid this problem use type that is 14 point or larger for "fine print" content, and at least 24 point for content that the viewer needs to read on their television monitors.

Small Patterns   Small, regular areas of high contrast, such as small checkerboard or dot patterns, will appear to wiggle or move on a television display. This is due to both the sharp contrast problem and the scan line problem seen in single-pixel lines. To avoid this problem use anti-aliasing or dithering on images, which include small pattern areas.

Safe Areas   Televisions are typically set to overscan so that the edges of the screen cannot be seen, while computer monitors underscan so that the entire screen is displayed. If you display a computer screen on a television, you frequently lose up to 20% of the computer screen to the overscan. The "Action Safe" zone is defined as the area within which action should be confined to ensure that it is visible on most televisions. Typically Action Safe is defined as the center area of the display out to within 5% of each edge. The "Title Safe" zone is defined as the area within which a title or graphical element will be visible on most televisions. Typically Title Safe is defined as the center area of the display out to within 10% of each edge. When you create still images or graphics for DVD-Video titles make sure that all of the important information is at least 10% away from any edge of the image. Figure 3.8 shows an example of the Safe Area you should use when creating still images or graphics for use on an NTSC DVD-Video title. Please feel free to download a Photoshop template that includes these safe zones from http://www.DVDToday.com.

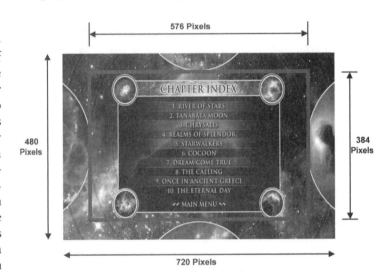

Figure 3.8   Safe Areas for NTSC 4:3 Still Images or Graphics (See color insert for color version of this figure.)

Subpicture Generation

Subpictures are graphics that are overlaid on top of the video image by the DVD-Video player. They are used to create the button highlights in menus as well as for subtitles. There are several elements that need to be defined for subpictures used on DVD-Video titles. While the vast majority of DVD-Video titles that include subpicture streams use these to display subtitles, subpictures can also be used to display simple graphics or animations. Subpictures are stored as run-length coded bitmaps, which is a lossless compression technique. Subpicture graphics used for DVD-Video titles use only four colors. These colors are referred to as Background (B), Pattern (P), Emphasis 1 (E1), and Emphasis 2 (E2). The Background color is a

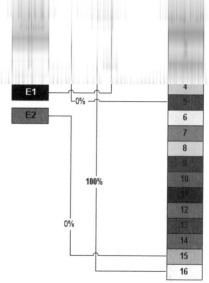

level definitions. The B, P, E1 and E2 colors are simply defined as the colors used in the original subpicture image. At run time the DVD-Video player can change the B, P, E1 and E2 colors to a different color defined in a 16-color palette. This 16-color palette can contain any colors from a 24-bit color universe. In addition to specifying the display color, you can also define the level of transparency the display color will take when overlaid on top of a video clip or still image by the DVD-Video player. There are 16 possible transparency levels that can be defined for each subpicture color (B, P, E1 and E2). Transparency levels are usually defined as percentages with 0% representing full transparency and 100% representing fully opaque.

Figure 3.9   Subpicture Color, Transparency and Palette Definitions

This ability to change the display color and assign a transparency value provides a level of abstraction between the colors used to create each subpicture element, and the actual colors displayed by the DVD-Video player. Figure 3.9 shows a typical definition of colors for B, P, E1, and E2 as well as their associated transparency levels and mapping to the 16-color display palette. Figure 3.10 shows how a DVD-Video player would use these color assignments to create the desired display of subpicture and still image graphic elements. It should be noted that some DVD authoring tools have slightly different names for the B, P, E1 and E2 color definitions of a subpicture. For example in Daikin's Scenarist tools these are called BG, PA, E1 and E2. As long as you understand the concepts for subpicture color definitions the actual naming convention used by an authoring tool is not important.

Still Image   Subpicture   DVD-Video Display

Figure 3.10   DVD-Video Display of Subpicture & Still Image Data
(See color insert for color version of this figure.)

Another required element for subpictures is the definition of starting and ending time in relation to the video or still images that will be displayed by the DVD-Video player. DVD-Video subpicture data can be displayed for as short as one frame, and as long as the underlying video or still image content lasts. For each subpicture element created you will also need to define a starting and ending time code for that subpicture. This can be a time consuming and boring process, particularly if you have to manually enter the start and stop time codes for every subpicture element. Fortunately most DVD-Video authoring tools that support the use of subpictures will allow you to store the start time code, stop time code, B, P, E1, E2, transparency level, color palette assignment, and the file name of the subpicture graphic in a script file that can be imported into the authoring system. The use of subpicture script files can save you a lot of time, and effort during the DVD authoring phase of a project.

Each DVD-Video authoring system that supports subpicture script files has its own unique file format for the script. While in general these files all contain ASCII data, they are not transferable from one authoring system to another.

A few additional characteristics about each subpicture element need to be defined. Subpictures can be forced to be displayed by the DVD-Video player, or they can be turned on or off by the viewer. Subpicture graphics can also be animated on screen through the use of the Fade, Scroll and Wipe effects. We will discuss these issues in more detail in Chapter 5 ("Mid-Range DVD Authoring") and Chapter 6 ("Professional DVD Authoring").

Menu Generation

Menus are used on DVD-Video titles as the primary method for the viewer to interact with the content. For example menus will allow the viewer to access each chapter of the title, turn subtitles on or off, specify which audio track they want to listen to, or to watch a preview of a coming attraction. DVD-Video menus are made up of two unique graphic elements, called the menu background and the highlight overlay, as well as a set of definitions for the shape and size of the menu buttons, the colors used to represent the state of each button, and the navigation parameters defined for each button. Menu backgrounds can either be still images or motion video clips. For the creation of the background and overlay graphics you will need to apply the same rules as outlined earlier in this chapter for still images and subtitles. Menu background graphics should be the correct resolution as defined in Table 3.11, should be designed to accommodate Action and Title Safe zones, and should have adjustments made in their color, intensity and contrast for display on television monitors. Menu overlay graphics are essentially full screen subpicture graphics, and use the same concepts of B, P, E1 and E2 colors, transparency levels and a display color palette. In addition to the basic subpicture graphic properties, menu overlays also have color definitions the various states a menu button can have, default, selected and activated.

It is important for a graphic artist who is creating a DVD menu to understand how DVD menus work, so that each menu button is easy for the viewer to identify, and navigation between menu buttons is intuitive using the remote control's menu navigation buttons. It is also important to provide the viewer with feedback on which button is currently selected, as well as to provide feedback when the user activates a specific button by using the Enter key. All DVD-Video players have five buttons defined specifically for use with interactive menus. These are called the Up, Down, Left, Right and Enter buttons. Using these buttons the viewer can select a specific button on a menu, and then by pressing the Enter key activate that menu button to either start the playback of a video clip, jump to another menu, etc.

subpicture overlay is used for each aspect ratio to highlight the correct button areas on the screen.

DVD-Video menus can include up to 36 different buttons. When more than one subpicture overlay is used to support multiple menu aspect ratios, the maximum number of buttons is decreased. If two different menu aspect ratios are used then only 18 buttons can be defined, while if three different aspect ratios are used only 12 buttons can be defined. It is important to keep these restrictions in mind when designing menus for DVD-Video titles that can be displayed in more than one aspect ratio.

Figure 3.11 shows how one background graphic and three overlay graphics can be used to create a menu for three different aspect ratios (4:3 letterbox, 4:3 Pan/Scan and 16:9 widescreen). As you can see from Figure 3.10 in the 4:3 Pan/Scan mode, the DVD-Video player will automatically crop the background image to create a full screen 4:3 menu. If the DVD-Video player is set to display in letterbox mode then the full background graphic will be displayed with black bars on the top and bottom to fill out the 4:3 display. Finally, if the DVD-Video player is set to display in widescreen (16:9) mode, then the full background graphic is displayed along with the widescreen overlay graphic.

Some DVD-Video authoring tools can import menu backgrounds and overlays stored in the Adobe Photoshop (.psd) format. In this case the background and each button highlight are stored in separate layers of the PhotoShop file. Most DVD-Video authoring systems can accept menu background and overlay graphics in the .tif and .bmp formats.

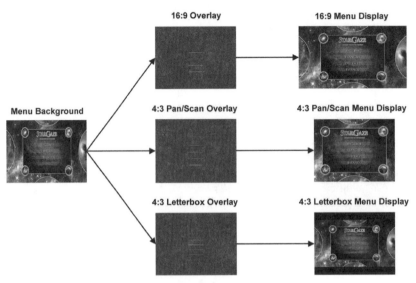

Figure 3.11   Multiple Aspect Ratio DVD-Video Menus
            (See color insert for color version of this figure.)

Tips, Tricks & Techniques

Designing DVD-Video menus requires a blend of artistic talent and logic. The trick is to create menus that are interesting and attractive, while still being intuitively easy for the general consumer to use. The axiom of "Less is More" applies quite well to DVD-Video menu design. A simple, clean menu design with a minimum number of buttons is usually better than a complex, intricate menu with lots of buttons. You should always design menus for an average consumer, who may only watch the title once.

Step 5: Authoring, Formatting & Layout

The term "DVD Authoring" is commonly used to describe the process of taking digital media assets and a project flowchart to create a valid DVD-Video disc image. Some people object to use of "authoring" in this context, as there are no traditional authoring activities involved, like the creative process used in writing a book. Others have suggested the use of the term "DVD Premastering" for this effort, but this is just as confusing as "DVD Authoring" since premastering is usually associated with the process of converting a final disc image into a glass master at a replication facility. "DVD Production" has also been offered up as a generic term for this step of the process, although quite a few people object to this terminology since it blurs the lines between content creation which are typically pre-production and production tasks, and content distribution which is a post-production task. Since DVD-Video is just another distribution vehicle for content, it should not be considered part of the production process. Finally "DVD Programming" has also been suggested as an appropriate description for this effort. Naturally, people who develop software for a living have objected to this terminology. They argue that you can't call something programming unless it actually requires a computer science background.

There are problems with all of the names used to describe this process, and I find each term equally bad. However we have to call this process something, and since DVD Authoring is by far the most common term in use today, that is what I will use in this book to describe the process of converting digital media assets into a DVD disc image.

The actual steps involved in the DVD Authoring process depend on the type of DVD Authoring tool you are using. Regardless of which authoring tool you use there are some

- Generation of a valid disc image suitable for replication.

These tasks can be grouped into three general categories, DVD Authoring, DVD Formatting and DVD Layout.

DVD Authoring

The DVD Authoring process includes the following steps, Media Identification, Media Association and Media Organization, as shown in Figure 3.12. These steps have been generalized so that they are applicable to all DVD-Video authoring systems.

In general there are three different types of DVD-Video authoring systems on the market today. The professional systems allow the developer to take advantage of all of the features defined in the DVD-Video specification such as motion menus, multiple camera angles, multiple audio tracks, subpicture streams, and the use of the System and General Purpose Registers. The mid-range or corporate systems provide some advanced features such as multiple audio tracks or subpictures, but won't allow the developer to use all of the features of the DVD-Video specification. The consumer systems, provide only support for the basic features of DVD-Video generally limiting the developer to one audio track, one camera angle, and no access to system or general purpose registers. The lines between professional, mid-range, and entry-level DVD-Video authoring systems are blurring as more features are added to the lower cost systems to make them more powerful, while professional systems maintain their rich feature sets but offer lower prices to attract a larger segment of the market.

Media Identification

In the Media Identification step audio, still image, subpicture and video media elements are imported into the DVD authoring system software. In some cases, the authoring system will process the media element file to determine critical information required for the media association steps. For example, MPEG video files will be processed to determine the location of all I frames so that scene or chapter points can be created within that video element. Subpicture elements will be converted to run-length coded bitmaps so that they can be integrated with

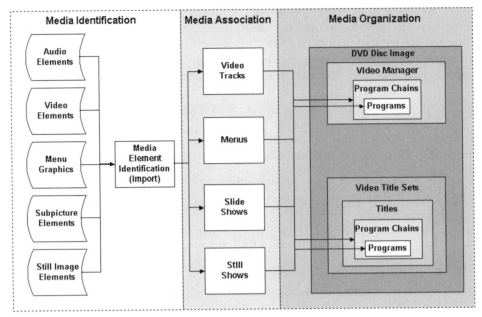

Figure 3.12   The DVD Authoring Process

disc note:

Real World Example

StarGaze was authored on a Scenarist NT 2.0 system. While I have practical experience using authoring tools from Apple, Daikin, Minerva, Sonic Solutions and Spruce Technologies, I generally use Scenarist to author my DVD-Video titles. I am "agnostic" when it comes to DVD authoring tools. I believe that products from all major DVD authoring tool vendors can be used to create excellent DVD titles. There are three reasons why I chose to use Scenarist NT for my authoring needs; (1) Daikin (recently bought by Sonic Solutions) was the only vendor offering DVD-Video authoring tools when I started developing DVD titles in 1996, (2) Scenarist was the first professional DVD authoring tool to support the Windows NT platform, which is my preferred OS, and (3) Scenarist provides support for all features defined in the DVD-Video specification. Since I tend to develop very interactive titles I need a bit more authoring power and flexibility than the average DVD title developer. Chapter 10 provides an in-depth look at most of the DVD-Video authoring tools on the market today. I am sure no matter which tool you choose to purchase and use, you will be able to develop great DVD-Video titles (with the help of this book of course!)

other media elements to create interactive menus, or be used as subpicture streams associated with a video or still image sequence. Still images will be compressed into MPEG I frames so they can be used as menu backgrounds, or included in slide shows or still shows.

Most DVD-Video authoring systems use a drag-and-drop process of identifying all the media assets for a DVD project. Essentially you use either Windows Explorer or the Mac Finder to select one or more media files, and then drop these files into the DVD authoring software. Some DVD-Video authoring systems will allow you to create "place-holders" for media elements that have not been created. Using this technique it is possible, although not recommend, to start authoring a DVD-Video title before all of the media elements have been created.

Most projects will have many unique media elements, so it is important to develop a logical structure for how media elements are identified and organized within the DVD-Video

on computers that support long file names and multiple nested directory structures, so it is a good idea to create media file names that will describe the contents of the file, and to store them in directories or subdirectories with other media files of the same type.

disc note:

Real World Example

Figure 3.13 shows some of the directories and files for media elements used on the Star-Gaze title. As you can see each media element has been given a descriptive file name such as "Once_In_Ancient_Greece.ac3". Nested directories are used to organize similar media elements, for example there is an "Audio" directory, with subdirectories for each audio track.

The second consideration is how media elements are organized within the authoring tool. When you drag-and-drop a media element into the authoring tool it is really only creating a link to that file on one of the system's storage devices. Most DVD-Video authoring systems will allow you to create directories and subdirectories within the authoring tool's graphical user interface to organize the media elements so that they are easier to work with. I recommend that you develop one consistent approach for organizing media elements, and that you use that approach on the physical media as well as within the authoring tool. Figure 3.14 shows one method for organizing media elements in a directory and subdirectory structure that will make it easier to manage the elements over the life of a project. There are many different methods for organizing media elements on your systems storage devices and within your authoring software. You should find a method that works best for you, and then use it consistently on all your projects.

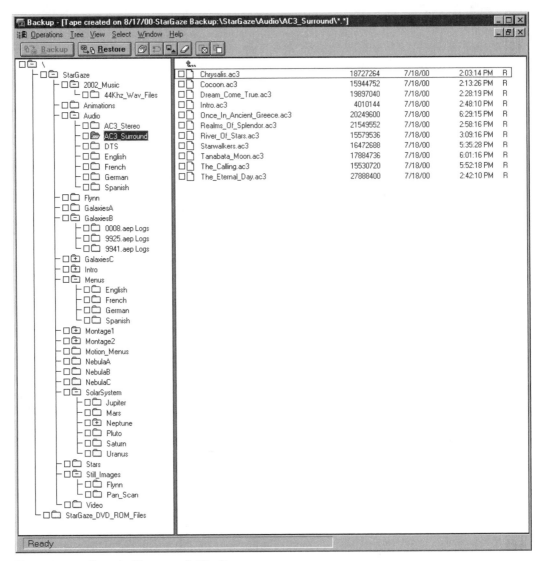

Figure 3.13 Sample Directory & File Structure

Media Association

In the Media Association step individual media elements are combined into logical groups or tracks that are presented in a synchronized fashion. The DVD-Video format supports the creation of multimedia elements with up to nine different camera angles, up to 8 different multi-channel audio tracks, and up to 32 different subpicture streams. Interactive menus can be created with up to 36 buttons distributed among one, two or three different aspect ratios. The Media Association step is where you combine all the various media elements to create the interactive menus and multimedia presentation groups for the title.

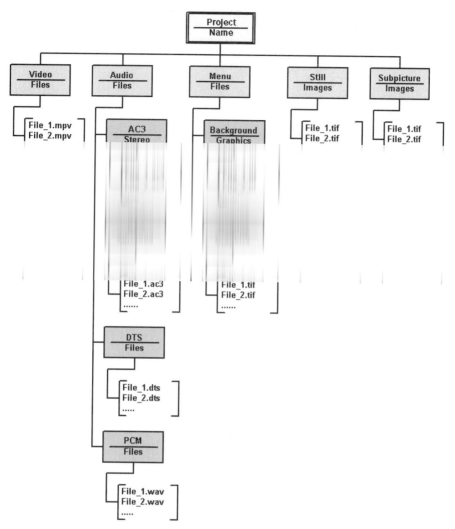

Figure 3.14   Sample Media Element Organization Structure

Many DVD-Video authoring tools use a timeline metaphor for associating media elements. Figure 3.15 shows a sample timeline structure for one of the StarGaze tracks. This particular track has a single video camera angle, seven unique audio tracks and 8 unique subpicture streams. Due to the complexity of this track it is not possible to display all the media elements on the screen at the same time, so some of the subpicture streams are not displayed in this figure. To give you an idea of how complex it can be to create a track for a DVD-Video title the timeline shown in Figure 3.15 includes one MPEG-2 video file, 6 Dolby Digital audio files, one DTS audio file and 368 unique subpicture graphic files.

The timeline metaphor also allows you to create scene or chapter indexes for a media track. This is used when you have long video segments that contain individual chapters or scenes that require direct access from a DVD menu. While each authoring tool is a bit different

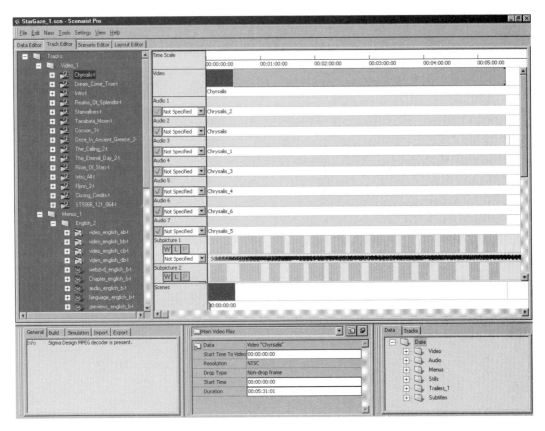

Figure 3.15   Sample Media Track Timeline
(See color insert for color version of this figure.)

most of them will allow you to add scene or chapter in-points to a media track using the time code that is part of the timeline structure. In the example shown in Figure 3.15 the media track starts at time code 0:00:00:00 and ends at 0:05:31:01, and there is only a single chapter defined at time code 0:00:00:00. Most DVD-Video authoring systems will restrict the creation of a scene or chapter index point to the location of the MPEG I frame nearest to the specified time code. This is usually within 1/2 second of the specified time code, so for most projects this is acceptable. If you need to be frame accurate for scene or chapter indexes, then use an MPEG encoder that allows you to force I frames at specific time codes, or use a DVD authoring system that can create forced I frames at desired index points in your media track.

Creating DVD menus is a two-step process. First you create a media track by associating video, still images and overlay graphics. Then you create the menu highlight information by defining the button size, shape and location, as well as the navigation options between buttons. Figure 3.16 shows a sample menu media track from the StarGaze title. In this example you will see that a still image is used for the menu background, and a single 4:3 aspect ratio graphic is used for the menu overlay.

Figure 3.17 shows a detailed screen of this menu showing all of the buttons defined on the menu, as well as the navigation commands to allow the user to move around the menu. This

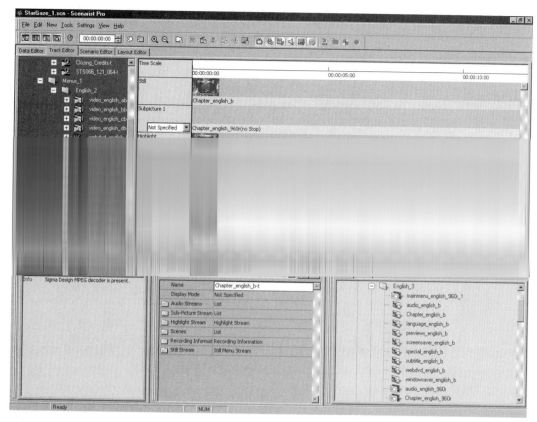

Figure 3.16   Sample Menu Track
(See color insert for color version of this figure.)

menu has a total of 11 buttons, arranged vertically. The Up and Down navigation buttons have been programmed to allow the user to move up or down through the menu, with a wrap-around feature at the top and bottom button (pressing Up from the top button takes the user to the bottom button). Since all the buttons are arranged vertically, the Left and Right navigation commands are not used on this menu.

Many DVD-Video authoring tools include a feature to automatically generate the button navigation commands (Left, Right, Up and Down). In general these "auto-route" features work well on menus with buttons arranged in vertical or horizontal patterns. If the menus are designed in a "free-form" fashion where buttons are not aligned either vertically or horizontally, it's best to enter the individual navigation commands for each button manually.

Menu buttons have display properties that also need to be configured when the track is created. Essentially a button can have three states: Unselected, Selected, and Activated. Only one menu button can be selected at a time, and this button is generally highlighted in some manner to indicate to the viewer that pressing the Enter key will activate that button. When the Enter key is pressed the Selected button can change color to provide feedback to the user that their choice has been accepted and is being acted upon.

Figure 3.17   Sample Menu Button and Navigation Design
(See color insert for color version of this figure.)

Figure 3.18 shows the display properties information for the StarGaze menu described earlier in this section. Pure blue is used as the key color (BG), while Gold, Black and Red are used for the highlight colors (P, E1 and E2). When the button is in the unselected mode, none of these colors will be displayed. A selected button will have a white underline (P at 100%). When a button is activated the underline changes to a gold color. Transparency levels for the white and gold underlines, as well as a black drop shadow are set to 100%.

Media Organization

Media organization is the process of defining the structure of how the various media tracks will be stored on the DVD-Video disc, as well as how the media tracks are connected and controlled by menus on the disc. Many DVD-Video authoring tools call this organization either a scenario or a project. Some authoring tools organize the media elements through the use of a time line, while most use a project flow chart metaphor. StarGaze includes over 12 unique video tracks, over 80 unique menu tracks, and over 150 unique slide show tracks that are combined into the scenario.

Figure 3.19 shows a portion of the StarGaze scenario. From this figure you can see how intricate the design of a DVD-Video title can be. Actually the StarGaze title is only moderately complicated, pri-

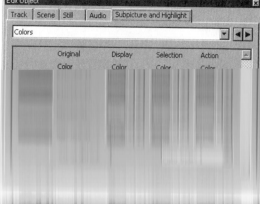

Figure 3.18 Menu Button Display Properties (See color insert for color version of this figure.)

2-5, which include the English, French, German, and Spanish menus. Video Title Set 6 include previews of other DVD titles and the last section, Video Title Set 7 is for the Video Screen Saver feature, which displays a random selection of high quality still images from a collection of over 150 graphics stored on the disc. The directional lines on Figure 3.19 indicate linkage from a menu button to a specific program chain, or to indicate the presence of a "Next," "Previous," and "GoUp" link between program chains.

Compare the StarGaze scenario with the StarGaze Project Flow Chart described earlier in this chapter, you'll see that the scenario closely matches the Flow Chart. The scenario includes significantly more detail than the Project Flow Chart, but in general these two documents should track fairly closely on all your DVD projects. If they don't then you have either made changes to the design of the DVD title without updating the Project Flow Chart, or you have implemented the title in a manner that is not consistent with your original project design.

During the DVD Authoring the following navigation commands are programmed for each media element:

First Play PGC   This is the starting point for a disc when it is inserted into a DVD-Video player. The First Play PGC can not contain any media elements and is generally used simply to set up any system registers or general purpose registers to correct initial values and then to pass control to the program chain that contains the first media elements to be played, such as an FBI warning, production company logo, or even the start of the program.

Title PGC   This is the top level, or main menu for the DVD disc, and is displayed whenever the viewer presses the Title key on their remote control. The Title PGC resides in the Video Manager Area and usually holds the Main Menu for the disc.

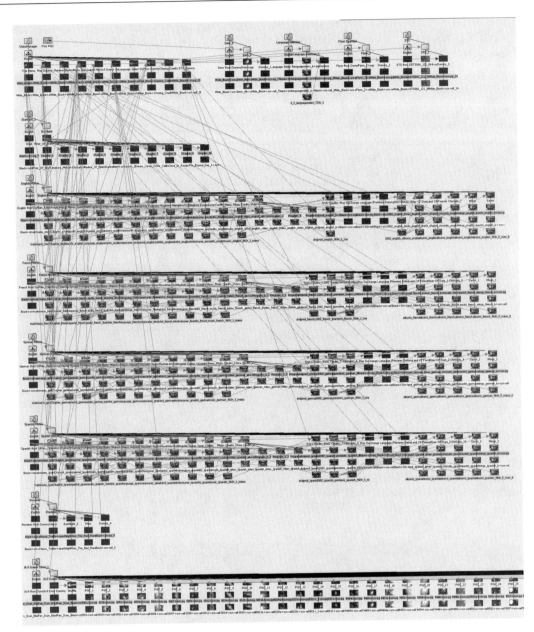

Figure 3.19   Expanded StarGaze Scenario

Root PGC(s)   This is a menu that can be associated with individual titles on the disc, and is displayed when the viewer presses the Menu Key on their remote control. There is a Root PGC for every Video Title Set defined on the disc. The Root PGC can be used to route control to a specific program chain in either the Video Manager Area, or a program chain in its own Video Title Set.

Next The Next link defines what program chain should be executed after completion of the current program chain. When the viewer presses the Next button on their remote control the player will stop playing the current program chain and start playing the program chain that is defined by the Next link.

Previous The Previous link defines what program chain should be executed when the is

playing the current program chain and start playing the program chain defined by the GoUp link. This button can be labeled Go Up, Return or Go Back depending on the specific DVD player manufacturer.

Menu Button Links Each menu button must be programmed to link to a single program chain when the button is activated. Menu buttons can only be linked to program chains within the same Video Title Set as the Menu program chain, or to program chains that reside in the Video Manager area.

Chapters 4–6 discuss the process of authoring a DVD-Video title in detail. Please refer to these chapters for additional information on this topic.

The DVD formatting step is where your authoring tool will convert all the media elements you use in your DVD title, along with the organizational structure that you defined in the Media Organization step, and create valid DVD-Video files. While DVD-Video uses video in the MPEG format, audio in the Dolby Digital, PCM or DTS formats and still images and graphics in various bitmap formats, all of these media elements are converted into a new file format for storage on a DVD disc. Thus the DVD formatting step converts all these media elements into the VOB file format and also creates the required information files (IFO) that tell DVD-Video players how to access the data stored in the VOB file. Backup files (BUP) are also created during the formatting process. The DVD Formatting process is done entirely by the authoring tool.

Some DVD authoring tools will only allow you to play back a media element once it has been stored in the Video Object format, so in many cases the DVD Formatting step must precede any Quality Assurance (QA), emulation and testing steps. Other DVD-Video authoring systems will let you play media elements back in their native (.mpv, .ac3, .tif, .bmp, .dts, .cpt, etc) formats so that you can perform some QA, emulation and testing tasks prior to this step. There are a number of potential timing and compatibility problems when you create Video Object files from individual media elements. Simulating playback using the raw media element files will not allow you to ensure that these potential timing and compatibility problems have been addressed and solved. Even if your authoring system allows you to play back media elements in their raw formats, you will want to go through the DVD Formatting step before you start the final QA, emulation and testing process.

DVD Layout is the process of taking the Video Object files created in the Formatting step and creating a complete disc image that can be used to test the project. The layout process is done entirely by the DVD authoring tool. The amount of time required to format and layout a DVD project depends on several different factors, including:

- Processing speed and power of the authoring system computer

- Efficiency of the authoring tool

- Size and complexity of the DVD title

Most DVD authoring tools will be able to complete the formatting and layout steps in real time, by that I mean it will take about an hour to format and layout a DVD title that has an hour's worth of video content.

Tips, Tricks & Techniques

DVD Formatting & Layout require a lot of hard drive space. As a general rule you will need 9 Gbytes of free space for a DVD-5 project, and 18 Gbytes of free space for a DVD-9 project. This is in addition to the space required for the media files, so when you start a project you will need free space equal to three times the capacity of the DVD disc type you intend to publish the project on.

Step 6: Simulation, Emulation & Quality Assurance

Simulation, and Emulation are essential steps in the QA process to insure that a DVD-Video title has been designed and implemented correctly. Simulation involves testing the DVD project from within a DVD-Video authoring tool. Emulation involves testing the DVD project outside of a DVD-Video authoring tool, usually with a third party hardware or software DVD-Video emulator. Both Simulation and Emulation are part of an overall Quality Assurance program that you should implement for all DVD projects. Essentially a Quality Assurance program is designed to insure that the implementation of the DVD title meets all of the requirements called out in the DVD Requirements document.

Simulation

Most DVD-Video authoring tools provide built-in testing hardware or software that can be used to make sure a DVD-Video title will work correctly. Many professional authoring tools also include software that compares a DVD-Video title implementation against a set of known player compatibility problems and generates warning messages if a particular design may not work correctly on various consumer DVD-Video players. In general this compatibility check software works well, although it won't catch every possible problem. Chapter 6 includes a detailed list of known compatibility problems that you will want to avoid when developing a DVD title.

Figure 3.20 shows the built-in simulation display of a Scenarist NT 2.5 authoring system. As you can see this simulation software provides buttons for all of the standard DVD remote control keys including Title, Menu, Return, Left, Right, Up, Down, Enter, Angle, Audio, Sub-picture, Play, Pause, Stop, Next, Previous, Fast Forward and Reverse. This simulation display can also be used to check the quality of the video and audio playback. MPEG-2 video is decompressed using a software decoder and displayed directly on the computer monitor. An optional hardware MPEG-2 decoder card can be used to display the video content on an external television monitor.

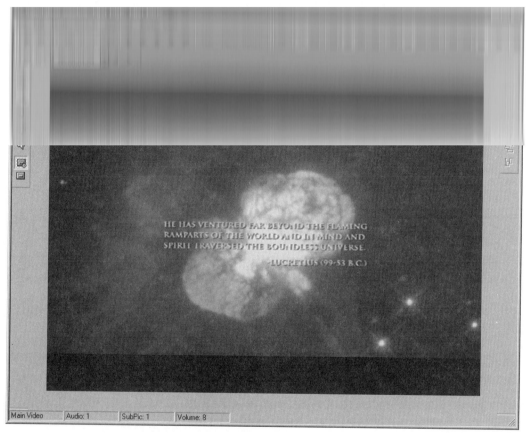

Figure 3.20   Scenarist NT 2.5 Simulation Display
(See color insert for color version of this figure.)

Figure 3.21 shows the Scenarist NT 2.5 simulation display for language settings, menu controls, system parameter registers and general parameter registers. This is extremely useful when you are debugging a complex or highly interactive DVD title and need to see the settings of each SPRM and GRPM register. Many simulation tools will allow you to single step through navigation commands so you can verify that each individual command is being executed properly, and is affecting the SPRM and GPRM registers in the way that you intended.

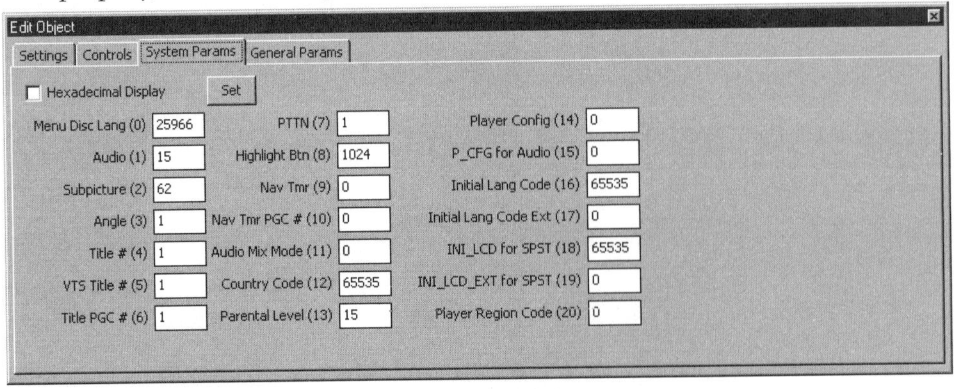

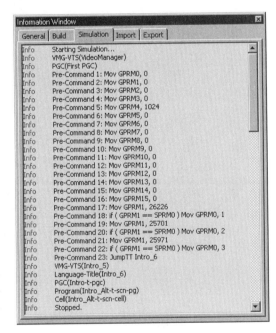

Figure 3.21   Scenarist NT 2.5 SPRM Register Display

Figure 3.22 shows the Scenarist NT 2.5 display showing the step-by-step operation of the simulation tool. This display can be used to debug the interactivity and automatic branching designed into a DVD title. A detailed list of every navigation command executed, and every program chain displayed helps you test the title for all valid presentation configurations.

In the Scenarist authoring tool each of these displays are used together to simulate and test a DVD project. Most professional DVD authoring tools provide similar simulation features and displays that will allow you to thoroughly simulate the operation of a DVD title. Many mid-range or entry-level tools do not provide simulation capabilities at all, so you will be limited to testing titles using DVD emulation hardware or software, which is discussed in the next section.

Figure 3.22   Scenarist NT 2.5 Simulation Status Display

Emulation

There is a subtle yet important difference between simulation and emulation. As shown in Figures 3.20–3.22, simulation involves the playback of a DVD title while providing the DVD author as much information and control over the inner-workings of the playback environment as possible. Thus using a simulator you can not only test a title to make sure it works properly, but also debug the title when it is not working correctly. This is particularly important for titles that make use of complex navigation schemes, or use the SPRM and GPRM registers.

Emulation on the other hand involves testing a DVD title with only the playback controls and displays offered by a traditional DVD-Video player. Emulation attempts to recreate the viewer playback environment in both form and function. Some hardware DVD emulators are actually modified consumer DVD-Video players that allow you to play a disc image from a hard drive rather than a recorded or mass-produced DVD disc. Most emulators used in DVD-Video production are actually off-the-shelf hardware or software DVD decoders and playback

title are tested at some point in this process, and it is not particularly important if the tests are performed on a DVD simulator or a DVD emulator. The following items should be verified in the DVD-Video title simulation and/or emulation process:

Video Quality All video elements should be checked to insure that they meet the minimum acceptable quality levels set out by the Project Requirements document. Video segments should be reviewed for correct start and stop times, the presence of digital compression artifacts, color blooming or bleeding, and the correct use of video and title safe zones. I recommend that a television monitor, rather than a computer monitor be used to review video quality, since computer monitors will not show color or safe zone problems. A great way to look for digital compression artifacts it to display the video on a black & white television monitor. The presence of blocking, fringing or ringing artifacts in compressed video is easy to detect on monochrome monitors.

Audio Quality All audio tracks should be checked to insure that they meet the minimum acceptable quality levels set out by the Project Requirements document. Audio tracks should be reviewed for correct start and stop times, the presence of digital compression artifacts, clipping, and appropriate audio levels across all audio tracks. I recommend you use a surround sound decoder and properly matched surround sound speakers to review audio quality. Most DVD-Video authoring systems that include a hardware DVD decoder card will allow you to route the playback audio to a surround sound receiver for testing. Make sure you test your audio using both the surround sound and stereo modes of your receiver, as surround sound audio often sounds much different when played through a stereo receiver.

Audio/Video Synchronization All video segments that include audio tracks should be checked to insure that the video and audio are properly synchronized. This synchronization should be verified for the entire length of each video segment, and for each unique audio track. It is entirely possible for the video and audio to be in-sync at the start of the segment and out of sync at the end of the segment.

Subpicture Quality   All subpicture streams should be checked to insure that all subpicture elements meet the minimum acceptable quality levels set out by the Project Requirements document. The brightness, color, contrast, start and stop times, and the content of each subpicture element should be checked, as well as the correct operation of the subpicture on and off controls for the title, either through the viewer remote control or via menus. It is important to review subpicture streams on a television monitor so that you can verify that each element is within the title safe area on the TV, and the display colors are appropriate for use on television displays.

Menu Quality   All menus should be checked to insure that they meet the minimum acceptable quality levels set out by the Project Requirements document. It is important to review menus on a television monitor so that you can verify that critical graphics are within the title safe area on the TV, and the display colors are appropriate for use on television displays.

Menu Operation   Every button on every menu must be tested to insure that they are working properly. This includes testing the Up, Down, Left, and Right navigation properties, the Display, Selected, and Activated overlay properties, and the Link property of every button. For complicated titles this can be tedious and time consuming, but it is essential to test every parameter of every button. Menus that include video or audio elements should also be tested to ensure that these meet the minimum quality requirement for video and audio. Menus that are displayed for a fixed amount of time also need to be tested to ensure that after the specified display period the menu will pass control to the correct program chain in the title.

SPRM & GPRM Register Usage   On DVD titles that use them, the SPRM and GRPM registers must be tested to ensure that each register is being read or written to correctly, and the programming logic being implemented through use of these registers is correct. For complex titles this may require rigorous testing of all possible paths through the logic of the DVD title, with single step testing to verify that registers are being set to the correct values at each pre, post and cell command defined in the title.

User Operations (UOP)   All user operations must be tested to make sure that they are working correctly. This includes the use of the Title, Menu, Return (GoUp), Angle, Audio, and Subpicture buttons, as well as the playback controls such as Play, Pause, Stop, Next, Previous, Search Forward and Search Backward buttons. If your title has been designed to prevent the use of specific user operations at certain times, such as the lockout of all user operations during the playback of an FBI Warning screen, then you need to make sure that the UOP's are being disabled and enabled at the correct places in the DVD title.

During the early days of DVD-Video, the emulation process was typically performed using a DVD disc image stored on a hard drive. Over the past several years as the cost of DVD-R recorders has decreased, and the capacity of DVD-R discs has increased, testing has shifted to using disc images stored on DVD-R media. I strongly recommend that you create DVD-R versions of all your DVD titles, using either DVD-R for General or DVD-R for Authoring media. These DVD-R versions of your titles should be tested on as many consumer DVD-Video players as possible to identify any compatibility problems that may have been missed by the DVD authoring software, or the emulation and simulation testing efforts. Since DVD-

R media can't be used to store CSS encrypted data, this testing effort is performed before CSS is added to a title.

Quality Assurance

The goal of simulation and emulation is simple, to verify that the DVD title has been correctly designed and implemented. Toward that end it is important to have an impartial staff member or outside service organization involved in this process. Many DVD authoring companies have a separate quality assurance department that is responsible for testing each title

process you are not required to pay for any spoiled or non-working production discs. Make sure you provide room on the QA form for feedback in case a problem is found. QA forms should be living documents that are completed as the project goes from one stage of the development process to the next. Thus one column should be completed and signed off by the DVD Authoring staff member that has completed work on the title. When the QA department has verified that the title meets all the project requirements then they will sign off the next column. Finally when the content owner or client has reviewed and approved the title they should complete the last column. The completed QA form should be filed with the original Project Requirements document, Project Flow Chart, Project Budget and Project Schedule. It may be necessary to refer to all these documents after the title has been submitted for replication. Please feel free to download a blank copy of this form from http://www.DVDToday.com.

Table 3.12 DVD Quality Assurance Approval Form			
DVD Element	Authoring Approval	QA Approval	Customer Approval
Video			
No Video Compression Artifacts			
Video Start & Stop Points OK			
Video Safe Zones OK			
Seamless Video Angle Transition OK			
Overall Video Quality OK			

Table 3.12 DVD Quality Assurance Approval Form (Continued)

DVD Element	Authoring Approval	QA Approval	Customer Approval
Audio			
No Audio Compression Artifacts			
Audio Formats and Data Rates OK			
Seamless Audio Track Transition OK			
Overall Audio Quality OK			
Audio/Video Synchronization OK			
Surround Sound Playback OK			
Stereo Playback OK			
Subpictures			
Subpicture Timing OK			
Subpicture Color, Brightness & Contrast OK			
Seamless Subpicture Transition OK			
Title Safe Zones OK			
Menus			
No Video/Audio/Still Compression Artifacts			
Overlay Highlight Color & Transparency OK			
Display, Selected, & Active Highlights OK			
Menu Button Operation OK			
Action Safe & Title Safe Zones OK			
Registers			
SPRM Register Usage OK			
GPRM Register Usage OK			
User Operations			
Title, Menu, Return Buttons OK			

Table 3.12 DVD Quality Assurance Approval Form (Continued)			
DVD Element	Authoring Approval	QA Approval	Customer Approval
Next, Previous Buttons OK			
Left, Right, Up, Down, Enter Buttons OK			

Client: Name: Date:

Step 7: Copy Protection & Region Coding

Since it is difficult, if not impossible, to create DVD disc images on hard drives or DVD-R discs with CSS encrypted content, the addition of CSS information is generally done after the title has been through QA, just before the final disc image is transferred to DLT tape. Many DVD authoring facilities also choose to turn on or off the appropriate region codes at this step since it is easier to test a region free disc image, than one that is limited to one or more specific regions. Most DVD authoring tools allow you to enter the CSS encryption and Region Code information at any step of the authoring process, but this data won't actually be used until the final disc image is created and stored on DLT tape. In the past if you wanted to use CSS encryption or region coding you had to submit a DLT tape in DDP 2.0 format to the replication facility. Some replication facilities accept disc images on DVD-R media rather than DLT tape, but in general these could not be used for CSS encrypted or region coded titles. With the recent release of the new "Cutting Master Format" it is now possible to use a DVD-R for Authoring disc to transfer the final disc image for a CSS encrypted or region coded title to a replication facility. One of the new features of the Cutting Master Format is that it can store the ancillary data files required by replicators for content protection and region coding. The disc image is not actually stored in an encrypted format on the DVD-R disc, but most of the information required by a replication facility to make a CSS protected disc is stored on the DVD-R. The replication facility will need to get the disc and title keys from the content owner in order to create the final CSS encrypted disc. Of course your DVD-Video authoring system must support the new Cutting Master Format, and your DVD-R drive must be able to write to DVD for Authoring media in order to use the feature.

Several different aspects of copyright protection and region coding must be configured during this last step of the DVD authoring process.

Copy Guard Management System (CGMS)   If CGMS is to be enabled on the title then it must be set to the appropriate level (no copies, one copy, or infinite copies)

Analog Protection System (APS)   If APS is to be enabled on the title then it must be set to the appropriate level (Macrovision AGC, Macrovision AGC + ColorStripe Type 1, or Macrovision AGC + ColorStripe Type 2). It is important to note that while most professional DVD-Video authoring systems provide the ability to select the appropriate level of APS protection, it is incumbent on the DVD authoring company to make sure they are authorized by Macrovision to use this feature. The DVD Analog Protection System includes technology that is licensed from Macrovision and a royalty must be paid by the content owner to Macrovision in order to use APS. When a DVD title that incorporates Macrovision APS technology is manufactured, the replication facility will provide Macrovision with a report providing the client name and the number of disc made. This report assists Macrovision in collecting any license fees due for the use of their patented technology.

Content Scrambling System (CSS)   There are three unique keys required by CSS, a Disc Key, Video Manager Key and Title Key(s). Each Title on a DVD-Video disc has its own key if it is to have CSS encryption enabled. In general the actual keys used for CSS protection are not provided directly to the DVD authoring facility, but are sent to the replication facility by the content owner. Many replication facilities act as a clearinghouse for CSS keys, since there is a fairly significant ($10,000) up-front license fee to become approved to hold CSS keys. If you want to use CSS encryption on one of your titles talk to your replication facility to see if they can provide all the keys you will need.

Region Codes   There are currently 7 different regions of the world defined for DVD-Video Region Codes. Support for different regions is independent, that is you can enable or disable playback support for each region, and create any custom region configuration you want. Figure 3.23 shows the Region Code selection screen from Scenarist, where you can see that each region code can be enabled or disabled independently. The currently defined regions codes are as follows.

- Region 1 — U.S., Canada, U.S. Territories

- Region 2 — Japan, Europe, South Africa, and Middle East, Egypt

- Region 3 — Southeast Asia and East Asia, Hong Kong

- Region 4 — Australia, New Zealand, Pacific Islands, Central America, Mexico, South America, the Caribbean

- Region 5 — Eastern Europe, Indian subcontinent, Africa, North Korea, Mongolia

- Region 6 — China

- Region 7 — Reserved for future use

- Region 8 — Special international venues such as airplanes, or cruise ships.

Once the copyright protection and region code properties have been set correctly in your DVD-Video authoring tool you can generate the final disc image and output it to either DLT tape, DVD-R for General media or DVD-R for Authoring media. If you have a small disc image that is only intended

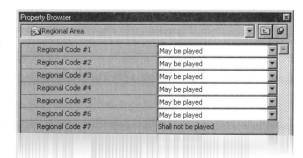

I recommend you use DLT tapes in the DDP 2.0 format to send completed disc images to DVD replication facilities. While DVD-R discs are robust, and have excellent error detection and correction features, in practice DLT tapes are much less prone to errors than DVD-R discs. I have completed over 200 DVD titles that were submitted to a replication facility on DLT tape, and I can honestly say that there has never been a problem caused by a DLT tape error. If you decide to use DVD-R media to send a disc image to a replication facility, I recommend you use blank media from Pioneer, TDK or Verbatim. From my experience these three vendors produce DVD-R media with low error rates, and are generally compatible with all DVD-ROM drives used by replication facilities.

Step 8: Replication

DVD disc replication is similar to the process used for CD replication although DVD discs require much more stringent manufacturing tolerances, and also require a bonding step that is not required by CD replication. Most DVD replication facilities will provide the DVD title developer with a "Check-Disc". A Check-Disc is essentially a limited run version of the final production discs, although most of the time the final disc label artwork is not printed on the check disc. The purpose of a Check-Disc is simple, to allow the DVD title developer to verify that the production disc does what it is supposed to do before they commit to a large production run. DVD replicators do not generally test DVD discs to ensure that they work properly. Some replicators will put samples of their replicated discs into a DVD-Video player just to make sure that they start to play, but they are not in a position to know if all aspects of the disc are working correctly.

It is up to the DVD title developer to verify that the Check-Disc is fully functional. This is the last line of Quality Assurance for a DVD title developer. Replicated Check-Discs should be tested in as many DVD-Video players and DVD-ROM enabled personal computers as possible. By testing the Check-Disc in a wide variety of DVD playback devices you will increase your odds of finding any potential compatibility problems before the start of a large production run. Surprisingly, despite the fact that most DVD replicators send Check-Discs to the title developers, there are still projects that have been released to the market that have not been thoroughly tested. During early 2001 the Disney film Dinosaur came to market with both a standard edition and collector's edition DVD release, both of which had significant problems that prevented them from working correctly in a large number of consumer DVD-Video players.

There are eight basic steps in the DVD Replication process, as shown in Figure 3.24.

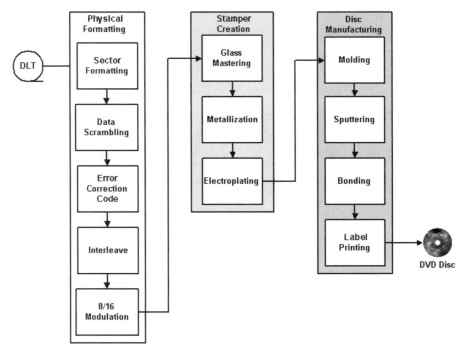

Figure 3.24   DVD Replication Process

1. Physical Formatting   In the physical formatting step the disc image stored on a DLT tape or DVD-R is converted into a bit stream suitable for use with a Laser Beam Recorder (LBR). The original disc image undergoes sector formatting, scrambling (if CSS encryption is required), generation of the proper error correction codes, interleaving, and finally 8/16 modulation and synchronization. There is a common misperception that the pits on a DVD disc represent individual data bits. Individual pits are simply parts of an 8/16 modulated signal created in this step. When a disc is read by the laser in a DVD-Video player or DVD-ROM drive, individual data bits are reconstructed through a process of 8/16 demodulation, de-interleaving, error detection and correction, and finally unscrambling (if CSS encryption was used).

2. Glass Mastering   The bit stream from Physical Formatting is sent to a Laser Beam Recorder, which uses a laser to write the information onto a 240 mm Soda-Lime Glass master with a 100 nm photoresist coating. The laser writes information to the glass master by burning away the photoresist coating on some areas of the disc, and leaving the coating intact on others. After completion of the recording session the glass master is "developed" using a Sodium Metasilicate developing solution. This developing process creates a master disc that has the required "pits and tracks" of the DVD disc to be manufactured.

3. Metallization   A thin layer of metal is applied to the developed glass master to provide a conductive layer for the electroplating process.

Substrate is made with an inverse copy of the pits and tracks stored on the stamper, thus creating an identical copy of the glass master.

6. Sputtering   An aluminum reflective layer, or gold semi-reflective layer (for DVD-9 discs) is sputtered onto the polycarbonate substrate to create half of the final manufactured DVD disc.

7. Bonding   Using hot melt glue, or ultraviolet cured glue, the two halves of the DVD disc are bonded together to create the final disc. DVD-5 discs include a "blank" half that contains no data. DVD-10 and DVD-18 discs include two halves each with a valid disc image. A DVD-9 disc can either have one data layer recorded on each disc half, or both layers on one half, which is then bonded to a blank.

8. Labeling   Finished discs can be labeled using a variety of printing techniques:

Pit Art   A stamper is produced with pits and tracks used to create molded artwork or printing. This process can be used only on DVD-5 discs.

Screen Print   Spot or process print similar to CD industry. Between one and five colors can be applied to the topside of a DVD-5 or DVD-9 disc.

Reverse Screen Print   Printing on an internal surface of an unused side for a wet appearance. This process can only be used for single sided discs.

Offset Printing   Full color picture printing similar to how magazines are printed. The low ink mass and minimal shrinkage properties of this process are beneficial for DVD balance and tilt.

Flexographic Printing   A new disc printing process similar to offset printing but with spot print capability.

Tips, Tricks & Techniques

I recommend that you have at least five DVD-Video players in-house for testing Check-Discs. Testing your Check-Discs on current models from Panasonic, Pioneer, Sony and Toshiba will allow you to detect compatibility problems before you commit to a large production run. You should also use the cheapest DVD-Video player you can find in addition to the name brands listed above. Cheap DVD-Video players generally have a higher number of compatibility problems than name brand players. In addition to in-house resources you may want to contract out with a 3rd party testing facility that has hundreds of different DVD-Video players in their test lab. These 3rd party testing services are not cheap, but they are a lot less expensive than recalling thousands, or even millions of DVD-Video discs that don't work properly.

Step 9: Packaging

Figure 3.25   Sample DVD Disc Label Artwork

The DVD-Video industry has settled on a few different styles of packages for the vast majority of consumer titles. The three most popular package styles are the Amaray case, the Warner Snapper case and the Super Jewell Box case. Each of these products conforms to the general recommendations issued by the Video Software Dealer's Association (VSDA) for DVD packaging. This recommendation states that a consumer DVD-Video package should be the same height as a VHS tape (7 3/8"), the same width as a CD jewel case (5 5/8"), with a depth between 3/8" and 5/8" for a single disc package. Additionally DVD-Video packages should have tamper proof design, include a UPC code on the top right of the back of the package, and provide for the implementation of a variety of security measures such as source tagging.

In general there are three different items that are combined to form a consumer DVD-Video title: the DVD disc, a plastic or cardboard case, and printed material for both the outside and inside of the package. The Warner Snapper design eliminates the need for one item since the case is actually made from a cardboard material that includes printing options for both the outside and inside of the package. In my experience the differences between package formats does not appear to significantly influence purchasing decisions by consumers.

For DVD title developers the important factors to keep in mind regarding packaging is how to create the artwork for the outside cover, the inside insert and the disc label. Most DVD replication facilities have templates in a variety of graphics formats for use in developing the final artwork for a DVD project. It is important to note that there are many different replication and printing processes for DVD discs, so you should consult with your DVD replication facility to get the correct templates you need to design the artwork for your DVD project. The specific template you use will depend on what type of DVD disc you are making (DVD-5, DVD-9, DVD-10, or DVD-18), what package style you choose (Amaray, Snapper or Super Jewell Case) and other factors.

designing your disc label. Star Gaze is printing a four color color outside cover shown in Figure 3.26, as well as a four color insert, shown in Figure 3.27.

Figure 3.26   Sample DVD Package Cover Artwork
(See color insert for color version of this figure.)

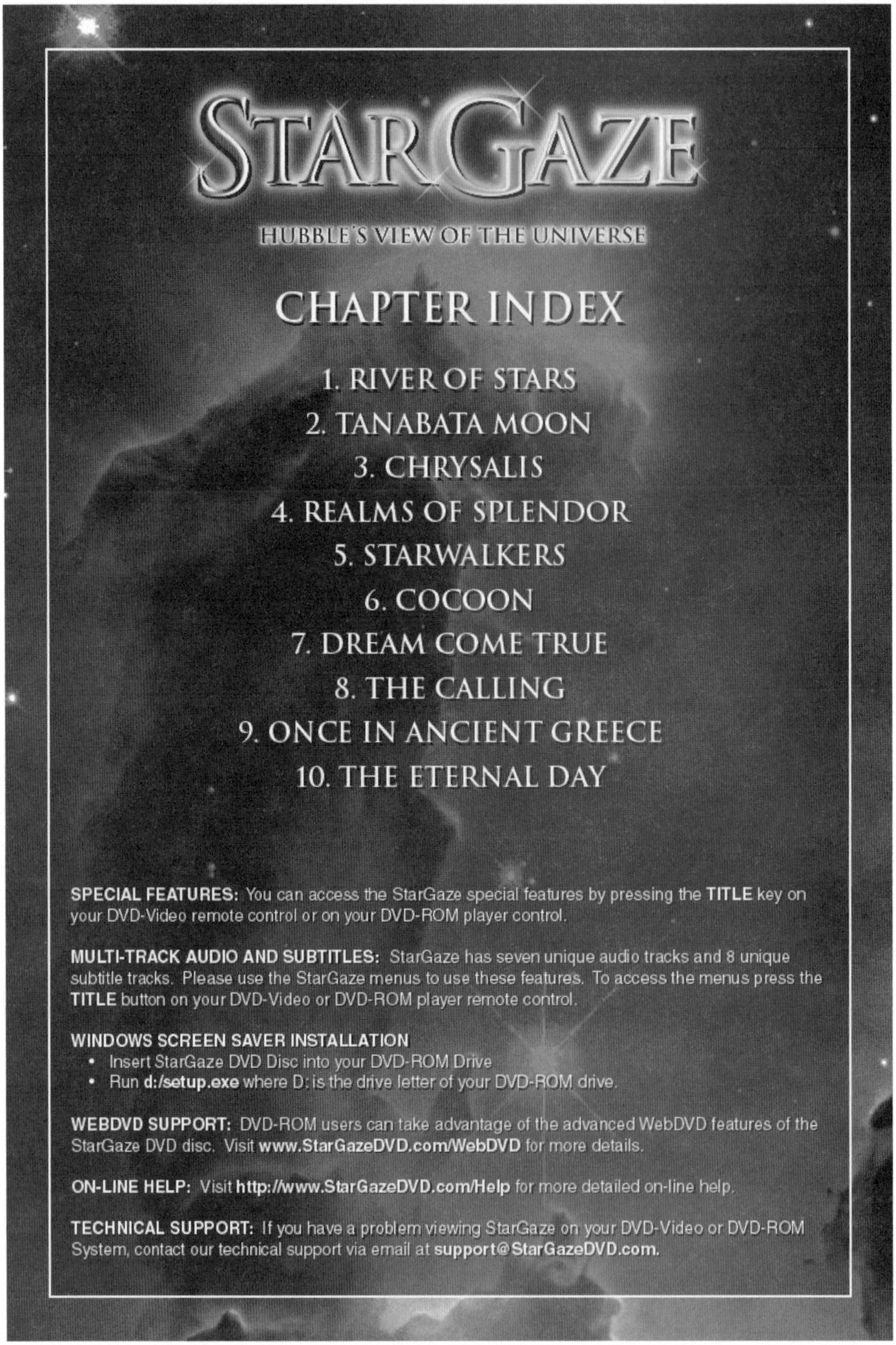

StarGaze
HUBBLE'S VIEW OF THE UNIVERSE

CHAPTER INDEX

1. RIVER OF STARS
2. TANABATA MOON
3. CHRYSALIS
4. REALMS OF SPLENDOR
5. STARWALKERS
6. COCOON
7. DREAM COME TRUE
8. THE CALLING
9. ONCE IN ANCIENT GREECE
10. THE ETERNAL DAY

SPECIAL FEATURES: You can access the StarGaze special features by pressing the **TITLE** key on your DVD-Video remote control or on your DVD-ROM player control.

MULTI-TRACK AUDIO AND SUBTITLES: StarGaze has seven unique audio tracks and 8 unique subtitle tracks. Please use the StarGaze menus to use these features. To access the menus press the **TITLE** button on your DVD-Video or DVD-ROM player remote control.

WINDOWS SCREEN SAVER INSTALLATION
- Insert StarGaze DVD Disc into your DVD-ROM Drive
- Run **d:/setup.exe** where D: is the drive letter of your DVD-ROM drive.

WEBDVD SUPPORT: DVD-ROM users can take advantage of the advanced WebDVD features of the StarGaze DVD disc. Visit **www.StarGazeDVD.com/WebDVD** for more details.

ON-LINE HELP: Visit **http://www.StarGazeDVD.com/Help** for more detailed on-line help.

TECHNICAL SUPPORT: If you have a problem viewing StarGaze on your DVD-Video or DVD-ROM System, contact our technical support via email at **support@StarGazeDVD.com**.

Figure 3.27   Sample DVD Insert Artwork
(See color insert for color version of this figure.)

Since every replication facility has its own unique collection of replication, printing and packaging systems, it is impossible to provide you with a single concise recommendation on the sizes, file formats, and delivery media you should use for package artwork. In general each replication facility will provide you with a template that you can use to create graphics that will work with their printing and packaging systems. Many replication facilities provide these templates on their web sites.

While there are few specific requirements called out for packaging by the DVD-Video specification, there are a number of industry standards that you should attempt to follow.

Dolby Digital, and DTS Logos   If your title includes either Dolby Digital or DTS audio tracks it is a good idea to include these logos on the package as well. You can obtain copies of each logo from Dolby Labs (http://www.dolby.com) and DTS (http://www.dtsonline.com) respectively.

NTSC and PAL   It is a good idea to identify the video television standard used on the disc (NTSC or PAL). DVD-Video players are popular throughout the world and consumers deserve to know what format disc they are purchasing.

DVD-5, DVD-9, DVD-10, and DVD-18   It is a good idea to identify the type of DVD disc(s), as well as how many discs are included in the package. DVD-9 titles have more perceived value than DVD-5 or DVD-10 titles so it is worthwhile to mention the presence of a dual layer disc on the package. DVD logo graphics can be obtained from the DVD Format/Logo Licensing Corporation (http://www.dvdfllc.co.jp).

Region Code   Region Codes are generally identified using a small icon of the world, with one or more numbers inside the globe. A Region 1 disc has a world icon with a "1" in it, Region 2 discs have a world icon with a "2" in it and so on. Discs that support all regions should have a world icon with "All" or "0" in it. Region logo graphics can be obtained from the DVD Format/Logo Licensing Corporation (http://www.dvdfllc.co.jp).

Aspect Ratio   The aspect ratio of the video content should be included somewhere on the back of the package. 16:9 content has a higher perceived value than 4:3 content, so it is important to highlight the presence of widescreen content. This information can be communicated to the consumer in a variety of ways, but there is no industry standard logo.

Display Mode (Normal, Pan/Scan, Letterbox, and Widescreen)   The display mode of the video content should also be included on the back of the package. Widescreen and Letterbox content have a higher perceived value than normal or Pan/Scan content, so this information should be highlighted on the package. This information can be communicated to the consumer in a variety of ways, but there is no industry standard logo.

Rating Level   Many countries require that the rating level of the content be included in a specific format on the package. In the US rating level logos can be obtained from the Motion Picture Association (http://www.mpaa.org).

UPC Code   The UPC code should be placed in the upper right portion of the back cover of the package. Titles that do not have UPC codes in general will not sell as well as titles with UPC codes. This is because many of the large DVD retailers will not carry titles that do not have UPC codes, thus sales of these titles will be limited to specialty and on-line retailers. In the United States UPC codes can be obtained from the Uniform Code Council (http://www.uc-council.org) and in Canada they may be obtained from the Electronic Commerce Council of Canada (http://www.eccc.org).

Special or Added Features   It is a good idea to describe any special or added features such as THX certification, multiple audio tracks, director commentary, actor biographies, theatrical trailers, etc. on the back cover. Many consumers make their purchasing decisions on the number and quality of "extras" included on the disc in addition to the quality of the main program, especially if they already own a VHS version of the title.

The front cover of a DVD-Video package generally includes the title of the program, a small number of additional graphics such as the DVD-Video icon, Dolby Digital or DTS icons, and one or more full color graphics designed to create an attractive cover. Most retail stores stock DVD titles on shelves that show only the front cover of the package, thus the front cover must be designed to stand out among the crowd of other DVD titles to grab the attention of the consumer. A few retailers stock DVD titles so that only the spine of the package is displayed to the consumer, thus it is important to include the name of the title as well as a few small logos on the spine as well as the front cover.

The vast majority of DVD retailers require that titles be shrink-wrapped prior to shipment. In addition to shrink-wrap there are a number of optional security devices that are popular for DVD titles. Most studios now include one or more plastic tapes on the top, side or bottom of the DVD case. These plastic tapes serve two purposes, first they include the title name and in some cases UPC code, and second they make it more difficult to steal the disc out of the case since one or more tapes must be cut to open the case. Other security devices such as magnetic source tags can be attached to the inside of the DVD case so that magnetic anti-theft systems can detect if a disc is being stolen.

Decisions on what security measures to include inside a DVD package as well as how many security tapes to include prior to shrink wrap should be made in consultation with the company that will act as the distributor for the title. Many large retailers have their own unique security requirements, but many smaller retailers are happy with shrink-wrapped cases with a single security tape.

Step 10: Distribution & Sales

While Distribution & Sales is listed towards the end of the DVD Production process, in many respects it should be one of the first tasks undertaken for a DVD project. This is particularly true for a DVD title that will be sold to consumers. The distribution timeline for consumer DVD titles, shown in Figure 3.28, has many levels and it can take between 60 and 90 days to get copies of a DVD title from the replication facility to the shelves of a DVD retailer. If you are developing a consumer DVD title it is always a good idea to know how the title will be distributed and sold before you actually start work on the title. It is also a good idea to

4	Disc Packaging	2/12/2001	2/16/2001	5d
5	Ship Review Copies	2/19/2001	2/23/2001	5d
6	Distributor Order	2/26/2001	2/27/2001	2d
7	Ship to Distributor	2/28/2001	3/6/2001	5d
8	Aggregator Order	3/7/2001	3/8/2001	2d
9	Ship to Aggregator	3/9/2001	3/15/2001	5d
10	Retailer Order	3/16/2001	3/19/2001	2d
11	Ship to Retailer	3/20/2001	3/26/2001	5d
12	Stock Shelves with DVD Titles	3/27/2001	3/28/2001	2d

Figure 3.28   Distribution Pipeline for Consumer DVD Titles

Consumer DVD titles generally have a four level distribution path, shown in Figure 3.29, with the content owner selling to a master distributor, who in turn sells to general distributors, who then sell to on-line and traditional retailers, who finally sell the disc to consumers. In some cases large DVD retailers, such as Best Buy, can purchase directly from a master distributor and eliminate one level of the distribution channel. Generally this is done to provide a large retailer with better service, as well as a higher margin on the products they purchase. The closer the product gets to the consumer the more choices they have, for example there are literally thousands of on-line and traditional retail stores where consumers can purchase DVD titles. Moving up the distribution channel, there are less than 100 distributors, and less than 20 master distributors that carry DVD titles. While there are hundreds of content owners who publish DVD titles, the vast majority of consumer titles come from less than 10 studios, or their home entertainment distribution companies.

Most DVD-Video titles have a suggested retail price of $25 or less. With up to four different companies involved in getting a DVD title from the replication facility to the shelves of a retail store, the cost of processing and shipping orders can become a significant percentage of the total sales price. Replication facilities typically ship DVD titles in boxes of 30 units, which weigh about 10 pounds each. In order to minimize shipping costs, DVD discs are typically shipped via ground transport, so it can take as much as a week to ship product from a

disc note:

Real World Example

To illustrate this concept lets take a look at how StarGaze is sold. Alpha DVD is the content owner for StarGaze and has granted a worldwide license to DVD International, which acts as the Master Distributor for the title. DVD International sells StarGaze to many different distribution companies such as Image Entertainment, who then sell the title to on-line and brick & mortar retail customers, such as Tower Records. Larger retail customers, such as DVD Express or Best Buy, purchase StarGaze directly from DVD International. Both DVD International and Alpha DVD offer copies of StarGaze directly to consumers via their web sites. Thus consumers can purchase StarGaze from a wide variety of on-line and traditional retail stores, from a master distributor (DVD International) as well as from the content owner (Alpha DVD).

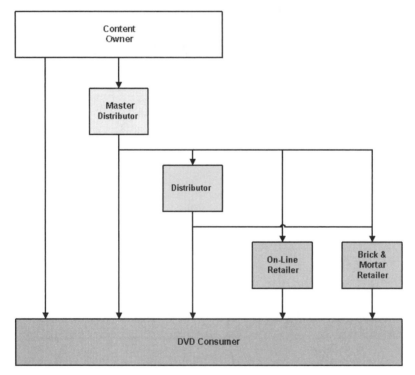

Figure 3.29   Consumer DVD Distribution Channel

replication facility to a distributor's warehouse. Many distributors act as fulfillment agents for retail stores, so they will maintain a small amount of stock for popular titles and then ship a consolidated order, which may include many different titles, to a retail store once a week or so. Consolidated orders are also shipped via ground transport to minimize shipping costs. Once the order arrives at the retail store it can either be placed directly onto the retail shelves, or into an on-site storage facility where current stock is held until it is needed on the sales floor.

Selling DVD titles also requires time and effort. There are actually two different selling efforts required for DVD titles. The first and most obvious sales effort is to convince consumers to purchase the title when it becomes available. Generating consumer awareness and interest in a DVD-Video title is usually done through advertising and marketing programs designed to educate consumers in an effort to convince them to make a purchase. Another popular technique is to provide advance copies of a DVD-Video title to the dozens of web sites that post reviews of consumer DVD titles. It is difficult to gauge how effective a good

video displays in a minimum amount of time. Specialty retailers like Best Buy have larger selections of DVD titles, but still only carry about 500 unique titles. Finally, on-line retailers will add almost any DVD-Video title to their product database, but they may not actually place an order until one of their customers has purchased a copy of the title.

Generally the process of selling a DVD-Video title to a distributor or retailer begins about three months prior to the title's official street date. Copies of the title cover art, along with a sell sheet, which provides a synopsis of the title as well as important information a customer needs to make an informed purchase decision are sent to each distributor and retailer. If available, DVD-R "review" copies should be provided, as well as a description of the marketing and advertising plans for the title. Finally, production copies of the title should be sent to each prospective customer as soon as they are available. A "pre-book" or "pre-order" sales period of about six weeks is used to secure the initial orders for a title and get them into the distribution pipeline prior to the official title street date.

Many content owners who don't have a large catalog of DVD titles will find that orders during the pre-book period will be negligible until they send production copies of the title to each distributor and retailer. Distributors and retailers have been burned in the past by content owners who announce a street date for a DVD title, accept pre-book orders, and then fail to deliver production copies on time. This can leave retailers with a hole on their shelves since they were planning on stocking a title starting on the announced street date.

The vast majority of DVD distributors and retailers will only purchase product that they can return if the title does not sell well. These "return privileges" offered to distributors and retailers usually have some restrictions such as a time (within one year of purchase), condition (factory sealed product only), and volume (up to 20% of a single order may be returned). In some cases a distributor may charge a restocking fee to a retailer who returns unsold product.

Tips, Tricks & Techniques

Every one knows that in North America the fourth quarter (October, November and December) is the best time to sell a consumer DVD-Video title. DVD retailers will generate up to 40% of their annual sales revenue during this three-month period. If you are a DVD-Video title developer trying to sell consumer titles you also need to know that most returns for the year come in January and February.

Step 11: Customer Support

The last step in the DVD Production process is Customer Support. If you have done a good job in QA, most DVD projects require a minimal level of customer support. In general most DVD-Video titles will play on most DVD-Video players with little or no problems. However even the simplest of DVD-Video titles can experience playback problems when it gets out into the real world. While the vast majority of DVD-Video playback problems are actually caused by player incompatibilities, the general consumer will blame the content owner or title developer when they encounter a problem. This is an understandable reaction by a consumer who may have hundreds of DVD-Video titles that work just fine on his or her home entertainment system. When a new title does not work correctly the consumer naturally assumes that the title is at fault, since they have all these other titles that work just fine.

There are several different approaches to providing customer support for DVD-Video titles. Unfortunately, the most common approach is to simply ignore the problem. Many content owners who publish DVD-Video titles do not provide the consumer with any mechanism to report problems. In this case the only solution the consumer has is to return the product for a refund. This approach is obviously bad for the consumer who must return the product and argue with the retailer to get a refund on an opened title. It is bad for retailers who are essentially stuck in the middle. They have to deal with an irate customer who wants their money back, and then they have to deal with a distributor or content owner who does not want to accept a return of an opened item. Finally, I would argue, that this is also bad for the content owner. Ignoring problems caused by DVD-Video player compatibility issues, or DVD authoring errors may in the short run make economic sense, but in the long run it can only damage the reputation of everyone involved.

Another common approach to customer support is a satisfaction guaranteed policy that allows consumers to return a DVD-Video title for a refund or store credit for any reason, no questions asked. This approach is much better for the consumer since they don't have to prove that the title does not work on their equipment. It is also a better for the retailer since they are not stuck in the middle between an irate consumer and a content owner who wont take an opened product back. Finally this approach is a little better for the content owner since their reputation will not suffer from a satisfaction guaranteed policy, but they will still have to deal with the problem of repackaging and reselling the returned items.

The last approach, which is not very common at all in the DVD industry, is to offer direct customer support to any consumer that has a problem. In this case the content owner or DVD publisher will provide a toll free number, as well as technical support section of their web site so that consumers can report a problem directly. This approach requires a significant amount of effort on the part of the content owner since they will have to deal with customers who have problems with one of their titles. I believe that this approach is the best long-term solution for all parties. The consumer has a direct line of communication to the content owner to report the problem and find a satisfactory resolution. Distributors and retailers are completely removed from the customer support function, which allows them to concentrate on what they do best, sell DVD-Video titles. Finally the content owner is in the best position to solve the customer's problem to begin with so this approach will yield the most efficient resolution for the majority of customer problems, and in the long-run consumers will have a higher opinion of the content owner due to the level of support provided.

connected to a PAL only TV. Connect it to a dual-standard TV and you will see a color picture". I can tell you from experience that consumers who get an honest and straightforward answer to their problem are very likely to become a repeat customer.

ENTRY-LEVEL DVD AUTHORING

This chapter will discuss "entry-level" authoring, systems, and techniques, generally found in entry-level DVD authoring systems such as DVDit!, iDVD, and SpruceUp. The design of entry-level DVD authoring systems, as shown in Figure 4.1, is primarily driven by cost factors. In general an entry-level DVD authoring system must be based on a low-cost personal computer platform, and use software to perform MPEG video compression. Most entry-level DVD authoring systems use PCM or MPEG audio, and Dolby Digital and DTS formats are generally not supported.

As shown in Figure 4.1, video and audio from a DV camera are transferred to a personal computer using an IEEE-1394 (FireWire) link. The video and audio can be edited using a software non-linear editing tool such as Apple iMovie or Adobe Premiere. The video is compressed into the MPEG format using a software encoder, which generally operates at less than real-time. An off-the-shelf graphics package, like Adobe PhotoShop, is used to create menu graphics, or the menus are created entirely within the DVD-Video authoring software. DVD-Video authoring software is used to combine the MPEG video, PCM or MPEG audio, and simple menu graphics to create a valid DVD-Video disc image. DVD disc images are either stored on a local hard drive, written to a CD-R or CD-RW disc, or written to DVD-R for general media using a relatively inexpensive DVD-R/RW drive. If DVD-R media are produced, the production system should also include one or more DVD-Video players connected to video and audio monitoring equipment to provide some quality assurance capabilities.

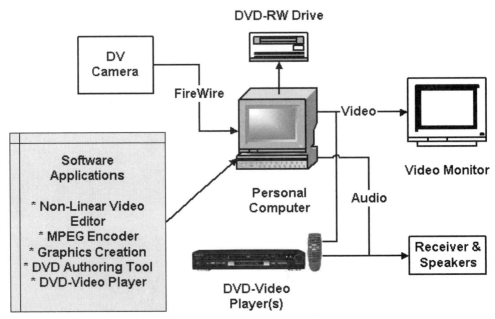

Figure 4.1   Block Diagram of an Entry-Level DVD-Video Authoring System

Entry-Level DVD-Video Authoring Systems & Software

As of the publication date of this book several entry-level DVD-Video authoring systems and third-party software tools were on the market. The following sections will provide background information on each of these systems and products. Over the next few years it is likely that DVD-Video authoring capabilities will become standard features on higher-end multimedia computers. A number of inexpensive after-market products will also become available combining DV capture boards, a DVD-R/RW drive and low-cost DVD authoring software. Apple has recently made a major commitment to the DVD-Video format with the release of the iDVD product line, and several major PC vendors, including Compaq, have made similar commitments for the Windows platform. One enabling technology that has made entry-level DVD-Video systems affordable is the new DVR-103 Pioneer DVD-R drive, also known as the Apple SuperDrive. The after-market version of the DVR-103 is priced below $1,000, while the OEM version, called the DVR-A03, is even cheaper when included as part of a turnkey system.

Apple iDVD

Apple's entry-level DVD system, called iDVD, is based on a 733 MHz PowerMac G4 platform, with 256 Mb of RAM, a 60 Gb IDE hard drive, and an Apple DVD-R SuperDrive. The iDVD system uses Mac OS 9 and includes Mac iTunes, iDVD, iMovie, and QuickTime 4 software.

The iDVD system is very tightly integrated which is essential for an entry-level PC. The system has two 400 Mbps FireWire ports that can be used to capture video and audio directly from most DV cameras. Once the video and audio elements are captured they can be edited using the iMovie software to create QuickTime files, which can be imported directly into the iDVD software. The iDVD graphical users interface, shown in Figure 4.2, is surprisingly simple. Apple has distilled the process of creating a DVD title down to five easy steps,

1. Select a Theme
2. Create and Fill Media Folders

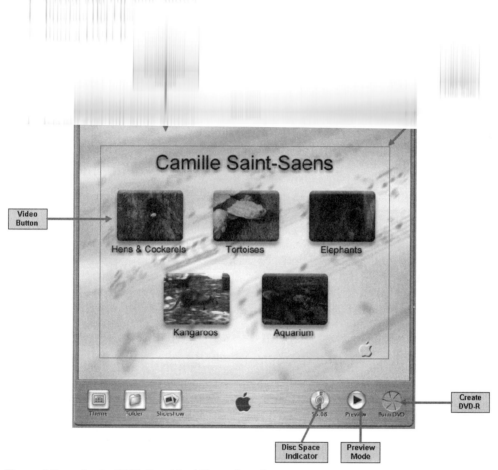

Figure 4.2   Apple iDVD Graphical Users Interface
(See color insert for color version of this figure.)

iDVD uses "Themes" to create a common look and feel for the DVD title. Approximately 20 predefined Themes come standard with iDVD, and you can create custom Themes as well. A Theme consists of a background image, a specific font style, color, and size, and a specific button shape and size. Buttons are used to launch the playback of video clips and slide shows or to branch to Folders.

"Folders" are used by iDVD as containers for media elements, and to organize the presentation of the content on the DVD disc. A Folder can hold additional Folders or individual media elements. iDVD Folders can have up to six buttons each, and there can be no more than 99 media elements used in the title. iDVD arranges the buttons in each Folder, and automatically creates the Left, Right, Up, and Down navigation commands as well. Each Folder can use the common project Theme, have its own unique Theme, or use a different background image if required. The DVD Menu key is programmed to take the user up one level in the Folder structure, and the DVD Title key is programmed to take the user to the top-level Folder.

"Slide Shows" are collection of still images that are presented in a linear fashion. Individual images can be displayed for a fixed amount of time, or indefinitely waiting for a user action. Previous (<<) and Next (>>) buttons are automatically created on each still image by iDVD to allow the viewer to navigate through the slideshow in a sequential fashion.

Adding video clips or photographs to a title is a simple process of selecting them in the Apple Finder and dropping them into the appropriate iDVD Folder. iDVD only accepts QuickTime video, so if you have files in any other format you will have to convert them to QuickTime before using them. Buttons are created in the order that the elements are dropped in, but you can change a button's position by clicking on it and dragging it to a different position on the screen. When video clips or slide shows are associated with a button, you can select which frame of video, or still image to use as a thumbnail image on the button.

iDVD has a Preview Mode that allows you to check your work at any time during the title creation process. Pressing the Preview button brings up a small remote control that allows you to navigate through the title. Video clips, slide shows, and folders are displayed just as they will be on the final disc image. The quality of the video clips may be different in Preview Mode than it is on the final disc, since the Preview Mode displays the uncompressed media elements, rather than the MPEG-2 encoded versions used on a DVD disc.

The beauty of iDVD is its simplicity. Just about any consumer who can use a Mac, can now create a DVD title — it really is that simple. DVD discs created by iDVD will work in over 90 percent of the DVD-Video players, and near 100% of the DVD-ROM computer installed base. With a suggested retail price of $3,499 the iDVD system is not cheap. Due to its price tag, only high-end consumers will buy this system. If you want to develop corporate or professional DVD titles you will need to upgrade to DVD Studio Pro, as the iDVD software is really not suited for anything more complicated than putting home movies on DVD.

Compaq MyMovieStudio

Compaq MyMovieStudio is a turnkey, consumer-oriented Windows PC that can be used for a wide variety of multimedia functions, including entry-level DVD-Video title authoring. MyMovieStudio Pro is included with the Presario 7000T, as well as other models from Compaq. These models include several third-party hardware and software items required for DVD-Video title development including the following.

Digital Video Center   Standard on every Presario 7000 series PC, the Digital Video Center provides a standard IEEE 1394 port, making it easily to plug in video peripherals, such as DV cameras.

Pinnacle StudioDV With the StudioDV non-linear video editing software, digital video can be captured directly from a DV camera to the PC hard drive. With a drag-and-drop interface it is easy to select only the scenes you want, and combine them with transitions to create professional looking video segments. Additional features include the ability to add voice-over narrations, titles, custom soundtracks, transitions between scenes, etc.

Sonic Solutions DVDit! DVDit! is used to author DVD-Video titles using AVI files, MPEG files, and digital still images. DVDit! can also be used to create buttons, links, and menus. It

The heart of the Compaq MyMovieStudio system, at least as far as DVD-Video title development is concerned, is the Sonic Solutions DVDit! software. Figure 4.3 shows the graphical users interface for DVDit!.

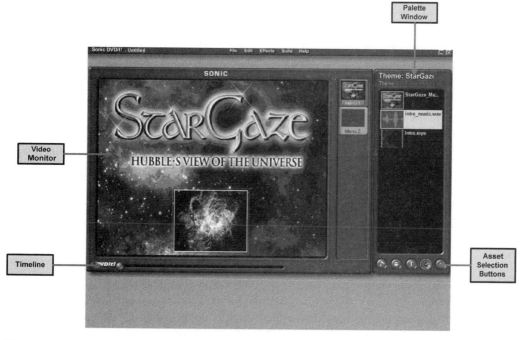

Figure 4.3   Sonic Solutions DVDit! Graphical User Interface
(See color insert for color version of this figure.)

The process of developing a DVD title using DVDit! is simple, and includes the following steps.

1. Import Media Assets The first step is to import all unique media elements (video, audio, and graphics) into the Palette window. DVDit! has a collection of background images and button graphics so it may only be necessary to import the video and audio clips. Sonic Solutions offers several "Theme Packs" to add additional background and button graphics to DVDit!.

2. Create Menus The next step is to create the interactive menus required for a project. Creating a menu is simple. Drag a background graphic from the Palette window into a menu box of the Video window. Add interactive buttons by dragging graphics from the Palette window on top of the menu graphic. Buttons can be repositioned and resized, as well as have custom text added to the menu. Text can be created in any installed font, and can be positioned and resized easily. Once the "look" of the menu is set up right, actions associated with each menu button are defined by dragging a media element or another menu icon on top of the desired menu button. Menu buttons can be used to jump to other menus, to play still images, or to play video clips. Unlike other entry-level DVD authoring tools DVDit! can't import menus in the Photoshop (.psd) format.

3. Simulate the Operation After you have created all the menus and assigned the appropriate actions to each menu button, you can begin testing the title using the Remote Control window. This real time preview feature is one of the strength's of DVDit!. Using the Remote Control window to test a project as it is created can save you a lot of time and effort.

4. Build Final Disc Image Once the title has been tested you can begin to build the final DVD disc image. This non real-time process converts all the media elements into the format required by the DVD-Video specification. The final disc image can be written directly to a DVD-R using a Pioneer DVD-R writer. If the final playback device is a personal computer, the disc image can be written to a CD-R, CD-RW, DVD-R, DVD-RW or DVD-RAM disc.

DVDit! uses the same basic internal scripting language used by all Sonic Solutions DVD authoring tools. Thus projects can be imported into professional tools like DVD Creator or DVD Fusion if they need additional features that are not directly supported by DVDit!. DVDit! also includes a non real-time MPEG video encoder that converts AVI files into the MPEG-1 or MPEG-2 video streams required by the DVD-Video specification.

SpruceUp

Spruce Technologies SpruceUp is a software program designed to run on Microsoft Windows 98 SE, Millennium Edition (ME), NT 4.0, and 2000. It imports MPEG video and audio files from third-party equipment such as video capture applications and non-linear editors. SpruceUp provides tools to design entry-level DVD-Video titles with menus and up to 99 multimedia segments. Completed projects are compiled to create a final disc image that can be used with set-top DVD players, as well as personal computers with CD-ROM and DVD-ROM drives.

SpruceUp is designed to take DVD-compliant MPEG video and audio files, combine them with menus, and create DVD titles that can be played back on PCs and set-top DVD players. Video sources can be from a wide variety of non-linear editors, video-capture cards, and

MPEG encoders. SpruceUp provides tools to add chapter points, providing the ability to provide random access to scenes within a video segment. SpruceUp is not an editor, and so it cannot directly link the end of one video segment to the start of another. Any effects, such as transitions between scenes or text graphics must be added using a video editing application, such as from Adobe or Ulead. Figure 4.4 shows the SpruceUp user interface with four main work areas.

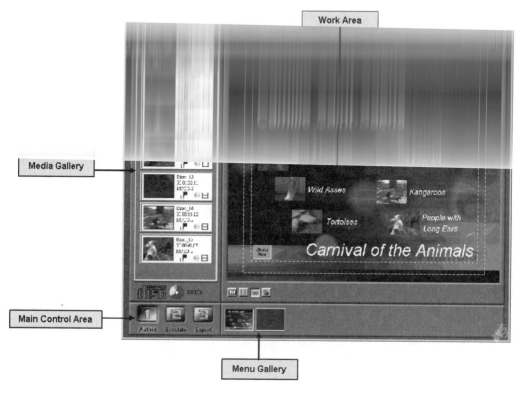

Figure 4.4   SpruceUp's Graphical User Interface
(See color insert for color version of this figure.)

Creating a DVD title using SpruceUp consists of the following steps.

1. Load Assets SpruceUp uses three types of assets: video movies (with audio), backgrounds, and buttons. These assets are managed in the Main window's Media Gallery, each with its own tab along the top.

2. Create Menus Most DVD titles contain at least one menu, and it is generally the first thing to appear when the title starts playing. A menu is made up of a background image, one or more buttons linked to movies, and optionally some text explaining what to do.

3. Define Clip Properties The Clip Properties window provides tools to perform a number of movie related functions, including play the movie, either at real time or by manually "scrubbing" through it, set a frame to use as a thumbnail image on menus, add chapter points and set thumbnail points for each, capture a frame from the movie to use as a background, create buttons automatically from chapter points, and add URLs and other items to the chapter points.

4. Simulate the Operation SpruceUp has a built in simulation mode in which the operation of the title can be fully tested.

5. Export Exporting a title is the process of having SpruceUp compile it into a DVD-compliant format and write it to CD-R/RW, DVD-R or to a hard drive. If necessary SpruceUp includes a royalty-free DVD player called Syzygy that, when included with a title, allows it to be played back on all Windows systems with a CD-ROM drive.

Entry-Level DVD Authoring Tool Summary

Each of the three major entry-level DVD authoring tools has their own unique strengths and weaknesses. Apple iDVD is the only product that will work on a Mac, and it is clearly the easiest tool for entry-level authors to use. The process of creating a DVD title using iDVD has been simplified so much that there are a number of things that simply can't be done with the tool, so professional developers will find its features somewhat lacking. Sonic Solutions has sold over 500,000 copies of DVDit!, mostly through bundles with third-party video capture and editing products. This makes DVDit! the best selling DVD authoring tool ever. However most of the copies of DVDit! sold to date are the LE version, which has a limited feature set. Sonic offers more capabilities in the SE and PE versions of DVDit!, but authors will have to pay an upgrade fee to gain access to the more powerful versions of the product. SpruceUp is perhaps the most powerful of the three entry-level DVD authoring tools, but it is the least well known. Spruce has not done as good a job as Sonic in licensing SpruceUp to third parties for bundling with video capture and editing products. SpruceUp's $129 price tag is a little high for most authors who are used to paying less than $100 for off the shelf software products.

Entry-Level DVD-Video Authoring Process

Figure 4.5 shows a block diagram of the entry-level DVD-Video authoring process. The three major steps in the process are Import Assets, Create Menus, and Simulation and Disc Image Build.

Generally most entry-level DVD-Video authoring systems are designed to hide as much of the DVD-Video complexity and terminology from the author as possible. Most entry-level systems also severely restrict DVD-Video features, such as multi-angle video, multi-track audio, and subpicture streams. This chapter will illustrate the entry-level DVD-Video production process using SpruceUp. Entry-level DVD-Video authoring tools from Apple, Sonic Solutions, and others have very similar features and essentially use the same basic concepts to transform video, audio, and still image elements into a working DVD-Video title.

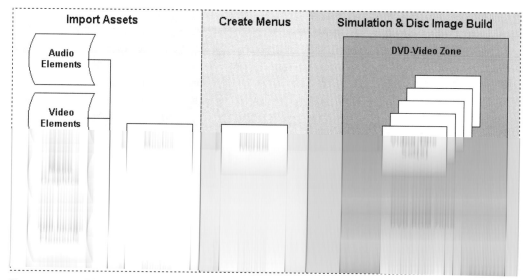

Figure 4.5   Block Diagram of the Entry-Level DVD-Video Authoring Process

Typically an entry-level DVD-Video authoring system will ask a few basic questions each time a new project is started, and in general the information required is limited to the type of video (NTSC or PAL), the type of output media (hard disk, CD-R, DVD-R, etc.), and the location of the working directory and files for the project. Figure 4.6 shows the Project Preferences screen from SpruceUp, in which this information is defined prior to starting a new DVD project.

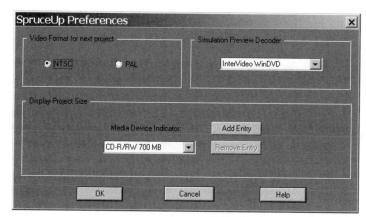

The DVD-Video specification does not allow the use of both NTSC and PAL video assets in the same project, so if you have different media types you will need to convert all of them into a consistent format before you start the DVD authoring process.

Figure 4.6   SpruceUp's Project Preferences Screen

Import Assets

Once a new DVD project has been created and its basic parameters defined, the next step is to import all of the media elements into the authoring tool. Media elements can include video,

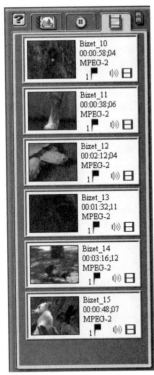

Figure 4.7   SpruceUp's Media Element
             Gallery Display

Figure 4.8   SpruceUp Movie Properties
             Selection (See color insert
             for color version of these two
             figures.)

audio, still image, and graphic files. Typically this is done with a drag-and-drop process in which media files are highlighted in Windows Explorer or the Mac Finder and then dropped on top of the DVD authoring tool. In general entry-level DVD-Video authoring tools will automatically segregate different types of media elements, and organize them as Backgrounds, Buttons, and Multimedia Elements. Background and Button graphics are used to create interactive menus, while Multimedia Elements are used to create individual movie clips that can be played back. Figure 4.7 shows an example of how video elements that have been imported into SpruceUp are organized and presented to the author.

Video Elements

The DVD-Video specification requires that all video be compressed in either the MPEG-1 or MPEG-2 formats. Some entry-level DVD-Video authoring tools, such as Sonic Solutions DVDit! and Apple's iDVD, include software for MPEG transcoding. These transcoders allow video files in the AVI or MOV formats to be imported into the authoring tool, where they will eventually be encoded into the MPEG format. Other entry-level tools, such as SpruceUp, require the video files to be in the MPEG format before they can be imported into the authoring tool. All video elements should be edited before they are imported into the authoring tool. Most entry-level DVD authoring tools do not provide any video editing functions, although some will allow you to define chapter or scene indexes within a video clip after it has been imported. Figure 4.8 shows how chapter points can be defined within a video clip using SpruceUp.

Audio Elements

According to the DVD-Video specification, all DVD-Video titles must have at least one audio track in either the Dolby Digital or Linear PCM format. Most entry-level DVD-Video authoring tools support audio in both the Linear PCM format (.wav) as well as the MPEG format

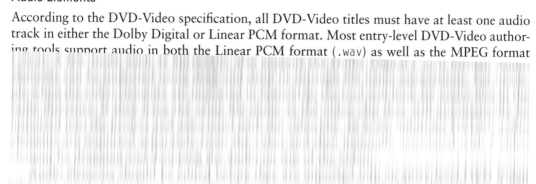

authoring tool. An audio element should be the same length as the video element that it be paired with. Most tools will not provide any mechanism to edit the audio once it has been imported, and even the volume levels of audio elements can't be changed within most entry-level DVD-Video authoring tools. If audio and video elements with different lengths are combined the results may not be what the author intends. If the audio is shorter than the video, the combined segment may end as soon as the audio is over, even if there are video frames that have not been displayed.

Still Image Elements

According to the DVD-Video specification, all still images used in menus or slide shows must be stored as MPEG I frames on the disc. Thus when a still image is imported into an entry-level DVD-Video authoring tool it will eventually be converted to the MPEG format. Generally this conversion process is done after all the menus and still image slide show movies have been created, so that only those still images actually used in the project need to be converted. Most entry-level DVD-Video authoring tools will accept a variety of still image file formats including .bmp, .tga, .tif, and .jpg. If possible use .bmp or .tif files, as these are uncompressed file formats that will deliver the highest level of quality. Still images that are to be displayed full screen should have a resolution of at least 720×540 pixels for NTSC and 768×576 for PAL, and a 4:3 aspect ratio. Images with different resolutions or different aspect ratios will be automatically converted to the correct size for a DVD-Video title by the authoring tool, which may result in poor quality results. While most entry-level DVD-Video authoring tools will accept JPEG files, it is not a good idea to use a compressed image since it will be compressed again when the tool converts it to the MPEG format.

Still images can be used as menu backgrounds, menu buttons, or as elements in a still image slide show. Once a still image element is imported into the authoring tool it can be used many different times, and for different purposes, so it is possible to have a single image used as a menu background, a menu button and an element in a slide show.

Create Menus

Once all the video, audio, and still image elements have been imported into the authoring tool, the process of designing the menus can start. DVD-Video menus are designed to allow the viewer to interact with the title and control the presentation order of media elements. Menus are not required for a DVD-Video title, but most consumers expect a DVD-Video title to have at least one chapter menu, which will allow them to jump directly to specific items of content. A DVD-Video menu is created using a background image, one or more button graphics, and text to provide additional information to the viewer. One popular technique for menu buttons is to display a single frame from the video clip to which the button is linked. This display frame along with some descriptive text provides enough information to the viewer to tell them what the button will do.

Figure 4.9 shows a sample menu created using SpruceUp. In this sample I used one of the predefined background images available in SpruceUp, along with single frames from each video clip linked to a button, and text that describes the purpose of the menu as well as the purpose of each button. Each text element includes a drop shadow to make it look more attractive.

Figure 4.9   Sample DVD-Video Menu Created Using SpruceUp
(See color insert for color version of this figure.)

This sample menu has a total of six buttons, with each button linked to a specific video clip. The addition of the "Camille Saint-Saens" and "Carnival of the Animals" text at the top and bottom of the menu along with the names of each song to the right of the button provide all the information the viewer needs to understand the menu organization.

Most entry-level DVD-Video authoring tools restrict what you can accomplish with menus. The Up, Down, Left, and Right

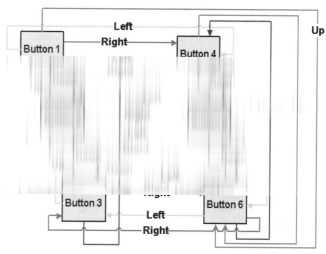

much easier to design and implement DVD-Video menus, although it also means that the author has less control over how the menus will work. For example, in the sample menu shown in Figure 4.9 there are six buttons that are

Figure 4.10   Button Navigation Commands Automatically Created by an Entry-Level DVD Authoring Tool (See color insert for color version of this figure.)

arranged in a diagonal pattern. When this menu was created SpruceUp automatically assigned Left, Right, Up, and Down commands as shown in Figure 4.10. Since the alignment of the menu buttons is quite regular in the vertical dimension the assignment of the Left and Right commands to each button makes sense. However, the alignment of the menu buttons in the horizontal dimension is not regular, so the assignments of the Up and Down commands are not what most viewers would expect. For example pressing the Up key while button 1 is highlighted will jump to button 6, and pressing the Up key while button 4 is highlighted will also jump to button 6. This button navigation implementation is inconsistent, and the only way to correct it is to move the button positions around until the automatic button navigation routing algorithm yields the desired results.

This is an excellent example of the limitations of entry-level DVD authoring tools. In an effort to hide the concept of button navigation commands (Left, Right, Up, and Down) and thus simplify the authoring process, entry-level tools can create menus with inconsistent user interfaces. The best way to avoid this problem is to design menus with buttons aligned in both the vertical and horizontal directions.

Simulation, Disc Image Build & Disc Burn

The last step in the entry-level DVD authoring process is to simulate the operation of the project, build a disc image, and then transfer it to the desired media. Most entry-level DVD authoring tools include built in simulation features to test the operation of the project. These simulation tools essentially turn the authoring PC into a DVD-Video player for playback testing. Generally a software MPEG-2 decoder is used, so the quality of video playback may be poor in emulation mode. Playback quality depends on the power and speed of the host systems CPU, as well as the number of other application programs running at the same time. The emulation program should be used to test every button on every menu, and to review every media element used on the project. Figure 4.11 shows SpruceUp's simulation mode.

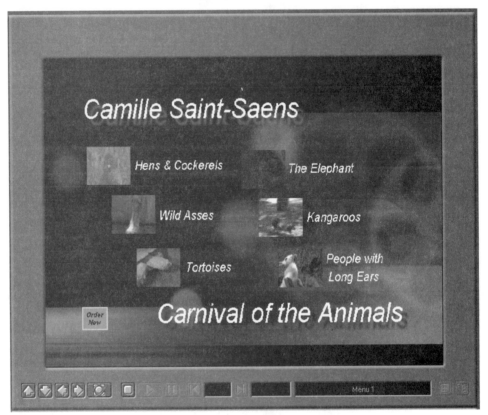

Figure 4.11   Entry-Level DVD Authoring Tool Simulation Display
(See color insert for color version of this figure.)

At the bottom of the Simulation user interface there are controls for the Up, Down, Left, Right, and Enter buttons, as well as Play, Pause, Stop, Next, Previous, Title, and Menu buttons. Using these controls, it is fairly easy to test the DVD project to ensure that it will work correctly on a DVD-Video player.

Once simulation has been completed the process of building the final disc image can be started. This process is required even if the project will not be transferred to optical media. The disc build process takes all of the media elements used in the project and puts them into the DVD-Video format. At the end of the disc build project a `Video_TS` directory will be created on the authoring system's local hard drive, and it will contain all of the DVD files created for the project. The project can be played back on the authoring system simply by using a DVD-Video player application and pointing it to the `Video_TS` directory that was created.

Most entry-level DVD-Video titles will be distributed on some form of removable optical media, such as DVD-R, DVD-RAM, or CD-R, as opposed to professional authoring for mass replicated discs. In general entry-level DVD authoring tools can be used to transfer the final disc image to a variety of removable media.

Figure 4.12 shows an example of the SpruceUp's Disc Build user interface. In this example,

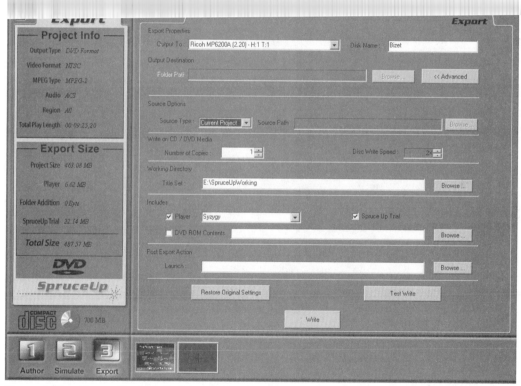

Figure 4.12   SpruceUp Disc Build and Disc Creation Process Window
(See color insert for color version of this figure.)

Special Features

Some entry-level DVD authoring tools provide special features to enhance the playback of the project on personal computers. Several authoring tools can put DVD-Video playback application programs on the target disc so that the project can be played back on computer systems that do not have DVD-ROM drives or DVD-Video playback software. For example SpruceUp includes an option to include the Syzygy DVD player on the output media along with the final disc image. An Autorun file is also placed on the disc to automatically launch the Syzygy player, which then starts playing the DVD-Video image from the disc. The ability to store DVD-Video disc images and a free DVD-Video player application on a CD-R is key to inexpensive distribution of projects. This is generally called a "DVD on CD" application and it can be used on most Windows personal computers that have a CD-ROM drive. "DVD on CD" applications can't be used on DVD-Video players, since these players will only play Audio-CD or Video-CD content from a CD-R disc. Figure 4.13 shows a "DVD on CD" application, being played back using the Syzygy player.

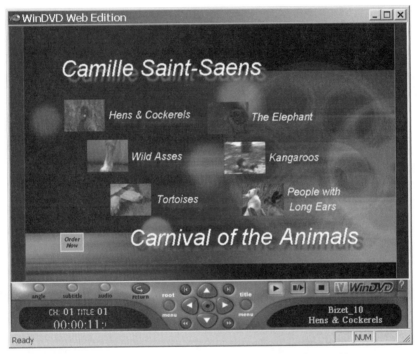

Figure 4.13   "DVD on CD" Application Created Using SpruceUp
(See color insert for color version of this figure.)

In addition to the "DVD on CD" capability offered by many entry-level DVD authoring tools, some tools also offer WebDVD support. WebDVD is simply the integration of the DVD-Video format with the Internet. WebDVD titles can deliver broadcast quality video and audio elements stored on an optical disc (CD or DVD) along with graphics, text, and real-time data delivered from the Internet. Some entry-level DVD authoring tools can be used to assign an `http:` address to a button, menu, or media element. During playback, a web browser can be automatically launched and pointed to the associated URL.

Entry-Level DVD Authoring Summary

This chapter has covered the steps required to author a DVD-Video title, using entry-level DVD authoring tools. There are a number of different entry-level DVD-Video authoring tools on the market today, and they all have slightly different user interfaces, features, and

2. Media Association

    a. Create Menus

    b. Associate Video, Audio, and Still Image Elements with Menu Buttons

3. Media Organization and Simulation

    a. Link Menu Buttons and Media Elements

    b. Test and verify correct operation via Emulation program

4. Export

    a. Add WebDVD or DVD-ROM files

    b. Build DVD Disc Image

    c. Write Disc Image to Media

Over the past five years the cost of developing DVD-Video titles has dropped dramatically. With the release of the Pioneer DVR-A03 DVD-R (repackaged as the Apple DVD-R Super-Drive) it is now possible for the average person to publish DVD titles that will work in the vast majority of DVD-Video players installed throughout the world (Table 6.9 provides a detailed list of DVD-Video players that have problems playing DVD-R discs). Prices will continue to drop over the next several years, and at some point in the near future DVD-R drives will be a standard feature on personal computers, and DVD-Video authoring tools will be as easy to use as today's word processing programs.

Many DVD developers and industry insiders have predicted that lowering the cost of DVD-Video authoring hardware and software will put them out of business, as the average person will be able to develop their own titles and thus not require an independent developer. I disagree with this conclusion. I believe that the need for independent DVD developers will increase dramatically over the next several years as more and more consumers want their existing VHS, BetaMax, SVHS, Hi-8 and film content transferred to DVD. DVD offers the average consumer better quality than any previous home entertainment format, although it will never be better than the original source material, as well as a longer life than any tape-based format. When consumers start to create DVD titles from their own home movie con-

MID-RANGE DVD AUTHORING

This chapter will discuss mid-range DVD-Video authoring systems and techniques. Mid-range DVD-Video production systems, as shown in Figure 5.1, try to strike a balance between quality, efficiency, and cost. Mid-range DVD-Video production systems are designed to support the internal development requirements of a large or mid-size company, which generally also has internal video and audio production systems. Thus the DVD production process is simply an extension of the video production process, and DVD-Video is just another media for delivering the desired message. Mid-range DVD-Video titles often have the same high level of production qualities as titles produced on professional systems, but generally they are targeted at a very different set of viewers. Professional DVD production systems are used to create consumer DVD titles, typically from content created in Hollywood. Mid-range DVD production systems are used to create limited distribution DVD titles, typically from content created outside Hollywood.

Mid-range DVD production systems are generally less complex and less expensive than professional production systems. This does not mean that they are not capable of delivering the same level of quality as a professional system, but in general a mid-range production system can't sustain the same level of workflow as a professional system. In a mid-range production system digital or analog tape decks, typically Digital Beta or BetaSp, deliver video and audio signals to a single workstation that creates encoded MPEG video and Dolby Digital or PCM audio streams. A separate graphics workstation is used to create the menu background and overlay graphics, as well as any required subpicture elements. The MPEG/AC3 workstation and the graphics workstation are usually connected to a DVD-Video authoring workstation by a high-speed network. The DVD authoring workstation includes one or more external hard drives, a DVD-R or DVD-RW recorder, and a DLT tape drive. It's also connected to video and audio monitoring equipment, used to verify the quality and performance of the DVD title.

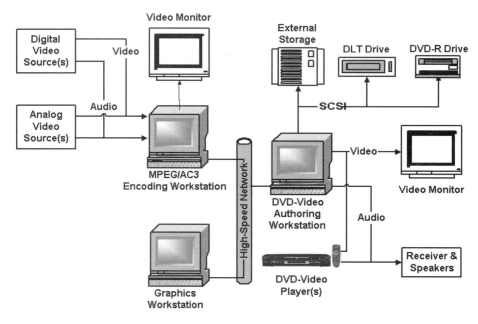

Figure 5.1   Mid-Range DVD-Video Authoring System

The components of a mid-range authoring system can be spread among several different departments within a single organization. For example the graphics workstation might reside in the Graphics Department, the MPEG/AC3 workstation could be in the A/V Department, while the DVD-Video authoring workstation could be located in the Programming Department. Alternatively all three workstations could be located in the same room, and simply be staffed by employees from different departments.

To reduce the cost of a mid-range DVD production system, many components found in professional systems are generally left out. These "optional" items can be included in a mid-range production system if there is sufficient budget, facilities, and staff for them. However most mid-range DVD production systems do not include a DTS encoder, DVNR, dedicated server, and a separate QA/QC workstation. Since the mid-range production system has a distributed architecture as well as a high-speed network, it is possible to upgrade them to support higher workloads, and to provide improvements in overall quality.

Mid-Range DVD Authoring Process

Figure 5.2 shows a block diagram of the mid-range DVD-Video authoring process. As outlined in Chapter 3 this process includes three major areas: Media Identification, Media Association, and Media Organization. One of the major differences between mid-range and entry-level DVD authoring systems is the ability to develop complex as well as highly interactive titles. Mid-range authoring tools will support the use of multiple title sets, multiple program chains, multiple audio tracks, multiple video camera angles, and multiple subpicture streams, while the entry-level tools provided only a bare minimum of DVD-Video features.

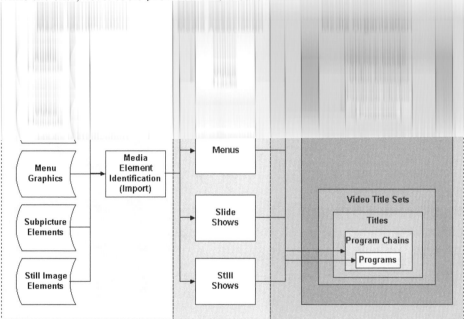

Figure 5.2   The DVD-Video Authoring Process

Generally most mid-range DVD-Video authoring systems are designed to support the concept of a DVD project or scenario. Each unique DVD-Video title is associated with a unique project or scenario within the DVD-Video authoring tool. Typically you can only work on one project or scenario at a time, and most authoring tools provide very limited abilities to copy and paste data or structures from one project to another. Some professional tools offer some "template" functions, which can be beneficial when you are developing a series of DVD-Video titles that have the same basic design.

When you start a new DVD-Video project you will enter a number of key parameters about the project so that the authoring system can process each media element correctly. Depending on the sophistication of your authoring tool this can be a simple or a fairly complex process. For example, defining a new project in Scenarist requires setting more than 40 different parameters using 12 different screens. Conversely, defining a new project using Sonic Solutions DVDit! requires setting only 1 parameter on a single screen. Figure 5.3 shows the screens used by Scenarist NT to enter the parameters for a new project. Figure 5.4 shows the new project setup screen for DVDit!.

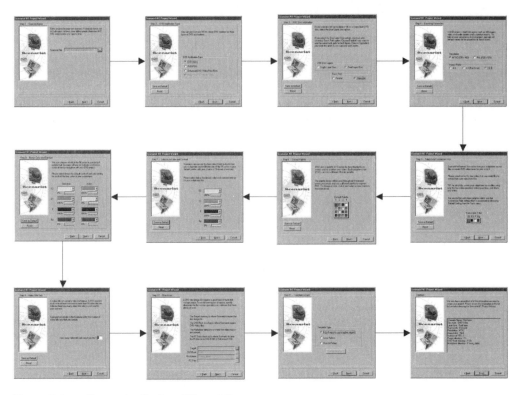

Figure 5.3 Scenarist Project Wizard Screens
(See color insert for color version of this figure and Figure 5.4 below.)

Figure 5.4 Sonic Solutions DVDit! New Project Screen

The type of information to be defined for each new DVD project or scenario includes the following.

Project or Scenario Name This information is used by the DVD-Video authoring system to keep track of a project and all its media assets. Some DVD-Video authoring systems will also use the project or scenario name to create the volume name for the final disc image.

DVD Type Define the type of content that will go on the DVD disc including DVD-Video, DVD-Audio, DVD-ROM, Hybrid, or WebDVD.

DVD Disc Information   Define the type of DVD disc to be created. This includes the size of the disc (DVD-5, DVD-9, DVD-10, DVD-14, or DVD-18) and, if the disc will be dual layered, whether it use the parallel track or opposite track configuration.

Video Format   Define the type of video content to be used throughout the disc including aspect ratio (4:3 Pan/Scan, 4:3 Letterbox, and 16:9) as well as the television standard (NTSC or PAL).

Subpicture Conversion Colors   Define the default values for the four subpicture colors (BG, P

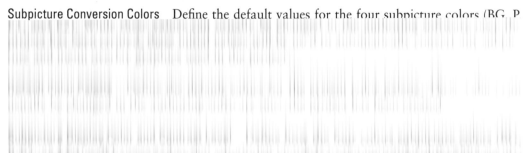

1, E1, and E2) will be mapped to the color palette, and the transparency level (0–100%) to be assigned to each color. These values can usually be changed in the authoring software once the project has been created.

Button Display Color and Contrast Level   Define how to map the four colors used in a menu overlay graphic (BG, P, E1, and E2) to the color palette, and the transparency level (0–100%) to be assigned to each color. Values must be defined for the unselected, selected, and activated mode for menu buttons. These values can usually be changed in the authoring software once the project has been created.

Video Title Sets   Define how many unique video title sets are required for the project. Additional title sets can be defined manually in the authoring system after the project creation step has been completed.

File Locations   Define where the authoring software should store work files generated in the DVD disc formatting process, as well as where the final disc image files should be stored.

Templates   Many mid-range authoring systems provide the ability to use predefined or custom templates to make the authoring process a little easier and faster. If the current project is similar to a project that has already been completed, it may be possible to use a template to complete the project faster.

Media Identification

As discussed in Chapter 3, Media Identification is the process of telling the DVD-Video authoring system the location and properties of each media element to be used in a DVD project. While the specific methods of importing media elements into a mid-range tool can be quite different from an entry-level tool, the basic concept is the same. One nice feature that is included in most mid-range and professional authoring systems is the ability to organize

Tips, Tricks & Techniques

It is a good idea to define standard RGB values for all subpicture and menu overlay colors (BG, P, E1, and E2). Using the same RGB values on all your projects will make it a lot easier and faster to author DVD titles. It is also a good idea to use primary colors for each of the four subpicture colors. Some easy colors to work with are Blue (RGB=0,0,255), Green (RGB=0,255,0), Red (RGB=255,0,0), White (RGB=255,255,255), and Black (RGB=0,0,0). Since these will not actually be displayed on the monitor it is acceptable to use colors that are outside the NTSC Color Safe range.

media elements once they have been identified by the authoring system. Figure 5.5 shows the Data Editor screen of Scenarist 2.5. As you can see from this figure Scenarist allows you to create custom folders to organize media elements, and it also allows you to manually set all of the important parameters for each media element. The ability to organize media elements once they have been brought into the authoring tool is of critical importance when you start to work on larger and more complicated titles. DVD titles can easily have hundreds, if not thousands, of unique media elements, and it is very difficult to work with an authoring tool that does not allow these elements to be organized in a logical fashion.

Video Elements

Most mid-range authoring tools will accept video in the MPEG-1 or MPEG-2 formats, while some will also accept uncompressed QuickTime (.mov) or Video for Windows (.avi) files and transcode them into the MPEG format (.mpv). When MPEG video files are dropped into the authoring tool the file is analyzed to determine its compression parameters and the location of the I frames so that chapter points can be added if needed. There are a number of compression parameters that can be automatically detected from the MPEG file.

- Video Format (NTSC or PAL)

- Aspect Ratio (4:3 or 16:9)

- Start Time Code

- End Time Code

- File Name and Path

- Resolution (720×480, 704×480, 720×576, 704×576, 352×480, 352×576, 352×240, or 352×288)

- Compressed Bit Rate

- Compression Format (MPEG-1, MPEG-2)

- Compression Method (Constant or Variable)

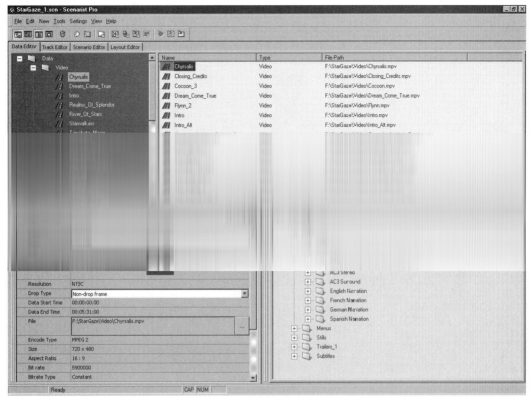

Figure 5.5   Scenarist Data Editor

Additional parameters may be entered by the developer.

- Media Element Name

- Media Element Location

- Time Code Format (Drop-Frame, Non-Drop Frame)

Figure 5.6 shows that properties of an MPEG video clip are imported into Scenarist, and are ready for use within the project.

Audio Elements

Audio elements used in a DVD-Video title can be in a variety of formats including linear PCM, Dolby Digital, DTS, MPEG, and SDDS. Linear PCM audio files generally end in .wav or .aiff extensions. Dolby Digital files usually end with the .ac3 extension, while DTS files can end in either a .dts or a .cpt extension. MPEG audio files can end with either the .mpa or .mpg extension. When an audio file is dropped into most DVD authoring tools, the file is analyzed to determine its encoding parameters.

A number of encoding parameters can be automatically detected from the file.

- Start Time Code

- End Time Code

- File Name and Path

- Audio Format (PCM, Dolby Digital, DTS, or SDDS)

- Bit Rate

- Number of Channels

- Quantization Level (16, 20, or 24 bit)

- Sample Rate (48 KHz or 96 KHz)

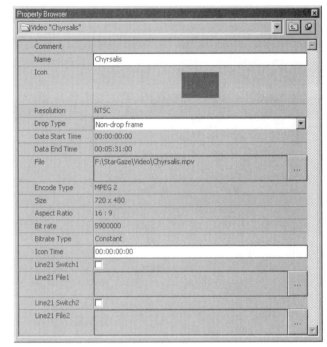

Figure 5.6   Scenarist Video Element Properties

Additional parameters may be entered by the developer.

- Media Element Name

- Video Format (NTSC or PAL)

- Time Code Format (Drop Frame or Non-Drop Frame)

- Emphasis, Mute, and Dynamic Range Settings

Figure 5.7 shows the properties of a linear PCM audio clip imported into Scenarist. As you can see from the figure, all of the important compression and audio format parameters are available for use by the authoring tool.

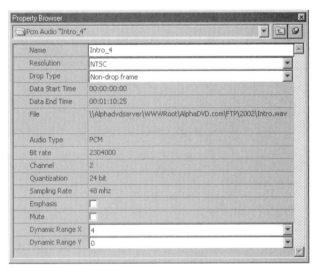

Figure 5.7   Scenarist Audio Element Properties Display

Still Image Elements

All still image elements used in a DVD-Video title are stored as MPEG I frames. Typically the authoring system will perform the required MPEG compression. Most authoring tools will accept still images or graphics in a variety of formats, such as TIF and BMP. It is a good idea to used uncompressed versions of these graphic file formats to maximize the quality of the final DVD title. When still images are dropped into the authoring tool there are a number of key parameters that can automatically be determined from the graphic file.

- File Name and Location

- Image Resolution Size

- Compression Bit Rate

- Compressed Image Resolution Size

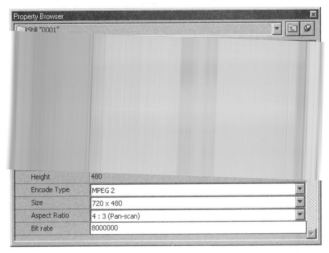

Figure 5.8 shows the properties of a still image imported into Scenarist. As you can see from the figure all of the important compression and image format parameters are available for use by the authoring tool.

Figure 5.8   Sonic Scenarist Still Image Properties

Subpicture Elements

Subpicture elements are static graphics used for subtitles or menu highlights. All subpicture elements used in a DVD-Video title are stored as run-length coded bitmaps. Authoring systems will automatically convert each subpicture element into a run-length coded bitmap. As with still images most authoring tools can accept subpicture elements in either the TIF or BMP format. When subpicture elements are dropped into the authoring tool, a number of key parameters can automatically be determined from the graphic file.

- File Name and Location

- Image Resolution Size

Additional parameters may be entered by the developer.

- Media Element Name

- MPEG encoding format (MPEG-1 or MPEG-2)

- Compression Bit Rate

- Compressed Image Resolution Size

- Forced or Non-Forced Start

- Color Conversion Rules

- DCS Stream Information

Figure 5.9 shows the properties of a subpicture element imported into Scenarist. As you can see from the figure all of the important compression and image format parameters are available for use by the authoring tool.

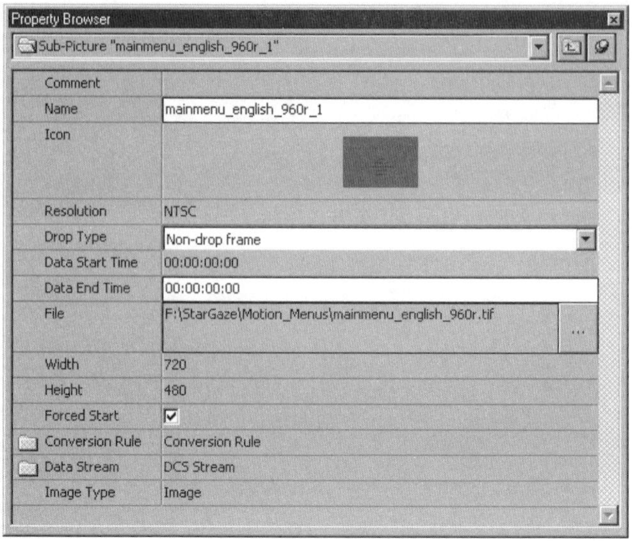

Figure 5.9   Scenarist Subpicture Element Properties Display

Media Association

Once the media elements have been identified by the authoring system, and the various parameters associated with each element have either been automatically detected or manually entered, you can start the process of combining media elements to form media tracks. A media track is a combination of video, audio, subpicture, and still image elements that are displayed by the DVD-Video player. There are three basic kinds of media tracks that can be used in a DVD title: video tracks, still tracks, and menu tracks.

Video Tracks

Video tracks are by far the most common track type used in a DVD title. They consist of at least one video camera angle. As many as nine video camera angles, eight audio streams, and 32 subpicture streams can be included in a single video track, although it is rare to see a track with the maximum number of camera angles, audio tracks, and subpicture streams. Most DVD-Video authoring tools use a time-line display to associate the video, audio, and subpicture elements to form a video track.

Subpicture streams are formed by the combination of one or more subtitle elements, which are synchronized to the video through the use of start and stop time codes. Subpicture elements can also have special effects, such as fades or wipes, associated with them and triggered at specific time codes. Subpicture streams have aspect ratio parameters associated with them to tell the DVD-Video player if the stream should be used in normal, letterbox, or wide-screen display modes.

Video tracks can also have scene indexes defined to allow direct access to a specific time code in the video. Most authoring tools will allow you to place a scene index at an MPEG I frame location. Some authoring tools will create an I frame if one does not already exist at the desired scene index point.

A sample video track is shown in Figure 5.10, with a single video audio streams and subpictures

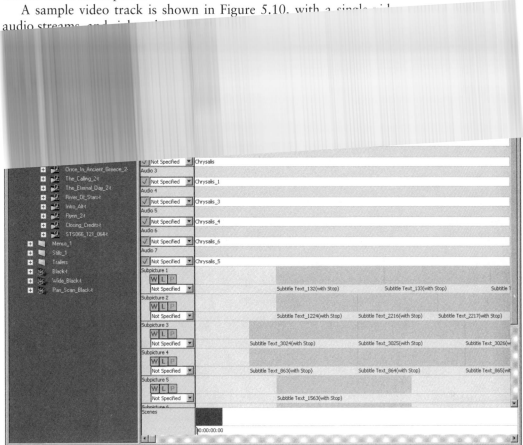

Figure 5.10   Scenarist Video Track Display

Audio and subpicture streams can have languages associated with them, which are used to identify the spoken or written language of a specific audio or subpicture stream. Table 5.1 lists the different languages that can be used to identify audio or subpicture streams. Many title developers choose to set the languages for audio and subpicture streams as Not Specified. This is primarily due to compatibility problems with older DVD-Video players and DVD-ROM decoders that can't interpret language codes correctly. Many mid-range and entry-level DVD authoring systems don't support the full range of languages for menus, audio, and subpicture streams.

Table 5.1		Valid DVD-Video Audio, Menu, and Subpicture Languages		
Afan (Oromo)	Dutch	Javanese	Oriya	Swedish
Abkhazian	English	Kannada	Panjabi	Tagalog
Afar	Esperanto	Kashmiri	Pashto (Pushto)	Tajik
Afrikaans	Estonian	Kazakh	Persian	Tamil
Albanian	Faroese	Kinyarwanda	Poush	Tatar
Ameharic	Fiji	Kirghiz	Portugeuse	Telugu
Arabic	Finnish	Kirundi	Quechua	Thai
Armenian	French	Korean	Rhaeto-Romano	Tibetan
Assamese	Frisian	Kurdish	Romanian	Tigrinya
Aymara	Galician	Laothian	Russian	Tonga
Azerbaijani	Georgian	Latin	Samoan	Tsonga
Bashkir	German	Latvian (Lettish)	Sangho	Turkish
Basque	Greek	Lingala	Sanskrit	Turkmen
Bengali (Bangla)	Greenlandic	Lithuanian	Scots Gaelic	Twi
Bhutani	Guarani	Macedonian	Serbo-Croatian	Ukranian
Bihari	Gujarati	Malagasy	Serbian	Urdu
Bislama	Hausa	Malay	Sesotho	Uzbek
Breton	Hebrew	Malayalam	Setwana	Vietnamese
Bulgarian	Hindi	Maltese	Shona	Volapuk
Burmese	Hungarian	Maori	Sindhi	Welsh
Byelorussian	Icelandic	Marathi	Singhalese	Wolof
Cambodian	Indonesian	Moldavian	Siswati	Xhosa
Catalan	Interlingua	Mongolian	Slovak	Yiddish
Chinese	Interlingue	Nauru	Slovenian	Yoruba
Corsican	Inupiak	Nepali	Somali	Zulu
Croatian	Irish	Norwegian	Spanish	
Czech	Italian	Not Specified	Sundanese	
Danish	Japanese	Occitan	Swahili	

Still Image Tracks

Still images can be presented individually or in a predefined series. Individual still images can be displayed on a timed basis, with a minimum display time of 0.4 seconds, or they can be displayed indefinitely until a specific user operation is initiated. Still show tracks can only include still images, with no accompanying audio or subpicture streams.

disc note:

Real World Example

StarGaze has ten distinct video tracks, or chapters. Each of these video tracks includes seven audio streams (Dolby Digital 5.1 music, DTS music, Dolby Digital 2.0 music, English narration, French narration, German narration, and Spanish narration) as well as eight subpicture streams (English, French, German, and Spanish subtitles and English, French, German, and Spanish nomenclature). Over 4,000 unique media elements (video, audio, and subpicture) were required to create these 10 video tracks.

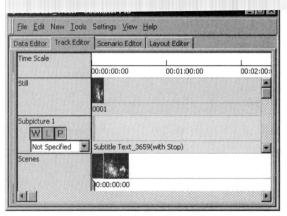

enabled personal computers that have problems playing back still show and slide show tracks. Some of these systems will display each still image for a fraction of a second, and then jump to the next image in the sequence, essentially ignoring the display time data authored into the DVD-Video disc. In Figure 5.11 a sample slide show track is shown with a single still image and an associated subpicture stream.

Figure 5.11   Scenarist Slide Show Track with
Still Image and Subpicture Stream

disc note:

Real World Example

StarGaze includes a "DVD-Video Screen Saver" mode that display over 140 different still images in a random order. Each of these still images was created as a slide show with eight subpicture streams, but no audio. To activate the DVD-Video screen saver mode of *StarGaze* go to the Special Features Menu, select the Screen Saver Menu and then select the DVD-Video Screen Saver button.

Menus

Menus are created in much the same way that a video track or a still image track is created, except that there is an extra layer of information associated with the menu buttons. This is generally called the Highlight layer and it is used to define the size, color and display properties of buttons on the menu. Static menus have still images as their background graphics while motion menus use video clips in the background. Static and motion menus can include a single audio stream, and up to three subpicture streams, which are used to create the button highlights. Not all mid-range authoring tools will support the use of multiple aspect ratio menus, or the use of a video background to create a motion menu.

Depending on your authoring tool there can be several steps in the process of creating a menu.

1. Create an empty menu track.
2. Add a still image or video clip as a background.
3. Add an audio stream if required.
4. Define the playback stop time if required.
5. Create one, two, or three subpicture streams as required. Each subpicture stream can be used to define highlight information for a specific display mode (4:3 normal, 4:3 letterbox, and 16:9 widescreen).
6. Insert the appropriate subpicture graphic into each subpicture stream.
7. Define the size and location of the menu buttons for each display mode.
8. Create the Up, Down, Left, and Right navigational links for each button in each display mode.
9. Define the default button to be enabled when the menu is first accessed.

Menus that include audio or video elements will only be displayed until the user takes action or when the audio or video element ends. Figure 5.12 shows a menu track with a still image background, a single subpicture stream, and the highlight stream that contains the button information.

Figure 5.13 shows the buttons and navigation commands for this sample menu track. In this example there are a total of five menu buttons defined, aligned vertically. The arrows indicate that an UP and Down navigation command has been programmed for each button. This menu uses a "wrap-around" naviga-

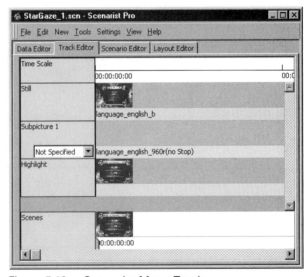

Figure 5.12   Scenarist Menu Track

tion scheme. Since all the buttons are aligned vertically, this menu does not make use of the Left and Right navigation commands.

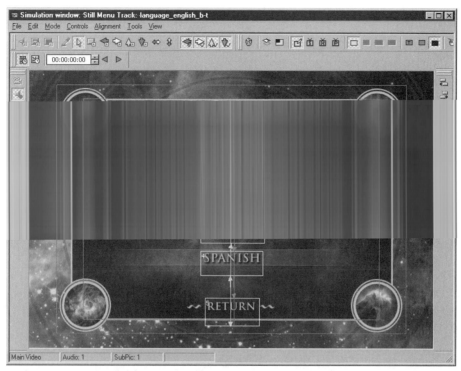

Figure 5.13   Scenarist Menu Buttons and Navigation Information
(See color insert for color version of this figure.)

DVD menu buttons can only be square or rectangular in shape. While it is possible to overlap buttons, it is not recommended since this may result in strange menu behavior on some DVD-Video players, or DVD-ROM computers.

It is possible to create "hidden" buttons on a menu by defining a button in an area where there is no P, E1, or E2 color on the subpicture graphic. Figure 5.14 shows a menu with two hidden buttons, located at the top left and top right of the menu. To select the hidden buttons the user simply has to press the Left or Right keys on the remote control. In this example the two hidden buttons have been given a "forced activate" property — once the button is selected, it will also be activated. Using a forced activation property for a hidden button will prevent the user from being confused by a menu where no specific button is selected.

For DVD-Video menus that use a single aspect ratio there can be up to 36 different buttons defined on a single menu. Menus with two aspect ratios have two groups of 18 buttons, with one group for each display mode. For menus with three aspect ratios there are three groups of 12 buttons defined. This concept of menu button groups is fairly difficult for some people to grasp, and in general only advanced DVD title developers will need to work with them. The key thing to remember is the maximum number of buttons for menus with 1, 2, or 3 different aspect ratios. Human factors engineers will tell you that menus should have seven buttons or less to make them easy to use, so in most cases having three button groups of 12 buttons is not a limitation for implementing a DVD-Video title.

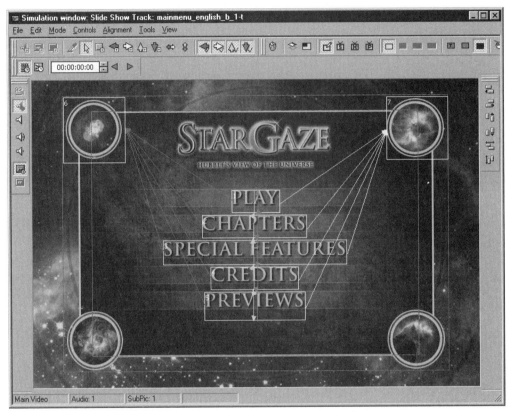

Figure 5.14   Menu with "Hidden" Buttons
(See color insert for color version of this figure.)

disc note:

Real World Example

All menus on the *StarGaze* disc are designed to provide simple and immediate feedback to the viewer. Selected buttons are indicated by the presence of a white line under the button. When a button is activated the white line changes to gold while the DVD-Video player is executing the appropriate button command. There are two hidden buttons on the Main Menu that have forced-activation properties. Press the Left key while on the Main Menu and *StarGaze* will set a loop mode flag so the main program is played forever. Press the Right key while on the Main Menu and a bonus video track is displayed. A hidden button on the DVD Production Credits Menu will play an "Easter Egg" track with video of Mount St. Helens (after the explosion).

Media Organization

Media Organization is the process of defining the playback order for all of the video, still show, slide show, and menu tracks on the disc, as well as programming the operation of each menu button. Most mid-range DVD-Video authoring tools use a flow chart metaphor to allow the developer to organize media elements into a functional DVD title, although some DVD tools use a timeline metaphor. In either case the goal of this step is simply to tell the authoring tool how to organize all of the media tracks to create the desired flow and operation of the DVD title.

authoring.

Tips, Tricks & Techniques

While it is not essential to understand how DVD-Video titles are organized in order to author them, it can be very beneficial. I have found using an analogy of a book helps most people understand the hierarchical organization of DVD-Video. If we ignore how books are published and concentrate on how they are organized we can see the following hierarchical structure.

```
Library
    Book(s)
        Chapter(s)
            Paragraph(s)
                Sentence(s)
                    Word(s)
                        Letter(s)
```

This organizational structure is independent of publishing medium and language. Using the structure of books to understand the structure of DVD-Video titles yields the following analogy:

```
Video Manager
    Video Title Set(s)
        Title(s)
            Program Chain(s)
                Program(s)
                    Cell(s)
                        VOBU(s)
```

Domains & Spaces

DVD-Video titles can include several domains and spaces. Domains and spaces are logical constructs that help to understand how media elements are organized on a DVD title, and how they can be presented to the viewer. Figure 5.15 shows the possible domains and spaces that can be found on a DVD-Video title. Some domains and spaces are optional, while others are mandatory. There are restrictions on movement directly between certain domains and spaces. To control the flow of a title you need to understand how to move from one domain or space to another.

Mid-range authoring tools from Spruce and Apple hide the concept of domains from the title developer. While this simplifies the authoring process, it also creates inherent limitations in the authoring tool. For example, DVD Studio Pro stores each video segment in its own Video Title Set, thus the maximum number of video segments in a project is limited to 99. Scenarist provides full access to all domains defined by the DVD-Video specification, so it can include over 98,000 unique video segments in a project. Providing the title

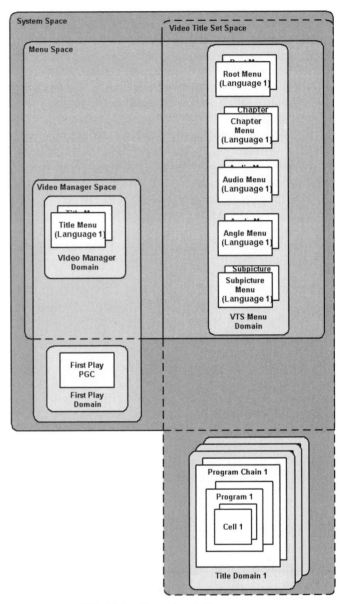

Figure 5.15   DVD-Video Domains & Spaces

developer access to all of the domains and spaces defined in the DVD-Video specification will require some additional knowledge to use these features to their full extent. Therefore mid-range authoring tools that provide access to domains and spaces are generally more difficult to use than tools that hide this level of the DVD-Video specification from the title developer.

Title Domain

The Title Domain generally includes all of the media elements to be presented to the viewer. A DVD disc can have as many as 99 different Title Domains, and each title can include up to 999 program chains. Program chains can be made up of a single media track, or multiple media tracks. If the Title Domain includes just one program chain, then it is called a "One_Sequential_PGC" title, which means that the DVD-Video player will have access to time-table information during playback of that PGC. If you want the viewer to see a time display on their DVD-Video player front panel, you will need to author your discs using

discussed in detail in Chapter 6.

Menu Space

The Menu Space includes all items stored in the Video Manager Domain and the Video Title Set Menu Domain. It is fairly easy to move from an element stored in the Video Title Set Menu Domain to an element in the Video Manager Domain. Moving from an element in the Video Manager Domain to an element in the Video Title Set Menu Domain is limited to the Root, Angle, Audio, Chapter, and Subpicture Menus.

While it is possible to create a DVD-Video title that has no items in the menu space, this is not recommended. DVD titles that have no menus are little better than linear VHS titles, and will not be seen favorably by consumers.

Video Title Set Space

The Video Title Set Space includes all items stored in the Video Title Set Domain and the Title Domain within the same Video Title Set. Movement within the Video Title Set Space is fairly easy. It is possible to jump directly from any program chain in the Video Title Set Menu Domain to any program chain in the Title Domain, and vice versa. It is not possible to jump directly from a program chain in either the Video Title Set Menu or Title Domains to a program chain in a different Video Title Set. If you need to jump from a program chain in one Video Title Set to a program chain in another Video Title Set, you will have to do it indirectly through program chains located in the Video Manager Domain. The concept of indirect jumping will be discussed in more detail in Chapter 6.

First Play Domain

The First Play Domain is optional and contains a single program chain that can't include any media elements. This is called the First Play PGC in most authoring tools. Whenever a DVD-Video player is turned on or a new disc is inserted, control automatically passes to the First Play PGC. Essentially this is a standard method to bootstrap a title so that it starts playing automatically when it is inserted into a DVD-Video player. While the First Play PGC is optional, I strongly recommend that you include one on every DVD title you develop. If you do not include a First Play PGC, some consumers will be confused when they insert your DVD title into their DVD-Video player and nothing happens. On many entry-level DVD-Video authoring systems the use of a First Play PGC is mandatory.

When using a First Play PGC you must include a Pre or Post Command to instruct the DVD-Video player where to jump at the end of the First Play PGC. You can only jump directly to the entry point of a Video Title Set or to another program chain within the System Space from the First Play PGC. Chapter 6 will discuss Pre and Post Commands in more detail.

Tips, Tricks & Techniques

The First Play PGC should only be played when a DVD disc is first inserted into the player, or when the player is turned on with a disc already in it. Generally the First Play PGC is used to start playback of a sequence of media elements that only need to be viewed once, such as an FBI warning or company logos. Some title developers have created DVD titles in which pressing the Title or Menu key forces the DVD-Video player to jump to the First Play PGC. In general this is not a good design practice as the Title and Menu keys have specific functions that are different from the First Play PGC.

Video Manager Menu Domain

The Video Manager Domain stores the disc's Title Menu(s). While most DVD-Video discs have only one Title Menu, it is possible to create a disc with a large number of Title Menus, each with their own unique language. When the viewer presses the Title button on their remote control the DVD-Video player will locate the appropriate Title Menu program chain in the Video Manager Domain, based on the default language setting of the DVD-Video player. As with the First Play PGC, the use of a Title Menu is optional. However I strongly recommend that you include one on every DVD title you develop. If you do not include a Title Menu, some consumers will be confused when they press the Title button on their remote control and nothing happens. Note that on some DVD-Video players the Title Menu button is labeled as "Top Menu".

It is a common practice, to include some video, still show, or slide show tracks in the Video Manager Domain. Generally media elements like an FBI warning screen and the distributors logos are included in the Video Manager Domain since they can be directly linked to from the First Play PGC. Media tracks stored in the Video Manager Domain can't be directly accessed from the DVD-Video player's remote control using the Title and Chapter number keys. Thus if you want to include hidden content, such as Easter Egg tracks, the Video Manager Domain is a good place to hide these tracks.

Video Title Set Menu Domain

The Video Title Set Menu Domain stores the disc's Root, Angle, Audio, Chapter, and Subpicture Menus. These menus are all optional, and as with the Title Menu there can be multiple copies of each menu with different languages. Some DVD-Video players will allow the viewer to press a combination of keys to directly access these menus. For example on some players pressing the Audio and Menu buttons will cause the player to jump directly to the audio menu, while pressing the Angle and Menu buttons results in the angle menu being displayed, if it exists. Unfortunately many players don't work this way, and most consumers are not aware that pressing two buttons at once will yield different results from pressing the same two buttons in sequence. If you choose to use Angle, Audio, Chapter, and Subpicture Menus in the Video Title Set Domain, make sure that these menus are accessible from buttons on the Title Menu or Root Menu of the disc.

there are a number of excellent authoring tools that will allow you to quickly and efficiently develop mid-range DVD-Video titles. However if you want to develop advanced DVD-Video titles or take advantage of DVD-Video features such as multi-angle video or multiple language menus, then you will need to understand how DVD-Video was designed to handle these advanced features. You will also need to use a mid-range or professional authoring tool that will allow you to use all the features of the DVD-Video specification. DVD-Video titles are organized into a hierarchical structure with seven distinct levels, as shown in Figure 5.16.

Many DVD-Video authoring tools hide some of the lower levels of this hierarchy to simplify the authoring process.

Video Object Unit (VOBU)

A VOBU is the smallest unit of multimedia content stored on a DVD disc, and holds between 0.4 and 1.2 second of video data. Most VOBUs hold exactly one GOP of video data, but there are some special cases in which they can hold slightly more. DVD-Video authoring systems will convert all multimedia data (video, audio, and images) into VOBUs so the DVD-Video title developer generally does not have to work at this lowest level of the organizational hierarchy.

Cell

A Cell is a combination of VOBUs that forms the basic unit of media presented to the viewer. Cells include video, audio, still images, and Pre and Post Commands to provide control of navigation both before and after a Cell is played. More than one program, or program chain can share cells.

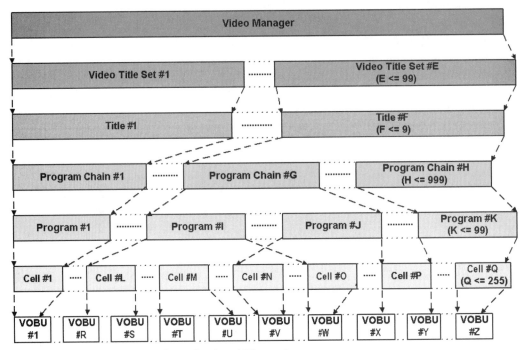

Figure 5.16   The DVD-Video Organizational Hierarchy

Program

A program is a collection of up to 255 cells, which can be presented to the viewer in a seamless fashion. For video tracks, programs can be equivalent to individual scenes defined in the track. Through the use of Pre and Post Commands as well as menu button commands it is possible to jump directly to the start of a program. For movies published on DVD-Video, each scene is generally assigned to a program so that the viewer can jump directly to the start of the scene.

Program Chain

A Program Chain is a collection of up to 99 programs, which can be presented to the viewer in a seamless fashion. For movies published on DVD-Video the entire length of the film is generally stored in a single program chain with as many as 99 programs used to provide random access to scene index points. Program chains can also be used to hold still shows, slide shows, and menus. Through the use of Pre and Post Commands as well as menu button commands it is possible to jump directly to the start of any program within a program chain, as long as the command is executed internally to the program chain.

Title

A Title is a collection of up to 999 program chains, which can be accessed through the use of Pre and Post Commands as well as menu button commands. Any program chain or program defined in a Title can be accessed directly from within that Title. One program chain in each Title is defined as the Entry PGC, which can be accessed directly from the Video Manager

Domain. Titles with a single program chain are called One_Sequential_PGC, while titles with more than one program chain are called Non_Sequential_PGC titles.

Video Title Set

A Video Title Set is a collection of up to nine titles defined in the Video Title Set Menu Domain. Any program chain or program defined in any Title within the Video Title Set can be accessed directly from within that Video Title Set Menu Domain. One program chain within the Video Title Set Menu Domain must be designated the Root PGC, and other program chains can be designated as the angle menu, audio menu, Chapter Menu

designated as the Title Menu. Separate copies of the Title Menu can be created with different languages. The Video Manager acts as the Table of Contents for all of the data stored on the DVD-Video disc. Direct access from any program chain in the Video Manager is possible to the Angle, Audio, Chapter, Root, and Subpicture Menus and the Title Entry PGC in all Video Title Sets.

Navigation Commands

There are three different types of navigational commands possible using the DVD-Video player remote control. These navigational commands allow the viewer to skip to the next or previous chapter, jump to the previous menu, and control the playback speed and direction of the content. Some of these navigation commands must be programmed into the DVD-Video title by the developer, while others will always work unless specifically prevented by the developer.

Next, Previous & Go-Up

The Next and Previous keys on the remote control allow the user to move between program chains, and between programs within the same program chain. Within a program chain pressing the Next key will instruct the DVD-Video player to jump to the start of the next program. If the Next key is pressed while the last program is being played it will have no effect. Pressing the Previous key within a program chain will instruct the DVD-Video player to jump to the start of the previous program. Many DVD-Video players will jump to the start of the current program when the Previous key is pressed, and to the start of the previous program when the key is pressed twice. It is generally not necessary to program the Next and Previous navigation functions within a program chain that has more than one program.

For Non-Sequential-PGC titles, which are titles with more than one program chain, the Next and Previous keys allow the user to navigate between the various program chains included in the title. While some DVD-Video authoring tools will automatically insert Next and Previous commands when you create multiple program chains in a title, this is generally a manual step that must be performed by the DVD developer. Next and Previous commands can only be created between program chains within a single Title Domain. It is not possible to link program chains in different Title Domains using the Next and Previous commands, nor is it possible to link program chains within the Video Title Set Menu Domain or the Video Manager Domain using Next and Previous commands.

The Go-Up command, called Return on many DVD-Video players, is used to allow the viewer to move between program chains within a Title. Generally the Go-Up command is used to navigate between Menu program chains, while Next and Previous are used to navigate between program chains that hold video, audio, or still image data. Using the Go-Up command to link Menu program chains allows the user to quickly return to a previous menu or a parent menu, although this key can be programmed to jump to any program chain in the title even if it does not contain a menu. The Go-Up command can't be used to link programs within a program chain to other programs. The Go-Up command can be used in the Video Title Set Menu Domain as well as the Video Manager Domain. Figure 5.17 shows a portion of a DVD-Video title design with program chains connected using the Next, Previous, and Go-Up commands.

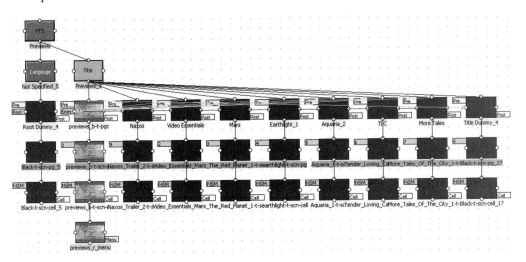

Figure 5.17   Next, Previous, and Go-Up Command Examples

In this example a Video Title Set has been created with a single Title, which includes seven program chains with video tracks, one program chain with a menu, and a dummy program chain. The Video Title Set Menu Domain has a single Root Menu program chain. The purpose of this VTS is to present the viewer with previews of seven different DVD-Video titles. The user can select any of the previews from the menu, which is defined as the Title Entry PGC. Once a preview is selected the DVD-Video player jumps directly to the start of that preview and starts playing the video and audio content. When the preview is over control passes back to the Menu PGC. If the viewer decides they don't want to watch any more of a specific preview they can press the Next, Previous, or Go-Up buttons to be taken directly to the Preview Menu program chain. So in this example, the seven previews program chains are programmed to support the use of the Next, Previous, and Go-Up buttons. The Next and

Previous commands are not programmed for the Menu PGC, but it does have a Go-Up command associated with it. If the viewer presses the Go-Up command while the Preview Menu is displayed, the DVD-Video player will jump directly to the Title Menu, which is this menu's parent menu.

Tips, Tricks & Techniques

While most DVD-Video titles make use of the Next and Previous commands to allow the viewer to jump between programs

Each button on every menu of a DVD-Video title must be programmed so that the desired effect is achieved when the viewer selects that button and presses the Enter key on the player's remote control. While there are some very sophisticated things that can be programmed for a menu button, the vast majority of DVD-Video titles have menu buttons that are programmed to jump to a specific program chain when activated. Figure 5.18 shows an example of how menu buttons are programmed. This menu includes buttons to allow the user to return to the Main Menu (Title Menu) or jump directly to any of the other major menus on the title (Chapters, Options, and Credits).

Buttons 1–7 on this sample menu are programmed to jump directly to the seven program chains that contain the different previews. Button 8 is programmed to jump to the Title Menu, button 9 will take the user to the Chapter Menu, button 10 will take the user to the Options menu, button 11 will take the user to the Credits Menu, and button 12 will instruct the DVD-Video player to remain on the Previews Menu with button 1 highlighted. The lines shown connecting the menu buttons are the Left, Right, Up, and Down navigation commands programmed for this menu.

This sample menu is designed without a default button highlight, so that different buttons will be highlighted each time the user returns to the menu. The first time the user sees this menu button 1 will be highlighted. If the user presses button 1, the player will start to play the first preview. When the preview ends or the user presses the Next, Previous, or Go-Up buttons, the Previews Menu will be displayed with the second button highlighted. Every time the user goes to a new menu the button he or she is most likely to use can be highlighted automatically. Including this type of menu button intelligence in your design allows the viewer to navigate through menus and buttons easier and faster. Some DVD-Video authoring systems, such as Spruce DVD-Maestro, can automatically generate the commands necessary to implement this intelligent menu structure, but most systems require the developer to implement a combination of Pre and Post Commands, as well as menu button commands.

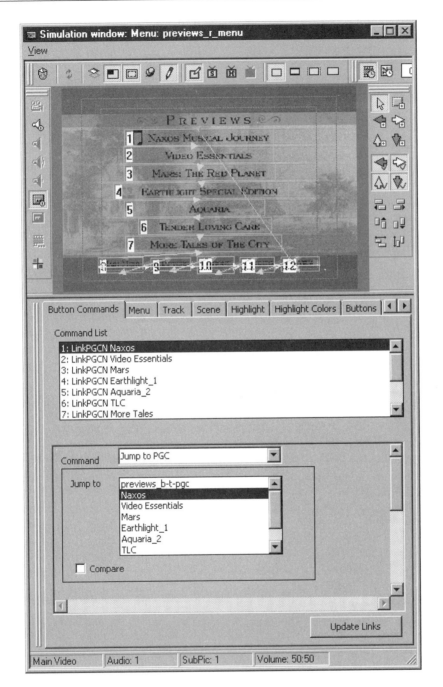

Figure 5.18   Sample Menu Button Commands
(See color insert for color version of this figure.)

Playback Controls

Most DVD-Video players include a variety of playback controls on their remote controls, including Play, Pause, Stop, Fast Forward, and Reverse. In general DVD-Video title developers do not need to program these functions into their title in order to support these keys. In fact unless the DVD-Video developer specifically prohibits these functions the viewer will be able to use these keys to navigate forwards and backwards through the title. Methods for prohibiting the use of playback controls will be discussed in Chapter 6.

1. Media Identification
   a. Import Video Elements
   b. Import Audio Elements
   c. Import Subpicture Elements
   d. Import Still Image & Graphic Elements
2. Media Association
   a. Create Video Tracks
   b. Create Still Show & Slide Show Tracks
   c. Create Menus
3. Media Organization
   a. Create First Play PGC
   b. Create Video Title Sets
   c. Create Titles
   d. Create Program Chains
   e. Insert Video, Still Show, Slide Show & Menu Tracks into Program Chains
   f. Create Next, Previous & Go-Up Navigation Commands
   g. Create Title, Root, Angle, Audio, Chapter & Subpicture Menus
   h. Program Menu Buttons

PROFESSIONAL DVD AUTHORING

Figure 6.1 shows a functional block diagram of a Professional DVD-Video Production environment, which as you can see includes many different components. The primary differences between professional and mid-range systems are the quality of the individual components and a multi-workstation design that allows professional systems to be used for many tasks at once.

Professional DVD-Video production systems generally have a number of different computer workstations, each designed to perform a specific step in the DVD production process. These systems also include a number of professional video and audio playback and monitoring devices so that the quality of the multimedia elements can be checked at each step of the production process.

Typically each video and audio playback device is synchronized through the use of a black burst signal generator or some other form of house sync that provides a consistent reference signal to all devices. Digital or analog video is fed from each playback device to an MPEG encoding workstation through a digital video noise reduction (DVNR) unit. Some professional facilities use a DVNR that is part of their MPEG encoder, while other have a stand-alone DVNR. The DVNR is used to eliminate noise from the video signal prior to MPEG compression. It can also be used to soften the video by removing high frequency components, thus making it easier to compress the video at low bit rates without visible digital artifacts. Digital or Analog audio signals are sent to either a Dolby Digital or DTS encoder, or to an Audio workstation. Some professional facilities use stand-alone Dolby Digital and DTS encoders, while others have software encoders that run in an Audio Workstation. The Audio

Workstation is also used to create new surround sound mixes for the audio streams, to sweeten the audio, or to make sure that all audio elements have the same levels throughout a DVD title.

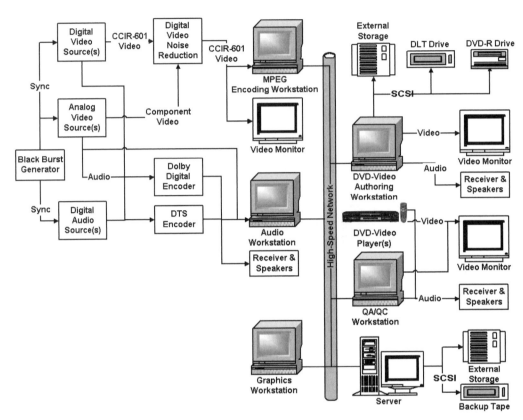

Figure 6.1   Professional DVD-Video Authoring System Block Diagram

Compressed video and audio data are sent to the DVD-Video authoring system via a high-speed network. This network can be fiber, 100 MBit, or faster Ethernet. In some cases the compressed video and audio files can be stored on network hard drives, but this will generally lead to slower network performance during the production process. A separate graphics workstation is used to generate menu background and overlay images, as well as any subpictures required for a DVD title. These image files are also transferred to the DVD-Video authoring system via a high-speed network connection.

The DVD-Video authoring workstation includes enough local hard drive storage to support the development of many different DVD titles at the same time, as well as output devices to create DLT tapes and DVD-R discs. Professional video and audio monitoring equipment is connected to the DVD-Video authoring workstation so that video and audio quality can be checked during the authoring process. At least one QA/QC workstation is also connected via the high-speed network, and is used to verify the overall quality of a completed DVD title. DVD disc images can be sent over the network for testing off the local hard drive of the QA/QC workstation. The QA/QC workstation should also have a number of consumer

DVD-Video players with DVD-R or DVD Check-Discs capability for quality testing. Video and audio monitoring equipment is connected to both the QA/QC workstation and the DVD-Video players to allow playback of DVD titles in an environment that mimics the typical consumer home entertainment system.

Many professional DVD-Video production systems will include a file server for storage and archival of the vast amounts of data created by a DVD production facility. The server keeps a backup copy of all media files used on a DVD title until the project has been completed and approved for replication or distribution. Backup copies can be stored on large hard drives connected to the server, internal RAID drives, or even on rewriteable optical

both of these goals. In general high-end MPEG encoders, Digital Video Noise Reduction units, Dolby Digital and DTS encoders, and Audio Workstations are sold as stand-alone units. Thus, the manufacturer can control all of the hardware and software elements that are used in each of these systems, allowing them to configure their products for optimal operation. Many professional DVD-Video authoring systems are also sold as stand-alone items that can be easily integrated into a production environment. Stand-alone units, which can each be connected via a high-speed network, are a key element in a robust and efficient DVD production system design. As a professional DVD production facility grows it will need additional workstations to support a larger workload. With a distributed system design it is relatively easy to add a new MPEG encoder, audio workstation, or DVD-Video authoring workstation to support additional workflow requirements. A distributed system design also makes it easier to upgrade specific equipment items when required. Improvements are constantly being made in MPEG video encoding, DVNR, DVD authoring, and DVD recordable media. Most professional DVD production systems undergo modifications and additions to their hardware and software components on a regular basis. A distributed system design makes it easier to upgrade individual components to improve overall quality or operational efficiency.

Navigation

The major functional difference between mid-range and professional DVD authoring software tools is support for the navigation features of the DVD-Video specification. While all authoring tools offer support for features like the Next, Previous, Up, Down, Left, and Right buttons, only advanced systems allow the DVD title developer to access the built in SPRM and general parameter registers (GPRM), and use them to develop complicated and highly interactive titles.

System Parameter Registers (SPRM)

All DVD-Video players have 24 SPRM registers that hold information about playback of a DVD title as well as user-specified default playback settings. Each SPRM is held in a 16-bit register, which can be accessed by a DVD title during playback. All SPRM registerss can be read, and some can also be written to during title playback. Advanced DVD authoring tools will provide a mechanism for the title developer to read and write to the SPRM registers during the playback of the title. Using SPRM registers, you can develop complex DVD titles.

SPRM 0 — Menu Description Language Code

When DVD menus are created a specific language code can be associated with each menu. Language codes are two bytes of data coded as lower case ASCII characters. DVD-Video uses the language codes defined in ISO-639, which are shown in Table 6.1.

Table 6.1	Language Codes for DVD Menus, Audio and Subpictures				
Language Code	Country	Language Code	Country	Language Code	Country
aa	Afar	ia	Interlingua	qu	Quechua
ab	Abkhazian	ie	Interlingue	rm	Rhaeto-Romance
af	Afrikaans	ik	Inupiak	rn	Kirundi
am	Amharic	in	Indonesian	ro	Romanian
ar	Arabic	is	Icelandic	ru	Russian
as	Assamese	it	Italian	rw	Kinyarwanda
ay	Aymara	iw	Hebrew	sa	Sanskrit
az	Azerbaijani	ja	Japanese	sd	Sindhi
ba	Bashkir	ji	Yiddish	sg	Sangro
be	Byelorussian	jw	Javanese	sh	Serbo-Croatian
bg	Bulgarian	ka	Georgian	si	Singhalese
bh	Bihari	kk	Kazakh	sk	Slovak
bi	Bislama	kl	Greenlandic	sl	Slovenian
bn	Bengali & Bangla	km	Cambodian	sm	Samoan
bo	Tibetan	kn	Kannada	sn	Shona
br	Breton	ko	Korean	so	Somali
ca	Catalan	ks	Kashmiri	sq	Albanian
co	Corsican	ku	Kurdish	sr	Serbian
cs	Czech	ky	Kirghiz	ss	Siswati
cy	Welsh	la	Latin	st	Sesotho
da	Danish	ln	Lingala	su	Sudanese
de	German	lo	Laothian	sv	Swedish
dz	Bhutani	lt	Lithuanian	sw	Swahili
el	Greek	lv	Latvian & Lettish	ta	Tamil
en	English	mg	Malagasy	te	Tegulu
eo	Esperanto	mi	Maori	tg	Tajik
es	Spanish	mk	Macedonian	th	Thai
et	Estonian	ml	Malayalam	ti	Tigrinya

Table 6.1	Language Codes for DVD Menus, Audio and Subpictures (Continued)				
Language Code	Country	Language Code	Country	Language Code	Country
eu	Basque	mn	Mongolian	tk	Turkmen
fa	Persian	mo	Moldavian	tl	Tagalog
fi	Finnish	mr	Marathi	tn	Setswana
fj	Fiji	ms	Malay	to	Tonga
	Gujarati		Oriya	vo	Volapuk
hi	Hausa	pa	Punjabi	wo	Wolof
hr	Hindi	pl	Polish	xh	Xhosa
hu	Croatian	ps	Pashto & Pushto	yo	Yoruba
hy	Hungarian	pt	Portuguese	zh	Chinese
	Armenian			zu	Zulu

DVD-Video players generally allow the viewer to specify a default display language for menus. If a DVD title is developed with menus in more than one language, then the player will automatically display the menus that have a language code matching the value set in SPRM 0. In Region 2 (Europe) many players are set at the factory to have a default menu language code of English. This is fine for the United Kingdom, but consumers in the rest of Europe who do not speak English may need to manually change the menu language code for their player. Unfortunately many consumers don't configure their player's default menu language setting, so a player's menu description language code may not be set correctly. So when developing a DVD-Video title with menus in more than one language it is a good idea to provide a menu that allows the user to manually select the menu languages.

SPRM 1 — Audio Stream Number

DVD-Video titles can include up to eight different audio streams (tracks). SPRM 1 stores the current selected audio stream number, with values between 0 and 7. SPRM 1 can also be set to a value of 16, which indicates that no audio stream has been selected. The default value for SPRM 1 is 16. DVD title developers can change the audio stream that is being played back by changing the value of SPRM 1. If the viewer changes audio streams by using the Audio key on the remote control, SPRM 1 will be updated with the new stream number.

In some cases the selected audio stream may not actually be the audio stream that is played back by the player. DVD-Video players use a fairly complicated algorithm to determine which audio stream should be played back at any given time. When more than one audio stream is present in a program chain, the player attempts to determine the correct audio stream to play back based on the value stored in SPRM 1 and the language code and language code extension associated with each audio stream. Within a single title domain, the player will always use SPRM 1 to determine which audio stream should be played. However when switching between different title domains, or between a title domain and the video manager domain, the player may play an audio stream that is different from the value in SPRM 1. Essentially when the player enters a new title domain or the video manager domain it tries to determine the correct audio stream number to play by evaluating the language code and language code extension settings.

This concept is best illustrated by an example, as shown in Figure 6.2. Let's assume that we have developed a DVD title with two video title sets (VTS). Each VTS contains a single program chain with three audio streams. In VTS #1 the first audio stream has the language code en (English), the second has the code fr (French) and the third has the code es (Spanish). In VTS #2 the first audio stream has the code en (English), the second has the code fr

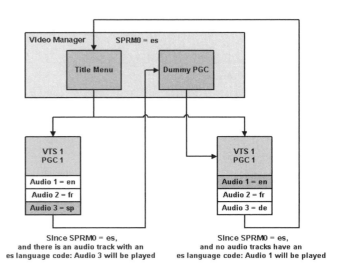

Figure 6.2   Default Audio Language Code Example

(French) and the third has the code de (German). Now assume that the viewer has configured their DVD player so that Spanish is their default audio language. When VTS #1 is played the DVD player will see that the user has selected Spanish as their default audio language and the third audio stream will be played. If the user then jumps from VTS #1 to VTS #2 the player will see that no Spanish audio stream is available, and so the first audio stream will be played. The algorithm for audio stream selection says that if no audio stream is found that matches the viewer-selected initial audio language code or audio language code extension, then the lowest numbered audio stream should be played.

SPRM 2 — Subpicture Stream Number

DVD-Video titles can include up to 32 different subpicture streams. SPRM 2 stores the currently selected audio stream number, with valid values of 0–31, 62, and 63. When SPRM 2 has a value of 0–31, subpictures are enabled and the corresponding subpicture stream will be displayed.

When SPRM 2 has the value of 62 (the default value), the display of subpictures is disabled. SPRM 2 can also have a value of 63, which is called the Dummy Stream value. When this occurs the DVD player will try to display the subpicture stream that matches the users default subpicture language setting. If no subpicture streams are available that match the

Tips, Tricks & Techniques

Be careful when assigning language codes and language code extensions to audio streams. If your DVD title has more than one VTS, try to assign audio streams with the same language codes to the same stream number across all VTS. The first audio stream should hold the audio that is most likely to be selected by the viewer since this is the stream that will be played if the player can not match the stream language codes with the viewers default audio language code.

SPRM 3 — Angle Number

DVD-Video titles can include up to 9 different video angles. SPRM 3 stores the currently selected video angle number, with values between 1 and 9. The default value for SPRM 3 is 1. If the viewer changes camera angles by using the Angle key on the remote control, SPRM 3 will be updated with the new stream number.

SPRM 4 — Title Number

DVD-Video titles can include up to 99 Titles. SPRM 4 stores the current title number with values between 1 and 99. If the viewer changes titles by using the Title, Menu, or numeric keys on the remote control, SPRM 4 will be updated with the new title number. Whenever SPRM 4 is updated with a new Title number, the values of SPRM 5 and SPRM 6 will also be updated. The default value for SPRM 4 is 1.

SPRM 5 — VTS Title Number

DVD-Video titles can include up to 99 VTS. SPRM 5 stores the current VTS number with values between 1 and 99. If the viewer changes the VTS by using the Title, Menu, or numeric keys on the remote control, SPRM 5 will be updated with the new title number. Whenever SPRM 5 is updated with a new VTS number, the values of SPRM 4 and SPRM 6 will also be updated. The default value for SPRM 5 is based on the value of SPRM 4.

SPRM 6 — Title PGC Number

DVD-Video titles can include up to 999 Program Chains within a title. SPRM 6 stores the current PGC number with values between 1 and 999. If the viewer changes Program Chains by using the Next, Previous, GoUp, or numeric keys on the remote control, SPRM 6 will be updated with the new PGC number. Whenever SPRM 6 is updated with a new PGC number, the values of SPRM 4 and SPRM 5 will also be updated. The default value for SPRM 6 is undefined.

SPRM 7 — Part_of_Title Number

DVD-Video titles can include up to 99 Part_of_Title (scenes) within a PGC. SPRM 7 stores the current Part_of_Title number with values between 1 and 99. If the viewer changes scenes by using the Next, Previous, GoUp, or numeric keys on the remote control, SPRM 7 will be updated with the new Part_of_Title number. The default value for SPRM 7 is 1. Note that SPRM 7 is only valid for One_Sequential_PGC titles

SPRM 8 — Highlighted Button Number

DVD-Video titles can include up to 36 buttons on each menu. SPRM 8 stores the currently highlighted button number. If the viewer changes menu buttons using the Up, Down, Left, Right, or numeric keys on the remote control, SPRM 8 will be updated with the new button highlight number. The default value for SPRM 8 is 1024. The value of SPRM 8 is maintained even when there are no valid buttons. DVD title developers can force a particular menu button to be highlighted by setting SPRM 8 to that button's number.

Button highlight numbers are stored in the upper half of SPRM 8, thus the values indicating which button should be highlighted are actually the button number multiplied by 1,024. Table 6.2 provides a cross reference for button numbers and SPRM 8 values.

Table 6.2   Button Highlight Cross Reference

Button #	SPRM 8 Value	Button #	SPRM 8 Value
1	1,024	19	19,456
2	2,048	20	20,480
3	3,072	21	21,504
4	4,096	22	22,528
5	5,120	23	23,552
6	6,144	24	24,576
7	7,168	25	25,600
8	8,192	26	26,624
9	9,216	27	27,648
10	10,240	28	28,672
11	11,264	29	29,696
12	12,288	30	30,720
13	13,312	31	31,744
14	14,336	32	32,768
15	15,360	33	33,792
16	16,384	34	34,816
17	17,408	35	35,840
18	18,432	36	36,864

SPRM 9 — Navigation Timer

SPRM 9 and SPRM 10 are used together to form a navigation timer that passes control to a specific program chain when the timer has expired. SPRM 9 is the navigation timer that can be set to any value between 1 and 65,535 seconds (approximately 18.2 hours). Once SPRM 9 is set to any non-zero value it will be automatically decremented by 1 every second. When SPRM 9 changes from a value of 1 to a value of 0, control automatically passes to the program chain number specified in SPRM 10 and the navigation timer is stopped.

The default value for SPRM 9 is 0, and its value is reset to 0 any time playback control passes into a new Title or Video Title Set. If control passes to the Video Manager domain the navigation timer is frozen at its current value, and the countdown will be restarted when control returns to the title domain. If the viewer presses the Pause key on the remote control, the navigation timer is also paused and will be automatically restarted when playback is resumed.

timer will be off by ten percent or more on personal computer systems. If the use of an accurate navigation timer is critical to the operation of your DVD title, its best to tell the viewer to use a DVD-Video player, rather than a DVD-ROM PC for playback.

SPRM 10 — PGC Pointer for Navigation Timer

SPRM 10 works in conjunction with SPRM 9 to form a navigation timer that passes control to a specific program chain when the timer has expired. SPRM 10 holds the number of the program chain that will be jumped to when the navigation timer expires. The program chain must be within the current Title domain. The default value for SPRM 10 is undefined.

SPRM 11 — Player Audio Mixing Mode for Karaoke

Many DVD-Video players support Karaoke features, in which audio channels 2, 3, and 4 can be mixed into channels 0 and 1. SPRM 11 is used to indicate the capabilities of the DVD-Video player with regard to audio mixing for Karaoke. SPRM 11 is defined as a 16-bit binary number with specific bits indicating the mixing characteristics for specific audio channels. If the bit is set to 0, mixing is not supported; if the bit is set to 1, the corresponding mixing mode is supported. The bit assignments are as follows.

Bit 0 – Reserved
Bit 1 – Reserved
Bit 2 – Audio Channel 2 mixed into Audio Channel 0 Flag
Bit 3 – Audio Channel 3 mixed into Audio Channel 0 Flag
Bit 4 – Audio Channel 4 mixed into Audio Channel 0 Flag
Bit 5 – Reserved
Bit 6 – Reserved
Bit 7 – Reserved
Bit 8 – Reserved

Bit 9 – Reserved
Bit 10 – Audio Channel 2 mixed into Audio Channel 1 Flag
Bit 11 – Audio Channel 3 mixed into Audio Channel 1 Flag
Bit 12 – Audio Channel 4 mixed into Audio Channel 1 Flag
Bit 13 – Reserved
Bit 14 – Reserved
Bit 15 – Reserved

The default value for SPRM 11 is 0. The viewer can't change SPRM 11. When the value of SPRM 11 is changed as a result of a DVD-Video navigation command, the audio mixing mode for Karaoke is immediately changed. SPRM 11 is only valid when the Karaoke capability flag (SPRM 15) is set and the current audio stream has been defined as Karaoke data.

SPRM 12 — Country Code for Parental Management

SPRM 12 holds the country code value for parental management features of DVD-Video titles. The DVD-Video specification requires that SPRM 12 hold a two-digit alphabetical country code as defined by ISO-3166 (Alpha 2). Valid country codes for SPRM 12 are shown in Table 6.3. The default value for SPRM 12 is "not specified", which is a value of 65,535.

Table 6.3   Valid Parental Management Country Codes

Afghanistan	AF	Lesotho	LS
Albania	AL	Liberia	LR
Algeria	DZ	Libya	LY
American Samoa	AS	Liechtenstein	LI
Andorra	AD	Lithuania	LT
Angola	AO	Luxembourg	LU
Anguilla	AI	Macau	MO
Antarctica	AQ	Macedonia	MK
Antigua And Barbuda	AG	Madagascar	MG
Argentina	AR	Malawi	MW
Armenia	AM	Malaysia	MY
Aruba	AW	Maldives	MV
Australia	AU	Mali	ML
Austria	AT	Malta	MT
Azerbaijan	AZ	Marshall Islands	MH
Bahamas	BS	Martinique	MQ
Bahrain	BH	Mauritania	MR
Bangladesh	BD	Mauritius	MU
Barbados	BB	Mayotte	YT
Belarus	BY	Mexico	MX
Belgium	BE	Micronesia	FM

Table 6.3   Valid Parental Management Country Codes (Continued)

Belize	BZ	Moldova	MD
Benin	BJ	Monaco	MC
Bermuda	BM	Mongolia	MN
Bhutan	BT	Montserrat	MS
Bolivia	BO	Morocco	MA
Bosnia And Herzegowina	BA	Mozambique	MZ
Burundi	BI	New Zealand	NZ
Cambodia	KH	Nicaragua	NI
Cameroon	CM	Niger	NE
Canada	CA	Nigeria	NG
Cape Verde	CV	Niue	NU
Cayman Islands	KY	Norfolk Island	NF
Central African Republic	CF	Northern Mariana Islands	MP
Chad	TD	Norway	NO
Chile	CL	Oman	OM
China	CN	Pakistan	PK
Christmas Island	CX	Palau	PW
Cocos (Keeling) Islands	CC	Palestinian Territory	PS
Colombia	CO	Panama	PA
Comoros	KM	Papua New Guinea	PG
Congo	CG	Paraguay	PY
Congo	CD	Peru	PE
Cook Islands	CK	Philippines	PH
Costa Rica	CR	Pitcairn	PN
Cote D'ivoire	CI	Poland	PL
Croatia	HR	Portugal	PT
Cuba	CU	Puerto Rico	PR
Cyprus	CY	Qatar	QA
Czech Republic	CZ	Reunion	RE
Denmark	DK	Romania	RO
Djibouti	DJ	Russian Federation	RU

Table 6.3   Valid Parental Management Country Codes (Continued)

Dominica	DM	Rwanda	RW
Dominican Republic	DO	Saint Kitts And Nevis	KN
East Timor	TP	Saint Lucia	LC
Ecuador	EC	Saint Vincent	VC
Egypt	EG	Samoa	WS
El Salvador	SV	San Marino	SM
Equatorial Guinea	GQ	Sao Tome And Principe	ST
Eritrea	ER	Saudi Arabia	SA
Estonia	EE	Senegal	SN
Ethiopia	ET	Seychelles	SC
Falkland Islands (Malvinas)	FK	Sierra Leone	SL
Faroe Islands	FO	Singapore	SG
Fiji	FJ	Slovakia	SK
Finland	FI	Slovenia	SI
France	FR	Solomon Islands	SB
France Metropolitan	FX	Somalia	SO
French Guiana	GF	South Africa	ZA
French Polynesia	PF	South Georgia	GS
French Southern Territories	TF	Spain	ES
Gabon	GA	Sri Lanka	LK
Gambia	GM	St. Helena	SH
Georgia	GE	St. Pierre And Miquelon	PM
Germany	DE	Sudan	SD
Ghana	GH	Suriname	SR
Gibraltar	GI	Svalbard And Jan Mayen Islands	SJ
Greece	GR	Swaziland	SZ
Greenland	GL	Sweden	SE
Grenada	GD	Switzerland	CH
Guadeloupe	GP	Syrian Arab Republic	SY
Guam	GU	Taiwan	TW
Guatemala	GT	Tajikistan	TJ
Guinea	GN	Tanzania	TZ
Guinea-bissau	GW	Thailand	TH
Guyana	GY	Togo	TG
Haiti	HT	Tokelau	TK
Heard And Mc Donald Islands	HM	Tonga	TO
Holy See (Vatican)	VA	Trinidad And Tobago	TT
Honduras	HN	Tunisia	TN

Table 6.3   Valid Parental Management Country Codes (Continued)

Hong Kong	HK	Turkey	TR
Hungary	HU	Turkmenistan	TM
Iceland	IS	Turks And Caicos Islands	TC
India	IN	Tuvalu	TV
Indonesia	ID	Uganda	UG
Iran	IR	Ukraine	UA
Kazakhstan	KZ	Venezuela	VE
Kenya	KE	Viet Nam	VN
Kiribati	KI	Virgin Islands (British)	VG
Korea, North	KP	Virgin Islands (U.S.)	VI
Korea, South	KR	Wallis And Futuna Islands	WF
Kuwait	KW	Western Sahara	EH
Kyrgyzstan	KG	Yemen	YE
Laos	LA	Yugoslavia	YU
Latvia	LV	Zambia	ZM
Lebanon	LB	Zimbabwe	ZW

SPRM 13 — Parental Level

SPRM 13 holds the parental level value associated with the parental management country code defined in SPRM 12. Each country has its own unique movie rating levels. These are translated to one of eight possible rating levels (1–8) supported by the DVD-Video specification. SPRM 13 can also have a value of 16, which means "not specified". The default value for SPRM 13 is undefined.

SPRM 14 — Video Aspect Ratio & Display Mode Configuration

SPRM 14 is used to hold the initial display aspect ratio and current display mode data for the DVD-Video player. The initial display aspect ratio data is stored in bits 10 and 11 of SPRM 14, while the current display mode data is stored in bits 8 and 9. SPRM 14 can be manually set by the viewer through the built in user interface of the DVD-Video player. The value stored in SPRM 14 can be read by a DVD-Video title using appropriate navigation commands. Possible values for the initial display aspect ratio and current display mode parameters are shown in Table 6.4

Table 6.4   Initial Aspect Ratio and Current Display Ratio Settings – SPRM 14

Initial Aspect Ratio	Bit 11	Bit 10
4:3 Aspect Ratio	0	0
Not Specified	0	1
Reserved	1	0
16:9 Aspect Ratio	1	1
Current Display Mode	**Bit 9**	**Bit 8**
Normal (4:3) or Wide (16:9)	0	0
Pan/Scan	0	1
Letterbox	1	0
Reserved	1	1

SPRM 15 — Player Audio Capabilities

SPRM 15 is used to hold the DVD player audio playback capabilities data. Information about the player's ability to play back AC3, DTS, MPEG, SDDS, and Linear PCM audio in normal and Karaoke modes is held in SPRM 15. Some of this information is set by the player manufacturer when the player is built, and other values are entered by the viewer through the built in user interface of the DVD-Video player. SPRM 15 is a 16-bit binary number, in which each bit is used as a flag to indicate support for a specific audio playback mode. If an audio playback mode is supported, the corresponding bit of SRPM 15 will be set to a 1; if the audio mode is not supported, the bit will be set to 0. The audio mode flags and their corresponding bit positions within SPRM 15 are shown in Table 6.5.

Table 6.5   Audio Capabilities Flags

SPRM 15 Bit #	Audio Mode Support Flag
0	Reserved
1	Reserved
2	SDDS Karaoke
3	DTS Audio
4	MPEG Karaoke
5	MPEG Karaoke (always set to 0)

Table 6.5   Audio Capabilities Flags (Continued)

SPRM 15 Bit #	Audio Mode Support Flag
6	Dolby Digital Karaoke
7	Linear PCM Karaoke
8	Reserved
9	Reserved
15	Reserved

SPRM 16 — Initial Audio Language Code

SPRM 16 is used to hold the initial audio language code, which can be configured by the viewer via the DVD-Video players built in user interface. Initial audio language codes for DVD-Video are defined in ISO-639, which are shown in Table 6.1. The default initial audio language code is "not specified", which has a value of 65,535.

SPRM 17 — Initial Audio Language Code Extension

SPRM 17 is used to hold the initial audio language code extension, which can be configured by the viewer via the DVD-Video players built in user interface. Initial audio language codes are 8-bit values stored in the lower byte of SPRM 17. Valid values for SPRM 17 are shown in Table 6.6. The default initial audio language code is "not specified", which has a value of 0.

Table 6.6   Initial Audio Language Code Extensions

SPRM 17	Audio Language Code Extensions
0	Not Specified
1	Normal Captions
2	Audio for Visually Impaired
3	Director's Comments 1
4	Director's Comments 2
5–112	Reserved
113–255	Provider Defined

SPRM 18 — Initial Subpicture Language Code

SPRM 18 is used to hold the initial subpicture language code, which can be configured by the viewer via the DVD-Video players built in user interface. Initial subpicture language codes for DVD-Video are defined in ISO-639, which are shown in Table 6.1. The default initial subpicture language code is "not specified", which has a value of 65,535.

SPRM 19 — Initial Subpicture Language Code Extension

SPRM 19 is used to hold the initial subpicture language code extension, which can be configured by the viewer via the DVD-Video player's built in user interface. Initial subpicture language codes are 8-bit values stored in the lower byte of SPRM 19. Valid values for SPRM 19 are shown in Table 6.7. The default initial subpicture language code is "not specified", which has a value of 0.

Table 6.7   Subpicture Audio Language Code Extensions

SPRM 19	Subpicture Language Code Extensions
0	Not Specified
1	Caption with Normal Size Characters
2	Caption with Larger Size Characters
3	Caption for Children
4	Reserved
5	Closed Caption with Normal Size Characters
6	Closed Caption with Larger Size Characters
7	Closed Caption for Children
8	Reserved
9	Forced Caption
10	Reserved
11	Reserved
12	Reserved
13	Director's Comments with Normal Size Characters
14	Director's Comments with Larger Size Characters
15	Director's Comments for Children
16–112	Reserved
113–255	Provider Defined

SPRM 20 — Player Region Code

SPRM 20 holds the region code data for the DVD-Video player. Region code information is stored in the lower byte of SPRM 20. When a DVD title is inserted into the player the region code setting of the title is compared to the region code setting of the player. If the player and title region codes match, the title can be played; if not, the player will display an error message.

Code-free, or "chipped", players are quite common throughout the world, particularly in Europe. A code-free player is one that has been modified to enable playback of all region-coded titles on the player, regardless of what regions the title was designed to support.

General Parameter Registers (GPRM)

The DVD-Video specification requires that all DVD-Video players include 16 GPRM registers that can be used by the DVD title author to control the presentation and playback of a DVD-Video title. GPRM registers are 16-bits in length and can be configured in either a register mode or a counter mode. In register mode the GPRM can be used to store and retrieve any 16-bit data value. In counter mode the GPRM will increase its stored value by 1 every second. Each GPRM is placed in register mode and set to 0 when any of the following conditions occur:

- initial insertion of a DVD-Video disc into the player;

- execution of Title Play, PTT Play and Time Play commands from all domains or from a Stop State; or

- execution of a Menu Call from the Stop State.

Values stored in each GPRM register are not changed when a title goes from one domain to another, thus a GPRM register can be used to store system-wide data, acting as variables that can be accessed from all domains within the title.

Navigation Command Areas

Navigation commands are used to develop complex or highly interactive DVD-Video titles. Essentially all DVD-Video players include a limited function microprocessor that can read and write to the SPRM and GPRM registers and can execute a small number of commands. Navigation commands can be stored in four different areas of a DVD-Video title. These area include the following.

Button Command Area   Navigation commands can be associated with menu buttons and executed whenever the viewer activates the button. Only a single navigation command can be associated with a menu button.

Pre Command Area   Single and compound navigation commands can be associated with a program chain and will be executed immediately before the contents of the program chain are accessed. Up to 128 different navigation commands can be included in the Pre command area of a PGC.

Post Command Area   Single and compound navigation commands can be associated with a program chain and will be executed immediately after the contents of the program chain are accessed. Up to 128 different navigation commands can be included in the Post command area of a PGC.

Cell Command Area   Single navigation commands can be associated with a Cell and will be executed when the Cell contents are accessed. Only a single navigation command can be associated with a Cell.

Every professional DVD-Video authoring tool that supports the use of Button, Pre, Post, and Cell commands has a slightly different syntax for how these commands are identified within the authoring tool. Some authoring tools, such as Scenarist, provide support for all of the navigation commands and access to all SPRM and GPRM registers. Other tools, such as Apple DVD Studio Pro, provide support for most of the navigation commands, access to all SPRM registers, and access to a limited number of GPRM registers. Authoring tools may also use a proprietary scripting language to implement navigation commands, rather than providing access to the specific commands called out by the DVD-Video specification. Thus it is not possible to provide specific instructions on how to implement navigation commands for all of the professional DVD-Video authoring systems currently available. Within this chapter I'll provide examples of navigation commands, using a Scenarist NT Professional system.

Instruction Groups

Navigation commands for DVD-Video titles are broken down into six basic instruction groups.

- The GoTo instruction group includes commands that can be used to change the execution order of other navigation commands in the Pre command and Post command areas. GoTo instruction group commands can't be used in the Button command area or the Cell command area.

- The Link instruction group includes navigation commands that transfer control within the current domain, and can be included in the Pre, Post, Button, and Cell command areas.

- The Jump instruction group includes navigation commands that transfer control outside the current domain, and can be used in the Pre, Post, Button, and Cell command areas.

- The Compare instruction group includes navigation commands that allow comparison operations between SPRM and GPRM registers and static values. Compare instruction group commands can be included in the Pre, Post, Button, or Cell command areas. Compare instruction group commands are always used in conjunction with commands from other instruction groups to form a compound command.

- The SetSystem instruction group includes commands used to set SPRM and GPRM register modes and values, and can be used in the Pre, Post, Button, and Cell command areas.

- The Set instruction group includes commands to perform simple arithmetic and logic operations on GPRM registers, and can be used in the Pre, Post, Button, and Cell command areas.

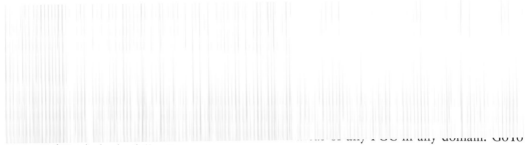

commands include the following.

GoTo   Pass control to another navigation command in the same command area.

Break   Terminate the execution of navigation commands in the Pre or Post command areas. If a Break command is encountered in a Pre command area the player will terminate the execution of any remaining Pre commands, and then start to display the content stored in the PGC. If a Break command is encountered in a Post command area the player will terminate the execution of any remaining Post commands and then proceed to the next PGC.

Nop   This is a no operation command, which essentially does nothing. In general the use of the Nop command should be avoided since many DVD-Video players interpret a Nop command as a Stop command.

SetTmpPML   Temporarily changes the parental management level of the player. This command may be necessary if there are no Titles on the disc matching the parental management level specified by SPRM 13. In this case using the SetTmpPML command can allow the viewer to change the player's parental management level in order to play the title that is in the player.

Link Group

The Link group includes navigation commands for starting playback at a specific point within the current domain. Link commands may be used in any Pre, Post, Button, and Cell command area. Link commands include the following.

LinkPGCN   Jumps directly to a specific program chain within the current domain. The DVD player immediately stops displaying the current program chain, skips over any additional navigation commands within the same command area, and jumps directly to the program chain specified in the navigation command.

LinkPTTN   Jumps directly to a specific Part_of_Title within the current Domain. The DVD player immediately stops displaying the current program chain, skips over any additional navigation commands within the same command area, and jumps directly to the Part_of_Title specified in the navigation command. The LinkPTTN command can also include an optional parameter to set the Highlight Button. This is useful when jumping to a menu and you want to highlight a specific button on the target menu.

LinkPGN   Jumps directly to a specific program within the current domain. The DVD player immediately stops displaying the current program chain, skips over any additional navigation commands within the same command area, and jumps directly to the program specified in the navigation command. The LinkPGN command can also include an optional parameter to set the Highlight Button.

LinkCN   Jumps directly to a specific Cell within the current domain. The DVD player immediately stops displaying the current program chain, skips over any additional navigation commands within the same command area, and jumps directly to the Cell specified in the navigation command. The LinkCN command can also include an optional parameter to set the Highlight Button.

LinkSIns   Jumps directly to a specific part of the current domain. LinkSIns commands can only be stored in the Button and Cell command areas. There are 13 different LinkSIns commands that can be used. These are as follows.

> **LinkNoLink**   Transfers the value stored in SPRM 8 into the current Highlight Button value, but does not transfer control to a different part of the current domain.
>
> **LinkTopC**   Jumps directly to the start of the current Cell. The current Highlight Button number may also be set at the same time.
>
> **LinkNextC**   Jumps directly to the start of the next Cell. The current Highlight Button number may also be set at the same time.
>
> **LinkPrevC**   Jumps directly to the start of the previous Cell. The current Highlight Button number may also be set at the same time.
>
> **LinkTopPG**   Jumps directly to the start of the current program. The current Highlight Button number may also be set at the same time.
>
> **LinkNextPG**   Jumps directly to the start of the next program. The current Highlight Button number may also be set at the same time.
>
> **LinkPrevPG**   Jumps directly to the start of the previous program. The current Highlight Button number may also be set at the same time.
>
> **LinkTopPGC**   Jumps directly to the start of the current program chain. The current Highlight Button number may also be set at the same time.

LinkNextPGC Jumps directly to the start of the next program chain. The current Highlight Button number may also be set at the same time.

LinkPrevPGC Jumps directly to the start of the previous program chain. The current Highlight Button number may also be set at the same time.

LinkGoUpPGC Jumps directly to the start of the program chain defined by the GoUp link. The current Highlight Button number may also be set at the same time.

LinkTailPGC Jumps directly to the Post command area of the current program chain. The current Highlight Button number may also be set at the same time.

Exit Stops playback of the title and clears the information used for the RSM command. In general the use of the Exit command should be avoided since the player will enter the Stop state, clear the GPRM registers, and clear the resume information.

JumpTT Jumps directly to a specific Title. The player immediately stops the presentation of the current program chain, clears the resume data and navigation timer, resets the audio and subpicture streams if required, and then starts the presentation of the specified Title.

JumpVTS_TT Jumps directly to a specific Title within the current VTS. The player immediately stops the presentation of the current program chain, clears the resume data and navigation timer, resets the audio and subpicture streams if required, and then starts the presentation of the specified Title.

JumpVTS_PTT Jumps directly to a specific Part_of_Title within the current VTS. The player immediately stops the presentation of the current program chain, clears the resume data and navigation timer, resets the audio and subpicture streams if required, and then starts the presentation of the specified Part_of_Title.

JumpSS Jumps directly to a specific program chain within the First Play, Video Manager, or Video Title Set Manager domains. The player immediately stops the presentation of the current program chain, stops the countdown of the navigation timer, stops the count up of any GPRM registers in counter mode, and then starts the presentation of the specified program chain. The current values of the navigation timer and all GPRM registers are left unchanged.

CallSS Jumps directly to a specific program chain within the First Play, Video Manager, or Video Title Set Manager Domains. The player immediately stops the presentation of the current program chain, stops the countdown of the navigation timer, stops the count up of any GPRM registers in counter mode, and then starts the presentation of the specified program chain. The current values of the navigation timer and all GPRM registers are left unchanged, and the Cell Number, first navigation pack address of the current Cell, PGC playback control status, Video Title Set Number, and SPRM registers 4–8 are also saved.

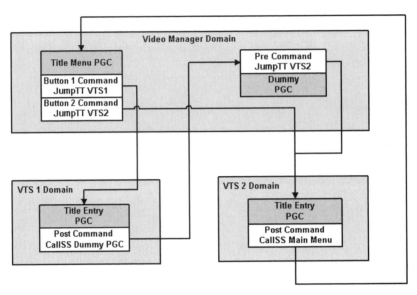

Figure 6.3   Jump Command Example

Compare Group

The Compare Group includes navigation commands for comparing two values. The first value is stored in one of the GPRM registers. The second value can be stored in a SPRM or GPRM register, or it can be a number between 0 and 65,535. Compare commands may be used in any Pre, Post, Button, and Cell command area. When a Compare command is encountered the player will execute the specified comparison. If the result of the compare is true, the remaining portions of the compound navigation command will be executed; if false, the player will skip to the next navigation command in the current command area, if it exists. Compare commands include the following.

BC   Performs a Bitwise Compare. Any GPRM can be compared to another GPRM, any SPRM, or any fixed value between 0 and 65,535. A Bitwise Compare is the equivalent of the logical And between the two values. If the result of the Bitwise Compare operation is non-zero then the remaining portions of the compound navigation command will be executed.

EQ (Equal To)   Compares any GPRM to another GPRM, SPRM, or a fixed value between 0 and 65,535. If the two values are equal, the remaining portions of the compound navigation command will be executed.

NE (Not Equal To)   Compares any GPRM to another GPRM, SPRM, or a fixed value between 0 and 65,535. If the two values are not equal, the remaining portions of the compound navigation command will be executed.

GE (Greater Than or Equal To)   Compares any GPRM to another GPRM, SPRM, or a fixed value between 0 and 65,535. If the first value is greater than or equal to the second value, the remaining portions of the compound navigation command will be executed.

GT (Greater Than)   Compares any GPRM to another GPRM, SPRM, or a fixed value between

and 65,535. If the first value is less than the second value, the remaining portions of the compound navigation command will be executed.

Figure 6.4 shows how compare commands can be used to jump directly to a specific chapter (or scene) within a program chain. In this example GPRM0 is used to hold the desired chapter number. Three Pre commands are used to compare GPRM0 to specific values (2, 3, and 4) and if the comparison is true the player will jump directly to the appropriate chapter. If GPRM0 is not equal to 2, 3, or 4, the first chapter will be played.

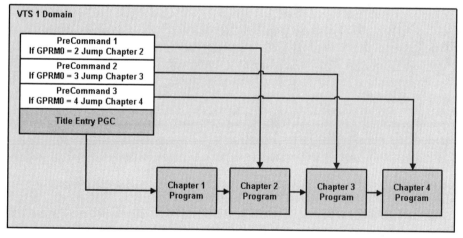

Figure 6.4   Compare Command Example

SetSystem Group

The SetSystem group includes navigation commands to set the values of various SPRM registers and to define the modes of GPRM registers. SetSystem commands may be used in any Pre, Post, Button, and Cell command area. SetSystem commands include the following.

SetSTN Sets the current audio, subpicture, and video angle streams. Streams can either be set to a specific value or to a value stored in a GPRM register. Values for audio streams must be between 0 and 7. Values for subpicture streams must be between 0 and 31, or 63. Values for video camera angles must be between 1 and 9. The SetSTN command can only be executed in the Video Title Set Manager and Title domains.

SetNVTMR Sets an initial value for the Navigation Timer and to assign the target Title and program chain that is to be jumped to when the Navigation Timer expires. The Navigation Timer will automatically be decremented by one every second, and when it changes from 1 to 0 control will automatically pass to the location specified in the SetNVTMR command.

SetGPRMMD Changes the operational mode of a GPRM register. Valid operational modes for GPRM registers are register mode and counter mode.

SetAMXMD Changes the audio mixing mode for Karaoke audio.

SetHL_BTNN Changes the Highlight button number. The Highlight button can either be set to a specific value or to a value stored in a GPRM register. Valid values for the Highlight button are between 1 and 36 if set to a specific value. If the Highlight button is set to the contents of a GPRM register, that register should contain values between 1024 and 36,864 in multiples of 1,024 as described in Table 6.2.

Figure 6.5 provides an example of how to use the SetSystem commands. In this example the Root Menu PGC of VTS 1 contains a Chapter Selection Menu with five buttons. Buttons 1–4 are used to jump directly to Chapters 1–4, while button 5 is used to return to the Title Menu. Pre commands are used to set the Menu Highlight button to match the last chapter that was played, so that if the viewer presses the Menu key in the middle of playback the Chapter Selection Menu will be displayed and the button associated with the chapter they were watching will be highlighted.

Set Group

The Set commands are used to perform arithmetic or logical operations on two values and to assign the result to a GPRM register. The first value can be any GPRM register. The second value can be any GPRM or SPRM register, or it can be a number between 0 and 65,535. Set commands can be included in any Pre, Post, Button, or Cell command area. Set commands include the following.

Mov (Move) Assigns a value to a GPRM. The target GPRM is set equal to the contents of a source GPRM, SPRM, or a specific value between 0 and 65,535.

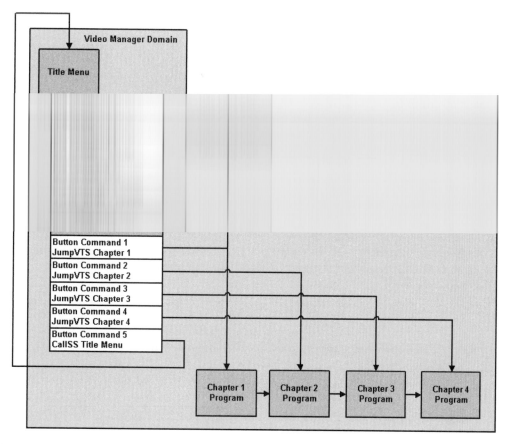

Figure 6.5   SetSystem Command Example

Swp (Swap) Swaps the values stored in two GPRMs. The value stored in the source GPRM will be stored in the target GPRM, and the value stored in the target GPRM will be stored in the source GPRM. This command can't be used if either GPRM is in counter mode.

Add Adds the first and second values and stores the result in the first GPRM. This command can't be used if the target GPRM is in counter mode.

Sub (Subtract) Subtracts the second value from the first value and stores the result in the first GPRM. This command can't be used if the target GPRM is in counter mode.

Mul (Multiply) Multiplies the first and second values and stores the result in the first GPRM. This command can't be used if the target GPRM is in counter mode.

Div (Divide)   Divides the first and second values and stores the result in the first GPRM. This command can't be used if the target GPRM is in counter mode. The second value can't be 0.

Mod (Modulo)   Finds the remainder when the first value is divided by the second value, and stores the result in the first GPRM. This command can't be used if the target GPRM is in counter mode. The second value can't be 0.

Rnd (Random)   Assigns a random number between 1 and x to the target GPRM. The value of x can either be stored in another GPRM or it can be provided as a fixed number between 0 and 65,535. This command can't be used if the target GPRM is in counter mode.

And (Logical And)   Performs a Bitwise Product (And) between the first and second values and stores the result in the target GPRM. This command can't be used if the target GPRM is in counter mode.

Or (Logical Or)   Performs a Bitwise Sum (Or) between the first and second values and stores the result in the target GPRM. This command can't be used if the target GPRM is in counter mode.

Xor (Logical Exclusive Or)   Performs a Bitwise Exclusive (Or) between the first and second values and store the result in the target GPRM. This command can't be used if the target GPRM is in counter mode.

Figure 6.6 shows an example of how to use Set Group commands. In this example a "random playback" mode is created so that the program chains in VTS1 can be played back in a random order endlessly. The random value is compared to the current chapter number so that the same chapter will not be played back twice in a row. After each chapter has been played control returns to the random number generator PGC to select the next chapter to play.

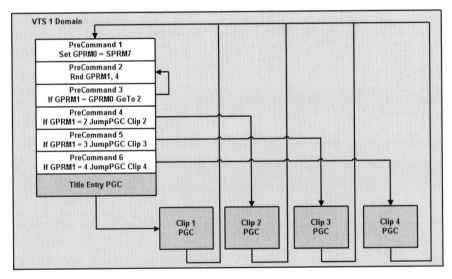

Figure 6.6   Set Command Example

Navigation Error Conditions

In some cases it is possible to cause an error condition through the execution of a navigation command. The DVD-Video specification requires the player to perform the following actions when an error condition occurs.

Divide by Zero If a navigation command attempts to divide a GPRM by zero, then the target GPRM will be set to 65,535.

Overflow If a navigation command results in an overflow, then the target GPRM will be set to 65,535. If the overflow occurred while a GPRM ·····

GPRM will be set to 0

...gation command is executed in an invalid command area, the player may not work correctly.

Navigation Command Examples

Using DVD-Video navigation commands requires an understanding of simple computer programming techniques. Essentially the set of DVD-Video navigation commands are an "assembly language" that allows you to instruct the DVD-Video player to perform a set of operations, and to read and write to a small number of memory locations (SPRM and GPRM registers). While many people are comfortable with programming computers, relatively few people still write software in low-level languages such as assembly. Today most programmers use a high-level language like C++ or Java to develop their applications.

High-level programming languages support more complex logical constructs than the DVD-Video navigation commands allow. For example Java has a `Switch` command that evaluates a system variable and executes a section of code based on the value of the variable. If the variable has ten possible values, there would be ten different sections of code that can be executed. When `Switch` is called, only a single section of code will be executed based on the value of the variable when `Switch` was initially called. `Switch` is a handy way to write code to perform a number of different operations based on the value of a system variable.

When you develop complex or highly interactive DVD-Video titles you will want to use high-level programming commands like `SWITCH`, `IF THEN ELSE`, `WHILE`, and `FOR`. When developing an educational title that includes an interactive test with scoring, it would be nice to use a `SWITCH` statement to evaluate the score the viewer received on the test, and then branch to an appropriate section of the title. If they scored 90 percent or better then they can go on to the next section of the title. If they scored between 70 percent and 90 percent you may want to have them review the material covered and then take the test again. If the viewer scored less than 70 percent you may want to require them to go through a remedial learning process to cover the material in more detail. While it is possible to implement this type of advanced logic in a DVD-Video title, it requires several navigation commands organized to perform the desired result. In the following sections I will show how you can use the available DVD-Video navigation commands to perform high-level programming functions.

If you don't understand these examples, or you find it difficult to use DVD-Video navigation commands to implement the interactive features you need in your titles, you have a few options. One option is to purchase a professional DVD authoring tool that provides a scripting language, which implements high-level programming statements for you. Authoring tools such as Spruce DVD Maestro and Apple DVD Studio Pro have internal scripting languages that allow you to add interactive features. In general scripting languages are much easier to use for people who do not have a programming background. An alternative is to hire a DVD title developer who is comfortable with the DVD-Video navigation commands and can implement the interactive features you require for your title.

Dummy PGC

DVD-Video titles have four basic domains, the First Play domain, the Video Manager domain, the Video Title Set Manager domain, and the Title domain. Using DVD navigation commands it is not always possible to transition directly from one domain to another domain. For example you can't use the Jump or Link commands to go from a program chain in one Title to a program chain in another Title.

Using dummy program chains is an excellent technique to transition from one domain to another within a DVD title. A dummy program chain is simply a program chain that does not include media elements that will ever be presented to the viewer. The First Play PGC, which is used to provide a starting location for a DVD title, is in effect a dummy PGC, since the First Play PGC does not include media elements for presentation. In general, a dummy PGC will include Pre commands that instruct the DVD-Video player to jump to a specific location within the DVD title.

Another use of a Dummy PGC is to execute additional navigation commands when a menu button is pressed. Navigation commands in the Button Highlight area are limited to a single command. If you need to execute more than one command when a button is pressed, you can accomplish this by having the button link to a dummy PGC. You can then use the Pre command area of the dummy PGC to execute up to 128 additional navigation commands. A Dummy PGC can be used in the Video Manager, Video Title Set Manager, and Title domains. It is a good idea to actually store a still image or static menu background in each Dummy PGC. Program chains that include some media content have more flexibility when it comes to executing navigation commands than program chains that are empty. Figure 6.7 shows how a Dummy PGC can be used to transition between two different Title domains.

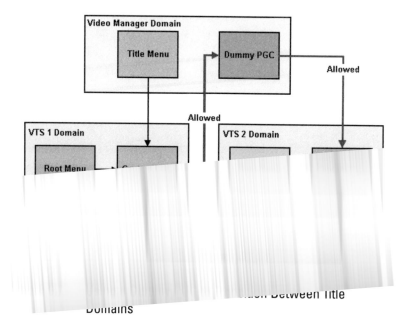

Video Manager Domain
Title Menu
Dummy PGC
Allowed
Allowed
VTS 1 Domain
VTS 2 Domain
Root Menu

...ن ween Title
Domains

FOR

A FOR statement executes a series of commands a specific number of times. Generally a FOR statement includes a counter variable (and initial value), an increment value, an ending value, and a block of code to be executed. A traditional computer program FOR statement looks something like this.

```
FOR (I=1, I<=100, I++)
    {
        Statement 1
        Statement 2
    }
End FOR
```

In this example Statement 1 and Statement 2 will be executed 100 times. After each time Statement 2 is executed the counter variable I will be incremented by 1. When I becomes greater than 100, the FOR statement execution will stop. The following code shows how a FOR statement can be implemented using DVD-Video navigation commands. In this example GPRM0 will be used as the counter variable.

Command #	Navigation Command	// Comments
1	Mov GPRM0, 0	// Initialize counter variable
2	if (GPRM0 >= 100) GoTo 7	// 100 is FOR loop end value
3	Nop	// Statement 1
4	Nop	// Statement 2
5	Add GRPM0, 1	// Increment counter
6	GoTo 3	// Return to top of FOR loop
7	Break	// End of FOR Statement

IF

The IF statement executes a block of code if a test is true. Generally an IF statement includes a statement that can be either true or false, and a block of code. A traditional computer program IF statement looks something like this.

```
IF (counter <= 10)
    {
        Statement 1
        Statement 2
    }
End IF
```

In this example Statement 1 and Statement 2 will be executed if the variable counter is less than or equal to 10 at the moment the IF statement is executed. If counter is greater than 10, Statement 1 and Statement 2 will not be executed. The following code shows how an IF statement can be implemented using DVD-Video navigation commands. In this example GPRM0 will be used as the counter variable. You should note that I have reversed the test in the DVD navigation command IF statement, as it is easier to implement the high-level IF statement using negative logic. For this example, I have used Nop commands as place holders for Statement 1 and Statement 2.

Command #	Navigation Command	// Comments
1	if (GPRM0 > 10) GoTo 4	// Compare "counter" to 10
2	Nop	// Statement 1
3	Nop	// Statement 2
4	Break	// End of IF Statement

IF THEN ELSE

The IF THEN ELSE statement executes one block of code if a statement is true, or a second block of code if the statement is false. Generally an IF THEN ELSE statement includes a statement that can be either true or false, and two blocks of code. A traditional computer program IF THEN ELSE statement looks something like this.

```
IF (counter <= 10) THEN
    {
        Statement 1
        Statement 2
```

In this example Statement 1 and Statement 2 will be executed if the variable counter is less than or equal to 10 when the IF statement is executed. If counter is greater than 10, Statement 3 and Statement 4 will be executed. The following code shows how an IF THEN ELSE statement can be implemented using DVD-Video navigation commands. In this example GPRM0 will be used as the counter variable.

Command #	Navigation Command	// Comments
1	if (GPRM0 > 10) GoTo 5	// Compare "counter" to 10
2	Nop	// Statement 1
3	Nop	// Statement 2
4	Break	// End of IF block
5	Nop	// Statement 3
7	Nop	// Statement 4
8	Break	// End of ELSE block

Navigation Timer

The DVD-Video Navigation Timer is roughly equivalent to a software timer interrupt in a personal computer. You can set up the Navigation Timer with any value between 1 and 65,535 seconds. While the DVD title is being played back the Navigation Timer is decremented once every second. When the Navigation Timer changes from 1 to 0 the DVD-Video player will automatically jump directly to the program chain specified in the initial Navigation Timer command. The Navigation Timer has a number of potential uses in a DVD-Video title.

For example if you are developing an educational title that includes a testing section, you may want to limit the amount of time that the viewer has to answer all the questions. The Navigation Timer works only in the Title domain, so you should set up the Navigation Timer using a Pre command in the Entry PGC of the Title. Figure 6.8 shows an example of how to use the Navigation Timer. In this example when the viewer has been playing the Title for one hour control will automatically pass to the designated program chain, which will tell the user that their time is up.

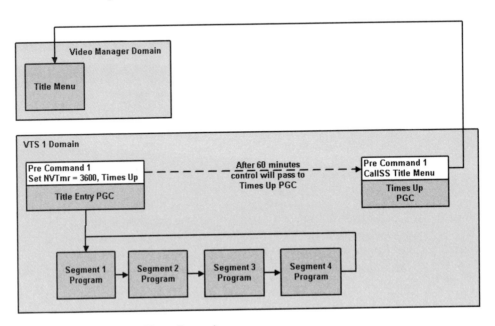

Figure 6.8   Navigation Timer Example

SWITCH

The SWITCH statement includes different blocks of code that are each executed when a variable has a specific value. Generally a SWITCH statement includes a statement or variable that can assume a range of values, blocks of code for each value range, and a default block of code to execute if the variable does not match any specific values. A traditional computer program SWITCH statement looks something like the following.

```
SWITCH ( variable)
CASE 1
    {
        Statement 1
        Statement 2
    }
```

```
Case 2
    {

        Statement 3
        Statement 4

    }
Case 3
    {

        Statement 5
        Statement 6

    }
```

In the previous example `variable` is evaluated when the `SWITCH` statement is initially called. If `variable` has a value of 1, `Statement 1` and `Statement 2` will be executed. If `variable` has a value of 2, `Statement 3` and `Statement 4` will be executed. If `variable` has a value of 3, `Statement 5` and `Statement 6` are executed. If "variable" has any other value than 1, 2, or 3, `Statement 7` and `Statement 8` are executed. The following code shows how a `SWITCH` statement can be implemented using DVD-Video navigation commands. In this example `GPRM0` will be used as the `variable`.

Command #	Navigation Command	// Comments
1	if (GPRM0 = 1) GoTo 7	// Case "1" Test
2	if (GPRM0 = 2) GoTo 8	// Case "2" Test
3	if (GPRM0 = 3) GoTo 11	// Case "3" Test
4	Nop	// Statement 7
5	Nop	// Statement 8
6	Break	// End Default Case
7	Nop	// Statement 1
8	Nop	// Statement 2
9	Break	// End Case 1
10	Nop	// Statement 3
11	Nop	// Statement 4

Command #	Navigation Command	// Comments
12	Break	// End Case 2
13	Nop	// Statement 5
14	Nop	// Statement 6
15	Break	// End Case 3

WHILE

The WHILE statement executes one block of code repeatedly until a statement is false. Generally a WHILE statement includes a statement that can be either true or false and one block of code. A traditional computer program WHILE statement looks something like this.

```
WHILE (counter <= 10)
    {
        Statement 1
        Statement 2
    }
```

In this example Statement 1 and Statement 2 will be executed if counter is less than or equal to 10 at the moment that the IF statement is executed. If counter is greater than 10, the WHILE function will be ended. In general at least one of the statements inside the WHILE loop will directly impact at least one of the variables used to determine when to stop execution of the block of code. The following code shows how a WHILE statement can be implemented using DVD-Video navigation commands. In this example GPRM0 will be used as the counter variable. In this example GPRM0 has been placed in counter mode so that it will automatically increase by one every second.

Command #	Navigation Command	// Comments
1	SetGPRMMD GPRM0, 0, 1	// Set GPRM0 in Counter Mode
2	Nop	// Statement 1
3	Nop	// Statement 2
4	If(GPRM0 <= 10) GoTo 2	// End WHILE

User Operations (UOP)

The DVD-Video specification defines a number of different User Operations (UOP). UOP are performed by pressing one or more buttons on the DVD-Video player remote control, or by clicking on a specific button in a PC DVD-Video navigation graphical users interface. All UOP can be enabled or disabled by the DVD-Video title author, and these properties can be changed during the playback of the title. For example on Hollywood titles it is common practice to disable all UOP during the playback of the FBI warning segment. Once this segment has been played UOP are enabled. Thus the viewer is prevented from jumping out of the FBI warning segment, but after that segment has been played the viewer can use the remote control to jump directly to the disc menus, use the fast forward function, or jump directly to any chapter in the title. The following UOP are defined for DVD-Video.

Title_Play(Title_Number)   Plays a specific title indicated by a Title_Number between 1 and 99.

PTT_Play(Title_Number, PTT_Number)   Plays a specific chapter from a specific Title indicated by the Title_Number and PTT_Number between 1 and 999. PTT_Play is an optional feature and may not be supported by all DVD-Video players.

Time_Play(Title_Number, Time)   S

(Time)   Starts playback at a specific time code within the current title, indicated by the Time (hours, minutes, seconds, frames). This user operation is only allowed for one-sequential-PGC titles. Time_Search is an optional feature and may not be supported by all DVD-Video players.

PTT_Search(PTT_Number)   Starts play at a specific chapter number within the current title, indicated by a PTT_Number between 1 and 999. PTT_Search is an optional feature and may not be supported by all DVD-Video players.

PrevPG_Search   Starts play from the beginning of the previous program.

TopPG_Search   Starts play from the start of the current program. TopPG_Search is an optional feature and may not be supported by all DVD-Video players.

NextPG_Search   Starts play from the beginning of the Next program.

Forward_Scan(Speed)   Changes the speed of playback to values faster or slower than the normal speed. Forward_Scan is an optional feature and may not be supported by all DVD-Video players.

Backward_Scan(Speed)   Changes the speed and reverses the direction of playback. Backward_Scan is an optional feature and may not be supported by all DVD-Video players.

Menu_Call(Menu_ID)   Jumps directly to the menu specified by Menu_ID. Valid Menu_ID values are Title, Root, Audio, Subpicture, Angle, and PTT. Menu_Call is an optional feature for Audio, Subpicture, Angle, and PTT menus, and may not be supported by all DVD-Video players.

Resume   Returns from the Video Manager or Video Title Set menu domains to the Title domain, and resumes playback at the last playback point.

Upper_Button_Select   Moves from the current button on a menu to the button defined by the Up link.

Lower_Button_Select   Moves from the current button on a menu to the button defined by the Down link.

Left_Button_Select   Moves from the current button on a menu to the button defined by the Left link.

Right_Button_Select   Moves from the current button on a menu to the button defined by the Right link.

Button_Activate   Executes the navigation command associated with the current button.

Button_Select_&_Activate(Button_Number)   Jumps directly to the specified button and then executes the navigation command associated with it. Button_Select_&_Activate is an optional feature and may not be supported by all DVD-Video players.

Still_Off   Releases the player from an infinite display of a VOBU, PGC, or Cell Still Image.

Pause_On   Pauses playback of the title. Pause_On is an optional feature and may not be supported by all DVD-Video players.

Pause_Off   Resumes playback of a paused title. Pause_Off is an optional feature and may not be supported by all DVD-Video players.

Menu_Language_Select(Language_Code)   Selects a specific language for menus indicated by the Language_Code.

Audio_Stream_Change(Audio_Stream_Number)   Changes the current audio stream to a new one indicated by the Audio_Stream_Number.

Subpicture_Stream_Change(Subpicture_Stream_Number)   Changes the current subpicture stream to a new one indicated by the Subpicture_Stream_Number.

Angle_Change(Angle_Number)   Changes the current video angle to a new one specified by the Angle_Number.

Parental_Level_Select(Parental_Level)   Changes the current Parental Level to a new one specified by Parental_Level. Parental_Level_Select is an optional feature and may not be supported by all DVD-Video players.

Parental_Country_Select(Country_Code)   Changes the current Parental Level Country Code to a new one specified by Country_Code. Parental_Country_Select is an optional feature and may not be supported by all DVD-Video players.

Karaoke_Audio_Presentation_Mode_Change(Mode)   Changes the current Karaoke mode to a new one specified by Mode. Karaoke_Audio_Presentation_Mode_Change is an optional feature and may not be supported by all DVD-Video players.

Video_Presentation_Mode_Change(Mode)   Changes the current video presentation mode to a new one specified by Mode.

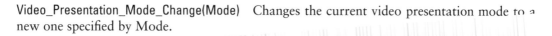

....c uomain.
....g ......ae set in both the Video Manager and Title ...., within the Title domain the UOP must be permitted at both the PGC and program levels. Table 6.8 shows the flags supported by DVD-Video players, the UOP with which they are associated, and the levels at which the flags may be set.

Table 6.8   DVD-Video User Operation Flags & Associate Operations

UOP Flag	User Operation	UOP Flag Set Allowed?		
		Video Manager	Program Chain	Program
UOP0	Time_Play Time_Search	Yes	Yes	No
UOP1	PTT_Play PTT_Search	Yes	Yes	No
UOP2	Title_Play	No	Yes	No
UOP3	Stop	No	Yes	Yes
UOP4	GoUp	No	No	Yes
UOP5	Time_Search PTT_Search	No	Yes	Yes
UOP6	Prev_PGC_Search Top_PGC_Search	No	Yes	Yes
UOP7	NextPGC_Search	No	Yes	Yes
UOP8	Forward_Scan	No	Yes	Yes
UOP9	Backward_Scan	No	Yes	Yes
UOP10	Menu_Call(Title)	No	Yes	Yes

Table 6.8   DVD-Video User Operation Flags & Associate Operations

UOP Flag	User Operation	UOP Flag Set Allowed?		
		Video Manager	Program Chain	Program
UOP11	Menu_Call(Root)	No	Yes	Yes
UOP12	Menu_Call(Subpicture)	No	Yes	Yes
UOP13	Menu_Call(Audio)	No	Yes	Yes
UOP14	Menu_Call(Angle)	No	Yes	Yes
UOP15	Menu_Call(PTT)	No	Yes	Yes
UOP16	Resume	No	Yes	Yes
UOP17	Upper_Button_Select Lower_Button_Select Left_Button_Select Right_Button_Select Button_Activate Button_Select_&_Activate	No	Yes	No
UOP18	Still_Off	No	Yes	Yes
UOP19	Pause_On, Pause_Off Menu_Language_Select	No	Yes	Yes
UOP20	Audio_Stream_Change	No	Yes	Yes
UOP21	Subpicture_Stream_Change	No	Yes	Yes
UOP22	Angle_Change Parental_Level_Select Parental_Country_Select	No	Yes	Yes
UOP23	Karaoke_Audio_Presentation_Mode_Change	No	Yes	Yes
UOP24	Video_Presentation_Mode_Change	No	Yes	Yes

Dual Layer Issues

Dual layer, or DVD-9, discs are very popular for publishing DVD titles that include a large amount of content. In general professional DVD authoring systems will allow you to develop dual layer titles, while few entry-level and only some mid-range authoring systems support dual layer titles. There are two basic methods of developing a dual layer titles: Parallel track and Opposite track, as shown in Figure 6.9.

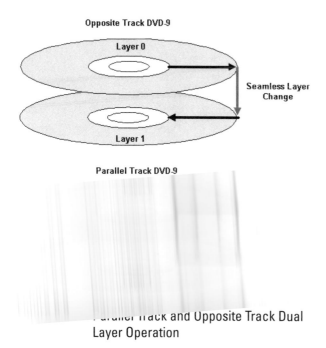

Opposite Track DVD-9

Layer 0

Seamless Layer Change

Layer 1

Parallel Track DVD-9

Parallel Track and Opposite Track Dual Layer Operation

In a parallel track dual layer title each data layer is independent,. When a DVD-Video player or DVD-ROM drive is instructed to change data layers there will be a noticeable pause in the playback of content. Most DVD-Video players take about 0.5 seconds to refocus the laser to read a different layer. If the laser also has to be repositioned at a different radius, the pause can take even longer. Thus a parallel track dual layer disc cannot change layers in a seamless fashion. When developing a parallel track dual layer disc the only thing you need to do is specify the location of the layer break, and make sure that the total amount of data stored on either layer is less than 4,269,998,080 bytes. For Parallel track dual layer titles there are no requirements on how large, or small each layer needs to be.

Opposite track dual layer titles are designed for the playback of content that requires a seamless transition between one layer and the next. Thus a movie that is too long to fit on a single layer, single sided disc (DVD-5) can be broken up into two pieces and stored on a dual layer (DVD-9) disc. When the player reaches the end of Layer 0 it will automatically refocus to start reading data from Layer 1 and continue playback of the content in an uninterrupted fashion. Because a seamless transition is needed between the two layers, there are some additional requirements for dual layer titles. Most importantly, the amount of data stored on Layer 0 must be larger than the amount on Layer 1 so that the laser won't have to be repositioned when it changes layers, but will only have to refocus. As with parallel track dual layer titles, there is a limit of 4,269,998,080 bytes that can be stored on either layer. Opposite track dual layer discs are played starting from the inner data-ring using Layer 0. When the player reaches the last data byte on Layer 0, which will be near the outer edge of the disc, it refocuses the laser to Layer 1 and starts reading data in the reverse direction, from the outer to inside edges of the data on the disc. Opposite track dual layer discs are also called Reverse Spiral Dual Layer (RSDL) discs.

Here are a few guidelines on where to position the layer change so that it will not be visible to the viewer.

1. Ideally the layer change should be positioned so that it occurs when the video is black and the audio is silent. Thus even if a DVD-Video player freezes for a short time during the layer break, it will not be noticeable to the viewer.

2. When developing an Opposite Track dual layer title you want to include as much data as possible on Layer 0. Since Layer 0 must be larger than Layer 1, you will not be able to store any data on the portion of Layer 1 that is beyond the last data sector of Data 0. Thus if Layer 0 is too small you may not be able to fit everything on the disc since you will have unusable space on both Layer 0, and Layer 1.

3. Many older DVD-Video players have a limited amount of buffer storage, which means that these players will "freeze" on layer changes that may be perfectly acceptable on newer players. Since you can't control the make and model of DVD player used to play the title, you should design for the worst case. Its a good idea to test the layer break on your dual layer titles on an older player to make sure it works correctly.

4. If you can't locate the layer change during a fade to black, you should choose a scene in which the video is as static as possible. A layer change during the middle of a high action scene will be noticeable on most DVD players. If the layer change has to occur during a non-black video sequence, there are some tricks you can use to minimize the visibility to the viewer. One technique is to lower the data rate of the compressed video stream a second or two before the layer change. Keep the video data rate low until a second or two after the layer change. Lowering the video data rate before the layer change will allow the internal buffer in the DVD-Video player to store the maximum amount of video frames and thus give the player more time to actually perform the layer change before it runs out of data to display. Keeping the data rate low just after the layer change will allow the player to load new frames quickly so that it can resume video playback as soon as possible.

5. Last, but not least, you need to plan for the layer break before you start encoding the video and audio elements or authoring the title. Once you decide where the layer break will be, you can perform the bit budget calculations discussed in Chapter 3 on each layer. When you perform the bit budget calculations for a dual layer disc don't forget that the maximum data storage on either layer of a dual layer disc is about ten percent less than the amount that can be stored on a single layer disc.

Multiple Angle Video Issues

A common misperception is that the total data rate of a multiple angle video stream can't exceed the maximum data rate for a single video stream, which is 9.8 Mbps. This however is not true; in fact multiple angle video streams can each have data rates as high as 8 Mbps, although in some cases maximum data rates can be restricted to 7 Mbps to ensure seamless branching between different video angles. Most professional DVD authoring tools support multiple camera angles and will provide a warning if the data rate of any video angle stream exceeds the maximum amount. There are a number of other restrictions that apply to multiple camera angles including the following.

- The audio streams must be the same format for all video angles in a specific segment.

- The subpicture streams must be the same format for all video angles in a specific segment.

- Each video angle must have the same number of GOPs.

- The number of audio packets must be the same for each video angle.

- The number of subpicture packets must be the same for each video angle.

- The Highlight information, with the exception of button commands, must be the same for each video angle.

- The individual data rates for each video angle must be close enough so that the maximum distance between data sectors of individual video angles is no more than 20,000 sectors and takes no more than 0.31 seconds.

Tips, Tricks & Techniques

A good rule of thumb for develop...

...players must support up to 32 subpicture streams. In theory it is possible to update a subpicture stream 30 times per second, and there are some DVD-Video players that will support this rate. However many DVD-Video players will not work properly when presented with one or more subpicture streams that are updated at a rate of 30 frames per second.

Subpicture images are stored as run-length coded bit maps, and can have resolutions as large as 720×480 for NTSC titles and 720×576 for PAL titles. It is possible to generate a subpicture image that is so complicated it can't be compressed to fit into the maximum space allocated for a single subpicture. This will only happen when you are generating subpictures that fill the entire screen and have a fair amount of detail.

Subpicture images must stay within the traditional video-safe areas for NTSC and PAL television signals. In general a subpicture image should contain no critical information within ten percent of the edges of the image.

Several advanced features can be used with subpictures such as fade in and out, scroll up and down, and movement of the subpicture display location. Some professional DVD authoring systems do not support these advanced features, and there are also many entry-level DVD-Video players that can't play back subpictures using these advanced features. Hopefully this is an area in which the DVD authoring tools and players will improve over the next few years.

Tips, Tricks & Techniques

A good rule of thumb for subpicture streams is to update them no faster than twice a second. Subpicture streams with new images that occur only twice per second will work on the vast majority of DVD-Video players.

Educational Title Issues

Educational titles have some unique requirements that must be addressed during the DVD-Video authoring process. Many educational titles are designed to work with the Pioneer V7300 or V7400 players. These are industrial-strength DVD-Video players that have been designed with mouse, RS-232, and bar code interfaces needed for educational or industrial applications. The Pioneer players provide a number of features that can be used by educators to develop customized presentations using DVD-Video titles. These customized presentations may include the playback of short segments of video stored on the DVD-Video disc, with a requirement for frame-accurate access to any frame of video. The primary command and control mechanism for the bar code interface to the Pioneer V7300/7400 players is based on an interface that Pioneer designed for their line of industrial laser disc players. This bar code interface provides educators with the ability to enter specific frames as in and out points for a playback sequence, or they can jump directly to any title or chapter stored on the disc. There are a few restrictions to the DVD-Video authoring process that must be accommodated if the title is to be played back using a Pioneer V7300/7400 player with a bar code interface. These restrictions include the following.

All content should be stored in one-sequential-PGC titles. The Pioneer players require time code information in order to provide frame-accurate in and out points. Only one-sequential-PGC titles will have the timetable information included on the DVD-Video to support this frame-accurate feature.

Dummy PGCs should be used in the Video Manager and Video Title Set Manager domains. These Dummy PGCs should include Pre commands that direct the DVD-Video player to jump back into a Title domain. The bar code interface of the Pioneer V7300/7400 players will not work when the player is in either the Video Manager or Video Title Set Manager domains. Essentially this means that you need to design the DVD title so that all of the menus are stored as program chains within one or more titles, rather than storing them in their traditional Video Manager or Video Title Set Manager locations. Dummy PGCs can be used to allow the viewer to press the Title and Menu buttons, but when these buttons are pushed control will pass through the Dummy PGC to a program chain within a Title domain. This somewhat backwards method of authoring a DVD title will ensure that the bar code interface can be used from any point within the DVD-Video title.

DVD-Video Player Compatibility Issues

The DVD-Video specification is an extremely complex document that leaves many details subject to interpretation. This has led to compatibility problems between some DVD-Video players and some DVD-Video titles. In general the vast majority of DVD-Video players will be able to play simple or basic DVD-Video titles. These titles usually have all of the content stored in a one-sequential-PGC title, with a single video stream, a single audio stream, and a limited number of subpicture streams. Simple titles generally include fewer than 20 menu screens in a single language. If you want to avoid player compatibility problems, you need to design your DVD title to be as simple as possible.

For many professional developers, designing a simple DVD title is not going to be good enough. Many title developers want to use advanced features such as multiple video angles, multiple audio tracks, menus in several different languages, slide shows, and DVD navigation commands to implement a highly interactive title. Professional DVD title developers need to know about compatibility problems with DVD-Video players and how they can be avoided.

No list of player compatibility problems can possibly include every problem on every player. New players are released every quarter. As DVD developers push the limits of their authoring tools and the specification, new compatibility problems are found on a routine basis. The best advice I can give you on this subject is to design your titles to avoid the known compatibility issues, and then test the final disc image on as many DVD-Video players as possible before you commit to the production run. In general, compatibility problems are more likely to occur on ch

Audio Compatibility Issues

There are a number of known compatibility issues with audio playback, including the following.

Audio Format Transitions   Some Dolby Digital and DTS receivers take several seconds to detect and react to a change in the format of the audio signal from a DVD-Video player. In some cases the receiver will not play the audio after the format has been changed, while in other cases the viewer will not hear the first few seconds of sound. The solution to this problem is to minimize the number of times the title automatically changes audio modes. You may also want to add a dummy PGC with a few seconds of silent audio in the new format to give the receiver time to sync up to the new format. For example, to transition between a menu with Dolby Digital 2.0 audio and the main program with Dolby Digital 5.1 audio, you can transition through the dummy PGC (with 5.1 audio).

Audio Language Definitions   Some DVD players will fail to play an audio stream if the stream's language code is different from the language code specified in the Video Manager or Video Title Set Manager domains. The solution to this problem is to make sure the audio language codes used in a Video Title Set are the same as the language codes used in the Video Manager and Video Title Set Manager domains.

Changing Audio Streams   Some DVD players will not allow you to change the audio stream number to a value that is higher than the number of streams in the current domain. There are several possible solutions to this problem. When you are in the same domain as the content, you can change the audio stream number. You can include Pre commands that set the audio stream number each time you enter a new domain. You could also add dummy audio tracks so that each domain in the title includes the same number of audio streams.

Dolby Digital Audio   Some DVD players will fail to play an audio stream when the last byte of audio data has a hex value of 0x0b77 in the last audio pack of a cell. This is a valid value for audio data and it can occur in a valid audio stream. While there is no way to predict when this problem will occur, the solution is to change the audio slightly and re-encode it so the last data value is not 0x0b77.

Slide Show Audio   Some DVD players will fail to play an audio stream in a slide show if the audio data is not present at the start of the slide show. The solution to this problem is to make sure that the audio stream has valid data throughout the entire slide show. If necessary you may need to add silent audio to the portions of the slide show that do not have active audio data.

Disc Structure Compatibility Issues

There are a number of known compatibility issues with DVD disc structures, including the following.

One-Second Cell   Some DVD players will fail to play a title that includes a cell that is less than one second long, except for menus.

More than 128 PGC in Video Manager or Video Title Set Manager Domains   Some DVD players will fail when they try to play a title that has more than 128 program chains in any individual language section of the Video Manager or Video Title Set Manager domains.

More than 243 PGC in VTS   Some DVD players will fail to play a title that has more than 243 program chains in a single VTS.

Three-Second Tracks   Some DVD players will fail to play a title that includes a track that is less than three seconds long.

More than 38 Files in the Root Directory   Some DVD players will fail to play a title that has more than 38 files in the root directory of the disc. This can only occur with hybrid DVD titles that include both DVD-Video and DVD-ROM data. If you have more than 38 files in the root directory you should consider moving some DVD-ROM files to their own directory on the disc.

More than 511 PTT in VTS   Some DVD players will fail to play a title that has more than 511 PTT (chapters) within a single VTS.

More than 75 Cells in a Program Chain   Some DVD players will fail when the try to play a title with more than 75 cells in a single program chain.

Forced Activation Button   Some DVD players will fail when they encounter a title that uses forced activation buttons.

Disc Image Size   Some DVD players will fail when they try to play a title that has more than 2,293,760 sectors for a single layer disc or more than 2,097,152 sectors for a dual layer disc. Make sure the size of any individual layer of a disc is approximately 24 Mb less than the maximum capacity called out by the DVD-Video specification.

Repeated Cells   Some DVD players will go into an infinite loop condition if a cell is repeated within a program chain. This can happen when you use the same track or scene in chain more than once.

Video M

... can t read DVD-R discs. Table 6.9 provides a list of players and the results of DVD-R compatibility tests. DVD-Video player models are released every quarter, and vendors occasionally change player firmware during a units manufacturing life. Please visit http://www.dvdtoday.com for an updated DVD-R compatibility list.

Table 6.9   DVD-R Compatibility

DVD-Video Vendor	DVD-R Capable Models	DVD-R Incapable Models
Aiwa	XDDV290	XDD370
Apex	AD660	AD500A
	AD703	AD600A
Denon	DVD3000	DVD1500
	DVD3300	
	DVM3700	
Emerson	DVD2000	
Go! Video		DVS3000
		DVR5000
Harmon Kardon	DVD5	
Hitachi		GD3000
		GD5000
		GVD305

Table 6.9   DVD-R Compatibility (Continued)

DVD-Video Vendor	DVD-R Capable Models	DVD-R Incapable Models
JVC	XV511BK	XV501
	XV723	XV523
	XVD55	XV1000
	XVM567	XVD701
Kenwood		DV402
		DV403
KLH		DVD1000
Konka	KD1800U1	
Magnavox	DVD711/171	
Memorex		MVD2026
Mitsubishi	DD6000	DD2000
		DD3000
		DD4001
Oritron	DVD100	
	DVD200	
	DVD600	
Panasonic	DVDA7	DVDA110
	DVDA10	DVDA120
	DVDA100	DVDCV50
	DVDA300	
	DVDA310	
	DVDL10D	
	DVDL110	
	DVDL50D	
	DVDT2000	
	DVDCV50	
	DVDRV20	
	DVDRV30	
	DVDRV55	
	DVDK520	
	CT27DC50	
Pioneer	DVC503	
	DV414	
	DV301	
	DV333	
	DV434	
	DVD-V7100	

Table 6.9   DVD-R Compatibility (Continued)

DVD-Video Vendor	DVD-R Capable Models	DVD-R Incapable Models
	DVD-V7200	
	DVD-V7300	
	DVD-V7400	
	Elite05	
	Elite DVF07	
	DV500	
	DV505	
		DVD170
		DVD400
		DVD405
		DVD751
		DVD825AT
		DVD850
		DVD950
Proscan	P8610P	
	P8680Z	
Raite	RDP715	
RCA	RC5200	RC5910
	RC5220P	
	RC5215P	
Sampo		DVE520
Samsung	DVD511	DVD839
	DVD611	DVD709/XAA
	DVD905	DVD739
		DVDC600
Sharp	DV750U	
	DVL70U	
SMC	DVD330S	
Sony	DAVS300	DVPS3000TP
	DVPC600	DVPS7000
	DVPC650D	DVPS3000

Table 6.9   DVD-R Compatibility (Continued)

DVD-Video Vendor	DVD-R Capable Models	DVD-R Incapable Models
	DVPC660	PVDV30
	DVPC670D	
	DVPCX850D	
	DVPCX860	
	DVPCX870D	
	DVPS300	
	DVPS330	
	DVPS350	
	DVPS360	
	DVPS500	
	DVPS530D	
	DVPS520	
	DVPS550D	
	DVPS560D	
	DVPS570D	
	DVP660	
	DVP670D	
	DVP680	
	DVPS7700	
	DVPS9000ES	
	PlayStation 2	
Technics	A10D	
Toshiba	SD1200	SD2006
	SD1600	SD2107U
	SD2150	SD2108U
	SD2200	SD2109
	SD2300	SD3006
	SD3205	SD3107
	SD4205	SD3109
	SD6200	SD5109
		SD6109C
		SD9000
Tredex	TX8303	
X-Wave		B171-L9
Yamaha	DVDC996	DVDC900
	DVDS700	
	DVDS796	

Table 6.9   DVD-R Compatibility (Continued)

DVD-Video Vendor	DVD-R Capable Models	DVD-R Incapable Models
Zenith	DVC2200	IQDVD2300
	DVC2250	
	DVC2515	

Menu Compatibility Issues

There are a number of known compatibility issues with

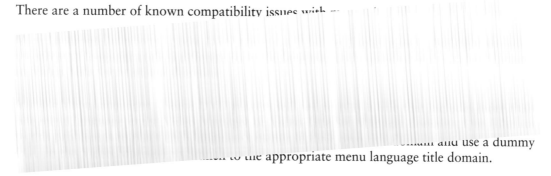

...um and use a dummy ...... .o the appropriate menu language title domain.

Navigation Command Compatibility Issues

There are a number of known compatibility issues with navigation commands, including the following.

Post Command in Last Cell   Some DVD players will not execute a Post command in the last cell of a PGC if the cells are connected seamlessly and the PGC resides in the Video Manager or Video Title Set Manager domains. The solution to this problem is to either use single-cell PGCs in the Video Manager and Video Title Set Manager domains, or to use the Link-TailPGC navigation command in each cell of the PGC.

Random Number Generation   Some DVD players will generate the same number when the RND (Random) command is executed more than once within a single PGC. You should only use the RND command once within the Pre or Post command areas of a PGC.

Reset Navigation Timer   Some DVD players will fail to play a title correctly if the Navigation Timer is reset. When the timer is reset, control could pass to the PGC specified as the target for when the Navigation Timer expires. When using the Navigation Timer you should specify a dummy PGC as the target of the Navigation Timer when the reset is performed. The dummy PGC should link to the same location as the PGC that is to be executed after the reset, so that even if the reset fails to work correctly, control will pass to the correct PGC.

Slide Show Compatibility Issues

There are a number of known compatibility issues with slide shows, including the following.

Fast Forward during Slide Show   Some DVD players will not work correctly when using the fast forward feature during a slide show. Using fast forward may cause the player to display each slide in the slide show for a fraction of a second, rather than for a 2×, 4×, or 8× period as required. There is no solution to this problem other than to avoid using slide shows entirely.

Slide Show with Audio   Some DVD players will not play an audio track that is part of a slide show. The only way to solve this problem is to avoid using audio tracks in slide shows.

Subpicture Compatibility Issues

There are a number of known compatibility issues with subpicture streams, including the following.

Disable Subpicture   Some DVD players will not turn off the subpicture stream if the current stream number is set to 63 (which is the default). The solution to this problem is to change the subpicture stream number to something other than 63 before you turn it off.

Forced Subpicture Display   Some DVD players can't display forced subpictures if the subpicture stream number is set from 0–31 and the subpicture stream is turned off. The solution to this problem is to set the subpicture stream number to 63 whenever subpictures are turned off.

SPRM 2 = 62   Some DVD players will display the subpicture stream that has the same language code as the DVD players setup menu default language when SPRM 2 is set equal to 62. The solution to this problem is to avoid setting SPRM 2 equal to 62.

Subpicture Displayed across Track Boundaries   Some DVD players will display a subpicture across a track boundary if the last subpicture in the track ends fewer than two seconds before the end of that track. The solution to this problem is to make sure that the final subpicture in a track ends at least two seconds before the end of the track.

Video Compatibility Issues

There are a number of known compatibility issues with video streams, including the following.

Half D1 MPEG-2 Video Resolution   Some DVD players can't correctly display video encoded at Half D1 MPEG-2 resolutions (352×480 for NTSC and 352×576 for PAL).

High Bit Rate Video   Some DVD players will not play a title correctly that includes video streams with the maximum video bit rate of 9.8 Mbps. A good rule of thumb is to use video with bit rates that are less than 9.0 Mbps.

Last Video Frame   Some DVD players will not play the last frame of video if there is no padding packet at the end of the video stream. This can happen on rare occasions when the last video packet is the same length as the other video packets in the video object. The solution to this problem is to re-encode the video or still image so that it will have a different number of bytes and thus require a padding packet at the end of the stream.

Jacket Pictures

Jacket pictures are a rather obscure feature of the DVD-Video specification that allows you to associate one or more still images with a DVD-Video volume. A DVD-Video volume is a single side of a DVD-Video disc. DVD-5 and DVD-9 discs have one volume. DVD-10, DVD-14, and DVD-18 discs have two volumes. With the introduction of multi-disc players the use of jacket pictures has become more popular because it all...

play of im...

Jacket Picture Description	Image Size	File Name
Large Jacket Picture for NTSC	720×480	J00___5L.mp2
Medium Jacket Picture for NTSC	176×112	J00___5M.mp2
Small Jacket Picture for NTSC	96×64	J00___5S.mp2
Large Jacket Picture for PAL	720×576	J00___6L.mp2
Medium Jacket Picture for PAL	176×144	J00___6M.mp2
Small Jacket Picture for PAL	96×80	J00___6S.mp2

If any jacket pictures are provided for either NTSC or PAL formats, all three sizes of jacket pictures for that format must be provided. It is not necessary to provide PAL jacket picture for NTSC titles, or to provide NTSC jacket pictures for PAL titles, but you can do so if you want. Not all professional DVD authoring systems support the use of jacket pictures, however it may be possible to use jacket pictures even if they are not supported by your authoring system. Most professional authoring systems will allow you to include DVD-ROM content on a disc image in addition to the DVD-Video data. If you can create the required jacket image pictures outside of your authoring tool, give them the correct file names, and then include them on the disc image as DVD-ROM data in the Jacket_P directory, then you can include this feature on your DVD title.

AUTHORING

There is an interesting dichotomy in the DVD world today. With over 8,000 titles already on the market, and another 2,000 due out before the end of 2001, DVD-Video has become a very popular consumer home entertainment format. Market research companies predict an installed base of about 20 million consumer players by the end of 2001. Sales of personal computers with DVD-ROM drives are running about three times higher than the rate of DVD-Video players sold, with a projected installed base of over 60 million by the end of 2001. Perhaps the most interesting statistic is that there are fewer than 200 titles on the market that have been designed specifically for these DVD-ROM systems.

Companies are always looking for opportunities in a rapidly-growing market with little competition. We can calculate an "opportunity index" for DVD-Video and DVD-ROM by dividing the number of available titles by the installed base of playback devices. Thus, the opportunity index for DVD-Video is 2,500 while the opportunity index for DVD-ROM is 300,000. In other words, developers who publish DVD-ROM titles have a larger installed base and less competition than developers who publish DVD-Video titles.

This significant disparity between the consumer-preferred DVD playback platform (DVD-ROM) and the industry-preferred DVD publishing format (DVD-Video) creates a unique business opportunity for developers. DVD titles that offer features for both DVD-Video players and DVD-ROM enabled personal computers will attract a wider segment of consumers. In short, enhanced DVD titles will have significant market penetration over the next several years due to the disparity between the number of consumer DVD-ROM systems and the number of available DVD-ROM titles.

Hollywood studios have recognized this opportunity and are now adding DVD-ROM content, such as web links, screen savers, games, and other extras, to their DVD-Video titles. Some of the best selling DVD-Video titles to date have been hybrid titles that offer the consumer extra content when played back on their DVD-ROM PC.

In May of 2001 the DVD Forum Steering Committee unanimously approved the creation of a working group to study the creation of a DVD Interactive format. This new working group is under WG-1, the DVD-Video format working group, so at some point in the future we may see a revision to the DVD-Video specification that includes optional, recommended, and possibly even required support for enhanced DVD features.

Several different methods are used to add DVD-ROM content to a DVD-Video title.

PC Friendly   DVD-ROM features can be added through the use of third-party tools, such as PC Friendly. These tools allow developers to wrap a DVD-ROM user interface around the DVD-Video content and offer new features, such as web links, games, screen savers, chat rooms, and on-line registration. Using PC Friendly to add DVD-ROM content is the most popular method in use today, since it offers fairly rapid development times at a moderate price tag.

Spinware   DVD-ROM features can also be added through the use of third-party tools from Spinware. Spinware PortaNet allows the addition of Internet content as well as conditional access content to a standard DVD-Video title. Spinware's iControl allows users to embed DVD-Video content for playback in standard web browsers or other ActiveX-compliant applications, such as PowerPoint.

WebDVD   DVD-ROM features can be added through the use of Microsoft's WebDVD software developers kit. Using WebDVD developers can access content stored on a DVD-Video title from standard web pages. Thus high quality (i.e., high bandwidth) video, audio, and graphics can be delivered from the DVD disc, while low bandwidth content such as time sensitive data is delivered from the Internet. Using WebDVD to add DVD-ROM content is still in the experimental stages, but since WebDVD is free it is likely that more title developers will embrace this method in the future.

DVD is the Key to Digital Convergence

Digital convergence is the integration of computers, communications, and consumer electronics. Data and text were converted into digital form for the computer years ago. With the advent of CD and DVD, all forms of information, both for business and entertainment, can be managed together. Music, movies, video games, and other interactive programs can be requested on demand using cable TV, satellite dish, optical fiber, or telephone, along with the Internet's inexhaustible array of offerings.

DVD-Video is the fastest growing consumer electronics product ever. DVD-ROM is quickly becoming a standard item in personal computers for the consumer market. Enhanced DVD devices already exist, including products such as the Internet connected DVD-ROM ~~~~ (~~~~)

~~~~ televisions and VCR

As you can see from Figure 7.1 more than 600 million households are expected to have DVD devices by the end of this decade. Is broadband Internet an alternative solution to delivering high quality digital video content? Internet bandwidth is constantly increasing; in the United States consumers are rapidly adopting cable and DSL modems. Outside the United States bandwidth capacity is also increasing rapidly. However, Internet bandwidth is not increasing fast enough to keep up with advances in multimedia formats. DVD-Video requires an average bandwidth of 4.5 Mbps, and a worst case burst rate of 10.08 Mbps. High definition DVD will require an average bandwidth of 16 Mbps and a worst case burst rate of 40 Mbps. By way of example, let's see how long it would take for a consumer to download a popular movie using a variety of data rates available today. For this example lets assume that a consumer wants to download a copy of *The Matrix*, one of the most popular DVD-Video titles ever released. *The Matrix* is a dual layer DVD-Video disc with 8,393,390,060 bytes of data (67,147,120,640 bits). If the consumer had a standard dial-up modem that can deliver approximately 28,800 bits per second of data over the Internet, it will take about 28 days to download all the data required for *The Matrix*. An ISDN link to the Internet that can deliver 56,000 bits per second would required 14 days of download time. Even a high-speed DSL link at 960,000 bits per second would require a full day to download this two-hour movie. These times assume the communication line is running at full speed, and there are no dropped connections during the file transfer — a somewhat unlikely scenario when connecting to the Internet. Thus it is easy to see that for the vast majority of consumers in the world the Internet is just not fast enough to use as a reliable delivery mechanism for DVD quality multimedia content.

Many experts have argued that it will only be a matter of time before the Internet is improved enough to deliver high quality multimedia content into the home. While this argument seems plausible, there is a problem with one of its underlying assumptions. It is not fair to assume that technological advances will deliver new capabilities to the Internet, but at the same time assume that DVD, and other optical disc technologies will not benefit from advances in technology during the same period of time. So while it is true that new technology will deliver increasingly faster connections to the Internet, it is also true that new technology will result in removable storage media, such as DVD discs, having much higher data capacities in the future.

Let's compare the growth of communications bandwidth to the growth of removable storage capacity over the past 30 years. This comparison, shown in Figure 7.2, indicates that both communications bandwidth and removable storage capacity have grown tremendously over the past 30 years. In growing from 300-baud modems to full T1 lines delivering 1,500,000 bits per second, we have seen a growth rate of more than 500,000 percent in communications bandwidth.

Over the same period of time removable media storage capacity has grown from 300,000 byte 8" floppy diskettes to 17 Gb dual-layer, dual-sided DVD discs, which translates into a growth rate of more than 5,000,000 percent. While it is reasonable to assume that communications bandwidth will increase over the next decade, we must also assume that the capacity of removable media will increase as

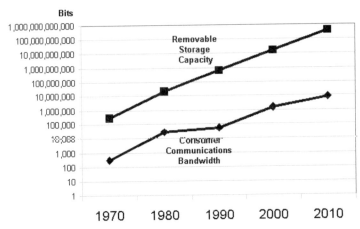

Figure 7.2　Projected Increases in Bandwidth and Storage Capacity

well. If the rate of increase continues as shown in Figure 7.2, removable media capacity will increase as much as ten times faster than communications bandwidth.

Both DVD and the Internet have some pretty compelling attributes. How can we take advantage of both? The answer is called enhanced or WebDVD. Simply put, WebDVD is a process more than a product. High quality (i.e., high bandwidth) static multimedia content is stored on a DVD disc and accessed on a local PC. Low quality (i.e., low bandwidth) dynamic content is stored on a web server and accessed through an Internet connection. Both the DVD and Internet content are accessed through a standard web browser in a seamless fashion. WebDVD utilizes the strengths of both technologies, but is not limited by their weaknesses.

The primary strength of DVD is its ability to deliver high quality multimedia content and its large storage capacity, while its fundamental weakness is that content can not be updated once it has been published. The primary strength of the Internet is its ability to deliver real time updateable content over large distances and from a wide variety of sources, while its fundamental weakness is its moderate to low bandwidth makes it difficult to download high quality multimedia content. WebDVD has the best of both worlds — the capacity to deliver large amounts of high quality multimedia content as well as the ability to deliver real time updateable content from a wide variety of sources.

Interactual Technologies

Interactual Technologies has been a leader in the development of enhanced DVD titles over the past several years. InterActual's PC Friendly software has helped a number of Hollywood studios create new home entertainment products in which the unprecedented quality of DVD-Video connects seamlessly to the World Wide Web. Interactual's clients include Artisan, Columbia Tristar, DreamWorks, Elektra Records, HBO, MGM, Miramax, New Line Home Video, Paramount Pictures, 20th Century Fox, Universal, and Warner Home Video to name just a few.

PC Friendly

... screenplays, and ... of the available enhancements on PCFriendly DVDs. All ...riendly DVDs can also connect the audience in new ways, such as "virtual theater" events that combine real-time chat sessions while simultaneously watching a synchronized DVD Video presentation. Contact information for InterActual can be found in Chapter 10.

The primary features of PCFriendly include the following.

Enhanced Multimedia Features PCFriendly integrates graphics, animations, and videos with the latest information from the Internet. The content on a DVD-Video title can be used for wallpaper, screen savers, and sound bytes as well as custom application programs. Some PCFriendly titles include a copy of the original web site as it appeared when the title was released, ensuring that this content is always available to the viewer even if they are not connected to the Internet, or if the web site's server is down.

Virtual Theaters, Games & Chat Rooms PCFriendly titles can include PC centric applications such as games, screenplays, online events, and chat-rooms. Some studios have arranged for actors, directors, and special effects artists to answer questions during an on-line event that includes unlocking bonus material from the DVD disc.

Hidden Video & Content PCFriendly titles can include keys to provide the viewer access to locked or special areas of a studios web site. Some discs also contain bonus video segments that can only be played from a specific web page or during a live event.

Secure Online Shopping PCFriendly titles can connect automatically to sites at which the viewer can purchase more titles and movie related merchandise in a secure area.

Automatic Updates PCFriendly checks for new or updated software releases and can download and install them automatically.

Free Technical Support   Interactual provides free end-user technical support for titles that use the PCFriendly software. Support is provided via their web site, e-mail, or telephone. Most problems are resolved in one day or less.

Interactual Player 2.0

InterActual Player 2.0 is the latest enhanced DVD product from InterActual Technologies. Interactual Player 2.0 plays DVD-Video and CD-Audio titles integrated with HTML content stored on either the disc or the Internet. InterActual Player 2.0 is a media playback architecture that allows the content to be authored once and delivered across multiple platforms with a consistent user interface. It supports the vast majority of hardware and software DVD decoders available for the Windows PC, as well as the Apple Macintosh. InterActual Player 2.0 also supports a number of Internet connected set-top DVD players and video appliances. Figure 7.3 shows the InterActual Player 2.0 GUI with one of the standard player skins. Player skins can be customized by the title developer or by the viewer to provide a content specific look and feel for the Player 2.0 GUI.

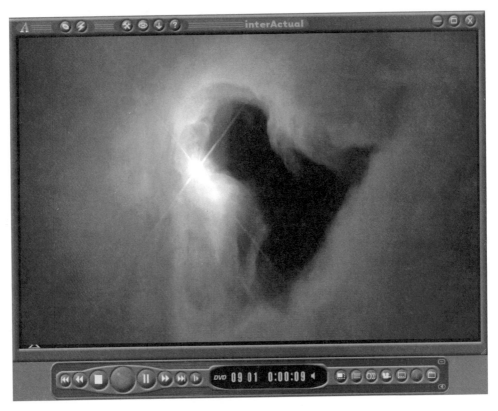

Figure 7.3   Interactual Player 2.0 GUI
(See color insert for color version of this figure.)

InterActual Player 2.0 allows the content owner to control the look and feel of the user's experience, providing several methods to transparently connect to the Internet. Internet or web content can be authored directly onto the DVD-Video disc or embedded within HTML available on a live web server. These connections can be based on events that are user initiated or triggered by the content itself. The primary features of InterActual Player 2.0 include the following.

Cross Platform Support   Microsoft Windows 95, 98, ME, NT, and 2000 based PCs, Macintosh, and Internet connected DVD set-top players are all supported.

DVD Decoder Support   All

PCFriendly-

and retention of investment in PCFriendly title development.

Forward Compatibility   InterActual Player 2.0 works with any DVD-Video or CD-Audio disc and can be the default player for all discs — not just enhanced DVD-Video titles.

Autorun & Autoplay   InterActual Player 2.0 can be configured to automatically start up when a DVD or CD-Audio disc is inserted into the drive.

Scaleable Playback   Content runs in a scaleable PC or Mac window or in full-screen mode. This option can be authored into the content by the developer. The user has total control of the media experience.

Customizable   The content developer can "wrap" the experience in a customized look and feel using custom skins for the player GUI. The user can use the theme provided on the disc or select an alternative. The developer is able to add value to the user experience, providing an environment or theme that enhances the content.

WebDVD Integration   Seamless playback of Internet links is authored into the content. InterActual Player 2.0 can launch HTML content based on "events" authored into the DVD video or embedded in the HTML. A rich variety of web content can be integrated with DVD-Video, combining the high quality media experience of DVD with the immediacy of the web.

DVD Authoring Tool Support   DVD-Video title developers can incorporate InterActual Player 2.0 features with their titles using the Scenarist and DVD Creator authoring tools from Sonic Solutions.

Tips, Tricks & Techniques

If you are looking for a simple yet effective way to enhance a DVD-Video title by adding DVD-ROM content or Internet connectivity, consider using PC Friendly or Player 2.0 from InterActual. The vast majority of enhanced DVD titles released to date use one of these products. Perhaps one of the best services provided by InterActual is their end-user support for enhanced DVD titles. DVD title developers who don't want to deal with providing technical support to consumers, but want to deliver advanced features like DVD-ROM content and Internet connectivity, will find Interactual's support program invaluable.

Figure 7.4 shows a detailed block diagram of the InterActual Player 2.0 playback environment. As you can see from this diagram InterActual has included support for a wide variety of playback platforms and operating systems, as well as support for the majority of hardware and software DVD decoders in use today. InterActual Player 2.0 is designed to be cross-platform as well as decoder agnostic, and in my experience it does the best job of meeting these goals of any third-party enhanced DVD tool on the market today.

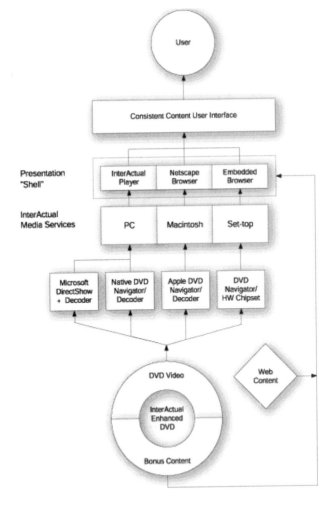

Figure 7.4   InterActual Player 2.0 Playback

SpinWare

SpinWare has two products that can be used to create enhanced DVD titles with integrated Internet support. SpinWare PortaNet is used to store additional or bonus content on a DVD disc with a conditional access file protocol. SpinWare iControl is a media playback technology that allows clients to play and control media elements, such as DVD movies, MP3 music, and video files in a variety of formats, such as PowerPoint slides and HTML documents served over the Internet. Contact information for SpinWare can be found in Chapter 10.

PortaNet

While there are several ways to use PortaNet to enhance a DVD-Video title, some of the most popular methods include the following.

- PortaNet can provide ancillary content to the viewer in return for something of value. This can be as simple as letting the user see some behind-the-scenes footage after they complete a user registration form on your web site. Hidden content on the disc can also be unlocked when the viewer pays an additional fee, thus providing an after market revenue stream from an enhanced DVD title.

- PortaNet can be used to build brand awareness and customer loyalty through a program of timed-release content stored on an enhanced DVD disc. Additional content can be stored on the disc and unlocked over a period of time, thus encouraging the viewer to visit a web site many times.

- PortaNet can also be used to implement a pay-per-view business model. Entire DVD-Video titles can be encrypted and stored on an enhanced DVD title. Decryption and playback of this locked content can be done easily over the Internet after the viewer has paid a "rental fee". Once the playback session has been completed the content on the disc will revert back to its locked condition.

iControl

SpinWare iControl is a media playback technology that allows viewers to play and control media elements, such as DVD-Video movies, MP3 music, and video files in a variety of PC applications. These applications include PowerPoint, Word, and HTML documents served over the Internet.

iControl is available in three formats:

- iControl PE for controlling DVD Playback in PowerPoint,

- iControl WE for creating WebDVD functionality over HTML, and

- iControl MP for controlling encrypted music over the Internet.

iControl PE

SpinWare iControl Personal Edition (PE) provides control of DVD-Video content with PowerPoint presentations. iControl PE is a DirectShow-based ActiveX control that works with most major software DVD decoders. iControl PE offers a sophisticated set of features that allow the viewer to script the playback of DVD-Video content in several ways. The main features of iControl PE include the following.

Title and Chapter Stop Playback   iControl PE can be scripted to play selected DVD-Video chapters from within a PowerPoint presentation.

Time Play   iControl PE can be scripted to play select time sequences from within a DVD-Video disc.

Custom PlayLists   iControl PE makes it easy to segment a DVD-Video title so the viewer can play just the scenes they want. Segments of a DVD-Video disc can be selected based on either the movie's time code or its chapters.

PlayList Wizard   iControl PE lets you playback your DVD-Video content while you are designing a PowerPoint presentation. The PlayList Wizard helps you set the scenes' start and stop points in your custom playlist without using a separate application or knowing the correct in and out time codes in advance.

Window Control   iControl PE allows the viewer to control the size of the DVD-Video playback window, so text and other graphics can be displayed on the same slide with DVD-Video content

Web-Based Transitions   In either chapter or time play mode, iControl PE can insert custom transitions between chapters or time codes. These transitions can be either custom JPEGs or remote web pages.

iControl WE

SpinWare iControl Web Edition (WE) can also be used to create a WebDVD title. The iControl WE ActiveX controller can be embedded into an HTML page, and can then provide control of various aspects of DVD-Video playback from a remote server. iControl WE offers several levels of sophisticated interactivity without requiring knowledge of scripting languages, such as VB Script and JavaScript. Some of the major features of iControl WE are as follows.

Script Jumping   As the user clicks on various sections of a script or other textual description, the web page will jump directly to that section of the DVD-Video title and display the multimedia content.

Original Image	4:3 Display			16:9 Display
	Normal	Pan & Scan	Letterbox	
	Original Image	Original Image	Original Image	Pillarboxed Image

Video Manager (VMG) video_ts.ifo	
Data Table Name	Required?
VMGI_MAT Video Manager Information Table	**Mandatory**
TT_SRPT Title Search Pointer Table	**Mandatory**
VMGM_PGCI_UT Video Manager Menu PGCI Unit Table	**Mandatory If video present**
PTL_MAIT Parental Management Information Table	**Optional**
VTS_ATRT Video Title Set Attribute Table	**Mandatory**
TXTDT_MG Text Data Manager	**Optional**
VMGM_C_ADT Video Manager Menu Cell Address Table	**Mandatory if video present**
VMGM_VOBU_ADMAP Video Manager Menu Video Object Unit Address Map	**Mandatory if video present**

Figure 2.13   DVD Video Manager (VMG) Structure

Video Manager (VMG) video_ts.ifo	
Data Table Name	Required?
VMGI_MAT Video Manager Information Table	**Mandatory**
TT_SRPT Title Search Pointer Table	**Mandatory**
VMGM_PGCI_UT Video Manager Menu PGCI Unit Table	**Mandatory If video present**
PTL_MAIT Parental Management Information Table	**Optional**
VTS_ATRT Video Title Set Attribute Table	**Mandatory**
TXTDT_MG Text Data Manager	**Optional**
VMGM_C_ADT Video Manager Menu Cell Address Table	**Mandatory if video present**
VMGM_VOBU_ADMAP Video Manager Menu Video Object Unit Address Map	**Mandatory if video present**

Figure 2.14   DVD Video Title Set Information (VTSI) File Structure

StarGaze Video Compressed in MPEG-2 @ 2.0 Mbps

Figure 3.5   Digital Video Compression Artifact Examples

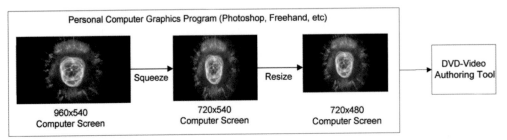

Personal Computer Graphics Program (Photoshop, Freehand, etc)

960x540
Computer Screen

Squeeze

720x540
Computer Screen

Resize

720x480
Computer Screen

DVD-Video
Authoring Tool

Figure 3.7   The Process of Creating a 16:9 NTSC Still Image

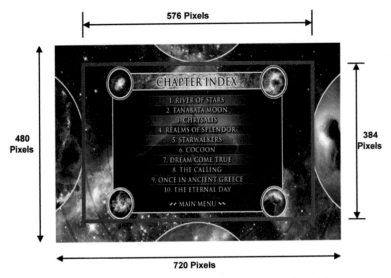

576 Pixels

480 Pixels

384 Pixels

720 Pixels

Figure 3.8   Safe Areas for NTSC 4:3 Still Images or Graphics

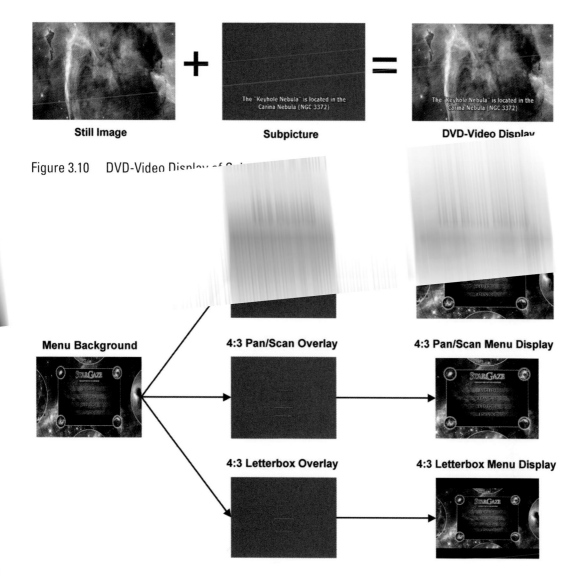

Still Image **Subpicture** **DVD-Video Display**

Figure 3.10   DVD-Video Display of S...

Menu Background   **4:3 Pan/Scan Overlay**   **4:3 Pan/Scan Menu Display**

4:3 Letterbox Overlay   **4:3 Letterbox Menu Display**

Figure 3.11   Multiple Aspect Ratio DVD-Video Menus

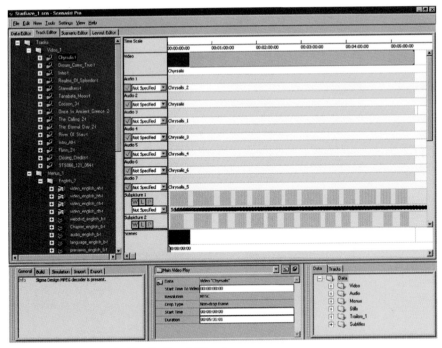

Figure 3.15   Sample Media Track Timeline

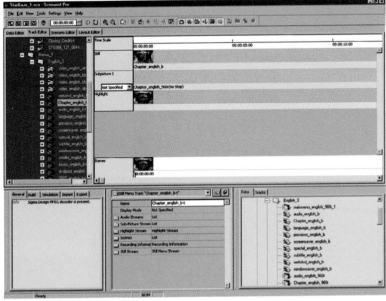

Figure 3.16   Sample Menu Track

Figure 3.17   Sample Menu Button and Navigation
               Design

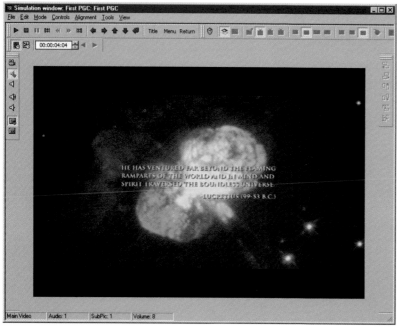

Figure 3.20   Scenarist NT 2.5 Simulation Display

Figure 3.26   Sample DVD Package Cover Artwork

StarGaze

HUBBLE'S VIEW OF THE UNIVERSE

5. STARWALKERS
6. COCOON
7. DREAM COME TRUE
8. THE CALLING
9. ONCE IN ANCIENT GREECE
10. THE ETERNAL DAY

SPECIAL FEATURES: You can access the StarGaze special features by pressing the **TITLE** key on your DVD-Video remote control or on your DVD-ROM player control.

MULTI-TRACK AUDIO AND SUBTITLES: StarGaze has seven unique audio tracks and 8 unique subtitle tracks. Please use the StarGaze menus to use these features. To access the menus press the **TITLE** button on your DVD-Video or DVD-ROM player remote control.

WINDOWS SCREEN SAVER INSTALLATION
- Insert StarGaze DVD Disc into your DVD-ROM Drive
- Run **d:/setup.exe** where D: is the drive letter of your DVD-ROM drive.

WEBDVD SUPPORT: DVD-ROM users can take advantage of the advanced WebDVD features of the StarGaze DVD disc. Visit **www.StarGazeDVD.com/WebDVD** for more details.

ON-LINE HELP: Visit **http://www.StarGazeDVD.com/Help** for more detailed on-line help.

TECHNICAL SUPPORT: If you have a problem viewing StarGaze on your DVD-Video or DVD-ROM System, contact our technical support via email at **support@StarGazeDVD.com**.

Figure 3.27   Sample DVD Insert Artwork

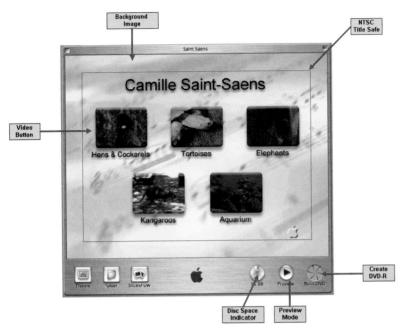

Figure 4.2   Apple iDVD Graphical Users Interface

Figure 4.3   Sonic Solutions DVDit! Graphical User Interface

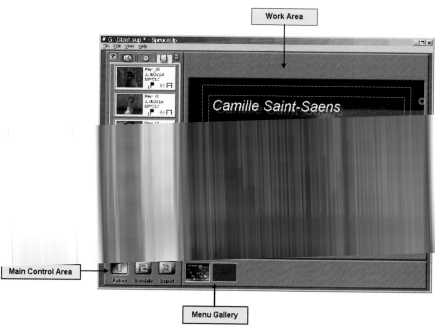

Figure 4.4   SpruceUp's Graphical User Interface

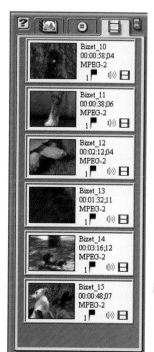

Figure 4.7   SpruceUp's
              Media Element
              Gallery Display

Figure 4.8   SpruceUp Movie
              Properties
              Selection

Figure 4.9   Sample DVD-Video Menu Created Using SpruceUp

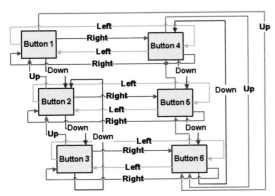

Figure 4.10   Button Navigation Commands Automatically Created by an Entry-Level DVD
               Authoring Tool

Figure 4.11   Entry-Level DVD Authoring Tool Simulation Display

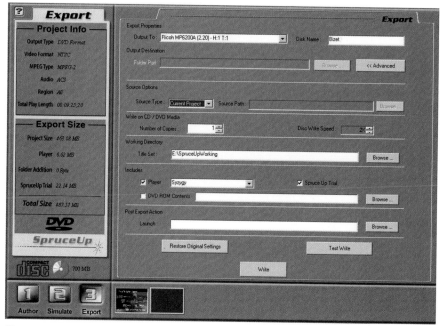

Figure 4.12   SpruceUp Disc Build and Disc Creation Process Window

Figure 4.13 "DVD on CD" Application Created Using SpruceUp

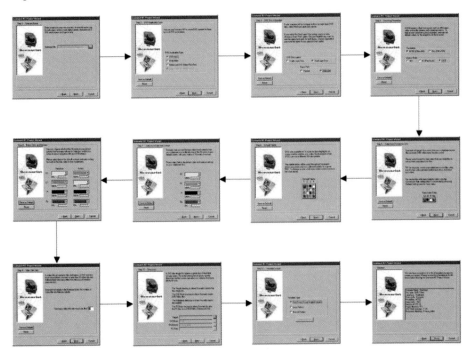

Figure 5.3 Scenarist Project Wizard Screens

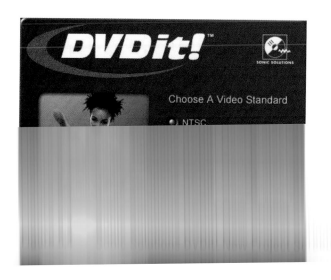

Figure 5.13   Scenarist Menu Buttons and Navigation Information

Figure 5.14   Menu with "Hidden" Buttons

Figure 5.18   Sample Menu Button Commands

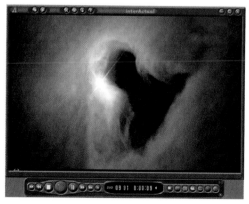

Figure 7.3   Interactual Player 2.0 GUI

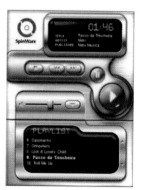

Figure 7.5   Spinware iControl ME

Figure 7.6   *StarGaze* WebDVD Menu

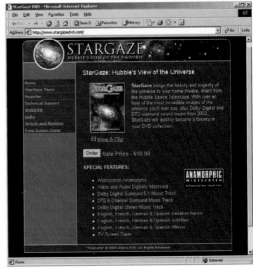

Figure 7.7   *StarGaze* Home Page

Figure 7.8   *StarGaze* WebDVD Page

Keyword Jumping You can define and associate keywords with specific scenes or chapters in the DVD-Video title. When a viewer enters a keyword the program can jump directly to the location on the disc at which the relevant content is stored.

Web-Based Transitions iControl WE provides a scripting method to play selected time codes of a DVD-Video title and to use web pages as transitions between each scene and chapter.

DVD-Video Linking iControl WE provides control over most aspects of the DVD-Video playback, such as scene jumping, angle changes, and subtitle selection, with the click of a m

additional information about the artist. iControl MP can be used to allow the viewer to enjoy high-quality music for free, in exchange for viewing ads. Figure 7.5 shows the graphical users interface for Spinware iControl ME.

Figure 7.5   Spinware iControl ME (See color insert for color version of this figure.)

Tips, Tricks & Techniques

Consumers with DVD-ROM enabled PCs are potential sources of after-market revenues for DVD title publishers. In appropriate situations, I recommend title developers include additional content on their DVD discs that can be used to generate additional revenues or to drive customers to their web sites. I have developed several titles that include SpinWare PortaNet encrypted files in the DVD-ROM portion of the disc. Consumers who register with us get some free additional screen saver images, and many of them will purchase even more images for a small fee. The benefits of using SpinWare PortaNet are an increased number of on-line customer registrations (great for direct sales of future titles) as well as an after-market revenue stream.

Microsoft WebDVD

In January 1999 Microsoft released an API called WebDVD that was designed to allow rapid development of enhanced DVD titles featuring playback of DVD content through standard web pages. Microsoft released an updated version of the WebDVD SDK (Software Developers Kit) in July of 1999, and then in November of 2000 Microsoft released a new version of DirectShow that included even more features for creating enhanced DVD titles. Essentially three different methods can be used to create enhanced DVD titles using Microsoft's DirectShow API. The first is the original method outlined in the Microsoft WebDVD SDK published in 1999, which uses an embedded version of the Windows Media Player. The second method, which is documented in the 2000 release of the DirectX 8.0 SDK, uses an embedded version of an MSWebDVD object. The third method is to develop custom Visual Basic or C++ programs making direct calls to individual `DirectShow` functions.

Perhaps the biggest advantage of Microsoft's WebDVD approach to creating enhanced DVD titles is that it is free. Microsoft distributes the WebDVD and DirectX 8.0 SDK at no charge, and there are no licensing or royalty charges for using WebDVD or DirectX 8.0. Both the original WebDVD SDK and the latest DirectX SDK make it fairly easy to create interactive HTML pages that can play back content stored on a DVD-Video disc. In both cases the basic approach is to embed a media play-back object into an HTML page and then use a scripting language, such as JavaScript, to issue play-back commands to the media object, based on viewer interactivity.

The biggest disadvantage of Microsoft's WebDVD approach is that it will only work on Windows 98, Windows 2000, and Windows ME systems that have Internet Explorer 5.0 or higher, as well as a hardware or software DVD decoder that supports DirectShow. While most new Windows systems support DirectShow, there are still many viewers who prefer to use Netscape instead of Internet Explorer as their default web browser. Microsoft's WebDVD API will not work with any of Netscape's browsers, and Netscape has not announced any plans to support WebDVD or any other embedded COM objects in the future.

Tips, Tricks & Techniques
The best way to determine if a PC is capable of playing back a Microsoft WebDVD title is to look for a "Designed for Microsoft Windows" sticker. If a PC has one of these stickers for Windows 98, Windows ME, or Windows 2000, the system must support DirectShow. A DVD-ROM PC with any of these stickers will most likely be fully compatible with a WebDVD title.

Windows Media Player Approach

The Microsoft Windows Media Player control provides a variety of methods and properties for controlling multimedia play-back from a web page or application. The main features of Windows Media Player include the following.

- The ability to create custom user interfaces on top of the Windows Media Player control. Buttons, boxes, and menus can be incorporated into an HTML page for controlling play-back.

- The ability to include DVD-Video play-back functions, such as start, stop, pause, fast-for-ward, rewind, mute, volume adjustment, and menus.

- The ability to retrieve information about the DVD-Video title, such as the number of titles, chapters, audio streams, camera angles and subpicture streams.

to create a user interface unique to your content, to process any type of script commands, and to integrate multimedia presentations into larger web applications. It also provides a large selection of DVD specific methods, properties, and events to allow precise playback control of content from a DVD-Video disc.

The OBJECT tag is used to embed the Windows Media Player control into an HTML page. The following code is an example of using the OBJECT tag to insert the Windows Media Player control.

```
<HTML>
<OBJECT CLASSID="CLSID:22D6F312-B0F6-11D0-94AB-0080C74C7E95" WIDTH="652"
    HEIGHT="382" ID="MediaPlayer1">
</OBJECT>
</HTML>
```

The following OBJECT tag attributes are required.

- ID is the name used to reference this instance of the control.

- CLSID is the class identifier of the Windows Media Player control. A CLSID is a COM object identifier.

One option for setting the properties of a Media Player object is adding PARAM tags between the OBJECT tags. This is an ideal way to set design time properties. The following code is an example of the Media Player OBJECT tag with PARAM tags added.

```
<HTML>
<OBJECT CLASSID="CLSID:22D6F312-B0F6-11D0-94AB-0080C74C7E95" WIDTH="652"
    HEIGHT="382" ID="MediaPlayer1">
<PARAM NAME="AutoStart" VALUE="0">
<PARAM NAME="FileName" VALUE="DVD:">
<PARAM NAME="ShowControls" VALUE="0">
</OBJECT>
</HTML>
```

The PARAM tags used in this example have two attributes; the first is the name of the property being set, and the second specifies the value of the property. In this example, the first PARAM tag sets the AUTOSTART property to false. The remaining PARAM tags change the default values of the FILENAME property to DVD: and the SHOWCONTROLS property to false. Note that DVD-Video specific properties can't be set using a PARAM tag. It is critical to note that DVD-Video play back is triggered by setting the FILENAME property to DVD:, which instructs the Windows Media Player control to search for the DVD drive on the local system. In this case Windows Media Player will locate the first system drive with a VIDEO_TS directory located in the root of the drive. That drive is then assumed to be the DVD-ROM drive. Thus it is possible to fool Windows Media Player into thinking that a local hard drive, or even a network drive that has been assigned a local drive letter, is actually a DVD-ROM drive. This can be accomplished by simply copying a valid DVD-Video disc image consisting of all the files in the VIDEO_TS directory to a VIDEO_TS directory located on the desired hard drive. If the AUTOSTART property is set to true (the default value), the Windows Media Player control will then begin DVD play back; otherwise, an event must be associated with DVD play back, such as the selection of a button.

You can create a simple user interface by adding button controls to the body of an HTML page. The following code creates the button controls to handle the selection of menu items from the DVD menu screen.

```
<HTML>
<INPUT TYPE="BUTTON" STYLE="WIDTH:70" NAME="cmdTopSelect" VALUE="Top">
<INPUT TYPE="BUTTON" STYLE="WIDTH:70" NAME="cmdLeftSelect" VALUE="Left">
<INPUT TYPE="BUTTON" STYLE="WIDTH:70" NAME="cmdRightSelect" VALUE="Right">
<INPUT TYPE="BUTTON" STYLE="WIDTH:70" NAME="cmdBottomSelect" VALUE="Bottom">
<INPUT TYPE="BUTTON" STYLE="WIDTH:70" NAME="cmdButtonActivate" VALUE="Select">
</HTML>
```

The following code creates the button controls that will handle basic play back (play, pause, and stop), as well as chapter searching and scanning.

```html
<HTML>
<INPUT TYPE="BUTTON" STYLE="WIDTH:60" NAME="cmdPlay" VALUE="Play">
<INPUT TYPE="BUTTON" STYLE="WIDTH:60" NAME="cmdPause" VALUE="Pause">
<INPUT TYPE="BUTTON" STYLE="WIDTH:60" NAME="cmdStop" VALUE="Stop">
<INPUT TYPE="BUTTON" STYLE="WIDTH:60" NAME="cmdResume" VALUE="Resume">
```

```vbscript
<SCRIPT LANGUAGE="VBScript">
<!--
Dim isScanning
isScanning = False
Sub cmdPlay_OnClick()
    If isScanning Then
            MediaPlayer1.DVD.ForwardScan(1)
    Else
            MediaPlayer1.Play()
    End If
    isScanning = False
End Sub
Sub cmdPause_OnClick()
        MediaPlayer1.Pause()
End Sub
Sub cmdStop_OnClick()
        MediaPlayer1.Stop()
End Sub
Sub cmdResume_OnClick()
        MediaPlayer1.DVD.ResumeFromMenu()
End Sub
Sub cmdShowMenu_OnClick()
        MediaPlayer1.DVD.MenuCall(3)
End Sub
```

```
Sub cmdPrevChapter_OnClick()
        MediaPlayer1.DVD.PrevPGSearch()
End Sub
Sub cmdNextChapter_OnClick()
        MediaPlayer1.DVD.NextPGSearch()
End Sub
Sub cmdFastForward_OnClick()
    isScanning = True
        MediaPlayer1.DVD.ForwardScan(5)
End Sub
Sub cmdRewind_OnClick()
    isScanning = True
        MediaPlayer1.DVD.BackwardScan(5)
End Sub
Sub cmdTopSelect_OnClick()
        MediaPlayer1.DVD.UpperButtonSelect()
End Sub
Sub cmdLeftSelect_OnClick()
        MediaPlayer1.DVD.LeftButtonSelect()
End Sub
Sub cmdRightSelect_OnClick()
        MediaPlayer1.DVD.RightButtonSelect()
End Sub
Sub cmdBottomSelect_OnClick()
        MediaPlayer1.DVD.LowerButtonSelect()
End Sub
Sub cmdButtonActivate_OnClick()
        Dim buttonNumber
        buttonNumber = MediaPlayer1.DVD.CurrentButton
        MediaPlayer1.DVD.ButtonSelectAndActivate(buttonNumber)
End Sub
-->
</SCRIPT>
</HTML>
```

DVD-specific properties and methods are passed to the Microsoft Windows Media Player control, which is then directed to the appropriate MediaPlayer object. An event code is generated when an event occurs. An event is an action, recognized by the DVD object, for which you can write code to respond. Events can be generated by a user action, such as clicking the mouse or pressing a key on the keyboard. Events are also generated by the system itself, for example, in the case of timers. Table 7.1 lists DVD-Video specific properties, methods, and events for the Windows Media Player control.

Table 7.1   DVD-Video Specific Properties, Methods and Events

AnglesAvailable	Retrieves a value specifying the number of available angles.
AudioStreamsAvailable	Retrieves a value specifying the number of available audio streams.
BackwardScan	Searches backward through the current disc at the specified speed.
ButtonActivate	Activates the selected ...
	... play the number of chapters specified.
ChapterSearch	Halts playback of the current chapter and starts playback from the specified chapter within the same title.
ColorKey	Sets or retrieves the color key being used by the DVD playback.
CurrentAngle	Sets or retrieves a value specifying the current angle.
CurrentAudioStream	Sets or retrieves a value specifying the current audio stream.
CurrentButton	Retrieves a value specifying the number of the currently selected button.
CurrentCCService	Sets or retrieves a value specifying the current closed captioning service.
CurrentChapter	Retrieves a value specifying the chapter number currently being played.
CurrentDiscSide	Retrieves a value specifying the current disc side.
CurrentDomain	Retrieves a value specifying the current DVD domain of the DVD player.
CurrentSubpictureStream	Sets or retrieves a value specifying the current subpicture stream.
CurrentTime	Retrieves a value specifying the current playback time.
CurrentTitle	Retrieves a value specifying the title number currently being played.
CurrentVolume	Retrieves a value specifying the volume number for the current root directory.
EC_DVD_ANGLE_CHANGE	Signals that either the number of available angles has changed, or the current user angle number has changed.
EC_DVD_ANGLES_AVAILABLE	Occurs when an angle block is being played and angle changes can be performed.
EC_DVD_AUDIO_STREAM_CHANGE	Signals that the current user audio stream number has changed for the main title.

Table 7.1   DVD-Video Specific Properties, Methods and Events (Continued)

EC_DVD_BUTTON_CHANGE	Signals that either the number of available buttons has changed, or the currently selected button number has changed.
EC_DVD_CHAPTER_AUTOSTOP	Indicates that playback has stopped as the result of a call to the ChapterPlayAutoStop method.
EC_DVD_CHAPTER_START	Signals that the DVD player has started playback of a new program in the TT_DOM domain.
EC_DVD_CURRENT_TIME	Signals the beginning of each VOBU, which occurs every 0.4 to 1.0 second.
EC_DVD_DOMAIN_CHANGE	Indicates the DVD-Video player's new domain.
EC_DVD_ERROR	Signals a DVD-Video error condition.
EC_DVD_NO_FP_PGC	Signals that the DVD-Video disc does not have a First Play Program Chain (FP_PGC) and that the DVD Navigator will not automatically load any program chain (PGC) or start playback.
EC_DVD_PLAYBACK_RATE_CHANGE	Signals that a rate change in the playback has been initiated.
EC_DVD_PLAYBACK_STOPPED	Indicates that playback has been stopped. The DVD Navigator has completed playback of the PGC and did not find any other branching instruction for subsequent playback.
EC_DVD_STILL_OFF	Signals the end of any still (PGC, Cell, or VOBU).
EC_DVD_STILL_ON	Signals the beginning of any still (PGC, Cell, or VOBU).
EC_DVD_SUBPICTURE_STREAM_CHANGE	Signals that the current user subpicture stream number has changed for the main title.
EC_DVD_TITLE_CHANGE	Occurs when the current title number changes.
EC_DVD_VALID_UOPS_CHANGE	Signals that the available set of DVD methods has changed.
EC_DVD_WARNING	Signals a DVD-Video disc warning condition.
FramesPerSecond	Retrieves a value specifying the number of frames per second used by the DVD title.
ForwardScan	Searches forward through the current disc at the specified speed.
GetAllGPRMs	Retrieves the current contents of all GPRMs.
GetAllSPRMs	Retrieves the current contents of all SPRMs.
GetAudioLanguage	Retrieves a value specifying the language of the specified audio stream within the current title.
GetNumberOfChapters	Retrieves the number of chapters defined for the specified title.
GetSubpictureLanguage	Retrieves a value specifying the language for the specified subpicture stream.
GoUp	Halts playback of the current media file and starts playback of the designated previous PGC.
LeftButtonSelect	Selects the left directional button from the displayed menu.
LowerButtonSelect	Selects the lower directional button from the displayed menu.

Table 7.1 DVD-Video Specific Properties, Methods and Events (Continued)

MenuCall	Displays the specified menu on the screen.
NextPGSearch	Halts playback of the current program and starts playback from the next program within the PGC.
PrevPGSearch	Halts playback of the current program and starts playback from the previous program within the PGC.
ResumeFromMenu	Returns to playing back a title from a menu.
TimePlay	Plays the media file with the specified title index, starting at the specified time.
TimeSearch	Halts playback of the current chapter and starts playback from the specified time in the same media file.
TitlePlay	Finds the media file with the specified title index and plays it back.
TitlesAvailable	Retrieves a value specifying the number of titles available in the current volume.
TopPGSearch	Halts playback of the current program and restarts playback of the current program within the PGC.
TotalTitleTime	Retrieves a value specifying the total playback time for the current title.
UniqueID	Retrieves a value specifying the unique identifier associated with the DVD volume.
UOPValid	Retrieves a value indicating whether the specified user operation is currently valid.s
UpperButtonSelect	Selects the upper directional button from the displayed menu.
VolumesAvailable	Retrieves a value specifying the number of volumes in the volume set.

Enhanced DVD applications, including web pages that control DVD play back, can be created in HTML using the Windows Media Player ActiveX control. This is simpler and faster than using C++, which is only required for more specialized applications, such as games, programs that overlay graphics on video, custom ActiveX controls or DLLs, and so on. DirectShow provides all the filters necessary to navigate and play DVD-Video except the MPEG-2 and Dolby Digital decoders. To play DVD-Video content using an HTML application based on DirectShow, users must have installed on their system a third-party hardware or software DVD decoder that is DirectShow-compatible.

Additional details on how to use the Windows Media Player Active X control to create enhanced DVD titles can be found in the Microsoft Interactive DVD Toolkit SDK, which can be obtained from Microsoft. You can get a copy of the Microsoft DVD SDK disc by sending an e-mail request to dvd@microsoft.com.

MSWebDVD Object Approach

The MSWebDVD object is an ActiveX control that handles all DVD-Video navigation commands as well as the display of DVD-Video content in an embedded window. The MSWebDVD control can be embedded within an HTML document's BODY element, as shown in the following script.

```
<HTML>
<OBJECT CLASSID=clsid:38EE5CEE-4B62-11D3-854F-00A0C9C898E7 ID=DVD
    STYLE="height:369px; width:740px">
    <PARAM NAME="BackColor" VALUE="1048592">
    <PARAM NAME="EnableResetOnStop" VALUE="-1">
    <PARAM NAME="ColorKey" VALUE="1048592">
</OBJECT>
</HTML>
```

To enable viewers to control the play back of content stored in the DVD-video zone of the disc, an HTML user interface is created with buttons for issuing specific DVD commands, such as stop and play. The following HTML code and JavaScript shows how to hook up basic buttons to the MSWebDVD object methods.

```
<HTML>
<INPUT ID=button1 NAME="button1" TYPE=button VALUE="Play"
    OnClick='Play();'>
<INPUT ID=button2 NAME="button2" TYPE=button VALUE="Pause"
    OnClick='Pause();'>
```

```
<SCRIPT LANGUAGE="JavaScript">
    function Play(){
        DVD.Play();
    }
    function Pause(){
        DVD.Pause();
    }
</SCRIPT>
```

about to enter an angle block, etc. The event parameters can contain additional information related to the event. Error messages and warnings are also generated in this matter.

The MSWebDVD object sends notifications when a specific UOP has been enabled or disabled by the disc. Each user operation has its own event, with a single Boolean parameter indicating whether that operation is enabled or disabled. By handling time code events from the disc, a web application can synchronize HTML content to the video. For example, you can cause images or text on the page to change at specified points in the video. (Text continues on page 261.)

Tips, Tricks & Techniques

Synchronizing the display of text, graphics, animations, or even video play back within a WebDVD page will require that the DVD-Video title be authored as a one-sequential-PGC title. Only one-sequential-PGC titles include time table data in the DVD-Video IFO file that is required for frame accurate access to content on the disc, as well as status information on what frame is currently being displayed. Some DVD-Video authoring tools are not capable of creating one-sequential-PGC titles, so make sure your authoring tool can do this if you want to make a WebDVD title with synchronization.

The MSWebDVD methods and properties act on the current state of the DVD Navigator, the information on a disc, or both. To store and retrieve various types of application-specific information in the registry, such as user preferences for parental levels and default language, use the methods of the MSDVDADM object. Table 7.2 describes the MSWebDVD properties, methods, and events.

Table 7.2   MSWebDVD Properties, Methods and Events

AcceptParentalLevelChange	Instructs the DVD Navigator to accept or reject the new temporary parental management level.
ActivateAtPosition	Activates the menu button at the specified position.
ActivateButton	Activates the selected menu button.
AnglesAvailable	Retrieves the number of angles available.
AspectRatio	Retrieves the aspect ratio of the current video stream as authored on the disc.
AudioStreamsAvailable	Retrieves the number of audio streams available in the current title.
BackColor	Sets or retrieves the color of the bars that appear around the edges of the video rectangle when the aspect ratio of the native video is not the same as that of the object's display area.
Balance	Sets or retrieves the speaker balance for the audio stream output.
ButtonsAvailable	Retrieves the total number of buttons on the current menu.
CanStep	Determines whether the MPEG-2 decoder on the local system can perform frame stepping.
Capture	Captures a still image from the video frame when the MSWebDVD object is in windowless mode.
CCActive	Sets or retrieves the current status of closed captioning.
ChangeCurrentAngle	Sent when the disc enables or disables changing the angle.
ChangeCurrentAudioStream	Sent when the disc enables or disables changing the audio stream.
ChangeCurrentSubpictureStream	Sent when the ChangeCurrentSubpictureStream command has been enabled or disabled.
ColorKey	Sets or retrieves the color key used in closed captioning.
CurrentAngle	Sets or retrieves the current angle in an angle block.
CurrentAudioStream	Sets or retrieves the number of the enabled audio stream.
CurrentButton	Retrieves the number of the selected button.
CurrentCCService	Sets or retrieves the current closed-captioned service.
CurrentChapter	Retrieves the number of the chapter currently playing.
CurrentDiscSide	Retrieves the current side of the DVD.
CurrentDomain	Retrieves the DVD domain that the DVD Navigator is in.
CurrentSubpictureStream	Retrieves the selected subpicture stream.
CurrentTime	Retrieves the current playback time.

Table 7.2   MSWebDVD Properties, Methods and Events (Continued)

CurrentTitle	Retrieves the number of the title currently playing.
CurrentVolume	Retrieves the volume number for the current root directory.
CursorType	Sets or retrieves the current cursor type.
DefaultAudioLanguage	Retrieves the default audio language from the disc.
DefaultAudioLanguageExt	Retrieves the default audio language extension from the disc.
DVDDirectory	Retrieves or sets the root directory of the current DVD volume.
DVDNotify	Notifies an application of many different DVD events and disc instructions.
DVDTimeCode2bstr	Retrieves a String indicating the current time on the disc.
DVDUniqueID	Retrieves a system-generated number that uniquely identifies the current DVD.
Eject	Ejects or inserts a disc from or into the drive.
EnableResetOnStop	Sets or retrieves a value that determines how play will resume when the filter graph transitions out of a stopped state.
FramesPerSecond	Retrieves the video frame rate for the current DVD title.
FullScreenMode	Sets or retrieves a value indicating whether the display is in full-screen mode.
GetAudioLanguage	Retrieves a string indicating which language is available on the specified audio stream.
GetButtonAtPosition	Retrieves the number of the button at the specified coordinates without selecting or activating it.
GetButtonRect	Retrieves the rectangle for the specified button, in window coordinates.
GetClipVideoRect	Retrieves the clipping rectangle defined for the video display.
GetDelayTime	Retrieves the delay time for the ToolTip associated with the MSWebDVD object.
GetDVDTextLanguageLCID	Retrieves the locale identifier (LCID) for the specified text string block.
GetDVDTextNumberOfLanguages	Retrieves the number of text languages available in the current DVD directory.
GetDVDTextNumberOfStrings	Retrieves the number of text strings available for the specified language.

Table 7.2   MSWebDVD Properties, Methods and Events (Continued)

GetDVDTextString	Retrieves the specified text string from the disc.
GetDVDTextStringType	Retrieves a value that indicates the type of information contained in the specified DVD text string.
GetGPRM	Retrieves the specified general parameter register.
GetKaraokeChannelAssignment	Retrieves a value that indicates how the karaoke channels are assigned to the left and right speakers.
GetKaraokeChannelContent	Retrieves a value that indicates the type of content in the specified karaoke channel in the specified stream.
GetLangFromLangID	Retrieves a human-readable string when given a primary language identifier (ID).
GetNumberOfChapters	Retrieves the number of chapters in the specified title.
GetPlayerParentalCountry	Retrieves the current country as set in the DVD Navigator.
GetPlayerParentalLevel	Retrieves the parental management level set in the DVD Navigator.
GetSPRM	Retrieves the specified system parameter register.
GetSubpictureLanguage	Retrieves the language for the specified subpicture stream.
GetTitleParentalLevels	Retrieves the parental management levels for the specified title.
GetVideoSize	Retrieves the native video dimensions.
IsAudioStreamEnabled	Retrieves a value indicating whether the specified audio stream is enabled in the current title.
IsSubpictureStreamEnabled	Retrieves a value indicating whether the specified subpicture stream is enabled in the current title.
KaraokeAudioPresentationMode	Sets or retrieves the right-left speaker mix for the auxiliary karaoke channels.
Mute	Turns the audio stream output on or off.
NotifyParentalLevelChange	Enables or disables the event handling for temporary parental management level commands.
Pause	Pauses playback at the current location.
PauseOn	Sent when the Pause command has been enabled or disabled.
Play	Plays the current DVD title.
PlayAtTime	Starts playback in the current title at the specified time.
PlayAtTimeInTitle	Starts playback at the specified time within the specified title.
PlayBackwards	Starts backward playback from the current location at the specified speed.
PlayChapter	Starts playback from the specified chapter in the current title.
PlayChapterInTitle	Plays the specified chapter in the specified title.
PlayChaptersAutoStop	Starts playback at the specified chapter in the specified title, for the number of chapters specified.

Table 7.2   MSWebDVD Properties, Methods and Events (Continued)

PlayForwards	Starts forward playback from the current location at the specified speed.
PlayNextChapter	Starts playback from the next chapter in the current title.
PlayPeriodInTitleAutoStop	Starts playback at the specified time in the specified title until the specified stop time.
PlayPrevChapter	Starts playback from the previous chapter in the current title.
RegionChange	Displays a system dialog box that enables the user to change the region associated with the DVD drive.
Render	Initializes the DVD filter graph.
ReplayChapter	Starts playback at the beginning of the current chapter.
RestoreBookmark	Moves the DVD Navigator to the point on the DVD as specified in the current bookmark, with all audio, video and subpicture settings restored.
Resume	Resumes playback after a menu has been displayed.
ReturnFromSubmenu	Returns display from a submenu to its parent menu, or to the current title if the menu is a top-level menu.
SaveBookmark	Saves the current disc position and state of the DVD Navigator to disc so that the user can return to the same place later.
SelectAndActivateButton	Selects and activates the specified button.
SelectAtPosition	Selects the menu button at the specified position.
SelectDefaultAudioLanguage	Sets the current default audio language in the DVD Navigator.
SelectDefaultSubpictureLanguage	Sets the current default subpicture language in the DVD Navigator.
SelectLeftButton	Selects the left directional button from the displayed menu.
SelectLowerButton	Selects the lower directional button from the displayed menu.
SelectParentalCountry	Sets the specified parental country for subsequent playback.
SelectParentalLevel	Sets the specified parental level for subsequent playback.
SelectRightButton	Selects the right directional button from the displayed menu.
SelectUpperButton	Selects the upper directional button from the displayed menu.
SetClipVideoRect	Sets the clipping rectangle occupied by the video display.

Table 7.2   MSWebDVD Properties, Methods and Events (Continued)

SetDelayTime	Sets the delay time for the ToolTip associated with the MSWebDVD object.
SetGPRM	Sets the specified general parameter register to the specified value.
ShowCursor	Makes the mouse pointer visible when the DVD Navigator is in full-screen mode.
ShowMenu	Displays the specified menu on the screen.
Step	Advances the DVD-Video stream by the specified number of frames.
StillOff	Resumes playback, canceling still mode.
Stop	Stops playback.
SubpictureOn	Sets or retrieves the current subpicture state (on or off).
SubpictureStreamsAvailable	Retrieves the number of subpicture streams available in the current title.
TitlesAvailable	Retrieves the number of titles available on the DVD.
ToolTip	Sets the text for the ToolTip that will appear when the mouse pointer is over the MSWebDVD video rectangle.
ToolTipMaxWidth	Sets or retrieves the maximum width for the ToolTip associated with the MSWebDVD object.
TotalTitleTime	Retrieves the total playback time for the current title.
UOPValid	Retrieves a value that indicates whether the specified user operation is currently valid.
UpdateOverlay	Sent when the overlay surface has been moved or resized or its color key has changed.
Volume	Sets or retrieves the audio volume level.
VolumesAvailable	Retrieves a value specifying the number of volumes in the disc set.
WindowlessActivation	Initializes the MSWebDVD object at design time for either windowed or windowless mode.
Zoom	Zooms the video display in or out, centered on a given set of screen coordinates.

Additional details on how to use the MSWebDVD Active X control to create enhanced DVD titles can be found in the Microsoft DirectX 8.0 SDK, which can be obtained directly from Microsoft.

disc note:

Real World Example

www.StarGazeDVD.com is an online web site that allows viewers to interact with the content on the *StarGaze* DVD using a WebDVD-based interface. I have found the best way to understand how to develop a WebDVD title is to review an existing WebDVD

One of the requirements defined at the start of the *StarGaze* project was that it would include an on-line WebDVD-enabled web site to allow consumers to interact with the video and still image content on the disc through a standard web browser. There were four major efforts needed to meet this requirement. First, the *StarGaze* DVD-Video title had to be designed and developed in a manner that would allow all the content on the disc to be accessed from a WebDVD-enabled web site. Second, an on-line web site needed to be developed with a unique GUI that would allow the integration of multimedia content stored on the *StarGaze* DVD-Video disc with traditional text and graphic data stored on various other web sites on the Internet. Next, a series of Java scripts had to be developed to link buttons on the HTML-based GUI with the content stored on the *StarGaze* DVD-Video disc. Finally, the *StarGaze* web site needed to be hosted on a live web server, and maintained and updated for as long as the *StarGaze* DVD-Video title is available to consumers.

StarGaze DVD-Video Development Issues

StarGaze includes video and still images from over 200 celestial objects. There is a wealth of textual and graphic data available on the Internet describing each celestial object in detail. Since much of this data is changing as astronomers learn more about the heavens, it did not make sense to include it on the *StarGaze* DVD disc, as it would most likely become out of date within a few months after the disc was released. Once the design decision was made to keep time-sensitive information off the DVD-Video portion of the disc, it was relatively easy to implement *StarGaze*. All of the video and still image content on *StarGaze* were placed in one-sequential-PGC titles to allow synchronous access to the content from a WebDVD page, or from educational DVD-Video players like the Pioneer V7400 using a bar code reader. Menu graphics were designed, and DVD-Video menus were created (see Figure 7.6) to tell consumers that *StarGaze* was designed to support WebDVD, and how they could access those features.

Figure 7.6   *StarGaze* WebDVD Menu
            (See color insert for color version of this figure.)

Finally, the packaging for *StarGaze* was designed to include a description of the minimum system requirements necessary to take advantage of the WebDVD features of the title.

StarGaze Web Site Development Issues

The *StarGaze* web site (http://www.StarGazeDVD.com) is designed to provide a variety of information and services to our customers. First it needs to provide sales and marketing information for prospective customers who are interested, but not ready to buy the product. Next it needs to provide an e-commerce solution so that customers can order the product on-line. The *StarGaze* web site also serves as the first line of technical support for the product, so when customers have a problem they need to be able to jump directly to the support pages to find an answer to their problem, or to request individual technical support. Last, but by no means least, the *StarGaze* web site should provide an integrated multimedia display incorporating high quality multimedia content from the DVD disc with traditional text and graphics from a variety of Internet sites.

Figure 7.7 show the default home page for the *StarGaze* web site. The site has a standard set of navigation buttons on the left side of the page providing direct links to all major areas of the web site. These buttons provide links to individual pages on the web site for on-line sales, customer registration, technical support, WebDVD features, links to other web sites, articles and product reviews, and a free download area.

Since WebDVD support requires a specific set of hardware and software, we created an entry page to the WebDVD section of the *StarGaze* web site. This entry page displayed the minimum hardware and software requirements for using the WebDVD features of *StarGaze*,

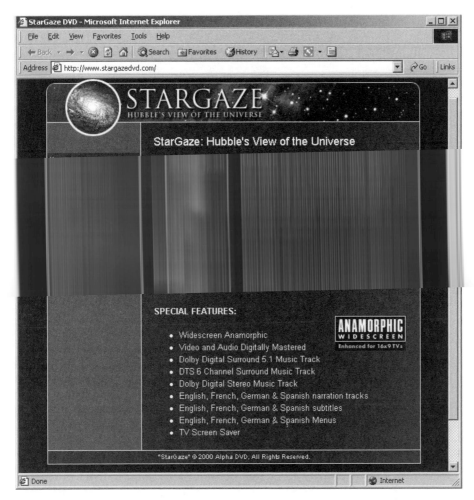

Figure 7.7   *StarGaze* Home Page
(See color insert for color version of this figure.)

and provided links for viewers to download the latest Microsoft Windows Media Player and DirectShow drivers. This entry page provided the following information to the viewer.

- WebDVD is a new technology developed by Microsoft Corporation. With WebDVD we can combine TV quality video, audio, and still image content delivered from a DVD disc, with rapidly changing graphic and text content delivered from the Internet.

- StarGazeDVD.com is one of the first operational WebDVD sites in the world. To use the WebDVD features of *StarGaze* you will need the following.

  1. A copy of the *StarGaze* DVD disc in your DVD-ROM drive.

  2. Internet Explorer 5.0 or higher — click here to get IE 5.0.

  3. A Pentium II (or better) PC with the Microsoft "Designed for Windows 98" logo.

  4. WebDVD works best with Windows Media Player 6.4 or later. If you don't have it, you can download it by clicking on the Media Player logo or here.

  5. Please note that Netscape browsers currently do not support WebDVD!

WebDVD specific features are only included on one HTML page of the *StarGaze* web site. We designed this page to work best with a display resolution of 1024×768 pixels or higher. Since the video content on *StarGaze* is wide screen (16:9) we needed to dedicate a fairly large section of the screen area to the Windows Media Player object display. The basic layout of the *StarGaze* WebDVD page is shown in Figure 7.8. It includes navigation buttons on the left side to allow viewers to jump directly to any section of the *StarGaze* web site, a multimedia display area in the center in which video and still images from the *StarGaze* DVD disc are shown, a link area on the right of the screen for jumping directly to specific chapters or items of interest, and a control area along the bottom that allows the viewer to select specific playback features such as music format, audio language, narration subtitles, and nomenclature subtitles. The media display area can also be expanded to full screen. A synchronized link button is just below the media display area. This button and its associated hyperlinks are synchronized to the content in the media display area, and allow the viewer to surf the Internet for more information on the celestial body being shown in the media display window.

As you can see from Figure 7.8 there are well over 40 unique buttons defined on the *StarGaze* WebDVD page and the GUI is significantly different from the menu and navigation structure implemented on the *StarGaze* DVD-Video disc. Simply put, it would be impossible to implement a GUI with this level of complexity in the DVD-Video portion of the disc. Too many buttons are required, the video is displayed in a window or in full screen mode, and many of the buttons are associated with context-sensitive hyperlinks to live web sites. Clearly the only way this type of user interface could have been implemented for *StarGaze* is as a WebDVD page.

All of the web pages in the *StarGaze* web site were developed using Microsoft FrontPage 2000. Graphics for each page were created by James Cave, the same artist who created all the graphics and menus for the *StarGaze* DVD-Video title, as well as the artwork for the product package. Using the same graphic artist on all aspects of the project enabled us to develop a consistent look and feel that we could use on both the DVD-Video and the WebDVD user interfaces.

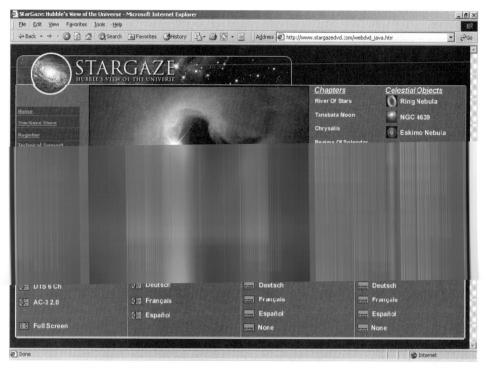

Figure 7.8   *StarGaze* WebDVD Page
(See color insert for color version of this figure.)

StarGaze WebDVD Java Script Development

Once the basic HTML page development was completed for the *StarGaze* WebDVD page, the next step was to write the Java scripts for each unique DVD play-back function that a user could invoke by pressing any of the buttons on the page. First the Windows Media Player Control was embedded into the page, configured to fit into the correct position with the page, and initialized to start playing a specific video sequence from the *StarGaze* DVD disc as soon as the page was launched. All of the scripts discussed in the following text are contained in a single JavaScript declaration of the *StarGaze* WebDVD page. It is possible to break each script up into its own unique declaration, but that makes it harder to read the code, and thus harder to maintain.

Tips, Tricks & Techniques
The best way to write your own WebDVD JavaScript is to not write them at all. Wherever possible you should "borrow" WebDVD scripts from public pages on the Internet, and modify them to do what you want. Please feel free to "borrow" any of the WebDVD JavaScript on the *StarGaze* web site located at http://www.StarGazeDVD.com/webdvd_Java.htm.

The following code is used to embed the Media Player control into the HTML page, and to configure it correctly.

```
<HTML>
<object classid="clsid:22D6F312-B0F6-11D0-94AB-0080C74C7E95"
    height="300" id="MediaPlayer1" name="MediaPlayer1" style="LEFT: 0px;
    TOP: 0px" width="480" border="0" align="absmiddle">
    <param name="AudioStream" value="-1">
    <param name="AutoSize" value="0">
    <param name="AutoStart" value="-1">
    <param name="AnimationAtStart" value="-1">
    <param name="AllowScan" value="-1">
    <param name="AllowChangeDisplaySize" value="-1">
    <param name="AutoRewind" value="-1">
    <param name="Balance" value="0">
    <param name="BaseURL" value>
    <param name="BufferingTime" value="5">
    <param name="CaptioningID" value>
    <param name="ClickToPlay" value="-1">
    <param name="CursorType" value="0">
    <param name="CurrentPosition" value="-1">
    <param name="CurrentMarker" value="0">
    <param name="DefaultFrame" value>
    <param name="DisplayBackColor" value="0">
    <param name="DisplayForeColor" value="16777215">
    <param name="DisplayMode" value="0">
    <param name="DisplaySize" value="4">
    <param name="Enabled" value="-1">
    <param name="EnableContextMenu" value="-1">
    <param name="EnablePositionControls" value="-1">
    <param name="EnableFullScreenControls" value="-1">
    <param name="EnableTracker" value="-1">
    <param name="Filename" value="DVD:">
    <param name="InvokeURLs" value="-1">
    <param name="Language" value="-1">
    <param name="Mute" value="0">
    <param name="PlayCount" value="1">
    <param name="PreviewMode" value="0">
    <param name="Rate" value="1">
    <param name="SAMILang" value>
```

```
<param name="SAMIStyle" value>
<param name="SAMIFileName" value>
<param name="SelectionStart" value="-1">
<param name="SelectionEnd" value="-1">
<param name="SendOpenStateChangeEvents" value="-1">
<param name="SendWarningEvents" value="-1">
<param name="SendErrorEvents" value="-1">
<param name="SendKeyboardEvents" value="0">
```

```
<param name="ShowGotoBar" value="0">
<param name="ShowPositionControls" value="-1">
<param name="ShowStatusBar" value="0">
<param name="ShowTracker" value="-1">
<param name="TransparentAtStart" value="0">
<param name="VideoBorderWidth" value="0">
<param name="VideoBorderColor" value="0">
<param name="VideoBorder3D" value="0">
<param name="Volume" value="-330">
<param name="WindowlessVideo" value="0">
</object>
</HTML>
```

To automatically start the Media Player control playing a specific item of content from the DVD-Video disc, the following Java script was inserted in the HTML page immediately after the `object` declarations. This script tells Media Player to open the DVD-Video title and play chapter number 1 from title 10. Once chapter number 10 has finished Media Player will simply wait for further instructions from the viewer.

```
<SCRIPT LANGUAGE="JavaScript">
<!--Begin
    // Start playback of the bonus track
    MediaPlayer1.DVD.ChapterPlayAutoStop(10,1,1);
// End -->
</SCRIPT>
```

Individual Java scripts were written for each HTML button that had a specific function related to DVD-Video play back. The following script is used to support the context-sensitive button that allows the user to search the Internet for additional content related to the content currently being displayed in the Media Player window. These scripts define the text that is displayed in the button, the size, shape, and position of a new instance of a web browser that is created when the button is pressed, and the full URL pathname of the a web page on the Internet that the new browser window should display.

```javascript
<SCRIPT LANGUAGE="JavaScript">
<!—Begin
typeWriterWait=120                      // Typewriter delay
blinkTextWait=1000                      // Blinking delay
blinkSpacesWait=300                     // Blinking 'blank-spaces' delay
blinkMax=5                              // how many times to blink
expandWait=100                          // expanding headliner delay
scrollWait=90                           // scrolling headliner delay
scrollWidth=35                          // characters in scroll display
randomLines=false                   // randomly choose lines? (true or false)
lineMax = 11                            // how many lines you have
lines=new Array(lineMax)
lines[1] = new Line("Space Telescope Science Institute",
                "http://www.stsci.edu/top.html", "", Static, 10000);
lines[2] = new Line("Ring Nebula",
                "http://oposite.stsci.edu/pubinfo/pr/1999/01/index.html",
                "", Static, 10000);
lines[3] = new Line("NGC 4639",
                "http://oposite.stsci.edu/pubinfo/PR/96/21/B.html",
                "", Static, 10000);
lines[4] = new Line("Eskimo Nebula",
                "http://oposite.stsci.edu/pubinfo/pr/2000/07/index.html",
                "", Static, 10000);
lines[5] = new Line("NGC 604",
                "http://oposite.stsci.edu/pubinfo/PR/96/27/A.html",
                "", Static, 10000);
lines[6] = new Line("Helix Nebula",
                "http://oposite.stsci.edu/pubinfo/pr/96/13/A.html",
                "", Static, 10000);
lines[7] = new Line("NGC 4414",
                "http://oposite.stsci.edu/pubinfo/PR/1999/25/index.html",
                "", Static, 10000);
lines[8] = new Line("Keyhole Nebula",
                "http://oposite.stsci.edu/pubinfo/pr/2000/06/index.html",
                "", Static, 10000);
```

```
lines[9] = new Line("NGC 3132",
                    "http://oposite.stsci.edu/pubinfo/pr/1998/39/index.html",
                    "", Static, 10000);
lines[10] = new Line("Trifid Nebula",
                    "http://oposite.stsci.edu/pubinfo/pr/1999/42/index.html",
                    "", Static, 10000);
lines[11] = new Line("Cats Eye Nebula",
                    "http://oposite.stsci.edu/pubinfo/gif/NGC6543a.txt",
                    "", Static, 10000);
```

```
lineNo=1
lineWait=0
function Line(text, url, frame, type, wait)
{
    this.text=text
    this.url=url
    this.frame=frame
    this.Display=type
    this.wait=wait
}
function StringFill(c, n)
{
    var s=""
    while (--n >= 0) {
        s+=c
    }
    return s
}
function GotoUrl(url, frame)
{
    windowprops = "height=485,width=710,location=no,left=142,
                   top=170,scrollbars=yes,menubars=no,toolbars=no,resizable=yes"
    window.open(url, "Popup", windowprops)
}
```

```
function Static()
{
    document.formDisplay.buttonFace.value=this.text
}
function StartHeadliner()
{
    StopHeadliner()
    timerID=setTimeout("ShowNextLine()", 2000)
    timerRunning=true
}
function StopHeadliner()
{
    if (timerRunning) {
        clearTimeout(timerID)
        timerRunning=false
    }
}
function ShowNextLine()
{
    lines[lineNo].Display()
}
function ShowLine(lineNo)
{
    lines[lineNo].Display()
}
function LineClick(lineNo)
{
    document.formDisplay.buttonFace.blur()
    if (lineNo > 0) GotoUrl(lines[lineNo].url, lines[lineNo].frame)
}
with (document)
{
    write('<center><form name="formDisplay"><input type="button"')
    write('name="buttonFace" style="cursor:hand"
            value="Space Telescope Science Institute"')
    write('onClick="LineClick(lineNo)"></input></form></center>')
}
// End -->
</SCRIPT>
```

The following script is a general-purpose subroutine to play a chapter from the *StarGaze* DVD. If the chapter is in the same DVD-Video domain as the current chapter being played, a `ChapterSearch` command is issued. If we are changing domains, a `ChapterPlay` command is issued. We need to keep track of the DVD-Video domain to make sure user selections of audio format, subtitle language, and audio language are retained when the user selects a new chapter within the same domain. The `ChapterSearch` command does not reset any of these playback parameters. The `ChapterPlay` command resets the default audio and subtitle tracks selections since it forces the DVD-Video player on the PC to go back through the Video Manager domain to find the correct title and chapter to be played.

```
ShowLine(1);
domain = MediaPlayer1.DVD.CurrentTitle;
if (domain == '1'){
    MediaPlayer1.DVD.ChapterSearch(chapter);
}
else {
    MediaPlayer1.DVD.ChapterPlay(title,chapter);
}
}
// End -->
</SCRIPT>
```

The following scripts define the title and chapter number of the *StarGaze* media element to be played, and the index for the synchronized link button.

```
<SCRIPT LANGUAGE="JavaScript">
<!-Begin
//Play Ring Nebula
function Ring_Nebula()
{
    MediaPlayer1.DVD.ChapterPlayAutoStop(7,105,1);
    lineNo = 2;
    ShowLine(2);
}
```

```
//Play NGC 4639
function NGC_4639()
{
    MediaPlayer1.DVD.ChapterPlayAutoStop(7,45,1);
    lineNo = 3;
    ShowLine(3);
}
//Play Eskimo Nebula
function Eskimo_Nebula()
{
    MediaPlayer1.DVD.ChapterPlayAutoStop(7,7,1);
    lineNo = 4;
    ShowLine(4);
}
//Play NGC 604
function NGC_604()
{
    MediaPlayer1.DVD.ChapterPlayAutoStop(7,48,1);
    lineNo = 5;
    ShowLine(5);
}
//Play Helix Nebula
function Helix_Nebula()
{
    MediaPlayer1.DVD.ChapterPlayAutoStop(7,41,1);
    lineNo = 6;
    ShowLine(6);
}
//Play Keyhole Nebula
function Keyhole_Nebula()
{
    MediaPlayer1.DVD.ChapterPlayAutoStop(7,6,1);
    lineNo = 8;
    ShowLine(8);
}
```

```
//Play Trifid Nebula
function Trifid_Nebula()
{
    MediaPlayer1.DVD.ChapterPlayAutoStop(7,103,1);
    lineNo = 10;
    ShowLine(10);
}
//Play NGC 4414
```

```
function NGC_3132()
{
    MediaPlayer1.DVD.ChapterPlayAutoStop(7,76,1);
    lineNo = 9;
    ShowLine(9);
}
//Play Cat's Eye Nebula
function Cats_Eye_Nebula()
{
    MediaPlayer1.DVD.ChapterPlayAutoStop(7,24,1);
    lineNo = 11;
    ShowLine(11);
}
// End -->
</SCRIPT>
```

The following script allows the user to turn on the subtitles within the DVD-Video display window, and to select the language (English, French, German, or Spanish) they want.

```
<SCRIPT LANGUAGE="JavaScript">
<!—Begin
//Select Subtitles
function Subtitles(stream)
{
    switch (stream)
    {
        case "0" :
            MediaPlayer1.DVD.CurrentSubpictureStream = 0;
            MediaPlayer1.DVD.SubpictureOn = 1;
            break;
        case "1" :
            MediaPlayer1.DVD.CurrentSubpictureStream = 1;
            MediaPlayer1.DVD.SubpictureOn = 1;
            break;
        case "2" :
            MediaPlayer1.DVD.CurrentSubpictureStream = 2;
            MediaPlayer1.DVD.SubpictureOn = 1;
            break;
        case "3" :
            MediaPlayer1.DVD.CurrentSubpictureStream = 3;
            MediaPlayer1.DVD.SubpictureOn = 1;
            break;
        case "4" :
            MediaPlayer1.DVD.CurrentSubpictureStream = 4;
            MediaPlayer1.DVD.SubpictureOn = 1;
            break;
        case "5" :
            MediaPlayer1.DVD.CurrentSubpictureStream = 5;
            MediaPlayer1.DVD.SubpictureOn = 1;
            break;
        case "6" :
            MediaPlayer1.DVD.CurrentSubpictureStream = 6;
            MediaPlayer1.DVD.SubpictureOn = 1;
            break;
```

```
            case "7" :
                MediaPlayer1.DVD.CurrentSubpictureStream = 7;
                MediaPlayer1.DVD.SubpictureOn = 1;
                break;
            case "8" :
                MediaPlayer1.DVD.SubpictureOn = 0;
                break;
        }
```

```
<SCRIPT LANGUAGE="JavaScript">
<!—Begin
//Select Audio
function Audio(stream)
{
    switch (stream)
    {
        case "0" :
            MediaPlayer1.DVD.CurrentAudioStream = 0;
            break;
        case "1" :
            MediaPlayer1.DVD.CurrentAudioStream = 1;
            break;
        case "2" :
            MediaPlayer1.DVD.CurrentAudioStream = 2;
            break;
        case "3" :
            MediaPlayer1.DVD.CurrentAudioStream = 3;
            break;
        case "4" :
            MediaPlayer1.DVD.CurrentAudioStream = 4;
            break;
```

```
        case "5" :
            MediaPlayer1.DVD.CurrentAudioStream = 5;
            break;
        case "6" :
            MediaPlayer1.DVD.CurrentAudioStream = 6;
            break;
    }
}
// End -->
</SCRIPT>
```

The following script tells Media Player to make the display window go to full screen. Media Player has been configured so that pressing the Esc key will return the display window to its original size.

```
<SCRIPT LANGUAGE="JavaScript">
<!—Begin
//player goes to fullscreen
function full()
{
    MediaPlayer1.DisplaySize = '3';
}
// End -->
</SCRIPT>
```

StarGaze Web Site Hosting, Maintenance & Upgrades

The *StarGaze* web site is hosted on a 300 Mhz Pentium II Windows NT 4.0 server, which is connected to the Internet via a dedicated T1 (1.544 Mbps) line. This same system also hosts another dozen or so web and FTP sites, as well as my e-mail server. Even though the server hardware is a few years old it is more than powerful enough to handle all the traffic demands of these web and FTP sites, and the dedicated T1 connection to the Internet usually runs at about two percent of capacity. Since all of the high bandwidth content delivered by the *Star-Gaze* WebDVD site is actually coming from the local DVD disc, and not my server, I could probably use a 56 Kbps dedicated modem line instead of the T1 connection to the Internet. WebDVD pages are very easy to serve since the majority of the communications and processing requirements are handled in the viewers PC rather than over the Internet.

The *StarGaze* web site is updated on a regular basis. Most of the updates are related to new data related to the celestial objects included on the *StarGaze* DVD-Video disc. Another common maintenance function is to update the links to other web sites since these tend to change frequently.

Tips, Tricks & Techniques

Developing an enhanced or WebDVD enabled DVD-Video title includes ongoing web

DVD-ROM AUTHORING
THE FORGOTTEN FORMAT

When this book was published in July 2001, there were less than 200 consumer DVD-ROM titles on the market. The disparity between the numbers of DVD-Video titles available, which exceeds 8,000, and the small number of DVD-ROM titles available is due to several factors. First the DVD-Forum has done an excellent job in promoting brand awareness of the DVD-Video format. In the United States nearly 75 percent of a recent survey of consumers were aware of DVD-Video and associated it with high quality home entertainment. The DVD Forum has done such an excellent job at building brand awareness for DVD-Video that many consumers who own DVD-ROM enabled personal computers think they can only use their DVD-ROM drive to play movies on their PC.

An equally important reason for the lack of DVD-ROM titles is the low level of demand from consumers for these products. Since all DVD-ROM drives can read standard CD-ROM, CD-R, CD-RW, and Audio-CD discs, many consumers are quite happy choosing from the thousands of titles already available in these formats. So even though there is a worldwide installed base of more than 20,000,000 DVD-ROM enabled personal computers, there is not enough consumer demand for DVD-ROM titles to entice title developers to jump into this market.

Also the development of titles has been hampered by some compatibility problems that prevent the universal playback of a DVD-ROM disc on all personal computer systems. DVD-ROM titles can be classified into three different types. Level 0 titles use the DVD disc to store vast amounts of data, but make no attempt to use any of the high quality multimedia data formats used in the DVD-Video specification. In general the only compatibility problems found in a Level 0 DVD-ROM title are related to the support by the operating system for the Micro-UDF file format. Level 1 DVD-ROM titles include high quality multimedia data in the MPEG-1 or MPEG-2 formats, but do not use the Video Object format used in DVD-Video discs. Most compatibility problems with Level 1 DVD-ROM discs are related to support by the operating system and third party drivers for playing back MPEG-1 or MPEG-2 video streams. Last, but not least, a Level 2 DVD-ROM disc uses high quality multimedia data stored in the DVD-Video VOB format, so each Level 2 disc includes both a DVD-Video zone and a DVD-ROM zone. Compatibility problems with Level 2 discs are generally related to the operating system's support for the DVD-Video format, and the built in DVD-Video navigation decoder software on the system.

In general the recommended method of developing a DVD-ROM title is to use either the Level 0 or Level 2 approaches. Since a Level 0 DVD-ROM is not intended to deliver high quality multimedia data, and it is also not designed to work in a DVD-Video player, the vast majority of compatibility problems can be avoided entirely. I recommend that all Level 0 DVD-ROM discs include a small DVD-Video zone that will display a static screen listing the minimum system requirements for the title. Since most consumers don't know there is a difference between a DVD-ROM and DVD-Video title, you will find that many try to put a DVD-ROM title into their DVD-Video player. If they get a "disc read error" or nothing happens at all, then they may return the title without ever knowing that it would work just fine had they put it in a DVD-ROM computer.

Using an autorun or autoload program on a DVD-ROM title is also something that I recommend. The vast majority of DVD-ROM personal computers include a DVD-Video navigation program, and many of these systems are configured to automatically launch the DVD-Video playback program as soon as they detect a disc with a DVD-Video zone in the DVD-ROM drive. If you include a small DVD-Video zone on your DVD-ROM disc, the viewer will see the minimum system requirements screen when the disc is inserted into the drive. If you use an autorun or autoload program on the DVD-ROM disc, this takes precedence over the automatic launching of the DVD-Video navigation program and your custom DVD-ROM application can start up automatically whenever the disc is inserted into the drive.

DVD-ROM for Microsoft Windows Systems

Developing Level 0 titles for Windows is almost identical to developing a CD-ROM title for Windows. You can use any application development tool or programming language and store any type of data you want on the disc. Essentially a Level 0 DVD-ROM is just a bigger CD-ROM. The only extra step required for publishing a Level 0 DVD-ROM is to format the disc image using the Micro-UDF file format. There are several off-the-shelf tools you can use to format the disc image in the Micro-UDF format, including products from Sonic, Gear, Prassi, Software Architects, and others. DVD replication facilities still require a DLT tape in DDP 2.0 format or a DVD-R in Cutting Master Format to replicate a Level 0 DVD-ROM disc, and most of these tools will also be able to generate the DLT tape or DVD-R you will need to send to the replication facility.

There are three basic methods to develop a Level 2 DVD-ROM title for Windows. Since the multimedia content stored on the disc is in the DVD-Video VOB format, your DVD-ROM application will need to access data stored in the DVD-Video zone of the disc. This can be done by

1. using the Windows Media Control Interface (MCI) API,
2. using the Windows DirectShow API, or
3. using a third-party tool that uses either the MCI or DirectShow APIs.

MCI

some nagging compatibility issues that can still cause problems, particularly with applications that use the Windows MCI API (application program interface).

In the fall of 1997 the SPA formed a Technical Working Group (TWG) to investigate the DVD-ROM Compatibility problems and to develop recommendations to ensure that any DVD-ROM title would work correctly on all DVD-ROM enabled personal computer systems. The SPA DVD-ROM Interactive Media Format TWG looked at Windows applications, since the vast majority of title developers were targeting their products for standard Windows platforms. Most of the compatibility problems were caused by differences in the way that standard MCI drivers had been implemented by each DVD-ROM vendor. The working group recommended a standard set of MCI calls that should be supported by all DVD-ROM hardware and software vendors. DVD title developers should use these standard calls to ensure that their titles will work on all Windows platforms. Since time was of the essence, it was decided to base the SPA recommendation on a subset of the OM-1 MCI Recommendations for MPEG-1 issued in 1995.

The SPA DVD-ROM working group recommended the following standard MCI calls be supported by all DVD-ROM vendors, and be used in the development of all Windows DVD-ROM titles. The use of the MCI API is not recommended for Windows 98, 2000, or ME applications, as Microsoft has developed the DirectShow API for these operating systems.

Table 8.1   Recommended MCI Calls for DVD-ROM Titles

MCI Command String	Message	MCI Command String	Message
capability	MCI_GETDEVCAPS	set	MCI_SET
close	MCI_CLOSE	setaudio	MCI_SETAUDIO
cue	MCI_CUE	setvideo	MCI_SETVIDEO
info	MCI_INFO	signal	MCI_SIGNAL
open	MCI_OPEN	status	MCI_STATUS
pause	MCI_PAUSE	stop	MCI_STOP

Table 8.1   Recommended MCI Calls for DVD-ROM Titles (Continued)

MCI Command String	Message	MCI Command String	Message
play	MCI_PLAY	update	MCI_UPDATE
put	MCI_PUT	where	MCI_WHERE
resume	MCI_RESUME	window	MCI_WINDOW
seek	MCI_SEEK		

Development of DVD-ROM titles under Windows 95 typically requires making several different MCI calls, particularly if the title includes any multimedia content. Microsoft has made it clear that they do not intend to provide MCI support in future versions of Windows. Figure 8.1 shows the standard playback environment for DVD-ROM titles using the MCI API. As you can see from Figure 8.1, Level 2 DVD-ROM titles will make calls to the DirectX and DirectSound drivers through the MCI API. These calls will allow the DVD-ROM title to open a VOB file, play a VOB file, check status, etc. It should be noted that none of the advanced features of the DVD-Video specification, such as multiple video angles, subpicture streams, or multiple audio tracks can be controlled through the MCI API. Thus Level 2 DVD-ROM titles that use MCI calls can use only a small subset of the content stored on a DVD-Video disc.

Developing Level 2 DVD-ROM titles using the MCI API usually requires writing custom application software in either Visual Basic or C++. Either language can be used to make the required MCI calls. Since the MCI calls used to access content stored on the DVD-Video portion of the disc are extensions to the standard MCI calls supported by Microsoft, you may find that off-the-shelf development tools such as Macromedia Director, AuthorWare, and others can't be used for Level 2 DVD-ROM development efforts.

Another potential problem with developing Level 2 DVD-ROM applications is that while many DVD decoder drivers support the extended MCI API, several drivers have bugs. For example, there are several early software decoders that have memory leaks in their DVD drivers. A memory leak occurs when a program fails to release all of the system memory resources that it uses. Over a long period of time a driver with a memory leak will use up all of the available system memory, and the system can lock up as a result. Level 2 DVD-ROM application programs that can run for long periods of time, such as a screen saver, may experience poor performance and system lock ups when using older software DVD decoders that use the MCI API.

DirectShow

DirectShow is a streaming media architecture for Windows that provides high-quality capture and playback of multimedia streams. It supports a wide variety of formats, including Advanced Streaming Format (ASF), Motion Picture Experts Group (MPEG), Audio-Video Interleaved (AVI), MPEG Audio Layer-3 (MP3), and WAV files. It automatically detects and uses video and audio acceleration hardware when available, but also supports systems without acceleration hardware. DirectShow does not include an embedded MPEG-2 video decoder or Dolby Digital audio decoder, so for DVD applications, third-party MPEG-2 and AC-3 decoders are required.

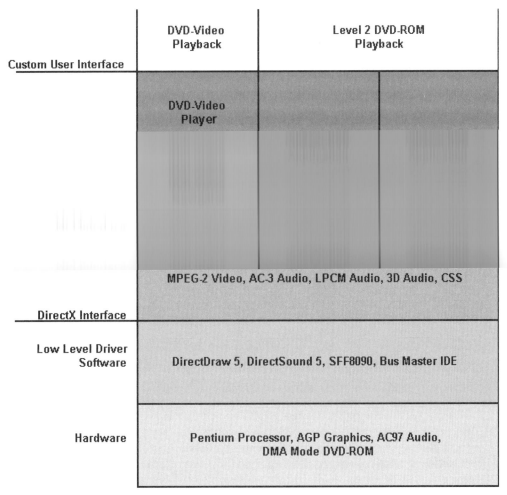

Figure 8.1   MCI Interface Block Diagram

Tips, Tricks & Techniques

I highly recommend that you develop Level 2 DVD-ROM applications using Microsoft DirectShow. However, you may need to develop your application so that they support the MCI API, as well. During the early days of DVD-ROM consumers bought a large number of hardware DVD decoder boards that did not include support for DirectShow. Even today the Creative Labs Encore DVD board does not include DirectShow drivers for either Windows 95 or Windows 98. If part of your market includes legacy systems, or personal computers with Creative Labs Encore boards, you may need to develop an MCI version of your application software to support these platforms.

for proper operation. DirectShow was developed for Windows 98, is supported on Windows 2000 and Windows ME, and can be installed on Windows 95 systems. DirectShow will not work on Windows NT platforms. Figure 8.2 provides a detailed block diagram of the Microsoft DirectShow environment.

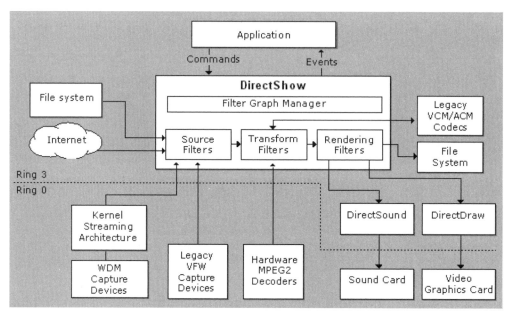

Figure 8.2   Microsoft DirectShow Environment Block Diagram

Examples of the types of applications you can write with DirectShow include DVD players, video-editing applications, AVI to ASF converters, MP3 players, and digital video capture applications. DirectShow is based on the component object model (COM), so to write a DirectShow application you must understand COM client programming. For most applications, you do not need to implement your own COM objects. DirectShow provides the components you need.

DirectShow is designed to work with a wide variety of multimedia data types. Its main design goal is to simplify the task of creating multimedia applications on the Windows platform by isolating applications from the complexities of data transports, hardware differences, and synchronization issues.

DirectShow uses DirectDraw and DirectSound to render data efficiently to the personal computer's graphics and sound cards, respectively. Synchronization is achieved by encapsulating the multimedia data in time-stamped media samples. To handle a variety of media sources, formats, and hardware devices, DirectShow uses a modular architecture in which operating system components called filters can be mixed and matched to provide support for many different scenarios.

DirectShow includes a DVD Navigator Filter that supports playback of content stored on a DVD-Video disc. The DVD Navigator filter is the source filter for a DVD-Video playback filter graph. It opens all necessary files in a DVD-Video volume, navigates through the content stored on a DVD-Video disc, and parses the resulting MPEG-2 program stream, splitting the stream into three outputs (video, audio, and subpicture).

The DVD Navigator filter is used to control the `IDvdControl2` and `IDvdInfo2` interfaces, enabling a DVD playback application to control DVD-Video playback. `IDvdControl2` provides the full functionality required by the DVD-Video specification, as well as methods for playback, menu navigation, and parental control. `IDvdInfo2`, which is a companion to `IDvdControl2`, groups the DVD Navigator's `get` methods and `IDvdControl2` groups the `set` methods. Together they provide DVD navigation and playback functionality beyond the DVD-Video specification.

The DVD Navigator includes all the capabilities found on full-featured stand-alone DVD players, plus additional capabilities specific to playing DVDs on personal computers. Using

it exposes. Developers using a scripting language or Microsoft Visual Basic control the DVD Navigator indirectly through the MSWebDVD ActiveX control.

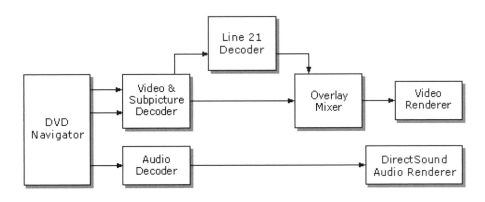

Figure 8.3   DirectShow DVD Filter Graph

When writing a DVD-ROM application for Windows, you develop the code for the user interface, and call the Microsoft DirectShow API to issue all DVD playback and navigation commands. This involves calling the COM `CoCreateInstance` method on the `DVDGraph-Builder` object, which does the actual work of creating the DVD filter graph. After the filter graph is created, you can obtain pointers to the `IDvdControl2` and `IDvdInfo2` interfaces of the DVD Navigator source filter. After you have the interface pointers, you can connect your user interface to the DVD navigation commands. This basic process is quite simple and is similar to the creation of other types of DirectShow applications. Figure 8.3 shows a typical DVD filter graph.

The DVD Navigator is the first filter in a DVD playback filter graph; it performs several tasks.

- Reads the navigation and video data from the disc.

- Demultiplexes the video, audio, and subpicture data into separate streams.

- Pumps the streams into the graph for further processing and eventual rendering.

- Informs your application of DVD-related events.

For the audio stream, the DVD Navigator connects to an audio decoder, which connects to the default audio renderer. On the video and subpicture streams, the downstream filters are the third-party video decoder, the overlay mixer, and the video renderer. Your custom application communicates with and controls the DVD Navigator through the custom interfaces that the DVD Navigator exposes: IDvdControl2 (the set methods) and IDvdInfo2 (the get methods). It also must communicate with the filter graph manager to stop, start, and otherwise control the graph.

Tips, Tricks & Techniques

DVD producers and developers who need to create custom application programs for Windows OS platforms should use the DirectShow API rather than the older MCI API. Microsoft no longer supports the MCI API, and it is only included as legacy support in the newer Microsoft operating systems, such as Windows 2000 and Windows ME.

disc note:

Real World Example

StarGaze includes a Level 2 DVD-ROM application in addition to its DVD-Video and WebDVD features. A Windows screen saver program, which supports the Windows 95, 98, 98SE, NT 4, 2000, and ME operating systems, is included on the *StarGaze* disc. The screen saver software supports both the MCI and DirectShow APIs. MCI support was included so that legacy DVD-ROM systems that do not support DirectShow could still use the *StarGaze* screen saver program. A custom InstallShield setup program was developed to install the screensaver code and the screen saver images onto the hard drive so that the program can operate even when the *StarGaze* disc is not in the DVD-ROM drive. You can install the *StarGaze* screensaver program on your Windows system by running the setup.exe program that is located in the root directory of the *StarGaze* disc.

Third-Party Development Tools

An alternative to using Visual Basic or C++ with either the MCI or DirectShow APIs is to use a third-party tool, such as Macromedia Director. While Director does not currently support direct access to content stored in DVD-Video VOB files, there are several Director Xtras that can be used for this. The two most popular Director Xtras for DVD are MPEGXtra from

Tabulerio Producoes and OnStageDVD from Visible Light. Contact information for both companies is provided in Chapter 10.

The Tabulerio Producoes MPEGXtra extension lets you incorporate videos directly into your Director cast, and adds several new scripting commands that allow precise control of MPEG videos. MPEGXtra is designed for use on Windows 95, NT, and 98 systems.

The Visible Light OnStage DVD Xtra extension includes a number of configurable options, and supports full screen or windowed playback. OnStageDVD is designed for use on Windows NT, 95, and 98 systems, and provides Lingo control of DVD-Video playback content as well as some WebDVD feature support.

will need to create a DVD-ROM disc image in the Micro-UDF file format. There are several tools you can use to do this, including Roxio Toast Titanium and most Mac-based DVD-Video authoring tools from Sonic Solutions.

Developing a Level 2 DVD-ROM application for the Mac is very difficult. Apple has not released an API that provides access to content stored on a DVD-Video disc through a custom application program. It is possible to use simple scripting commands from a custom application program to launch the Apple DVD-Video navigator program and instruct it to perform some basic playback functions. This scripting method does not allow you to develop an integrated application program in which video or audio content from the DVD-Video zone of the disc are seamlessly combined with content generated by the application program. Using this scripting technique the Apple DVD-Video navigator will launch in its own window and the user will be able to use the navigator controls outside of your custom application program. Apple has not announced a target date for supporting access to DVD-Video content from custom application programs on any of the operating systems. If Apple does decide to provide support for Level 2 DVD-ROM software developers, it will most likely come in a future release of QuickTime.

THE DVD AUTHORING & PRODUCTION BUSINESS

This chapter will offer insight into how companies work together to bring DVD titles to market, what services and products should be offered by DVD production and authoring companies, how these products should be priced and sold, and what it takes to set up and run a profitable DVD production and authoring company. Publishing a DVD title typically involves several different companies, including a content owner or studio, one or more DVD authoring facilities, a DVD replication facility, a DVD title distributor, and a number of DVD retailers. To stay in business, each of these companies needs to make a profit on each DVD title in which they are involved. Figure 9.1 shows the various relationships involved in bringing a DVD title to market.

Who Are the Players?

As you can see from Figure 9.1, there are several different types of companies involved in bringing a DVD title to market. Each company is responsible for a different aspect of the DVD authoring, production, replication, distribution, and sales process.

Authoring Tool Vendors

Authoring tool vendors develop the hardware and software tools required to produce a DVD title. DVD authoring tools on the market today fall into four general categories.

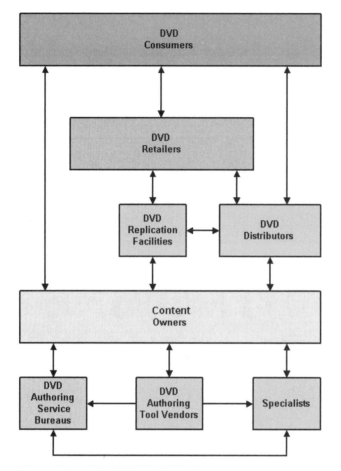

Figure 9.1   The DVD Food Chain

Professional Authoring Tools   Used to develop Hollywood entertainment titles and highly interactive or complex titles.

Corporate Authoring Tools   Used to develop entertainment or corporate titles with a moderate amount of interactivity and complexity.

Consumer Authoring Tools   Used to develop low-end corporate titles with little or not interactivity or complexity, and to allow consumers to transfer their home movies onto DVD.

Ancillary Tools   Used to provide optional and add-on features to a DVD title, including Dolby Digital or DTS audio, web connectivity, subtitles, etc.

Content Owners

A common misperception in the DVD industry is that the only content owners publishing on DVD are major motion picture studios. While DVD titles from major motion picture studios account for more than 90 percent of the total number of DVD discs sold, the total number of studio titles released is only about 3,500 titles. With over 8,000 titles released to date, you can see that studios only account for about 45 percent of the total titles released. Thus, many other content owners are involved in DVD than just studios. Content owners publishing products on DVD include:

- consumers publishing home movies on DVD.

DVD Authoring Service Bureaus

Historically, the acquisition cost of the hardware and software required to create a DVD title has been quite high, so authoring service bureaus have created most of the DVD titles released to date. These companies have the required equipment and skilled staff to create a finished DVD program from a disparate set of video, audio, text, and graphics media elements. Generally, a DVD authoring service bureau will generate the DLT tape that goes to the replication facility. There are a number of different types of DVD authoring service bureaus:

- studio affiliates, including Universal DVCC, Warner CVC, and Sony, who specialize in transferring DVD titles from their parent company motion picture studio's collections of films;

- distribution companies who license programs from content owners and then release them on DVD using in-house authoring equipment and personnel;

- DVD replication facilities that offer both authoring and mastering services to their clients;

- Video post production facilities that have added DVD authoring services to their traditional video and audio post, telecine, and color correction services; and

- DVD authoring service bureaus that offer services directly related to creating a DVD title. Many DVD authoring service bureaus have formed strategic alliances with studios, distributors, replication facilities, and post production houses.

Specialists

The DVD authoring business has now matured to the point at which it can sustain companies that provide niche or specialized services required on some, but not all, DVD titles. These specialized services include:

- audio mixing for stereo and surround sound, as well as compression in the Dolby Digital, DTS, and SDDS formats;

- menu graphic design for both static and dynamic (motion) menus;

- package graphic design for the disc label, inserts, and outside cover artwork;

- translation services to generate content for menus, audio tracks, and subpicture streams for multi-language DVD titles;

- subtitle services to generate the individual graphic files required for each subtitle, as well as a script file with in and out time codes that can be imported into the authoring system;

- video processing and compression services, which can include noise reduction, and high quality variable bit rate MPEG-2 compression; and

- WebDVD and DVD-ROM feature development for inclusion on DVD-Video titles.

Replication Facilities

In the early days of DVD there were only a few replication facilities that could actually produce a DVD disc that would work correctly on consumer DVD-Video players. Today there are at least 20 replication facilities offering DVD products and services. Typical services offered by a DVD replication facility include:

- glass mastering, which is the process of creating the glass master and molds from a DLT tape;

- Check Disc Package, which is delivering a limited quantity of production discs to allow the content owner or DVD authoring company to verify that the disc is working properly before committing to a large production run;

- mass duplication services, including short runs of 1,000 discs or less, moderate runs of between 1,000 and 50,000 discs, and large runs that may require millions of discs to be made in just a few weeks of production;

- packaging services, including assembly of the finished disc, printed materials, and the disc case, application of security measures and shrink-wrap, and boxing discs in standard quantities ready for shipment; and

- warehousing and direct to retail shipping services.

Distributors

Distributors purchase large quantities of DVD product from content owners and then sell smaller quantities to a variety of secondary distributors, retailers, and in some cases directly to the consumer. There are several different types of distributors in the DVD business including the following.

- Master distributors have the exclusive right to one or more specific DVD titles. Many studios have their own in-house distribution companies. Companies like Image Entertainment, DVD International, and others act as master distributors for titles not carried directly by a studio distribution company.

- Aggregators purchase DVD titles from one or more distributors and sell to large retailers, such as Best Buy, Kmart, and others. An aggregator will combine all the titles ordered by a

cent of the total sales of DVD titles. In general, superstores sell DVD titles at a ten to 20 percent discount off Suggested Retail Price (SRP).

- Specialty stores, such as Tower Records, Virgin Records, and others, sell DVD titles at SRP or with a slight discount.

- Internet retailers offer titles from all genres to consumers, but they may stock only the top 1,000 selling titles. In general, Internet retailers offer DVD titles at a 20 to 40 percent discount off SRP.

The old adage that "Content is King" is just as true in the DVD business as it is in the movie business. With over 8,000 DVD titles available to consumers, the market for DVD titles is quite crowded. In order for a DVD title to be a commercial success, it must include content that is of interest to at least a segment of consumers. In today's market the top 100 DVD titles from the major motion pictures studios generate almost 90 percent of the total sales of DVD titles worldwide. With blockbuster hits like *The Matrix* selling upwards of 10,000,000 copies on DVD, it is easy for an unknown title to get lost in the shuffle. While there is a thriving market for back catalog movies, special interest, and niche titles, the average sales volume for these titles is less than 50,000 copies per year. More than half the DVD titles on the market today sell less than 10,000 copies per year, so it is very important to bring titles to market in an efficient and cost effective manner.

Since "Content is King" in the DVD world, the content owner is generally involved in each step of the DVD authoring and production process. The content owner will initiate the process of bringing a DVD title to market by deciding which of their video properties will be released on DVD. Once a decision has been made to bring out a new DVD title, the content owner must also decide when the title will be available, what the SRP will be, what companies will be involved in authoring, producing, replicating and distributing the title, and how much money will be allocated to each step of the process.

The typical path for a new DVD title starts with the content owner, winds its way through a DVD authoring service bureau, with an optional stop-over at a DVD specialist for custom audio processing, motion menu design, or other features that are not offered by the DVD authoring facility. Once the title has been completed by the DVD authoring facility, and approved by the content owner, a DLT tape is sent to a replication facility. When DVD check discs are approved by the content owner, and in many cases the authoring facility as well, the replication facility will start the disc production process. For many DVD titles this means making 5,000 to 10,000 discs, while for a few titles it can mean making 5,000,000 to 10,000,000 discs. Obviously the price and level of service that a content owner gets from a replication facility is directly related to the number of discs produced for a specific title. You can bet when Lucas Films sells 25,000,000 copies of *Star Wars* on DVD that they will get better pricing and service from their replication facility than I have received on *StarGaze*, which has sold approximately 25,000 copies to date. Don't get me wrong — Panasonic Disc Services Corporation (PDSC), who handles the replication for *StarGaze*, has done a great job. However, PDSC, and all other replicators, naturally provide their best prices and level of service to their largest clients.

Once the replication facility has completed the manufacturing process, finished goods are shipped to distribution companies. Each major motion picture studio has either an in-house distribution company or works closely with another studio to get their products into the market. In some cases content owners will sell direct to retailers, or even direct to consumers, but in most cases the product will go from the replication facility to a distributor, and then on to retailers who sell to consumers. Approximately 70 percent of the DVD titles sold in the United States go through a few large retail chains. In general each of these major retailers has a few distributors with whom they prefer to work. These preferred distributors provide ancillary services to their customers, such as warehousing, direct shipment of aggregated orders to individual retail stores, and coordination of product returns at the end of their shelf life.

Follow the Money

Before you can make money in the DVD authoring and production business, you need to understand how money flows from the sale of a DVD title. They key items that you need to understand are the suggested retail price (SRP), wholesale price, cost of goods, production costs, and any royalty costs that are paid on a per disc basis.

SRP is quite simply the list price for the title. Some titles are sold to consumers at SRP, but retailers discount many titles.

The wholesale price is what retailers and distributors pay for copies of the title. In general, a DVD title's wholesale price is between 40 and 60 percent less than the SRP, depending on a variety of factors.

Cost of goods is simply the total net cost of manufacturing and shipping the DVD title to a distributor or retailer. Cost of goods will include separate fees for disc replication, disc printing, package costs, assembly of the disc and the package, warehousing, and shipment of finished goods.

Production costs will include one-time fees paid to video post-production facilities, graphic art shops, and DVD authoring facilities that are directly related to creating the final DVD disc image and sending a DLT tape to the replication facilities. In some cases the replication facility will charge a one-time fee for creating the glass masters and negatives for printing the disc label, so these can also be included in the disc production cost.

Last, but not least, many content owners are required to pay a royalty for each copy of a title sold, whether it is on VHS, Laserdisc, Audio CD, DVD-Video, DVD-Audio, or SACD. Royalties are generally paid on a quarterly basis for discs that have actually been sold and shipped to retailers or distributors. In some cases a small portion of the royalty due will be set aside as a reserve against future returns.

Another key factor is a DVD title's break-even point, which is the number of discs that must be sold to recover the production costs. A large part of the decision to publish a title on DVD is determining if, and when, it will sell enough copies to reach the break-even point. For the top 100 selling DVD titles this is not a major concern since they will generate millions of

involved in a DVD title is through an example. Here are the key price and cost parameters for *StarGaze*.

- Suggested Retail Price = $24.98

- Average Retail Sale Price = $19.98

- Average Wholesale Price = $10.00

- Cost of Goods = $2.00 per disc

    - Disc Replication = $1.20 per disc

    - Packaging = $0.50 per disc

    - Warehousing & Shipping = $0.30 per disc

- Production Costs = $47,000 (including music royalty advance)

- Royalties

    - Music Synchronization Rights = $1.50 per disc

- Break Even Point = 13,500 copies sold

Now lets take a look at how the revenues generated by *StarGaze* are distributed. As of the publication date of this book, *StarGaze* had sold approximately 25,000 copies worldwide at an average retail price of $19.98.

- Total revenues from retail sales = $499,500

    - Less wholesale cost of $249,500

    - Net revenues for retailers = $249,750

- Total revenues for distributor = $249,750
  - Less cost of goods of $50,000
  - Less royalty paid to content owner of $87,412
  - Net revenues for distributor = $112,338
- Total revenues for content owner = $87,412
  - Less production costs of $47,000
  - Less music royalties of $17,500
  - Net revenues for content owner = $22,912

So as you can see that *StarGaze* has already exceeded its break-even point and is now generating profits for the content owner, distributor, and retailers.

DVD Authoring & Production Business Models

Most of the people who are reading this book are either in the DVD authoring and production business or want to get into this business. Developing DVD titles for content owners, or for your own company, can be a rewarding and profitable business. Unfortunately, for every DVD authoring and production company success story there are also examples of failed businesses. There are several different business models that can be adopted by a DVD authoring and production facility including

- the horizontal business model,
- the specialist business model, and
- the vertical business model.

Each business model has its own unique rewards and challenges, and there are examples of successful and failed DVD authoring and production companies that have used each model. There is no single best way to run a DVD authoring and production business, so I can't tell you which model is right for your company. Your client base, skill set, and location will determine which business model makes the most sense for your company. The best advice is to offer high-quality services at a fair price and to provide your clients with the best level of customer service you can. This is a proven formula for success in many different business areas, and it works just as well in the DVD authoring and production business.

Horizontal Business Model

In the horizontal business model a specific DVD product or service is offered to a broad segment of the market. For example, a DVD authoring and production company using the horizontal business model will offer a full range of DVD authoring services to clients in the entertainment, corporate, government, and education markets. The keys to success using the horizontal business model are to automate the production process, provide quality products and services, provide good customer service, and keep your equipment, facility and staff up to the latest standards. Most major video post-production facilities that offer DVD authoring and production services use the horizontal business model. Successful companies can leverage their existing customer base to offer a wide variety of services, thus generating more revenue from each client than would be possible by offering them only a single service. In addition to offering each client whatever services they need, a horizontal business model company will also attract and retain customers from a variety of business areas, thus reducing the risk that losing one or two clients will significantly affect the company's business.

DVD authoring and production companies that use a horizontal business model need to be able to develop all different types of DVD titles, including movies from their entertainment customers, sales or marketing presentations from the corporate customers, and training titles from the educational institution customers. This diversity in the type of DVD title that must

duction is selected and marketed to a broad segment of the market. The specific product or service offered can be only a piece of the DVD authoring and production process, such as translation services, 5.1 surround mixing, or just DVD authoring. The keys to success for a DVD authoring and production company using the specialist business model are to be the best at what you do, deliver a high-quality product on time, provide good customer service, and develop a captive client base who use only your services.

Over the past few years a number of companies using the specialist business model has increased. Many studios routinely farm out the tasks of menu creation, audio mixing and compression, and translation and subtitle graphic generation to small specialist companies. The advantage to the studios is a better quality product, and in some cases a lower price than from a DVD production company offering all the services required to develop a DVD title.

DVD authoring and production companies that employ the specialist business model do not need to buy high end DVD authoring tools. They can generally use a subset of the hardware and software required to develop a complete DVD title. Specialist companies should develop relationships with Horizontal DVD authoring companies who may be able to take advantage of their unique services on some of their projects.

Vertical Business Model

In the vertical business model all aspects of developing, manufacturing, and selling a DVD product are brought in-house, including content acquisition and creation, authoring, replication, and distribution. The keys to success for the vertical business model include bringing every aspect of the DVD production process in-house to minimize cost and maximize profit, maintaining access to a deep product catalog, and developing a consistent look and feel for all titles so that authoring templates can be used to reduce cost and time required for development.

The vertical business model is the most difficult method of developing DVD titles since it requires the most investment in authoring and replication hardware and software, and the largest staff in order to perform each of the required tasks. Many motion picture studios have adopted the vertical business model as it offers them the maximum amount of revenues and profits on each of the DVD titles they publish. Since a single company controls each step of the process, the vertical business model can offer the most cost effective and efficient method of developing DVD titles. This is a powerful argument in favor of this approach. The one major risk in using the Vertical business model is what happens when the catalog of titles available have already been released on DVD. If this happens DVD authoring and production companies that use a vertical business model may need to shift to one of the other models to find work from other sources.

DVD Authoring & Production Equipment

DVD authoring and production companies need a fair amount of equipment in order to offer professional products and services. As outlined in Chapter 10 there are wide variety of tools and equipment available for use in DVD authoring. Table 9.1 shows the approximate cost of each item of equipment or software required for a consumer, corporate or professional DVD authoring and production system. DVD authoring systems are available for Windows, Mac, and SGI platforms. In general I recommend that you only look at DVD authoring tools that work on the platform that you are already using in your organization. If you are a Mac shop you should only look at products from Sonic Solutions or Apple, while if you are an SGI shop you will want to look at Sonic's tools. Windows shops have the most choices with at least a half dozen excellent vendors for DVD authoring and production tools. There are two reasons I recommend that you restrict your search to only those products that work on the platform you normally use. First there are excellent DVD authoring tools available in a variety of price ranges for the Mac, Windows, and SGI platforms. Second you will want to connect your DVD authoring and production equipment to your internal network so that you can share data easily among your production systems. While it is possible to connect Mac, Windows, and SGI systems to the same network, it is much easier and more efficient to run the same operating system and maintain and upgrade your systems if all of your network workstations run the same operating system.

As you can see from Table 9.1 there are wide price ranges for professional, corporate and consumer DVD authoring and production systems. A large percentage of the cost of each of these systems is related to the video source equipment, computer workstation, and output devices that are common to all platforms. Typically only about 33 percent of the cost of a DVD authoring and production system is actually spent on the hardware and software items required to author a DVD title.

Table 9.1   DVD Authoring & Production System Costs

Item Description	Professional System Cost	Corporate System Cost	Consumer System Cost
Black Burst Generator	$500–$1,000	NA	NA
Digital Video Source	$10,000–$100,000	$20,000–$50,000	$500–$5,000
Analog Video Source	$5,000–$50,000	$5,000–$25,000	$200–$1,000

Table 9.1   DVD Authoring & Production System Costs

Item Description	Professional System Cost	Corporate System Cost	Consumer System Cost
MPEG-2 Encoder	$5,000–$50,000	$1,000–$20,000	$200–$1,000
AC3 Encoder	$1,000–$5,000	$500–$5,000	NA
DTS Encoder			
	$2,000–$10,000	$1,000–$5,000	$200–$500
Total Cost Range	$46,000–$254,500	$34,000–$127,500	$3,700–$13,000

DVD Authoring & Production Staff

Authoring and producing a DVD title can require many different staff members, as shown in Figure 9.2. A typical DVD authoring and production company may have video compressionist, audio compressionist, DVD author, graphic artist, producer, sales and marketing, and quality assurance staff members assigned to a specific DVD project. While each staff member can work on several projects at once, there are distinct skill sets involved in performing each function.

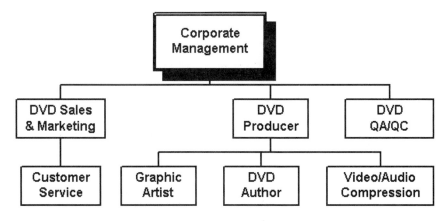

Figure 9.2   DVD Authoring & Production Staff Members

The functions performed by each of the staff members shown in Figure 9.2 are as follows.

The customer service staff member is the primary interface with the customer once the order has been received. The customer service representative coordinates receipt of all media assets, gets client approvals, schedules internal resources to complete a job, coordinates external resources required for a job, communicates with the customer on a regular basis, is involved in problem identification and resolution, and keeps the project schedule updated. This function can be combined with the sales and technical support functions in smaller organizations.

The DVD author operates the DVD authoring system to combine all the digital media assets to create the final DVD program desired by the client. A computer programming background is beneficial for development of sophisticated DVD titles, as well as familiarity with workstation computers, networks, and a variety of operating systems. It is very important that the DVD author attend training classes for the various software tools that will be used. The DVD author takes direction from the producer, will work with customer service and QA/QC representatives, but should have minimal direct contact with the client. This function can be combined with the video/audio compression function in smaller organizations.

The graphic artist designs and develops all graphics required for the project, including the background and overlay graphics for each menu, graphics for any still images or slide shows, and graphics for package art and disc label art. The graphic artist may also create graphics for associated WebDVD HTML pages. He or she must understand how graphics are displayed by DVD players; know the limitations of various TV displays, display resolutions, menu highlights, NTSC/PAL safe zones, and NTSC color-safe colors; and be comfortable with computer-based graphics programs to generate still images as well as animated graphics. The graphic artist takes direction from the producer, will work with customer service and QA/QC staff, and may need to work with client's graphics department to maintain the desired look and feel for the title.

The producer must have a working knowledge of the DVD-Video format, and is responsible for overall design of the DVD title. He or she takes the client's list of requirements and turns them into specific menus, media elements, and navigation flow for the DVD title; coordinates with the Graphic Artist to get menus and graphics completed; determines start and stop points for all video and audio content used on the title; and works closely with the client to ensure that the finished product is what they want. The producer is responsible for delivering a completed DVD title to the client on time, within budget, and within all the specifications.

The quality assurance staff member is responsible for ensuring that the final product meets all the client's requirements. He or she should be involved in every step of the DVD production process, including the review of incoming media elements, DVD-R check discs, compressed video and audio elements, navigation implementation, and menus. The quality assurance team member works with the producer, DVD author, graphic artist and video/audio compressionist to ensure a good product. In smaller organizations it is common for staff members to QA/QC their own work — this is not a good idea!

The sales and marketing staff member is responsible for selling and marketing all DVD services, and for setting prices for all services. He or she should work closely with the producer to determine the appropriate price for each service, set standard prices for typical services, and publish a rate card. Custom pricing should be generated for jobs that require extraordinary services, custom authoring, or quantity discounts. Sales and marketing should work closely with customer service to make sure that the client is informed and that jobs are being completed in a timely manner. In some organizations the same person handles customer service and sales functions.

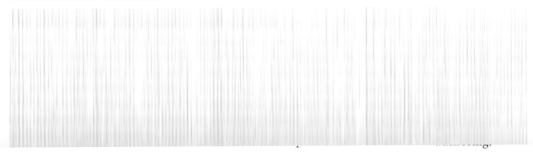

DVD Authoring & Production Pricing

If you are going to offer DVD authoring and production services to entertainment, corporate, government, or education clients, you will need to develop a standard rate card that you can give out to prospective customers. A rate card lists the standard services you provide for DVD title development as well as the price range for those services. It is customary in the DVD business to publish a rate card with prices that vary by both quantity and required delivery times. In general, prices go lower as quantity increases, and prices go higher as the required delivery time decreases.

Your rate card should include the following services. I have included typical price ranges for these services in the United States. These prices are based on my experience in working with DVD authoring service bureaus throughout the country. In general, prices tend to be higher in the Los Angeles and New York City markets, although many service bureaus in these markets must match prices from companies outside their geographical location in order to stay competitive.

- MPEG Video Compression
  - Constant Bit Rate Compression ($5–$10 per finished minute)
  - Variable Bit Rate Compression ($10–$15 per finished minute)
- Dolby Digital (AC3) Audio Compression
  - Stereo (2.0) Format ($5–$10 per finished minute)
  - Surround (5.1) Format ($10–$20 per finished minute)
- DTS Audio Compression ($10–$20 per finished minute)
- DVD Authoring
  - Simple Title ($1,000–$2,000 per title)

- Moderate Title ($2,000–$4,000 per title)
- Complex Title ($4,000–$8,000 per title)
- Ala Carte ($100–$200 per hour)
- DVD Consulting Services ($100–$200 per hour)
- Subtitle Graphics Generation
  - European Languages ($5–$10 per minute of subtitles)
  - Asian Languages ($10–$15 per minute of subtitles)
- Menu Design
  - Static Menus ($50–$100 per hour)
  - Motion Menus ($500–$2,000 per menu)
- DVD Packaging and Label Art Design ($50–$100 per hour)
- DVD-R Replication ($25–$50 per disc)
- DLT Tape Generation ($50–$100 per tape)
- DVD Check Disc Package ($1,000–$2,000)
- Short Run DVD Replication (i.e., less than 1,000 copies, $1.50–$5 per disc)
- Long Run DVD Replication (i.e., more than 1,000 copies, $1.00–$3.00 per disc)

In addition to a rate card you will need to have published prices for several different standard DVD development efforts, and a description of what services are provided at that price. Some typical package deals on DVD-Video titles include the following.

Simple DVD-Video Title Package ($2,000–$5,000)   This package includes up to 90 minutes of CBR MPEG-2 video, 90 minutes of Dolby Digital 2.0 audio, static menus (main menu, chapter menu, and credits menu), a single layer, single side disc (DVD-5) layout, one DVD-R check disc, and a DLT for replication. The client provides the video and audio masters, and gives guidance on menu design.

Moderate DVD-Video Title Package ($5,000–$10,000)   This package includes up to 120 minutes of VBR MPEG-2 video, up to 120 minutes of Dolby Digital 5.1 audio, up to 120 minutes of Dolby Digital 2.0 audio, a dynamic main menu and static secondary menus (chapter menu, audio menu, subtitle, menu, and credits menu) up to 120 of minutes English subtitles, a single layer, single side disc (DVD-5) layout, one DVD-R check disc and a DLT for replication. The client provides the video and audio masters, and gives guidance on menu design.

Complex DVD-Video Title Package ($10,000–$15,000)   This package includes up to 200 minutes of VBR MPEG-2 video including multiple angle or multiple story-line content, up to 120 minutes of Dolby Digital 5.1 audio, up to 240 minutes of Dolby Digital 2.0 audio, dynamic menus (main menu, chapter menu, audio menu, subtitle menu, credits menu), up to 200 minutes of subtitles in two languages, a dual layer, single side disc (DVD-9) layout, a replicated DVD check disc, and a DLT for replication. The client provides video and audio masters, and gives guidance on menu design.

In addition to a standard rate card and package prices for DVD title development you will often have to provide custom proposals for potential clients if their requirements do not fit into the standard pricing categories you have prepared. Having a rate card and package pricing will get you in the door to see many prospective clients, but you will need to prepare custom proposals and offer them discounts over your "published" prices to win their projects. The DVD authoring and production services business is quite competitive, so be prepared to match other offers that your prospective client may receive.

Over the past several years industry-wide prices for DVD authoring services have

Alpha DVD Business Model

From 1990 to 1996 my company (NB Engineering) was a leading provider of off-line digital video compression services, and we developed custom multimedia CD-ROM titles for corporate, government, and educational clients. We opened the first digital video compression service bureau in the United States back in 1990 offering Intel Digital Video Interactive video compression using a $500,000 supercomputer and professional video equipment. Over a six-year period we upgraded our equipment and software to support new digital video compression codecs as they became popular. Over time our services gradually changed from Intel DVI compression, to Cinepak and Indeo compression, to MPEG-1 compression, and finally to MPEG-2 compression. Each time a new video compression codec came on the market we upgraded our equipment and software to accommodate the new technology. While we made enough money to pay for the required video compression equipment and software, and to pay our staff, we were never able to make a significant profit as a service bureau during this period of time.

During 1994 and 1995 we worked closely with Toshiba as they developed their new MMCD format, and saw it become an integral part of the DVD-Video specification that was released in 1996. Our extensive background in digital video compression and the development of high-end multimedia CD-ROM titles made us uniquely qualified to become an early adopter of DVD-Video technology. We formed a partnership with a video post-production facility in Los Angeles called The Post Group, and together we spent more than $500,000 and several man-years of effort becoming one of the first facilities to actually author a DVD-Video title. Unfortunately we were a bit ahead of the curve and even though we had the ability to develop high-end DVD titles, there were few clients who wanted to actually pay for DVD development services at that time.

From 1996 through 1998 my company completed over 100 DVD projects for a diverse set of entertainment, corporate, government, and education clients. After three years of work we made enough money to pay for the equipment and software needed to develop high-end DVD titles, and to pay the salaries of the staff required to develop DVD titles. Even though we had an excellent reputation in the DVD industry, provided quality products and services at reasonable prices, and delivered excellent customer support, we struggled to make a profit on our DVD business. As DVD became more popular we had to compete with companies that offered essentially the same products and services we did. Since most of these companies had waited for the DVD market to mature, they were able to purchase their DVD authoring equipment and software at a fraction of the cost we paid just a few years earlier, and thus it was easy for them to offer lower prices for DVD services than we could.

In early 1998 NB Engineering was closed due to a merger between our parent company and an Internet services company. The newly merged companies were going to concentrate on the new and exciting field of Internet advertising, so management decided to close all divisions that did not offer products and services directly related to the Internet. This was a difficult time as I was forced to lay-off about 20 full-time staff members, many of whom had worked for me for the past 10 years. I also had to sell off all the video compression and DVD authoring equipment we had accumulated, and tell our client base that they would have to find a new partner to fill their DVD authoring and production requirements.

So after 12 years of running my own company, and being responsible for the success of up to 30 friends and co-workers, I found myself without a job. As an expert in video compression and DVD title development I had several offers for new positions within the DVD authoring and production business. However my recent experience in having to lay off all my staff had left a bad taste in my mouth. I decided to take a few months off and figure out what I really wanted to do before jumping back into a full time job. Looking back I realized that over the past 12 years I had started and grown a company that was able to keep pace with the rapidly changing technology of digital video compression, and experience the launch of an entirely new home entertainment format, DVD-Video. Despite being a leader in these technologies, and winning our share of business, NB Engineering was unable to make consistent profits offering video compression or DVD authoring and production services to other companies. While I wanted to continue to work in the field of DVD authoring and production, I realized that I needed to make a fundamental change in the way I approached the business. Either I had such poor management skills that I was incapable of running a profitable company, or there was a basic flaw with DVD authoring and production service bureaus that prevented them from ever achieving profitability. The constant cycle of adopting new technologies every two or three years, and then competing with companies who would wait a year or two and acquire the same equipment and software for less than half the cost, seemed to me to be a losing proposition.

So in May of 1998 I came up with a new business model for DVD authoring, and I started a new company called Alpha DVD that is based on this model. I don't have a name for this model, but it has a few guiding principals that I would like to share with you. The proof of any business model is always in the results, and I am happy to say that over the past three years Alpha DVD has made a profit every year, and each of the DVD projects we have worked on continue to generate revenues long after the project has been completed. Here are the guiding principles for the business model I use at Alpha DVD.

1. Get Paid in Royalties The first and most important principal is to own a small piece of every DVD title I work on. In the long run getting paid a royalty from every disc sold generates far more revenues than charging a fixed price for providing authoring services. I typically get a royalty between ten and 40 percent of the gross wholesale price of my DVD titles. I get a larger royalty on titles for which I create and produce the content, such as *StarGaze*, and smaller royalties on titles for which I simply provide the required DVD authoring services.

2. Quality & Quantity This principal is key to the success of my business model. Every title that gets released has to include the highest quality media elements possible. The flip side of this principal is that I need to release as many titles as possible. It is impossible to determine which DVD titles are going to be marginal and which are will be popular with consumers, so to insure success it is a good idea to put out as many titles as possible.

4. Include Advanced Features I am not sure if this principal is essential, but in the long run I think it makes sense to author and produce DVD titles that take advantage of as many DVD-Video features as possible. Thus all my titles include some, if not all, of the advanced DVD-Video feature set. My experience over the past three years has shown that consumers prefer to buy titles that have advanced features. The law of diminishing returns does apply to this principal, so you want to balance the use of advanced features against the cost of producing them. In general I like to include advanced DVD-Video features such as multiple audio tracks, subtitles, and multiple language menus first. If there is enough development budget left over, I will consider adding DVD-ROM and WebDVD features as well.

5. Break Even in Less than Twelve Months This last principal is key to actually making a profit on my titles. Most DVD titles have a sales life of two to three years so if I only release titles that break even in a year or less I cant help but make money in the long run.

Even though this business model sounds simple, and is actually fairly easy to set up and run, there are some requirements of which you need to be aware. Before you embark on a similar business model you will need to have enough working capital to last at least six months, you will need to either purchase or lease all the DVD authoring hardware and software required to develop the kinds of titles you might publish, and you need to locate a DVD distributor who will license your titles and get them into the retail channel. Let's talk about each of these requirements in more detail.

Working Capital A typical DVD-Video title takes about three months to go from the concept stage to completed DLT. Some projects can be done faster and others will take longer, but I have found 3 months to be about what it takes from the day I acquire new content to the day I can send a DLT out for replication. You may be able to complete projects in less time, but if you license content from someone else they will generally have the right to approve the final DVD disc image before replication. Having another company involved in any aspect of the DVD design and production process will slow things down. Unless you are lucky and can negotiate an advance with a distributor, you won't have any cash flow while you are developing your first DVD title. To make matters worse most distributors negotiate payment terms for your royalty so that it will be 60–90 days after the title is available to consumers before you receive your first royalty check. Thus having at least six months of working capital available when you start your first title is essential.

DVD Authoring System   While it may seem obvious that you will need a DVD authoring system to actually develop your first DVD title, I know several people who have tried to follow this business model without having the required hardware and software. If you don't have a DVD authoring system at your disposal you will either have to have the title developed by someone else (which violates my third principal) or you simply will never release your first title. It is not necessary to spend $100,000 or more to buy a professional authoring system before you start your first title. In fact I recommend against that course of action as it is far too risky for most people. If you want to become a DVD developer following my business model I suggest you purchase (or lease) a Mac G4 system with DVD Studio Pro and the Apple Super Drive, or a Compaq Presario 7000 system with the same Pioneer DVD-R drive and Sonic ReelDVD. Both of these systems can be connected to high-end DV cameras and will allow you to generate professional looking DVD titles, for less than $5,000 in capital expenditures.

DVD Distributor   Unless you are already involved in distributing and selling DVD titles to consumers you will be totally unprepared for the arcane way DVD titles are sold to the public. Many large retailers purchase DVD titles from only one or two distributors, who in turn purchase product from the studios and other distributors. In my opinion it is best to turn over the sales, marketing, advertising, and distribution of your titles to someone who does that for a living. There are a number of good DVD distributors who are always looking for new titles to license. Finding a distributor who will get your titles into the retail channel, pay you on time, and help you locate content for future titles is an essential component to using my business model.

Does this business model really work? If you stop and think about it you will see that this is essentially the same business model that is used by the major motion picture studios as well as several large DVD distribution companies. Each of these companies makes money by getting a royalty when someone buys a copy of any of their titles. I have simply adapted the Hollywood business model to work on a much smaller scale, and I can assure you that it works quite well for my company. By the time this book goes to print I will have over 30 DVD titles from which I receive royalties. My royalties vary from $0.50–$5.00 per disc, and I get royalty checks every month based on the number of units sold to the retail channel. During 2001 I will release approximately 25 new DVD titles, and by the end of 2002 I should have a total of 75 DVD titles from which I receive royalties. None of these titles will generate vast amounts of royalties, but when you add them all up it works out to be a good business. In addition to the financial benefits of this business model I have found it quite rewarding to go into Best Buy, Virgin Records, or Tower Records and see my titles on the shelves.

I am sure that the business model I use is not right for everyone. It requires a fair amount of working capital, access to DVD tools, the ability and knowledge to use those tools to produce quality DVD titles, a working relationship with an established DVD distributor, and a lot of hard work and perseverance. In my opinion the financial rewards from a royalty-based DVD business far outweigh the risks. Developing DVD titles in my basement is the most fun I have had at work in over 20 years, and I would recommend this approach to any DVD developer who has the skills and desire to make it work.

DVD PRODUCTION SERVICES & TOOLS

This chapter provides a brief summary of production services and tools that are available to help you complete a DVD project. While I have used many of the tools and services listed here, I am not recommending one specific tool or service provider over another. Every DVD production tool or service has its own unique strengths and weaknesses so it is impossible to recommend a single product or service that is right for everyone.

Audio Encoding Tools

This section covers products to encode audio into one or more of the formats supported by the DVD-Video specification. Audio formats that can be used in DVD-Video titles include Linear PCM, Dolby Digital, DTS, MPEG and SDDS. Each vendor that offers audio encoding tools is listed, along with the specific audio encoding products that they offer.

Digital Vision

Digital Vision's BitPack Multichannel Audio Encoding Workstation is designed for DVD premastering and other applications such as audio archiving. It provides a complete audio solution supporting Dolby Digital, MPEG and PCM formats. Encoding can be done from multichannel audio tape recorders or from digital files. Integrated machine control allows automatic frame accurate encoding and playback. A Windows user interface enables project management including project information exchange with BitPack Video Workstations to speed up operation. The workstation is based on a rack mounted Windows NT, Pentium III PC with a 9 pin RS-232 machine control interface for deck control. For more information contact:

Digital Vision (US) Inc
11835 West Olympic Blvd, Suite 1275
Los Angeles, CA 90064
(310) 914-5200 (Voice)
(310) 914-0011 (Fax)
sales@digitalvisionusa.com (E-Mail)
http://www.digitalvision.se (Web)

Dolby Labs

The Dolby Labs DP569 is the industry standard for Dolby Digital multichannel audio encoding systems. It supports encoded bit rates from 56 to 640 kbps and channel configurations from mono to 5.1-channel surround sound. The DP569 was designed for digital TV, cable, and disc authoring applications, including automated broadcast installations and mastering for DVD and other recorded media. The DP569 provides three pairs of AES-3 digital audio inputs and a single AES-3 output. A separate AES-3 input may be used for a clock reference signal. The suggested retail price of the DP569 is $5,000. For more information contact:

Dolby Laboratories
100 Potrero Avenue
San Francisco, CA 94103-4813
(415) 558-0200 (Voice)
(415) 863-1373 (Fax)
info@dolby.com (E-Mail)
http://www.dolby.com (Web)

Kind of Loud Technologies

Kind of Loud Technologies has two audio encoding tools that can be used for DVD production. Their SmartCode Pro products work with DigiDesign ProTools systems to provide software encoding of surround sound audio. SmartCode Pro is available in two versions to accommodate the two most widely used surround formats: Dolby Digital™ and DTS™. Both versions of SmartCode Pro are AudioSuite software programs that allow Pro Tools users to preview their 5.1 surround mixes in real time 5.1, then encode and decode the mix to create a 6-channel surround master. Both SmartCode Pro tools only work on Macintosh computers with Pro Tools LE or TDM version 5.0 or higher software. SmartCode Pro Dolby has a suggested retail price of $795, while Smart Code Pro DTS has an SRP of $1,495. For more information contact:

Kind of Loud Technologies, LLC
2125 Delaware Avenue, Suite A

Santa Cruz, CA, 95060
(831) 466-3737 (Voice)
(831) 466-3775 (Fax)
info@kindofloud.com (E-Mail)
http://www.kindofloud.com (Web)

Microboards

- Fully customizable Surround Mixers
- Automatic 5.1 bussing
- Fully automated Surround Panning for every channel
- Midi time code generation
- Automatic 6 track master creation to hard disk
- User adjusted Surround Sound Panning Algorithm
- True Center / Virtual Center Blend Control
- Per Channel Subbass Crossover with user defined parameter

- Author: The MASS 5.1 authoring software can be used to premaster and create DVD Audio Discs using DVD R media.

  - Creates DVD Audio compliant discs from your `Audio_TS` directories or from an image file
  - Records DVD ROMS using UDF structures
  - Masters to DLT tape using the DCA 2.0 specification,
  - Verifies audio data ensuring accurate disc geometry
  - Creates global, images for replication
  - Supports Windows 95 / 98 / NT / 2000
  - Includes `Audio_TS` directories for testing

- Record: The M.A.S.S. 5.1 system can use a Pioneer S201 DVD R Recorder to burn professional DVD R discs.

  - Features - 4.7 Gb Capacity SCSI II interface, Half Height, external desktop configuration
  - Disc at Once or Incremental recording, DVD R media compatible with all DVD playback devices

The M.A.S.S 5.1 system has a suggested retail price of $8,995, including the Pioneer DVR-S201 drive. For more information contact:

Jim Speich
Microboards Technology, LLC
Western Regional Sales Manager
ProVideo Group
(952) 556-1636 (Voice)
(952) 556-1620 (Fax)
jims@microboards.com (E-Mail)
http://www.microboards.com (Web)

Minnetonka Audio

Minnetonka Audio has two audio encoding products that can be used in DVD production. SurCode for Dolby Digital encodes 5.1 Surround Sound or stereo files into Dolby Digital (.ac3) files. The tool accepts up to 6 .wav or .AIFF input files, provides stereo mix down for auditioning Surround sound files prior to encoding, and supports all Dolby encoding options. SurCode for DTS encodes 5.1 Surround Sound or stereo files into DTS (.dts or .cpt) files. The tool accepts 6 .wav or .AIFF input files, provides stereo mix down for auditioning surround sound files prior to encoding, and supports all DTS encoding options. Both SurCode for Dolby Digital and SurCode for DTS are software encoders that run on Windows systems. SurCode for Dolby Digital has a suggested retail price of $995 for a full 5.1 channel version, and $599 for a stereo version. SurCode for DTS has a suggested retail price of $1,995. For more information contact:

Minnetonka Audio Software
17113 Minnetonka Blvd. Suite 300
Minnetonka, MN 55345
(952) 449-6481 (Voice)
(952) 449-0318 (Fax)
info@minnetonkaaudio.com (E-Mail)
http://www.minnetonkaaudio.com (Web)

Sonic Solutions

SonicStudio HD is an advanced audio editing and CD premastering system that supports CD, DVD-Audio, audio for DVD-Video, and EMD mastering. SonicStudio HD systems offer up to eight channels of 24-bit 96kHz audio, or four channels of 24-bit 192 kHz audio, and supports both DVD-Audio and Audio for DVD-Video publishing with Sonic OneClick DVD or Sonic's advanced DVD-Audio authoring technology. SonicStudio HD requires a Power Macintosh G3, G4, or dual-processor G4 system, with Mac OS 9.04 operating system software. SonicStudio HD requires a minimum of 128Mb of internal CPU memory with 256 MB or more preferred. For the Sonic DVD-Audio Workstation (HD-2100) and Sonic DVD AV Workstation (HD-2200), a minimum of 256 Mb RAM is required, with 384 Mb recommended. For more information contact:

Sonic Solutions
101 Rowland Way
Novato, CA 94945
415-893-8000 (Voice)
415-893-8008 (Fax)
info@sonic.com (E-Mail)
http://www.sonic.com (Web)

San Jose, CA 95129
(888) 355-MPEG (Voice)
info@spruce-tech.com (E-Mail)
http://www.spruce-tech.com (Web)

Zapex

Zapex's has two audio encoding products that can be used in DVD production. The ZP-100 (2 channel) and the ZP-100 (5.1 channel) Dolby Digital audio encoders are full sized PCI boards providing real-time capture and encoding for DVD and HDTV applications. Both ZP-100 cards provide frame accurate deck control and start/stop control. An integrated "Playback Tool" provides a sound peak wave display, region save and bitstream analysis for Dolby Digital (AC-3), MPEG Audio Layer2, and Linear PCM streams. For more information contact:

Zapex Technologies, Inc.
2432 Charleston Road
Mountain View, CA 94043
(650) 930-1300 (Voice)
(650) 930-1399 (Fax)
info@zapex.com (E-Mail)
http://www.zapex.com (Web)

DVD Authoring Services

There are hundreds, if not thousands, of companies who provide DVD production and authoring services. Most of these companies are DVD authoring service bureaus, who provide a complete line of services designed to create finished DVD titles ready for production.

This section provides basic information on approximately 100 companies that offer DVD production services, along with contact information you will need to learn more about them.

Abbey Road Interactive

Abbey Road Interactive is a full service DVD production facility dedicated to the new media needs of the entertainment industry — from DVD to enhanced CD and web. Abbey Road Interactive offers services in each step of the DVD production process, from interactive and graphic design, encoding, and DVD authoring. Working in conjunction with Abbey Road Studios they also offer audio restoration, surround sound remixing and faux surround production. Abbey Road Interactive accepts all popular video and audio formats, although they prefer to work from Digital Beta source. DVD authoring equipment includes Scenarist SGI, Scenarist NT 2.5, Sonic DVD Creator, and Spruce DVD Maestro systems. Abbey Road Interactive has completed more than 200 DVD projects to date. For more information contact:

> Abbey Road Interactive
> 3 Abbey Road
> ST Johns Wood, London, NW8 9AY
> United Kingdom
> +44 (0) 20 7266 7282 (Voice)
> +44 (0) 20 7266 7321 (Fax)
> interactive@abbeyroad.co.uk (E-Mail)
> http://www.abbeyroad.co.uk (Web)

Alpha DVD

Alpha DVD is a full service DVD production facility specializing in the development of consumer DVD-Video, DVD-ROM and WebDVD titles. Alpha DVD generally works on projects where they receive a royalty on sales of the DVD title to the public. Input video and audio formats supported include Digital Beta, BetaSP, DA88, QuickTime and AVI. DVD authoring equipment includes Spruce MPX3000 video encoder, and Sonic Scenarist NT systems. Alpha DVD has completed more than 200 DVD-Video, DVD-ROM and WebDVD projects to date. For more information contact:

> Alpha DVD
> 3109 Arrowhead Farms Road
> Gambrills, MD 21054
> (410) 721-9460 (Voice)
> (410) 721-9461 (Fax)
> rlabarge@alphadvd.com (E-Mail)
> http://www.alphadvd.com (Web)

Aludra

Aludra is a full service DVD authoring company providing DVD based solutions to address various business opportunities such as creating Training Programs, Product Catalogues, Sales

Presentations, Kiosks, Video Documentaries and Films. Aludra also possess expertise in CD Duplication and Replication thereby providing various Digital Solutions under one roof. Input video and audio formats supported include DV, Mini DV, DAT, CD, DVD, Umatic, VHS, SVHS, 1 Inch, BetaSP, and Digital Beta. DVD authoring equipment includes Pinnacle MiroDC 1000 and Avid Express systems. Aludra has completed more than 10 DVD projects to date. For more information contact:

Aludra Inc.
1 Woodborough Avenue

Angel DVD Scandinavia is a full service DVD production facility owned by Angel Facility House, a division of Angel Films. The company was formed spring 1999 to provide a one-stop DVD solution for distributors and film production companies. Input video and audio formats supported include Digital Beta, BetaSP, DVCam, DA88, DAT, OMF, WAV and QuickTime. Both PAL and NTSC video formats are supported. DVD Authoring equipment includes Sonic DVDCreator, and Spruce DVDMaestro systems. Angel DVD Scandinavia has completed more than 200 DVD projects to date. For more information contact:

Angel DVD Scandinavia
Rentemestervej 2
2400 Copenhagen NV
Denmark
+45 3581 4777 (Voice)
+45 3581 4778 (Fax)
INFO@DVDSCANDINAVIA.COM (E-Mail)
http://www.DVDSCANDINAVIA.COM (Web)

Animation Dynamics, Inc.

Animation Dynamics is a full service DVD production facility providing consultation, menu design and production, DVD Video, Hybrid DVD, DVD-ROM, MPEG 1, and MPEG 2 encoding services. Input video and audio formats supported include Digital Beta, Beta SP, and DV. DVD authoring equipment includes Astarte DVD Director, Media Press video encoding and DPS reality encoding systems. Animation Dynamics has completed more than 40 DVD projects to date. For more information contact:

Animation Dynamics, Inc.
1720 NW Lovejoy St,

Suite 120
Portland, OR 97209
(503) 227-5914 (Voice)
(503) 227-5956 (Fax)
kate@flypixels.com (E-Mail)
http://www.flypixels.com (Web)

asv multimedia

asv multimedia is a German company that specializes in high quality MPEG encoding and DVD authoring. All input video and audio formats are supported. DVD authoring equipment includes Astarte DVD Director and Apple DVD Studio Pro. asv multimedia has completed numerous DVD-Video, DVD-ROM, Mini-DVD and SVCD projects to date. For more information contact:

asv multimedia
Goethestr.24
88512 Mengen
Germany
049 7572 78361 (Voice)
asvid@gmx.de (E-Mail)

BCD Associates

BCD is full service DVD production facility offering MPEG-2 video encoding, AC-3 audio encoding, program design, graphics design, animation design, authoring, premastering, and short-run duplication services. Input video and audio formats supported include BetaSP, DV, Laserdisc, VHS, and AVI files. DVD authoring equipment includes MTC DVDMotion R7 systems. BCD Associates has completed more than 20 DVD projects to date. For more information contact:

BCD Associates, Inc.
128 N.W. 67th Street
Oklahoma City, OK 73116
(405) 843-4574 (Voice)
(405) 840-3147 (Fax)
bob@bcdusa.com (E-Mail)
http://www.bcdusa.com (Web)

Beretta Designs

Beretta Designs specializes in the design and development of static and motion menus for DVD titles. Menus are developed using Macintosh computers running Aftereffects, Photoshop, and Illustrator. Input video and audio formats supported include Digital Beta, BetaSP,

QuickTime, AVI, Wave, and AIFF. Beretta Designs does not provide any DVD authoring services, so they don't have any in-house DVD authoring equipment. Beretta Designs has developed menus for over 50 DVD projects to date. For more information contact:

Beretta Designs
1810 West 16th Avenue
Vancouver, BC V6J 2M2
Canada
(604) 729-7394 (Voice)

mastering for compact disc and DVD and audio restoration. Blue City Digital specializes in serving independent producers and extending the capabilities of video post facilities and recording studios. Input video and audio formats supported include Digital Beta, BetaSP, DVCam, DAT, and DA-88. DVD authoring equipment includes Sonic Solutions Creator with SonicStudioHD. Blue City Digital has completed more than 20 DVD projects to date, primarily in the kiosk and trade show markets. For more information contact:

Blue City Digital
1900 Swift, Suite 209C
North Kansas City, MO 64116
(816) 300-0441 (Voice)
dvd@rbw.net (E-Mail)
http://www.rbw.net (Web)

BroadcastDVD

BroadcastDVD is a leading developer of web connected DVD titles. Founders James Volk and Scott Epstein began producing original content for DVD in 1997 with the SHORT cinema journal series. They were among the first to use multiple angles, motion menus, web enhancements and 360-degree video in DVD titles. In 1998 with the formation of BroadcastDVD, they branched out into Corporate DVD title development. BroadcastDVD is a full service DVD production facility offering concept development, production, post-production, menu design, authoring and encoding services. Input video and audio formats supported include Digital Beta, BetaSP, Mini DV, and DA88. DVD authoring equipment includes Sonic DVD-Creator systems. BroadcastDVD has completed more than 50 DVD-Video and WebDVD projects to date. For more information contact:

BroadcastDVD
5700 Wilshire Blvd., #203
Los Angeles, CA 90036
(323) 302-0010 (Voice)
(323) 302-0020 (Fax)
scott@broadcastdvd.com (E-Mail)
http://www.broadcastdvd.com (Web)

California DVD

California DVD is a full service DVD Authoring and Post Production facility offering uncompressed Non-Linear Video Editing, Motion Graphics Design, 5.1 Surround Sound Mixing/Mastering, DVD Authoring and Encoding to Corporate, Government, Educational, and Entertainment sectors. Input video and audio formats supported include Digital Beta, Beta-SP, DVCPRO, DVCam, MiniDV, S-VHS, Hi-8, QuickTime, AVI, DA-88, DAT, .WAV, and .AIFF. DVD authoring equipment includes Spruce DVD Maestro, Spruce MPX3000 video encoder and Dolby Digital ACX5100 audio encoder systems. California DVD has completed over 150 DVD projects to date. For more information contact:

California DVD
221 11th Street
San Francisco, CA 94103
(800) 864-1957 (Voice)
(415)-621-3733 (Fax)
makedvds@caldvd.com (E-Mail)
http://www.caldvd.com (Web)

Cine-Magnetics

Cine-Magnetics provides complete DVD authoring & compression services, In house art & graphics development, Video on Demand (VOD), Video Streaming Services, DVD replication, DVD custom packaging & distribution services, inbound 800# order capturing and e-commerce integration. Input video and audio formats supported include Beta SP, Beta SX, Digital Beta, D-2, DA-88, and DAT. DVD authoring equipment includes Sonic Solutions DVD "3100" Creator Workstations, Digital Vision DVNR 500, Minerva Compressionist, Media 100 suite, BTS MNR-10 noise reduction unit, and Pioneer DVD-R writers. DVD and MPEG compliance testing is performed using MProbe and DVD Surveyor. Cine-Magnetics has completed approximately 100 theatrical, educational, corporate, and special interest DVD titles to date. For more information contact:

Cine Magnetics Video & Digital Laboratories
100 Business Park Drive
Armonk, NY 10504
(800) 431-1102 (Voice)
(914) 273-7575 (Fax)

cminfo@cinemagnetics.com (E-Mail)
www.cinemagnetics.com (Web)

Cinram POP DVD Center

Cinram/POP DVD Center is a full service compression, authoring, design and post-production facility located in Santa Monica, California. Services include DVD design, premastering, video and audio encoding, static and dynamic menu design, formatting, layout and testing. Input video and audio formats supported include D1, Digital Betacam, and Betacam SP

(310) 899-7250 (Fax)
info@dvdinfo.com (E-Mail)
http://www.dvdinfo.com (Web)

ComChoice

ComChoice offers several DVD authoring services including *BizChoice DVD*, a business card sized DVD with storage capability of 280 Mbytes that utilizes the full spectrum of DVD capabilities, and *ShowChoice DVD*, a full size DVD featuring auto-looping which allows content to play continuously for trade shows, demonstrations, presentations, etc. Video and audio input formats supported include PAL, NTSC, Dolby AC 35.1, Stereo, Digital Beta, and Beta SP. DVD authoring equipment includes Sonic Solutions and Toshiba systems. ComChoice has completed over 200 DVD projects to date. For more information contact:

ComChoice Corporation
1025 W. 190Th ST., Suite 200
Gardena, CA 90248
(310) 630-1360 (Voice)
(310) 630-1365 (Fax)
CHOICES@COMCHOICE.COM (E-Mail)
HTTP://WWW.COMCHOICE.COM (Web)

COTOC AB

COTOC AB provides DVD authoring, video compression, editing, compositing, 3D, VFx, and graphics services. All Digital formats and BetaSP video formats are supported. DVD authoring equipment includes Sonic Solutions DVDCreator systems. COTOC AB has completed over 20 DVD projects to date. For more information please contact:

COTOC AB
Sodra Hamnvagen 22
Stockholm 115 41
SWEDEN
+46 8 54568780 (Voice)
+46 8 54568781 (Fax)
herman@cotoc.se (E-Mail)
http://www.cotoc.com (Web)

Crush Digital

Crush Digital is a full service DVD Authoring facility providing a complete range of DVD services for DVD-Video, DVD-Audio and Corporate DVD solutions. Services include video and audio compression in MPEG-2 and streaming formats, surround sound 5.1 mixing, static and dynamic menu design, interactive ROM design and programming, project management and consulting, and authoring and premastering for both DVD-Video and DVD-Audio formats. All major Video and Audio formats are accepted. DVD authoring equipment includes Scenarist NT 2.0, Sonic DVD-Creator, Sonic HD Audio, Panasonic DVD-Audio System, Sony Encoder (DVA-V1100), Minerva Encoder, Dolby Digital and Meridian Audio Compression systems. Crush Digital Video has completed over 750 DVD projects to date. For more information contact:

Crush Digital
147 West 25th Street
New York, NY 10001
(212) 989-6500 (Voice)
(212) 645-9093 (Fax)
info@crushdigital.com (E-Mail)
http://www.crushdigital.com (Web)

CruSh Interactive

CruSh Interactive provides turnkey DVD authoring services catering to the corporate market. Additional services include video editing, MPEG encoding, animation, broadcast graphics and menu design. Input video and audio formats supported include Digital Beta, BetaSP, DVCam, DV, and S-Video. DVD authoring equipment includes a Sonic DVD Creator v2.1.2 system with 16×9 and Dolby 5.1 Support. CruSh Interactive has completed over 100 DVD projects to date. For more information contact:

CruSh Interactive, Inc.
2400 Augusta, Suite 340
Houston, TX 77057
713-972-1133 (Voice)
713-972-1588 (Fax)
info@crushinteractive.com (E-Mail)
http://www.crushdvd.com (Web)

Cubist Post & Effects

Cubist Post & Effects is a Philadelphia-based digital project studio offering a full range of DVD services including: title planning, encoding, authoring, pre-mastering, static and motion menu design. They have developed web-enabled DVD-Video titles, custom DVD-ROM applications and multimedia kiosks. Cubist has developed DVDconnect™, a web-enabled DVD interface. Cubist Post & Effects is focused on creating highly interactive DVD solutions for the corporate, museum, advertising, and educational markets. Input video and audio formats supported include Digital Beta, BetaSP, DA88, DVCAM, DVCPRO, and Mini DV. DVD

http://www.cubistpost.com (Web)
http://www.DVDconnect.net (Web)

CVC, A Time Warner Entertainment Company

CVC, a corporate cousin of Warner Bros., offers digital video compression and authoring services for DVD, Video On Demand, and Streaming Media for the Internet. The facility acts as the digital video distribution center for clients such as Warner Home Video, Fox Home Video International, MGM Home Video, The WB Television Network, and Time Warner Cable. Notable DVD titles produced by CVC include The Matrix, Casablanca, Gone With The Wind, Titanic, The Green Mile, Unforgiven, and The Perfect Storm. Input video and audio formats supported include DCT, Digital Beta, Beta SP, D-1, DA88, DAT, DVD-RAM, DVD-R, CD-R, Jazz and Zip. DVD authoring equipment includes encoding and authoring systems co-developed by CVC and Toshiba Corporation. Similar systems are used by CVC's authoring affiliate companies, which include ComChoice Corporation (Gardena, CA), Mercury Entertainment (Singapore), Videolar (Brazil), and Planet Optical Disc (Dubai, UAE). CVC has completed over 2,500 DVD projects to date. For more information contact:

CVC, A Time Warner Entertainment Company
5432 W. 102nd Street
Los Angeles, CA 90045
(818) 972-0200 (Voice)
(818) 972-0212 (Fax)
dvdsales@calvid.com (E-Mail)
http://www.cvcdigital.com (Web)

Designlab Systems

Designlab Systems provide video graphics development and video compression products and services for the broadcast, blue chip corporate, communications, and professional multimedia markets, and also the emerging convergence of the Internet & Television. Services include video compression and authoring for DVD, VideoCD, and CD/DVD-ROM, manufacturers of streaming video for the Internet, and broadband hosting for private/secure VOD in interactive MPEG-4 format. Video and audio input formats supported include Digital Betacam and Betacam SP, with other options arranged as required. DVD authoring tools includes Spruce DVD-Maestro systems. Designlab Systems has completed over 20 Feature Film DVD-Video projects for major Hollywood studio clients, and over 50 Corporate DVD projects to date. For more information contact:

Designlab Systems Limited
9 D'Arblay Street, Soho
London W1F 8DR
England
+44 20 7437 5621 (Voice)
+44 20 7734 1582 (Fax)
hilary@medialab.demon.co.uk (E-Mail)
www.designlab.co.uk (Web)

DGP

DGP is a full service DVD authoring facility. Their services include; an experienced & creative interactive design team for stunning moving menus, Avid uncompressed editing, Discreet graphics (Flint & Smoke), 3D & animation, VBR MPEG2 encoding for maximum quality compression, Dolby digital 5.1 surround sound, DVD-audio, Multi camera angle options, web links & DVD-ROM content including games, mastering & replication, full proofing, QC and verification services. Input video and audio formats supported include Digital Beta, BetaSP and DA88. DVD Authoring equipment includes Sonic Solutions DVD Creator systems. DGP has completed over 100 DVD-Video, DVD-ROM and WebDVD projects to date. For more information contact:

DGP
Portland House, 12-13 Greek Street
London, W1D 4DL
United Kingdom
(0) 20 7734 4501 (Voice)
(0) 20 7734 7034 (Fax)
mail@dgpsoho.co.uk (E-Mail)
http://www.dgpsoho.co.uk (Web)

Digidisc

Digidisc offers a variety of DVD authoring and MPEG compression services. Additional services include DVD replication for DVD-5, DVD-9, and DVD-10. Conversion of "General" DVD's from DVD Studio Pro or DVDit!, to "Authoring" format for replication. They also offer high quality MPEG-1 encoding for VCD, Internet, CD-i, SVCD, and Macromedia Director, DVD menu graphics design using Adobe Photoshop. Uncompressed video editing (Digital Beta on-line or Avid Symphony) services are also available. Digidisc has proprietary software to convert DVD content to streaming QuickTime, Windows Media, and Real Net-

Atlanta, GA., 30312
(770) 925-1839 (Voice)
(404) 584-5247 (Fax)
jbrooke@digi-disc.com (E-Mail)
www.digi-disc.com (Web)

Digital Farm

Digital Farm is a full service DVD production facility offering project consultation, title design/storyboarding, scripting/shooting (film or video), video editing/sound editing, 2D/3D animation and special effects, graphic/menu design (motion and static), video and audio encoding, authoring, formatting, output to DVD-R or DLT, and DVD replication management. Input video and audio formats supported include Digital Beta, BetaSP, QuickTime, AIFF, S-VHS and VHS. DVD authoring equipment includes Sonic DVDCreator and Apple DVD Studio Pro systems. Digital Farm has completed more than 100 DVD projects to date for clients such as Nickelodeon, HBO Family, Philip Morris, and Atom Films. For more information contact:

Digital Farm
3800 Aurora Ave. N., Suite 280
Seattle, WA 98103
(206) 634-2677 (Voice)
(206) 634-2676 (Fax)
info@digitalfarm.com (E-Mail)
http://www.digitalfarm.com (Web)

Digital Images GmbH

Digital Images is one of the largest digital production centers in Europe, and one of the first companies to be founded specifically for DVD production services. Their services include high-end DVD mastering for home entertainment and marketing communication, digital filing, non-linear editing, image and sound restoration, and digital high-end imaging technology (HDTV). Input video and audio formats supported include Digital Betacam, BetaSP, D1, DVCAM, MiniDV, DVCPRO 25/50, SonyHD HDCAM, VoodooHD, 1" Type B, 1" Type C (PAL/NTSC), CD, Cord (16,17,35 mm), DAT, DTRS/DA88, and Senkel (1/2, 1/4). DVD authoring equipment includes Spruce DVD Maestro, Sonic Scenarist Professional, Sonic Solutions DVD Creator, BitPack Video Encoder, BitPackHD Encoder, and Sonic DVD Creator Encoder systems. Digital Images GmbH has completed more than 300 DVD projects to date. For more information contact:

> Digital Images GmbH
> Waisenhausring 9
> Halle / Saale, 06108
> Germany
> +49 (0) 345-2175-0 (Voice)
> +49 (0) 345-2175-111 (Fax)
> info@digim.de (E-Mail)
> http://www.digim.de (Web)

digital Outpost

digital OutPost offers a full range of services for DVD production including, Digital Betacam video production, serial digital post-production, graphics and motion menu design, sound design, encoding, authoring and mastering. digital OutPost has been encoding video since 1991 for clients such as Warner Bros, DreamWorks, Nissan, Disney and Sun Microsystems. Video and audio input formats supported include D-1, Digital Betacam, BetaSP, DV, 3/4" Umatic, S-VHS, QuickTime, DAT, DA-88, and ProTools. DVD authoring equipment includes a variety of systems from Sonic Solutions, Spruce, Sonic and Apple. Digital Outpost has completed more than 350 DVD-Video and DVD-ROM projects to date. For more information contact:

> digital OutPost
> 2385 Camino Vida Roble, suite 200
> Carlsbad, CA 92009
> 800/464-6434 (Voice)
> 760/431-3575 (Voice)
> 760/431-8717 (Fax)
> sales@dop.com (E-Mail)
> www.dop.com (Web)

Digital Video Compression Corporation (DVCC)

Digital Video Compression Corporation (DVCC) is a full service DVD production facility offering MPEG2 Video Compression, DVD authoring for simple and complex titles including multi-angle and multi-story authoring, quality control, emulation and disc testing, and static/dynamic menu design. Input video and audio formats supported include D5, D1, Digital Beta, DAT, DA88, DLT, Jazz and CD-R. DVD authoring equipment includes Panasonic authoring systems, as well as Panasonic video and audio encoders. DVCC has completed more than 1,000 DVD projects to date. For more information contact:

Digital Video Masters

Digital Video Masters is a full service DVD authoring facility in operation for the past five years. Their services include DVD authoring, video and audio encoding, static and dynamic menu creation, and support for DVD-Video, DVD-Audio, DVD-ROM and WebDVD formats. All DVD projects undergo a thorough quality-control process and discounts and generous credit terms are available for new customers. Input video and audio formats supported include Digital Beta, BetaSP, DVCam, Laserdisc, VHS, D2, DAT, and DA88. Conversion services are provided for any video or audio formats not directly supported. DVD Authoring equipment includes Sonic Scenarist (SGI), and Sonic DVD-Creator systems. Digital Video Masters has completed more than 400 DVD projects to date. For more information contact:

Digital Video Masters
3807 9th Street SE
Calgary, Alberta, T2G 3C7
Canada
(403) 543-8998 (Voice)
(403) 543-8230 (Fax)
bfoote@digital-video-masters.com (E-Mail)
http://www.digital-video-masters.com (Web)

Digital Video Services (DVS)

Digital Video Services (DVS) is a video, CD, DVD, and web service bureau offering development, duplication, and distribution services. Established in 1993, DVS has worked with interactive CD, DVD, and web technologies since their inception. Input video and audio formats supported include Digital Beta, Betacam SP, Betacam, DVCPro, DVCAM, MiniDV, DVD, Laserdisc, 1"c, 3/4"SP, Hi8mm, S-VHS, R-Dat, and CD-Audio. DVD authoring equipment includes Minerva Publisher 300 Encoder, Sonic SD-2000 Encoder, Scenarist NT Professional, Sonic DVD Creator, and Sonic AutoDVD systems. DVS has completed over 60 DVD projects to date. For more information contact:

Paul E. La Vigne - Principal
Digital Video Services
4592 40th Street S.E.
Grand Rapids, MI 49512
800 747-8273 (Toll Free Voice)
616 975-9911 (Voice)
616 975-9696 (Fax)
paul@dvs.cc (E-Mail)
http://www.dvs.cc (Web)

Directorsite

Directorsite is a full service DVD authoring facility specializing in innovative high quality DVD disks for both major film studios and corporate clients. Input video and audio formats supported include HD-5, HD-6, D1, Digital Betacam, Betacam SP, DA-88, DAT, MiniDV, DV-CAM, 3/4 Umatic, and VHS. DVD Authoring equipment includes a Sony MPEG encoder, Spruce Maestro DVD authoring & encoding system, and a Sonic DVD authoring & encoding system. Directorsite has completed over 500 DVD-Video and DVD-ROM projects to date. For more information contact:

Directorsite DVD Company
1600 Rosecrans Avenue, Building 2B
Manhattan Beach, CA 90266
(310) 727-2770 (Voice)
(310) 727-2601 (Fax)
dvd@directorsite.com (E-Mail)
http://www.directorsite.com (Web)

Dockhouse Film & Television AB

Dockhouse is a full service production company specializing in corporate films, based in Sweden. Their DVD facilities were initially included in the business as a media for distribution, but now are used to add new dimensions to most of their productions. Typical DVD projects include standard films with traditional menus, language and sound options, to synchronized multi plasma displays at international automotive exhibitions. Input video and audio formats supported include Digital Beta and BetaSP. DVD authoring equipment includes Spruce MPX 3000 video and audio encoder and Spruce DVDMaestro systems. Dockhouse has completed more than 40 DVD projects to date. For more information contact:

Dockhouse Film & Television AB
Sjöportsgatan 4
S-417 64 Gothenburg

Sweden
+46-31-651600 (Voice)
+46-31-651601 (Fax)
info@dockhouse.se (E-Mail)
http://www.dockhouse.se (Web)

DownStream Digital

DownStream Digital is a full service DVD production facility offering encoding, authoring

(503) 226-1283 (Fax)
info@downstream.com (E-Mail)
http://www.downstream.com (Web)

DVD Labs

DVD Labs is a full-service DVD creation facility, offering encoding, mastering, authoring and replication services. They place special emphasis on feature film and state-of-the-art multimedia presentations for corporate, government and institutional installations. Additional services include WebDVD integration, custom DVD-ROM applications, high-end audio services, interactive title planning, award-winning art direction, and professional project management. Input video and audio formats supported include D1, Digital Beta, BetaSP, DA98HR, GENEX, Sonic Solutions, ProTools and SADIE file formats, AC3 and DTS, (up to 192Khz). DVD authoring equipment includes Scenarist NT and Sonic DVD Creator, Sony DVA V700 Video Encoder, Sonic SD200 Video Encoder, Dolby DP569 AC3 Encoder, MLP Encoder, and DTS Encoding systems. DVD Labs has completed over 1,000 DVD-Video, DVD-Audio, DVD-ROM and WebDVD projects to date. For more information please contact:

DVD Labs
432 Columbia St Suite 17B
Cambridge, MA. 02141
(888) DVD-LABS (Voice)
(617) 577-0098 (Fax)
webmail@dvdlabs.com (E-Mail)
http://www.dvdlabs.com (Web)

DVD Master

DVD Master is a full service DVD production facility offering DVD-Video and DVD-ROM title development. DVD Master serves the museum, corporate, presentation, educational and entertainment markets. Notable credits include DVD titles for the J. Paul Getty Museum, the Los Angeles County Museum of Art's, National Aquarium of Baltimore, Drexel University, and many others. Input video and audio formats supported include Digital Betacam, BetaSP, DVCPRO25, DVCAM, 3/4' Umatic, Mini-DV, DA88, sequential Targa & Tiff on hard drives or DLT. DVD authoring equipment includes Scenarist Pro NT, and Minerva Impression systems. DVD Master has completed more than 200 DVD-Video, DVD-ROM and WebDVD projects to date. For more information contact:

DVD Master
18437 Mt Langley St Suite E
Fountain Valley, CA, 92708
(714) 962-4098 (Voice)
(714) 962-4198 (Fax)
info@dvdmaster.com (E-Mail)
http://www.dvdmaster.com (Web)

DVD Power

DVD Power is worldwide digital media publishing company with headquarters in Auckland, New Zealand, offering one of Asia Pacific's most well-rounded and experienced team of DVD authoring professionals. DVD Power specializes in providing both regional and worldwide solutions for consumer, educational, government and corporate digital DVD publishing solutions for both small and large clients. Input video and audio formats supported include D1, D2, Digital Beta, BetaSP, CD, DA88, and ProTools files. DVD authoring equipment includes Sonic Scenarist NT Professional, Spruce DVDMaestro, and Spruce MPX3000 video encoding systems. DVD Power and its affiliates have completed more than 500 DVD projects to date. For more information contact:

DVD Power Limited
PO Box 98823, SAMC
Auckland
New Zealand
+64 (9) 415 5601 (Voice)
+64 (9) 415 5639 (Fax)
inquiries@dvdpower.co.nz (E-Mail)
http://www.dvdpower.co.nz (Web)

DVD Recording Center

DVD Recording Center, a division of Questa Interactive Group, is a full service DVD authoring company capable of implementing all DVD-Video features including Laserdisc emulated DVD, line 21 closed captions, subtitles, Dolby AC3, DTS, MPEG and PCM, 16:9, Pan &

Scan, web-enable coding. MPEG encoding is done with a patented proprietary system with options for video clean up, conversion to progressive, inverse telecine, dropout repair, sync tear repair, film dust/scratch removal, etc. Direct transfer & matching to/from laser videodisc. DVD Recording Center has in-house computer graphic designers for motion menu compositing. DVD playback hardware, players & touchscreen systems are also available. DVD authoring equipment includes Scenarist Professional and proprietary video encoding technology. Input video tape formats supported include D1, Digital Beta, D2, 1"C, DVCAM, Hi8, DVCPro, MiniDV, M2, 3/4Umatic, S-VHS, and VHS. DVD Recording Center has completed over 1,000 DVD projects to date. For more information contact:

DVD Technologies

DVD Technologies is one of the premiere DVD Authoring facilities in Australia. DVD Technologies was designed from the ground up to meet the growing needs of digital technology in the fields of entertainment, publishing and business. A leader in the industry, DVD Technologies was formed in 1997, as the first company created specifically to service the DVD community. DVD Technologies was the first independent facility in existence to create a DVD product for corporate use. Input video and audio formats supported include Digital Beta

BetaSP, and DA98. DVD authoring equipment includes Sonic Solutions DVD Creator, Sonic Scenarist NT 2.5, Minerva Compressionist C250, Dolby DP569 Encoder, Dolby Dp567 Encoder, and Sony Professional Video Encoder systems. DVD Technologies has completed more than 250 DVD-Video, DVD-ROM and WebDVD projects to date. For more information contact:

DVD Technologies II Pty Ltd
Level 7, 122 Arthur St
North Sydney NSW 2060
Australia
+61 2 9929-3339 (Voice)
+61 2 9929 3335 (Fax)
jeffs@dvdtech.com.au (E-Mail)
http://www.dvdtech.com.au (Web)

DVD Transfer.com

DVDTransfer.com offers professional encoding, authoring, and replication services for corporate, museum, and entertainment industries. From simple authoring for tradeshows to complex authoring including motion menus, multiple camera angles, multiple language tracks, and AC-3 Audio for feature films. Prices are available online. In-house DVD-Authoring systems include Spruce DVD Maestro. Input videotape formats supported include Digital Betacam, Beta SP, DVCPro, DVCam, D-1, D-2, MiniDV, SVHS, VHS and PAL BetaSP. DVD Transfer.com has completed hundreds of DVD projects to date. For more information contact:

DVDTransfer.com, LLC
1313 5th St SE #324B
Minneapolis, MN 55414
(866) 383-3831 (Voice)
(612) 676-1165 (Fax)
Jason@DVDTransfer.com (E-Mail)
www.DVDTransfer.com (Web)

EagleVision

EagleVision is a full service DVD authoring, design and production company catering to the entertainment, arts, documentary, educational, and corporate markets. Typical DVD projects include documentary and independent films, concert and performing arts programs, classic and special interest titles, trade show presentations, interactive presentations and corporate training and information kiosks. EagleVision offers project management services, verification of all incoming assets, graphics and menu creation and creative services, constant and variable bit rate MPEG 2 encoding, DVD project authoring, emulation and DVD-R Quality Control, 3.95GB and 4.7GB DVD-R check discs, DLT production and coordination, and verification and testing of check discs from glass master. Input video and audio formats supported include Digital Beta, BetaSP, DA88, R-DAT, VHS, S-VHS, Ω" and other formats on request. DVD authoring equipment includes Spruce DVD Maestro, Heuris software encoder, and DigiDesign ProTools 5.1. EagleVision has completed over 60 DVD projects to date. For more information contact:

EagleVision, Inc.
880 Canal Street
Stamford, CT 06902
(203) 359-8777 (Voice)
(203) 348-6000 (Fax)
sales@eaglevisiontv.com (E-Mail)
www.DVDAuthors.com (Web)

EDR/Beachwood Studios

EDR/Beachwood Studios is a full service DVD production facility offering original music and sound design, video production, sound stage, uncompressed Avid/Unity and Smoke editing, graphic design, motion menu development, CBR and VBR MPEG-2 encoding, transcoding from QuickTime, DVD-Video authoring, hybrid/Director authoring, cDVD development, and WebDVD development. Input video and audio formats supported include Digital Betacam, Beta SP, D2, DVC-Pro, 1", Hi8, S-VHS, VHS, DA-88/98, and DAT. DVD authoring equipment includes Sonic Solutions DVD Creator systems. EDR/Beachwood Studios has completed more than 60 DVD projects to date. For more information contact:

EDR/Beachwood Studios
23330 Commerce Park Road
Beachwood, OH 44122
(216) 292-7300 (Voice)
(216) 292-0545 (Fax)
hammes@edr.com (E-Mail)

date. For more information contact:

Electric Switch Limited.
7-11 Lexington Street,
London, W1F 9AF
United Kingdom
020 7437 4402 (Voice)
020 7437 4403 (Fax)
dvd@bydeluxe.com (E-Mail)
http://www.byedeluxe.com (Web)

EMA Multimedia, Inc.

EMA Multimedia is a full-service interactive design and production company that produces interactive campaigns, designs, content and products. Having emerged as a leading entertainment design studio soon after its launch in 1992, EMA has worked with every major Hollywood studio in interactive new media, especially for major motion picture DVD products. EMA's clients include Disney, HBO, Paramount, Sony, Universal and Warner Bros. EMA's DVD services include compression, authoring and replication services, DVD Video and ROM "Special Feature" development incorporating proprietary technology from InterActual Technologies and content development solutions from BroadcastDVD. In association with Chicago-based HyperLOCK Technologies, Inc., EMA also develops and markets HyperDVD(TM)-enabled DVD titles, adding an online component to clients' DVD titles and positioning EMA as the premier provider of secure DVD hybrids. For more information contact:

EMA Multimedia, Inc.
1800 Ave. of the Stars

Suite #430
Century City, CA 90067
(310) 277-7379 (Voice)
(310) 277-7378 (Fax)
http://www.emamultimedia.com (Web)

Escape Lab

Escape Lab is a full service DVD production facility offering video production and post-production, filming, editing, sound mixing and special effects services. They develop DVD titles for entertainment industry (film, video) as well as for internal and/or external corporate communications. Input video and audio formats supported include Digital Beta, BetaSP, BetaSX, IMX, DV, DVCAM, VHS, S-VHS in both NTSC and PAL standards. DVD Authoring equipment includes Scenarist NT 2.5, and Sony DVA-V700 MPEG-2 encoder. Escape Lab was launched on the 25 April 2001 and are currently working on a number of DVD projects. For more information contact:

Escape Lab
28 rue Vilain XIIII
B-1000 Brussels
Belgium
+32 2 644 99 62 (Voice)
+32 2 644 99 62 (Fax)
info@escapelab.com (E-Mail)
http://www.escapelab.com (Web)

Evideo

Evideo provides DVD authoring, encoding, web-enablement, and video streaming services, as well as DVD training. Training classes on Sonic Creator, Sonic Fusion, and Apple DVD Studio Pro are provided at their sister company, Video Symphony. DVD equipment rental services are provided for Sonic authoring and encoding systems, both at their facility and for portable systems. Ancillary services include Avid editing, editing bays & rentals, menu graphics, ProTools audio editing & mixing. Input video and audio formats supported include Digital Beta, BetaSP, DV, SVHS, Hi8, 3/4", D2, and most audio formats. DVD authoring equipment includes Sonic Creator, Sonic Fusion, and Apple DVD Studio Pro systems. EVideo has completed more than 20 DVD projects to date. For more information contact:

Evideo, Inc.
731 N. Hollywood Way
Burbank, CA 91505
(818) 557-7200 (Voice)
(818) 845-1951 (Fax)
info@evideoinc.com (E-Mail)
http://www.evideoinc.com (Web)

EXILOG

EXILOG is a full service DVD authoring facility offering specializing in films and documentaries about tourism and wildlife, which may or may not already be on videocassette. EXILOG creates a complete bonus environment, adding an arborescence of original menus, interviews of actors, film directors or specialists of the subject, animated photo albums, varied relevant documentation, trailers, film clips, quizzes. All elements can be gathered from a variety of sources or made from scratch by EXILOG. EXILOG has their own recording studio where

36 500 Vendoeuvres
France
+33 (0) 2 54 38 30 95 (Voice)
+33 (0) 2 54 38 30 31 (Fax)
exilog.jml@wanadoo.fr (E-Mail)

FATdisc

FATdisc is a full service DVD authoring facility providing a wide variety of services including: preproduction planning and consultation, asset preparation and management, interactive menu design for static and motion menus, digital video encoding, DVD authoring and premastering, porting of CD-ROM titles to DVD-ROM and DVD-Hybrid formats, WebDVD site integration, CD-ROM title development and new media authoring with MPEG-1 or MPEG-2. Input video and audio formats supported include HD, D1, D2, Digital Beta, BetaSP, DVCAM, DVPRO, MiniDV, DA88, and DAT. DVD authoring equipment includes Sonic Scenarist SGI, Sonic Solutions DVD Creator, Apple DVD Studio Pro, Minerva Compressionist, and Heuris MPEG Power Pro systems. FATDisc has completed more than 50 DVD projects to date. For more information contact:

FATDisc, Inc.
3002 233rd Ave SE
Sammamish, WA 98075
(425) 837-1791 (Voice)
info@fatdisc.com (E-Mail)
http://www.fatdisc.com (Web)

Forest New Media Services

Forest New Media Services offers high quality compression and Internet media services for DVD, cDVD, eDVD, MPEG-1, MPEG-2, QuickTime, AVI, Windows Media, Wave, MP3, as well as HTML and JavaScript coding and other internet solutions. Video input formats include 3/4", 1", BetaSP, Digital Beta, D2, and D5. Audio input formats include DAT, DA88 and 1/4". Computer file formats are also accepted for video and audio data. DVD authoring equipment includes Sonic DVDCreator, Pioneer DVR-S201 DVD-R writers and Pioneer DVD-V7400 Players. Forest New Media Services has completed hundreds of DVD and new media projects over the past four years. For more information contact:

Forest New Media Services
31400 Northwestern Hwy. Suite G
Farmington Hills, MI 48334
(248) 855-4333, Ext. 178 (Voice)
(248) 855-3640 (Fax)
BigDan@ForestPost.com (E-Mail)
http://www.ForestPost.com (Web)

Full Circle Studios

Full Circle Studios is a multimedia production company offering DVD authoring and production services. FCS provides all services related to DVD, including (but not limited to) scriptwriting, video & audio production, menu & graphic design, and 2D & 3D animation. DVD projects can be output to DVD-R or DLT tape for mass replication. FCS can also directly incorporate DVD with other media formats, such as PowerPoint and the Internet. Combining these applications with the visual quality, access speed, and durability of DVD provides clients with enhanced multimedia experiences for entertainment, corporate, training, or educational purposes. Their preferred video and audio input format is Betacam SP. Shorter video materials and separate audio materials may be provided in digital form (QuickTime, AIFF, etc.) Materials can be provided on a number of other analog or digital formats, which will be transferred either to Betacam SP for encoding, or to a digital format for transcoding. In-house DVD authoring equipment includes Sonic DVD Creator systems. Full Circle Studios has completed more than 20 corporate DVD projects to date for clients such as Lojocano Inc., City of Niagara Falls, N.Y., Ronco Communications and Electronics, Inc, Electrical Contractors Foundation, St. John's Lutheran Church, Buffalo City Mission, and Syracuse University. For more information contact:

Full Circle Studios
100 River Rock Drive, Suite 304
Buffalo, NY 14207
(716) 875-7740 (Voice)
(716) 875-7162 (Fax)
jerry@fullcirclestudios.com (E-Mail)
http://www.fullcirclestudios.com (Web)

Future Disc Systems

Future Disc Systems provides surround sound editing and mastering, surround sound reproving (2 channel to 6 channel), Dolby Digital audio encoding, and MLP audio encoding. Additional services include MPEG-2 and MPEG-1 video encoding, DVD-Video & DVD-Audio navigation design and authoring, web-enabled & hybrid DVD authoring, menu graphics design, audio & video & still file conversion, sample rate conversion, noise removal and restoration. Video and audio input formats supported include Digital Betacam, DLT tape, DA-88, DVD-ROM, HR-45 24 bit DAT, Masterlink, 1/2" Analog tape, 1630 U-matic, Exabyte

(323) 876-8733 (Voice)
(323) 876-8143 (Fax)
email@futurediscsystems.com (E-Mail)
http://www.FutureDiscSystems.com (Web)

Gnome Digital Media

Gnome Digital Media is a full service DVD production offering DVD authoring, video compression, and DVD production services. They specialize in creating innovative DVDs that push the envelope of the DVD specification. Input video and audio formats supported include Digital Beta, BetaSP, DA88 and DAT. DVD authoring tools include Sonic DVDCreator, Sonic DVDFusion, and Apple DVD Studio Pro systems. Gnome Digital Media has completed more than 100 DVD projects to date. For more information contact:

Gnome Digital Media
3727 W. Magnolia Blvd, Suite 812
Burbank, CA 91505
(818) 563-6539 (Voice)
(818) 563-6264 (Fax)
gome@gnomedigital.com (E-Mail)
http://www.gnomedigital.com (Web)

GTN

GTN is a digital full service post production, visual effects, new media, and distribution company, with the capability to master new material and repurpose legacy material for release through standard tape, high definition, electronic file and interactive disc formats. GTN New

Media services include complete development of DVD-Video, DVD-ROM, WebDVD, standard and mini CD-ROM formats. Encoding services include MPEG-2 Variable Bit Rate and Constant Bit Rate, MPEG-1, JPEG, AVI, QuickTime and Real/Windows Media for the Internet. Input video and audio formats supported include Digital Betacam, D1, D2, D5, HD-D5, DV, mini-DV, Betacam SP, 1", DA88, DAT, and CD. DVD authoring equipment includes Sonic Solution DVD-Creator and Digital Vision Noise Reducer systems. GTN has completed over 750 DVD-Video, DVD-ROM and WebDVD projects to date. For more information contact:

GTN New Media
13320 Northend Ave.
Oak Park, MI 48237 United States
(248) 548-2500 (Voice)
(248) 548-1916 (Fax)
rsovis@gtninc.com (E-Mail)
http://www.gtninc.com (Web)

Hammer & Pixel

Hammer & Pixel is a full service post-production facility specializing in Green Screen Shooting, Stereo Videography, Microvideography, animation, show openings, as well as multi-thread authoring for DVD and specialized graphics and EFX for DVD authoring and interactivity, and Multi-synchronized DVD playback for special venue. Input video and audio formats supported include SDI, Digital Betacam, Betacam, DV, specialized Hi-Res digital imaging. DVD Authoring equipment includes Sonic DVD Creator, Quantel HAL graphic support, Mac/PC based graphics/FX systems, motion control, and virtual reality systems. Hammer & Pixel has completed more than 150 DVD projects to date. For more information contact:

Hammer & Pixel
800 North Wells St. 3rd Floor
Chicago, Illinois 60610
(312) 587-1550 (Voice)
(312) 751-8452 (Fax)
Steve@HammerandPixel.com (E-Mail)
http://www.HammerandPixel.com (Web)

HAVE, Inc.

HAVE is a full service DVD production company offering services, from expert assistance in pre-project planning, to audio/video asset preparation, to finished, packaging design; DVD replication and order fulfillment services. Input video and audio formats supported include D-2, 1" Type C, Digital Beta, Beta SP, MII, 3/4" SP, 3/4", S-VHS, Stereo Hi-Fi VHS, 8MM, Hi8, DVC-Pro, DVCAM, Mini DV, R-DAT, CD-R, 1/4" and Open Reel. DVD authoring equipment includes Spruce DVDMaestro systems. HAVE has completed more than more than

20 DVD projects for corporations, trainers, and special interest video producers. For more information contact:

HAVE, Inc.
309 Power Avenue
Hudson, NY 12534
(518) 828-2000 (Voice)
(518) 828-2008 (Fax)
have@haveinc.com (E-Mail)

ment includes full featured Sonic DVD-Creator systems. HDMG has completed more than 40 DVD titles to date. For more information contact:

HDMG
6573 City West Parkway
Minneapolis, MN 55344
(952) 943-1711 (Voice)
(952) 943-1957 (Fax)
dvd@hdmg.com (E-Mail)
http://www.hdmg.com (Web)

Henninger Interactive Media

Henninger Interactive Media is an award winning DVD authoring services provider. DVD Services include telecine transfer, menu design, DVD-Video, DVD-ROM, DVD-Audio and WebDVD authoring, surround audio mixing, video compression, and project management. Subtitling, captioning, and foreign translation services are also offered. Input video formats supported include Film, Hi-Def, D1, Digital Beta, 1", Ω" Umatic, VHS, S-VHS, 8mm Videotape, Betacam, Betacam SP, D2, DVC Pro, DV Cam, and Mini DV. Non-digital sources are bumped or transferred to a digital source prior to MPEG encoding. PAL sources are also supported. Input audio formats supported include DAT and DA-88 and many computer formats such as .wav, .aiff, .bwav, and .sdII. In-house DVD authoring equipment includes Sonic DVD Encoder, DTS Encoder, Sonic DVD-Audio Encoder, Sonic DVD Creator and Spruce DVD Maestro systems. Located in one of the top ten video post-production houses in the United States, Henninger Interactive Media has been in the DVD business for three years, and has completed over 200 DVD projects for museums, corporate clients, producers, and film distributors. For more information contact:

Wendy H. Chinn
Henninger Interactive Media
2601-A Wilson Boulevard
Arlington, VA 22201
(703) 908-4101 (Voice)
(888) 243-3444 (Voice)
(703) 243-5697 (Fax)
wchinn@henninger.com (E-Mail)
http://www.DVDexperts.com (Web)

Ibis Multimedia

Ibis Multimedia is a full service DVD production facility specializing in the creation of DVD titles for the display of information to the public. Past projects have included kiosk, touch-screen interfaces, bar code readers and other innovative control devices. All video and audio input formats are supported. DVD authoring equipment includes Optibase MovieMaker 200 video encoder and Scenarist NT Professional authoring systems. Ibis Multimedia has completed over 200 DVD projects to date. For more information contact:

Ibis Multimedia Ltd
The Rutherford Centre
4 Dunlop Road
Ipswich, Suffolk, IP2 0UG
United Kingdom
+01473 288865 Voice
+01473 288866 Fax
ibism@btinternet.com (E-Mail)
http://www.ibismultimedia.co.uk (Web)

IBT Media

IBT Media provides custom DVD production services for corporate marketing, training, and informational DVD programs, including encoding, authoring, graphic development, and disc replication. They accept input video in the Avid, Beta SP, Digital Beta, Beta SX, Beta IMX, Beta oxide, D-2, 3/4", S-VHS, and VHS formats. DVD authoring equipment includes Spruce DVD Maestro systems. IBT Media has completed over 50 DVD projects to date. For more information contact:

IBT Media Group
9400 W. 55th St.
Merriam, KS 66203
(913) 677-3151 (Voice)
(913) 677-1996 (Fax)
craig@ibtmedia.com (E-Mail)
http://www.ibtmedia.com (Web)

Imagesource

Imagesource is a full service DVD authoring company that specializes in both corporate and entertainment titles. Input video and audio formats supported include BetaSP, Digital Beta, D-2, VHS, 3/4 inch Umatic. DVD authoring equipment includes Spruce DVD Maestro systems. Imagesource has completed more than 50 DVD projects to date. For more information contact:

Imagesource

Island Post & Graphics is a full-service production and post-production facility located in Honolulu, Hawaii. Their facility includes 4 edit suites, including an Accom Affinity, Avid XL 1000, Apple Final Cut Pro, and traditional online composite BetaCam playback and record. Input video and audio formats supported include Digital Betacam, Betacam SP, DVCam, DVCPro, MiniDV, VHS, DAT, and Audio CD. DVD authoring equipment includes Sonic DVD-Creator, Apple DVD Studio Pro. Island Post & Graphics has completed over 10 DVD projects to date. For more information contact:

Island Post & Graphics
875 Waimanu Street, Suite 600
Honolulu, HI 96813
(808) 596-0933 (Voice)
(808) 596-0934 (Fax)
info@islandpost.net (E-Mail)
http://www.islandpost.net (Web)

JamSync

JamSync has developed proprietary techniques to up mix stereo audio assets to 5.1 channels. They can repurpose existing stereo audio to 5.1 channel surround sound. JamSync's audio mastering and encoding services include optimization and enhancement of audio for stereo and multi-channel DVD audio tracks, as well as complete audio post production services for mixing and sound design. For more information contact:

KK Proffitt/Joel Silverman
1232 17th Ave. South
Nashville, TN 37212
615-320-5050 (Voice)

info@jamsync.com (E-Mail)
www.jamsync.com (Web)

Javanni Digital Video

Javanni Digital Video is a full service DVD production company offering custom graphics and animation production to intense interactive menu mapping, and digital MPEG2 encoding. Services also include VideoCD and Digital Business Card services. Javanni Digital Video supports all professional NTSC and PAL tape formats. DVD authoring equipment includes a Galaquest MPEG Encoder and Sonic Solutions DVD authoring systems. Over 200 DVD projects have been completed to date including work for Paramount Pictures and Dolby Laboratories. For more information contact:

JAVANNI, INC.
4091 DEERFIELD DRIVE
CONCORD, NC 28027
(704) 425-3287 (Voice)
(704) 795-7708 (Fax)
dvd@javanni.com (E-Mail)
http://www.javanni.com (Web)

Jumby Bay Studios

Jumby Bay Studios is a full service DVD production company located in St. Louis, Missouri. Their 20,000 square foot facility houses a full-service video production company and a post-production company. They offer creative concepting, scripting, storyboarding, flow-charting, location and studio shooting, set design and building, video and audio editing, DVD authoring and burning, and video tape duplication. Input video and audio formats supported include Digital Beta, BetaSP, DV, mini DV, 1 inch, 3/4 inch, VHS, DAT, 1/4 inch and most common audio file formats. DVD authoring equipment includes Spruce DVD Maestro systems. Jumby Bay Studios has completed more than 50 DVD projects to date. For more information contact:

Jumby Bay Studios
11783 Borman Drive
St. Louis, MO 63146
(314) 569-1771 (Voice)
(314) 569-1909 (Fax)
keane@jumbybaystudios.com (E-Mail)
http://www.jumbybaystudios.com (Web)

LaserPacific Media Corporation

LaserPacific Media Corporation offers comprehensive post-production services to the motion picture, television and digital media industries. The company is a leading provider of advanced high definition services to the entertainment industry, and opened the world's first digital high definition facility in March of 1998. LaserPacific opened Hollywood's first MPEG compression facility in 1991, encoded the first DVD-ROM title, and helped Philips create some of the first DVD-Video titles ever seen. Some LaserPacific digital media firsts became industry standards: Artisan's Truth or Dare featured the first animated menus seen in a DVD for a feature film, Terminator 2 pioneered the use of dual layer technology, and New Line's Lost In Space offered web connectivity to DVD users for the first time. Input video and audio formats supported include D1, Digital Beta, Beta SP, PCM-800/DA-88, DAT and all high definition formats. DVD authoring equipment includes Sonic Scenarist with in-house developed

http://www.laserpacific.com (Web)

M Works Mastering

M Works Mastering is a full service DVD production facility offering DVD-Video, DVD-Audio and WebDVD development services. Services include audio sweetening, video and audio encoding, and DVD authoring. Input video and audio formats supported include Digital Beta, Beta-SP, DA-88, DA-98HR, and all AIFF and WAV File Formats. DVD authoring equipment includes Sonic DVD Creator and SONY-1100A Video encoding systems. M Works Mastering has completed more than 30 DVD projects to date. For more information contact:

M Works Mastering
432 Columbia St, Suite 17B
Cambridge, MA 02141
(617) 577-0089 (Voice)
(617) 577-0098 (Fax)
studio@m-works.com (E-Mail)
http://www.m-works.com (Web)

Mares Multimedia

Mares Multimedia is a full service DVD production facility specializing in video encoding, authoring, pre-mastering and menu creation. Additional services include creation of graphics for still and motion menus, design for disc packaging, digital audio creation services, 5.1 surround mixing and mastering, WebDVD development, and cDVD development. Input video and audio formats supported include Beta SP, D1, DV, S-VHS, DA-88, DAT, Pro tools sessions. DVD authoring equipment includes Sonic DVD creator systems. Mares Multimedia has completed more than 20 DVD projects to date. For more information contact:

Mares Multimedia Inc.
3004 Hillmeade Court
Nashville, TN 37221
(615) 396 3905 (Voice)
info@maresmultimedia.com (E-Mail)
http://www.maresmultimedia.com (Web)

Masterdisk

Masterdisk is a full-service DVD production facility. Their services include DVD-Video, DVD- Audio and DVD-ROM production, 5.1 mastering, and creation, DTS and AC-3 encoding, MPEG-1 and MPEG-2 compression, high-end motion graphics, and DVD authoring. Input video and audio formats supported include Digital Beta, Betacam SP, mini-DV, D-1, D-2, DVCAM, DAT, DA-88, Genex, Sonic Solutions Files, and Pro Tools Files. DVD authoring equipment includes Scenarist NT 2.0 and Sonic DVD-Creator systems. Masterdisk has completed more than 100 DVD-Video titles and over 25 DVD-ROM titles to date. For more information contact:

Masterdisk Studios
545 West 45th Street
New York, NY 10036
(212) 541-5022 (Voice)
(212) 265-5645 (Fax)
info@masterdisk.com (E-Mail)
http://www.masterdisk.com (Web)

Matinée Sound & Vision

Matinée Sound and Vision is a full service media agency offering video digitization, Avid Video Editing, audio editing, music composition, sound for games and entertainment (including our own commercially available Sound FX CD), translation, foreign language versions, animations, web sites, e-commerce, database integration, DVD and CD-ROM development. Matinée offers complete DVD production services, taking projects from concept, through design and programming, to duplication of the finished master. Input video and audio formats supported include Digital Betacam, Betacam SP, Mini DV, Ω" U-Matic, Tascam TRS (DA98), and DAT. DVD authoring equipment includes Sonic Solutions DVD Creator, Digital Vision BitPack, Avid Xpress Elite, Soundscape, and Logic Audio systems. Matinée Sound and Vision has completed more than 20 DVD projects to date. For more information contact:

Matinée Sound & Vision
132-134 Oxford Road,
Reading, RG1 7NL
United Kingdom
+44 (0) 118 957 5876 (Voice)
+44 (0) 118 959 4936 (Fax)

dvd@matinee.co.uk (E-Mail)
http://www.matinee.co.uk (Web)

Media Galleries, Inc.

Media Galleries, Inc. is one of the first authoring and DVD production studios in the United States. Their DVD production facility opened in 1997, and they specialize in Region Code 2 PAL format as well as complex presentation titles. Clients include C-Cube, NASA, San Jose Tech Museum, VISION Films, and Kit Parker Films. Input video and audio formats

Santa Cruz, CA 95003
(831) 662-0612 (Voice)
(831) 685-0340 (Fax)
arthur@mediagalleries.com (E-Mail)
http://www.mediagalleries.com (Web)

Media Tech

Media Tech is a full service DVD authoring facility with over 3 years of experience. Services include full video & film production, post-production, compression and authoring, audio, graphic and print design services. Media Tech has a 10,000 square foot studio, with Beta SP, 16mm and 35mm film capabilities. Input video formats include Digital Beta, BetaSP and Ω" Umatic. DVD authoring tools include Sonic Solutions DVD-Creator. Media Tech has completed over 300 DVD projects to date. For more information contact:

Media Tech
12999 East Jamison Circle Suite 250
Englewood, CO 80112
(303) 741-6878 (Voice)
(303) 773-0265 (Fax)
projects@mediatech1.com (E-Mail)
http://www.mediatech1.com (Web)

MEP Medienhaus GmbH

MEP medienhaus GmbH is a full service DVD authoring facility that provides DVD preproduction and mastering, Avid Composer based video editing, Pro Tools for sound editing, Maja for 3D productions, and in-house designers and programmers for WebDVD productions. Supported video and audio formats include Digital Beta, DA 88 and all other digital formats. DVD Authoring equipment includes Sonic Scenarist NT 2.0 systems, and Optibase Encoders. MEP Medienhaus GmbH has completed more than 100 DVD projects to date. For more information contact:

MEP medienhaus GmbH
Alt Hausen 34
Frankfurt, 60488
Germany
+49(69) 7896 0202 (Voice)
+49(69) 7896 0404 (Fax)
info@mep-ffm.de (E-Mail)
http://www.mep-ffm.de (Web)

Metropolis DVD

Metropolis DVD is the interactive studio of the Metropolis Group, offering a fully integrated DVD encoding, authoring, and design service. They produce a full range of DVD formats (video, audio, ROM) plus many complementary services such as 5.1 mixing and mastering, web design, video editing and ROM authoring, comprehensive project management and consultancy services. Input video and audio formats supported include Digital Beta, Beta SP, DA88, DAT and Genex. DVD authoring equipment includes Sonic DVD Creator and Spruce DVD Maestro systems. Metropolis DVD has completed more than 50 DVD projects to date. For more information contact:

Metropolis DVD
The Powerhouse
70 Chiswick High Road
London, W4 1SY
United Kingdom
+44(0) 20 8742 1111 (Voice)
+44(0) 20 8742 1616 (Fax)
dvd@metropolis-group.co.uk (E-Mail)
www.metropolis-group.co.uk (Web)

Mirage Video Productions

Mirage Video Productions offers a complete range of DVD authoring services. Final output can be created on DLT tape for replication, or to DVD-R for small quantities. Additional services include full video productions services including non-linear digital editing, After Effects motion graphics and Director interactive presentation development. They also offer MPEG-2 digitizing from any format, MPEG-1 digitizing and VideoCD or SVCD authoring. Input video formats supported include Digital Beta, BetaSP, DVCAM, DV, SVHS, Hi8 and VHS. DVD authoring equipment includes Spruce Virtuoso and Canopus Amber MPEG-2 encoder. Mirage Video Productions has completed more than 10 DVD projects to date. For more information contact:

Mirage Video Production
3635 Conifer Ct
Boulder, CO 80304
(303) 786-7800 (Voice)
(303) 938-9706 (Fax)
sales@miragevideo (E-Mail)
http://www.miragevideo.com (Web)

Theresienstr. 27
Munich, Bavaria, D-80333
Germany
+49/89/28 66 92-0 (Voice)
+49/89/28 66 92-30 (Fax)
info@msm-studios.com (E-Mail)
http://www.msm-studios.com (Web)

OASIS DVD

Oasis Post is one of the first full service DVD production facilities in Australia. Their services include design, video and audio encoding, authoring, formatting and layout of DVD-Video, DVD-ROM and DVD-Audio titles. They support all NTSC and PAL video and audio input formats. DVD authoring equipment includes Sonic Solutions DVD Creator systems. OASIS DVD has completed more than 50 DVD-Video, DVD-ROM, WebDVD and DVD-Audio projects to date. For more information contact:

OASIS DVD
21 DICKSON AVENEUE ARTARMON
SYDNEY NEW SOUTH WALES 2064
AUSTRALIA
+61-2-94374939 (Voice)
+61-2-94363953 (Fax)
david@oasisdvd.com.au (E-Mail)
http://www.oasisdvd.com.au (Web)

Phaebus Communications Group

Phaebus Communications Group is a full DVD production company offering services from concept through replication. Their multimedia, graphics, video facilities, broadcast production and post-production divisions are all used to achieve dynamic cross platform discs. Services include design of the disc navigation, design and creation of still and moving graphics, editing of source material where necessary, broadcast transfers and standards conversion to enable titles to be authored in NTSC or PAL, digital video noise reduction and scratch removal where required. All video and audio formats are supported. DVD authoring equipment includes Sonic Solutions DVD Creator systems. For more information contact:

Phaebus Communications Group
Olympic House, 17-19 Whitworth Street West,
Manchester, M1 5WG
United Kingdom
0044 (0) 161 950 8105 (Voice)
0044 (0) 161 950 8105 (Fax)
DVD@Phaebus.co.uk (E-Mail)
http://www.phaebus.co.uk (Web)

Provac Disc Media

Provac Disc Media is a full sevice DVD production facility offering authoring, encoding, mastering and replication services. Provac owns and operates the only DVD facility in Canada that replicated DVD-5, DVD-9 and DVD-10 format discs. Input video and audio formats supported include Digital Beta, BetaSP and DA88. DVD Authoring equipment includes Sonic Solutions and Sony systems. Provac has completed more than 200 DVD projects to date. For more information contact:

Provac Disc Media
224 Lesmill Road
Toronto, M3B 2T5
Canada
(416) 447-0707 (Voice)
(888) 876-9013 (Toll Free Voice)
(416) 447-3803 (Fax)
provac@idirect.ca (E-Mail)

RGB Productions

RGB Productions offers DVD authoring for retail distribution, commercial, industrial, and trade show use as well as for home video archiving. They produce hybrid DVD-Video, DVD-ROM, WebDVD, and DVDonCD titles. Input video and audio formats supported include DVCam, DVC Pro, Mini-DV, BetaCam SP, D-2, 1" Type C, 3/4" Umatic, SVHS and Hi-8. DVD authoring equipment includes Spruce Technologies DVD Maestro systems. RGB Productions has completed more than 30 DVD projects to date. For more information contact:

RGB Productions, Inc.
1678 Lance Pointe Drive
Maumee, OH 43537
(419) 891-2120 (Voice)
(419) 891-2130 (Fax)
info@rgb-productions.com (E-Mail)
http://www.RGB-Productions.com (Web)
http://www.DVDauthor.net (Web)

equipment includes several Sonic DVD-Creator systems. RISE has completed more than 100 DVD titles to date for corporate, education and government clients. For more information contact:

RISE Int'l.
2501 Parkview Dr., Suite 206
Fort Worth, TX 76102
(817) 336-0404 (Voice)
(817) 336-1430 (Fax)
Richardf@riseintl.com (E-Mail)
http://www.riseintl.com (Web)

Scream DVD

ScreamDVD is a full service DVD production facility offering video and audio encoding, authoring, static, and dynamic 2D and 3D menu creation, formatting and layout. Input video and audio formats supported include D-1, Digital Beta, Beta, 1", D-2, DV, MiniDV, Hi-8, VHS, DA-88, and DAT. DVD authoring equipment includes Sonic DVD Creator systems. Scream DVD has completed more than 200 DVD projects to date. For more information contact:

ScreamDVD, LLC
99 Madison Ave.
7th Floor
New York, NY 10016
(212) 951-7171 (Voice)
(212) 685-8686 (Fax)
mark@screamdvd.com (E-Mail)
http://www.screamdvd.com (Web)

Skyline Interactive

Skyline Interactive is a full service DVD production company providing custom design, authoring, encoding and replication services for kiosks, trade shows, marketing, and educational titles. Chris Ammen, Director of Technology at Skyline Interactive, has over 30 years experience in Post Production and Multimedia. Having created titles on Laserdisc, CD-i and VideoCD, Chris Ammen brings his creativity and experience to all of Skyline Interactive's DVD projects. Skyline Interactive can handle projects as simple as tradeshow loops to complex projects requiring unique user interfaces such as touch-screen, barcode or web browsers. Input video and audio formats supported include Digital Betacam, D2, Betacam SP, DV Cam, DV, Type C-1", Umatic 3/4", SVHS. DVD authoring equipment includes Minerva Compressionist 255 with SDI, pre-processing, 16:9, VBR and ITC options and Sonic Solutions DVD Creator systems. Skyline Interactive has completed more than 75 DVD projects to date. For more information contact:

> Skyline Interactive
> 1032 Elwell Ct., Suite 100
> Palo Alto, CA 94303
> (650) 965-2829 (Voice)
> (650) 988-8710 (Fax)
> cammen@skylineinteractive.com (E-Mail)
> http://www.skylineinteractive.com (Web)

Sony Digital Authoring Services

Sony Digital Authoring Services, a unit of Sony Disc Manufacturing, provides content preparation services for audio, video and multimedia content holders, including project planning, bit budgeting, asset capture, graphic interface design, authoring, emulation and formatting for CD, DVD, broadcast, or the web. For more information contact:

> Shelly Dawn Keel
> Manager Market Development
> Sony Digital Authoring Services
> 2689 Chatham Woods Drive
> Grand Rapids, MI 49546
> 541-988-7750 (Voice)
> WebSDM@disc.sony.com (E-Mail)
> http://sdm.sony.com/das (Web)

Sony DVD Center Europe GmbH

Located within the Sony DADC replication facility, Sony DVD Center Europe GmbH (Sony DCE) is the first Sony DVD authoring facility in Europe and offers a complete DVD solution to clients. Services of the new facility include Audio & Video compression, DVD authoring, menu design and content development. In addition, Sony DCE will offer integration of Internet and web links, e-commerce convergence and other multimedia hybrid applications. Input video and audio formats supported include D1, Digital Beta, BetaSP, DV, MiniDV, D2, PCM-800/DA-88, DA-98HR, and DASH-3324. DVD authoring equipment includes Sony Authoring and Video encoding, and Digital Vision Noise Reduction systems. Sony DADC Center Europe has completed more than 300 DVD projects to date. For more information contact:

Sony DVD Center Europe GmbH
Sonystrasse 20
A-5081 Anif/Salzburg
AUSTRIA

sentations. Utilizing Director and Flash, they integrate DVD video into presentations that can be distributed on CD-ROM. They also can create full feature DVD projects for training, sales, and marketing purposes. Input video and audio formats supported include BetaSP, DV, DVCAM, DAT, ADAT, CD, AIF, and WAV. DVD authoring equipment includes Spruce Technologies' DVD Conductor systems. Stone Studio Productions has completed over 20 DVD project to date. For more information contact:

Stone Studio Productions, Inc.
110 West Kinzie St Suite 300
Chicago, IL 60610
(312) 455-8021 (Voice)
(312) 455-8022 (Fax)
rob@stonestudio.com (E-Mail)
http://www.stonestudio.com (Web)

Stream AV

Stream AV is a full service DVD authoring facility based in Melbourne Australia. Their services include high quality MPEG II encoding, DVD-Video authoring, 2D and 3D static and motion menu design, audio preparation including 5.1 recording, mixing and mastering, and audio encoding in the Dolby Digital, DTS and MPEG formats. Input video and audio formats supported include Digital Betacam, Betacam SP, MiniDV, VHS, DA88/98, and most computer formats such as SDII, AIFF, mp3, .wav, and MPEG. DVD authoring equipment includes Sonic DVD Creator, Snell & Wilcox CPP-100 MPEG pre-processor, and DigiDesign Pro Tools systems. Stream AV has completed more than 40 DVD projects to date. For more information contact:

Stream AV
95 Lambeth Street

Kensington, Victoria, 3031
Australia
61 3 9376 6444 (Voice)
61 3 9376 6081 (Fax)
info@streamav.com.au (E-Mail)
http://www.streamav.com.au (Web)

Syzygy Media Works, Inc.

Syzygy Media Works, Inc. is a full service DVD production facility offering services to corporate clients, and independent filmmakers. They also provide on-site training at their customer's facilities. Services include production, post-production, encoding, authoring, and mastering. Input video and audio formats supported include BetaSP, DVCAM, SVHS, VHS, DVCPro, 16 mm, DV audio, DAT, Mini Disc, and Audio CD. DVD authoring equipment includes Sonic Solutions Authoring, Mediapress encoding, and Apple DVD Studio Pro systems. Syzygy Media Works, Inc. has completed more than 10 DVD projects to date. For more information contact:

Syzygy Media Works, Inc.
P.O. Box 252
Wakefield, MA 01880

The Machine Room, Ltd.

The Machine Room is a full service DVD-VIDEO production facility offering pre-mastering, encoding, authoring and emulation services. They have produced a wide variety of projects including corporate, feature films, ad agency titles and broadcast programming. Input video and audio formats supported include D1, D2, D3, D5, Digital Betacam, Betacam SP, Beta SX, DVCPro, DVCam, Mini DV, DA88, DAT, and graphics and subtitles from external suppliers in all standard formats. DVD authoring equipment includes Spruce DVD Maestro, Dolby Digital (AC-3) encoding and Sony MPEG video encoding systems. The Machine Room has completed over 100 DVD projects to date. For more information contact:

The Machine Room Limited
54-58 Wardour Street
London, W1V 3HN
United Kingdom
+44 20 7734 3433 (Voice)
+44 20 7287 3773 (Fax)
info@themachineroom.co.uk (E-Mail)
http://www.themachineroom.co.uk (Web)

The Pavement

The Pavement is a full service DVD production facility whose services include audio mixing and conforming for music and film, non-linear video editing and compositing, 2D, and 3D animation for static and motion menus, and traditional graphic design for packaging artwork and other forms of print design. Audio compression services include Dolby Digital, DTS, LPCM, MPEG and MLP. Video compression services include MPEG-1, MPEG-2, QuickTime and AVI for video. The Pavement develops DVD-Video, DVD-Audio, and WebDVD titles, as also provides web design and production services. CD and DVD-ROM programming services are provided using traditional tools like Director & Visual Basic. Input video and audio formats supported include Digital Beta, BetaSP, DA-88, and DAT. DVD authoring equipment includes Sonic Scenarist NT Professional, Sonic ReelDVD, Spruce DVDMaestro and Spruce Pre-Mastering systems. The Pavement has completed over 300 DVD projects to date. For

info@the-pavement.com (E-Mail)
http://www.the-pavement.com (Web)

The Wizard.be

The Wizard.be is a full service DVD production facility offering consulting, project management, dynamic AV-archiving, studio, post-production, translation, subtitling, encoding, authoring, and replication services. They specialize in developing entertainment, corporate and educational DVD titles. Input video and audio formats supported include all PAL and NTSC formats, DA88, DAT, JAZ, ZIP, DVD-RAM, and DLT. DVD authoring equipment includes Spruce MPX3000 encoding and DVD Maestro systems. The Wizard.be has completed more than 100 DVD projects to date. For more information contact:

The Wizard.be
Machelsesteenweg 67, 1820 Melsbroek, Belgium
Ind. Zone, Zandvoortstraat C8
2800 Mechelen
Belgium
+32/ (0) 15-28 73 00 (Voice)
+32/ (0) 15-28 73 01 (Fax)
info@option-av.be (E-Mail)
http://www.option-av.be (Web)

US DVD

US DVD is a full service DVD production facility specializing in MPEG-2 encoding, authoring, mastering, and replication. Services include Dolby 5.1 surround encoding, multiple angle support, multiple language subtitles, multiple audio languages, closed caption, scripting, and karaoke. Input video and audio formats supported include BetaSP, Digital Betacam,

DVCAM, DVC Pro, Mini-DV, and PCM 800 Digital Audio Player/Recorder. Other consumer formats such as VHS, S-VHS, 8 mm, Hi-8, Ω" Umatic are also supported. DVD authoring equipment includes Spruce DVDMaestro systems. US DVD has completed more than 40 DVD projects to date. For more information contact:

US DVD
1222 Flickinger Avenue,
San Jose, CA 95131
(408) 259-1495 (Voice)
(253) 399-7282 (Fax)
info@usdvd.tv (E-Mail)
http://www.usdvd.tv (Web)

Valkieser Solutions

Valkieser Solutions is a full service DVD developer specializing in both the corporate and entertainment markets. Corporate clients include Sony Europe, Philips, Mitsubishi, and Ahold. Entertainment clients include Warner Home Video, Buena Vista, and RCV Home Entertainment. Their services include DVD authoring, video compression, Dolby Digital 5.1 post production, high end video, film & commercial post production, camera facilities, satellite broadcasting, streaming video & broadband internet, and content management systems. Input video and audio formats supported include Digital Beta, BetaSP, DA88 and DA98. DVD authoring equipment includes Sonic Scenarist NT and Sonic Solutions DVD-Creator systems. Valkieser Solutions has completed over 20 DVD projects to date. For more information contact:

Valkieser Solutions
Marathon 9 B
Hilversum 1200 CE
The Netherlands
+31 (0) 35 671 43 00 (Voice)
+31 (0) 35 671 43 33 (Fax)
solutions@valkieser.nl (E-Mail)
http://www.valkieser.com (Web)

Video Transfer

Video Transfer Inc. is a full service DVD production company staffed with a team of producers, graphic designers, DVD compresionists, and multimedia authors. They can handle everything from Pre-production to replication including graphic design and packaging. Video and audio input format supported include D1, D2, D3, D5, Digital Betacam, DVCPRO, DV, DVCAM, Digital-S, Digital 8, Beta SP, Betacam, MII, 1", S-VHS, W-VHS, VHS, Ω", Hi-8, and 8mm. DVD authoring equipment includes Sonic Solutions Creator systems. Video Transfer Inc. has produced over 75 DVD-Video features and over 700 total DVD projects to date. For more information contact:

Video Transfer Inc.
580 Harrison Ave.
Boston, MA 02118
(617) 247-0100 (Voice)
(617) 247-1365 (Fax)
mgrady@vtiboston.com (E-Mail)
http://www.vtiboston.com (Web)

BetaSP, DV, DVCAM, SVHS, VHS, QuickTime, and AVI. DVD Authoring equipment includes Scenarist NT Professional 2.0 systems. Visible Light Digital has completed over 50 DVD projects to date. For more information contact:

Visible Light DIGITAL, Inc.
195 West State Road 434
Winter Springs, Florida 32708
(407) 327-7804 (Voice)
(407) 327-5006 (Fax)
info@VLDIGITAL.com (E-Mail)
http://www.VLDIGITAL.com (Web)

Vision Wise Inc

Vision Wise is a full service DVD production facility serving a wide range of entertainment, corporate, and institutional customers. Input video and audio formats supported include Digital Beta, BetaSP, D2, DVCAM, DVCPRO, 1" Type C, and DA88. DVD Authoring equipment includes Sonic Scenarist NT authoring systems with Sony and Optibase MPEG-2 video encoders. Vision Wise has completed over 500 DVD projects to date. For more information contact:

Vision Wise Inc
6305 N O'Connor rd #111 Bldg 4
Irving TX 75039
(972) 401 3320 (Voice)
(972) 401 2393 (Fax)
tcapper@visionwise.com (E-Mail)
http://www.visionwise.com (Web)

Visom Digital

Visom Digital provides turnkey DVD Authoring in both the NTSC and PAL formats. Their services include fully interactive static and dynamic menu creation, subtitling, language dubbing, 5.1 mixing for AC-3, DTS and DVD-Audio (96Khz/192Khz), full sound restoration, and audio pre-mastering. Visom Digital also specializes in the nationalization of international titles for Brazil. In addition to authoring services, Visom Digital also provides sales, importation, commissioning, training, technical support and maintenance of Sonic Solutions DVD Authoring Systems. Video and audio formats supported include Sony Digital and SP Beta video formats, NTSC and PAL (SP). Tascam DA-88, Genex-8500, ADAT - XT, Studer 24Tk 2" Machines, Euphonix R-1 Multitrack machines, Tascam MX 24242 Hard Disk 24 Tk machines, WAV, SounDesigner and AIFF files, DLT, Exabyte and DVD-R formats. DVD authoring equipment includes Sonic Solutions DVD Creator Systems with DVD-Audio capability, CEDAR, Sonic NoNoise and Spectral Design Audio Cube for Sound Restoration and Pre-mastering, Euphonix CS-2000 and Sony DMX-R100 surround mixing consoles. Visom Digital has completed over 300 DVD titles to date, including 12 DVD-ROM titles, more than 100 corporate titles and more than 200 movie titles, among them Caetano Veloso "Prenda Minha", Brazil's Best Selling DVD Title (80,000 copies) and first DTS title in Latin America. For more information contact:

> Visom Digital
> Rua Sarapui 8, Humaita
> Rio de Janeiro, RJ, 22260-170
> Brazil
> (5521) 539-7312 (Voice)
> (5521) 539-7312 (Fax)
> visom@visomdigital.com.br (E-Mail)
> www.visomdigital.com.br (Web)

Westport Media Resources

Westport Media Resources is a full service DVD authoring facility specializing in both feature films and corporate projects. Their services include menu design, video and audio encoding, web connectivity, and project management. Westport Media Resources is a small boutique shop that prefers to work with independent filmmakers, often on a participation basis. Each DVD project must meet the same rigorous Quality Control requirements as a major Hollywood release. Input video and audio formats supported include Digital Beta and Beta SP, with other formats supported based on as needed basis. DVD authoring equipment includes DVD-Composer video encoder, Dolby DP561B audio encoder and Sonic Scenarist SGI systems. Westport Media Resources has completed over 40 DVD projects to date. For more information contact:

> Westport Media Resources
> 1895 Park Ave Suite 201
> San Jose, CA 95126
> (408) 246-4949 (Voice)
> (408) 246-7371 (Fax)

pam@wmr.com (E-Mail)
http://www.wmr.com (Web)

Zomax

Zomax is a global leader in software production and distribution services, offering a complete solution to publishers and content developers for DVD-Video, DVD-ROM, and multimedia products. Zomax has a full service DVD authoring facility located at their replication plant. Input video and audio formats supported include Digital Beta, Beta-SP, Hi-8, S-VHS,

(800) 525-6575 (Voice)
(612) 553-0826 (Fax)
contactus@zomax.com (E-Mail)
http://www.zomax.com (Web)

DVD Authoring Tools & Systems

Apple

Apple offers two DVD authoring tools, iDVD for the consumer market and DVD Studio Pro for the professional market.

iDVD

Currently iDVD is sold only with Mac G4 systems that include the new Apple DVD-R Super-Drive. The iDVD graphical users interface is surprisingly simple. Apple has distilled the process of creating a DVD title down to five easy steps, (1) Select a Theme, (2) Create and fill Media Folders, (3) Create and fill Slide Shows, (4) Preview the Disc, and (5) Burn a DVD-R.

IDVD uses "Themes" to create a common look and feel for the DVD title. Approximately 20 predefined Themes come standard with iDVD, and you can create custom Themes as well. A Theme consists of a background image, a specific font style, color and size, and a specific button shape and size. Buttons are used to launch the playback of video clips or slideshows, or to branch to Folders.

"Folders" are used by iDVD as containers for media elements, and to organize the presentation of the content on the DVD disc. A Folder can hold additional Folders or individual media elements. IDVD Folders can have up to six buttons each, and there can be no more than 99 media elements used in the title. IDVD automatically arranges the buttons in each

Folder, and creates the Left, Right, Up and Down navigation commands as well. Each Folder can use the common project Theme, have it's own unique Theme, or use different background image if required. The DVD Menu key is automatically programmed to take the user up one level in the Folder structure, and the DVD Title key is programmed to take the user to the top-level Folder.

"Slideshows" are collection of still images that are presented in a linear fashion. Individual images can be displayed for a fixed amount of time, or indefinitely waiting for a user action. Previous (<<) and Next (>>) buttons are automatically created on each still image by iDVD to allow the viewer to navigate through the slideshow in a sequential fashion.

Adding video clips or photographs to a title is a simple process of selecting them in the Apple Finder and dropping them into the appropriate iDVD Folder. IDVD only accepts QuickTime video, so if you have files in any other format you will have to convert them to QuickTime before using them. Buttons are created in the order that the elements are dropped in, but you can change a button's position by clicking on it and dragging it to a different position on the screen. When video clips or slide shows are associated with a button, you can select which frame of video, or still image to use as a thumbnail image on the button.

IDVD has a Preview Mode that allows you to check your work at any time during the title creation process. Pressing the Preview Button brings up a small remote control, shown in Figure 2, that allows you to navigate through the title. Video clips, slideshows and folders are displayed just as they will be on the final disc image. The quality of the video clips may be different in Preview Mode than it is on the final disc, since the Preview Mode displays the uncompressed media elements, rather than the MPEG-2 encoded versions used on a DVD disc.

The last step of the DVD creation process is Burn DVD. During this step all of the Quick-Time video files used on the title are converted into the MPEG-2 format using an integrated software MPEG-2 encoder. IDVD can only create constant bit rate MPEG-2 video streams, and can fit about one hours worth of video on a DVD disc. There is a disc capacity indicator on the bottom of the iDVD users interface that displays the total time used on the disc, or total time left. IDVD can't be used to create a "DVD on CD" disc or store a DVD disc image on the hard drive; it only can store the final disc image on a DVD-R disc. IDVD uses "DVD-R for General" media, which can be purchased directly from Apple for $10 each. For more information contact:

Apple
1 Infinite Loop
Cupertino, CA, 95014
(408) 996-1010 (Voice)
info@apple.com (E-Mail)
http://www.apple.com (Web)

DVD Studio Pro

DVD Studio Pro user's interface includes a variety of different display areas and windows, which are all individually configurable. The *Graphical View* shows a flowchart like display of the DVD project. The *Property Inspector* is used to set properties related to specific assets or media elements used in the project. The *Project View* window shows all of the assets that can be used in the project. There are also various *Editors, Matrix Views, Troubleshooting Windows* and a *Preview Mode* display.

DVD Studio Pro's workflow is similar to most corporate or professional DVD authoring tools. Video, audio, and graphics assets are brought into the *Project View* area in a variety of formats. MPEG video files can be directly imported, and DVD Studio Pro includes a software MPEG compression utility to convert QuickTime video clips into the MPEG format. Audio can be imported in the PCM, Dolby Digital and MPEG formats. DVD Studio Pro includes a feature called A.Pack, which allows AIFF, SoundDesigner II, WAV or QuickTime audio streams to be converted to into the Dolby Digital format. DVD Studio Pro does not support

added to video tracks once they have been created in the *Graphical View* area. Only 99 video or slide show tracks can be used in a single project since DVD Studio Pro stores each of these elements in their own Video Title Set (VTS).

Adobe Photoshop files are dropped into the Graphical View area to create menus. Both static and dynamic menus can be created, and the tool supports multiple aspect ratio menus (4:3 and 16:9). There are several different ways to implement menus in DVD-Studio Pro. If the PhotoShop file has full color background and button graphics, then the menu is implemented as an "auto-activate" menu where multiple copies of the menu are stored for each combination of selected and activated buttons. If the PhotoShop file includes a full color background and a four-color highlight overlay, then the menu is implemented as a traditional DVD menu where the highlight information is displayed when a button is selected or activated. If only a background graphic is included in the PhotoShop file then the menu is implemented as a traditional DVD menu where the color of the button area on the screen is changed to indicate the selected or activated button states. DVD Studio Pro automatically assigns the Left, Right, Up and Down button navigation commands when each button is created. These assignments can be manually overridden if necessary.

Links between tracks, slideshows and menus are defined by setting properties in the *Property Inspector*. For each track, specific actions can be assigned for the Next, Previous, Title, Menu, Return and Enter buttons on the DVD player remote control. DVD Studio Pro provides access to SPRM and GPRM registers, along with a scripting language to create scripts that can be executed before or after a track is played. Only 8 GPRM registers can be used, but the scripting language provides support for all of the commands defined by the DVD-Video specification.

DVD Studio Pro includes a Preview Mode to review individual media elements, or the entire project. This is an excellent tool for checking the project before starting to build a disc image. Once the project has been created, and previewed, the next step is to build the disc image, and if desired output it to either DVD-R or DLT tape. The disc image build process is executed faster than real time using DVD Studio Pro, and with the 2X writing speed of the Apple SuperDrive it took about an hour to build a full 4.7 GByte disc image and write it to a

DVD-R. DVD Studio Pro supports single or dual layer disc images, Macrovision Analog Copy Protection, Content Scrambling System, and Region Coding, features normally found only on professional authoring tools.

DVD Studio Pro is a full featured, yet inexpensive professional DVD authoring tool. When combined with an off-the-shelf Apple iDVD system, DVD Studio Pro can be used as a stand-alone professional DVD authoring system, with a price tag of less than $5,000. DVD Studio Pro could be improved by adding support for DTS audio, although most DVD developers will not use this capability. Expert DVD authors may find it difficult to implement very complex DVD-Video titles using DVD Studio Pro due to the support for only 8 GRPM registers, and only 99 unique video tracks.

DVD Studio Pro has a suggested retail price of $1,000 and requires a Mac PowerPC G4 system with Apple AGP graphics card, 128 Mbytes RAM, 10 Gbytes available hard drive space, Mac OS 9.0.4 or 9.1, QuickTime Pro 4.1 or later, Apple DVD Player 2.3 or later, and Adobe Photoshop 4.0 or later. For more information contact:

Apple
1 Infinite Loop
Cupertino, CA, 95014
(408) 996-1010 (Voice)
info@apple.com (E-Mail)
http://www.apple.com (Web)

Authoringware

Authoringware offers several DVD authoring tools, both as stand-alone products or for OEM bundle deals. All of their tools work on Windows 98/ME/NT/2K platforms and require a DirectShow compatible hardware or software DVD decoder.

DVD Quick Builder accepts MPEG-2 video, WAV, AIFF, AC-3, and MPEG1, Layer 2 audio files and can be used to generate a valid DVD-Video disc image. Projects are limited to 2 menus, 2 titles, up to 99 chapters for each title, up to 36 buttons on each menu, and up to 8 audio streams and audio languages. DVD Quick Builder has a suggested retail price of $299.

DVD Wise accepts MPEG-2 video, WAV, AIFF, AC-3, and MPEG1, Layer 2 audio files and can be used to generate a valid DVD-Video disc image. Projects can include 99 menus, 99 titles, up to 99 chapters for each title, up to 36 buttons on each menu, up to 8 subtitles for each title, and up to 8 audio streams and audio languages. DVD Quick Builder has a suggested retail price of $2,250. For more information contact:

AuthoringWare Company
21514 Talisman Street
Torrance, CA 90503
(310) 540-5248 (Voice)
(310) 316-5804 (Fax)
sales@authoringware.com (E-Mail)
http://www.authoringware.com (Web)

Avid

Available on select Dell Precision and IBM IntelliStation workstations, Avid Xpress DV offers professional video editing with the ability to output content to the web, CDs, DVDs, in presentations, and to DV tape. Major features of Avid Xpress DV include professional DV editing, effects, audio, titling, graphics, composition and interoperability, and web and DVD publishing in the same application. More than 80 built-in digital video effects are included. A copy of Sonic Solutions DVDIt! LE authoring software is included for DVD authoring. For more information contact:

Blossom Technologies

Blossom Technologies offers several DVD authoring products. All of their products are designed to work on Windows systems.

DaViD Suite LE can be used to create simple DVD-Video titles. It includes an MPEG 2 encoder/decoder PCI card, a DVD Emulator PCI Card, video/audio capture software and a simple DVD authoring tool. David Suite LE has a suggested retail price of $3,995.

DaViD Suite can be used to create moderately complex DVD-Video titles. It includes an MPEG 2 encoder/decoder PCI card, a DVD Emulator PCI Card, video/audio capture software and a copy of the Sonic ReelDVD authoring software. David Suite has a suggested retail price of $6,995.

DaViD Suite Station LE is a turnkey workstation for creating simple DVD-Video titles. It includes a dual Intel PIII processor workstation running Windows NT 4.0, hard drive storage for up to 6 hours of video, an MPEG 2 encoder/decoder PCI card, a DVD Emulator PCI Card, video/audio capture software and a simple DVD authoring tool. David Suite Station LE has a suggested retail price of $9,995.

DaViD SUITE STATION is a turnkey workstation for creating moderately completed DVD-Video titles. It includes a dual Intel PIII processor workstation running Windows NT 4.0, hard drive storage for up to 6 hours of video, an MPEG 2 encoder/decoder PCI card, a DVD Emulator PCI Card, video/audio capture software and a copy of the Sonic ReelDVD authoring software. David Suite Station has a suggested retail price of $12,995.

DaViD Pro is a turnkey workstation for creating advanced DVD-Video titles. It includes a dual Intel PIII processor workstation running Windows NT 4.0, hard drive storage for up to 6 hours of video, an MPEG 2 encoder/decoder PCI card, a DVD Emulator PCI Card, video/audio capture software and a copy of the Sonic Scenarist NT authoring software. David Suite Station has a suggested retail price of $27,995. For more information contact:

Blossom Technologies Corporation
(305) 266-2800 (Voice)

(800) 378-3057 (Toll Free Voice)
(305) 261-2544 (Fax)
blossom@blossomvideo.com (E-Mail)
http://www.blossomvideo.com (Web)

Canopus

Amber for DVD combines the real-time MPEG encoding capabilities of Amber, with the DVD authoring capabilities of Spruce DVDVirtuoso authoring software. The Amber hardware encodes MPEG-1 and MPEG-2 video in real time using constant or variable bit rates. Spruce's DVDVirtuoso software supports NTSC and PAL, 4:3 and 16:9 aspect ratios, 48 KHz PCM 16-bit, AC-3 2-channel, and MPEG1 (Layer I and II) audio. Up to 99 chapter points can be defined in each video segment. DVDVirtuoso has a built-in subtitle generator, built-in menu editor, and provides real-time preview and navigation simulation.

The Amber encoder is a single PCI board that provides MPEG2 video and audio capture up to 15 Mb/s, with a simultaneous high quality VGA video overlay and analog video output. Real time encoding of MPEG-2 D1, Half-D1, and MPEG-1 formats is supported, as well as MPEG Layer I and II audio encoding. Amber provides S-Video and composite video inputs and outputs. Amber for DVD requires a Windows NT 4.0 system with 400 MHz Pentium II CPU, and 128 Mbytes of system RAM. Amber for DVD has a suggested retail price of $2,995. For more information contact:

Canopus Corporation
711 Charcot Ave.
San Jose, CA, 95131
(408) 954-4500 (Voice)
(408) 954-4504 (Fax)
info@canopuscorp.com (E-Mail)
http://www.canopuscorp.com (Web)

DV Studio

DV Studio has two products that can be used to product DVD-Video titles. Apollo Expert Plus is a real time hardware MPEG-2 encoder that includes a DVD authoring tool for generating simple DVD-Video titles. The encoder provides constant or variable bit rate real time MPEG-2 encoding & decoding at bit rates from 2 to 25 Mbps. The DVD authoring tool can accept MPEG video, PCM MPEG-1 or Dolby Digital audio files. Limitations of the authoring tool include a single level of menus, and a maximum of 8 audio files.

Apollo d2d is a software MPEG transcoder that includes the same DVD authoring tool as Apollo Expert Plus. Apollo d2d is designed for systems that have DV capture and editing software using IEEE 1394 FireWire interfaces. For more information contact:

DV Studio Technologies, LLC
23671 Via Del Rio
Yorba Linda, California, 92887
(714) 692.7220 (Voice)

(714) 692.7221 (Fax)
sales@dv-studio.com (E-Mail)
http://www.dv-studios.com (Web)

Intec

INTEC, INC., a Japanese company who developed the "Video-CD Writing Tool" has also developed DVDAuthorQUICK, a Windows NT based DVD authoring tool. DVDAuthorQUICK masks the complexity of the DVD-Video specification behind a simple interface

menus, submenus, chapters, subtitles & automatic button linking in only a few hours is possible with DVDAuthorQUICK. DVDAuthorQUICK's build process creates the DVD-Video disc image for output to either DVD-R or DLT. DVDAuthorQUICK is available in three versions with increased functionality at each level.

* DVDAuthorQUICK Pro (Suggested Retail Price of $7,900)

* DVDAuthorQUICK Desktop (Suggested Retail Price of $2,500)

* DV Author (Suggested Retail Price of $399)

For more information contact:

June H. Tanaka
INTEC America, Inc.
1010 El Camino Real, Suite 370
Menlo Park, CA 94025
650-327-9402 (Voice)
dvd@inteca.com (E-Mail)
http://www.inteca.com (Web)

Matrox

The Matrox RT2000 is a real-time video editing card that include a copy of Sonic Solutions DVDit! for authoring of simple DVD-Video titles. Major features of the RT2000 board include real-time editing with two video layers plus a graphics layer, native DV and MPEG-2 editing, analog and digital video input/outputs including Y/C, composite, and IEEE-1394 FireWire, and MPEG-2 output for DVD and CD authoring. A variety of software products are bundled with the RT2000 product including Adobe Premiere, Inscriber TitleExpress, Pixélan Video SpiceRack Lite, Sonic Foundry ACID Music, Sonic DVDit! LE, and Ulead Cool

3D. The suggested retail price for the RT2000 product is $1,099. For more information contact:

Matrox Electronic Systems Ltd
1055 St. Regis Blvd
Dorval, Quebec, H9P 2T4
Canada
(514) 685-2630 (Voice)
(514) 685-2853 (Fax)
video.info@matrox.com (E-Mail)
http://www.matrox.com (Web)

Panasonic

The Panasonic LQ-VD2000S is a compact, highly integrated system designed for authoring DVD-Video, DVD-ROM and Hybrid DVD discs. All functions required for DVD authoring have been integrated into a single Windows NT based personal computer. The system includes four items of hardware, the host computer, a video encoder board, and audio encoder board, and a decoder board.

There are six different primary user interfaces. The Project Manager allows you to launch all DVD authoring applications, backup and restore projects or make copies of projects. The Reelset Editor allows you to set global parameters for video, audio and subtitles within a project, and define the start and stop timecodes for controlling the video and audio encoders. DA Author is the program where menus, buttons and navigation commands are defined for a DVD title, including support for parental levels, seamless branching, and single or dual layer disc definitions. The A/V Encode tool provides automatic variable bit rate MPEG-2 video and Dolby Digital audio compression from source tape. The Disc Image Creator program generates the final DVD disc image, providing support for DVD-Video, DVD-ROM and Hybrid DVD disc layouts. The Output Disc Image program is used to output the final disc image to DLT or DVD-R.

The LQ-VD2000S has a suggested retail price of $120,000 which includes the host computer, video encoder, audio encoder, decoder card and the LQ-VD3000 emulator. For more information contact:

Panasonic
3330 Cahuenga Blvd
West Los Angeles, CA 90068
(323) 436-3500 (Voice)
dvdauthoring@panasonic.com (E-Mail)
http://www.panasonic.com/pbds/products (Web)

Pinnacle

The Pinnacle DVD2000 is videotape, CD-ROM, DVD, and Internet video delivery production system. It combines frame accurate dual stream MPEG-2 video editing and a complete DVD authoring solution. The DVD2000 encodes directly in the DVD format and can edit or immediately author the video. DVD2000 features DV and Component Video inputs and outputs, and includes copies of Adobe Premiere 6.0, Title Deko, Pinnacle Impression 2.0 DVD authoring software, Hollywood FX Bronze and Alpha Magic, Pipeline ProVTR, Smart Sound Quicktracks and Total Training Introduction to Premiere 6.0.

For DVD authoring the Pinnacle DVD2000 system uses the Pinnacle Impression 2.0 software, which was developed by Minerva Systems and recently purchased by Pinnacle. Impression 2.0 has lots of great features, including support for multiple camera angles, multiple audio tracks, subpicture streams, and static and motion menus. Impression's graphical user interface is clean and intuitive. It consists of three major areas, the Timeline, Library, and

menu graphics into the Library, drag them onto the Timeline and then define individual menu buttons. (5) Link menu buttons to specific media assets on the Timeline. (6) Create any required control links on the Timeline. (7) Use the Monitor area to preview the title in real time to make sure it is correct. (8) Build a DVD disc image and output it to a DVD-R or DLT.

Another neat feature is the way you create DVD Menus graphics.

Impression can import Adobe Photoshop files that have unique layers defined for each section of a menu graphic. The first layer is the background graphic, and subsequent layers are used for defining the DVD overlay palette, menu buttons, and highlights for those buttons. Once you get used to creating DVD menus in this Photoshop format you will wish that all DVD authoring tools had this feature.

There are some areas of the DVD specification that Impression does not support, such as access to the general-purpose registers (GRPM), region coding, or CSS content protection.

The DVD2000 requires a 400 MHz Pentium II system with one free 32 bit PCI slot, 64 MByte RAM, 500 MByte free hard disk space for system files, a 4 GByte SCSI video hard disk, a 16-bit display adapter with DirectDraw drivers, a CD-ROM drive, and sound board. DVD2000 can work under the Windows 98, Windows 2000, or Windows NT 4.0 operating systems. The suggested retail price for DVD2000 is $3,499, including the Impression software. A copy of Impression 2.0 can be purchased separately for $999. For more information contact:

Pinnacle Systems
280 North Bernardo Avenue
Mountain View, California 94043
(650) 526-1600 (Voice)
(650) 526-1601 (Fax)
sales@pinnaclesys.com
http://www.pinnaclesys.com (Web)

Pioneer

Pioneer's DVDesigner is a design tool, rather than a DVD authoring tool. DVDesigner is intended for producers and content owners who want to put their content on DVD. Designing the title using DVDesigner allows them to get a good idea of how the final product will look and feel, before starting the DVD authoring process.

There are four basic work areas of the DVDesigner Graphical Users Interface (GUI); Properties Dialogs, Layout, MenuMaker, and Simulation. Properties Dialogs are areas where you enter values for various DVD-Video parameters.

The Layout section is the main work area for DVDesigner. This is where you define the various titles, chapters, multiple video angles and decision points that are required for your DVD-Video title.

DVDesigner allows you to associate a thumbnail image, in JPEG or GIF format, with each unique Title, Chapter or Scene. This makes it easy to keep track of each element since you can use a frame from the real video clip as your thumbnail. If you right click on any of the items in the Layout section a drop down menu is displayed that allows you to insert, add, collapse/expand, edit properties, simulate and add a decision associated with the item. A left click on an item in the Layout section allows you to insert cell level commands.

The MenuMaker section of DVDesigner allows you to create mock-ups of the various menus in your DVD-Video title. You can import a background image as well as a Subpicture overlay image and then create the various interactive buttons. You can enter the up, down, left and right navigation commands for each button, as well as specify the colors used for the overlay graphic.

The Simulation section of DVDesigner allows you to preview the logical flow of the Titles, Chapters and Scenes defined in the Layout section as well as the navigation commands selected in MenuMaker. It is important to note that DVDesigner does not use the real media elements that are required for the final DVD-video title; it simply uses a still image, in JPEG or GIF format, to represent each unique media element.

When you finish creating a detailed project storyboard, and assign the appropriate navigation actions and commands you are ready to export the project. Sonic Solutions and Spruce Technologies have announced support for DVDesigner. Once you define all the media elements in your title, and fill in a few basic parameters like the length of each video clip and the average bit rate for MPEG compression, DVDesigner will tell you how much disc space is used.

DVDesigner is an excellent tool for producers and content owners who want to participate directly in the process of creating a DVD-Video title. DVDesigner is easy to use, works on just about any computer platform, and can be used to accurately storyboard the vast majority of DVD-Video titles being published today. Used correctly DVDesigner should save money by allowing the DVD Authoring facilities to concentrate on the actual implementation of a DVD title, rather than hold the hands of a producer or content owner through the definition stage of a project.

Pioneer provides DVDesigner to developers at no charge. To get a copy of DVDesigner you need to send a letter to Pioneer with the following information:

• Name

• Company/Organization Name

- Address

- E-Mail Address

- Company web site URL

- Telephone number

- Fax number

- Description of your companies business

SimpleDVD is a software utility that encodes an AVI video/audio file into DVD single chapter files that play on a PC DVD player or, when written to a DVD disc, play on a set-top DVD. The program generates disc images or files that will play on a DVD enabled PC, either from the hard disk or CD. Copies made on a standard PC CDR writer will play on any DVD compliant PC, simplifying wide scale distribution. SimpleDVD offers single button operation to convert AVI to DVD. It outputs VOB files, a DVD disc simulation, or DVD multiplexed files, and interfaces with all cameras, frame grabbers, video editors, and animator tools that generate AVI video. Minimum system requirements are a Pentium II MMX 266 MHz CPU with 128 MB RAM, a 4 GB hard drive and the Windows 95, 98, 2000 or NT operating systems. SimpleDVD has a suggested retail price of $495. For more information contact:

PixelTools Corporation
10721 Wunderlich Drive
Cupertino, CA 95014
(408) 374-5327 (Voice)
(408) 374-8074 (Fax)
pixeltools@pixeltools.com (E-Mail)
http://www.pixeltools.com (Web)

SmartDisk Corporation

In January 2001 SmartDisk Corporation acquired the DVD authoring products developed by Multimedia Technology Center (MTC). The MTC DVDMotion and tools are now being sold and serviced by SmartDisk. All of the DVDMotion tools are designed for use on Windows 98, NT4, 2000 and ME systems.

DVDMotion CE is a DVD-Video authoring tool used for simple DVD-Video titles. It is designed for people who want to experiment with the DVD-Video format but only need simple non-interactive or single menu interactive titles. DVDMotion CE is now as shareware from SmartDisk's web site where you can download a fully operational copy of DVDMotion CE and try it out. The download version provides 15 days of free use, and the cost to upgrade to an unlimited version is $95. DVDMotion CE titles are limited to one video angle, one chapter per video clip, 60 video clips, one audio track per video, and one menu.

DVDMotion SE is designed for the corporate and prosumer DVD-Video developer. It is designed to support the needs of MIS, presentations, training and education departments of corporations, as well as small businesses or individuals who produce wedding, graduation, anniversary, family albums and other similar consumer DVD-Video applications. DVDMotion SE has a suggested retail price of $395. DVDMotion SE titles are limited to one video angle, 99 chapters per video clip, 99 video clips per title, 2 audio tracks per video clip, and unlimited menus. DVDMotion SE supports linear PCM, MPEG and Dolby Digital audio.

DVDMotion Pro is designed for high-end corporate DVD-Video developers working on movie, business, kiosk, industrial, education, and training titles. DVDMotion Pro has a suggested retail price of $895. DVDMotion Pro titles can have one video angle, 99 video clips with 99 chapters each, 8 audio tracks, 32 subpicture streams per, and unlimited menus. DVDMotion Pro supports linear PCM, MPEG and Dolby Digital audio. For more information contact:

SmartDisk Corporation
Attn: Rick Hallock
3506 Mercantile Avenue
Naples, FL 34104
(941) 436-2500 (Voice)
http://www.mtc2000.com (Web)

Sonic Solutions

With its recent acquistion of Daikin's products, Sonic Solutions is the undisputed leader in consumer, corporate and professional DVD authoring tools. Sonic has a DVD authoring tool in just about every price range ($100 to $50,000+), as well as for almost every computer platform (Mac, SGI, & Windows). For more information on any Sonic product contact:

Sonic Solutions
101 Rowland Way
Novato, CA 94945
(415) 893-8000 (Voice)
(415) 893-8008 (Fax)
info@sonic.com (E-Mail)
http://www.sonic.com (Web)

AutoDVD

AutoDVD is a DVD production tool for post-production facilities that want a simple process of producing a DVD-Video title from a video source. Its major features include:

- One-step user interface

- Automated operation, Video to final DVD

- MPEG-2 VBR and CBR video encoding

- Dolby-Certified Dolby Digital encoding

- Direct DVD-R recording

- UDF ISO 9660 volume formatting

- 16:9 aspect ratio support

AutoDVD requires a Power Macintosh G3 system with 512 MB Memory, a 2 GB hard disk for system files and a 18 GB hard disk for content files, a 24-bit color graphics card with at least 1024 x 768 pixel resolution. DVD-ROM drive and Mac OS 9.0 or later.

- Up to 9 Camera Angles

- Up to 8 Audio Tracks

- Single Layer (DVD-5) and Dual Layer (DVD-9) support

- 4:3 and 16:9 Aspect Ratio Support

- Region Code, Analog Copy Protection and Digital Copy Protection (CSS) support.

- Parental Block support

- PCM, MPEG, Dolby Digital and DTS audio support

- Dolby Digital 2.0 and 5.1 channel software encoder

- MPEG-2 software encoder

- Output to DVD-R and DLT

DVD-Video titles are created using a five-step process using Sonic DVD Creator:

1. Open the authoring template. Sonic DVD Creator use custom templates for each project. Similar projects can use the same template, resulting in a more efficient use of time on the authoring system

2. Define encoding parameters. Specific video and audio encoding parameter are added to the template. Start and stop time code locations and encoding parameters for the source material is entered in this step. The AutoSonic option for DVD Creator will automatically manage the video encoder to capture content and encode into MPEG-2 video and Dolby Digital audio.

3. Build menus. Create menus by dragging PhotoShop files, or TIFF bitmaps, into the DVD Creator Menu Editor.

4. Check the title. Check your title using the integrated Proof function, which allows you to view your title just as the viewer would see it on a DVD-Video player.

5. Write the title. Write the final project out to DVD-R or DLT. With Direct-to-DVD formatting, a full-length movie can be written to DVD-R, without storing a disc image on the hard drive, saving system resources and development time.

DVD Creator requires a Power Macintosh G3 system with at least 384 MB Memory, a 2GB hard disk for system files, an 18GB hard disk for content files, a 24-bit color graphics adaptor with at least 1024 x 768 pixel resolution, a DVD-ROM drive, and Mac OS 8.6 or later.

DVDit!

Sonic Solutions DVDit! is the fastest selling DVD authoring tool on the market today. Since its introduction in May 2000 over 150,000 copies of DVDit! have been shipped, giving DVDit! the largest installed base of any DVD authoring tool. There are three different versions of DVDit!. DVDit! Limited Edition (LE) is available as a bundled product from several vendors, such as Matrox, NEC, Sony, Sigma Designs and others. DVDit! Standard Edition (SE) is available as an upgrade to the LE version, as a stand-alone product, or as a bundle with Avid and Media 100 products. DVDit! Professional Edition (PE) was announced at the NAB 2000 conference and is now shipping.

DVDit! has a clean, attractive, and functional users interface that allows authors to quickly develop simple DVD titles. When you launch DVDit! an introduction screen called the "Project Planner" asks a few simple questions about the DVD title to be created or edited, such as the required video format (NTSC or PAL). The main interface for DVDit! consists of just three areas, the "Palette Window", the "Video Monitor", and the "Remote Control".

The Palette Window is used to access media elements that are to be used in your DVD title. Sonic has included a selection of background images, and button graphics that can be used to create semi-custom menus. If you want to use your own background graphics and buttons, then you can import them into the Palette Window using the Media button. The Media button is also used to import AVI or MPEG video clips, and WAV or MPEG audio clips. DVDit! supports several popular multimedia video file formats, including AVI, MPEG-1 and MPEG-2, as well as the WAV and MPEG-1 audio file formats. Background graphics, buttons and still images can be imported in a wide variety of formats including .bmp and .tif. It should be noted that DVDit! can't import AC-3 compressed audio files, so those readers who are used to working with Dolby Digital (AC-3) DVD titles will have to switch over to MPEG-1 or linear PCM (.wav) audio formats to use DVDit! The DVDit! PE version does support the stereo Dolby Digital (AC-3) format.

DVDit! includes a non real time MPEG video encoder that converts AVI files into MPEG-1 or MPEG-2 video streams required by the DVD-Video specification. As with all non real-time MPEG video encoders, the time required to convert the AVI file into MPEG depends on the power and speed of your computer.

The process of developing a DVD title using DVDit! is fairly simple. First you import all of the unique media elements (video, audio & graphics) that are used in the project. DVDit! has a collection of background images and button graphics so you may only need to import your own video and audio clips. Sonic Solutions offers several "Theme Packs" to add additional background and button graphics to DVDit!.

Next you create the interactive menus required for the project. Creating a menu is simple, drag a background graphic from the Palette Window into a Menu box of the Video Window. To add interactive buttons you simply drag the button graphics from the Palette Window on top of the Menu graphic. You can position and resize the buttons, as well as add custom text to the menu. Text can be created in any font supported by your system, and can be positioned and resized easily. Once you have the "look" of your menu set up right, you associate actions with each menu button by dragging a media element or another menu icon on top of the desired menu button. Menu buttons can be used to jump to other menus, to play still images, or to play video clips.

the same basic internal scripting language used by all Sonic Solutions DVD authoring tools. Thus projects can be imported into higher end tools like DVD Creator or DVD Fusion if they need additional features that are not directly supported by DVDit!.

DVD Fusion

Sonic DVD Fusion is designed for NLE-based, professional DVD authoring environments such as post-production facilities and multimedia producers. DVD Fusion integrates the DVD production process: Encoding, authoring, formatting, and writing to DVD-R and DLT. Real time hardware video and audio encoding is provided, plus real-time project proofing and playback of discs. Simple DVD-Video titles can be authored quickly, creating navigation with drag-and-drop editing. DVDFusion also includes many advanced features and fine-tuning controls to create the complex DVD-Video titles. DVD Fusion includes advanced features like motion menu support, interactive programming and a subtitle generator. DVD Fusion includes the Sonic DVD Transcoder, a software MPEG encoder that takes QuickTime and AVI files and converts them to MPEG-2 video and Dolby Digital audio.

DVD Fusion can work on either a Mac or PC platform. For the Mac version the system requirements are a Power Macintosh G3 with at 384 MB RAM, a 2GB hard disk for system files, a 18GB hard disk for content files, a 24 bit color graphics adaptor with 1024 x 768 pixel resolution, a DVD-ROM drive, and Mac OS 9.0 or later. For the Windows version the system requirements are a 600 MHz Pentium III with 256 MB RAM, 200 MB available hard disk space for the DVD Fusion application, an 18 GB hard disk for content files, and a 24 bit color graphics adaptor with 1024 x 768 pixel resolution, a DVD-ROM drive. The Windows version of DVD Fusion will work on Windows 98, ME, Windows NT 4 with Service Pack 6, or Windows 2000 systems with Microsoft DirectShow 7.0 and Microsoft Internet Explorer 5.x.

MyDVD

MyDVD is Sonic Solutions most inexpensive consumer DVD-Video authoring tool. Like most consumer DVD authoring tools, MyDVD provides a limited set of capabilities for authoring DVD titles, and is primarily designed to allow consumers to transfer home videos to DVD, using CD-R as the primary storage medium.

MyDVD can directly import MPEG-2 or MPEG-1 files. It can also import native AVI or QuickTime video files and then automatically converts these files to MPEG before the DVD disc image is created. MyDVD also supports WAV and MPEG-1 audio formats as well as most of the common image formats, including Windows or OS/2 Bitmap (.bmp, .rle), JPEG (.jpg, .jpeg), Macintosh PICT (.pct, .pic), Portable Network Graphic (.png), TIFF (.tif), and Targa (.tga, .vda, .ich, .vst).

MyDVD supports an unlimited number of DVD menus, each with up to 36 menu buttons. Dragging video clips or images onto a menu creates individual buttons. MyDVD automatically links button to clips, and creates a thumbnail image of the video frame or image as the button. Images used as menu backgrounds, buttons, and text can color-adjusted to make them more attractive or more visible. MyDVD includes a text section of the palette that includes dozens of fonts. DVD disc images created with MyDVD can be output to a CD-R disc, or stored on the computers local hard drive.

MyDVD requires a Pentium 233 MHz system with 64MB RAM, 80MB disk space for the MyDVD application, 4GB hard disc space for content, 16-bit color display adaptor with 1024 x 768 pixel resolution, and a CD-R drive. MyDVD will work on systems with Windows 98, 2000, NT or Millennium Edition operating system software. The suggested retail price of MyDVD is $99.

ReelDVD

ReelDVD is an entry level DVD-Video authoring tool, and is designed to run on Windows NT 4.0, or 2000 systems. ReelDVD has a simple Graphical Users Interface (GUI), and a Drag-and-Drop philosophy for DVD authoring. The ReelDVD GUI is formed by three main windows; the Storyboard Editor, the Track Editor, and the Preview Window. The authoring process begins by importing MPEG video clips, menu graphics and still images, dragging them from Windows Explorer and dropping them into the Storyboard Editor. ReelDVD does not include an MPEG transcoder so video content must already be in the MPEG-1 or MPEG-2 format before starting the authoring process. Up to three audio tracks can be added to each video by dragging them on top of the clip in the Storyboard Editor. ReelDVD includes a Dolby Digital software encoder so 48Khz WAV or MPEG audio files can be converted into the Dolby Digital format. ReelDVD also supports the use of Still Shows and Slide Shows, two popular methods of displaying still images (with or without audio) on DVD-Video titles.

ReelDVD hides most of the DVD-Video specification from the title author, although a few key concepts remain. The Storyboard Editor includes icons for AutoPlay, Title and Menu. The AutoPlay icon is essentially the DVD-Video First Play PGC, which defines a starting point for playback when a disc is inserted into a DVD-Video player. The Title icon maps to the Title Menu in the Video Manager space, while the Menu icon maps to the Root Menu in the VTS Manager space. This simplified approach limits ReelDVD titles to a single Video Title Set, but this is more than adequate to handle the vast majority of corporate or prosumer titles.

The Track Editor can be used to define chapter access points within a video segment, to add up to three subpicture streams, and to create specific subtitle graphics. Adding a subtitle stream to a video segment is easy, just click on the subtitle button at the bottom of the Track Editor. This brings up a subtitle generation window where you enter the text information for the subtitle, and set the font type, size and color, as well as the duration of the subtitle. Additional subtitles can be created in the same manner. As you create new subtitles they appear in the Preview window, giving you immediate feedback on how the text will appear over the video. You can also use a script file to import a series of subtitle graphics that have been created outside of ReelDVD.

The Preview Window serves several purposes. When you are working with menus the Preview Window is where you define the number and location of menu buttons, create the button navigation properties (left, right, up and down) as well as the button color properties (display, select and activation colors). Both background and overlay menu graphics need to

navigation.

DVD navigation parameters such as Next, Previous, GoUp, and Menu Buttons are programmed in the Storyboard Editor. Each video, still image, still show, slide show or menu item has icons for navigation parameters. For example, to define the next item to be displayed after a video clip is done, click on the "Next" icon, drag the mouse to the center of the object you want to play next, and then release the mouse.

Scenarist NT

Scenarist NT is one of the most popular DVD authoring tools on the market. It comes in three different configurations, Basic, Advanced and Professional. I use a Scenarist NT Professional system to develop all of my DVD-Video titles.

Scenarist NT Basic is used for corporate, kiosk, or simple DVD title creation. Scenarist NT Basic supports basic DVD features and is limited to one Video Title Set, one subtitle track, and one audio track. Scenarist NT Advanced is used by DVD title developers, DVD publishers, post-production facilities, and content providers to create simple to moderately complex DVD-Video titles. In addition to supporting all the Scenarist NT Basic features, Scenarist NT Advanced supports more DVD features such as 99 Video Title Sets, 32 subtitle tracks, 8 audio tracks, compound navigation commands, parental management, Line 21 data, 16:9 aspect ratio menus, and multi-channel MPEG audio.

Scenarist NT Professional is perhaps the most advanced DVD authoring tool on the market today. The Professional version provides all of the same features as the Advanced product with many additional features such as the creation of title templates, reusing data from one title to the next, sharing data assets, and simultaneously accessing DVD projects by using Scenarist NT's high-performance, cross-platform database engine. Scenarist NT checks compatibility between driver functions (such as MCI) and DVD playback boards; interfaces with PC authoring tools; and includes a software encoder for still pictures, MPEG (2ch) and AC-3

(2ch) audio. Scenarist NT seamlessly integrates with all Sonic DVD software. Scenarist NT Professional provides the following major features:

- Navigation Editing

  - Simple operation for simple titles
  - Comprehensive navigation editing for complex titles
  - Template Wizard allows use of templates for common DVD title designs
  - Copy and paste functions for navigation and menu information
  - Editing with place holder & dummy data
  - Flexible scene creation with the Track Editor
  - Intuitive visual navigation editing with the Scenario Editor
  - Slide and still show support
  - Seamless and non-seamless navigation links
  - Easy highlight still and moving menu creation with Menu Editor

- Simulation

  - Simulation of DVD VOB streams with the Track Editor, including multiple sub-pictures, audio tracks and multi-angles
  - Complete menu simulation including highlight information within the Track Editor
  - Complete emulation using optional Sonic Informer
  - Complete navigation simulation within the Scenario Editor including parental and regional information
  - Software and hardware playback
  - Playback on TV and/or PC monitors
  - S/PDIF digital audio output

- Efficient Work Flow

  - Subtitle text editor and fast subtitle import
  - Script import and export capabilities for the remaking or sharing of DVD projects
  - Validation and verification during the entire authoring process
  - Shared database of DVD projects among several authors
  - Software two-channel Dolby Digital (AC-3) audio encoding and optional Dolby Digital 5.1 (AC-3 5.1)

Scenarist SGI

Scenarist SGI (formerly Scenarist II) is an integrated DVD authoring solution for Silicon Graphics workstations, offering content providers and multimedia developers a complete authoring and premastering solution. With features specifically designed to support the full set of the DVD specifications, Scenarist SGI is on of the most advanced DVD authoring systems available. This platform independent, fully distributed authoring system is compatible all popular video and audio encoders. Scenarist SGI imports MPEG-2 video, TIFF files, still files and audio formats such as AC-3, MPEG-1, MPEG-2, and PCM for professional DVD premastering and authoring. Scenarist SGI provides program chain editing, DVD simulation, DVD Video and ISO/UDF Bridge Formatting, tape premastering (DDP) to DLT tape or DVD-R. Major Scenarist SGI features are:

- Complete support of the DVD-Video 1.0 specification

- DVD stream assembly and layout

- Support for up to 32 subtitle and subpicture streams

- Micro UDF/ISO-9660 file formatting for DVD-ROM

- DVD stream verification against specs

- Slide show support

- Seamless playback

- Karaoke Mode

- DVD copy protection support

- Overlay video and still highlighting

- DVD formatting, layout, and premastering to DLT and DVD-R

- Hybrid DVD-Video/DVD-ROM: Supports creation of hybrid content that can be played on a PC or a DVD player.

- Optional add-ons for VCD authoring support

Scenarist SGI requires an SGI O2 or Octane system with at least 64 MB system RAM, and the IRIX operating system. 18 Gbytes of free hard drive space is required for development of single layer (DVD-5) titles, and 27 Gbytes of free hard drive space is required for dual layer (DVD-9) titles.

Sony

The Sony Vizaro DVD Authoring system (DVA-S700), offers an intuitive and powerful DVD production toolkit. When combined with the Sony Vizaro encoder, the result is a turnkey DVD authoring system that meets the needs of a wide range of applications including corporate training material, and feature film distribution. There are two configurations of the Vizaro system, one for non-technical DVD authors called the "Standard" DVA-S700 system. The DVA-S700+BZDA-S701 system includes additional features such as dual layer support as well as multi-angle support. Incorporating all the power of earlier Sony systems, the Vizaro DVD Authoring system comes as a scaleable and affordable solution that is designed to overcome first time users' cost and complexity concerns. Vizaro is Microsoft Windows 2000 compatible, and integrates video and audio encoding with DVD authoring features supported by a single graphic user interface (GUI).

The Vizaro system removes the complexity associated with the DVD-Video specification by incorporating a comprehensive set of pre-programmed macros, which eliminate the need for any detailed DVD-Video specification or computer programming knowledge. Referred to as 'Nature Commands,' these can be dragged and dropped into the DVD project to create an item appropriate to the need. 'Behaviour Icons' are pre-programmed navigation command sequences that let the user construct sophisticated DVD projects in an intuitive fashion.

A major feature of the Vizaro User Interface is the 'Scenario Preview Window,' which gives the user an overview of the project throughout all the creation stages. Inside the window, icons represent each video section and DVD menu, and together with links illustrate the project's interactivity. For more information contact:

Sony Electronics, Inc
1 Sony Drive
Park Ridge NJ, 07656
(201) 930-1000 (Voice)
(201) 930-6307 (Fax)
kevin.george@am.sony.com (E-Mail)
http://www.sony.com/professional (Web)

Spruce Technologies

Spruce Technologies has four different DVD-Video authoring tools, all working on Windows platforms. Spruce has also developed a proprietary technology called Convergence, that enables DVD-Video titles to include Internet links associated with individual menu screens or media elements. Convergence enabled titles include a customized copy of the InterVideo WinDVD player software that runs directly off the DVD or CD disc, eliminating the need for the installation of custom software on the viewers PC. Convergence is included with all of Spruce's DVD-Video authoring products. For more information contact:

Spruce Technologies, Inc.
1054 S. De Anza Blvd. Suite 200
San Jose, CA 95129
(888) 355-MPEG (Voice)
info@spruce-tech.com (E-Mail)
http://www.spruce-tech.com (Web)

DVDConductor

DVDConductor is a mid-range DVD authoring tool targeted at the corporate market. Based on the DVDMaestro core, DVDConductor provides all the features required for basic, to moderately complex DVD-Video titles, with DVD-ROM and WebDVD feature support. Its major features include:

- Easy to use graphical interface
- "Drag & drop" interface
- Support for up to 2 video camera angles
- Support for up to 8 audio tracks
- Support for up to 32 subtitle streams
- Support for multiple chapters per segment

- WebDVD support
- Support for Motion Menus

Minimum system requirements for DVD Conductor include Pentium II or better PC, Windows NT 4.0 Operating System Software, 128 MB RAM, 9 Gb hard disk, DVD ROM drive, and an AGP VGA card.

DVDMaestro

DVDMaestro is an award-winning professional DVD authoring tool that supports all of the features of the DVD-Video specification, including the ability to create complete hybrid video and data titles that play in and recognize the differences between DVD players and DVD-ROM computers. Its major features include:

- Easy to use graphical interface
- "Drag & drop" interface with complete flexibility for title navigation and interactivity
- Support for up to 9 video camera angles
- Support for up to 8 audio tracks
- Support for up to 32 subtitle streams
- Menu Editor: full "motion menu" support
- Photoshop file import with smart layer recognition
- Support for multiple chapters per segment
- Subtitle text import with editing capability
- Preview System: real time preview of audio/video/subtitle streams
- DVD Emulator for full title verification

- DVD Layout Tools for disc-image layout and production of DVD-ROM and hybrid titles

- Region coding support

- Dual layer support

- Copy scrambling system (CSS)

- Parental block support

- WebDVD support

- Forced I-frame insertion

Minimum system requirements for DVD Conductor include Pentium II or better PC, Windows NT 4.0 Operating System Software, 128 MB RAM, 9 GB hard disk, DVD ROM drive, and an AGP VGA card.

DVDPerformer

DVDPerformer is an entry level corporate DVD authoring and encoding solution for Windows NT. Its major features include the following.

- Integrated system with both DVD Authoring and Encoding

- Real-time Hardware-based MPEG Encoding with Analog Inputs

- Support for Multiple Camera Angles,

- Support for up to 8 Audio tracks

- Support for up to 32 Subtitle streams

- Integrated DVD Proofing and Debugging features

- Support for Cutting Master Format (CMF) for DVD-R to replication

- Support for Motion Menus

- Support for Slide Shows

- Support for 4:3 and 16:9 content

- Support for DVD-Video, DVD-ROM and DVD-Hybrid titles

- Support for Spruce DVDonCD titles with Integrated Web Links

Minimum system requirements for DVD Conductor include Pentium II or better PC, Windows NT 4.0 Operating System Software, 128 MB RAM, 9 GB hard disk, DVD ROM drive, and an AGP VGA card.

SpruceUp

As with most consumer authoring tools, SpruceUp hides the complexity and terminology of the DVD-Video specification from the author. Creating DVD titles with SpruceUp is a three-step process: Author, Simulate and Export. The graphical users interface is clean, easy to understand, and simple to use.

The Media Gallery is used to identify and store background images, button graphics, and video clips. SpruceUp includes a number of predefined background and button images. Custom graphics can be imported in a variety of formats such as .bmp, .tif, .jpg and .tga files. MPEG-1 or MPEG-2 video elements can be imported in the m1v, .m2v, .mpv, .vbs, .mpg, .mpe, .mpeg, .mp2, .m2p, and .avi (MPEG only) formats. Audio elements are associated with video elements through their file name. When importing a video element if there is an audio file in the same directory, with the same name, it is attached to the video element. Audio elements can be imported in the MPEG-1 Layer 2 audio (.m1a, .mpa, or .abs), Dolby Digital

cific frame to use as the thumbnail image by double-clicking on the element in the Media Gallery, and changing its parameters. Buttons, media elements and text can be positioned anywhere on the menu, and properties such as the font color, size, and drop-shadow can be adjusted as required. Each button can be associated with a media element, or another menu. SpruceUp includes integrated support for WebDVD functions so http: addresses can be assigned to menu buttons or media elements. The Menu Gallery is a handy way to keep track of, and select, the various menus created for a project. The Main Control Area allows you navigate through the three main authoring steps, Author, Simulate and Export.

The Simulation step of the authoring process allows you to test each menu, and play back each media element, to verify that the DVD title is working correctly. SpruceUp automatically assigns the Left, Right, Up and Down navigation properties to each menu button. The algorithm used to assign these links appears to work best when menu buttons are aligned in horizontal or vertical patterns. Navigation controls are provided in the Work Area so that buttons can be selected and activated. SpruceUp creates a unique DVD Video Title Set for each video element used in a title, so you can only have up to 99 different video elements in a project.

The third and final step in the authoring process is Export where a valid DVD-Video disc image is created and stored on a hard drive, or on recordable media such as CD-R, DVD-R, DVD-RAM and DVD+RW. SpruceUp has a built in disc space calculator, so it will provide a warning if the final project is larger than the media you are trying to store it on. Exporting creates the various DVD-Video volume and file structures, and records them on the selected media type.

Spruce has included several advanced features as part of the Export step. A custom, royalty free version of the InterVideo WinDVD player, called Syzygy, can be included with the final DVD disc image. This is very important when the project is published on CD-R or CD-RW media, and may be played back on a personal computer that does not support DVD-Video playback. When the Syzygy player is included with the DVD disc image, SpruceUp also creates an Autorun file that automatically launches the Syzygy player when the disc is inserted into the CD-ROM drive. The Syzygy player also provides WebDVD playback features that launch a web browser when a button or media element has a URL associated with it. Last, but not least, SpruceUp also allows you to include DVD-ROM data along with the DVD-Video title on the final disc image. Thus it is possible to create DVD-Video, DVD-ROM and WebDVD titles using SpruceUp.

SpruceUp has a suggested retail price of $129, and is being bundled with a number of video encoding products, such as Heuris MPEG Power Professional 2 (MPP2). Minimum system requirements for SpruceUp are Windows' 98SE, Millennium (ME), NT 4.0 (Service Pack 4 minimum), and 2000 operating systems, Intel Pentium II 300Mhz, Intel Celeron 333Mhz (with L2 cache), or AMD K6 (350Mhz minimum) CPU, 128MB RAM and an 8MB RAM Video Card with 1024 by 768 pixel resolution at 65,536 colors.

Vitec

Vitec DVD Toolbox™ is a collection of six programs including an AVI to MPEG-2 compression engine, an MPEG-2 editor, DVD authoring software, a VOB to MPEG file converter, an MPEG audio remixer and a software DVD player. The MPEG Maker 2 program is used to convert video stored in the AVI format into the MPEG format. Source video files can be in either NTSC or PAL, and can be compressed into MPEG-1 or MPEG-2. Variable bit rate encoding is supported for native MPEG-1 or MPEG-2 formats, but only constant bit rate encoding is supported for DVD and Video-CD formats. Audio can be compressed at the same time as the video, but only in the MPEG-1 audio format.

The Video Clip MPEG-2 SE program is used to edit MPEG-2 streams. Edit functions are limited to simple trimming and splicing operations with accuracy to the nearest I frame for in-points and the nearest P or I frame for out points.

DVDMaker is used to create the DVD-Video disc image. Each chapter of the title should have an MPEG-2 video stream and an associated MPEG-1 audio stream. The process of creating the DVD title is deceptively simple. You drag MPEG-2 video streams into a chapter list, then associate the correct MPEG-1 audio stream. You can move the video clips up or down in the chapter list to control the playback order. If you want the DVD title to repeat after the end of the last chapter you can click on the "Do Loop" button.

DVDMaker has some severe limitations when it comes to making DVD titles. The final disc image is limited to a collection of chapters in a single title within a single title set. DVD menus are not supported, thus there is no way to make an interactive DVD title with this tool. AC-3 audio, multiple camera angles, multiple audio tracks, and subpicture streams are not supported. In summary you can use DVDMaker to create a DVD title that looks and feels just like a VHS title.

DVD Toolbox includes a licensed copy of Ravisent's Cinemaster software DVD player. You can use Cinemaster to play back the DVD disc image created with DVDMaker. Since Cinemaster uses the Microsoft DirectShow API it will find the first hard drive or optical disc drive with a Video_TS directory in the root, and will start playing the DVD title stored in that location. DVDMaker can output the DVD disc image in the UDF format, and if you have access to a Pioneer DVD-R writer then you can create a DVD title that will work on most, but not all, consumer DVD-Video players.

The VOBtoMPEG utility can be used to strip out the elementary MPEG-2 video stream and MPEG-1 audio streams from a DVD Video Object (VOB) file. This is handy if you want to reuse some content from a DVD title you previously developed with DVD Toolbox. This utility will not work on CSS encrypted VOB files, unless you run the infamous DeCSS utility first. It also will not be able to strip out the AC-3 audio stream from the VOB file since DVD Toolbox only supports MPEG-1 audio streams. The MPEG Remix utility can convert a standard WAV audio stream into MPEG-1 audio. Once the audio has been converted to the MPEG-1 format it can be inserted into an MPEG-1 or MPEG-2 multiplexed video file, essentially allowing you to replace the existing audio streams with any WAV audio files. The suggested retail price for DVD Toolbox is $400. For more information contact:

VITEC MULTIMEDIA, USA
556 Weddell Drive, Suite 3

DVD-ROM formatting tools are used to create DVD-ROM only disc images, or to create hybrid discs with both DVD-Video and DVD-ROM data areas.

GEAR

Based on the well-known GEAR product line, GEAR PRO DVD supports DVD-R, DVD-RAM, DLT and CD-R(W) creation. It is compatible with most recorders and a variety of jukeboxes. GEAR PRO DVD supports the new technologies for DVD/UDF and CD-rewriteable. GEAR PRO DVD provides a reliable, versatile and cost effective solution for producing a single DVD-R copy, or forwarding a project to a replication facility for manufacturing. Software Developers Toolkits (API) are available for W/NT/200, Linux and Unix. To master DVD-ROM titles, GEAR PRO DVD also supports the creation of a pre-master tape, optionally in DDP format. Tape output can be performed to DLT tape units, Exabyte 8 mm tape drives or DAT. In addition to creating Digital Versatile Discs (DVD-RAM and DVD-R) in Universal Disc Format (UDF), GEAR PRO DVD can also be used to create hybrid ISO 9660 / UDF discs. GEAR PRO DVD is designed for fast data transfer rates while ensuring data integrity. For DVD-ROM titles GEAR PRO DVD supports the standard UDF file system. UDF can be combined with the ISO 9660 file system (ISO/UDF hybrid) for backwards compatibility. The Windows version of Gear Pro DVD sells for $500, the Unix version is $1,500 and the Linux version is $699. For more information contact:

Sam Plummer
GEAR Software
1061 East Indiantown Road
Suite 500
Jupiter, Florida 33477
877-237-4327 x 4120 (Voice)
(561) 575-3026 (Fax)
http://www.gearsoftware.com (Web)

Prassi

DVD Rep™ is a Windows software application for DVD-R mastering. DVD Rep is UDF compliant, and can master on the fly, using the UDF/ISO Bridge or pure UDF file system formats. Key features of DVD Rep include the ability to copy data directly from a hard drive to a DVD-R, support for DVD-Video disc images, support for CD-RW devices, file system integrity verification. DVD Rep is sold only through OEM agreements, and in the past has been provided with Pioneer DVD-R drives. For more information contact:

> Prassi Software
> 1731 Technology Dr., Suite 490
> San Jose CA 95110
> (408) 573-9100 (Voice)
> (888) 477-2774 (Voice)
> (408) 573-8100 (Fax)
> info@prassi.com (E-Mail)
> http://www.prassi.com (Web)

Roxio

Toast™ 5 Titanium is a comprehensive, all-in-one CD and DVD mastering product that enables you to create, organize, share and store all of your digital content on CDs or DVDs. Toast 5 Titanium includes, Toast 5 Titanium CD Recording Software, CD Spin Doctor™, QDesign MVP™, iView Multimedia™, Magic Mouse Discus™, Toast Audio Extractor, Photos by professional photographer James Beal, and free music samples by various artists. Toast 5 Titanium allows you to burn DVD disc images on DVD-R, DVD-RW and DVD-RAM media. Toast 5 Titanium requires a CD or DVD recorder to use this software, a Power Macintosh with Mac OS 8.6 or later, 12 MB of RAM, minimum 100 MB free hard disk space, and QuickTime 4.0 or later. The suggested retail price of Toast 5 Titanium is $89.95. For more information contact:

> Roxio, Inc.
> 461 S. Milpitas Blvd.
> Milpitas, CA 95035
> (408) 635-7694) (Voice)
> sales@roxio.com (E-Mail)
> http://www.roxio.com (Web)

SmartDisk

ForDVD is a premastering tool used for DVD-ROM development. Premastering is the process by which data files of various types and sizes are compiled into a disc image file suitable for storage on DVD disc. ForDVD is a Windows based application that supports UDF, ISO-9660, and Joliet formats, long file names, DVD-5, DVD-9, DVD-10 and DVD-18 disc sizes. Completed disc images can be written directly to removable DVD media, or to a DLT tape in DDP 2.0 format for use by a DVD replication facility. Up to 10,000 unique folders can be defined on a single disc image, with up to 20,000 unique files per folder. ForDVD can be purchased directly from SmartDisk Corporation for $1,195. For more information contact:

SmartDisk Corporation
Attn: Rick Hallock
3506 Mercantile Avenue
Naples, FL 34104
(941) 436-2500 (Voice)
http://www.mtc2000.com (Web)

for creation of check discs. Effective March 31, 2001 SmartDVD Maker will no longer be offered by Smart Storage, although they will continue to support the product through December 31, 2001.

Sonic Solutions

DVD ROM Formatter is a Windows NT based DVD-ROM formatting and layout tool. It's primary features include support for DVD-5, DVD-9, DVD-10 and DVD-18 discs, generation of disc images that are fully compliant with the DVD specification, output to DDP 2.0 DLT tape or directly to DVD-R, and cross-platform support for both PC and Mac files. For more information contact:

Sonic Solutions
101 Rowland Way
Novato, CA 94945
(415) 893-8000 (Voice)
(415) 893-8008 (Fax)
info@sonic.com (E-Mail)
http://www.sonic.com (Web)

Software Architects

WriteDVD! Pro for Windows can be used to set up, run, test & repair DVD-RAM drives and media on a PC running Windows OS. The world's first and most widely used UDF file system based DVD utility for PC's, WriteDVD! Pro includes FixDVD!^{TM} the world's first disk diagnostic and repair utility designed specifically for UDF formatted DVD disks. WriteDVD! Features include support for 4.7 gig DVD-RAM drives, drive letter access to your DVD-RAM for "drag & drop" convenience and optimized performance on Windows systems. WriteDVD!

Pro supports all manufacturers' drives and models, including SCSI, ATAPI. WriteDVD! Can be purchased directly from Software Architects for $89.95. For more information contact:

Software Architects Inc.
Attn: Bryan Love
1702-H Meridian Avenue #301
San Jose, California 95125
(831) 768-7440 (Voice)
(831) 768-7211 (Fax)
bryanl@softarch.com (E-Mail)
Http://www.softarch.com (Web)

Spruce Technologies

DVD Premaster Tool (DVD PMT) is a stand-alone DVD formatter, working with DVD-R recorders and DLT tape drives to format any data set on local or networked volumes to fully compliant DVD-ROM disc images on DVD-R, or on DDP-format DLT tape ready for mass replication. DVD PMT includes a verifier that performs a bit-level verification of DVD-R or DLT masters for total confidence. The major features of DVD PMT include:

- Compilation of any project prepared with Spruce DVD authoring tools into a valid DVD data set (Video_TS directory).

- Formatting of DVD Video, DVD ROM, or Hybrid data sets into an ISO-9660/micro-UDF bridge disc image on hard disc, DVD-R, or DLT tape (DDP format) for replication.

- Transfer of formatted DVD disc image to DVD-R.

- Transfer of formatted DVD disc image to DLT in DDP format for replication.

- Bit-for-bit verify of disc image on hard disc against DLT tape for quality assurance prior to mastering and replication.

For more information contact:

Spruce Technologies, Inc.
1054 S. De Anza Blvd. Suite 200
San Jose, CA 95129
(888) 355-MPEG (Voice)
info@spruce-tech.com (E-Mail)
http://www.spruce-tech.com (Web)

Veritas

PrimoDVD is a DVD Mastering and Duplication software package designed for the professional market. PrimoDVD from, Prassi Europe SARL a division of Veritas, is a multitasking DVD-Mastering application. Using PrimoDVD, you can record to 16 DVD-R drives simultaneously. PrimoDVD also provides features needed for creating single DVD's, while providing advanced functions for DVD replication. Its major features include:

- `Video_TS` and `Audio_TS` formatting – Creates DVD-Video compliant discs from your `Video_TS` and `Audio_TS` directories or from an image file.

- Triple Tree for DVD Bridge – Records DVD-ROMs using ISO, Joliet and UDF structures.

- Master to 16 DVD recorders

- Record Multiple Different Jobs Simultaneously

- DLT Support for DDP 2.0 format

- Disc Verify

Prassi Europe SARL
75 Bd. Oyon, Technopôle Novaxis
72100 Le Mans
FRANCE
info@prassieurope.com (E-Mail)
http://www.prassieurope.com (Web)

VOB Information Systems, Inc

VOB Information Systems, Inc. has two products for recordable DVD, InstantBackup and Instant CD/DVD SDK. InstantBackup utilizes the reliable storage capability of DVD-RAM drives, and the efficiency and control of custom backup software to ensure your data will be safe and easily accessible in case of a problem. The CD/DVD-WIZARD SDK is a sophisticated CD/DVD-Recording toolkit that can easily be included in custom applications. Custom applications can be ported in almost any programming language for Microsoft Windows95, Windows98, Windows ME, Windows NT4.x and 2000. For more information contact:

Rick Huhnke
VOB Information Systems, Inc.
66E. Laurel Ave
Sierra Madre, CA 91024
(626) 836 5467 (Voice)
Rhuhnke@vobinc.com (E-Mail)
www.vobinc.com (Web)

Young Minds

DVD Studio is a complete hardware and software solution for recording DVD-ROMs. DVD Studio combines MakeDisc Plus for DVD premastering software, with the DVD Studio intelligent controller and a Pioneer DVD-R recorder. MakeDisc for DVD orchestrates and controls the process of picking and formatting files. The intelligent controller provides the buffering and completely isolates the writer from the workstation. DVD Studio creates cross platform compatible DVD discs on NT and most of the widely available UNIX platforms including Sun, Linux, IBM, HP and Digital UNIX. DVD Studio can be purchased from authorized Young Minds resellers, or direct from Young Minds if you do not have a reseller located near you. For more information contact:

Young Minds. Inc
1906 Orange Tree Lane, #220
Redlands, CA 92374
(909) 335-1350 (Voice)
(909) 798-0488 (Fax)
info@ymi.com (E-Mail)
http://www.ymi.com (Web)

Distributors

There are only a handful of independent DVD distribution companies serving the US market. Most major motion picture studios have their own home video distribution companies, and these distributors only carry their parent studios products. Here are a few independent DVD distributors that can help you get your title into the retail channel.

DVD International

DVD International is a leading distributor of non-theatrical DVD titles throughout the world. With distribution channels set up in the US, Canada, Europe, Australia, Taiwan and New Zealand markets, DVD International can help you get your DVD title exposure worldwide. For more information contact:

DVD International
35 Sherwood Dr.
Mountain Lakes, NJ 07046
(973) 335-1837 (Voice)
(973) 335-3414 (Fax)
david@dvdinternational.com (E-Mail)
http://www.dvdinternational.com (Web)

Image Entertainment

Image Entertainment acquires rights to film, video and DVD titles and distributes them to US retailers, including Best Buy and Amazon.com. Its joint venture Aviva International (50%-owned) sells its products overseas. In addition, the company sells its titles directly to consumers through its online subsidiary DVDPlanet.com (about 15% of sales). The company also sells broadcast rights to cable and satellite channels and is moving to produce more original content. For more information contact:

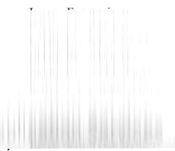

DVD replication services are offered throughout the world. Generally a DVD replication facility will accept a DVD disc image on DLT tape in the DDP 2.0 format or on a DVD-R, either as a valid disc image or in the new Cutting Master Format (CMF). Replicators will make a glass master from the disc image data, create molds from the glass master, and then make production copies of the disc through an injection molding process. Most replication facilities will provide a limited number of check discs so that the developer can verify the correct operation of the disc before committing to a large production run. In most cases the cost of the check disc is waived if at least 1,000 production discs are made using the glass master and molds created for the check disc. Many replication facilities also will print color labels on the DVD discs, package them in a variety of DVD package designs, and ship them directly to wholesale or retail customers.

Americ Disc

Americ Disc is a major North American provider of DVD manufacturing services and other optical disc media. Americ Disc is partly owned by MPO of France, the largest independent optical disc manufacturer in Europe. Together, MPO and Americ Disc form the worlds largest independent CD/DVD manufacturing groups with facilities in Europe, Asia and North America. Americ Disc has manufacturing facilities in California, Florida, Tennessee and Canada, as well as service and distribution centers in Minnesota, Tennessee and Montreal. Americ Disc offers DVD-5, DVD-9, DVD-10 and DVD-18 replication services as well as authoring, printing, assembly, packaging, fulfillment, shipping and distribution. For more information contact:

Luis Betances
Director, DVD sales
655 Joost Avenue
San Francisco, CA, 94127

(415) 334-8198 (Voice)
luis.betances@americdisc.com (E-Mail)
http://www.americdisc.com (Web)

CD-ROM-Works

CD-ROM Works is a full service CD and DVD replication facility located in Portland, Oregon. The offer DVD-5, DVD-9 and DVD-10 replication services. 8 check discs can be delivered within five days of receipt of source disc image. There is no charge for check discs as long as a replication order is placed using the same disc image. CD-ROM Works will accept short run (less than 1000 units) orders, and delivery is typically within 8-10 days of reciept of all input materials. Input formats accepted include DLT and DVD-R. Packaging options include Amarary, Digipak, Flip-Pak, and Jewel cases. For more information contact:

CD-ROM Works
139 NW Second
Portland, OR 97209
(503) 219-9331 (Voice)
(503) 254-4830 (Fax)
sales@cd-rom-works.com (E-Mail)
http://www.cd-rom-works.com (Web)

Cinram

Cinram International Inc. was founded in 1969 and is one of the world's largest independent providers of pre-recorded multimedia products and services, and custom-order downloadable and optical disc digital content. With facilities in the United States, Canada, Europe, and Latin America, Cinram manufactures and distributes pre-recorded VHS videocassettes, audio cassettes, music CDs, CD-ROM and DVD for motion picture studios, music labels, publishers and computer software companies around the globe. Cinram manufactures DVD-5, DVD-9 and DVD-10 format discs, and accepts disc images in the DLT (DDP 2.0) and DVD-R formats. For more information contact:

Cinram, Inc.
4905 Moores Mill Road
Huntsville, AL 35811
(800) 433-3472 (Voice)
(256) 852-8706 (Fax)
sales@cinram.com (E-Mail)
http://www.cinram.com (Web)

Crest National

Crest National's is a full service DVD replication facility offering services for the preparation, replication and distribution of optical media. Their services include pre-mastering, mastering, replication (CD-Audio, CD-ROM, CD+G, CD-I, CD-V, DVD 5, DVD 10, DVD 9, HDCD), serialization, six-color disc printing, tray card/booklet printing, graphic design services, customized packaging, shrink-wrapping, inventory management, and global distribution. For more information contact:

Crest National
6721 Romaine St
Hollywood, CA 90038
(800) 309-DISC (Voice)
(323) 466-7128 (Fax)

tomer, product assembly and disassembly, POP construction and special promotional program fulfillment. For more information contact:

Deluxe Video Services
555 Huehl Road
Northbrook, IL 60062
(847) 291-1150 (Voice)
videoinfo@bydeluxe.com (E-Mail)
http://www.rank.com (Web)

Disctronics

Disctronics is a multinational optical disc replicator with facilities in the US, UK, France and Italy. Their facilities are equipped with the latest Laser Beam Recorders and DVD manufacturing lines, enabling quick turn-times and highly reliable manufacturing. A full range of test equipment also insures the highest level of quality and playability. Disctronics provide glass-mastering services, DVD-5, DVD-9 and DVD-10 replication, and they have a wide range of packaging options at competitive prices. For more information contact:

Andrew DaPuzzo
2800 Summit Ave
Plano, TX 75074
(800) 929-8100 ext 7890 (Voice)
andrewd@discusa.com (E-Mail)
Http://www.discusa.com (Web)

DOCdata

DOCdata is a full service video cassette, CD and DVD replication company with facilities throughout the world. Services include mastering, replication, packaging and fulfillment. DOCdata can replicate DVD-5, DVD-9 and DVD-10 format discs. For more information contact:

DOCdata Ablex
Harcourt Halesfield 14
Telford Shropshire TF7 4QR
United Kingdom
+44 1952 680 131 (Voice)
+44 1952 583 501 (Fax)
http://www.docdata.com (Web)

Future Media Productions

Future Media Productions is one of the largest independent CD/DVD replication plants on the West Coast and offers replication services for the DVD-5, DVD-9 and DVD-10 formats. Their services include Pre-mastering, Glass Mastering, Film Production for DVD and CD label artwork from digital files, DVD and CD Replication, Assembly, Print Outsourcing, Complete Turnkey Operations, Inventory Control, Warehousing, and Shipping. Replication capacity exceeds 550,000 CDs and 120,000 DVDs per day, and a wide variety of packaging formats are supported. For more information contact:

Dave Moss
Future Media Productions
24811 Avenue Rockefeller
Valencia, CA. 91355
(661) 294-5575 (Voice)
(661) 294-5583 (Fax)
dmoss@fmpi.com (E-Mail)
http://www.fmpi.com (Web)

Infodisc

Infodisc is an ISO 9002 certified, full service CD and DVD replication facility located in Taiwan. Infodisc can replicate DVD-5, DVD-9 and DVD-10 format discs. Services include mastering, replication, packaging and distribution. Infodisc is an authorized Warner Advanced Media Operations (WAMO) DVD Affilliate. For more information contact please review their web site at http://www.infodiscusa.com.

IPC Communication Services

IPC Communication Services is an ISO 9002 certified, full service CD and DVD replication facility providing global manufacturing and distribution services. Their services include printing, CD and DVD mastering and replication, diskette duplication, assembly, and complete product fulfillment and distribution worldwide. IPC can replicate DVD-5, DVD-9 and DVD-10 format discs. For more information contact:

IPC Communication Services
501 Colonial Drive
St. Joseph, MI 49085
888-563-3220 (Voice)
Sales@ipcjci.com (E-Mail)
http://www.ipc-world.com (Web)

been authorized to replicate DVD discs for Microsoft Xbox 3rd party developers. For more information contact:

JVC Disc America, Co.
3443 Laguna Blvd.
Elk Grove, CA 95758
(916) 399-4098 (Voice)
(916) 399-4000 (Fax)
rmontgomery@sac.jvcdiscusa.com (E-Mail)
http://www.jvcdiscusa.com (Web)

JVC Disc America, Co.
2 JVC Road
Tuscaloosa, AL 95405
(205) 556-7111 (Voice)
sheiberger@jvcdiscusa.com (E-Mail)
http://www.jvcdiscusa.com (Web)

Lena Optical Disc

Lena Optical Disc is a full service DVD replication facility located in Hong Kong. Services include audio/video editing, AC-3 audio editing, MPEG 2 encoding, pre-mastering, mastering, replication, bonding, and printing. Lena Optical Disc can replicate DVD-5, DVD-9 and DVD-10 format discs. For more information contact:

Lena Optical Disc
4106, 41/F, Office Tower, Convention Plaza,
No. 1 Harbour Road, Hong Kong.
(852) 2556-8198 (Voice)
(852) 2556-1536 (Fax)

info@lenaoptical.com (E-Mail)
http://www.lenaoptical.com (Web)

Media Group, Inc.

Media Group, Inc. is a world wide ISO 9002, WAMO Certified replicator of DVD-5 DVD-9, & DVD-10 discs, as well as CDs. With factories on 2 continents, they offer world wide shipping capabilities. Media Group, Inc. offers Mini DVDs & CDs, as well as Business Card DVDs & CDs. Media Group is a manufacturer, not a broker, so they offer competitive pricing and direct communication. For more information contact:

Damon S. Martin
Dir. Sales & Marketing
Media Group, Inc.
44799 Industrial Drive
Fremont, CA 94538
510.683.0188 ext. 123 (Voice)
510.683.0189 (Fax)
damonm@mediagrpusa.com (E-Mail)

Metatec

Metatec is an ISO 9002 certified, full service CD and DVD production company with facilities in Ohio, California and The Netherlands. Their services include premastering, mastering, DVD-5, DVD-9 and DVD-10 replication, packaging, and printing. For more information contact:

Metatec
7001 Metatec Blvd.
Dublin, OH 43017
(614) 761-2000 (Voice)
(614) 766-3146(Fax)
http://www.metatec.com (Web)

MRT Technology

MRT Technology is a full service CD and DVD production facility located in California. Services include DVD-5, DVD-9 and DVD-10 replication, printing, and packaging. For more information contact:

MRT Technology LLC
18560 San Jose Avenue
City of Industry, California 91748
(626) 839-5555 (Voice)
(626) 810-1365 (Fax)

robynt@mrttech.com (E-Mail)
http://www.mrttech.com (Web)

Optical Disc Corporation

Optical Disc Corporation (ODC) provides DVD mastering and stamper services to DVD replicator facilities worldwide. This service fills an industry need allowing replicators to offer DVDs without having in-house mastering equipment. ODC currently provides stampers for DVD-5, DVD-9, DVD-10, and DVD-18 formats. Stampers from the ODC DVD mastering

(562) 946.6030 (Fax)
omcdowell@optical-disc.com (E-Mail)
http://www.optical-disc.com (Web)

Panasonic Disc Services Corporation

Panasonic Disc Services Corporation (PDSC) is a full service DVD production company with facilities througout the world. Services include premastering, mastering, replication, printing, packaging, fulfilment and distribution. PDSC replicates DVD-5, DVD-9, and DVD-10 format discs. For more information contact:

Panasonic Disc Services Corporation
20608 Madrona Ave.
Torrance, CA 90503
(310) 783-4800 (Voice)
(310) 783-4804 (Fax)
sales@dvd.panasonic.com (E-Mail)
http://www.panasonicdvd.com (Web)

Provac Disc Media

Provac Disc Media launched the first DVD replication line in Canada in February 2000, and underwent an expansion in February 2002. Provac owns and operates the only DVD facility in Canada that replicates DVD-5, DVD-9 and DVD-10 format discs. Provac services the entertainment industry (movies and games) and corporate customers (premium and promotional discs, directories, catalogs and product showcases). Provac's services include authoring, glass mastering, DVD-5, DVD-9 and DVD-10 replication, on-disc screen-printing up to 5 colors, and automated clamshell packaging. For more information contact:

Provac Disc Media
224 Lesmill Road
Toronto, M3B 2T5
Canada
(416) 447-0707 (Voice)
(888) 876-9013 (Toll Free Voice)
(416) 447-3803 (Fax)
provac@idirect.ca (E-Mail)

Ritek Global Media

Ritek Global Media is a full service DVD production facility located in Taiwan. Services include premastering, mastering, replication, printing and packaging. Ritek can replicate DVD-5, DVD-9 and DVD-10 format discs. For more information contact:

Ritek Global Media
No. 42, Kuang-Fu N. Rd.,
Hsin-Chu Industrial Park, 303
Taiwan R.O.C
+886-2-85215555 (Voice)
+886-2-85217904 (Fax)
http://www.ritek.com.tw (Web)

Sonopress

Sonopress is a full service CD and DVD production company offering premastering, mastering, replication, printing, packaging, and distribution services. DVD-5, DVD-9, and DVD-10 discs can be replicated in their worldwide facilities. For more information contact:

Sonopress LLC
108 Monticello Road
Weaverville, NC 28787-9442
(828) 658-2000 (Voice)
(828) 658-2008 (Fax)
www.sonopress.com (Web)

Sony DADC

Sony DADC is a full service CD, DVD, MiniDisc and PlayStation production company with facilities located in Europe. Sony DADC can replicate DVD-5, DVD-9, DVD-10 and DVD-18 format discs. Their services include premastering, mastering, replication, printing, packaging and distribution. For more information contact:

Sony DADC Austria AG
Sonystrasse 20, A-5081
Anif/Salzburg Austria

+43 (0) 6246-880-555 (Voice)
+43 (0) 6246-880-509 (Fax)
sales@sonydadc.com (E-Mail)
http://www.sonydadc.com (Web)

Sony Disc Manufacturing

As the world's largest producer of pre-recorded optical discs, Sony Disc Manufacturing (SDM) offers high-quality products and services to serve the growing needs of the education

63 Spit Brook Road, Suite 200
Nashua, NH 03060
Phone: 1-800-358-7316
WebSDM@disc.sony.com (E-Mail)
http://sdm.sony.com (Web)

Technicolor

Technicolor is the world's largest independent DVD replicator. With more than a dozen manufacturing and distribution operations worldwide, Technicolor replicates nearly 175,000 DVD units daily and has the capacity to produce almost 65 million annually. The company enhanced its DVD capabilities when it merged with Nimbus CD International, Inc., a leading international optical disc manufacturer. Services include premastering, mastering, replication, printing, packaging and distribution. Technicolor can replicate DVD-5, DVD-9, DVD-10, and DVD-18 format discs. For more information contact:

Technicolor
623 Welsh Run Road
Ruckersville, VA 22968
(804) 985-1100 (Voice)
(804) 985-4692 (Fax)
http://www.technicolor.com (Web)

Utech Media Corporation

UTECH is the largest DVD/CD manufacturer in Asia; offering a variety of services, including Compression, Authoring, Pre-mastering, Mastering, Replication, Printing, Packaging, Warehousing, Distribution, Single and Worldwide Distribution Services. UTECH's DVD Studio provides computer graphics, editing, AV encoding and authoring, recording, CD pre-mastering, audio mastering with Dolby and DTS 5.1 surround sound technology. Besides DVD/CD replication, U-TECH also offers diversified service, including FreeCut CD and NameCard CD, Colorful CD and DVD, CD-Single (8cm CD), Semi CD and DVD, and 24K gold CD.

UTECH replicates DVD-5, DVD-9 and DVD-10 format discs. Input data is accepted on DLT in the DDP 2.0 format or on DVD-R in the Cutting Master (CMF) format. DVD replication capacity is over 3,000,000 discs per month. For more information contact:

UTECH Media Corporation
No. 222, Hwa-Ya 2Rd., Kuei-Shan Hsiang
Tao-Yuan Shien, 333
Taiwan, R.O.C.
+886-3-3961111 (Voice)
+886-396-0830 (Fax)
service@utechmedia.com.tw (E-Mail)
http://www.utechmedia.com.tw (Web)

Warner Media Services

Warner Media Services is one of the largest DVD production companies in the world. Their services include premastering, mastering, replication, printing, packaging, and distribution of DVD-5, DVD-9, DVD-10 and DVD-18 format discs. For more information contact:

Warner Media Services
1400 East Lackawwana Avenue
Olyphant, PA 18448
http://www.ivyhill-wms.com (Web)

Zomax

Zomax is a full service DVD facility offering DVD-5, DVD-9, and DVD-10 replication services. Input formats accepted are DLT (DDP format) and DVD-R. Their standard check disc package includes 100 replicated disc with a single color label, delivered in 5-7 days from receipt of the input media. Screen printing in up to six colors is available. Packaging options include Amaray, Alpha, Warner, Jewel Box, Super Jewel Box, Multi Jewel Box, Tyvex sleeve, binder sleeve, and bulk discs on spindles. Zomax also offers warehouse and complete fulfillment services including RMA processing. Zomax has completed more than 1,000 DVD replication projects to date, including titles for Microsoft MSDN, the US Patent Office, Apple, Dell, Gateway, Cisco, Novell, AutoDesk, and AOL. For more information contact:

Zomax, Inc.
5353 Nathan Lane
Plymouth, MN 55442
(800) 525-6575 (Voice)
(612) 553-0826 (Fax)

contactus@zomax.com (E-Mail)
http://www.zomax.com (Web)

Testing & Verification Products & Services

While DVD-Video players and DVD-Video authoring tools are all supposed to be designed to meet the requirements of the DVD-Video specification, there are a few compatibility problems with many consumer players. There are a number of independent testing facilities and

the MPEG encoding. DVD Plus is a complete system based on the proven CDA DVD analysis architecture. The software has many features and functions, including simple multiple reference set auto-calibration, and many automated functions such as preset data printing configurations, user-configurable default data views, and highly configurable testing options and graph configurations. The user can tile windows to view multiple graphical and/or digital data streams while testing. For more information contact:

CD Associates
15-A Marconi
Irvine, CA 92618
(949) 588-3800 (Voice)
(949) 588-3805 (Fax)
http://www.cdassociates.com (Web)

ContentWise

SecondSight is an automated DVD-Video test system designed to replace much of the current in-process content QC in the DVD authoring process. The system enables verification of video content and navigational command compliance across the full spectrum of available DVD players and drives, allowing authoring houses to check multiple devices from various manufacturers simultaneously. SecondSight was developed in conjunction with the California Video Center, the DVD production affiliate of Warner Bros. and the largest producer of DVD titles in the world. For more information see the ContentWise web site at http://www.content-wise.com.

DVD Forum Verification Labs

The DVD Forum has established a number of Verification Labs throughout the world. These Labs are generally located at one of the DVD Forum members facilities and are responsible for testing DVD hardware and discs to insure that they comply with the appropriate DVD Format Book. Services provide by the DVD Verification Labs includes physical disc testing, logical disc testing, player testing and market inspections. Contact information for each DVD Forum Verification Lab is listed below.

- USA Lab (Crest National) Fax: 323-466-7128

- USA Lab (Panasonic Disc Service Center) Fax: 310-783-4849

- USA Lab (WAMO) Fax: 717-383-0328

- Europe Lab (Philips) Fax: +31-40-273-2113

- China Lab (3rd Institute) Fax: +86-10-6438-2911

- Korea Lab (LGE) Fax: +82-333-610-5355

- Korea Lab (Samsung) Fax: +82-331-200-8666

- Taiwan Lab (ITRI) Fax: +88-6-3-591-7531

- Japan Lab (Hitachi) Fax: +81-3-3506-1603

- Japan Lab (JVC) Fax: +81-45-450-1639

- Japan Lab (Matsushita) Fax: +81-6-6909-5027

- Japan Lab (Mitsibushi) Fax: +81-75-958-3731

- Japan Lab (Pioneer) Fax: +81-42-990-2831

- Japan Lab (Sony) Fax: +81-3-5769-5890

- Japan Lab (Toshiba) Fax: +81-3-5444-9403

Intellikey Labs

Intellikey Labs provides comprehensive testing involving Compatibility, Functionality, and Linear Playback for all DVD and DVD-ROM applications. The lab consists of over 100 different DVD players (set top and portable machines) that cover all existing region codes as well as over 35 different DVD-ROM equipped computers. As manufacturers release new DVD drives and models, they continuously integrate them into their testing matrix. Check discs are used to detect programming, player, replication, and media errors using our patent-pending testing methodology. Early detection of these problems saves thousands of dollars while increasing the number of DVD titles compliant with DVD players. Clients are usually provided with complete analysis of their project within 24-48 hours. Intellikey's testing equipment consists of over 100 DVD players for Regions 1-6 and Region 8, and over 35 DVD-ROM equipped computers. Their hardware ranges from first generation players and DVD-ROM drives released in 1996 to the latest model players available. Since Intellikey

Labs' inception, they have tested approximately 7,000 titles including DVD, CD-ROM, DVD-ROM, DVD-Audio and web-enabled DVD projects. For more information contact:

Intellikey Labs Inc.
2777 Ontario Street
Burbank CA, 91504
(818) 953-9116 (Voice)
(818) 953-9144 (Fax)
info@intellikeylabs.com (E-Mail)

forms comprehensive data analysis and compliance checking of DVD-Video content against the specification and bitstream standards. Surveyor performs an assortment of tests, including checks of: elementary video (MPEG) and audio (MPEG and Dolby Digital) bit streams, navigation data and commands, copy protection settings, system and general parameters, and DVD file structure. The various tests can be selected and deselected under user control where applicable to the particular type of object under analysis. Surveyor can analyze MPEG-1 and MPEG-2 video, MPEG audio, Dolby Digital audio, MPEG stills, multiplexed video objects (VOBs), titles and title sets, zero directories, and disc images. Surveyor has a suggested retail price of $6,000. For more information contact:

Interra Digital Video Technologies, Inc.
2001 Gateway Place, Suite # 440W
San Jose, CA 95110
(408) 573-1400 (Voice)
(800) 646-4434 (Toll Free Voice)
(408) 573-1430 (Fax)
info_dvt@interra.com (E-Mail)
http://www.interra.com (Web)

Philips

DVD-Video Verifier, designed to run on a Windows NT platform is specially constructed to simplify the release procedures for DVD-Video titles by checking the structures and formats against the relevant specifications: DVD Specifications for Read-Only Discs part 2 (file system specifications) and part 3 (video specifications). The recommended system configuration for DVD-Video Verifier is a 300 MHz Pentium Pro or Pentium II system running Windows NT 4.0 with 64MB internal memory and a SCSI connection for external (DLT) drive with DDP disc image or a DVD drive. For more information contact:

Philips System Standards & Licensing
Licensing Support
Building SFF-8
PO Box 80002
5600 JB Eindhoben
The Netherlands
http://www.licensing.philips.com (Web)

PMTC

PMTC provides compliance testing services to insure that a DVD-Video disc complies with all appropriate DVD standards. To ensure compatibility between DVD Video playback systems and DVD Video titles, PMTC has set up a DVD Logical Verification laboratory. DVD Video discs and disc images are submitted to a test that examines their compliance with all the DVD Video related standards by means of a specialist tool. The three primary tests run include a Stream check where every stream in the title (audio, video, subtitles) is checked to verify encoding quality and synchronization. Compatibility check tests look for conflicts between specific titles and playback systems. PMTC offers compatibility tests on more than 40 playback systems. Finally functionality checks are run to verify the interactive structure of each title. For more information contact:

Professional Multimedia Test Centre
Wetenschapspark 5
3590 Diepenbeek
BELGIUM
+32 11 30 36 96 (Fax)
http://www.pmtctest.com (Web)

Testronic Labs

Testronic Labs provides independent QA testing of VHS tape, and DVD titles for a variety of customers. They have a Matrix of over 120 DVD players including dedicated DVD Region players for all six regions. They perform independent DVD title Emulation for DVD Authoring houses as well as DVD publishers. Testronic uses a combination of set-top and PC DVD playback equipment, as well as PlayStation2 systems for Region 1 and 2, and Aeco DVDQ analysis systems for electrical testing of DVD discs and stampers. For more information contact:

Testronic Labs
3619 W. Magnolia St.,
Burbank, CA, 91505
(818) 845-3223 (Voice)
(818) 845-3236 (Fax)
testronic@earthlink.net (E-Mail)
http://www.testroniclabs.com (Web)

Training Products & Services

There are a few companies and education institutions that providing training products, services or classes for DVD-Video. Most of these companies specialize in one or two DVD authoring system, so make sure you locate a training facility that can teach you how to use the authoring system you will use to develop DVD titles. Each major DVD-Video authoring tool vendor also provides detailed training classes on their products, although only third party vendors are listed in this section.

projects. The cost of a single day crash course is $399, while the cost of a three-day workshop is $999. For more information contact:

all4dvd
428 32nd Street,
Newport Beach, CA 92663
(949) 566-9246 (Voice)
(949) 566-9248 (Fax)
training@all4dvd.com (E-Mail)
http://www.all4dvd.com (Web)

DVD.learn

DVD.learn is the Rocky Mountain regional DVD authoring training center for Sonic Solutions' DVD Creator, Fusion and DVDIT! authoring systems, as well as the Interactual Technologies PC Friendly software. Located next to downtown Denver, DVD.learn offers full service training for the development and authoring of DVD applications and web-enabled DVD applications. The DVD.learn instructional staff is comprised of faculty and adjunct faculty from the Department of Technical Communications at the Metropolitan State College of Denver. Housed at Metro's Center for Business Success, DVD.learn also offers customized training packages to businesses. DVD.learn offers three different training courses.

1. DVD Authoring is a two-day course designed for anyone who wants to create DVD applications. This course teaches you how use DVD technology to create high quality media applications that are interactive and playback with full screen video and multiple audio tracks. When you complete the course you'll be able to author DVD applications. This course costs $800

2. Advanced DVD Authoring is a one-day course that builds on the concepts learned in the DVD authoring course. You'll learn how to work with system and general parameters to create if/then statements, change audio, subpicture and angle streams and create password applications and scored quizzes. This course will also address 4:3 vs. 16:9 aspect ratio considerations. This course costs $400.

3. The Web-Connected DVD course introduces you to the process of integrating DVD Video with HTML that is stored either on the DVD disc or on the web. Using the Interactual 2.0 player, you will learn how to connect to the web from within a DVD disc, or by embedding DVD Video within HTML content. Web connections can be based on user initiated events or initiated by content triggers. This course costs $800.

For course schedules and more information contact:

The Metropolitan State College of Denver
P.O. Box 173362 Campus Box 35
Denver, CO 80217-3362
303.556.5387 (Voice)
303.556.8135 (Fax)
training@dvdlearn.com (E-Mail)
http://www.dvdlearn.com (Web)

DVDMadeEasy.com

DVDMadeEasy.com, developed by award-winning DVD author, Mark Johnson, is a web site providing hands-on technical information for DVD authors around the world. Members receive full access to all of the site's services, including articles, tutorials, reviews, tips & tricks, media and player compatibility tables & workarounds, file downloads, an electronic mailing list, and real-time chat system, all of which is maintained by leading experts in the field, including Ralph LaBarge, Dana Parker, Phil De Lancie, and Mark Johnson. For more information contact:

DVDMadeEasy.com
448 Ignacio Blvd. #179
Novato, CA 94949
415-883-0923 (Voice)
561-423-3752 (Fax)
mark@DVDMadeEasy.com (E-Mail)
http://www.DVDMadeEasy.com (Web)

Ex'pression Center for New Media

Ex'pression Center for New Media is an authorized Sonic solutions training site offering a weekend course in DVD Authoring. Students explore current DVD videos with an emphasis on the advantages and differences between DVD and VHS. Over 4 instruction days, students participate in every aspect of DVD authoring from the initial project planning and bit budgeting, discussions in menu design and the processes of creating menus for DVD video, to the actual assembly of all video, audio, and sub-picture assets. In addition to a full exploration of the Authoring tool and navigation of DVD video, students also focus on the MPEG-2 video compression standard and Dolby Digital (AC3) encoding, as well as formatting and disc imaging. A basic knowledge of Macintosh computers is required for this course. The class is held on four consecutive Saturdays, and costs $795. For class schedules and more information contact:

Ex'pression Center for New Media
6601 Shellmound Street
Emeryville, CA 94608

course in DVD Production, as well as workshops for professionals. Students explore the full spectrum of DVD from an understanding of the DVD-Video specifications through the details of assembling assets, encoding and transcoding, navigation and instructional design implications, authoring, proofing, and then burning a DVD-R. Current tuition for is $180 per credit for Michigan residents, $380 per credit for nonresidents, and $265 per credit for Midwest Compact students. Workshop rates are competitive with other such learning opportunities. Full semester courses are targeted toward full-time students who have already acquired video production and image creation skills and who want to expand their skill set into an area of knowledge with recognized growth potential. Workshops are targeted at professionals who purchase Sonic Solutions products. DVD authoring systems include six Sonic DVDit! systems and two Sonic DVDFusion systems. For more information contact:

Fred Wyman
Ferris State University
Television and Digital Media Production Program,
1301 S. State Street,
Big Rapids, MI 49307
231 591-2714 (Voice)
231 591-2060 (Fax)
wymanf@ferris.edu (E-Mail)
http://www.ferris.edu (Web)

Gnome Digital Media

Gnome Digital Media is an authorized Sonic Solutions training facility, and also offers training courses on the Apple DVD Studio Pro system. The following training courses are offered on a regular basis.

- Apple DVD Studio Pro, One-day seminar on "How to use DVD Studio Pro". The cost of this course is $250.

- Apple DVD Studio Pro, 2-day hands on training. The cost of this course is $695.

- Sonic DVD Fusion, 1-day overview. The cost of this course is $250.

- Sonic DVD Creator, 1-day overview. The cost of this course is $250.

- Sonic DVD Creator, 3-day hands-on training. The cost of this course is $950.

Gnome Digital Media also maintains a web site dedicated to helping new DVD authors develop their first titles. This web site is called "Recipe 4 DVD" and can be found at http://www.recipe4dvd.com. For more information contact:

Gnome Digital Media
3727 W. Magnolia Blvd, Suite 812
Burbank, CA 91505
(818) 563-6539 (Voice)
(818) 563-6264 (Fax)
gome@gnomedigital.com (E-Mail)
http://www.gnomedigital.com (Web)

New Constellation Technologies

New Constellation Technologies has created several DVD training discs; "DVD from A to Z, A DVD-Video Production Primer" and "Inside DVD Studio Pro". DVD authoring training and consulting services are provided on-site or by phone. Their primary markets are corporate, government and educational A/V departments; as well as broadcast and project studios. For more information contact:

Trai Forrester
New Constellation Technologies
645 Penfield Ave.
Havertown, PA 19083
800-213-2297 (Phone)
http://www.dvdconsultants.com (Web)

Ngee Ann Polytechnic Digital Media Authoring Studio

Digital Media Authoring Studio (DMAS) is the first full-scale DVD training center in Asia based at the Centre for Film and Media Studies, NgeeAnn Polytechnic - the only educational institution in Singapore. DMAS is a collaborative project by NgeeAnn Polytechnic and A.C.E. Daikin (Singapore) Pte Ltd, funded by Ministry of Education and supported by Economic Development Board. DMAS has offered seven different course in DVD Authoring including (1) Introduction to DVD Authoring, (2) DVD Authoring, (3) Advanced DVD Authoring, (4) Enhanced DVD Authoring, (5) DVD: A Producers Course, (6) Audio for DVD: Premastering Dolby Digital, and (7) Video for DVD: Motion Menu Creation. For more information contact:

The DMAS Course Coordinator
Centre for Film and Media Studies
Ngee Ann Polytechnic
Block 52, #08-08
535, Clementi Road
Singapore 599489
4608058 (Voice)
4686218 (Fax)
tch5@np.edu.sg (E-Mail)

the basic Multi Media skills, which are developed simultaneously to ensure a full understanding of their interrelation. Once this foundation has been built, both the DVD and Advanced Internet and E-Commerce applications are covered. A student may choose to learn both skills or favor one over the other, although basic comprehension of both must be achieved. The course culminates in a logical combination of all skills where the students operate as a team for the Advanced New Media curriculum. This reinforces the individual skills, while exploring the full potential of the synergy between these technologies. This course costs NZ$7,260, which includes GST. For more information contact:

South Seas Film And Television School
Unit 3/75 Ellice Road, Glenfield, Auckland, New Zealand
PO Box 34-579, Birkenhead, Auckland,
New Zealand
64+9+444-3253 (Voice)
64+9+444-7821 (Fax)
info@southseas.co.nz (E-Mail)
http://www.southseas.co.nz (Web)

Texas State Technical College

Texas State Technical College is an authorized Sonic Solutions DVD training facility offering a three-day hands-on workshop. This workshop provides training in DVD Fusion and Sonic Creator authoring systems. Students learn to build interactive menus, kiosks, DVD movies, and develop DVD presentations. The three-day course costs $1,200. For more information contact:

Texas State Technical College
IDEAS/DVD Training
3801 Campus Drive

Waco, TX 76705
(254) 867-3300 (Voice)
(254) 867-3326 (Fax)
whudson@tstc.edu (E-Mail)
http://waco.tstc.edu/dvd/ (Web)

Video Symphony

Video Symphony is an industry-leading digital media center located in Burbank, California. Thousands of professionals in the Hollywood entertainment industry have trained at Video Symphony since 1994 in nonlinear film, video and audio editing, 3D animation, DVD production, streaming video, and digital imaging. Video Symphony offers an Introduction to DVD Production with Sonic Creator/Fusion. This three-day course teaches students how to create DVD titles from start to finish. Key classes cover all aspects of design, authoring, video and audio encoding, proofing and pre-mastering. This course costs $995. For class schedules and additional information contact:

Video Symphony
731 N. Hollywood Way
Burbank, CA 91505
(818) 557-7200 (Voice)
info@videosymphony.com (E-Mail)
http://www.videosymphony,com (Web)

Video Encoding Tools

All video used in a DVD-Video title must be in either the MPEG-1 or MPEG-2 format. There are a number of excellent hardware and software MPEG encoders on the market, most of which can be used to create video streams for DVD titles. This section covers the major hardware and software MPEG encoding products on the market today.

Brent Beyeler

bbMPEG and AVI2MPG2 are Windows programs that convert AVI files to MPEG-2 or MPEG-1 files. Each program is freeware, and the source code is available on Brent Beyeler's web site. The programs generate MPEG-2 (ISO/IEC 13818-2) or MPEG-1 (ISO/IEC 11172-2) video streams, MPEG-1 (ISO/IEC 11172-3, layer 1 and 2 only) audio streams and MPEG-2 (ISO/IEC 13818-1) or MPEG-1 (ISO/IEC 11172-1) program streams. bbMPEG requires Win95, Win98 or WinNT with at least a Pentium processor. AVI2MPG2 requires Microsoft's DirectShow. For more information visit http://members.home.net/beyeler/bbmpeg.html.

Canopus

The Canopus Amber and Amber for DVD products are real time Single slot PCI MPEG capture cards that provide MPEG-2 D1, Half-D1 and MPEG1 real-time encoding. The Amber cards support constant and variable bit rate, user adjustable encoding at 1-15Mb/s. Both NTSC and PAL video can be captured with S and composite video input and outputs. The Amber cards require Windows 9x, 2000, or NT4.0 compatible systems, and provide simultaneous high quality VGA video overlay and analog video output. The Amber card has a suggested retail price of $2,300 and Amber For DVD has a suggested retail price of $2,998. For more information contact:

Canopus Corporation
711 Charcot Ave.

Cinema Craft Encoder Lite is a stand-alone MPEG encoder supporting AVI and MOV input file formats and generating MPEG-1 and MPEG-2 output files. It is designed to work on Windows 98, 98SE, Me, NT4.0, and 2000 systems, and it supports Intel Pentium and Celeron processors as well as AMD processors. The Cinema Craft Encoder Lite can also be uses as an Adobe Premier plug-in if stand-alone operation is not desired.

Cinema Craft Encoder Lite only supports constant bit rate encoding (CBR) and provides limited control over MPEG compression parameters. Compression parameters that can be set via the Cinema Craft Encoder Lite user interface include output format (MPEG-1, Half Resolution MPEG-2 and full resolution MPEG-2), progressive or interlaced frames, DVD compliant streams, compressed bit rate, image quality, noise-filtering and audio compression data rates. Cinema Craft Encoder Lite has a suggested retail price of $250. For more information contact:

Cinema Craft Inc
17744 Skypark Blvd. Suite# 265
Irvine, CA 92614
info@cinemacraft.com (E-Mail)
http://www.cinemacraft.com (Web)

Darim

MPEGator2 is a single slot PCI real-time MPEG-2 capture card for Windows 95/98 or NT 4.0 Operating systems. Its major features include composite, S-video, and component (YUV) video inputs, unbalanced and balanced stereo audio inputs, and D1 video capture resolution (720×480 for NTSC or 720×576 for PAL). Constant bit rate encoding is provided at bit rates between 3 and 15 Mbps. Real time source video preview to the computer screen is provided during encoding. MPEG editing software and other MPEG tools are provided with the product. MPEGator2 has a suggested retail price of $1,799. For more information contact:

Darim Vision Corp
5976 W. Las Positas Blvd., Suite 106
Pleasanton, CA 94588
http://www.darvision.com (Web)

Dazzle

Digital Video Creator II is a single slot PCI MPEG-2 capture card for Windows 98, 2000 or Me systems. The card can create constant bit rate MPEG-2 streams with bit rates between 2.0 and 10.0 Mbps, from either NTSC or PAL composite video inputs. The product comes bundled with Dazzle MovieStar Software, Sonic Solutions DVDit!™ LE, Mediamatics Software DVD Player, Sonic Desktop SmartSound™, Microsoft Media Player, Microsoft Internet Explorer™, Sample MPEG Video Clips, and RealPlayer 8. Minimum system requirements are 400MHz or higher Intel Pentium II, Intel Celeron, or AMD K6-2 with 64MB RAM, and an 800 x 600, DirectDraw compatible graphics card. The suggested retail price of Digital Video Creator II is $299. For more information contact:

Dazzle Incorporated
47211 Bayside Parkway
Fremont, CA 94538
(510) 360-2300 (Voice)
(510) 360-0211 (Fax)
lisat@dazzle.com (E-Mail)
http://www.dazzle.com (Web)

Digital Ventures Diversified

DVDComposer is a high-end, stand-alone MPEG-2 compression system based on C-Cube MPEG compression chips and an SGI platform. The system supports NTSC and PAL analog composite, analog component and digital component (SDI) inputs. CBD, 1-pass VBR, 2-pass VBR or 3-pass VBR encoding is supported, with selective re-encoding for correcting small sections of a large encoded file. It supports open and closed GOP structures, and is designed to work easily with a Dolby Labs DP569 encoder and Sonic Scenarist SGI authoring software. Suggested retail price for DVDComposer is $45,000. For more information contact:

Digital Ventures Diversified
51 Sutteer St.
San Francisco, CA
(408) 246-4949 (Voice)
info@dvdcomposer.com (E-Mail)
http://www.dvdcomposer.com (Web)

Digital Vision

Digital Vision's BitPack-SD Pre-mastering Workstation is a stand-alone MPEG-2 encoding system with integrated pre-processing, based on MPEG2 Main Level using 4:2:0 or 4:2:2 formats. BitPack-SD is based on Digital Vision's proprietary, non-chip set based MPEG2 engine, which provides excellent picture quality and system flexibility. Integrated machine control provides automatic frame accurate encoding as well as playback. The Windows NT user interface enables project management, graphical encoding control and quality analyses. It supports CBR or VBR encoding from 2.0 to 50.0 Mbps. An optional DVNR processor can be used to preprocess the video prior to compression. The suggested retail price of the BitPack-SD Pre-mastering Workstation range from $59,000 to $125,000 depending on system configuration and options. For more information contact:

Digital Vision (US) Inc

MegaPeg is a software MPEG-1 and MPEG-2 encoder. MegaPEG Batch Encoder converts AVI and MOV files into ISO-compliant MPEG-1 and MPEG-2 streams. MegaPEG is also available as a movie compiler plug-in for Adobe Premiere. MegaPEG is available in versions for MacOS 8.x, 9.x, Windows 95/98/NT/ME/2000, and Adobe Premiere 5.x & 6.x. It creates CBR or VBR encoded MPEG-2 streams at bit rates up to 10.0 Mbps. The suggested retail price of MegaPEG is $495, while the suggested retail price for the MegaPEG Adobe Plug-in is $395. For more information contact:

Digigami, Inc.
906-10th Ave. #104
San Diego, CA 92101
(619) 231-2600 (Voice)
(619) 231-2773 (Fax)
http://www.digigami.com (Web)

DreamCom

The MPEGRich MPEG-2 Encoder/Decoder is a real time MPEG-2 single slot PCI capture card. It encodes at bit rates up to 15 Mbits per second. It supports NTSC & PAL composite (BNC) and S-Video (MiniDIN Adapter Cable) inputs. Minimum system requirements are a 233 MHz Pentium II with PCI version 2.1, 64MB RAM, 4GB SCSI ultra-wide hard disk, Windows Workstation NT 4.0, and one full size PCI slot. For more information contact:

DreamCom Co., Ltd. (Gunzameory)
Dae-Ah Building 10 Floor, 707-7,
Yeoksam-Dong, Kangnam-Ku, Seoul,
Korea
+822-561-6071~3 (Voice)

+822-561-6074 (Fax)
sales@gunzam.co.kr (E-Mail)
http://www.gunzam.co.kr (Web)

Heuris

Heuris MPEG Power Professional (MPP2) provides a number of improvements over the original MPP product, including faster performance, improved image quality, image processing capabilities, source file concatenation, and closed GOP support.

The main user interface for MPP2 allows you to define one or more video segments for a project. Double clicking on a video segment brings up a dialog box where you define the basic parameters for that segment such as input and output file names, the type of encoding process (video, audio, still or multiplexed), and what template to use for the encoder parameters. You can control a wide variety of compression parameters in the "Encoder Settings" dialog box, and save them as a template for use with other segments in the same project, or even other projects.

You can control a wide variety of compression parameters, probably more than you will ever need. Supported formats include MPEG-1, MPEG-2 and Half-D1 MPEG-2, at the full range of resolutions, frame rates, and television standards called out by the MPEG standard. Both constant bit rate and variable bit rate compression are supported, and there is a good selection of motion vector search techniques (Auto, Logarithmic, Hybrid, Two-Pass and Complete) and search distances (Auto, Short, Medium and Long). Four different global filter settings are provided (Auto, Median, Non-Linear and FIR) as well as support for Inverse Telecine processing. The Source Crop option allows you to remove unwanted content from the source prior to compression. Finally, you can control detailed compression parameters such as GOP size, closed or open GOP, reference interval, aspect ratios, VBV size, frame rate, and field/frame (Interlaced or Progressive) encoding.

In the Multiplex window you can control the target data rate to match your delivery media (CD, DVD, or custom), set the type of multiplexing used (System, Program, Transport or DVD VOB), set stream IDs and even control the Initial Clock Reference. If you are not sure what any of these compression parameters are used for then you should just use the default settings. Since MPP2 is a software encoder, its performance depends on several different variables, including how fast the CPU in your computer is, and what specific compression parameters you are using. MPP2 has a suggested retail price of $1,500 and comes in versions for both Windows and Mac systems. Heuris customers who own a previous release of MPEG Power Professional can update to MPP2 for $525. Optional support for DVD Video Object multiplexing is offered in the MPP2-DVD product that has a list price of $2,500 and an update price of $895. For more information contact:

Heuris
555 Washington Avenue, 1st Floor
St. Louis, MO 63101
(314) 534-1514 (Voice)
(314) 534-4351 (Fax)
sales@heuris.com (E-Mail)
http://www.heuris.com (Web)

InnovaCom

The TP-EWS is an integrated MPEG encoding, editing, and assembly work station. Encoding supports MP@ML MPEG from SIF to full D1, in CBR or VBR mode. Analog composite, S-video and component video input is standard with balanced or unbalanced analog audio. SDI video and AES/EBU audio is optional. The TP-EWS video encoder includes VTR control and other video sources with frame accuracy. The authoring suite permits output to network devices and includes a combination DVD-ROM, CD-RW as standard input and output storage. A high capacity, removable hard drive, such as 60 GByte, can also be added. Constant or

(408) 727-6625 (Fax)
http://www.transpeg.com (Web)

Ligos

The LSX-MPEG Encoder is a standalone AVI-to-MPEG transcoder for the Windows platform, taking advantage of Intel's MMX technology to deliver reasonably fast software MPEG encoding. In addition to being fast, the LSX-MPEG Encoder is also full featured. The users interface is simple, yet powerful, providing control over every major MPEG-2 compression parameter. Both constant-bit-rate (CBR) and variable-bit-rate (VBR) encoding are supported. The LSX-MPEG Encoder comes with 18 predefined profiles to create MPEG files for a variety of applications, from streaming Internet video all the way up to DVD-Video.

The LSX-MPEG for Adobe Premiere is a plug-in that provides Adobe Premiere™ users the same features available in the standalone LSX-MPEG Encoder. It can output MPEG streams directly from Adobe Premiere, exporting for media types such as AVI, MOV, DV, and others. It produces fully compliant MPEG video, MPEG Layer 2 audio, and multiplexed video/audio streams for MPEG-1, MPEG-2, VideoCD, Super VideoCD, and DVD applications.

LSX-MPEG Encoder has a suggested retail price of $179, while LSX-MPEG for Adobe Premiere has a suggested retail price of $179. Both products require an Intel Pentium CPU, Windows 95/98, ME, or Windows NT 3.51, 16 MB RAM, 16-bit VGA display adaptor, and 9 MB free hard drive space for installation of the software. For more information contact:

Ligos Technology
55 Stockton St. Suite 450
San Francisco, CA 94108
(415) 249-0100 (Voice)
(415) 249-0150 (Fax)
sales@ligos.com (E-Mail)
http://www.ligos.com (Web)

Media100

MediaPress is a Mac based real-time MPEG encoder that supports both NTSC and PAL formats. CBR and VBR encoding at data rates up to 15.0 Mbps are supported with S-video and Composite video inputs. The suggested retail price of MediaPress is $2,499.

MediaPress Pro YUV has the same features as MediaPress while adding features suited to video professionals with legacy analog equipment and QuickTime-based nonlinear editing systems such as Media 100 i, or Avid Composer. MediaPress Pro YUV includes the Media-Press component analog input, so can accept analog video from a Beta or BetaSP deck and convert it directly to MPEG-2 in real-time. MediaPress Pro YUV also ships with the Quick-Time Transcoder, allowing the export of QuickTime files directly from a nonlinear editor and transcode them to MPEG-2 at accelerated speeds (currently 6X real-time). The suggested retail price of MediaPress Pro YUV is $3,999.

MediaPress Pro SDI takes all of the features of MediaPress Pro YUV and adds serial digital interface complete with S/PDIF and AES/EBU audio connections. The suggested retail price of MediaPress Pro SDI is $5,499.

Digital MediaPress is a Macintosh hardware transcoder that offers real-time transcoding from DV to MPEG-2. Digital MediaPress includes an easy-to-understand software package for controlling the encoding process. A built-in preview window even lets you see your material as it's captured. Data rates range from 2 mbps to 8 mbps in either NTSC or PAL standards, and audio can be captured at either 44.1 or 48 kHz. The suggested retail price of Digital MediaPress is $499. For more information on any of the MediaPress products contact:

> Media 100
> 290 Donald Lynch Blvd.
> Marlboro, MA 01752
> (508) 460-1600 (Voice)
> sales@media100.com (E-Mail)
> http://www.media100.com (Web)

Nanocosmos

MPEG SoftEngine is a digital audio and video encoder supporting the MPEG1- and MPEG-2- Standards. SoftEngine reads Digital Video / Audio Files in AVI and WAV formats as compresses them into MPEG through an easy-to-use graphical user interface (GUI). Major features of MPEG SoftEngine include full support for Digital Video / TV / HDTV (interlaced PAL/NTSC), nanoDVR real-time capture included, Adobe Premiere MPEG plugins included. MPEG SoftEngine is available for the Windows, Linux and Solaris Operating systems. The suggested retail price for the Windows and Solaris versions is $299, while the Linux version is priced at $199. For more information contact:

> nanocosmos Informationstechnologien GmbH
> Hamann
> Am Borsigturm 40
> D-13507 Berlin
> Germany

+49 (30) 43 03 24 11 (Voice)
+49 (30) 43 03 24 13 (Fax)
info@nanocosmos.de (E-Mail)
http://www.nanocosmos.de (Web)

Optibase

MPEG MovieMaker 200 Publisher is a real time MPEG-1 and MPEG-2 encoder designed for
the content creation broadcast market, where high quality and Dolby Digital audio

application. For product prices or more information contact:

Optibase Inc.
3031 Tisch Way
Plaza West, Suite 1
San Jose, CA., 95128
(408) 260-6760 (Voice)
(408) 244-0545 (Fax)

PixelTools

Expert-DVD is a multi-pass MPEG-2 software encoder that creates constant or variable bit-
rate content for DVD authoring. Expert-DVD includes extensive control of compression
parameters that facilitate the generation of feature length compressed video segments for
DVD production at a high level of quality. An analysis pass evaluates encoding complexity
and scene changes. The final encoding pass can be customized for scene complexity and entry
points.

Expert-DVD's analysis pass coupled with the Expert-DVD's Edit Decision List (EDL) file
utilization permit optimization of encoding bits throughout an entire DVD disk. The optional
preliminary analysis pass provides detailed graphical and textual information into the encoding complexity of the subject content on a frame-by-frame and scene-by-scene basis. Expert-
DVD is optimized for speed on all Pentium processors. The suggested retail price of Expert-
DVD is $1,995. For more information contact:

PixelTools Corporation
10721 Wunderlich Drive
Cupertino, CA 95014
(408) 374-5327 (Voice)
(408) 374-8074 (Fax)

pixeltools@pixeltools.com (E-Mail)
http://www.pixeltools.com (Web)

Sony

The DVA-V700 system consists of two essential elements; the video encoding hardware, which is packaged on a standard PCI board, and the software that controls the encoding process. The encoded MPEG date stream is output in the NTFS file format, which allows the DVA-V700 to be used with most major DVD authoring systems. The optional advanced encoding software (BZDA-V701) permits the operator to perform such tasks as Auto Bit Budget, segment bit-rate adjustment, multi-angle encoding, pull-down detection and more. This encoder should be pre-configured with the optional Windows NT-based PC, model DVAPC800/256 in order to ensure the highest level of customer satisfaction and support. The suggested retail price of the DVA-V700 encoder is $19,995. For more information contact:

Sony Electronics, Inc
1 Sony Drive
Park Ridge NJ, 07656
(201) 930-1000 (Voice)
(201) 930-6307 (Fax)
kevin.george@am.sony.com (E-Mail)
http://www.sony.com/professional (Web)

Spruce Technologies

The MPX3000 is a real time MPEG encoder for Windows NT systems. The MPX-3000 uses the latest C-Cube MPEG encoding chips, which has consistently been rated as superior to other solutions. The major features of the MPX3000 include multipass VBR with inverse telecine, automatic scene detection with I frame insertion, forced I frame insertion, one pass, two pass and three pass VBR recording, simultaneous video and audio encoding with full preview, and batch encoding. For pricing or more information contact:

Spruce Technologies, Inc.
1054 S. De Anza Blvd. Suite 200
San Jose, CA 95129
(888) 355-MPEG (Voice)
info@spruce-tech.com (E-Mail)
http://www.spruce-tech.com (Web)

Zapex

The ZP 200 / 300 audio - video encoder boards offer features that ensure the highest quality output at the lowest possible bit rates. Zapex boards are PCI bus compatible, and can be installed in most PC systems. The ZP series supports both PCM and Dolby Digital audio, and MPEG 2 video encoding. Video inputs supported include D1 serial digital, Component analog and digital, and S - Video. Encoded streams created by the Zapex ZP 200 / 300 series are

DVD compliant, and can be imported into most DVD authoring tools. For pricing or more information contact:

Zapex Technologies, Inc.
2432 Charleston Road
Mountain View, CA 94043
(650) 930-1300 (Voice)
(650) 930-1399 (Fax)
info@zapex.com (E-Mail)

DVD ACRONYMS & TERMS

This chapter provides definitions for the common acronyms and terms used in DVD authoring and production. The author would like to thank Jim Taylor, author of DVD Demystified, for contributing many of the definitions provided in this chapter, as well as Mark Johnson of DVDMadeEasy.com who reviewed, added and modified this extensive list of DVD terms.

1080i   1080 lines of interlaced video (540 lines per field). Usually refers to 1920×1080 resolution in 1.78 aspect ratio.

1080p   1080 lines of progressive video (1080 lines per frame). Usually refers to 1920×1080 resolution in 1.78 aspect ratio.

2-2 pulldown   The process of transferring 24-frame-per-second film to video by repeating each film frame as two video fields. When 24-fps film is converted via 2-2 pulldown to 25-fps 625/50 (PAL) video, the film runs 4 percent faster than normal.

2-3 pulldown   The process of converting 24-frame-per-second film to video by repeating one film frame as three fields, then the next film frame as two fields.

3-2 pulldown   An uncommon variation of 2-3 pulldown, where the first film frame is repeated for 3 fields instead of two. Most people mean 2-3 pulldown when they say 3-2 pulldown.

4:1:1 The component digital video format with one C_b sample and one C_r sample for every four Y samples. 4:1 horizontal downsampling with no vertical downsampling. Chroma is sampled on every line, but only for every four luma pixels (i.e., 1 pixel in a 1 ∞ 4 grid). This amounts to a subsampling of chroma by a factor of two compared to luma (and by a factor of four for a single C_b or C_r component). DVD uses 4:2:0 sampling, not 4:1:1 sampling.

4:2:0 The component digital video format used by DVD, where there is one C_b sample and one C_r sample for every four Y samples (i.e., 1 pixel in a 2 ∞ 2 grid). 2:1 horizontal downsampling and 2:1 vertical downsampling. Cb and Cr are sampled on every other line, in between the scan lines, with one set of chroma samples for each two luma samples on a line. This amounts to a subsampling of chroma by a factor of two compared to luma (and by a factor of four for a single C_b or C_r component).

4:2:2 The component digital video format commonly used for studio recordings, where there is one C_b sample and one C_r sample for every two Y samples (i.e., 1 pixel in a 1 ∞ 2 grid). 2:1 horizontal downsampling with no vertical downsampling. This allocates the same number of samples to the chroma signal as to the luma signal. The input to MPEG-2 encoders used for DVD is typically in 4:2:2 format, but the video is subsampled to 4:2:0 before being encoded and stored.

4:4:4 A component digital video format for high-end studio recordings, where Y, C_b, and C_r are sampled equally.

480i 480 lines of interlaced video (240 lines per field). Usually refers to 720 x 480 (or 704 x 480) resolution.

480p 480 lines of progressive video (480 lines per frame). 480p60 refers to 60 frames per second; 480p30 refers to 30 frames per second; and 480p24 refers to 24 frames per second (film source). Usually refers to 720 x 480 (or 704 x 480) resolution.

4C The four-company entity: IBM, Intel, Matsushita, and Toshiba.

525/60 The scanning system of 525 lines per frame and 60 interlaced fields (30 frames) per second. Used by the NTSC television standard.

5C The five-company entity: IBM, Intel, Matsushita, Toshiba, and Sony.

625/50 The scanning system of 625 lines per frame and 50 interlaced fields (25 frames) per second. Used by PAL and SECAM television standards.

720p 720 lines of progressive video (720 lines per frame). Higher definition than standard DVD (480i or 480p). 720p60 refers to 60 frames per second; 720p30 refers to 30 frames per second; and 720p24 refers to 24 frames per second (film source). Usually refers to 1280 x 720 resolution in 1.78 aspect ratio.

8/16 modulation   The form of modulation block code used by DVD to store channel data on the disc. See modulation.

AAC   Advanced Audio Coder. An audio-encoding standard for MPEG-2 that is not backward-compatible with MPEG-1 audio.

AC   Alternating Current. An electric current that regularly reverses direction. Adopted as a video term for a signal of non-zero frequency. Compare to DC.

and begin transferring data to the host system.

ActiveMovie   The former name for Microsoft's DirectShow technology.

ADPCM   Adaptive Differential Pulse Code Modulation. A compression technique, which encodes the difference between one sample and the next. Variations are lossy and lossless.

Advanced Technology Attachment Packet Interface   An interface between a computer and its internal peripherals such as DVD-ROM drives. ATAPI provides the command set for controlling devices connected via an IDE interface. ATAPI is part of the Enhanced IDE (E-IDE) interface, also known as ATA-2. ATAPI was extended for use in DVD-ROM drives by the SFF 8090 specification.

Advanced Television   TV with significantly better video and audio than standard TV. Sometimes used interchangeably with HDTV, but more accurately encompasses any improved television system, including those beyond HDTV. Also sometimes used interchangeably with the final recommended standard of the ATSC, which is more correctly called DTV.

Advanced Television Systems Committee   In 1978, the Federal Communications Commission (FCC) empanelled the Advisory Committee on Advanced Television Service (ACATS) as an investigatory and advisory committee to develop information that would assist the FCC in establishing an advanced broadcast television (ATV) standard for the United States. This committee created a subcommittee, the ATSC, to explore the need for and to coordinate development of the documentation of Advanced Television Systems. In 1993, the ATSC recommended that efforts be limited to a digital television system (DTV), and in September 1995 issued its recommendation for a Digital Television System standard, which was approved with the exclusion of compression format constraints (picture resolution, frame rate, and frame sequence).

AES Audio Engineering Society.

AES/EBU A digital audio signal transmission standard for professional use, defined by the Audio Engineering Society and the European Broadcasting Union. S/P DIF is the consumer adaptation of this standard.

AGC See Automatic Gain Control.

aliasing A distortion (artifact) in the reproduction of digital audio or video that results when the signal frequency is more than twice the sampling frequency. The resolution is insufficient to distinguish between alternate reconstructions of the waveform, thus admitting additional noise that was not present in the original signal.

AMGM Audio Manager Menu.

AMGM_VOBS Video Object Set for Audio Manager Menu.

analog A signal of (theoretically) infinitely variable levels. Compare to digital.

anchor point One of a specified set of logical sector numbers at which descriptor, that identify an extent of a volume descriptor sequence, may be recorded.

angle menu Menu used to select the angle number.

angle An angle is a scene recorded from different viewpoints. Each angle is equal in time length and an Angle Block may contain up to nine (9) angles.

ANSI American National Standards Institute (see http://www.ansi.org).

AOB Audio Object.

AOBS Audio Object Set.

AOTT_AOBS Audio Object Set for Audio Only Title.

A PCK Audio packs.

application format A specification for storing information in a particular way to enable a particular use.

artifact An unnatural effect not present in the original video or audio, produced by an external agent or action. Artifacts can be caused by many factors, including digital compression, film-to-video transfer, transmission errors, data readout errors, electrical interference, analog signal noise, and analog signal crosstalk. Most artifacts attributed to the digital compression of DVD are in fact from other sources. Digital compression artifacts will always occur in the same place and in the same way. Possible MPEG artifacts are mosquitoes, blocking, and video noise.

aspect ratio   The width-to-height ratio of an image. A 4:3 aspect ratio means the horizontal size is a third again wider than the vertical size. Standard television ratio is 4:3 (or 1.33:1). Widescreen DVD and HTDV aspect ratio is 16:9 (or 1.78:1). Common film aspect ratios are 1.85:1 and 2.35:1. Aspect ratios normalized to a height of 1 are often abbreviated by leaving off the :1.

ATSC   See Advanced Television Systems Committee.

ATT   Audio Title.

ATV   See Advanced Television.

Audio_TS   UDF filename used for audio directory on disc volume.

audio channel number   These are consecutive numbers assigned to the Audio channel of the audio stream. They range from '0' to '7' in the description are of the video title set manager area. ACH0 and ACH1 are assigned to Left channel and Right channel respectively for 2 channel stereo audio signals.

audio menu   Menu used to select the audio stream

Audio Still Video   A still picture on a DVD-Audio disc.

audio stream number   These are consecutive numbers assigned to the Audio streams for a Title in a VTS. These range from '0' to '7' in the order described in the video title set manager area. For menus the number of audio streams is limited to 0 or 1.

authoring   For DVD-Video, authoring refers to the process of designing, creating, collecting, formatting, and encoding material. For DVD-ROM, authoring usually refers to using a specialized program to produce multimedia software.

automatic gain control   A circuit designed to boost the amplitude of a signal to provide adequate levels for recording. See also Macrovision.

autoplay (or automatic playback) A feature of DVD players, which automatically begins playback of a disc if so, encoded.

B picture (or B frame) One of three picture types used in MPEG video. B pictures are bi-directional predicted, based on both previous and following pictures. B pictures usually use the least number of bits. B pictures do not propagate coding errors since they are not used as a reference by other pictures.

bandwidth Strictly speaking, the range of frequencies (or the difference between the highest and the lowest frequency) carried by a circuit or signal. Loosely speaking, the amount of information carried in a signal. Technically, bandwidth does not apply to digital information; the term data rate is more accurate.

BCA See Burst Cutting Area.

bi-directional prediction A form of compression in which the codec uses information not only from frames that have already been decompressed, but also from frames yet to come. The codec looks in two directions: ahead as well as back. This helps avoid large spikes in data rate caused by scene changes or fast movement, improving image quality.

birefringence An optical phenomenon where light is transmitted at slightly different speeds depending on the angle of incidence. Also light scattering due to different refractions created by impurities, defects, or stresses within the media substrate.

bit A binary digit. The smallest representation of digital data: zero/one, off/on, no/yes. Eight bits make one byte.

bit rate The volume of data measured in bits over time. Equivalent to data rate.

bitmap An image made of a two-dimensional grid of pixels. Each frame of digital video can be considered a bitmap, although some color information is usually shared by more than one pixel.

bits per pixel The number of bits used to represent the color or intensity of each pixel in a bitmap. One bit allows only two values (black and white), two bits allows four values, and so on. Also called color depth or bit depth.

bitstream recorder A device capable of recording a stream of digital data but not necessarily able to process the data.

bitstream Digital data, usually encoded, designed to be processed sequentially and continuously.

BLER See block error rate.

block   In video encoding, an 8 ∞ 8 matrix of pixels or DCT values representing a small chunk of luma or chroma. In DVD MPEG-2 video, a macroblock is made up of 6 blocks: 4 luma and 2 chroma.

block error rate   A measure of the average number of raw channel errors when reading or writing a disc.

blocking   A term referring to the occasional blocky appearance of compressed video (an artifact). Caused when the compression ratio is high enough that the averaging of pixels in 8 ∞ 8

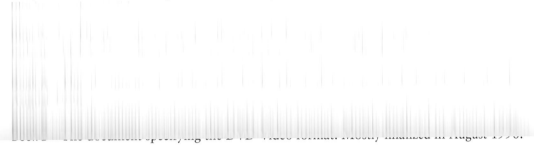

Book B   The document specifying the DVD-Video format. Mostly finalized in August 1996.

Book C   The document specifying the DVD-Audio format.

Book D   The document specifying the DVD record-once format (DVD-R). Finalized in August 1997.

Book E   The document specifying the Rewritable DVD format (DVD-RAM). Finalized in August 1997.

bps   Bits per second. A unit of data rate.

brightness   Defined by the CIE as the attribute of a visual sensation according to which area appears to emit more or less light. Loosely, the intensity of an image or pixel, independent of color; that is, its value along the axis from black to white.

buffer   Temporary storage space in the memory of a device. Helps smooth data flow.

burst   A short segment of the color subcarrier in a composite signal, inserted to help the composite video decoder regenerate the color subcarrier.

burst cutting area   A circular section near the center of a DVD disc where ID codes and manufacturing information can be inscribed in bar-code format.

button   This is a rectangular area in the Sub-picture display area highlighted by the Highlight Information (HLI) that is used to define the active area on a menu associated with a specific action.

button number These are consecutive numbers assigned to each button on a menu, ranging from 1 to 36.

B-Y, R-Y The general term for color-difference video signals carrying blue and red color information, where the brightness (Y) has been subtracted from the blue and red RGB signals to create B-Y and R-Y color-difference signals.

byte A unit of data or data storage space consisting of eight bits, commonly representing a single character. Digital data storage is usually measured in bytes, kilobytes, megabytes, and so on.

caption A textual representation of the audio information in a video program. Captions are usually intended for the hearing impaired, and therefore include additional text to identify the person speaking, off screen sounds, and so on.

CAV See constant angular velocity.

C_b, C_r The components of digital color-difference video signals carrying blue and red color information, where the brightness (Y) has been subtracted from the blue and red RGB signals to create B-Y and R-Y color-difference signals.

CBEMA Computer and Business Equipment Manufacturers Association.

CBR See constant bit rate.

CCI See copy control information.

CCIR Rec. 601 A standard for digital video. The CCIR changed its name to ITU-R, and the standard is now properly called ITU-R BT.601.

CD Compact disc. An optical disc storage format developed by Philips and Sony.

CD+G Compact disc plus graphics. A variation of CD, which embeds graphical data in with the audio data, allowing video pictures to be displayed periodically as music is played. Primarily used for karaoke.

CD-DA Compact disc digital audio. The original music CD format, storing audio information as digital PCM data. Defined by the Red Book standard.

CD-i Compact disc interactive. An extension of the CD format designed around a set-top computer that connects to a TV to provide interactive home entertainment, including digital audio and video, video games, and software applications. Defined by the Green Book standard.

CD-Plus A type of Enhanced CD format using stamped multisession technology.

CD-R   An extension of the CD format allowing data to be recorded once on a disc by using dye-sublimation technology. Defined by the Orange Book standard.

CD-ROM XA   CD-ROM extended architecture. A hybrid version of CD allowing interleaved audio and video.

CD-ROM   Compact disc read-only memory. An extension of the Compact disc digital audio (CD-DA) format that allows computer data to be stored in digital format. Defined by the Yellow Book standard.

cell command   A Navigation command executed when the presentation of a cell has been completed.

CEMA   Consumer Electronics Manufacturers Association. A subsidiary of the Electronics Industry Association (EIA).

CGMS   See copy guard management system.

challenge key   Data used in the authentication key exchange process between a DVD-ROM drive and a host computer, where one side determines if the other side contains the necessary authorized keys and algorithms for passing encrypted (scrambled) data.

channel   A part of an audio track. Typically there is one channel allocated for each loudspeaker.

channel bit   The bits stored on the disc, after being modulated.

channel data   The bits physically recorded on an optical disc after error-correction encoding and modulation. Because of the extra information and processing, channel data is larger than the user data contained within it.

chapter   In DVD-Video, a division of a title. Technically called a part of title (PTT).

chroma (C¢)   The nonlinear color component of a video signal, independent of the luma. Identified by the symbol C ¢ (where ¢ indicates nonlinearity) but usually written as C because it's never linear in practice.

chroma subsampling   Reducing color resolution by taking fewer color samples than luminance samples.

chrominance (C) The color component (hue and saturation) of light, independent of luminance. Technically, chrominance refers to the linear component of video, as opposed to the transformed nonlinear chroma component.

CIE Commission Internationale de l'Éclairage/International Commission on Illumination.

CIF Common intermediate format. Video resolution of 352×288.

CIRC Cross-interleaved Reed Solomon code. An error-correction coding method, which overlaps small frames of data.

clamping area The area near the inner hole of a disc where the drive grips the disc in order to spin it.

closed caption Textual video overlays that are not normally visible, as opposed to open captions, which are a permanent part of the picture. Captions are usually a textual representation of the spoken audio. In the United States, the official NTSC Closed Caption standard requires that all TVs larger than 13 inches include circuitry to decode and display caption information stored on line 21 of the video signal. DVD-Video can provide closed caption data, but the subpicture format is preferred for its versatility.

CLUT Color Lookup Table. An index that maps a limited range color values to a full range of values such as RGB or YUV.

CLV See constant linear velocity.

CMF Cutting Master Format is a protocol, similar to DDP, which describes data that will be recorded onto an optical disc. Developed by Pioneer, CMF can now be recorded directly to DVD-R for Authoring (4.7G byte) media using the Pioneer DVR-S201 recorder. This allows a single DVD-R disc to serve as both a check disc for testing playback, and as the replication master, saving time and ensuring accuracy of the data. DVD-R Cutting Master Format is written to the "lead in" area, which has been specially reserved for mastering applications and is defined in version 2.0 of the DVD-R for Authoring specification. Special software and some handling at a press facility are required to use the DVD-R Cutting Master. Most DVD copyright protection mechanisms, including CSS encryption, Copy Guard Management System (CGMS), and Region Management (RMA) cannot currently be used with CMF.

CMI Content Management Information. General information about copy protection and allowed use of protected content. Includes CCI.

codec Coder/decoder. Circuitry or computer software that encodes and decodes a signal.

color depth The number of levels of color (usually including luma and chroma) that can be represented by a pixel. Generally expressed as a number of bits or a number of colors. The color depth of MPEG video in DVD is 24 bits, although the chroma component is shared across 4 pixels (averaging 12 actual bits per pixel).

color difference A pair of video signals that contain the color components minus the brightness component, usually B-Y and R-Y (G-Y is not used, since it generally carries less information). The color-difference signals for a black-and-white picture are zero. The advantage of color-difference signals is that the color component can be reduced more than the brightness (luma) component without being visually perceptible.

color model Any of several means of specifying colors according to their individual components. See RGB, YUV.

component video A video system containing three separate color component signals, either red/green/blue (RGB) or chroma/color difference (YC_bC_r, YP_bP_r, YUV), in analog or digital form. The MPEG-2 encoding system used by DVD is based on color-difference component digital video. Very few televisions have component video inputs.

composite video An analog video signal in which the luma and chroma components are combined (by frequency multiplexing), along with sync and burst. Also called CVBS. Most televisions and VCRs have composite video connectors, which are usually colored yellow.

compression The process of removing redundancies in digital data to reduce the amount that must be stored or transmitted. Lossless compression removes only enough redundancy so that the original data can be recreated exactly as it was. Lossy compression sacrifices additional data to achieve greater compression.

constant angular velocity Refers to rotating disc systems in which the rotation speed is kept constant, where the pickup head travels over a longer surface as it moves away from the center of the disc. The advantage of CAV is that the same amount of information is provided in one rotation of the disc. Contrast with CLV and ZCLV.

constant bit rate Data compressed into a stream with a fixed data rate. The amount of compression (such as quantization) is varied to match the allocated data rate, but as a result quality may suffer during high compression periods. In other words, data rate is held constant while quality is allowed to vary. Compare to VBR.

constant data rate See constant bit rate.

constant linear velocity Refers to a rotating disc system in which the head moves over the disc surface at a constant velocity, requiring that the motor vary the rotation speed as the head travels in and out. The further the head is from the center of the disc, the slower the rotation.

The advantage of CLV is that data density remains constant, optimizing use of the surface area. Contrast with CAV and ZCLV.

Content Protection for Prerecorded Media   Copy protection for DVD-Audio.

Content Scrambling System   In DVD-Video, an encryption scheme designed to protect copyrighted material that resides on a disc by periodically scrambling the data using encryption keys.

contrast   The range of brightness between the darkest and lightest elements of an image.

control area   A part of the lead-in area on a DVD containing one ECC block (16 sectors) repeated 192 times. The repeated ECC block holds information about the disc.

copy control information   Information specifying if content is allowed to be copied.

copy guard management system   A method of preventing copies or controlling the number of sequential copies allowed. CGMS/A is added to an analog signal (such as line 21 of NTSC). CGMS/D is added to a digital signal, such as IEEE 1394.

copyrighted material flag   In DVD-Video, a 1-bit value stored in the CPR_MAI that indicates if the corresponding sector includes any copyrighted material.

CPM   See copyrighted material flag.

CPPM   See Content Protection for Prerecorded Media.

CPRM   Content Protection for Recordable Media. Copy protection for writeable DVD formats.

CPR_MAI   Copyright Management Information. In DVD-Video, an extra 6 bytes per sector that includes the Copyright Protection System Type (CPS_TY) and Region Management information (RMA) in the Contents provider section of the Control data block; and Copyrighted Material flag (CPM), Copyright Protection System flag (CP_SEC) and Copy Guard Management System (CGMS) flags in the Data Area.

CPSA   Content Protection System Architecture. An overall copy protection design for DVD.

CPTWG   Copy Protection Technical Working Group. The industry body responsible for developing or approving DVD copy protection systems.

CPU   Central Processing Unit. The integrated circuit chip that forms the brain of a computer or other electronic device. DVD-Video players contain rudimentary CPUs to provide general control and interactive features.

CP_SEC   Copyright Protection System flag. In DVD-Video, a 1-bit value stored in the CPR_MAI that indicates if the corresponding sector has implemented a copyright protection system. See Content Scrambling System (CSS).

CPS_TY   Copyright Protection System Type. In DVD-Video, an 8-bit (1 byte) value stored in the CPR_MAI that defines the type of copyright protection system implemented on a disc.

crop   To trim and remove a section of the video picture in order to make it conform to a different shape. Cropping is used in the pan & scan process, but not in the letterbox process.

Cyclic Redundancy Check   A method for computing a signature of a sequence of bytes used to detect the presence of errors in the data.

DAC   Digital-to-Analog Converter. Circuitry that converts digital data (such as audio or video) to analog data.

DAE   Digital Audio Extraction. Reading digital audio data directly from a CD audio disc.

DAT   Digital Audio Tape. A magnetic audio tape format that uses PCM to store digitized audio or digital data.

data area   The physical area of a DVD disc between the lead in and the lead out (or middle area) which contains the stored data content of the disc.

data rate   The volume of data measured over time; the rate at which digital information can be conveyed. Usually expressed as bits per second with notations of kbps (thousand/sec), Mbps (million/sec), and Gbps (billion/sec). Digital audio date rate is generally computed as the number of samples per second times the bit size of the sample. For example, the data rate of uncompressed 16-bit, 48-kHz, two-channel audio is 1536 kbps. Digital video bit rate is generally computed as the number of bits per pixel times the number of pixels per line times the number of lines per frame times the number of frames per second. For example, the data rate of a DVD movie before compression is usually $12 \times 720 \times 480 \times 24 = 99.5$ Mbps. Compression reduces the data rate. Digital data rate is sometimes inaccurately equated with bandwidth.

Data Search Information   Information for Fast Forward/Fast Backward and seamless playback. This is real time control data spread throughout the DVD-Video data stream. Along with PGCI, these packets are part of the 1.00 Mbit/sec overhead in video applications (Book B). These packets contain navigation information, which makes it possible to search and maintain seamless playback of the Video Object Unit (VOBU). The most important field in this packet is the sector address where the first reference frame of the video object begins. Advanced angle change and presentation timing are included to assist seamless playback.

dB See decibel.

DBS See Digital Broadcast Satellite.

DC See Direct Current.

DCC See Digital Compact Cassette.

DCT See Discrete Cosine Transform. *Also* Digital Component Technology, a videotape format.

DDP See Disc Description Protocol.

DDWG Digital Display Working Group. (See Digital Visual Interface.)

decibel A unit of measurement expressing ratios using logarithmic scales related to human aural or visual perception. Many different measurements are based on a reference point of 0 dB; for example a standard level of sound or power.

decimation A form of subsampling, which discards existing samples (pixels, in the case of spatial decimation, or pictures, in the case of temporal decimation). The resulting information is reduced in size but may suffer from aliasing.

decode To reverse the transformation process of an encoding method. Decoding processes are usually deterministic.

decoder 1) A circuit that decodes compressed audio or video, taking an encoded input stream and producing output such as audio or video. DVD players use the decoders to recreate information that was compressed by systems such as MPEG-2 and Dolby Digital; 2) a circuit that converts composite video to component video or matrixed audio to multiple channels.

delta picture (or delta frame) A video picture based on the changes from the picture before (or after) it. MPEG P pictures and B pictures are examples. Contrast with key picture.

deterministic A process or model whose outcome does not depend upon chance, and where a given input will always produce the same output. Audio and video decoding processes are mostly deterministic.

digital Expressed in digits. A set of discrete numeric values, as used by a computer. Sampling can digitize analog information.

Digital Broadcast Satellite   The general term for 18-inch digital satellite systems.

Digital Compact Cassette   A digital audio tape format based on the popular compact cassette. Abandoned by Philips in 1996.

Digital Linear Tape   A digital archive standard using half-inch tapes, commonly used for submitting a premastered DVD disc image to a replication service.

mat and logical/file structures. They differ only content. Physical differences between erasable (Book E), write-once read many times (Book D), and ROM (Book A) may emerge.

Digital Video   Usually refers to the digital videocassette standard developed by Sony and JVC.

Digital Video Broadcast   A European standard for broadcast, cable, and digital satellite video transmission.

Digital Video Noise Reduction   Digitally removing noise from video by comparing frames in sequence to spot temporal aberrations.

Digital Visual Interface   The digital video interface standard developed by the Digital Display Working Group (DDWG). A replacement for analog VGA monitor interface.

digitize   To convert analog information to digital information by sampling.

DIN   Deutsches Institut für Normung/German Institute for Standardization.

Direct Current   Electrical current flowing in one direction only. Adopted in the video world to refer to a signal with zero frequency. Compare to AC.

Direct Stream Digital   An uncompressed audio bitstream coding method developed by Sony. An alternative to PCM.

directory   The part of a disc that indicates what files are stored on the disc and where they are located.

directory structure   For the video specification (Book B), this defines a common set of files that must be present on all DVD discs. Components include Root and `Video_TS`.

DirectShow   A software standard developed by Microsoft for playback of digital video and audio in the Windows operating system. Replaces the older MCI and Video for Windows software.

Disc Description Protocol   Identifies and describes collections of data that will be recorded onto a compact disc (CD) or digital versatile disc (DVD). DDP allows for automated transfer of data from data publishers to disc manufacturers. DDP is the de facto standard in the DVD industry for delivering disc image data to the replication plant for manufacturing. Originally developed by Doug Carson & Associates (DCA), Inc. for CD manufacturing, DDP provides descriptive information about the disc to be manufactured, such as the physical size, number of sides, etc. DVD utilizes version 2.0 of this specification, which can be requested via the DCA web site (http://www.dcainc.com).

disc key   A value used to encrypt and decrypt (scramble) a title key on DVD-Video discs.

disc menu   The main menu of a DVD-Video disc, from which titles are selected. Also called the system menu or title selection menu. Sometimes confusingly called the title menu, which more accurately refers to the menu within a title from which audio, subpicture, chapters, and so forth can be selected.

Discrete Cosine Transform   An invertible, discrete, orthogonal transformation. Got that? A mathematical process used in MPEG video encoding to transform blocks of pixel values into blocks of spatial frequency values with lower-frequency components organized into the upper-left corner, allowing the high-frequency components in the lower-right corner to be discounted or discarded.

discrete surround sound   Audio in which each channel is stored and transmitted separate from and independent of other channels. Multiple independent channels directed to loudspeakers in front of and behind the listener allow precise control of the sound field in order to generate localized sounds and simulate moving sound sources.

display rate   The number of times per second the image in a video system is refreshed. Progressive scan systems such as film or HDTV change the image once per frame. Interlace scan systems such as standard television change the image twice per frame, with two fields in each frame. Film has a frame rate of 24 fps, but each frame is shown twice by the projector for a display rate of 48 fps. 525/60 (NTSC) television has a rate of 29.97 frames per second (59.94 fields per second). 625/50 (PAL/SECAM) television has a rate of 25 frames per second (50 fields per second).

Divx   Digital Video Express. A short-lived pay-per-viewing-period variation of DVD.

DLT   See Digital Linear Tape.

Dolby Digital   A perceptual coding system for audio, developed by Dolby Laboratories and accepted as an international standard. Dolby Digital is the most common means of encoding audio for DVD-Video and is the mandatory audio compression system for 525/60 (NTSC) discs.

Dolby Pro Logic   The technique (or the circuit which applies the technique) of extracting surround audio channels from a matrix-encoded audio signal. Dolby Pro Logic is a decoding technique only, but is often mistakenly used to refer to Dolby Surround audio encoding.

Dolby Surround   The standard for matrix encoding surround-sound channels in a stereo sig-

Domain, Video Manager Menu Domain, VTS Menu Domain and Title Domain.

downmix   To convert a multichannel audio track into a two-channel stereo track by combining the channels with the Dolby Surround process. All DVD players are required to provide downmixed audio output from Dolby Digital audio tracks.

downsampling   See subsampling.

DRC   See Dynamic Range Compression.

driver   A software component that enables an application to communicate with a hardware device.

DSD   See Direct Stream Digital.

DSI   See Data Search Information.

DSP   See Digital Signal Processor (or Processing).

DSVCD   Double Super Video Compact. Long-playing (100-minute) variation of SVCD.

DTS   Digital Theater Sound. A perceptual audio-coding system developed for theaters. A competitor to Dolby Digital and an optional audio track format for DVD-Video and DVD-Audio.

DTS-ES   A version of DTS decoding that is compatible with 6.1-channel Dolby Surround EX. DTS-ES Discrete is a variation of DTS encoding and decoding that carries a discrete rear center channel instead of a matrixed channel.

DTV   See Digital Television.

duplication   The reproduction of media. Generally refers to producing discs in small quantities, as opposed to large-scale replication.

DV   See Digital Video.

DVB   See Digital Video Broadcast.

DVC   Digital Video Cassette — an early name for DV.

DVCAM   Sony's proprietary version of DV.

DVCD   Double Video Compact Disc. Long-playing (100-minute) variation of VCD.

DVCPro   Matsushita's proprietary version of DV.

DVD   See Digital Versatile Disc.

DVDA   DVD Association, a non-profit industry trade association representing DVD authors, producers, and vendors throughout the world.

DVD-A (DVD-Audio)   The audio-only format of DVD. Primarily uses PCM audio with MLP encoding, along with an optional subset of DVD-Video features.

DVD Forum   An international association of hardware and media manufacturers, software firms and other users of Digital Versatile Discs, created for the purpose of exchanging and disseminating ideas and information about the DVD Format.

DVD Multi   DVD Multi is a logo program that promotes compatibility with DVD-RAM and DVD-RW. It is not a drive, but defines a testing methodology which, when passed, ensures the drive product can in fact read RAM and -RW. It puts the emphasis for compatibility on the reader, not the writer.

DVD-R (DVD Recordable)   The authoring use drive (635nm laser) was introduced in 1998 by Pioneer, and the general use format (650nm laser) was authorized by DVD Forum in 2000. DVD-R offers a write-once, read-many storage format akin to CD-R and is used to master DVD-Video and DVD-ROM discs, as well as for data archival and storage applications.

DVD-RW (DVD Rewritable)   A Rewritable DVD format, introduced by Pioneer that is similar to DVD+RW. It has a read-write capacity of 4.38 GB.

DVD-RAM (DVD Random Access Memory)   A Rewritable DVD disc endorsed by Panasonic, Hitachi and Toshiba. It is a cartridge-based, and more recently, bare disc technology for data recording and playback. The first DVD-RAM drives were introduced in Spring 1998 and had a capacity of 2.6GB (single sided) or 5.2GB (double sided). DVD-RAM Version 2 discs with

4.38GB arrived in late 1999, and double-sided 9.4GB discs in 2000. DVD-RAM drives typically read DVD-Video, DVD-ROM and CD media. The current installed base of DVD-ROM drives and DVD-Video players cannot read DVD-RAM media.

DVD-ROM (DVD Read Only Memory)   The base format of DVD. Standard DVD-ROM and DVD-Video discs can't be recorded on. A DVD-ROM can store essentially any form of digital data.

DVD+RW (DVD Rewritable)   Developed in cooperation by Hewlett-Packard, Mitsubishi Chem-

DVI   See Digital Visual Interface.

DVNR   See Digital Video Noise Reduction.

DVS   Descriptive Video Services. Descriptive narration of video for blind or sight-impaired viewers.

dye polymer   The chemical used in DVD-R and CD-R media that darkens when heated by a high-power laser.

dye-sublimation   Optical disc recording technology that uses a high-powered laser to burn readable marks into a layer of organic dye. Other recording formats include magneto-optical and phase-change.

dynamic range   The difference between the loudest and softest sound in an audio signal. The dynamic range of digital audio is determined by the sample size. Increasing the sample size does not allow louder sounds; it increases the resolution of the signal, thus allowing softer sounds to be separated from the noise floor (and allowing more amplification with less distortion). Dynamic range refers to the difference between the maximum level of distortion-free signal and the minimum limit reproducible by the equipment.

Dynamic Range Compression   A technique of reducing the range between loud and soft sounds in order to make dialogue more audible, especially when listening at low volume levels. Used in the downmix process of multichannel Dolby Digital sound tracks.

EBU   European Broadcasting Union.

ECC   See error-correction code.

ECC Constraint Length   The number of sectors that are interleaved to combat bursty error characteristics of discs. 16 sectors are interleaved in DVD. Interleaving takes advantage of typical disc defects such as scratch marks by spreading the error over a larger data area, thereby increasing the chance that the error correction codes can conceal the error.

ECD   Error-detection and correction code. See error-correction code.

ECMA   European Computer Manufacturers Association (see http://www.ecma.org).

ECMA-262   An ECMA standard that specifies the core JavaScript language, which is expected to be adopted shortly by the International Standards Organization (ISO) as ISO 16262. ECMA-262 is roughly equivalent to JavaScript 1.1.

EDC   A short error-detection code applied at the end of a DVD sector.

edge enhancement   When films are transferred to video in preparation for DVD encoding, they are commonly run through digital processes that attempt to clean up the picture. These processes include noise reduction (DVNR) and image enhancement. Enhancement increases contrast (similar to the effect of the "sharpen" or "unsharp mask" filters in PhotoShop), but can tend to overdo areas of transition between light and dark or different colors, causing a "chiseled" look or a ringing effect like the haloes you see around streetlights when driving in the rain. Video noise reduction is a good thing, when done well, since it can remove scratches, spots, and other defects from the original film. Enhancement, which is rarely done well, is a bad thing. The video may look sharper and clearer to the casual observer, but fine tonal details of the original picture are altered and lost.

EDS   Enhanced Data Services. Additional information in NTSC line such as a time signal.

EDTV   Enhanced-Definition Television. A system which uses existing transmission equipment to send an enhanced signal which looks the same on existing receivers but carries additional information to improve the picture quality on new enhanced receivers. PALPlus is an example of EDTV. Contrast with HDTV and IDTV.

EFM   Eight-to-Fourteen Modulation. This low-level and very critical channel coding technique maximizes pit sizes on the disc by reducing frequent transitions from 0 to 1 or 1 to 0. CD employs pulse width modulation, representing 1's as Land-pit transitions along the track. The 8/14 code maps 8 user data bits into 14 channel bits. In the 1982 compact disc standard (IEC 908 standard), 3 merge bits are added to the 14 bit block to further eliminate 1-0 or 0-1 transitions between adjacent 8/14 blocks.

EFM Plus   DVD's EFM+ method is a derivative of EFM. It folds the merge bits into the main 8/16 table. EFM+ may be covered by U.S. Patent 5,206,646.

EIA   Electronics Industry Association.

E-IDE Enhanced Integrated Drive Electronics. Extensions to the IDE standard providing faster data transfer and allowing access to larger drives, including CD-ROM and tape drives, using ATAPI. E-IDE was adopted as a standard by ANSI in 1994. ANSI calls it Advanced Technology Attachment-2 (ATA-2) or Fast ATA.

elementary stream A general term for a coded bitstream such as audio or video. Elementary streams are made up of packs of packets.

emulate To test the function of a DVD disc on a computer after formatting a complete disc

circuit that converts component digital video to composite analog video. DVD players include TV encoders to generate standard television signals from decoded video and audio; 3) a circuit that converts multichannel audio to two-channel matrixed audio.

Enhanced CD A general term for various techniques that add computer software to a music CD, producing a disc, which can be played in a music player or read by a computer. Also called CD Extra, CD Plus, hybrid CD, interactive music CD, mixed-mode CD, pre-gap CD, or track-zero CD.

entropy coding Variable-length, lossless coding of a digital signal to reduce redundancy. MPEG-2, DTS and Dolby Digital apply entropy coding after the quantization step. MLP also uses entropy coding.

EQ Equalization of audio.

error-correction code Additional information added to data to allow errors to be detected and possibly corrected.

Error Detection Code (EDC) 32-bit (4 byte) CRC-like code appended at the end of the data sector.

ETSI European Telecommunications Standards Institute.

Extent (1) For the volume structure and the ISO 9660 file structure, an extent is defined as a set of logical sectors, the logical sector numbers of which form a continuous ascending sequence. The address, or location, of an extent is the number of the first logical sector in the sequence. (2) For the UDF file structure an extent is defined as a set of logical blocks, the logical block numbers of which form a continuous ascending sequence. The address, or location, of an extent is the number of the first logical block in the sequence.

father   The metal master disc formed by electroplating the glass master. The father disc is used to make mother discs, from which multiple stampers (sons) can be made.

field   A set of alternating scan lines in an interlaced video picture. A frame is made of a top (odd) field and a bottom (even) field.

file set   A collection of files and directories.

file system   A defined way of storing files, directories, and information about them on a data storage device.

file   A collection of data stored on a disc, usually in groups of sectors.

filter   (verb) To reduce the amount of information in a signal. (noun) A circuit or process that reduces the amount of information in a signal. Analog filtering usually removes certain frequencies. Digital filtering (when not emulating analog filtering) usually averages together multiple adjacent pixels, lines, or frames to create a single new pixel, line, or frame. This generally causes a loss of detail, especially with complex images or rapid motion. See letterbox filter. Compare to interpolate.

FireWire   A standard for transmission of digital data between external peripherals, including consumer audio and video devices. The official name is IEEE 1394, based on the original FireWire design by Apple Computer.

First Play PGC   This Program Chain (PGC) is described in the Video Manager Information table, and has no corresponding video objects (VOB). The First Play PGC is executed at initial access, e.g. just after disc loading.

fixed rate   Information flow at a constant volume over time. See CBR.

forced activation button   Menu buttons that automatically perform the specified action as soon as the button has been highlighted on the menu.

forced selected button   Menu button that is automatically selected when the menu is displayed.

forced display   A feature of DVD-Video allowing subpictures to be displayed even if the player's subpicture display mode is turned off. Designed for showing subtitles in a scene where the language is different from the native language of the film.

formatting   1) Creating a disc image. 2) Preparing storage media for recording.

fps   Frames per second. A measure of the rate at which pictures are shown for a motion video image. In NTSC and PAL video, each frame is made up of two interlaced fields.

fragile watermark   A watermark designed to be destroyed by any form of copying or encoding other than a bit-for-bit digital copy. Absence of the watermark indicates that a copy has been made.

frame doubler   A video processor that increases the frame rate (display rate) in order to create a smoother-looking video display. Compare to line doubler.

frame rate   The frequency of discrete images. Usually measured in frames per second (fps). Film has a rate of 24 frames per second, but usually must be adjusted to match the display

Full motion video   Video that plays at thirty frames per second (NTSC) or 25 frames per second (PAL).

G byte   One billion (10^9) bytes. Not to be confused with GB or gigabyte (2^{30} bytes).

G Giga   An SI prefix for denominations of 1 billion (10^9).

Galaxy Group   The group of companies proposing the Galaxy watermarking format. (IBM/NEC, Hitachi/Pioneer/Sony.)

Gb   Gigabyte.

Gbps   Gigabits/second. Billions (10^9) of bits per second.

General Parameters   GPRMs are used to store the users operational history and to modify a player's behavior. DVD-Video players have 16 unique GPRMs. Each GRPM may store a fixed length, two-byte numerical value.

gigabyte   1,073,741,824 (2^{30}) bytes.

GOF   Group of Audio Frames. The data area of 1/30 second, which is composed of 20 audio frames of Linear PCM Audio.

GOP   Group of Pictures. In MPEG video, one or more I pictures followed by P and B pictures. A GOP is the atomic unit of MPEG video access. GOPs are limited in DVD-Video to 18 frames for 525/60 and 15 frames for 625/50.

GPRM   See General Parameters.

gray market Dealers and distributors who sell equipment without proper authorization from the manufacturer.

Green Book The document developed in 1987 by Philips and Sony as an extension to CD-ROM XA for the CD-i system.

H/DTV High-definition/digital television. A combination of acronyms that refers to both HDTV and DTV systems.

Half D1 An MPEG-2 video encoding mode in which half the horizontal resolution is sampled (352∞480 for NTSC, 352∞576 for PAL).

HAVi A consumer electronics industry standard for interoperability between digital audio and video devices connected via a network in the consumer's home.

HDCD High-Definition Compatible Digital. A proprietary method of enhancing audio on CDs.

HDTV High-definition television. A video format with a resolution approximately twice that of conventional television in both the horizontal and vertical dimensions, and a picture aspect ratio of 16:9. Used loosely to refer to the U.S. DTV System. Contrast with EDTV and IDTV.

Hertz See Hz.

hexadecimal Representation of numbers using base 16.

HFS Hierarchical File System. A file system used by Apple Computer's Mac OS operating system.

Highlight Information (HLI) This is used to specify button highlights for menus. HLI contains information on the button number, highlight timing, palette for sub-picture highlights, coordinates of the button, etc.

High Sierra The original file system standard developed for CD-ROM, later modified and adopted as ISO 9660.

horizontal resolution See lines of horizontal resolution.

HQ-VCD High-quality Video Compact Disc. Developed by the Video CD Consortium (Philips, Sony, Matsushita and JVC) as a successor to VCD. Evolved into SVCD.

HRRA Home Recording Rights Association.

HSF See High Sierra.

HTML   HyperText Markup Language. A tagging specification, based on SGML (standard generalized markup language), for formatting text to be transmitted over the Internet and displayed by client software.

hue   The color of light or of a pixel. The property of color determined by the dominant wavelength of light.

Huffman coding   A lossless compression technique of assigning variable-length codes to a known set of values. Values occurring most frequently are assigned the shortest codes. MPEG uses a

point for dependent P pictures and B pictures and allow random access into the compressed video stream.

i.Link   Trademarked Sony name for IEEE 1394.

ID Error Correction (IEC)   2 special error correction bytes (IEC) that are added to each sector header.

IDE   Integrated Drive Electronics. An internal bus, or standard electronic interface between a computer and internal block storage devices. IDE was adopted as a standard by ANSI in November 1990. ANSI calls it Advanced Technology Attachment (ATA). Also see E-IDE and ATAPI.

Identification Data (ID)   32-bit field identifying the sector number within the disc volume.

IDTV   Improved-Definition Television. A television receiver that improves the apparent quality of the picture from a standard video signal by using techniques such as frame doubling, line doubling, and digital signal processing. Contrast with EDTV and HDTV.

IEC   International Electrotechnical Commission.

IED   ID Error Correction. An error-detection code applied to each sector ID on a DVD disc.

IEEE 1394   A standard for transmission of digital data between external peripherals, including consumer audio and video devices. Also known as FireWire.

IEEE   Institute of Electrical and Electronics Engineers. An electronics standards body.

IFE   In-Flight Entertainment.

I-MPEG   Intraframe MPEG. An unofficial variation of MPEG video encoding that uses only Intraframe compression. I-MPEG is used by DV equipment.

Interframe   Something that occurs between multiple frames of video. Interframe compression takes temporal redundancy into account. Contrast with Intraframe.

interlace   A video scanning system in which alternating lines are transmitted, so that half a picture is displayed each time the scanning beam moves down the screen. An interlaced frame is made of two fields.

interleave   To arrange data in alternating chunks so that selected parts can be extracted while other parts are skipped over, or so that each chunk carries a piece of a different data stream. In DVD, used for seamless multi-angle and Director's cut features, in which multiplexed streams are subsequently interleaved to allow seamless playback of alternate program material.

interpolate   To increase the pixels, scan lines, or pictures when scaling an image or a video stream by averaging together adjacent pixels, lines, or frames to create additional inserted pixels or frames. This generally causes a softening of still images and a blurriness of motion images because no new information is created. Compare to filter.

Intraframe   Something that occurs within a single frame of video. Intraframe compression does not reduce temporal redundancy, but allows each frame to be independently manipulated or accessed. (See I picture.) Compare to Interframe.

inverse Telecine   The reverse of 3:2 pulldown, where frames, which were duplicated to create 60-fields/second video from 24-frames/second film, are removed. MPEG-2 video encoders usually apply an inverse Telecine process to convert 60-fields/second video into 24-frames/second encoded video. The encoder adds information enabling the decoder to recreate the 60-fields/second display rate.

ISO 2202   Information Processing – ISO 7-bit and 8-bit coded character sets – Code extension techniques

ISO 3166   Codes for the representation of names of countries.

ISO 3901   Documentation – International Standard Recording Code (ISRC).

ISO 639   Codes for the representation of names of languages.

ISO 8859-1   Information Processing – 8-bit single-byte coded graphic character sets.

ISO 9660   The international standard for the file system used by CD-ROM. Allows filenames of only 8 characters plus a 3-character extension.

ISO/IEC 11172 Information technology coding of moving pictures and associated audio for digital storage media up to about 1.5 Mbit/s.

ISO/IEC 13818 Information technology- generic coding of moving pictures and associated audio.

ISO/IEC DIS 13818-3 Information technology- generic coding of moving pictures and associated audio.

Java A highly portable, object-oriented programming language developed by Sun Microsystems. Not to be confused with JavaScript.

JavaScript A programming language originally created by Netscape with specific features designed for use with the Internet and HTML, and syntax resembling that of Java and C++. Now standardized as ECMA-262.

JCIC Joint Committee on Intersociety Coordination.

JEC Joint Engineering Committee of EIA and NCTA.

jewel box The plastic clamshell case that holds a CD or DVD.

jitter Temporal variation in a signal from an ideal reference clock. There are many kinds of jitter, including sample jitter, channel jitter, and interface jitter.

JPEG Joint Photographic Experts Group. The international committee which created its namesake standard for compressing still images.

Jscript A proprietary Microsoft variant of JavaScript.

k byte One thousand (10^3) bytes. Not to be confused with Kb or kilobyte (2^{10} bytes). Note the small "k."

k kilo An SI prefix for denominations of one thousand (10^3). Also used, in capital form, for 1024 bytes of computer data (see kilobyte).

karaoke Literally empty orchestra. The social sensation from Japan where sufficiently inebriated people embarrass themselves in public by singing along to a music track. Karaoke was largely responsible for the success of laserdisc in Japan, thus supporting it elsewhere.

Kb Kilobyte.

kbps Kilobits/second Thousands (10^3) of bits per second.

key picture (or key frame) A video picture containing the entire content of the image (Intraframe encoding), rather than the difference between it and another image (Interframe encoding). MPEG I pictures are key pictures. Contrast with delta picture.

kHz Kilohertz A unit of frequency measurement. One thousand cycles (repetitions) per second or 1000 hertz.

kilobyte 1024 (2^{10}) bytes.

land The raised area of an optical disc.

laserdisc A 12-inch (or 8-inch) optical disc that holds analog video (using an FM signal) and both analog and digital (PCM) audio. A precursor to DVD.

layer The plane of a DVD disc on which information is recorded in a pattern of microscopic pits. Each substrate of a disc can contain one or two layers.

Layer 0 In a dual layer disc, this is the layer closest to the optical pickup beam and surface of the disc. Dual layer discs are 10% less dense than single layer discs due to crosstalk between the layers.

Layer 1 In a dual layer disc, this is the deeper of the two layers.

lead in The physical area 1.2 mm or wider preceding the data area on a disc. The lead in contains sync sectors and control data including disc keys and other information.

lead out On a single-layer disc or PTP dual-layer disc, the physical area 1.0 mm or wider toward the outside of the disc following the data area. On an OTP dual-layer disc, the physical area 1.2 mm or wider at the inside of the disc following the recorded data area (which is read from the outside toward the inside on the second layer).

legacy A term used to describe a hybrid disc that can be played in both a DVD player and a CD player.

letterbox The process or form of video where black horizontal mattes are added to the top and bottom of the display area in order to create a frame in which to display video using an aspect ratio different than that of the display. The letterbox method preserves the entire video picture, as opposed to pan & scan. DVD-Video players can automatically letterbox a wide-screen picture for display on a standard 4:3 TV.

letterbox filter   Circuitry in a DVD player that reduces the vertical size of anamorphic wide-screen video (combining every 4 lines into 3) and adds black mattes at the top and bottom. Also see filter.

level   In MPEG-2, levels specify parameters such as resolution, bit rate, and frame rate.

lines of horizontal resolution   Sometimes abbreviated as TVL (TV lines) or LoHR. A common but subjective measurement of the visually resolvable horizontal detail of an analog video system, measured in half-cycles per picture height. Each cycle is a pair of vertical lines, one black and one white. The measurement is usually made by viewing a test pattern to determine where the black and white lines blur into gray. The resolution of VHS video is commonly gauged at 240 lines of horizontal resolution, broadcast video at 330, laserdisc at 425, and DVD at 500 to 540. Because the measurement is relative to picture height, the aspect ratio must be taken into account when determining the number of vertical units (roughly equivalent to pixels) that can be displayed across the width of the display. For example, an aspect ratio of 1.33 multiplied by 540 gives 720 pixels.

L_o/R_o   Left only/right only. Stereo signal (no matrixed surround information). Optional downmixing output in Dolby Digital decoders. Does not change phase, simply folds surround channels forward into L_f and R_f.

locale   See regional code.

logical unit   A physical or virtual peripheral device, such as a DVD-ROM drive.

logical   An artificial structure or organization of information created for convenience of access or reference, usually different from the physical structure or organization. For example, the application specifications of DVD (the way information is organized and stored) are logical formats.

lossless compression   Compression techniques that allow the original data to be recreated without loss. Contrast with lossy compression.

lossy compression   Compression techniques that achieve very high compression ratios by permanently removing data while preserving as much significant information as possible. Lossy compression includes perceptual coding techniques that attempt to limit the data loss to that which is least likely to be noticed by human perception.

LP   Long-playing record. An audio recording on a plastic platter turning at 33 1/3 rpm and read by a stylus.

LPCM   See linear PCM.

L_t/R_t   Left total/right total. Four surround channels matrixed into two channels. Mandatory downmixing output in Dolby Digital decoders.

luma ($Y¢$)   The brightness component of a color video image (also called the grayscale, monochrome, or black-and-white component). Nonlinear luminance. The standard luma signal is computed from nonlinear RGB as $Y¢ = 0.299\ R¢ + 0.587\ G¢ + 0.114\ B¢$.

luminance (Y)   Loosely, the sum of RGB tristimulus values corresponding to brightness. May refer to a linear signal or (incorrectly) a nonlinear signal.

m byte   One million (10^6) bytes. Not to be confused with MB or megabyte (2^{20} bytes).

m mega   An SI prefix for denominations of one million (10^6).

Mac OS   The operating system used by Apple Macintosh computers.

macroblock   In MPEG MP@ML, the four 8 ∞ 8 blocks of luma information and two 8 ∞ 8 blocks of chroma information form a 16 ∞ 16 area of a video frame.

macroblocking   An MPEG artifact. See blocking.

Macrovision   An antitaping process that modifies a signal so that it appears unchanged on most televisions but is distorted and unwatchable when played back from a videotape recording. Macrovision takes advantage of characteristics of AGC circuits and burst decoder circuits in VCRs to interfere with the recording process.

magneto-optical   Recordable disc technology using a laser to heat spots that are altered by a magnetic field. Other formats include dye-sublimation and phase-change.

Main data   User data portion of each sector. 2048 bytes.

main level (ML)   A range of proscribed picture parameters defined by the MPEG-2 video standard, with maximum resolution equivalent to ITU-R BT.601 (720 ∞ 576 ∞ 30). (Also see level.)

main profile (MP)   A subset of the syntax of the MPEG-2 video standard designed to be supported over a large range of mainstream applications such as digital cable TV, DVD, and digital satellite transmission. (Also see profile.)

mark   The non-reflective area of a writeable optical disc. Equivalent to a pit.

master   The metal disc used to stamp replicas of optical discs. The tape used to make additional recordings.

Mb   Megabyte.

Mbps   Megabits/second. Millions (10^6) of bits per second.

megabyte   1,048,576 (2^{20}) bytes. See p. 12 for more information.

megapixel   A term referring to an image or display format with a resolution of approximately 1 million pixels.

memory   Data storage used by computers or other digital electronics systems. Read-only memory (ROM) permanently stores data or software program instructions. New data cannot be written to ROM. Random-access memory (RAM) temporarily stores data—including digital audio and video—while it is being manipulated, and holds software application programs while they are being executed. Data can be read from and written to RAM. Other long-term memory includes hard disks, floppy disks, digital CD formats (CD-ROM, CD-R, and CD-RW), and DVD formats (DVD-ROM, DVD-R, and DVD-RAM).

menu   In DVD-Video there are two kinds of menus, System Menus and Interactive Menus. There are six types of System Menus: Title Menu, Root Menu, Audio Menu, Sub-picture Menu, Angle Menu and PTT or Chapter Menu.

MHz   One million (10^6) Hz.

Microsoft Windows   The leading operating system for Intel CPU-based computers. Developed by Microsoft.

middle area   Unused physical area that marks the transition from layer 0 to layer 1. Middle Area only exists in dual layer discs where the tracks of each layer are in opposite directions.

Millennium Group   The group of companies proposing the Galaxy watermarking format. (Macrovision, Philips, Digimarc)

mixed mode   A type of CD containing both Red Book audio and Yellow Book computer data tracks.

MKB   Media Key Block. Set of keys used in CPPM and CPRM for authenticating players.

MLP   Meridian Lossless Packing. A lossless compression technique (used by DVD-Audio) that removes redundancy from PCM audio signals to achieve a compression ratio of about 2:1 while allowing the signal to be perfectly recreated by the MLP decoder.

MO   Magneto-optical rewriteable discs.

modulation   Replacing patterns of bits with different (usually larger) patterns designed to control the characteristics of the data signal. DVD uses 8/16 modulation, where each set of 8 bits is replaced by 16 bits before being written onto the disc.

mosquitoes   A term referring to the fuzzy dots that can appear around sharp edges (high spatial frequencies) after video compression. Also known as the Gibbs Effect.

mother   The metal discs produced from mirror images of the father disc in the replication process. Mothers are used to make stampers, often called sons

motion compensation   In video decoding, the application of motion vectors to already-decoded blocks to construct a new picture.

motion estimation   In video encoding, the process of analyzing previous or future frames to identify blocks that have not changed or have only changed location. Motion vectors are then stored in place of the blocks. This is very computation-intensive and can cause visual artifacts when subject to errors.

motion vector   A two-dimensional spatial displacement vector used for MPEG motion compensation to provide an offset from the encoded position of a block in a reference (I or P) picture to the predicted position (in a P or B picture).

MP@ML   Main Profile at Main Level. The common MPEG-2 format used by DVD (along with SP@SL).

MP3   MPEG-1 Layer III audio. A perceptual audio coding algorithm. Not supported in DVD-Video or DVD-Audio formats.

MPEG audio   Audio compressed according to the MPEG perceptual encoding system. MPEG-1 audio provides two channels, which can be in Dolby Surround format. MPEG-2 audio adds data to provide discrete multichannel audio. Stereo MPEG audio is the mandatory audio compression system for 625/50 (PAL/SECAM) DVD-Video.

MPEG video   Video compressed according to the MPEG encoding system. MPEG-1 is typically used for low data rate video such as on a Video CD. MPEG-2 is used for higher-quality video, especially interlaced video, such as on DVD or HDTV.

MPEG   Moving Pictures Expert Group. An international committee that developed the MPEG family of audio and video compression systems.

MPEG-1 video   Video encoded in accordance with the ISO/IEC 11172 specification.

scene to be selected during playback.

multichannel   Multiple channels of audio, usually containing different signals for different speakers in order to create a surround-sound effect.

multilanguage   A DVD-Video program containing sound tracks and subtitle tracks for more than one language.

multimedia   Information in more than one form, such as text, still images, sound, animation, and video. Usually implies that a computer presents the information.

Multi_PGC Title   In DVD-Video, a Title within a Video Title Set (VTS) that contains more than one Program Chain (PGC). Contrast with One_Sequential_PGC Title and One_Random_PGC Title.

multiplexing   Combining multiple signals or data streams into a single signal or stream. Usually achieved by interleaving at a low level.

MultiRead   A standard developed by the Yokohama group, a consortium of companies attempting to ensure that new CD and DVD hardware can read all CD formats.

multisession   A technique in write-once recording technology that allows additional data to be appended after data written in an earlier session.

mux   Short for multiplex.

mux_rate   In MPEG, the combined rate of all packetized elementary streams (PES) of one program. The mux_rate of DVD is 10.08 Mbps.

NAB   National Association of Broadcasters.

Native resolution   The resolution at which the video file was captured.

Navigation Data   In DVD-Video there are five types of navigation data: Video Manager Information (VMGI), Video Title Set Information (VTSI), Program Chain Information (PGCI), Presentation Control Information (PCI) and Data Search Information (DSI).

Navigation Timer   In DVD-Video a system timer used during navigation operations.

NCTA   National Cable Television Association.

nighttime mode   Name for Dolby Digital dynamic range compression feature to allow low-volume nighttime listening without losing legibility of dialog.

noise floor   The level of background noise in a signal or the level of noise introduced by equipment or storage media below which the signal can't be isolated from the noise.

noise   Irrelevant, meaningless, or erroneous information added to a signal by the recording or transmission medium or by an encoding/decoding process. An advantage of digital formats over analog formats is that noise can be completely eliminated (although new noise may be introduced by compression).

NRZI   Non-Return to Zero, Inverted. A method of coding binary data as waveform pulses. Each transition represents a one, while lack of a transition represents a run of zeros.

NTSC   National Television Systems Committee. A committee organized by the Electronic Industries Association (EIA) that developed commercial television broadcast standards for the United States. The group first established black-and-white TV standards in 1941, using a scanning system of 525 lines at 60 fields per second. The second committee standardized color enhancements using 525 lines at 59.94 fields per second. NTSC refers to the composite color-encoding system. The 525/59.94 scanning system (with a 3.58-MHz color subcarrier) is identified by the letter M, and is often incorrectly referred to as NTSC. The NTSC standard is also used in Canada, Japan, and other parts of the world. NTSC is facetiously referred to as meaning *never the same color* because of the system's difficulty in maintaining color consistency.

NTSC-4.43   A variation of NTSC where a 525/59.94 signal is encoded using the PAL subcarrier frequency and chroma modulation. Also called 60-Hz PAL.

numerical aperture (NA)   A unitless measure of the ability of a lens to gather and focus light. NA = n sin q, where q is the angle of the light as it narrows to the focal point. A numerical aperture of 1 implies no change in parallel light beams. The higher the number, the greater the focusing power and the smaller the spot.

OEM   Original Equipment Manufacturer. Computer maker.

One_Random_PGC Title   In DVD-Video, a Title within a Video Title Set (VTS) that contains a single Program Chain (PGC), but does not meet the requirements of a One_Sequential_PGC Title. Contrast with One_Sequential_PGC Title and Multi_PGC Title.

One_Sequential_PGC Title   In DVD-Video, a Title within a Video Title Set (VTS) that contains a single Program Chain (PGC) with the following attributes: 1) PG Playback mode is Sequential, 2) no Next PGC, Previous PGC or Go Up PGCs are defined, and 3) the Navigation Timer is neither set, nor referred to. Contrast with One_Random_PGC Title and Multi_PGC Title.

session capabilities to the CD-ROM XA format.

OS   Operating System.

OSTA   Optical Storage Technology Association.

Opposite Track Path (OTP)   Dual-layer disc where Layer 0 and Layer 1 have opposite track directions. Layer 0 reads from the inside to the outside of the disc, whereas Layer 1 reads from the outside to the inside. The disc always spins clockwise, regardless of track structure or layers. This mode facilitates movie playback by allowing seamless (or near-seamless) transition from one layer to another. In computer applications (DVD-ROM), it usually makes more sense to use the Parallel Track Path (PTP) format where random access time is more important.

Outer diameter   Width of the disc. This is 12 cm for "normal" CDs and DVDs, and 8 cm for small CDs and DVDs.

overscan   The area at the edges of a television tube that is covered to hide possible video distortion. Overscan typically covers about 4 or 5 percent of the picture.

P picture (or P frame)   In MPEG video, a "predicted" picture based on difference from previous pictures. P pictures (along with I pictures) provide a reference for following P pictures or B pictures.

pack   A group of MPEG packets in a DVD-Video program stream. Each DVD sector (2048 bytes) contains one pack.

packet   A low-level unit of DVD-Video (MPEG) data storage containing contiguous bytes of data belonging to a single elementary stream such as video, audio, control, and so forth. Packets are grouped into packs.

packetized elementary stream (PES)   The low-level stream of MPEG packets containing an elementary stream, such as audio or video.

PAL Phase Alternate Line   A video standard used in Europe and other parts of the world for composite color encoding. Various version of PAL use different scanning systems and color subcarrier frequencies (identified with letters B, D, G, H, I, M, and N), the most common being 625 lines at 50 fields per second, with a color subcarrier of 4.43 MHz. PAL is also said to mean "picture always lousy" or "perfect at last," depending on which side of the ocean the speaker comes from.

palette   A table of colors that identifies a subset from a larger range of colors. The small number of colors in the palette allows fewer bits to be used for each pixel. Also called a color look-up table (CLUT).

pan and scan   The technique of reframing a picture to conform to a different aspect ratio by cropping parts of the picture. DVD-Video players can automatically create a 4:3 pan and scan version from widescreen video by using a horizontal offset encoded with the video.

parallel path   See PTP.

parental management   An optional feature of DVD-Video that prohibits programs from being viewed or substitutes different scenes within a program depending on the parental level set in the player. Parental control requires that parental levels and additional material (if necessary) be encoded on the disc.

part of title   In DVD-Video, a division of a title representing a scene. Also called a chapter. Parts of titles are numbered 1 to 99 in a One_Sequential_PGC title and 1 to 999 in a non_sequential_PGC title.

PCI   Presentation Control Information. A DVD-Video data stream containing details of the timing and presentation of a program (aspect ratio, angle change, menu highlight and selection information, and so on). PCI and DSI together make up an overhead of about 1 Mbps.

PCM   An uncompressed, digitally coded representation of an analog signal. The waveform is sampled at regular intervals and a series of pulses in coded form (usually quantized) are generated to represent the amplitude.

PC-TV   The merger of television and computers. A personal computer capable of displaying video as a television.

pel   See pixel.

perceived resolution   The apparent resolution of a display from the observer's point of view, based on viewing distance, viewing conditions, and physical resolution of the display.

perceptual coding   Lossy compression techniques based on the study of human perception. Perceptual coding systems identify and remove information that is least likely to be missed by the average human observer.

PES   Packetized Elementary Stream. A single video or audio stream in MPEG format.

PGCI   Program Chain Information. Data describing a chain of cells (grouped into programs) and their sector locations, thus composing a sequential program. PGCI data is contained in

Photo CD   Kodak's Photo CD for representing 24-bit 4:2:0 YCbCr images hierarchically at resolutions of up to 3072×2048 pixels. Thumbnails image representation is also part of the Photo CD spec. Built upon CD-ROM XA.

physical format   The low-level characteristics of the DVD-ROM and DVD-Video standards, including pits on the disc, location of data, and organization of data according to physical position.

physical sector number   Serial number assigned to physical sectors on a DVD disc. Serial incremented numbers are assigned to sectors from the head sector in the Data Area as 30000h from the start of the Lead In Area to the end of the Lead Out Area.

picture stop   A function of DVD-Video where a code indicates that video playback should stop and a still picture be displayed.

picture   In video terms, a single still image or a sequence of moving images. Picture generally refers to a frame, but for interlaced frames may refer instead to a field of the frame. In a more general sense, picture refers to the entire image shown on a video display.

PIP   Picture In Picture. A feature of some televisions that shows another channel or video source in a small window superimposed in a corner of the screen.

pit   The depressed area of an optical disc. A microscopic depression in the recording layer of a disc. Pits are usually 1/4 of the laser wavelength so as to cause cancellation of the beam by diffraction.

pit art   A pattern of pits to be stamped onto a disc to provide visual art rather than data. A cheaper alternative to a printed label.

Pit length   Arc length of pit along the direction of the track.

pixel aspect ratio   The ratio of width to height of a single pixel. Often means sample pitch aspect ratio (when referring to sampled digital video). Pixel aspect ratio for a given raster can be calculated as $y/x \infty w/h$ (where x and y are the raster horizontal pixel count and vertical pixel count, and w and h are the display aspect ratio width and height). Pixel aspect ratios are also confusingly calculated as $x/y \infty w/h$, giving a height-to-width ratio.

pixel depth   See color depth.

pixel   The smallest picture element of an image (one sample of each color component). A single dot of the array of dots that makes up a picture. Sometimes abbreviated to pel. The resolution of a digital display is typically specified in terms of pixels (width by height) and color depth (the number of bits required to represent each pixel).

Player   Embodiment of a DVD decoder system, which executes the Navigation system and performs all decoding from the channel layer at least up to the track buffer layer. In future, external MPEG decoders may perform the actual video and audio reconstruction, but copyright issues currently prevent this.

Player Reference Model   Defines the ideal behavior of a DVD (compliant) Player.

PMMA   Polymethylmethacrylate. A clear acrylic compound used in laserdiscs and as an intermediary in the surface transfer process (STP) for dual-layer DVDs. PMMA is also sometimes used for DVD substrates.

POP   Picture Outside Picture. A feature of some widescreen displays that uses the unused area around a 4:3 picture to show additional pictures.

Post-command   In DVD-Video a navigation command to be executed after the presentation of a Program Chain (PGC) has been completed.

Pre-command   In DVD-Video a navigation command to be execute before the presentation of a Program Chain (PGC) has been started.

premastering   The process of preparing data in the final format to create a DVD disc image for mastering. Includes creating DVD control and navigation data, multiplexing data streams together, generating error-correction codes, and performing channel modulation. Often includes the process of encoding video, audio, and subpictures.

presentation data   DVD-Video information such as video, menus, and audio, which is presented to the viewer. (See PCI.)

profile   In MPEG-2, profiles specify syntax and processes such as picture types, scalability, and extensions. Compare to level.

program   In a general sense, a sequence of audio or video. In a technical sense for DVD-Video, a group of cells within a program chain (PGC).

program chain   In DVD-Video, a collection of programs, or groups of cells, linked together to create a sequential presentation.

progressive scan   A video scanning system that displays all lines of a frame in one pass. Contrast with interlaced scan.

PTT Menu   Menu used to access special
referred to as Chapter Menu.

PUH   PickUp Head. The assembly of optics and electronics that reads data from a disc.

QCIF   Quarter Common Intermediate Format. Video resolution of 176×144.

quantization levels   The predetermined levels at which an analog signal can be sampled as determined by the resolution of the analog-to-digital converter (in bits per sample); or the number of bits stored for the sampled signal.

quantize   To convert a value or range of values into a smaller value or smaller range by integer division. Quantized values are converted back (by multiplying) to a value, which is close to the original but may not be exactly the same. Quantization is a primary technique of lossless encoding.

QuickTime   A digital video software standard developed by Apple Computer for Macintosh (Mac OS) and Windows operating systems. QuickTime is used to support audio and video from a DVD.

QXGA   A video graphics resolution of 2048×1536.

RAM   Random-Access Memory. Generally refers to solid-state chips. In the case of DVD-RAM, the term was borrowed to indicate ability to read and write at any point on the disc.

RAMbo drive   A DVD-RAM drive capable of reading and writing CD-R and CD-RW media. (A play on the word "combo.")

random access   The ability to jump to a point on a storage medium.

raster   The pattern of parallel horizontal scan lines that makes up a video picture.

read-modify-write   An operation used in writing to DVD-RAM discs. Because data can be written by the host computer in blocks as small as 2 Kb, but the DVD format uses ECC blocks of 32 Kb, an entire ECC block is read from the data buffer or disc, modified to include the new data and new ECC data, then written back to the data buffer and disc.

Red Book   The document first published in 1982 that specifies the original compact disc digital audio format developed by Philips and Sony.

Reed-Solomon   An error-correction encoding system that cycles data multiple times through a mathematical transformation in order to increase the effectiveness of the error correction, especially for burst errors (errors concentrated closely together, as from a scratch or physical defect). DVD uses rows and columns of Reed-Solomon encoding in a two-dimensional lattice, called Reed-Solomon product code (RS-PC).

reference picture (or reference frame)   An encoded frame that is used as a reference point from which to build dependent frames. In MPEG-2, I pictures and P pictures are used as references.

reference player   A DVD player that defines the ideal behavior as specified by the DVD-Video standard.

regional code   A code identifying one of the world regions for restricting DVD-Video playback.

regional management   A mandatory feature of DVD-Video to restrict the playback of a disc to a specific geographical region. Each player and DVD-ROM drive includes a single regional code, and each disc side can specify in which regions it is allowed to be played. Regional coding is optional—a disc without regional codes will play in all players in all regions.

replication   1) The reproduction of media such as optical discs by stamping (contrast with duplication); 2) a process used to increase the size of an image by repeating pixels (to increase the horizontal size) and/or lines (to increase the vertical size) or to increase the display rate of a video stream by repeating frames. For example, a 360 ∞ 240 pixel image can be displayed at 720 ∞ 480 size by duplicating each pixel on each line and then duplicating each line. In this case the resulting image contains blocks of four identical pixels. Obviously, image replication can cause blockiness. A 24-fps video signal can be displayed at 72 fps by repeating each frame three times. Frame replication can cause jerkiness of motion. Contrast with decimation. Also see interpolate.

resampling   The process of converting between different spatial resolutions or different temporal resolutions. This may be based on simple sampling of the source information at higher or lower resolution or may include interpolation to correct for differences in pixel aspect ratios or to adjust for differences in display rates.

reserved (or reserved field)   The field indicated by the term "reserved" may be used in future revisions of the DVD specifications. Unless otherwise indicated all reserved bits shall be set to zero.

Reserved bytes   6 bytes in the header of each DVD sector reserved for future use.

resolution   1) A measurement of relative detail of a digital display, typically given in pixels of ~~width and height.~~ 2) the ability of an imaging system to make clearly distinguishable or ~~resolution (the clarity of a single~~

RGB   Video information in the form of red, green, ~~and blue. The combina~~tion of three values representing the intensity of each of the three colors can represent the entire range of visible light.

RMA   Region Management information. In DVD-Video, an 8-bit (1 byte) value that appears in the CPR_MAI and is used to indicate which regions of the world a disc is permitted to play in. See regional management.

ROM   Read-Only Memory.

Root Menu   Menu used to access other interactive menus in the Video Tile Set Manager domain, or to make a selection, which is not defined, by other system menus such as Angle Menu, Audio, Menu, PTT Menu and Sub-picture Menu.

rpm   Revolutions per minute. A measure of rotational speed.

RS   Reed-Solomon. An error-correction encoding system that cycles data multiple times through a mathematical transformation in order to increase the effectiveness of the error correction. DVD uses rows and columns of Reed-Solomon encoding in a two-dimensional lattice, called Reed-Solomon product code (RS-PC).

RS-CIRC   See CIRC.

RSDL   Reverse-Spiral Dual-layer. See OTP.

RS-PC   Reed-Solomon Product Code. An error-correction encoding system used by DVD employing rows and columns of Reed-Solomon encoding to increase error-correction effectiveness.

run-length coding   Lossless compression method that exploits contiguous samples with same value.

R-Y, B-Y   The general term for color-difference video signals carrying red and blue color information, where the brightness (Y) has been subtracted from the red and blue RGB signals to create R-Y and B-Y color-difference signals.

S/N (or SNR)   Signal-to-Noise Ratio.

S/P DIF   Sony/Philips Digital Interface. A consumer version of the AES/EBU digital audio transmission standard. Most DVD players include S/P DIF coaxial digital audio connectors providing PCM and encoded digital audio output.

sample   A single digital measurement of analog information. A snapshot in time of a continuous analog waveform. See sampling.

sample rate   The number of times a digital sample is taken, measured in samples per second, or Hertz. The more often samples are taken, the better a digital signal can represent the original analog signal. Sampling theory states that the sampling frequency must be more than twice the signal frequency in order to reproduce the signal without aliasing. DVD PCM audio allows sampling rates of 48 and 96 kHz.

sample size   The number of bits used to store a sample. Also called resolution. In general, the more bits allocated per sample, the better the reproduction of the original analog information. Audio sample size determines the dynamic range. DVD PCM audio uses sample sizes of 16, 20, or 24 bits.

sampling   Converting analog information into a digital representation by measuring the value of the analog signal at regular intervals, called samples, and encoding these numerical values in digital form. Sampling is often based on specified quantization levels. Sampling may also be used to adjust for differences between different digital systems (see resampling and subsampling).

saturation   The intensity or vividness of a color.

scaling   Altering the spatial resolution of a single image to increase or reduce the size; or altering the temporal resolution of an image sequence to increase or decrease the rate of display. Techniques include decimation, interpolation, motion compensation, replication, resampling, and subsampling. Most scaling methods introduce artifacts.

scan line   A single horizontal line traced out by the scanning system of a video display unit. 525/60 (NTSC) video has 525 scan lines, about 480 of which contain actual picture. 625/50 (PAL/SECAM) video has 625 scan lines, about 576 of which contain actual picture.

scanning velocity   The speed at which the laser pickup head travels along the spiral track of a disc.

SCMS   Serial Copy Management System. Used by DAT, MiniDisc, and other digital recording systems to control copying and limit the number of copies that can be made from copies.

SCSI   Small Computer Systems Interface. An electronic interface and command set for attaching and controlling internal or external peripherals, such as a DVD-ROM drive, to a computer. The command set of SCSI was extended for DVD-ROM devices by the SFF 8090 specification.

ᵗ ᵢ ᵉᵈ fᵒʳ serial digital

SDI   see serial d g

of 2000 was still not available on DVD other than as boot g y

SDMI   Secure Digital Music Initiative. Efforts and specifications for protecting digital music.

SDTV   Standard-Definition Television. A term applied to traditional 4:3 television (in digital or analog form) with a resolution of about 700 × 480 (about one-third of a megapixel). Contrast with HDTV.

seamless playback   A feature of DVD-Video where a program can jump from place to place on the disc without any interruption of the video. Allows different versions of a program to be put on a single disc by sharing common parts.

SECAM   Séquential Couleur Avec Mémoire (sequential color with memory). A composite color standard similar to PAL, but currently used only as a transmission standard in France and a few other countries. Video is produced using the 625/50 PAL standard and is then transcoded to SECAM by the player or transmitter.

sector   A logical or physical group of bytes recorded on the disc — the smallest addressable unit. A DVD sector contains 38,688 bits of channel data and 2048 bytes of user data.

sector information   Header field providing the sector number.

sector number   A number that uniquely identifies the physical sector on a disc.

seek time   The time it takes for the head in a drive to move to a data track.

Serial Digital Interface (SDI)   The professional digital video connection format using a 270 Mbps transfer rate. A 10-bit, scrambled, polarity-independent interface, with common scrambling for both component ITU-R 601 and composite digital video and four groups each of four channels of embedded digital audio. SDI uses standard 75-ohm BNC connectors and coax cable.

SFF 8090   Specification number 8090 of the Small Form Factor Committee, an ad hoc group formed to promptly address disk industry needs and to develop recommendations to be passed on to standards organizations. SFF 8090 (also known as the Mt. Fuji specification), defines a command set for CD-ROM– and DVD-ROM–type devices, including implementation notes for ATAPI and SCSI.

SI   Système International (d'Unités)/International System (of Units). A complete system of standardized units and prefixes for fundamental quantities of length, time, volume, mass, and so on.

signal-to-noise ratio   The ratio of pure signal to extraneous noise, such as tape hiss or video interference. Signal-to-noise ratio is measured in decibels (dB). Analog recordings almost always have noise. Digital recordings, when properly prefiltered and not compressed, have no noise.

simple profile (SP)   A subset of the syntax of the MPEG-2 video standard designed for simple and inexpensive applications such as software. SP does not allow B pictures. See profile.

simulate   To test the function of a DVD disc in the authoring system, without actually formatting an image.

SMPTE   The Society of Motion Picture and Television Engineers. An international research and standards organization. The SMPTE time code, used for marking the position of audio or video in time, was developed by this group.

son   The metal discs produced from a mother discs in the replication process. Fathers or sons are used in molds to stamp discs.

SP@ML   Simple Profile at Main Level. The simplest MPEG-2 format used by DVD. Most discs use MP@ML. SP does not allow B pictures.

space   The reflective area of a writeable optical disc. Equivalent to a land.

spatial   Relating to space, usually two-dimensional. Video can be defined by its spatial characteristics (information from the horizontal plane and vertical plane) and its temporal characteristics (information at different instances in time).

spatial resolution   The clarity of a single image or the measure of detail in an image. See resolution.

squeezed video   See anamorphic.

stamping   The process of replicating optical discs by injecting liquid plastic into a mold containing a stamper (father or son). Also (inaccurately) called mastering.

STP   Surface Transfer Process. A method of producing dual-layer DVDs that sputters the reflective (aluminum) layer onto a temporary substrate of PMMA, then transfers the metallized layer to the already-molded layer 0.

...lly digitally encoded, designed to be processed

subsampling   The process ... areas than the original samples or of reducing temporal resolution ... cover more time than the original samples. See chroma subsampling. Also called downsampling.

substrate   The clear polycarbonate disc onto which data layers are stamped or deposited.

subtitle   A textual representation of the spoken audio in a video program. Subtitles are often used with foreign languages and do not serve the same purpose as captions for the hearing impaired. See subpicture.

surround sound   A multichannel audio system with speakers in front of and behind the listener to create a surrounding envelope of sound and to simulate directional audio sources.

SVCD   Super Video Compact Disc. MPEG-2 video on CD. Used primarily in Asia.

SVGA   A video graphics resolution of 800×600 pixels.

S-VHS   Super VHS (Video Home System). An enhancement of the VHS videotape standard using better recording techniques and Y/C signals. The term S-VHS is often used incorrectly to refer to s-video signals and connectors.

s-video   A video interface standard that carries separate luma and chroma signals, usually on a four-pin mini-DIN connector. Also called Y/C. The quality of s-video is significantly better than composite video since it does not require a comb filter to separate the signals, but it's not quite as good as component video. Most high-end televisions have s-video inputs. S-video is often erroneously called S-VHS.

SXGA   A video graphics resolution of 1280×1024 pixels.

sync   A video signal (or component of a video signal) containing information necessary to synchronize the picture horizontally and vertically. Also, specially formatted data on disc, which helps the readout system identify location and specific data structures.

sync frame   Physical record unit of 1488 channel bits length comprising data (91 bytes) and a SYNC code. One physical sector consists of 26 sync frames.

syntax   The rules governing construction or formation of an orderly system of information. For example, the syntax of the MPEG video encoding specification defines how data and associated instructions are used by a decoder to create video pictures.

system menu   The main menu of a DVD-Video disc, from which titles are selected. Also called the title selection menu or disc menu.

T Tera   An SI prefix for denominations of one trillion (10^{12}).

Telecine   The process (and the equipment) used to transfer film to video. The Telecine machine performs 3:2 pulldown by projecting film frames in the proper sequence to be captured by a video camera.

Telecine artist   The operator of a Telecine machine. Also called a colorist.

temporal   Relating to time. The temporal component of motion video is broken into individual still pictures. Because motion video can contain images (such as backgrounds) that do not change much over time, typical video has large amounts of temporal redundancy.

temporal resolution   The clarity of a moving image or moving object, or the measurement of the rate of information change in motion video. See resolution.

TIF (or TIFF)   Tag Image File Format. A common graphic file format supported by most DVD-Video authoring tools for the importation of still images, menu backgrounds and highlight overlay images.

tilt   A mechanical measurement of the warp of a disc. Usually expressed in radial and tangential components: radial indicating dishing and tangential indicating ripples in the perpendicular direction.

time code   Information recorded with audio or video to indicate a position in time. Usually consists of values for hours, minutes, seconds, and frames. Also called SMPTE time code. Some DVD-Video material includes information to allow the player to search to a specific time code position.

title   The largest unit of a DVD-Video disc (other than the entire volume or side). Usually a movie, TV program, music album, or so on. A disc can hold up to 99 titles, which can be selected from the disc menu. Entire DVD volumes are also commonly called titles.

title key   A value used to encrypt and decrypt (scramble) user data on DVD-Video discs.

track   1) A distinct element of audiovisual information, such as the picture, a sound track for a specific language, or the like. DVD-Video allows one track of video (with multiple angles), up to 8 tracks of audio, and up to 32 tracks of subpicture; 2) one revolution of the continuous spiral channel of information recorded on a disc.

... (including memory) in a DVD player that provides a variable stream ... ... at a constant

... a D... ... ond or bytes per second. Sometimes confusingly used to re... dent of the actual transfer system.

transform   The process or result of replacing a set of values with another set of values. A mapping of one information space onto another.

trim   See crop.

tristimulus   A three-valued signal that can match nearly all colors of visible light in human vision. This is possible because of the three types of photoreceptors in the eye. RGB, YC_bC_r, and similar signals are tristimulus, and can be interchanged by using mathematical transformations (subject to possible loss of information).

TVL   Television Line. See lines of horizontal resolution.

TWG   Technical Working Group. A general term for an industry working group. Specifically, the predecessor to the CPTWG.

twos complement   The number calculated so that each bit of a binary number is inverted (ones are replaced with zeros and vice versa), then one (=000...0001b) is added ignoring the overflow.

UDF Bridge   A combination of UDF and ISO 9660 file system formats that provides backward-compatibility with ISO 9660 readers while allowing full use of the UDF standard.

UDF Universal Disc Format   A standard developed by the Optical Storage Technology Association designed to create a practical and usable subset of the ISO/IEC 13346 recordable, random-access file system and volume structure format.

Unidirectional prediction A form of compression in which the codec uses information only from frames that have already been decompressed.

universal DVD A DVD designed to play in DVD-Audio and DVD-Video players (by carrying a Dolby Digital audio track in the DVD-Video zone).

universal DVD player A DVD player that can play both DVD-Video and DVD-Audio discs.

user data The data recorded on a disc independent of formatting and error-correction overhead. Each DVD sector contains 2048 bytes of user data.

UXGA A video graphics resolution of 1600×1200.

VBI Vertical Blanking Interval. The scan lines in a television signal that do not contain picture information. These lines are present to allow the electron scanning beam to return to the top and are used to contain auxiliary information such as closed captions.

VBR Variable Bit Rate. Data that can be read and processed at a volume that varies over time. A data compression technique that produces a data stream between a fixed minimum and maximum rate. A constant level of compression is generally maintained, with the required bandwidth increasing or decreasing depending on the complexity (the amount of spatial and temporal energy) of the data being encoded. In other words, data rate is held constant while quality is allowed to vary. Compare to CBR.

VBScript A proprietary Visual Basic-based programming language defined by Microsoft for use in their Internet Explorer web browser. (See also, JavaScript and JScript.)

VBV Video Buffering Verifier. A hypothetical decoder that is conceptually connected to the output of an MPEG video encoder. Provides a constraint on the variability of the data rate that an encoder can produce.

VCAP Video Capable Audio Player. An audio player that can read the limited subset of video features defined for the DVD-Audio format. (Contrast with universal DVD player.)

VCD Video Compact Disc. Near-VHS-quality MPEG-1 video on CD. Used primarily in Asia.

VfW See Video for Windows.

VGA Video Graphics Array. A standard analog monitor interface for computers. Also a video graphics resolution of 640×480 pixels.

VHS Video Home System. The most popular system of videotape for home use. Developed by JCV.

Video CD   An extension of CD based on MPEG-1 video and audio. Allows playback of near-VHS-quality video on a Video CD player, CD-i player, or computer with MPEG decoding capability.

Video for Windows   The system software additions used for motion video playback in Microsoft Windows. Replaced in newer versions of Windows by DirectShow (formerly called

Object Set for the Menu (VTSM_...
and a backup of the VTSI (VTSI_BUP).

VIDEO_TS   UDF filename used for video directory on disc volume. Files under this directory name contain pointers to the sectors on the disc which hold the program streams.

videophile   Someone with an avid interest in watching videos or in making video recordings. Videophiles are often very particular about audio quality, picture quality, and aspect ratio to the point of snobbishness.

VLC   Variable Length Coding. See Huffman coding.

VMGI   Video Manager Information. Information required to manage one or more Video Title Sets and Video Manager Menu areas. This is non real time data located at the start of the Video Manager area.

VOB   Video Object. A single, complete presentation stream composed of multiplexed Video, Audio, Sub-picture, PCI and DSI elementary streams, and consisting of an integer number of VOBUs.

VOBS   Video Object Set. A collection of one or more VOBs. There are three types: 1) VMGM_VOBS for the Video Manager Menu (VMGM) area, 2) VTSM_VOBS for the Video Titles Set Menu (VTSM) area, and 3) VTST_VOBS for the Video Title Set Title (VTST) area.

VOBU   Video Object Unit. A small (between 0.4 and 1.0 seconds) physical unit of DVD-Video data storage, usually the length of one GOP, that begins with a Navigation pack (NV_PCK) and usually includes an integer number of GOPs.

Volume Management Information   Identifies disc side and content type.

Volume Space   Collection of sectors that make the volume. Not all sectors on the disc comprise the volume. Some near the inner and out spiral are used as leader.

volume   A logical unit representing all the data on one side of a disc.

VSDA   Video Software Dealers Association.

VTSI   Video Title Set Information. Information required to manage one or more Titles and Video Title Set Menus. This is non real time data located at the start of the Video Title Set.

WAEA   World Airline Entertainment Association. Discs produced for use in airplanes contain extra information in a WAEA directory. The in-flight entertainment working group of the WAEA petitioned the DVD Forum to assign region 8 to discs intended for in-flight use.

watermark   Information hidden as "invisible noise" or "inaudible noise" in a video or audio signal.

White Book   The document from Sony, Philips, and JVC, begun in 1993 that extended the Red Book compact disc format to include digital video in MPEG-1 format. Commonly called Video CD.

widescreen   A video image wider than the standard 1.33 (4:3) aspect ratio. When referring to DVD or HDTV, widescreen usually indicates a 1.78 (16:9) aspect ratio.

window   A usually rectangular section within an entire screen or picture.

Windows   See Microsoft Windows.

XA   See CD-ROM XA.

XGA   A video graphics resolution of 1024×768 pixels.

XVCD   A non-standard variation of VCD.

Y   The luma or luminance component of video: brightness independent of color.

Y/C   A video signal in which the brightness (luma, Y) and color (chroma, C) signals are separated. Also called s-video.

YC_bC_r   A component digital video signal containing one luma and two chroma components. The chroma components are usually adjusted for digital transmission according to ITU-R BT.601. DVD-Video MPEG-2 encoding is based on 4:2:0 YC_bC_r signals. YC_bC_r applies only to digital video, but is often incorrectly used in reference to the YP_bP_r analog component outputs of DVD players.

Yellow Book   The document produced in 1985 by Sony and Philips that extended the Red Book compact disc format to include digital data for use by a computer. Commonly called CD-ROM.

YP$_b$P$_r$ A component analog video signal containing one luma and two chroma components. Often referred to loosely as YUV or Y, B-Y, R-Y.

INDEX

Revamped and Enhanced, DV.com Gives Users the Tools and Technologies to Power Projects.

 Interactive Community Forums

Product Reviews, Features, Opinions

 User-Focused Tutorials

Web-Exclusive Articles

 DV Product Information Guide

Weekly Newsletters

 Daily News

Visit DV.com Today for a Whole New User Experience

DV.com   DV   DVexpo   DVWebVideo.com   3Dgate   CMP DV Media Group

Take Your Talents to the Next Level

DV Expo provides practical solutions in digital video, Web video, and 3D. Learn how to use the evolving tools and technologies essential to dynamic media production, postproduction, and delivery.

DVexpo.com

(Contact by phone: 415-947-6135)

Acquire new tips, tricks, and groundbreaking techniques to power your digital video projects. Test drive cutting-edge products showcsed on the expo floor.

Prepare to master new skills!

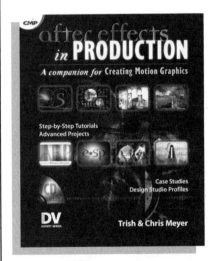

What's on the DVD?

A copy of *StarGaze*, a DVD title developed by the author, is included to provide real-world examples of the DVD authoring and production process. This disc will work in any DVD-Video player, or DVD-ROM enabled PC.

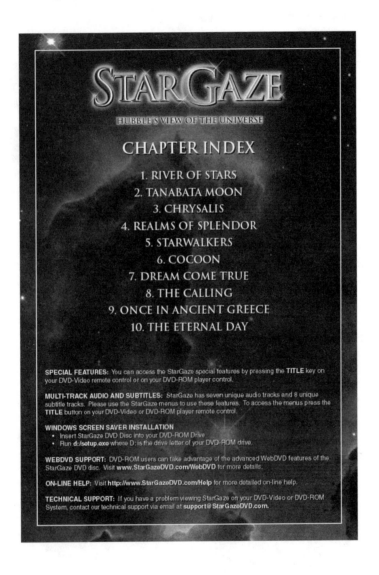

COLLECTOR'S EDITIONS

Grace

Livingston Hill

Collection

Three Books in One
Marcia Schuyler
Phoebe Dean
Miranda

A BARBOUR BOOK

THE GRACE LIVINGSTON HILL COLLECTION #2

ISBN 1-55748-531-3

Marcia Schuyler

Book One in the *Miranda* Trilogy

of dew, as Marcia stepped from the kitchen door.

She wore a chocolate calico with little sprigs of red and white scattered over it, her hair was in smooth brown braids down her back, and there was a flush on her round cheeks that might have been but the reflection of the rosy light in the East. Her face was as untroubled as the Summer morning, in its freshness, and her eyes as dreamy as the soft clouds that hovered upon the horizon uncertain where they were to be sent for the day.

Marcia walked lightly through the grass, and the way behind her sparkled again like that of the girl in the fairy tale who left jewels wherever she passed.

A rail fence stopped her, which she mounted as though it had been a steed to carry her onward, and sat a moment looking at the beauty of the morning, her eyes taking on that far-away look that annoyed her stepmother when she wanted her to hurry with the dishes, or finish a long seam before it was time to get supper.

She loitered but a moment, for her mind was full of business, and she wished to accomplish much before the day was done. Swinging easily down to the other side of the fence she moved on through the meadow, over another fence, and another meadow, skirting the edge of a cool little strip of woods which lured her with its green mysterious shadows, its whispering leaves, and twittering birds. One wistful glance she gave into the sweet silence, seeing a clump of maiden-hair ferns rippling their feathery locks in the breeze. Then resolutely turning away she sped on to the slope of Blackberry Hill.

It was not a long climb to where the blackberries grew, and she was soon at work, the great luscious berries dropping into her pail almost with a touch. But while she worked the vision of the hills, the sheep meadow below, the river winding between the neighboring farms, melted away, and she did not even see the ripe fruit before her, because she was planning the new frock she was to buy with these berries she had come to pick.

Pink and white it was to be; she had seen it in the store the last time she went for sugar and spice. There were dainty sprigs of pink over the white ground, and every berry that dropped into her bright pail was no longer a berry but a sprig of pink chintz. While she worked she went over her plans for the day.

There had been busy times at the old house during the past weeks. Kate, her elder sister, was to be married. It was only a few days now to the wedding.

There had been a whole year of preparation: spinning and weaving and fine sewing. The smooth white linen lay ready, packed between rose leaves and lavender. There had been yards and yards of tatting and embroidery made by the two girls for the trousseau, and the village dressmaker had spent days at the house, cutting, fitting, shirring, till now there was a goodly array of gorgeous apparel piled high upon bed, and chairs, and hanging in the closets of the great spare bedroom. The outfit was as fine as that made for Patience Hartrandt six months before, and Mr. Hartrandt had given his one daughter all she had asked for in the way of a "setting out." Kate had seen to it that her things were as fine as Patience's—but—they were all for Kate!

Of course, that was right! Kate was to be married, not Marcia, and everything must make way for that. Marcia was scarcely more than a child as yet, barely seventeen. No one thought of anything new for her just then, and she did not expect it. But into her heart there had stolen a longing for a new frock herself amid all this finery for Kate. She had her best one of course. That was good, and pretty, and quite nice enough to wear to the wedding, and her stepmother had taken much relief in the thought that Marcia would need nothing during the rush of getting Kate ready.

But there were people coming to the house every day, especially in the afternoons, friends of Kate, and of her stepmother, to be shown Kate's wardrobe, and to talk things over curiously. Marcia could not wear her best dress all the time. And *he* was coming! That was the way Marcia always denominated the prospective bridegroom in her mind.

His name was David Spafford, and Kate often called him Dave, but Marcia, even to herself, could never bring herself to breathe the name so familiarly. She held him in great awe. He was so fine and strong and good, with a face like a young saint in some old picture, she thought. She often wondered how her wild, sparkling sister Kate dared to be so familiar with him. She had ventured the thought once when she watched Kate dressing to go out with some young people and preening herself like a bird of Paradise before the glass. It all came over her, the vanity and frivolousness of the life that Kate loved, and she spoke out with conviction:

"Kate, you'll have to be very different when you're married." Kate had faced about amusedly and asked why.

"Because *he is so* good," Marcia had replied, unable to explain further.

"Oh, is that all?" said the daring sister, wheeling back to the glass. "Don't you worry, I'll soon take that out of him."

But Kate's indifference had never lessened her young sister's awe of her prospective brother-in-law. She had listened to his conversations with her father during the brief visits he had made, and she had watched his face at church while he and Kate sang together as the minister lined it out: "Rock of Ages cleft for me, Let me hide myself in Thee," a new song which had just been written. And she had mused upon the charmed life Kate would lead. It was about it, for she knew it would be useless; neither did she think it worth while to go to her father, for she knew that both his wife and Kate would find it out and charge her with useless expense just now when there were so many other uses for money, and they were anxious to have it all flow their way. She had an independent spirit, so she took the time that belonged to herself, and went to the blackberry patch which belonged to everybody.

Marcia's fingers were nimble and accustomed, and the sun was not very high in the heavens when she had finished her task and turned happily toward the village. The pails would not hold another berry.

Her cheeks were glowing with the sun and exercise, and little wisps of wavy curls had escaped about her brow, damp with perspiration. Her eyes were shining with her purpose, half fulfilled, as she hastened down the hill.

Crossing a field she met Hanford Weston with a rake over his shoulder and a wide-brimmed straw hat like a small shed over him. He was on his way to the South meadow. He blushed and greeted her as she passed shyly by. When she had passed he paused and looked admiringly after her. They had been in the same classes at school all winter, the girl at the head, the boy at the foot. But Hanford Weston's father owned the largest farm in all the country round about, and he felt that did not so much matter. He would rather see Marcia at the head anyway, though there never had been the slightest danger that he would take her place. He felt a sudden desire now to follow her. It would be a pleasure to carry those pails that she bore as if they were mere featherweights.

He watched her long, elastic step for a moment, considered the sun in the sky, and his father's command about the South meadow, and then strode after her.

It did not take long to reach her side, swiftly as she had gone.

As well as he could, with the sudden hotness in his face and the tremor in his throat, he made out to ask if he might carry her burden for her. Marcia stopped annoyed. She had forgotten all about him, though he was an attractive fellow, sometimes called by the girls "handsome Hanford."

She had been planning exactly how that pink sprigged chintz was to be made, and which parts she would cut first in order to save time and material. She did not wish to be interrupted. The importance of the matter was too great to be marred by the appearance of just a schoolmate whom she might meet every day, and whom she could so easily "spell down." She summoned her thoughts from the details of mutton-leg sleeves and looked the boy over, to his great confusion. She did not want him along, and she was considering how best to get rid of him. "Weren't you going somewhere else?" she asked sweetly. "Wasn't there a rake over your shoulder? What have you done with it?" The culprit blushed deeper. "Where were you going?" she demanded. "To the South meadow," he stammered out. "Oh, well, then you must go back. I shall do quite well, thank you. Your father will not be pleased to have you neglected your work for me, though I'm much obliged I'm sure."

Was there some foreshadowing of her womanhood in the decided way she spoke, and the quaint, prim set of her head as she bowed him good morning and went on her way once more? The boy did not understand. He only felt abashed, and half angry that she had ordered him back to work; and, too, in a tone that forbade him to take her memory with him as he went. Nevertheless her image lingered by the way, and haunted the South meadow all day long as he worked.

Marcia, unconscious of the admiration she had stirred in the boyish heart, went her way on fleet feet, her spirit one with the sunny morning, her body light with anticipation, for a new frock of her own choice was yet an event in her life.

She had thought many times as she spent long hours putting delicate stitches into her sister's wedding garments, how it would seem if they were being made for her. She had whiled away many a dreary seam by thinking out, in a sort of dream-story, how she would put on this or that at will if it were her own, and go here or there, and have people love and admire her as they did Kate. It would never come true, of course. She never expected to be admired and loved like Kate. Kate was beautiful, bright and gay. Everybody loved her, no matter how she treated them. It was a matter of course for Kate to have everything she wanted. Marcia felt that she never could attain to such heights. In the first place she considered her own sweet serious face with its pure brown eyes as exceedingly plain. She could not catch the lights that played at hide and seek in her eyes when she talked with animation. Indeed few saw her at her best, because she seldom talked freely. It was only with certain people that she could forget herself.

She did not envy Kate. She was proud of her sister, and loved her, though there was an element of anxiety in the love. But she never thought of her many faults. She felt that they were excusable because Kate was Kate. It was as if you should find fault with a wild rose because it carried a thorn. Kate was set about with many a thorn, but amid them all she bloomed, her fragrant pink self, as apparently unconscious of the many pricks she gave, and unconcerned, as the flower itself

So Marcia never thought to be jealous that Kate had so many lovely things, and was going out into the world to do just as she pleased, and lead a charmed

A whole long day she had to herself, for Kate and her stepmother were gone up to the neighboring town on the packet to make a few last purchases. She had told no one of her plans, and was awake betimes in the morning to see the travellers off, eager to have them gone that she might begin to carry out her plan. Just at the edge of the village Marcia put down the pails of berries by a large flat stone and sat down for a moment to tidy herself. The lacing of one shoe had come untied, and her hair was rumpled by exercise. But she could not sit long to rest, and taking up her burdens was soon upon the way again.

Mary Ann Fothergill stepped from her own gate lingering till Marcia should come up, and the two girls walked along side by side. Mary Ann had stiff, straight, light hair, and high cheek bones. Her eyes were light and her eyelashes almost white. They did not show up well beneath her checked sunbonnet. Her complexion was dull and tanned. She was a contrast to Marcia with her dear red and white skin. She was tall and awkward and wore a linsey-woolsey frock as though it were a meal sack temporarily appropriated. She had the air of always trying to hide her feet and hands. Mary Ann had some find qualities, but beauty was not one of them. Beside her Marcia's delicate features showed clear-cut like a cameo, and her every movement spoke of patrician blood.

Mary Ann regarded Marcia's smooth brown braids enviously. Her own sparse hair barely reached to her shoulders, and straggled about her neck helplessly and hopelessly, in spite of her constant efforts.

"It must be lots of fun at your house these days," said Mary Ann wistfully. "Are you most ready for the wedding?"

Marcia nodded. Her eyes were bright. She could see the sign of the village store just ahead and knew the bolts of new chintz were displaying their charms in the window.

"My, but your cheeks do look pretty," admired Mary Ann impulsively. "Say, how many of each has your sister got?"

"Two dozens," said Marcia conscious of a little swelling of pride in her breast. It was not every girl that had such a setting out as her sister.

"My!" sighed Mary Ann. "And outside things, too. I 'spose she's got one of every color. What are her frocks? Tell me about them. I've been up to Dutchess county and just got back last night, but Ma wrote Aunt Tilly that Mis' Hotchkiss said her frocks was the prettiest Miss Hancock's ever sewed on."

"We think they are pretty," admitted Marcia modestly. "There's a sprigged chin —" here she caught herself, remembering and laughed. "I mean muslin-de-laine, and a blue delaine, and a blue silk —"

"My! silk!" breathed Mary Ann in an ecstasy of wonder. "And what's she going to be married in?"

"White," answered Marcia, "white satin. And the veil was mother's — our own mother's, you know."

Marcia spoke it reverently, her eyes shining with something far away that made Mary Ann think she looked like an angel.

"Oh, my! Don't you just envy her?"

"No," said Marcia slowly; "I think not. At least — I hope not. It wouldn't be right, you know. And then she's my sister and I love her dearly, and it's nearly as nice to have one's sister have nice things and a good time as to have them one's self."

"You're good," said Mary Ann decidedly as if that were a foregone conclusion. "But I should envy her, I just should. Mis' Hotchkiss told Ma there wa'nt many lots in life so all honey-and-dew-prepared like your sister's. All the money she wanted to spend on clo'es, and a nice set out, and a man as handsome as you'll find anywhere, and he's well off too, ain't he? Ma said she heard he kept a horse and lived right in the village too, not as how he needed to keep one to get anywhere, either. That's what I call luxury — a horse to ride around with. And then Mr. What's-his-name? I can't remember. Oh, yes, Spafford. He's good, and everybody says he won't make a bit of fuss if Kate does go around and have a good time. He'll just let her do as she pleases. Only old Grandma Doolittle says she doesn't believe it. She thinks every man, no matter how good he is, wants to manage his wife, just for the name of it. She says your sister'll have to change her ways or else there'll be trouble. But that's Grandma! Everybody knows her. She croaks! Ma says Kate's got her nest feathered well if ever a girl had. My! I only wish I had the same chance!"

Marcia held her head a trifle high when Mary Ann touched upon her sister's personal character, but they were nearing the store, and everybody knew Mary Ann was blunt. Poor Mary Ann! She meant no harm. She was but repeating the village gossip. Besides, Marcia must give her mind to sprigged chintz. There was no time for discussions if she would accomplish her purpose before the folks came home that night.

"Mary Ann," she said in her sweet, prim way that always made the other girl stand a little in awe of her, "you mustn't listen to gossip. It isn't worth while. I'm sure my sister Kate will be very happy. I'm going in the store now, are you?" And the conversation was suddenly concluded.

Mary Ann followed meekly watching with wonder and envy as Marcia made her bargain with the kindly merchant, and selected her chintz. What a delicious swish the scissors made as they went through the width of cloth, and how

...y had reached the turn of the road and Mary Ann hoped that Marcia would ask her out to "help," but Marcia had no such purpose.

"Well, good-bye! Will you wear it next Sunday?" she asked.

"Perhaps," answered Marcia breathlessly, and sped on her homeward way, her cheeks bright with excitement.

In her own room she spread the chintz out upon the bed and with trembling fingers set about her task. The bright shears clipped the edge and tore off the lengths exultantly as if in league with the girl. The bees hummed outside in the clover, and now and again buzzed between the muslin curtains of the open window, looked in and grumbled out again. The birds sang across the meadows and the sun mounted to the zenith and began its downward march, but still the busy fingers worked on. Well for Marcia's scheme that the fashion of the day was simple, wherein were few puckers and plaits and tucks, and little trimming required, else her task would have been impossible.

Her heart beat high as she tried it on at last, the new chintz that she had made. She went into the spare room and stood before the long mirror in its wide gilt frame that rested on two gilt knobs standing out from the wall like giant rosettes. She had dared to make the skirt a little longer than that of her best frock. It was almost as long as Kate's, and for a moment she lingered, sweeping backward and forward before the glass and admiring herself in the long graceful folds. She caught up her braids in the fashion that Kate wore her hair and smiled at the reflection of herself in the mirror. How funny it seemed to think she would soon be a woman like Kate. When Kate was gone they would begin to call her "Miss" sometimes. Somehow she did not care to look ahead. The present seemed enough. She had so wrapped her thoughts in her sister's new life that her own seemed flat and stale in comparison.

The sound of a distant hay wagon on the road reminded her that the sun was near to setting. The family carryall would soon be coming up the lane from the evening packet. She must hurry and take off her frock and be dressed before they arrived.

Marcia was so tired that night after supper that she was glad to slip away to bed, without waiting to hear Kate's voluble account of her day in town, the beauties she had seen and the friends she had met.

She lay down and dreamed of the morrow, and of the next day, and the next. In strange bewilderment she awoke in the night and found the moonlight streaming full into her face. Then she laughed and rubbed her eyes and tried to go to sleep again; but she could not, for she had dreamed that she was a bride herself, and the words of Mary Ann kept going over and over in her mind. "Oh, don't you envy her?" *Did* she envy her sister? But that was wicked. It troubled her to think of it, and she tried to banish the dream, but it would come again and again with a strange sweet pleasure.

She lay wondering if such a time of joy would ever come to her as had come to Kate, and whether the spare bed would ever be piled high with clothes and fittings for her new life. What a wonderful thing it was anyway to be a woman and be loved!

Then her dreams blended again with the soft perfume of the honeysuckle at the window, and the hooting of a young owl.

The moon dropped lower, the bright stars paled, dawn stole up through the edges of the woods far away and awakened a day that was to bring a strange transformation over Marcia's life.

...haste, not even taking time to glance toward the new folds of her chintz that drew thoughts closetward. She dared not say anything about it yet. There was much to be done, and not even Kate had time for an idle word with her. Marcia was called upon to run errands, to do odds and ends of things, to fill in vacant places, to sew on lost buttons, to do everything for which nobody else had time. The household had suddenly become aware that there was now but one more intervening day between them and the wedding.

It was not until late in the afternoon that Marcia ventured to put on her frock. Even then she felt shy about appearing in it.

Madam Schuyler was busy in the parlor with callers, and Kate was locked in her own room whither she had gone to rest. There was no one to notice if Marcia should "dress up," and it was not unlikely that she might escape much notice even at the supper table, as everybody was so absorbed in other things.

She lingered before her own little glass looking wistfully at herself. She was pleased with the frock she had made and liked her appearance in it, but yet there was something disappointing about it. It had none of the style of her sister's garments, newly come from the hand of the village mantua-maker. It was girlish, and showed her slip of a form prettily in the fashion of the day, but she felt too young. She wanted to look older. She searched her drawer and found a bit of black velvet which she pinned about her throat with a pin containing the miniature of her mother, then with a second thought she drew the long braids up in loops and fastened them about her head in older fashion. It suited her well, and the change it made astonished her. She decided to wear them so and see if others would notice. Surely, some day she would be a young woman, and perhaps then she would be allowed to have a will of her own occasionally.

She drew a quick breath as she descended the stairs and found her step-mother and the visitor just coming into the hall from the parlor.

They both involuntarily ceased their talk and looked at her in surprise. Over Madam Schuyler's face there came a look as if she had received a revelation. Marcia was no longer a child, but had suddenly blossomed into young womanhood. It was not the time she would have chosen for such an event. There was enough going on, and Marcia was still in school. She had no desire to steer another young soul through the various dangers and follies that beset a pretty girl from the time she puts up her hair until she is safely married to the right man — or the wrong one. She had just begun to look forward with relief to having Kate well settled in life. Kate had been a hard one to manage. She had too much will of her own and a pretty way of always having it. She had no deep sense of reverence for old, staid manners and customs. Many a long lecture had Madam Schuyler delivered to Kate upon her unseemly ways. It did not please her to think of having to go through it all so soon again, therefore upon her usually complacent brow there came a look of dismay.

"Why!" exclaimed the visitor, "is this the bride? How tall she looks! No! Bless me! it isn't, is it? Yes, — Well! I'll declare. It's just Marsh! What have you got on, child? How old you look!"

Marcia flushed. It was not pleasant to have her young womanhood questioned, and in a tone so familiar and patronizing. She disliked the name of "Marsh" exceedingly, especially upon the lips of this woman, a sort of second cousin of her stepmother's. She would rather have chosen the new frock to pass under inspection of her stepmother without witnesses, but it was too late to turn back now. She must face it.

Though Madam Schuyler's equilibrium was a trifle disturbed, she was not one to show it before a visitor. Instantly she recovered her balance, and perhaps Marcia's ordeal was less trying than if there had been no third person present. "That looks very well, child!" she said critically with a shade of complacence in her voice. It is true that Marcia had gone beyond orders in purchasing and making garments unknown to her, yet the neatness and fit could but reflect well upon her training. It did no harm for cousin Maria to see what a child of her training could do. It was, on the whole, a very creditable piece of work, and Madam Schuyler grew more reconciled to it as Marcia came down toward them.

"Make it herself?" asked cousin Maria. "Why, Marsh, you did real well. My Matilda does all her own clothes now. It's time you were learning. It's a trifle longish to what you've been wearing them, isn't it? But you'll grow into it, I dare say. Got your hair a new way too. I thought you were Kate when you first started down stairs. You'll make a good-looking young lady when you grow up; only don't be in too much hurry. Take your girlhood while you've got it, is what I always tell Matilda."

Matilda was well on to thirty and showed no signs of taking anything else.

Madam Schuyler smoothed an imaginary pucker across the shoulders and again pronounced the work good.

"I picked berries and got the cloth," confessed Marcia.

Madam Schuyler smiled benevolently and patted Marcia's cheek.

"You needn't have done that, child. Why didn't you come to me for money? You needed something new, and that is a very good purchase, a little light, perhaps, but very pretty. We've been so busy with Kate's things you have been neglected."

Marcia smil...

...er to get the money by ...an to ask for it, and later, as he passed through ...om where she was helping to remove the dishes from the table, he paused and handed her a crisp five-dollar note. It had occurred to him that one daughter was getting all the good things and the other was having nothing. There was a pleasant tenderness in his eyes, a recognition of her rights as a young woman, that made Marcia's heart exceedingly light. There was something strange about the influence this little new frock seemed to have upon people.

Even Kate had taken a new tone with her. Much of the time at supper she had sat staring at her sister. Marcia wondered about it as she walked down toward the gate after her work was done. Kate had never seemed so quiet. Was she just beginning to realize that she was leaving home forever, and was she thinking how the home would be after she had left it? How she, Marcia, would take the place of elder sister, with only little Harriet and the boys, their stepsister and brothers, left? Was Kate sad over the thought of going so far away from them, or was she feeling suddenly the responsibility of the new position she was to occupy and the duties that would be hers? No, that could not be it, for surely that would bring a softening of expression, a sweetness of anticipation, and Kate's expression had been wondering, perplexed, almost troubled. If she had not been her own sister Marcia would have added, "hard," but she stopped short at that.

It was a lovely evening. The twilight was not yet over as she stepped from the low piazza that ran the length of the house bearing another above it on great white pillars. A drapery of wisteria in full bloom festooned across one end and half over the front. Marcia stepped back across the stone flagging and driveway to look up the purple clusters of graceful fairy-like shape that embowered the house, and thought how beautiful it would look when the wedding guests should arrive the day after the morrow. Then she turned into the gravel path, box-bordered, that led to the gate. Here and there on either side luxuriant blooms of dahlias, peonies and roses leaned over into the night and peered at her. The yard had never looked so pretty. The flowers truly had done their best for the occasion, and they seemed to be asking some word of commendation from her. They nodded their dewy heads sleepily as she went on.

To-morrow the children would be coming back from Aunt Eliza's, where they had been sent safely out of the way for a few days, and the last things would arrive,—and *he* would come. Not later than three in the afternoon he ought to arrive, Kate had said, though there was a possibility that he might come in the morning, but Kate was not counting upon it. He was to drive from his home to Schenectady and, leaving his own horse there to rest, come on by coach. Then he and Kate would go back in fine style to Schenectady in a coach and pair, with a black coachman, and at Schenectady take their own horse and drive on to their home, a long beautiful ride, so thought Marcia half enviously. How beautiful it would be! What endless delightful talks they might have about the birds and things they saw in passing only Kate did not love to talk about such things. But then she would be with David, and he talked beautifully about nature or anything else. Kate would learn to love it if she loved him. Did Kate love David? Of course she must or why should she marry him? Marcia resented the thought that Kate might have other objects in view, such as Mary Ann Fothergill had suggested for instance. Of course Kate would never marry any man unless she loved him. That would be a dreadful thing to do. Love was the greatest thing in the world. Marcia looked up to the stars, her young soul thrilling with awe and reverence for the great mysteries of life. She wondered again if life would open sometime for her in some such great way, and if she would ever know better than now what it meant. Would some one come and love her? Some one whom she could love in return with all the fervor of her nature?

She had dreamed such dreams before many times, as girls will, while lovers and future are all in one dreamy, sweet blending of rosy tints and joyous mystery, but never had they come to her with such vividness as that night. Perhaps it was because the household had recognized the woman in her for the first time that evening. Perhaps because the vision she had seen reflected in her mirror before she left her room that afternoon had opened the door of the future a little wider than it had ever opened before.

She stood by the gate where the syringa and lilac bushes leaned over and arched the way, and the honeysuckle climbed about the fence in a wild pretty way of its own and flung sweetness on the air in vivid, erratic whiffs.

The sidewalk outside was brick, and whenever she heard footsteps coming she stepped back into the shadow of the syringa and was hidden from view. She was in no mood to talk with anyone.

She could look out into the dusty road and see dimly the horses and carryalls as they passed, and recognize an occasional laughing voice of some village maiden out with her best young man for a ride. Others strolled along the sidewalk, and fragments of talk floated back. Almost every one had a word to say about the wedding as they neared the gate, and if Marcia had been in another mood it would have been interesting and gratifying to her pride. Every one had a good word for Kate, though many disapproved of her in a general way for principle's sake.

.... s mouth, so he slouched on, not
.... his goddess held her breath behind a lilac bush not three feet away,
her heart beating in annoyed taps to be again interrupted by him in her pleasant
thoughts.

Merry, laughing voices mingling with many footsteps came sounding down
the street and paused beside the gate. Marcia knew the voices and again slid
behind the shrubbery that bordered all the way to the house, and not even a
gleam of her light frock was visible. They trooped in, three or four girl friends
of Kate's and a couple of young men.

Marcia watched them pass up the box-bordered path from her shadowy
retreat, and thought how they would miss Kate, and wondered if the young men
who had been coming there so constantly to see her had no pangs of heart that
their friend and leader was about to leave them. Then she smiled at herself in
the dark. She seemed to be doing the retrospect for Kate, taking leave of all the
old friends, home, and life, in Kate's place. It was not her life anyway, and why
should she bother herself and sigh and feel this sadness creeping over her for
some one else? Was it that she was going to lose her sister? No, for Kate had
never been much of a companion to her. She had always put her down as a little
girl and made distinct and clear the difference in their ages. Marcia had been
the little maid to fetch and carry, the errand girl, and unselfish, devoted slave
in Kate's life. There had been nothing protective and elder-sisterly in her
manner toward Marcia. At times Marcia had felt this keenly, but no expression
of this lack had ever crossed her lips, and afterwards her devotion to her sister
had been the greater, to in a measure compensate for this reproachful thought.

But Marcia could not shake the sadness off. She stole in further among the
trees to think about it till the callers should go away. She felt no desire to meet
any of them.

She began again to wonder how she would feel if day after to-morrow were
her wedding day, and she were going away from home and friends and all the
scenes with which she had been familiar since babyhood. Would she mind very
much leaving them all? Father? Yes, father had been good to her, and loved
her and was proud of her in a way. But one does not lose one's father no matter
how far one goes. A father is a father always; and Mr. Schuyler was not a
demonstrative man. Marcia felt that her father would not miss her deeply, and
she was not sure she would miss him so very much. She had read to him a great

deal and talked politics with him whenever he had no one better by, but aside from that her life had been lived much apart from him. Yet stepmother? Yes, she would miss her as one misses a perfect mentor and guide. She had been used to looking to her for direction. She was thoroughly conscious that she had a will of her own and would like a chance to exercise it, still, she knew that in many cases without her stepmother she would be like a rudderless ship, a guideless traveller. And she loved her stepmother too, as a young girl can love a good woman who has been her guide and helper, even though there never has been great tenderness between them. Yes, she would miss her stepmother, but she would not feel so very sad over it. Harriet and the little brothers? Oh, yes she would miss them, they were dear little things and devoted to her.

Then there were the neighbors, and the schoolmates, and the people of the village. She would miss the minister, – the dear old minister and his wife. Many a time she had gone with her arms full of flowers to the parsonage down the street, and spent the afternoon with the minister's wife. Her smooth white hair under its muslin cap, and her soft wrinkled cheek were very dear to the young girl. She had talked to this friend more freely about her innermost thoughts than she had ever spoken to any living being. Oh, she would miss the minister's wife very much if she were to go away.

The names of her schoolmates came to her. Harriet Woodgate, Eliza Buchanan, Margaret Fletcher, three girls who were her intimates. She would miss them, of course, but how much? She could scarcely tell. Margaret Fletcher more than the other two. Mary Ann Fothergill? She almost laughed at the thought of anybody missing Mary Ann. John Middleton? Hanford Weston? There was not a boy in the school she would miss for an instant, she told herself with conviction. Not one of them realized her ideal. There was much pairing off of boy and girl in school, but Marcia, like the heroine of "Comin' thro' the Rye," was good friends with all the boys and intimate with none. They all counted it an honor to wait upon her, and she cared not a farthing for any. She felt herself too young, of course, to think of such things, but when she dreamed her day dreams the lover and prince who figured in them bore no familiar form or feature. He was a prince and these were only schoolboys.

The merry chatter of the young people in the house floated through the open windows, and Marcia could hear her sister's voice above them all. Chameleon-like she was all gaiety and laughter now, since her gravity at supper.

They were coming out the front door and down the walk. Kate was with them. Marcia could catch glimpses of the girls' white frocks as they came nearer. She saw that her sister was walking with Captain Leavenworth. He was a handsome young man who made a fine appearance in his uniform. He and Kate had been intimate for two years, and it might have been more than friendship had not Kate's father interfered between them. He did not think so well of the handsome young captain as did either his daughter Kate or the

....u David Spafford had appeared and promptly fallen in love with the beautiful girl, and the Schuyler mind was relieved. So it came about that, upon the reappearance of the handsome young captain wearing the insignia of his first honors, the Squire received him graciously. He even felt that he might be more lenient about his moral character, and told himself that perhaps he was not so bad after all, he must have something in him or the United States government would not have seen fit to honor him. It was easier to think so, now Kate was safe.

Marcia watched her sister and the captain go laughing down to the gate, and out into the street. She wondered that Kate could care to go out to-night when it was to be almost her last evening at home; wondered, too, that Kate would walk with Captain Leavenworth when she belonged to David now. She might have managed it to go with one of the girls. But that was Kate's way. Kate's ways were not Marcia's ways.

Marcia wondered if she would miss Kate, and was obliged to acknowledge to herself that in many ways her sister's absence would be a relief to her. While she recognized the power of her sister's beauty and will over her, she felt oppressed sometimes by the strain she was under to please, and wearied of the constant, half-fretful, half-playful faultfinding.

The gay footsteps and voices died away down the village street, and Marcia ventured forth from her retreat. The moon was just rising and came up a glorious burnished disk, silhouetting her face as she took a moment listening to the stirring of a bird among the branches. It was her will to-night to be alone and let her fancies wander where they would. The beauty and the mystery of a wedding was upon her, touching all her deeper feelings, and she wished to dream it out and wonder over it. Again it came to her what if the day after the morrow were her wedding day and she stood alone thinking about it. She would not have gone off down the street with a lot of giggling girls nor walked with another young man. She would have stood here, or down by the gate—and she moved on toward her favorite arch of lilac and syringa—yes, down by the gate in the darkness looking out and thinking how it would be when he should come. She felt sure if it had been herself who expected David she would have begun to watch for him a week before the time he had set for coming, heralding it again and again to her heart in joyous thrills of happiness, for who knew but he might come sooner and surprise her? She would have rejoiced that to-night she was alone, and would have excused herself from everything else to come down there in the stillness and watch for him, and think how it would be when he would really get there. She would hear his step echoing down the street and would recognize it as his. She would lean far over the gate to listen and watch, and it would come nearer and nearer, and her heart would beat faster and faster, and her breath come quicker, until he was at last by her side, his beautiful surprise for her in his eyes. But now, if David should really try to surprise Kate by coming that way to-night he would not find her waiting nor thinking of him at all, but off with Captain Leavenworth.

With a passing pity for David she went back to her own dream. With one elbow on the gate and her cheek in her hand she thought it all over. The delayed evening coach rumbled up to the tavern not far away and halted. Real footsteps came up the street, but Marcia did not notice them only as they made more vivid her thoughts.

Her dream went on and the steps drew nearer until suddenly they halted and some one appeared out of the shadow. Her heart stood still, for form and face in the darkness seemed unreal, and the dreams had been most vivid. Then with tender masterfulness two strong arms were flung about her and her face was drawn close to his across the vine-twined gate until her lips touched his. One long clinging kiss of tenderness he gave her and held her head close against his breast for just a moment while he murmured: "My darling! My precious, precious Kate, I have you at last!"

The spell was broken! Marcia's dream was shattered.

Her mind awoke. With a scream she sprang from him, horror and a wild but holy joy mingling with her perplexity. She put her hand upon her heart, marvelling over the sweetness that lingered upon her lips, trying to recover her senses as she faced the eager lover who opened the little gate and came quickly toward her, as yet unaware that it was not Kate to whom he had been talking.

, ... was on having a good time with some one else. He had mistaken her for Kate. Her long dress and her put-up hair had deceived him in the moonlight. She tried to summon some womanly courage, and in her earnestness to make things right she forgot her natural timidity.

"It is not Kate," she said gently; "it is only Marcia. Kate did not know you were coming to-night. She did not expect you till to-morrow. She had to go out,—that is—she has gone with—" the truthful, youthful, troubled sister paused. To her mind it was a calamity that Kate was not present to meet her lover. She should at least have been in the house ready for a surprise like this. Would David not feel the omission keenly? She must keep it from him if she could about Captain Leavenworth. There was no reason why he should feel badly about it, of course, and yet it might annoy him. But he stepped back laughing at his mistake.

"Why! Marcia, is it you, child? How you have grown! I never should have known you!" said the young man pleasantly. He had always a grave tenderness for this little sister of his love. "Of course your sister did not know I was coming," he went on, "and doubtless she has many things to attend to. I did not expect her to be out here watching for me, though for a moment I did think she was at the gate. You say she is gone out? Then we will go up to the house and I will be there to surprise her when she comes."

Marcia turned with relief. He had not asked where Kate was gone, nor with whom.

The Squire and Madam Schuyler greeted the arrival with elaborate welcome. The Squire like Marcia seemed much annoyed that Kate had gone out. He kept fuming back and forth from the window to the door and asking: "What did she go out for to-night? She ought to have stayed at home!"

But Madam Schuyler wore ample satisfaction upon her smooth brow. The bridegroom had arrived. There could be no further hitch in the ceremonies. He had arrived a day before the time, it is true; but he had not found *her* unprepared. So far as she was concerned, with a few extra touches the wedding might proceed at once. She was always ready for everything in time. No one could find a screw loose in the machinery of her household.

She bustled about, giving orders and laying a bountiful supper before the young man, while the Squire sat and talked with him and Marcia hovered watchfully, waiting upon the table, noticing with admiring eyes the beautiful wave of his abundant hair, tossed back from his forehead. She took a kind of pride of possession in his handsome face, — the far removed possession of a sister-in-law. There was his sunny smile, that seemed as though it could bring joy out of the gloom of a bleak December day, and there were the two dimples — not real dimples, of course men never had dimples — but hints, suggestions of dimples, that caught themselves when he smiled, here and there like hidden mischief well kept under control, but still merrily ready to come to the surface. His hands were white and firm, the fingers long and shapely, the hands of a brain worker. The vision of Hanford Weston's hands, red and bony, came up to her in contrast. She had not known that she looked at them that day when he had stood awkwardly asking if he might walk with her. Poor Hanford! He would ill compare with this cultured scholarly man who was his senior by ten years, though it is possible that with the ten years added he would have been quite worthy of the admiration of any of the village girls.

The fruit cake and raspberry preserves and doughnuts and all the various viands that Madam Schuyler had ordered set out for the delectation of her guest had been partaken of, and David and the Squire sat talking of the news of the day, touching on politics, with a bit of laughter from the Squire at the man who thought he had invented a machine to draw carriages by steam in place of horses.

"There's a good deal in it, I believe," said the younger man. "His theory is all right if he can get some one to help him carry it out."

"Well maybe, maybe," said the Squire shaking his head dubiously, "but it seems to me a very fanciful scheme. Horses are good enough for me. I shouldn't like to trust myself to an unknown quantity like steam, but time will tell."

"Yes, and the world is progressing. Something of the sort is sure to come. It has come in England. It would make a vast change in our country, binding city to city and practically eradicating space."

"Visionary schemes, David, visionary schemes, that's what I call them. You and I'll never see them in our day, I'm sure of that. Remember this is a new country and must go slow." The Squire was half laughing, half in earnest.

Amid the talk Marcia had quietly slipped out. It had occurred to her that perhaps the captain might return with her sister.

She must watch for Kate and warn her. Like a shadow in the moonlight she stepped softly down the gravel path once more and waited at the gate. Did not that sacred kiss placed upon her lips all by mistake bind her to this solemn duty? Had it not been given to her to see as in a revelation, by that kiss, the love of one man for one woman, deep and tender and true?

In the fragrant darkness her soul stood still and wondered over Love, the marvellous. With an insight such as few have who have not tasted years of wedded joy, Marcia comprehended the possibility and joy of sacrifice that made even sad things bright because of Love. She saw like a flash how Kate could give up her gay life, her home, her friends, everything that life had heretofore

The night crept slowly for the anxious little watcher at the gate. Had she been sure where to look for her sister, and not afraid of the tongues of a few interested neighbors who had watched everything at the house for days that no item about the wedding should escape them, she would have started on a search at once. She knew if she just ran into old Miss Pemberton's, whose house stood out upon the street with two straight-backed little, high, white seats each side of the stoop, a most delightful post of observation, she could discover at once in which direction Kate had gone, and perhaps a good deal more of hints and suggestions besides. But Marcia had no mind to make gossip. She must wait as patiently as she could for Kate. Moreover Kate might be walking even now in some secluded, rose-lined lane arm in arm with the captain, saying a pleasant farewell. It was Kate's way and no one might gainsay her.

Marcia's dreams came back once more, the thoughts that had been hers as she stood there an hour before. She thought how the kiss had fitted into the dream. Then all at once conscience told her it was Kate's lover, not her own, whose arms had encircled her. And now there was a strange unwillingness to go back to the dreams at all, a lingering longing for the joys into whose glory she had been for a moment permitted to look. She drew back from all thoughts and tried to close the door upon them. They seemed too sacred to enter. Her maidenhood was but just begun and she had much yet to learn of life. She was glad, glad for Kate that such wonderfulness was coming to her. Kate would be sweeter, softer in her ways now. She could not help it with a love like that enfolding her life.

At last there were footsteps! Hark! Two people — only two! Just what Marcia had expected. The other girls and boys had dropped into other streets or gone home. Kate and her former lover were coming home alone. And, furthermore, Kate would not be glad to see her sister at the gate. This last thought came with sudden conviction, but Marcia did not falter.

"Kate, David has come!" Marcia said it in low, almost accusing tones, at least so it sounded to Kate, before the two had hardly reached the gate. They had been loitering along talking in low tones, and the young captain's head was bent over his companion in an earnest, pleading attitude. Marcia could not bear to look, and did not wish to see more, so she had spoken.

Kate, startled, sprang away from her companion, a white angry look in her face.

"How you scared me, Marsh!" she exclaimed pettishly. "What if he has come? That's nothing. I guess he can wait a few minutes. He had no business to come to-night anyway. He knew we wouldn't be ready for him till to-morrow."

Kate was recovering her self-possession in proportion as she realized the situation. That she was vexed over her bridegroom's arrival neither of the two witnesses could doubt. It stung her sister with a deep pity for David. He was not getting as much in Kate as he was giving. But there was no time for such thoughts, besides Marcia was trembling from head to foot, partly with her own daring, partly with wrath at her sister's words.

"For shame, Kate!" she cried. "How can you talk so, even in fun! David came to surprise you, and I think he had a right to expect to find you here so near to the time of your marriage."

There was a flash in the young eyes as she said it, and a delicate lifting of her chin with the conviction of the truth she was speaking, that gave her a new dignity even in the moonlight. Captain Leavenworth looked at her in lazy admiration and said:

"Why, Marsh, you're developing into quite a spitfire. What have you got on to-night that makes you look so tall and handsome? Why didn't you stay in and talk to your fine gentleman? I'm sure he would have been just as well satisfied with you as your sister."

Marcia gave one withering glance at the young man and then turned her back full upon him. He was not worth noticing. Besides he was to be pitied, for he evidently cared still for Kate.

But Kate was fairly white with anger. Perhaps her own accusing conscience helped it on. Her voice was imperious and cold. She drew herself up haughtily and pointed toward the house.

"Marcia Schuyler," she said coldly, facing her sister, "go into the house and attend to your own affairs. You'll find that you'll get into serious trouble if you attempt to meddle with mine. You're nothing but a child yet and ought to be punished for your impudence. Go! I tell you!" she stamped her foot, "I will come in when I get ready."

Marcia went. Not proudly as she might have gone the moment before, but covered with confusion and shame, her head drooping like some crushed lily on a bleeding stalk. Through her soul rushed indignation, mighty and forceful; indignation and shame, for her sister, for David, for herself. She did not stop to analyze her various feelings, nor did she stop to speak further with those in the house. She fled to her own room, and burying her face in the pillow she wept until she fell asleep.

The moon-shadows grew longer about the arbored gateway where the two she had left stood talking in low tones, looking furtively now and then toward the house, and withdrawing into the covert of the bushes by the walk. But Kate dared not "

...good-night
...y ...ed and was going straight to bed
.. ...orrow. Then she ran lightly across the hall to the stairs.

She knew they would call her back, and that they would all come into the hall with David to see the effect of his surprise upon her. She had planned to a nicety just which stair she could reach before they got there, and where she would pause and turn and poise, and what pose she would take with her round white arm stretched to the handrail, the sleeve turned carelessly back. She had ready her countenances, a sleepy indifference, then a pleased surprise, and a climax of delight. She carried it all out, this little bit of impromptu acting, as well as though she had rehearsed it for a month.

They called her, and she turned deliberately, one dainty, slippered foot, with its crossed black ribbons about the slender ankle, just leaving the stair below, and showing the arch of the aristocratic instep. Her gown was blue and she held it back enough for the stiff white frill of her petticoat to peep below. Well she read the admiration in the eyes below her. Admiration was Kate's life: she thrived upon it. She could not do without it.

David stood still, his love in his eyes, looking upon the vision of his bride, and his heart swelled within him that so great a treasure should be his. Then straightway they all forgot to question where she had been or to rebuke her that she had been at all. She had known they would. She ever possessed the power to make others forget her wrong doings when it was worth her while to try.

The next morning things were astir even earlier than usual. There was the sound of the beating of eggs, the stirring of cakes, the clatter of pots and pans from the wide, stoneflagged kitchen.

Marcia, fresh as a flower from its morning dew in spite of her cry the night before, had arisen to new opportunities for service. She was glad with the joyous forgetfulness of youth when she looked at David's happy face, and she thought no more of Kate's treatment of herself.

David followed Kate with a true lover's eyes and was never for more than a few moments out of her sight, though it seemed to Marcia that Kate did not try very hard to stay with him. When afternoon came she dismissed him for what she called her "beauty nap." Marcia was passing through the hall at the time and she caught the tender look upon his face as he touched her brow with reverent fingers and told her she had no need for that. Her eyes met Kate's as they were going up the stairs, and in spite of what Kate had said the night before

Marcia could not refrain from saying: "Oh, Kate! how could you when he loves you so? You know you never take a nap in the daytime!"

"You silly girl!" said Kate pleasantly enough, "don't you know the less a man sees of one the more he thinks of her?" With this remark she closed and fastened her door after her.

Marcia pondered these words of wisdom for some time, wondering whether Kate had really done it for that reason, or whether she did not care for the company of her lover. And why should it be so that a man loved you less because he saw you more? In her straightforward code the more you loved persons the more you desired to be in their company.

Kate had issued from her "beauty nap" with a feverish restlessness in her eyes, an averted face, and ink upon one finger. At supper she scarcely spoke, and when she did she laughed excitedly over little things. Her lover watched her with eyes of pride and ever increasing wonder over her beauty, and Marcia, seeing the light in his face, watched for its answer in her sister's, and finding it not was troubled.

She watched them from her bedroom window as they walked down the path where she had gone the evening before, decorously side by side, Kate holding her light muslin frock back from the dew on the hedges. She wondered if it was because Kate had more respect for David than for Captain Leavenworth that she never seemed to treat him with as much familiarity. She did not take possession of him in the same sweet imperious way.

Marcia had not lighted her candle. The moon gave light enough and she was very weary, so she undressed in the dim chamber and pondered upon the ways of the great world. Out there in the moonlight were those two who to-morrow would be one, and here was she, alone. The world seemed all circling about that white chamber of hers, and echoing with her own consciousness of self, and a loneliness she had never felt before. She wondered what it might be. Was it all sadness at parting with Kate, or was it the sadness over inevitable partings of all human relationships, and the aloneness of every living spirit?

She stood for a moment, white-robed, beside her window, looking up into the full round moon, and wondering if God knew the ache of loneliness in His little human creatures' souls that He had made, and whether He had ready something wherewith to satisfy. Then her meek soul bowed before the faith that was in her and she knelt for her shy but reverent evening prayer.

She heard the two lovers come in early and go upstairs, and she heard her father fastening up the doors and windows for the night. Then stillness gradually settled down and she fell asleep. Later, in her dreams, there echoed the sound of hastening hoofs far down the deserted street and over the old covered bridge, but she took no note of any sound, and the weary household slept on.

David had driven the day before with his own horse and chaise to a town some twenty miles away, and there left his horse at a tavern to rest for the return trip, for Kate would have it that they must leave the house in high style. So the finest equipage the town afforded had been secured to bear them on the first stage of their journey, with a portly negro driver and everything according to the custom of the greatest of the land. Nothing that Kate desired about the arrangements had been left undone.

The household was fully astir by half past four, for the family breakfast was to be at six promptly, that all might be cleared away and in readiness for the early arrival of the various aunts and uncles and cousins and friends who would "drive over" from the country round about. It would have been something Madam Schuyler would never have been able to get over if aught had been awry when a single uncle or aunt appeared upon the scene, or if there seemed to be the least evidence of fluster and nervousness.

The rosy sunlight in the East was mixing the morning with fresher air, and new odors for the new day that was dawning, when Marcia awoke. The sharp click of spoons and dishes, the voices of the maids, the sizzle, sputter, odor of frying ham and eggs, mingled with the early chorus of the birds, and calling to life of all living creatures, like an intrusion upon nature. It seemed not right to steal the morning's "quiet hour" thus rudely. The thought flitted through the girl's mind, and in an instant more the whole panorama of the day's excitement was before her, and she sprang from her bed. As if it had been her own wedding day instead of her sister's, she performed her dainty toilet, for though there was need for haste, she knew she would have no further time beyond a moment to slip on her best gown and smooth her hair.

Marcia hurried downstairs just as the bell rang for breakfast, and David, coming down smiling behind her, patted her cheek and greeted her with, "Well, little sister, you look as rested as if you had not done a thing all day yesterday."

She smiled shyly back at him, and her heart filled with pleasure over his new name for her. It sounded pleasantly from his happy lips. She was conscious of a gladness that he was to be so nearly related to her. She fancied how it would seem to say to Mary Ann: "My brother-in-law says so and so." It would be grand to call such a man "brother."

They were all seated at the table but Kate, and Squire Schuyler waited with pleasantly frowning brows to ask the blessing on the morning food. Kate was often late. She was the only member of the family who dared to be late to breakfast, and being the bride and the centre of the occasion more leniency was granted her this morning than ever before. Madam Schuyler waited until every one at the table was served to ham and eggs, coffee and bread-and-butter, and steaming griddle cakes, before she said, looking anxiously at the tall clock: "Marcia, perhaps you better go up and see if your sister needs any help. She ought to be down by now. Uncle Joab and Aunt Polly will be sure to be here by eight. She must have overslept, but we made so much noise she is surely awake by this time."

Marcia left her half-eaten breakfast and went slowly upstairs. She knew her sister would not welcome her, for she had often been sent on like errands before, and the brunt of Kate's anger had fallen upon the hapless messenger, wearing itself out there so that she might descend all smiles to greet father and mother and smooth off the situation in a most harmonious manner.

Marcia paused before the door to listen. Perhaps Kate was nearly ready and her distasteful errand need not be performed. But though she held her breath to listen, no sound came from the closed door. Very softly she tried to lift the latch and peep in. Kate must still be asleep. It was not the first time Marcia had found that to be the case when sent to bring her sister.

But the latch would not lift. The catch was firmly down from the inside. Marcia applied her eye to the keyhole, but could get no vision save a dim outline of the window on the other side of the room. She tapped gently once or twice and waited again, then called softly: "Kate, Kate! Wake up. Breakfast is ready and everybody is eating. Aunt Polly and Uncle Joab will soon be here."

She repeated her tapping and calling, growing louder as she received no answer. Kate would often keep still to tease her thus. Surely though she would not do so upon her wedding morning!

She called and called and shook the door, not daring, however, to make much of an uproar lest David should hear. She could not bear he should know the shortcomings of his bride.

But at last she grew alarmed. Perhaps Kate was ill. At any rate, whatever it was, it was time she was up. She worked for some minutes trying to loosen the catch that held the latch, but all to no purpose. She was forced to go downstairs and whisper to her stepmother the state of the case.

Madam Schuyler, excusing herself from the table, went upstairs, purposeful decision in every line of her substantial body, determination in every sound of her footfall. Bride though she be, Kate would have meted out to her just dues this time. Company and a lover and the nearness of the wedding hour were things not to be trifled with even by a charming Kate.

But M⸺

⸺ ⸺tter see if you can

⸺⸺u calm in her voice, but her face belied her words. She ⸺us anxious lest Kate was playing one of her pranks. She knew Kate's careless, fun-loving ways. It was more to her that all things should move decently and in order than that Kate should even be perfectly well. But Marcia's white face behind her stepmother's ample shoulder showed a dread of something worse than a mere indisposition. David Spafford took alarm at once. He put down the silver syrup jug from which he had been pouring golden maple syrup on his cakes, and pushed his chair back with a click.

"Perhaps she has fainted!" he said, and Marcia saw how deeply he was concerned. Father and lover both started up the stairs, the father angry, the lover alarmed. The Squire grumbled all the way up that Kate should sleep so late, but David said nothing. He waited anxiously behind while the Squire worked with the door. Madam Schuyler and Marcia had followed them, and halting curiously just behind came the two maids. They all loved Miss Kate and were deeply interested in the day's doings. They did not want anything to interfere with the well-planned pageant.

The Squire fumbled nervously with the latch, all the time calling upon his daughter to open the door; then wrathfully placed his solid shoulder and knee in just the right place, and with a groan and wrench the latch gave way, and the solid oak door swung open, precipitating the anxious group somewhat suddenly into the room.

Almost immediately they all became aware that there was no one there. David had stood with averted eyes at first, but that second sense which makes us aware without sight when others are near or absent, brought with it an unnamed anxiety. He looked wildly about.

The bed had not been slept in; that they all saw at once. The room was in confusion, but perhaps not more than might have been expected when the occupant was about to leave on the morrow. There were pieces of paper and string upon the floor and one or two garments lying about as if carelessly cast off in a hurry. David recognized the purple muslin frock Kate had worn the night before, and put out his hand to touch it as it lay across the foot of the bed, vainly reaching after her who was not there.

They stood in silence, father, mother, sister, and lover, and took in every detail of the deserted room, then looked blankly into one another's white faces, and in the eyes of each a terrible question began to dawn. Where was she?

Madam Schuyler recovered her senses first. With her sharp, practical system she endeavored to find out the exact situation. "Who saw her last? Has she been downstairs this morning?" she looked straight at Marcia this time, but the girl shook her head.

"I went to bed last night before they came in," she said, looking questioningly at David, but a sudden remembrance and fear seized her heart. She turned away to the window to face it where they could not look at her.

"We came in early," said David, trying to keep the anxiety out of his voice, as he remembered his well-beloved's good-night. Surely, surely, nothing very dreadful could have happened just over night, and in her father's own house. He looked about again to see the natural, every-day, little things that would help him drive away the thoughts of possible tragedy.

"Kate was tired. She said she was going to get up very early this morning and wash her face in the dew on the grass." He braved a smile and looked about on the troubled group. "She must be out somewhere upon the place," he continued, gathering courage with the thought; "she told me it was an old superstition. She has maybe wandered further than she intended, and perhaps got into some trouble. I'd better go and search for her. Is there any place near here where she would be likely to be?" He turned to Marcia for help.

"But Kate would never delay so long I'm sure," said the stepmother severely. "She's not such a fool as to go traipsing through the wet grass before daylight for any nonsense. If it were Marcia now, you might expect anything, but Kate would be satisfied with the dew on the grass by the kitchen pump. I know Kate."

Marcia's face crimsoned at her stepmother's words, but she turned her troubled eyes to David and tried to answer him.

"There are plenty of places, but Kate has never cared to go to them. I could go out and look everywhere." She started to go down, but as she passed the wide mahogany bureau she saw a bit of folded paper lying under the corner of the pincushion. With a smothered exclamation she went over and picked it up. It was addressed to David in Kate's handwriting, fine and even like copperplate. Without a word Marcia handed it to him and then stood back where the wide draperies of the window would shadow her.

Madam Schuyler, with sudden keen prescience, took alarm. Noticing the two maids standing wide-mouthed in the hallway, she summoned her most commandatory tone, stepped into the hall, half closing the door behind her, and cowed the two handmaidens under her glance.

"It is all right!" she said calmly. "Miss Kate has left a note, and will return soon. Go down and keep her breakfast warm, and not a word to a soul! Dolly,

...solemn conclave in Kate's room the preparations for the wedding moved steadily forward below stairs, and only two solemn maids, of all the helpers that morning, knew that a tragedy was hovering in the air and might burst about them.

David had grasped for the letter eagerly, and fumbled it open with trembling hand, but as he read, the smile of expectation froze upon his lips and his face grew ashen. He tottered and grasped for the mantel shelf to steady himself as he read further, but he did not seem to take in the meaning of what he read. The others waited breathless, a reasonable length of time, Madam Schuyler impatiently patient. She felt that long delay would be perilous to her arrangements. She ought to know the whole truth at once and be put in command of the situation. Marcia with sorrowful face and drooping eyelashes stood quiet behind the curtain, while over and over the echo of a horse's hoofs in a silent street and over a bridge sounded in her brain. She did not need to be told, she knew intuitively what had happened, and she dared not to look at David.

"Well, what has she done with herself?" said the Squire impatiently. He had not finished his plate of cakes, and now that there was word he wanted to know at once and go back to his breakfast. The sight of his daughter's handwriting relieved and reassured him. Some crazy thing she had done of course, but then Kate had always done queer things, and probably would to the end of time. She was a hussy to frighten them so, and he meant to tell her so when she returned, if it was her wedding day. But then, Kate would be Kate, and his breakfast was getting cold. He had the horses to look after and orders to give the hands before the early guests arrived.

But David did not answer, and the sight of him was alarming. He stood as one stricken dumb all in a moment. He raised his eyes to the Squire's—pleading, pitiful. His face had grown strained and haggard.

"Speak out, man, doesn't the letter tell?" said the Squire imperiously. "Where is the girl?"

And this time David managed to say brokenly: "She's gone!" and then his head dropped forward on his cold hand that rested on the mantel. Great beads of perspiration stood out upon his white forehead, and the letter fluttered gaily, coquettishly to the floor, a reminder of the uncertain ways of its writer.

The Squire reached for it impatiently, and wiping his spectacles laboriously put them on and drew near to the window to read, his heavy brows lowering in a frown. But his wife did not need to read the letter, for she, like Marcia, had divined its purport, and already her able faculties were marshalled to face the predicament.

The Squire with deepening frown was studying his elder daughter's letter, scarce able to believe the evidence of his senses that a girl of his could be so heartless.

Dear David, — the letter ran, — written as though in a hurry, done at the last moment, — which indeed it was: —

I want you to forgive me for what I am doing. I know you will feel bad about it, but really I never was the right one for you. I'm sure you thought me all too good, and I never could have stayed in a strait-jacket, it would have killed me. I shall always consider you the best man in the world, and I like you better than anyone else except Captain Leavenworth. I can't help it, you know, that I care more for him than anyone else, though I've tried. So I am going away to-night and when you read this we shall have been married. You are so very good that I know you will forgive me, and be glad I am happy. Don't think hardly of me for I always did care a great deal for you.

Your loving
Kate

It was characteristic of Kate that she demanded the love and loyalty of her betrayed lover to the bitter end, false and heartless though she had been. The coquette in her played with him even now in the midst of the bitter pain she must have known she was inflicting. No word of contrition spoke she, but took her deed as one of her prerogatives, just as she had always taken everything she chose. She did not even spare him the loving salutation that had been her custom in her letters to him, but wrote herself down as she would have done the day before when all was fair and dear between them. She did not hint at any better day for David, or give him permission to forget her, but held him for all time as her own, as she had known she would by those words of hers, "I like you better than anyone else except!—" Ah! That fatal "except!" Could any knife cut deeper and more ways? They sank into the young man's heart as he stood there those first few minutes and faced his trouble, his head bowed upon the mantel-piece.

Meantime Madam Schuyler's keen vision had spied another folded paper beside the pincushion. Smaller it was than the other, and evidently intended to be placed further out of sight. It was addressed to Kate's father, and her stepmother opened it and read with hard pressure of her thin lips, slanted down at the corners, and a steely look in her eyes. Was it possible that the girl, even in the midst of her treachery, had enjoyed with a sort of malicious glee the thought of her stepmother reading that note and facing the horror of a wedding

[illegible] as she could
[illegible] note read:

Dear Father:—I am going away to-night to marry Captain Leavenworth. You wouldn't let me have him in the right way so I had to take this. I tried very hard to forget him and get interested in David but it was no use. You couldn't stop it. So now I hope you will see it the way we do and forgive us. We are going to Washington and you can write us there and say you forgive us and then we will come home. I know you will forgive us Daddy dear. You know you always loved your little Kate and you couldn't really want me to be unhappy. Please send my trunks to Washington. I've tacked the card with the address on the envelope.

Your loving girl
Kate

There was a terrible stillness in the room, broken only by the crackling of the paper as the notes were turned in the hands of their readers. Marcia felt as if centuries were passing. David's soul was pierced by one awful thought. He had no room for others. She was gone! Life was a blank for him stretching out into interminable years. Of her treachery and false-heartedness in doing what she had done in the way she had done it, he had no time to take account. That would come later. Now he was trying to understand this one awful fact.

Madam Schuyler handed the second note to her husband, and with set lips quickly skimmed through the other one. As she read, indignation rose in her, and a great desire to outwit everybody. If it had been possible to bring the erring girl back and make her face her disgraced wedding alone, Madam Schuyler would have been glad to do it. She knew that upon her would likely rest the re-arrangements, and her ready brain was already taking account of her servants and the number of messages that would have to be sent out to stop the guests from arriving. She waited impatiently for her husband to finish reading that she might consult with him as to the best message to send, but she was scarcely prepared for the burst of anger that came with the finish of the letters. The old man crushed his daughter's note in his hand and flung it from him. He had great respect and love for David, and the sight of him broken in grief, the deed of his daughter, roused in him mighty indignation. His voice shook, but there was a deep note of command in it that made Madam Schuyler step aside and wait. The Squire had arisen to the situation, and she recognized her lord and master.

"She must be brought back at once at all costs!" he exclaimed. "That rascal shall not outwit us. Fool that I was to trust him in the house! Tell the men to saddle the horses. They cannot have gone far yet, and there are not so many roads to Washington. We may yet overtake them, and married or unmarried the hussy shall be here for her wedding!"

But David raised his head from the mantel-shelf and steadied his voice:

"No, no, you must not do that—father—" the appellative came from his lips almost tenderly, as if he had long considered the use of it with pleasure, and now he spoke it as a tender bond meant to comfort.

The older man started and his face softened. A flash of understanding and love passed between the two men.

"Remember, she has said she loves some one else. She could never be mine now."

There was a terrible sadness in the words as David spoke them, and his voice broke. Madam Schuyler turned away and took out her handkerchief, an article of apparel for which she seldom had use except as it belonged to every well-ordered toilet.

The father stood looking hopelessly at David and taking in the thought. Then he too bowed his head and groaned.

"And my daughter, my little Kate has done it!" Marcia covered her face with the curtains and her tears fell fast.

David went and stood beside the Squire and touched his arm.

"Don't!" he said pleadingly. "You could not help it. It was not your fault. Do not take it so to heart!"

"But it is my disgrace. I have brought up a child who could do it. I cannot escape from that. It is the most dishonorable thing a woman can do. And look how she has done it, brought shame upon us all! Here we have a wedding on our hands, and little or no time to do anything! I have lived in honor all my life, and now to be disgraced by my own daughter!"

Marcia shuddered at her father's agony. She could not bear it longer. With a soft cry she went to him, and nestled her head against his breast unnoticed.

"Father, Father, don't!" she cried.

But her father went on without seeming to see her.

"To be disgraced and deserted and dishonored by my own child! Something must be done. Send the servants! Let the wedding be stopped!"

He looked at Madam and she started toward the door to carry out his bidding, but he recalled her immediately.

"No, stay!" he cried. "It is too late to stop them all. Let them come. Let them be told! Let the disgrace rest upon the one to whom it belongs!"

Madam stopped in consternation! A wedding without a bride! Yet she knew it was a serious thing to try to dispute with her husband in that mood. She paused to consider.

agony of the knowledge of David's part coming to him.

"No, I cannot go home," said David hopelessly, a look of keen pain darting across his face, "for the house will be all ready for her, and the table set. The friends will be coming in, and we are invited to dinner and tea everywhere. They will all be coming to the house, my friends, to welcome us. No, I cannot go home." Then he passed his hand over his forehead blindly, and added, in a stupefied tone, "and yet I must—sometime—I must—go—home!"

Chapter 5

The room was very still as he spoke. Madam Schuyler forgot the coming guests and the preparations, in consternation over the thought of David and his sorrow. Marcia sobbed softly upon her father's breast, and her father involuntarily placed his arm about her as he stood in painful thought.

"It is terrible!" he murmured, "terrible! How could she bear to inflict such sorrow! She might have saved us the scorn of all our friends. David, you must not go back alone. It must not be. You must not bear that. There are lovely girls in plenty elsewhere. Find another one and marry her. Take your bride home with you, and no one in your home need be the wiser. Don't sorrow for that cruel girl of mine. Give her not the satisfaction of feeling that your life is broken. Take another. Any girl might be proud to go with you for the asking. Had I a dozen other daughters you should have your pick of them, and one should go with you, if you would condescend to choose another from the home where you have been so treacherously dealt with. But I have only this one girl. She is but a child as yet and cannot compare with what you thought you had. I blame you not if you do not wish to wed another Schuyler, but if you will she is yours. And she is a good girl, David, though she is but a child. Speak up, child, and say if you will make amends for the wrong your sister has done!"

The room was so still one could almost hear the heartbeats. David raised his head once more and was looking at Marcia. Sad and searching was his gaze, as if he fain would find the features of Kate in her face, yet it seemed to Marcia, as she raised wide tear-filled eyes from her father's breast where her head still lay, that he saw her not. He was looking beyond her and facing the home-going alone, and the empty life that would follow.

Her thoughts the last few days had matured her fully. She understood and pitied, and her woman-nature longed to give comfort, yet she shrunk from going unasked. It was all terrible, this sudden situation thrust upon her, yet she felt a willing sacrifice if she but felt sure it was his wish.

But David did not seem to know that he must speak. He waited, looking earnestly at her, through her, beyond her, to see if Heaven would grant this small relief to his sufferings. At last Marcia summoned her voice:

"If David wishes I will go."

She spoke the words solemnly, her eyes lifted slightly above him as if she were speaking to Another One higher than he. It was like an answer to a call from God. It had come to Marcia this way. It seemed to leave her no room for drawing back, if indeed she had wished to do so. Other considerations were not present. There was just one great desire in her heart to make amends in

g at him through the lashes and
.... for recognition. She did not feel that she was pleading for anything for
herself, only for the chance to help him.

Her voice had broken the spell. David looked down upon her kindly, a
pleasant light of gratitude flashing through the sternness and sorrow in his face.
Here was comradeship in trouble, and his voice recognized it as he said:

"Child, you are good to me, and I thank you. I will try to make you happy
if you will go with me, and I am sure your going will be a comfort in many ways,
but I would not have you go unwillingly."

There was a dull ache in Marcia's heart, its cause she could not understand,
but she was conscious of a gladness that she was not counted unworthy to be
accepted, young though she was, and child though he called her. His tone had
been kindness itself, the gentle kindness that had won her childish sisterly love
when he first began to visit her sister. She had that answer to remember for
many a long day, and to live upon, when questionings and loneliness came upon
her. But she raised her face to her father now, and said: "I will go, father!"

The Squire stooped and kissed his little girl for the last time. Perhaps he
realized that from this time forth she would be a little girl no longer, and that
he would never look into those child-eyes of hers again, unclouded with the
sorrows of life, and filled only with the wonder-pictures of a rosy future. She
seemed to him and to herself to be renouncing her own life forever, and to be
taking up one of sacrificial penitence for her sister's wrong doing.

The father then took Marcia's hand and placed it in David's, and the
betrothal was complete.

Madam Schuyler, whose reign for the time being was set aside, stood silent,
half disapproving, yet not interfering. Her conscience told her that this
wholesale disposal of Marcia was against nature. The new arrangement was a
relief to her in many ways, and would make the solution of the day a less trying
one for every one. But she was a woman and knew a woman's heart. Marcia
was not having her chance in life as her sister had, as every woman had a right
to have. Then her face hardened. How had Kate used her chances? Perhaps
it was better for Marcia to be well placed in life before she grew headstrong
enough to make a fool of herself as Kate had done. David would be good to
her, that was certain. One could not look at the strong, pleasant lines of his well
cut mouth and chin and not be sure of that. Perhaps it was all for the best. At
least it was not her doing. And it was only the night before that she had been

looking at Marcia and worrying because she was growing into a woman so fast. Now she would be relieved of that care, and could take her ease and enjoy life until her own children were grown up. But the voice of her husband aroused her to the present.

"Let the wedding go on as planned, Sarah, and no one need know until the ceremony is over except the minister. I myself will go and tell the minister. There will need to be but a change of names."

"But," said the Madam, with housewifely alarm, as the suddenness of the whole thing flashed over her, "Marcia is not ready. She has no suitable clothes for her wedding."

"Not ready! No clothes!" said the Squire, now thoroughly irritated over this trivial objection, as a fly will sometimes ruffle the temper of a man who has kept calm under fire of an enemy. "And where are all the clothes that have been making these weeks and months past? What more preparation does she need? Did the hussy take her wedding things with her? What's in the trunk?"

"But those are Kate's things, father," said Marcia in gentle explanation. "Kate would be very angry if I took her things. They were made for her, you know."

"And what if they were made for her?" answered the father, very angry now at Kate. "You are near of a size. What will do for one is good enough for the other, and Kate may be angry and get over it, for not one rag of it will she get, nor a penny of my money will ever go to her again. She is no daughter of mine from henceforth. That rascal has beaten me and stolen my daughter, but he gets a dowerless lass. Not a penny will ever go from the Schuyler estate into his pocket, and no trunk will ever travel from here to Washington for that heartless girl. I forbid it. Let her feel some of the sorrow she has inflicted upon others more innocent. I forbid it, do you hear?" He brought his fist down upon the mahogany bureau until the prisms on a candle-stand in front of the mirror jangled discordantly.

"Oh, Father!" gasped Marcia, and turned with terror to her stepmother. But David stood with his back toward the rest looking out the window. He had forgotten them all.

Madam Schuyler was now in command again. For once the Squire had anticipated his wife, and the next move had been planned without her help, but it was as she would have it. Her face had lost its consternation and beamed with satisfaction beneath its mask of grave perplexity. She could not help it that she was glad to have the terrible ordeal of a wedding without a bride changed to something less formidable.

At least the country round about could not pity, for who was to say but that David was as well suited with one sister as with the other? And Marcia was a good girl; doubtless she would grow into a good wife. Far more suitable for so good and steady a man as David than pretty, imperious Kate.

...that I hove takes your place and then come back."

David and Squire went out like two men who had suddenly grown old, and had not the strength to walk rapidly. No one thought any more of breakfast. It was half past seven by the old tall clock that stood upon the stair-landing. It would not be long before Aunt Polly and Uncle Joab would be driving up to the door.

Straight ahead went the preparations, just as if nothing had happened, and if Mistress Kate Leavenworth could have looked into her old room an hour after the discovery of her flight she would have been astonished beyond measure.

Up in her own room stood poor bewildered Marcia. She looked about upon her little white bed, and thought she would never likely sleep in it again. She looked out of the small-paned window with its view of distant hill and river, and thought she was bidding it good-bye forever. She went toward her closet and put out her hand to choose what she would take with her, and her heart sank. There hung the faded old ginghams short and scant, and scorned but yesterday, yet her heart wildly clung to them. Almost would she have put one on and gone back to her happy care-free school life. The thought of the new life frightened her. She must give up her girlhood all at once. She might not keep a vestige of it, for that would betray David. She must be Kate from morning to evening. Like a sword thrust came the remembrance that she had envied Kate, and God had given her the punishment of being Kate in very truth. Only there was this great difference. She was not the chosen one, and Kate had been. She must bear about forever in her heart the thought of Kate's sin.

The voice of her stepmother drew nearer and warned her that her time alone was almost over, and out on the lawn she could hear the voices of Uncle Joab and Aunt Polly who had just arrived.

She dropped on her knees for one brief moment and let her young soul pour itself out in one great cry of distress to God, a cry without words borne only on the breath of a sob. Then she arose, hastily dashed cold water in her face, and dried away the traces of tears. There was no time to think. With hurried hand she began to gather a few trifles together from closet and drawer.

One last lingering look she took about her room as she left it, her arms filled with the things she had hastily culled from among her own. Then she shut the door quickly and went down the hall to her sister's room to enter upon her new life. She was literally putting off herself and putting on a new being as far as it was possible to do so outwardly.

There on the bed lay the bridal outfit. Madam Schuyler had just brought it from the spare room that there might be no more going back and forth through the halls to excite suspicion. She was determined that there should be no excitement or demonstration or opportunity for gossip among the guests at least until the ceremony was over. She had satisfied herself that not a soul outside the family save the two maids suspected that aught was the matter, and she felt sure of their silence.

Kate had taken very little with her, evidently fearing to excite suspicion, and having no doubt that her father would relent and send all her trousseau as she had requested in her letter. For once Mistress Kate had forgotten her fineries and made good her escape with but two frocks and a few other necessaries in a small hand-bag.

Madam Schuyler was relieved to the point of genuine cheerfulness, over this, despite the cloud of tragedy that hung over the day. She began to talk to Marcia as if she had been Kate, as she smoothed down this and that article and laid them back into the trunk, telling how the blue gown would be the best for church and the green silk for going out to very fine places, to tea drinkings and the like, and how she must always be sure to wear the cream undersleeves with the Irish point lace with her silk gown as they set it off to perfection. She recalled, too, how little experience Marcia had in the ways of the world, and all the while the girl was being dressed in the dainty bridal garments she gave her careful instructions in the art of being a success in society, until Marcia felt that the green fields and the fences and trees to climb and the excursions after blackberries, and all the joyful merry-makings of the boys and girls were receding far from her. She could even welcome Hanford Weston as a playfellow in her near future, if thereby a little fresh air and freedom of her girlhood might be left. Nevertheless there gradually came over her an elation of excitement. The feel of the dainty garments, the delicate embroidery, the excitement lest the white slippers would not fit her, the difficulty in making her hair stay up in just Kate's style—for her stepmother insisted that she must dress it exactly like Kate's and make herself look as nearly as possible as Kate would have looked,—all drove sadness from her mind and she began to take a little delight in the pretty clothes, the great occasion, and her own importance. The vision in the looking glass, too, told her that her own face was winsome, and the new array not unbecoming. Something of this she had seen the night before when she put on the new chintz; now the change was complete, as she stood in the white satin and lace with a string of seed pearls that had been her mother's tied about her soft white throat. She thought about the tradition of the pearls that Kate's girlfriends had laughingly reminded her of a few days before when they were looking at the bridal garments. They had said that each pearl a bride wore to look with half-closed eyes at the effect, deciding that very few would notice that the bride was other than they had expected until the ceremony was over and the veil thrown back. The sisters had never looked alike, yet there was a general family resemblance that was now accentuated by the dress; perhaps only those nearest would notice that it was Marcia instead of Kate. At least the guests would have the good grace to keep their wondering to themselves until the ceremony was over.

Then Marcia was left to herself with trembling hands and wildly throbbing heart. What would Mary Ann think? What would all the girls and boys think? Some of them would be there, and others would be standing along the shady streets to watch the progress of the carriage as it drove away. And they would see her going away instead of Kate. Perhaps they would think it was all a great joke and that she had going to be married all the time and not Kate. But no; the truth would soon come out. People would not be astonished at anything Kate did. They would only say it was just what they had all along expected from her, and pity her father, and pity her perhaps. But they would look at her and admire her and for once she would be the centre of attraction. The pink of pride swelled up into her cheeks, and then realizing what she was thinking she crushed the feeling down. How could she think of such things when Kate had done such a dreadful thing, and David was suffering so terribly? Here was she actually enjoying, and delighting in the thought of being in Kate's place. Oh, she was wicked, wicked! She must not be happy for a moment in what was Kate's shame and David's sorrow. Of her future with David she did not now think. It was of the pageant of the day that her thoughts were full. If the days and weeks and months that were to follow came into her mind at all between the other things it was always that she was to care for David and to help him, and that she would have to grow up quickly; and remember all the hard housewifely things her stepmother had taught her; and try to order his house well. But that troubled her not at all at present. She was more concerned with the ceremony, and the many eyes that would be turned upon her. It was a relief when a tap came on the door and the dear old minister entered.

Chapter 6

He stood a moment by the door looking at her, half startled. Then he came over beside her, put his hands upon her shoulders, looking down into her upturned, veiled face.

"My child!" he said tenderly, "my little Marcia, is this you? I did not know you in all this beautiful dress. You look as your own mother looked when she was married. I remember perfectly as it were but yesterday, her face as she stood by your father's side. I was but a young man then, you know, and it was my first wedding in my new church, so you see I could not forget it. Your mother was a beautiful woman, Marcia, and you are like her both in face and life."

The tears came into Marcia's eyes and her lips trembled.

"Are you sure, child," went on the gentle voice of the old man, "that you understand what a solemn thing you are doing? It is not a light thing to give yourself in marriage to any man. You are so young yet! Are you doing this thing quite willingly, little girl? Are you sure? Your father is a good man, and a dear old friend of mine, but I know what has happened has been a terrible blow to him, and a great humiliation. It has perhaps unnerved his judgment for the time. No one should have brought pressure to bear upon a child like you to make you marry against your will. Are you sure it is all right, dear?"

"Oh, yes, sir!" Marcia raised her tear-filled eyes. "I am doing it quite of myself. No one has made me. I am glad I might. It was so dreadful for David!"

"But child, do you love him?" the old minister said, searching her face closely.

Marcia's eyes shone out radiant and childlike through her tears.

"Oh, yes, sir! I love him of course. No one could help loving David."

There was a tap at the door and the Squire entered. With a sigh the minister turned away, but there was trouble in his heart. The love of the girl had been all too frankly confessed. It was not as he would have had things for a daughter of his, but it could not be helped of course, and he had no right to interfere. He would like to speak to David, but David had not come out of his room yet. When he did there was but a moment for them alone and all he had opportunity to say was:

"Mr. Spafford, you will be good to the little girl, and remember she is but a child. She has been dear to us all."

David looked at him wonderingly, earnestly, in reply:

"I will do all in my power to make her happy," he said.

The hour had come, and all things, just as Madam Schuyler had planned, were ready. The minister took his place, and the impatient bridesmaids were

... ... scarcely felt the presence of the guests she had so much dreaded, for to her the ceremony was holy. She was giving herself as a sacrifice for the sin of her sister. She was too young and inexperienced to know all that would be thought and said as soon as the company understood. She also felt secure behind that film of lace. It seemed impossible that they could know her, so softly and so mistily it shut her in from the world. It was like a kind of moving house about her, a protection from all eyes. So sheltered she might go through the ceremony with composure. As yet she had not begun to dread the afterward. The hall was wide through which she passed, and the day was bright, but the windows were so shadowed by the waiting bridesmaids that the light did not fall in full glare upon her, and it was not strange they did not know her at once. She heard their smothered exclamations of wonder and admiration, and one, Kate's dearest friend, whispered softly behind her: "Oh, Kate, why did you keep us waiting, you sly girl! How lovely you are! You look like an angel straight from heaven."

There were other whispered words which Marcia heard sadly. They gave her no pleasure. The words were for Kate, not her. What would they say when they knew all?

There was David in the distance waiting for her. How fine he looked in his wedding clothes! How proud Kate might have been of him! How pitiful was his white face! He had summoned courage and put on a mask of happiness for the eyes of those who saw him, but it could not deceive the heart of Marcia. Surely not since the days when Jacob served seven years for Rachel and then lifted the bridal veil to look upon the face of her sister Leah, walked there sadder bridegroom on this earth than David Spafford walked that day.

Down the stairs and through the wide hall they came, Marcia not daring to look up, yet seeing familiar glimpses as she passed. That green plaid silk lap at one side of the parlor door, in which lay two nervous little hands and a neatly folded pocket handkerchief, belonged to Sabrina Bates, she knew; and the round lace collar a little farther on, fastened by the brooch with a colored daguerreotype encircled by a braid of faded brown hair under glass, must be about the neck of Aunt Polly. There was not another brooch like that in New York state, Marcia felt sure. Beyond were Uncle Joab's small meek Sunday boots, toeing in, and next were little feet covered by white stockings and slippers fastened with crossed black ribbons, some child's, not Harriet—Marcia dared not raise her eyes to identify them now. She must fix her mind upon the great things before her. She wondered at herself for noticing such trivial things when she was walking up to the presence of the great God, and there before her stood the minister with his open book!

Now, at last, with most of the audience behind her, shut in by the film of lace, she could raise her eyes to the minister's familiar face, take David's arm without letting her hand tremble much, and listen to the solemn words read out to her. For her alone they seemed to be read. David's heart she knew was crushed, and it was only a form for him. She must take double vows upon her for the sake of the wrong done to him. So she listened:

"Dearly beloved, we are gathered together" – how the words thrilled her! – "in the sight of God and in the presence of this company to join together this man and woman in the bonds of holy matrimony;" – a deathly stillness rested upon the room and the painful throbbing of her heart was all the little bride could hear. She was glad she might look straight into the dear face of the old minister. Had her mother felt this way when she was being married? Did her stepmother understand it? Yes, she must, in part at least, for she had bent and kissed her most tenderly upon the brow just before leaving her, a most sentimental thing for her to do. It touched Marcia deeply, though she was fond of her stepmother at all times.

She waited breathless with drooped eyes while the minister demanded, "If any man can show just cause why they may not be lawfully joined together, let him now declare it, or else hereafter hold his peace." What if some one should recognize her and, thinking she had usurped Kate's place, speak out and stop the marriage! How would David feel? And she? She would sink to the floor. Oh, did any of them know? How she wished she dared raise her eyes to look about and see. But she must not. She must listen. She must shake off these worldly thoughts. She was not hearing for idle thinking. It was a solemn, holy vow she was taking upon herself for life. She brought herself sharply back to the ceremony. It was to David the minister was talking now:

"Wilt thou love her, comfort her, honor and keep her, in sickness and in health, and forsaking all other, keep thee only unto her, so long as ye both shall live?"

It was hard to make David promise that when his heart belonged to Kate. She wondered that his voice could be so steady when it said, "I will," and the white glove of Kate's which was just a trifle too large for her, trembled on David's arm as the minister next turned to her:

"Wilt thou, Marcia" – Ah! It was out now! and the sharp rustle of silk and stiff linen showed that all the company were aware at last of who was the bride; but the minister went steadily on. He cared not what the listening assembly thought. He was talking earnestly to his little friend, Marcia, – "have this man to be thy wedded husband, to live together after God's ordinance in the holy estate of matrimony? Wilt thou obey him, and serve him, love, honor, and keep

...And the dear old minister's wife, sitting sweet and dove-like in her soft grey poplin, fine white kerchief, and cap of book muslin, smiled to herself at the music in Marcia's voice and nodded approval. She felt that all was well with her little friend.

They waited, those astonished people, till the ceremony was concluded and the prayer over, and then they broke forth. There had been lifted brows and looks passing from one to another, of question, of disclaiming any knowledge in the matter, and just as soon as the minister turned and took the bride's hand to congratulate her the heads bent together behind fans and the soft buzz of whispers began.

What does it mean? Where is Kate? She isn't in the room! Did he change his mind at the last minute? How old is Marcia? Mercy me! Nothing but a child! Are you sure? Why, my Mary Ann is older than that by three months, and she's no more able to become mistress of a home than a nine-days-old kitten. Are you sure that's Marcia? Didn't the minister make a mistake in the name? It looked to me like Kate. Look again. She's put her veil back. No, it can't be! Yes, it is! No, it looks like Kate! Her hair's done the same, but, no, Kate never had such a sweet innocent look like that. Why, when she was a child her face always had a sharpness to it. Look at Marcia's eyes, poor lamb! I don't see how her father could bear it, and she so young. But Kate! Where can she be? What has happened? You don't say! Yes, I did see that captain about again last week or so. Do you believe it? Surely she never would. Who told you? Was he sure? But Maria and Janet are bridesmaids and they didn't see signs of anything. They were over here yesterday. Yes, Kate showed them everything and planned how they would all walk in. No, she didn't do anything queer, for Janet would have mentioned it. Janet always sees everything. Well, they say he's a good man and Marcia'll be well provided for. Madam Schuyler'll be relieved about that. Marcia can't ever lead her the dance Kate has among the young men. How white he looks! Do you suppose he loves her? What on earth can it all mean? Do you s'pose Kate feels bad? Where is she anyway? Wouldn't she come down? Well, if 'twas his choosing it serves her right. She's too much of a flirt for a good man and maybe he found her out. She's probably got just what she deserves, and I think Marcia'll make a good little wife. She always was a quiet, grown-up child and Madam Schuyler trained her well! But what will Kate do now? Hush! They are coming this way. How do you suppose we can find out? Go ask Cousin Janet, perhaps they've told her, or Aunt Polly. Surely she knows.

But Aunt Polly sat with pursed lips of disapproval. She had not been told, and it was her prerogative to know everything. She always made a point of being on hand early at all funerals and weddings, especially in the family circle, and learning the utmost details, which she dispensed at her discretion to late comers in fine sepulchral whispers.

Now she sat silent, disgraced, unable to explain a thing. It was unhandsome of Sarah Schuyler, she felt, though no more than she might have expected of her, she told herself. She had never liked her. Well, wait until her opportunity came. If they did not wish her to say the truth she must say something. She could at least tell what she thought. And what more natural than to let it be known that Sarah Schuyler had always held a dislike for Marcia, and to suggest that it was likely she was glad to get her off her hands. Aunt Polly meant to find a trail somewhere, no matter how many times they threw her off the scent.

Meantime for Marcia the sun seemed to have shined out once more with something of its old brightness. The terrible deed of self-renunciation was over, and familiar faces actually were smiling upon her and wishing her joy. She felt the flutter of her heart in her throat beneath the string of pearls, and wondered if after all she might hope for a little happiness of her own. She could climb no more fences nor wade in gurgling brooks, but might there not be other happy things as good? A little touch of the pride of life had settled upon her. The relatives were coming with pleasant words and kisses. The blushes upon her cheeks were growing deeper. She almost forgot David in the pretty excitement. A few of her girl friends ventured shyly near, as one might look at a mate suddenly and unexpectedly translated into eternal bliss. They put out cold fingers in salute with distant, stiff phrases belonging to a grown-up world. Not one of them save Mary Ann dared recognize their former bond of playmates. Mary Ann leaned down and whispered with a giggle: "Say, you didn't need to envy Kate, did you? My! Ain't you in clover! Say, Marsh," wistfully, "do invite me fer a visit sometime, won't you?"

Now Mary Ann was not quite on a par with the Schuylers socially, and had it not been for a distant mutual relative she would not have been asked to the wedding. Marcia never liked her very much, but now, with the uncertain, dim future it seemed pleasant and home-like to think of a visit from Mary Ann and she nodded and said childishly: "Sometime, Mary Ann, if I can."

Mary Ann squeezed her hand, kissed her, blushed and giggled herself out of the way of the next comer.

They went out to the dining room and sat around the long table. It was Marcia's timid hand that cut the bridecake, and all the room full watched her. Seeing the pretty color come and go in her excited cheeks, they wondered that they had never noticed before how beautiful Marcia was growing. A handsome couple they would make! And they looked from Marcia to David and back again, wondering and trying to fathom the mystery.

...... questions as possible himself, and not to know too much before undertaking this task for his old friend the Squire.

And so Kate's marriage went into the annals of the village, at least so far as that morning was concerned, quietly, and with little exclamation before the family. The Squire and his wife controlled their faces wonderfully. There was an austerity about the Squire as he talked with his friends that was new to his pleasant face, but Madam conversed with her usual placid self-poise, and never gave cause for conjecture as to her true feelings.

There were some who dared to offer their surprised condolences. To such the stepmother replied that of course the outcome of events had been a sore trial to the Squire, and all of them, but they were delighted at the happy arrangement that had been made. She glanced contentedly toward the child-bride.

It was a revelation to the whole village that Marcia had grown up and was so handsome.

Dismay filled the breasts of the village gossips. They had been defrauded. Here was a fine scandal which they had failed to discover in time and spread abroad in its due course.

Everybody was shy of speaking to the bride. She sat in her lovely finery like some wild rose caught as a sacrifice. Yet every one admitted that she might have done far worse. David was a good man, with prospects far beyond most young men of his time. Moreover he was known to have a brilliant mind, and the career he had chosen, that of journalism, in which he was already making his mark, was one that promised to be lucrative as well as influential.

It was all very hurried at the last, Madam Schuyler and Dolly the maid helped her off with the satin and lace finery, and she was soon out of her bridal attire and struggling with the intricacies of Kate's travelling costume.

Marcia was not Marcia any longer, but Mrs. David Spafford. She had been made to feel the new name almost at once, and it gave her a sense of masquerading pleasant enough for the time being, but with a dim foreboding of nameless dread and emptiness for the future, like all masquerading which must end sometime. And when the mask is taken off how sad if one is not to find one's real self again: or worse still if one may never remove the mask, but must grow to it and be it from the soul.

All this Marcia felt but dimly of course, for she was young and light hearted naturally, and the excitement and pretty things about her could not but be pleasant.

To have Kate's friends stand about her, half shyly trying to joke with her as they might have done with Kate, to feel their admiring glances, and half envious references to her handsome husband, almost intoxicated her for the moment. Her cheeks grew rosier as she tied on Kate's pretty poke bonnet whose nodding blue flowers had been brought over from Paris by a friend of Kate's. It seemed a shame that Kate should not have her things after all. The pleasure died out of Marcia's eyes as she carefully looped the soft blue ribbons under her round chin and drew on Kate's long gloves. There was no denying the fact that Kate's outfit was becoming to Marcia, for she had that complexion that looks well with any color under the sun, though in blue she was not at her best.

When Marcia was ready she stood back from the little looking-glass, with a frightened, half-childish gaze about the room.

Now that the last minute was come, there was no one to understand Marcia's feelings nor help her. Even the girls were merely standing there waiting to say the last formal farewell that they might be free to burst into an astonished chatter of exclamations over Kate's romantic disappearance. They were Kate's friends, not Marcia's, and they were bidding Kate's clothes goodbye for want of the original bride. Marcia's friends were too young and too shy to do more than stand back in awe and gaze at their mate so suddenly promoted to a life which but yesterday had seemed years away for any of them.

So Marcia walked alone down hall — yet, no, not all the way alone. A little wrinkled hand was laid upon her gloved one, and a little old lady, her true friend, the minister's wife, walked down the stairs with the bride arm in arm. Marcia's heart fluttered back to warmth again and was glad for her friend, yet all she had said was: "My dear!" but there was that in her touch and the tone of her gentle voice that comforted Marcia.

She stood at the edge of the steps, with her white hair shining in the morning, her kind-faced husband just behind her during all the farewell, and Marcia felt happier because of her motherly presence.

The guests were all out on the piazza in the gorgeousness of the summer morning. David stood on the flagging below the step beside the open coach door, a carriage lap-robe over his arm and his hat on, ready. He was talking with the Squire. Every one was looking at them, and they were entirely conscious of the fact. They laughed and talked with studied pleasantness, though there seemed to be an undertone of sadness that the most obtuse guest could not fail to detect.

Harriet, as a small flower-girl, stood upon the broad low step ready to fling posies before the bride as she stepped into the coach.

... the tears, and the bride came back most decorously to where her stepmother stood awaiting her with a smile of complacent—almost completed—duty upon her face.

She wore the sense of having carried off a trying situation in a most creditable manner, and she knew she had won the respect and awe of every matron present thereby. That was a great deal to Madam Schuyler.

The stepmother's arms were around her and Marcia remembered how kindly they had felt when they first clasped her little body years ago, and she had been kissed, and told to be a good little girl. She had always liked her stepmother. And now, as she came to say good-bye to the only mother she had ever known, who had been a true mother to her in many ways, her young heart almost gave way, and she longed to hide in that ample bosom and stay under the wing on one who had so ably led her thus far along the path of life.

Perhaps Madam Schuyler felt the clinging of the girl's arms about her, and perchance her heart rebuked her that she had let so young and inexperienced a girl go out to the cares of life all of a sudden in this way. At least she stooped and kissed Marcia again and whispered: "You have been a good girl, Marcia."

Afterwards, Marcia cherished that sentence among memory's dearest treasures. It seemed as though it meant that she had fulfilled her stepmother's first command, given on the night when her father brought home their new mother.

Then the flowers were thrown upon the pavement, to make it bright for the bride. She was handed into the coach behind the white-haired negro coachman, and by his side Kate's fine new hair trunk. Ah! That was a bitter touch! Kate's trunk! Kate's things! Kate's husband! If it had only been her own little moth-eaten trunk that had belonged to her mother, and filled with her own things—and if he had only been her own husband! Yet she wanted no other than David—only if he could have been her David.

Then Madam Schuyler, her heart still troubled about Marcia, stepped down and whispered:

"David, you will remember she is young. You will deal gently with her?"

Gravely David bent his head and answered:

"I will remember. She shall not be troubled. I will care for her as I would care for my own sister." And Madam Schuyler turned away half satisfied. After all, was that what woman wanted? Would she have been satisfied to have been cared for as a sister?

Then gravely, with his eyes half unseeing her, the father kissed his daughter good-bye, David got into the coach, the door was slammed shut, and the white horses arched their necks and stepped away, amid a shower of rice and slippers.

...people of the village ...upon their doorsteps to watch the ...face of the bride was a puzzle and a surprise. They ...ected to see another coach coming with the other bride behind.

Marcia nodded brightly to those she knew, and threw flowers from the great nosegay that had been put upon her lap by Harriet. she felt for a few minutes like a girl in a fairy tale riding in this fine coach in grand attire. She stole a look at David. He certainly looked like a prince, but gravity was already settling about his mouth. Would he always look so now, she wondered, would he never laugh and joke again as he used to do? Could she manage to make him happy sometimes for a little while and help him to forget?

Down through the village they passed, in front of the store and post-office where Marcia had bought her frock but three days before, and they turned up the road she had come with Mary Ann. How long ago that seemed! How light her heart was then, and how young! All life was before her with its delightful possibilities. Now it seemed to have closed for her and she was some one else. A great ache came upon her heart. For a moment she longed to jump down and run away from the coach and David and the new clothes that were not hers. Away from the new life that had been planned for some one else which she must live now. She must always be a woman, never a girl any more.

Out past Granny McVane's they drove, the old lady sitting upon her front porch knitting endless stockings. She stared mildly, unrecognizingly at Marcia and paused in her rocking to crane her neck after the coach.

The tall corn rustled and waved green arms to them as they passed, and the cows looked up munching from the pasture in mild surprise at the turnout. The little coach dog stepped aside from the road to give them a bark as he passed, and then pattered and pattered his tiny feet to catch up. The old school house came in sight with its worn playground and dejected summer air, and Marcia's eyes searched out the window where she used to sit to eat her lunch in winters, and the tree under which she used to sit in summers, and the path by which she and Mary Ann used to wander down to the brook, or go in search of butternuts, even the old door knob that her hand would probably never grasp again. She searched them all out and bade them good-bye with her eyes. Then once she turned a little to see if she could catch a glimpse of the old blackboard through the window where she and Susanna Brown and Miller Thompson used to do arithmetic examples. The dust of the coach, or the bees in the sunshine, or something in her eyes blurred her vision. She could only see a long slant ray of a sunbeam crossing the wall where she knew it must be. Then the road wound around through a maple grove and the school was lost to view.

They passed the South meadow belonging to the Westons, and Hanford was plowing. Marcia could see him stop to wipe the perspiration from his brow, and her heart warmed even to this boy admirer now that she was going from him forever.

Hanford had caught sight of the coach and he turned to watch it thinking to see Kate sitting in the bride's place. He wondered if the bride would notice him, and turned a deeper red under his heavy coat of tan.

And the bride did notice him. She smiled the sweetest smile the boy had ever seen upon her face, the smile he had dreamed of as he thought of her, at night standing under the stars all alone by his father's gatepost whittling the cross bar of the gate. For a moment he forgot that it was the bridal party passing, forgot the stern-faced bridegroom and saw only Marcia—his girl love. His heart stood still, and a bright light of response filled his eyes. He took off his wide straw hat and bowed her reverence. He would have called to her, and tried three times, but his dry throat gave forth no utterance, and when he looked again the coach was passed and only the flutter of a white handkerchief came back to him and told him the beginning of the truth.

Then the poor boy's face grew white, yes, white and stricken under the tan, and he tottered to the roadside and sat down with his face in his hands to try and comprehend what it might mean, while the old horse dragged the plow whither he would in search of a bite of tender grass.

What could it mean? And why did Marcia occupy that place beside the stranger, obviously the bridegroom? Was she going on a visit? He had heard of no such plan. Where was her sister? Would there be another coach presently, and was this man then not the bridegroom but merely a friend of the family? Of course, that must be it. He got up and staggered to the fence to look down the road, but no one came by save the jogging old gray and carryall, with Aunt Polly grim and offended and Uncle Joab meek and depressed beside her. Could he have missed the bridal carriage when he was at the other end of the lot? Could they have gone another way? He had a half a mind to call to Uncle Joab to enquire only he was a timid boy and shrank back until it was too late.

But why had Marcia as she rode away wafted that strange farewell that had in it the familiarity of the final? And why did he feel so strange and weak in his knees?

Marcia was to help his mother next week at the quilting bee. She had not gone away to stay, of course. He got up and tried to whistle and turn the furrows evenly as before, but his heart was heavy, and, try as he would, he could not understand the feeling that kept telling him Marcia was gone out of his life forever.

... stood by her front gate in the dusk of the summer evening, the halo of her unusual wedding finery upon her, for she had taken advantage of being dressed up to make two or three visits since the wedding, and so prolong the holiday. The light of the sunset softened her plain features, and gave her a gentler look than was her wont. Was it that, and an air of lonesomeness akin to his own, that made Hanford stop and speak to her?

And then she told him. She could not keep it in long. It was the wonder of her life, and it filled her so that her thought had no room for anything else. To think of Marcia taken in a day, gone from their midst forever, gone to be a grown-up woman in a new world! It was as strange as sudden death, and almost as terrible and beautiful.

There were tears in her eyes, and in the eyes of the boy as they spoke about the one who was gone, and the kind dusk hid the sight so that neither knew, but each felt a subtle sympathy with the other, and before Hanford started upon his desolate way home under the burden of his first sorrow he took Mary Ann's slim bony hand in his and said quite stiffly: "Well, good-night, Miss Mary Ann. I'm glad you told me," and Mary Ann responded, with a deep blush under her freckles in the dark, "Good-night, Mr. Weston, and—call again!"

Something of the sympathy lingered with the boy as he went on his way and he was not without a certain sort of comfort, while Mary Ann climbed to her little chamber in the loft with a new wonder to dream over.

Meanwhile the coach drove on, and Marcia passed from her childhood's home into the great world of men and women, changes, heartbreakings, sorrows and joys.

David spoke to her kindly now and then; asked if she was comfortable; if she would prefer to change seats with him; if the cushions were right; and if she had forgotten anything. He seemed nervous, and anxious to have this part of the journey over and asked the coachman frequent questions about the horses and the speed they could make. Marcia thought she understood that he was longing to get away from the painful reminder of what he had expected to be a joyful trip, and her young heart pitied him, while yet it felt an undertone of hurt for herself. She found so much unadulterated joy in this charming ride with the beautiful horses, in this luxurious coach, that she could not bear to have it spoiled by the thought that only David's sadness and pain had made it possible for her.

Constantly as the scene changed, and new sights came upon her view, she had to restrain herself from crying out with happiness over the beauty and calling David's attention. Once she did point out a bird just leaving a stalk of goldenrod, its light touch making the spray to bow and bend. David had looked with unseeing eyes, and smiled with uncomprehending assent. Marcia felt she might as well have been talking to herself. He was not even the old friend and brother he used to be. She drew a gentle little sigh and wished this might have been only a happy ride with the ending at home, and a longer girlhood uncrossed by this wall of trouble that Kate had put up in a night for them all.

The coach came at last to the town where they were to stop for dinner and a change of horses.

Marcia looked about with interest at the houses, streets, and people. There were two girls of about her own age with long hair braided down their backs. They were walking with arms about each other as she and Mary Ann had often done. She wondered if any such sudden changes might be coming to them as had come into her life. They turned and looked at her curiously, enviously it seemed, as the coach drew up to the tavern and she was helped out with ceremony. Doubtless they thought of her as she had thought of Kate but last week.

She was shown into the dim parlor of the tavern and seated in a stiff hair-cloth chair. It was all new and strange and delightful.

Before a high gilt mirror set on great glass knobs like rosettes, she smoothed her wind-blown hair, and looked back at the reflection of her strange self with startled eyes. Even her face seemed changed. She knew the bonnet and arrangement of hair were becoming, but she felt unacquainted with them, and wished for her own modest braids and plain bonnet. Even a sunbonnet would have been welcome and have made her feel more like herself.

David did not see how pretty she looked when he came to take her to the dining room ten minutes later. His eyes were looking into the hard future, and he was steeling himself against the glances of others. He must be the model bridegroom in the sight of all who knew him. His pride bore him out in this. He had acquaintances all along the way home.

They were expecting the bridal party, for David had arranged that a fine dinner should be ready for his bride. Fine it was, with the best cooking and table service the mistress of the tavern could command, and with many a little touch new and strange to Marcia, and therefore interesting. It was all a lovely play till she looked at David.

David ate but little, and Marcia felt she must hurry through the meal for his sake. Then when the carryall was ready he put her in and they drove away.

Marcia's keen intuition told her how many little things had been thought of and planned for, for the comfort of the one who was to have taken this journey with David. Gradually the thought of how terrible it was for him, and how

... the sweet young face ... from him as much as possible that he might ... so they must have driven for half an hour through a dim sweet wood before he happened to catch a sight of the tear-wet face, and knew suddenly that there were other troubles in the world beside his own.

"Why, child, what is the matter?" he said, turning to her with grave concern. "Are you so tired? I'm afraid I have been very dull company," with a sigh. "You must forgive me child, to-day."

"Oh, David, don't," said Marcia putting her face down into her hands and crying now regardless of the roses. "I do not want you to think of me. It is dreadful, dreadful for you. I am so sorry for you. I wish I could do something."

"Dear child!" he said, putting his hand upon hers. "Bless you for that. But do not let your heart be troubled about me. Try to forget me and be happy. It is not for you to bear, this trouble."

"But I must bear it," said Marcia, sitting up and trying to stop crying. "She was my sister and she did an awful thing. I cannot forget it. How could she, how *could* she do it? How could she leave a man like you that—" Marcia stopped, her brown eyes flashing fiercely as she thought of Captain Leavenworth's hateful look at her that night in the moonlight. She shuddered and hid her face in her hands once more and cried with all the fervor of her young and undisciplined soul.

David did not know what to do with a young woman in tears. Had it been Kate his alarm would have vied with a delicious sense of his own power to comfort, but even the thought of comforting anyone but Kate was now a bitter thing. Was it always going to be? Would he always have to start and shrink with sudden remembrance of his pain at every turn of his way? He drew a deep sigh and looked helplessly at his companion. Then he did a hard thing. He tried to justify Kate, just as he had been trying all the morning to justify her to himself. The odd thing about it all was that the very deepest sting of his sorrow was that Kate could have done this thing! His peerless Kate!

"She cared for him," he breathed the words as if they hurt him.

"She should have told you so before then. She should not have let you think she cared for you—*ever!*" said Marcia fiercely. Strangely enough the plain truth was bitter to the man to hear, although he had been feeling it in his soul ever since they had discovered the flight of the bride.

"Perhaps there was too much pressure brought to bear upon her," he said lamely. "Looking back I can see times when she did not second me with regard to hurrying the marriage, so warmly as I could have wished. I laid it to her shyness. Yet she seemed happy when we met. Did you—did she—have you any idea she had been planning this for long, or was it sudden?"

The words were out now, the thing he longed to know. It had been writing its fiery way through his soul. Had she meant to torture him this way all along, or was it the yielding to a sudden impulse that perhaps she had already repented? He looked at Marcia with piteous, almost pleading eyes, and her tortured young soul would have given anything to have been able to tell him what he wanted to know. Yet she could not help him. She knew no more than he. She steadied her own nerves and tried to tell all she knew or surmised, tried her best to reveal Kate in her true character before him. Not that she wished to speak ill of her sister, only that she would be true and give this lover a chance to escape some of the pain if possible, by seeing the real Kate as she was at home without varnish or furbelows. Yet she reflected that those who knew Kate's shallowness well, still loved her in spite of it, and always bowed to her wishes.

Gradually their talk subsided into deep silence once more, broken only by the jog-trot of the horse or the stray note of some bird.

The road wound into the woods with its fragrant scents of hemlock, spruce and wintergreen, and out into a broad, hot, sunny way.

The bees hummed in the flowers, and the grasshoppers sang hotly along the side of the dusty road. Over the whole earth there seemed to be the sound of a soft simmering, as if nature were boiling down her sweets, the better to keep them during the winter.

The strain of the day's excitement and hurry and the weariness of sorrow were beginning to tell upon the two travellers. The road was heavy with dust and the horse plodded monotonously through it. With the drone of the insects and the glare of the afternoon sun, it was not strange that little by little a great drowsiness came over Marcia and her head began to droop like a poor wilted flower until she was fast asleep.

David noticed that she slept, and drew her head against his shoulder that she might rest more comfortably. Then he settled back to his own pain, a deeper pang coming as he thought how different it would have been if the head resting against his shoulder had been golden instead of brown. Then soon he too fell asleep, and the old horse, going slow, and yet more slowly, finding no urging voice behind her and seeing no need to hurry herself, came at last on the way to the shade of an apple tree, and halted, finding it a pleasant place to remain and think until the heat of the afternoon was passed. Awhile she ate the tender grass that grew beneath the generous shade, and nipped daintily at an apple or two that hung within tempting reach. Then she too drooped her white lashes, and nodded and drooped, and took an afternoon nap.

A farmer, trund... curiously

...made him somewhat ...hushed over the insinuation, and ...hung out guiltily upon the way as if to make up ...driver, however, was soon lost in his own troubles, which ...turned upon him with redoubled sharpness as new sorrow always does after brief sleep.

But Marcia slept on.

Chapter 8

Owing to the horse's nap by the roadside, it was quite late in the evening when they reached the town and David saw the lights of his own neighborhood gleaming in the distance. He was glad it was late, for now there would be no one to meet them that night. His friends would think, perhaps, that they had changed their plans and stopped over night on the way, or met with some detention.

Marcia still slept.

David as he drew near the house began to feel that perhaps he had made a mistake in carrying out his marriage just as if nothing had happened and everything was all right. It would be too great a strain upon him to live there in that house without Kate, and come home every night just as he had planned it, and not to find her there to greet him as he had hoped. Oh, if he might turn even now and flee from it, out into the wilderness somewhere and hide himself from human kind, where no one would know, and no one ever ask him about his wife!

He groaned in spirit as the horse drew up to the door, and the heavy head of the sweet girl who was his wife reminded him that he could not go away, but must stay and face the responsibilities of life which he had taken upon himself, and bear the pain that was his. It was not the fault of the girl he had married. She sorrowed for him truly, and he felt deeply grateful for the great thing she had done to save his pride.

He leaned over and touched her shoulder gently to rouse her, but her sleep was deep and healthy, the sleep of exhausted youth. She did not rouse nor even open her eyes, but murmured half audibly, "David has come, Kate, hurry!"

Half guessing what had passed the night he arrived, David stooped and tenderly gathered her up in his arms. He felt a bond of kindliness far deeper than brotherly love. It was a bond of common suffering, and by her own choice she had made herself his comrade in his trouble. He would at least save her what suffering he could.

She did not waken as he carried her into the house, nor when he took her upstairs and laid her gently upon the white bed that had been prepared for the bridal chamber.

The moonlight stole in at the small-paned windows and fell across the floor, showing every object in the room plainly. David lighted a candle and set it upon the high mahogany chest of drawers. The light flickered and played over the sweet face and Marcia slept on.

David

...the jaunty poke bonnet
..., unused to the confinement of combs, fell
...p-flushed face. Contentedly she nestled down, the bonnet
...of her way, her red lips parted the least bit with a half-smile, the black lashes lying upon her rosy cheek, one childish hand upon which gleamed the new wedding ring—that was not hers,—lying relaxed and appealing upon her breast, rising and falling with her breath. A lovely bride!

David, stern, true, pained and appreciative, suddenly awakened to what a dreadful thing he had done.

Here was this lovely woman, her womanhood not yet unfolded from the bud, but lovely in promise even as her sister had been in truth, her charms, her dreams, her woman's ways, her love, her very life, taken by him as ruthlessly and as thoughtlessly as though she had been but a wax doll, and put into a home where she could not possibly be what she ought to be, because the place belonged to another. Thrown away upon a man without a heart! That was what she was! A sacrifice to his pride! There was no other way to put it.

It fairly frightened him to think of the promises he had made. "Love, honor, cherish," yes, all those he had promised, and in a way he could perform, but not in the sense that the wedding ceremony had meant, not in the way in which he would have performed them had the bride been Kate, the choice of his love. Oh, why, why had this awful thing come upon him!

And now his conscience told him he had done wrong to take this girl away from the possibilities of joy in the life that might have been hers, and sacrifice her for the sake of saving his own sufferings, and to keep his friends from knowing that the girl he was to marry had jilted him.

As he stood before the lovely, defenseless girl her very beauty and innocence arraigned him. He felt that God would hold him accountable for the act he had so thoughtlessly committed that day, and a burden of responsibility settled upon his weight of sorrow that made him groan aloud. For a moment his soul cried out against it in rebellion. Why could he not have loved this sweet self-sacrificing girl instead of her fickle sister? Why? Why? She might perhaps have loved him in return, but now nothing could ever be! Earth was filled with a black sorrow, and life henceforth meant renunciation and one long struggle to hide his trouble from the world.

But the girl he had selfishly drawn into the darkness of his sorrow with him, she must not be made to suffer more than he could help. He must try to make her happy, and keep her as much as possible from knowing what she had missed by coming with him! His lips in stern resolve, and a purpose, half prayer, went up on record before God, that he would save her as much as he knew how.

Lying helpless so, she appealed to him. Asking nothing she yet demanded all from him in the name of true chivalry. How readily she had given up all for him! How sweetly she had said she would fill the place left vacant by her sister, just to save him pain and humiliation!

A desire to stoop and kiss the fair face came to him, not for affection's sake, but reverently, as if to render to her before God some fitting sign that he knew and understood her act of self sacrifice, and would not presume upon it.

Slowly, as though he were performing a religious ceremony, a sacred duty laid upon him on high, David stooped over her, bringing his face to the gentle sleeping one. Her sweet breath fanned his cheek like the imperceptible fragrance of a bud not fully opened yet to give forth its sweetness to the world. His soul, awake and keen through the thoughts that had just come to him, gave homage to her sweetness, sadly, wistfully, half wishing his spirit free to gather this sweetness for his own.

And so he brought his lips to hers, and kissed her, his bride, yet not his bride. Kissed her for the second time. That thought came to him with the touch of the warm lips and startled him. Had there been something significant in the fact that he had met Marcia first and kissed her instead of Kate by mistake?

It seemed as though the sleeping lips clung to his lingeringly, and half responded to the kiss, as Marcia in her dreams lived over and over again the kiss she had received by her father's gate in the moonlight. Only the dream lover was her own and not another's. David, as he lifted up his head and looked at her gravely, saw a half smile illuminating her lips as if the sleeping soul within had felt the touch and answered to the call.

With a deep sigh he turned away, blew out the candle, and left her with the moonbeams in her chamber. He walked sadly to a rear room of the house and lay down upon the bed, his whole soul crying out in agony at his miserable state.

Kate, the careless one, who had made all this heart-break and misery, had quarreled with her husband already because he did not further some expensive whim of hers. She had told him she was sorry she had not stayed where she was and carried on her marriage with David as she had planned to do. Now she sat sulkily in her room alone, too angry to sleep; while her husband smoked sullenly in the barroom below, and drank frequent glasses of brandy to fortify himself against Kate's moods.

Kate was considering whether or not she had been a fool in marrying the captain instead of David, though she called herself by a much milder word than that. The romance was already worn away. She wished for her trunk and her pretty furb___

_____ ___, and
_____ ___ captain ever would.
_____ ___ sure, and perhaps, by and by, when
_____ forgotten and forgiven, she might establish a pleasant
_____nship with him again. It would be charming to coquet with him. He made love so earnestly, and his great eyes were so handsome when he looked at one with his whole soul in them. Yes, she certainly must keep in with him, for it would be good to have a friend like that when her husband was off at sea with his ship. Now that she was a married woman she would be free of all such childish trammels as being guarded at home and never going anywhere alone. She could go to New York, and she would let David know where she was and he would come up on business and perhaps take her to the theatre. To be sure, she had heard David express views against theatre-going, and she knew he was as much of a church man, almost, as her father, but she was sure she could coax him to do anything for her, and she had always wanted to go to the theatre. His scruples might be strong, but she knew his love for her, and thought it was stronger. She had read in his eyes that it would never fail her. Yes, she thought, she would begin at once to make a friend of David. She would write him a letter asking forgiveness, and she would keep him under her influence. There was no telling what would happen with her husband off at sea so much. It was well to be foresighted, besides, it would be wholesome for the captain to know she had another friend. He might be less stubborn. What a nuisance the marriage vows had to be taken for life! It would be much nicer if they could be put off as easily as they were put on. Rather hard on some women, perhaps, but she could keep any man as long as she chose, and then—she snapped her pretty thumb and finger in the air to express her utter disdain for the man she chose to cast off.

It seemed that Kate, in running away from her father's house and her betrothed bridegroom, and in breaking the laws of respectable society, had with that act given over all attempt at any principle.

So she set herself down to write her letter, with a pout here and a dimple there, and as much pretty gentleness as if she had been talking with her own bewitching face and eyes quite near to his. She knew she could bewitch him if she chose, and she was in the mood just now to choose very much, for she was deeply angry with her husband.

She had ever been utterly heartless when she pleased, knowing that it needed but her returning smile, sweet as a May morning, to bring her much abused subjects fondly to her feet once more. It did not strike her that this time she had sinned not only against her friends, but against heaven, and God-given love, and that a time of reckoning must come to her,—had come, indeed.

She had never believed they would be angry with her, her father least of all. She had no thought they would do anything desperate. She had expected the wedding would be put off indefinitely, that the servants would be sent out hither and yon in hot haste to unbid the guests, upon some pretext of accident or illness, and that it would be left to rest until the village had ceased to wonder and her real marriage with Captain Leavenworth could be announced.

She had counted upon David to stand up for her. She had not understood how her father's righteous soul would be stirred to the depths of shame and utter disgrace over her wanton action. Not that she would have been in the least deterred from doing as she pleased had she understood, only that she counted upon too great power with all of them.

When the letter was written it sounded quite pathetic and penitent, putting all the blame of her action upon her husband, and making herself out a poor, helpless, sweet thing, bewildered by so much love put upon her, and suggesting, just in hint, that perhaps after all she had made a mistake not to have kept David's love instead of a wilder, fiercer one. She ended by begging David to be her friend forever, and leaving an impression with him, though it was slight, that already shadows had crossed her path that made her feel his friendship might be needed some day.

It was a letter calculated to drive such a lover as David had been, half mad with anguish, even without the fact of his hasty marriage added to the situation.

And in due time, by coach, the letter came to David.

...sunbeams fell across the floor when Marcia awoke suddenly to a sense of her new surroundings. For a moment she could not think where she was or how she came there. She looked about the unfamiliar walls, covered with paper decorated in landscapes—a hill in the distance with a tall castle among the trees, a blue lake in the foreground and two maidens sitting pensively upon a green bank with their arms about one another. Marcia liked it. She felt there was a story in it. She would like to imagine about the lives of those two girls when she had more time.

There were no pictures in the room to mar those upon the paper, but the walls did not look bare. Everything was new and stiff and needed a woman's hand to bring the little homey touches, but the newness was a delight to the girl. It was as good as the time when she was a little girl and played house with Mary Ann down on the old flat stone in the pasture, with acorns for cups and saucers, and bits of broken china carefully treasured upon the mossy shelves in among the roots of the old elm tree that arched over the stone.

She was stiff from the long ride, but her sleep had wonderfully refreshed her, and now she was ready to go to work. She wondered as she rose how she got upon that bed, how the blue bonnet got untied and laid upon the chair beside her. Surely she could not have done it herself and have no memory of it. Had she walked upstairs by herself, or did some one carry her? Did David perhaps? Good kind David! A bird hopped upon the window seat and trilled a song, perked his head knowingly at her and flitted away. Marcia went to the window to look after him, and was held by the new sights that met her gaze. She could catch glimpses of houses through bowers of vines, and smoke rising from chimneys. She wondered who lived near, and if there were girls who would prove pleasant companions. Then she suddenly remembered that she was a girl no longer and must associate with married women hereafter.

But suddenly the clock on the church steeple across the way warned her that it was late, and with a sense of deserving reprimand she hurried downstairs.

The fire was already lighted and David had brought in fresh water. So much his intuition had told him was necessary. He had been brought up by three maiden aunts who thought that a man in the kitchen was out of his sphere, so the kitchen was an unknown quantity to him.

Marcia entered the room as if she were not quite certain of her welcome. She was coming into a kingdom she only half understood.

"Good morning," she said shyly, and a lovely color stole into her cheeks. Once more David's conscience smote him as her waking beauty intensified the impression made the night before.

"Good morning," he said gravely, studying her face as he might have studied some poor waif whom he had unknowingly run over in the night and picked up to resuscitate. "Are you rested? You were very tired last night."

"What a baby I was!" said Marcia deprecatingly, with a soft little gurgle of a laugh like a merry brook. David was amazed to find she had two dimples located about where Kate's were, only deeper, and more gentle in their expression.

"Did I sleep all the afternoon after we left the canal? And did you have hard work to get me into the house and upstairs?"

"You slept most soundly," said David, smiling in spite of his heavy heart. "It seemed a pity to waken you, so I did the next best thing and put you to bed as well as I knew how."

"It was very good of you," said Marcia, coming over to him with her hands clasped earnestly, "and I don't know how to thank you."

There was something quaint and old-fashioned in her way of speaking, and it struck David pitifully that she should be thanking her husband, the man who had pledged himself to care for her all his life. It seemed that everywhere he turned his conscience would continually be reproaching him.

It was a dainty breakfast to which they presently sat down. There was plenty of bread and fresh butter just from the hands of the best butter-maker in the county; the eggs had been laid the day before and the bacon was browned just right. Marcia well knew how to make coffee, there was cream rich and yellow as ever came from the cows at home and there was blackberries as large and fine every bit as those Marcia picked but a few days before for the purchase of her pink sprigged chintz.

David watched her deft movements and all at once keen smiting conscience came to remind him that Marcia was defrauded of all the loving interchange of mirth that would have been if Kate had been here. Also, keener still the thought that Kate had not wanted it: that she had preferred the love of another man to his, and that these joys had not been held in dear anticipation with her as they had with him. He had been a fool. All these months of waiting for his marriage he had thought that he and Kate held feelings in common, joys and hopes and tender thoughts of one another; and, behold, he was having these feelings all to himself, fool and blind that he was! A bitter sigh came to his lips, and Marcia, eager in the excitement of getting her first breakfast upon her own responsibility, heard and forgot to smile over the completed work. She could hardly eat what she had prepared, her heart felt David's sadness so keenly.

...ы at twelve.

...ьлg, as she must be weary yet. Then

...ьш out and closed the door behind him. He waited again on the door stone outside and opened the door to ask:

"You won't be lonesome, will you, child?" He had the feeling of troubled responsibility upon him.

"Oh, no!" said Marcia brightly, smiling back. She thought it so kind of him to take the trouble to think of her. She was quite anticipating a trip of investigation over her new domain, and the pleasure of feeling that she was mistress and might do as she pleased. Yet she stood by the window after he was gone and watched his easy strides down the street with a feeling of mingled pride and disappointment. It was a very nice play she was going through, and David was handsome, and her young heart swelled with pride to belong to him, but after all there was something left out. A great lack, a great unknown longing unsatisfied. What was it? What made it? Was it David's sorrow?

She turned with a sigh as he disappeared around a curve in the sidewalk and was lost to view. Then casting aside the troubles which were trying to settle upon her, she gave herself up to a morning of pure delight.

She flew about the kitchen putting things to rights, washing the delicate sprigged china with its lavender sprays and buff bands, and putting it tenderly upon the shelves behind the glass doors; shoving the table back against the wall demurely with dropped leaves. It did not take long.

There was no need to worry about the dinner. There was a leg of lamb beautifully cooked, half a dozen pies, their flaky crusts bearing witness to the culinary skill of the aunts, a fruit cake, a pound cake, a jar of delectable cookies and another of fat sugary doughnuts, three loaves of bread, and a sheet of puffy rusks with their shining tops dusted with sugar. Besides the preserve closet was rich in all kinds of preserves, jellies and pickles. No, it would not take long to get dinner.

It was into the great parlor that Marcia peeped first. It had been toward that room that her hopes and fears had turned while she washed the dishes.

The Schuylers were one of the few families in those days that possessed a musical instrument, and it had been the delight of Marcia's heart. She seemed to have a natural talent for music, and many an hour she spent at the old spinet drawing tender tones from the yellowed keys. The spinet had been in the family for years and very proud had the Schuyler girls been of it. Kate could rattle off gay waltzes and merry, rollicking tunes that fairly made the feet of the sedate village maidens flutter in time to their melody, but Marcia's music had always been more tender and spiritual. Dear old hymns, she loved, and some of the old classics. "Stupid old things without any tune," Kate called them. But Marcia persevered in playing them until she could bring out the beautiful passages in a way that at least satisfied herself. Her one great desire had been to take lessons of a real musician and be able to play the wonderful things that the old masters had composed. It is true that very few of these had come her way. One somewhat mutilated copy of Haydn's "Creation," a copy of Handel's "Messiah," and a few fragments of an old book of Bach's Fugues and Preludes. Many of these she could not play at all, but others she had managed to pick out. A visit from a cousin who lived in Boston and told of the concerts given there by the Handel and Haydn Society had served to strengthen her deeper interest in music. The one question that had been going over in her mind ever since she awoke had been whether there was a musical instrument in the house. She felt that if there was not she would miss the old spinet in her father's house more than any other thing about her childhood's home.

So with fear and trepidation she entered the darkened room, where the careful aunts had drawn the thick green shades. The furniture stood about in shadowed corners, and every footfall seemed a fearsome thing.

Marcia's bright eyes hurried furtively about, noting the great glass knobs that held the lace curtains with heavy silk cords, the round mahogany table, with its china vase of "everlastings," the high, stiff-backed chairs all decked in elaborate antimacassars of intricate pattern. Then, in the furthest corner, shrouded in dark coverings she found what she was searching for. With a cry she sprang to it, touched its polished wood with gentle fingers, and lovingly fell for the keyboard. It was closed. Marcia pushed up the shade to see better, and opened the instrument cautiously.

It was a pianoforte of the latest pattern, and with exclamations of delight she sat down and began to strike chords, softly at first, as if half afraid, then more boldly. The tone was sweeter than the old spinet, or the harpsichord owned by Squire Hartrandt. Marcia marvelled at the volume of sound. It filled the room and seemed to echo through the empty halls.

She played soft little airs from memory, and her soul was filled with joy. Now she knew she would never be lonely in the new life, for she would always have this wonderful instrument to flee to when she felt homesick.

Across the hall were two rooms, the front one furnished as a library. Here were rows of books behind glass doors. Marcia looked at them with awe. Might she read them all? She resolved to cultivate her mind that she might be a fit companion for David. She knew he was wise beyond his years for she had heard her father say so. She went nearer and scanned the titles, and at once there looked out to her from the rows of bindings a few familiar faces of books she had read and re-read. *Thaddeus of Warsaw, the Scottish Chiefs, Mysteries of*

... sunny sitting room, or breakfast room,—or dining room" as it would be called at the present time. In Marcia's time the family ate most of their meals in one end of the large bright kitchen, that end furnished with a comfortable lounge, a few bookshelves, a thick ingrain carpet, and a blooming geranium in the wide window seat. But there was always the other room for company, for "high days and holidays."

Out of this morning room the pantry opened with its spicy odors of preserves and fruit cake.

Marcia looked about her well pleased. The house itself was a part of David's inheritance, his mother's family homestead. Things were all on a grand scale for a bride. Most brides began in a very simple way and climbed up year by year. How Kate would have liked it all! David must have had in mind her fastidious tastes, and spent a great deal of money in trying to please her. The piano must have been very expensive. Once more Marcia felt how David had loved Kate and a pang went through her as she wondered however he was to live without her. Her young soul had not yet awakened to the question of how *she* was to live with *him,* while his heart went continually mourning for one who was lost to him forever.

The rooms upstairs were all pleasant, spacious, and comfortably furnished. There was no suggestion of bareness or anything left unfinished. Much of the furniture was old, having belonged to David's mother, and was in a state of fine preservation, a possession of which to be justly proud.

There were four rooms besides the one in which Marcia had slept: a front and back on the opposite side of the hall, a room just back of her own, and one at the end of the hall over the large kitchen.

She entered them all and looked about. The three beside her own in the front part of the house were all large and airy, furnished with high four-posted bedsteads, and pretty chintz hangings. Each was immaculate in its appointments. Cautiously she lifted the latch of the back room. David had not slept in any of the others, for the bedcoverings and pillows were plump and undisturbed. Ah! It was here in the back room that he had carried his heavy heart, as far away from the rest of the house as possible!

The bed was rumpled as if some one had thrown himself heavily down without stopping to undress. There was water in the washbowl and a towel lay carelessly across a chair as if it had been hastily used. There was a newspaper on the bureau and a handkerchief on the floor. Marcia looked sadly about at the signs of occupancy, her eyes dwelling upon each detail. It was here that David had suffered, and her loving heart longed to help him in his suffering.

But there was nothing in the room to keep her, and remembering the fire she had left upon the hearth, which must be almost spent and need replenishing by this time, she turned to go downstairs.

Just at the door something caught her eye under the edge of the chintz valence round the bed. It was but the very tip of the corner of an old daguerreotype, but for some reason Marcia was moved to stoop and draw it from its concealment. Then she saw it was her sister's saucy, pretty face that laughed back at her in defiance from the picture.

As if she had touched something red hot Marcia dropped it, and pushed it with her foot far back under the bed. Then shutting the door quickly she went downstairs. Was it always to be thus? Would Kate ever blight all her joy from this time forth?

As he stood in the doorway of the wide kitchen and caught the odor of the steaming platter of green corn she was putting on the table, David suddenly realized that he had scarcely eaten anything for breakfast.

Also, he felt a certain comfort from the sweet steady look of wistful sympathy in Marcia's eyes. Did he fancy it, or was there a new look upon her face, a more reserved bearing, less childish, more touched by sad knowledge of life and its bitterness? It was mere fancy of course, something he had just not noticed. He had seen so little of her before.

In the heart of the maiden there stirred a something which she did not quite understand, something brought to life by the sight of her sister's daguerreotype lying at the edge of the valence, where it must have fallen from David's pocket without his knowledge as he lay asleep. It had seemed to put into tangible form the solid wall of fact that hung between her and any hope of future happiness as a wife, and for the first time she too began to realize what she had sacrificed in thus impetuously throwing her young life into the breach that it might be healed. But she was not sorry, — not yet, anyway, — only frightened, and filled with dreary forebodings.

The meal was a pleasant one, though constrained. David roused himself to be cheerful for Marcia's sake, as he would have done for any stranger, and the girl, suddenly grown sensitive, felt it, and appreciated it, yet did not understand why it made her unhappy.

She was anxious to please him, and kept asking if the potatoes were seasoned right and if his corn were tender, and if he wouldn't have another cup of coffee. Her cheeks were quite red with the effort at matronly dignity when David was finally through his dinner and gone back to the office, and two big tears came and sat in her eyes for a moment, but were persuaded with a determined effort to sink back again into the unfathomable wells that lie in the depths of a woman's eyes. She longed to get out of doors and run wild and free in the old South pasture for relief. She did not know how different it all was from the first dinner of the ordinary young married couple; so stiff and formal, with no gentle touches, no words of love, no glances that told more than words. And yet, child as she was, she felt it, a lack somewhere, she knew not what.

But training is a great thing. Marcia had been trained to be on the alert for the next duty and to do it before she gave herself time for any of her own thoughts. The dinner table was awaiting her attention, and there was company coming.

She glanced at the tall clock in the hall and found she had scarcely an hour before she might expect David's aunts, for David had brought her word that they would come and spend the afternoon and stay for tea.

She shrank from the ordeal and wished David had seen fit to stay and introduce her. It would have been a relief to have had him for a shelter. Somehow she knew that he would have stayed if it had been Kate, and the thought pained her, with a quick sharpness like the sting of an insect. She wondered if she were growing selfish, that it should hurt to find herself of so little account. And, yet, it was to be expected, and she must stop thinking about it. Of course, Kate was the one he had chosen and Kate would always be the only one to him.

It did not take her long to reduce the dinner table to order and put all things in readiness for tea time; and in doing her work Marcia's thoughts flew to pleasanter themes. She wondered what Dolly and Debby, the servants at home, would say if they could see her pretty china and the nice kitchen. They had always been fond of her, and naturally her new honors made her wish to have her old friends see her. What would Mary Ann say? What fun it would be to have Mary Ann there sometime. It would be almost like the days when they had played house under the old elm on the big flat stone, only this would be a real house with real sprigged china instead of bits of broken things. Then she fell into a song, one they sang in school,

> "Sister, thou wast mild and lovely,
> Gentle as the summer breeze,
> Pleasant as the air of evening
> When it floats among the trees."

But the first words set her to thinking of her own sister, and how little the song applied to her, and she thought with a sigh how much better it would have been, how much less bitter, if Kate had been that way and had lain down to die and they could have laid her away in the little hilly graveyard under the weeping willows, and felt about her as they did about the girl for whom that song was written.

The work was done, and Marcia arrayed in one of the simplest of Kate's afternoon frocks, when the brass knocker sounded through the house, startling her with its unfamiliar sound.

Breathlessly she hurried downstairs. The crucial moment had come when she must stand to meet her new relatives alone. With her hand trembling she opened the door, but there was only one person standing on the stoop, a girl of about her own age, perhaps a few months younger. Her hair was red, her face

I was jest crazy to see how you looked. I've ben watchin' out o' the window all the morning, but I couldn't ketch a glimpse of you. When David came out this morning I thought you'd sure be at the kitchen door to kiss him good-bye, but you wasn't, and I watched every chance I could get, but I couldn't see you till you ran out in the garden fer corn. Then I saw you good, fer I was out hangin' up the dish towels. You didn't have a sunbonnet on, so I could see real well. And when I saw how young you was I made up my mind I'd get acquainted in spite of Grandma. You don't mind my comin' over this way without bein' dressed up, do you? There wouldn't be any way to get here without Grandma seeing me, you know, if I'd put on my Sunday clo'es."

"I'm glad you came!" said Marcia impulsively, feeling a rush of something like tears in her throat at the relief of delay from the aunts. "Come in and sit down. Who are you, and why wouldn't your Grandmother like you to come?"

The strange girl laughed a mirthless laugh.

"Me? Oh, I'm Mirandy. Nobody ever calls me anything but Mirandy. My pa left ma when I was a baby an' never come back, an' ma died, and I live with Grandma Heath. An' Grandma's mad 'cause David didn't marry Hannah Heath. She wanted him to an' she did everything she could to make him pay 'tention to Hannah, give her fine silk frocks, two of 'em, and a real pink parasol, but David he never seemed to know the parasol was pink at all, fer he'd never offer to hold it over Hannah even when Grandma made him walk with her home from church ahead of us. So when it came out that David was really going to marry, and wouldn't take Hannah, Grandma got as mad as mad could be and said we never any of us should step over his door sill. But I've stepped, I have, and Grandma can't help herself."

"And who is Hannah Heath?" questioned the dazed young bride. It appeared there was more than a sister to be taken into account.

"Hannah? Oh, Hannah is my cousin, Uncle Jim's oldest daughter, and she's getting on toward thirty somewhere. She has whitey-yellow hair and light blue eyes and is tall and real pretty. She held her head high fer a good many years waitin' fer David, and I guess she feels she made a mistake now. I noticed she bowed real sweet to Hermon Worcester last Sunday and let him hold her parasol all the way to Grandma's gate. Hannah was mad as hops when she heard that you had gold hair and blue eyes, for it did seem hard to be beaten by a girl of the same kind? but you haven't, have you? Your hair is almost black and your eyes are brownie-brown. You're years younger than Hannah, too. My! Won't she be astonished when she sees you! But I don't understand how it got around about your having gold hair. It was a man that stopped at your father's house once told it—"

"It was my sister!" said Marcia, and then blushed crimson to think how near she had come to revealing the truth which must not be known.

"Your sister? Have you got a sister with gold hair?"

"Yes, he must have seen her," said Marcia confusedly. She was not used to evasion.

"How funny!" said Miranda. "Well, I'm glad he did, for it made Hannah so jealous it was funny. But I guess she'll get a set-back when she sees how young you are. You're not as pretty as I thought you would be, but I believe I like you better."

Miranda's frank speech reminded Marcia of Mary Ann and made her feel quite at home with her curious visitor. She did not mind being told she was not up to the mark of beauty. From her point of view she was not nearly so pretty as Kate, and her only fear was that her lack of beauty might reveal the secret and bring confusion to David. But she need not have feared: no one watching the two girls, as they sat in the large sunny room and faced each other, but would have smiled to think the homely crude girl could suggest that the other calm, cool bud of womanhood was not as near perfection of beauty as a bud could expect to come. There was always something childlike about Marcia's face, especially her profile, something deep and other-world-like in her eyes, that gave her an appearance so distinguished from other girls that the word "pretty" did not apply, and surface observers might have passed her by when searching for prettiness, but not so those who saw soul beauties.

But Miranda's time was limited, and she wanted to make as much of it as possible.

"Say, I heard you making music this morning. Won't you do it for me? I'd just love to hear you."

Marcia's face lit up with responsive enthusiasm, and she led the way to the darkened parlor and folded back the covers of the precious piano. She played some tender little airs she loved as she would have played them for Mary Ann, and the two young things stood there together, children in thought and feeling, half a generation apart in position, and neither recognized the difference.

"My land!" said the visitor, " 'f I could play like that I wouldn't care ef I had freckles and no father and red hair," and looking up Marcia saw tears in the light blue eyes, and knew she had a kindred feeling in her heart for Miranda.

They had been talking a minute or two when the knocker suddenly sounded through the long hall again making both girls start. Miranda boldly tiptoed over to the front window and peeped between the green slats of the Venetian blind to see who was at the door, while Marcia started guiltily and quickly closed the instrument.

"But you haven't been to the store," said Marcia in a dismayed whisper.

"Oh, well, that don't matter! I'll tell her they didn't have what she sent me for. Good-bye. You better hurry." So saying, she disappeared into the kitchen; and Marcia, startled by such easy morality, stood dazed until the knocker sounded forth again, this time a little more peremptorily, as the elder aunt took her turn at it.

And so at last Marcia was face to face with the Misses Spafford.

They came in, each with her knitting in a black silk bag on her slim arm, and greeted the flushed, perturbed Marcia with gentle, righteous, rigid inspection. She felt with the first glance that she was being tried in the fire, and that it was to be no easy ordeal through which she was to pass. They had come determined to sift her to the depths and know at once the worst of what their beloved nephew had brought upon himself. If they found aught wrong with her they meant to be kindly and loving with her, but they meant to take it out of her. This had been the unspoken understanding between them as they wended their dignified, determined way to David's house that afternoon, and this was what Marcia faced as she opened the door for them.

She gasped a little, as any girl overwhelmed thus might have done. She did not tilt her chin in defiance as Kate would have done. The thought of David came to support her, and she grasped for her own little part and tried to play it creditably. She did not know whether the aunts knew of her true identity or not, but she was not left long in doubt.

"My dear, we have long desired to know you, of whom we have heard so much," recited Miss Amelia, with slightly agitated mien, as she bestowed a cool kiss of duty upon Marcia's warm cheek. It chilled the girl, like the breath of a funeral flower.

"Yes, it is indeed a pleasure to us to at last look upon our dear nephew's wife," said Miss Hortense quite precisely, and laid the sister kiss upon the other cheek. In spite of her there flitted through Marcia's brain the verse, "Whosoever shall smite thee on thy right cheek, turn to him the other also." Then she was shocked at her own irreverence and tried to put away a hysterical desire to laugh.

The aunts, too, were somewhat taken aback. They had not looked for so girlish a wife. She was not at all what they had pictured. David had tried to describe Kate to them once, and this young, sweet, disarming thing did not in the least fit their preconceived ideas of her. What should they do? How could they carry on a campaign planned against a certain kind of enemy, when lo, as they came upon the field of action the supposed enemy had taken another and more bewildering form than the one for whom they prepared. They were for the moment silent, gathering their thoughts, and trying to fit their intended tactics to the present situation.

During this operation, Marcia helped them to remove their bonnets and silk capes and to lay them neatly on the parlor sofa. She gave them chairs, suggested palm-leaf fans, and looked about, for the moment forgetting that this was not her old home plentifully supplied with those gracious breeze wafters.

They watched her graceful movements, those two angular old ladies, and marvelled over her roundness and suppleness. They saw with appalled hearts what a power youth and beauty might have over a man. Perhaps she might be even worse than they had feared, though if you could have heard them talk about their nephew's coming bride to their neighbors for months beforehand, you would have supposed they knew her to be a model in every required direction. But their stately pride required that of them, an outward loyalty at least. Now that loyalty was to be tried, and Marcia had two old, narrow and well-fortified hearts to conquer ere her way would be entirely smooth.

Well might Madam Schuyler have been proud of her pupil as alone and unaided she faced the trying situation and mastered it in a sweet and unassuming way.

They began their inquisition at once, so soon as they were seated, and the preliminary sentences uttered. The gleaming knitting needles seemed to Marcia like so many swarming, vindictive bees, menacing her peace of mind.

"You look young, child, to have the care of so large a house as this," said Aunt Amelia, looking at Marcia over her spectacles as if she were expected to take the first bite out of her. "It's a great responsibility!" she shut her thin lips tightly and shook her head, as if she had said: "It's a great *impossibility*."

"Have you ever had the care of a house?" asked Miss Hortense, going in a little deeper. "David likes everything nice, you know, he has always been used to it."

There was something in the tone, and in the set of the bow on Aunt Hortense's purple trimmed cap that roused the spirit in Marcia.

"I think I rather enjoy housework," she responded coolly. This unexpected statement somewhat mollified the aunts. They had heard to the contrary from some one who had lived in the same town with the Schuylers. Kate's reputation was widely known, as that of a spoiled beauty, who did not care to work, and would do whatever she pleased. The aunts had entertained many forebodings from the few stray hints an old neighbor of Kate's had dared utter in their hearing.

The talk drifted at once to household matters, as though that were the first division of the examination the young bride was expected to undergo. Marcia

The question was flung out by Aunt Hortense like a challenge, and the very set of her nostrils gave Marcia warning. But it was in a relieved voice that ended almost in a ripple of a laugh that she answered quite assuredly: "Oh, yes, indeed. I can make beautiful bread. I just love to make it, too!"

"But how do you make it?" quickly questioned Aunt Amelia, like a repeating rifle. If the first shot had not struck home, the second was likely to. "Do you use hop yeast? Potatoes? I thought so. Don't know how to make salt-rising, do you? It's just what might have been expected."

"David has always been used to salt-rising bread," said Aunt Hortense with a grim set of her lips as though she were delivering a judgement. "He was raised on it."

"If David does not like my bread," said Marcia with a rising color and a nervous little laugh, "then I shall try to make some that he does like."

There was an assurance about the "if" that did not please the oracle.

"David was raised on salt-rising bread," said Aunt Hortense again as if that settled it. "We can send you down a loaf or two every time we bake until you learn how."

"I'm sure it's very kind of you," said Marcia, not at all pleased, "but I do not think that will be necessary. David has always seemed to like our bread when he visited at home. Indeed he often praised it."

"David would not be impolite," said Aunt Amelia, after a suitable pause in which Marcia felt disapprobation in the air. "It would be best for us to send it. David's health might suffer if he was not suitably nourished."

Marcia's cheeks grew redder. Bread had been one of her stepmother's strong points, well infused into her young pupil. Madam Schuyler had never been able to say enough to sufficiently express her scorn of people who made salt-rising bread.

"My stepmother made beautiful bread," she said quite childishly; "she did not think salt-rising bread was so healthy as that made from hop yeast. She disliked the odor in the house from salt-rising bread."

Now indeed the aunts exchanged glances of "On to the combat." Four red spots flamed giddily out in their four sallow cheeks, and eight shining knitting needles suddenly became idle. The moment was too momentous to work. It was as they feared, even the worst. For, be it known, salt-rising bread was one of their tender points, and for it they would fight to the bitter end. They looked at her with four cold, forbidding, steely, spectacled eyes, and Marcia felt that their looks said volumes: "And she so young too! To be so out of the way!" was what they might have expressed to one another. Marcia felt she had been unwise in uttering her honest, indignant sentiments concerning salt-rising bread.

The pause was long and impressive, and the bride felt like a naughty little four-year-old.

At last Aunt Hortense took up her knitting again with the air that all was over and an unrevokable verdict was passed upon the culprit.

"People have never seemed to stay away from our house on that account," she said dryly. "I'm sure I hope it will not be so disagreeable that it will affect your coming to see us sometimes with David."

There was an iciness in her manner that seemed to suggest a long line of offended family portraits of ancestors frowning down upon her.

Marcia's cheeks flamed crimson and her heart fairly stopped beating.

"I beg your pardon," she said quickly, "I did not mean to say anything disagreeable. I am sure I shall be glad to come as often as you will let me." As she said it Marcia wondered if that were quite true. Would she ever be glad to go to the home of those two severe-looking aunts? There were three of them. Perhaps the other one would be even more withered and severe than these two. A slight shudder passed over Marcia, and a sudden realization of a side of married life that had never come into her thoughts before. For a moment she longed with all the intensity of a child for her father's house and the shelter of his loving protection, amply supported by her stepmother's capable, self-sufficient, comforting countenance. Her heart sank with the fear that she would never be able to do justice to the position of David's wife, and David would be disappointed in her and sorry he had accepted her sacrifice. She roused herself to do better, and bit her tongue to remind it that it must make no more blunders. She praised the garden, the house and the furnishings, in voluble, eager, girlish language until the thin lines of lips relaxed and the drawn muscles of the aunt's cheeks took on a less severe aspect. They liked to be appreciated, and they certainly had taken a great deal of pains with the house — for David's sake — not for hers. They did not care to have her deluded by the idea that they had done it for her sake. David was to them a young god, and with this one supreme idea of his supremacy they wished to impress his young wife. It was a foregone conclusion in their minds that no mere pretty young girl was capable of appreciating David, as could they, who had watched him from babyhood, and pampered and petted and been severe with him by turns, until if he had not had the temper of an angel he would surely have been spoiled.

"We did our best to make the house just as David would have wished it," said Aunt Amelia at last, a self-satisfied shadow of what answered for a smile with her, passing over her face for a moment.

"We did not at all approve of this big house, nor indeed of David's setting up in a separate establishment for himself," said Aunt Hortense, taking up her daily under the scrutiny of these two, and she blest David for his thoughtfulness, even though it had not been meant for her. She went into pleased ecstasies once more over the house, and its furnishings, and ended by her pleasure over the piano.

There was a grim stillness when she touched upon that subject. The aunts did not approve of that musical instrument, that was plain. Marcia wondered if they always paused so long before speaking when they disapproved, in order to show their displeasure. In fact, did they always disapprove of everything?

"You will want to be very careful of it," said Aunt Amelia, looking at the disputed article over her glasses, "it cost a good deal of money. It was the most foolish thing I ever knew David to do, buying that."

"Yes," said Aunt Hortense, "you will not want to use it much, it might get scratched. It has a fine polish. I'd keep it closed up only when I had company. You ought to be very proud to have a husband who could buy a thing like that. There's not many has them. When I was a girl my grandfather had a spinet, the only one for miles around, and it was taken great care of. The case hadn't a scratch on it."

Marcia had started toward the piano intending to open it and play for her new relatives, but she halted midway in the room and came back to her seat after that speech, feeling that she must just sit and hold her hands until it was time to get supper, while these dreadful aunts picked her to pieces, body, soul and spirit.

It was with great relief that at last she heard David's step and knew she might leave the room and put the tea things upon the table.

Chapter 11

They got through the supper without any trouble, and the aunts went home in the early twilight, each with her bonnet strings tied precisely, her lace mitts drawn smoothly over her bony hands, and her little knitting bag over her right arm. They walked decorously up the shaded, elm-domed street, each mindful of her aristocratic instep, and trying to walk erect as in the days when they were gazed upon with admiration, knowing that still an air of former greatness hovered about them wherever they went.

They had brightened considerably at the supper table, under the genial influence of David's presence. They came as near to worshiping David as one can possibly come to worshiping a human being. David, desirous above all things of blinding their keen, sure-to-say-"I-told-you-so" old eyes, roused to be his former gay self with them, and pleased them so that they did not notice how little lover-like reference he made to his bride, who was decidedly in the background for the time, the aunts, perhaps purposely, desiring to show her a wife's true place, — at least the true place of a wife of a David.

They had allowed her to bring them her things and help them on with capes and bonnets, and, when they were ready to leave, Aunt Amelia put out a lifeless hand, that felt in its silk mitt like a dead fish in a net, and said to Marcia:

"Our sister Clarinda is desirous of seeing David's wife. She wished us most particularly to give you her love and say to you that she wishes you to come to her at the earliest possible moment. You know she is lame and cannot easily get about."

"Young folks should always be ready to wait upon their elders," said Aunt Hortense, grimly. "Come as soon as you can, — that is, if you think you can stand the smell of salt-rising."

Marcia's face flushed painfully, and she glanced quickly at David to see if he had noticed what his aunt had said, but David was already anticipating the moment when he would be free to lay aside his mask and bury his face in his hands and his thoughts in sadness.

Marcia's heart sank as she went about clearing off the supper things. Was life always to be thus? Would she be forever under the espionage of those two grim specters of women, who seemed, to her girlish imagination, to have nothing about them warm or loving or woman-like?

She seemed to herself to be standing outside a married life and looking on at it as one might gaze on a panorama. It was all new and painful, and she was one of the central figures expected to act on through all the pictures, taking another's place, yet doing it as if it were her own. She glanced over at David's

window looking out on
been some sort of a meeting at the church across
way, and the people were filing out and taking their various ways home,
calling pleasant good nights, and speaking cheerily of the morrow. The moon,
though beginning to wane, was bright and cast sharp shadows. Marcia longed
to get out into the night. If she could have got downstairs without being heard
she would have slipped out into the garden. But downstairs she could hear
David pacing back and forth like some hurt, caged thing. Steadily, dully, he
walked from the front hall back into the kitchen and back again. There was no
possibility of escaping his notice. Marcia felt as if she might breathe freer in the
open air, so she leaned far out of her window and looked up and down the street,
and thought. Finally, — her heart swelled to bursting, as young hearts with their
first little troubles will do, — she leaned down her dark head upon the window
seat and wept and wept, alone.

It was the next morning at breakfast that David told her of the festivities
that were planned in honor of their home coming. He spoke as if they were a
great trial through which they both must pass in order to have any peace, and
expressed his gratitude once more that she had been willing to come here with
him and pass through it. Marcia had the impression, after he was done speaking
and had gone away to the office, that he felt she had come merely for these few
days of ceremony and after they were passed she was dismissed, her duty done,
and she might go home. A great lump arose in her throat and she suddenly
wished very much that it were so. For if it were, how much, how very much she
would enjoy queening it for a few days — except for David's sadness. But
already, there had begun to be an element to her in that sadness which in spite
of herself she resented. It was a heavy burden which she began dimly to see
would be harder and harder to bear as the days went by. She had not yet begun
to think of the time before her in years.

They were to go to the aunts' to tea that evening, and after tea a company
of David's old friends — or rather the old friends of David's aunts — were coming
to meet them. This the aunts had planned: but it seemed they had not counted
her worthy to be told of the plans, and had only divulged them to David. Marcia
had not thought that a little thing could annoy her so much, but she found it
vexed her more and more as she thought upon it going about her work.

There was not so much to be done in the house that morning after the
breakfast things were cleared away. Dinners and suppers would not be much

of a problem for some days to come, for the house was well stocked with good things.

The beds done and the rooms left in dainty order with the sweet summer breeze blowing the green tassels on the window shades, Marcia went softly down like some half guilty creature to the piano. She opened it and was forthwith lost in delight of the sounds her own fingers brought forth.

She had been playing perhaps half an hour when she became conscious of another presence in the room. She looked up with a start, feeling that some one had been there for some time, she could not tell just how long. Peering into the shadowy room lighted only from the window behind her, she made out a head looking in at the door, the face almost hidden by a capacious sunbonnet. She was not long in recognizing her visitor of the day before. It was like a sudden dropping from a lofty mountain height down into a valley of annoyance to hear Miranda's sharp metallic voice:

"Morning!" she curtsied, coming in as soon as she perceived she was seen. "At it again? I ben listening sometime. It's as pretty as Silas Drew's harmonicker when he comes home evenings behind the cows."

Marcia drew her hands sharply from the keys as if she had been struck. Somehow Miranda and music were inharmonious. She scarcely knew what to say. She felt as if her morning were spoiled. But Miranda was too full of her own errand to notice the clouded face and cool welcome. "Say, you can't guess how I got over here. I'll tell you. You're going over to the Spafford house to-night, ain't you? and there's going to be a lot of folks there. Of course we all know all about it. It's been planned for months. And my cousin Hannah Heath has an invite. You can't think how fond Miss Amelia and Miss Hortense are of her. They tried their level best to make David pay attention to her, but it didn't work. Well, she was talking about what she'd wear. She's had three frocks made last week, all frilled and fancy. You see she don't want to let folks think she is down in the mouth the least bit about David. She'll likely make up to you, to your face, a whole lot, and pretend she's the best friend you've got in the world. But I've just got this to say, don't you be too sure of her friendship. She's smooth as butter, but she can give you a slap in the face if you don't serve her purpose. I don't mind telling you for she's given me many a one," and the pale eyes snapped in unison with the color of her hair. "Well, you see I heard her talking to Grandma, and she said she'd give anything to know what you were going to wear to-night."

"How curious!" said Marcia surprised. "I'm sure I do not see why she should care!" There was the coolness born of utter indifference in her reply that filled the younger girl with admiration. Perhaps too there was the least mite of haughtiness in her manner, born of the knowledge that she belonged to an old and honored family, and that she had in her possession a trunk full of clothes that could vie with any that Hannah Hearth could display. Miranda wished silent...

...ow if you'd accept a jar
...could find out about your clothes. The
...the kitchen table. I left it when I came through. It's good, but
there ain't any love in it." And Miranda laughed a hard mirthless laugh, and
then settled down to her subject again.

"Now, you needn't be a mite afraid to tell me about it. I won't tell it straight,
you know. I'd just like to see what you are going to wear so I could keep her out
of her tricks for once. Is your frock blue?"

Now it is true that the trunk upstairs contained a goodly amount of the color
blue, for Kate Schuyler had been her bonniest in blue, and the particular frock
which had been made with reference to this first very significant gathering was
blue. Marcia had accepted the fact as unalterable. The garment was made for
a purpose, and its mission must be fulfilled however much she might wish to
wear something else, but suddenly as Miranda spoke there came over her mind
the thought of rebellion. Why should she be bound down to do as Kate would
do in her place? If she had accepted the sacrifice of living Kate's life for her,
she might at least have the privilege of living it in the pleasantest possible way,
and surely the matter of the dress was one she might be allowed to settle for
herself if she was old enough at all to be trusted away from home. Among the
pretty things Kate had made was a sweet rose-pink silk tissue. Madam Schuyler
had frowned upon it as frivolous, and besides she did not think it becoming to
Kate. She had a fixed theory that people with blue eyes and gold hair should
never wear pink or red, but Kate as usual had her own way, and with her wild
rose complexion had succeeded in looking like the wild rose itself in spite of
blue eyes and golden hair. Marcia knew in her heart, in fact she had known
from the minute the lovely pink thing had come into the house, that it was the
very thing to set her off. Her dark eyes and hair made a charming contrast with
the rose, and her complexion was even fresher than Kate's. Her heart grew
suddenly eager to don this dainty, frilly thing and outshine Hannah Heath
beyond any chance of further trying. There were other frocks, too, in the trunk.
Why should she be confined to the stately blue one that had been marked out
for this occasion? Marcia, with sudden inspiration, answered calmly, just as
though all these tumultuous possibilities of clothes had not been whirling
through her brain in that half second's hesitation: "I have not quite decided what
I shall wear. It is not an important matter, I'm sure. Let us go and see the

piccalilli. I'm very obliged to your grandmother, I'm sure. It was very kind of her."

Somewhat awed, Miranda followed her hostess into the kitchen. She could not reconcile this girl's face with the stately little airs that she wore, but she liked her and forthwith she told her so.

"I like you," she said fervently. "You remind me of one of Grandma's sturtions, bright and independent and lively, with a spice and a color to 'em, and Hannah makes you think of one of them tall spikes of gladiolus all fixed up without any smell."

Marcia tried to smile over the doubtful compliment. Somehow there was something about Miranda that reminded her of Mary Ann. Poor Mary Ann! *Dear* Mary Ann! For suddenly she realized that everything that reminded her of the precious life of her childhood, left behind forever, was dear. If she could see Mary Ann at this moment she would throw her arms about her neck and call her "Dear Mary Ann," and say, "I love you," to her. Perhaps this feeling made her more gentle with the annoying Miranda than she might have been.

When Miranda was gone the precious play hour was gone too. Marcia had only time to steal hurriedly into the parlor, close the instrument, and then fly about getting her dinner ready. But as she worked she had other thoughts to occupy her mind. She was becoming adjusted to her new environment and she found many unexpected things to make it hard. Here, for instance, was Hannah Heath. Why did there have to a Hannah Heath? And what was Hannah Heath to her? Kate might feel jealous, indeed, but not she, not the unloved, unreal, wife of David. She would rather pity Hannah that David had not loved her instead of Kate, or pity David that he had not. But somehow she did not, somehow she could not. Somehow Hannah Heath had become a living, breathing enemy to be met and conquered. Marcia felt her fighting blood rising, felt the Schuyler in her coming to the front. However little there was in her wifehood, its name at least was hers. The tale that Miranda had told was enough, if it were true, to put any woman, however young she might be, into battle array. Marcia was puzzling her mind over the question that has been more or less of a weary burden to every woman since the fatal day that Eve made her great mistake.

David was silent and abstracted at the dinner table, and Marcia absorbed in her own problems did not feel cut by it. She was trying to determine whether to blossom out in pink, or to be crushed and set aside into insignificance in blue, or to choose a happy medium and wear neither. She ventured a timid little question before David went away again: Did he, would he, — that is, was there any thing, — any word he would like to say to her? Would she have to do anything to-night?

David looked at her in surprise. Why, no! He knew of nothing. Just go and speak pleasantly to every one. He was sure she knew what to do. He had

...y, unless, perhaps — I don't suppose you know what it would be proper for me to wear."

"Oh, that does not matter in the least," he replied promptly. "Anything. You always look nice. Why, I'll tell you, wear the frock you had on the night I came." Then he suddenly remembered the reason why that was a pleasant memory to him, and that it was not for her sake at all, but for the sake of one who was lost to him forever. His face contracted with sudden pain, and Marcia, cut to the heart, read the meaning, and felt sick and sore too.

"Oh, I could not wear that," she said sadly, "it is only chintz. It would not be nice enough, but thank you. I shall be all right. Don't trouble about me," and she forced a weak smile to light him from the house, and shut from his pained eyes the knowledge of how he had hurt her, for with those words of his had come the vision of herself that happy night as she stood at the gate in the stillness and moonlight looking from the portal of her maidenhood into the vista of her womanhood, which had seemed then so far away and bright, and was now upon her in sad reality. Oh, if she could but have caught that sentence of his about her little chintz frock to her heart with the joy of possession, and known that he said it because he too had a happy memory about her in it, as she had always felt the coming, misty, dream-expected lover would do!

She spread the available frocks out upon the bed after the other things were put neatly away in closet and drawer, and sat down to decide the matter. David's suggestion while impossible had given her an idea, and she proceeded to carry it out. There was a soft sheer white muslin, whereon Kate had expended her daintiest embroidering, edged with the finest of little lace frills. It was quaint and simple and girlish, the sweetest, most simple affair in all of Kate's elaborate wardrobe, and yet, perhaps, from an artistic point of view, the most elegant. Marcia soon made up her mind.

She dressed herself early, for David had said he would be home by four o'clock and they would start as soon after as he could get ready. His aunts wished to show her the old garden before dark.

When she came to the arrangement of her hair she paused. Somehow her soul rebelled at the style of Kate. It did not suit her face. It did not accord with her feeling. It made her seem unlike herself, or unlike the self she would ever wish to be. It suited Kate well, but not her. With sudden determination she pulled it all down again from the top of her head and loosened its rich waves about her face, then loosely twisted it behind, low on her neck, falling over her delicate ears, until her head looked like that of an old Greek statue. It was not fashion, it was pure instinct the child was following out, and there was enough conformity to one of the fashionable modes of the day to keep her from looking odd. It was lovely. Marcia could not help seeing herself that it was much more becoming than the way she had arranged it for her marriage, though then she had had the wedding veil to soften the tightly drawn outlines of her head. She put on the sheer white embroidered frock then, and as a last touch pinned the bit of black velvet about her throat with a single pearl that had been her mother's. It was the bit of black velvet she had worn the night David came. It gave her pleasure to think that in so far she was conforming to his suggestion.

She had just completed her toilet when she heard David's step coming up the walk.

David, coming in out of the sunshine and beholding this beautiful girl in the coolness and shadow of the hall awaiting him shyly, almost started back as he rubbed his eyes and looked at her again. She was beautiful. He had to admit it to himself, even in the midst of his sadness, and he smiled at her, and felt another pang of condemnation that he had taken this beauty from some other man's lot perhaps, and appropriated it to shield himself from the world's exclamation about his own lonely life.

"You have done it admirably. I do not see that there is anything left to be desired," he said in his pleasant voice that used to make her girl-heart flutter with pride that her new brother-to-be was pleased with her. It fluttered now, but there was a wider sweep to its wings, and a longer flight ahead of the thought.

Quite demurely the young wife accepted her compliment, and then she meekly folded her little white muslin cape with its dainty frills about her pretty shoulders, drew on the new lace mitts, and tied beneath her chin the white strings of a shirred gauze bonnet with tiny rosebuds nestling in the ruching of tulle about the face.

Once more the bride walked down the world the observed of all observers, the gazed at of the town, only this time it was brick pavement not oaken stairs she trod, and most of the eyes that looked upon her were sheltered behind green jalousies. None the less, however, she was conscious of them as she made her way to the house of solemn feasting with David by her side. Her eyes rested upon the ground, or glanced quietly at things in the distance, when they were not lifted for a moment in wifely humility to her husband's face at some word of his. Just as she imagined a hundred times in her girlish thoughts that her sister Kate would do, so did she, and after what seemed to her an interminable walk, though in reality it was but four village blocks, they arrived at the house of Spafford.

It seemed to Marcia that she wished to remind her that all her old life and relations were passed away, and she had nothing now but David's, especially David's relatives. She shrank from lifting her eyes, expecting to find the third aunt, who was older, as much sourer and sharper in proportion to the other two, but she controlled herself and lifted her flower face to meet a gentle, meek old face set in soft white frills of a cap, with white ribbons flying, and though the old lady leaned upon a crutch she managed to give the impression that she had fairly flown in her gladness to welcome her new niece. There was the lighting of a repressed nature let free in her kind old face as she looked with true pleasure upon the lovely young one, and Marcia felt herself folded in truly loving arms in an embrace which her own passionate, much repressed, loving nature returned with heartiness. At last she had found a friend!

She felt it every time she spoke, more and more. They walked out into the garden almost immediately, and Aunt Clarinda insisted upon hobbling along by Marcia's side, though her sisters both protested that it would be too hard for her that warm afternoon. Every time Marcia spoke she felt the kind old eyes upon her, and she knew that at least one of the aunts was satisfied with her as a wife for David, for her eyes would travel from David to Marcia and back again to David, and when they met Marcia's there was not a shade of disparagement in them.

It was rather a tiresome walk through a tiresome old garden, laid out in the ways of the past generation, and bordered with much funereal box. The sisters, Amelia and Hortense, took the new member of the family, conscientiously, through every path, and faithfully told her how each spot was associated with some happening in the family history. Occasionally there was a solemn pause for the purpose of properly impressing the new member of the house, and Amelia wiped her eyes with her carefully folded handkerchief. Marcia felt extremely like laughing. She was sure that if Kate had been obliged to pass through this ordeal she would have giggled out at once and said some shockingly funny thing that would have horrified the aunts beyond forgiveness. The thought of this nerved her to keep a sober face. She wondered what David thought of it all, but when she looked at him she wondered no longer, for David stood as one waiting for a certain ceremony to be over, a ceremony which he knew to be inevitable, but which was wholly and familiarly uninteresting. He did not even see how it must strike the girl who was going through it all for him, for David's thoughts were out on the flood-tide of sorrow, drifting against the rocks of the might-have-been.

They went in to tea presently, just when the garden was growing loveliest with a tinge of the setting sun, and Marcia longed to run up and down the little paths like a child and call to them all to catch if they could. The house was dark and stately and gloomy.

"You are coming up to my room for a few minutes after supper," whispered Aunt Clarinda encouragingly as they passed into the dark hall. The supper table was alight with a fine old silver candelabra whose wavering lights cast a solemn, grotesque shadow on the different faces.

Beside her plate the young bride saw an ostentatious plate of puffy soda biscuits, and involuntarily her eyes searched the table for the bread plate.

Aunt Clarinda almost immediately pounced upon the bread plate and passed it with a smile to Marcia, and as Marcia with an answering smile took a generous smile she heard the other two aunts exclaim in chorus: "Oh, don't pass her the bread, Clarinda; take it away sister, quick! She does not like salt-rising! It is unpleasant to her!"

Then with blazing cheeks the girl protested that she wished to keep the bread, that they were mistaken, she had not said it was obnoxious to her, but had merely given them her stepmother's opinion when they asked. They must excuse her for her seeming rudeness, for she had not intended to hurt them. She presumed salt-rising bread was very nice; it looked beautiful. This was a long speech for shy Marcia to make before so many strangers, but David's wondering, troubled eyes were upon her, questioning what it all might mean, and she felt she could do anything to save David from more suffering or annoyance of any kind.

David said little. He seemed to perceive that there had been an unpleasant prelude to this, and perhaps knew from former experience that the best thing to do was to change the subject. He launched into a detailed account of their wedding journey. Marcia on her part was grateful to him, for when she took the first brave bite into the very puffy, very white slice of bread she had taken, she perceived that it was much worse than that which had been baked for their home-coming, and not only justified all her stepmother's execrations, but in addition it was sour. For an instant, perceiving down the horoscope of time whole calendars full of such suppers with the aunts, and this bread, her soul shuddered and shrank. Could she ever learn to like it? Impossible! Could she ever tolerate it? Could she? She doubted. Then she swallowed bravely and perceived that the impossible had been accomplished once. It could be again, but she must go slowly else she might have to eat two slices instead of one. David was kind. He had roused himself to help his helper. Perhaps something in her girlish beauty and helplessness, helpless here for his sake, appealed to him. At least his eyes sought hers often with a tender interest to see if she were

took a big bite from the
swallowed it. There were worse things in the world,
after all, than salt-rising, and, when one could smother it in Aunt Amelia's peach
preserves, it was quite bearable.

Aunt Clarinda slipped her off to her own room after supper, and left the
other two sisters with their beloved idol, David. In their stately parlor lighted
with many candles in honor of the occasion, they sat and talked in low tones with
him, their voices suggesting condolence with his misfortune of having married
out of the family, and disapproval with the married state in general. Poor souls!
How their hard, loving hearts would have been wrung could they but have known
the true state of the case! And, strange anomaly, how much deeper would have
been their antagonism toward poor, self-sacrificing, loving Marcia! Just because she had dared to think herself fit for David, belonging as she did to her
renegade sister Kate. But they did not know, and for this fact David was
profoundly thankful. Those were not the days of rapid transit, of telegraph and
telephone, nor even much letter writing, else the story would probably have
reached the aunts even before the bride and bridegroom arrived at home. As
it was, David had some hope of keeping the tragedy of his life from the ears of
his aunts forever. Patiently he answered their questions concerning the wedding, questions that were intended to bring out facts showing whether David
had received his due amount of respect, and whether the family he had so greatly
honored felt the burden of that honor sufficiently.

Upstairs in a quaint old-fashioned room Aunt Clarinda was taking Marcia's
face in her two wrinkled hands and looking lovingly into her eyes; then she kissed
her on each rosy cheek and said:

"Dear child! You look just as I did when I was young. You wouldn't think
it from me now, would you? But it's true. I might not have grown to be such a
dried-up old thing if I had somebody like David. I'm so glad you've got David.
He'll take good care of you. He's a dear boy. He's always been good to me.
But you mustn't let the others crush the roses out of your cheeks. They crushed
mine out. They wouldn't let me have my life the way I wanted it, and the pink
in my cheeks all went back into my heart and burst it a good many years ago.
But they can't spoil your life, for you've got David and that's worth every-thing."

Then she kissed her on the lips and cheeks and eyes and let her go. But
that one moment had given Marcia a glimpse into another life-story and put her

in touch forever with Aunt Clarinda, setting athrob the chord of loving sympathy.

When they came into the parlor the other two aunts looked up with a quick, suspicious glance from one to the other and then fastened disapproving eyes upon Marcia. They rather resented it that she was so pretty. Hannah had been their favorite, and Hannah was beautiful in their eyes. They wanted no other to outshine her. Albeit they would be proud enough before their neighbors to have it said that their nephew's wife was beautiful.

After a chilling pause in which David was wondering anew at Marcia's beauty, Aunt Hortense asked, as though it were an omission from the former examination, "Did you ever make a shirt?"

"Oh, plenty of them!" said Marcia, with a merry laugh, so relieved that she fairly bubbled. "I think I could make a shirt with my eyes shut."

Aunt Clarinda beamed on her with delight. A shirt was something she had never succeeded in making quite right. It was one of the things that her sisters had against her that she could not make good shirts. Any one who could not make a good shirt was deficient. Clarinda was deficient. She could not make a shirt. Meekly she had tried year after year. Humbly had she ripped out gusset and seam and band, having put them on upside down or inside out. Never could she learn the ins and outs of a shirt. But her old heart trembled with delight that the new girl, who was going to take the place in her heart of her old dead self and live out all the beautiful things which had been lost to her, had mastered this one great accomplishment in which she had failed so supremely.

But Aunt Hortense was not pleased. True, it was one of the seven virtues in her mind which a young wife should possess, and she had carefully instructed Hannah Heath for a number of years back, while Hannah bungled out a couple for her father occasionally, but Aunt Hortense had been sure that if Hannah ever became David's wife she might still have the honor of making most of David's shirts. That had been her happy task ever since David had worn a shirt, and she hoped to hold the position of shirt-maker to David until she left this mortal clay. Therefore Aunt Hortense was not pleased, even though David's wife was not lacking, and, too, even though she foreheard herself telling her neighbors next day how many shirts David's wife had made.

"Well, David will not need any for some time," she said grimly. "I made him a dozen before he was married."

Marcia reflected that it seemed to be impossible to make any headway into the good graces of either Aunt Hortense or Aunt Amelia. Aunt Amelia then took her turn at a question.

"Hortense," said she, and there was an ominous inflection in the word as if the question were portentous, "have you asked our new niece by what name she desires us to call her?"

...gathered itself to brave

...ow to her cheeks, and rose slowly in David's,

...y veins that swelled in his neck till he could feel their pulsation against his stock, but his smooth shaven lips were white. He felt that a moment had come which he could not bear to face.

Then with a hesitation that was but pardonable, and with a shy sweet look, Marcia answered; and though her voice trembled just the least bit, her true, dear eyes looked into the battalion of steel ones bravely.

"I would like you to call me Marcia, if you please."

"Marcia!" Miss Hortense snipped the word out as if with scissors of surprise.

But there was a distinct relaxation about Miss Amelia's mouth. She heaved a relieved sigh. Marcia was so much better than Kate, so much more classical, so much more to be compared with Hannah, for instance.

"Well, I'm glad!" she allowed herself to remark. "David has been calling you Kate till it made me sick, such a frivolous name and no sense in it either. Marcia sounds quite sensible. I suppose Katherine is your middle name. Do you spell it with a K or a C?"

But the knocker sounded on the street door and Marcia was spared the torture of a reply. She dared not look at David's face, for she knew there must be pain and mortification mingling there, and she hoped that the trying subject would not come up again for discussion.

The guests began to arrive. Old Mrs. Heath and her daughter-in-law and grand-daughter came first.

Hannah's features were handsome and she knew exactly how to manage her shapely hands with their long white fingers. The soft delicate undersleeves fell away from arms white and well moulded, and she carried her height gracefully. Her hair was elaborately stowed upon the top of her head in many puffs, ending in little ringlets carelessly and coquettishly straying over temple, or ears, or gracefully curved neck. She wore a frock of green, and its color sent a pang through the bride's heart to realize that perhaps it had been worn with an unkindly purpose. Nevertheless Hannah Heath was beautiful and fascinated Marcia. She resolved to try to think the best of her, and to make her a friend if possible. Why, after all, should she be to blame for wanting David? Was he not a man to be admired and desired? It was unwomanly, of course, that she had let it be known, but perhaps her relatives were more to blame than herself. At least Marcia made up her mind to try to like her.

Hannah's frock was of silk, not a common material in those days, soft and shimmery and green enough to take away the heart from anything blue that was ever made, but Hannah was stately and her skin was white as the lily she resembled, in her bright leaf green.

Hannah chose to be effusive and condescending to the bride, giving the impression that she and David had been like brother and sister all their lives and that she might have been his choice if she had chosen, but as she had not chosen, she was glad that David had found some one wherewith to console himself. She did not say this in so many words, but Marcia found that impression left after the evening was over.

With sweet dignity Marcia received her introductions, given in Miss Amelia's most commanding tone, "Our niece, Marcia!"

"Marshy, Marshy!" the bride heard old Mrs. Heath murmur to Miss Spafford. "Why, I thought 'twas to be Kate!"

"Her name is Marcia," said Miss Amelia in a most satisfied tone; "you must have misunderstood."

Marcia caught a look in Miss Heath's eyes, alert, keen, questioning, which flashed all over her like something searching and bright but not friendly.

She felt a painful shyness stealing over her and wished that David were by her side. She looked across the room at him. His face had recovered its usual calmness, though he looked pale. He was talking on his favorite theme with old Mr. Heath: the newly invented steam engine and its possibilities. He had forgotten everything else for the time, and his face lighted with animation as he tried to answer William Heath's arguments against it.

"Have you read what the Boston *Courier* said, David? 'Long in June it was I think," Marcia heard Mr. Heath ask. Indeed his voice was so large that it filled the room, and for the moment Marcia had been left to herself while some new people were being ushered in. "It says, David, that the project of a railroad from Bawston to Albany is impracticable as everybody knows who knows the simplest rule of arithmetic, and the expense would be little less than the market value of the whole territory of Massachusetts; and which, if practicable, every person of common sense knows would be as useless as a railroad from Bawston to the moon. There, David, what do ye think o' that?" and William Heath slapped David on the knee with his broad, fat fist and laughed heartily, as though he had him in a tight corner.

Marcia would have given a good deal to slip in beside David on the sofa and listen to the discussion. She wanted with all her heart to know how he would answer this man who could be so insufferably wise, but there was other work for her, and her attention was brought back to her own uncomfortable part by Hannah Heath's voice:

...... his high cheek bones was ...... tight as if it were a trifle too close a fit for the genial cushion beneath. He did not look brilliant, and he certainly was not handsome, but there was an inoffensive desire to please about him. He was introduced as Mr. Lemuel Skinner. He bowed low over Marcia's hand, said a few embarrassed, stiff sentences and turned to Hannah Heath with relief. It was evident that Hannah was in his eyes a great and shining light, to which he fluttered as naturally as does the moth to the candle. But Hannah did not scruple to singe his wings whenever she chose. Perhaps she knew, no matter how badly he was burned he would only flutter back again whenever she scintillated. She had turned her back upon him now, and left him to Marcia's tender mercies. Hannah was engaged in talking to a younger man. "Harry Temple, from New York," Lemuel explained to Marcia.

The young man, Harry Temple, had large lazy eyes and heavy dark hair. There was a discontented look in his face, and a looseness about the set of his lips that Marcia did not like, although she had to admit that he was handsome. Something about him reminded her of Captain Leavenworth, and she instinctively shrank from him. But Harry Temple had no mind to talk to any one but Marcia that evening, and he presently so managed it that he and she were ensconced in a corner of the room away from others. Marcia felt perturbed. She did not feel flattered by the man's attentions, and she wanted to be at the other end of the room listening to the conversation.

She listened as intently as she might between sentences, and her keen ears could catch a word or two of what David was saying. After all, it was not so much the new railroad project that she cared about, though that was strange and interesting enough, but she wanted to watch and listen to David.

Harry Temple said a great many pretty things to Marcia. She did not half hear some of them at first, but after a time she began to realize that she must have made a good impression, and the pretty flush in her cheeks grew deeper. She did little talking. Mr. Temple did it all. He told her of New York. He asked if she were not dreadfully bored with this little town and its doings, and bewailed her lot when he learned that she had not had much experience there. Then he asked if she had ever been to New York and began to tell of some of its attractions. Among other things he mentioned some concerts, and immediately Marcia was all attention. Her dark eyes glowed and her speaking face gave eager response to his words. Seeing he had interested her at last, he kept on, for he was possessor of a glib tongue, and what he did not know he could fabricate without the slightest compunction. He had been about the world and gathered up superficial knowledge enough to help him do this admirably, therefore he was able to use a few musical terms, and to bring before Marcia's vivid imagination the scene of the performance of Handel's great "Creation" given in Boston, and of certain musical events that were to be attempted soon in New York. He admitted that he could play a little upon the harpsichord, and, when he learned that Marcia could play also and that she was the possessor of a piano, one of the latest improved makes, he managed to invite himself to play upon it Marcia found to her dismay that she actually seemed to have invited him to come some afternoon when her husband was away. She had only said politely that she would like to hear him play sometime, and expressed her great delight in music, and he had done the rest, but in her inexperience somehow it had happened and she did not know what to do.

It troubled her a good deal, and she turned again toward the other end of the room, where the attention of most of the company was riveted upon the group who were discussing the railroad, its pros and cons. David was the center of that group.

"Let us go over and hear what they are saying," she said, turning to her companion eagerly.

"Oh, it is all stupid politics and arguments about that ridiculous fairy-tale of a railroad scheme. You would not enjoy it," answered the young man disappointedly. He saw in Marcia a beautiful young soul, the only one who had really attracted him since he had left New York, and he wished to become intimate enough with her to enjoy himself.

It mattered not to him that she was married to another man. He felt secure in his own attractions. He had ever been able to while away the time with whom he chose, why should a simple village maiden resist him? And this was an unusual one, the contour of her head was like a Greek statue.

Nevertheless he was obliged to stroll after her. Once she had spoken. She had suddenly become aware that they had been in their corner together a long time, and that Aunt Amelia's cold eyes were fastened upon her in disapproval.

"The farmers would be ruined, man alive!" Mr. Heath was saying. "Why, all the horses would have to be killed, because they would be wholly useless if this new fandango came in, and then where would be a market for the wheat and oats?"

"Yes, an' I've heard some say the hens wouldn't lay, on account of the noise," ventured Lemuel Skinner in his high voice. "And think of the fires from the sparks of the engine. I tell you it would be dangerous." He looked over at Hannah triumphantly, but Hannah was endeavoring to signal Harry Temple to her side and did not see nor hear.

....ere were others by, and
.... contusion to think what she had done. The aunts,
Amelia and Hortense, were shocked. It was so unladylike. A woman should
not speak on such subjects. She should be silent and leave such topics to her
husband.

"Deah me, she's strong minded, isn't she?" giggled Hannah Heath to
Lemuel, who had taken the signals to himself and come to her side.

"Quite so, quite so!" murmured Lemuel, his lips looking puffier and more
cherry-fied than ever and his chin flattened itself back till he looked like a
frustrated old hen who did not understand the perplexities of life and was
clucking to find out, after having been startled half out of its senses.

But Marcia was not wholly without consolation, for David had flashed a
look of approval at her and had made room for her to sit down by his side on
the sofa. It was almost like belonging to him for a minute or two. Marcia felt
her heart glow with something new and pleasant.

Mr. William Heath drew his heavy grey brows together and looked at her
grimly over his spectacles, poking his bristly under-lip out in astonishment,
bewildered that he should have been answered by a gentle, pretty woman, all
frills and sparkle like his own daughter. He had been wont to look upon a
woman as something like a kitten, — that is, a young woman, — and suddenly the
kitten had lifted a velvet paw and struck him squarely in the face. He had felt
there were claws in the blow, too, for there had been a truth behind her words
that set the room a mocking him.

"Well, Dave, you've got your wife well trained already!" he laughed, concluding it was best to put a smiling front upon the defeat. "She knows just when
to come in and help when your side's getting weak!"

They served cake and raspberry vinegar then, and a little while after
everybody went home. It was later than the hours usually kept in the village,
and the lights in most of the houses were out, or burning dimly in upper stories.
The voices of the guests sounded subdued in the misty waning moonlight air.
Marcia could hear Hannah Heath's voice ahead giggling affectedly to Harry
Temple and Lemuel Skinner, as they walked one on either side of her, while her
father and mother and grandmother came more slowly.

David drew Marcia's hand within his arm and walked with her quietly down
the street, making their steps hushed instinctively that they might so seem more
removed from the others. They were both tired with the unusual excitement

and the strain they had been through, and each was glad of the silence of the other.

But when they reached their own doorstep David said: "You spoke well, child. You must have thought about these things."

Marcia felt a sob rising in a tide of joy into her throat. Then he was not angry with her, and he did not disapprove as the two aunts had done. Aunt Clarinda had kissed her good-night and murmured, "You are a bright little girl, Marcia, and you will make a good wife for David. You will come soon to see me, won't you?" and that made her glad, but these words of David's were so good and so unexpected that Marcia could hardly hide her happy tears.

"I was afraid I had been forward," murmured Marcia in the shadow of the front stoop.

"Not at all, child, I like to hear a woman speak her mind,—that is, allowing she has any mind to speak. That can't be said of all women. There's Hannah Heath, for instance. I don't believe she would know a railroad project from an essay on ancient art."

After that the house seemed a pleasant place aglow as they entered it, and Marcia went up to her rest with a lighter heart.

But the child knew not that she had made a great impression that night upon all who saw her as being beautiful and wise.

The aunts would not express it even to each other—for they felt in duty bound to discountenance her boldness in speaking out before the men and making herself so prominent, joining in their discussions,—but each in spite of her convictions felt a deep satisfaction that their neighbors had seen what a beautiful and bright wife David had selected. They even felt triumphant over their favorite Hannah, and thought secretly that Marcia compared well with her in every way, but they would not have told this even to themselves, no, not for worlds.

So the kindly gossipy town slept, and the young bride became a part of its daily life.

pleasant household duties and she enjoyed them.

There were many other gatherings in honor of the bride and groom, tea-drinkings and evening calls, and a few called in to a neighbor's house to meet them. It was very pleasant to Marcia as she became better acquainted with the people and grew to like some of them, only there was the constant drawback of feeling that it was all a pain and weariness to David.

But Marcia was young, and it was only natural that she should enjoy her sudden promotion to the privileges of a matron, and the marked attention that was paid her. It was a mercy that her head was not turned, living as she did to herself, and with no one in whom she could confide. For David had shrunk within himself to such an extent that she did not like to trouble him with anything.

It was only two days after the evening at the old Spafford house that David came home to tea with ashen face, haggard eyes and white lips. He scarcely tasted his supper and said he would go and lie down, that his head ached. Marcia heard him sigh deeply as he went upstairs. It was that afternoon that the post had brought him Kate's letter.

Sadly Marcia put away the tea things, for she could not eat anything either, though it was an unusually inviting meal she had prepared. Slowly she went up to her room and sat looking out into the quiet, darkening summer night, wondering what additional sorrow had come to David.

David's face looked like death the next morning when he came down. He drank a cup of coffee feverishly, then took his hat as if he would go to the office, but paused at the door and came back saying he wold not go if Marcia would not mind taking a message for him. His head felt badly. She need only tell the man to go on with things as they had planned and say he was detained. Marcia was ready at once to do his bidding with quiet sympathy in her manner.

She delivered her message with the frank straightforward look of a school girl, mingled with a touch of matronly dignity she was trying to assume, which added to her charm; and she smiled her open smile of comradeship, such as she would have dispensed about the old red school house at home, upon boys and girls alike, leaving the clerk and type-setters in a most subjected state, and ready to do anything in the service of their master's wife. It is to be feared that they almost envied David. They watched her as she moved gracefully down the street, and their eyes had a reverent look as they turned away from the window to their work, as though they had been looking upon something sacred.

Harry Temple watched her come out of the office.

She impressed him again as something fresh and different from the common run of maidens in the village. He lazily stepped from the store where he had been lounging and walked down the street to intercept her as she crossed and turned the corner.

"Good morning, Mrs. Spafford," he said, with a courtly grace that was certainly captivating, "are you going to your home? Then our ways lie together. May I walk beside you?"

Marcia smiled and tried to seem gracious, though she would rather have been alone just then, for she wanted to enjoy the day and not be bothered with talking.

Harry Temple mentioned having a letter from a friend in Boston who had lately heard a great chorus rendered. He could not be quite sure of the name of the composer because he had read the letter hurriedly and his friend was a blind-writer, but that made no difference to Harry. He could fill in facts enough about the grandeur of the music from his own imagination to make up for the lack of a little matter like the name of a composer. He was keen enough to see that Marcia was more interested in music than in anything he said, therefore he racked his brains for all the music talk he had ever heard, and made up what he did not know, which was not hard to do, for Marcia was very ignorant on the subject.

At the door they paused. Marcia was eager to get in. She began to wonder how David felt, and she longed to do something for him. Harry Temple looked at her admiringly, noted the dainty set of chin, the clear curve of cheek, the lovely sweep of eyelashes, and resolved to get better acquainted with this woman, so young and lovely.

"I have not forgotten my promise to play for you," he said lightly, watching to see if the flush of rose would steal into her cheek, and that deep light into her expressive eyes. "How about this afternoon? Shall you be at home and disengaged?"

But welcome did not flash into Marcia's face as he had hoped. Instead a troubled look came into her eyes.

"I am afraid it will not be possible this afternoon," said Marcia, the trouble in her eyes creeping into her voice. "That is—I expect to be at home, but—I am not sure of being disengaged."

"Ah! I see!" he raised his eyebrows archly, looking her meanwhile straight in the eyes; "some one else more fortunate than I. Some one else coming?"

Although Marcia did not in the least understand his insinuation, the color flowed into her cheeks in a hurry now, for she instinctively felt that there was something unpleasant in his tone, something below her standard of morals or culture, she did not quite know what. But she felt she must protect herself at any cost. She drew up a little mantle of dignity.

"I understand perfectly," he said, with another meaning smile as though he and she had a secret together; "I'll come some other time," and he took himself very quickly away, much to Marcia's relief. But the trouble did not go out of her eyes as she saw him turn the corner. Instead she went in and stood at the dining room window a long time looking out on the Heaths' hollyhocks beaming in the sun behind the picket fence, and wondered what he could have meant, and why he smiled in that hateful way. She decided she did not like him, and she hoped he would never come. She did not think she would care to hear him play. There was something about him that reminded her of Captain Leavenworth, and now that she saw it in him she would dislike to have him about.

With a sigh she turned to the getting of a dinner which she feared would not be eaten. Nevertheless, she put more dainty thought in it than usual, and when it was done and steaming upon the table she went gently up and tapped on David's door. A voice hoarse with emotion and weariness answered. Marcia scarcely heard the first time.

"Dinner is ready. Isn't your head any better, — David?" There was caressing in his name. It wrung David's heart. Oh, if it were Kate, his Kate, his little bride that were calling him, how his heart would leap with joy! How his headache would disappear and he would be with her in an instant.

For Kate's letter had had its desired effect. All her wrong doings, her crowning outrage of his noble intentions, had been forgotten in the one little plaintive appeal she had managed to breathe in a minor wail throughout that treacherous letter, treacherous alike to her husband and to her lover. Just as Kate had always been able to do with every one about her, she had blinded him to her faults, and managed to put herself in the light of an abused, troubled maiden, who was in a predicament through no fault of her own, and sat in sorrow and a baby-innocence that was bewilderingly sweet.

There had been times when David's anger had been hot enough to waft away this filmy mist of fancies that Kate had woven about herself and let him see the true Kate as she really was. At such times David would confess that she must be wholly heartless. That bright as she was it was impossible for her to have been so easily persuaded into running away with a man she did not love. He had never found it so easy to persuade her against her will. Did she love him? Had she truly loved him, and was she suffering now? His very soul writhed in agony to think of his bride the wife of another against her will. If he might but go and rescue her. If he might but kill that other man! Then his soul would be confronted with the thought of murder. Never before had he felt hate, such hate, for a human being. Then again his heart would soften toward him as he felt how the other must have loved her, Kate, his little wild rose! and there was a fellow feeling between them too, for had she not let him see that she did not half care aright for that other one? Then his mind would stop in a whirl of mingled feeling and he would pause, and pray for steadiness to think and know what was right.

Around and around through this maze of arguing he had gone through the long hours of the morning, always coming sharp against the thought that there was nothing he could possibly do in the matter but bear it, and that Kate, after all, the Kate he loved with his whole soul, had done it and must therefore be to blame. Then he would read her letter over, burning every word of it upon his brain, until the piteous minor appeal would torture him once more and he would begin again to try to get hold of some thread of thought that would unravel this snarl and bring peace.

Like a sound from another world came Marcia's sweet voice, its very sweetness reminding him of that other lost voice, whose tantalizing music floated about his imagination like a string of phantom silver bells that all but sounded and then vanished into silence.

And while all this was going on, this spiritual torture, his living, suffering, physical self was able to summon its thoughts, to answer gently that he did not want any dinner; that his head was no better; that he thanked her for her thought of him; and that he would take the tea she offered if it was not too much trouble.

Gladly, with hurried breath and fingers that almost trembled, Marcia hastened to the kitchen once more and prepared a dainty tray, not even glancing at the dinner table all so fine and ready for its guest, and back again she went to his door, an eager light in her eyes, as if she had obtained audience to a king.

He opened the door this time and took the tray from her with a smile. It was a smile of ashen hue, and fell like a pall upon Marcia's soul. It was as if she had been permitted for a moment to gaze upon a martyred soul upon the rack. Marcia fled from it and went to her own room, where she flung herself on her knees beside her bed and buried her face in the pillows. There she knelt, unmindful of the dinner waiting downstairs, unmindful of the bright day that was droning on its hours. Whether she prayed she knew not, whether she was weeping she could not have told. Her heart was crying out in one great longing to have this cloud of sorrow that had settled upon David lifted.

She might have knelt there until night had there not come the sound of a knock upon the front door. It startled her to her feet in an instant, and she hastily smoothed her rumpled hair, dashed some water on her eyes, and ran down.

ᵣₑ took his departure with a series of bows and smiles, and Marcia flew up to her room to read her letter. It was in the round unformed hand of Mary Ann. Marcia tore it open eagerly. Never had Mary Ann's hand-writing looked so pleasant as at that moment. A letter in those days was a rarity at all times, and this one to Marcia in her distress of mind seemed little short of a miracle. It began in Mary Ann's abrupt way, and opened up to her the world of home since she had left it. But a few short days had passed, scarcely yet numbering into weeks, since she left, yet it seemed half a life-time to the girl promoted so suddenly into womanhood without the accompanying joy of love and close companionship that usually makes desolation impossible.

Dear Marsh, —the letter ran:

—*I expect you think queer of me to write you so soon. I ain't much on writing you know, but something happened right after you leaving and has kept right on happening that made me feel I kinder like to tell you. Don't you mind the mistakes I make. I'm thankful to goodness you ain't the school teacher or I'd never write 'slong s' I'm living, but ennyhow I'm going to tell you all about it. The night you went away I was standing down by the gate under the old elm. I had on my best things yet from the wedding, and I hated to go in and have the day over and have to begin putting on my old calico tomorrow morn-ing again, and washing dishes just the same. Seemed as if I couldn't bear to have the world just the same now you was gone away. Well, I heard someone coming down the street, and who do you think it was? Why, Hanford Weston. He came right up to the gate and stopped. I don't know's he ever spoke two words to me in my life except that time he stopped the big boys from snow-balling me and told me to run along quick and git in the school house while he fit 'em. Well, he stopped and spoke, and he looked so sad, seemed like I knew just what he was feeling sad about, and I told him all about you getting married instead of your sister. He looked at me like he couldn't move for a while and his face was as white as that marble man in the cemetery over Squire Hancock's grave. He grabbed the gate real hard and I thought he was going to fall. He couldn't even move his lips for a while. I felt just awful sorry for him. Something came in my throat like a big stone and my eyes got all blurred with the moonlight. He looked real handsome. I just couldn't help thinking you ought to see him. By and by he got his voice back again, and we talked a lot about you. He told me how he used to watch you when you was a little girl wearing pantalettes. You used to sit in the church pew across from his father's and he could just see your big eyes over the top of the door. He says he always thought to himself he would marry you when he grew up. Then when you began to go to school and was so bright he tried hard to study and keep up just to have you think him good enough for you. He owned up he was a bad speller and he'd tried his level best to do better but it didn't seem to come natural, and he thought maybe if he was a good farmer you wouldn't mind about the spelling. He hired out to his father for the summer and he was trying with all his might to get to be the kind of man t'would suit you, and then when he was plowing and planning all what kind of a house with big columns to the front he would build, here comes the coach driving by and you in it! He said he thought the sky and fields was all mixed up and his heart was going out of him. He couldn't work any more and he started out after supper to see what it all meant.*

That wasn't just the exact way he told it, Marsh, it was more like poetry, the kind in our reader about Lord Ullin's daughter— you know. We used to recite it on examination exhibition. I didn't know Hanford could talk like that. His words were pretty, kind of sorrowful you know. And it all come over me that you ought to know about it. You're married of course, and can't help it now, but 'taint every girl that has a boy care for her like that from the time she's a baby with a red hood on, and you ought to know 'bout it, fer it wasn't Hanford's fault he didn't have time to tell you. He's just been living fer you fer a number of years, and its kind of hard on him. 'Course you may not care, being you're married and have a fine house and lots of clo'es of your own and a good time, but it does seem hard for him. It seems as if somebody ought to comfort him. I'd like to try if you don't mind. He does seem to like to talk about you to me, and I feel so sorry for him I guess I could comfort him a little, for it seems as if it would be the nicest thing in the world to have some one like you that way for years, just as they do in books, only every time I think about being a comfort to him I think he belongs to you and it ain't right. So Marsh, you just speak out and say if your willing I should try to comfort him a little, and make up to him fer what he lost in you, being as you're married and fixed so nice yourself. Of course, I know I ain't pretty like you, nor can't hold my head proud and step high as you always did, even when you was little, but I can feel, and perhaps that's something. Anyhow Hanford's been down three times to talk about you to me, and if you don't mind I'm going to let him come some more. But if you mind the leastest little bit I want you should say so, for things are mixed in this world and I don't want to get to trmpl any other person's feelings, much less you who have always been my best friend and always will be as long as I live I guess. 'Member how we used to play house on the old flat stone in the orchard, and you give me all the prettiest pieces of china with sprigs on 'em? I ain't forgot that, and never will. I shall always say you made the prettiest bride I ever saw, no matter how many more I see, and I hope you won't forget me. It's lonesome here without you. If it wasn't for comforting Hanford I shouldn't care much for anything. I can't think of you a grown up woman. Do you feel any different? I spose you wouldn't climb a fence nor run through the pasture lot for anything now. Have you got a lot of new

Marcia laid down the letter and buried her face in her hands. To her too had come a thrust which must search her life and change it. So while David wrestled with his sorrow Marcia entered upon the knowledge of her own heart.

There was something in the revelation by Mary Ann of Hanford Weston's feelings toward her that touched her immeasurably. Had it all happened before she left him, had Hanford come to her and told her of his love, she would have turned from him in dismay, almost disgust, and have told him that they were both but children, how could they talk of love. She could never have loved him. She would have felt it instantly, and her mocking laugh might have done a good deal toward saving him from sorrow. But now, with miles between them, with the wall of the solemn marriage vows to separate them forever, with her own youth locked up as she supposed until the day of eternity should perhaps set it free, with no hope of any bright dream of life such as girls have, could she turn from even a school boy's love without a passing tenderness, such as she would never have felt if she had not come away from it all? Told in Mary Ann's blunt way, with her crude attempts at pathos, it reached her as it could not otherwise. With her own new view of life she could sympathize better with another's disappointments. Perhaps her own loneliness gave her pity for another. Whatever it was, Marcia's heart suddenly turned toward Hanford Weston with a great throb of gratitude. She felt that she had been loved, even though it had been impossible for that love to be returned, and that whatever happened she would not go unloved down to the end of her days. Suddenly, out of the midst of the perplexity of her thoughts, there formed a distinct knowledge of what was lacking in her life, a lack she had never felt before, and probably would not have felt now had she not thus suddenly stepped into a place much beyond her years. It seemed to the girl as she sat in the great chintz chair and read and re-read that letter, as if she lived years that afternoon, and all her life was to be changed henceforth. It was not that she was sorry that she could not go back, and live out her girlhood and have it crowned with Hanford Weston's love. Not at all. She knew, as well now as she ever had known, that he could never be anything to her, but she knew also, or thought she knew, that he could have given her some-thing, in his clumsy way, that now she could never have from any man, seeing she was David's and David could not love her that way, of course.

Having come to this conclusion, she arose and wrote a letter giving and bequeathing to Mary Ann Fothergill all right, title, and claim to the affections of Hanford Weston, past, present, and future — sending him a message calculated to smooth his ruffled feelings, with her pretty thanks for his youthful adoration; comfort his sorrow with the thought that it must have been a hallucination, that some day he would find his true ideal which he had only thought he had found in her; and send him on his way rejoicing with her blessings and good wishes for a happy life. As for Mary Ann, for once she received her need of Marcia's love, for homesick Marcia felt more tenderness for her than she had ever been able to feel before; and Marcia's loving messages set Mary Ann in a flutter of delight, as she laid her plans for comforting Hanford Weston.

...—.....ᴜᴵᴄ, impenetrable wall
..—possibility he stood helpless, his misery eating upon his soul, but there still remained the fact that there was nothing, absolutely nothing, which he could possibly do. At times the truth rose to the surface, the wretched truth, that Kate was at fault, that having done the deed she should abide by it, and not try to keep a hold upon him, but it was not often he was able to think in this way. Most of the time he mourned over and for the lovely girl he had lost.

As for Marcia, she came and went unobtrusively, making quiet comfort for David which he scarcely noticed. At times he roused himself to be polite to her, and made a labored effort to do something to amuse her, just as if she had been visiting him as a favor and he felt in duty bound to make the time pass pleasantly, but she troubled him so little with herself, that nearly always he forgot her. Whenever there was any public function to which they were bidden he always told her apologetically, as though it must be as much of a bore to her as to him, and he regretted that it was necessary to go in order to carry out their mutual agreement. Marcia, hailing with delight every chance to go out in search of something which would keep her from thinking the new thoughts which had come to her, demurely covered her pleasure and dressed herself dutifully in the robes made for her sister, hating them secretly the while, and was always ready when he came for her. David had nothing to complain of in his wife, so far as outward duty was concerned, but he was too busy with his own heart's bitterness to even recognize it.

One afternoon, of a day when David had gone out of town not expecting to return until late in the evening, there came a knock at the door.

There was something womanish in the knock, Marcia thought, as she hastened to answer it, and she wondered, hurriedly smoothing her shining hair, if it could be the aunts come to make their fortnightly-afternoon penance visit. She gave a hasty glance into the parlor hoping all was right, and was relieved to make sure she had closed the piano. The aunts would consider it a great breach of housewifely decorum to allow a moment's dust to settle upon its sacred keys.

But it was not the aunts who stood upon the stoop, smiling and bowing with a handsome assurance of his own welcome. It was Harry Temple.

Marcia was not glad to see him. A sudden feeling of unreasoning alarm took possession of her.

"You're all alone this time, sweet lady, aren't you?" he asked with easy nonchalance, as he lounged into the hall without waiting her bidding.

"Sir!" said Marcia, half frightened, half wondering.

But he smiled reassuringly down upon her and took the door knob in his own hands to close the door.

"Your good man is out this time, isn't he?" he smiled again most delightfully. His face was very handsome when he smiled. He knew this fact well.

Marcia did not smile. Why did he speak as if he knew where David was, and seemed to be pleased that he was away?

"My husband is not in at present," she said guardedly, her innocent eyes searching his face, "did you wish to see him?"

She was beautiful as she stood there in the wide hall, with only the light from the high transom over the door, shedding an afternoon glow through its pleated Swiss oval. She looked more sweet and little-girlish than ever, and he felt a strong desire to take her in his arms and tell her so, only he feared, from something he saw in those wide, sweet eyes, that she might take alarm and run away too soon, so he only smiled and said that his business with her husband could wait until another time, and meantime he had called to fulfill his promise to play for her.

She took him into the darkened parlor, gave him the stiffest and stateliest hair-cloth chair; but he walked straight over to the instrument, and with not at all the reverence she liked to treat it, flung back the coverings, threw the lid open, and sat down.

He had white fingers, and he ran them over the keys with an air of being at home among them, light little airs dripping from his touch like dew from a glistening grass blade. Marcia felt there were butterflies in the air, and buzzing bees, and fairy flowers dancing on the slightest of stems, with a sky so blue it seemed to be filled with the sound of lily bells. The music he played was of the nature of what would be styled to-day "popular," for this man was master of nothing but having a good time. Quick music with a jingle he played, that to the puritanic-bred girl suggested nothing but a heart bubbling over with gladness, but he meant it should make her heart flutter and her foot beat time to the tripping measure. In his world feet were attuned to gay music. But Marcia stood with quiet dignity a little away from the instrument, her lips parted, her eyes bright with the pleasure of the melody, her hands clasped, and her breath coming quickly. She was all absorbed with the music. All unknowingly Marcia had placed herself where the light from the window fell full across her face, and every flitting expression as she followed the undulant sounds was visible. The young man gazed, almost as much pleased with the lovely face as Marcia was with the music.

At last he drew a chair quite near his own seat.

"Come and sit down," he said, "and I will sing to you. You did not know I could sing, too, did you? Oh, I can. But you must sit down for I couldn't sing right when you are standing."

birds and the sunny sky, rather than the wild whirly kind that seemed all a mad scramble.

She meant to ask him to play over again what he played at the beginning, but he struck into a Scotch love ballad. The melody intoxicated her fancy, and her face shone with pleasure. She had not noticed the words particularly, save that they were of love, and she thought with pain of David and Kate, and how the pleading tenderness might have been his heart calling to hers not to forget his love for her. But Harry Temple mistook her expression for one of interest in himself. With his eyes still upon hers, as a cat might mesmerize a bird, he changed into a minor wail of heart-broken love, whose sadness brought great tears to Marcia's eyes, and deep color to her already burning cheeks, while the music throbbed out her own half-realized loneliness and sorrow. It was as if the sounds painted for her a picture of what she had missed out of love, and set her sorrow flowing tangibly.

The last note died away in an impressive diminuendo, and the young man turned toward her. His eyes were languishing, his voice gentle, persuasive, as though it had but been the song come a little nearer.

"And that is the way I feel toward you, dear," he said, and reached out his white hands to where hers lay forgotten in her lap.

But his hands had scarcely touched hers, before Marcia sprang back, in her haste knocking over the chair.

Erect, her hands snatched behind her, frightened, alert, she stood a moment bewildered, all her fears to the front.

Ah! but he was used to shy maidens. He was not to be baffled thus. A little coaxing, a little gentle persuasion, a little boldness — that was all he needed. He had conquered hearts before, why should he not this unsophisticated one?

"Don't be afraid, dear; there is no one about. And surely there is no harm in telling you I love you, and letting you comfort my poor broken heart to think that I have found you too late —"

He had arisen and with a passionate gesture put his arms about Marcia and before she could know what was coming had pressed a kiss upon her lips.

But she was aroused now. Every angry force within her was fully awake. Every sense of right and justice inherited and taught came flocking forward. Horror unspeakable filled her, and wrath, that such a dreadful thing should come to her. There was no time to think. She brought her two strong supple hands up and beat him in the face, mouth, cheeks, and eyes, with all her might, until he turned blinded; and then she struggled away crying, "You are a wicked man!" and fled from the room.

Out through the hall she sped to the kitchen, and flinging wide the door before her, the nearest one at hand, she fairly flew down the garden walk, past the nodding dahlias, past the basking pumpkins, past the whispering corn, down through the berry bushes, at the lower end of the lot, and behind the currant bushes. She crouched a moment looking back to see if she were pursued. Then imagining she heard a noise from the open door, she scrambled over the low back fence, the high comb with which her hair was fastened falling out unheeded behind her, and all her dark waves of hair coming about her shoulders in wild disarray.

She was in a field of wheat now, and the tall shocks were like waves all about her, thick and close, kissing her as she passed with their bended stalks. Ahead of her it looked like an endless sea to cross before she could reach another fence, and a bare field, and then another fence and the woods. She knew not that in her wake she left a tracks clear as if she had set up signals all along the way. She felt that the kind wheat would flow back like real waves and hide the way she had passed over. She only sped on, to the woods. In all the wide world there seemed no refuge but the woods. The woods were home to her. She loved the tall shadows, the whispering music in the upper branches, the quiet places underneath, the hushed silence like a city of refuge with cool wings whereunder to hide. And to it, as her only friend, she was hastening. She went to the woods as she would have flown to the minister's wife at home, if she only had been near, and buried her face in her lap and sobbed out her horror and shame. Breathless she sped, without looking once behind her, now over the next fence and still another. They were nothing to her. She forgot that she was wearing Kate's special sprigged muslin, and that it might tear on the rough fences. She forgot that she was a matron and must not run wild through strange fields. She forgot that some one might be watching her. She forgot everything save that she must get away and hide her poor shamed face.

At last she reached the shelter of the woods, and, with one wild furtive look behind her to assure herself that she was not pursued, she flung herself into the lap of mother earth, and buried her face in the soft moss at the foot of a tree. There she sobbed out her horror and sorrow and loneliness, sobbed until it seemed to her that her heart had gone out with great shudders. Sobbed and sobbed and sobbed! For a time she could not even think clearly. Her brain was confused with the magnitude of what had come to her. She tried to go over the whole happening that afternoon and see if she might have prevented anything. She blamed herself most unmercifully for listening to the foolish music and, too, after her own suspicions had been aroused, though how could she dream any man in his senses would do a thing like that! Not even Captain Leavenworth would stoop to that, she thought. Poor child! She knew so little of the world, why had not the aunts come that afternoon! Why had they not arrived before this man came! And yet, oh, horror! if they had come after he was there! How disgusting he seemed to her with his smirky smile, and slim white fingers! How utterly unfit beside David did he seem to breathe the same air even. David, her David—no, Kate's David! Oh, pity! What a pain the world was!

There was nowhere to turn that she might find a trace of comfort. For what would David say, and how could she ever tell him? Would he find it out if she did not? What would he think of her? Would he blame her? Oh, the agony of it all! What would the aunts think of her! Ah! that was worse than all, for even now she could see the tilt of Aunt Hortense's head, and the purse of Aunt Amelia's lips. How dreadful if they should have to know of it. They would not believe her, unless perhaps Aunt Clarinda might. She did not look wise, but she seemed kind and loving. If it had not been for the other two she might have fled to Aunt Clarinda. Oh, if she might but flee home to her father's house! How could she ever play on that dreadful piano again? She would always see that hateful, smiling face sitting there and think how he had looked at her. Then she shuddered and sobbed harder than ever. And mother earth, true to all her children, received the poor child with open arms. There she lay upon the resinous pine needles, at the foot of the tall trees, and the trees looked down tenderly upon her and consulted in whispers with their heads bent together. The winds blew sweetness from the buckwheat fields in the valley about her, murmuring delicious music in the air above her, and even the birds hushed their loud voices and peeped curiously at the tired, sorrowful creature of another kind that had come among them.

Marcia's overwrought nerves were having their revenge. Tears had their way until she was worn out, and then the angel of sleep came down upon her. There upon the pine-needle bed, with tear-wet cheeks she lay, and slept like a tired child come home to its mother from the tumult of the world.

Harry Temple, recovering from his rebuff, and left alone in the parlor, looked about him with surprise. Never before in all his short and brilliant career as a heart breaker had he met with the like, and this from a mere child! He could not believe his senses! She must have been in play. He would sit still and presently she would come back with eyes full of mischief and beg his pardon. But even as he sat down to wait her coming, something told him he was mistaken and that she would not come. There had been something beside mischief in the smart raps whose tingle even now his cheeks and lips felt. The house, too, had grown strangely hushed as though no one else besides himself were in it. She must have gone out. Perhaps she had been really frightened and would tell somebody! How awkward if she should presently return with one of those grim aunts, or that solemn puritan-like husband of hers. Perhaps he had better decamp while the coast was still clear. She did not seem to be returning and there was no telling what the little fool might do.

With a deliberation which suddenly became feverish in his haste to be away, he compelled himself to walk slowly, nonchalantly out through the hall. Still as a thief he opened and closed the front door and got himself down the front steps, but not so still but that a quick ear caught the sound of the latch as if flew back into place, and the scrape of a boot on the path; and not so invisibly nor so quickly but that a pair of keen eyes saw him.

When Harry Temple had made his way toward the Spafford house that afternoon, with his dauntless front and conceited smile, Miranda had been sent out to pick raspberries along the fence that separated the Heath garden from the Spafford garden.

Harry Temple was too new in the town not to excite comment among the young girls wherever he might go, and Miranda was always having her eye out for anything new. Not for herself! Bless you! No! Miranda never expected anything from a young man for herself, but she was keenly interested in what befell other girls.

So Miranda, crouched behind the berry bushes, watched Harry Temple saunter down the street and saw with surprise that he stopped at the house of her new admiration. Now, although Marcia was a married woman, Miranda felt pleased that she should have the attention of others, and a feeling of pride in her idol, and of triumph over her cousin Hannah that he had not stopped to see her, swelled in her brown calico breast.

She managed to bring her picking as near to the region of the Spafford parlor windows as possible, and much did her ravished ear delight itself in the music that tinkled through the green shaded window, for Miranda had tastes that were greatly appealed to by the gay dance music. She fancied that her idol was the player. But then she heard a man's voice, and her picking stopped short insomuch that her grandmother's strident tones mingled with the liquid tenor or Mr. Temple, calling to Miranda to "be spry there or the sun'll catch you 'fore you get a quart." All at once the music ceased, and then in a minute or two Miranda hear the Spafford kitchen door thrown violently open and saw Marcia rush forth.

She gazed in astonishment, too surprised to call out to her, or to remember to keep on picking for a moment. She watched her as she fairly flew down between the rows of currant bushes, saw the comb fly from her hair, saw the glow of excitement on her cheek, and the fire in her eye, saw her mount the first fence. Then suddenly a feeling of protection arose within her, and, with a hasty glance toward her grandmother's window to satisfy herself that no one else saw

...gate, she hastened to the end of the lot and watched Marcia; watched her as she climbed the fences, held her breath at the daring leaps from the top rails, expecting to see the delicate muslin catch on the rough fence and send the flying figure to the ground senseless perhaps. It was like a theatre to Miranda, this watching the beautiful girl in her flight, the long dark hair in the wind, the graceful untrammeled bounds. Miranda watched with unveiled admiration until the dark of the green-blue wood had swallowed her up, then slowly her eyes traveled back over the path which Marcia had taken, back through the meadow and the wheat, to the kitchen door left standing wide. Slowly, painfully, Miranda set herself to understand it. Something had happened! That was flight with fear behind it, fear that left everything else forgotten. What had happened?

Miranda was wiser in her generation than Marcia. She began to put two and two together. Her brows darkened, and a look of cunning came into her honest blue eyes. Stealthily she crept with cat-like quickness along the fence near to the front, and there she stood like a red-haired Nemesis in a sunbonnet, with irate red face, confronting the unsuspecting man as he sauntered forth from the unwelcoming roof where he had whiled away a mistaken hour.

"What you ben sayin' to her?"

It was as if a serpent had stung him, so unexpected, so direct. He jumped aside and turned deadly pale. She knew her chance arrow had struck the truth. But he recovered himself almost immediately when he saw what a harmless looking creature had attacked him.

"Why, my dear girl," he said patronizingly, "you quite startled me! I'm sure you must have made some mistake!"

"I ain't your girl, thank goodness!" snapped Miranda, "and I guess by your looks there ain't anybody 'dear' to you but yourself. But I ain't made a mistake. It's you I was asking. *What you bin in there for?*" There was a blaze of defiance in Miranda's eyes, and her stubby forefinger pointed at him like a shotgun. Before her the bold black eyes quailed for an instant. The young man's hand sought his pocket, brought a piece of money and extended it.

"Look here my friend," he said trying another line, "you take this and say nothing more about it. That's a good girl. No harm's been done."

Miranda looked him in the face with noble scorn, and with a sudden motion of her brown hand sent the coin flying on the stone pavement.

"I tell you I'm not your friend, and I don't want your money. I wouldn't trust its goodness any more than your face. As fer keepin' still I'll do as I see fit about it. I intend to know what this means, and if you've made her any trouble you'd better leave this town, for I'll make it too unpleasant fer you to stay here!"

With a stealthy glance about him, cautious, concerned, the young man suddenly hurried down the street. He wanted no more parley with this loud-voiced avenging maiden. His fear came back upon him in double force, and he was seen to glance at his watch and quicken his pace almost to a run as though a forgotten engagement had suddenly come to mind. Miranda, scowling, stood and watched him disappear around the corner, than she turned back and began to pick raspberries with a diligence that would have astonished her grandmother had she not been for the last hour engaged with a calling neighbor in the room at the other side of the house, where they were overhauling the character of a fellow church member.

Miranda picked on, and thought on, and could not make up her mind what she ought to do. From time to time she glanced anxiously toward the woods, and then at the lowering sun in the West, and half meditated going after Marcia, but a wholesome fear of her grandmother held her hesitating.

At length she heard a firm step coming down the street. Could it be? Yes, it was David Spafford. How was it he happened to come so soon? Miranda had heard in a round-about-way, as neighbors hear and know these things, that David had taken the stage that morning, presumably on business to New York, and was hardly expected to return for several days. She had wondered if Marcia would stay all night alone in the house or if she would go to the aunts. But now here was David!

Miranda looked again over the wheat, half expecting to see the flying figure returning in haste, but the parted wheat waved on and sang its song of the harvest, unmindful and alone, with only a fluttering butterfly to give life to the landscape. A little rusty-throated cricket piped a doleful sentence now and then between the silences.

David Spafford let himself in at his own door, and went in search of Marcia.

He wanted to find Marcia for a purpose. The business which had taken him away in the morning, and which he had hardly expected to accomplish before late that night, had been partly transacted at a little tavern where the coach horses had been changed that morning, and where he had met most unexpectedly the two men whom he had been going to see, who were coming straight to his town. So he turned him back with them and came home, and they were at this minute attending to some other business in the town, while he had come home to announce to Marcia that they would take supper with him and perhaps spend the night.

Marcia was nowhere to be found. He went upstairs and timidly knocked at her door, but no answer came. Then he thought she might be asleep and knocked louder, but only the humming-bird in the honeysuckle outside her window sent back a little humming answer through the latch-hole. Finally he brick path that led to the garden. Ah! what was that? Something gleamed in the sun with a spot of blue behind it. The bit of blue ribbon she had down at her throat, with a tiny gold brooch unclasped sticking in.

Miranda caught sight of him coming, and crouched behind the currants.

David came on searching the path every side. A bit of branch had been torn from a succulent, tender plant that leaned over the path and was lying in the way. It seemed another blaze along the trail. Further down where the bushes almost met a single fragment of a thread waved on a thorn as though it had snatched for more in the passing and had caught only this. David hardly knew whether he was following these little things or not, but at any rate they were apparently not leading him anywhere for he stopped abruptly in front of the fence and looked both ways behind the bushes that grew along in front of it. Then he turned to go back again. Miranda held her breath. Something touched David's foot in turning, and, looking down, he saw Marcia's large shell comb lying there in the grass. Curiously he picked it up and examined it. It was like finding fragments of a wreck along the sand.

All at once Miranda arose from her hiding place and confronted him timidly. She was not the same Miranda who came down upon Harry Temple, however.

"She ain't in the house," she said hoarsely. "She's gone over there!"

David Spafford turned surprised.

"Is that you, Miranda? Oh, thank you! Where do you say she has gone? Where?"

"Through there, don't you see?" and again the stubby forefinger pointed to the rift in the wheat.

David gazed stupidly at the path in the wheat, but gradually it began to dawn upon him that there was a distinct line through it where some one must have gone.

"Yes, I see," he said thinking aloud, "but why should she have gone there? There is nothing over there."

"She went on further, she went to the woods," said Miranda, looking fearfully around lest even now her grandmother might be upon her, "and she was scared, I guess. She looked it. He hair all come tumblin' down when she clum the fence, an' she just went flyin' over like some bird, didn't care a feather if she did fall, an' she never once looked behind her till she come to the woods."

David's bewilderment was growing uncomfortable. There was a shade of alarm in his face and of the embarrassment one feels when a neighbor divulges news about a member of one's own household.

"Why, surely, Miranda, you must be mistaken. Maybe it was some one else you saw. I do not think Mrs. Spafford would be likely to run over there that way, and what in the world would she have to be frightened at?"

"No, I ain't mistaken," said Miranda half sullenly, nettled at his unbelief. "It was her all right. She came flyin' out the kitchen door when I was picking raspberries, and down that path to the fence, and never stopped fer fence ner wheat, ner medder lot, but went into them woods there, right up to the left of them tall pines, and she,—she looked plum scared to death 's if a whole circus menagerie was after her, lions and 'nelefunts an' all. An' I guess she had plenty to be scared at ef I ain't mistaken. That dandy Temple feller went there to call on her, an' I heard him tinklin' that music box, and it's my opinion he needs a wallupin'! You better go after her! It's gettin' late and you'll have hard times finding her in the dark. Just you foller her path in the wheat, and then make fer them pines. I'd a gone after her myself only grandma'd make sech a fuss, and hev to know it all. You needn't be afraid o' me. I'll keep still."

By this time David was thoroughly alive to the situation and much alarmed. He mounted the fence with alacrity, gave one glance with "thank you" at Miranda, and disappeared through the wheat. Miranda watched him till she was sure he was making for the right spot, then with a sigh of relief she hastened into the house with her now brimming pail of berries.

he experienced a series of sensations. For the first time since his wedding day he was aroused to entirely forget himself and his pain. What did it mean? Marcia frightened! What at? Harry Temple at their house! What did he know of Harry Temple? Nothing beyond the mere fact that Hannah Heath had introduced him and that he was doing business in the town. But why had Mr. Temple visited the house? He could have no possible business with himself, David was sure; moreover he now remembered having seen the young man standing near the stable that morning when he took his seat in the coach, and knew that he must have heard his remark that he would not return till the late coach that night, or possibly not till the next day. He remembered as he said it that he had unconsciously studied Mr. Temple's face and noted its weak points. Did the young man have a purpose in coming to the house during his absence? A great anger rose within him at the thought.

There was one strange thing about David's thoughts. For the first time he looked at himself in the light of Marcia's natural protector—her husband. He suddenly saw a duty from himself to her, aside from the mere feeding and clothing her. He felt a personal responsibility, and an actual interest in her. Out of the whole world, now, he was the only one she could look to for help.

It gave him a feeling of possession that was new, and almost seemed pleasant. He forgot entirely the errand that had made him come to search for Marcia in the first place, and the two men who were probably at that moment preparing to go to his house according to their invitation. He forgot everything but Marcia, and strode into the purply-blue shadows of the wood and stopped to listen.

The hush there seemed intense. There were no echoes lingering of flying feet down that pine-padded pathway of the aisle of the woods. It was long since he had had time to wander in the woods, and he wondered at their silence. So much whispering above, the sky so far away, the breeze so quiet, the bird notes so subdued, it seemed almost uncanny. He had not remembered that it was thus in the woods. It struck him in passing that here would be a good place to bring his pain some day when he had time to face it again, and wished to be alone with it.

He took his hat in his hand and stepped firmly into the vast solemnity as if he had entered a great church when the service was going on, on an errand of life and death that gave excuse for profaning the holy silence. He went a few paces and stopped again, listening. Was that a long-drawn sighing breath he heard, or only the wind coughing through the waving tassels overhead? He summoned his voice to call. It seemed a great effort, and sounded weak and feeble under the grandeur of the vaulted green dome. "Marcia!" he called,— and "Marcia!" realizing as he did so that it was the first time he had called her by her name, or sought after her in any way. He had always said "you" to her, or "child," or spoken of her in company as "Mrs. Spafford," a strange and far-off mythical person whose very intangibility had separated her from himself immeasurably.

He went further into the forest, called again, and yet again, and stood to listen. All was still about him, but in the far distance he heard the faint report of a gun. With a new thought of danger coming to mind he hurried further into the shadows. The gun sounded again more clearly. He shuddered involuntarily and looked about in all directions, hoping to see the gleam of her gown. It was not likely there were any wild beasts about these parts, so near the town and yet, they had been seen occasionally,—a stray fox, or even a bear,—and the sun was certainly very low. He glanced back, and the low line of the horizon gleamed the gold of the intensified shining that is the sun's farewell for the night. The gun again! Stray shots had been known to kill people wandering in the forest. He was growing nervous as a woman now, and went this way and that calling, but still no answer came. He began to think he was not near the clump of pines of which Miranda spoke, and went a little to the right and then turned to look back to where he had entered the wood, and there, almost at his feet, she lay!

She slept as soundly as if she had been lying on a couch of velvet, one round white arm under her cheek. Her face was flushed with weeping, and her lashes still wet. Her tender sensitive mouth still quivered slightly as she gave a long-drawn breath with a catch in it that seemed like a sob, and all her lovely dark hair floated about her as if it were spread upon a wave that upheld her. She was beautiful indeed as she lay there sleeping, and the man, thus suddenly come upon her, anxious and troubled and every nerve quivering, stopped, awed with the beauty of her as if she had been some heavenly being suddenly confronting him. He stepped softly to her side and bending down observed her, first anxiously, to make sure she was alive and safe, then searchingly, as though he would know every detail of the picture before him because it was his, and he not only had a right but a duty to possess it, and to care for it.

She might have been a statue or a painting as he looked upon her and noted the lovely curve of her flushed cheek, but when his eyes reached the firm brown hand and the slender finger on which gleamed the wedding ring that was not really hers, something pathetic in the tear-wet lashes, and the whole sorrowful, beautiful figure touched him with a great tenderness, and he stooped down gently and put his arm about her.

speaking gently. Then Marcia opened her eyes bewildered, and with a start, sprang back and looked at David, as though she would be sure it was he and not that other dreadful man from whom she had fled.

"Why, child! What's the matter?" said David, brushing her hair back from her face. Bewildered still, Marcia scarcely knew him, his voice was so strangely sweet and sympathetic. The tears were coming back, but she could not stop them. She made one effort to control herself and speak, but her lips quivered a moment, and then the flood-gates opened again, and she covered her face with her hands and shook with sobs. How could she tell David what a dreadful thing had happened, now, when he was kinder to her than he had ever thought of being before! He would grow grave and stern when she had told him, and she could not bear that. He would likely blame her too, and how could she endure more?

But he drew her to him again and laid her head against his coat, trying to smooth her hair with unaccustomed passes of his hand. By and by the tears subsided and she could control herself again. She hushed her sobs and drew back a little from the comforting rough coat where she had lain.

"Indeed, indeed, I could not help it, David," – she faltered, trying to smile like a bit of rainbow through the rain.

"I know you couldn't, child." His answer was wonderfully kind and his eyes smiled at her as they had never done before. Her heart gave a leap of astonishment and fluttered with gladness over it. It was so good to have David care. She had not known how much she wanted him to speak to her as if he saw her and thought a little about her.

"And now what was it? Remember I do not know. Tell me quick, for it is growing late and damp, and you will take cold out here in the woods with that thin frock on. You are chilly already."

"I better go at once," she said reservedly, willing to put off telling him as long as possible, peradventure to avoid it altogether.

"No, child," he said firmly drawing her back again beside him, "you must rest a minute yet before taking that long walk. You are weary and excited, and besides it will do you good to tell me. What made you run off up here? Are you homesick?"

He scanned her face anxiously. He began to fear with sudden compunction that the sacrifice he had accepted so easily had been too much for the victim, and it suddenly began to be a great comfort to him to have Marcia with him, to help him hide his sorrow from the world. He did not know before that he cared.

"I was frightened," she said with drooping lashes. She was trying to keep her lips and fingers from trembling, for she feared greatly to tell him all. But though the woods were growing dusky he saw the fluttering little fingers and gathered them firmly in his own.

"Now, child," he said in that tone that even his aunts obeyed, "tell me all. What frightened you, and why did you come up here away from everybody instead of calling for help?"

Brought to bay she lifted her beautiful eyes to his face and told him briefly the story, beginning with the night when she had first met Harry Temple. She said as little about music as possible, because she feared that the mention of the piano might be painful to David, but made the whole matter quite plain in a few words, so that David could readily fill in between the lines.

"Scoundrel!" he murmured clenching his fists, " he ought to be strung up!" Then quite gently again, "Poor child! How frightened you must have been! You did right to run away, but it was a dangerous thing to run out here! Why, he might have followed you!"

"Oh!" said Marcia, turning pale, "I never thought of that. I only wanted to get away from everybody. It seemed so dreadful I did not want anybody to know. I did not want you to know. I wanted to run away and hide, and never come back!" She covered her face with her hands and shuddered. David thought the tears were coming back again.

"Child, child!" he said gently, "you must not talk that way. What would I do if you did that?" and he laid his hand softly upon the bowed head.

It was the first time anything like a personal talk had passed between them, and Marcia felt a thrill of delight at his words. It was like heavenly comfort to her wounded spirit.

She stole a shy look at him under her lashes, and wished she dared say something, but no words came. They sat for a moment in silence, each feeling a sort of comforting sense of the other's presence, and each clasping the hand of the other with clinging pressure, yet neither fully aware of the fact.

The last rays of the sun which had been lying for a while at their feet upon the pine needles suddenly slipped away unperceived, and behold! the world was in gloom, and the place where the two sat was almost utterly dark. David became aware of it first, and with sudden remembrance of his expected guests he started in dismay.

"Child!" said he,—but he did not let go of her hand, nor forget to put tenderness in his voice, "the sun has gone down, and here have I been forgetting what I came to tell you in the astonishment over what you had to tell me. We must hurry and get back. We have guests to-night to supper, two gentlemen, very distinguished in their lines of work. We have business together, and I must make haste. I doubt not they are at the house already, and what they think of me I cannot tell; let us hurry as fast as possible."

...gentlemen will delay
...er of a Temple and suggesting that
...morning stage. I should like to give him what Miranda
...a good 'wallupin,' but perhaps that would be undignified."

He laughed as he said it, a hearty laugh with a ring to it like his old self. Marcia felt happy at the sound. How wonderful it would be if he would be like that to her all the time! Her heart swelled with the great thought of it.

He helped her to her feet and taking her hand led her out to the open field where they could walk faster. As he walked he told her about Miranda waiting for him behind the currant bushes. They laughed together and made the way seem short.

It was quite dark now, with the faded moon trembling feebly in the West as though it meant to retire early, and wished they would hurry home while she held her light for them. David had drawn Marcia's arm within his, and then, noticing that her dress was thin, he pulled off his coat and put it firmly about her despite her protest that she did not need it, and so, warmed, comforted, and cheered Marcia's feet hurried back over the path she had taken in such sorrow and fright a few hours before.

When they could see the lights of the village twinkling close below them David began to tell her about the two men who were to be their guests, if they were still waiting, and so interesting was his brief story of each that Marcia hardly knew they were home before David was helping her over their own back fence.

"Oh, David! There seems to be a light in the kitchen! Do you suppose they have gone in and are getting their own supper? What shall I do with my hair? I cannot go in with it this way. How did that light get there?"

"Here!" said David, fumbling in his pocket, "will this help you?" and he brought out the shell comb he had picked up in the garden.

By the light of the feeble old moon David watched her coil her long wavy hair and stood to pass his criticism upon the effect before they should go in. They were just back of the tall sunflowers, and talked in whispers. It was all so cheery, and comradely, and merry, that Marcia hated to go in and have it over, for she could not feel that this sweet evening hour could last. Then they took hands and swiftly, cautiously, stole up to the kitchen window and looked in. The door stood open as both had left it that afternoon, and there seemed to be nobody in the kitchen. A candle was burning on the high little shelf over the table, and the tea kettle was singing on the crane above the hearth, but the room was without occupant. Cautiously, looking questioningly at each other, they stole into the kitchen, each dreading lest the aunts had come by chance and discovered their lapse. There was a light in the front part of the house and they could hear voices, two men were earnestly discussing politics. They listened longer, but no other presence was revealed.

David in pantomime outlined the course of action, and Marcia, understanding perfectly flew up the back stairs as noiselessly as a mouse, to make her toilet after her nap in the woods, while David with much show and to-do of opening and shutting the wide-open kitchen door walked obviously into the kitchen and hurried to greet his guests wondering,—not suspecting the least,— what good angel had been there to let them in.

Good fortune had favored Miranda. The neighbor had stayed longer than usual, perhaps in hopes of an invitation to stay to tea and share in the gingerbread she could smell being taken from the oven by Hannah, who occasionally varied her occupations by a turn at the culinary art. Hannah could make delicious gingerbread. Her grandmother had taught her when she was but a child.

Miranda stole into the kitchen when Hannah's back was turned and picked over the berries so fast that when Hannah came into the pantry to set her gingerbread to cool Miranda had nearly all her berries in a big yellow bowl ready to wash, and Hannah might conjecture if she pleased that Miranda had been some time picking them over. It is not stated how thoroughly those berries were picked over. But Miranda cared little for that. Her mind was upon other things. The pantry window overlooked the hills and the woods. She could see if David and Marcia were coming back soon. She wanted to watch her play till the close, and had no fancy for having the curtain fall in the middle of the most exciting act, the rescue of the princess. But the talk in the sitting room went on and on. By and by Hannah Heath washed her hands, untied her apron, and taking her sunbonnet slipped over to Ann Bertram's for a pattern of her new sleeve. Miranda took the opportunity to be off again.

Swiftly down behind the currants she ran, and standing on the fence between the corn she looked off across the wheat, but no sign of anybody yet coming out of the woods was granted her. She stood so a long time. It was growing dusk. She wondered if Harry Temple had shut the front door when he went out. But David went in that way, and he would have closed it, of course. Still, he went away in a hurry, maybe it would be as well to go and look. She did not wish to be caught by her grandmother, so she stole along like a cat close to the dark berry bushes, and the gathering dusk hid her well. She thought she could see from the front of the fence whether the door looked as if it were closed. But there were people coming up the street. She would wait until they had passed before she looked over the fence.

_____ _____, _ _____. _ was here once before."

"There doesn't seem to be a light in the house," said the other, looking up to the windows over the street. "Are you sure? Brother Spafford said he was coming directly home to let his wife know of our arrival."

"A little strange there's no light yet, for it is quite dark now, but I'm sure this must be the house. Maybe they are all in the kitchen and not expecting us quite so soon. Let's try anyhow," said the other, setting down his carpet-bag on the stoop and lifting the big brass knocker.

Miranda stood still debating but a moment. The situation was made plain to her in an instant. Not for nothing had she stood at Grandma Heath's elbow for years watching the movements of her neighbors and interpreting exactly what they meant. Miranda's wits were sharpened for situations of all kinds. Miranda was ready and loyal to those she adored. Without further ado she hastened to a sheltered spot she knew and climbed the picket fence which separated the Heath garden from the Spafford side yard. Before the brass knocker had sounded through the empty house the second time Miranda had crossed the side porch, thrown her sunbonnet upon a chair in the dark kitchen, and was hastening with noisy encouraging steps to the front door.

She flung it wide open, saying in a breezy voice, "Just wait till I get a light, won't you, the wind blew the candle out."

There wasn't a particle of wind about that soft September night, but that made little difference to Miranda. She was part of a play and she was acting her best. If her impromptu part was a little irregular, it was at least well meant, boldly and bravely presented.

Miranda found a candle on the shelf and, stooping to the smoldering fire upon the hearth, blew and coaxed it into flame enough to light it.

"This is Mr. Spafford's home, is it not?" questioned the old gentleman whom Miranda had heard speak first on the sidewalk.

"Oh, yes, indeed," said the girl glibly. "Jest come in and set down. Here, let me take your hats. Jest put your bags right there on the floor."

"You are—Are you—Mrs. Spafford?" hesitated the courtly old gentleman.

"Oh, landy sakes, no, I ain't her," laughed Miranda well pleased. "Mis' Spafford had jest stepped out a bit when her husband come home, an' he's gone after her. You see she didn't expect her husband home till late to-night. But you set down. They'll be home real soon now. They'd oughter ben here before this. I 'spose she'd gone on further'n she thought she'd go when she stepped out."

"It's all right," said the other gentleman, "no harm done, I'm sure. I hope we shan't inconvenience Mrs. Spafford any coming so unexpectedly."

"No, indeedy!" said quick-witted Miranda. "You can't ketch Mis' Spafford unprepared if you come in the middle o' the night. She's allus ready fer comp'ny." Miranda's eyes shone. She felt she was getting on finely doing the honors.

"Well, that's very nice. I'm sure it makes one feel at home. I wonder now if she would mind if we were to go right up to our room and wash our hands. I feel so travel stained. I'd like to be more presentable before we meet her," said the first gentleman, who looked very weary.

But Miranda was not dashed.

"Why, that's all right. 'Course you ken go right up. Jest you set in the keepin' room a minnit while I run up'n be sure the water pitcher's filled. I ain't quire sure 'bout it. I won't be long."

Miranda seated them in the parlor with great gusto and hastened up the back stairs to investigate. She was not at all sure which room would be called the guest room and whether the two strangers would have a room apiece or occupy the same together. At least it would be safe to show them one till the mistress of the house returned. She peeped into Marcia's room, and knew it instinctively before she caught sight of a cameo brooch on the pin cushion, and a rose colored ribbon neatly folded lying on the foot of the bed where it had been forgotten. That question settled, she thought any other room would do, and chose the large front room across the hall with its high four-poster and the little ball fringe on the valance and canopy. Having lighted the candle which stood in a tall glass candlestick on the high chest of drawers, she hurried down to bid her guests come up.

Then she hastened back into the kitchen and went to work with swift skillful fingers. Her breath came quickly and her cheeks grew red with the excitement of it all. It was like playing fairy. She would get supper for them and have everything all ready when the mistress came, so that there would be no bad breaks. She raked the fire and filled the tea kettle, swinging it from the crane. Then she searched where she thought such things should be and found a table cloth and set the table. Her hands trembled as she put out the sprigged china that was kept in the corner cupboard. Perhaps this was wrong, and she would be blamed for it, but at least it was what she would have done, she thought, if she were mistress of this house and had two nice gentlemen come to stay to tea. It was not often that Grandmother Heath allowed her to handle her sprigged china, to be sure, so Miranda felt the joy and daring of it all the more. Once a delicate cup slipped and rolled over on the table and almost reached the edge. A little more and it would have rolled off to the floor and been shivered into a dozen fragments, but Miranda spread her apron in front and caught it fairly as it started and then hugged it in fear and delight for a moment as she might have

...pped into the pantry
...stores. It was not hard to find all that was needed; cold ham, cheese, pickles, seed cakes, gingerbread, fruit cake, preserves and jelly, bread and raised biscuit, then she went down cellar and found the milk and cream and butter. She had just finished the table and set out the tea pot and caddy of tea when she heard the two gentlemen coming down the stairs. They went into the parlor and sat down, remarking that their friend had a pleasant home, and then Miranda heard them plunge into a political discussion again and she felt that they were safe for a while. She stole out into the dewy dark to see if there were yet signs of the home-comers. A screech owl hooted across the night. She stood a while by the back fence looking out across the dark sea of whispering wheat. By and by she thought she heard subdued voices above the soft swish of the parting wheat, and by the light of the stars she saw them coming. Quick as a wink she slid over the fence into the Heath back-yard and crouched in her old place behind the currant bushes. So she saw them come up together, saw David help Marcia over the fence and watched them till they had passed up the walk to the light of the kitchen door. Then swiftly she turned and glided to her own home, well knowing the reckoning that would be in store for her for this daring bit of recreation. There was about her, however, an air of triumphant joy as she entered.

"Where have you ben to, Miranda Griscom, and what on airth you ben up to now?" was the greeting she received as she lifted the latch of the old green kitchen door of her grandmother's house.

Miranda knew that the worst was to come now, for her grandmother never mentioned the name of Griscom unless she meant business. It was a hated name to her because of the man who had broken the heart of her daughter. Grandma Heath always felt that Miranda was an out and out Griscom with not a streak of Heath about her. The Griscoms all had red hair. But Miranda lifted her chin high and felt like a princess in disguise.

"Ben huntin' hen's eggs down in the grass," she said, taking the first excuse that came into her head. "Is it time to get supper?"

"Hen's eggs? This time o' night an' dark as pitch. Miranda Griscom, you ken go up to your room an' not come down tell I call you!"

It was a dire punishment, or would have been if Miranda had not had her head full of other things, for the neighbor had been asked to tea and there would have been much to hear at the table. Besides, it was apparent that her disgrace was to be made public. However, Miranda did not care. She hastened to her little attic window, which looked down, as good fortune would have it, upon the dining-room windows of the Spafford house. With joy Miranda observed that no one had thought to draw down the shades and she might sit and watch the supper served over the way, — the supper she had prepared, — and might think how delectable the doughnuts were, and let her mouth water over the currant jelly and the quince preserves and pretend she was a guest, and forget the supper downstairs she was missing.

David made what apology he could for his absence on the arrival of his guests, and pondered in his heart who it could have been that they referred to as "the maid," until he suddenly remembered Miranda, and inwardly blessed her for her kindliness. It was more than he would have expected from any member of the Heath household. Miranda's honest face among the currant bushes when she had said, "You needn't be afraid of me, I'll keep still," came to mind. Miranda had evidently scented out the true state of the case and filled in the breach, taking care not to divulge a word. He blest her kindly heart and resolved to show his gratitude to her in some way. Could poor Miranda, sitting supperless in the dark, have but known his thought, her lonely heart would have fluttered happily. But she did not, and virtue had to bring its own reward in a sense of duty done. Then, too, there was a spice of adventure to Miranda's monotonous life in what she had done, and she was not altogether sad as she sat and let her imagination revel in what the Spaffords had said and thought, when they found the house lighted and supper ready. It was better than playing house down behind the barn when she was a little girl.

Marcia was the most astonished when she slipped down from her hurried toilet and found the table decked out in all the house afforded, fairly groaning under its weight of pickles, preserves, doughnuts, and pie. In fact, everything that Miranda had found she had put upon that table, and it is safe to say that the result was not quite as it would have been had the preparation of the supper been left to Marcia.

She stood before it and looked, and could not keep from laughing softly to herself at the array of little dishes of things. Marcia thought at first that one of the aunts must be here, in the parlor, probably entertaining the guests, and that the supper was a reproof to her for being away when she should have been at home attending to her duties, but still she was puzzled. It scarcely seemed like the aunts to set a table in such a peculiar manner. The best china was set out, it is true, but so many little bits of things were in separate dishes. There was half a mould of currant jelly in a large china plate, there was a fresh mould of quince jelly quivering on a common dish. All over the table in every available inch there was something. It would not do to call the guests out to a table like that. What would David say? And yet, if one of the aunts had set it and was going to stay to tea, would she be hurt? She tiptoed to the door and listened, but heard no sound save of men's voices. If an aunt had been here she was surely gone now and would be none the wiser if a few dishes were removed.

With swift fingers Marcia weeded out the things, and set straight those that were to remain, and then made the tea. She was so quick about it David had scarcely time to begin to worry because supper was not announced before she stood in the parlor door, shy and sweet, with a brilliant color in her cheeks. His little comrade, David felt her to be, and again it struck him that she was beautiful as he arose to introduce her to the guests. He saw their open admiration as they greeted her, and he found himself wondering what they would have thought of Kate, wild-rose Kate with her graceful witching ways. A tinge of sadness came into his face, but something suggested to him the thought that Marcia was even more beautiful than Kate, more like a half-blown bud of a thing. He wondered that he had never noticed before how her eyes shone. He gave her a pleasant smile as they passed into the hall, which set the color flaming in her cheeks again. David seemed different somehow, and that lonely, set-apart feeling that she had had ever since she came here to live was gone. David was there and he understood, at least a little bit, and they had something—just something, even though it was but a few minutes in a lonely woods and some gentle words of his,—to call their very own together. At least that experience did not belong to Kate, never had been hers, and could not have been borrowed from her. Marcia sighed a happy sigh as she took her seat at the table.

The talk ran upon Andrew Jackson, and some utterances of his in his last message to Congress. The elder of the two gentlemen expressed grave fears that a mistake had been made in policy and that the country would suffer.

Governor Clinton was mentioned and his policy discussed. But all this talk was familiar to Marcia. Her father had been interested in public affairs always, and she had been brought up to listen to discussions deep and long, and to think about such things for herself. When she was quite a little girl her father had made her read the paper aloud to him, from one end to the other, as he lay back in his big chair with his eyes closed and his shaggy brows drawn thoughtfully into a frown. Sometimes as he read he would burst forth with a tirade against this or that man or set of men who were in opposition to his own pronounced views, and he would pour out a lengthy reply to little Marcia as she sat patient, waiting for a chance to go on with her reading. As she grew older she became proud of the distinction of being her father's *confidante* politically, and she was able to talk on such matters as intelligently and as well if not better than most of the men who came to the house. It was a position which no one disputed with her. Kate had been much too full of her own plans and Madam Schuyler too busy with household affairs to bother with politics and newspapers, so Marcia had always been the one called upon to read when her father's eyes were tired. As a consequence she was far beyond other girls of her age in knowledge on public affairs. Well she knew what Andrew Jackson thought about the tariff, and about the system of canals, and about improvements in general. She knew which men in Congress were opposed to and which in favor of certain bills. All

through the struggle f...
observer. T...

...a teacups and
...en said, and she drew her
...ne was deeply excited, as at last the
...great subject of interest which to her seemed of
...the country at the present day, the project of a railroad run

Nothing was too great for Marcia to believe. Her father had been inclined to be conservative in great improvements. He had favored the Erie Canal, though had feared it would be impossible to carry so great a project through, and Marcia in her girlish mind had rejoiced with a joy that to her was unspeakable when it had been completed and news had come that many packets were travelling day and night upon the wonderful new water way. There had been a kind of triumph in her heart to think that men who could study out these big schemes and plan it all, had been able against so great odds to carry out their project and prove to all unbelievers that it was not only possible but practicable.

Marcia's brain was throbbing with the desire for progress. If she were a man with money and influence she felt she would so much like to go out into the world and make stupid people do the things for the country that ought to be done. Progress had been the keynote of her upbringing, and she was teeming with energy which she had no hope could ever be used to help along that for which she felt her ambitions rising. She wanted to see the world alive, and busy, the great cities connected with one another. She longed to have free access to cities, to great libraries, to pictures, to wonderful music. She longed to meet great men and women, the men and women who were making the history of the world, writing, speaking, and doing things that were moulding public opinion. Reforms of all sorts were what helped along and made possible her desires. Why did not the people want a steam railroad? Why were they so ready to say it could never succeed, that it would be an impossibility; that the roads could not be made strong enough to bear so great weights and so constant wear and tear? Why did they interpose objections to every suggestion made by inventors and thinking men? Why did even her dear father who was so far in advance of his times in many ways, why did even he too shake his head and say that he feared it would never be in this country, at least not in his day, that it was impracticable?

The talk was very interesting to Marcia. She ate bits of her biscuit without knowing, and she left her tea untasted till it was cold. The younger of the two guests was talking. His name was Jervis. Marcia thought she had heard the name somewhere, but had not yet placed him in her mind.

"Yes," said he, with an eager look on his face, "it is coming, it is coming sooner than they think. Oliver Evans said, you know, that good roads were all we could expect one generation to do. The next must make canals, the next might build a railroad which should run by horse power, and perhaps the next would run a railroad by steam. But we shall not have to wait so long. We shall have steam moving railway carriages before another year."

"What!" said David, "you don't mean it! Have you really any foundation for such a statement?" He leaned forward, his eyes shining and his whole attitude one of deep interest. Marcia watched him, and a great pride began to glow within her that she belonged to him. She looked at the other men. Their eyes were fixed upon David with a heightening pleasure and pride.

The older man watched the little tableau a moment and then he explained: "The Mohawk and Hudson Company have just made an engagement with Mr. Jervis as chief engineer of their road. He expects to run that road by steam!"

He finished his fruit cake and preserves under the spell of astonishment he had cast upon his host and hostess.

David and Marcia turned simultaneously toward Mr. Jervis for a confirmation of this statement. Mr. Jervis smiled in affirmation.

"But will it not be like all the rest, no funds?" asked David a trifle sadly. "It may be years even yet before it is really started."

But Mr. Jervis' face was reassuring.

"The contract is let for the grading. In fact work has already begun. I expect to begin laying the track by next Spring, perhaps sooner. As soon as the track is laid we shall show them."

David's eyes shone and he reached out and grasped the hand of the man who had the will and apparently the means of accomplishing this great thing for the country.

"It will make a wonderful change in the whole land," said David musingly. He had forgotten to eat. His face was aglow and a side of his nature which Marcia did not know was uppermost. Marcia saw the man, the thinker, the writer, the former of public opinion, the idealist. Heretofore David had been to her in the light of her sister's lover, a young man of promise, but that was all. Now she saw something more earnest, and at once it was revealed to her what a man he was, a man like her father. David's eyes were suddenly drawn to meet hers. He looked on Marcia and seemed to be sharing his thought with her, and smiled a smile of comradeship. He felt all at once that she could and would understand his feelings about this great new enterprise, and would be glad too. It pleased him to feel this. It took a little of his loneliness away. Kate would never have been interested in these things. He had never expected such sympathy from her. She had been something beautiful and apart from his world, and as such he had adored her. But it was pleasant to have some one who could understand and feel as he did. Just then he was not thinking of his lost Kate.

So he smiled ...

...u will soon be

...ng.

...vis, closing his lips firmly in a way that made

...or he spoke.

...now tell me about it," said David, with his most engaging smile, as a child will ask to have a story. David could be most fascinating when he felt he was in a sympathetic company. At other times he was wont to be grave, almost to severity. But those who knew him best and had seen him thus melted into childlike enthusiasm, felt his lovableness as the others never dreamed.

The table talk launched into a description of the proposed road, the road bed, the manner of laying the rails, their thickness and width, and the way of bolting them down to the heavy timbers that lay underneath. It was all intensely fascinating to Marcia. Mr. Jervis took knives and forks to illustrate and then showed by plates and spoons how they were fastened down.

David asked a question now and then, took out his note book and wrote down some things. The two guests were eager and plain in their answers. They wanted David to write it up. They wanted the information to be accurate and full.

"The other day I saw a question in a Baltimore paper, sent in by a subscriber, 'What is a railroad?'" said the old gentleman, "and the editor's reply was, 'Can any of our readers answer this question and tell us what is a railroad?'"

There was a hearty laugh over the unenlightened unbelievers who seemed to be only too willing to remain in ignorance of the march of improvement.

David finally laid down his note book, feeling that he had gained all the information he needed at present. "I have much faith in you and your skill, but I do not quite see how you are going to overcome all the obstacles. How, for instance, are you going to overcome the inequalities in the road? Our country is not a flat even one like those abroad where the railroad has been tried. There are sharp grades, and many curves will be necessary," said he.

Mr. Jervis had shoved his chair back from the table, but now he drew it up again sharply and began to move the dishes back from his place, a look of eagerness gleaming in his face.

Once again the dishes and cups were brought into requisition as the engineer showed a crude model, in china and cutlery, of an engine he proposed to have constructed, illustrating his own idea about a truck for the forward wheels which should move separately from the back wheels and enable the engine to conform to curves more readily.

Marcia sat with glowing cheeks watching the outline of history that was to be, not knowing that the little model before her, made from her own teacups and saucers, was to be the model for all the coming engines of the many railroads of the future.

Finally the chairs were pushed back, and yet the talk went on. Marcia slipped silently about conveying the dishes away. And still the guests sat talking. She could hear all they said even when she was in the kitchen washing the china, for she did it very softly and never a clink hid a word. They talked of Governor Clinton again and of his attitude toward the railroad. They spoke of Thurlow Weed and a number of others whose names were familiar to Marcia in the papers she had read to her father. They told how lately on the Baltimore and Ohio railroad Peter Cooper had experimented with a little locomotive, and had beaten a gray horse attached to another car.

Marcia smiled brightly as she listened, and laid the delicate china teapot down with care lest she should lose a word. But ever with her interest in the march of civilization, there were other thoughts mingling. Thoughts of David and of how he would be connected with it all. He would write it up and be identified with it. He was brave enough to face any new movement.

David's paper was a temperance paper. There were not many temperance papers in those days. David was brave. He had already faced a number of unpleasant circumstances in consequence. He was not afraid of sneers or sarcasms, nor of being called a fanatic. He had taken such a stand that even those who were opposed had to respect him. Marcia felt the joy of a great pride in David to-night.

She sang a happy little song at the bottom of her heart as she worked. The new railroad was an assured thing, and David was her comrade, that was the song, and the refrain was, "David, David, David!"

Later, after the guests had talked themselves out and taken their candles to their rooms, David with another comrade's smile, and a look in his eyes that saw visions of the country's future, and for this one night at least promised not to dream of the past, bade her good night.

She went up to her white chamber and lay down upon the pillow, whose case was fragrant of lavender blossoms, dreaming with a smile of to-morrow. She thought she was riding in a strange new railroad train with David's arm about her and Harry Temple running along at his very best pace to try to catch them, but he could not.

Miranda, at her supperless window, watched the evening hours and thought many thoughts. She wondered why they stayed in the dining room so late, and why they did not go into the parlor and make Marcia play the "music box" as she called it; and why there was a light so long in that back chamber over the kitchen. Could it be they had put one of the guests there? Surely not. Perhaps

that was David's stud..
David was si..

...a his

...uld appear in his paper in
...y doubters that a railroad was at last
...

...or two points which he must ask the skilled engineer in the
..., but as he reviewed what he had written he felt a sense of deep
satisfaction, and a true delight in his work. His soul thrilled with the power of
his gift. He loved it, exulted in it. It was pleasant to feel that delight in his work
once more. He had thought since his marriage that it was gone forever, but
perhaps by and by it would return to console him, and he would be able to do
greater things in the world because of his suffering.

Just as he dropped to sleep there came a thought of Marcia, pleasantly, as
one remembers a flower. He felt that there was a comfort about Marcia, a
something helpful in her smile. There was more to her than he had supposed.
She was not merely a child. How her face had glowed as the men talked of the
projected railroad, and almost she seemed to understand as they described the
proposed engine with its movable trucks. She would be a companion who would
be interested in his pursuits. He had hoped to teach Kate to understand his life
work and perhaps help him some, but Kate was by nature a butterfly, a bird of
gay colors, always on the wing. He would not have wanted her to be troubled
with deep thoughts. Marcia seemed to enjoy such things. What if he should
take pains to teach her, read with her, help cultivate her mind? It would at least
be an occupation for leisure hours, something to interest him and keep away
the awful pall of sadness.

How sweet she had looked as she lay asleep in the woods with the tears on
her cheek like the dew-drops upon a rose petal! She was a dear little girl and
he must take care of her and protect her. That scoundrel Temple! What were
such men made for? He must settle him to-morrow.

And so he fell asleep.

Chapter 17

Harry Temple sat in his office the next morning with his feet upon the table and his wooden armed chair titled back against the wall.

He had letters to write, a number of them, that should go out with the afternoon coach, to reach the night packet. There were at least three men he ought to go and see at once if he would do the best for his employers, and the office he sat in was by no means in the best of order. But his feet were elevated comfortably on the table and he was deep in the pages of a story of the French Court, its loves and hates and intrigues.

It was therefore with annoyance that he looked up at the opening of the office door.

But the frown changed to apprehension, as he saw who was his visitor. He brought the chair legs suddenly to the floor and his own legs followed them swiftly. David Spafford was not a man before whom another would sit with his feet on a table, even to transact business.

There was a look of startled enquiry on Harry Temple's face. For an instant his self-complacency was shaken. He hesitated, wondering what tack to take. Perhaps after all his alarm was unnecessary. Marcia likely had been too frightened to tell of what had occurred. He noticed the broad shoulder, the lean, active body, the keen eye, and the grave poise of his visitor, and thought he would hardly care to fight a duel with that man. It was natural for him to think at once of a duel on account of the French court life from which his mind had just emerged. A flash of wonder passed through his mind whether it would be swords or pistols, and then he set himself to face the other man.

David Spafford stood for a full minute and looked into the face of the man he had come to shame. He looked at him with a calm eye and brow, but with a growing contempt that did not need words to express it. Harry Temple felt the color rise in his cheek, and his soul quaked for an instant. Then his habitual conceit arose and he tried to parry with his eye that keen piercing gaze of the other. It must have lasted a full minute, though it seemed to Mr. Temple it was five at least. He made an attempt to offer his visitor a chair, but it was not noticed. David Spafford looked his man through and through, and knew him for exactly what he was. At last he spoke, quietly, in a tone that was too courteous to be contemptuous, but it humiliated the listener more even than contempt:

"It would be well for you to leave town at once."

That was all. The listener felt that it was a command. His wrath arose hotly, and beat itself against the calm exterior of his visitor's gaze in a look that was brazen eno...

...

... ...ut to his chin which usually
...ment. Once he could break that steady, iron,
...would have the best of things. He could easily persuade
...Spatford that everything was all right if he could get him off his guard
and make him angry. An angry man could do little but bluster.

"You understand very well," replied David, his voice still, steady and his
gaze not swerving.

"Indeed! Well, this is most extraordinary," said Harry, losing control of
himself again. "Of what do you accuse me, may I enquire?"

"Of nothing that your own heart does not accuse you," said David. And
somehow there was more than human indignation in the gaze now: there was
pity, a sense of shame for another soul who could lower himself to do unseemly
things. Before that look the blood crept into Harry's cheek again. An uncomfortable sensation entirely new was stealing over him. A sense of sin—no, not
that exactly,—a sense that he had made a mistake, perhaps. He never was very
hard upon himself even when the evidence was clear against him. It angered
him to feel humiliated. What a fuss to make about a little thing! What a tiresome
old cad to care about a little flirtation with his wife! He wished he had let the
pretty baby alone entirely. She was of no finer stuff than many another who had
accepted his advances with pleasure. He stiffened his neck and replied with
much haughtiness:

"My heart accuses me of nothing, sir. I assure you I consider your words
an insult! I demand satisfaction for your insulting language, sir!" Harry Temple
had never fought a duel, and had never been present when others fought, but
that was the language in which a challenge was usually delivered in French
novels.

"It is not a matter for discussion!" said David Spafford, utterly ignoring the
other's blustering words. "I am fully informed as to all that occurred yesterday
afternoon, and I tell you once more, it would be well for you to leave town at
once. I have nothing further to say."

David turned and walked toward the door, and Harry stood, ignored, angry,
crestfallen, and watched him until he reached the door.

"You would better ask your informant further of her part in the matter!" he
hissed, suddenly, an open sneer in his voice and a covert implication of deep
meaning.

David turned, his face flashing with righteous indignation. The man who was withered by the scorn of that glance wished heartily that he had not uttered the false sentence. He felt the smallness of his own soul, during the instant of silence in which his visitor stood looking at him.

Then David spoke deliberately:

"I knew you were a knave," said he, "but I did not suppose you were also a coward. A man who is not a coward will not try to put the blame upon a woman, especially upon an innocent one. You, sir, will leave town this evening. Any business further than you can settle between this and that I will see properly attended to. I warn you, sir, it will be unwise for you to remain longer than till the evening coach."

Perfectly courteous were David's tones, keen command was in his eye and determination in every line of his face. Harry could not recover himself to reply, could not master his frenzy of anger and humiliation to face the righteous look of his accuser. Before he realized it, David was gone.

He stood by the window and watched him go down the street with rapid, firm tread and upright bearing. Every line in that erect form spoke of determination. The conviction grew within him that the last words of his visitor were true, and that it would be wise for him to leave town. He rebelled at the idea. He did not wish to leave, for business matters were in such shape, or rather in such chaos, that it would be extremely awkward for him to meet his employers and explain his desertion at that time. Moreover there were several homes in the town open to him whenever he chose, where were many attractions. It was a lazy pleasant life he had been leading here, fully trusted, and wholly disloyal to the trust, troubled by no uneasy overseers, not even his own conscience, dined and smiled upon with lovely languishing eyes. He did not care to go, even though he had decried the town as dull and monotonous.

But, on the other hand, things had occurred—not the unfortunate little mistake of yesterday, of course, but others, more serious things—that he would hardly care to have brought to the light of day, especially through the keen sarcastic columns of David Spafford's paper. He had seen other sinners brought to a bloodless retribution in those columns by dauntless weapons of sarcasm and wit which in David Spafford's hands could be made to do valiant work. He did not care to be humiliated in that way. He could not brazen it out. He was convinced that the man meant what he said, and from what he knew of his influence he felt that he would leave no stone unturned till he had made the place too hot to hold him. Only Harry Temple himself knew how easy that would be to do, for no one else knew how many "mistakes" Harry had made, and he, unfortunately for himself, did not know how many of them were not known, by any who could harm him.

He stood a long time clinking some sixpences and shillings together in his pocket, and scowling down the street after David had disappeared from sight.

"Blame that li**
on his b**

...presented a whole week's
...were cleared away, and reflected how
...be to get up a good excuse and go away, leaving
...poor drudge who should be sent here in his place. He looked
...again and his eyes lighted upon his book. He remembered the exciting crisis in which he had left the heroine and down he sat to his story again. At least there was nothing demanding attention this moment. He need not decide what he would do. If he went there were few preparations to make. He would toss some things into his carpet-bag and pretend to have been summoned to see a sick and dying relative, a long-lost brother, something. It would be easy to invent one when the time came. Then he could leave directions for the rest of his things to be packed if he did not return, and get rid of the trouble of it all. As for the letters, if he was going what use to bother with them? Let them wait till his successor should come. It mattered little to him whether his employers suffered for his negligence or not so long as he finished his story. Besides, it would not do to let that cad think he had frightened him. He would pretend he was not going, at least during his hours of grace. So he picked up his book and went on reading.

At noon he sauntered back to his boarding house as usual for his dinner, having professed an unusually busy morning to those who came in to the office on business and made appointments with them for the next day. This had brought him much satisfaction as the morning wore away and he was left free to his book, and so before dinner he had come to within a very few pages of the end.

After a leisurely dinner he sauntered back to the office again, rejoicing in the fact that circumstances had so arranged themselves that he had passed David Spafford in front of the newspaper office and given him a most elaborate and friendly bow in the presence of four to five bystanders. David's look in return had meant volumes, and decided Harry Temple to do as he had been ordered, not, of course, because he had been ordered to do so, but because it would be an easier thing to do. In fact he made up his mind that he was weary of this part of the country. He went back to his book.

About the middle of the afternoon he finished the last pages. He rose up with alacrity then and began to think what he should do. He glanced around the room, sought out a few papers, took some daguerreotypes of girls from a drawer of his desk, gave a farewell glance around the dismal little room that had seen so much shirking for the past few months, and then went out and locked the door.

He paused at the corner. Which way should he go? He did not care to go back to the office, for his book was done, and he scarcely needed to go to his room at his boarding place yet either, for the afternoon was but half over and he wished his departure to appear to be entirely unpremeditated. A daring thought came into his head. He would walk past David Spafford's house. He would let Marcia see him if possible. He would show them that he was not afraid in the least. He even meditated going in and explaining to Marcia that she had made a great mistake, that he had been merely admiring her, and that there was no harm in anything he had said or done yesterday, that he was exceedingly grieved and mortified that she should have mistaken his meaning for an insult, and so on and so on. He knew well how to make such honeyed talk when he chose, but the audacity of the thing was a trifle too much for even his bold nature, so he satisfied himself by strolling in a leisurely manner by the house.

When he was directly opposite to it he raised his eyes casually and bowed and smiled with his most graceful air. True, he did not see any one, for Marcia had caught sight of him as she was coming out upon the stoop and had fled into her own room with the door buttoned, she was watching unseen from behind the folds of her curtain, but he made the bow as complete as though a whole family had been greeting him from the windows. Marcia, poor child, thought he must see her, and she felt frozen to the spot, and stared wildly through the little fold of her curtain with trembling hands and weak knees till he was passed. Well pleased at himself the young man walked on, knowing that at least three prominent citizens had seen him bow and smile, and that they would be witnesses, against anything David might say to the contrary, that he was on friendly terms with Mrs. Spafford.

Hannah Heath was sitting on the front stoop with her knitting. She often sat there dressed daintily of an afternoon. Her hands were white and looked well against the blue yarn she was knitting. Besides there was something domestic and sentimental in a stocking. It gave a cozy, homey air to a woman, Hannah considered. So she sat and knitted and smiled at whomsoever passed by, luring many in to sit and talk with her, so that the stockings never grew rapidly, but always kept at about the same stage. If it had been Miranda, Grandmother Heath would have made some sharp remarks about the length of time it took to finish that blue stocking, but as it was Hannah it was all right.

Hannah sat upon the stoop and knitted as Harry Temple came by. Now, Hannah was not so great a favorite with Harry as Harry was with Hannah. She was of the kind who was conquered too easily, and he did not consider it worth his while to waste time upon her simperings usually. But this afternoon was different. He had nowhere to go for a little while, and Hannah's appearance on the stoop was opportune and gave him an idea. He would lounge there with her. Perchance f...

pass ...

...hat
...hat retribution
...new it would be severe.

...., Harry Temple stepped daintily across ... came and sat down beside her. He toyed with her ...ught one of her plump white hands, the one on the side away ..om the street, and held it, while Hannah pretended not to notice, and dropped her long eyelashes in a telling way. Hannah knew how. She had been at it a good many years.

So he sat, toward five o'clock, when David came by, and bowed gravely to Hannah, but seemed not to see Harry. Harry let his eyes follow the tall figure in an insolent stare.

"What a dough-faced cad that man is!" he said lazily, "no wonder his little pink-cheeked wife seeks other society. Handsome bady, though, isn't she?"

Hannah pricked up her ears. Her loss of David was too recent not to cause her extreme jealousy of his pretty young wife. Already she fairly hated her. Her upbringing in the atmosphere of Grandmother Heath's sarcastic, ill-natured gossip had prepared her to be quick to see meaning in any insinuation.

She looked at him keenly, archly for a moment, then replied with dropping gaze and coquettish manner:

"You should not blame any one for enjoying your company."

Hannah stole sly glances to see how he took this, but Harry was an old hand and proof against such scrutiny. He only shrugged his shoulder carelessly, as though he dropped all blame like a garment that he had no need for.

"And what's the matter with David?" asked Hannah, watching David as he mounted his own steps, and thinking how often she had watched that tall form go down the street, and thought of him as destined to belong to her. The mortification that he had chosen some one else was not yet forgotten. It amounted almost to a desire for revenge.

Harry lingered longer than he intended. Hannah begged him to remain to supper, but he declined, and when she pressed him to do so he looked troubled and said he was expecting a letter and must hurry back to see if it came in the afternoon coach. He told her that a dear friend, a beloved cousin, was lying very ill, and he might be summoned at any moment to his bedside, and Hannah said some comforting little things in a caressing voice, and hoped he would find the letter saying the cousin was better. Then he hurried away.

It was easy at his boarding house to say he had been called away, and he rushed up to his room and threw some necessaries into his carpet-bag, scattering things around the room and helping out the impression that he was called away in a great hurry. When he was ready he looked at this watch. It was growing late. The evening coach left in half an hour. He knew its route well. It started at the village inn, and went down the old turnpike, stopping here and there to pick up passengers. There was always a convocation when it started. Perhaps David Spafford would be there and witness his obedience to the command given him. He set his lips and made up his mind to escape that at least. He would cheat his adversary of that satisfaction.

It would involve a sacrifice. He would have to go without his supper, and he could smell the frying bacon coming up the stairs. But it would help the illusion and he could perhaps get something on the way when the coach stopped to change horses.

He rushed downstairs and told his landlady that he must start at once, as he must see a man before the coach went, and she, poor lady, had no chance to suggest that he leave her a little deposit on the sum of his board which he already owed her. There was perhaps some method in his hurry for that reason also. It always bothered him to pay his bills, he had so many other ways of spending his money.

So he hurried away and caught a ride in a farm wagon toward the Cross Roads. When it turned off he walked a little way until another wagon came along; finally crossed several fields at a breathless pace and caught the coach just as it was leaving the Cross Roads, which was the last stopping place anywhere near the village. He climbed up beside the driver, still in a breathless condition, and detailed to him how he had received word, just before the coach started, by a messenger who came across-country on horseback, that his cousin was dying.

After he had answered the driver's minutest questions, he sat back and reflected upon his course with satisfaction. He was off, and he had not been seen nor questioned by a single citizen, and by to-morrow night his story as he had told it to the driver would be fully known and circulated through the place he had just left. The stage driver was one of the best means of advertisement. It was well to give him full particulars.

The driver after he had satisfied his curiosity about the young man by his side, and his reasons for leaving town so hastily, began to wax eloquent upon the one theme which now occupied his spare moments and his fluent tongue, the subject of a projected railroad. Whether some of the sentiments he uttered were his own, or whether he had but borrowed from others, they were at least uttered with force and apparent conviction, and many a traveller sat and listened as they were detailed and viewed the subject from the standpoint of the loud-mouthed coachman.

A little later Tony Weller, called by some one "the best beloved of all coachmen," uttered much the same sentiments in the following words:

"T...

..., ... you

... vere can that be without a coach-
... coachmen as is sometimes forced to go by it, but
... an hinsult? As to the ingen, a nasty, wheezin', gapsin', puffin',
bustin' monster always out o' breath, with a shiny green and gold back like an
onpleasant beetle; as to the ingen as is always a pourin' out red 'ot coals at night
an' black smoke in the day, the sensiblest thing it does, in my opinion, is ven
there's somethin' in the vay, it sets up that 'ere frightful scream vich seems to
say, 'Now 'ere's two 'undred an' forty passengers in the werry greatest extremity
o' danger, an' 'ere's their two 'undred an' forty screams in vun!'"

But such sentiments as these troubled Harry Temple not one whit. He
cared not whether the present century had a railroad or whether it travelled by
foot. He would not lift a white finger to help it along or hinder. As the talk went
on he was considering how and where he might get his supper.

Chapter 18

The weather turned suddenly cold and raw that Fall, and almost in one day, the trees that had been green, or yellowing in the sunshine, put on their autumn garments of defeat, flaunted them for a brief hour, and dropped them early in despair. The pleasant woods, to which Marcia had fled in her dismay, became a mass of finely penciled branches against a wintry sky, save for the one group of tall pines that hung out heavy above the rest, and seemed to defy even snowy blasts.

Marcia could see those pines from her kitchen window, and sometimes as she worked, if her heart was heavy, she would look out and away to them, and think of the day she laid her head down beneath them to sob out her trouble, and awoke to find comfort. Somehow the memory of that little talk that she and David had then grew into vast proportions in her mind, and she loved to cherish it.

There had come letters from home. Her stepmother had written, a stiff, not unloving letter, full of injunctions to be sure to remember this, and not do that, and on no account to let any relative or neighbor persuade her out of the ways in which she had been brought up. She was attempting to do as many mothers do, when they see the faults in the child they have brought up, try to bring them up over again. At some of the sentences a wild homesickness took possession of her. Some little homely phrase about one of the servants, or the mention of a pet hen or cow, would bring the longing tears to her eyes, and she would feel that she must throw away this new life and run back to the old one.

School was begun at home. Mary Ann and Hanford would be taking the long walk back and forth together twice a day to the old school-house. She half envied them their happy, care-free life. She liked to think of the shy courting that she had often seen between scholars in the upper classes. Her imagination pleased itself sometimes when she was going to sleep, trying to picture out the school goings and home comings, and their sober talk. Not that she ever looked back to Hanford Weston with regret, not she. She knew always that he was not for her, and perhaps, even so early as that in her new life, if the choice had been given her whether she would go back to her girlhood again and be as she was before Kate had run away, or whether she would choose to stay here in the new life with David, it is likely she would have chosen to stay.

There were occasional letters from Squire Schuyler. He wrote of politics, and sent many messages to his son-in-law which Marcia handed over to David at the tea table to read, and which always seemed to soften David and bring a sweet sadness into his eyes. He loved and respected his father-in-law. It was

... a mention of the bright, beautiful, ... whom the old home life used to centre and who seemed now, judging from the home letters, to be worse than dead to them all. But since the afternoon upon the hill a new and pleasant intercourse had sprung up between David and Marcia. True it was confined mainly to discussions of the new railroad, the possibilities of its success, and the construction of engines, tracks, etc. David was constantly writing up the subject for his paper, and he fell into the habit of reading his articles aloud to Marcia when they were finished. She would listen with breathless admiration, sometimes combating a point ably, with the old vim she had used in her discussion over the newspaper with her father, but mainly agreeing with every word he wrote, and always eager to understand it down to the minutest detail.

He always seemed pleased at her praise, and wrote on while she put away the tea-things with a contented expression as though he had passed a high critic, and need not fear any other. Once he looked up with a quizzical expression and made a jocose remark about "our article," taking her into a sort of partnership with him in it, which set her heart to beating happily, until it seemed as if she were really in some part at least growing into his life.

But after all their companionship was a shy, distant one, more like that of a brother and sister who had been separated all their lives and were just beginning to get acquainted, and ever there was a settled sadness about the lines of David's mouth and eyes. They sat around one table now, the evenings when they were at home, for there were still occasional tea-drinkings at their friends' houses; and there was one night a week held religiously for a formal supper with the aunts, which David kindly acquiesced in—more for the sake of his Aunt Clarinda than the others,—whenever he was not detained by actual business. Then, too, there was the weekly prayer meeting held at "early candle light" in the dim old shadowed church. They always walked down the twilighted streets together, and it seemed to Marcia there was a sweet solemnity about that walk. They never said much to each other on the way. David seemed preoccupied with holy thoughts, and Marcia walked softly beside him as if he had been the minister, looking at him proudly and reverently now and then. David was often called upon to pray in meeting and Marcia loved to listen to his words. He seemed to be more intimate with God than the others, who were mostly old men and prayed with long, rolling, solemn sentences that put the whole community down into the dust and ashes before their Creator.

Marcia rather enjoyed the hour spent in the somberness of the church, with the flickering candle-light making grotesque forms of shadows on the wall and among the tall pews. The old minister reminded her of the one she had left at home, though he was more learned and scholarly, and when he had read the Scripture passages he would take his spectacles off and lay them across the great Bible where the candle-light played at glances with the steel bows, and say: "Let us pray!" Then would come that soft stir and hush as the people took the attitude of prayer. Marcia sometimes joined in the prayer in her heart, uttering shy little petitions that were vague and indefinite, and had to do mostly with the days when she was troubled and homesick, and felt that David belonged wholly to Kate. Always her clear voice joined in the slow hymns that quavered out now and again, lined out to the worshippers.

Marcia and David went out from that meeting down the street to their home with the hush upon them that must have been upon the Israelites of old after they had been to the solemn congregation.

But once David had come in earlier than usual and had caught Marcia reading the Scottish Chiefs, and while she started guiltily to be found thus employed he smiled indulgently. After supper he said: "Get your book, child, and sit down. I have some writing to do, and after it is done I will read it to you." So after that, more and more often, it was a book that Marcia held in her hands in the long evenings when they sat together, instead of some useful employment, and so her education progressed. Thus she read Epictetus, Rasselas, *The Deserted Village*, *The Vicar of Walkfield*, *Paradise Lost*, the *Mysteries of the Human Heart*, Marshall's *Life of Columbus*, *The Spy*, *The Pioneers*, and *The Last of the Mohicans*.

She had been asked to sing in the village choir. David sang a sweet high tenor there, and Marcia's voice was clear and strong as a blackbird's, with the plaintive sweetness of the wood-robin's.

Hannah Heath was in the choir also, and jealously watched her every move, but of this Marcia was unaware until informed of it by Miranda. With her inherited sweetness of nature she scarcely credited it, until one Sunday, a few weeks after the departure of Harry Temple, Hannah leaned forward from her seat among the altos and whispered quite distinctly, so that those around could hear—it was just before the service—"I've just had a letter from your friend Mr. Temple. I thought you might like to know that his cousin got well and he has gone back to New York. He won't be returning here this year. On some accounts he thought it was better not."

It was all said pointedly, with double emphasis upon the "your friend," and "some accounts." Marcia felt her cheeks glow, much to her vexation, and tried to control her whisper to seem kindly as she answered indifferently enough.

_____ own word—and quite coldly, "I should have thought differently from what Harry himself told me," and there was that in her tone which deepened the color in Marcia's cheeks and caused it to stay there during the entire morning service as she sat puzzling over what Hannah could have meant. It rankled in her mind during the whole day. She longed to ask David about it, but could not get up the courage.

She could not bear to revive the memory of what seemed to be her shame. It was at the minister's donation party that Hannah planted another thorn in her heart,—Hannah, in a green plaid silk with delicate undersleeves of lace, and a tiny black velvet jacket.

She selected a time when Lemuel was near, and when Aunt Amelia and Aunt Hortense, who believed that all the young men in town were hovering about David's wife, sat one on either side of Marcia, as if to guard her for their beloved nephew—who was discussing politics with Mr. Heath—and who never seemed to notice, so blind he was in his trust of her.

"I've had another letter from New York, from your friend Mr. Temple," she said it with the slightest possible glance over her shoulder to get the effect of her words upon the faithful Lemuel, "and he tells me he has met a sister of yours. By the way, she told him that David used to be very fond of her before she was married. I suppose she'll be coming to visit you now she's so near as New York."

Two pairs of suspicious steely eyes flew like stinging insects to gaze upon her, one on either side, and Marcia's heart stood still for just one instant, but she felt that here was her trying time, and if she would help David and do the work for which she had become his wife, she must protect him now from any suspicions or disagreeable tongues. By very force of will she controlled the trembling of her lips.

"My sister will not likely visit us this winter, I think," she replied as coolly as if she had had a letter to that effect that morning, and then she deliberately looked at Lemuel Skinner and asked if he had heard of the offer of prizes of four thousand dollars in cash that the Baltimore and Ohio railroad had just made for the most approved engine delivered for trial before June first, 1831, not to exceed three and a half tons in weight and capable of drawing, day by day, fifteen tons inclusive of weight of wagons, fifteen miles per hours. Lemuel looked at her blankly and said he had not heard of it. He was engaged in thinking over what Hannah had said about a letter from Harry Temple. He cared nothing about railroads.

"The second prize is thirty-five hundred dollars," stated Marcia eagerly, as though it were of the utmost importance to her.

"Are you thinking of trying for one of the prizes?" sneered Hannah, piercing her with her eyes, and now indeed the ready color flowed into Marcia's face. Her ruse had been detected.

"If I were a man and understood machinery I believe I would. What a grand thing it would be to be able to invent a thing like an engine that would be of so much use to the world," she answered bravely.

"They are most dangerous machines," said Aunt Amelia disapprovingly. "No right-minded Christian who wishes to live out the life his Creator has given him would ever ride behind one. I have heard that boilers always explode."

"They are most unnecessary!" said Aunt Hortense severely, as if that settled the question for all time and all railroad corporations.

But Marcia was glad for once of their disapproval and entered most heartily into a discussion of the pros and cons of engines and steam, quoting largely from David's last article for the paper on the subject, until Hannah and Lemuel moved slowly away. The discussion served to keep the aunts from inquiring further that evening about the sister in New York.

Marcia begged them to go with her into the kitchen and see the store of good things that had been brought to the minister's house by his loving parishioners. Bags of flour and meal, pumpkins, corn in the ear, eggs, and nice little pats of butter. A great wooden tub of doughnuts, baskets of apples and quinces, pounds of sugar and tea, barrels of potatoes, whole hams, a side of pork, a quarter of beef, hanks of yarn, and strings of onions. It was a goodly array. Marcia felt that the minister must be beloved by his people. She watched him and his wife as they greeted their people, and wished she knew them better, and might come and see them sometimes, and perhaps eventually feel as much at home with them as with her own dear minister.

She avoided Hannah during the remainder of the evening. When the evening was over and she went upstairs to get her wraps from the high four-poster bedstead, she had almost forgotten Hannah and her ill-natured, prying remarks. But Hannah had not forgotten her. She came forth from behind the bed curtains where she had been searching for a lost glove, and remarked that she should think Marcia would be lonely this first winter away from home and want her sister with her for a while.

But the presence of Hannah always seemed a mental stimulus to the spirit of Marcia.

"Oh, I'm not in the least lonely," she laughed merrily. "I have a great many interesting things to do, and I love music and books."

"Oh, yes, I forgot you are very fond of music. Harry Temple told me about it," said Hannah. Again there was that disagreeable hint of something more behind her words, that aggravated Marcia almost beyond control. For an instant

...oad construction, quite ....p, while she, poor child, much perturbed in spirit, wondered how he would feel if he knew what Hannah had said.

David fell into a deep study with a book and his papers about him, after they had reached home. Marcia went up to her quiet, lonely chamber, put her face in the pillow and thought and wept and prayed. When at last she lay down to rest she did not know anything she could do but just to go on living day by day and helping David all she could. At most there was nothing to fear for herself, save a kind of shame that she had not been the first sister chosen, and she found to her surprise that that was growing to be deeper than she had supposed.

She wished as she fell asleep that her girl-dreams might have been left to develop and bloom like other girls', and that she might have had a real lover,— like David in every way, yet of course not David because he was Kate's. But a real lover who would meet her as David had done that night when he thought she was Kate, and speak to her tenderly.

One afternoon David, being wearied with an unusual round of taxing cares, came home to rest and study up some question in his library.

Finding the front door fastened, and remembering that he had left his key in his other pocket, he came around to the back door, and much preoccupied with thought went through the kitchen and nearly to the hall before the unusual sounds of melody penetrated to his ears. He stopped for an instant amazed, forgetting the piano, then comprehending he wondered who was playing. Perhaps some visitor was in the parlor. He would listen and find out. He was weary and dusty with the soil of the office upon his hands and clothes. He did not care to meet a visitor, so under cover of the music he slipped into the door of his library across the hall from the parlor and dropped into his great arm-chair.

Softly and tenderly stole the music through the open door, all about him, like the gentle dropping of some tender psalms or comforting chapter in the Bible to an aching heart. It touched his brow like a soft soothing hand, and seemed to know and recognize all the agonies his heart had been passing through, and all the weariness his body felt.

He put his head back and let it float over him and rest him. Tinkling brooks and gentle zephyrs, waving of forest trees, and twitterings of birds, calm lazy clouds floating by, a sweetness in the atmosphere, bells far away, lowing herds, music of the angels high in heaven, the soothing strain from each extracted and brought to heal his broken heart. It fell like dew upon his spirit. Then, like a fresh breeze with zest and life borne on, came a new strain, grand and fine and high, calling him to better things. He did not know it was a strain of Handel's music grown immortal, but his spirit recognized the higher call, commanding him to follow, and straightway he felt strengthened to go onward in the course he had been pursuing. Old troubles seemed to grow less, anguish fell away from him. He took new lease of life. Nothing seemed impossible.

Then she played by ear one or two of the old tunes they sang in church, touching the notes tenderly and almost making them speak the words. It seemed a benediction. Suddenly the playing ceased and Marcia remembered it was nearly supper time.

He met her in the doorway with a new look in his eyes, a look of high purpose and exultation. He smiled upon her and said: "That was good, child. I did not know you could do it. You must give it to us often." Marcia felt a glow of pleasure in his kindliness, albeit she felt that the look in his eyes set him apart and above her, and made her feel the child she was. She hurried out to get the supper between pleasure and nameless unrest. She was glad of this much, but she wanted more, a something to meet her soul and satisfy.

_____ Kate Leavenworth, and she _____. She had not succeeded in turning her father's heart toward herself as she had confidently expected to do when she ran away with her sea captain. She had written a gay letter home, taking for granted, in a pretty way, the forgiveness she did not think it necessary to ask, but there had come in return a brief harsh statement from her father that she was no longer his daughter and must cease from further communication with the family in any way; that she should never enter his house again and not a penny of his money should ever pass to her. He also informed her plainly that the trousseau made for her had been given to her sister who was now the wife of the man she had not seen fit to marry.

Over this letter Mistress Kate at first stormed, then wept, and finally sat down to frame epistle after epistle in petulant, penitent language. These epistles following each other by daily mail coaches still brought nothing further from her irate parent, and my lady was at least forced to face the fact that she must bear the penalty of her own misdeeds; a lesson she should have learned much earlier in life.

The young captain, who had always made it appear that he had plenty of money, had spent his salary, and most of his mother's fortune, which had been left in his keeping as administrator of his father's estate; so he had really very little to offer the spoiled and petted beauty, who simply would not settle down to the inevitable and accept the fact she had brought upon herself and others. Day after day she fretted and blamed her husband until he heartily wished her back from whence he had taken her; wished her back with her straitlaced lover from whom he had stolen her; wished her anywhere save where she was. Her brightness and beauty seemed all gone: she was a sulky child insisting upon the moon or nothing. She wanted to go to New York and be established in a fine house with plenty of servants and a carriage and horses, and the young captain had not the wherewithal to furnish these accessories to an elegant and luxurious life.

He had loved her so far as his shallow nature could love, and perhaps she had returned it in the beginning. He wanted to spend his furlough in quiet places where he might have a honeymoon of his ideal, bantering Kate's sparkling sentences, looking into her beautiful eyes, touching her rosy lips with his own as often as he chose. But Mistress Kate had lost her sparkle. She would not be kissed until she had gained her point, her lovely eyes were full of disfiguring tears and angry flashes, and her speech scintillated with cutting sarcasms, which were none the less hard to bear that they pressed home some disagreeable truths to the easy, careless spendthrift. The rose had lost its dew and was making its thorns felt.

And so they quarreled through their honeymoon, and Captain Leavenworth was not sorry when a hasty and unexpected end came to his furlough and he was ordered off with his ship for an indefinite length of time.

Even then Kate thought to get her will before he left, and held on her sullen ways and her angry, blameful talk until the last minute, so that he hurried away without even one good-bye kiss, and with her angry sentences sounding in his ears.

True, he repented somewhat on board the ship and sent her back more money than she could reasonably have expected under the circumstances, but he sent it without one word of gentleness, and Kate's heart was hard toward her husband.

Then with bitterness and anguish,—that was new and fairly astonishing that it had come to her who had always had her way,—she sat down to think of the man she had jilted. He would have been kind to her. He would have given her all she asked and more. He would even have moved his business to New York to please her, she felt sure. Why had she been so foolish! And then, like many another sinner who is made at least to see the error of his ways, she cast hard thoughts at a Fate which had allowed her to make so great a mistake, and pitied her poor little self out of all recognition of the character she had formed.

But she took her money and went to New York, for she felt that there only could she be at all happy, and have some little taste of the delights of true living.

She took up her abode with an ancient relative of her own mother's, who lived in a quiet respectable part of the city, and who was glad to piece out her small annuity with the modest sum that Kate agreed to pay for her board.

It was not long before Mistress Kate, with her beautiful face, and the pretty clothes which she took care to provide at once for herself, spending lavishly out of the diminishing sum her husband had sent her, and thinking not of the morrow, nor the day when the board bills would due, became well known. The musty little parlor of the ancient relative was daily filled with visitors, and every evening Kate held court, with the old aunt nodding in her chair by the fireside.

Neither did the poor old lady have a very easy time of it, in spite of the promise of weekly pay. Kate laughed at the old furniture and the old ways. She demanded new things, and got them, too, until the old lady saw little hope of any help from the board money when Kate was constantly saying: "I saw this in a shop down town, auntie, and as I knew you needed it I just bought it. My board this week will just pay for it." As always, Kate ruled. The little parlor took on an air of brightness, and Kate became popular. A few women of fashion took her up, and Kate launched herself upon a gay life, her one object to have as good a time as possible, regardless of what her husband or anyone else might think.

carriage and all, just as the sun was setting.

The view was marvelous. The water a flood of pink and green and gold; the sails of the vessels along the shore lit up resplendently; the buildings of the city beyond sent back occasional flashes of reflected light from window glass or church spire. It was a picture worth looking upon, and Kate's companion was absorbed in it.

Not so Kate. She loved display above all things. She sat up stately, aware that she looked well in her new frock with the fine lace collar she had extravagantly purchased the day before, and her leghorn bonnet with its real ostrich feather, which was becoming in the extreme. She enjoyed sitting back of the colored coachman, her elegant friend by her side, and being admired by the two ladies and the little girl who sat in the ladies' cabin and occasionally peeped curiously at her from the window. She drew herself up haughtily and let her soul "delight itself in fatness"—borrowed fatness, perhaps, but still, the long desired. She told herself she had a right to it, for was she not a Schuyler? That name was respected everywhere.

She bore a grudge at a man and woman who stood by the railing absorbed in watching the sunset haze that lay over the river showing the white sails in gleams like flashes of white birds here and there.

A young man well set up, and fashionably attired, sauntered up to the carriage. He spoke to Kate's friend, and was introduced. Kate felt in her heart it was because of her presence there he came. His bold black eyes told her as much and she was flattered.

They fell to talking.

"You say you spent the summer near Albany, Mr. Temple," said Kate presently, "I wonder if you happen to know of any of my friends. Did you meet a Mr. Spafford? David Spafford?"

"Of course I did, knew him well," said the young man with guarded tone. But a quick flash of dislike, and perhaps fear had crossed his face at the name. Kate was keen. She analyzed that look. She parted her charming red lips and showed her sharp little teeth like the treacherous pearls in a white kitten's pink mouth.

"He was once a lover of mine," said Kate carelessly, wrinkling her piquant little nose as if the idea were comical, and laughing out a sweet ripple of mirth that would have cut David to the heart.

"Indeed!" said the ever ready Harry, "and I do not wonder. Is not every one that at once they see you Madam Leavenworth? How kind of your husband to stay at sea for so long a time and give us other poor fellows a chance to say pleasant things."

Then Kate pouted her pretty lips in a way she had and tapped the delighted Harry with her carriage parasol cross the fingers of his hand that had taken familiar hold of the carriage beside her arm.

"Oh, you naughty man!" she exclaimed prettily. "How dare you! Yes, David Spafford and I were quite good friends. I almost gave in at one time and became Mrs. Spafford, but he was too good for me!"

She uttered this truth in a mocking tone, and Harry saw her lead and hastened to follow. Here was a possible chance for revenge. He was ready for any. He studied the lady before him keenly. Of what did that face remind him? Had he ever seen her before? "I should judge him a little straitlaced for your merry ways," he responded gallantly, "but he's like all the rest, fickle, you know. He's married. Have you heard?"

Kate's face darkened with something hard and cruel, but her voice was soft as a cat's purr: "Yes," she sighed, "I know. He married my sister. Poor child! I am sorry for her. I think he did it out of revenge, and she was too young to know her own mind. But they, poor things, will have to bear the consequences of what they have done. Isn't it a pity that that has to be, Mr. Temple? It is dreadful to have the innocent suffer. I have been greatly anxious about my sister." She lifted her large eyes swimming in tears, and he did not perceive the insincerity in her purring voice just then. He was thanking his lucky stars that he had been saved from any remarks about young Mrs. Spafford, whom her sister seemed to love so deeply. It had been on the tip of his tongue to suggest that she might be able to lead her husband a gay little dance if she chose. How lucky he had not spoken! He tried to say some pleasant comforting nothings, and found it delightful to see her face clear into smiles and her blue eyes look into his so confidingly. By the time the boat touched the New York side the two felt well acquainted, and Harry Temple had promised to call soon, which promise he lost no time in keeping.

Kate's heart had grown bitter against the young sister who had dared to take her place, and against the lover who had so easily solaced himself. She could not understand it.

She resolved to learn all that Mr. Temple knew about David, and to find out if possible whether he were happy. It was Kate's nature not to be able to give up anything even though she did not want it. She desired the life-long devotion of every man who came near her, and have it she would or punish him.

Harry Temple, meanwhile, was reflecting upon his chance meeting that afternoon and wondering if in some way he might not yet have revenge upon the man who had humbled him. Possibly this woman could help him.

After some thought he sat down and penned a letter to Hannah Heath, beginning it here and there with devoted sentences which caused that young been a success. Gold hair! Ah! Hannah had heard of gold hair before, and in connection with David's promised wife. Here was a mystery and Hannah resolved to look into it. It would at least be interesting to note the effect of her knowledge upon the young bride next door. She would try it.

Meantime, the acquaintance of Harry Temple and Kate Leavenworth had progressed rapidly. The second sight of the lady proved more interesting than the first, for now her beautiful gold hair added to the charm of her handsome face. Harry ever delighted in beauty of whatever type, and a blonde was more fascinating to him than a brunette. Kate had dressed herself bewitchingly, and her manner was charming. She knew how to assume pretty child-like airs, but she was not afraid to look him boldly in the eyes, and the light in her own seemed to challenge him. Here was a delighful new study. A woman fresh from the country, having all the charm of innocence, almost as child-like as her sister, yet with none of her prudishness. Kate's eyes held latent wickedness in them, or he was much mistaken. She did not droop her lids and blush when he looked boldly and admiringly into her face, but stared him back, smilingly, merrily, daringly, as though she would go quite as far as he would. Moreover with her he was sure he need feel none of the compunctions he might have felt with her younger sister who was so obviously innocent, for whether Kate's boldness was from lack of knowledge, or from lack of innocence, she was quite able to protect herself, that was plain.

So Harry settled into his chair with a smile of pleasant anticipation upon his face. He not only had the prospect before him of a possible ally in revenge against David Spafford, but he had the promise of a most unusually delightful flirtation with a woman who was worthy of his best efforts in that line.

Almost at once it began, with pleasant banter, adorned with personal compliments.

"Lovelier than I thought, my lady," said Harry, bowing low over the hand she gave him, in a courtly manner he had acquired, perhaps from the old-world novels he had read, and he brushed her pink finger tips with his lips in a way that signified he was her abject slave.

Kate blushed and smiled, greatly pleased, for though she had held her own little court in the village where she was brought up, and queened it over the young men who had flocked about her willingly, she had not been used to the fulsome flattery that breathed from Harry Temple in every word and glance.

He looked at her keenly as he stood back a moment, to see if she were in any wise offended with his salutation, and saw as he expected that she was pleased and flattered. Her cheeks had grown rosier, and her eyes sparkled with pleasure as she responded with a pretty, gracious speech.

Then they sat down and faced one another. A good woman would have called his look impudent—insulting. Kate returned it with a look that did not shrink, nor waver, but fearlessly, recklessly accepted the challenge. Playing with fire, were these two, and with no care for the fearful results which might follow. Both knew it was dangerous, and liked it the better for that. There was a long silence. The game was opening on a wider scale than either had every played before.

"Do you believe in affinities?" asked the devil, through the man's voice.

The woman colored and showed she understood his deeper meaning. Her eyes drooped for just the shade of an instant, and then she looked up and faced him saucily, provokingly:

"Why?"

He admired her with his gaze, and waited, lazily watching the color play in her cheeks.

"Do you need to ask why?" he said at last, looking at her significantly. "I knew that you were my affinity the moment I laid my eyes upon you, and I hoped you felt the same. But perhaps I was mistaken." He searched her face.

She kept her eyes upon his, returning their full gaze, as if to hold it from going too deep into her soul.

"I did not say you were mistaken, did I?" said the rosy lips coquettishly, and Kate drooped her long lashes till they fell in becoming sweeps over her burning cheeks.

Something in the curve of cheek and chin, and sweep of dark lash over velvet skin, reminded him of her sister. It was so she had sat, though utterly unconscious, while he had been singing, when there had come over him that overwhelming desire to kiss her. If he should kiss this fair lady would she slap him in the face and run into the garden? He thought not. Still, she was brought up by the same father and mother in all likelihood, and it was well to go slow. He reached forward, drawing his chair a little nearer to her, and then boldly took one of her small unresisting hands, gently, that he might not frighten her, and smoothed it thoughtfully between his own. He held it in a close grasp and looked into her face gain, she meanwhile watching her hand amusedly, as though it were something apart from herself, a sort of distant possession, for which she was in no wise responsible.

"I feel that you belong to me," he said boldly looking into her eyes with a languishing gaze. "I have known it from the first moment."

Kate let her hand lie in his as if she liked it, but she said:

"And what makes you think that, most audacious sir? Did you not know that I am married?" Then she swept her gaze up provokingly at him again and smiled, showing her dainty, treacherous, little teeth. She was so bewitchingly

, you are mine! By all the power
Can any other man keep my soul from yours, can he keep
my eyes from looking into yours, or my thoughts from hovering over you, or—"
he hesitated and looked at her keenly, while she furtively watched him, holding
her breath and half inviting him—"or my lips from drinking life from yours?"
He stooped quickly and pressed his lips upon hers.

Kate gave a quick little gasp like a sob and drew back. The aunt nodding
over her Bible in the next room had not heard,—she was very deaf,—but for an
instant the young woman felt that all the shades of her worthy patriarchal
ancestors were hurrying around and away from her in horror. She had come of
too good Puritan stock not to know that she was treading in the path of
unrighteousness. Nevertheless it was a broad path, and easy. It tempted her.
It was exciting. It lured her with promise of satisfying some of her untamed
longings and impulses.

She did not look offended. She only drew back to get breath and consider.
The wild beating of her heart, the tumult of her cheeks and eyes were all a part
of a new emotion. Her vanity was excited, and she thrilled with a wild pleasure.
As a duck will take to swimming so she took to the new game, with wonderful
facility.

"But I didn't say you might," she cried with a bewildering smile.

"I beg your pardon, fair lady, may I have another?"

His bold, bad face was near her own, so that she did not see the evil triumph
that lurked there. She had come to the turning of another way in her life, and
just here she might have drawn back if she would. Half she knew this, yet she
toyed with the opportunity, and it was gone. The new way seemed so alluring.

"You will first have to prove your right!" she said decidedly, with that pretty
commanding air that had conquered so many times.

And in like manner on they went through the evening, frittering the time
away at playing with edged tools.

A friendship so begun—if so unworthy an intimacy may be called by that
sweet name—boded no good to either of the two, and that evening marked a
decided turn for the worse in Kate Leavenworth's career.

Chapter 20

David had found it necessary to take a journey which might keep him away for several weeks.

He told Marcia in the evening when he came home from the office. He told her as he would have told his clerk. It meant nothing to him but an annoyance that he had to start out in the early winter, leave his business in other's hands for an indefinite period, and go among strangers. He did not see the whitening of Marcia's lips, nor the quick little movement of her hand to her heart. Even Marcia herself did not realize all that it meant to her. She felt as if a sudden shock had almost knocked her off her feet. This quiet life in the big house, with only David at intervals to watch and speak to occasionally, and no one to open her true heart to, had been lonely; and many a time when she was alone at night she had wept bitter tears upon her pillow,—why she did not quite know. But now when she knew that it was to cease, and David was going away from her for a long time, perhaps weeks, her heart suddenly tightened and she knew how sweet it had been growing. Almost the tears came to her eyes, but she made a quick errand to the hearth for the teapot, busying herself there till they were under control again. When she returned to her place at the table she was able to ask David some commonplace question about the journey which kept her true feeling quite hidden from him.

He was to start the next evening if possible. It appeared that there was something important about railroading coming up in Congress. It was necessary that he should be present to hear the debate, and also that he should see and interview influential men. It meant much to the success of the great new enterprises that were just in their infancy that he should go and find out all about them and write them up as only he whose heart was in it could do. He was pleased to have been selected for this; he was lifted for the time above himself and his life troubles, and given to feel that he had a work in the world that was worth while, a high calling, a chance to give a push to the unrolling of the secret possibilities of the universe, and help them on their way.

Marcia understood it all, and was proud and glad for him, but her own heart which beat in such perfect sympathy with the work felt lonely and left out. If only she could have helped too!

There was no time for David to take Marcia to her home to stay during his absence. He spoke of it regretfully just as he was about to leave, and asked if she would like him to get some one to escort her by coach to her father's house until he could come for her; but she held back the tears by main force and shook her head. She had canvassed that question in the still hours of the night. She

The only other alternative was to go to the aunts. David expected it, and the aunts spoke of it as if nothing else were possible. Marcia would have preferred to remain alone in her own house, with her beloved piano, but David would not consent, and the aunts were scandalized at the suggestion. So to the aunts went Marcia, and they took her in with a hope in their hearts that she might get the same good from the visit that the sluggard in the Bible is bidden to find.

"We must do our duty by her for David's sake," said Aunt Hortense, with pursed lips and capable, folded hands that seemed fairly to ache to get at the work of reconstructing the new niece.

"Yes, it is our opportunity," said Aunt Amelia with a snap as though she thoroughly enjoyed the prospect. "Poor David!" and so they sat and laid out their plans for their sweet young victim, who all unknowingly was coming to one of those tests in her life whereby we are tried for greater things and made perfect in patience and sweetness.

It began with the first breakfast—the night before she had been company, at supper—but when the morning came they felt she must be counted one of the family. They examined her thoroughly on what she had been taught with regard to housekeeping. They made her tell her recipes for pickling and preserving. They put her through a catechism of culinary lore, and always after her most animated account of the careful way in which she had been trained in this or that housewifely art she looked up with wistful eyes that longed to please, only to be met by the hard set lips and steely glances of the two mentors who regretted that she should not have been taught their way which was so much better.

Aunt Hortense even went so far once as to suggest that Marcia write to her stepmother and tell her how much better it was to salt the water in which potatoes were to be boiled before putting them in, and was much offended by the clear girlish laugh that bubbled up involuntarily at the thought of teaching her stepmother anything about cooking.

"Excuse me," she said, instantly sobering as she saw the grim look of the aunt, and felt frightened at what she had done. "I did not mean to laugh, indeed I did not; but it seemed so funny to think of my telling Mother how to do anything."

"People are never too old to learn," remarked Aunt Hortense with offended mien, "and one ought never to be too proud when there is a better way."

"But Mother thinks there is no better way I am sure. She says that it makes potatoes soggy to boil them in salt. All that grows below the ground should be salted after it is cooked and all that grows above the ground should be cooked in salted water, is her rule."

"I am surprised that your stepmother should uphold any such superstitious ideas," said Aunt Amelia with a self-satisfied expression.

"One should never be too proud to learn something better," Aunt Hortense said grimly, and Marcia retreated in dire consternation at the thought of what might follow if these three notable housekeeping gentlewomen should come together. Somehow she felt a wicked little triumph in the thought that it would be hard to down her stepmother.

Marcia was given a few light duties ostensibly to "make her feel at home," but in reality, she knew, because the aunts felt she needed their instruction. She was asked if she would like to wash the china and glass; and regularly after each meal a small wooden tub and a mop were brought in with hot water and soap, and she was expected to handle the costly heirlooms under the careful scrutiny of their worshipping owners, who evidently watched each process with strained nerves lest any bit of treasured pottery should be cracked or broken. It was a trying ordeal.

The girl would have been no girl if she had not chafed under this treatment. To hold her temper steady and sweet under it was almost more than she could bear.

There were long afternoons when it was decreed that they should knit.

Marcia had been used to take long walks at home, over the smooth crust of the snow, going to her beloved woods, where she delighted to wander among the bare and creaking trees; fancying them whispering sadly to one another of the summer that was gone and the leaves they had borne now dead. But it would be a dreadful thing in the aunts' opinion for a woman, and especially a young one, to take a long walk in the woods alone, in winter too, and with no object whatever in view but a walk! What a waste of time!

There were two places of refuge for Marcia during the weeks that followed. There was home. How sweet that word sounded to her! How she longed to go back there, with David coming home to his quiet meals three times a day, and with her own time to herself to do as she pleased. With housewifely zeal that was commendable in the eyes of the aunts, Marcia insisted upon going down to her own house every morning to see that all was right, guiltily knowing that in her heart she meant to hurry to her beloved books and piano. To be sure it was cold and cheerless in the empty house. She dared not make up fires and leave them, and she dared not stay too long lest the aunts would feel hurt at her absence, but she longed with an inexpressible longing to be back there by herself, away from that terrible supervision and able to live her own glad little life and think her own thoughts untrammeled by primness.

...place of refuge was Aunt Clarinda's room. Thither she would betake herself after supper, to the delight of the old lady. Then the other two occupants of the house were left to themselves and might unbend from their rigid surveillance for a little while. Marcia often wondered if they ever did unbend.

There was a large padded rocking chair in Aunt Clarinda's room and Marcia would laughingly take the little old lady in her arms and place her comfortably in it, after a pleasant struggle on Miss Clarinda's part to put her guest into it. They had this same little play every evening, and it seemed to please the old lady mightily. Then when she was conquered she always sat meekly laughing, a fine pink color in her soft peachy cheek, the candle light from the high shelf making flickering sparkles in her old eyes that always seemed young; and she would say: "That's just as David used to do."

Then Marcia drew up the little mahogany stool covered with the worsted dog which Aunt Clarinda had worked when she was ten years old, and snuggling down at the old lady's feet exclaimed delightedly: "Tell me about it!" and they settled down to solid comfort.

There came a letter from David after he had been gone a little over a week. Marcia had not expected to hear from him. He had said nothing about writing, and their relations were scarcely such as to make it necessary. Letters were an expensive luxury in those days. But when the letter was handed to her, Marcia's heart went pounding against her breast, the color flew into her cheeks, and she sped away home on feet swift as the wings of a bird. The postmaster's daughter looked after her, and remarked to her father: "My, but don't she think a lot of him!"

Straight to the cold, lonely house she flew, and sitting down in his big chair read it.

It was a pleasant letter, beginning formally: *My dear Marcia,* and asking after her health. It brought back a little of the unacquaintedness she had felt when he was at home, and which had been swept away in part by her knowledge of his childhood. But it went on quite happily telling all about his journey and describing minutely the places he had passed through and the people he had met on the way; detailing every little incident as only a born writer and observer could do, until she felt as if he were talking to her. He told her of the men whom he had met who were interested in the new project. He told of new plans and described minutely his visit to the foundry at West Point and the machinery he had seen. Marcia read it all breathlessly, in search of something, she knew not what, that was not there. When she had finished and found it not, there was a sense of aloofness, a sad little disappointment which welled up in her throat. She sat back to think about it. He was having a good time, and he was not lonely. He had no longing to be back in the house and everything running as before he had gone. He was out in the big glorious world having to do with progress, and coming in contact with men who were making history. Of course he did not dream how lonely she was here, and how she longed, if for nothing else, just to be back here alone and do as she pleased, and not to be watched over. If only she might steal Aunt Clarinda and bring her back to live here with her while David was away! But that was not to be thought of, of course. By and by she mustered courage to be glad of her letter, and to read it over once more.

That night she read the letter to Aunt Clarinda and together they discussed the great inventions, and the changes that were coming to pass in the land. Aunt Clarinda was just a little beyond her depth in such a conversation, but Marcia did most of the talking, and the dear old lady made an excellent listener, with a pat here, and a "Dearie me! Now you don't say so!" there, and a "Bless the boy! What great things he does expect. And I hope he won't be disappointed."

That letter lasted them for many a day until another came, this time from Washington, with many descriptions of public men and public doings, and a word picture of the place which made it appear much like any other place after all if it was the capitol of the country. And once there was a sentence which Marcia treasured. It was, *I wish you could be here and see everything. You would enjoy it I know.*

There came another letter later beginning, *My dear little girl.* There was nothing else in it to make Marcia's heart throb, it was all about his work, but Marcia carried it many days in her bosom. It gave her a thrill of delight to think of those words at the beginning. Of course it meant no more than that he thought of her as a girl, his little sister that was to have been, but there was a kind of ownership in the words that was sweet to Marcia's lonely heart. It had come to her that she was always looking for something that would make her feel that she belonged to David.

_____ was standing listlessly by the window looking into the street. She was cross and felt a great depression settling over her. The flirtation with Harry Temple had begun to pall upon her. She wanted new worlds to conquer. She was restless and feverish. There was not excitement enough in the life she was living. She would like to meet more people, senators and statesmen—and to have plenty of money to dress as became her beauty, and be admired publicly. She half wished for the return of her husband, and meditated making up with him for the sake of going to Washington to have a good time in society there. What was the use of running away with a naval officer if one could not have the benefit of it? She had been a fool. Here she was almost to the last penny, and so many things she wanted. No word had come from her husband since he sent her the money at sailing. She felt a bitter resentment toward him for urging her to marry him. If she had only gone on and married David she would be living a life of ease now—plenty of money—nothing to do but what she pleased and no anxiety whatever, for David would have done just what she wanted.

Then suddenly she looked up and David passed before her!

He was walking with a tall splendid-looking man, with whom he was engaged in most earnest conversation, and his look was grave and deeply absorbed. He did not know of Kate's presence in New York, and passed the house in utter unconsciousness of the eyes watching him.

Kate's lips grew white, and her limbs seemed suddenly weak, but she strained her face against the window to watch the retreating figure of the man who had almost been her husband. How well she knew the familiar outline. How fine and handsome he appeared now! Why had she not thought so before? Were her eyes blind, or had she been under some strange enchantment? Why had she not known that her happiness lay in the way that had been marked out for her? Well, at least she knew it now.

She sat all day by that window and watched. She professed to have no appetite when pressed to come to the table, though she permitted herself to languidly consume the bountiful tray of good things that was brought her, but her eyes were on the street. She was watching to see if David would pass that way again. But though she watched until the sun went down and dusk sifted through the streets, she saw no sign nor heard the sound of his footsteps. Then she hastened up to her room, which faced upon the street also, and there, wrapped in blankets she sat in the cold frosty air, waiting and listening. And while she watched she was thinking bitter feverish thoughts. She heard Harry Temple knock and knew that he was told that she was not feeling well and had retired early. She watched him pause on the stoop thoughtfully as if considering what to do with the time thus unexpectedly thrown upon his hands, then saw him saunter up the street unconcernedly, and she wondered idly where he would go, and what he would do.

It grew late, even for New York. One by one the lights in the houses along the street went out, and all was quiet. She drew back from the window at last, weary with excitement and thinking, and lay down on the bed, but she could not sleep. The window was open and her ears were on the alert, and by and by there came the distant echo of feet ringing on the pavement. Some one was coming. She sprang up. She felt sure he was coming. Yes, there were two men. They were coming back together. She could hear their voices. She fancied she heard David's long before it was possible to distinguish any words. She leaned far out of her upper window till she could discern dim forms under the starlight, and then just as they were under the window she distinctly heard David say:

"There is no doubt but we shall win. The right is on our side, and it is the march of progress. Some of the best men in Congress are with us, and now that we are to have your influence, I do not feel afraid of the issue."

They had passed by rapidly, like men who had been on a long day's jaunt of some kind and were hastening home to rest. There was little in the sentence that Kate could understand. She had no more idea whether the subject of their discourse was railroads or the last hay crop. The sentence meant to her but one thing. It showed that David companioned with the great men of the land, and his position would have given her a standing that would have been above the one she now occupied. Tears of defeat ran down her cheeks. She had made a bad mistake and she saw no way to rectify it. If her husband should die,—and it might be, for the sea was often treacherous—of course there were all sorts of possibilities,—but even then there was Marcia! She set her sharp little teeth into her red lips till the blood came. She could not get over her anger at Marcia. It would not have been so bad if David had remained her lone lorn lover, ready to fly to her if others failed. Her self-love was wounded sorely, and she, poor silly soul, mistook it for love of David. She began to fancy that after all she had loved him, and that Fate had somehow played her a mad trick and tied her to a husband she had not wanted.

Then out of the watchings of the day and the fancies of the night, there grew a thought—and the thought widened into a plan. She thought of her intimacy with Harry and her new found power. Might she perhaps exercise it over others as well as Harry Temple? Might she possibly lead back this man who had once been her lover, to bow at her feet again and worship her? If that might be she could bear all the rest. She began to long with intense craving to see David grovel at her feet, to hear him plead for a kiss from her, and tell her once more

By and by she lighted a candle and drew her writing materials toward her to write, but it was long she sat and thought before she finally wrote the hastily scrawled note, signed and sealed it, and blowing out her candle lay down to sleep.

The letter was addressed to David, and it ran thus:

Dear David:

I have just heard that you are in New York. I am in great distress and do not know where to turn for help. For the sake of what we have been to each other in the past will you come to me?

Hastily, your loving Kate.

She did not know where David was but she felt reasonably sure she could find out his address in the morning. There was a small boy living next door who was capable of ferreting out almost anything for money. Kate had employed him more than once as an amateur detective in cases of minor importance. So, with a bit of silver and her letter she made her way to his familiar haunts and explained most carefully that the letter was to be delivered to no one but the man to whom it was addressed, naming several stopping places where he might be likely to be found, and hinting that there was more silver to be forthcoming when he should bring her an answer to the note. With a minute description of David the keen-eyed urchin set out, while Kate betook herself to her room to dress for David's coming. She felt sure he would be found, and confident that he would come at once.

The icy wind of the night before blowing on her exposed throat and chest had given her a severe cold, but she paid no heed to that. Her eyes and cheeks were shining with fever. She knew she was entering upon a dangerous and unholy way. The excitement of it stimulated her. She felt she did not care for anything, right or wrong, sin or sorrow, only to win. She wanted to see David at her feet again. It was the only thing that would satisfy this insatiable longing in her, this wounded pride of self.

When she was dressed she stood before the mirror and surveyed herself. She knew she was beautiful, and she defied the glass to tell her anything else. She raised her chin in haughty challenge to the unseen David to resist her charms. She would bring him low before her. She would make him forget Marcia, and his home and his staid Puritan notions, and all else he held dear but herself. He should bend and kiss her hand as Harry had done, only more warmly, for instinctively she felt that his had been the purer life and therefore his surrender would mean more. He should do whatever she chose. And her eyes glowed with an unhallowed light.

She had chosen to array herself regally, in velvet, but in black, without a touch of color or of white. From her rich frock her slender throat rose daintily, like a stem upon which nodded the tempting flower of her face. No enameled complexion could have been more striking in its vivid reds and whites, and her mass of gold hair made her seem more lovely than she really was, for in her face was love of self, alluring, but heartless and cruel.

The boy found David, as Kate had thought he would, in one of the quieter hostelries where men of letter were to stop when in New York, and David read the letter and came at once. She had known that he would do that, too. His heart beat wildly, to the exclusion of all other thoughts save that she was in trouble, his love, his dear one. He forgot Marcia, and the young naval officer, and everything but her trouble, and before he had reached her house the sorrow had grown in his imagination into some great danger to protect her from which he was hastening.

She received him alone in the room where Harry Temple had first called, and a moment later Harry himself came to knock and enquire for the health of Mistress Leavenworth, and was told she was very much engaged at present with a gentleman and could not see any one, whereupon Harry scowled, and set himself at a suitable distance from the house to watch who should come out.

David's face was white as death as he entered, his eyes shining like dark jewels blazing at her as if he would absorb the vision for the lonely future. She stood and posed, — not by any means the picture of broken sorrow he had expected to find her from her note, — and let the sense of her beauty reach him. There she stood with the look on her face he had pictured to himself many a time when he had thought of her as his wife. It was a look of love unutterable, bewildering, alluring, compelling. It was so he had thought she would meet him when he came home to her from his daily business cares. And now she was there, looking that way, and he stood here, so near her, and yet a great gulf fixed! It was heaven and hell met together, and he had no power to change either.

He did not come over to her and bow low to kiss the white hand as Harry had done, — as she had thought she could compel him to do. He only stood and looked at her with the pain of an anguish beyond her comprehension, until the look would have burned through to her heart — if she had had a heart.

"You are in trouble," he spoke hoarsely, as if murmuring an excuse for having come.

She melted at once into the loveliest sorrow, her mobile features taking on a wan cast only enlivened by the glow of her cheeks.

dainty, lace bordered kerchief that suppressed a well-timed sob.

Kate had wisely calculated how she could reach David's heart. If she had looked up then and seen his white, drawn look, and the tense grasp of his hands that only the greatest self-control kept quiet on his knee, perhaps even her mercilessness would have been softened. But she did not look, and she felt her part was well taken. She sobbed quietly, and waited, and his hoarse voice asked once more, as gently as a woman's though his pain:

"Will you tell me what it is and how I can help you?" He longed to take her in his arms like a little child and comfort her, but he might not. She was another's. And perhaps that other had been cruel to her! His clenched fists showed how terrible was the thought. But still the bowed figure in its piteous black sobbed and did not reply anything except, "Oh, I am so unhappy! I cannot bear it any longer."

"Is—your—your—husband unkind to you?" The words tore themselves from his tense lips as though they were beyond his control.

"Oh, no—not exactly unkind—that is—he was not very nice before he went away," wailed out a sad voice from behind the linen cambric and lace, "and he went away without a kind word, and left me hardly any money—and he hasn't sent me any word since—and fa-father won't have anything to do with me any more—but—but—it's not that I mind, David. I don't think about those things at all. I'm so unhappy about you. I feel you do not forgive me, and I cannot stand it any longer. I have made a fearful mistake, and you are angry with me—I think about it at night"—the voice was growing lower now, and the sentences broken by sobs that told better than words what distress the sufferer would convey.

"I have been so wicked—and you were so good and kind—and now you will never forgive me—I think it will kill me to keep on thinking about it—" her voice trailed off in tears again.

David white with anguish sprang to his feet.

"Oh, Kate," he cried, "my darling! Don't talk that way. You know I forgive you. Look up and tell me you know I forgive you."

Almost she smiled her triumph beneath her sobs in the little lace border, but she looked up with real tears on her face. Even her tears obeyed her will. She was a good actress, also she knew her power over David.

"Oh, David," she cried, standing up and clasping her hands beseechingly, "can it be true? Do you really forgive me? Tell me again."

She came and stood temptingly near to the stern, suffering man wild with the tumult that raged within him. Her golden head was near his shoulder where it had rested more than once in time gone by. He looked down at her from his suffering height his arms folded tightly and said, as though taking oath before a court of justice:

"I do."

She looked up with her pleading blue eyes, like two jewels of light now, questioning whether she might yet go one step further. Her breath came quick and soft, he fancied it touched his cheek, though she was not tall enough for that. She lifted her tear-wet face like a flower after a storm, and pleaded with her eyes once more, saying in a whisper very soft and sweet:

"If you really forgive me, then kiss me, just once, so I may remember it always."

It was more than he could bear. He caught her to himself and pressed his lips upon hers in one frenzied kiss of torture. It was as if wrung from him against his will. Then suddenly it came upon him what he had done, as he held her in his arms, and he put her from him gently, as a mother might put away the precious child she was sacrificing tenderly, agonizingly, but finally. He put her from him thus and stood a moment looking at her, while she almost sparkled her pleasure at him through the tears. She felt that she had won.

But gradually the silence grew ominous. She perceived he was not smiling. His mien was like one who looks into an open grave, and gazes for the last time at all that remains of one who is dear. He did not seem like one who had yielded a moral point and was ready now to serve her as she would. She grew uneasy under his gaze. She moved forward and put out her hands inviting, yielding, as only such a woman could do, and the spell which bound him seemed to be broken. He fumbled for a moment in his waistcoat pocket and brought out a large roll of bills which he laid upon the table, and taking up his hat turned toward the door. A cold wave of weakness seemed to pass over her, stung here and there by mortal pride that was in fear of being wounded beyond recovery.

"Where are you going?" she asked weakly, and her voice sounded to her from miles away, and strange.

He turned and looked at her again and she knew the look meant farewell. He did not speak. Her whole being rose for one more mighty effort.

"You are not going to leave me — now?" There was angelic sweetness in the voice, pleading, reproachful, piteous.

"I must!" he said, and his voice sounded harsh. "I have just done that for which, were I your husband, I would feel like killing any other man. I must protect you against yourself, — against myself. You must be kept pure before God if it kills us both. I would gladly die if that could help you, but I am not even free to do that, for I belong to another."

Then he turned and was gone.

was seeing her own sinful heart as it was.

But the devil was there also. He whispered to her now the last sentence that David had spoken: "I belong to another!"

Up to that moment Marcia had been a very negative factor in the affair to Kate's mind. She had been annoyed and angry at her as one whose ignorance and impertinence had brought her into an affair where she did not belong, but now she suddenly faced the fact that Marcia must be reckoned with. Marcia the child, who had for years been her slave and done her bidding, had arisen in her way, and she hated her with a sudden vindictive hate that would have killed without flinching if the opportunity had presented at that moment. Kate had no idea how utterly uncontrolled was her whole nature. She was at the mercy of any passing passion. Hate and revenge took possession of her now. With flashing eyes she rose to her feet, brushing her tumbled hair back and wiping away angry tears. She was too much agitated to notice that some one had knocked at the front door and been admitted, and when Harry Temple walked into the room he found her standing so with hands clenched together, and tears flowing down her cheeks unchecked.

Now a woman in tears, when the tears were not caused by his own actions, was Harry's opportunity. He had ways of comforting which were as unscrupulous as they generally proved effective, and so with affectionate tenderness he took Kate's hand and held it impressively, calling her "dear." He spoke soothing words, smoothed her hair, and kissed her flushed cheeks and eyes. It was all very pleasant to Kate's hurt pride. She let Harry comfort her, and pet her a while, and at last he said:

"Now tell me all about it, dear. I saw Lord Spafford trail dejectedly away from here looking like death, and I come here and find my lady in a fine fury. What has happened? If I mistake not the insufferable cad has got badly hurt, but it seems to have ruffled the lady also."

This helped. It was something to feel that David was suffering. She wanted him to suffer. He had brought shame and humiliation upon her. She never realized that the thing that shamed her was that he thought her better than she was.

"He is offensively good. I *hate* him!" she remarked as a kitten might who had got hurt at playing with a mouse in a trap.

The man's face grew bland with satisfaction.

"Not so good, my lady, but that he has been making love to you, if I mistake not, and he with a wife at home." The words were said quietly, but there was more of a question in them than the tone conveyed. The man wished to have evidence against his enemy.

Kate colored uneasily and drooped her lashes.

Harry studied her face keenly, and then went on cautiously:

"If his wife were not your sister I should say that one might punish him well through her."

Kate cast him a hard, scrutinizing look.

"You have some score against him yourself," she said with conviction.

"Perhaps I have, my lady. Perhaps I too hate him. He is offensively good, you know."

There was silence in the room for a full minute while the devil worked in both hearts.

"What did you mean by saying one might punish him through his wife? He does not love his wife."

"Are you sure?"

"Quite sure."

"Perhaps he loves some one else, my lady."

"He does." She said it proudly.

"Perhaps he loves you, my lady." He said it softly like the suggestion from another world. The lady was silent, but he needed no other answer.

"Then indeed, the way would be even clearer,—were not his wife your sister."

Kate looked at him, a half knowledge of his meaning beginning to dawn in her eyes.

"How?" she asked laconically.

"In case his wife should leave him do you think my lord would hold his head so high?"

Kate still looked puzzled.

"If some one else should win her affection, and should persuade her to leave a husband who did not love her, and who was bestowing his heart"—he hesitated an instant and his eye travelled significantly to the roll of bills still lying where David had left them—"and his gifts," he hazarded, "upon another woman—"

Kate grasped the thought at once and an evil glint of eagerness showed in her eyes. She could see what an advantage it would be to herself to have Marcia removed from the situation. It would break one more cord of honor that bound David to a code which was hateful to her now, because its existence shamed her. Nevertheless, unscrupulous as she was she could not see how this was a possibility.

"But she is offensively good too," she said as if answering her own thoughts.

she wished this might be. She looked her co-operation in the plan even before her hard voice answered:

"You need not stop because she is my sister."

He felt he had her permission, and he permitted himself a glance of admiration for the depths to which she could go without being daunted. Here was evil courage worthy of his teaching. She seemed to him beautiful enough and daring enough for Satan himself to admire.

"And may I have the pleasure of knowing that I would by so doing serve my lady in some wise?"

She drooped her shameless eyes and murmured guardedly, "Perhaps." Then she swept him a coquettish glance that meant they understood one another.

"Then I shall feel well rewarded," he said gallantly, and bowing with more than his ordinary flattery of look bade her good day and went out.

Chapter 22

David stumbled blindly out the door and down the street. His one thought was to get to his room at the tavern and shut the door. He had an important appointment that morning, but it passed completely from his mind. He met one or two men whom he knew, but he did not see them, and passed them swiftly without a glance of recognition. They said one to another, "How absorbed he is in the great themes of the world!" but David passed on in his pain and misery and humiliation and never knew they were near him.

He went to the room that had been his since he had reached New York, and fastening the door against all intrusion fell upon his knees beside the bed, and let the floodtide of his sorrow roll over him. Not even when Kate had played him false on his wedding morning had he felt the pain that now cut into his very soul. For now there was mingled with it the agony of consciousness of sin. He had sinned against heaven, against honor and love, and all that was pure and good. He was just like any bad man. He had yielded to sudden temptation and taken another man's wife in his arms and kissed her! That the woman had been his by first right, and that he loved her: that she had invited the kiss, indeed pleaded for it, his sensitive conscience told him in no wise lessened the offense. He had also caused her whom he loved to sin. He was a man and knew the world. He should have shielded her against herself. And yet as he went over and over the whole painful scene through which he had just passed his soul cried out in agony and he felt his weakness more and more. He had failed, failed most miserably. Acted like any coward!

The humiliation of it was unspeakable. Could any sorrow be like unto his? Like a knife flashing through the gloom of his own shame would come the echo of her words as she pleaded with him to kiss her. It was a kiss of forgiveness she had wanted, and she had put her heart into her eyes and begged as for her very life. How could he have refused? Then he would parley with himself for a long time trying to prove to himself that the kiss and the embrace were justified, that he had done no wrong in God's sight. And ever after this round of confused arguing he would end with the terrible conviction that he had sinned.

Sometimes Marcia's sweet face and troubled eyes would appear to him as he wrestled all alone, and seemed to be longing to help him, and again would come the piercing thought that he had harmed this gentle girl also. He had tangled her into his own spoiled web of life, and been disloyal to her. She was pure and true and good. She had given up everything to help him and he had utterly forgotten her. He had promised to love, cherish, and protect her! That was another sin. He could not love and cherish her when his whole heart was

...nau been

...g ... give it!

... aloud at the thought of his helplessness to help her helplessness. Was there not some way he could find out and help her without doing wrong?

Over and over he went through the whole dreadful day, until his brain was weary and his heart failed him. The heavens seemed brass and no answer came to his cry, — the appeal of a broken soul. It seemed that he could not get up from his knees, could not go out into the world again and face life. He had been tried and had failed, and yet though he knew his sin he felt an intolerable longing to commit it over again. He was frightened at his own weakness, and with renewed vigor he began to pray for help. It was like the prayer of Jacob of old, the crying out of a soul that would not be denied. All day long the struggle continued, and far into the night. At last a great peace began to settle upon David's soul. Things that had been confused by his passionate longings grew clear as day. Self dropped away, and sin, conquered, slunk out of sight. Right and Wrong were once more clearly defined in his mind. However wrong it might or might not be he was here in this situation. He had married Marcia and promised to be true to her. He was doubly cut off from Kate by her own act and by his. That was his punishment, — and hers. He must not seek to lessen it even for her, for it was God-sent. Henceforth his path and hers must be apart. If she were to be helped in any way from whatsoever trouble was hers, it was not permitted him to be the instrument. He had shown his unfitness for it in his interview that morning, even if in the eyes of the world it could have been at all. It was his duty to cut himself off from her forever. He must not even think of her any more. He must be as true and good to Marcia as was possible. He must do no more wrong. He must grow strong and suffer.

The peace that came with conviction brought sleep to his weary mind and body.

When he awoke it was almost noon. He remembered the missed appointment of the day before, and the journey to Washington which he had planned for that day. With a start of horror he looked at his watch and found he had but a few hours in which to try to make up for the remissness of yesterday before the evening coach left for Philadelphia. It was as if some guardian angel had met his first waking thoughts with business that could not be delayed and so kept him from going over the painful events of the day before. He arose and hastened out into the world once more.

Late in the afternoon he found the man he was to have met the day before, and succeeded in convincing him that he ought to help the new enterprise. He was standing on the corner saying the last words as the two separated, when Kate drove by in a friend's carriage, surrounded by parcels. She had been on a shopping tour spending the money that David had given her, for silks and laces and jewelry, and now she was returning in high glee with her booty. The carriage passed quite near to David who stood with his back to the street, and she could see his animated face as he smiled at the other man, a fine looking man who looked as if he might be some one of note. The momentary glance did not show the haggard look of David's face nor the lines under his eyes, and Kate was angered to see him so unconcerned and forgetful of his pain of yesterday. Her face darkened with spite, and she resolved to make him suffer yet, and to the utmost, for the sin of forgetting her.

But David was in the way of duty, and he did not see her, for his guardian angel was hovering close at hand.

As the Fall wore on and the winter set in Harry's letters became less frequent and less intimate. Hannah was troubled, and after consultation with her grandmother, to which Miranda listened at the latch hole, duly reporting quotations to her adored Mrs. Spafford, Hannah decided upon an immediate trip to the metropolis.

"Hannah's gone to New York to find out what's become of that nimshi Harry Temple. She thought she had him fast, an' she's been holdin' him over poor Lemuel Skinner's head like thet there sword hangin' by a 'air I heard the minister tell about last Sunday, till Lemuel, he don't know but every minute's gone'll be his last. You mark my words, she'll hev to take poor Lem after all, an' be glad she's got him, too,—and she's none too good for him neither. He's ben faithful to her ever since she wore pantalets, an' she's ben keepin' him off'n on an' hopin' an' tryin fer somebody bigger. It would jes' serve her right ef she'd get that fool of a Harry Temple, but she won't. He's too sharp for that ef he *is* a fool. He don't want to tie himself up to no woman's aprun strings. He rather dandle about after 'em all an' say pretty things, an' keep his earnin's fer himself."

Hannah reached New York the week after David left for Washington. She wrote beforehand to Harry to let him know she was coming, and made plain that she expected his attentions exclusively while there, and he smiled blandly as he read the letter and read her intentions between the lines. He told Kate a good deal about her that evening when he went to call, told her how he had heard she was an old flame of David's, and Kate's jealousy was immediately aroused. She wished to meet Hannah Heath. There was a sort of triumph in the thought that she had scorned and flung aside the man whom this woman had "set her cap" for, even though another woman was now in the place that neither had. Hannah went to visit a cousin in New York who lived in a quiet

...... women friends

...... choose in this case, for it occurred to her

...... to have a friend in the town where lived her sister and her former lover. There might be reasons why, sometime. She opened her heart of hearts to Hannah, and Hannah, quite discreetly, and without wasting much of her scanty store of love, entered, and the friendship was sealed. They had not known each other many days before Kate had confided to Hannah the story of her own marriage and her sister's, embellished of course as she chose. Hannah, astonished, puzzled, wondering, curious, at the tragedy that had been enacted at her very home door, became more friendly than ever and hated more cordially than ever the young and innocent wife who had stepped into the vacant place and so made her own hopes and ambitions impossible. She felt that she would like to put down the pert young thing for daring to be there, and to be pretty, and now she felt she had the secret which would help her to do so.

As the visit went on and it became apparent to Hannah Heath that she was not the one woman in all the world to Harry Temple, she hinted to Kate that it was likely she would be married soon. She even went so far as to say that she had come away from home to decide the matter, and that she had but to say the word and the ceremony would come off. Kate questioned eagerly, and seeing her opportunity asked if she might come to the wedding. Hannah, flattered, and seeing a grand opportunity for a wholesale triumph and revenge, assented with pleasure. Afterward as Hannah had hoped and intended, Kate carried the news of the impending decision and probable wedding to the ears of Harry Temple.

But Hannah's hint had no further effect upon the redoubtable Harry. Two days later he appeared, smiling, congratulatory, deploring the fact that she would be lost in a certain sense to his friendship, although he hoped always to be looked upon as a little more than a friend.

Hannah covered her mortification under a calm and condescending exterior. She blushed appropriately, said some sentimental things about hoping their friendship would not be affected by the change, told him how much she had enjoyed their correspondence, but gave him to understand that it had been mere friendship of course from her point of view, and Harry indulgently allowed her to think that he had hoped for more and was grieved but consolable over the outcome.

They waxed a trifle sentimental at the parting, but when Harry was gone, Hannah wrote a most touching letter to Lemuel Skinner which raised him to the seventh heaven of delight, causing him to feel that he was treading upon air as he walked the prosaic streets of his native town where he had been going about during Hannah's absence like a lost spirit without a guiding star.

Dear Lemuel: she wrote: —
I am coming home. I wonder if you will be glad? (Artful Hannah, as if she did not know!)
It is very delightful in New York and I have been having a gay time since I came, and everybody has been most pleasant, but —
"Mid pleasures and palaces though we may roam, Still, be it ever so humble, there's no place like home. A charm from the skies seems to hallow it there, which, go through the world, you'll not meet elsewhere. Home, home, sweet home! There's no place like home."
That is a new song, Lemuel, that everybody here is singing. It is written by a young American named John Howard Payne who is in London now acting in a great playhouse. Everybody is wild over this song. I'll sing it for you when I come home.
I shall be at home in time for singing school next week, Lemuel. I wonder if you'll come to see me at once and welcome me. You cannot think how glad I shall be to get home again. It seems as though I had been gone a year at least. Hoping to see you soon, I remain

Always your sincere friend,
Hannah Heath.

And thus did Hannah make smooth her path before her, and very soon after inditing this epistle she bade good-bye to New York and took her way home resolved to waste no further time in chasing will-o'-the-wisps.

When Lemuel received that letter he took a good look at himself in the glass. More than seven years had he served for Hannah, and little hope had he had of a final reward. He was older by ten years than she, and already his face began to show it. He examined himself critically, and was pleased to find with that light of hope in his eyes he was not so bad looking as he feared. He betook himself to the village tailor forthwith and ordered a new suit of clothes, though his Sunday best was by no means shiny yet. He realized that he if did not win now he never would, and he resolved to do his best.

On the way home, during all the joltings of the coach over rough roads Hannah Heath was planning two campaigns, one of love with Lemuel, and one of hate with Marcia Spafford. She was possessed of knowledge which she felt would help her in the latter, and often she smiled vindictively as she laid her neat plans for the destruction of the bride's complacency.

That night the fire in the Heath parlor burned high and glowed, and the candles in their silver holders flickered across fair Hannah's face as she dimpled

Hannah had not been at home many days before she called upon Marcia.

Marcia had just seated herself at the piano when Hannah appeared to her from the hall, coming in unannounced through the kitchen door according to old neighborly fashion.

Marcia was vexed. She arose from the instrument and led the way to the little morning room which was sunny and cozy, and bare of music or books. She did not like to visit with Hannah in the parlor. Somehow her presence reminded her of the evil face of Harry Temple as he had stooped to kiss her.

"You know how to play, too, don't you?" said Hannah as they sat down. "Your sister plays beautifully. Do you know the new song, 'Home, Sweet Home?' She plays it with so much feeling and sings it so that one would think her heart was breaking for her home. You must have been a united family." Hannah said it with sharp scrutiny in voice and eyes.

"Sit down, Miss Heath," said Marcia coolly, lowering the yellow shades that her visitor's eyes might not be troubled by a broad sunbeam. "Did you have a pleasant time in New York?"

Hannah could not be sure whether or not the question was an evasion. The utterly child-like manner of Marcia disarmed suspicion.

"Oh, delightful, of course. Could any one have anything else in New York?" Hannah laughed disagreeably. She realized the limitations of life in a town.

"I suppose," said Marcia, her eyes shining with the thought, "that you saw all the wonderful things of the city. I should enjoy being in New York a little while. I have heard of so many new things. Were there any ships in the harbor? I have always wanted to go over a great ship. Did you have opportunity of seeing one?"

"Oh, dear me. No!" said Hannah. "I shouldn't have cared in the least for that. I'm sure I don't know whether there were any ships in or not. I suppose there were. I saw a lot of sails on the water, but I did not ask about them. I'm not interested in dirty boats. I liked visiting the shops best. Your sister took me about everywhere. She is a most charming creature. You must miss her greatly. You were a sly little thing to cut her out."

Marcia's face flamed crimson with anger and amazement. Hannah's dart had hit the mark, and she was watching keenly to see her victim quiver.

"I do not understand you," said Marcia with girlish dignity.

"Oh, now don't pretend to misunderstand. I've heard all about it from headquarters," she said it archly, laughing. "But then I don't blame you. David was worth it." Hannah ended with a sigh. If she had ever cared for any one besides herself that one was David Spafford.

"I do not understand you," said Marcia again, drawing herself up with all the Schuyler haughtiness she could muster, till she quite resembled her father.

"Now, Mrs. Spafford," said the visitor, looking straight into her face and watching every expression as a cat would watch a mouse, "you don't mean to tell me your sister was not at one time very intimate with your husband."

"Mr. Spafford has been intimate in our family for a number of years," said Marcia proudly, her fighting fire up, "but as for my having 'cut my sister out' as you call it, you certainly have been misinformed. Excuse me, I think I will close the kitchen door. It seems to blow in here and make a draft."

Marcia left the room with her head up and her fine color well under control, and when she came back her head was still up and a distant expression was in her face. Somehow Hannah felt she had not gained much after all. But Marcia, after Hannah's departure, went up to her cold room and wept bitter tears on her pillow alone.

After that first visit Hannah never found the kitchen door unlocked when she came to make a morning call, but she improved every little opportunity to torment her gentle victim. She had had a letter from Kate and had Marcia heard? How often did Kate write her? Did Marcia know how fond Harry Temple was of Kate? And where was Kate's husband? Would he likely be ordered home soon? These little annoyances were almost unbearable sometimes and Marcia had much ado to keep her sweetness of outward demeanor.

People looked upon Lemuel with new respect. He had finally won where they had considered him a fool for years for hanging on. The added respect brought added self-respect. He took on new manliness. Grandmother Heath felt that he really was not so bad after all, and perhaps Hannah might as well have taken him at first. Altogether the Heath family were well pleased, and preparations began at once for a wedding in the near future.

And still David lingered, held here and there by a call from first one man and then another, and by important doings in Congress. He seemed to be rarely fitted for the work.

Once he was called back to New York for a day or two, and Harry Temple happened to see him as he arrived. That night he wrote to Hannah a friendly letter—Harry was by no means through with Hannah yet—and casually remarked that he saw David Spafford was in New York again. He supposed now that Mrs. Leavenworth's evenings would be fully occupied and society would see little of her while he remained.

The day after Hannah received that letter was Sunday.

The weeks had gone by rapidly since David left his home, and now the Spring was coming on. The grass was already green as summer and the willow tree by the graveyard gate was tender and green like a spring-plume. All the their own home, in public no two could have appeared more adoring than Amelia and Hortense Spafford. They hovered near Marcia and delighted to show how very close and intimate was the relationship between themselves and their new and beautiful niece, of whom in their secret hearts they were prouder than they would have cared to tell. In their best black silks and their fine lace shawls they walked beside her and talked almost eagerly, if those two stately beings could have anything to do with a quality so frivolous as eagerness. They wished it understood that David's wife was worthy of appreciation and they were more conscious than she of the many glances of admiration in her direction.

Hannah Heath encountered some of those admiring glances and saw jealously for whom they were meant. She hastened to lean forward and greet Marcia, her spiteful tongue all ready for a stab.

"Good morning, Mrs. Spafford. Is that husband of yours not home yet? Really! Why, he's quite deserted you. I call that hard for the first year, and your honeymoon scarcely over yet."

"He's been called back to New York again," said Marcia annoyed over the spiteful little sentences. "He says he may be at home soon, but he cannot be sure. His business is rather uncertain."

"New York!" said Hannah, and her voice was annoyingly loud. "What! Not again! There must be some great attraction there," and then with a meaning glance, "I suppose your sister is still there!"

Marcia felt her face crimsoning, and the tears starting from angry eyes. She felt a sudden impulse to slap Hannah. What if she should! What would the aunts say? The thought of the tumult she might make roused her sense of humor and a laugh bubbled up instead of the tears, and Hannah, watching, cat-like, could only see eyes dancing with fun though the cheeks were charmingly red. By Hannah's expression Marcia knew she was baffled, but Marcia could not get away from the disagreeable suggestion that had been made.

Yes, David was in New York, and Kate was there. Not for an instant did she doubt her husband's nobleness. She knew David would be good and true. She knew little of the world's wickedness, and never thought of any blame, as other women might, in such a suggestion. But a great jealousy sprang into being that she never dreamed existed. Kate was there, and he would perhaps see her, and all his old love and disappointment would be brought to mind again. Had she, Marcia, been hoping he would forget it? Had she been claiming something of him in her heart for herself? She could not tell. She did not know what all this tumult of feeling meant. She longed to get away and think it over, but the solemn Sunday must be observed. She must fold away her church things, put on another frock and come down to the oppressive Sunday dinner, hear Deacon Brown's rheumatism discussed, or listen to a long comparison of the morning's sermon with one preached twenty years ago by the minister, now long dead, upon the same text. It was all very hard to keep her mind upon, with these other thoughts rushing pell-mell through her brain; and when Aunt Amelia asked her to pass the butter, she handed the sugar bowl instead. Miss Amelia looked as shocked as if she had broken the great-grandmother's china teapot.

Aunt Clarinda claimed her after dinner and carried her off to her room to talk about David, so that Marcia had no chance to think even then. Miss Clarinda looked into the sweet shadowed eyes and wondered why the girl looked so sad. She thought it was because David stayed away so long, and so she kept her with her all the rest of the day.

When Marcia went to her room that night she threw herself on her knees beside the bed and tried to pray. She felt more lonely and heartsick than she ever felt before in her life. She did not know what the great hunger in her heart meant. It was terrible to think David had loved Kate. Kate never loved him in return in the right way. Marcia felt very sure of that. She wished she might have had the chance in Kate's place, and then all of a sudden the revelation came to her. She loved David herself with a great overwhelming love. Not just a love that could come and keep house for him and save him from the criticisms and comments of others; but with a love that demanded to be loved in return; a love that was mindful of every dear lineament of his countenance. The knowledge thrilled through her with a great sweetness. She did not seem to care for anything else just now, only to know that she loved David. David could never love her of course, not in that way, but she would love him. She would try to shut out the thought of Kate from him forever.

And so, dreaming, hovering on the edge of all that was bitter and all that was sweet, she fell asleep with David's letter clasped close over her heart.

...ng very early. She
... come. Her soul was in torment between
...p out of her mind the hateful things Hannah Heath had said,
and reproaching herself for what seemed to her unseemly feeling toward David,
who loved another and could never love her. It was not a part of her life-dream
to love one who belonged to another. Yet her heart was his and she was
beginning to know that everything belonging to him was dear to her. She went
and sat in his place at the table, she touched with tenderness the books upon
his desk that he had used before he went away, she went up to his room and laid
her lips for one precious daring instant upon his pillow, and then drew back with
wildly beating heart ashamed of her emotion. She knelt beside his bed and
prayed: "Oh, God, I love him, I love him! I cannot help it!" as if she would
apologize for herself, and then she hugged the thought of her love to herself,
feeling its sweet pain drift through her like some delicious agony. Her love had
come through sorrow to her, and was not as she would have had it could she
have chosen. It brought no ray of happy hope for the future, save just the
happiness of loving in secret, and of doing for the object she loved, with no
thought of a returned affection.

Then she went slowly down the stairs, trying to think how it would seem
when David came back. He had been so long gone that it seemed as if perhaps
he might never return. She felt that it had been no part of the spirit of her
contract with David that she should render to him this wild sweet love that he
had expected Kate to give. He had not wanted it. He had only wanted a wife
in name.

Then the color would sweep over her face in a crimson drift and leave it
painfully white, and she would glide to the piano like a ghost of her former self
and play some sad sweet strain and sometimes sing.

She had no heart for her dear old woods in these days. She had tried it one
day in Spring; slipped over the back fence and away through the ploughed field
where the sea of silver oats had surged, and up into the hillside and the woods;
but she was so reminded of David that it only brought heart aches and tears.
She wondered if it was because she was getting old that the hillside did not seem
so joyous now, and she did not care to look up into the sky just for the pure joy
of sky and air and clouds, nor to listen to the branches whisper to the robins
nesting. She stooped and picked a great handful of Spring beauties, but they
did not seem to give her pleasure, and by and by she dropped them from listless
fingers and walked sedately down to the house once more.

On this morning she did not even care to play. She went into the parlor and touched a few notes, but her heart was heavy and sad. Life was growing too complex.

Last week there had come a letter from Harry Temple. It had startled her when it arrived. She feared it was some ill-news about David, coming as it did from New York and being written in a strange hand.

It had been a plea for forgiveness, representing that the writer had experienced nothing but deep repentance and sorrow since the time he had seen her last. He set forth his case in a masterly way, with little touching facts of his childhood, and lonely upbringing, with no mother to guide. He told her that her noble action toward him had but made him revere her the more, and that, in short, she had made a new creature of him by refusing to return his kiss that day, and leaving him alone with so severe a rebuke. He felt that if all women were so good and true men would be a different race, and now he looked up to an angel, and he felt he could never be happy again on this earth until he had her written word of forgiveness. With that he felt he could live a new life, and she must rest assured that he would never offer other than reverence to any woman again. He further added that his action had not intended any insult to her, that he was merely expressing his natural admiration for a spirit so good and true, and that his soul was innocent of any intention of evil. With sophistry in the use of which he was an adept, he closed his epistle, fully clearing himself, and assuring her that he could have made her understand it that day if she had not left so suddenly, and he had not been almost immediately called away to the dying bed of his dear cousin. This contradictory letter had troubled Marcia greatly. She was keen enough to see that his logic was at fault, and that the two pages of his letter did not hang together, but one thing was plain, that he wished her forgiveness. The Bible said that one must forgive, and surely it was right to let him know that she did, though when she thought of the fright he had given her it was hard to do. Still, it was right, and if he was so unhappy, perhaps she had better let him know. She would rather have waited until David returned to consult him in the matter, but the letter seemed so insistent that she had finally written a stiff little note, in formal language, *Mrs. Spafford sends herewith her full and free forgiveness to Mr. Harry Temple, and promises to think no more of the matter.*

She would have liked to consult some one. She almost thought of taking Aunt Clarinda into her confidence, but decided that she might not understand. So she finally sent off the brief missive, and let her troubled thoughts wander after it more than once.

She was standing by the window looking out into the yard perplexing herself over this again when there came a loud knocking at the front door. She started, half frightened, for the knock sounded through the empty house so insistently. It seemed like trouble coming. She felt nervous as she went down the hall.

... she realized that

DEAR MADAM: the letter read, *I bring you news of your husband, and having met with with an accident I am unable to come further. You will find me at the Green Tavern two miles out on the corduroy road. As the business is private, please come alone.*

A Messenger

Marcia trembled so that she sat down on the stairs. A sudden weakness went over her like a wave, and the hall grew dark around her as though she were going to faint. But she did not. She was strong and well and had never fainted in her life. She rallied in a moment and tried to think. Something had happened to David. Something dreadful, perhaps, and she must go at once and find out. Still it must be something mysterious, for the man had said it was private. Of course that meant David would not want it known. David had intended that the man would come to her and tell her by herself. She must go. There was nothing else to be done. She must go at once and get rid of this awful suspense. It was a good day for the message to have come, for she had brought her lunch expecting to do some Spring cleaning. David had been expected home soon, and she liked to make a bustle of preparation as if he might come in any day, for it kept up her good cheer.

Having resolved to go she got up at once, closed the doors and windows, put on her bonnet and went out down the street toward the old corduroy road. It frightened her to think what might be at the end of her journey. Possibly David himself, hurt or dying, and he had sent for her in this way that she might break the news gently to his aunts. As she walked along she conjured various forms of trouble that might have come to him. Now and then she would try to take a cheerful view, saying to herself that David might have needed more important papers, papers which he would not like everyone to know about, and had sent by special messenger to her to get them. Then her face would brighten and her step grow more brisk. But always would come the dull thud of possibility of something more serious. Her heart beat so fast sometimes that she was forced to lessen her speed to get her breath, for though she was going through town, and must necessarily walk somewhat soberly lest she call attention to herself, she found that her nerves and imagination were fairly running ahead, and waiting impatiently for her feet to catch up at every turning place.

At last she came to the corduroy road—a long stretch of winding way overlaid with logs which made an unpleasant path. Most of the way was swampy, and bordered in some places by thick, dark woods. Marcia sped on from log to log, with a nervous feeling that she must step on each one or her errand would not be successful. She was not afraid of the loneliness, only of what might be coming at the end of her journey.

But suddenly, in the densest part of the wood, she became conscious of footsteps echoing hers, and a chill laid hold upon her. She turned her head and there, wildly gesticulating and running after her, was Miranda!

Annoyed, and impatient to be on her way, and wondering what to do with Miranda, or what she could possibly want, Marcia stopped to wait for her.

"I thought—as you was goin' 'long my way" — puffed Miranda, "I'd jes' step along beside you. You don't mind, do you?"

Marcia looked troubled. If she should say she did then Miranda would think it queer and perhaps suspect something.

She tried to smile and ask how far Miranda was going.

"Oh, I'm goin' to hunt fer wild strawberries," said the girl nonchalantly clattering a big tin pail.

"Isn't it early yet for strawberries?" questioned Marcia.

"Well, mebbe, an' then ag'in mebbe 'tain't. I know a place I'm goin' to look anyway. Are you goin' 's fur 's the Green Tavern?"

Miranda's bright eyes looked her through and through, and Marcia's truthful ones could not evade. Suddenly as she looked into the girl's homely face, filled with a kind of blind adoration, her heart yearned for counsel in this trying situation. She was reminded of Miranda's helpfulness the time she ran away to the woods, and the care with which she had guarded the whole matter so that no one ever heard of it. An impulse came to her to confide in Miranda. She was a girl of sharp common sense, and would perhaps be able to help with her advice. At least she could get comfort from merely telling her trouble and anxiety.

"Miranda," she said, "can you keep a secret?"

The girl nodded.

"Well, I'm going to tell you something, just because I am so troubled and I feel as if it would do me good to tell it." She smiled and Miranda answered the smile with much satisfaction and no surprise. Miranda had come for this, though she did not expect her way to be so easy.

"I'll be mum as an oyster," said Miranda. "You jest tell me anything you please. You needn't be afraid Hannah Heath'll know a grain about it. She'n' I are two people. I know when to shut up."

"Well, Miranda, I'm in great perplexity and anxiety. I've just had a note from a messenger my husband has sent asking me to come out to that Green Tavern you were talking about. He was sent to me with some message and has

...looked troubled.

...do, Miranda, for the note says it is a private matter and I must come alone. You know Mr. Spafford has matters to write about that are very important, railroads, and such things, and sometimes he doesn't care to have any one get hold of his ideas before they appear in the paper. His enemies might use them to stop the plans of the great improvements he is writing about."

"Let me see that note!" demanded Miranda. "Got it with you?" Marcia hesitated. Perhaps she ought not to show it, and yet there was nothing in the note but what she had already told the girl, and she felt sure she would not breathe a word to a living soul after her promise. She handed Miranda the letter, and they stopped a moment while she slowly spelled it out. Miranda was no scholar. Marcia watched her face eagerly, as if to gather a ray of hope from it, but she was puzzled by Miranda's look. A kind of satisfaction had overspread her homely countenance.

"Should you think from that that David was hurt — or ill — or — or — killed or anything?" She asked the question as if Miranda were a wizard, and hung anxiously upon her answer.

"Naw, I don't reckon so!" said Miranda. "Don't you worry. David's all right somehow. I'll take care o' you. You go 'long up and see what's the business, an' I'll wait here out o' sight o' the tavern. Likely's not he might take a notion not to tell you ef he see me come along with you. You jest go ahead, and I'll be on hand when you get through. If you need me fer anything you jest holler out 'Randy!' good and loud an' I'll hear you. Guess I'll set on this log. The tavern's jest round that bend in the road. Naw, you needn't thank me. This is a real pretty mornin' to set an' rest. Good-bye."

Marcia hurried on, glancing back happily at her protector in a calico sunbonnet seated stolidly on a log with her tin pail beside her.

Poor stupid Miranda! Of course she could not understand what a comfort it was to have confided her trouble. Marcia went up to the tavern with almost a smile on her face, though her heart began to beat wildly as a slatternly girl led her into a big room at the right of the hall.

As Marcia disappeared behind the bend in the road, Miranda stealthily stole along the edge of the woods, till she stood hidden behind a clump of alders where she could peer out and watch Marcia until she reached the tavern and passed safely by the row of lounging, smoking men, and on into the doorway. Then Miranda waited just an instant to look in all directions, and sped across the road, mounting the fence and on through two meadows, and the barnyard to the kitchen door of the tavern.

"Mornin'! Mis' Green," she said to the slovenly looking woman who sat by the table peeling potatoes. "Mind givin' me a drink o' water? I'm terrible thirsty, and seemed like I couldn't find the spring. Didn't thare used to be a spring 'tween here'n town?"

"Goodness sakes! Randy! Where'd you come from? Water! Jes' help yourself. There's the bucket jes' from the spring five minutes since, an' there's the gourd hanging up on the wall. I can't get up, I'm that busy. Twelve to dinner to-day, an' only me to do the cookin'. 'Melia she's got to be upstairs helpin' at the bar."

"Who all you got here?" questioned Miranda as she took a draught from the old gourd.

"Well, got a gentleman from New York fur one. He's real pretty. Quite a beau. His clo'es are that nice you'd think he was goin' to court. He's that particular 'bout his eatin' I feel flustered. Nothin' would do but he hed to hev a downstairs room. He said he didn't like goin' upstairs. He don't look sickly, neither."

"Mebbe he's had a accident an' lamed himself," suggested Miranda cunningly. "Heard o' any accidents? How'd he come? Coach or horseback?"

"Coach," said Mrs. Green. "Why do you ask? Got any friends in New York?"

"Not many," responded Miranda importantly, "but my cousin Hannah Heath has. You know she's ben up there fer a spell visitin' an' they say there was lots of gentlemen in love with her. There's one in particular used to come round a good deal. It might be him come round to see ef it's true Hannah's goin' to get married to Lem Skinner. Know what this fellow's name is?"

"You don't say! Well now it might be. No, I don't rightly remember his name. Seems though it was something like Church er Chapel. 'Melia could tell ye, but she's busy."

"Where's he at? Mebbe I could get a glimpse o' him. I'd jest like to know ef he was coming to bother our Hannah."

"Well, now. Mebbe you could get a sight of him. There's a cupboard between his room an' the room back. It has a door both sides. Mebbe ef you was to slip in there you might see him through the latch hole. I ain't usin' that back room fer anythin' but a store-room this Spring, so look out you don't stumble over nothin' when you go in fer it's dark as a pocket. You go right 'long in, I reckon you'll find the way. Yes, it's on the right hand side o' the hall. I've got to set here an' finish these potatoes er dinner'll be late. I'd like to know real well ef he's one o' Hannah Heath's beaux."

Miranda needed no second bidding. She slipped through the hall and store room, and in a moment stood before the door of the closet. Softly she opened

.... with a broken nose, a row of bottles, a bunch
of seed corn with the husks braided together and hung on a nail, an old coat on
another nail.

Down on her knees beside the crack of light went Miranda. First her eye
and then her ear were applied to the small aperture. She could see nothing but
a table directly in front of the door about a foot away on which were quills, paper,
and a large horn inkstand filled with ink. Some one evidently had been writing,
for a page was half done, and the pen was laid down beside a word.

The limits of the latch hole made it impossible for Miranda to make out any
more. She applied her ear and could hear a man's voice talking in low insinuat-
ing tones, but she could make little of what was said. It drove her fairly frantic
to think that she was losing time. Miranda had no mind to be balked in her
purpose. She meant to find out who was in that room and what was going on.
She felt a righteous interest in it.

Her eyes could see quite plainly now in the dark closet. There was a big
button on the door. She no sooner discovered it than she put up her hand and
tried to turn it. It was tight and made a slight squeak in turning. She stopped
but the noise seemed to have no effect upon the evenly modulated tones inside.
Cautiously she moved the button again, holding the latch firmly in her other
hand lest the door should suddenly fly open. It was an exciting moment when
at last the button was turned entirely away from the door frame and the lifted
latch swung free in Miranda's hand. The door opened outward. If it were
allowed to go it would probably strike against the table. Miranda only allowed
it to open a crack. She could hear words now, and the voice reminded her of
something unpleasant. The least little bit more she dared open the door, and
she could see, as she had expected, Marcia's bonnet and shoulder cape as she
sat at the other side of the room. This then was the room of the messenger who
had sent for Mrs. Spafford so peremptorily. The next thing was to discover the
identity of the messenger. Miranda had suspicions.

The night before she had seen a man lurking near the Spafford house when
she went out in the garden to feed the chickens. She had watched him from
behind the lilac bush, and when he had finally gone away she had followed him
some distance until he turned into the old corduroy road and was lost in the
gathering dusk. The man she had seen before, and had reason to suspect. It
was not for nothing that she had braved her grandmother and gone hunting wild
strawberries out of season.

With the caution of a creature of the forest Miranda opened the door an inch further, and applied her eye to the latch hole again. The man's head was in full range of her eye then, and her suspicion proved true.

When Marcia entered the big room and the heavy oak door closed behind her her heart seemed almost choking her, but she tried with all her might to be calm. She was to know the worst now.

On the other side of the room in a large arm-chair, with his feet extended on another and covered by a travelling shawl, reclined a man. Marcia went toward him eagerly, and then stopped:

"Mr. Temple!" There was horror, fear, reproach in the way she spoke it.

"I know you are astonished, Mrs. Spafford, that the messenger should be one so unworthy, and let me say at the beginning that I am more thankful than I can express that your letter of forgiveness reached me before I was obliged to start on my sorrowful commission. I beg you will sit down and be as comfortable as you can while I explain further. Pardon my not rising. I have met with a bad sprain caused by falling from my horse on the way, and was barely able to reach this stopping place. My ankle is swollen so badly that I cannot step upon my foot."

Marcia, with white face, moved to the chair he indicated near him, and sat down. The one thought his speech had conveyed to her had come through those words "my sorrowful commission." She felt the need of sitting down, for her limbs would no longer bear her up, and she felt she must immediately know what was the matter.

"Mrs. Spafford, may I ask you once more to speak your forgiveness? Before I begin to tell you what I have come for, I long to hear you say the words 'I forgive you.' Will you give me your hand and say them?"

"Mr. Temple, I beg you will tell me what is the matter. Do not think any further about that other matter. I meant what I said in the note. Tell me quick! Is my husband—has anything happened to Mr. Spafford? Is he ill? Is he hurt?"

"My poor child! How can I bear to tell you? It seems terrible to put your love and trust upon another human being and then suddenly find—But wait. Let me tell the story in my own way. No, your husband is not hurt, physically. Illness, and death even, are not the worst things that can happen to a mortal soul. It seems to me cruel, as I see you sit there so young and tender and beautiful, that I should have to hurt you by what I have to say. I come from the purest of motives to tell you a sad truth about one who should be nearest and dearest to you of all the earth. I beg you will look upon me kindly and believe that it hurts me to have to tell you these things. Before I begin I pray you will tell me that you forgive me for all I have to say. Put you hand in mine and say so."

Marcia had listened to this torrent of words unable to stop them, a choking sensation in her throat, fear gripping her heart. Some terrible thing had he continued ... she stumbled toward him and laid her hand in his. He grasped it and thanked her profusely. He looked at the little cold hand in his own, and his lying tongue went on:

"Mrs. Spafford, you are good and true. You have saved me from a life of uselessness, and your example and high noble character have given me new inspiration. It seems a poor gratitude that would turn and stab you to the heart. Ah! I cannot do it, and yet I must."

This was torture indeed! Marcia drew her hand sharply away and held it to her heart. She felt her brain reeling with the strain. Harry Temple saw he must go on at once or he would lose what he had gained. He had meant to keep that little hand and touch it gently with a comforting pressure as his story went on, but it would not do to frighten her or she might take sudden alarm.

"Sit down," he begged, reaching out and drawing a chair near to his own, but she stepped back and dropped into the one which she had first taken.

"You know your husband has been in New York?" he began. She nodded. She could not speak.

"Did you never suspect why he is there and why he stays so long?" A cold vise gripped Marcia's heart, but though she turned white she said nothing, only looked steadily into the false eyes that glowed and burned at her like two hateful coals of fire that would scorch her soul and David's to a horrid death.

"Poor child, you cannot answer. You have trusted perfectly. You thought he was there on business connected with his writing, but did it never occur to you what a very long time he has been away and that — that there might be some other reason also which he has not told? But you must know it now, my child. I am sorry to say it, but he has been keeping it from you, and those who love you think you ought to know. Let me explain. Very soon after he reached New York he met a lady whom he used to know and admire. She is a very beautiful woman, and though she is married is still much sought after. Your husband, like the rest of her admirers, soon lost his heart completely, and his head. Strange that he could so easily forget the pearl of women he had left behind! He went to see her. He showed his affection for her in every possible way. He gave her large sums of money. In fact, to make a long story short, he is lingering in New York just to be near her. I hesitate to speak the whole truth, but he has surely done that which you cannot forgive. You with your lofty ideas — Mrs. Spafford — he has cut himself off from any right to your respect or love.

"And now I am here to-day to offer to do all in my power to help you. From what I know of your husband's movements, he is likely to return to you soon. You cannot meet him knowing that the lips that will salute you have been pressed upon the lips of another woman, and that woman *your own sister,* dear Mrs. Spafford!

"Ah! Now you understand, poor child. Your lips quiver! You have reason to understand. I know, I know you cannot think what to do. Let me think for you." His eyes were glowing and his face animated. He was using all his persuasive power, and her gaze was fixed upon him as though he had mesmerized her. She could not resist the flood-tide of his eloquence. She could only look on and seem to be gradually turning to stone—frozen with horror.

He felt he had almost won, and with demoniacal skill he phrased his sentences.

"I am here for that purpose. I am here to help you and for no other reason. In the stable are horses harnessed and a comfortable carriage. My advice to you is to fly from here as fast as these fleet horses can carry you. Where you go is for you to say. I should advise going to your father's house. That I am sure is what will please him best. He is your natural refuge at such a time as this. If, however, you shrink from appearing before the eyes of the village gossips in your native town, I will take you to the home of a dear old friend of mine, hidden among the quiet hills, where you will be cared for most royally and tenderly for my sake, and where you can work out your life problem in the way that seems best to you. It is there that I am planning to take you to-night. We can easily reach there before evening if we start at once."

Marcia started to her feet in horror.

"What do you mean?" she stammered in a choking voice. "I could never go anywhere with you Mr. Temple. You are a bad man! You have been telling me lies! I do not believe one word of what you have said. My husband is noble and good. If he did any of those things you say he did he had a reason for it. I shall never distrust him."

Marcia's head was up grandly now and her voice had come back. She looked the man in the eye until he quailed, but still he sought to hold his power over her.

"You poor child!" and his voice was gentleness and forbearance itself. "I do not wonder in your first horror and surprise that you feel as you do. I anticipated this. Sit down and calm yourself and let me tell you more about it. I can prove everything that I have said. I have letters here—" and he swept his hand toward a pile of letters lying on the table; Miranda in the closet marked well the position of those letters. "All that I have said is only too true, I am sorry to say, and you must listen to me—"

Marcia interrupted him, her eyes blazing, her face excited. "Mr. Temple, I shall not listen to another word you say. You are a wicked man and I was wrong shall not leave this room except in my company. Do you not know that you are in my power? You have spent nearly an hour alone in my bedchamber, and what will your precious husband have to do with you after this is known?"

Chapter 24

Miranda's time had come. She had seen it coming and was prepared.

With a movement like a flash she pushed open the closet door, seized the pot of ink from the table, and before the two excited occupants of the room had time to even hear her or realize that she was near, she hurled the ink pot full into the insolent face of Harry Temple. The inkstand itself was a light affair of horn and inflicted only a slight wound, but the ink came into his eyes in a deluge blinding him completely, as Miranda had meant it should do. She had seen no other weapon of defense at hand.

Harry Temple dropped Marcia's wrists and groaned in pain, staggering back against the wall and sinking to the floor. But Miranda would not stay to see the effect of her punishment. She seized the frightened Marcia, dragged her toward the cupboard door, sweeping as she passed the pile of letters, finished and unfinished, into her apron, and closed the cupboard doors carefully behind her. Then she guided Marcia through the dark mazes of the store room to the hall, and pushing her toward the front door, whispered: "Go quick 'fore he gets his eyes open. I've got to go this way. Run down the road fast as you can an' I'll be at the meetin' place first. Hurry, quick!"

Marcia went with feet that shook so that every step seemed like to slip, but with beating heart she finally traversed the length of the piazza with a show of dignity, passed the loungers, and was out in the road. Then indeed she took courage and fairly flew.

Miranda, breathless, but triumphant, went back into the kitchen: "I guess 'tain't him after all," she said to the interested woman who was putting on the potatoes to boil. "He's real interested to look at though. I'd like to stop and watch him longer but I must be goin'. I come out to hunt fer"—Miranda hesitated for a suitable object before this country-bred woman who well knew that strawberries were not ripe yet—"wintergreens fer Grandma," she added cheerfully, not quite sure whether they grew around these parts, "and I must be in a hurry. Good-bye! Thank you fer the drink."

Miranda whizzed out of the door breezily, calling a good morning to one of the hostlers as she passed the barnyard, and was off through the meadows and over the fence like a bird, the package of letters rustling loud in her bosom where she had tucked them before she entered the kitchen.

Neither of the two girls spoke for some minutes after they met, but continued their rapid gait, until the end of the corduroy road was in sight and they felt comparatively safe.

...gently as a mother might have done, and smoothed her hair back from the hot cheek, speaking tenderly:

"There now, you poor pretty little flower. Jest you cry 's hard 's you war to. I know how good it makes you feel to cry. I've done it many a time up garret where nobody couldn't hear me. That old Satan, he won't trouble you fer a good long spell again. When he gets his evil eyes open, if he ever does, he'll be glad to get out o' these parts or I miss my guess. Now don't you worry no more. He can't hurt you one mite. An' don't think a thing about what he said. He's a great big liar, that's what he is."

"Miranda, you saved me. Yes, you did. I never can thank you enough. If you hadn't come and helped me something awful might have happened!" Marcia shuddered and began to sob convulsively again.

"Nonsense!" said Miranda, pleased. "I didn't do a thing wortl. mentioning. Now you jest wipe your eyes and chirk up. We've got to go through town an' you don't want folks to wonder what's up."

Miranda led Marcia up to the spring whose location had been known to her all the time of course, and Marcia bathed her eyes and was soon looking more like herself, though there was a nervous tremor to her lips now and then. But her companion talked gaily, and tried to keep her mind from going over the events of the morning.

When they reached the village Miranda suggested they go home by the back street, slipping through a field of spring wheat and climbing the garden fence. She had a mind to keep out of her grandmother's sight for a while longer.

"I might's well be hung for a sheep 's a lamb," she remarked as she slid in at Marcia's kitchen door in the shadow of the morning-glory vines. "I'm goin' to stay here a spell an' get you some dinner while you go upstairs an' lie down. You don't need to go back to your aunt's till near night, an' you can wait till dusk an' I'll go with you. Then you needn't be out alone at all. I know how you feel, but I don't believe you need worry. He'll be done with you now forever, er I'll miss my guess. Now you go lie down till I make a cup o' tea."

Marcia was glad to be alone, and soon fell asleep, worn out with the excitement, her brain too weary to go over the awful occurrences of the morning. That would come later. Now her body demanded rest.

Miranda, coming upstairs with the tea, tiptoed in and looked at her, — one round arm thrown over her head, and her smooth peachy cheek resting against it. Miranda, homely, and with no hope of ever attaining any of the beautiful things of life, loved unselfishly this girl who had what she had not, and longed with all her heart to comfort and protect the sweet young thing who seemed so ill-prepared to protect herself. She stooped over the sleeper for one yearning moment, and touched her hair lightly with her lips. She felt a great desire to kiss the soft round cheek, but was afraid of wakening her. Then she took the cup of tea and tiptoed out again, her eyes shining with satisfaction. She had a self-imposed task before her, and was well pleased that Marcia slept, for it gave her plenty of opportunity to carry out her plans.

She went quickly to David's library, opened drawers and doors in the desk until she found writing materials, and sat down to work. She had a letter to write, and a letter, to Miranda, was the achievement of a lifetime. She did not much expect to ever have to write another. She plunged into her subject at once.

Dear Mr. David: (she was afraid that sounded a little stiff, but she felt it was almost too familiar to say "David" as he was always called.)

I ain't much on letters, but this one has got to be writ. Something happened and somebody's got to tell you about it. I'm most sure she wont, and nobody else knows cept me.

Last night 'bout dark I went out to feed the chickens, an' I see that nimshi Harry Temple skulkin round your house. It was all dark there, an he walked in the side gate and tried to peek in the winders, only the shades was down an he couldn't see a thing. I thought he was up to some mischief so I followed him down the old corduroy road. It was dark by then an I come home, but I was on the watchout this morning, and after Mis' Spafford come down to the house I heard a horse gallopin by an I looked out an saw a boy get off an take a letter to the door an ride away, an pretty soon all in a hurry your wife come out tyin her bonnet and hurrin along lookin scared. I grabbed my sunbonnet an clipped after her, but she went so fast I didn't get up to her till she got on the old corduroy road. She was awful scared lookin an she didn't want me much I see, but pretty soon she up an told me she had a note sayin there was a messenger with news from you out to the old Green Tavern. He had an accident an couldn't come no further. He wanted her to come alone cause the business was private, so I stayed down by the turn of the road till she got in an then I went cross lots an round to the kitchen an called on Mis' Green a spell. She was tellin me about her boarders an I told her I thought mebbe one of em was a friend o' Hannah Heath's so she said I might peek through the key hole of the cubberd an see. She was busy so I went alone.

Well sir, I jest wish you'd been there. That lying nimshi was jest goin' on the sweetest, as respectful an nice a thankin your wife fer comin, an excusin himself fer sendin fer her, and sayin he couldn't bear to tell her what he'd come fer, an pretty soon when she was scared 's death he up an told her a awful fib bout you an a woman called Kate, whoever she is, an he jest poured the words out fast so she couldn't speak, an he said things about you he shouldn't uv, an you could see he was makin it up as he went along, an he said he had proof. So he pointed at a pile y ... ... wouldn't go a step with him anywhere.

An then he forgets all about the lame ankle he had kept covered up on a chair pertendin it was hurt fallin off his horse when the coach brought him all the way fer I asked Mis' Green — and he ketches her by the wrists, and he says she can't go without him, and she needn't be in such a hurry fer you wouldn't have no more to do with her anyway after her being shut up there with him so long, an then she looked jest like she was going to faint, an I bust out through the door an ketched up the ink pot, it want heavy enough to kill him, an I slung it at him, an the ink went square in his eyes, an we slipped through the closet an got away quick fore anybody knew a thing.

I brought all the letters along so here they be. I havn't read a one, cause I thought mebbe you'd ruther not. She aint seen em neither. She dont know I've got em. I hid em in my dress. She's all wore out with cryin and hurryin, and being scared, so she's upstairs now asleep, an she dont know I'm writing. I'm goin to send this off fore she knows, fer I think she wouldn't tell you fear of worryin you. I'll look after her es well's I can till you get back, but I think that feller ought to be strung up. But you'll know what to do, so no more at present from your obedient servent,

Miranda Griscom.

Having at last succeeded on sealing her packet to her satisfaction and the diminishing of the stick of sealing wax she had found in the drawer, Miranda slid out the front door, and by a detour went to David Spafford's office.

"Good afternoon, Mr. Clark," she said to the clerk importantly. "Grandma sends her respects and wants to know if you'd be so kind as to back this letter fer her to Mr. David Spafford. She's writin' to him on business an' she don't rightly know his street an' number in New York."

Mr. Clark willingly wrote the address, and Miranda took it to the post office, and sped back to Marcia, happy in the accomplishment of her purpose.

In the same mail bag that brought Miranda's package came a letter from Aunt Clarinda. David's face lit up with a pleased smile. Her letters were so infrequent that they were a rare pleasure. He put aside the thick package written in this clerk's hand. It was doubtless some business papers and could wait.

Aunt Clarinda wrote in a fine old script that in spite of her eighty years was clear and legible. She told about the beauty of the weather, and how Amelia and Hortense were almost done with the house cleaning, and how Marcia had been going to their house every day putting it in order. Then she added a paragraph which David, knowing the old lady well, understood to be the *raison d'etre* of the whole letter:

I think your wife misses you very much, Davie, she looks sort of peaked and sad. It is hard on her being separated from you so long this first year. Men don't think of those things, but it is lonely for a young thing like her here with three old women, and you know Hortense and Amelia never try to make it lively for anybody. I have been watching her, and I think if I were you I would let the business finish itself up as soon as possible and hurry back to put a bit of cheer into that child. She's whiter than she ought to be.

David read it over three times in astonishment with growing, mingled feelings which he could not quite analyze.

Poor Aunt Clarinda! Of course she did not understand the situation, and equally of course she was mistaken. Marcia was not sighing for him, though it might be dull for her at the old house. He ought to have thought of that; and a great burden suddenly settled down upon him. He was not doing right by Marcia. It could not be himself of course that Marcia was missing, if indeed Aunt Clarinda was right and she was worried about anything. Perhaps something has occurred to trouble her. Could that snake of a Temple have turned up again? No, he felt reasonably sure he would have heard of that, besides he saw him not long ago on the street at a distance. Could it be some boy-lover at home whose memory came to trouble her? Or had she discovered what a sacrifice she had made of her young life? Whatever it was, it was careless and cruel of him to have left her alone with his aunts all this time. He was a selfish man, he told himself, to have accepted her quiet little sacrifice of all for him. He read the letter over again, and suddenly there came to him a wish that Marcia *was* missing him. It seemed a pleasant thought to have her care. He had been trying to train himself to the fact that no one would ever care for him again, but now it seemed dear and desirable that his sweet young companion should like to have him back. He had vision of home as it had been, so pleasant and restful, always the food that he liked, always the thought for his wishes, and he felt condemned. He had not noticed or cared. Had she thought him ungrateful?

He read the letter over again, noting every mention of his wife in the account of the daily living at home. He was searching for some clue that would give him more information about her. And when he reached the last paragraph about missing him, a little tingle of pleasure shot through him at the thought. He did not understand it. After all she was his, and if it was possible he must help to make up to her for what she had lost in giving herself to him. If the thought of

...went to work at an article, to absorb his mind. He had several times arisen in the night to write because he could not sleep, and must think.

When he was obliged to be in New York he had steadily kept away from the house where Kate lived, and never walked through the streets without occupying his mind as fully as possible so that he should not chance to see her. In this way his sorrow was growing old without having been worn out, and he was really regaining a large amount of the former happiness and interest in life. Not so often now did the vision of Kate come to trouble him. He thought she was still his one ideal of womanly beauty and grace and perfection of course, and always would be, but she was not for him to think upon any more. A strong true man he was growing, out of his sorrow. And now when the thought of Marcia came to him with a certain sweetness he could be glad that it was so, and not resent it. Of course no one could ever take the place of Kate, that was impossible.

So reflecting, with a pleasant smile upon his face, he opened Miranda's epistle.

Puzzled and surprised he began to read the strange chirography, and as he read his face darkened and he drew his brows in a heavy frown. "The scoundrel!" he muttered as he turned the sheet. Then as he went on his look grew anxious. He scanned the page quickly as if he would gather the meaning from the crooked ill-spelled words without taking them one by one. But he had to go slowly, for Miranda had not written with as much plainness as haste. He fairly held his breath when he thought of the gentle girl in the hands of the unscrupulous man of the world. A terrible fear gripped his heart. Marcia, little Marcia, so sweet and pure and good. A vision of her face as she lay asleep in the woods came between him and the paper. Why had he left her unprotected all these months? Fool that he was! She was worth more than all the railroads put together. As if his own life was in the balance, he read on, growing sick with horror. Poor child! What had she thought? And how had his own sin and weakness been found out, or was it merely Harry Temple's wicked heart that had evolved these stories? The letter smote him with terrible accusation, and all at once it was fearful to him to think that Marcia had heard such things about him. When he came to her trust in him he groaned aloud and buried his face in the letter, and then raised it quickly to read to the end.

When he had finished he rose with sudden determination to pack his carpet-bag and go home at once. Marcia needed him, and he felt a strong desire to be near her, to see her and know she was safe. It was overwhelming. He had not known he could ever feel strongly again. He must confess his own weakness of course, and he would. She should know all and know that she might trust him after all.

But the motion of rising had sent the other papers to the floor, and in falling the bundle of letters that Miranda had enclosed, scattered about him. He stooped to pick them up and saw his own name written in Kate's handwriting. Old association held him, and wondering, fearful, not wholly glad to see it, he picked up the letter. It was an epistle of Kate's, written in intimate style to Harry Temple and speaking of himself in terms of the utmost contempt. She even stooped to detail to Harry an account of her own triumph on that miserable morning when he had taken her in his arms and kissed her. There were expressions in the letter that showed her own wicked heart, as nothing else could ever have done, to David. As he read, his soul growing sick within him,—read one letter after another, and saw how she had plotted with this bad man to wreck the life of her young sister for her own triumph and revenge,—the beautiful woman whom he had loved, and whom he had thought beautiful within as well as without, crumbled into dust before him. When he looked up at last with white face and firmly set lips, he found that his soul was free forever from the fetters that had bound him to her.

He went to the fireplace and laid the pile of letters among the embers, blowing them into a blaze, and watched them until they were eaten up by the fire and nothing remained but dead grey ashes. The thought came to him that that was like his old love. It was burnt out. There had not been the right kind of fuel to feed it. Kate was worthless, but his own self was alive, and please God he would yet see better days. He would go home at once to the child wife who needed him, and whom now he might love as she should be loved. The thought became wondrously sweet to him as he rapidly threw the things into his travelling bag and went about arrangements for his trip home. He determined that if he ever came to New York again Marcia should come with him.

Once there she could do nothing but go over and over the dreadful things that Harry Temple had said. In vain did she try to work. She went into the library and took up a book, but her mind would wander to David. She sat down at the piano and played a few tender chords and sang an Old Italian song which somebody had left at their house several years before:

> Dearest, believe,
> When e'er we part:
> Lonely I grieve,
> In my sad heart:—

With a sob her head dropped upon her hands in one sad little crash of wailing tones, while the sound died away in reverberation after reverberation of the strings till Marcia felt as if a sea of sound were about her in soft ebbing, flowing waves.

The sound covered the lifting of the side door latch and quiet step of a foot. Marcia was absorbed in her own thoughts. Her smothered sobs were mingling with the dying sounds of the music, still audible to her fine ear.

David had come by instinct to his own home first. He felt that Marcia would be there, and now that he was come and the morning sun flooded everything and made home look so good he felt that he must find her first of all before his relationship with home had been re-established. He passed through kitchen, dining room and hall, and by the closed parlor door. He never thought of her being in there with the door closed. He glanced into the library and saw the book lying in his chair as she had left it, and it gave a touch of her presence which pleased him. He went softly toward the stairs thinking to find her. He had stopped at a shop the last thing and bought a beautiful creamy shawl of China crepe heavily embroidered, and finished with long silken fringe. He had taken it from his carpet-bag and was carrying it in its rice paper wrapping lest it should be crushed. He was pleased as a child at the present he had brought her, and felt strangely shy about giving it to her.

Just then there came a sound from the parlor, sweet and tender and plaintive. Marcia had conquered her sobs and was singing again with her whole soul, singing as she were singing to David. The words drew him strangely, wonderingly toward the parlor door, yet so softly that he heard every syllable.

> Dearest, believe,
> When e'er we part
> Lonely I grieve
> In my sad heart:
> Thy faithful slave,
> Languishing sighs,
> Haste then and save —

Here the words trailed away again into a half sob, and the melody continued in broken, halting chords that flickered out and faded into the shadows of the room.

David's heart was pierced with a belief that Aunt Clarinda was right and something was the matter with Marcia. A great trouble and tenderness, and almost jealousy, leaped up in his heart which were incomprehensible to him. Who was Marcia singing this song for? That it was a true cry from a lonely soul he could but believe. Was she feeling her prison-bars here in the lonely old house with only a forlorn man whose life and love had been thrown away upon another? Poor child! Poor child! If he might but save her from suffering, cover her with his own tenderness and make her content with that. Would it be possible if he devoted himself to it to make her forget the one for whom she was sighing; to bring peace and a certain sort of sweet forgetfulness and interest in other things into her life? He wanted to make a new life for her, his little girl whom he had so unthinkingly torn from the home nest and her future, and compelled to take up his barren way with him. He would make it up to her if such a thing were possible. Then he opened the door.

In the soft green light of the noonday coming through the shades Marcia's color did not show as it flew into her cheeks. Her hands grew weak and dropped upon the keys with a soft little tinkle of surprise and joy. She sprang up and came a step toward him, then clasped her hands against her breast and stopped shyly. David coming into the room, questioning, wondering, anxious, stopped midway too, and for an instant they looked upon one another. David saw a new look in the girl's face. She seemed older, much older than when he had left her. The sweet round cheeks were thinner, her mouth drooped sadly, pathetically. For an instant he longed to take her in his arms and kiss her. The longing startled him. So many months he had thought of only Kate in that way, and then had tried to teach himself never to think of Kate or any woman as one to be caressed by him, that it shocked him. He felt that he had been disloyal to himself, to honor, — to Kate — no — not to Kate, he had no call to be loyal to her. She had not been loyal to him ever. Perhaps rather he would have put it loyalty to Love for Love's sake, love that is worthy to be crowned by a woman's love.

.... as to what it could mean. Their hands clung together longer than either had meant, and there was something pleasant to each in the fact that they were together again. David thought it was just because it was home, rest, and peace, and a relief from his anxiety about Marcia now that he saw she was all right. Marcia knew it was better to have David standing there with his strong fingers about her trembling ones, than to have anything else in the world. But she would not have told him so.

"That was a sweet song you were singing," said David. "I hope you were singing it for me, and that it was true! I am glad I am come home, and you must sing it again for me soon."

It was not in the least what he intended to say, and the words tumbled themselves out so tumultuously that he was almost ashamed and wondered if Marcia would think he had lost his mind in New York. Marcia, dear child, treasured them every word and hugged them to heart, and carried them in her prayers.

They went out together and got dinner as if they had been two children, with a wild excited kind of glee; and they tried to get back their natural ways of doing and saying things, but they could not.

Instead they were forever blundering and halting in what they said; coming face to face and almost running over one another as they tried to help each other; laughing and blushing and blundering again.

When they each tried to reach for the tea kettle to fill the coffee pot and their fingers touched, each drew back and pretended not to notice, but yet had felt the contact sweet.

They were lingering over the dinner when Hannah Heath came to the door. David had been telling of some of his adventures in detail and was enjoying the play of expression on Marcia's face as she listened eagerly to every word. They had pushed their chairs back a little and were sitting there talking, — or rather David was talking, Marcia listening. Hannah stood for one jealous instant and saw it all. This was what she had dreamed for her own long years back, she and David. She had questioned much just what feeling there might be between him and Marcia, and now more than ever she desired to bring him face to face with Kate and read for herself what the truth had been. She hated Marcia for that look of intense delight and sympathy upon her face; hated her that she had the right to sit there and hear what David had to say—some stupid stuff about railroads. She did not see that she herself would have made an ill companion for a man like David.

As yet neither Marcia nor David had touched upon the subjects which had troubled them. They did not realize it, but were so suddenly happy in each other's company they had forgotten for the moment. The pleasant converse was broken up at once. Marcia's face hardened into something like alarm as saw who stood in the doorway.

"Why, David, have you got home at last?" said Hannah. "I did not know it." That was an untruth. She had watched him from behind Grandmother Heath's rose bush. "Where did you come from last? New York? Oh, then you saw Mrs. Leavenworth. How is she? I fell in love with her when I was there."

Now David had never fully taken in Kate's married name. He knew it of course, but in his present state of happiness at getting home, and his absorption in the work he had been doing, the name "Mrs. Leavenworth" conveyed nothing whatever to David's mind. He looked blankly at Hannah and replied indifferently enough with a cool air. "No, Miss Hannah, I had no time for social life. I was busy every minute I was away."

David never expected Hannah to say anything worth listening to, and he was so full of his subject that he had not noticed that she made no reply.

Hannah watched him curiously as he talked, his remarks after all were directed more to Marcia than to her, and when he paused she said with a contemptuous sneer in her voice, "I never could understand, David, how you who seem to have so much sense in other things will take up with such fanciful, impractical dreams as this railroad. Lemuel says it'll never run."

Hannah quoted her lover with a proud bridling of her head as if the matter were settled once and for all. It was the first time she allowed the world to see that she acknowledged her relation to Lemuel. She was not averse to having David understand that she felt there were other men in the world besides himself. But David turned merry eyes on her.

"Lemuel says?" he repeated, and he made a sudden movement with his arm which sent a knife and spoon from the table in a clatter upon the floor. "And how much does Lemuel know about the matter?"

"Lemuel has good practical common sense," said Hannah, vexed, "and he knows what is possible and what is not. He does not need to travel all over the country on a wild goose chase to learn that."

Now that she had accepted him Hannah did not intend to allow Lemuel to be discounted.

"He has not long to wait to be convinced," said David thoughtfully and unaware of her tart tone. "Before the year is out it will be a settled fact that every one can see."

"Well, it's beyond comprehension that you care, anyway," said Hannah contemptuously. "Did you really spend all your time in New York on such things? It seems incredible. There certainly must have been other attractions?"

"It is strange you did not stay with Mrs. Leavenworth," she said. "She told me you were one of her dearest friends, and you used to be quite fond of one another."

Then it suddenly dawned upon David who Mrs. Leavenworth was, and a sternness overspread his face.

"Mrs. Leavenworth, did you say? Ah! I did not understand. I saw her but once and that for only a few minutes soon after I first arrived. I did not see her again." His voice was cool and steady. Marcia coming from the pantry with set face, ready for defence if there was any she could give, marvelled at his coolness. Her heart was gripped with fear, and yet leaping with joy at David's words. He had not seen Kate but once. He had known she was there and yet had kept away. Hannah's insinuations were false. Mr. Temple's words were untrue. She had known it all the time, yet what sorrow they had given her!

"By the way, Marcia," said David, turning toward her with a smile that seemed to erase the sternness in his voice but a moment before. "Did you not write me some news? Miss Hannah, you are to be congratulated I believe. Lemuel is a good man. I wish you much happiness."

And thus did David, with a pleasant speech, turn aside Hannah Heath's dart. Yet while she went from the house with a smile and a sound of pleasant wishes in her ears, she carried with her a bitter heart and a revengeful one.

David was suddenly brought face to face with the thing he had to tell Marcia. He sat watching her as she went back and forth from pantry to kitchen, and at last he came and stood beside her and took her hands in his looking down earnestly into her face. It seemed terrible to him to tell this thing to the innocent girl, no, just when he was growing anxious to win her confidence, but it must be told, and better now than later lest he might be tempted not to tell it at all.

"Marcia!" He said the name tenderly, with an inflection he had never used before. It was not lover-like, nor passionate, but it reached her heart and drew her eyes to his and the color to cheeks. She thought how different his clasp was from Harry Temple's hateful touch. She looked up at him trustingly, and waited.

"You heard what I said to Hannah Heath just now, about—your—" He paused, dissatisfied—"about Mrs. Leavenworth"—it was as if he would set the subject of his words far from them. Marcia's heart beat wildly, remembering all that she had been told, yet she looked bravely, trustingly into his eyes.

"It was true what I told her. I met Mrs. Leavenworth but once while I was away. It was in her own home and she sent for me saying she was in trouble.

She told me that she was in terrible anxiety lest I would not forgive her. She begged me to say that I forgave her, and when I told her I did she asked me to kiss her once to prove it. I was utterly overcome and did so, but the moment my lips touched hers I knew that I was doing wrong and I put her from me. She begged me to remain, and I now know that she was utterly false from the first. It was but a part she was playing when she touched my heart until I yielded and sinned. I have only learned that recently, within a few days, and from words written by her own hand to another. I will tell you about it all sometime. But I want to confess to you this wrong I have done, and to let you know that I went away from her that day and have never seen her since. She had said she was without money, and I left her all I had with me. I feel that all this was a sin against you. I would like you to forgive me if you can, I want you to know that this other woman who was the cause of our coming together, is no longer anything to me. Even if she and I were both free as we were when we first met, we could never be anything but strangers. Can you forgive me now, Marcia, and can you ever trust me after what I told you?"

Marcia looked into his eyes, and loved him but the more for his confession. She felt she could forgive him anything, and her whole soul in her countenance answered with her voice, as she said: "I can." It made David think of their wedding day, and suddenly it came over him with a thrill that this sweet womanly woman belonged to him. He marvelled at her sweet forgiveness. The joy of it surprised him beyond measure.

"You have had some sad experiences yourself. Will you tell me now all about it?" He asked the question wistfully still holding her hands in a firm close grasp, and she let them lie nestling these feeling safe as birds in the nest.

"Why, how did you know?" questioned Marcia, her whole face flooded with rosy light for joy at his kind ways and relief that she did not have to open the story.

"Oh, a little bird, or a guardian angel whispered the tale," he said pleasantly. "Come into the room where we can be sure no Hannah Heaths will trouble us," and he drew her into the library and seated her beside him on the sofa.

"But, indeed, Marcia," and his face sobered, "it is no light matter to me, what has happened to you. I have been in an agony all the way home lest I might not find you safe and well after having escaped so terrible a danger."

He drew the whole story from her bit by bit, tenderly questioning her, his face blazing with righteous wrath, and darkening with his wider knowledge as she told on to the end, and showed him plainly the black heart of the villain who had dared so diabolical a conspiracy; and the inhumanity of the woman who had helped in the intrigue against her own sister, — nay even instigated it. His feeling were too deep for utterance. He was shaken to the depths. His new comprehension of Kate's character was confirmed at the worst. Marcia could only guess his deep feelings from his shaken countenance and the earnest way

...........rered."

But the old clock striking in the hall suddenly reminded David that he should go at once to the office, so he hurried away and Marcia set about her work with energy, a happy song of praise in her heart.

There was much to be done. David had said he would scarcely have time to go over to his aunts that night, so she had decided to invite them to tea. She would far rather have had David to herself this first evening, but it would please them to come, especially Aunt Clarinda. There was not much time to prepare supper to be sure, but she would stir up a gingerbread, make some puffy cream biscuits, and there was lovely white honey and fresh eggs and peach preserves.

So she ran to Deacon Appleby's to get some cream for her biscuits, and to ask Tommy Appleby to harness David's horse and drive over for Aunt Clarinda. Then she hurried down to the aunts to give her invitation.

Aunt Clarinda sat down in her calico-covered rocking chair, wiped her dear old eyes and her glasses, and said, over and over again: "Dear child! Bless her! Bless her!"

It was a happy gathering that evening. David was as pleased as they could have desired, and looked about upon the group in the dining-room with genuine boyish pleasure. It did his heart good to see Aunt Clarinda there. It had never occurred to him before that she could come. He turned to Marcia with a light in his eyes that fully repaid her for the little trouble she had had in carrying out her plan. He began to feel that home meant something even though he had lost the home of his long dreams and ideals.

He talked a great deal about his trip, and in between the sentences, he caught himself watching Marcia, noting the curve of her round chin, the dimple on her left cheek when she smiled, the way her hair waved off from her forehead, the pink curves of her well-shaped ears. He found a distinct pleasure in noting these things and he wondered at himself. It was as if he had suddenly been placed before some great painting and become possessed of the knowledge wherewith to appreciate art to its fullest. It was as if he had heard a marvellous piece of music and had the eyes and ears of his understanding opened to take in the gracious melodies and majestic harmonies.

Aunt Clarinda watched his eyes, and Aunt Clarinda was satisfied. Aunt Hortense watched his eyes, jealously and sighed. Aunt Amelia watched his eyes and set her lips and feared to herself. "He will spoil her if he does like that. She will think she can walk right over him." But Aunt Clarinda knew better. She recognized the eternal right of love.

They took the three old ladies home in the rising of an early moon, Marcia walking demurely on the sidewalk with Aunt Amelia, while David drove the chaise with Aunt Clarinda and Aunt Hortense.

As he gently lifted Aunt Clarinda down and helped her to her room David felt her old hands tremble and press his arm, and when he had reached her door he stooped and kissed her.

"Davie," she said in the voice that used to comfort his little childish troubles, or tell him of some nice surprise she had for him, "Davie, she's a dear child! She's just as good as gold. She's the princess I used to put in all your fairy-tales. David, she's just the right one for you!" and David answered earnestly, solemnly, as if he were discovering a truth which surprised him but yet was not unwelcome. "I believe she is, Aunt Clarinda."

They drove to the barn and Marcia sat in the chaise in the sweet hay-scented darkness while David put up the horse by the cobwebby light of the lantern; then they walked quietly back to the house. David had drawn Marcia's hand through his arm and it rested softly on his coat sleeve. She was silently happy, she knew not why, afraid to think of it lest to-morrow would show her there was nothing out of the ordinary monotony to be happy about.

David was silent, wondering at himself. What was this that had come to him? A new pleasure in life. A little trembling rill of joy bubbling up in his heart; a rift in the dark clouds of fate; a show of sunshine where he had expected never to see the light again. Why was it so pleasant to have that little hand resting upon his arm? Was it really pleasant or was it only a part of the restfulness of getting home again away from strange faces and uncomfortable beds, and poor tables?

They let themselves into the house as if they were walking into a new world together and both were glad to be there again. When she got up to her room Marcia went and stood before the glass and looked at herself by the flickering flame of the candle. Her eyes were bright and her cheeks burned red in the centre like two soft deep roses. She felt she hardly knew herself. She tried to be critical. Was this person she was examining a pretty person? Would she be called so in comparison with Kate and Hannah Heath? Would a man,—would David,—if his heart were not filled,—think so? She decided not. She felt she was too immature. There was too much shyness in her glance, too much babyishness about her mouth. No, David could never have thought her beautiful, even if he had seen her before he knew Kate. But perhaps, if Kate had been married first and away and then he had come to their home, perhaps if he knew no one else well enough to love,—could he have cared for her?

Oh, it was a dreadful, beautiful thought. It thrilled through and through her till she hid her face from her own gaze. She suddenly kissed the hand that

...ppiness had died, but ...g with pleasure over the look in a girl's soft eyes, and the touch of her hand. And that girl was his wife. It was enough to keep him awake to try to understand himself.

Chapter 26

Hannah Heath's wedding day dawned bright enough for a less calculating bride.

David did not get home until half past three. He had been obliged to drive out to the starting place of the new railroad, near Albany, where it was important that he get a few points correctly. On the morrow was to be the initial trip, by the Mohawk and Hudson Railroad, of the first train drawn by a steam engine in the state of New York.

His article about it, bargained for by a New York paper, must be on its way by special post as soon after the starting of the train as possible. He must have all items accurate; technicalities of preparation; description of engine and coaches; details of arrangements, etc.; before he added the final paragraphs describing the actual start of the train. His article was practically done now, save for these few items. He had started early that morning on his long drive, and, being detained longer than he had expected, arrived at home with barely time to put himself into wedding garments, and hasten in at the last moment with Marcia who stood quietly waiting for him in the front hall. They were the last guests to arrive. It was time for the ceremony, but the bride, true to her nature to the last, still kept Lemuel waiting; and Lemuel, true to the end, stood smiling and patient awaiting her pleasure.

David and Marcia entered the wide parlor and shook hands here and there with those assembled, though for the most part a hushed air pervaded the room, as it always does when something is about to happen.

Soon after their arrival some one in purple silk came down the stairs and seated herself in a vacant chair close to where the bride was to stand. She had gold hair and eyes like forget-me-nots. She was directly opposite to David and Marcia. David was engrossed in a whispered conversation with Mr. Brentwood about the events of the morrow, and did not notice her entrance, though she paused in the doorway and searched him directly from amongst the company before she took her seat. Marcia, who was talking with Rose Brentwood, caught the vision of purple and gold and turned to face for one brief instant the scornful, half-merry glance of her sister. The blood in her face fled back to her heart and left it white.

Then Marcia summoned all her courage and braced herself to face what was to come. She forced herself to smile in answer to Rose Brentwood's question. But all the while she was trying to understand what it was in her sister's look that had hurt her so. It was not the anger,—for that she was prepared. It was not the scorn, for she had often faced that. Was it the almost merriment?

... could bear all things for ... play well her part of wife this day. The happy two months that had passed since David came back from New York had made her almost feel as if she was really his and he hers. For this hour she would forget that it was otherwise. She would look at him and speak to him as if he had been her husband for years, as if there were the truest understanding between them, — as indeed, of a certain wistful, pleasant sort there was. She would not let the dreadful thought of Kate cloud her face for others to see. Bravely she faced the company, but her heart under Kate's blue frock sent up a swift and pleading prayer demanding of a higher Power something she knew she had not in herself, and must therefore find in Him who had created her. It was the most trustful, and needy prayer that Marcia ever uttered and yet there were no words, not even the closing of an eyelid. Only her heart took the attitude of prayer.

The door upstairs opened in a business-like way, and Hannah's composed voice was heard giving a direction. Hannah's silken tread began to be audible. Miranda told Marcia afterward that she kept her standing at the window for an hour beforehand to see when David arrived, and when they started over to the house. Hannah kept herself posted on what was going on in the room below as well as if she were down there. She knew where David and Marcia stood, and told Kate exactly where to go. It was like Hannah that in the moment of her sacrifice of the long cherished hopes of her life she should have planned a dramatic revenge to help carry her through.

The bride's rustle became at last so audible that even David and Mr. Brentwood heard and turned from their absorbing conversation to the business in hand.

Hannah was in the doorway when David looked up, very cold and beautiful in her bridal array despite the years she had waited, and almost at once David saw the vision in purple and gold like a saucy pansy, standing near her.

Kate's eyes were fixed upon him with their most bewitching, dancing smile of recognition, like a naughty little child who had been in hiding for a time and now peeps out laughing over the discomfiture of its elders. So Kate encountered the steadfast gaze of David's astonished eyes.

But there was no light of love in those eyes as she had expected to see. Instead there grew in his face such a blaze of righteous indignation as the lord of the wedding feast might have turned upon the person who came in without a wedding garment. In spite of herself Kate was disconcerted. She was astonished. She felt that David was challenging her presence there. It seemed to her he was looking through her, searching her, judging her, sentencing her, and casting her out, and presently his eyes wandered beyond her through the open hall door and out into God's green world; and when they came back and next rested upon her his look had frozen into the glance of a stranger.

Angry, ashamed, baffled, she bit her lips in vexation, but tried to keep the merry smile. In her heart she hated him, and vowed to make him bow before her smiles once more.

David did not see the bride at all to notice her, but the bride, unlike the one of the psalmist's vision whose eyes were upon "her dear bridegroom's face," was looking straight across the room with evident intent to observe David.

The ceremony proceeded, and Hannah went through her part correctly and calmly, aware that she was giving herself to Lemuel Skinner irrevocably, yet perfectly aware also of the discomfiture of the sweet-faced girl-wife who sat across the room bravely watching the ceremony with white cheeks and eyes that shone like righteous lights.

Marcia did not look at David. She was with him in heart, suffering with him, feeling for him, quivering in every nerve for what he might be enduring. She had no need to look. Her part was to ignore, and help to cover.

They went through it all well. Not once did Aunt Amelia or Aunt Hortense notice anything strange in the demeanor of their nephew or his wife. Aunt Clarinda was not there. She was not fond of Hannah.

As soon as the service was over and the relatives had broken the solemn hush by kissing the bride, David turned and spoke to Rose Brentwood, making some smiling remark about the occasion. Rose Brentwood was looking her very prettiest in a rose-sprigged delaine and her wavy dark hair in a beaded net tied round with a rose-colored lute-string ribbon.

Kate flushed angrily at this. If it had been Marcia to whom he had spoken she would have judged he did it out of pique, but a pretty stranger coming upon the scene at this critical moment was trying. And then, too, David's manner was so indifferent, so utterly natural. He did not seem in the least troubled by the sight of herself.

David and Marcia did not go up to speak to the bride at once. David stepped back into the deep window seat to talk with Mr. Brentwood, and seemed to be in no hurry to follow the procession who were filing past the calm bride to congratulate her. Marcia remained quietly talking to Rose Brentwood. At last David turned toward his wife with a smile as though he had known she was there all the time, and had felt her sympathy. Her heart leaped up with new strength at that look, and her husband's firm touch as he drew her hand within his arm to lead her over to the bride gave her courage. She felt that she could face the battle, and with a bright smile that lit up her whole lovely face she marched bravely to the front to do or to die.

It was an impetuous, childish thing to say, and Marcia scarcely realized what words she meant to speak until they were out, and then she blushed rosy red. Was she happy? Why was she happy? Yes, even in the present trying circumstances she suddenly felt a great deep happiness bubbling up in her heart. Was it David's look and his strong arm under her hand?

Hannah darted a look at her. She was stung by the words. But did the girl-bride before her mean to flaunt her own triumphs in her face? Did she fully understand? Or was she trying to act a part and make them believe she was happy? Hannah was baffled once more as she had been before with Marcia.

Kate turned upon Marcia for one piercing instant again, that look of understanding, mocking merriment, which cut through the soul of her sister.

But did Marcia imagine it, or was it true that at her words to Hannah, David's arm had pressed hers closer as they stood there in the crowd? The thought thrilled through her and gave her greater strength.

Hannah turned toward Kate.

"David," she said, as she had always called him, and it is possible that she enjoyed the triumph of this touch of intimacy before her guest, "you knew my friend Mrs. Leavenworth!"

David bowed gravely, but did not attempt to put out his hand to take the one which Kate offered in greeting. Instead he laid it over Marcia's little trembling one on his arm as if to steady it.

"We have met before," said David briefly in an impenetrable tone, and turning passed out of the room to make way for the Brentwoods who were behind him.

Hannah scarcely treated the Brentwoods with decency, so vexed was she with the way things were turning out. To think that David should so completely baffle her. She turned an annoyed look at Kate, who flashed her blue eyes contemptuously as if to blame Hannah.

Soon the whole little gathering were in the dining-room and wide hall being served with Grandmother Heath's fried chicken and currant jelly, delicate soda biscuits, and fruit cake baked months before and left to ripen.

The ordeal through which they were passing made David and Marcia feel, as they sat down, that they would not be able to swallow a mouthful, but strangely enough they found themselves eating with relish, each to encourage the other perhaps, but almost enjoying it, and feeling that they had not yet met more than they would be able to withstand.

Kate was seated on the other side of the dining-room, by Hannah, and she watched the two incessantly with that half merry contemptuous look, toying with her own food, and apparently waiting for their acting to cease and David to put on his true character. She never doubted for an instant that they were acting.

The wedding supper was over at last. The guests crowded out to the front stoop to bid good-bye to the happy bride-groom and cross-looking bride, who seemed as if she left the gala scene reluctantly.

Marcia, for the instant, was separated from David, who stepped down upon the grass and stood to one side to let the bridal party pass. The minister was at the other side. Marcia had slipped into the shelter of Aunt Amelia's black silk presence and wished she might run out the back door and away home.

Suddenly a shimmer of gold with the sunlight through it caught her gaze, and a glimpse of sheeny purple. There, close behind David, standing upon the top step, quite unseen by him, stood her sister Kate.

Marcia's heart gave a quick thump and seemed to stop, then went painfully laboring on. She stood quite still watching for the moment to come when David would turn around and see Kate that she might look into his face and read there what was written.

Hannah had been put carefully into the carriage by the adoring Lemuel, with many a pat, and shaking of cushions, and adjustment of curtains to suit her whim. It pleased Hannah, now in her last lingering moment of freedom, to be exacting and show others what a slave her husband was.

They all stood for an instant looking after the carriage, but Marcia watched David. Then, just as the carriage wound around the curve in the road and was lost from view, she saw him turn, and at once knew she must not see his face as he looked at Kate. Closing her eyes like a flash she turned and fled upstairs to get her shawl and bonnet. There she took refuge behind the great white curtains, and hid her face for several minutes, praying wildly, she hardly knew what, thankful she had been kept from the sight which yet she had longed to behold.

As David turned to go up the steps and search for Marcia he was confronted by Kate's beautiful, smiling face, radiant as it used to be when it had first charmed him. He exulted, as he looked into it, that it did not any longer charm him.

"David, you don't seem a bit glad to see me," blamed Kate sweetly in her pretty, childish tones, looking into his face with those blue eyes so like to liquid skies. Almost there was a hint of tears in them. He had been wont to kiss them when she looked like that. Now he felt only disgust as some of the flippant sentences in her letters to Harry Temple came to his mind.

His face was stern and unrecognizing.

"David, you are angry with me yet! You said you would forgive!" The gentle reproach minimized the crime, and enlarged the punishment. It was Kate's way.

... pretty face into a thousand dimples and looked her most bewitching like a naughty child who knew she was loved in spite of anything, and coquettishly putting her head on one side, added, in the tone she used of old to cajole him:

"You know you never could refuse me anything, David."

David did not smile. He did not answer the look. With a voice that recognized her only as a stranger he said gravely: "I have an important engagement to-morrow morning."

"But you will put off the engagement." She said it confidently.

"It is impossible!" said David decidedly. "I am starting quite early to drive over to Albany. I am under obligation to be present at the starting of the new steam railroad."

"Oh, how nice!" said Kate, clapping her hands childishly, "I have wanted to be there, and now you will take me. Then I—we—can talk on the way. How like old times that will be!" She flashed him a smile of molten sunshine, alluring and transforming.

"That, too, is impossible, Mrs. Leavenworth. My wife accompanies me!" he answered her promptly and clearly and with a curt bow left her and went into the house.

Kate Leavenworth was angry, and for Kate to be angry, meant to visit it upon some one, the offender if possible, if not the nearest to the offender. She had failed utterly in her attempt to win back the friendship of her former lover. She had hoped to enjoy his attention to a certain extent and bathe her sad heart in the wistful glances of the man she had jilted; and incidentally perhaps be invited to spend a little time in his house, by which she would contrive to have a good many of her own ways. A rich brother-in-law who adored one was not a bad thing to have, especially when his wife was one's own little sister whom one had always dominated. She was tired of New York and at this season of the year the country was much preferable. She could thus contrive to hoard her small income, and save for the next winter, as well as secure a possible entrance finally into her father's good graces again through the forgiveness of David and Marcia. But she had failed. Could it be that he cared for Marcia! That child! Scout the idea! She would discover at once.

Hurriedly she searched through the rooms downstairs and then went stealthily upstairs. Instinctively she went to the room where Marcia had hidden herself.

Marcia, with that strong upward breath of prayer had grown steady again. She was standing with her back to the door looking out of the window toward her own home when Kate entered the room. Without turning about she felt Kate's presence and knew that it was she. The moment had come. She turned around, her face calm and sweet, with two red spots upon her cheeks, and her bonnet,—Kate's bonnet and shawl, Kate's fine lace shawl sent from Paris—grasped in her hands.

They faced each other, the sisters, and much was understood between them in a flash without a word spoken. Marcia suddenly saw herself standing there in Kate's rightful place, Kate's things in her hands, Kate's garments upon her body, Kate's husband held by her. It was as if Kate charged her with all these things, as she looked her through and over, from her slipper tips to the ruffle around the neck. And oh, the scorn that flamed from Kate's eyes playing over her, and scorching her cheeks into crimson, and burning her lips dry and stiff! And yet when Kate's eyes reached her face and charged her with the supreme offense of taking David from her, Marcia's eyes looked bravely back, and were not burned by the fire, and she felt that her soul was not even scorched by it. Something about the thought of David like an angelic presence seemed to save her.

The silence between them was so intense that nothing else could be heard by the two. The voices below were drowned by it, the footstep on the stair was as if it were not.

At last Kate spoke, angered still more by her sister's soft eyes which gazed steadily back and did not droop before her own flashing onslaught. Her voice was cold and cruel. There was nothing sisterly in it, nothing to remind either that the other had ever been beloved.

"Fool!" hissed Kate. "Silly fool! Did you think you could steal a husband as you stole your clothes? Did you suppose marrying David would make him yours, as putting on my clothes seemed to make them yours? Well I can tell you he will never be a husband to you. He doesn't love you and he never can. He will always love me. He's as much mine as if I had married him, in spite of all your attempts to take him. Oh, you needn't put up your baby mouth and pucker it as if you were going to cry. Cry away. It won't do any good. You can't make a man yours, any more than you can make somebody's clothes yours. They don't fit you any more than he does. You look horrid in blue, and you know it, in spite of all your prinking around and pretending. I'd be ashamed to be tricked out that way and know that every dud I had was made for somebody else. As for going around and pretending you have a husband—it's a lie. You know he's nothing to you. You know he never told you he cared for you. I tell you he's mine, and he always will be."

"Kate, you're married!" cried Marcia in shocked tones. "How can you talk like that?"

word to-day. He would kiss me if I asked him. He is weak as water in my hands."

Marcia's cheeks burned with shame and anger. Almost she felt at the limit of her strength. For the first time in her life she felt like striking, – striking her own sister. Horrified over her feelings, and the rage which was tearing her soul, she looked up, and there stood David in the doorway, like some tall avenging angel!

Kate had her back that way and did not see at once, but Marcia's eyes rested on him hungrily, pleadingly, and his answered hers. From her sudden calmness Kate saw there was some one near, and turning, looked at David. But he did not glance her way. How much or how little he had heard of Kate's tirade, which in her passion had been keyed in a high voice, he never let them know and neither dared to ask him, lest perhaps he had not heard anything. There was a light of steel in his eyes toward everything but Marcia, and his tone had in it kindness and a recognition of mutual understanding as he said:

"If you are ready we had better go now, dear, had we not?"

Oh how gladly Marcia followed her husband down the stairs and out the door! She scarcely knew how she went through the formalities of getting away. It seemed as she looked back upon them that David had sheltered her from it all, and said everything needful for her, and all she had done was to smile an assent. He talked calmly to her all the way home; told her Mr. Brentwood's opinion about the change in the commerce of the country the new railroad was going to make; told her though he must have known she could not listen. Perhaps both were conscious of the bedroom window over the way and a pair of blue eyes that might be watching them as they passed into the house. David took hold of her arm and helped her up the steps of their own home as if she had been some great lady. Marcia wondered if Kate saw that. In her heart she blessed David for this outward sign of their relationship. It gave her shame a little cover at least. She glanced up toward the next house as she passed in and felt sure she saw a glimmer of purple move away from the window. Then David shut the door behind them and led her gently in.

Chapter 27

He made her go into the parlor and sit down and she was all unnerved by his gentle ways. The tears would come in spite of her. He took his own fine wedding handkerchief and wiped them softly off her hot cheeks. He untied the bonnet that was not hers, and flung it far into a corner in the room. Marcia thought he put force into the fling. Then he unfolded the shawl from her shoulders and threw that into another corner. Kate's beautiful thread lace shawl. Marcia felt a hysterical desire to laugh, but David's voice was steady and quiet when he spoke as one might speak to a little child in trouble.

"There now, dear," he said. He had never called her dear before. "There, that was an ordeal, and I'm glad it's over. It will never trouble us that way again. Let us put it aside and never think about it any more. We have our own lives to live. I want you to go with me to-morrow morning to see the train start if you feel able. We must start early and you must take a good rest. Would you like to go?"

Marcia's face like a radiant rainbow answered for her as she smiled behind her tears, and all the while he talked David's hand, as tender as a woman's, was passing back and forth on Marcia's hot forehead and smoothing the hair. He talked on quietly to soothe her, and give her a chance to regain her composure, speaking of a few necessary arrangements for the morning's ride. Then he said, still in his quiet voice: "Now dear, I want you to go to bed, for we must start rather early, but first do you think you could sing me that little song you were singing the day I came home? Don't if you feel too tired, you know."

Then Marcia, an eager light in her eyes, sprang up and went to the piano, and began to play softly and sing the tender words she had sung once before when he was listening and she knew it not.

Dearest, believe,
Whene'r we part,
Lonely I grieve,
In my sad heart:—

Kate, standing within the chintz curtains across the yard shedding angry tears upon her purple silk, heard presently the sweet tones of the piano, which might have been hers; heard her sister's voice singing, and began to understand that she must bear the punishment of her own rash deeds.

The room had grown from a purple dusk into quiet darkness while Marcia was singing, for the sun was almost down when they walked home. When the

... this eyes as well
... Marcia felt that she was moving up the stairs under a spell of some gentle loving power that surrounded her and would always guard her.

And it was about this time that Miranda, having been sent over to take a forgotten piece of bride's cake to Marcia, and having heard the piano, and stolen discreetly to the parlor window for a moment, returned and detailed for the delectation of that most unhappy guest Mrs. Leavenworth why she could not get in and would have to take it over in the morning:

"The window was open in the parlor and they were in there, them two, but they was so plum took up with their two selves, as they always are, that there wasn't no use knockin' fer they'd never hev heard."

Miranda enjoyed making those remarks to the guest. Some keen instinct always told her where best to strike her blows.

When Marcia had reached the top stair she looked down and there was David smiling up to her.

"Marcia," said he in a tone that seemed half ashamed and half amused, "have you, any — that is — things — that you had before — all your own I mean?" With quick intuition Marcia understood and her own sweet shame about her clothes that were not her own came back upon her with double force. She suddenly saw herself again standing before the censure of her sister. She wondered if David had heard. If not, how then did he know? Oh, the shame of it!

"Yes," said she, trying to think. "Some old things, and one frock."

"Wear it then to-morrow, dear," said David, in a compelling voice and with the sweet smile that took the hurt out of his most severe words.

Marcia smiled. "It is very plain," she said, "only chintz, pink and white. I made it myself."

"Charming!" said David. "Wear it, dear. Marcia, one thing more. Don't wear any more things that don't belong to you. Not a dud. Promise me? Can you get along without it?"

"Why, I guess so," said Marcia laughing joyfully. "I'll try to manage. But I haven't any bonnet. Nothing but a pink sunbonnet."

"All right, wear that," said David.

"It will look a little queer, won't it?" said Marcia doubtfully, and yet as if the idea expressed a certain freedom which was grateful to her.

"Never mind," said David. "Wear it. Don't wear any more of those other things. Pack them all and send them where they belong, just as quick as we get home."

There was something masterful and delightful in David's voice, and Marcia with a happy laugh took her candle and got up saying, with a ring of joy in her voice: "All right!" She went to her room with David's second good-night ringing in her ears and her heart so light she wanted to sing.

Not at once did Marcia go to her bed. She set her candle upon the bureau and began to search wildly in a little old haircloth trunk, her own special old trunk that had contained her treasures and which had been sent her after she left home. She had scarcely looked into it since she came to the new home. It seemed as if her girlhood were shut up in it. Now she pulled it out from the closet.

What a flood of memories rushed over her as she opened it! There were relics of her school days, and of her little childhood. But she had no time for them now. She was in search of something. She touched them tenderly, but laid them all out one after another upon the floor until down in the lower corner she found a roll of soft white cloth. It contained a number of white garments, half a dozen perhaps in all, finished, and several others cut out barely begun. They were her own work, every stitch, the first begun when she was quite a little girl, and her stepmother started to teach her to sew. What pride she had taken in them! How pleased she had been when allowed to put real tucks in some of them! She had thought as she sewed upon them at different times that they were to be a part of her own wedding trousseau. And then her wedding had come upon her unawares, with the trousseau ready-made, and everything belonged to some one else. She had folded her own poor little garments away and thought never to take them out again, for they seemed to belong to her dead self.

But now that dead self had suddenly come to life again. These hated things that she had worn for a year that were not hers were to be put away, and, pretty as they were, many of them, she regretted not a thread of them.

She laid the white garments out upon a chair and decided that she would put on what she needed of them on the morrow, even though they were rumpled with long lying away. She even searched out an old pair of her own stockings and laid them on a chair with the other things. They were neatly darned as all things had always been under her stepmother's supervision. Further search brought a pair of partly worn prunella slippers to light, with narrow ankle ribbons.

Then Marcia took down the pink sprigged chintz that she had made a year ago and laid it near the other things, with a bit of black velvet and the quaint old brooch. She felt a little dubious about appearing on such a great occasion, almost in Albany, in a chintz dress and with no wrap. Stay! There was the white crepe shawl, all her own, that David had brought her. She had not felt like

...ain... only in an unusual fit of benevolence had given her.

Then, as if to make the change complete, she searched out an old night robe, plain but smooth and clean and arrayed herself in it, and so, thankful, happy, she lay down as she had been bidden and fell asleep.

David in the room below pondered, strange to say, the subject of dress. There was some pride beneath it all, of course; there always is behind the great problem of dress. It was the rejected bonnet lying in the corner with its blue ribbons limp and its blue flowers crushed that made that subject paramount among so many others he might have chosen for his night's meditation.

He was going over to close the parlor window, when he saw the thing lying innocent and discarded in the corner. Though it bore an injured look, it yet held enough of its original aristocratic style to cause him to stop and think.

It was all well enough to suggest that Marcia wear a pink sunbonnet. It sounded deliciously picturesque. She looked lovely in pink and a sunbonnet was pretty and sensible on any one; but the morrow was a great day. David would be seen of many and his wife would come under strict scrutiny. Moreover it was possible that Kate might be upon the scene to jeer at her sister in a sunbonnet. In fact, when he considered it he would not like to take his wife to Albany in a sunbonnet. It behoved him to consider. The outrageous words which he had heard Mistress Leavenworth speak to his wife still burned in his brain like needles of torture: revelation of the true character of the woman he had once longed to call his own.

But that bonnet! He stood and examined it. What was a bonnet like? The proper kind of a bonnet for a woman in his wife's position to wear. He had never noticed a woman's bonnet before except as he had absent-mindedly observed them in front of him in meeting. Now he brought his mind to bear upon that bonnet. It seemed to be made up of three component parts—a foundation; a girdle apparently to bind together and tie on the head; and a decoration. Straw, silk and some kind of unreal flowers. Was that all? He stooped down and picked the thing up with the tips of his fingers, held it at arms length as though it were contaminating, and examined the inside. Ah! There was another element in its construction, a sort of frill of something thin,—hardly lace,—more like the foam of a cloud. He touched the tulle clumsily with his thumb and finger and then he dropped the bonnet back into the corner again. He thought he understood well enough to know one again. He stood pondering a moment, and looked at his watch.

Yes, it was still early enough to try at least, though of course the shop would be closed. But the village milliner lived behind her little store. It would be easy enough to rouse her, and he had known her all his life. He took his hat as eagerly as he had done when as a boy Aunt Clarinda had given him a penny to buy a top and permission to go to the corner and buy it before Aunt Amelia woke up from her nap. He went quietly out of the door, fastening it behind him and walked rapidly down the street.

Yes, the milliner's shop was closed, but a light in the side windows shining through the veiling hop-vines guided him, and he was presently tapping at Miss Mitchell's side door. She opened the door cautiously and peeped over her glasses at him, and then a bright smile overspread her face. Who in the whole village did not welcome David whenever he chanced to come? Miss Mitchell was resting from her labors and reading the village paper. She had finished the column of gossip and was quite ready for a visitor.

"Come right in, David," she said heartily, for she had known him all the years, "it does a body good to see you though your visits are as few and far between as angels' visits. I'm right glad to see you! Sit down." But David was too eager about his business.

"I haven't any time to sit down to-night, Miss Susan," he said eagerly, "I've come to buy a bonnet. Have you got one? I hope it isn't too late because I want it very early in the morning."

"A bonnet! Bless me! For yourself?" said Miss Mitchell from mere force of commercial habit. But neither of them saw the joke, so intent upon business were they. "For my wife, Miss Mitchell. You see she is going with me over to Albany to-morrow morning and we start quite early. We are going to see the new railroad train start, you know, and she seems to think she hasn't a bonnet that's suitable."

"Going to see a steam engine start, are you! Well, take care, David, you don't get too near. They do say they're terrible dangerous things, and fer my part I can't see what good they'll be, fer nobody'll ever be willin' to ride behind 'em, but I'd like to see it start well enough. And that sweet little wife of yours thinks she ain't got a good enough bonnet. Land sakes! What is the matter with her Dunstable straw, and what's become of that one trimmed with blue lutestrings, and where's the shirred silk one she wore last Sunday? They're every one fine bonnets and ought to last her a good many years yet if she cares fer 'em. The mice haven't got into the house and et them, hev they?"

"No, Miss Susan, those bonnets are all whole yet I believe, but they don't seem to be just the suitable thing. In fact, I don't think they're over-becoming lo her, do you? You see they're mostly blue—"

"That's so!" said Miss Mitchell. "I think myself she'd look better in pink. How'd you like white? I've got a pretty thing that I made fer Hannah Heath an' when it was done Hannah thought it was too plain and wouldn't have it. I sent things, and was superior to most of the bonnets produced in the village.

It was trimmed with plain white taffeta ribbon, soft and silky. That was all on the outside. Around the face was a soft ruching of tulle, and clambering among it a vine of delicate green leaves that looked as if they were just plucked from a wild rose bank. David was delighted. Somehow the bonnet looked like Marcia. He paid the price at once, declining to look at anything else. It was enough that he liked it and that Hannah Heath had not. He had never admired Hannah's taste. He carried it home in triumph, letting himself softly into the house, lighted three candles, took the bonnet out and hung it upon a chair. Then he walked around it surveying it critically, first from this side, then from that. It pleased him exceedingly. He half wished Marcia would hear him and come down. He wanted to see it on her, but concluded that he was growing boyish and had better get himself under control.

The bonnet approved, he walked back and forth through the kitchen and dining-room thinking. He compelled himself to go over the events of the afternoon and analyze most carefully his own innermost feelings. In fact, after doing that he began further back and tried to find out how he felt toward Marcia. What was this something that had been growing in him unaware through the months; that had made his homecoming so sweet, and had brightened every succeeding day; and had made this meeting with Kate a mere common-place? What was this precious thing that nestled in his heart? Might he, had he a right to call it love? Surely! Now all at once his pulses thrilled with gladness. He loved her! It was good to love her! She was the most precious being on earth to him. What was Kate in comparison with her? Kate who had shown herself cold and cruel and unloving in every way?

His anger flamed anew as he thought of those cutting sentences he had overheard, taunting her own sister about the clothes she wore. Boasting that he still belonged to her! She, a married woman! A woman who had of her own free will left him at the last moment and gone away with another! His whole nature recoiled against her. She had sinned against her womanhood, and might no longer demand from man the homage that a true woman had a right to claim.

Poor little bruised flower! His heart went out to Marcia. He could not bear to think of her having to stand and listen to that heartless tirade. And he had been the cause of all this. He had allowed her to take a position which threw her open to Kate's vile taunts.

Up and down he paced till the torrent of his anger spent itself, and he was able to think more calmly. Then he went back in his thoughts to the time when he had first met Kate and she had bewitched him. He could see now the heartlessness of her. He had met her first at the house of a friend where he was visiting, partly on pleasure, partly on business. She had devoted herself to him during the time of her stay in a most charming way, though now he recalled that she had also been equally devoted to the son of the house whom he was visiting. When she went home she had asked him to come and call, for her home was but seven miles away. He had been so charmed with her that he had accepted the invitation, and, rashly he now saw, had engaged himself to her, after having known her in all face to face but a few days. To be sure he had known of her father for years, and he took a good deal for granted on account of her fine family. They had corresponded after their engagement which had lasted for nearly a year, and in that time David had seen her but twice, for a day or two at a time, and each time he had thought her grown more lovely. Her letters had been marvels of modesty, and shy admiration. It was easy for Kate to maintain her character upon paper, though she had had little trouble in making people love her under any circumstances. Now as he looked back he could recall many instances when she had shown a cruel, heartless nature.

Then, all at once, with a throb of joy, it came to him to be thankful to God for the experience through which he had passed. After all it had not been taken from him to love with a love enduring, for though Kate had been snatched from him just at the moment of his possession, Marcia had been given to him. Fool that he was! He had been blind to his own salvation. Suppose he had been allowed to go on and marry Kate! Suppose he had had her character revealed to him suddenly as those letters of hers to Harry Temple had revealed it—as it surely would have been revealed in time, for such things cannot be hid,—and she had been his *wife!* He shuddered. How he would have loathed her! How he loathed her now!

Strangely enough the realization of that fact gave him joy. He sprang up and waved his hands about in silent delight. He felt as if he must shout for gladness. Then he gravely knelt beside his chair and uttered an audible thanksgiving for his escape and the joy he had been given. Nothing else seemed fitting expression of his feelings.

There was one other question to consider—Marcia's feelings. She had always been kind and gentle and loving to him, just as a sister might have been. She was exceedingly young yet. Did she know, could she understand what it meant to be loved the way he was sure he could love a woman? And would she ever be able to love him in that way? She was so silent and shy he hardly knew whether she cared for him or not. But there was one thought that gave him unbounded joy and that was that she was his wife. At least no one else could take her from him. He had felt condemned that he had married her when his naᴅ turned when she was out of his sight. Still there were instances of strong union of hearts of those who had loved from early childhood. It might be that Marcia's sometime-sadness was over a companion of her girlhood.

A great longing took possession of him to rush up and waken her and find out if she could ever care for him. He scarcely knew himself. This was not his dignified contained self that he had lived with for twenty-seven years.

It was very late before he finally went upstairs. He walked softly lest he disturb Marcia. He paused before her door listening to see if she was asleep, but there was only the sound of the katydids in the branches outside her window, and the distant tree-toads singing a fugue in an orchard not far away. He tiptoed to his room but he did not light his candle, therefore there was no light in the back room of the Spafford house that night for any watching eyes to ponder over. He threw himself on the bed. He was weary in body yet his soul seemed buoyant as a bird in the morning air. The moon was casting long bars of silver across the rag carpet and white counterpane. It was almost full moon. Yes, to-morrow it would be entirely full. It was full moon the night he had met Marcia down by the gate, and kissed her. It was the first time he had thought of that kiss with anything but pain. It used to hurt him that he had made the mistake and taken her for Kate. It had seemed like an ill-omen of what was to come. But now, it thrilled him with a great new joy. After all he had given the kiss to the right one. It was Marcia to whom his soul bowed in the homage that a man may give to a woman. Did his good angel guide him to her that night? And how was it he had not seen the sweetness of Marcia sooner? How had he lived with her nearly a year, and watched her dainty ways, and loving ministry and not known that his heart was hers? How was it he had grieved so long over Kate, and now since he had seen her once more, not a regret was in his heart that she was not his; but a beautiful revelation of his own love to Marcia had been wrought in him? How came it?

And the importunate little songsters in the night answered him a thousand times: "Kate-did-it! Kate-she-did-it! Yes she did! I say she did. Kate did it!"

Had angel voices reached him through his dreams, and suddenly given him the revelation which the little insects had voiced in their ridiculous colloquy? It was Kate herself who had shown him how he loved Marcia.

Chapter 28

Slowly the moon rode over the house, and down toward its way in the West, and after its vanishing chariot the night stretched wistful arms. Softly the grey in the East tinged into violet and glowed into rose and gold. The birds woke up and told one another that the first of August was come and life was good.

The breath that came in the early dawn savored of new-mown hay, and the bird songs thrilled Marcia as if it were the day of her dreams.

She forgot all her troubles; forgot even her wayward sister next door; and rose with the song of the birds in her heart. This was to be a great day. No matter what happened she had now this day to date from. David had asked her to go somewhere just because he wanted her to. She knew it from the look in his eyes when he told her, and she knew it because he might have asked a dozen men to go with him. There was no reason why he need have taken her to-day, for it was distinctly an affair for men, this great wonder of machinery. It was a privilege for a woman to go. She felt it. She understood the honor.

With fingers trembling from joy she dressed. Not the sight of her pink calico sunbonnet lying on the chair, nor the thought of wearing it upon so grand an occasion, could spoil the pleasure of the day. Among so large a company her bonnet would hardly be noticed. If David was satisfied why what difference did it make? She was glad it would be early when they drove by the aunts, else they might be scandalized. But never mind! Trill! She hummed a merry little tune which melted into the melody of the song she had sung last night.

Then she smiled at herself in the glass. She was fastening the brooch in the bit of velvet round her neck, and she thought of the day a year ago when she had fastened that brooch. She had wondered then how she would feel if the next day was to be her own wedding day. Now as she smiled back at herself in the glass all at once she thought it seemed as if this was her wedding day. Somehow last night had seemed to realize her dreams. A wonderful joy had descended upon her heart. Maybe she was foolish, but was she not going to ride with David? She did not long for the green fields and a chance to run wild through the wood now. This was better than those childish pleasures. This was real happiness. And to think it should have come through David!

She hurried with the arrangement of her hair until her fingers trembled with excitement. She wanted to get downstairs and see if it were all really true or if she were dreaming it. Would David look at her as he had done last night? Would he speak that precious word "dear" to her again to-day? Would he take her by the hand and lead her sometimes, or was that a special gentleness because he knew she had suffered from her sister's words? She clasped her hands with tor breakfast. He was sitting by the hearth impatient for her coming, with a bandbox by his side.

It was like another sunrise to watch their eyes light up as they saw one another. Their glances rushed together as though they had been a long time withholden from each other, and a rosy glow came over Marcia's face that made her long to hide it for a moment from view. Then she knew in her heart that her dream was not all a dream. David was the same. It had lasted, whatever this wonderful thing was that bound them together. She stood still in her happy bewilderment, looking at him, and he enjoying the radiant morning vision of her, stood too.

David found that longing to take her in his arms overcoming him again. He had made strict account with himself and was resolved to be careful and not frighten her. He must be sure it would not be unpleasant to her before he let her know his great deep love. He must be careful. He must not take advantage of the fact that she was his and could not run away from him. If she dreaded his attentions, neither could she any more say no.

And so their two looks met, and longed to come closer, but were held back, and a lovely shyness crept over Marcia's sweet face. Then David bethought himself of his bandbox.

He took up the box and untied it with unaccustomed fingers, fumbling among the tissue paper for the handle end of the thing. Where did they take hold of bonnets anyway? He had no trouble with it the night before, but then he was not thinking about it. Now he was half afraid she might not like it. He remembered that Hannah Heath had pronounced against it. It suddenly seemed impossible that he should have bought a bonnet that a pretty woman had said was not right. There must be something wrong with it after all.

Marcia stood wondering.

"I thought maybe this would do instead of the sunbonnet," he said at last, getting out the bonnet by one string and holding it dangling before him.

Marcia caught it with deft careful hands and an exclamation of delight. He watched her anxiously. It had all the requisite number of materials, — one, two, three, four, — like the despised bonnet he threw on the floor — straw, silk, lace and flowers. Would she like it? Her face showed that she did. Her cheeks flushed with pleasure, and her eyes danced with joy. Marcia's face always showed it when she liked anything. There was nothing half-way about her.

"Oh, it is beautiful!" she said delightedly. "It is so sweet and white and cool with that green vine. Oh, I am glad, glad, glad! I shall never wear that old blue bonnet again." She went over to the glass and put it on. The soft ruching settled about her brown hair, and made a lovely setting for her face. The green vine twined and peeped in and out under the round brim and the ribbon sat in a prim bow beneath her pretty chin.

She gave one comprehensive glance at herself in the glass and then turned to David. In that glance was revealed to her just how much she had dreaded wearing her pink sunbonnet, and just how relieved she was to have a substitute.

Her look was shy and sweet as she said with eyes that dared and then drooped timidly:

"You—are—very—good to me."

Almost he forgot his vow of carefulness at that, but remembered when he got half across the room toward her, and answered earnestly:

"Dear, *you* have been very good to *me.*"

Marcia's eyes suddenly sobered and half the glow faded from her face. Was it then only gratitude? She took off the bonnet and touched the bows with wistful tenderness as she laid it by till after breakfast. He watched her and misinterpreted the look. Was she then disappointed in the bonnet? Was it not right after all? Had Hannah known better than he? He hesitated and then asked her:

"Is there—Is it—That is—perhaps you would rather take it back and choose another. You know how to choose one better than I. There were others I think. In fact, I forgot to look at any but this because I liked it, but I'm only a man—" he finished helplessly.

"No! No! No!" said Marcia, her eyes sparkling emphatically again. "There couldn't be a better one. This is just exactly what I like. I do not want anything else. And I—like it all the better because you selected it," she added daringly, suddenly lifting her face to his with a spice of her own childish freedom.

His eyes admired her.

"She told me Hannah Heath thought it too plain," he added honestly.

"Then I'm sure I like it all the better for that," said Marcia so emphatically that they both laughed.

It all at once became necessary to hurry, for the old clock in the hall clanged out the hour and David became aware that haste was imperative.

Early as Marcia had come down, David had been up long before her, his heart too light to sleep. In a dream, or perchance on the borders of the morning, an idea had come to him. He told Marcia that he must go out now to see about the horse, but he also made a hurried visit to the home of his office clerk and another to the aunts, and when he returned with the horse he had left things in such train that if he did not return that evening he would not be greatly missed. But he said nothing to Marcia about it. He laughed to himself as he thought of another trip away from the village for a few days with good grace. Aunt Hortense asked Aunt Amelia if she had ever feared that Marcia would have a bad effect upon David by making him frivolous. Perhaps he would lose interest in his business with all his careering around the country. Aunt Amelia agreed that Marcia must be to blame in some way, and then discovering they had a whole hour before their usual rising time, the two good ladies settled themselves with indignant composure to their interrupted repose.

Breakfast was ready when David returned. Marcia supposed he had only been to harness the horse. She glanced out happily through the window to where the horse stood tied to the post in front of the house. She felt like waving her hand to him, and he turned and seemed to see her; rolling the whites of his eyes around, and tossing his head as if in greeting.

Marcia would scarcely have eaten anything in her excitement if David had not urged her to do so. She hurried with her clearing away, and then flew upstairs to arrange her bonnet before the glass and don the lovely folds of the creamy crepe shawl, folding it demurely around her shoulders and knotting it in front. She put on her mitts, took her handkerchief folded primly, and came down ready.

But David no longer seemed in such haste. He made a great fuss fastening up everything. She wondered at his unusual care, for she thought everything quite safe for the day.

She raised one shade toward the Heath house. It was the first time she had permitted herself this morning to think of Kate. Was she there yet? Probably, for no coach had left since last night, and unless she had gone by private conveyance there would have been no way to go. She looked up to the front corner guest room where the windows were open and the white muslin curtains swayed in the morning breeze. No one seemed to be moving about in the room. Perhaps Kate was not awake. Just then she caught the flutter of a blue muslin down on the front stoop. Kate was up, early as it was, and was coming out. A sudden misgiving seized Marcia's heart, as when a little child, she had seen her sister coming to eat up the piece of cake or sweetmeat that had been given to her. Many a time had that happened. Now, she felt that in some mysterious way Kate would contrive to take from her her new-found joy.

She could not resist her, — David could not resist her, — no one could ever resist Kate. Her face turned white and her hand began to tremble so that she dropped the curtain she had been holding up.

Just then came David's clear voice, louder than would have been necessary, and pitched as if he were calling to some one upstairs, though he knew she was just inside the parlor where she had gone to make sure of the window fastening.

"Come, dear! Aren't you ready? It is more than time we started."

There was a glad ring in David's voice that somehow belied the somewhat exacting words he had spoken, and Marcia's heart leaped up to meet him.

"Yes, I'm all ready, dear!" she called back with a hysterical little laugh. Of course Kate could not hear so far, but it gave her satisfaction to say it. The final word was unpremeditated. It bubbled up out of the depths of her heart and made the red rush back into her cheeks when she realized what she had said. It was the first time she had ever used a term of endearment toward David. She wondered if he noticed it and if he would think her very—bold,—queer,—immodest, to use it. She looked shyly up at him, enquiring with her eyes, as she came out to him on the front stoop, and he looked down with such a smile she felt as if it were a caress. And yet neither was quite conscious of this little real by-play they were enacting for benefit of the audience of one in blue muslin over the way. How much she heard, or how little they could not tell, but it gave satisfaction to go through with it inasmuch as it was real, and not acting at all.

David fastened the door and then helped Marcia into the carriage. They were both laughing happily like two children starting upon a picnic. Marcia was serenely conscious of her new bonnet, and it was pleasant to have David tuck the linen lap robe over chintz frock so carefully. She was certain Kate could not identify it now at that distance, thanks to the lap robe and her crepe shawl. At least Kate could not see any of her own trousseau on her sister now.

Kate was sitting on the little white seat in the shelter of the honeysuckle vine facing them on the stoop of the Heath house. It was impossible for them to know whether she was watching them or not. They did not look up to see. She was talking with Mr. Heath who, in his milking garb, was putting to rights some shrubs and plants near the walk that had been trampled upon during the wedding festivities. But Kate must have seen a good deal that went on.

David took up the reins, settled himself with a smile at Marcia, touched the horse with the tip of the whip, which caused him to spring forward in astonishment—that from David! No horse in town would have expected it of him. They had known him from babyhood, most of them, and he was gentleness itself. It must have been a mistake. But the impression lasted long enough to carry them a rod or two past the Heath house at swift pace, with only time for a lifting of David's hat, prolonged politely,—which might or might not have included Kate, and they were out upon their way together.

Marcia could scarcely believe her senses that she was really here beside David, riding with him swiftly through the village and leaving Kate behind. She felt a passing pity for Kate. Then she looked shyly up at David. Would his gaiety pass when they were away, and would he grow grave and sad again as soon as country. It was a day much as that other one, just as bright, just as warm, yet oh, so much more radiant to both! Then they were sad and fearful of the future. All their life seemed in the past. Now the darkness had been led through, and they had reached the brightness again. In fact, all the future stretched out before them that fair morning and looked bright as the day.

They were conscious of the blueness of the sky, of the soft clouds that hovered in haziness on the rim of the horizon, as holding off far enough to spoil no moment of that perfect day. They were conscious of the waving grains and of the perfume of the buckwheat drifting like snow in the fields beyond the wheat; conscious of the meadow-lark and the wood-robin's note; of the whir of a locust; and the thud of a frog in the cool green of a pool deep with brown shadows; conscious of the circling of mated butterflies in the simmering gold air; of the wild roses lifting fair pink petals from the brambly banks beside the road; conscious of the whispering pine needles in a wood they passed; the fluttering chatter of leaves and silver flash of the lining of poplar leaves, where tall trees stood like sentinels, apart and sad; conscious of a little brook that tinkled under a log bridge they crossed, then hurried on its way unmindful of their happy crossing; conscious of the dusty daisy beside the road, closing with a bumbling bee who wanted honey below the market price; conscious of all these things; but most conscious of each other, close, side by side.

It was all so dear, that ride, and over so soon. Marcia was just trying to get used to looking up into the dazzling light of David's eyes. She had to droop her own almost immediately for the truth she read in his was overpowering. Could it be? A fluttering thought came timidly to her heart and would not be denied.

"Can it be, can it be that he cares for me? He loves me. He loves me!" It sang its way in with thrill after thrill of joy and more David's eyes told the story which his lips dared not risk yet. But eyes and hearts are not held by the conventions that bind lips. They rushed into their inheritance of each other and had that day ahead, a day so rare and sweet that it would do to set among the jewels of fair days for all time and for any one.

All too soon they began to turn into roads where were other vehicles, many of them, and all going in the same direction. Men and women in gala day attire all laughing and talking expectantly and looking at one another as the carriages passed with a degree of familiar curiosity which betokens a common errand. Family coaches, farm wagons, with kitchen chairs for accommodation of the family; old one-horse chaises, carryalls, and even a stage coach or two wheeled

into the old turnpike. David and Marcia settled into subdued quiet, their joy
not expressing itself in the ripples of laughter that had rung out earlier in the
morning when they were alone. They sought each other's eyes often and often,
and in one of these excursions that David's eyes made to Marcia's face he
noticed how extremely becoming the new bonnet was. After thinking it over he
decided to risk letting her know. He was not shy about it now.

"Do you know, dear," he said,—there had been a good many "dear's"
slipping back and forth all unannounced during that ride, and not openly
acknowledged either. "Do you know how becoming your new bonnet is to you?
You look prettier than I ever saw you look but once before." He kept his eyes
upon her face and watched the sweet color steal up to her drooping eyelashes.

"When was that?" she asked coyly, to hide her embarrassment, and sweeping him one laughing glance.

"Why, that night, dear, at the gate, in the moonlight. Don't you remember?"

"Oh-h-h-h!" Marcia caught her breath and a thrill of joy passed through
her that made her close her eyes lest the glad tears should come. Then the little
bird in her heart set up the song in earnest to the tune of Wonder: "He loves
me, He loves me, He loves me!"

He leaned a little closer to her.

"If there were not so many people looking I think I should have to kiss you
now."

"Oh-h-h-h!" said Marcia drawing in her breath and looking around
frightened on the number of people that were driving all about them, for they
were come almost to the railroad now, and could see the black smoke of the
engine a little beyond as it stood puffing and snorting upon its track like some
sulky animal that had been caught and chained and harnessed and was longing
to leap forward and upset its load.

But though Marcia looked about in her happy fright, and sat a trifle
straighter in the chaise, she did not move her hand away that lay next to David's,
underneath the linen lap robe, and he put his own hand over it and covered it
close in his firm hold. Marcia trembled and was so happy she was almost faint
with joy. She wondered if she were very foolish indeed to feel so, and if all love
had this terrible element of solemn joy in it that made it seem too great to be
real.

They had to stop a number of times to speak to people. Everybody knew
David, it appeared. This man and that had a word to speak with him, some bit
of news that he must not omit to notice in his article, some new development
about the attitude of a man of influence that was important; the change of two
or three of those who were to go in the coaches on this trial trip.

To all of them David introduced his wife, with a ring of pride in his voice as
he said the words "My wife," and all of them stopped whatever business they
had in hand and stepped back to bow most deferentially to the beautiful woman

Many of them stood for some time and talked with her. Mr. Thurlow Weed was the last one to leave them before the train was actually ready for starting, and he laid an urging hand upon David's arm as he went. "Then you think you cannot go with us? Better come. Mrs. Spafford will let you I am sure. You're not afraid are you, Mrs. Spafford? I am sure you are a brave woman. Better come, Spafford."

But David laughingly thanked him again as he had thanked others, and said that he would not be able to go, as he and his wife had other plans, and he must go on to Albany as soon as the train had started.

Marcia looked up at him half worshipfully as he said this, wondering what it was, instinctively knowing that it was for her sake he was giving up this honor which they all wished to put upon him. It would naturally have been an interesting thing to him to have taken this first ride behind the new engine "Dewitt Clinton."

Then, suddenly, like a chill wind from a thunder cloud that has stolen up unannounced and clutched the little wild flowers before they have time to bind up their windy locks and duck their heads under cover, there happened a thing that clutched Marcia's heart and froze all the joy in her veins.

Chapter 29

A coach was approaching filled with people, some of them Marcia knew; they were friends and neighbors from their own village, and behind it plodding along came a horse with a strangely familiar gait drawing four people. The driver was old Mr. Heath looking unbelievingly at the scene before him. He did not believe that an engine would be able to haul a train any appreciable distance whatever, and he believed that he had come out here to witness this entire company of fanatics circumvented by the ill-natured iron steed who stood on the track ahead surrounded by gaping boys and a flock of quacking ganders, living symbol of the people who had come to see the thing start; so thought Mr. Heath. He told himself he was as much of a goose as any of them to have let this chit of a woman fool him into coming off out here when he ought to have been in the hay field to-day.

By his side in all the glory of shimmering blue with a wide white lace bertha and a bonnet with a steeple crown wreathed about heavily with roses sat Kate, a blue silk parasol shading her eyes from the sun, those eyes that looked to conquer, and seemed to pierce beyond and through her sister and ignore her. Old Mrs. Heath and Miranda were along, but they did not count, except to themselves. Miranda was all eyes, under an ugly bonnet. She desired above all things to see that wonderful engine in which David was so interested.

Marcia shrunk and seemed to wither where she sat. All her bright bloom faded in an instant and a kind of frenzy seized her. She had a wild desire to get down out of the carriage and run with all her might away from this hateful scene. The sky seemed to have suddenly clouded over and the hum and buzz of voices about seemed a babble that would never cease.

David felt the arm beside his cringe, and shrink back, and looking down saw the look upon her sweet frightened face; following her glance his own face hardened into what might have been termed righteous wrath. But not a word did he say, and neither did he apparently notice the oncoming carriage. He busied himself at once talking with a man who happened to pass the carriage, and when Mr. Heath drove by to get a better view of the engine he was so absorbed in his conversation that he did not notice them, which seemed but natural.

But Kate was not to be thus easily foiled. She had much at stake and she must win if possible. She worked it about that Squire Heath should drive around to the end of the line of coaches, quite out of sight of the engine and where there was little chance of seeing the train and its passengers,—the only thing Squire Heath cared about. But there was an excellent view of David's carriage and horse. Miranda, at that, had insisted upon changing seats, thereby getting herself nearer the horse, and the scene of action. Miranda did not like to miss seeing the engine start.

At last word to start was given. A man ran along by the train and mounted into his high seat with his horn in his hand ready to blow. The fireman ceased his raking of the glowing fire and every traveller sprang into his seat and looked toward the crowd of spectators importantly. This was a great moment for all interested. The little ones whose fathers were in the train began to call good-bye and wave their hands, and one old lady whose only son was going as one of the train assistants began to sob aloud.

A horse in the crowd began to act badly. Every snort of the engine as the steam was let off made him start and rear. He was directly behind Marcia, and she turned her head and looked straight into his fiery frightened eyes, red with fear and frenzy, and felt his hot breath upon her cheek. A man was trying most ineffectually to hold him, but it seemed as if in another minute he would come plunging into the seat with them. Marcia uttered a frightened cry and clutched at David's arm. He turned, and seeing instantly what was the matter, placed his arm protectingly about her and at once guided his own horse out of the crowd, and around nearer to the engine. Somehow that protecting arm gave Marcia a steadiness once more and she was able to watch the wonderful wheels begin to turn and the whole train slowly move and start on its way. Her lips parted, her breath came quick, and for the instant she forgot her trouble. David's arm was still about her, and there was a reassuring pressure in it. He seemed to have forgotten that the crowd might see him — if the crowd had not been too busy watching something more wonderful. It is probable that only one person in that whole company saw David sitting with his arm about his wife — for he soon remembered and put it quietly on the back of the seat, where it would call no one's attention — and that person was Kate. She had not come to this hot dusty place to watch an engine creak along a track, she had come to watch David, and she was vexed and angry at what she saw. Here was Marcia flaunting her power over David directly in her face. Spiteful thing! She would pay her back yet and let her know that she could not touch the things that she, Kate, had put her own sign and seal upon. For this reason it was that at the last minute Kate allowed poor Squire Heath to drive around near the front of the train, saying that as David Spafford seemed to find it safe she supposed she ought not to hold them back for her fears. It needed but the word to send the vexed and curious Squire around through the crowd to a spot directly behind David's carriage, and there

Miranda could see quite well, and Kate could sit and watch David and frame her plans for immediate action so soon as the curtain should fall upon this ridiculous engine play over which everybody was wild.

And so, amid shouts and cheers, and squawking of the geese that attempted to precede the engine like a white frightened body-guard down the track; amid the waving of handkerchiefs, the shouts of excited little boys, and the neighing of frightened horses, the first steam engine that ever drew a train in New York state started upon its initial trip.

Then there came a great hush upon the spectators assembled. The wheels were rolling, the carriages were moving, the train was actually going by them, and what had been so long talked about was an assured fact. They were seeing it with their own eyes, and might be witnesses of it to all their acquaintances. It was true. They dared not speak nor breathe lest something should happen and the great miracle should stop. They hushed simultaneously as though at the passing of some great soul. They watched in silence until the train went on between the meadows, grew smaller in the distance, slitted into the shadow of the wood, flashed out into the sunlight beyond again, and then was lost behind a hill. A low murmur growing rapidly into a shout of cheer arose as the crowd turned and faced one another and the fact of what they had seen.

"By gum! She kin do it!" ejaculated Squire Heath, who had watched the melting of his skeptical opinions in speechless amazement.

The words were the first intimation the Spaffords had of the proximity of Kate. They made David smile, but Marcia turned white with sudden fear again. Not for nothing had she lived with her sister so many years. She knew that cruel nature and dreaded it.

David looked at Marcia for sympathy in his smile at the old Squire, but when he saw her face he turned frowning toward those behind him.

Kate saw her opportunity. She learned forward with honeyed smile, and wily as the serpent addressed her words to Marcia, loud and clear enough for all those about them to hear.

"Oh, Mrs. Spafford! I am going to ask a great favor of you. I am sure you will grant it when you know I have so little time. I am extremely anxious to get a word of advice from your husband upon business matters that are very pressing. Would you kindly change places with me during the ride home, and give me a chance to talk with him about it? I would not ask it but that I must leave for New York on the evening coach and shall have no other opportunity to see him."

Kate's smile was roses and cream touched with frosty sunshine, and to onlookers nothing could have been sweeter. But her eyes were coldly cruel as sharpened steel, and they said to her sister as plainly as words could have spoken: "Do you obey my wish, my lady, or I will freeze the heart out of you."

her throat, the great tears beating at the portals of her eyes, and she suddenly still waiting for her leaden tongue to speak, David answered:

All gracefully 'twas done, with not much as a second's hesitation, —though it had seemed so long to Marcia, —nor the shadow of a sign that he was angry:

"Mrs. Leavenworth," he said in his masterful voice, "I am sure my wife would not wish to seem ungracious, or unwilling to comply with your request, but as it happens it is impossible. We are not returning home for several days. My wife has some shopping to do in Albany, and in fact we are expecting to take a little trip. A sort of second honeymoon, you know," —he added, smiling toward Mrs. Heath and Miranda; "it is the first time I have had leisure to plan for it since we were married. I am sorry I have to hurry away, but I am sure that my friend Squire Heath can give as much help in a business way as I could, and furthermore, Squire Schuyler is now in New York for a few days as I learned in a letter from him which arrived last evening. I am sure he can give you more and better advice than any I could give. I wish you good morning. Good morning, Mrs. Heath. Good morning, Miss Miranda!"

Lifting his hat David drove away from them and straight over to the little wayside hostelry where he was to finish his article to send by the messenger who was even then ready mounted for the purpose.

"My! Don't he think a lot of her though!" said Miranda, rolling the words as a sweet morsel under her tongue. "It must be nice to have a man so fond of you." This was one of the occasions when Miranda wished she had eyes in the back of her head. She was sharp and she had seen a thing or two, also she had heard scraps of her cousin Hannah's talk. But she sat demurely in the recesses of her deep, ugly bonnet and tried to imagine how the guest behind her looked.

All trembling sat Marcia in the rusty parlor of the little hostelry, while David at the table wrote with hurried hand, glancing up at her to now and then, and passing over the sheets as he finished them for her criticism. She thought she had seen the Heath wagon drive away in the home direction, but she was not sure. She half expected to see the door open and Kate walk in. Her heart was thumping so she could scarcely sit still and the brightness of the world outside seemed to make her dizzy. She was glad to have the sheets to look over, for it took her thoughts away from herself and her nameless fears. She was not quite sure what it was she feared, only that in some way Kate would have power over David to take him away from her. As he wrote she studied the dear lines of his face and knew, as well as human heart may ever know, how dear another soul had grown to hers.

David had not much to write and it was soon signed, approved, and sealed. He sent his messenger on the way and then coming back closed the door and went and stood before Marcia.

As though she felt some critical moment had come she arose, trembling, and looked into his eyes questioningly.

"Marcia," he said, and his tone was grave and earnest, putting her upon an equality with him, not as if she were a child any more. "Marcia, I have come to ask your forgiveness for the terrible thing I did to you in allowing you, who scarcely knew what you were doing then, to give your life away to a man who loved another woman."

Marcia's heart stood still with horror. It had come then, the dreadful thing she had feared. The blow was going to fall. He did not love her! What a fool she had been!

But the steady voice went on, though the blood in her neck and temples throbbed in such loud waves that she could scarcely hear the words to understand them.

"It was a crime, Marcia, and I have come to realize it more and more during all the days of this year that you have so uncomplainingly spent yourself for me. I know now, as I did not think in my careless, selfish sorrow, that I was as cruel to you, with your sweet young life, as your sister was cruel to me. You might already have given your heart to some one else; I never stopped to inquire. You might have had plans and hopes for your own future; I never even thought of it. I was a brute. Can you forgive me? Sometimes the thought of the responsibility I took upon myself has been so terrible to me that I felt I could not stand it. You did not realize what it was then that you were giving, perhaps, but somehow I think you have begun to realize now. Will you forgive me?" He stopped and looked at her anxiously. She was drooped and white as if a blast had suddenly struck her and faded her sweet bloom. Her throat was hot and dry and she had to try three times before she could frame the words, "Yes, I forgive."

There was no hope, no joy in the words, and sudden fear descended upon David's heart. Had he then done more damage than he knew? Was the child's heart broken by him, and did she just realize it? What could he do? Must he conceal his love from her? Perhaps this was no time to tell it. But he must. He could not bear the burden of having done her harm and not also tell her how he loved her. He would be very careful, very considerate, he would not press his love as a claim, but he must tell her.

"And Marcia, I must tell you the rest," he went on, his own words seeming to stay upon his lips, and then tumble over one another; "I have learned to love you as I never loved your sister. I love you more and better that I ever could have loved her. I can see how God has led me away from her and brought me to you. I can look back to that night when I came to her and found you there waiting for me, and kissed you,—darling. Do you remember?" He took her that meeting was not all ours; that it should be shadowed for us by the heart-lessness of another. It gives me much joy now to think how I took you in my arms and kissed you. I cannot bear to think it was mistake. Yet glad as I am that God sent you down to that gate to meet me, and much as I love you, I would rather have died than feel that I have brought sorrow into your life, and bound you to one whom you cannot love. Marcia, tell me truly, never mind my feelings, tell me! Can you ever love me?"

Then did Marcia lift her flowerlike face, all bright with tears of joy and a flood of rosy smiles, the light of seven stars in her eyes. But she could not speak, she could only look, and after a little whisper, "Oh, David, I think I have always loved you! I think I was waiting for you that night, though I did not know it. And look!"— with sudden thought—

She drew from the folds of her dress a little old-fashioned locket hung by a chain about her neck out of sight. She opened it and showed him a soft gold curl which she touched gently with her lips, as though it were something very sacred.

"What is it, darling?" asked David perplexed, half happy, half afraid as he took the locket and touched the curl more thrilled with the thought that she had carried it next her heart than with the sight of it.

"It is yours," she said, disappointed that he did not understand. "Aunt Clarinda gave it to me while you were away. I've worn it ever since. And she gave me other things, and told me all about you. I know it all, about the tops and marbles, and the spelling book, and I've cried with you over your punish-ments, and —I—love it all!"

He had fastened the door before he began to talk, but he caught her in his arms now, regardless of the fact that the shades were not drawn down, and that they swayed in the summer breeze.

"Oh, my darling! My wife!" he cried, and kissed her lips for the third time.

The world was changed then for those two. They belonged to each other they believed, as no two that ever walked through Eden had ever belonged. When they thought of the precious bond that bound them together their hearts throbbed with a happiness that well-nigh overwhelmed them.

A dinner of stewed chickens and little white soda biscuits was served them, fit for a wedding breakfast, for the barmaid whispered to the cook that she was sure there was a bride and groom in the parlor they looked so happy and seemed to forget anybody else was by. But it might have been ham and eggs for all they knew what it was they ate, these two who were so happy they could but look into each other's eyes.

When the dinner was over and they started on their way again, with Albany shimmering in the hot sun in the distance, and David's arm sliding from the top of the seat to circle Marcia's waist, David whispered:

"This is our real wedding journey, dearest, and this is our bridal day. We'll go to Albany and buy you a trousseau, and then we will go wherever you wish. I can stay a whole week if you wish. Would you like to go home for a visit?"

Marcia, with shining eyes and glowing cheeks, looked her love into his face and answered: "Yes, now I would like to go home,—just for a few days—and then back to our home."

And David looking into her eyes understood why she had not wanted to go before. She was taking her husband, her husband, not Kate's, with her now, and might be proud of his love. She could go among her old comrades and be happy, for he loved her. He looked a moment, comprehended, sympathized, and then pressing her hand close—for he might not kiss her, as there was a load of hay coming their way—he said: "Darling!" But their eyes said more.

Phoebe Deane

Book Two in the *Miranda* Trilogy

upper room patiently rocking Emmeline's baby to sleep in the little wooden cradle.

She had washed the supper dishes. The tea towels hung smoothly on the little line in the wood-shed, the milk pans stood in a shining row ready for the early milking, and the kitchen, swept and garnished and dark, had settled into its nightly repose. The day had been long and full of hard work, but now as soon as the baby slept Phoebe would be free for a while before bedtime.

Unconsciously her foot tapped faster on the rocker in her impatience to be out, and the baby stirred and opened his round eyes at her, murmuring sleepily: "Pee-bee, up-e-knee! Pee-bee, up-e-knee!" Which being interpreted was a demand to be taken up on Phoebe's knee. But Phoebe, knowing from experience that she would be tied for the evening if she acceded to this request, toned her rocking into a sleepy motion, and the long lashes suddenly dropped again upon the fat little cheeks. At last the baby was asleep.

With careful touch Phoebe slowed the rocking until the motion was scarcely perceptible, waiting a minute in hushed attention to hear the soft regular breathing after the cradle had stopped. Then she rose noiselessly from her chair, and posed on tiptoe over the cradle to listen once more and be sure, before she stole softly from the room.

As she reached the door the baby heaved a long, deep sigh, doubtless of satisfaction with its toys in dreamland, and Phoebe paused, her heart standing still for an instant lest, after all, that naughty baby would waken and demand to be taken up. How many times had she just reached the door, on other hot summer nights, and been greeted by a loud cry which served to bring Emmeline to the foot of the stairs, with: "I declare, Phoebe Deane! I should think if you would half try you could keep that poor child from crying all night!" and Phoebe would be in for an hour or two of singing, and rocking and amusing the fretful baby.

But the baby slept on, and Phoebe stepped cautiously over the creaking boards in the floor, and down the stairs lightly, scarcely daring yet to breathe. Like a fairy she slipped past the sitting-room door, scarcely daring to glance in lest she would be seen, yet carrying with her the perfect mental picture of the room and its occupants as she glided out into the night.

Albert, her half-brother, was in the sitting-room. She could see his outline through the window: Albert, with his long, thin, kindly-careless face bent over the village paper he had brought home just before supper. Emmeline sat over by the table close to the candle, with her sharp features intent upon the hole in Johnny's stocking. She had been threading her needle as Phoebe passed the door, and the fretful lines between her eyes were intensified by the effort to get the thread into the eye of the needle.

Hiram Green was in the sitting-room also. He was the neighbor whose farm adjoined Albert Deane's on the side next the village. He was sitting opposite the hall door, his lank form in a splint-bottomed chair tilted back against the wall. His slouch hat was drawn down over his eyes and his hands were in his pockets. He often sat so with Albert in the evening. Sometimes Emmeline called Phoebe in and gave her some darning or mending, and then Phoebe had to listen to Hiram Green's dull talk, to escape which she had fallen into the habit of slipping out into the orchard after her work was done. But it was not always that she could elude the vigilance of Emmeline, who seemed to be determined that Phoebe should not have a moment to herself, day or night.

Phoebe wore a thin white frock—that was one of Emmeline's grievances, those thin white frocks that Phoebe would insist on wearing afternoons, so uneconomical and foolish; besides, they would wear out sometime. Emmeline felt that Phoebe should keep her mother's frocks till she married, and so save Albert having to spend so much on her setting out. Emmeline had a very poor opinion of Phoebe's dead mother; her frocks had been too fine and too daintily trimmed to belong to a sensible woman, Emmeline thought.

Phoebe flashed across the path of light that fell from the door and into the orchard like some winged creature. She loved the night with its sounds and its scents and its darkness—darkness like velvet, with depths for hiding and a glimpse of the vaulted sky set with far-away stars. Soon the summer would be gone, the branches would be bare against the stark whiteness of the snow, and all her solitude and dreaming would be over until the spring again. She cherished every moment of the summer as if it were worth rich gold. She loved to sit on the fence that separated the orchard from the meadow, and wonder what the rusty-throated crickets were saying as they chirped or moaned. She liked to listen to the argument about Katy, and wonder over and over again what it was that Katy-did and why she did it, and whether she really did it at all as the little green creatures in the branches declared, for all the world the way people were picked to pieces at the sewing bees. That was just the way they used to talk about young Mrs. Spafford. Nobody was safe from gossip—for they said Mrs. Spafford belonged to the old Schuyler family. When she came a bride to the town, how cruel tongues were, and how babbling and irresponsible, like the katydids!

The girl seated herself in h... ... ...

... ...Green stepped heavily out from the shadows and stood beside her.

Phoebe had never liked Hiram Green since the day she had seen him shove his wife out of his way and say to her roughly, "Aw, shut up, can't you? Women are forever talking about what they don't understand!" She had watched the faint color flicker into the white-cheeked wife's face and then flicker out whitely again as she tried to laugh his roughness off before Phoebe, but the girl had never forgotten it. She had been but a little girl, then, very shy and quiet, almost a stranger in the town, for her mother had just died and she had come to live with the half-brother who had been married so long that he was almost a stranger to her. Hiram Green had not noticed the young girl then, and had treated his wife as if no one were present. But Phoebe had remembered. She had grown to know and love the sad wife, to watch her gentle, patient ways with her boisterous boys, and her blowsy little girl who looked like Hiram and had none of her mother's delicacy; and her heart used to fill with indignation over the rude ways of the coarse man with his wife.

Hiram Green's wife had been dead a year. Phoebe had been with her for a week before she died, and watched the stolid husband with never a shadow of anxiety in his eyes while he told the neighbors that "Annie would be all right in a few days. It was her own fault, anyway, that she got down sick. She *would* drive over to see her mother when she wasn't able." He neglected to state that she had been making preserves and jelly for his special benefit, and had prepared dinner for twelve men who were harvesting for a week. He did not state that she only went to see her mother once in six months, and it was her only holiday.

Phoebe had listened, and inwardly fumed over the blindness and hardness of his nature. When Annie died he blamed her as he had always done, and hinted that he guessed now she was sorry she hadn't listened to him and been content at home. As if any kind of heaven wouldn't be better than Hiram Green's house to his poor disappointed wife.

But Phoebe had stood beside the dying woman as her life flickered out and heard her say: "I ain't sorry to go, Phoebe, for I'm tired. I'm that tired that I'd rather rest through eternity than do anything else. I don't think Hiram'll miss me much, and the children ain't like me. They never took after me, only the baby that died. They didn't care when I went away to Mother's. I don't think anybody in the world'll miss me, unless it's Mother, and she has the other girls, and never saw me much anyway now. Maybe the baby that died'll want me."

And so the weary eyes had closed, and Phoebe had been glad to fold the thin, work-worn hand across her breast and feel that she was at rest. The only expression of regret that Hiram gave was, "It's going to be mighty unhandy, her dying just now. Harvesting ain't over yet, and the meadow lot ought to be cut before it rains or the hull thing'll be lost." Then Phoebe felt a fierce delight in the fact that everything had to stop for Annie. Whether Hiram would or no, for very decency's sake, the work must stop and the forms of respect must be gone through with even though his heart was not in it. The rain came, too, to do Annie honor, and before the meadow lot was cut.

The funeral over, the farm work had gone on with doubled vigor, and Phoebe overheard Hiram tell Albert that "burying Annie had been mighty expensive 'count o' that thunder-storm coming so soon, it spoiled the whole south meadow; and it was just like Annie to upset everything. If she had only been a little more careful and not gone off to her mother's on pleasure, she might have kept up a little longer till harvest was over."

Phoebe had been coming into the sitting-room with her sewing when Hiram said that—it was a fall evening, not six weeks after Annie had been laid to rest—and she looked indignantly at her brother to see if he would not give Hiram a rebuke; but he only leaned back against the wall and said, "Such things were to be expected in the natural course of life," he supposed. Phoebe turned her chair so that she would not have to look at Hiram. She despised him. She wished she knew how to show him what a despicable creature he was, but as she was only a young girl she could do nothing but turn her back. Perhaps Phoebe never realized how effective that method might be. At least she never knew that all that evening Hiram Green watched the back of her shining head, its waves of bright hair bound about with a ribbon, and conforming to the beautiful shape of her head with exquisite grace. He studied the shapely shoulders and graceful movements of the indignant girl as she patiently mended Johnny's stockings, let down the hem of Alma's linsey-woolsey, and set a patch on the seat of Bertie's trousers, with her slender capable fingers. He remembered that Annie had been "pretty" when he married her, and it gratified him to feel that he had given her this tribute in his thoughts. He felt himself to be a truly sorrowful widower. At the same time he could see the good points in the girl Phoebe, even though she sat with her indignant shoulders toward him. In fact, the very sauciness of those shoulders, as the winter went by, attracted him more and more. Annie had never dared be saucy nor indifferent. Annie had loved him from the first and had unfortunately let him know it too soon and too often. It was a new experience to have someone indifferent to him. He rather liked it, knowing as he did that he had always had his own way when he got ready for it.

went by for Phoebe full of hard work, and constant companionship, and the evenings also with no leisure, and no seclusion. Phoebe had longed and longed for the spring to come, when she might get out into the night alone, and take long deep breaths that were all her own, for it seemed as if even her breathing were ordered and supervised.

But through it all, strange to say, it had never once entered Phoebe's head that Hiram was turning his thoughts toward her, and so, when he came and stood there beside her in the darkness he startled her merely because he was something she disliked, and she shrank from him as one would shrink from a snake in the grass.

Then Hiram came closer to her and her heart gave one warding thud of alarm as she shrank away from him.

"Phoebe," he said, boldly, putting out his hand to where he supposed her hands would be in the darkness—though he did not find hers, "ain't it about time you and I was comin' to an understandin'?"

Phoebe slid off the fence and backed away in the darkness. She knew the location of every apple-tree and could have led him a chase through their labyrinths if she had chosen. Her heart froze within her for fear of what might be coming, and she felt she must not run away, but stay and face it whatever it was.

"Whatever do you mean?" asked Phoebe, her voice full of antagonism.

"Mean?" said Hiram, sidling after her. "I mean it's time we set up a partnership. I've waited long enough. I need somebody to look after the children. You suit me pretty well, and I guess you'd be well enough fixed with me."

Hiram's air of assurance made Phoebe's heart chill with fear. For a moment she was speechless with horror and indignation.

Taking her silence as a favorable indication, Hiram drew near her and once more tried to find her hands in the darkness.

"I've always liked you, Phoebe," he said, insinuatingly. "Don't you like me?"

"No, No, No!" almost screamed Phoebe, snatching her hands away. "Don't ever dare to think of such a thing again!"

Then she turned and vanished in the dark like a wraith of mist, leaving the crestfallen Hiram alone, feeling very foolish and not a little astonished. He had not expected his suit to be met quite in this way.

"Phoebe, is that you?" called Emmeline's metallic voice, as she lifted her sharp eyes to peer into the darkness of the entry. "Albert, I wonder if Hiram went the wrong way and missed her?"

But Phoebe, keen of instinct, light of foot, drifted like a breath past the door, and was up in her room before Emmeline decided whether she had heard anything or not, and Albert went on reading his paper.

Phoebe sat alone in her little kitchen chamber, with the button on the door fastened, and faced the situation, looking out into the night. She kept very still that Emmeline might not know she was there. She almost held her breath for a time, for it seemed as if Hiram had so much assurance that he almost had the power to draw her from her room against her will. Her indignation and fear were beyond all possible need of the occasion. Yet every time she thought of the hateful sound of his voice as he made his cold-blooded proposition, the fierce anger boiled within her, so that she wished over and over again that she might have another opportunity to answer him and make her refusal more emphatic. Yet, when she thought of it, what could she say more than "No"? Great waves of hate surged through her soul for the man who had treated one woman so that she was glad to die, and now wanted to take her life and crush it out. With the intensity of a very young girl she took up the cause of the dead Annie, and felt like fighting for her memory.

By and by she heard Albert and Emmeline shutting up the house for the night. Hiram did not come back as she feared he might.

He half started to come, then thought better of it, and felt his way through the orchard to the other fence and climbed lumberingly over it into the road. His self-love had been wounded and he did not care to appear before his neighbors to-night. Moreover, he felt a little dazed and wanted to think things over and adjust himself to Phoebe's point of view. He felt a half resentment toward the Deanes for Phoebe's action, as if the rebuff she had given him had been their fault somehow. They should have prepared her better. They understood the situation fully. There had often been an interchange of remarks between them on the subject and Albert had responded by a nod and wink. It was tacitly understood that it would be a good thing to have the farms join, and keep them "all in the family." Emmeline, too, had often given some practical hints about Phoebe's capabilities as a housewife and mother to his wild little children. It was Emmeline who had given the hint tonight as to Phoebe's hiding-place. He began to feel as if Emmeline had somehow tricked him. He resolved to stay away from the Deanes for a long time—perhaps a week, or at any rate two or three days—certainly one day, at least. Then he began to wonder if perhaps after all Phoebe was not just flirting with him. Surely she could not

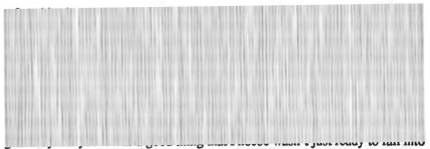

his arms, the minute he asked her, then she wouldn't be always bothering around, clinging to him and sobbing in that maddening way that Annie had.

By the time he had reached home he had reasoned himself into complaisance again, and was pretty well satisfied with himself. As he closed the kitchen door he reflected that perhaps he might fix things up a bit in the house in view of a new mistress. That would probably please Phoebe, and he certainly did need a wife. Then Hiram went to bed and slept soundly.

Emmeline came to Phoebe's door before she went to bed, calling softly, "Phoebe, are you in there?" and tapping on the door two or three times. When no answer came from the breathless girl in the dark behind the buttoned door, Emmeline lifted the latch and tried to open the door, but when she found it resisted her, she turned away and said to Albert in a fretful tone:

"I s'pose she's sound asleep, but I don't see what call she has to fasten her door every night. It looks so unsociable, as if she was afraid we weren't to be trusted. I wonder you don't speak to her about it."

But Albert only yawned good-naturedly, and said: "I don't see how it hurts you any."

"It hurts my self-respect," said Emmeline in an injured tone, as she shut her own door with a click.

Far into the night sat Phoebe, looking out of the window on the world which she loved, but could not enjoy any more. The storm of rage and shame and hatred passed, and left her weak and miserable and lonely. At last she put her head down on the window-sill and cried out softly: "Oh, Mother, Mother, Mother! If you were only here tonight! You would take me away where I would never see his hateful face again."

The symphony of the night wailed on about her, as if echoing her cry in sobbing, throbbing chords, growing fainter as the moon arose, with now and then a hint of a theme of comfort, until there came a sudden hush. Then softly, tenderly, the music changed into the night's lullaby. All the world slept, and Phoebe slept, too.

Chapter 2

Phoebe was late coming downstairs the next morning. Emmeline was already in the kitchen rattling the pots and pans significantly. Emmeline always did that when Phoebe was late, as her room was directly over the kitchen, and the degree of her displeasure could be plainly heard.

She looked up sharply as Phoebe entered, and eyed the girl keenly. There were dark circles under Phoebe's eyes, but otherwise her spirits had arisen with the morning light, and she almost wondered at the fear that had possessed her the night before. She felt only scorn now for Hiram Green, and was ready to protect herself. She went straight at her work without a word. Emmeline had long ago expressed herself with regard to the "Good-morning" with which the child Phoebe used to greet her when she came down in the morning. Emmeline said it was "a foolish waste of time, and only stuck-up folks use it. It was all of a piece with dressing up at home with no one to see you, and curling your hair"—this with a meaning look at Phoebe's bright waves. Emmeline's light, fady hair was straight as a die.

They worked in silence. The bacon was spluttering to the eggs, and Phoebe was taking up the mush when Emmeline asked:

"Didn't Hiram find you last night?" She cast one of her sideways searching looks at the girl as if she would look her through and through.

Phoebe started and dropped the spoon back into the mush where it sank with a sigh and a mutter. There was something enlightening in Emmeline's tone. Phoebe saw it at once. The family had been aware of Hiram's intention! Her eyes flashed one spark of anger, then she turned abruptly back to the kettle and went on with her work.

"Yes," she answered, inscrutably. Emmeline was always irritated at the difficulty with which she found out anything from Phoebe.

"Well, I didn't hear you come in," she complained, "you must have been out a long time."

Wary Emmeline. She had touched the spring that opened the secret.

"I wasn't out five minutes in all."

"You don't say!" said Emmeline, in surprise. "Why, I thought you said Hiram found you."

Phoebe put the cover on the dish of mush and set it on the table before she deigned any reply. Then she came over and stood beside Emmeline calmly and spoke in a cool, clear voice:

"Emmeline, did Hiram Green tell you what he was coming out to the orchard for last night?"

and did you...

Her voice was very calm and low. It reminded one of some river, with unknown depths in its shadowed bosom. Emmeline was awed by it for a moment. She laid down the bread-knife and stood and stared. Phoebe was small and dainty, with features cut like a cameo, and a singularly sweet, childlike expression when her face was in repose. That she was rarely beautiful her family had never noticed, though sometimes Albert liked to watch her as she sat sewing. She seemed to him a pleasant thing to have around, like a bright posy-bed. Emmeline thought her too frail-looking and pale. But for the moment the delicate girl was transformed. Her face shone with a light of righteous anger, and her eyes blazed dark with feeling. Two spots of lovely rose-color glowed upon her cheeks. The morning sun had just reached the south window by the table where Emmeline had been cutting bread, and it laid its golden fingers over the bright waves of brown hair in a halo round her head, as if the sun would sanction her righteous wrath. She looked like some beautiful, injured saint, and before the intensity of the maiden's emotion her sister-in-law fairly quailed.

"Fer the land! Phoebe! Now don't!" said Emmeline, in a tone conciliatory. "What if I did know? Was that any sin? You must remember your brother and I are looking to your best interests, and Hiram is considered a real fine ketch."

Slowly Phoebe's righteous wrath sank again into her heart. The fire went out of her eyes, and in its place came ice that seemed to pierce Emmeline till she felt like shrinking away.

"You're the queerest girl I ever saw," said Emmeline, fretfully restive under Phoebe's gaze. "What's the matter with you? Didn't you ever expect to have any beaux?"

Phoebe shivered as if a north blast had struck her at that last word.

"Did you mean, then," she said, coldly, in a voice that sounded as if it came from very far away, "that you thought that I would ever be willing to marry Hiram Green? Did you and Albert talk it over and think that?"

Emmeline found it hard to answer the question, put in a tone which seemed to imply a great offence. Phoebe lived on a plane far too high for Emmeline to even try to understand without a great effort. The effort wearied her.

"Well, I should like to know why you shouldn't marry him!" declared Emmeline, impatiently. "There's plenty of girls would be glad to get him."

Emmeline glanced hurriedly out of the window and saw Albert and the hired man coming to breakfast. It was time the children were down. Alma came lagging into the kitchen, asking to have her frock buttoned, and Johnny and Bertie were heard scuffling in the rooms overhead. There was no time for further conversation. Emmeline was about to dismiss the subject, but Phoebe stepped between her and the little girl and laid her small supple hands on Emmeline's stout rounding shoulders, looking her straight in the eyes.

"Emmeline, how can you possibly be so unkind as to think such a thing for me when you know how Annie suffered?"

"Oh, fiddlesticks!" said Emmeline, shoving the girl away roughly. "Annie was a milk-and-water baby who wanted to be coddled. The right woman could wind Hiram Green around her little finger. You're a little fool if you think about that. Annie's dead and gone and you've no need to trouble with her. Come, put the things on the table while I button Alma. I'm sure there never was as silly a girl as you are in this world. Anybody'd think you were a princess in disguise instead of a poor orphan dependent on her brother, and he only a *half* at that!" With which parting shot Emmeline slammed the kitchen door and called to the two little boys in a loud, harsh tone.

The crimson rose in Phoebe's cheeks till it covered face and neck in a sweet, shamed tide and threatened to bring the tears into her eyes. Her very soul seemed wrenched from its moorings at the cruel reminder of her dependence upon the bounty of this coarse woman and her husband. Phoebe felt as if she must leave the house at once never to return, only there was no place—no place in this wide world for her to go.

Then Albert appeared in the kitchen door with the hired man behind him, and the sense of her duty made her turn to work, that old, blessed refuge for those who are turned out of their bits of Eden for a time. She hurried to take up the breakfast, while the two men washed their faces at the pump and dried them on the long roller-towel that hung from the inside of the door.

"Hello, Phoebe," called Albert, as he turned to surrender his place at the comb and the looking-glass. "I say, Phoebe, you're looking like a rose this morning. What makes your cheeks so red? Anybody been kissing you this early?"

This pleasantry was intended as a joke. Albert had never said anything of the sort to her before. She felt instinctively that Emmeline had been putting ideas about her and Hiram into his head. It almost brought the tears to have Albert speak in this way. He was so uniformly kind to her and treated her as if she were still almost a child. She hated jokes of this sort, and it was all the worse because of the presence of Alma and the hired man. Alma grinned knowingly, and went over where she could look into Phoebe's face. Henry Williams, with the freedom born of his own social equality—he being the son of a neighboring

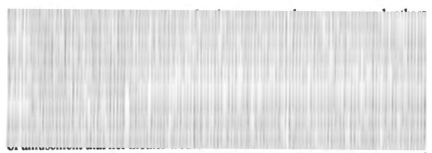

toward her, and she realized that it trifled with the most sacred and personal relations of life, it filled her with horror.

"Please don't, Albert!" she said, with trembling lips in a low voice. "Don't! I don't like it." And Alma saw with wonder, and gloated over the fact, that there were tears in Aunt Phoebe's eyes. That would be something to remember and tell. Aunt Phoebe usually kept her emotions to herself with the door shut too tight for Alma to peep in.

"No?" said Albert, perplexed. "Well, course I won't if you don't like it. I was only telling you how bright and pretty you looked and making you know how nice it was to have you around. Sit down, child, and let's have breakfast. Where's your mother, Alma?"

Emmeline entered with a flushed face, and a couple of cowed and dejected small boys held firmly by the shoulders.

Somewhat comforted by Albert's assurance, Phoebe was able to finish her work and sit down at the table; but although she busied herself industriously in putting on the baby's bib, spreading Johnny's bread, handing Alma the syrupjug, and preventing her from emptying its entire contents over her personal breakfast, inside and out, she ate nothing herself, for every time she raised her eyes she found a battalion of other eyes staring at her.

Emmeline was looking her through, in puzzled annoyance and chagrin, taking in the fact that her well-planned match-making was not running as smoothly as had been expected. Albert was studying her in the astonishing discovery that the thin, sad little half-sister he had brought into his home, who had seemed so lifeless and colorless and unlike the bouncing pretty girls of the neighborhood, had suddenly become beautiful, and was almost a woman. Several times he opened his mouth to say this in the bosom of his family, and then the dignified poise of the lovely head, or a something in the stately set of the small shoulders, or a pleading look in the large soft eyes raised to him, held him quiet; and his own eyes tried to tell her again that he would not say it if she did not like it.

Alma was staring at her between mouthfuls of mush, and, thinking how she would tell about those tears, and how perhaps she would taunt Aunt Phoebe with them sometime when she tried to "boss," when Ma was out to a sewing bee.

"Ehh! I saw you cry once, Aunt Phoebe! Ehh! Right before folks. *EHH-HH!* Cry baby! You had great big tears in your eyes, when my pa teased you. I saw um. Eh-hh-hh!" How would that sound? Alma felt the roll of the taunt now, and wished it were time to try it. She knew she could make Aunt Phoebe writhe sometime, and that was what she had always wanted to do, for Aunt Phoebe was always discovering her best laid plans and revealing them to Emmeline, and Alma longed sorely for revenge.

But the worst pair of eyes of all were those of Henry Williams, bold, and intimate, who sat directly opposite her. He seemed to feel that the way had been opened to him by Albert Deane's words, and was only waiting his opportunity to enter in. He had been admiring Phoebe ever since he came there, early in the spring, and wondering that no one seemed to think her of much account, but somehow her quiet dignity had always kept him at a distance. But now he felt he was justified in making more free with her.

"Did you hear that singing-school was going to open early this fall, Phoebe?" he asked, after many clearings of his throat.

"No," said Phoebe, without looking up. That was rather disappointing to him, for it had taken him a long time to think up that subject, and it was too much to have it disposed of so quickly, without even a glimpse of her eyes.

"Do you usually 'tend?" he asked again, after a pause filled in by Alma and the little boys in a squabble for the last scrap of mush and molasses.

"No!" said Phoebe again, her eyes still down.

"Phoebe didn't go because there wasn't anyone for her to come home with, before, Hank, but I guess there'll be plenty now," said Emmeline, with a meaningful laugh.

"Yes," said Phoebe, now looking up calmly without a flicker of the anger she was feeling. "Hester McVane and Polly said they were going this winter. If I decide to go I'm going with them. Emmeline, if you're going to dry those apples today I'd better begin them. Excuse me, please."

"You haven't eaten any breakfast, Aunt Phoebe! Ma, Aunt Phoebe never touched a bite!" announced Alma, gleefully.

"I'm not hungry this morning," said Phoebe truthfully, and went in triumph from the room, having baffled the gaze of the man and the child, and wrested the dart from her sister-in-law's arrow. It was hard on the man, for he had decided to ask Phoebe if she would go to singing-school with him. He had been a long time making up his mind as to whether he wouldn't rather ask Harriet Woodgate, but now he had decided on Phoebe he did not like to be balked in the asking. He sought her out in the wood-shed where she sat, and gave his invitation, but she only made her white fingers fly the faster round the apple she was peeling as she answered: "Thank you, it won't be necessary for you to go with me if I decide to go." Then as she perceived by his prolonged "H'm-m-m!" that he was about to urge his case she arose hastily, exclaiming: "Emmeline, did

you call me? I'm coming," and vanished into the h...
after her...

...culture had been hers that these new relatives did not know nor understand. What to her had been necessities were to them foolish nonsense. She looked at Albert wistfully sometimes, for she felt if it were not for Emmeline she might perhaps in time make him understand and change a little in some ways. But Emmeline resented any suggestions she made to Albert, especially when he good-naturedly tried to please her. Emmeline resented almost everything about Phoebe. She had resented her coming in the first place. Albert was grown up and living away from home when his father married Phoebe's mother, a delicate, refined woman, far different from himself. Emmeline felt that Albert had no call to take the child in at all for her to bring up when she was not a "real relation." Besides, Emmeline had an older sister of her own who would have been glad to come and live with them and help with the work, but of course there was no room nor excuse for her with Phoebe there, and they could not afford to have them both, although Albert was ready to take in any stray chick or child that came along. It was only Emmeline's forbidding attitude that kept him from adopting all the lonely creatures, be they animal or human, that appealed to his sympathy. There were a great many nice points about Albert, and Phoebe recognized them gratefully, the more as she grew older, though he *would* come to the table in his shirt-sleeves and eat his pie with his knife.

But in spite of her nature this morning Phoebe had much ado to keep from crying. The annoyances increased as the day grew, and if it had not been for her work she would have felt desperate. As it was she kept steadily at it, conquering everything that came in her way. The apples fairly flew out of their coats into the pan, and Emmeline, glancing into the back shed, noting the set of the forbidding young shoulders, and the undaunted tilt of the head, also the fast diminishing pile of apples on the floor and the multiplying quarters in the pans, forbore to disturb her. Emmeline was far-seeing, and she was anxious to have those apples off her mind. With Phoebe in that mood she knew it would be done before she could possibly get around to help. There was time enough for remarks later; meantime perhaps it was just as well to let my lady alone until she came to her senses a little.

The old stone sun-dial by the side door shadowed the hour of eleven, and the apples were almost gone from the pile on the floor, when Emmeline came into the back shed with a knife and sat down to help. She looked at Phoebe sharply as she seated herself with a show of finishing things up in a hurry, but she intended, and Phoebe knew she did, to have it out with the girl before her.

Phoebe did not help her to begin. Her fingers flew faster than ever, though they ached with the motion, and the juicy knife against her sensitive skin made every nerve cry out to be released. With set lips she went on with her work, though she longed to fling the apple away and run out to the fields for a long, deep breath.

Emmeline had pared two whole apples before she began, in a conciliatory tone. She had eyed Phoebe furtively several times, but the girl might have been a sphinx, or some lovely mountain wrapped about with mist, for all she could read of her mood. This was what Emmeline could not stand, this distant, proud silence that would not mix with other folk. She longed to break through it by force, and reduce the pride to dust. It would do her heart good to see Phoebe humbled for once, she often told herself.

"Phoebe, I don't see what you find to dislike so in Hiram Green," she began. "He's a good man. He always attends church on Sundays."

"I would respect him more if he was a good man in his home on week-days. Anybody can be good once a week before people. A man needs to be good at home in his family."

"Well, now, he pervides well for his family. Look at his comfortable home, and his farm. There isn't a finer in this county. He has his name up all round this region for the fine stock he raises. You can't find a barn like his anywhere. It's the biggest and most expensive in this town."

"He certainly has a fine barn," said Phoebe, "but I don't suppose he expects his family to live in it. He takes better care of his stock than he does of his family. Look at the house —"

Phoebe's eyes waxed scornful, and Emmeline marvelled. She was brought up to think a barn a most important feature of one's possessions.

"His house is away back from the road out of sight," went on Phoebe, "Annie used to hunger for a sight of people going by on the road when she sat down to sew in the afternoon, but there was that great barn right out on the road, and straight in front of the house. He ought to have put the barn back of the house. And the house is a miserable affair. Low, and ugly, and with two steps between the kitchen and the shed, enough to kill one who does the work. He ought to have built Annie a pleasant home up on that lovely little knoll of maples, where she could have seen out and down the road, and have had a little company now and then. She might have been alive today if she had one-half the care and attention that Hiram gave the stock!" Phoebe's words were bitter and vehement.

"It sounds dreadful . . .

. . . . back her chair and left the room. Emmeline felt that she had failed again to make any impression on her sister-in-law. It maddened her almost to distraction to have a girl like that around her, a girl who thought everything beneath her and who criticized the customs of the entire neighborhood. She was an annoyance and a reproach. Emmeline felt she would like to get rid of her if it could be done in a legitimate way.

At dinner, Henry Williams looked at Phoebe meaningly and asked if she made the pie. Phoebe had to own that she did.

"It tastes like you, nice and sweet," he declared, gallantly. Whereat Albert laughed, and Alma leaned forward to look into her aunt's flaming face, impudently.

"Betsy Green says she thinks her pa is going to get her a new ma," she remarked, knowingly, when the laugh had subsided. "And Betsy says she bet she knows who 'tis, too!"

"You shut up!" remarked Emmeline to her offspring, in a low tone, giving Alma a dig under the table. But Phoebe hastily drew back her chair and fled from the table.

There was a moment of uncomfortable silence after Phoebe left the room. Emmeline felt that things had gone too far. Albert asked what was the matter with Phoebe, but instead of answering him Emmeline yanked Alma from the table and out into the wood-shed, where a whispered scolding was administered as a sort of obligato solo to the accompaniment of some stinging cuts from a little switch that hung conveniently on the wall.

Alma returned to the table chastened outwardly, but inwardly vowing vengeance on her aunt, her anger in no wise softened by the disappearance of her piece of pie with Bertie. Her mother told her she deserved to lose her pie, and she determined to get even with Aunt Phoebe even if another switching happened.

Phoebe did not come downstairs again that afternoon. Emmeline hesitated about sending for her, and finally decided to wait until she came. The unwilling Alma was pressed into service to dry the dishes, and the long, yellow, sunny afternoon dragged drowsily on, while Phoebe lay upon her bed up in her kitchen chamber, and pressed her aching eyeballs hard with her cold fingers, wondering why so many tortures were coming to her all at once.

Chapter 3

Hiram Green kept his word to himself and did not go to see Phoebe for two evenings. By that time Emmeline had begun to wonder what in the world Phoebe had said to him to keep him away when he seemed so anxious to get her; and Phoebe, with the hopefulness of youth, had decided that her trouble in that direction was over. But the third evening he arrived promptly, attired with unusual care, and asked Emmeline if he might see Phoebe alone.

It happened that Phoebe had finished her work in the kitchen and gone up to rock the baby to sleep. Emmeline swept the younger children out of the sitting-room with alacrity, and called Albert sharply to help her with something in the kitchen, sending Alma up at once with a carefully worded message to Phoebe. Emmeline was relieved to see Hiram again. She knew by his face that he meant business this time, and she hoped to see Phoebe conquered at once.

"Ma says you please"—the word sounded strangely on Alma's unloving lips—"come down to the settin'-room now—*to once,*" she added.

The baby was just dropping asleep and roused of course at Alma's boisterous tone. Phoebe nodded, and shoved the child from the room, keeping the cradle going all the time. The naughty little girl delighted to have authority behind her evil doing, and called loudly:

"Well, ma wants you RIGHT OFF, *so,* and I don't care!" as she thumped down stairs with her copper-toed shoes.

The baby gave a crow of glee and arose to the occasion in his cradle, but Phoebe resolutely disregarded the call below, and went on rocking until the little restless head was still on its pillow again. Then she stole softly down to the sitting-room, her eyes blinded by the darkness where she had been sitting, and explained quietly as she entered the room, "I couldn't come sooner. Alma woke the baby again."

Hiram, quite mollified by the gentle tone of explanation, arose, blandly answering: "Oh, that's all right. I'm glad to see you now you're here," and went forward with the evident intention of taking both her hands in his.

Phoebe rubbed her blinded eyes and looked up in horror! Knowing Alma stood behind the crack of the door and watched it all with wicked joy.

"I beg your pardon, Mr. Green, I thought Emmeline was in here. She sent for me. Excuse me, I must find her."

"Oh, that's all right!" said Hiram, easily, putting out his hand and shutting the door sharply in Alma's impudent face, thereby almost pinching her inquisitive nose in the crack. "She don't expect you, Emmeline don't. She sent for you to see me. I asked her could I see you alone. She understands all about us, good would it do to run away? She had tried that once and it did not work. She must speak to him decidedly and end the matter. She summoned all her dignity and courage and backed over to the other side of the room, where a single chair stood.

"Won't you sit down, Mr. Green?" she said, trying to get the tremble out of her voice.

"Why, yes, I will; let's sit right here together," he said, sitting down at one end of the couch and making room for her. "Come, you sit here beside me, Phoebe, and then we can talk better. It's more sociable."

Phoebe sat down on the chair opposite him.

"I would rather sit here, Mr. Green," she said.

"Well, of course, if you'd rather," he said, reluctantly, "but it seems to be kind of unsociable. And say, Phoebe, I wish you wouldn't 'mister' me any more. Can't you call me Hiram."

"I would rather not."

"Say, Phoebe, that sounds real unfriendly," blamed Hiram, in a tone which suggested he would not be trifled with much longer.

"Did you wish to speak to me, Mr. Green?" said Phoebe, her clear eyes looking at him steadily over the candle-light, with the bearing of a queen.

"Well, yes," he said, straightening up, and hitching a chair around to the side nearer to her. "I thought we better talk that matter over a little that I was mentioning to you several nights ago."

"I don't think that is necessary, Mr. Green," answered Phoebe, quickly; "I thought I made you understand that that was impossible."

"Oh, I didn't take account of what you said that night," said Hiram. "I saw you was sort of upset, not expecting me out there in the dark, so I thought I better come round again after you had plenty chance to think over what I said."

"I couldn't say anything different if I thought over it a thousand years," declared Phoebe, with characteristic emphasis. Hiram Green was not thin-skinned, and did not need saving. It was just as well to tell the truth and be done with it.

But the fellow was in no wise daunted. He rather admired Phoebe the more for her vehemence, for here was a prize that promised to be worth his winning.

For the first time as he looked at her he felt his blood stir with a sense of pleasure such as one feels in a well matched race, where one is yet sure of winning.

"Aw, git out!" scouted Hiram, pleasantly. "That ain't the way to talk. Course you're young yet, and ain't had much experience, but you certainly had time enough to consider the matter all this year I been comin' to see you."

Phoebe arose with two red spots burning on her cheeks.

"Coming to see me!" she gasped. "You didn't come to see me!"

"Aw, git out now, Phoebe. You needn't pertend you didn't know I was comin' to see you. Who did you s'pose I was comin' to see, then?"

"I supposed of course you were coming to see Albert," said Phoebe, her voice settling into that deep calm that betokened she was overwhelmed.

"Albert! You s'posed I was comin' to see Albert every night! Aw, yes, you did a whole lot! Phoebe, you're a sly one. You must of thought I was gettin' fond of Albert!"

"I did not think anything about it," said Phoebe, haughtily, "and you may be sure, Mr. Green, if I had dreamed of such a thing I would have told you it was useless."

There was something in her tone and manner that ruffled the self-assurance of Hiram Green. Up to this minute he had persuaded himself that Phoebe was but acting the part of a coy and modest maiden who wished to pretend that she never dreamed that he was courting her. Now a suspicion began to glimmer in his consciousness that perhaps, after all, she was honest, and had not suspected his attentions. Could it be possible that she did not care for them, and really wished to dismiss him? Hiram could not credit such a thought. Yet as he looked at the firm set of her lips he was bewildered.

"What on earth makes you keep sayin' that?" he asked, in an irritated tone. "What's your reason for not wantin' to marry me?"

"There are so many reasons that I wouldn't know where to begin," answered the girl, shortly.

Hiram gave his shoulders a little shake, as if to rouse himself. Had he heard her words aright?

"What reasons?" he growled, frowning. He began to feel that Phoebe was trifling with him. He would make her understand that he would not endure much of that.

Phoebe looked troubled. She wished he would not insist on further talk, but she was too honest and too angry not to tell the exact truth.

"The first and greatest reason of all is that I do not love you, and never could," she said vehemently, looking him straight in the eyes.

"Shucks!" said Hiram, laughing. "I don't mind that a mite. In fact, I think it's an advantage. Folks mostly get over it when they do feel that sentimental kind of way. It don't last but a few weeks, anyhow, and it's better to begin on a practical basis I think. That was the trouble with Annie, she was so blamed sentimental she hadn't time to get dinner. I think

better. You're

.....gs at home, but I can

.... wantin' to get ready more, only don't be long about

it. As I said, I don't mind about the love part. That'll come all right. And you remember, Phoebe, if I do say so as shouldn't, there's plenty of girls around here would be glad to marry me if they got the chance."

"Then by all means, let them marry you!" said Phoebe, grandly, steadying her trembling limbs for flight. "I shall never, never marry you! Good-night, Mr. Green."

She swept him a ceremonious bit of courtesy at the door, like a flutter of wings as a bird takes affright, and was gone before he fully took it in. He reached out detaining hands towards her in protest, but it was too late. The latch clicked behind her, and he could hear the soft stir of her garments on the stairs. She had fled to her room. He heard the button on her door creak and turn. He unfolded his lank limbs from their comfortable pose around the legs of his chair, and went after her as far as the door, but the stairway was quiet and dark. He could hear Albert and Emmeline in the kitchen. He stood a moment in puzzled chagrin, going over his interview and trying to make it all out. What mistake had he made? He had failed, that was certain. It was a new experience and one that angered him, but somehow the anger was numbed by the remembrance of the look of the girl's eyes, the dainty movements of her hands, the set of her shapely head. He did not know that he was fascinated by her beauty; he only knew that a dogged determination to have her for his own in spite of everything was settling down upon him.

Albert and Emmeline were conversing in low tones in the kitchen when the door was flung open and Hiram Green stepped in, his brow dark, his eyes sullen. He felt that Emmeline owned him some explanation of Phoebe's behavior. He had come for it.

"I can't make her out!" he muttered, as he flung himself into a kitchen chair, "she's just for all the world like a wild colt. When you think you have her she gives you the slip and is off further away than when you begun. I think mebbe ef I had her where she couldn't get away I'd be able to find out the difficulty."

"Better take her out riding," suggested Albert, slyly, "and drive fast. She couldn't get out very well then."

"I ain't sure," growled Hiram, "the way she looked she might jump over a precipice. What's the matter with her anyway?" turning to Emmeline, as though she were responsible for the whole of womankind. "Is there anybody else? She ain't got in with Hank Williams, has she?"

"She won't look at him," declared Emmeline positively. "He tried to get to go to singin'-school with her just today and she shut him off short. What reason did she give you?"

"She spoke about not havin' proper affection," he answered diffidently, "but if I was dead sure that was the hull trouble I think I could fix her up. I'd like to get things settled 'fore winter comes on. I can't afford to waste time like this."

"I think I know what's the matter of her," said Emmeline, mysteriously. "She isn't such a fool as to give up a good chance in life for reasons of affection, though it is mighty high-soundin' to say so. But there's somethin' back of it all. I shouldn't wonder, Hiram, if she's tryin' you to see if you want her enough to fix things handy the way she'd like em."

"What do you mean?" asked Hiram, gruffly, showing sudden interest. "Has she spoke of anything to you?"

"Well, she did let on that your house was too far back from the street to be pleasant, and she seemed to think the barn had the best situation. She spoke about the knoll being a good place for a house."

Hiram brightened. If Phoebe had taken interest in his affairs to say all this surely she was not so indifferent after all.

"You don't say!" said Hiram, meditatively. "When did she say that?"

"Just today," Emmeline answered.

"Well, if that's the hitch why didn't she say so? She didn't seem shy."

"Mebbe she was waitin' for you to ask her what she wanted."

"Well, she didn't wait long. She lit out before I had a chance to half talk things over."

"She's young yet, you know," said Emmeline, in a soothing tone. "Young folks take queer notions. I shouldn't wonder but she hates to go to that house and live way back from the road that way. She ain't much more than a child, anyway, in some things — though she's first class to work."

"Well," said Hiram, reluctantly, "I been thinkin' the house needed fixin' up some. I don't know as I should object to buildin' all new. The old house would come in handy fer the men. Bill would like to have his ma and keep house right well. It would help me out in one way, fer Bill is gettin' uneasy, and I'd rather spare any man I've got than Bill, he works so steady and good. Say, you might mention to Phoebe, if you like, that I'm thinkin' of buildin' a new house. Say I'd thought of the knoll for a location. Think that would ease her up a little?"

"All right, I'll see what can be done," said Emmeline, importantly.

...had been entrusted with a commission worthy of her best efforts, and surely Phoebe would listen now.

Up in her kitchen chamber the hum of their conversation came to Phoebe, as she sat with burning cheeks looking wildly into the darkness. She did not hear the nightly symphony as it sang on all about the house. She was thinking of what she had been through, and wondering if she had finally freed herself from the hateful attentions of Hiram Green. Would he take her answer as final, or not? She thought not, judging from his nature. He was one of those men who never give up what they have set themselves to get, be it sunny pasture lot, young heifer, or pretty wife. She shuddered at the thought of many more encounters such as she had passed through tonight. It was all dreadful to her. It touched a side of life that jarred her inexpressibly. It made the world seem an intolerable place to her.

She fell to wondering what her life would have been if her mother had lived — a quiet little home, of course, plain and sweet and cosy, with plenty of hard work, but always some one to sympathize. Her frail little mother had not been able to stand the rough world and the hard work, but she had left behind her a memory of gentleness and refinement that could never be wholly crushed out of her young daughter's heart, no matter how much she came in contact with the coarse, rude world. Often the girl in her silent meditations would take her mother into her thoughts and tell her all that had passed in her life that day. But tonight she felt that were her mother here, and helpless to help her, she could not bear to tell her of this torturing experience through which she was passing. She knew instinctively that a living mother such as hers had been would shrink with horror from the thought of seeing her child united to a man like Hiram Green —would rather see her dead than married to him.

Somehow she could not get the comfort from thinking of her mother tonight that she usually could. She wanted some close, tangible help, some one all-wise and powerful; someone that could tell what life meant, and what God meant her particular life to be, and make her sure she was right in her fierce recoil from what life now seemed to be offering. She felt sure she was right, yet she wanted another to say so also, to take her part against the world that was troubling her. There were perhaps people who could do that for her if she only dared to go to them, but what would they think!

Her young pride arose and bore her up. She must tell nobody but God. And so thinking, she knelt timidly down and tried to pour out her proud, hurt spirit in a prayer. She had always prayed, but had never felt that it meant anything to her until tonight; and when she arose, not knowing what she had asked, or if indeed she had asked anything for herself, she yet felt stronger to face her life, which somehow stretched out ahead in one blank of monotonous tortures.

Meantime the man who desired to have her, and the woman who desired to have him have her, were forming their plans for a regular campaign against her.

...was a perfect

...se, as though it did her good to push ...tient feet. She was not walking towards the village, ...open country, past the farm, where presently the road turned ...skirted a maple grove. But she did not pause here, though she dearly loved the crimson maple leaves that carpeted the ground alluringly. On she went, as though her only object was to get away, as though she would like to run if there were not danger she might be seen.

A farm wagon was coming. She strained her eyes ahead to see who was driving. If it should happen to be Hank, and he should stop to talk! Oh! She put her hand on her heart and hurried forward, for she would not go back. She wished she had worn her sunbonnet, for then she might hide her in its depths, but her coming away had been too sudden for that. She had merely untied her large apron, and flung it from her as she started. Even now she knew not whether it hung upon the chair where she had been sitting shelling dried beans, or whether it adorned the rosebush by the kitchen door. She had not looked back to see, and did not care.

No one knew it was her birthday, or, if they knew, they had not remembered. Perhaps that made it harder to stay and shell beans and bear Emmeline's talk.

Matters had been going on in much the way they had gone all summer — that is, outwardly; Hiram Green had spent the evenings regularly talking with Albert, while Emmeline darned stockings, and Phoebe escaped upstairs when she could, and sewed with her back to the guest when she could not. Phoebe had taken diligent care that Hiram should have no more tete-a-tetes with her, even at the expense of having to spend many evenings in her dark room when all outdooors was calling her with the tender lovely sounds of the dying summer. Grimly and silently she went through the days of work.

Emmeline, since the morning she attempted to discuss Hiram's proposed new house and found Phoebe utterly unresponsive, had held her peace. Not that she was by any means vanquished, but as she made so little headway in talking to the girl she concluded that it would be well to let her alone awhile. In fact Albert had advised that line of action in his easy, kindly way and Emmeline, partly because she did not know how else to move her sister-in-law, shut her lips and went around with an air of offended dignity. She spoke disagreeably whenever it was necessary to speak at all to Phoebe, and whenever the girl came downstairs in other than her working garments she looked her disapproval in unspeakable volumes.

Phoebe went about her daily routine without noticing, much as a bird might whose plumage was being criticized. She could not help putting herself in dainty array, even though the materials at hand might be only a hair brush and a bit of ribbon. Her hair was always waving about her lovely face, softly and smoothly, and a tiny rim of white collar outlined the throat, even in her homespun morning gown, which sat upon her like a young queen's garment.

It was all hateful to Emmeline—"impudent," she styled it, in speaking to herself. She had tried the phrase once in a confidence to Albert—for Phoebe was only a half- sister; why should Albert care?—but somehow Albert had not understood. He had almost resented it. He said he thought Phoebe always looked "real neat and pretty" and he "liked to see her round." This had fired Emmeline's jealousy, although she would not have owned it. Albert made so many remarks of this sort that Emmeline felt they would spoil his sister and make her unbearable to live with. Albert used to talk like that to her when they were first married, but she told him it was silly for married people to say such things, and he never gave her any more compliments. She had not missed them herself, but it was another thing to find him speaking that way about his sister—so foolish for a grown-up man to care about looks.

But Emmeline continued to meditate upon Phoebe's "impudent" attire, until this afternoon of her birthday the thoughts had culminated in words.

Phoebe had gone upstairs after the dinner work was done, and had come down arrayed in a gown that Emmeline had never seen. It was of soft buff merino, trimmed with narrow lines of brown velvet ribbon, and a bit of the same velvet around the white throat held a small plain gold locket that nestled in the white hollow of Phoebe's neck as if it loved to be there. The brown hair was dressed in its usual way except for a knot of brown velvet. It was a simple girlish costume, and Phoebe wore it with the same easy grace she wore her homespun, which made it doubly annoying to Emmeline, who felt that Phoebe had no right to act as if she was doing nothing unusual.

Years ago when the child Phoebe had come to live with them she had brought with her some boxes and trunks, and a few pieces of furniture for her own room. They were things of her mother's which she wished to keep. Emmeline had gone carefully over the collection with ruthless hand and critical tongue, casting out what she considered useless, laying aside what she considered unfit for present use, and freely commenting upon all she saw. Phoebe, fresh from her mother's grave, and the memory of that mother's living words, had stood by in stony silence, holding back by main force the angry tears that tried to get their way, and letting none of the storm of passion that surged

through her heart be seen. But when Emmeli~~
haircovered trunk and demanded the ~~
string that held it round h~~
her little sorr~~

~~ess I'm
~~ything about. I've
~~uis."

~~ she continued to talk steadily:
~~, Emmeline. My mother packed them all away carefully
~~ and rosemary for me. She did not wish them opened till I got ready
to open them myself. I do not want them opened."

Emmeline had been very angry at that, and told the little girl she would not have any such talk around her, and demanded the key at once, but Phoebe said:

"I have told you it is not necessary. These are my things and I will not have any more of them opened, and I will not give you the key."

That was open rebellion and Emmeline carried her in high dudgeon to Albert. Albert had looked at the pitiful little face with its pleading eyes under which dark circles sat mournfully, and—sided with Phoebe. He said that Phoebe was right, the things were hers, and he did not see for his part why Emmeline wanted to open them. From that hour Emmeline had hard work to tolerate her little half-sister-in-law, and the enmity between them had never grown less. Little did Phoebe know, whenever she wore one of the frocks from that unopened trunk, how she roused her sister-in-law's wrath.

The trunk had been stored in the deep closet in Phoebe's room, and the key had never left its resting-place against her heart, night or day. Sometimes Phoebe had unlocked it in the still hours of the early summer mornings when no one else was stirring, and had looked long and lovingly at the garments folded within. It was there she kept the daguerreotype of the mother who was the idol of her child heart. Her father she could not remember, as he died when she was but a year old. In the depths of that trunk were laid several large packages, labeled. The mother had told her about them before she died, and with her own hand had placed the boxes in the bottom of the trunk. The upper one was labeled, "For my dear daughter Phoebe Deane on her eighteenth birthday."

For several days before her birthday Phoebe had felt an undertone of excitement. It was almost time to open the box which had been laid there over eight years ago by that beloved hand. Phoebe did not know what was in that box, but she knew it was something her mother put there for her. It contained her mother's thought for her grown-up daughter. It was like a voice from the grave. It thrilled her to think of it.

On her birthday morning she had awakened with the light, and slipping out of bed had applied the little black key to the keyhole. Her fingers trembled as she turned the lock, and opened the lid, softly lest she should wake someone. She wanted this holy gift all to herself now, this moment when her soul would touch again the soul of the lost mother.

Carefully she lifted out the treasures in the trunk until she reached the box, then drew it forth, and placing the other things back closed the trunk and locked it. Then she took the box to her bed and untied it. Her heart was beating so fast she felt almost as if she had been running. She lifted the cover. There lay the buff merino in all its beauty, complete even to the brown knot for the hair, and the locket which had been her mother's at eighteen. And there on the top lay a letter in her mother's handwriting. Ah! This was what she had hoped for — a real word from her mother which should be a guide to her in this grown-up life that was so lonely and different from the life she had lived with her mother. She hugged the letter to her heart and cried over it and kissed it. She felt that she was nestling her head in her mother's lap as she cried, and it gave her aching, longing heart a rest just to think so.

But there were sounds of stirring in the house, and Phoebe knew that she would be expected in the kitchen before long, so she dried her tears and read her letter.

Before it was half done the clatter in the kitchen had begun, and Emmeline's strident voice was calling up the stairway: "Phoebe! Phoebe! Are you going to stay up there all day?"

Phoebe had cast a wistful look at the rest of her letter, patted the soft folds of her merino tenderly, swept it out of sight into her closet, and answered Emmeline pleasantly, "Yes, I'm coming!" Not even the interruption could quite dim her pleasure on this day of days. She sprang up conscience stricken. She had not meant to be so late.

It did not take long to dress, and with the letter tucked in with the key against her heart she hurried down, only to meet Emmeline's frowning words, and be ordered around like a little child. Emmeline had been very disagreeable ever since Hiram Green had proposed to Phoebe.

The morning had been crowded full of work and the letter had no chance, except to crackle lovingly against the blue homespun.

The thought of the buff merino upstairs made her thrill with pleasure, and the morning passed away happily in spite of Emmeline and hard work. Words from her mother's hastily read letter came floating to her, and calling. She longed to pull it out and read once more to be sure just how they had been phrased. But there was no time.

After dinner, however, as soon as she had finished the dishes, and while Emmeline was looking after something in the wood-shed, she slipped away upstairs, without, as usual, asking is there was anything else to be done. She had

decided that she would put on her new frock, for it had
in the letter, and go down to the village an
It was two years since Mrs. Sn
and she had never pl
something

her
a maple grove
ed; so with all haste she
knot, and put on the pretty frock. For
ont of the glass and looked at herself thrilling
this dress was planned by her dear mother, and that the
had set every perfect stitch in its place. And this girl in the glass
was the daughter her mother had wished her to be, at least in outward appearance.
Was she also in heart life? She looked earnestly at the face in the glass, longing
to ask herself many questions and unable to answer. Then with the letter safely
hidden she hurried down.

But her conscience would not let her go out the front door unobserved as
she had planned. It seemed a mean, sneaking thing to do on her birthday. She
would be open and frank. She would step into the kitchen and tell Emmeline
that she was going out for the afternoon. That would be the way her mother
would desire her to do. So, though much against her own desire, she went.

And there sat Emmeline with a large basket of dried beans to be shelled
and put away for the winter. Phoebe stood aghast, and hesitated.

"Well, really!" said Emmeline, looking up severely at the apparition in buff
that stood in the doorway. "Are you going to play the fine lady while I shell
beans? It seems to me that's rather taking a high hand for one who's dependent
on her relatives for every mouthful she eats, and seems likely to be for the rest
of her days. That's gratitude, that is. But I take notice you eat the beans —oh,
yes! the beans that Albert provides, and I shell, while you gallivant round in
party clo'es."

The hateful speech brought the color to Phoebe's cheeks.

"Emmeline," she broke in, "you know I didn't know you wanted those beans
shelled today. I would have done them this morning between times if you had
said so."

"You didn't know," sniffed Emmeline. "You knew the beans was to shell,
and you knew this was the first chance to do it. Besides, there wasn't any between
times this morning. You didn't get up till most noon. Everything was clear put
back, and now you wash your white hands and dress up, no matter what the
folks that keeps you have to do. That wasn't the way *I* was brought up, if
I *didn't* have a fine lady mother like yours. *My* mother taught me *gratitude*."

Phoebe reflected on the long hard days of work she had done for Emmeline without a word of praise or thanks, work as hard, and harder than any wage-earner in the house in the same position would have been expected to do. She had earned her board and more, and she knew it. Her clothes she made altogether from the stores her mother had left for her. She had not cost Albert a cent in that way. Nevertheless, her conscience hurt her because of the late hour of her coming down that morning. With one desperate glance at the size of the bean-basket, and a rapid calculation how long it would take her to finish them, she siezed her clean apron that hung behind the door and enveloped herself in it.

"I have wanted to go for a long time, but if those beans have got to be done this afternoon I can do them first."

She said it calmly, and went at the beans with determined fingers, that fairly made the beans shiver as they hustled out of their resisting withered pods.

Emmeline sniffed.

"You're a pretty figure shellin' beans in thay rig. I s'pose that's one of your ma's contoguments, but if she had any sense at all she wouldn't want you to put it on. It ain't fit for ordinary life. It might do to have your picture took in, or go to a weddin', but you do look like a fool in it now. Besides, if it's worth anything, an' it looks like there was good stuff in it, you'll spoil it shellin' beans."

Phoebe shelled away feverishly and said not a word. Her eyes looked as though ther might be anything behind their lower lashes, from tears to fire-flashes. Emmeline surveyed her angrily. Her wrath was on the boiling point and she felt the time had come to let it boil.

A little bird, perched on the roof of the barn, piped out: "Phoe-bee! Phoebee!" The girl lifted her head toward the outside door and listened. The bird seemed to be a reminder that there were other things in the world worthwhile besides having one's own way even on one's birthday. The paper in her bosom crackled, and Emmeline eyed her suspiciously, but the swift fingers shelled on unremittingly.

"I think the time has come to have an understandin'," said Emmeline, raising her voice harshly. "If you won't talk to me, Albert'll have to tend to you, but I'm the proper one to speak, and I'm goin' to do it. I won't have this sort of thing goin' on in my house. It's a disgrace. I'd like to know what you mean, treatin' Hiram Green in this way? He's a respectable man, and you've no call to keep him danglin' after you forever. People'll talk about you, and I won't have it!"

There was an angry flash in Emmeline's eyes. She had made up her mind to have her say.

Phoebe raised astonished eyes to her sister-in-law's excited face.

"I don't know what you mean, Emmeline. I h[...]
with Hiram Green. I can't prevent h[...]
I wish I could, for i[...]

[...] not
[...] ppose, that he comes
[...] not so much of a little fool as you
[...] well enough Hiram Green is just waitin' round on
[...], and I say it's high time you stopped this nonsense, keepin' a
respectable man danglin' after you forever just to show off your power over him,
and when all the time he needs a housekeeper, and his children are runnin' wild.
You'll get your pay, miss, when you do marry him. Those young ones will be
so wild you'll never get 'em tamed. They'll lead you a life of it. It's a strange
way for any decent girl to act. If it's a new house you're waiting' on I guess
you can have your way at once by just sayin' so. And I think it's time for you
to speak, for I tell you plainly it ain't likely another such good chance'll come
your way ever, and I don't suppose you want to be a hanger-on all your life on
people that can't afford to keep you."

Phoebe's fingers were still shelling beans rapidly, but her eyes were on
Emmeline's angry face.

"I thought I had told you," she said, and her voice was steady, "that I would
never marry Hiram Green. Nothing and nobody on earth could make me marry
him. I despise him. You know perfectly well that the things you are saying are
wrong. It is not my fault that he comes here. I do not want him to come and
he knows it. I have told him I will never marry him. I do not want him to build
a house nor do anything else, for nothing that he could do would make any
difference."

"You certainly are a little fool!" screamed Emmeline, "to let such a chance
go. If he wasn't entirely daft about you he'd give you up at once. Well, what
are you intendin' to do then? Answer me that! Are you layin' out to live on Albert
the rest of your life? It's best to know what to expect and be prepared. Answer
me!" she demanded again, as Phoebe dropped her eyes to hide the sudden tears
that threatened to overwhelm her calm.

"I don't know." The girl tried to say it quietly, but the angry woman snatched
the words from her lips and tossed them back:

"You don't know! You don't know! Well, you better know! I can tell you
right now that there's going' to be a new order of things. If you stay here any
longer you've got to do as I say. You're not goin' on your high and mighty way

doin' as you please an hour longer. And to begin with you can march upstairs and take off that ridiculous rig of your foolish mother's —"

Phoebe shoved the kitchen chair back with a sharp noise on the bare floor, and stood up, her face white with anger.

"Emmeline," said she, and her voice was low and controlled, but reminded Emmeline somehow of the first low rumbling of a storm, and when she looked at Phoebe's white face she fancied a flash like livid lightning passed over it. "Emmeline, don't you dare to speak my mother's name in that way! I will not listen to you!"

Then in the pause of the clashing voices the little bird from the weathervane on the barn called out again: "Phoebee! Phoe-bee!"

And it was then that Phoebe cast her apron from her and went through the kitchen door, into the golden glorious October afternoon, away from the pitiless tongue, and the endless beans, — and the sorrow of her life.

The little bird on the weathervane left his perch and flew along from tree to tree, calling joyously, "Phoe-bee! Phoe-bee!" as she went down the road. He seemed as glad as though she were a comrade come to roam the woods with him. The sunlight lingered lovingly on the buff merino, as though it were a piece of itself come out to meet it, and she flitted breathlessly down the way, she knew not whither, only to get out and away.

Queer, wintry-looking worms crawled lazily to their homes across the long white road, woolly caterpillars in early fur overcoats. Large leaves floated solemnly down to their long home. Patches of rank grass rose green and pert, passionately pretending that summer was not done, scorning the deadness all about them. All the air was filled with a golden haze and Phoebe in her golden, sunlit garments, seemed a part of it.

Th...

...ster-in-

... on her birthday; to feel so
... me where one was welcome, save that
...ram Green's house! Oh, why was it that one
...u become a torture?

...gone a long distance before her mind cleared sufficiently to think
...re she was going. The sight of a distant red farm-house made her pause in
her wild walk. If she went on she would be seen from the well-watched windows
of that red house, and the two women who lived there were noted alike for their
curiosity and for their ability to impart news.

In sudden panic Phoebe climbed a fence and struck out across the field
toward Chestnut Ridge, a small hill rising to the left of the village. There she
might hope to be alone a little while and think it out, and perhaps creep close
to her mother once more through the letter which she pressed against her heart.
She hurried over the rough stubble of the field, gathering her buff garments with
the other hand to hold them from any detaining briars. She seemed like some
bright golden leaf blowing across the pasture to frolic with the other leaves on
the nut-crowned hillside.

Breathless at last she reached the hill and found a great log where she sat
down to read her letter.

My dear little grown-up girl, it began, and as Phoebe read the previous words
again the tears burst from her smarting eyes, welling up from her aching heart,
and she buried her face in the letter and stained it with her tears.

It was some time before she could conquer herself and read farther.

*This is your eighteenth birthday, dear child, and I have thought so much about
you and how you will be when you are a young woman, that I want to be with you
a little while on your birthday and let you know how much, how very much, I love
you. I cannot look forward into your life and see how it will be with you. I do not
know whether you will have had sad years or bright ones between the time when I
said good-bye to you and now when you are reading this. I could not plan
positively, dear little girl, to have them bright ones, else you surely know I would.
I had to leave you in God's care, and I know you will be taken care of, whatever
comes. If there have been trials, somehow, Phoebe, little girl, they must have been*

good for you. Sometime you will learn why, perhaps, and sometime there will be a way out. Never forget that. God has His brightness ready somewhere for you if you are true to Him and brave. Somehow I am afraid that there will have been trials, perhaps very heavy ones, for you were always such a sensitive little soul, and you are going among people who may not understand.

In thinking about your life I have been afraid for you that you would be tempted because of unhappiness to take some rash impulsive step before God is ready to show you His plan for your life. I would like to give you a little warning through the years, and tell you to be careful.

You have entered young womanhood, and will perhaps be asked to give your life into the keeping of some man. If I were going to live I would try to train you through the years for this great crisis of your life. But when it comes, remember that I have thought about you and longed for you that you may find another soul who will love you better than himself, and whom you can love better than you love anything else in the world, and who will be grand and noble in every way. Dear child, hear your mother's voice, and don't take anything less. It will not matter so much if he is poor, if only he loves you better than himself and is worthy of your love. Never marry anyone for a home, or a chance to have your own way, or freedom from good honest work. There will be no happiness in it. Trust your mother, for she knows. Do not marry anyone to whom you cannot look up and give honor next to God. Unless you can marry such a man it is better not to marry at all, believe your mother, child. I say it lovingly, for I have seen much sorrow and would protect you.

And now, my sweet child, with a face like the dawn of the morning, and eyes so untroubled, if when you read this anything has come into your life to make you unhappy, just try to lay it all down for a little while and feel your mother's love about you. See, I have made this bright sunny dress for you, every stitch set with love, and I want you to wear it on your birthday to remind you of me. It is yellow, because that is the glory color, the color of the sunshine I have always loved so much. I want you to think of me in a bright, sunny happy way, and as in a glory of happiness, waiting for you; not as dead, and lying in the grave. Think of my love for you as a joy, and not a lost one, either, for I am sure that where I am going I shall love you just the same, and more.

I am very tired and must not write any more, for there are other letters yet to write and much to do before I can feel ready to go and leave you, but as I am writing this birthday letter for you I am praying God that He will bring some brightness into your life, the beginning of some great joy, on this your eighteenth birthday, that shall be His blessing, and my birthday gift to my child. I put a kiss here where I write my name and give you with it more love than you can ever understand.

Your Mother

The tears rained down upon her hands as ~~she~~
was finished she put her he~~ad~~
since her m~~other~~

~~they~~
~~g~~ray squirrels silently
~~of~~ gathering in the winter's store, then
~~away.~~ It was all quite still in the woods except for the
~~occasional~~ falling of a nut, or the stir of a leaf, or the skitter of a squirrel, for
Phoebe did not sob aloud. Her grief was deeper than that. Her soul was crying
out to one who was far away and yet who seemed so near to her that nothing
else mattered for the time.

She was thinking over all her sad little life, telling it to her mother in
imagination, trying to draw comfort from the letter, and to reconcile the realities
with what her mother had said. Would her mother have been just as sure that
it would all come out right if she had known the real facts? Would she have
given the same advice? Carefully she thought it over, washing the anger away
in her tears. Yes, she felt sure if her mother had known all she could not have
written more truly than she had done. She would have had her say "No" to
Hiram, just as she had done, and would have exhorted to patience with Emmeline, and to trust that brightness would sometime come.

She thought of her mother's prayer for her, and almost smiled through her
tears to think how impossible that could be. Yet—the day was not done—perhaps there might be some little pleasant thing yet, that she might consider as a
blessing and her mother's gift. She would look and wait for it and perhaps it
would come. It might be Albert would be kind—he was, sometimes-or if it were
not too late she might go down to the village and make her call on Mrs. Spafford.
That might be a beautiful thing and the beginning of a joy—but no, that was too
far away and her eyes were red with weeping. She must just take this quiet hour
in the woods as her blessing and be glad over it because her mother and God
had sent it to her to help her bear the rest of the days. She lifted her tear-wet
face to look around on the golden autumn world, and the sun caught the tears
on her lashes and turned them into flashing jewels, till the sweet, sad face looked
like a tired flower with the dew upon it.

Then quite suddenly she knew she was not alone.

A young man stood in the shadow of the tallest chestnut tree, regarding her
with troubled gaze. His hat was in his hand and his head slightly bowed in
deference, as if in the presence of something holy.

He was tall, well-formed, and his face fine and handsome. His eyes were deep and brown, with lights in them like those on the shadowed depths of a quiet woodland stream. His heavy dark hair was tossed back from a white forehead that had not been exposed to the summer sun of the hayfield, one could see at a glance, and the hand that held the hat was white and smooth also. There was a grace about his attitude that reminded Phoebe of David Spafford, who had seemed to her the ideal of a gentleman. He was dressed in dark brown and his black silk stock set off a finely cut clean-shaven chin of unusual strength and firmness. If it had not been for the lights in eyes, and the hint of smile behind the almost tender strength of the lips, Phoebe would have been afraid of him as she lifted shy, ashamed eyes to the intruder's face.

"I beg your pardon, I did not mean to intrude," he said, apologetically, "but a party of young people are coming up the hill. They will be here in a moment, and I thought perhaps you would not care to meet them. You seem to be in trouble."

"Oh, thank you!" said Phoebe, arising in sudden panic and dropping her mother's letter at her feet. She stooped to pick it up, but the young man had reached it first and their fingers met for one brief instant over the letter of the dead. In her confusion Phoebe did not know what to say but "Thank you," and then felt like a parrot repeating the same phrase.

Voices were distinctly audible now and the girl turned to flee, but ahead and around there seemed nowhere to go for hiding except a dense growth of mountain laurel that still stood green and shining amid the autumn brown. She looked for a way around it, but the young man caught her thought, and reaching forward with a quick motion of his arms he parted the strong branches and made a way for her.

"Here, jump right in there! Nobody will see you. Hurry, they are almost here!" he whispered, kindly.

The girl sprang quickly on the log, paused just an instant to gather her golden draperies about her, and then fluttered into the green hiding-place and settled down like a drift of yellow leaves.

The laurel swung back into place, nodding quite as if it understood the secret. The young man stooped and she saw him deliberately take from his pocket a letter and put it down behind the log that lay across her hiding-place.

The letter settled softly into place and looked at her knowingly as if it, too, were in the secret and were there to help her. For even a letter has an expression if one has but eyes to see and understand.

Up the hill-side came a troop of young people. Phoebe could not see them, for the growth of laurel was very dense, but she could hear their voices.

"Oh, Janet Bristol, how fast you go! I'm all out of breath. Why do you hurry so? The nuts will keep till we get there, and we have all the afternoon before us."

"Go slow as you like, Caroline," said a sweet
anywhere I like to get there. I wonde
minutes since he went out
us the best w

place came the voice

called. "There are plenty of nuts up there!"
toward her hiding-place, and pointed farther up the hill.
ging, scrambling over slippery leaves and protruding logs the gay
company frolicked past, and Phoebe was left, undiscovered, alone with the letter
that smiled back at her in a friendly way.

She stooped a little to look at it and read the address, "Nathaniel Graham,
Esq.," written in a fine commanding hand, a chirography that gave the impression of honoring the name it wrote.

The girl studied the beautiful name, till every turn of the pen was graven on
her mind, the fine, even clearness of the small letters, the bold downward stroke
in the capitals. It was unusual writing of an unusual name and the girl felt that
it belonged to an unusual man.

Then all of a sudden, while she waited and listened to the happy jingle of
voices, like bells of different tones, exclaiming over rich finds in nuts, the barren
loneliness of her own life came over her and brought a rush of tears. Why was
she here in hiding from those girls and boys that should have been her companions? Why did she shrink from meeting Janet Bristol, the sweetly haughty
beauty of the village? Why was she never invited to their pleasant tea-drinkings,
and their berry and nut gatherings? She saw them in church, and that was all.
They never seemed to see her. True, she had not been brought up from
childhood among them, but she had lived there long enough to have known them
intimately if her life had not always been so full of care. Janet Bristol had gone
away to school for several years, and was only at home in summer when Phoebe's
life was full of farm work—cooking for the hands, and for the harvesters. But
Maria Finch and Caroline Penfield had gone to school with Phoebe. She felt a
bitterness that they were in these good times and she was not. They were not
to blame, perhaps, for she had always avoided them, keeping much to herself
and her studies in school, and hurrying home at Emmeline's strict command.
They had never attracted her as had the tall, fair Janet, in the few summer
glimpses she had had of her. Yet she would never likely know Janet Bristol or
come any nearer to her than she was now, hidden behind God's screen of laurel
on the hill-side, while the gay company gathered nuts a few rods away. The

young man with the beautiful face and the kind ways would forget her and leave her to scramble out of her hiding-place as best she could while he helped Janet Bristol over the stile and carried her basket of nuts home for her. He would not cross her path again. Nevertheless she was glad he had met her this once, and she could know there was in the world one so kind and noble; it was a beautiful thing to have come into her life. She would stay here till they were all out of hearing, and then creep out and steal away as she had come. Her sad life and its annoyances, forgotten for the moment, settled down upon her, but with this change. They now seemed possible to bear. She could go back to Albert's house, to Emmeline where she was unwelcome, and work her way twice over. She could doff the golden garments, and take up her daily toil, even patiently perhaps, and bear Emmeline's hateful insinuations, Alma's impudence, the disagreeable attentions of Hank and the hateful presence of Hiram Green, but never again would she be troubled with the horrible thought that perhaps after all she was wrong and ought to accept the home that Hiram Green was offering her. *Never,* for now she had seen a man, who had looked at her as she felt sure God meant a man to look at a woman, with honor, and respect, and gentle helpfulness, and deference.

All at once she knew that her mother's prayer had been answered and that something beautiful had come into her life. It would not stay and grow as her mother had hoped. This stranger could be nothing to her, but the memory of his helpfulness and the smile of sympathy that had lighted his eyes would remain with her, a beautiful joy, always. It was something that had come to save her at the moment of her utter despair.

Meantime, under the chestnut-trees but a few rods away, the baskets were being filled rapidly, for the nuts were many and the squirrels had been idle, thinking they owned them all. Nathaniel Graham helped each girl impartially, and seemed to be especially successful in finding the largest and shiniest nuts. The laughing and joking went on, but Nathaniel said little. Phoebe, from her covert could watch them, and felt that the young man would soon pilot them farther away. She could hear bits of their talk.

"What's the matter with Nathaniel?" said Caroline Penfield. "He's hardly said a word since we started. What deep subject is your massive mind engaged upon, young man?"

"Oh, Nate is thinking about Texas," said Daniel Westgate, flippantly. "He has no thoughts or words for anything but setting Texas free. We'll hear of him joining the volunteers to help them fight Mexico the next thing. I wouldn't be one bit surprised."

"Don't, Daniel," said Janet Bristol, sharply. "Nathaniel has far more sense than that."

"I should hope so!" echoed Maria Finch. "Nathaniel isn't a hot-headed fanatic."

"Don't you be too sure!" said the irrep̶̶̶̶̶̶̶̶
fine heroics he w̶̶̶̶

̶̶ just loaded, and the
̶̶̶̶̶̶̶̶̶̶̶̶̶̶̶̶̶̶̶̶̶̶̶ of wind."

̶̶̶̶̶̶̶ Just look at that squirrel, leaning against his tail as if it were the back of an easy chair. He is mincing away at that nut as daintily as any lady," called Caroline.

The merry company picked up baskets and began to move out of sight, but the young man Nathaniel stood still thoughtfully and felt in his pockets, until Phoebe, from her hiding-place, could see none of the others. Then she heard him call in a pleasant voice, "Janet, I have dropped a letter. It cannot be far away. Go on without me for a moment. I will be with you right away."

Then came Janet's sweet, vexed tones:

"Oh, Nathaniel! How tiresome! Can't you let it go? Was it of any consequence? Shall we come and help you find it?"

"No, Janet, thank you. I know just where I dropped it, and I will be with you again before you have missed me. Keep right on."

Then he turned, swiftly, and came back to the laurel, before the startled Phoebe, who had intended running away at once, could realize that he was coming.

She sprang up with the instinct of fleeing from him, but as if the laurel were loath to part with her, it reached out detaining fingers and caught her by the strands of her fine brown hair; and down came the soft, shining waves of hair, in shameless, lovely disorder about the flushed face, and rippling far below the waist of the buff frock. The sun caught it and kissed it into a thousand lights and shadows of brown and red and purple and gold. A strand here and there clung to the laurel as if the charm were mutual, and made a fine veil of spun gold before her face. Thus she stood abashed, with her hair unbound before the stranger, her face in a beautiful confusion.

Now this young man had gazed upon many a maiden's hair with entire indifference. In the days of his boyhood he had even dared to attach a paper kite to the yellow braids of a girl who sat in front of him in school, and laughed with the rest at recess, as after carefully following her with hidden kite and wound-up cord they had succeeded in launching the paper thing in the breeze till it lifted the astonished victim's yellow plaits high in air and she cried out angrily upon them. He had even pulled many a girl's hair. He had watched his cousin Janet brush and plait and curl her abundant locks into the various changing fashions, and criticized the effect freely. He had once untied a hard knot in a bonnet-string among a mass of golden curls without a thrill. Why therefore did he feel such awe as he approached in deep embarrassment to offer his assistance! Why did his fingers tremble as he laid them reverently upon a strand of hair that had tangled itself in the laurel? Why did it bring a fine ecstasy into his being as the wind blew it across his face? Did all hair have that delicate, indescribable perfume about it?

When he had set her free from the entangling bushes, he marvelled at the dexterity with which she reduced the flying hair to order the imprisoned it meekly. It seemed like magic.

Then, before she had time to spring out of her covert, he took her hands, firmly, reverently, without undue familiarity, and helped her to the top of the log and thence to the ground. She liked him for the way he did it, so different from the way the other men she knew would have done it. She shuddered to think if it had been Hank, or Hiram Green.

"Come this way, it is nearer to the road," he said, quietly, parting the branches at his right to let her pass, and when she had gone a few steps, behold, not two rods below lay the cross road, which met the highway by which she had come, a quarter of a mile farther on.

"But you have forgotten your letter," she turned to say, as they came out of the woods and began to descend the hill; "and I can get out quite well now. You have been very kind—"

"I will get the letter presently," he said, with a smile."Just let me help you over the fence. I want to ask your pardon for my intrusion. I did not see you at first, the woods were so quiet, and you looked so much like the yellow leaves that lay all about—" and his eyes cast an admiring glance at the buff merino.

"Oh, it was not an intrusion," she exclaimed, her cheeks rosy with the remembrance, "and I am so grateful to you for telling me they were coming. I would not have liked to be found there—so." She looked shyly up. "I thank you very much!" He saw that her eyes were beautiful, with ripples of laughter and shadows of sorrow in their glance. He experienced a deep and unnecessary satisfaction that his first impression of her face was verified, and he stood looking down upon her as if she were something he was proud of having discovered and rescued from an unpleasant fate.

Phoebe felt a warm glow like sunshine breaking over her in the kindness of his look.

"Don't thank me," he said. "I felt like a criminal, intruding so upon your trouble."

"But you must not feel so. It was only that I had been reading a letter from my mother, and it made me feel so lonely that I cried."

"That is trouble enough," he said, with quick
away from home, or are you?"

"My mother is dead. Sh
quivering lips. "
aw

.road over
.y when they came out
.s ne answered:

.s, now I will understand. My mother has been
. I wish she had written me a letter to read today."

, as if he knew he must not stay longer, he lifted his hat, smiled, and walked quickly up the hill, while Phoebe sped swiftly down the road, not noticing the glories of the day, not thinking so much of her own troubles, but marvelling at what had happened and living it all over once more in imagination. She knew without thinking that a wagon was rumbling nearer and nearer, but she gave it no heed.

Nathaniel Graham, when he reached the edge of the wood, turned and looked back down the road; saw the girl in her yellow draperies moving in the autumn sunshine, and watched her intently. The driver of the farm wagon, now almost opposite to him, watched glumly from behind his bags of wheat, high piled, sneered under his breath at the fine attire, half guessed who he was; then wondered who the girl was who kept tryst so far from any houses, and with a last glance at the man just vanishing into the woods he whipped up his team, resolved to find out.

Chapter 6

Nathaniel Graham went to pick up the letter he had left behind the log, but as he did so his eye caught something brown, lying on the ground among the laurel near the letter. He reached out and took it. It was a bit of a bow of brown velvet, and seemed strangely a part of the girl who had been there but a few moments before. What part had this bit of velvet played in her make-up? Had it been worn at her throat, or in her wonderful hair? He never doubted that it was hers. As he raised it wonderingly in his hand to look at it more closely he fancied he caught the same subtle fragrance that had been in her hair. His fingers closed pleasantly about the soft little thing. For a moment he pondered whether he ought to go after her and give it to her. Then farther up the hill he heard the voices calling him, and with a pleasant smile he tucked it into his inner pocket beside the letter that had played so important a part in the little affair. He rather liked to think he had that bit of velvet himself, and perhaps it was not of much value to the owner. It might at least make another opportunity of seeing her. And so he passed on up the hill with something besides the freedom of Texas to think upon.

Meantime, the load of wheat went down the road after Phoebe at a lively pace, and its driver, in no pleasant mood because he had been all the way to Albany with his wheat and had been unable to sell it, studied the graceful sunlit figure ahead of him, and wondered what there was about it so strangely familiar.

Phoebe had just reached the highroad and paused to think which way she would go, when the wagon overtook her, and turning with her face bright with pleasure, and momentary forgetfulness, she faced the lowering astonishment of Hiram Green! Her face grew deadly white with the revulsion, and she caught at the fence to steady herself. She felt as if the earth were reeling under her unprotected feet. One hand flew to her heart and her frightened eyes, with a wild thought of her late protector, sought the way by which she had come; but the hill-side lay unresponsive in the late sunshine, and not a soul was to be seen. Nathaniel Graham had just picked up his cousin Janet's basket.

"Well, I swow!" said Hiram Green, pulling his horses up sharply. "It ain't *you* tricked out that way, away off here!" Then slowly his little pig eyes traveled to the lonely hill-side, gathered up an idea, came back to the girl's guilty face, and narrowed to a hateful slit through which shone a gleam of something that might be likely to illumine outer darkness. He brought his thin, cruel lips together with satisfaction. He felt that at last he had a hold upon the girl, but he could wait and use it to his best advantage.

She, poor child, never dreamed that he had ~~~~~
and was only frightened f~~ ~~
in an ~~~~

~~~~~~~~~ to him.

~~~~~ he responded. "Won't you get up and
~~~~ pretty seat, but I guess it's clean and comfortable. Sorry
I ain't got the carryall. You're a long piece from home."

"Oh, thank you, Mr. Green," she said, cordially. "I'm sure the seat would
be very comfortable, and just as nice as the carryall, but I'm out taking a
walk this beautiful afternoon, and I'm enjoying every minute of it. I would
much rather walk. Besides, I am not going directly home. I may stop at
Granny McVane's and perhaps another place before I get home. Thank you
for the invitation."

Then without waiting for a reply she flew lightly in front of the horses and
sped up the main highway toward the old red farm-house. It was not the direction
she would have chosen, but there was no time to do anything else, and her
frightened heart gave wings to her feet. She dared not look behind lest she was
being pursued.

Hiram Green, thus left alone after his attempt at gallantry, looked after the
flying maiden with venom in his little eyes. His mouth hardened once more into
its cruel lines and he took up the reins again and said to his horses in no pleasant
tones: "G'long there!" pointing his remark with a stinging cut of the whip, which
made the weary beasts leap forward at a lively gait.

He did not watch Phoebe any longer, but once he turned his head and looked
threateningly at the barren hill-side, and shook the fist that held his whip in a
menacing way.

When Phoebe neared the old red house, where lived the two women who
always saw and enlarged and told everything, she noted with relief that the
shades were drawn down and there was a general air of not-at-home-ness about
the place that betokened the inhabitants were away for the afternoon. With joy
she went on by the house and turned down another cross road which would lead
to a second road going into the village. On this road, just on the border of the
town, lived Granny McVane all alone save for her silent old husband. She was
a sweet old lady whom care and disappointment had not hardened, but only made
more humble and patient. Phoebe had been there on occasional errands, and her
kindness had won the girl's heart. From Granny McVane's it would be but a
short run home across the fields, and she would thus escape meeting any

more prying eyes. She was not accustomed to making calls on the neighbors without an errand, but the fancy came to her now that she would just stop and ask how Granny's rheumatism was, and wish her good-day. Perhaps, if she seemed glad to see her, she might tell her it was her birthday and this was the frock her mother had made. The girl had a longing to confide in some one.

As she walked along the country road, she began to think of home and the inevitable black looks that would be hers from Emmeline. But the day was good yet, though a chill was creeping into the air that made her cheeks tingle. The sun was dropping low now, and the rays were glowing deeper. The stubble in the cornfields that she passed was bathed in its light. The buff merino was touched with a ruddy glow and the girl, as she sped along, seemed like a living topaz in the golden setting of the day.

She reached the little double door of Granny McVane's cottage, and knocked. The old lady, in her white ruffled cap with its black band, and soft kerchief folded across her bosom, opened the upper half of the door, and on seeing Phoebe opened the lower door, too, and brought her in most cordially. She made her sit down, and looked her over with delight, her old eyes glowing with pleasure at the sweet picture the girl made sitting in the flowered calico rocking-chair. She seemed to catch the long sunbeams that slanted low across the kitchen floor, and reflect them with her gown and face till all the little room was filled with sunny brightness.

She made Phoebe tell about the frock, her birthday, her mother's letter, and her walk; and then she told her she must stay to tea with her, for the 'Squire was off to Albany on business and would not be back that night.

The old cat was winking cordially before the hearth, the pot of mush was sputtering sleepily on its crane over the fire, the kettle was singing cheerily beside it, and the old lady's face was so wistful that Phoebe put by her thought of home, and the supper that she ought to be getting this minute, and decided to stay just for once, as it was her birthday. The stiff white curtains shut the little room in cozily from the outside world, and a scarlet geranium bloomed happily on the broad window-seat. Phoebe looked around at the polished old mahogany, and the shining pewter dishes that adorned the shelf, touched the drowsy cat with gentle fingers that brought forth a purr, glanced up at the great old clock with its measured, unhurried tick-tock, tick-tock, and felt like a person who has turned her back upon life and all its duties and abandoned herself to pleasure pure and simple. Yes, for one short hour more she would have what her day offered her of joy, without a thought of trouble, and then she would go back to her duty and cherish the memory of her pleasure. Thus did Phoebe give herself over to the wild excitement of a birthday tea at Granny McVane's cottage.

Precisely at five o'clock the little round table was drawn out from the wall, and its leaves put up. A snow-white homespun cloth was laid upon it and lovely

blue dishes of quaint designs in blue set upon it;
for each; steel knives; a great
butte

.... of honor, than was
.... tea, all yellows and beautiful browns, with
...... the setting sun over all. The lazy cat got up, stretched, and
yawned, and came over by the table as they sat down. The cat, by the way, was
yellow, too.

It was a delicious meal, and Phoebe ate it with the appetite gained in her
long walk. After it was over she bade Granny McVane good-evening, kissed her
for the beautiful ending to her birthday, and hurried guiltily across the fields to
the farm-house she called home, not allowing herself to think of what was before
her until she reached the very door, for she would not have one moment of her
precious day spoiled.

The family had just sat down to supper when Phoebe opened the door and
came in. She had hoped this ceremony would be over, for the usual hour for
supper was half past five, but Emmeline had waited longer than usual, thinking
Phoebe would surely come back to help, and having it all to do herself had not
been able to get it ready as soon as usual. Moreover, an undertone of apprehension as to what Albert might say if Phoebe should be headstrong enough to
remain away after dark, kept her going to the window to look up the road for
the possible sight of a girlish figure in a curious yellow frock. Emmeline had
been angry, astonished, and bewildered all the afternoon. She had not been
able to decide what she would do about the way her young sister-in-law had
acted. She had been a little anxious, too, lest she had gone too far, and would
be blamed if the truth should be known. She would have been glad, many times
during the afternoon, to have seen Phoebe meekly returning, but now that she
had come, after staying away till the work was done and Albert had come home
and found out her absence, Emmeline's wrath was kindled anew. She stood at
the hearth taking up the second pan of johnnycake when the girl came in, and
when she saw Phoebe apparently as cheerful as if she had stayed at home and
done her duty all the afternoon, Emmeline set her lips in cold and haughty
disapproval.

Alma, with her mouth full of fried potatoes, stopped her fork midway with
another supply and stared. The little boys chorused in unison: "Hullo, Aunt
Phoebe! Where'd'ye get the clo'es!" Hank, who was just helping himself to a
slice of bread with his fork, turned full around and after the first glimpse of the

girl in her unfamiliar garments he sat in awed embarrassment. Only Albert sat in pleased surprise, his knife and fork akimbo on his plate, his chair tipped back, and a look of real welcome in his face.

"Well, now, Phoebe, I'm real glad you've got back. I was getting uneasy about you, off so long. It isn't like you to stay away from your meals. My, but you do look pretty in that rig! What took you, anyway? Where've you been?"

Not to the others would she have told for the world, but somehow Albert's pleasant tones and kindly eyes unsealed her lips and without a thought she spoke:

"I've just been for a walk in the woods this afternoon, and I stopped a few minutes to see Granny McVane. She made me stay to tea with her. I did not mean to stay so late."

"That sounds very sweet, I'm sure," broke in Emmeline's sharp voice, "but she forgets that she left me with all her work to do on top of my own."

Phoebe's cheeks flushed.

"I am sorry I did not get back in time to help get supper," she said, looking straight at Albert as if explaining to him alone, "but it was my birthday, and I thought I might take a little time to myself."

"Your birthday! To be sure you can. You don't go out half enough. Emmeline, you wouldn't want her to work all day on her birthday, of course. Sit down, child, and have some more supper. This is real good johnnycake; have a piece? You ought to have told us before that you had a birthday, and then we might have celebrated. Eh, Hank! What do you say?"

"I say yes," said Hank, chuckling in a vain endeavor to regain his usual composure. He had visions of a certain red ribbon at the village store that he might have bought her, or a green glass breastpin. He watched her furtively and wondered if it was too late yet to improve the occasion.

"Other people have birthdays too, and I don't see much fuss made over 'em either," sniffed Emmeline, flinging the tea towel up to its nail with an impatient movement. She had burned her finger, and her temper burned in sympathy.

"Thank you, Albert," said Phoebe, quietly, "I don't care for any more supper. I will go up and change my frock and be ready to wash the dishes."

She was going toward the door, but Albert detained her.

"Wait, Phoebe! You come here and sit down. I've got something to tell you. I'd clean forgot about the birthday myself, but now I remember all right. Let's see, you're eighteen today, aren't you? I thought so."

Hank lifted bold, admiring eyes to her face, and the girl, standing patiently behind her chair at the table waiting for her brother to finish, felt she would like to extinguish him for a little while till the conference was over.

"Well, now, child, I've got a surprise for you. You're eighteen, and of age, so you've got a right to know it."

"Wouldn't it be better for you to tell me _____
pleaded Phoebe, _____

_____ _____ eignteen, and then
_____ _____ to use it and be more likely to need it."

"_____ay, Aunt Phoebe," broke in Alma, tilting her turn-up nose to its most inquisitive point, and sticking out her chin in a grown-up manner she had copied after her mother, "does Hiram Green know you got a birthday?"

"Shut up!" said Emmeline, applying the palm of her hand in a stinging slap to her offspring's cheek.

"Sister! Sister!" said Albert, in gentle reproof. "Now, Emmeline, don't be so severe with the child! She doesn't realize how impertinent she is. Sister, you mustn't talk like that to Aunt Phoebe." Then in an aside to Hank, with a wink, "It does beat all how keen children will be sometimes."

Phoebe, with scarlet cheeks, felt as if she could bear no more. "Thank you, Albert," she said, with a voice that *would* tremble despite her best efforts. "Now if you will excuse me I'll change my frock."

"Wait a minute, child; that's a mighty pretty frock you've got on. Look pretty as a peach in it. Let's have a look at you. Where'd you get it? Make it yourself?"

"Mother made it for me to wear today," said Phoebe, in a low voice, and then she vanished into the hall, leaving somehow an impression of victory behind her, and a sense of embarrassment among the family.

"There'll be no livin' with her now," snapped Emmeline over the tea-cups. "I'm sure I thought you had better sense. You never told me there was any money left for her, or I'd've advised you about it. I'm sure we've spent for her, and if there's anything left her it belongs to you. Here she's had a good home, and paid not a cent for it, and had everything just the same as us. If she had any spirit of right she wouldn't touch a cent of that money!"

"Now look here, Emmeline," said Albert, in his kind, conciliatory tone. "You don't quite understand this matter. Not having known about it before of course you couldn't judge rightly. And as it was her ma's request that I didn't tell anybody. I couldn't very well tell you. Besides, I don't see why it should affect you any. The money was hers, and we'd nothing to do with it. As for her home here, she's been very welcome, and I'm sure she's earned her way. She's a good worker, Phoebe is."

"That's so, she is," assented Hank, warmly. "I don't know a girl in the county can beat her workin'."

"I don't know as anybody asked your opinion, Hank Williams. I'm able to judge of work a little myself, and if she works well, who taught her? She'd never done a stroke when she came here, and nobody thinks of the hard time I've had breakin' her in, and puttin' up with her mistakes when she was young and her hands lily white, and soft as a baby's."

"Now, Emmeline, don't go and get excited," said Albert, anxiously. "You know we ain't letting go a mite of what you've done. Only it's fair to the girl to say she's earned her way."

"H'm!" said Emmeline, contemptuously, "that depends on who's the judge!"

"Won't Aunt Phoebe do any more work now she's got some money, ma?" broke in Alma in a panic of what might be the possibilities in store for her small selfish self.

"Haven't I told you to keep still, Alma," reproved her mother, angrily. "If you say another word I'll send you to bed without any cake."

At this dire threat Alma retired temporarily from the conversation till the cake should be passed, and a kind of family gloom settled over the room. Hank felt the constraint and made haste to bolt the last of his supper and escape.

Phoebe came down shortly afterward, attired in her everyday garb, and looking meekly sensible. Albert felt somehow a relief to see her so, though he protested weakly.

"Say, Phoebe, it's too bad for you to wash dishes your birthday night. You go back and put on your pretty things, and Alma'll help her ma wash up this time."

"No, she won't, either," broke in Emmeline. "Alma ain't a bit well, and she's not goin' to be made to work at her age unless she likes. Here, honey, you may have this piece of ma's cake, she don't want it all. It seems to me you're kind of an unnatural father, Albert Deane. I guess it won't hurt Phoebe to wash a few dishes when she's been lyin' around havin' a good time all day, while I've worked my fingers half off doin' her work. We've all had to work on our birthdays, and I guess if Phoebe's goin' to stay here she'll have to put up with what the rest of us gets, unless she's got money to pay for better."

With that Albert looked helplessly about the room and retired to his newspaper in the sitting-room, while Phoebe went swiftly about the usual evening work. Emmeline yanked the boys away from the cake plate, and marched them and Alma out of the kitchen with her head held high and her chin in the air. She did not even do the usual little duties of putting away the cake and bread and pickles and jelly, but left it all for Phoebe. Of this Phoebe was glad.

Before the dishes were quite done, the front door opened and Hiram Green sauntered into the sitting-room. Phoebe heard him, and hurried to hang up her dish towels and flee to her own room.

And thus ended the birthday, though the girl
thinking over all its wonderful
upon the possib

Chapter 7

When little Rose Spafford was born the sweet girl-mother, who had been Marcia Schuyler, found no one so helpful and reliable in the whole town as Miranda Griscom, granddaughter and household drudge of her next door neighbor, Mrs. Heath. David Spafford "borrowed" her for the first three or four weeks, and Mrs. Heath gave reluctant consent, because the Heaths and the Spaffords had always been intimate friends; but Grandma Heath realized during that time just how many steps the eccentric Miranda saved her, and she began to look forward to her return with more eagerness than she cared to show. Miranda, as she revelled in doing as she pleased in the large well-furnished kitchen of the Spafford house, using the best sprigged china to send a pretty tray upstairs to Mrs. Spafford, used often to look triumphantly over toward her grandmother's house, and wonder if she was missed. One little gleam of appreciation would have started a flame of abounding love in the queer, lonely heart of Miranda. But the grim grandmother never appreciated anything that this unloved grandchild, the daughter of an undesired son-in-law, tried to do.

As the delightful days sped by in loving service Miranda began to dread the time when she must go back to her grandmother's house again, and Marcia and David dreaded it also. They set about planning how they might keep her, and presently they had it all arranged.

David suggested it first.

It was while they both hung over the little Rose's cradle, watching her wake up, like the opening of the little bud she was. Miranda had come to the door for a direction, and stood a moment, remarking "I thought I'd find you two a-worshippin'. Just keep right on. My heart's with you. I'll see to supper. Don't you give it a thought." And then a moment later they heard her high, nasal tones voicing something about a "Sweet, sweet rose on a garden wall," and they smiled at the quaint loving soul. Then David spoke.

"Marcia, we must contrive to keep her here. She has blossomed out in the last month. It would be cruel to send her back to that dismal house over there again. They don't need her in the least with Hannah's cousin there all the time. I mean to offer her wages to stay with us. You are not strong enough to care for baby and do the housework, anyway, and I would feel safer about you if Miranda were here. Wouldn't you like her?"

Marcia's sweet laugh rang out. "Oh, David, you will spoil me! I'm sure I'm perfectly able to do the work and look after this wee flower. But of course I'd like to have Miranda here. I think it would be a good thing if she could get away from her surroundings, and she is a comfort to me in a good many ways."

"Then it is settled, dear," said David

"Oh, but D

...doubtfully.

And then, there is Mrs. Heath. She never will consent."

"Leave that to me, my little wife, and don't worry about it. Let us first settle it with Miranda."

"Oh, but if Mrs. Heath wouldn't hear to it, Miranda would be so disappointed," suggested Marcia.

Just then Miranda presented herself at the door.

"Your supper's spoilin' on the table. Will you two just walk down and eat it while I have my try at that baby? I haven't seen scarcely a wink of her all this blessed day."

"Miranda," said David, not looking at his wife's warning eyes, "would you be willing to stay with us altogether?"

"H'm!" said Miranda. "Jes' gimme the try and see!" and she stooped over the cradle with such a wistful longing in her gaze that the young mother's heart went out to her with a real love.

"Very well, Miranda, then we'll consider it a bargain. I'll pay you wages so that we shall feel quite comfortable about asking you to do anything, and you shall call this your home from now on."

"What!" gasped the astonished girl, straightening up. "Did you mean what you said? I never knew you to do a mean thing like tease any one, David Spafford, but you can't mean what you say. It couldn't come around so nice as that fer me. Don't go to talk about wages. I'd work from mornin' to night fer one chance at that blessed baby there in the cradle. But I know it can't be."

The supper grew quite cold while they were persuading her that it was all true and that they really wanted her; and while they talked over the possibilities of having trouble with her grandmother; but at last with her sandy eyelashes wet with tears of joy and hope Miranda went downstairs and heated the supper all over again for them, and the two upstairs, beside the little bud of life that had bloomed for them, rejoiced that a heart so faithful and true would be her watchful attendant through babyhood.

Perhaps it was with a feeling that he desired to burn his bridges behind him before his maiden aunts should hear of the new arrangement, that David went over to see old Mrs. Heath that very evening. Perhaps it was to relieve the excitement of poor Miranda, who felt that though heaven had opened before her, it could not really be for her, and was counting on being put out of her Eden at once.

No one but Marcia ever heard what passed between David and old Mrs. Heath, and no one else quite knows what arguments he used to finally bring the determined old woman to terms. Miranda, with her nose flattened against the window pane of the dark kitchen chamber, watching the two blurred figures in the candlelight of Grandmother Heath's "settin room," wondered, and prayed, and hoped and feared, and prayed again.

It was well that David had gone over to see Mrs. Heath that night and made all arrangements, if he cared to escape criticism from his relatives. It was the very next afternoon that Miss Amelia, on her daily visit to the shrine of her new grandniece, remarked: "Well, Marcia, has Miranda gone home yet? I should think her grandmother would need her, all this time away, poor old lady. And you're perfectly strong and able now to attend to your own work again."

Marcia's fair face flushed delicately, and she gathered her baby closer as if to protect her from the chill that would follow the words that she must speak.

"Why, Aunt Amelia," she said, brightly, "what do you think! Miranda is not going home at all. David has a foolish notion that he wants her to stay with me, and help look after the baby. Besides, he wants me to go with him as I have been doing. I told him it was not necessary, but he wanted it, so he has arranged it all, and Mrs. Heath has given her consent."

"Miranda stay here!" The words fell like long slanting icicles that seemed to pierce as they fell. They lingered in the air until their full surprise and displeasure could be distinctly felt, and then followed more.

"I am *surprised* at you, Marcia. I thought you had more self-respect than that! It is a disgrace to a young strong woman to let her husband hire a girl to do her work while she gads about the country and leaves her house and her young child. If your own mother had lived she would have taught you better than that. And then, *Miranda,* of *all people to select!* The child of a renegade! A waif dependent, utterly thankless, and irresponsible! She is scatterbrained, and untrustworthy. I you needed anyone at any time to sit with the child while you were out for a legitimate cause to pay a call, or make an occasional visit, either Hortense or I would be glad to come and relieve you. Indeed, you must not think of leaving this wild, good-for-nothing Miranda Griscom with my nephew's child. I shall speak to my sister Hortense, and we will make it our business to come down every day, one or the other of us, and do anything that you find your strength is unequal to doing. We are still strong enough, I hope, to do anything for the family honor. I should be ashamed to have it known that David Spafford's wife was such a weakling that she had to have hired help in. The young wives of our family have always been proud of their housekeeping."

Now Miranda Griscom, whatever might be said of her, had no convictions against eavesdropping

she felt

since Rose

ping, approached the door, and applied her

rous crack. She could feel the subject of herself coming on, and her ready brain had devised a plan by which she thought she could relieve the pressure if it should become unduly heavy upon Marcia at any time.

So, just as Marcia lifted her face, white with control, and tried to take the angry flash out of her eyes and think what to reply to her tormentor, Miranda, without ceremony of approach, burst into the room, exclaiming, "Oh, Miss Amelia, 'scuse me fer interruptin', but *did* your nice old gray cat mebbe foller you down here, and *could* it a' ben her out on our front porch fightin' with Bob Sykes's yellow dog? 'Cause ef 'tis, sumpin' ought to be done right off, 'r he'll make hash out a' her. S'pose you come down an' look. I wouldn't like to make a mistake 'bout it."

Miss Amelia placed her hand upon her heart and looked helplessly at Marcia for an instant. "Oh, my dear, you don't suppose—" she began, in a trembling voice quite unlike her usual tones. Then she gathered up her shawl, which had slipped off her shoulders, and utterly unheeding that her bonnet was awry she hurried down the stairs after the sympathetic Miranda.

"Come right out here, softly," Miranda said, opening the front door cautiously. "Why, they must a' gone around the house!"

The old lady followed the girl out on the porch, and together they looked on both sides of the house, but there was no trace of dog or cat, any more than if, like the gingham dog and the calico cat of later days, they had "eaten each other up." "Where could they a' gone?" inquired Miranda, excitedly. "Mebbe I ought a' jus' called you and stayed here an' watched, but I was afraid to wake baby. You don't suppose that cat would a' run home, an' he after her? Is that them up the street? Don't you see a whirl o' dust in the road? Would you like me to go an' see? Cause I'm most afraid ef she's tried to run home; fer Bob Sykes hes trained thet dog to run races, an' he's a turrible fast runner, an' your cat is gettin' on in years. It might go hard with her." Miranda's sympathetic tone quite excited the old lady, whose old gray cat was very dear to her, being the last descendant of an ancient line of cats traditional in the family.

"No, Miranda, you just stay right here. Mrs. Spafford might need you after all this excitement. Tell her not to worry until I know the worst. I will go right home and see if anything has happened to Matthew. It really would be very distressing to me and my sister. If he has escaped from that dog he will need attention. Just tell Mrs. Spafford I will come down or send Hortense tomorrow as I promised." And the dignified old lady hurried off up the village street, for once unmindful of her dignity.

"Miranda!" called Marcia, when she had waited a reasonable time for the aunt's return and not even the girl presented herself.

Miranda appeared in a minute, with meek yet triumphant mien.

Marcia's eyes were laughing, but she tried to look grave.

"Miranda," she began, trying to suppress the merriment in her voice, "did you really see that cat out there?"

Miranda put on a dogged air and hesitated for a reply.

"Well, I heard a dog bark—" she began.

"Miranda was that quite honest!" protested Marcia who felt she ought to try to improve the moral standard of the girl thus under her charge and influence.

"I don't see anythin' wrong with that," asserted Miranda. "I didn't say a word that wasn't true. I'm always careful 'bout that sence I see how much you think of such things. I asked her ef it might a' ben her cat, an' how do I know but 'twas? And it would be easy to a' ben Bob Sykes's dog, ef she *was* round, fer that dog never lets a cat come on his block. Anyway I heard a dog bark, and I thought it sounded like Bob's dog's voice. I'm pretty good on sounds."

"But you shouldn't frighten Aunt Amelia. She's an old lady, and it isn't good for old people to get frightened. You know she thinks a great deal of her cat."

"Well, it ain't good fer you to be badgered, and Mr. David told me to look after you, an' I'm doin' it the best way I know how. If I don't do it right I s'pose you'll send me back to Grandma's an' then who'll take care of that blessed baby!"

When Marcia told it all to David he laughed until tears came.

"Good for Miranda!" he said. "She'll do, and Aunt Amelia'll never know what happened to poor old Matthew, who was probably sitting quietly by the hearth purring out his afternoon nap. Well, little girl, I'm glad you didn't have to answer Aunt Amelia's questions. Leave her to me. I'll shoulder all the blame and exonerate you. Don't worry."

"But, David," began Marcia, in her troubled tone, "Miranda ought not to tell things that are not exactly true. How can I teach her?"

"Well, Miranda's standards are not exactly right, and we must try little by little to raise them higher, but I'll miss my guess if she doesn't manage some way to protect you, even if she does have to tell the truth."

And thus it was that Miranda Griscom because a fixture in the household of David Spafford, and did about as she pleased with her master and mistress and the baby, because she usually pleased to do pretty well.

The years had gone by and little

[illegible]

David sat at the end of his pew, with Marcia, sweet and worshipful, beside him, and Miranda alert, one eye on her worship, the other on what might happen about her — or was it, quaint soul, but her way of watching for an opportunity to do good in her way?

Across the aisle the sweet face of Phoebe Deane attracted her attention. It was clouded with trouble. Miranda's keen eyes read that at once. Miranda had often noticed that about Phoebe Deane, and wondered, but there were so many other people that Miranda knew better to look after, that Phoebe Deane had heretofore not received her undivided attention.

But this particular morning Phoebe looked so pretty in her buff merino, which after much hesitation she had finally put on for church because her old church dress was so exceedingly shabby, that Miranda was all attention at once. Miranda, who had always been homely and red-haired and freckled, whose clothes had most of them been made over from Hannah Heath's cast-off wardrobe, yet loved beautiful things and beautiful people, and Phoebe, with her brown hair and deep, starry eyes, seemed like a lovely picture to her in the buff merino and with her face framed in its neat straw bonnet. The bonnet Miranda had seen for two or three summers past, but the frock was new, and a thing of beauty; therefore she studied its every detail and rejoiced that her position in the pew gave her a pretty good view of the young girl across the aisle, for something was wrong with the hinge of the door of Albert Deane's pew, and it stood wide open.

As her eyes travelled over Phoebe's frock they came finally to the face, so grave and sweet and troubled, as if already life was too filled with perplexities to have much joy left in it. Her keen gaze detected the droop to the pretty lips and the dark lines under the eyes; and then she looked at the sharp lines of Emmeline's sour face with its thin, pursed lips, and decided that Emmeline was not a pleasant woman to live with. Alma, preening herself in her Sunday clothes with her self-conscious smirk, was not a pleasant child, either, and she wondered if Phoebe could possibly take any pleasure in putting on her little garments for her, and planning surprises, and plays, the way she did for Rose. It seemed impossible. Miranda, the homely, looked down tenderly at the little Rose, and then gratefully toward David and Marcia at the end of the pew, and pitied the beautiful Phoebe, wishing for her the happiness that had come into her own barren life.

The service was about to commence when Judge Bristol, with his daughter Janet, and her cousin Nathaniel Graham, walked up the aisle to their pew, just in front of Albert Deane's.

Now there had been much debate in the heart of Phoebe Deane about coming to church that morning, for she could not keep out of her mind the thought of the stranger who had been so kind to her but a few days before, and it was impossible not to wonder if he would be there, and whether he would see her, and speak to her. It was in order to crucify this thought that she had half made up her mind not to wear the buff merino to church, and then nature triumphed and she put it on, realizing that her mother had made it for her to wear, and she had a perfect right to wear it, though Emmeline should disapprove. And Emmeline had disapproved in no uncertain tones. When she came downstairs ready for church Emmeline lifted her disagreeable eyebrows and exclaimed: "You're not going to wear that ridiculous rig to church, I hope? I should think you'd be ashamed to be decked out like that in the house of God! I'd sooner stay at home!"

And poor Phoebe would gladly have stayed at home if it had not been that Hank would have been there, and that she would have had to explain her reasons to Albert.

"I s'pose she wants people to know she's rich," piped in Alma, after a pause. This reference to her poor little pittance had been made almost hourly since Albert had told her of it, and it was growing unbearable to Phoebe. Altogether it was not with a very happy heart that she rode to church that morning, and she was half ashamed of herself for that undeniable wish to see the stranger once more. When she got out of the carryall at the church she would not look around nor even lift her eyes to see who was standing by the door. She had resolved not to think about him. If he came up the aisle, she would not know it, and her eyes should be otherwise occupied. No one should dare to say she was watching for him.

Nevertheless, as Janet and her cousin came up the aisle, Phoebe knew by the wild little beating of her heart that he was coming, and she commanded her eyes most strenuously that they should not lift from the psalm-book she had opened, albeit upside down. Yet, in spite of all resolves, when the occupants of the Bristol pew had entered it and were about to sit down, and while Nathaniel Graham stood so that his head and shoulders were just above the top of the high-back pew, those truant eyes fluttered up for one instant's glance, and in that instant were caught and held by the eyes of the young man in front in pleased recognition. 'Twas but a flash and Phoebe's eyes were back upon her book, and the young man was seated in the pew with only the top of his fine dark head showing, yet the pretty color flew into the cheek of the girl, and in the eyes of

the young man there was a light of ~~~~
The gl~~~~

~~~~ ~~~~, and if
~~~~ ~~~~son, There's somethin' doing
~~~~ whether to her shame or her praise, sat through the whole
long service, studied the faces of those two, and wove a pretty romance for herself
out of the golden fabric of a glance.

Chapter 8

When the service was ended Phoebe took good care of her eyes that they should not look toward the stranger. Nathaniel Graham was kept busy for the first few moments shaking hands with old friends, and talking with the minister, who came down from the pulpit on purpose to greet him, and when he turned, as he did on the first opportunity, the pew behind him was empty, and the eyes that had met his when he came in were nowhere to be seen. He looked anxiously over the receding audience towards the open door, and caught the glimmer of the buff merino. Hastily excusing himself to Janet on the plea that he wished to speak to someone and would join her later, Nathaniel made his way down the aisle, disappointing some good old ladies who had been friends of his mother, and who were lying in wait for him at various pew doors.

Miranda, who had been awaiting the pleasure of David and Marcia, saw it all, and her eager eyes watched to see if he would catch Phoebe. The way being open just then, she pressed out into the aisle, and, for once leaving Rose to follow with her mother, hurried to the door.

Nathaniel did not overtake Phoebe until she had gone down the church steps, and was on the path in front of the churchyard that led to the shed where many of the conveyances were tied. He stepped up beside her, taking off his hat with a cheery, "Good morning," and Phoebe's pink cheeks and smiling eyes welcomed him happily.

"I wanted to be quite sure you were all right after your adventure the other day," he said, looking down into the lovely face with real pleasure; and then, before she could even answer, Hiram Green stepped up airily as if he belonged, and looked at Nathaniel questioningly as though he were intruding, saying, "Well, here you are Phoebe; I lost track of you at the church door. We better step along. The carryall is waitin'."

Nathaniel looked up annoyed, then puzzled, recognized Hiram, with astonishment, and said, "I beg your pardon, I did not know I was keeping you from your friends," to Phoebe, and, lifting his hat with a courteous "Good morning, Mr. Green," to Hiram, stepped back among the little throng coming out of the church door.

Now Miranda had been close behind, for she was determined to read every chapter of her romance that appeared in sight. She saw the whole maneuver on Hiram Green's part, and the color the flamed angrily into Phoebe's cheek when she recognized Hiram's interference. She also saw the dismay that showed in the girl's face as Nathaniel left her and Hiram Green made as if to walk beside her. Phoebe looked wildly about. There seemed no escape from him as a

.... responded to the name, but she did not know that it was a light of satisfaction because he had found out her name without asking anyone. He stood a moment and looked after them. He saw quite plainly that Phoebe dismissed the sulky Hiram with a word and went off with Miranda. He saw that Hiram did not even raise his hat on leaving Phoebe, but slouched off angrily without a word.

"Say, Phoebe Deane," said Miranda, familiarly, "my Mrs. Spafford,"— this was Miranda's common way of speaking of Marcia in the possessive— "she's ben talkin' a long time 'bout you, and wishin' you'd come to see her, an' she's ben layin' out to ask you to tea, but things hes prevented. So, could you come Tuesday? You better come early and stay all afternoon, so you can play with Rose. She's the sweetest thing!"

"Oh, I'd love to come," said Phoebe, her face aglow with pleasure. "I've always admired Mrs. Spafford so much, and little Rose is beautiful, just like a rose. Yes, tell her I will come."

Just then came the strident voice of Emmeline.

"Phoebe! Phoebe Deane! Was you intendin' to go home with us, or had you calculated to ride with Hiram Green? If you're comin' with us we can't wait all day."

With scarlet cheeks, angry heart, and trembling limbs Phoebe bade Miranda a frightened good-bye and climbed into the carriage, not daring to look behind her to see who had heard the hateful words of her sister-in-law. Oh, had the stranger heard them? How dreadful if he had! How contemptible, how unforgivable in Emmeline! How could she endure this persecution any longer? She did not even dare lift her eyes as they drove by the church, but sat with drooping lashes and burning cheeks, so missing the glance of the young man Nathaniel as he stood on the sidewalk with his cousin, waiting for another opportunity to lift his hat. Perhaps it was as well, for she would have been most unmercifully teased and cross-questioned if Emmeline and Alma had seen him speak to her.

Miranda watched the Deanes drive away, and turned with a vindictive look of triumph to stare at Hiram Green getting into his chaise alone. Then she began to reflect upon what she had done.

About four o'clock that afternoon, the dinner dishes being well out of the way, and the Sunday quiet resting upon the house, Miranda presented herself before Marcia with the most guilty look upon her face that Marcia had ever seen her wear.

"Well, I've up an' done it now, Mrs. Marcia, an' no mistake. I expect I'll have to leave you, an' the thought of it jes' breaks my heart."

"Why, Miranda!" said Marcia, sitting up very suddenly from the couch where she had been reading Bible stories to Rose. "You're not—you're surely not going to get married!"

"Not by a jugful I ain't. Do you s'pose I'd hev enny man that would take up with freckles an' a turn-up nose in a wife? I've gone and done sumpin' you'll think is a heap worse'n gittin' married. But I didn't tell no lie. I was keerful enough 'bout that. I only told her you'd been talkin' 'long back 'bout askin' her, an' you hed all right 'nough, only I oughtn't to a ast her, an' set the day an' all 'thout you knowin'. I knowed it at the time well 'nough, but I hed to do it, 'cause the circumstances wuz sech. You see thet squint-eyed Hiram Green was makin' it out that she was somewhat great to him, a paradin' down the walk there from the church, an' a driven' off that nice city cousin of Janet Bristol's with his nice, genteel manners, an' his tippin's of his hat, an' her a lookin' like she'd drop from shame, so I called her to wait, an' I runs up an' talks to her, an' course then she tels Hiram Green he needn't to trouble to wait fer her, an' we goes off together in full sight of all. My, I was glad I beat that skin-flint of a Hiram Green, but I was that excited I jes' couldn't think of 'nother thing to do 'cept to invite her."

"Who in the world are you talking about, Miranda? And what terrible thing have you done?"

Marcia's laughing eyes reassured Miranda and she went on with her story.

"Why that pretty little Phoebe Deane," she explained. "I've invited her to tea Tuesday night. I thought that would suit you better than any other time. Monday night things ain't straight from wash-day yet, and I didn't want to put it off too long, an' I can make everything myself. But if you don't like it I'll go an' tell her the hull truth on't, only she did look so mortal pleased I hate to spoil her fun."

By degrees Marcia drew the whole story from Miranda, even to a voluble description of the buff merino, and its owner's drooping expression.

"Well, I don't see why you thought I would be displeased," said Marcia. "It is only right you should invite company once in a while. I am glad you invited her, and as you do most of the work, and know our plans pretty well, you knew it would likely be convenient. I am glad you invited her."

"But I didn't invite her," said Miranda, "leastways she doesn't know I did. She thinks you done it yourself, and she sent you a whole lots of thanks, and said she 'dmired you turrible. And I didn't tell a thing but the truth either," Miranda added, doggedly.

"You ....

....

..... afternoon, when she could not get away from the family because Emmeline had ordered her to "stay downstairs and mind the baby, and not prance off to her room like a royal lady," and through the trials of Monday with its heavy work, which did not even cease with the washing of the tea things, but continued in the form of a great basket of mending which Emmeline announced at the supper table were "all to be finished and put away that evening." Emmeline seemed to have made up her mind to be as disagreeable as possible. Phoebe sat beside the candle and sewed with weary fingers, and longed to be away from them all where she might think over quietly the pleasant things that had come into her life of late. Hiram Green came in, too, and seemed to have come with a purpose, for he was hardly seated in his usual chair with its back tilted against the wall, and the fore-legs tipped up, when he began with:

"Say, Albert, did you see that nincompoop of a nephew of Judge Bristol in the church? Does beat all how he takes on airs jest because he's been off to college. Gosh! I ken remember him goin' fishin' in his bare feet, and here he was bowin' round among the ladies like he'd always been a fine gentleman and never done a stroke of work in his life. His hands are ez white and soft ez a woman's. He strikes me very ladylike, indeed, he does. Smirkin round and takin' off his hat ez if he'd nothin' better to do. Fine feathers don't make fine birds, I say. I don't believe he could cut a swath o' hay now to save his precious little life. He makes me sick with his airs. Seems like Miss Janet better look after him ef she expects to marry him, er he'll lose his head to every girl he meets."

Something uncontrollable seemed to have stolen the blood out of Phoebe's heart for a moment, and all her strength was slipping away from her. Then a mighty anger rolled through her being, and surged to her very finger tips, yet she held those fingers steadily, as her needle pierced back and forth through the stocking she was darning with unnecessary care. She knew perfectly well that these remarks were entirely for her benefit and she resolved not to let Hiram see that she understood or cared.

"Is he going to marry his cousin Janet?" asked Albert interestedly. "I never heard that."

"You didn't? Well, where've you ben, all these years? It's ben common talk sence they was little tads. Their mothers 'lowed that was the way it was to be, and they was sent away to separate schools on that account; I s'pose they was afraid they'd take a dislike to each other ef they saw each other constant. 'Pon my word I think Janet could look higher, an' ef I was her I wouldn't be held by no promise of no dead mothers. But they do say she worships the very ground he walks on, an' she'll hold him to all right enough, so it's no sort o' use fer any other girls to go anglin' after him."

"I heard he was real bright," said Albert, genially. "They say he's taken honors, a good many of 'em. He was president of the Philomathean Society in Union College, you know, and that's a great honor."

Albert read a good deal, and knew more about the world's affairs than Hiram.

"Oh, bah! That's child's play!" sneered Hiram. "Who couldn't be president of a literary society? It don't take much spunk to preside. I take it I ran the town meeting last year 'bout's well 's ef I'd ben a college president. My opinion is Nate Graham would 'v' 'mounted to more ef he'd stayed t' home an' learned farmin', 'er studied law with his uncle an' worked fer his board. A feller thet's all give over to lyin' around makin' nuthin' of himself don't amount to a row o' pins."

"But they say Dr. Nott thinks he's got brains," persisted Albert. "I'm sure I'd like to see him come out on top. I heard he was studying law in New York now. He was always a pleasant-spoken boy when he was here."

"What's pleasant speakin'!" growled Hiram. "It can't sell a load o' wheat." His unsold wheat was bitterly in his thoughts.

"Well, I don't know 'bout that, Hiram." Albert felt pleasantly argumentative. "I don't know but if I was going to buy wheat I'd a little sooner buy off the man that was pleasant spoken than the man that wasn't."

Hiram sat glumly and pondered this saying for a few minutes, and Phoebe took advantage of the pause in conversation to lay down her work-basket, determinedly saying to Emmeline:

"I'll finish these stockings tomorrow, Emmeline. I feel tired and I'm going upstairs."

It was the first time that Phoebe had ever dared to take a stand against Emmeline's orders. Emmeline was too astonished to speak for a minute, but just as Phoebe reached the door she said:

"Well, really! Tired! I was down half an hour before you this mornin', and I'm not tired to speak of, but I suppose ef I was I'd have to keep right on. And who's to do your work tomorrow mornin' while you do this, I'd like to know?"

But Phoebe had escaped out of hearing, and Emmeline relapsed into vexed silence. Hiram, however, narrowed his cruel little eyes, and thought he understood why she had gone.

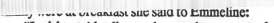

...y were at breakfast she said to Emmeline:

"I wish you'd tell me what work you want done besides the rest of the ironing. I'm invited out to tea this afternoon, and I want to get everything done this morning."

"Where to?" exploded Alma, her curiosity getting the better of her superiority to her aunt for once.

"Indeed!" said Emmeline, disdainfully. "Invited out to tea! What airs we are takin' on with our money! Pretty soon you won't have any time to give at home at all. If I was you I'd go and board somewhere, you have so many social engagements. I'm sure I don't feel like askin' a young lady like you to soil her hands washin' my dishes. I'll wash 'em myself after this. Alma, you go get your apern on and help ma this mornin'. Aunt Phoebe hasn't got time. She'll have to take all mornin' to curl her hair."

"Now, Emmeline!" said Albert, gently reproachful, "don't tease the child. It's real nice for her to get invited out. She don't get much change, that's sure."

"Oh, no, two tea-parties inside of a week's nothin'. I've heard of New York ladies goin' out as often as every other day," said Emmeline, sarcastically.

Albert never could quite understand his wife's sarcasm, so he turned to Phoebe and voiced the question that the rest were just bursting with curiosity to have answered.

"Who invited you, Phoebe?"

"Mrs. Spafford," said Phoebe, trying not to show how near she was to crying over Emmeline's hateful speeches.

"Well, now, that's real nice," said Albert, in genuine earnest. "There isn't a finer man in town than David Spafford. His paper's the best edited in the whole state of New York, and he's got a fine little wife. I don't believe she's many days older than you are, Phoebe, either. She looked real young when he brought her here, and she hasn't grown a day older that I can see."

"Good reason why," sniffed Emmeline; "she's nothin' to do but lie around and be waited on. I'm sure Phoebe's welcome to such friends if they suit her; fer my part I'd ruther go to see good self-respectin' women that did a woman's work in the world, and not let their husbands make babies of them, and go ridin' round in a carriage forever lookin' like a June mornin'. I call it *lazy*, I do. It's nothing' more'n or less—and she keepin' that poor good-fer-nothin' Miranda

Griscom slavin' from mornin' to night fer her. If Phoebe was my sister I shouldn't choose such friends fer her. Besides, she hasn't got very good manners not to invite your wife, too, Albert Deane, but I suppose you never thought o' that. I shouldn't think Phoebe would care to accept an invitation that was an insult to her relations, even if they wasn't just blood relations—they're all she's got, that's sure."

"Say, look here, Emmeline. Your speech don't hang together. You just said you didn't care to make friends of Mrs. Spafford, and now you're fussing because she didn't invite you, too. It looks like a case of sour grapes. Eh, Phoebe?"

Hank caught the joke and laughed uproariously, though Phoebe looked grave, knowing how bitter it would be to Emmeline to be laughed at. Two red spots flamed out on the wife's cheeks, and her eyes snapped.

"Seems to me things has gone pretty far, Albert Deane," she said, in a high, excited voice, "when you—*YOU*—can insult your wife in public, and then *LAUGH!* I shan't forget this of you, Albert Deane!" and with her head well up she shoved her chair back from the table and left the room, closing the door with loud decision behind her.

Albert's merry laugh came to an abrupt end. He looked after his wife with startled surprise. Never in all their one-sidedly-harmonious wedded life had Emmeline taken offence like that in the presence of others. He looked helplessly, inquiringly, from one to another.

"Well, now!" he began, aimlessly. "You don't suppose she thought I meant that, do you?"

"'Course!" said Alma, knowingly. "You've made her dreadful mad, pa. My! But you're goin' to get it!"

"Looks mighty like it," snickered Hank.

Albert continued to look at Phoebe for a reply.

"I'm afraid she thought you were in earnest, Albert. You better go and explain," said Phoebe, commiseratingly.

"You better not go fer a while, pa," called out Johnny, sympathetically. "Wait till she gets over it a little. Go hide in the barn. That's the way I do!"

But Albert was going heavily up the stairs after his offended wife and did not hear his young hopeful's voice. Albert was tender-hearted and could not bear to hurt any one's feelings. Besides, it never was pleasant to have Emmeline angry. He wished if possible to explain away the offence before it struck in too deep for healing and had to be lived down.

This state of things was rather more helpful to Phoebe than otherwise. Hank took himself off, finding a certain embarrassment in Phoebe's dignified silence. The children slipped away, glad to get rid of any little duties usually required by their mother. Phoebe went at her work unhindered and it vanished before her while her thoughts took happy flight away from the unhappy home to the afternoon that was before her. Upstairs the conference was long and

.... , ... way to say much about it. You just go out to tea and have a good time and don't think any more about this. It'll blow over, you know. Most things do."

Phoebe tried to smile, and felt a throb of gratitude toward the brother who was not really her brother at all.

"You're a good girl, Phoebe," he went on, patting her cheek. "You're like your mother. She was little, and pretty, and liked things nice, and had a quiet voice. I sometimes think maybe it isn't as pleasant here for you as it might be. You're made of different kind of stuff, that thinks and feels in a different way. Your mother was so. I've oftened wondered whether father understood her. Men don't understand women very well, I guess. Now, I don't really always understand Emmeline, and I guess it's pretty hard for her. Father was some rough and blunt, and maybe that was hard for your mother at times. I remember she used to look sad, though I never saw her much, come to think about it. I was off working for myself when they were married, you know. Say, Phoebe, you didn't for a minute think I meant what I said about sour grapes and Emmeline, did you? I told her you didn't, but I promised her I'd make sure about it. I knew you didn't. Well, I must go out and see if Hank's done everything."

He went out drawing a long breath as if he had accomplished an unpleasant task, and left Phoebe wondering about her own mother, and trying to get a little glimpse into her possible sorrows and joys through the words that Albert had spoken. Somehow that sentence in her birthday letter came back to her: "Unless you can marry a man to whom you can look up and honor next to God it is better not to marry at all, believe your mother, child. I say it lovingly, for I have seen much sorrow and would protect you."

Had her father been hard to live with? Phoebe put the thought from her and was half glad she could not answer it. Her own life was enough of a problem without going back and sorrowing for her mother's. But it made her heart throb with a sense of a fuller understanding of her mother's life and warnings.

Emmeline did not come downstairs until dinnertime, and her manner was freezing. Phoebe was glad that the work was all done carefully, even to the scrubbing of the back steps, and that the dinner was more than usually inviting. But Emmeline seemed not to see anything, and her manner remained as severe as when she first entered the kitchen. She poured the coffee, and drank a cup of it herself, and ate a bit of bread, but would not touch anything else on the table. She waited on the children with ostentatious care, but would not respond to the solicitations of her anxious husband, who urged this and that dainty upon her. Hank even suggested that the hot biscuits were nicer than usual. But that remark had to be lived down by Hank, for Emmeline usually made the biscuits, and Phoebe had made these. She did not condescend to even look at him in response.

Phoebe was glad when the last bit of pumpkin pie and cheese had disappeared and she could rise from her chair and go about the after-dinner work. Glad, too, that Emmeline went away again and left her to herself, for so she could more quickly finish up.

She was just hanging up her wiping towels when Emmeline came downstairs with the look of a martyr on her face, and the quilting frames in her hand. Over her shoulder was thrown her latest achievement in patchwork, a brilliant combination of reds and yellows and white known as the "rising sun" pattern. It was a large quilt, and would be quite a job to put on the frames. It was a herculean task for one person without an assistant.

Phoebe stopped with an exclamation of dismay.

"You're not going to put that on the frames today, Emmeline? I thought you were saving that for next month!"

Emmeline's grim mouth remained shut for several seconds. At last she snapped out: "I don't know that it makes any difference what you thought. This is a free country and I've surely a right to do what I please in my own house."

"But, Emmeline, I can't help you this afternoon!"

"I don't know that I've asked you!"

"But you can't do it alone!"

"Indeed! What makes you think I can't! Go right along to your tea-party and take your ease. I was brought up to work, thank fortune, and a few burdens more or less can't make much difference. I'm not a lady of leisure and means like you."

Phoebe stood a minute watching Emmeline's stubby, determined fingers as they fitted a wooden peg into its socket like a period to the conversation. It seemed dreadful to go away and leave Emmeline to put up that quilt alone, but what was she to do? There seemed to be no law in the universe that would compel her to give up her first invitation out to tea in order that Emmeline might finish that quilt this particular week. It was plain that she had brought it down on purpose to hold her at home. Indignation boiled within her. If she had slipped stealthily away this would not have happened, but she had done her duty in telling Emmeline, and she felt perfectly justified in going. It wasn't as if she had invited herself. It would not be polite, now she had accepted the invitation, putting up that sunrise bedquilt all alone. The thought of it seemed to cloud the sun and spoil anticipation of her precious afternoon.

Once out in the crisp autumn air she drew a long breath of relief. It was so good to get away from the gloomy atmosphere that had been cramping her life for so many years. In a lonely place in the road between farm-houses she uttered a soft little scream under her breath. She felt as if she *must* do something to let out the agony of wrath and longing and hurt and indignity that were trying to burst her soul. Then she walked on to the town with demure dignity, and the people in the passing carryalls and farm wagons never suspected that she was aught but a happy maiden with thoughts busy with the joys of life.

The autumn days were lingering in sunny deep-blue haze, though the reds were changing into brown, and in the fields were gathering huddled groups of cornshocks like old crones, waving skeleton arms in the breeze, and whispering weird gossip. A rusty-throated cricket in the thicket by the way piped out his monotonous dirge to the summer now deceased. A flight of birds sprang into sight across the sky, calling and chattering to one another of a warmer climate. An old red cow stood in her well-grazed meadow, snuffed the short grass, and, looking at Phoebe as she passed, bawled a gentle protest at the decline of fresh vegetables. Everything spoke of autumn and the winter that was to come. But Phoebe, every step she took from home, grew lighter and lighter hearted, and could only think of the happy time she was to have.

It was not that she was thinking of the stranger, for there was no possibility of meeting him. The Bristol place, a fine old Colonial house behind a tall white fence and high privet hedge with a glimpse of a wonderful garden set off with dark borders of box through the imposing gateway, was over near the Presbyterian church. It was not near the Spaffords' house. She felt the freer and happier because there was no question of him to trouble her careful conscience.

Miranda had gone to the window that looked up the road towards the Deanes at least twenty times since the dinner dishes were washed. She was more nervous over the success of this her first tea-party than over anything she had ever done. She was beginning to be afraid that her guest would not arrive.

Everything was in train for supper. There was to be stewed chicken, with "riz biscuits" and honey, raspberry preserves, spiced peaches, fruitcake and caraway-seed cookies with delectable sugary tops. The tea was to be served in the very thinnest of the blue china cups. It was with difficulty that Marcia had suppressed a multitude of varieties of pickles and jellies and preserves and cakes, for Miranda could not understand why it wasn't "skimpin" ' to have so few dishes upon the table.

"Gran'ma was never half satisfied ef you could see the tablecloth much between the dishes," she was wont to say, dubiously. But Marcia tried patiently to explain that it was not refined to load the table with too many varieties, and Miranda, half convinced, gave it up, thinking Marcia sweet, but "inexperienced."

Miranda, fidgeting from window to door and back again to the kitchen, came at last to the library where sat Marcia with her work, watching a frolic between Rose and her kitten outside the window.

"Say, Mrs. Marcia," she began, ingratiatingly, "you'll find out what troubles that poor little thing, and see ef you can't help her, won't you? She's your size an' kind, more'n she is mine, an' you ought to be able to give her some help. You needn't think you've got to tell out to me every thing you find out. I shan't ask. I can find out enough fer my own use when I'm needed, but I think she needs you this time. When there's any use fer me I seem always to kind o' feel it in the air."

"Bless your heart, Miranda, I don't believe you care for any one unless they need helping!" exclaimed Marcia, laughing. "What makes you so sure Phoebe Deane needs helping?"

"Oh, I know," said Miranda, mysteriously, "an' so will you when you look at her real hard. There she comes now. Don't you go an' tell I said nothing 'bout her. You jes' make her tell you. She's that sweet an' so are you that you two can't help pourin' out your perfume to each other like two flowers."

"But trouble isn't perfume, Miranda."

"H'm! Flowers smells all the sweeter when you crush 'em a little, don't they? There, you set right still where you be. I'll go to the door. Don't you stir. I want her to see you lookin' that way with the sun across the top o' your pretty hair. She'll like it, I know she will."

Marcia sat quite still as she was bidden with the madonna smile upon her lips that David loved so well, smiling over Miranda's strange fancies, yet never thinking of herself as a picture against the window-panes. In a moment more Phoebe Deane stood in the doorway, with Miranda beside her, looking from one to another of the two sweet girl-faces in deep admiration, and noting with delight that Phoebe fully appreciated the loveliness of her "Mrs. Marcia."

...., for Marcia, though she had grown in heart and intellect during her five years of beautiful companionship with David Spafford, had not lost the years she had skipped by her early marriage, but kept their memory fresh in her heart. Perhaps it was the girl in her that had attracted her to Phoebe Deane.

They fell into happy converse at once, Phoebe begging for a seam to sew on the frock of pale blue merino that Marcia was making for Rose, all exquisitely braided with white silk braid in a rosebud pattern.

They talked about their mothers, these two who had known so little of real mothering; and Marcia, because she had felt it herself, understood the wistfulness in Phoebe's tone when she spoke of her loneliness and her longing for her mother. Then Phoebe, with a half-apologetic flush, told of her mother's birthday letter and the buff merino, and Marcia smoothed down the soft folds of the skirt reverently, half wistfully, and told Phoebe it was beautiful, just like a present and a letter from heaven. Then she kissed her gently and made her come out where little Rose was playing. There they frolicked until the child was Phoebe's devoted slave, and then they all went back to the big stately parlor, where Miranda had a great fire of logs blazing, and there in a deep easy chair Phoebe was ensconced with Rose cuddled in her lap playing with her locket, and having it tied at will about her own dimpled neck.

While this was going on Marcia played exquisite music on her pianoforte, which to the ear of the girl, who had seldom heard any music in her life save the singing in church or singing-school, seemed entrancing. She almost forgot the charming child in her lap, forgot to look about on the beautiful room so full of interesting things, forgot even to think, as she listened, and her very soul responded to the music, which seemed to be calling a great comfort across the immense distances that separated her from things she loved.

Then suddenly the music ceased and Marcia sprang up, saying in a glad voice, "Oh, there is David!" and went to the door to let him in.

Phoebe exclaimed in dismay that it was so late, and the beautiful afternoon was at an end, but she forgot her disappointment in wonder over Marcia's joy at her husband's coming. It brought back to her the subject that had been uppermost in her thoughts ever since the night when Hiram Green had dared to follow her to the orchard. Somehow she had grown up with very little halo about the institution of marriage. It had seemed to her a kind of necessary arrangement, but never anything that gave great joy. The married people whom she knew did not seem greatly to rejoice in one another's presence. Indeed, they often seemed to be a hindrance each to the other. She had never cherished many bright dreams of any such state for herself, as most girls do. Life had been too dully tinted since her little girlhood for her to indulge fancies. Therefore it was a revelation to her to see how much these two rare souls cared for one another. It was not that they displayed their affection by any act of endearment, but she saw it in the glance of each, in a sudden lighting of the eye, the involuntary cadence of the voice, the evident pleasure of yielding each to the other, aye, rather preferring one another; the constant presence of joy as a guest in that house, because of the presence of the other. One could never feel that way about Hiram Green—no one could,—it would be impossible! Wait! Had not that been the very thing possessed by his poor crushed little wife? But how could she feel it when it was not returned? She began to think over the married households she knew, but then she knew so few of them intimately. There was Granny McVane. Did the old 'Squire feel so about her? And did she spring to meet him at the door after all these years of life with its hardness? There was something about the sweet meek face in its ruffled cap that made Phoebe think it possible. And there was Albert. Of course Emmeline did not feel so, for Emmeline was not that kind of a woman, but might not a different woman have felt that for Albert? He was kind and gentle to women. Too slow and easy to gain real respect, yet—yes, she felt that it might be possible for some women to feel real joy in his presence. There lurked a possibility that he felt so toward Emmeline, in some degree; but Hiram Green, with his chair tilted back against the wall, and his hat drawn down over his narrow eyes, above his cruel mouth! Never! He was utterly incapable of so beautiful a feeling. If he only might in some way pass out of her horizon forever it would be a great relief.

David Spafford when he entered the parlor not only filled it with pleasure for his wife and little girl, but he brought an added cheer for the guest as well, and Phoebe found herself talking with this man of literature and politics and science as easily as if she had known him well all her life. Afterward she wondered at herself for it. Somehow he took it for granted that she knew as much as he did, and made her feel at her ease at once. He had ready a bright story from the newspaper office that exactly fitted someone's remark, and a joke for his little one. He asked after Albert Deane as though he were an old friend, and seemed to know more about him than Phoebe dreamed. "He has a good head," he added in response to Phoebe's timid answer about the farm and some improvements that Albert had introduced. "I had a long talk with him the other day and enjoyed it." Somehow that little remark made Phoebe more at home. She knew Albert's short-comings keenly herself, and she was not deeply attached to him, yet he was all she had, and he had been kind to her. He stood

Deane family. But Marcia give the sign to be seated, and Miranda hastened to the door.

"It's just one of the boys from the office, I think, Marcia," said David Spafford. "I told him to bring up the mail if anything important came. The coach wasn't in when I left."

But a man's voice was heard conversing with Miranda.

"I won't keep him but a minute! I'm sorry to disturb him." A moment more and Miranda appeared with a guileless face.

"A man to see you, Mr. Spafford. I think it's that nevview of Jedge Bristol's. Shall I tell him you're eatin' supper?"

"What! Nathaniel Graham? No indeed, Miranda; just put on another plate and bring him right in. Come in, Nathaniel, and take tea with us while you tell your errand. You're just the one we need to complete our company."

Miranda, innocent and cheerful, hurried away to obey orders, while David helped the willing guest off with his overcoat, and brought him out to the table. She felt there was no need to say anything of a little conversation she had held with Judge Bristol's "nevview" about half past four that afternoon. It was while Marcia was playing the pianoforte in the parlor. Miranda had gone into the garden to pick a bunch of parsley for her chicken gravy, and as was her wont, to keep a good watch upon all outlying territory. She had sauntered up to the fence for a glance about to see if there was anything of interest happening, and Nathaniel Graham had happened. She had watched him coming, wistfully. Yet she dared not add another guest to her tea-party, though the very one she would have chosen had wandered her way.

He had tipped his hat to her and smiled. Miranda liked to have hats tipped to her even though she was freckled and red-haired. This young man had been in the highest grade of village school when she entered the lowest class, yet he remembered her enough to bow, freckled though she was, and working for her living. Her heart had swelled with pride in him, and she decided he would do for the part she wished him to play in life.

"Ah, Miss Miranda," he had paused when almost past, and stepped back a pace, "do you happen to know if Mr. Spafford will be at home this evening? I want to see him very much for a few minutes."

Now, though Miranda had dared not invite another guest, she saw no reason why she should not put him in the way of an invitation, so inclining her head thoughtfully on one side and squinting her eyes introspectively, as if she were the keeper of David Spafford's engagements, she had said, thoughtfully: "Let me see! Yes, I *think* he's at home tonight. Thur's one night this week I heerd him say he was goin' out, but I'm *pretty* sure it ain't this night. But I'll tell you what you better do ef you're real anxious to see him, you better jest stop 'long about six o'clock. He's always home then, 'thout fail, 'n' he'll tell you ef he ain't goin' to be in."

The young man's face had lighted gratefully.

"Thank you," he had said, quite as if he were speaking to a lady Miranda thought, "that will suit me very well. I need not keep him long and he can tell me if he will be in later in the evening. I shall be passing here about that time."

Then Miranda had hustled in with satisfaction to see if her biscuits were beginning to brown. If this plan worked well there was nothing further to be desired.

She had spent the remainder of the afternoon in stealthily vibrating between the kitchen and the parlor door, where, unseen, she could inspect the conversation from time to time and keep advised as to any possible developments. She had set out to see if Phoebe Deane needed any help, and she meant to leave no stone unturned to get at the facts.

So it all happened just as Miranda would have planned. Things were happening her way these days, mostly, she told herself with a chuckle and a triumphant glance over the lights in her grandmother's kitchen, as she went to get another sprigged plate for Nathaniel Graham. And when Marcia was not looking she slid another plate of quivering jelly, amber tinted to match Phoebe's frock, in between Phoebe's and Nathaniel's plates.

Meantime Phoebe's heart was in a great flutter over the introduction to her knight of the forest. The pretty color came into her cheeks, and her eyes shone like stars in the candle light as David said: "Nathaniel, let me make you acquainted with our friend Miss Phoebe Deane. I think she is a newcomer since you left us. Miss Deane, this is our friend Mr. Graham."

And then she found herself murmuring an acknowledgment as the young man took her hand and bowed low over it, saying: "Thank you, David, but I am not so far behind the times as you think. I have met Miss Deane before." That frightened her quite, so that she hardly could manage to seat herself with her chair properly drawn up to the table, and she fell to wondering if they had noticed how her cheeks burned. Ah! If they had they were keeping it to themselves, especially Miranda, who was dishing up the chicken. Wily Miranda! She had called them to supper without dishing it up, making due allowance for the digression of another guest which she had planned.

The meal moved along quite smoothl~~y~~ ~~th~~
around until Phoeb~~e had~~

~~.....~~ances by the present

~~... an~~ new and interesting to Phoebe, to whom had come but a stray
word now and again of all these wonderful happenings. Who, for instance, was
this "Santa Anna" whose name was spoken of so familiarly? Neither a saint nor
a woman, apparently. And what had he or she to do with affairs so grave?

And who was this brave Indian chief, Osceola, languishing in prison because he and his people could not bear to give up the home of their fathers?
Why had she never heard of it all before? O, life was very hard for everybody.
She had never thought of the Indians before as anything but terrible, blood-
thirsty savages, and lo! they had feelings and loves and homes like others. Her
cheeks glowed and her eyes were alight with feeling, and when young Nathaniel
turned to her now and again he thought how wondrously beautiful she was, and
marvelled that he had not heard her praises rung from every mouth so soon as
he had reached the town. He had been very little at home during his college life
and years of law study.

Then the conversation came nearer home, and David and Nathaniel talked
of their college days. Nathaniel spoke a great deal of Eliphalet Nott, the
honored president of his college, and told many a little anecdote of his wisdom
and wit.

"This chicken reminds me," he began, laughingly, as he held up a delicate
wishbone toward Phoebe, "of a story that is told of Dr. Nott. It seems a number
of students had planned a raid upon his chicken-house. Dr. Nott's family
consists of himself and wife and his daughter Miss Sally. Well, the rumor of this
plot against his chickens reached the good president's ears, and he prepared to
circumvent it.

"The students had planned to go to a tree where it was known that several
favorite fowls roosted, and one was to climb up while the others stood below
and took the booty. They waited until it was late, and the lights in the doctor's
study went out, and then they stole silently into the yard and made for the
hen-roost. The man who was to catch the chickens climbed carefully, silently,
into the tree so as not to disturb the sleeping birds, and the others waited in the
dark below.

"The first hen made a good deal of cackling and fuss as she was caught and while this was going on the students below the tree saw some one approaching them from the house. Very silently they scattered into the dark and fled, leaving the poor man in the tree alone. Dr. Nott, well muffled about his face, came quietly up and took his stand below the tree, and in a moment the man in the tree handed down a big white rooster.

"'This is Daddy Nott,' he said, in a whisper, and the man below received the bird without a word.

"In a moment more a second fowl was handed down. 'This is Mammy Nott,' whispered the irreverent student. Again the bird was received without comment. Then a third hen was handed down with the comment: 'This is Sally Nott.' The Doctor received the third bird and disappeared into the darkness and the student in the tree came down to find his partners fled, with no knowledge of who had taken the fowls. They were much troubled about the circumstance, but hoped that it was only a joke some fellow student had played upon them. They were however extremely anxious the next day when each one concerned in the affair received an invitation to dine with Dr. Nott that evening. Not daring to refuse, nor being able to find any suitable excuse, they presented themselves dubiously at Dr. Nott's house at the appointed hour, and were received courteously as usual. They were beginning to breathe more freely when they were ushered out to dinner, and there, before the Doctor's place, lay three large platters, each containing a fine fowl cooked to a turn. They dared not look at one another, but their embarrassment came to a climax when Dr. Nott looked up pleasantly at the student on his right, who had been the man to climb the tree, and asked, 'Hastings, will you have a piece of Daddy Nott, or Mommy Nott, or Sally Nott?' pointing in order to each platter. I think if it hadn't been for the twinkle in the Doctor's eye those boys would have taken their hats and left without making any adieus, for they say Hastings looked as if you could knock him over with a feather, but that twinkle broke the horror of it, and they all broke down and laughed until they were most heartily ashamed of themselves, and every man there was cured forever of robbing chicken-roosts. But do you know, the Doctor never said another word to those fellows about that, and they were his most loyal students from that time on."

Amid the laughter over this story they rose from the table. Little Rose, who had fallen asleep at the table, was whisked off to bed by the faithful Miranda, and the others went into the parlor where Marcia played exquisite melodies as David and Nathaniel called for them, and Phoebe, entranced, listened, and did not know how her charmed day was spending itself, until suddenly she realized that it was half past eight o'clock and she was some distance from home.

Now, for a maiden to be abroad after nine o'clock in those days was little short of a crime. It would be deemed most highly improper and disreputable by every good person; therefore, as Phoebe noted the time by the great clock

she started to her feet in a panic and ~~~~~
after h~~~

Chapter 11

Phoebe's heart, as she stepped out into the moonlight with the young man, fluttered so she scarcely could speak without letting her voice shake. It seemed so wonderful that she, of all the girls in the village, should be going home with this bright, handsome, noble man. There was nothing foolish or vain in her thought about it. He was not to be anything more to her for this walk, for his life was set otherwhere, and he belonged to others—notably, in all likelihood, to his cousin Janet. Nevertheless she felt highly honored that he should take the trouble to see her home, and she knew in her heart that the memory of this walk, her first alone with a young man who was not her brother, would remain long a pleasant spot in her life.

He seemed to enjoy her company as much as he had done David's, for he talked on about the things that had interested them in the evening. He told more college stories, and even spoke of his literary society, so that Phoebe, remembering Albert's words, asked if it was true that he had once been president of the Philomatheans, and he modestly acknowledged it, as though the office gave him honor, not he the office. She asked him shyly of the meetings and what they did and he gave her reminiscences of his college days. Their voices rang out now and then in a merry laugh, whereat all the little cornshock ladies huddled in the moonlight seemed to wave sinister arms and shake their heads mournfully to hear mirth at so unseemly an hour. Out in the quiet country road the young man suddenly asked her:

"Tell me, Miss Deane, suppose I knew of some people who were oppressed, suffering, and wanted their freedom; suppose they needed help to set them free, what do you think I ought to do? Think of myself and my career, or go and help set them free?"

Phoebe raised her sweet eyes to his earnest face in the moonlight and tried to understand.

"I am not wise," she said, "and perhaps I would not know what you ought to do, but I think I can tell you what you *would* do. I think you would forget all about yourself and go to set those people free."

He looked down into her face, and thought what it meant to a man to have a girl like this one believe in him.

"Thank you!" he said gravely. "I am honored by your opinion of me. You have told me where duty lies. I will remember your words when the time comes."

In the quiet of her chamber a few minutes later Phoebe remembered the words of the young people that day upon the hill-side, and wondered if it were the people of Texas whom he meant needed to be set free.

He had bade her good-night with a ╎
glad to ╎

╎ am Green like an angry
╎ ╎ made his face look fairly livid with unholy wrath. "Hev
yeh learned yer lesson, er d'yeh need another? 'Cause there's plenty more
where that come from!"

Nathaniel's senses had almost deserted him for an instant, but he was
master of the art of self-defence, and before the bully had finished his threat
with a curse he found himself lying in the ditch with Nathaniel towering over
him in righteous wrath.

"Coward," he said, looking down on him contemptuously, "you have made
a mistake, of course, and struck the wrong man, but that makes no difference.
A brave man does not strike in the dark."

"No, I haven't made no mistake, either," snarled Hiram, as he got up angrily
from the ground. "I seen you myself with my own eyes, Nate Graham. I seen
you trail down the hill out o' the woods after her, 'n I seen you try to get a kiss
from her, an' she run away. I was an eye-witness. *I* seen yeh. Then you tried to
get 'longside her after meetin' was out Sunday, tippin' yer hat so polite, as ef
that was everythin' a girl wanted; an' I seen yeh takin' her home tonight after
decent folks was a-bed, walkin' 'long a country road talkin' so sweet an' low
butter wouldn't melt in yer mouth. No, sir! I ain't made no mistake. An' I jest
want you to understand after this you're not to meddle with Phoebe Deane, for
she belongs to me!"

By this time Nathaniel had recognized Hiram Green, and his astonishment
and dismay knew no bounds. Could it be possible that a girl like that had aught
to do in any way with this coarse, ignorant man? Indignation filled him. He
longed to pound the insolent wretch before him and make him take back all he
had said, but he realized that this might be a serious matter for the young girl,
and it was necessary to proceed cautiously, therefore he drew himself up
haughtily and replied:

"There has never been anything between myself and Miss Deane to which
any one, no matter how close their relationship to her might be could object. I
met her in the woods while nutting with a party of friends, and had the good
fortune to help her out of a tangle of laurel that had caught in her hair, and to
show her the short cut to the road. I merely spoke to her on Sunday as I spoke

to my other acquaintances, and this evening I have been escorting her home from the house of a friend where we have both been taking tea."

"You lie!" snarled Hiram.

"What did I understand you to say, Mr. Green?"

"It don't make any matter what you understood me to say. I *said* YOU LIE, an' I'll say it again, too, ef I like. You needn't git off any more o' your fine words, fer they don't go down with me, even ef you have been to college. All I've got to say is *YOU LET MY GIRL ALONE FROM NOW ON!* D'yeh understand that? Ef yeh don't I'll take means to make ye!" And Hiram's big first was raised threateningly again.

But somehow the next instant Hiram was sprawling in the dust, and this time Nathaniel held something gleaming and sinister in his hand as he stood above him.

"I always go armed," said Nathaniel, in a cool voice. "You will oblige me by lying still where you are until I am out of sight down the road. Then it will be quite safe for you to rise to go home and wash you face. If I see you get up before that I shall shoot. Another thing. If I hear another word of this ridiculous nonsense from you I will have you arrested and brought before my uncle on charge of assault, and blackmail, and several other things perhaps. As for speaking to the young lady in question, or showing her any courtesy whatever that is ordinarily shown between young men and women in good society, that shall be as Miss Deane says, and not in any way as you say. You are not fit to speak her name."

Nathaniel stepped back slowly a few paces, and Hiram attempted to rise, pouring forth a volley of oaths and vile language. Nathaniel halted and raised the pistol, flashing in the moonlight.

"You will keep entirely still, Mr. Green. Remember that this is loaded."

Hiram subsided and Nathaniel walked deliberately backward until the man on the ground could see but a dim speck in the gray of the distance, and a night-hawk in the trees by his home mocked him in a clamorous tone.

Now all this happened not a stone's throw from Albert Deane's front gate, and might almost have been discerned from Phoebe's window if her room had not been upon the other side of the house.

After a little Hiram crawled stiffly up from the ground, looked furtively about, shook his fist menacingly at the distance where the flash of Nathaniel's pistol had disappeared, and slunk like a shadow close to the fence till he reached his house. Presently only a bit of white paper ground down with a great heel-mark, and a few footprints in the frosty dust, told where the encounter had been. The moon spread her obliterating white light over all, and Phoebe slept smiling in her dreams and living over her happy afternoon and evening again. But Nathaniel sat up far into the night till his candle burned low and sputtered out, and even the moon grew weary and bent low. He was thinking, and his thoughts were not all of t

[illegible] more evil was brewing.

The lights had been out, all save a candle in Emmeline's room, when she came home, but the door was left on the latch for her. She knew Emmeline wished to reprove her for the late hour of her return, and was fully prepared for the greeting next morning, spoken frigidly:

"Oh, so you did come home last night, after all! Or was it this morning? I'm surprised. I thought you had gone for good."

At breakfast things were uncomfortable. Albert persisted in asking Phoebe questions about her tea-party, in spite of Emmeline's disagreeable sarcasms. When Emmeline complained that Phoebe had "sneaked" away without giving her a chance to send for anything to the village, and that she needed thread for her quilting that very morning, Phoebe arose from her almost untasted breakfast and offered to go for it at once.

She stepped into the crisp morning with a sigh of relief, and walked briskly down the road feeling exultantly happy that she had escaped her prison for a little hour of the early freshness. Then she stopped suddenly, for there before her lay a letter ground into the dust, and about the writing there was something strangely familiar, as if she had seen it before, yet it was not anyone's she knew. It was not folded so that the address could be seen, as the manner of letters was in those days of no envelopes, but open and rumpled with the communication uppermost, and the words that stood out clearly to her vision as she stooped to pick it up were these: *It is most important that you present this letter or it will do no good to go but BE SURE THAT NO ONE ELSE SEE IT, or great harm may come to you!*

She turned the paper over with reverent fingers, for a bit of writing was not so common then as now and was treated with far more importance. And there on the other side lay the name that had gleamed at her pleasantly but a few days before through the laurel bushes as she lay in hiding, *Nathaniel Graham, Esq.* Did it look up at her confidingly now as if it would plead to be restored to its owner? Phoebe started at the foolish fancy, and was appalled with her responsibility.

Was this letter but an old one, useless now, and of no value to its owner? Surely it must be, and he had dropped it on his way home with her last night. The wind had blown it open and a passer-by had trodden upon it. That must be the explanation, for surely if it were important he would not have laid it down behind the log so carelessly in keeping of a stranger. Yet there were the words in the letter: *It is most important that you present it when you come.* Well, perhaps he had already "come," wherever that was, and the letter had seen its usefulness and passed out of value. But then it further stated that great harm might come to the owner if any one saw it. She might make sure no one would see it by destroying it, but how was she to know but that she was really destroying an important document? And she might not read further because of that caution, *Be sure that no one else sees it.* A less conscientious soul might not have heeded it, but Phoebe would not have read another word for the world. She felt it was a secret communication to which she had no right, and she must respect it.

More and more as this reasoning became clear to her, she saw that there was only one thing to do, and that was to go at once to the owner and give it to him, telling him that she had not read another word than those she saw at first, and making him understand that not a breath of it would ever pass her lips.

Her troubled gaze saw nothing of the morning beauties. Little jewels gemmed the fringes of the grass along the road, and the dull red and brown leaves that still lingered on their native branches were coated over with silver gauze. It would have given her joy at another time, but now it was as if it was not. She passed by Hiram Green's farm just as he was coming down to his barn near the road. He was in full view, and near enough for recognition. He quickened his pace as he saw her coming in her morning tidiness and beauty. She made a trim and dainty picture. But her eyes were straight ahead and she did not turn her head to look at him. He thought she did it to escape speaking, and he had had it in mind to imitate Nathaniel and call a good-morning. It angered him anew to have her pass him by unseeing, as if he were not good enough to treat with ordinary common politeness as between neighbors at least. If he had needed anything more to justify his heart in its evil plot he had it now. With lowering brow and ugly mien he raised his voice and called unpleasantly:

"Where you goin' this early, Phoebe?" but with her face set straight ahead and eyes that were studying perplexing questions she went on her way and never even heard him. Then the devil entered into Hiram Green.

He waited until she had passed beyond the red school house that marked the boundary line between the village and the country, and then slouched out from the shelter of the barn, and with long dogged steps followed her; keeping his little eyes narrowed and intent upon the blue of her frock in the distance. He would not let her see him, but he meant to know where she was going. She had a letter in her hand as she passed, at least it was a small white article much like a letter. Was she writing his rival a letter already? The thought brought a throb of hate—hate toward the man who was better than he, toward the girl who had scorned him, and toward the whole world, even the little weak caterpillar that crawled in a sickly ~~...~~

~~...~~ was something that must be done at once. ~~...~~ gave herself no time for thought of what would be said, but entered the great gate, which to her relief stood open. She held the letter tight in her cold trembling hand. Hiram had arrived at the church corner just in time to see her disappear within the white gates, and his jaw dropped down in astonishment. He had not dreamed she would go to his house. Yet after a moment's thought his eyes narrowed and gleamed with the satisfaction they always showed when he had thought out some theory, or seen through some possibility. The situation was one that was trying for the girl, and the fact of his being an eye-witness might some day give him power over her. He took his stand behind the trunk of a weeping willow tree in the church-yard to see what might happen.

Meantime Phoebe raised the great brass knocker held in the mouth of a lion. She felt as if all lions of the earth were come to meet her at this threshold, and her heart was beating in her throat now, so that she could scarcely speak. How hollow the sound of the knocker was as it reverberated through the great hall, not at all the cheerful thing it had been when Nathaniel knocked at Mrs. Spafford's door. A plump black woman in a large yellow turban and white apron opened the door, and was even more formidable than some of the family whom she had expected to meet might have been. She managed to ask if Mr. Graham were in.

"Missis Gra'm! Dere ain't no Missis Gra'm," ejaculated the old woman, looking her over carefully and it must be admitted rather scornfully. The young ladies who came to that house to visit did not dress as Phoebe was dressed just then, in working garb. "Dere's only jes' Mis' Brist'l. Mis' Janet, we calls her."

"Mr. Graham. Mr. Nathaniel Graham," corrected Phoebe, in trepidation. She thought she felt a rebuke in the black woman's words that she should call to see a young man. "I have a message for him," she added, bravely. "I will wait here, please. No, I'd rather not come in."

"I'll call Miss Janet," said the servant briefly, and swept away, closing the door with a bang in Phoebe's face.

She waited several minutes before it was opened again, this time by Janet Bristol.

Chapter 12

"You wished to see me?" questioned the tall, handsome girl in the doorway, scrutinizing Phoebe haughtily. There was nothing encouraging in her attitude.

"I wished to see Mr. Graham," said Phoebe, trying to look as if it were quite the natural thing for a young woman to call on a young man of a morning.

"I thought you had a message for him," said Janet sharply. She was wondering what business this very pretty girl could possibly have with her cousin.

"Yes, I have a message for him, but I must give it to him, if you please," she said with gentle emphasis. She lifted her eyes, and Janet could not help noticing the lovely face, and the beauty of the smile.

"Well, that will not be possible, for he is not here." Janet said it stiffly and Phoebe felt the disapproval in her glance.

"Oh!" said Phoebe, growing troubled. "He is not here? What shall I do? He ought to have it at once. When will he come? I might wait for him."

"He will not be at home until evening," said Janet, as if she were glad. "You will have to leave your message."

"I am sorry," said Phoebe, in troubled tone, "I cannot leave it. The one who sends it said it was private."

"That would not mean you could not tell it to his family," said Janet, in a superior tone. She was bristling with curiosity.

"I do not know," said Phoebe, turning to go.

"I can't understand how it is that you, a young girl, should be trusted with a message if it is so private that his own people are not to know." Her tone was vexed.

"I know," said Phoebe, "it is strange, and I am sorry that it happened so. But there is nothing wrong about it, really," and she looked up wistfully with her clear eyes so that Janet scarce could continue to think evil of her. "Perhaps Mr. Graham may be able to explain it to you. I would have no right." She turned and went down the steps. "I will come back this evening," she said, more as if she were making a resolve than as if it were a communication to Janet.

"Wait," said Janet sharply. "Who are you? I've seen you in church, haven't I?"

"Oh, yes," said Phoebe, glad to have something natural said. "I sit just behind you. I'm only Phoebe Deane."

"And who sends this message to my cousin."

Phoebe's face clouded over. "I do not know," she said, slowly.

...ng up nor noticing any more than when she had come. She passed Miranda on the other side of the street and never saw her, and Miranda wondered where she was going and why she looked so troubled. If she had not been hurrying to the store for something that was needed at once for the day's dinner, she would have followed her to find out, and perhaps have asked her point blank. It would have been a good thing, for when one is tracked by a devil it is well to be followed also by an angel, even if it be only one with a freckled face.

Without a thought for anything but her perplexities Phoebe made her way through the village and out on the country road, and in a very short time arrived in the kitchen of her home, where Emmeline had just finished the breakfast dishes.

"Well," she said, grimly, looking up as Phoebe entered, and noticing her empty hands, "where's the thread? Didn't they have any?"

"Oh!" said Phoebe, blankly. Her hands flew to her heart in dismay as she took in her situation. "I forgot it!" She murmured, humbly; "I'll go right back!" and without waiting for a word from the amazed Emmeline she turned and sped down the road again towards the village.

"Of all things!" ejaculated Emmeline, as she went to close the door that had blown open; "she needs a nurse! I didn't suppose going out to tea and a little money in the bank could make a girl lose her head like that! She has turned into a regular scatterbrain. The idea of her forgetting to get that thread when she hadn't another earthly thing to do! I'd like to know who 'twas brung her home last night. I don't know how I could hev missed him till he was way out in the road. It didn't look 'egzactly like David Spafford, an' yet who could it 'a' ben ef 't wasn't? She must 'a' went to Mis' Spafford's again this mornin' stead o' goin' to the store, er she never would 'a' forgot. I have to find out when she gits back. It's my duty!"

Emmeline snapped her lips together over the words as if she anticipated the duty would be a pleasant one.

Phoebe in her hasty flight down the road almost ran into Hiram Green who was sulkily plodding back from his fruitless errand to his belated chores.

"Gosh!" he said, as she started back with a hasty, "Excuse me, Mr. Green. I'm in such a hurry I didn't see you." She was gone on before her sentence was quite finished, and the breeze wafted it back to him from her flying figure.

"Gosh!" he said again, looking after her, "I wonder what's up now!" Then he turned doggedly and followed her again. If this kept up, detective business was going to be lively work. He was tired already and his morning's work not half done. Two trips to the village on foot in one morning were wearisome. Yet he was determined to know what all this meant.

Phoebe did her errand swiftly this time, and was so quick in returning with her purchase that she met Hiram face to face outside the store before he had had time to conceal himself.

He was thrown off his guard, but he rallied and tried to play the gallant.

"Thought I'd come 'long and see ef I couldn't carry yer bundle fer yeh."

"Oh, thank you, Mr. Green," said Phoebe, in new dismay at this un-wonted display of courtesy on his part. "But I can't wait, for Emmeline is in a great hurry for this. I shall have to run most of the way home. Besides it's very light. I couldn't think of troubling you." She had backed off as she spoke, and with the closing words she turned and flew up the street on feet as light as a thistle-down.

"Gosh!" said Hiram, under his breath, almost dazed at the rebuff. "Gosh! but she's a slippery one! But I'll catch her yet where she can't squirm out so easy. See ef I don't!" And with scowling brows he started slowly after her again. He did not intend any move on her part should go unwatched. He hated her for disliking him.

Miranda, from her watch-tower in the Spafford kitchen window, saw Phoebe's flying figure, and wondered. She did not know what it meant, but it meant something she was sure. She felt "stirrings" in her soul that usually called for some action on her part. Her alert soul was ready when the time should arrive and she felt it "arriving" fast, and sniffed the air like a trained war-horse. To be sure she sniffed nothing more dangerous than the fragrance of mince pies just out of the great brick oven, standing in a row on the shelf to cool.

The remainder of the morning was not pleasant for Phoebe. Her mind was too busy with her perplexity about how to get the letter to Nathaniel for her to spend much time in planning how to excuse her forgetfulness. She merely said: "I was thinking of something else, Emmeline, so came back without going to the store at all." Emmeline scolded, and sniffed, and scoffed to no purpose. Phoebe silently worked on, her brow thoughtful, her eyes far away, her whole manner showing she was paying little heed to what her sister-in-law said. This made Emmeline still more angry, so that she exhausted the vials of her wrath in fruitless words upon the girl. But Phoebe's lips were sealed. She answered questions when it was necessary and quietly worked on. The tasks disappeared

from under her hand as if by a sort of m...
she seated her...

... quilt
...me looked scrutinizingly at
... seemed to her there was something strange about
...obe. She would have given a good deal to know all about her afternoon at
the Spaffords', but Phoebe's monosyllabic answers brought forth little in the way
of information.

Albert looked at her in a troubled way, then glanced at Emmeline's forbidding face, and forbore to say anything.

The afternoon wore away in silence. Several times Emmeline opened her lips to ask a question, and snapped them shut again. She made up her mind that Phoebe must be thinking about Hiram Green, and if that was so she would better keep still and let her think. Nevertheless there was something serene and lofty about Phoebe's look that was hardly in keeping with a thought of Hiram Green, and there was something sphinx-like in her manner that made Emmeline feel it was useless to ask questions, though of course Emmeline had never heard of the sphinx.

Phoebe acted like one who was making up for lost time. The dishes seemed to marshal themselves into cleanly array on the shelves, and before the darkness came on she had caused a number of suns on the sunrise bedquilt to set forever behind a goodly roll of fine stitches set in most intricate patterns.

She arose like one who was wound up at five o'clock and without a word got the supper. Then, eating little or nothing herself, she cleared it rapidly away and went up to her room. Albert took his newspaper, and Emmeline went grimly at her basket of stockings. She was wondering whether the girl intended coming down to help her with them. After all it was rather profitable to have Phoebe work like that, things got done so quickly.

"Is Phoebe sick?" asked Albert, suddenly looking up from his paper.

Emmeline started and pricked her fingers with the needle.

"I should like to know what makes you think that," she snapped, frowning at the prick. "You seem to think she's made of some kind of perishable stuff that needs more'n ordinary care. You never seem to think I'm sick as I've noticed."

"Now, Emmeline!" he began pleasantly, "you know you aren't ever sick, and this is your home, and you like to stay in it, and you've got your own folks and all. But Phoebe's kind of different. She doesn't seem to quite belong, and I wouldn't want her to miss anything out of her life because she's living with us."

"Bosh!" said Emmeline. "Phoebe's made of no better stuff 'n I am. She ken do more work when the fit's on her than a yoke of oxen. The fit's ben on her today. She's got her spunk up. That's all the matter. She's tryin' to make up fer losin' yesterday afternoon, jes' to spite me fer what I said about her goin' out. I know her. She's done a hull lot on that there quilt this afternoon. At this rate we'll hev it off the frames before the week's out. She ain't et much 'cause she's mad, but she'll come out of it all right. You make me sick the way you fret about her doldrums."

Albert subsided and the darning-needle had it all its own way clicking in and out. They could hear Phoebe moving about her chamber quietly, though it was not directly over the sitting-room, and presently the sounds ceased altogether, and they thought she had gone to bed. A few minutes more and Hiram with his customary shuffle opened the sitting-room door and walked in.

"Where's Phoebe?" he asked, looking at the silent group around the candle; "she ain't out to another tea-party is she?"

"She's gone to bed," said Emmeline, shortly. "Is it cold out?"

Phoebe, upstairs by her window, arrayed in her plain brown delaine, brown shirred bonnet, and brown cape, with the letter safely pinned inside her cape, waited until the accustomed sounds downstairs told her Hiram had come and was seated. Then she softly, cautiously climbed out of her window to the roof of a shed a few feet below her window, crept out to the back edge of this and dropped like a cat to the ground. She had performed this feat many times as a child, but never since she wore long dresses. She was glad the moon was not up yet, and she hurried around the back of the house and across the side yard to the fence, which she climbed. Her feet had scarcely left the last rail ere she heard the door-latch click, and a broad beam of light was flung out across the path not far from her. To her horror she saw Hiram Green's tall form coming out and then the door slammed shut and she knew he was out in the night with her.

But she was in the road now with nothing to hinder her, and her light feet fairly flew over the ground, treading on the grassy spots at the edge so she would make no sound, and never turning her head to listen even if he were following. Somehow she felt he was coming nearer and nearer every step she took. Her heart beat wildly, and great tears started to her eyes. She tried to pray as she fled along. Added to her fear of Hiram was her dread of what he would think if he found her out there in the dark alone, and a third fear for the secret of the letter she carried, for instinctively she felt that of all people to find out a secret Hiram Green would be among the most dangerous. She put her hand upon the letter and clenched it fast as though it might be spirited away unless she held it. She was glad it was dark, and yet, if he had seen her, and were pursuing, how

dreadful it would be to reach the villa.... ...
help, her heart ....

... over
... ... un uke this much further.
...uge pavement, and could see the blessed friendly
... ... uie nouses all about her.

She hurried on, not daring to run so fast here, for people were coming ahead, and she tried to think and to still the wild fluttering of her heart. If Hiram Green were behind and really following her it would not do for her to go to Judge Bristol's at once. She could scarcely hope to reach there and hide from him now, for her strength for running was almost spent and not for anything must he of all people know where she was going.

This thought gave new wings to her feet, and she fled past the houses, scarcely stopping to realize where she was. She could hear the man's steps on the brick pavement now and his heavy boots rang out distinctly on the frosty air. She felt as if she had been running for years with an evil fate pursuing her. Her limbs grew heavy, and her feet seemed to drag behind. She half closed her eyes to stop the surging of the blood. Her ears rang, her cheeks were burning and perspiration was standing on her lips and brow. Her breath came hard and hurt her.

And then, quite naturally, as if it had all been planned, Miranda, with a little shawl around her shoulders and over her head, stepped out from behind the lilacs in the Spafford garden by the gate, and walked along beside her, fitting her large easy gait to Phoebe's weary, flying steps.

"I heard yeh comin' an' thought I'd go a piece with yeh!" she explained, easily, as if this were a common occurrence. "D'ye hev to hurry like this, 'r was yeh doin' it fer exercise?"

"Oh, Miranda!" gasped Phoebe, slowing down her going, and putting a plaintive hand out to reach the strong red friendly one in the dark, "I am so glad you are here!"

"So'm I!" said Miranda, confidently, "but you jest wait till you git your breath. Can't you come in and set a spell 'fore you go on?"

"No, Miranda, I must hurry. I had an errand and must get right back,—but I'm almost sure some one is following me. I don't dare look behind, but I heard footsteps and—I'm—so—frightened." Her voice trailed off, trembling into another gasp for breath.

"Well, all right, we'll fix 'em. You jest keep your breath fer walkin' an' I'll boss this pilgrimage a spell. We'll go down to the village store fer a spool o' cotton Mis' Spafford ast me t' get the fust thing in the mornin' to sew some sprigged calico curtains she's been gettin' up to the spare bed, an' while we're down to the store we'll jest natcherally lose sight o' that man till he don't know where he's at, an' then we'll meander on our happy way. Don't talk 'r he'll hear you. You jest foller me."

... Phoebe Deane wants ... ken she jest go right in and get it whilst I ...cotton?"

"Why certainly, certainly, young ladies, walk right in," said the affable Mr. Peebles, arising from a nail keg.

Miranda had Phoebe into the back room in no time, and was calmly debating over the virtues of different spools of thread when Hiram Green entered puffing and snorting like a porpoise, and gazed about him confidently. Then suddenly a blank look spread over his face. The one he was searching for was not there? Could he have been mistaken?

Miranda, innocently paying for her thread, eyed him furtively, and began her keen putting of two and two together, figuring out her problem with a relish. "Hiram Green, to be sure—Ah! It was Hiram who had tried to walk beside Phoebe on Sunday. Hiram Green"—contemptuously—"of all men! Umph!"

These were something like her thoughts. Then with wide-eyed good nature she paid for her thread, said good-evening to Mr. Peebles, and deliberately went out the door of the store to the street. Hiram had watched her suspiciously, but she held her head high as if she were going straight home, and slipped in the dark around to the side door where she walked in on Mrs. Peebles and the astonished Phoebe without ceremony.

"Did yeh get yer drink, Phoebe? Ev'nin Mis' Peebles. Thank yeh, no I can't set down. Mis' Spafford needs this thread t' oncet. She jest ast me wouldn't I run down and git it so's she could finish up some pillar-slips she's makin'. Come on, Phoebe, ef yer ready. Ken we go right out this door, Mis' Peebles; there's so many men in the store, an' I can't bear 'em to stare at my pretty red hair, you know." And in a moment more she had whisked Phoebe out the side door into the dark yard, where they could slip through the fence to the side street.

"Now, which way?" demanded Miranda, briefly, in a low tone, as they emerged from the shadow of the store to the sidewalk.

"Oh, Miranda, you're so kind," said Phoebe, hardly knowing what to do, for she dared not tell her errand to her. "I think I can go quite well by myself now. I'm not much afraid, and I'll soon be done and go home."

"See here, Phoebe Deane, d'yeh think I'm going' t' leave a little white-faced thing like you with them two star eyes t' go buffetin' round alone in the dark where there's liable to be lopsided nimshies follerin' round? Yeh can say what yeh like, but I'm goin' to foller yeh till I see yeh safe inside yer own door."

"Oh, you dear, good Miranda!" choked Phoebe, with a teary smile, clasping her arm tight. "If you only knew how glad I was to see you."

"I knowed all right. I cud see you was scared. But come 'long quick er that hound in there'll be trackin' us again. Which way?"

"To Judge Bristol's," breathed Phoebe, in a low frightened whisper.

"That's a good place to go," said Miranda, with satisfaction. "I guess you won't need me inside with you. I'm not much on fancy things, an' I'll fit better outside with the fence-posts, but I'll be thar to take yeh home. My! but you'd orter a' seen Hiram Green's blank look when he got in the store an' seen you want there. I'm calculatin' he'll search quite a spell 'fore he makes out which way we disappeared."

Phoebe's heart beat wildly at the thought of her escape. She felt as if an evil fate were dogging her every step.

"Oh, Miranda!" she shivered. "What if you hadn't come along just then!"

"Well, there ain't no use cipherin' on that proposition. I was thar, an' I generally calculate to be thar when I'm needed. Jest you rest easy. There ain't no long-legged, good-fer-nothin' bully like Hiram Green goin' to gather you in, not while I'm able to bob 'round. Here we be. Now I'll wait in the shadder behind this bush while you go in."

Phoebe timidly approached the house, while Miranda, as usual, selected her post of observation with discernment and a view to the lighted window of the front room where the family were assembled.

Janet did not keep Phoebe waiting long this time, but swept down upon her in a frock of ruby red with a little gold locket hung from a bit of black velvet ribbon about her neck. Her dark hair was arranged in clusters of curls each side of her sparkling face, and the glow on her cheek seemed reflected from the color of her garments. Phoebe almost spoke her admiration, so beautiful did this haughty girl seem to her.

"I am afraid my cousin is too busy to see you," she said, in a kindly, condescending tone. "He is very busy preparing to leave on the early stage in the morning. He finds he must go to New York sooner than he expected."

"I will not keep him," said Phoebe, earnestly, rising, "but I must see him for just a minute. Will you kindly tell him it is Phoebe Deane, and that she says she _MUST_ see him for just a moment?"

"You will find he will desire you to send the message by me," said Janet, quite confidently. "It does not do to say must to my cousin Nathaniel."

But contrary to Janet's expectation Nathaniel came down at once, with welcome in his face. Phoebe was standing with her hand upon the letter over her heart waiting for him breathlessly. The watching Miranda eyed him jealously through the front window-pane to see if his countenance would light up properly when he saw his visit...

...... to detain her, to thank her, to introduce her to his cousin, who had by this time entered and was watching them distantly, but Phoebe was in haste to leave; and Janet was haughtily irresponsive.

He followed her to the door and said in a low tone: "Miss Deane, you have done me a greater service than I can possibly repay. I have been hunting frantically for this letter all day. It is most important. I know I can trust you not to speak of it to a soul. I am deeply grateful. You may not know it, but not only my life and safety but that of others as well has been in your hands today with the keeping of that letter."

"Oh, then I am glad I have brought it safely to you. I have been frightened all day lest something would happen that I could not get it to you without its being found out. And if it has been of service I am more than glad, because then I have repaid your kindness to me in the woods that day."

Now that she was away from Janet's scrutinizing eyes Phoebe could dimple into a smile.

"Oh, what I did that day was a little, little thing beside your service," said he.

"A kindness is never a little thing," answered Phoebe, gently. "Good-night, Mr. Graham. Miranda is waiting for me," and she sped down the path without giving him opportunity for a reply. Miranda had wandered into the shaft of light down by the gate that streamed from the candle Nathaniel held, and Phoebe flew to her as if to a rock of refuge. They turned and looked back as they reached the gate. Nathaniel was still standing on the top step with the tall candle held above his head to give them light, and through the window they could dimly see Janet's slim figure standing by the mantelpiece toying with some ornaments. Phoebe gave a great sigh of relief that the errand was accomplished, and grasping Miranda's arm clung lovingly to her, and so they two walked softly through the village streets and out the country way into the road that was white with the new risen moon; while Hiram Green, perplexed and baffled, searched vainly through the village for a clue to Phoebe's whereabouts, and finally gave it up and dragged his weary limbs home. Excitement of this sort did not agree with his constitution and he was mortally tired.

Nathaniel turned back into the house again, his vision filled with the face of the girl who had just brought his letter back to him. His great relief at finding it was almost lost in his absorption in the thought of Phoebe Deane, and the sudden pang that came to him with his remembrance of Hiram Green. Could it be? Could it possibly be that she was bound in any way to that man?

Janet roused him from his thought by demanding to know what on earth the message was that made that girl so absurdly secretive.

Nathaniel smiled. "It was just a letter of mine she had found. A letter that I have searched everywhere for."

"How did she know it was your letter?" There was something offensive in Janet's tone. Nathaniel felt his color rising like a girl. He wondered what was the matter with Janet that she should be so curious.

"Why, it was addressed to me of course!"

"Then why in the world couldn't she give it to me? She was here in the morning and we had a long argument about it. She said it was a private message and the person who sent it did not wish any one but you to see it, and yet she professed not to know who the person was who sent it. I told her that was ridiculous; that of course you had no secrets from your family; but she was quite stubborn and went away. Who is she, anyway, and how does she happen to know you?"

Nathaniel could be haughty, too, when he liked, and now he drew himself to his greatest height.

"Miss Deane is quite a charming girl, Janet, and you would do well to make her acquaintance. She is a friend of Mrs. Spafford, and was visiting her last evening when I happened in on business and they made me stay to tea."

"That's no sign of where she belongs socially," said Janet, disagreeably; "Mrs. Spafford may have had to invite her just because she didn't know enough to go home before supper. Besides, Mrs. Spafford's choice in friends might not be mine at all."

"Janet, Mr. and Mrs. Spafford are unimpeachable socially and every other way. And I happen to know that Miss Deane was there by invitation. I heard her speaking of it as she bade her good-night."

"Oh, indeed!" sneered Janet, quite beside herself with jealously. " I suppose you were waiting to take her home!"

"Why, certainly," said Nathaniel, looking surprised. "What has come over you, Janet? You do not talk like your usual kind self."

His tone brought angry tears to Janet's eyes.

"I should think it was enough," she said, trying to hide the tears in her little lace handkerchief, "having you go off suddenly like this when we've scarcely had you a week, and you busy and absent-minded all the time; and then to have this upstart of a girl coming here with secrets that you will not tell me about. I want to know who wrote that letter, Nathaniel, and what it is about. I can't stand it

to have that girl smirking behind me in ~~~~~~
that I am ~~~~~~

~~~~~~ Deane's part, I am sure. ~~~~~~ your own pleasant, winning way, and say to her that I have explained to you that it was all right. That ought to satisfy both you and her. She asked me to explain it to you."

"Well, you haven't done so, at all. I am sure I can't see what possible harm it could do for you to tell me about it, inasmuch as that other girl knows all about it, too. I should think you would want me to watch and be sure that she doesn't tell—unless, indeed, the secret is between you two."

There was a hint in Janet's tone which seemed almost like an insinuation. Nathaniel grew quite stern.

"The secret is not between Miss Deane and myself," he said, "and she does not know it any more than you do. She found it open, and read only one line which told her it was absolutely private. She tells me she did not read another word."

"Very likely!" sneered Janet, coldly. "Do you think any woman would find it possible to read only one line of a secret? Your absolute faith in this stranger is quite childlike."

"Janet, would you have read further if it had fallen into your hands?"

"Well,—I—why—of course that would be different," said Janet, coloring and looking disconcerted, "but you needn't compare me—"

"Janet, you have no right to think she has a lower sense of honor than you have. I feel sure she has not read it."

But Janet, with haughty mien and flashing eyes in which tears were scarcely concealed, swept up the stairs and took refuge in her room, where a perfect storm of tears and mortification followed.

Nathaniel, confounded, dismayed, after vainly tapping at her door and begging her to come out and explain her strange conduct, went sadly to his packing, puzzling much over the strange ways of girls with one another. Here for instance were two well suited to friendship, and yet he could plainly see that they would have nothing to do with one another. He dearly loved his cousin. She had been his playmate and companion from childhood, and he could not understand why suddenly she had grown so disregardful of his wishes. He tried to put it away, deciding that he would say another little word about this charming Miss Deane to Janet in the morning before he left, but Miss Janet forestalled any such attempt by sending down word that she had a headache and would try to sleep a little longer to get rid of it. She would only call a cool little good-bye to her cousin through the closed door, as he, mildly distressed, was hurrying down to the stage waiting for him at the door.

Meantime Miranda and Phoebe had hurried out past the old red schoolhouse into the country road white with frosty moonlight, Phoebe all the time protesting that Miranda must not go with her.

"Why not, in conscience!" said Miranda. "I'll jest enjoy the walk. I was thinkin' of goin' on a lark this very evenin', only I hadn't picked out a companion."

"But you'll have to come all the way back alone, Miranda."

"Well, what's that? You don't s'pose anybody's goin' to chase *ME*, do yeh? If they want to they're welcome. I'd jest turn round an' say: 'Boo! I'm red-haired an' freckled, an' I don't want nothin' of you, nor you of me. Git 'long with yeh!' " Miranda's inimitable manner brought a merry laugh to Phoebe's lips and helped to relieve the tension of the heavy strain she had been under. She felt like laughing and crying all at once. Miranda seemed to understand and enter into her mood and kept her in ripples of laughter till they neared her home. Then, suddenly sobering, Phoebe attempted to make Miranda go back at once, but Miranda was stubborn. Not until she saw her charge safe inside her own door would the faithful soul budge an inch.

"Well, then, Miranda, I'll have to tell you how I got out," said Phoebe, confidentially. "There was a caller—some one I didn't care to see—so I went upstairs and they thought I'd gone to bed. I just slipped out my window to the low shed roof and dropped down. I'll have to be very still, for I wouldn't care to have them know I slipped away like that. It might make them ask me questions. You see I had found a letter that I knew Mr. Graham had dropped, and it ought to go to him at once. If I had asked Albert to take it there would have been a big fuss and Emmeline would have wanted to know all about it, and maybe read it, and I didn't think it would be best—"

"I see," said Miranda, comprehensively, "so you tuk it yourself. O' course. Who wouldn't, I'd like to know? All right, we'll jest slip in through the pasture and round to your shed, an' I'll give yeh a boost up. Two's better one fer a job like that, ef one is a red-head. I take it yer caller ain't present any longer. Reckon he made out to foller yeh a piece but we run him into a hole, an' he didn't make much. Hush, now; don't go to thankin', 'taint worth while till I git through, fer I've jest begun this job, an' I intend to see it through. Here, put yer hand on my shoulder. Now let me hold this foot, don't you be 'fraid, I'm good an' strong. There yeh go! Now yer up! Is that your winder up there? Wal, hope to see yeh again soon. Happy dreams!" and she slid around the corner to watch Phoebe till she disappeared into the little dark window above. Then Miranda made for the road, looking curiously in at the side window of the Deanes'

sitting-room on the way, to make sure she ~~~~~
and to ~~~~~

~~~~~, seen anythin' of a little ~~~~~ blue eye and one green one, an' a black tip to her tail, an' a pink nose? I've been up to see if she follered Phoebe Deane home from our house las' night, but she's gone to bed with the toothache an' I wouldn't disturb her fer the world. I thought I'd mebbe find her round this way? You ain't seen her, have yeh?"

"No," growled Hiram, suspiciously, "I'd a wrung her neck ef I had."

"Oh, thank you, Mr. Green. You're very kind," said Miranda, sweetly. "I'll remember that, next little kitten I lose. I'll know jest who t' apply to fer it. Lovely night, ain't it? Don't trouble yerself 'bout the kitten. I reckon it's safe somewheres. 'Taint every one's ez blood-thirsty's you be. Good-night." And Miranda flung off down the road before Hiram could decide whether she was poking fun at him or was extremely dull. At last he roused himself from his weary pondering, uttered his accustomed ejaculation, "Gosh!" looked up the road toward the Deanes, and down toward the vanishing Miranda, brought forth the expression he reserved for the perplexing crises in his life, "Gosh Ninety!" and went home to bed. He had not been able all day to quite fathom the mystery which he was attempting to control, and this new unknown quantity was more perplexing than all that had gone before. What, for instance, had Miranda Griscom to do with Phoebe Deane? His slow brain remembered that she had been in the store where Phoebe—it must have been Phoebe; for he did not believe he could have been mistaken—had disappeared. Had Miranda spirited her away somewhere? Ah! And it was Miranda who had come up to Phoebe after church and interrupted their walk together! What had Miranda to do with it all? Hang Miranda! He would like to wring her neck, too. With such charming meditations he fell asleep.

Chapter 14

Nathaniel sat inside the coach as it rolled through the village streets and out into the country road toward Albany, and tried to think. All remembrance of Janet and her foolish pet had passed from his mind. He had before him a problem to decide. It was the harder because the advice of his nearest and dearest friends was so at variance.

He took out two letters which represented the two sides of the question and began to reread. The first was the letter which Phoebe had brought, torn, disfigured by the dust, but still legible. It bore a Texas postmark and was brief and businesslike.

Dear nephew, (it read), *if you are keen as you used to be you have been keeping yourself informed about old Texas, and know the whole state of the case better than I can put it. Ever since Austin went to ask the admission of Texas as a separate state into the Mexican Republic and was denied and thrown into prison, our people have been gathering together; and now things are coming to a crisis. Something will be done and that right soon, perhaps in a few days. The troops are gathering near Gonzales. Resistance will be made. But we need help. We want young blood, and strong arms behind which are heads and hearts with a conviction for right and freedom. No one on earth has a right to deprive us of our property, and say we shall not own slaves which we have come honestly by. We will fight and win, as the United States has fought and won its right to govern itself. Now I call upon you, Nathaniel, to rise up and bring honor to your father's name by raising a company of young men to come down here and set Texas free. I know you are busy with your law studies but they will keep and Texas will not. Texas must be set free now or never. When you were a little chap you had strong convictions about what was right, and I feel pretty sure my appeal will not come to deaf ears. Your father loved Texas and came down here to make his fortune. If he had lived he would have been here fighting. He would have been a slave-owner, and have asserted his right as a free man in a free country to protect his property. He would have taught his son to do the same. I call upon you for your father's sake to come down here in the hour of your Texas' need—for it is the place where you were born—and help us. Use your utmost influence to get other young men to come with you.*

Your uncle the Judge will perhaps help you financially. He owns a couple of slaves himself I remember, house servants, does he not? Ask him how he would like the government of the United States to order him to set them free. I feel sure he will sympathize with Texas in her need and help you do this thing which I have asked.

I am a man of few words ~~~~~~~~~~~~~~~~~~~~~~~~~~~~~~~~

Your uncle,
ROYAL GRAHAM.

The other letter was kept waiting a long time while the young man read and reread this one, and then let his eyes wander through the window of the coach to the brown fields and dim hills in the distance. He was going over all he could remember of his boyhood life in that far-away Southern home. He could dimly remember the form of his father, who had been to him a great hero; who had taken him with him on horseback wherever he went and never been too weary or too busy for his little son. There came a blur of sadness over the picture, the death of his beloved father, and an interval of emptiness when the gentle mother was too full of sorrow to know how the baby heart had felt the utter loneliness, and then one day his Uncle Royal, so like yet not like his father, had lifted him in his arms and said: "Good-bye, little chap. Some day you'll come back to us and do your father's work, and take his place." Then he and his mother had ridden away in an endless succession of post-chaises and coaches, until one day they had come to Judge Bristol's great white house set among the green hedges, and there Nathaniel had found a new home. There, first his mother, and then Janet's mother, had slipped away into that mysterious door of death, and he had grown up in the home of his mother's brother, with Janet as a sister. From time to time he had received letters from this shadowy uncle in Texas, and once, when he was about twelve, there had been a brief visit from him which cleared the memory and kept him fresh in Nathaniel's mind; and always there had been some hint or sentence of expectation that when Nathaniel was grown and educated he would come back to the country which had been his father's and help to make it great. This had been a hazy undertone always in his life, in spite of the fact that his other uncle, Judge Bristol, was constantly talking of his future career as a lawyer in New York City, with a possibility of a political career also. Nathaniel had gone on with his life, working out the daily plan as it came, with all the time the feeling that these two plans were contending in him for supremacy. Sometimes during leisure moments lately he had wondered if the two could ever be combined, and if not how possibly they were to both work out. Gradually it had dawned upon him that a day was coming, indeed might not be far away, when he would have to choose. And now, since these two letters had reached him, he knew the time had come. And how was he to know how to choose?

His Uncle Royal's letter had reached him the afternoon of the nutting party on the hill. Pompey, his uncle's house servant, had brought it to him on a silver salver just as they were starting. He had glanced at the familiar writing, known it for his uncle's, and put it in his pocket for reading at his leisure. He always enjoyed his uncle's letters, yet they were not of deep moment to him. He had been too long separated from him to have keen interests in common with him. Hence he had not read the letter until after his return from the hill-side, which explains how he had carelessly left it behind the log by Phoebe, as an excuse to return and help her out of the laurel.

In the quiet of his own room after Janet and the others were sleeping he had remembered the letter, and, relighting his candle, which had been extinguished, he had read it, feeling a touch of reproach that he could have so lightly put off attending to his good relative's words. How, then, was he startled to discover its contents! The talk of the afternoon floated back to him, idle talk, about his going down to set Texas free. Talk that grew out of his own keen interest in all the questions of the day, and his readiness to argue them out. But he had never had a very definite idea of going to Texas to take part in the struggle that was going on until this letter brought him face to face with a possible duty.

Perhaps he would have had no question about his decision, if, following hard upon this letter, had not come the other one, the very next day in fact, which put an entirely new phase upon some sides of the question, and made duty seem an uncertain creature with more faces than one.

The coach was half way to Albany before Nathaniel finally folded away his uncle's letter and put it in his inner pocket with great care. Then he took up the other letter with a perplexed sigh, and read:

DEAR CHUM:

I am sitting on a high point of white sand, where I can look off at the blue sea. At my right is a great hairy, prickly cactus with a few gorgeous yellow blossoms in a glory of delicate petals and fringed stamens that look as out of place amid the sand as a diamond on a plank. Just now a green lizard peered curiously out from under one of the hairy balls that pass for leaves with a cactus, and then slid back out of sight. But the next time I looked he was blue, brilliant, and palpitating as a peacock's feathers, and sunning himself, not thinking of me at all. Then just as I moved he became a dull gray-brown, hardly discernible from the sand. And thus I know he is not a lizard at all, but a chameleon. The sun is very warm and bright, and everything about seems basking in it.

As I look off to sea the Gulf Stream is distinct today, a brilliant green ribbon in the brilliant blue of the sea. It winds along so curiously and so independently in the great ocean, keeping its own individuality in spite of storm and wind and tide. I went out in a small boat

...... sweet apathy that steals over one ...... which soothes, and rests.

I am having a holiday, for my little pupils are gone away on a visit. This is a delightful land to which I have come, and a charming family with whom my lot is cast. I am having an opportunity to study the South in a most ideal manner, and many of my former ideas of it are becoming much modified. For example, there is slavery. I am by no means so sure as I used to be that it was ordained of God. I wish you were here to talk it over with me, and to study it, too. There are possibilities in the institution that make one shudder. Perhaps, after all, Texas is in the wrong. As you have opportunity drop into an Abolition meeting now and then and see what you think. I have been reading the Liberator lately. I find much in it that is strong and appeals to my sense of right. You know what a disturbance it has made in the country recently. I hear some mails have even been broken into and burned on account of it. I wonder if this question of slavery will ever be an issue in our country. If it should be I cannot help wondering what the South will do. From what I have seen I feel sure they will never stand it to have their rights interfered with.

Now, I have to confess that much as I rebelled against giving up my work and coming down here I feel that it has already benefited me. I can take long walks without the least weariness, and can even talk and sing like any one else without becoming hoarse. I do not believe my lungs have ever been affected, and I feel I am going to get well and come back to my work. With that hope in my veins I can go joyfully through these sunny days and feel the new life creeping into me with every breath of balmy air. We shall yet work shoulder to shoulder, my friend—I feel it. God bless you and keep you, and show you the right.

Yours, faithfully,
MARTIN VAN RENSSELAER.

Nathaniel folded the letter, placed it in his pocket with the other, and leaned his head back to think. It was all perplexing.

This man Van Rensselaer had been his room-mate for four years. They had grown into one another's thoughts as two who are much together and love each other will grow until each had come to depend upon the other's decision as if it were nearly his own judgment. Nathaniel could not quite tell why it was that this letter troubled him, yet he felt breathing through the whole epistle the stirring of a new principle that seemed to antagonize his sympathy with Texas.

So, through the long cold journey the question was debated back and forth. His duty to his uncle demanded that he go to the address given and investigate the matter of helping Texas, else his uncle might think him exceedingly neglectful; and when he looked at the question from his uncle's stand-point, and thought of his father, and his own natural heritage, his sympathy was with Texas. On the other hand his love for his friend and his perfect trust in him demanded that he investigate the other side also. He felt intuitively that the two things could not go together.

Martin Van Rensselaer had been preparing for the Christian ministry. His zeal and earnestness were great, too great for his strength, and before he had finished his theological studies he had broken down and been sent South, as it was feared he had serious lung trouble. This separation had been a great trial to both young men. Martin was three years older than Nathaniel, and two years ahead of him in his studies, but in mind and spirit they were as one, so that the words of the letter had great influence.

The day had grown surly as the coach rumbled on. Sullen clouds lowered in the corners of the sky as if meditating mutiny. There was a hint of snow in the biting air that whistled around the cracks of the coach windows. Nature seemed to have suddenly put on a bare, brown look—hopeless, discouraging, cold.

Nathaniel shivered and drew his cloak close about him. He wished the journey were over, or that he had some one with whom to advise. Somehow the question troubled him as if it were of immediate necessity that it be decided, and he could not dismiss it, nor put it off. He had once or twice broached the subject with Judge Bristol, but had hesitated to show him either of the letters which had been the cause of his own perplexity. He felt that his uncle's letter might arouse antagonism in Judge Bristol on account of the claim it seemed to put upon himself, as his father's son, to come and give himself.

Judge Bristol was almost jealously fond of his sister's son, and felt that he belonged to the North. Aside from that, his sympathies would probably have been with Texas. Keeping a few slaves himself as house servants, and treating them as kindly as if they had been his own children, he saw no reason to object to slavery, and deemed it a man's right to do as he pleased with his own property.

Martin Van Rensselaer's letter the Judge would have been likely to look upon as the production of a sentimental, hot-headed fanatic, whose judgment was unsound. Nathaniel was morally certain that if the Judge should read those letters he would advise against having anything to do with either cause personally; yet, dearly as he loved and honored the Judge, who had been a second father to him, Nathaniel's conscience would not let him drop the matter thus easily.

So the coach thumped

.... with his old friend, or was he in love? ... coachman sat gloomily mile after mile, and tried to think what girl of his acquaintance was good enough for Nathaniel.

But all oblivious of his old friend's disquietude, Nathaniel sat inside with closed eyes and tried to think, and ever and anon there came a vision of a sweet-faced girl with brown hair and a golden gown sitting among the falling yellow leaves with bowed head; and somehow in his thoughts her trouble became tangled, and it seemed as if there were three instead of two who needed setting free, and he was to choose between them all.

Chapter 15

The cold weather had come suddenly and Phoebe felt like a prisoner. Emmeline's tongue became a daily torture, and the little ways in which she contrived to make Phoebe's life a burden were too numerous to count. Her paltry fortune in the bank was a source of continual trouble. Scarcely a morning passed but it was referred to in some unpleasant way. Every request was prefaced with some such phrase as: "If you're not too grand to soil your hands," or "I don't like to ask a rich lady to do such a thing," till Phoebe felt sometimes that she could bear it no longer and longed to take the few dollars and fling them into the lap of her disagreeable sister-in-law, if thereby she might but gain peace. Like the continual dropping that wears the stone, the unpleasant reference had worn upon a single nerve until the pain was acute.

But there was another source of discomfort still more trying to the girl than all that had gone before, and this was Hiram Green's new role. He had taken it upon himself to act the fine gentleman. It was somewhat surprising considering the fact that Hiram was known in the village as "near," and this new departure demanded an entirely new outfit of clothes. In his selection he aimed to emulate Nathaniel Graham. As he had neither Nathaniel's taste nor his New York tailor the effect was far from perfect, except perhaps in the eyes of Hiram, who felt quite set up in his fine raiment.

On the first Sunday of his proud appearance in church thus arrayed he waited boldly at the door until the Deanes came out and then took his place beside Phoebe and walked with her to the carryall as though he belonged there. Phoebe's thoughts were on other things and for a moment she had not noticed, but suddenly becoming conscious of measured footsteps by her own, she looked up and found the reconstructed Hiram strutting by her side as consciously as a peacock. In spite of her great annoyance her first impulse was to laugh, and that laugh probably did more than any other thing to turn the venom of Hiram Green's hate upon her own innocent head. After all the effort he had made to appear well before her, and before the congregation assembled she had laughed. She had dared to laugh aloud, and the hateful Miranda Griscom, who seemed to be always around in the way whenever he tried to walk with Phoebe had laughed back. A slow ugly red rolled into his sun-burned face, and his eyes narrowed with resolve to pay back all and more than he had received of scorn.

It happened that Miranda was holding Rose by the hand, and could not without greatly attracting attention get much nearer to Phoebe that morning, so the girl could do nothing to get away from her unpleasant suitor except to hasten to the carryall. And there before the open-eyed congregation Hiram Green

Thereafter Hiram Green was in attendance upon her at every possible public place. She could not go to church without finding him at her elbow the minute the service was over, ready to walk down the very aisle beside her. She could not go to singing-school but he would step out from behind his gate as she passed and join her, or if she evaded him he would sit beside her and manage to sing out of the same book. She could not go to the village on an errand but he would appear in the way and accompany her. He seemed to have developed a strange intuition as to her every movement. He was ever vigilant, and the girl began to feel like a hunted creature. Even if she stayed at home he appeared at the door ten minutes after the family had gone, a triumphant, unpleasant smile upon his face, and sauntered into the kitchen without waiting for her to bid him, and there, tilted back in a chair in his favorite attitude, he would watch her every movement, and drawl out an occasional remark. That happened only once, however; she never dared to stay again, lest it would be repeated. She had been busy preparing something for dinner, and she turned suddenly and caught a look upon his face that reminded her of a beast of prey. It flashed upon her that he was actually enjoying her annoyance. Without waiting to think she stepped into the wood-shed, and from there fairly fled across the backyard, and the meadows between and burst into the bright little room of Granny McVane.

The dear old lady sat there rocking by the fire, with her open Bible on her knee. Phoebe was relieved to find her alone, and in answer to the gentle: "Why, dearie, what can be the matter?" she flung herself on the floor at the old lady's feet and putting her head in her lap burst into tears.

It was only for a moment that she lost her self-control, but even that moment relieved the heavy strain on her nerves, and she was able to sit up and tell the old lady all about it. She had not intended to tell anything, when in her sudden panic she had beaten a hasty retreat from the enemy, but Granny McVane's sweet face showed so much tender sympathy that all at once it seemed good to tell some one of her trouble.

She listened, watched her sympathetically, smoothed back the damp tendrils of hair that had blown about her face, and then stooped over and kissed her.

"Don't you ever marry him, Phoebe. Don't you ever do it, if you don't love him child!" she said, solemnly, like a warning. "And just you run over here, dearie, whenever he bothers you. I'll take care of you."

Phoebe, with her natural reserve, had not drawn her family into the story except to say that they favored the suit of the would-be lover. But it comforted her greatly to have someone on her side, even if it were but this quiet old lady who could not really help her much.

They watched out the back windows until they saw Hiram emerge from the Deane house and saunter off down the road. Even then Phoebe was afraid to go back until she saw the carryall far down the road. Then she flew across the fields and entered the back door before they had turned in at the great gate. When they got out and came into the house she was demurely paring potatoes, and Emmeline eyed her suspiciously.

"Seems to me you're pretty late with your potatoes," she remarked, disagreeably. "I suppose you had a nice easy time all morning."

But Phoebe did not explain, only she did not stay at home again when the family were all to be away. She never knew whether Emmeline was aware of Hiram's Sunday morning visit or not.

Phoebe's state of mind after this occurrence was one of constant nervous alarm. She began to hate the thought of the man who seemed to haunt her at every turn.

Heretofore one of her greatest pleasures had been to walk to the village after the daily mail, or for an errand to the store. Now such walks became a dread. One afternoon in early November she had hurried away and gone around by Granny McVane's, hoping thus to escape the vigilance of Hiram Green. She managed to get safely to the village, and get her errands done, but just as she emerged from the post-office the long, lank figure of Hiram loomed before her and slouched into his dogged gait beside her. "Did you get a letter?" he asked, looking suspiciously at the one she held in her hand. Then as she did not answer he went on: "You must have a whole lot of folks writin' you quite constant; you seem to go to the post-office so much."

Phoebe said nothing. She felt too indignant to speak. How could she get away from her tormentor unless she deliberately ran away from him? And how could she do that right here in the village where every one was watching? She glanced up furtively. Hiram wore a look of triumph as he talked on, knowing he was annoying her.

"I s'pose you get letters from New York," he said, and there was a disagreeable insinuation in his tone. Phoebe did not know what he meant, but something in his tone made the color come into her cheeks. They were nearing the Spafford house. If only Miranda would come out and speak to her! She looked up at the great bully beside her and saw he was trying to calculate just how near to the mark he had come. She stopped short on the pavement.

Now Miranda was alone in the house that afternoon, and not much went on in the neighborhood that she did not keep herself informed concerning; therefore, when Phoebe, breathless, reached the front stoop the door swung open before her, and she stepped into her refuge with a gasp of relief and heard it close behind her as two strong freckled arms enclosed her and two honest lips greeted her with a resounding kiss.

"Ben waitin' quite a spell fer ye," she declared, as if it were the expected thing for Phoebe to fly into her arms unannounced in that way, "ever sence I see ye comin' down the street with that pleasant friend of yourn. Wonder you could tear yourself away. Take off yer bonnet and set a spell. Mis' Spafford's gone up t' th' aunts fer tea and took Rose. I'm all alone. You set down an' we'll have a real nice time an' then I'll take you home by 'n by."

"Oh, Miranda," gasped Phoebe, struggling hysterically between laughter and tears and trying to control the trembling that had taken possession of her body, "I'm such a miserable coward. I'm always running away when I get frightened!"

"H'm! I should hope you would!" said Miranda significantly. "Such a snake in the grass as that! Le's see ef he's gone!" and she crouched before the window and peered behind the curtain cautiously.

Hiram had watched Phoebe's sudden disappearance within the door with something like awe. It was almost uncanny having that door open and swallow her up. Besides, he had not expected that Phoebe would dare to run away from him. He stood a moment gazing after her, and then sauntered on undecidedly, calling himself a fool for having met her so near to the Spafford house. Another time he would choose his meeting-place away from her friends. He had lost this move in the game, but he by no means meant to lose the game, and the hate in his heart grew with determination to have this tempting young life in his power and crush out its resistance.

It goaded him to madness to have her dare to tell him she did not wish to walk with him. Why did she say that? Had he not always been respected, and thought well of? His farm was as good a spot of land as could be found in the whole New York state, and his barn was talked of through all the county. He was prosperous, everybody knew. Before he had married Annie any girl in the vicinity would have thought him a great catch, and he knew well, by all the indescribable signs, that many a girl as good as Phoebe would still be glad to accept his attentions. Why did this little nobody, who was after all merely a poor relation of his neighbor, presume to scorn him? He hated her for it, even while his heart was set upon having her. He wanted her at first because he admired her. Now he wanted her to conquer her and punish her for her scorn of him.

As he walked on alone his slow brain tried to form a new plan for revenge, and little by little an idea crept out of his thoughts and looked at him with its two snaky eyes until the poison of its fang had stolen into his heart. The post-office! Ah! He would watch to see if she had a letter from that fellow, for surely only the knowledge that another man was at her feet could make her scorn his attentions. If that was so he would crush the rival! He ground his teeth at the thought, and his eyes glittered with hate.

Meantime, Hiram Green's children and Alma Deane were playing together behind the big barn that had been one of the disappointments of Annie Green's married life, because it had not been a house instead of a barn. The children had dug houses in a hay-stack, and chased the few venturesome hens that had not learned to be wary when they were around; now, for the moment weary of their games, they mounted the fence to rest.

"There comes your pa," announced Alma from her perch on the top rail. The young Greens retired precipitately from the fence, and Alma was forced to follow them if she wished company. They hurried around the other side of the barn out of sight.

"Say," said Alma, after they had reached a spot of safety and ensconced themselves on the sunny exposure of a board across two logs, "my Aunt Phoebe went to the village a while ago. She'll be 'long pretty soon. Let's make up somethin' an' shout at her when she comes back. It'll make her mad as hops an' I'd just like to pay her back fer the way she acts sometimes."

"Ain't she good to you?" enquired the youngest Green, anxiously.

"Le's make up sumpin' 'bout her 'n your pa. There ain't nothin' 'll make her so mad. She's mad as mad can be when my ma says anythin' 'bout her gettin' married," went on Alma, ignoring the question.

"All right! What'll we make up?" agreed the three Greens. They were not anxious to have a step-mother who might make life's restrictions more strenuous than they were already. They were prepared to do battle valiantly if they only had a general, and Alma was thoroughly competent in their eyes to fill that position.

"It'll have to be to a song, you know," went on Alma. "Le's sing the Doxol'gy an' see how that goes." So they all stood in an enquiring row and droned out the Doxology, piping shrilly where they knew the words and filling in with home-made syllables where they did not. Alma had practiced the art of rhyming

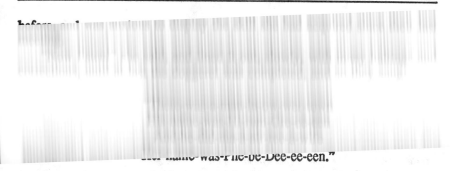

... . was-r nc-ve-Dee-ee-een."

Alma was no lax general. She drilled her little company again and again until they could shout the words at the top of their voices, to saying nothing of the way they murdered Old Hundred. The young scapegraces looked at their leader with wide-eyed admiration, and fairly palpitated for the moment when their victim should arrive and they might put their drill into practice. Between rehearsals they mounted the fence by the barn and kept a watch-out down the road. At last it was announced that she was coming.

"But there's somebuddy with 'er," said a disappointed little Green. "We won't dast, will we?"

Alma held up her undaunted chin and mounted the post of observation to see who it was.

"Aw! That's all right," she presently announced. "'Taint nobody but the red-headed girl down to Spafford's. She can't do nothin'. Come on, now, le's get ready."

She marshalled her forces behind the wide board fence next to the pig-sty and there they waited for the signal to begin. Alma thought it prudent to wait until Phoebe and Miranda had almost passed before they sang. Then she raised her hand and they piped out shrilly, making the words more than plain. Phoebe started at the first line and hurried her steps, but Miranda glanced back and said: "H'm! I thought 'es much. Like father, like child!"

Maddened by such indifference the children ran along inside the fence and continued to yell at the top of their lungs, regardless of time or tune until they reached the more open fields near the Deane house, where they dared go no further. Then they retired in triumph to the shelter of the pig-sty and the hay-stack to plume themselves upon their success, and recount the numerous faces they had made, and the times they had stuck their tongues out. They did not anticipate any trouble from the incident as they were too far away from the house for Hiram to hear, and they felt sure Phoebe would never tell on them, as it involved herself too closely.

Suddenly, in the midst of the gratulations, without the slightest warning, a strong hand seized the sturdy Alma from the rear and pinioned her arms so that she could not get away. She set up a yell that could have been heard for a half mile, and began to kick and squirm, but Miranda's hands held her fast, while she took in the surroundings at a glance, moved her captive toward a convenient seat on a log, and taking her calmly over her knee administered in full measure the spanking that child deserved, Alma, meanwhile yelling like a loon, unable to believe her senses that the despised "red-haired girl from Spafford's" had displayed so much ability and thoroughness in her methods of redress.

The valiant army of little Greens had retired with haste from the scene of action, and were even then virtuously combing their hair and washing their hands and faces with a view to proving an alibi should the avenger seek further retribution. Alma was left to the mercy of Miranda and though she kicked and yelled right lustily Miranda spanked on until she was tired.

"There!" she said, at last letting her go. "That ain't half you need, but I can't spend any more time on yeh today. Ef yeh ever do that er anythin' like it again I'll come in the night when everybody's asleep and give yeh the rest, an' I ken tell you now I won't let yeh off this easy next time. Mind you behave to yer Aunt Phoebe, er I'll hant yeh! D'yeh understand? Wherever yeh go in the dark I'll be there to hant yeh. And when red-haired people hants yeh at night their hair's all on fire in the dark an' it burns yeh, so yeh better watch out!"

She shook her fist decidedly at the child, who now thoroughly frightened began to cry in earnest and ran away home as fast as her fat legs could carry her, not daring to look back lest the supernatural creature with the fiery hair and the strong hand should be upon her again. It was the first time in her brief, impertinent life that Alma had ever been thoroughly frightened.

Her first act on reaching the house was to see how the land lay. She found that her mother had gone out to get some eggs and that Phoebe was up in her room with the door buttoned. No one else was about, so Alma stole noiselessly up to Phoebe's door, righteous innocence upon her tear-stained face, her voice smoother than butter with deceit.

"Aunt Phoebe!" she called, lovingly, "I hope you don't think I sung that mean song at you. I was real 'shamed of them Green children. I run after 'em an' tried to make 'em stop, but they jest wouldn't. I think their pa ought to be told, don't you? Say, Aunt Phoebe, you didn't think 'twas me, did you?"

There was no answer from the other side of the door for Phoebe was lying on her bed shaking with suppressed sobs, and could not control her voice to reply even if she had known what to say. Her heart was filled with pain, too, that this child whom she had tended and been kind to should be so hateful.

Alma, rather nonplussed at receiving no answer, tried once or twice and then calling out sweetly: "Well, I just thought I'd let you know 'twasn't me, Aunt Phoebe," stumped off downstairs to reflect upon the way of sinners. Her main fear was that Phoebe would "tell on her" to her father, and then she knew she would receive the other half of her spanking.

Chapter 16

Hiram Green began to put his new plan into practice the very next day. He took care to be on hand when the mail coach arrived, and as soon as the mail was distributed he presented himself at the post-office corner of the store.

"Any mail fer th' Deanes?" he enquired carelessly, after he had been told there was nothing for himself. "I'm goin' up there on business an' I'll save 'em the trouble o' comin' down."

This question he put in varied forms, until it grew to be a habit with the postmaster to hand over the Deanes' mail to Hiram every day. This was rather expensive business, for Albert frequently received letters from people who did not prepay the postage, and it went much against Hiram's grain to hand out eighteen cents or more for another man's letter, even though he were sure he would receive it again. He made prompt collections from Albert, however, and by this means Phoebe became aware of Hiram's daily visits to the post-office. Not that it made any difference to her, for she did not expect a letter from any one. There was no one to write to her.

This went on for about two weeks, and during that time Hiram had been able to see very little of Phoebe, for she kept herself well out of his way, when one day a letter bearing a New York post-mark, and closed with heavy seals, arrived, addressed to Miss Phoebe Deane.

Hiram grasped it as if it had been a long sought fortune, put it hastily in his pocket, looking furtively around lest any one had seen it, and slouched off toward home. When he reached there he went straight to his own room and fastened the door. Then he took out the letter and read the address again, written in a fine large hand of a man accustomed to handling the pen. He frowned and turned it over. The seals were stamped with a crest on which was a lion, rampant, that seemed to defy him. He held the letter up to the light, but could not make out any words. Then without hesitation he took out his knife and inserted the sharpest blade under the seals one by one, prying them up carefully so that they should not be broken more than could be helped. The letter lay open before him at last and he read with rising fury:

NEW YORK, December 20th, 1835.

MY DEAR MISS DEANE:

Will you pardon my presumption in daring thus to address you without permission? My pleasant memory of our brief acquaintance has led me to wish a continuance of it, and I am writing to ask you if you are free and willing to

was a terrible and beautiful sight.

I have just had the honor and privilege of meeting a noble and brave gentleman. His name is William Lloyd Garrison. I feel sure you would like to know about him and the work he is doing. If I am to have the pleasure of writing you again I shall be glad to tell you more of him, as I hope to meet him again, and to know him better.

Hoping that you are quite well, and that I shall soon have a favorable reply from you, I am,

Yours with esteem,
NATHANIEL GRAHAM.

Hiram Green was not a rapid reader, and in spite of Nathaniel's clear chirography it took him some time to take in all that the letter contained. The first thought that took form in his mind was that this rival of his was not out of his way yet. He had dared to write to her and ask if she was free. Ah! That showed he had taken note of what Hiram had said about her belonging to him, and he was going to find out for himself. Well, he would never find out by that letter, for Phoebe would never see it. That was easy enough. Of course it was against the law to open another person's mail, and was a state's prison offense, but who was to know that he had opened it? A letter could tell no tales when it was in ashes, and the ashes well buried. How else could they prove it? They could not. He was perfectly safe, and more and more was he getting power over these two whom he was coming to hate and to wish to crush. He congratulated himself on having been keen enough to have watched the mails. He had outwitted them, and he was pleased with himself beyond expression.

"H'm!" he ejaculated under his breath. "He's a goin' to get up a correspondence with her, is he? Like to see him! I rather think by the time she answers this letter he'll 'uv give it up. When he gets around again to give her another try—supposin' he ain't stumped at not hearin' from her this time—I reckon she'll be nicely established in my kitchen doin' my work. Yes, she's worth fightin' for, I guess, fer she ken turn off the work faster'n anybody I've seen. Wal, I guess there ain't any cause to worry 'bout this."

Then he read it over again, and yet again, noting down on an old bit of paper the date, and a few items about the fire in New York, also William Lloyd Garrison's name. After that he sent the old woman who was keeping house for him to the attic in search of a coat he knew was not there, while he carefully burned the letter on the hearth, gathering every scrap of its ashes and pulverizing them, to make sure not a trace remained to tell the tale.

As he walked away towards his barn he felt himself a man of consequence. His self-satisfaction fairly radiated from his lanky figure. For had he not outwitted a college man? And no thought of the crime had he just committed troubled his dull conscience for an instant.

That evening he took his eager way to Albert Deane's house and prepared to enjoy himself. The sunrise bedquilt was long since finished and rolled away in the chest of drawers in the spare bedroom. The spinning-wheel had taken the place of the quilting frames. And it happened that on this particular night Emmeline had demanded that Phoebe stay downstairs and spin, declaring that the yarn ought to have been ready long ago for more winter stockings.

Hiram noted this fact with satisfaction, and tilted his chair in pleasurable anticipation.

"Heard anythin' 'bout the big fire in New York?" he began, watching Phoebe's back narrowly to see if she would start. But Phoebe worked steadily on. She paid little heed to anything Hiram said, but as they talked of the fire she wondered whether Nathaniel Graham had been near it, and hoped in a maidenly way that he had been kept safe from harm.

"Why, no," said Albert, sitting up with interest, "I haven't looked at the paper yet —" unfolding it with zest. "How'd you come to know, Hiram? You say you never read the papers."

"Oh, I have better ways o' knowin' than readin' it in the papers," boasted Hiram, airily. "I had a letter from New York straight, an' the fire's goin' on yet, an' mebbe by this time it's all burnt up."

Phoebe stood so that he could see her face distinctly as he spoke about receiving a letter, but there was not a movement of a muscle to show she had heard. Hiram was disappointed. He had expected to catch some flitting expression that would show him she had interests in letters from New York. But Phoebe had no expectations of any letter from New York, so why should she start or look troubled?

"Yes," said Albert, bending over his paper, "an area of thirteen acres — six hundred and ninety-three houses burned!"

"Valued at eighteen millions!" remarked Hiram, dryly. He was enjoying the unique position of knowing more than Albert about something.

"Nonsense!" said Emmeline, sharply. "Thirteen acres! Why, that's not much bigger'n Hiram's ten-acre lot down by the old chestnut-tree. Think of

"Why, Emmeline, the paper says it was so cold the water froze in the hose-pipes and they couldn't put it out."

"Serves 'em right then fer dependin' on such new-fangled things as hosepipes. It's jest some more of their laziness. Why didn't they form a line and hand buckets? A good fire line with the women an' all in it would beat all the new lazy ways invented to save folks from liftin' their fingers to even put out a fire. I'm surprised some of 'em didn't jest sit still and expect some kind of a new machine to be made in time to wheel 'em away to safety 'stead of usin' their legs and runnin' out o' harm's way. Haven't they got a river in New York?"

"'Course," said Hiram, as if he knew it all. "The fire burned the whole line of the East River." He was glad to be reminded of the rest of his newly-acquired information.

"There, that just shows it!" exclaimed Emmeline. "That's just what I said. Shiftless lot, they are. Let their houses burn up right in front of a river! Well, I'm thankful to say I don't live in New York!"

The talk hummed on about her, but Phoebe heard no more. Somehow she kept her busy wheel whirring, but her thoughts had wandered off in a sunlit wood, and she was holding sweet converse with a golden day, and a stranger hovering on the pleasant horizon. It was not until near the close of the evening that her thoughts came back to listen to what was going on. Hiram had brought the front legs of his chair down to the floor with a thud. Phoebe thought he was going home, and she was glad they would soon be rid of his hated presence.

"Oh, by the way!" said Hiram, with a sway of conceit, "Albert, have you ever heard of a man named Garrison? William Lloyd Garrison, I believe it is."

He rolled the name out fluently, having practiced in the barn during the evening milking.

"Oh, yes," said Albert, interestedly. "You know who he is, Hiram. He's a smart fellow, though I'd hate to be in his boots!"

"Why!" Hiram's voice was sharp and his eyes narrowed as they always did when he was reaching out for clue.

"Why, don't you know about Garrison? He's had a price on his head for some time back. He gets mobbed every time he turns around, too, but I guess he's pretty plucky, for he keeps right on."

"What doing?"

"Why, he's the great Abolitionist. He publishes that paper, the *Liberator*, don't you know. You remember two years ago those anti-slavery meetings that were broken up and all the trouble they had? Well, he was the man that started it all. I don't know whether he's very wise or not, but he certainly has got a lot of courage."

Hiram's eyes were narrowing to a slit now with knowledge and satisfaction. "Oh, yes, I place him now," he drawled out. "He wouldn't be a very comfortable 'quaintance fer a man t' have, would he?"

"Well," considered Albert, thoughtfully, "I wouldn't like to have any of my relations in his place. I'd be afraid of what might happen. I think likely 'twould take a bit of courage to be friend to a man like that. But they say he has friends, a few of them."

"H'm!" said Hiram, and he rolled a thought like a sweet morsel under his tongue. "I guess I better be goin'. Night." And he shuffled away at last, casting a curious smile at Phoebe as he left.

The next morning while they were going about their work in the kitchen Emmeline remarked to Phoebe that Albert thought Hiram Green was changing for the better, he seemed to be growing real intellectual. Had Phoebe noticed how well he talked about that New York fire?

Phoebe had not noticed.

"What a queer girl you are!" exclaimed Emmeline, much vexed; "I should think you'd see he's takin' all this interest in things jest fer you. It ain't like him to care fer such things. He just thinks it will please you, and you are hard as nails not to 'preciate it."

"You are quite mistaken, Emmeline. Hiram Green never did anything to please any one but himself, I am sure," answered Phoebe, and taking her apron off went up to her room.

Phoebe was spending much more time in her room in these days than pleased Emmeline. Not that her work suffered, for Phoebe's swift fingers performed all the tasks required of her in the most approved manner, but so soon as they were done she was off. The fact that the room was cold seemed to affect her in no wise. Emmeline was in a state of chronic rage for this isolation from the rest of the family, though perhaps the only reason she liked to have her around was that she might make sarcastic remarks about her. Then, too, it seemed like an assumption of superiority on Phoebe's part. Emmeline could not bear superiority.

Phoebe's reason for hurrying to the seclusion of her own room on every possible occasion was that a new source of comfort and pleasure had been open to her through the kindness of Marcia Spafford. Miranda had reported promptly Phoebe's two escapes from Hiram Green and not only Marcia but David was greatly interested in the sweet-faced young girl. Shortly after the occasion of by Cooper.

Phoebe had naturally a bright mind, and during her days of school she had studied all that came in her way. Always she had stood at the head of her classes, sometimes getting up at the first peep of dawn to study a lesson or work over a problem, and sticking to her books until the very last minute. This had been a great source of trouble, because Emmeline objected most seriously to "taking her education so hard," as she expressed it. "Some children have measles and whooping-cough and chicken-pox and mumps real hard," she was wont to say, "but they most of 'em take learnin' easy. But Phoebe's got learnin' hard. She acts like there wasn't any use for anything else in the world but them books. Land! What good'll they do her? They won't make her spin a smoother thread, 'er quilt a straighter row, 'er sew a finer seam. She'll jest ferget everything she learnt when she's married. I'm sure I did." And no one ever disputed this convincing fact.

Nevertheless Phoebe had studied on, trying it is true to please Emmeline by doing all the work required of her, but still insisting on getting her lessons even if it deprived her of her rest, or her noon luncheon. She had acquired the habit of devouring every bit of information that came in her way, so that in spite of her environments she had a measure of true mind culture. It may have been this which so mystified and annoyed Emmeline.

So the afternoon was one of unalloyed delight to Phoebe. When she insisted that she must go home to help get supper, Miranda was sent with her, and the precious book went along to be read in odd moments. Since then Phoebe felt she had something to help her through the trying days.

These afternoons of reading with Marcia Spafford had become quite the settled thing every week or two, and always there was a book to carry home, or a new poem or article to think about.

Emmeline had grown wrathful about his constant going out, and had asked questions until she had in a measure discovered what was going on. She held her temper in for a while, for when she spoke to Albert he did not seem to sympathize with her irritation at Phoebe, but only asked the girl to let him see the book she had been reading, and became so delighted with it himself that he forgot to bring in the armful of wood Emmeline asked for until she called him the second time. After that Albert shared in the literary treasures that Phoebe brought to the house, and it became his habit to say when he came in to supper: "Been down to the village this afternoon, Phoebe? Didn't get anything new to read, did you?" This made Emmeline fairly furious, and she decided to express her mind once more freely to the girl.

She chose a morning when Phoebe was tied by a task which she could not well leave, and began:

"Now look here, Phoebe Deane, I must say you are goin' beyond all bounds. I think it's about time you stopped. I want you to understand that I think the way you're actin' is a downright sin. It isn't enough that you should scorn a good honest man that's eatin' his heart out fer yeh, an' you payin' no more 'tention to him 'n if he was the very dust o' your feet, an' him able to keep you well, too; an' you willin' to set round an' live on relations that ain't real relations at all; an' you with money in the bank a-plenty, an' never even offerin' to give so much as a little present to your little nephews and nieces that are all you've got in the world. It ain't enough that you should do all that, an' be a drug on our hands, but here you must get an' get up a 'quaintance with a woman I don't like n'er respect at all, an' let her send that poor, hard-workin', good-fer-nothin', red-headed girl after you every few days 'a takin' you away from your home, an' your good honest work that you ought to be willin' to do twice over fer all you've had. Phoebe Deane, d' you realize thet we let you go to school clear up to the top grade when other girls hed to stop an' go to work? It was all *his* doin's, I'd never hev allowed it. I think it jest spoils a girl to get so much knowledge. It's jest as I said 'twould be, too. Look at you! Spoiled. You want lily-white hands an' nothin' to do. You want to go to everlastin' tea-parties an' bring home books to read the rest o' the time. Now I stopped school when I was in the fourth reader 'n look at me. There ain't a woman round is better fixed 'n what I am. What do I need of more books? Answer that, Phoebe Deane! Answer me! Would it make me darn the children's stockin's, er cook his meals, er spin, er weave better, er would it make me any better anyway? Answer me?"

Emmeline had two bright red spots on her cheeks and she was very angry. When she was angry she always screamed her sentences at her opponent in a high key. Phoebe had the impulse to throw the wet dish-cloth at her sister-in-law, and it was hard indeed to restrain her indignation at this speech. There was the lovely Mrs. Spafford lending her books and helping her and encouraging her in every way to improve her mind by reading and study, and even Mr. Spafford seemed anxious she should have all the books to read that she desired; and here was this woman talking this way! It was beyond speech. There was nothing to say.

Emmeline stepped up close to the girl, grasped her white arm and shook it fiercely until the dish-cloth came near doing a rash deed of its own accord.

"Answer me!" she hissed in the girl's face.

"It might—" The exasperated girl hesitated ~~...~~ ~~...~~ it?

"Well ~~...~~

~~...~~ my husband ~~...~~ you mean understand you, you ~~...~~. Well, that ain't necessary! You're so different from ~~...~~body else on earth that an angel from heaven er a perfesser from college couldn't understand you, an' learnin' won't make you any different, no matter how much time you waste on it."

"Emmeline, listen!" said Phoebe, trying to stop this outburst; "I consider that I've worked for my board since I came here—"

"Consider! Consider! You consider! Well, really! Worked for your board, when you was scarcely more use 'n a baby when you come, an' think o' all the trouble o' raisin' ye! And you consider thet you've earned all you've got here! Well, I don't consider any such a thing, I ken tell you."

"Please let me finish, Emmeline. I was going to say that I have tried to make Albert take the money I have in the bank as payment for any expense and trouble I have been to him, but he says he promised my mother he wouldn't touch a cent of it, and he will not take it."

"Oh, yes, Albert is soft-hearted. Well, I didn't promise yer ma, by a long sight, an' I ain't bound to no such fool notions."

"Emmeline, I don't feel the money belongs to you. It was not you who brought me here, nor paid for whatever I have had. It was Albert. I cannot see why I should give you the money. You have done nothing for me but what you have had to do, and I am sure I have worked for you enough to pay for that, but I would much rather give the money to you than to have you talk in this way—"

"Oh, I wasn't askin' fer yer money. I wouldn't take it es a gift. I was only showin' yeh up to yourself, what a selfish good-fer-nothin' you are, settin' up airs to read books when there's good honest work goin' on."

It happened that Albert came in just then and the discussion dropped, but Phoebe with determined mien went on with her visits to Mrs. Spafford whenever Miranda came for her—never alone, lest she encounter Hiram Green—and so the winter dragged slowly on its way.

Chapter 17

Meanwhile Hiram Green still kept up his attention to the post-office, watching the Deanes so vigilantly that it was impossible for them to receive mail without his knowing it. This never annoyed Albert, as he was too good-natured to suspect any one of an ill turn, and he thought it exceedingly kind of Hiram to bring his mail up. As for Phoebe, it simply cut out all opportunity for her to go out, except when Miranda came for her.

"Why can't that Mirandy girl stay home an' mind her business an' let you come when you get ready?" asked Emmeline, in a loud tone one day when Miranda was waiting in the sitting-room for Phoebe to get ready to go with her. "She ac's 's if she was your nurse."

But Miranda continued her vigilance, and that without Phoebe's asking, and somehow Marcia always planned it that if Phoebe could stay to tea and she and David would walk home with her. It was all delightful for Phoebe, but everything that was done merely offended Emmeline the more.

Miranda, in these days, was enjoying herself. She lost no opportunity to observe the detestable Hiram and rejoice that she had foiled his attempts to bother Phoebe. One day, however, she happened to be in the post-office when the mail was distributed. She was buying sugar, and she loitered a moment after the package was handed her, watching Hiram Green who had slouched over to the counter and asked for his mail.

"Nothin' fer the Deanes?" she heard him ask in a low tone. "Nothin' fer Phoebe? She was 'spectin' somethin' I'm sure."

Miranda cast a sharp glance at him as she passed him. She was glad somehow that he received nothing. She wondered if Phoebe knew he was enquiring for her mail. Miranda laid it by in her mind as something that might be of use in the future, and went on her way.

That very day the old woman who kept house for Hiram, in sweeping out his room, came across a bit of red sealing-wax stamped with a part of a crest which bore a lion's head with the jaws apart. It was lying on a dark stripe in the rag carpet and had not been noticed before. She saw at once it was of no value and tossed it toward the open window, where it lodged upon the sill close up to the frame, and by and by when the window was closed it was shut in tight between sash and sill, the lion's head, erect and fierce, caught in the crack, a tiny thing and hidden, but reminding one of "truth crushed to earth."

The next day Nathaniel Graham made a flying visit to his home to have a serious conference with his uncle the Judge. His investigations concerning the two questions which had troubled him on his journey back to New York had involved him in matters that had

[illegible faded text]

...those who were opposed to slavery, and as yet that question was but in its infancy. Nathaniel had been put to it at last to decide definitely about Texas. He had been offered command of a company of men who were to sail soon, and he must say yes or no at once. The pressure was very strong, and sometimes he almost thought he ought to go. The time had come to speak to Judge Bristol. Nothing could be decided without his final word, for Nathaniel felt too much honor and love for the one who had been his second father to do anything without his sanction.

As was to be expected the Judge was seriously troubled at the thought of Nathaniel's going South to join in the conflict, and he argued long and seriously against any such project, telling his nephew that he had no right to even consider such questions until he had made a place for himself in the world. When Nathaniel admitted that he had been attending Abolition meetings, and was becoming intimate with some of the leaders, the Judge was roused into excited hostility.

"Nathaniel, how could you?" he exclaimed, in deep distress. "I thought your judgment was sound, but to be carried away by these wild, fanatical people is anything but evidence of sound judgment. Can you not see that this is a question that you have no business with? If your uncle in Texas chooses to keep slaves, you have no more right to meddle with his choice than if he chose to keep horses or sheep. And as for this bosh about slavery being such a terrible evil, look at Pompey and Caesar and Dianthe and the rest? Do you fancy they want to be free? Why, what would the poor things do if I didn't care for them as if they were my own children? It is all nonsense.

"Of course, there are a few bad masters, and probably will be as long as sin is in the world; but to condemn the whole system of slavery because a few men who happen to own slaves mistreat them would be like condemning marriage because a few men abused their wives. It is utmost nonsense for a few hot-headed fanatics to try to run the rest of the country into the moulds they have made and call it righteousness. Let other men alone, and they will let you go in peace is a better motto. Let every man look out to cast the beam from his own eyes before he attempts to find a mote in his brother's."

When his uncle quoted Scripture in this way Nathaniel was at a loss how to answer him.

"I wish you could hear Mr. Garrison talk, Uncle."

"I wouldn't listen to him for a moment," he answered, hotly. "He is a dangerous man! Keep away from all such gatherings, for they only breed discontent and uprisings. You will see that nothing but a lot of mobs will arise from this agitation. Slavery is a thing that cannot be overthrown, and all these meetings are mere talk to let a few men get into prominence. No man in his senses would do the things that that Garrison has done unless he wanted to get notoriety. That's what makes him so foolhardy. Keep away from him, my boy. There's a price on his head, and you'll do yourself and your prospects no good if you have anything to do with him."

They talked far into the night, Nathaniel trying to defend the man whom he had met but once or twice, but whom he had been compelled to admire. Janet pouted through the evening because Nathaniel did not come out to talk with her, and finally went to bed in a fit of the blues.

When at last Nathaniel pressed his uncle's hand at parting they both knew that he would not go to Texas. Indeed, as the young man had reflected during the night, he felt that his purpose of going there had been shaken before he came home to ask Judge Bristol's advice. However, he was not altogether sure that his uncle had considered the matter from the correct view-point either, but the talk had somehow helped to crystallize his own views. So now he felt free, nay bound, to return and complete his law course. As for the other matter, that must be left to develop in its time. He was by no means sure he was done with it yet, for his heart had been too deeply touched, and his reason stirred.

As Nathaniel climbed into the coach at the big white gate he felt that he had only put off all these questions for a time, but there was a certain relief in feeling that a decision had been reached at least for the present.

He was half a mind to ride on top with the driver, though it was a bitterly cold morning, but quite unexpectedly the driver suggested that he better sit inside this time, as the weather was so cold. Without giving it a passing thought he went inside, waving his hand and smiling at Janet, who stood at the front door with a fur-trimmed scarlet cloak about her shapely shoulders. Then the door closed and he sat down.

There was one other passenger, a girl, who sat far back in the shadows of the coach, but her eyes shone out from the heavy wrappings of cloak and bonnet and gave him welcome.

"Oh!" she said, catching her breath.

"And is it you?" he asked eagerly, reaching out to grasp her hand. Then each remembered, the girl that she was alone in the coach with this man, the man that this girl might belong to another. But in spite of it they were glad to see one another.

The coach rolled out into the main street again and as it lurched over the crossing Hiram Green, who was hurrying to his daily vigilance at the post-office, caught a good view of Nathaniel's .... for she felt sure that if he knew she was going that morning he would have found it possible to have accompanied her, and she would have found it impossible to get rid of his company. So when the day before Emmeline had suggested that somebody ought to go out to Miss Ann Jane Bloodgood's and get some dried saffron flowers she had promised them last fall, to dye the carpet-rags, Phoebe said nothing until after Hiram had left that night. Then as she was going upstairs with her candle she turned to Emmeline and said:

"I've been thinking Emmeline, I could go over to Bloodgood's by the morning coach if Albert could drive me down when he takes his corn to the mill. Then perhaps some of them would be coming over to the village, or I could catch a ride back, or if not I could come back by the evening coach."

Emmeline assented grimly. She wanted the dye and she did not relish the long cold ride in the coach. Ann Jane Bloodgood was too condescending to please her, anyway. So, as Albert was going to mill early, Phoebe made her simple preparations that night, and was ready bright and early. Moreover, she coaxed Albert to drive around by Granny McVane's that she might leave a bit of poetry for her which she had told her about. The poem could have waited, but Albert did not tell her that, and Phoebe did not explain to Albert that if they went around by Granny's Hiram would not know she was gone away and therefore would not try to follow her. It was a pity that Phoebe had not confided a little now and then in Albert, though he, poor soul, could do little against such odds as Emmeline and Hiram.

The ten-mile coach ride to Bloodgood's wide farm-house spun itself away into nothing in such company, and before Phoebe could believe it was half over she saw the distant roof, low-browed with overhanging snow, and the red barns glimmering warmly a little beyond. Nathaniel saw them, too, for she had told him at once where she was going and he might not think she had planned to go with him. He felt that the moments were precious.

"Do you remember what we talked of that night we walked to your home?" he asked.

"Oh, yes," she breathed, softly. "You were talking of some one who needed setting free. I have been reading some wonderful poems lately that made me think a great deal of what you said."

He looked at her keenly. How could a girl who read poems and talked so well belong to Hiram Green?

"I have been thinking much about it lately," he went on with just the breath of sign. "I may have to decide what I will do at no distant day now. I wonder if I may ask you to pray for me?"

He watched her, this girl with the drooping eyes and rosy-hued cheeks, the girl who had by her silence refused to answer his letter, and wondered if perhaps by his request he had offended her. The coach lurched up to the wide piazza and stopped, and the driver jumped heavily into the snowy road. They could hear his steps plowing through the drift by the back wheel. His hand was on the coach door. Then quickly, as if she might be too late, her eyes were lifted to his, and he saw her heart would be in those prayers, as she answered:

"Oh, I will."

Something like a flash of light went through them as they looked for that instant into one another's eyes, and lifted them above the mere petty things of earth. It was intangible. Nathaniel could not explain it to himself as he sat back alone in the empty coach and went over the facts of the case, why his heart felt light, and the day seemed brighter, just because a girl whom he knew ever so little had promised in that tone of voice to pray for him. It thrilled him anew as he thought it over, and his heart went soaring up into heavens of happiness, until he called himself a fool, and told himself nothing was changed, and that Phoebe had not even replied to his letter and politely declined the correspondence, as she would certainly have been justified in doing even if she were the promised wife of Hiram Green. Yet his heart refused to be anything but buoyant. He began to berate himself that he had not frankly spoken of his letter and heard what she had to say about the matter. Perhaps in some way it had never reached her, and yet after all that was scarcely possible. Letters clearly addressed were seldom lost. It might only have embarrassed her if he had spoken.

At the next stop he accepted the coach driver's invitation to "come up top a spell, there's a fine sun comin' up now," and he let old Michael babble on about the gossip of the town, until at last the sly old man asked him innocently enough: "And what did ye think av the other passenger, Mr. 'Than'el? An' ain't she a bonnie lassie?" And then he was treated to a list of Phoebe's virtues sounded forth by one who in reality knew very little of her save that as a child on the way home from school one day she had shyly handed him up a bunch of wayside posies as he drove by her on the road. That childish act had won his loyalty, and old Michael was not troubled with the truth. He was thoroughly capable of filling in virtues where he knew none. He went on the principle that what ought to be was. And so it was that when Nathaniel arrived in New York his heart was strangely light, and he wondered often if Phoebe Deane would remember to pray for him. It seemed as if the momentous question were now in better hands than his own.

Meantime Hiram Green, having found in th........
for Albert concern...........

.... she gone to the
.... she not know he was here? Perhaps his own
.... manipulating of the mail had nipped this miniature courtship in the bud, as it were, and there would be no further need of his vigilance.

But when Hiram reached the Deanes and looked about for Phoebe she was not there.

"Where's Phoebe?" he demanded, frowning.

"She's gone up to Ann Jane Bloodgood's t' get some saffron flowers," said Emmeline. "Won't you come in, Hiram? She'll be mighty sorry to know she missed you." Emmeline thought it was as well to keep up appearances for Phoebe.

"Yes, I'm sure," drawled Hiram. "How'd she go?" he asked her after an ominous silence in which Emmeline was meditating on what it would be best to say.

"She went in the coach, an' I reckon she'll come back that way by night ef there don't no one come over from Bloodgood's this way. You might meet the coach ef you was goin' in to the village again. I don't know's Albert'll feel he hes time after losin' so much o' the day t' mill."

Hiram said nothing, but Emmeline saw he was angry.

"I'd a sent you word she was goin' an' given you the chance to go 'long with her, only she didn't say a word till after you was gone home last night—" she began apologetically, but Hiram did not seem to heed her. He got up after a minute, his brows still lowering. He was thinking that Phoebe had planned to go with Nathaniel Graham.

"I'll be over t' th' village," he said, as he went out. "Albert needn't go." Emmeline looked after him meditatively.

"I shouldn't be a bit s'prised ef he give er up, the way she goes on. It's wonderful how he holds on to her. She's a fool, that's what she is, an' I've no pity on to her. I wish to goodness she was well married an' out o' the way. She does try me beyond all, with her books, an' her visitin's, an' her locked doors, an' notions."

Meantime, Phoebe, all unconscious of the plot that was thickening round her, accepted an invitation to remain over night and the next day with Ann Jane Bloodgood, and drive in to town in the afternoon when she went to missionary meeting. Ann Jane was interested in Christian missions and fascinated Phoebe with her tales of Eliot, Brainerd, Carey, Whiteman, and Robert Moffat. Phoebe, as she looked over Ann Jane's pile of missionary papers, began to wonder how many people of one sort and another there were in the world who needed setting free from something. It all seemed to be a part of the one great thing for which she was praying, the thing that Nathaniel Graham was trying to decide, and he was another just like those wonderful men who were giving their lives to save others. Phoebe was glad she had come, though perhaps she might not have been if she could have seen the thought that was working in Hiram Green's heart.

After some reflection Hiram harnessed his horses and took the long ride over to Bloodgood's that afternoon, arriving at the house just after Phoebe and Ann Jane were safely established in Ann Jane's second cousin's best room, a mile away, for a visit. Ann Jane's second cousin was an invalid and liked company, so Phoebe's bright face cheered what would otherwise have been a lonely afternoon, and she escaped the unpleasant encounter with Hiram.

Hiram, his suspicions confirmed, met the evening coach, but no Phoebe appeared. He stepped up to Albert Deane's in the evening long enough to make sure that she had not returned by any private conveyance, and the next day he drove over again, but again found the low farm-house closed and deserted, for Ann Jane had driven with Phoebe by another road to the village missionary meeting.

His temper not much improved with his two fruitless rides, Hiram returned, watched every passenger from the evening coach alight, and then betook himself to the Deanes again, where he was really surprised to find Phoebe had returned.

That evening when the saffron flowers were being discussed he remarked that there were mighty nice saffron flowers for sale in Albany, and he watched Phoebe narrowly, but the round cheek did not flush nor the long lashes flutter in any suspicious way. Nevertheless, Hiram's mind never let go an evil thought that once lodged there. He felt he had a new power over Phoebe that he might use if occasion demanded. He could bide his time.

...from him, save for ...y in the evening. Hiram took every opportunity possible to make it apparent that he was "keeping company" with Phoebe, through the medium of his nightly visit, and Phoebe made it plain upon every occasion that she did not consider his visit was for her. She got out of the way when she could, but Emmeline contrived to keep her unusually busy every evening, and her own room was so cold that escape was impossible.

Hiram had made several unsuccessful efforts to establish himself beside Phoebe in public, and he was getting desperate. Every Sunday when he tried to walk down the aisle with her he would find Miranda and Rose one on either side of her, Mrs. Spafford herself, sometimes all three, and all serenely unconscious of his presence. They attended her down to the carryall. She never went to the village any more that he could discover, unless Miranda came for her, or Albert took her back and forth, though once he had seen her flying across the fields from Granny McVane's house with a bundle that looked as if it came from the store. He complained to Emmeline at last and she agreed to help him. Albert was not taken into the scheme. For some reason it was deemed best not to tell Albert about it at all. He was apt to ask kindly, searching questions, and he always took it for granted that one did everything with the best motives. Besides, he was not quick at evasion and might let the cat out of the bag.

There was to be a barn raising about ten miles the other side of the village, and the whole country round about were invited. It happened that the Woodburys, whose barn was to be raised, were distant relatives of Emmeline, and of course the Deanes were going.

Emmeline had shown plainly that she would be offended if Phoebe did not go, though the girl would have much preferred remaining at home with the new book Mrs. Spafford had sent up the day before. It was a matter of selfishness with Emmeline. She wanted Phoebe to help with the big dinner and relieve her so that she could visit with the other women.

It was a part of the scheme that Albert should go in the chaise with Alma, and should start while Phoebe was still dressing. Emmeline had managed Albert very adroitly, telling him that Hiram wanted a change to "set in the front seat with Phoebe" in the carryall. Albert, always willing to do a good turn, acceded readily, though Alma was a somewhat reluctant passenger.

When Phoebe came downstairs she found Emmeline already seated in the back seat of the carryall with the other children. She gladly got into the front seat, as it was much pleasanter to be there than beside Emmeline, and she seldom had the opportunity of riding beside her brother, who was more congenial than the others. But in a moment Hiram Green appeared from around the corner of the house. He got quickly into the vacant seat beside Phoebe and whipped up the horses.

"Why, where is Albert?" asked Phoebe in dismay, wishing she could get out.

"He had to go on," explained Emmeline, blandly. "Drive fast, Hiram, we'll be late." This last because she fancied she saw a frightened sideways glance from Phoebe as if she might be going to get out.

Phoebe turned her head to the road-side and tried to watch for the chance wild flowers, and forget the talk of crops and gossip that was kept up between Emmeline and Hiram, but the whole pleasant day was clouded for her, and her annoyance was double when they passed through the village and Janet Bristol in dainty pink dimity stared at them with haughty sweetness from under her white shirred bonnet and pink-lined sunshade. Janet was not going to the barn-raising evidently. She had many interests outside of the village where she was born, and did not mingle freely with her fellow-townsmen. There were only a favored few who were her friends and had the privileges of the beautiful old house.

Her passing called forth unfavorable comment from Emmeline and Hiram, and Phoebe writhed at her sister-in-law's tone, loud enough for Janet to hear easily, if she had a mind.

"The idea of wearing such fancy things of a mornin'!" she exclaimed. "I didn't think the Judge was such a fool as to let his daughter come up like that, fixed up fit fer a party this early, an' a sunshade, too! What's she think it's for, I wonder! Her complexion's so dark a little more of this weak sunshine couldn't make much difference. Mebbe she thinks she looks fine, but she's much mistaken. A lazy girl all decked out never looks pretty to me."

"That's 'bout right," declared Hiram, as if he knew all about it. "Give me a good worker ev'ry time, I sez, in preference to one with ringlets an' a nosegay on her frock. But you couldn't expec' much of that one. She's goin' to marry that highfolutin' Nate Graham, an' they'll have money 'nough betwixt 'em to keep her in prettys all the rest of her life. Say, did you hear Nate Graham'd turned Abolitionist? Well, it's so; I heard it from a r'liable source. Hev a friend in Noo York writes me once in a while an' I know what I'm talkin' 'bout. Hed it from headquarters like, you know. Er it's so he may git into trouble enny time now. There's prices on them Abolitionists' heads!"

Hiram turned to look straight into Phoebe's startled face, with an ugly leer of a laugh. The girl's cheeks grew pink, and she turned quickly away; Hiram felt he had scored one against his

The day was one of noise and bustle and, for Phoebe, hard work. By instinct the women put tasks upon her young shoulders which they wished to shirk, knowing they would be well done. It was written large on Phoebe's face that she could be trusted. So they trusted her, and the fun and frolic and feasting went on, while she toiled in the kitchen, gladly taking extra burdens upon herself, only so it kept her out of any possibility of being troubled by Hiram.

She was washing dishes and meditating on how she could manage not to sit next to Hiram on the return trip when a little Woodbury entered the kitchen.

"Say, Phoebe Deane," she called out, "your brother says you're to go in the chaise with him this time, an' when you get ready you come out to the barn an' get in. He says you needn't hurry, fer he's busy yet a while."

The child was gone back to her play before Phoebe could thank her, and with lightened heart she went on washing the dishes. Perhaps Albert had surmised her dislike to riding with Hiram and had planned this for her sake. She made up her mind to confide in Albert during this ride and see if he could not help her to get rid of her obnoxious lover once and for all. Albert was usually slow and undecided, but when once in a great while he put his foot down about something things usually went as he said.

She wiped the last dish, washed her hands, and ran upstairs for her bonnet and mantilla. Everybody else was gone. The long, slant rays of the setting sun were streaming in at the window and touching the great four-poster bed where lay her wraps alone. She put them on quickly, glad that every one else was out of the way and she would not have to wait for a lot of good-byes. The day had been a weariness to her, and she was thankful to have it over.

Mr. and Mrs. Woodbury stood together by the great stepping-stone in front of the house. They had said good-bye to Albert and Emmeline an hour before, and had just been seeing off the last wagon-load of guests. They turned eagerly to thank Phoebe for her assistance. Indeed, the girl had many warm friends among older people who knew her kindly heart and willing hands.

"What! Your folks all gone and left you, Phoebe!" exclaimed Mrs. Woodbury in dismay! "Why, they must a' forgot you."

"No, they're not all gone, Mrs. Woodbury. Our chaise is out in the barn waiting for me. Albert sent word to me by your Martha that I needn't hurry, so I stopped to finish the dishes."

"Oh! Now that's so good of you, Phoebe Deane," said the tired farmer's wife, who expected she would have plenty of cleaning to do after the departure of her large company of guests. "You shouldn't ov done that. I could a' cleaned up. I'm 'fraid you're real tired. Wouldn't you like to stay over night and get rested?"

But Phoebe shook hands happily with them and hurried down to the chaise. Now the Woodbury barn was out near the road, and the chaise stood facing the road, the horse not tied, but waiting with turned head as if his master was not far away. Phoebe jumped in with a spring, calling "Come on, Albert. I'm here at last. Did I keep you waiting long?"

Then before she had time to look around or know what was happening Hiram Green stepped out from the barn door, sprang into the seat beside her, and with unwonted swiftness caught up the whip and gave the horse such a cut that it started off at a brisk trot down the road. It was he who had sent the message by little Martha Woodbury, just as it had been given. Emmeline had managed the rest.

"Oh!" gasped Phoebe. "Why, Mr. Green, Albert is here waiting for me somewhere. Please stop the horse and let me find him. He sent word he would wait for me."

"That's all right," said Hiram, nonchalantly. "Albert decided to go in the carryall. Your sister-in-law was in a great stew to get back fer milkin' time an' made him come, so I offered to bring ye back home."

Phoebe's heart froze within her. She looked wildly about her and knew not what to do. The horse was going very fast, and to jump would be dangerous. She had no idea that Hiram would stop and let her out if she should ask him. His talk the last time they had an encounter had shown her that she must not let him see he had her in his power. Besides, what excuse could she give for stopping save that she did not wish to go with him? And how otherwise could she get home that night? How she wished that she had accepted Mrs. Woodbury's kind invitation. Could she not, perhaps, manage it yet?

"That's very kind of you," she faltered, with white lips, as she tried to marshal her wits and contrive some way out of this predicament. Then she made a feint of looking about her in the seat.

"I wonder if I remembered to bring my apron," she said faintly. "Would you mind, Mr. Green, just driving me back to see?"

"Oh, I reckon you'll find it," Hiram said, easily. "Ef you don't you got a few more, ain't you? Here, ain't this it?" and he fished out a damp roll from under the seat.

Phoebe had hoped for one wild little ~~moment~~ ....

.... perhaps. She

.... courage and tried to talk pleasantly, although the countenance of the man beside her as she stole a swift glance at his profile, frightened her. There was both triumph and revenge upon it. "They had a pleasant day for the raising, Mr. Green," she began.

And then to her horror he slowed the horse to a walk and sat back close to her as if he intended to enjoy the tete a tete to its full.

It was an awful strain. Phoebe's cheeks blazed out in two red spots, and her eyes were bright with excitement. They dragged their slow way through a woods where the lights and shadows played in all the sweetness of spring odors. Phoebe sat up very straight, very much to her side of the chaise, and laughed and talked as if she were wound up.

Hiram did not say much. He sat watching her, almost devouring the changefulness of her face, fully understanding her horror of him and this ride, yet determined to make her suffer every minute of the time. It made his anger all the greater as he saw her bravely try to keep up a semblance of respect toward him and knew she did not feel it. Why could she not give it freely, and not against her will? What was there about him she disliked? Never mind, she should pay for her dislike. She should see that she would have to treat him as she would treat those she liked, whether she wished or no.

She suggested that they better drive faster, as it was getting late and would be dark. He said that did not matter, that Emmeline had said they were not to hurry. She told him she would be needed, but he told her it was right she should have a little rest once in a while, and he smiled grimly as he said it, knowing the present ride was anything but rest to the poor tired soul beside him. He seemed to delight in torturing her. The farther she edged away from him the nearer he came to her, until when they emerged from the woods and met a carryall with some people they both knew, he was sitting quite over on her side, and she was almost out of her seat, her face a piteous picture of rage and helplessness.

Emboldened by the expression on the faces of their acquaintances, Hiram threw his arm across the back of the chaise, until it quite encircled Phoebe's back, or would have if she had not sat upon the extreme front edge of the seat.

They had reached a settlement of three houses, where a toll-gate, spreading its white pole out across the way, and a little store and school-house, went by the name of The Crossroads. Hiram flung a bit of money out to the toll-man and drove on without stopping. Phoebe's heart was beating wildly. She could not sit thus on the edge of her seat another instant. Something must be done.

"Mr. Green, would you mind moving over just a little, I haven't quite enough room," she gasped.

"Oh, that's all right," said Hiram, as heartily as if he really did not understand the situation. "Just sit clos'ter. Don't be shy." His circling arm came round her waist and by brute strength drew her up to him, so that it looked from behind as if they were a pair of lovers. The top of the chaise was thrown back so that they could easily be seen.

They had just passed the last house. It was the home of old Mrs. Duzenberry and her elderly daughter Suzanna. Living so far from the village they made it a point not to miss anything that went by their door, and at this hour in the afternoon, when their simple tea was brewing, they both sat by the front window, ready to bob to the door the minute there was anything of interest. It is needless to say that they both bobbed on this occasion, the daughter with folded arms and alert beak like some old bird of prey, the mother just behind with quizzical exclamatory interrogations written in every curve of her cap-strings.

Phoebe, glancing back wildly, as she felt herself drawn beyond her power to stop it, saw them gaping at her in amaze, and her cheeks grew crimson with shame.

"Stop!" she cried, putting out her hands and pushing against him.

She might as well have tried to push off a mountain that was in her path. Hiram only laughed and drew her closer, till his ugly, grizzled face was near to her own. She could feel his breath upon her cheek, and the horse was going faster now. She did not know just how it happened, whether Hiram had touched him with the whip, or spoken a low word. They were down the road out of sight of the Duzenberrys' before she could wrench herself away from the scoundrel. Even then it was but that he might settle himself a little closer and more comfortably that he let go of her for a moment and then the strong, cruel arm came back as if it had a right around her waist, and Hiram's face came cheek to cheek with her own.

She uttered one terrible scream, and looked around, but there was no one in sight. The sun, which had been slowly sinking like a ball of burning opal, suddenly dropped behind a hill and left the world dull and leaden with a heavy sky of gray. Dark blue clouds seemed all around, which until now had not been noticed, and a quick uncertain wind was springing up; a low rumble behind them seemed to wrap them in a new dread. But the strong man's grasp held her fast, and her screams brought no help.

In the horror of the moment a thought of her mother came, and she wondered if that mother were where she could see her child, and whether it did not give her deep anguish even in the bliss of heaven to know she was in such straits. Then as the sharp stubble of Hi~~...~~

~~[text obscured by damage]~~

~~...~~ by a terrible crash of thunder.

With an oath of mingled rage and awe, Hiram pushed Phoebe from him and reached for the reins to try and soothe the frightened horse, who was plunging and snorting and trembling in fear.

The chaise was on the edge of a deep ditch half filled with muddy water. One wheel was almost over the edge. Hiram saw the danger, and reached for his whip. He cut the horse a frantic lash which brought his fore-feet to the ground again and caused him to start off down the road on a terrific gallop. But in that instant, while the chaise poised on the edge of the ditch, Phoebe's resolve had crystallized into action. She gave a wild spring, just as the cut from the whip sent the horse tearing headlong down the road. Her dress caught in the arm of the chaise, and for one instant she poised over the ditch. Then the fabric gave way and she fell heavily, striking her head against the fence, and lay huddled in the muddy depths. Down the hard road echoed the heavy hoof-beats of the horse in frenzied gallop with no abatement, and over all the majestic thunder rolled.

Chapter 19

Her senses swam off into the relief of unconsciousness for a moment, but the cold water creeping up through her clothing chilled her back to life again, and in a moment more she had opened her eyes in wonder that she was lying there alone, free from her tormentor. She fancied she could hear the echo of the horse's feet yet, or was it the thunder? Then came the awful thought, what would happen if he returned and found her lying here? He would be terribly angry at her for having frightened the horse and jumped out of the chaise. He would visit it upon her in some way she felt sure, and she would be utterly defenseless against him.

There was not a soul in sight and it was growing suddenly dark. She must be at least six or seven miles away from home. She did not come that way often enough to be sure of distances. With new fear she sat up, and crept out of the water. The mud was deep and it was difficult to step, but she managed to get away from the oozy soil, and into the road again. Then in a panic she sprang across the ditch and crept under the fence. She must fly from here. When Hiram succeeded in stopping the horse he would undoubtedly come back for her, and she must get away before he found her.

Which way should she go? She looked back upon the road, but feared to go that way, lest he would go to those houses and search for her. There was no telling what he would say. She had no faith in him. He might say she had given him the right to put his arms around her. She must get away from here at once where he could not find her. Out to the right, across the road, it was all open country. There was nowhere she could take refuge near by. But across this field and another there was a growth of trees and bushes. Perhaps she could reach there and hide and so make her way home after he had gone.

She fled across the spring-sodden field as fast as her soaked shoes and her trembling limbs could carry her; slipping now and then and almost falling, but catching at the fence and going on, wildly, blindly, till she reached the fence. Once she thought she heard the distant bellowing of a bull, but she crept to the other side of the fence and kept on her way, breathless. And now the storm broke into wild splashes of rain, pelting on her face and hair, for her bonnet had fallen back and was hanging around her neck by its ribbons. The net had come off from her hair, and the long locks blew about her face and lashed her in the eyes as she ran. It was dark as night and Phoebe could see but dimly where she was going. Yet this was a comfort to her rather than a source of fear. She felt it would the better cover her hiding. Her worst dread was to come under the power of Hiram Green again.

shelter of the wood; and though the shocks crashed about her, and seemed to be cleaving the giants of the forest, there she stayed until the storm had abated, and the genuine darkness had succeeded.

She was wet to the skin, and trembling like a leaf. Her strongest impulse was to sink to the earth and weep herself into nothingness, but her common-sense would not let her even sit down to rest. She knew she must start at once if she would hope to reach home. Yet by this time she had very little idea of where she was and how to get home. With another prayer for guidance she started out, keeping sharp lookout along the road with ears and eyes, that there might be no possibility of Hiram's coming upon her unaware. Twice she heard vehicles in the distance, and crept into the shelter of some trees until they passed. She heard pleasant voices talking of the storm and longed to cry out to them for help, yet dared not. What would they think of her, a young girl out alone at that time of night, and in a such condition? Besides, they were all strangers. She dared not speak. And neither to friends would she have spoken, for they would have been all the more astonished to find her so. She thought longingly of Mrs. Spafford, and Miranda, yet dreaded lest even Mrs. Spafford might think she had done wrong to allow herself to ride even a couple of miles with such a man as Hiram Green after all the experience she had had with him. Yet as she plodded along she wondered how she could have done differently, unless indeed she had dared to pull up the horse and jump out at once; yet very likely she would not have been able to make her escape from her tormentor as easily earlier in the afternoon as at the time when she had taken her unpremeditated leap into the ditch.

As she looked back upon the experience it seemed as though the storm had been sent by Providence to provide her a shield and a way of escape. If it had not been for the storm the horse would not have been easily frightened into running, and Hiram would soon have found her and compelled her to get into the chaise again. What could she have done against his strength! She shuddered, partly with cold and partly with horror.

A slender thread of pale moon had come up, but it gave a sickly light, and soon slipped out of sight again, leaving only the kindly stars whose lights looked brilliant but so far away tonight. Everywhere was a soft dripping sound, and the seething of the earth drinking in a good draught.

Once when it seemed as if she had been going for hours she sat down on the wet bank to rest, and a horse and rider galloped out of the blackness past her. She hid her white face in her lap and he may have thought her but a stump beside the fence. She was thankful he did not stop to see, but as yet nothing had given her a clue to her whereabouts, and she was cold, so terribly cold.

At last she passed a house she did not know, and then another, and another. Finally she made out that she was in a little settlement, about three miles from the Deanes' farm. She could not tell how she had wandered, nor how she came to be yet so far away when she must have walked at least twenty miles. But the knowledge of where she was brought her new courage.

There was a road leading from this settlement straight to Granny McVane's, and she would not need to go back by the road where Hiram would search for her, if indeed he had not already given up the search and gone home. The lights were out everywhere in this village, save in one small house at the farthest end, and she stole past that as if she had been a wraith. Then she breathed more freely as she came into the open country road again, and knew there were but two or three houses now between herself and home.

It occurred to her to wonder in a dull way if the horse had thrown Hiram out and maybe he was hurt, and whether she might not after all have to send a search party after him. She wondered what he would do when he could not find her, supposing he was not hurt. Perhaps he had been too angry to go back for her and her dread of him had been unnecessary. But she thought she knew him well enough to know he would not easily give her up.

She wondered if he would tell Albert, and whether Albert would be worried—she was sure he would be, good, kind Albert—and what would Emmeline say? Emmeline, who had been at the bottom of all this she was sure—and then her thoughts would trail on ahead of her in the wet, and her feet would lag behind and she would feel that she could not catch up. If only a kindly coach would appear! Yet she kept on, holding up her heavy head, and gripping her wet mantle close with her cold, cold hands, shivering as she went.

Once she caught herself murmuring: "Oh, mother, mother!" and then wondered what it meant. So stumbling on, slower and more slowly, she came at last to the little house of Granny McVane, all dark and quiet, but so kindly-looking in the night. She longed to crawl to the doorstep and lie down to die, but duty kept her on. No one must know of this if she could help it. That seemed to be the main thought she could grasp with her weary brain.

The fields behind Granny McVane's were very miry. Three times she fell, and the last time almost lay still, but some stirring of brain and conscience helped her up and on again, across the last hillock, over the last fence, through the garden and up to the back door of her home.

There was a light inside, but she was too f__ ___
She tried to open the door but the l___
and almost ____

_____you ben? You've
_____ Albert ain't got home yet. I tol' him
_____ likely gone in somewheres out o' the storm, an' you'd
_____ all right in the mornin', but it's just like your crazy ways to come home
in the middle o' th' night. Fer goodness sake, what a sight yeh are! You ain't
comin' in the house like that! Why, there'll be mud to clean fer a week. Stop
there till I get some water an' a broom."

But Phoebe, with deathly white face, and eyes that saw not, stumbled past
her without a word, the water and mud oozing out of her shoes at every step,
and dripping from her garments; her sodden bonnet dejectedly upon her shoulders, her hair once long drenched mantle of darkness. Emmeline, half awed by
the sight, stood still in the doorway and watched her go upstairs, realizing that
the girl did not know what she was doing. Then she shut the door sharply as
she had opened it, and followed Phoebe upstairs.

Phoebe held out until she reached her own door, and opened it. Then she
sank without a sound upon the floor and lay there as if dead. All breath and
consciousness had fluttered out, it seemed, with that last effort.

Emmeline set the candle down with a sudden, startled exclamation and went
to her. She felt her hands so cold, like ice, and her face like wet marble, and
hard as she was, she was frightened. Her conscience, so long enjoying a vacation,
leaped into a new life and became active. What part had she borne in this that
seemed as if it might yet be a tragedy?

She unlaced the clodded shoes, untied the soaked bonnet, pulled off the wet
garments one by one and wrapped the girl in thick warm blankets, dragging her
light weight to the bed; but still no sign of consciousness had come. She felt
her heart and listened for a breath, but she could not tell yet if she were alive
or not. Then she went downstairs with hurried steps, flapping over the kitchen
floor in the large carpet slippers, and stirred up the fire that had been banked
down, putting the kettle over it to heat. In a little while she had plenty of hot
water, and various remedies applied, but life seem scarcely yet to have crept
back to her, only a flutter of the eyelids now and then or a fleeting breath like
a sigh. The dawn was coming on and Albert's voice in low strained tones could
be heard outside:

"No, I'm not going to stop for anything to eat, Hiram, you may if you like, but I shall not stop till I find her. It's been a real bad night, an' to think of that little girl out in it, I can't bear it!" There seemed to be something like a sob in Albert's last words.

"Well, suit yerself," answered Hiram, gruffly. "I'm pretty well played out. I'll go home an' get a bite, an' then I'll come on an' meet yeh. You'll likely find her back at Woodbury's I reckon. She wanted to go back, I mind now. We'd ought to 'a' gone there in the first place."

The voices were under her window. Phoebe slowly opened her eyes and shuddering grasped Emmeline's hands so tightly that it hurt her.

"Oh, don't let him come; don't let him come!" she pleaded, and sank away into unconsciousness again.

It was a long time before they could rouse her, and when she finally opened her eyes she did not know them. A fierce and terrible fever had flamed up in her veins till her face was brilliant with color, and her long dark hair was scorched dry again in its fires.

Granny McVane came quietly over the next day and offered to nurse her. Then the long blank days of fever stretched themselves out for the unconscious girl, and a fight between life and death began.

Now, it happened that on that very afternoon of the barn raising, Mistress Janet Bristol, in all the bravery of her pink and white frills and furbelows, with a bunch of pink moss-roses at her breast, and her haughtiest air, drove over to the Deanes to call upon Phoebe, in long-delayed response to her cousin Nathaniel's most cousinly letter requesting her to do so. She had parleyed long with herself whether she would go or not, but at last curiosity to see what there was in this country girl to attract her handsome, brilliant cousin, led her to go.

One can scarcely conjecture what Emmeline would have said and thought if she had seen the grand carriage drive up before her door, with its colored coachman and footman in livery. But no one was at home to tell the tale save the white lilacs on the great bush near the front gate, who waved a welcome rich with fragrance. Perhaps they sent the essence of the welcome Phoebe would have gladly given to this favored girl whom she admired.

So half petulant at this reception when she had condescended to come, she scanned the house for some trace of the life of this unknown girl, and drove away with the memory of lilac fragrance floating about a dull and commonplace house. She drove away half determined she would tell her cousin she had done her best, and would not go again. There was no sign left behind to tell this other girl of the lost call. It is doubtful, if Janet had been able to carry out her purpose that afternoon and make her call upon Phoebe, whether either of the two would have been able to find and understand the other at that time.

Janet drove back to her own world again, and the door between the two closed. That very evening's mail brought a brief letter from Nathaniel, saying his dear friend and chum, Martin Van Rensselaer, would

in a few days, and he desired

Chapter 20

Miranda was out in the flower-bed by the side gate. She had gathered her hands full of spicy gray-green Southern wood and was standing by the fence looking wistfully down the street. The afternoon coach was in and she was idly watching to see who came in, but not with her usual vim. The spectre of the shadow of death was hovering too near to Phoebe for Miranda to take much interest in things in general.

Three days after Phoebe's midnight walk Miranda had gone out to see her and bring her down to take tea with Mrs. Spafford. What was her dismay to find that she was refused admittance, and that too very shortly.

"Phoebe's sick abed!" snapped Emmeline. She had been tried beyond measure over all the extra work that was thrown on her hands by Phoebe's illness, and she had no time for buttered words. "No, she can't see you today nor next day. She's got a fever an' she don't know nobody. The doctor says she mus' be kep' quiet. No, I can't tell yeh how she got it. The land only knows it! Ef she ever gits well mebbe she ken tell herself, but I doubt it. She'll uv forgot by that time. What she does know she fergets mostly. No, you can't go an' take care of her. She's got folks 'nough to do that now, more'n she needs. There ain't a livin' thing to do but let her alone till she comes out of it. You don't suppose *you* c'd take care o' her, do yeh? *H'm!* Wal, I ain't got time to talk," and the door was shut in her face.

Miranda, however, was not to be turned aside thus easily. With real concern in her face she marched around the wood-shed to the place under the little window of the kitchen chamber that she knew was Phoebe's room.

"Phoebe!" she called, softly; "Phoe-bee!"

And the sick girl tossing on her bed of fever called wildly, "Don't you hear that Phoebe-bird calling, mother! Oh, mother! It's calling me from the top of the barn. It says, 'Phoebe, I'm here! Don't be afraid!'" and the voice trailed off into incoherence again.

Granny McVane hobbled to the window, perplexed, for she too had heard the soft sound.

"Oh, is that you, Granny?" whispered Miranda. "Say, what's the matter with Phoebe? Is she bad?"

"Yes, real bad," whispered back Granny. "She don't know a soul, poor little thing. She thinks her mother's here with her. I don't know much about how it happened. There was an accident and the horse ran away. She was out in that awful storm the other night. She's calling and I must go back to her."

In much dismay Miranda had hurried b... ...
doctor's ...

... ...heart of Miranda
...gement as it had ever come in its dauntless life.

And now this afternoon she had just returned from a particularly fruitless journey to the farm. She had been unable to get sight or sound of anyone but Emmeline, who slammed the door in her face as usual after telling her she wished she would mind her own business and let folks alone that weren't troubling her, and Miranda felt as she trudged back to the village with tears in her homely eyes, as if she must cry out or do something. She had never quite come to a place before where her wits could not plan out some help for those she loved. Death was different. One could not outwit death.

Then, like a slowly dawning hope, she saw Nathaniel Graham coming up the street with his carpet-bag in his hand.

Nathaniel had come up for a day to tell his uncle and cousin all about this dear friend of his whom he so much desired to have made welcome for a week or two for his sake. He had been made junior partner in a law firm, the senior partner being an old friend of Judge Bristol's, and his work would be strenuous, else he would probably have planned to be at the old home all summer himself. As it was, he could hope for but a few days now and then when he could be spared.

Nathaniel came to a halt with his pleasant smile as he recognized Miranda. "How do you do, Miss Miranda? Are all your folks well? Are Mr. and Mrs. Spafford at home? I must try to run over and see them before I go back. I'm only here on a brief visit, must return tomorrow. How is the place getting on? All the old friends just the same? Do you ever see Miss Deane? She's well, I hope."

Nathaniel was running through these sentences pleasantly, as one will who has been away from a town for a time, and he did not note the replies carefully, as he thought he knew pretty well what they would be, having heard from home but a day or two before. He was just going on when something deep and different in Miranda's tone and clouded eyes made him pause and listen:

"No, she ain't well, Phoebe Deane ain't. She's way down sick, an' they don't nobody think she's goin' to get well, I'm sure o' that!" Then the unexpected happened. Two big tears welled up and rolled down the two dauntless, freckled cheeks. Nobody had ever seen Miranda Griscom cry before.

A sudden nameless fear gripped Nathaniel's heart. Phoebe Deane sick! Near to death! All at once the day seemed to have clouded over for him.

"Tell me, Miranda," he said, gently, "she is my friend, too, I think. I did not know—I had not heard. Has she been ill long? What was the cause?"

"'Bout two weeks," said Miranda, mopping her face with the corner of her clean apron, "an' I can't find out what made her sick, but it's my 'pinion she's bein' tormented to death by that long-legged blatherskite of a Hiram Green. He ain't nothin' but a big bully, fer he's really a coward at heart, an' what's more, folks 'll find it out some day ef I don't miss my guess. But he ken git up the low-downdest, pin-prickenist, soul-shakenest tormentin's that ever a saint hed to bear. An' ef Phoebe Deane ain't a saint I don't know who is 'cept my Mis' Spafford. Them tow's ez much alike's two pease—sweet-pease, I mean, pink an' white ones in blow."

Nathaniel warmed to Miranda's eloquence and kindled to her poetry. He felt that here was something that must be investigated.

"I believe that man is a scoundrel!" said Nathaniel, earnestly. "Do you say he really dares to annoy Miss Deane?"

"Well, I rather guess you'd think so! She can't stir without he's at her side, tendin' like he b'longs there. She can't bar the sight o' him, an' he struts up to her at the church door like he owned her, an' ef 'twant fer me an Rose an' Mis' Spafford she couldn't get red of 'im. She can't go to the post-office any more 'thout he hants the very road, though she's told him up 'n down she won't hev a thing to do 'ith him. I hev to go after her an' take her home when she comes to see us, fear he'll dog her steps, an' he's scared her most to death twice now, chasin' after her, once at night when she was comin' down to your house to bring some letter she'd found."

Nathaniel's face grew suddenly conscious, and a warm glow of indignation rolled over it. He set down his carpet-bag and came close to the fence to listen.

"Why, w'd you b'lieve it, thet feller found she liked to go to th' post-office fer a walk, and he jest follered her every time, an' when she quit goin' he hunted up other ways to trouble her. They tell a tale 'bout th' horse runnin' away an' her bein' out in a big storm the night she took sick, but I b'lieve in my soul he's t' th' bottom of it, an' I'd like to see him get his come-uppance right now."

"Miranda, do you happen to know—I don't suppose you ever heard Miss Deane speak of receiving a letter from me."

Miranda's alert eyes were on his face.

"Long 'bout when?" she demanded, keenly.

"Why last December, I think it was. I wrote her a note and I never received any reply. I wondered if it might have got lost, or whether she did not like my writing it, as I am almost a stranger."

"No, sir-ree, she never got that letter! I know fer sure, 'cause I happened to speak to her 'bout hearin' Hiram Green askin' pertick'ler fer her mail in the

post-office one day; and I found out he gets the Dea~~~
carries it out to 'em' an' I ~~~~~~~
~~~~~

~~~~~~~ person's
~~~~~ must know that's a crime. He could
~~~~ prison for that. It must have got lost if you are sure she never received it."

"Could he?" said Miranda, eagerly; "could he be put in prison? My! but I'd like to help get him lodged there fer a spell 'til he learned a little bit o' politeness toward th' angels thet walks the airth in mortal form. Dast! Hiram Green dast? He's got cheek enough to dast ennythin'. You don't know him. He wouldn't think enny one would find out! But say, I'll tell you what you ken do. You jest write that letter over again, ef you ken rem'mber 'bout what you wanted to say b'fore, an' I'll agree to git it to her first hand this time."

Nathaniel's face was alight with the eagerness of a boy. Somehow Miranda's childish proposal was pleasant to him. Her homely, honest face beamed at him expectantly, and he replied with earnestness:

"I'll do it, Miranda, I'll do it this very day, and trust it to your kindness to get it to her safely. Thank you for suggesting it."

Then suddenly a cloud came over the freckled face, and the gray eyes filled with tears again.

"But I mightn't ever git it to 'er, after all, yeh know. They say she's jest hangin' 'tween life 'n death today, an' t'night's the crisis."

A cloud seemed suddenly to have passed before the sun again, a chill almost imperceptible came in the air. What was that icy something gripping Nathaniel's heart? Why did all the forces of life and nature seem to hang upon the well-being of this young girl? He caught his breath.

"We must pray for her, Miranda, you and I," he said, gravely; "she once promised to pray for me."

"Did she?" said Miranda, looking up with solemn awe through her tears. "I'm real glad you tole me that. I'll try, but I ain't much on things like that. I could wallup Hiram Green a grea' deal better'n I could pray; but I s'pose that wouldn't do no good, so I'll do my best at the prayin'. Ef it's kind of botched up mebbe yours'll make up fer it. But say you better write that letter right off. I've heard tell there's things like thet'll help when crisises comes. I'm goin' t' make it a pint t' git up there t'night, spite o' that ole Mis' Deane, an' ef I see a chance I'll give it to her. I kind of think it might please her to have a letter t'git well fer."

"I'll do it, Miranda, I'll do it at once, and bring it around to you before dark. But you must be careful not to trouble her with it till she is able. You know it might make her worse to be bothered with any excitement like a letter from a stranger."

"I'll use my bes' jedgment," said Miranda, with happy pride. "I aint' runnin' no resks, so you needn't worry."

With a new interest in his face Nathaniel grasped his carpet-bag and hurried to his uncle's house. He found Janet ready with a joyful welcome, but he showed more anxiety to get to his room than to talk with her.

"I suppose it was dusty on the road today," she conceded, unwillingly, "but hurry back. I've a great deal to ask you, and to tell; and I want you all to myself before your friend comes."

But once in his room he forgot dust and sat down immediately to the great mahogany desk where paper and pens were just as he had left them when he went away. Janet had to call twice before he made his appearance, for he was deep in writing a letter.

My dear Miss Deane, he wrote. *They tell me you are lying very ill and I feel as if I must write a few words to tell you how anxious and sad I am about you. I want you to know that I am praying that you may get well.*

I wrote you sometime ago asking if you were willing to correspond with me, but I have reason now to think you never received my letter, so I have ventured to write again. I know it may be sometime before you are able even to read this, but I am sending it by a trusty messenger and I am sure you will let me know my answer when you are better. It will be a great source of pleasure and profit to me if you will write to me sometimes.

Yours faithfully,
NATHANIEL GRAHAM.

He folded and addressed it, sealing it with his crest, and then Janet called for the second time:

"Yes, Janet, I'm coming now, really. I had to write a letter. I am sorry, but it couldn't wait."

"Oh, how poky! Always business, business!" cried Janet. "It is well your friend is coming tonight for it is plain to be seen we shall have no good of you. How is it that you have grown old and grave so soon, Nathaniel? I thought you would stay a boy a long time."

"Just wait until I send my letter, Janet, and I will be as young as you please for two whole days."

"Let Caesar take it for you, then. There is no need for you to go."

"I would rather take it myself, cousin," he said, and she knew by his look that he would have his way.

"Well, then, I will go with you," she ...

... friend of yours. Is he nice? That is, will I like him? It isn't enough that you like him, for you like some very stupid people sometimes. I want to know if I will like him."

"And how should I be able to tell that, Janet? Of one thing I am sure, he will have to like you," and he surveyed his handsome cousin admiringly. "That's a very pretty sunshade you have. May I carry it for you?"

"Well, after that pleasant speech perhaps you may," she said, surrendering it. "About this young man, is it really true, Nathaniel, that he is a minister, and that he is to preach for Dr. MacFarlane while the doctor goes to visit his daughter? Father thought you had arranged for that. You see it is very important that I like him, because if I don't I simply cannot go to church and hear him preach. In fact I'm not sure but I shall stay away anyway. I should be so afraid he'd break down if I liked him, and if I didn't I should want to laugh. It will be so funny to see a minister at home every day, and know all his faults and his little peculiarities, and then see him get up and try to preach. I'm *sure* I should laugh."

"I am sure you would dare do nothing of the kind when Martin preaches."

"Oh, is he then so terribly grave and solemn? I shall not like him in the least."

"Wait until he comes, Janet. The evening coach will soon be in."

They had reached the Spafford house now, and Nathaniel's anxiety about delivering his letter was relieved by seeing Miranda hurry out to the flower-bed again with a manner as if the demand for fresh flowers had suddenly become greater than the supply. She was quite close to the fence as they came up, but she remained unconscious of their presence until Nathaniel spoke.

"Is that you, Miss Miranda?" he said, lifting his hat as though he had not seen her before that afternoon. "Will you kindly deliver this letter for me?"

He handed her the letter directly from his pocket, and Janet could not see the address. Miranda took it serenely.

"Yes, sir," she said, scrutinizing the address at a safe angle from Janet's vision, "I'll deliver it safe an' sure. Afternoon, Mis' Janet. Like a bunch o' pink columbine to stick in yer frock? Jes' matches them posies on the muslin delaine." And she snapped off a fine whirl of delicate pink columbine. Janet accepted it graciously and the two turned back home again.

"Now I can't see why Caesar couldn't have done that," grumbled Janet. "He's just as trustworthy as that funny red-haired girl."

"You would not have got your columbine," smiled Nathaniel, "and I'm sure it was just what you needed to complete the picture."

"Now for that pretty speech I'll say no more about it," granted Mistress Janet, well pleased.

And so they walked along the shaded street, where the sunlight was beginning to lie in long slant rays on the pavement and play strange yellow fancies with the smart new leaves of the maples. Nathaniel talked as he knew his cousin liked to have him do, and all the time she never knew that his heart had gone with the letter he had given to Miranda. Perhaps it was her interest in the stranger who was coming that kept her from missing something. Perhaps it was his light-hearted manner, so free from the perplexing problems that had filled his face with gravity on his recent visits. Perhaps it was just Janet's own happy heart, glad with the gladness of life and the summer weather, and the holiday guests.

Yet underneath Nathaniel's gay manner there ran two thoughts side by side—one, the fact that Miranda had said Phoebe had repulsed Hiram Green; the other, that she was lying at death's door; and all the time his strong heart was going out in a wild, hopeful pleading that her young life might yet be spared to joy. He felt that this mute pleading was her due, for had she not lifted her clear eyes and said, "Oh, I will," when he had asked her to pray for him? He must return it in full measure.

The evening coach was late, but it rolled in at last, bringing the eagerly-watched-for guest, bronzed from his months in the South. The dinner was served around a joyous board, the Judge beaming his pleasure upon the little company. The evening was prolonged far beyond the usual retiring hour, while laughter and talk floated on around him, and all the time Nathaniel was conscious of that other house but two miles away, where life and death were battling for a victim.

He went upstairs with Martin for another talk after the house was quiet, but at last they separated; and Nathaniel was free to sit by the window in his dark room looking out into the night now grown brilliant with the late rising moon, and keep tryst with one who was hovering on the brink of the other world.

...ways none o' gettin'
...make up my mind to git there you'll see I'll do it."

Marcia laughed.

"I suppose you will, Miranda. Well, go on. You may be needed. Poor Phoebe! I wish there was something I could do for her."

"Wal, thur is," said Miranda, with unexpected vim. "I've took a contrac' thet I don't seem to make much headway on. I'd like to hev you take a little try at it, an' see ef you can't do better. I 'greed t' pray fer Phoebe Deane, but t' save my life I can't think uv any more ways uv sayin' it thun jest to ast, an' after I've done it oncet it don't seem quite p'lite to keep at it, z' if I didn't b'lieve 'twas heard. The minister preached awhile back 'about the 'fectual fervent prayer uv a righteous man 'vailin' much, but he didn't say nothin' 'bout a red-headed woman. I reckon I ain't much good at prayin', fer I'm all wore out with it, but ef you'd jest spell me a while, an' lemme go see ef thur ain't sumpthin' to do, I think it would be a sight more 'availin' than fer me to set still an' jest pray; 'sides, ef you ain't better 'n most any righteous man I ever see, I'll miss my guess."

Thus the responsibility was divided, and Marcia with a smile upon her lips and a tear in her eye went away to pray, while Miranda tied on her bonnet, tucked the letter safely in her pocket after examining its seals and address most minutely, and went her way into the night.

She did not go to the front door, but stole around to the wood-shed where with the help of a milking-stool which stood there she mounted to the low roof. Strong of limb and courageous she found the climb nothing. She crept softly along the roof till she reached Phoebe's window, and crouched to listen. The window was open but a little way, though the night was warm and dry.

"Granny, Granny McVane," she called, softly, and Granny, startled from her evening drowsiness, stole over to the window wondering. A candle was burning behind the water pitcher and shed a weird and sickly light through the room. Granny looked old and tired as she came to the window, and it struck Miranda she had been crying.

"Fer the land sake! Is that you Mirandy?" she exclaimed, in horror. "Mercy! How'd you get there? Look out! You'll fall."

"Open the winder till I come in," whispered Miranda.

Granny opened the window cautiously.

"Be quick," she said, "I mustn't let the air get to the bed."

"I should think air was jes' what she'd want this night," whispered Miranda, as she emerged into the room and straightened her garments. "How's she seem? Any change?"

"I think she's failing, I surely do," moaned the old lady, softly, the tears running down her cheeks in slow uneven rivulets between the wrinkles. "I don't see how she can hold out till morning anyhow. She's jest burnt up with fever, and sometimes she seems to be gasping for breath. But how'd you get up there? Weren't you scairt?"

"I jes' couldn't keep away a minute longer. The doctor said this was the crisis an' I had to come. My Mrs. Spafford's home prayin' an' I come to see ef I couldn't help answer them prayers. You might need help tonight, an' I'm goin' to stay. Will any of her folks be in again tonight?"

"No, I reckon not. Emmeline's worn out. The baby's teething and hasn't given her a minute's let-up for two nights. She had his gums lanced today and she hopes to get a wink of sleep, for there's likely to be plenty doing tomorrow."

Miranda set her lips hard at this and turned to the bed, where Phoebe lay under heavy blankets and comfortables, a low moan, almost a gasp, escaping her parched lips now and then.

The fever seemed to have burnt a place for itself in the whiteness of her cheeks. Her beautiful hair had been cut short by Emmeline the second day because she could not be bothered combing it. It was as well, for it would not have withstood the fever, but to Miranda it seemed like a ruthless tampering with the sacred. Her wrath burned hot within her, even while she was considering what was to be done.

"My goodness alive," was her first word, "I should think she would hev a fever. It's hotter'n mustard in here. Why don't you open them winders wide? I should think you'd roast alive yerself. And land sakes! Look at the covers she's got piled on! Poor little thing!" Miranda reached out a swift hand and swept several layers off to the floor. A sigh of relief followed from Phoebe.

Miranda placed a firm cool hand on the burning forehead, and the sufferer seemed to take note of the touch eagerly.

"Oh, mercy me! Miranda, you mustn't take the covers off. She must be kept warm to try and break the fever. The doctor's orders were very strict. I wouldn't like to disobey him. It might be her death."

"Does he think she's any better?" questioned Miranda, fiercely. "No." The old lady shook her head sadly, "he said this morning there wasn't a thread of hope, poor little thing. Her fever hasn't let up a mite."

"Well, ef he said that, then I'm goin' to hev my try. She can't do more 'n die, an' ef I was goin' to die I'd like to hev a cool comf'table place to do it in, wouldn't you, Granny, an' not a furnace? Let's give her a few minutes' peace somethin' like in here pretty soon. Where's a towel? Is this fresh water? Say, Granny, couldn't you slip down to the spring without wakin' anyone an' bring us a good cold drink? I'm dyin' fer a dipper o' water, I come up here so fast, and it'll taste good to Phoebe, I know."

"Oh, she mustn't have a drop o' water," exclaimed the old lady, in horror. "Fever patients don't get a mite of water."

"Fever fiddlesticks! You git that water, please, an' then you kin lay down on that couch over there an' take a nap while I set by her."

After much whispered persuasion and bullying Miranda succeeded in getting the old lady to slip downstairs and go for the water, though the spring-house was almost as far as the barn and Granny was not used to prowling around alone at night. While she was gone Miranda boldly dipped a towel in the water pitcher and washed the fevered brow and face. The parched lips crept to the wetness eagerly, and Miranda began to feel assurance to the tips of her fingers. She calmly bathed the girl's hot face and hands, until the low moans became sounds of relief and content. Then quite unconscious that she was anticipating science she prepared to give her patient a sponge bath. In the midst of the performance she looked up to see Granny standing over her in horror.

"What are you doing, Mirandy Griscom? You'll kill her. The doctor said she mustn't have a drop of water touch her."

"I'm takin' the fever out uv her. Jes' feel her an' see," said Miranda, triumphantly. "Put yer lips on her forrid, thet's the way to tell. Ain't she coolin' off nice?"

"You're killing her, Miranda," said Granny, in a terrified tone, "and I've cared fer her so carefully all these weeks, and now to have her go like this! It's death coming that makes her cold."

"Death fiddlesticks!" said Miranda, wrathfully. "Well, ef 'tis, she'll die happy. Here, give me that water!" and she took the cup from the trembling hand of Granny and held it to Phoebe's dry lips. Eagerly the lips opened, and drank in the water as Miranda raised her head on her strong young arm. Then the sick girl lay back with a long sigh of content, and fell asleep.

It was the first natural sleep she had had since the awful beginning of the fever. She did not toss nor moan, and Granny hovered doubtingly above her, watching and listening to see if she still breathed, wondering at the fading of the crimson flames upon the white cheeks, dismayed at the cooling of the brow, even troubled at the quiet sleep.

"I fear she'll slip away in this," she said at last, in a sepulchral whisper. "That was an awful daresome thin you did. I wouldn't like them to find it out on you. They might say you caused her death."

"But she ain't dead yet," said Miranda, triumphantly, "an' ef she slips away in this it's a sight pleasanter 'n the way she was when I crep' in. Say now, Granny, don't you think so, honest?"

"Oh, I don't know," signed Granny, turning away sadly. "Mebbe I oughtn't to have let you."

"You couldn't a he'ped yerself, fer I'd come to do it, an' anyway, ef you'd made a fuss I'd hed to put you out on the roof er somethin' till I got done. Now, Granny, you're all tired out. You jes' go over an' lie down on thet couch an' I'll set by an' watch her a spell."

The conversation was carried on in close proximity to Granny's ear, for both nurses were anxious lest some of the sleeping household should hear. Granny knew she would be blamed for Miranda's presence in the sick room, and Miranda knew she would be ousted if discovery were made.

Granny settled down at last, with many protests, owned she was "jest the least mite tuckered out," and lay down for what she called a "cat-nap." Miranda, meantime, wide-eyed and sleepless, sat beside Phoebe and watched her every breath, for she felt more anxiety about what she had done than she cared to own to Granny. She had never had much experience in nursing, except in waiting upon Marcia, but her common sense told her that people were not so likely to get well as long as they were uncomfortable, therefore without much consideration she did for Phoebe what she would like to have had done for herself if she were ill. It seemed the right thing, and it seemed to be working, but supposing Granny were right, after all!

Then Miranda remembered the two who were praying.

"H'm" she said to herself, as she sat watching the still face on the pillow. "I reckon that's their part. Mine's to do the best I know. Ef the prayers is good fer anything they ought to piece out whar' I fail. An' I guess they will, too, with them two at it."

After that she got the wet towel and went to work again, bathing the brow and hands whenever the heat seemed to be growing in them again. She was bound to bring that fever down. Now and then the sleeper would draw a long sigh as of contentment, and comfort, and Miranda felt that she had received her thanks. It was enough to know that she had given her friend a little comfort, if nothing else.

The hours throbbed on. The moon went down; the candle began to sputter, and Miranda lighted another. Granny slept and actually snored, weary with her long vigil. Miranda had to touch her occasionally to stop the loud noise lest

some one should hear and come to see what it was. But ~~~
were weary, too, for it ~~~

~~~ and wakened her. The old lady started up with
a frightened look, guilty that she had slept so long, but Miranda reassured her.
"It's all right. I'm glad you slep', fer you wan't needed, an' I guess you'll feel all
the better fer it today. She's slep' real quiet all night long, ain't moaned once,
an' jes' feel her. Ain't she feelin' all right? I b'lieve the fever's gone."

Granny went over and touched her face and hands wonderingly. "She does
feel better," she admitted, "but I don't know. It mayn't last. I've seen 'em rally
toward the end," dubiously; "she'll be so powerful weak now, it'll be all we can
do to hold her to earth."

"What's she ben eatin'?" enquired Miranda.

"She hasn't eaten anything of any account for some time back."

"Well, she can't live on jest air an' water ferever. Say, Granny, I've got to
be goin' soon, er I'll hev to hide in the closet all day fer sure, but 'spose you slip
out to the barn now while I wait an' get a few drops o' new milk. Hank's out
there milkin'. I heard him go down an' git his milk pails an' stool 'fore I woke
you up. We'll give her a spoonful o' warm milk. Mebbe that'll hearten her up."

"It might," said Granny, doubtfully. She took the cup and hurried away,
Miranda taking the precaution to button the door after her the lest Emmeline
whom she could hear moving around in her room should take a notion to look
in.

When Granny got back Miranda took the cup and putting a few drops of
the sweet warm fluid in a spoon she touched it to Phoebe's lips. A slow sigh
followed, and then Phoebe's eyes opened and she looked straight at Miranda
and seemed to know her, for a flicker of a smile shone in her face.

"There, Phoebe, take this spoonful. You've ben sick, but it'll make you
well," crooned Miranda, softly.

Phoebe obediently swallowed the few drops and Miranda dipped up a few
more.

"It's all right, dear," she said softly. "I'll take care o' you. Jes' you drink
this, an' get well, fer I've got somethin' real nice in my pocket fer you when ye'
take yer milk an' go to sleep."

Thus Miranda fed her two or three spoonfuls, then the white lids closed
over the trusting eyes, and in a moment more she was sleeping again.

Miranda watched her a few minutes, and then cautiously stole away from the bed, to the astonished Granny who had been watching with a new respect for the domineering young nurse that had usurped her place.

"I guess she'll sleep most o' the day," Miranda whispered. "Ef she wakes up you jes' give her a spoonful o' fresh milk, er a sup o' water, an' tell her I'll be back bime-by. She'll understan' an' that'll keep her quiet. Tell her I said she mus' lie still an' get well. Don't you dast keep them winders shet up all day again, an' don't pile on the clo'es. She may need a light blanket ef she feels cool, but don't fer mercy's sake get her all het up again, er we might not be able to stop it off so easy next time. I'll be back's soon es it's dark. Bye-bye. I mus' go. I may get ketched es 'tis."

Miranda slid out the window and down the sloping roof, dropping over the eaves just in time to escape being seen by Emmeline, who opened the back door with a sharp click and came out to get a broom she had forgotten the night before. The morning was almost come now, and the long grass was dripping with dew as Miranda swept through it.

"Reckon they'll think there's ben a fox er somethin' prowlin' round the house ef they see my tracks," she said to herself, as she hurried through the dewy fields and out to the road.

Victory was written upon her countenance as she sped along, victory tempered with hope. Perhaps she was not judge enough of illness, and it might be that her hopes were vain ones, and apparent signs deceitful, but come what might she would always be glad she had done what she had. That look in Phoebe's eyes before she fell asleep again was reward enough. It made her heart swell with triumph to think of it.

Two hours later she brought a platter of delicately poached eggs on toast to the breakfast table just as Marcia entered the room.

"Good-morning, Miranda. How did it go last night? You evidently got in and found something to do."

Miranda set down the platter and stood with hands on her hips and face shining with morning welcome.

"I tell you, Mrs. Marcia, them prayers was all right. They worked fine. When I got mixed and didn't know what was right to do I just remembered them an' cast off all 'sponsibility. Anyhow, she's sleepin' an' the fever's gone."

Marcia smiled.

"I shouldn't wonder if your part was really prayer, too," she said, dreamily. "We are not all heard for our much speaking."

It was a glorious day. The sun shown in a perfect heaven without a cloud to blur it. A soft south breeze kept the air from being too warm. Miranda sang all the morning as she went about her belated work.

After dinner Marcia insisted she should go and take a nap. She obediently lay down for half an hour straight and stiff on her bright neat patchwork quilt,

scarcely relaxing a muscle lest she rumple the bed. Sl..........
however........................

..................................., and Miranda went
.... wanted, a great fear clutching her heart. But she was
reassured by the smile on his face, and the good will in the expressions of his
wife and her sister, who were riding with him.

"Say, Mirandy, I don't know but I'll take you into partnership. Where'd you
learn nursing? You did what I wouldn't have dared do, but it seemed to hit the
mark. I'd given her up. I've seen her slipping away for a week past, but she's
taken a turn for the better now, and I believe in my soul she's going to get well.
If she does it'll be you that'll get the honor."

Miranda's eyes shone with happy tears.

"You don't say, doctor," she said. "Why, I was real scared when Granny
told me you said she wasn't to hev a sup o' water, but it seemed like she must be
so turrible hot —"

"Well, I wouldn't have dared try it myself, but I believe it did the business,"
said the doctor, heartily.

"Yes, you deserve great credit, Miranda," said the doctor's wife. "You do,
indeed," echoed her sister, pleasantly.

"Granny ain't tole Mis' Deane I was there hes she?" asked Miranda, to
cover her embarrassment. She was not used to praise except from her own
household.

"No, she hasn't told her yet, but I think I shall tell her myself by tomorrow
if all goes well. Can you find time to run over tonight again? Granny might not
stay wide awake all the time. She's fagged out, and I think it's a critical time."

"Oh, I'll be there!" said Miranda, gleefully. "You couldn't keep me away."

"How'll you get in? Same way you did last night?" asked the doctor,
laughing. "Say, that's a good joke! I've laughed and laughed ever since Granny
told me, at the thought of you climbing in the window and the family all sleeping
calmly. Good for you, Miranda. You're made of the right stuff. Well, good-bye.
I'll fix it up with Mrs. Deane tomorrow so you can go in by the door."

The doctor drove on, laughing, and his wife and sister bowing and smiling.
Miranda, with high head of pride and heart full of joy, went in to get supper.

Supper was just cleared away when Nathaniel came over. He talked with
David in the dusk of the front stoop a few minutes and then asked diffidently if
Miranda was going up to see how Miss Deane was again soon.

David, because of his love for Marcia, half understood, and calling Miranda left the two together for a moment while he went to call Marcia, who was putting Rose to bed.

"She's better," said Miranda, entering without preamble into the subject nearest their hearts, "the doctor told me so this afternoon. But don't you stop prayin' yet, fer we don't want no half-way job, an' she's powerful weak. I kinder rely on them prayers to do a lot. I got Mrs. Spafford to spell me at mine while I went up to help nurse. She opened her eyes oncet last night when I was givin' her some milk, an' I tole her I had somethin' nice fer her if she'd lie still an' go to sleep an' hurry up an' git well. She kinder seemed to understand, I most think. I've got the letter all safe, an' jest ez soon ez she gits the least mite better, able to talk, I'll give it to her."

"Thank you, Miss Miranda," said Nathaniel, "and won't you take this to her? It will be better than letters for her for a while until she gets well. You needn't bother her telling anything about it now. Just give it to her. It may help her a little. Then later, if you think best, you may tell her I sent it."

He held out a single tea-rose, half blown, with delicate petals of pale saffron.

Miranda took it with awe. It was not like anything that grew in the gardens she knew.

"It looks like her," she said, reverently.

"It makes me think of her as I first saw her," he answered, in a low voice. "She wore a frock like that."

"I know," said Miranda, understandingly, "I'll give it to her, and tell her all about it when she's better."

"Thank you," said Nathaniel. Then Marcia and David entered, and Miranda went away to wonder over the rose, and prepare for her night's vigil.

_____ looked at her. Then at once she _____ that Phoebe's eyes had sought the rose, and a smile was hovering about her lips.

"It was sent to you," she answered the questioning eyes, putting the rose close down to the white cheek. Phoebe really smiled then faintly.

"She better have some milk now," said Granny, anxiously. "She's been asleep so long an' I didn't disturb her."

"Yes, take some milk," whispered Miranda, gently, "an' I'll tell you all 'bout the rose when you're better."

The night crept on in quiet exultation on Miranda's part. While Phoebe slept Miranda and the rose kept vigil, and Granny sank into the first restful sleep she had had since she came to nurse Phoebe. The house was quiet. There was nothing for the watcher to do much of the time but to watch. Now and then she drew the coverlet up a little higher when a fresh breeze came through the window; or again gave a drink of water, or a spoonful of milk. The candle was shaded by the water pitcher, and the frail sweet rose looked spectral in the weird light. Miranda looked at the flower, and it looked back at her. As the hours slowly passed Miranda found her lips murmuring:

"Thanks be! Thanks be!"

Suddenly she drew herself up with a new thought.

"Land sakes! That's sounds like prayin'. Wonder ef 'tis. Anyhow it's thanks-givin', an' that's what I feel. Guess it's my turn to give thanks."

The next day the doctor had a talk with Albert Deane. He told him how Miranda had crept in at the window and cared for Phoebe; and how he believed it had been Phoebe's salvation. Albert was deeply affected. He readily agreed that it would be a fine thing for Phoebe if Miranda could be got to come and help Granny care for her, now that she seemed to be on the fair road to recovery.

It was all arranged in a few minutes and Emmeline was not told until just before Miranda arrived.

"It's very queer," she said, with her nose in the air, "that I wasn't consulted. I'm sure it's my business more'n yours to look after such things, Albert Deane. An' I wouldn't uv had that sassy creature in the house fer a good deal. Hank's sister would 'a ben a sight better, an' could a' helped me between times with Phoebe's extry work. I'm sure it's bad enough havin' sickness this way in the midst o' hayin' season, an' me with all them men to feed, an' not havin' Phoebe to help. I could 'a' sent fer my own sister, when it comes to that, an' 'twould 'a' ben a sight pleasanter."

But before there was time for a protest or apology from Albert there came a knock at the door, and without waiting for ceremony Miranda walked in.

"Ev'nin', Miss Deane," she said, unconcernedly. "Everything goin' well? I'll go right up, shall I?" Her smiling insolence struck Emmeline dumb for the moment.

"Well, I vow!" declared Emmeline. "Will yeh listen to the impedence. 'Will I go right up?' es ef she was the Queen o' Sheby er the doctor himself."

But Miranda was marching serenely upstairs and if she heard she paid no heed.

"She doesn't mean any harm, Emmeline!" pleaded Albert. "She's jest Phoebe's friend, so don't you mind. It'll relieve you a lot, and if you want Hank's sister to come over too I guess we can manage it."

Thus was Miranda domiciled in Phoebe's room for a short space, much to the comfort of Phoebe and the satisfaction of Miranda.

Emmeline was only half mollified when she came upstairs to look around and "give that Griscom girl a settin' down," as she expressed it. But she who attempted to "sit" on Miranda usually arose unexpectedly.

"Where'd that come from?" was Emmeline's first question, as she pointed at the unoffending rose.

"Mirandy brought it," said Granny, proud of her colleague. "H'm!" said Emmeline, with a sniff. "It ain't healthy to hev plants round in a bedroom I've heard. D' you raise that kind down to Spaffords?"

"We ain't got just to say a-plenty yet," said Miranda, cheerfully, "but we might hev sometime. Would yeh like a slip?"

"No, thank yeh," said Emmeline, dryly, "I never had time to waste good daylight fussin' over weeds. I s'pose Mis' Spafford don't do much else."

"Oh, 'casionally!" answered Miranda, undisturbed. "This spring she put up a hundred glasses o' blueberry jelly, made peach preserves, spiced pears, an' crab-apple jam, crocheted a white bed-spread fer the spare bed, an' three antimacassars fer her Aunt Hortense's best parlor chairs, did up the second story curtains, tucked a muslin slip fer Rose, sewed carpet-rags enough fer a whole strip in Shorty Briscutt's new rag carpet, made a set o' shirts fer Mr. Spafford, knit nine pair o' stocking', spun the winter's yarn, cut out an' made Rose's flannel petticoats, an' went to missionary meetin', but o' course that ain't much, nothin' to what you'd do."

(Oh Miranda, Miranda! of the short prayers and the long tongue! telling all that off with a straight face to the sour-faced woman, Emmeline!)

"She must be a smart woman!" said Granny, much impressed.

"She is," said Miranda,

by pitching out the tea-rose into the yard below the window.

"I never seen such a fuss," complained Emmeline to Miranda, who stood over Phoebe and felt her fluttering pulse, "all about a dead weed. I declare I can't understand folks gettin' 'tached to trash."

Emmeline was somewhat anxious at the upset state of the patient, who was yet too weak to talk much, but who had roused herself to protest vigorously as the rose was hurled through the window, and then could not keep back the disappointed tears.

But Miranda, mindful of the weak state of her patient, and wishing to mollify Emmeline as much as possible, tried to pour oil on the troubled waters.

"Never mind, Mis' Deane, no harm done. Phoebe jest wanted to keep them leaves fer her han'kerchers, they smell real nice. I'll pick 'em up, Phoebe. They won't be hurt a mite. They're right on the green grass."

Miranda stole down and picked up the leaves tenderly, washing them at the spring, and brought them back to Phoebe. Emmeline had gone off sniffing with her chin in the air.

"I was silly to cry," murmured Phoebe, trying feebly to dry her tears, "but I loved that sweet rose. I wanted to keep it just as it was in a box. You haven't told me about it yet, Miranda, how did she come to send it?"

"It ain't hurt a mite, Phoebe, only jest three leaves come off. I'll lay it together in a box fer yeh. Now lemme put my bonnet off, an' you lay quiet an' shet your eyes while I tell you 'bout that rose. First, though, you must take your milk.

"It wan't her at all that sent you that rose, Phoebe Deane. You s'picioned 'twas Mrs. Marcia, didn't you? But 'twan't 't all. It was a man —"

"Oh, Miranda!" The words came in a moan of pain from the bed, "Not — not — Miranda, you would never have brought it if Hiram Green —"

"Land sake, child, what's took yeh? 'Course not. Why ef that nimshi'd undertake to send yeh so much ez a blade o' grass I'd fling it in his mean little face. Don't you worry, dearie, you jest listen. 'Twas Nathaniel Graham sent you that rose. He said I wan't to say nothin' 'bout it till you got better, an' then I could say 'twas from him ef I wanted to. I didn't say anythin' yet 'cause I hed more to tell, but I ain't sure you are strong 'nough to hear any more now. Better take a nap first."

"No, Miranda; do tell me now."

"Wal, I reckon I better. I've most busted wantin' to tell yeh sev'ral times. Say, did you ever get a letter from Nathaniel Graham, Phoebe?"

"Why no, of course not, Miranda. Why would I get a letter from him?"

"Wal, he said he wrote yeh one oncet, an' he ast me did I know ef you'd got it, and I said No, I was sure you didn't, cause you said oncet you hadn't ever got a letter 'cept from your mother, an' so he said he'd write it over again fer yeh, an' I've hed it in my pocket fer a long time waitin' till I dared give it to yeh. So her 'tis, but I won't give it to yeh 'thout you promise to go right to sleep 'fore you read it fer you've hed more goin's on now than 's good fer yeh."

Phoebe protested that she must read the letter first, but Miranda was inexorable, and would not even show it to her until she promised. So meekly Phoebe promised, and went to sleep with the precious missive clasped in her hands, the wonder of it helping her to get quiet.

She slept a long time, for the excitement about the rose had taken her strength. When she awoke, before she opened her eyes she felt the letter, pressing the seals with her fingers, to make sure she had not been dreaming. She almost feared to open her eyes lest it should not be true. A letter for her all her own! Somehow she almost dreaded to break the seal and have the first wonder of it over. She had not thought what it might contain.

Miranda had brought a little pail of chicken broth that Marcia had made for Phoebe, and she had some steaming in a china bowl when Phoebe at last opened her eyes. She made her eat it before she opened the letter, and Phoebe smiled and acquiesced.

She lay smiling and quiet a long time after reading the letter, trying to get used to the thought that Nathaniel had remembered her, and cared to write to her; cared to have her write to him, too; it was not merely passing kindness toward a stranger. He wanted to be friends, real friends. It was good to feel that one had friends.

Phoebe looked over at the alert figure of Miranda, sitting bolt upright, watching her charge with anxiety to see if the letter was all that it should be, and then she laughed a soft little ripple that sounded like a shadow of her former self.

"Oh, you dear, good Miranda! You don't know how nice it all is to have friends, and a real letter."

"Is it a good letter?" asked Miranda, wistfully.

"Read it," said Phoebe, handing it to her, smiling. "You certainly have a right to read it after all you have done to get it here."

Miranda took it shyly, and went over by the ~~~
made it a little less embarrassing. S~~
on her face when she ~~~

"I ~~

~~ing to worry them;
~~ be propped up with pillows for a
~~ length allowed her to write a few lines in reply
~~ this was the message that in a few days thereafter travelled to
~~ York.

My Dear Mr. Graham:

It was very pleasant to receive your letter and to know that you thought of me and prayed that I might get well. I think your prayers are being answered.

It will be good to have a friend to write to me, and I shall be glad to correspond with you. I want to thank you for the beautiful rose. It helped me to get well. Its leaves are sweet yet.

I have been a long time writing this, for I am very weak and tired yet, and Miranda will not let me write any more now, but you will understand and excuse me, will you not?

Your friend
Phoebe Deane.

Miranda had to go home soon after that, for it was plain Emmeline was wanting to get rid of her, and Marcia was to have guests for a couple of weeks. 'Squire Schuyler and his wife were coming to visit for the first time since little Rose's birth, for it was a long journey for an old man to take, and the 'Squire did not like to go away from home. Miranda felt that she must go, much as she hated to leave Phoebe, and so she bade her good-bye, and Phoebe began to take care of herself.

She was able to walk around her room, and soon to go downstairs, but somehow when she got down into the old atmosphere something seemed to choke her, she felt weary and wanted to creep back to bed again. So, much to Emmeline's disgust, she did not progress as rapidly as she ought to have done.

"You need to git some ambition," said Emmeline, in disgust, the first morning Phoebe came down to breakfast, and sat back after one or two mouthfuls. There was fried ham and eggs, and fried potatoes. Anybody ought to be glad to get that, Emmeline thought.

But somehow they did not appeal to Phoebe, and she left her plate almost untasted.

"I think ef you'd get some work and do somethin' mebbe you'd get your strength again. I never see anybody hang back like you do. There ain't any sense in it. What's the matter with yeh, anyway?"

"I don't know," said Phoebe, with an effort at cheerfulness. "I try, but somehow I feel so heavy and tired all the time."

"She isn't strong yet, Emmeline," pleaded Albert, kindly.

"Wal, don't I know that?" snapped Emmeline. "But how's she ever goin' to get strong ef she don't work it up?"

Such little pin-pricks were hard to bear when Phoebe felt well, and now that her strength was but a breath she seemed not to be able to bear them at all, and after a short effort would creep back to her room and lie down.

Miranda discovered her all huddled in a little heap on her bed late one afternoon when she came up to bring Phoebe her second letter, for Nathaniel had arranged that for the present he would send his correspondence to Phoebe through Miranda. Neither of them said aloud that it was because Hiram Green brought up the Deanes' mail so often, but both understood.

Miranda and the letter succeeded in cheering up Phoebe, but the ex-nurse felt that things were not going with her charge as prosperously as they should, and she took her trouble back to Marcia.

"Let's bring her down here, Miranda," proposed Marcia. "Father and mother are going home on Monday and it will be quiet and nice here. I think she might spend a month with us and get strong before she goes back and tries to work."

Miranda was delighted and took the first opportunity to convey the invitation to Phoebe, whose cheeks grew pink and eyes bright with anticipation. A whole month with Mrs. Spafford and Miranda! It was too good to be true.

It was Monday morning when they came for her with the big old chaise. Emmeline and Hank's sister were out hanging up clothes. Emmeline's mouth was full of clothespins, and her brow was dark, for Hank's sister talked much and worked slowly. Moreover, she made lumpy starch and could not be depended upon to keep the potatoes from burning if one went out to feed the chickens. It was hard to have trained up a good worker and then have her trail off in a thunder-storm and get sick and leave the work all on one's hands without ambition enough to get well. Emmeline was very ungracious to Marcia. She told Albert that she didn't see what business Mrs. Spafford had coming round to run their house. She thought Phoebe was better off at home, but Albert felt that Mrs. Spafford had been exceedingly kind.

So it was with little regret that Phoebe was carried away from her childhood's home, and into a sweet new world of loving kindness and joy, where the round cheeks and happiness of health might be coaxed back. Yet to Phoebe

it was not an unalloyed bliss, for always there was th
and by she must go back to th
thought of it

Chapter 23

Hiram Green had been exceedingly quiet since the night of the runaway.

The old plow-horse had kicked something loose about the chaise in his final lurch before he started to run, and it goaded his every step. He thought Hiram was striking him with a club. He thought the thunder was pursuing him; he thought the lightning was reaching for him as it darted through the livid sky; and down the road he flew, mile after mile, not slowing up for curves or excrescences in the road, but taking a short cut at the turns, rearing and shying at every flash of lightning. The chaise came lurching after, like one tied to a whirlwind, and Hiram, clinging, cursing, lashing out madly with his whip, was finally forced to spend his time in holding on, thinking every minute would be his last.

As the horse saw his own gate at last, however, he gave a final leap into the air, and bounded across the ditch, regardless of what was behind him, perhaps hoping to rid himself of it. The chaise lurched into the air and Hiram was tossed lightly over the fence and landed in the cow pasture. Something snapped, and the horse entered his own dooryard free at last from the thing which had been pursuing him.

The rain had begun to come down in driving sheets, now, and brought Hiram to his feet in spite of his dazed condition. He looked about him in the alternate dimness and vivid brightness, and perceived that he was close to the Deanes'. A moment's reflection made it plain that he must get up some kind of story, so he put on the best face that he could and went in.

"We've hed an axident," he explained, limping into the kitchen, where Emmeline was trying to get supper and keep the fretful baby quiet. "The blamed horse got scared at th' lightnin'. I seen what was goin' to happen an' I held him on his haunches fer a second while Phoebe jumped. She's back there a piece now, I reck'n, fer that blamed critter never stopped till he landed to home, an' he placed me in a awkword persition in the cow pasture, with the chaise all broke up. I guess Phoebe's all right, fer I looked back an' thought I saw her tryin' to wave her hand to me, but I 'spect we better go hunt her up soon 's this here storm lets up. She'll likely go in somewheres. We'd just got past old Mis' Duzenberry's."

That was all the explanation the Deanes had ever had of the adventure. Phoebe had been too ill to speak of it at first, and after she got well enough to come downstairs and Albert had questioned her at the table about it she had shuddered, and turned so white saying: "Please, don't, Albert, I can't bear to think of it," that he had never asked her again.

During her illness Hiram had been polit~~ely~~
taking the precaution t~~o~~

...~~per~~ reason for Phoebe's
...away. She was relieved that Phoebe said
...about it, if there had been trouble, and hoped it was forgotten.

The day after Phoebe went to the Spaffords to visit Hiram came up to see Emmeline in the afternoon when he knew Albert was out in the hayfield.

"Say, do you still favor livin' down to the village?" he asked, seating himself without waiting for an invitation.

Emmeline looked up keenly, and wondered what was in the air. "I hev said so," she remarked, tentatively, not willing to commit herself without further knowledge.

"Wal, you know that lot o' mine down there opposite the Seceder church? It has a big weepin' willer same 's in the church yard, an a couple o' plum-trees in bearin'. How'd you like to live on thet lot?"

"H'm!" said Emmeline, stolidly. "Much good 'twould do me to like it. Albert'll never buy that lot, Hiram Green, there ain't no use askin' him. You wasn't thinkin' of buildin' there yerself, was yeh?" Emmeline looked up sharply as this new thought entered her mind. Perhaps he wanted her to hold out the bait of a house in the village to Phoebe.

"Naw, I ain't goin' to build in no village at present, Mis' Deane," he remarked, dryly. "Too fur from work fer me, thank you. But I was thinkin' I'd heard you say you wanted to live in the village, an' I thought I'd make a bargain with you. Say, Emmeline, 'taint no use mincin' matters. I'm a' goin' to marry Phoebe Deane, an' I want you should help me to it. I'll make you this offer. It's a real generous one, too. The day I marry Phoebe Deane I'll give you a deed to that lot in the village. Now, what d'yeh say? Is't a bargain?"

"What to do?" questioned Emmeline. She would be caught in no trap. "I've done all I know now. I'd like my sister Mandy to come here to live, an' there ain't room fer her while Phoebe stays; but I don't see what I kin do, more'n what I've done a'ready. Wouldn't she make up to yeh none the day you come home from the barn raisin'?"

"Wal, I was gettin' on pretty well 'til that blamed horse took an' run," said Hiram, shifting his eyes from her piercing ones.

"Wal, I can't compel her to marry you," snapped Emmeline.

"You don't hev to," said Hiram. "I've got my plans laid, an' all you got to do is stand by me when the time comes. I ain't tellin' my plans jest yet, but you'll see what they be, an' all is, you remember my offer. Ef you want that village lot jest remember to stand by me."

He unfolded his length from the kitchen chair and went out. Emmeline said nothing. When he reached the door he turned back and said:

"I broke ground this mornin' fer a new house on the knoll. Me an' Phoebe'll be livin' there by this time next year."

"Well, I hope to goodness yeh will," responded Emmeline, heartily, "fer I've hed trouble 'nough a'ready with this business. I'll do what I ken, o' course, but do fer goodness' sake hurry up!"

The house on the knoll steadily progressed. Hiram came little to the Deane house during Phoebe's absence, but spent his time at the new building when his farm work did not demand his presence. He also came often to the village and hung around the post-office. He was determined that nothing should escape his vigilance in that direction. Seeing him there one day when the mail was being distributed Miranda took her place in the front ranks and asked in a clear cool voice:

"Anythin' fer Phoebe Deane? She's stayin t' our house fer a spell now an' I'll take her mail to her."

Miranda well knew that the only mail Phoebe was likely to receive came addressed to herself, so she was more than surprised when the postmaster with his spectacles on the end of his nose held up a letter whose address he carefully studied, and handed it to her rather reluctantly. He would have liked a chance to study that letter more closely.

But nothing fazed Miranda. She took the letter as composedly as if there ought to be two or three more forthcoming, and marched off. Hiram Green, however, got down scowling from his seat on the counter and stalked over to the postmaster.

"I sh'd think you'd hev to be keerful who you give letters to," he remarked, in a low tone. "Phoebe Deane might not like that harum-scarum girl bringin' her letters. Did you take notice ef that letter was from New York? She was expectin' quite a important letter from there."

The postmaster looked over his spectacles at Hiram patronizingly.

"I sh'd hope I know who to trust," he remarked, with dignity. "No, I didn't take notice. I hev too much to do to notice post-marks."

Hiram, however, was greatly shaken up by the sight of that letter in Miranda's triumphant hands, and betook himself to the hayloft to meditate. If he had known that the letter merely contained a clipping about the progress of missions in South Africa, which Ann Jane Bloodgood had sent thinking it might help Phoebe to recover from her illness, as she heard she was feeling "poorly" yet, and "hoped she would soon hear she was better!"

But Hiram had no thought but that the l...
his reflections ...

... we like, we *mob* 'em.
... we ask, we *mob* 'em. Heard 'bout the mob down in Chatham Street last summer—er it might have been two years ago. A lot of niggers met to hear a darkey preacher in a little chapel down there. We got wind of it, an' we ordered 'em to leave, but they wouldn't budge 'cause they'd paid their rent, so we just *put* 'em out. There was a man named Tappan who lived down in Rose Street, an' he was there. He was an Abolitionist, an' we didn't like him. He'd had somethin' to do with this meetin', so we follered him home with hoots and threats, and give his house a good stoning. Did him good. Oh, we do things up in great shape in New York. Next night we went down to the Bowery Theatre. Manager there's English, you know, and he'd said some imperlite things about America, we thought, something about our right to own slaves, so we give him a dose. Oh, we're not afraid of anything down in New York."

Hiram was greatly fascinated by this representative New Yorker, and after the crowd had begun to disperse he went to the stranger and buttonholed him.

"Say, look a'here!" he began, holding a five-dollar bill invitingly near to the New Yorker's hand. "I know a feller you ought to mob. I could give yeh his name an' address real easy. He's prominent down there, an' I reckon 'twould be worth somethin' to you folks to know his name. Fact is, I've an' interest in the matter myself, an' I'd like to see him come to justice, an' I'm willin' to subscribe this here bill to the cause ef you see your way clear to lookin' the matter up fer me."

"Why, certainly, certainly," said the stranger, grasping the bill affably, "I'll do anything I can for you. I'll hand this over to the treasurer of our side. In fact I'm the treasurer myself, and I thank you very much for your interest. Anything I can do I'm sure I'll be glad to. Can you tell me any more about this?"

Hiram toled him off to a quiet corner and before the interview was ended he had entered into a secret plot against Nathaniel Graham, and had pledged himself to give the stranger not only one but four more five-dollar bills when the work should be complete, and Nathaniel Graham stand revealed to the world an Abolitionist, a man who should be suppressed. It was all arranged before the stranger left on the evening stage-coach that he would write Hiram what day a move would be made in the matter, and just how far he felt they could go.

Hiram went home chuckling and felt that revenge was sweet. He would get the better of Nathaniel Graham now, and Nathaniel would never know who struck the blow.

A few days afterward there came a letter from the stranger saying that all things were prospering, but it would be impossible to get up a thoroughly organized mob and do the work without a little more money, for their funds were low; and would it be possible for Hiram to forward the twenty dollars now instead of waiting?

After a sleepless night Hiram doled out the twenty dollars. The stranger wrote that the time had been arranged, and he would let him know all about it soon. They thought they had their man pinned down tight. The night Hiram received that letter he slept soundly.

Meantime the world had been moving in an orbit of beauty for Phoebe. She was tended and guarded like a little child. They made her feel that her presence was a joy to them all. Every member of the family down to Rose made it a point to brighten her stay with them. Rose brought her flowers from the garden, David brought the latest books and poems for her to read, Marcia was her constant loving companion, and Miranda cooked the daintiest dishes known to the culinary art for her tempting. The letters went back and forth to New York every day or two, for as Phoebe was growing better she was able to write longer epistles, and Nathaniel seemed always to have something to say that needed an immediate answer. Phoebe was growing less shy of him, and more and more opened her heart to his friendship like a flower turning to a newly risen sun.

Janet Bristol had been away on a visit during Phoebe's illness, but while she was still with the Spaffords Janet returned, and one afternoon came to return Mrs. Spafford's call.

Phoebe wore a thin white frock whose dainty frills showed modestly her white throat and arms now taking on something of their old roundness. She was sitting in the cool parlor with Marcia when the caller arrived. Her mother's locket was tied about her throat with a bit of velvet ribbon, and her hair, now coming out in soft curls, made a lovely fluffy halo of brown all about her face.

Janet watched her while she talked with Marcia, and wondered at the sweet grace of form and feature. Somehow her former prejudice against this girl melted strangely as Phoebe raised her beautiful eyes and smiled at her. Janet felt drawn to her against her will, yet she could not tell why she held back, only that Nathaniel had been so strangely stubborn about that letter. To be sure that was long past, and her mind was fully occupied just now with Nathaniel's theological friend, Martin Van Renssaeler. She was attempting to teach him the ways of the world, and draw him out of his gravity. He seemed to be a willing subject, if one might judge from the number of visits he made to the Bristol home during the summer.

Then, one bright, beautiful day, just a week bef...
close, Nathaniel came up from Ne... ...

He reached th...

...ng the coach as it rolled down the
... great horses, enveloped in a cloud of dust, and
... the tavern with a flourish. Then suddenly he noticed that there were
passengers, two of them, and that one was Nathaniel himself.

Hiram felt weak in the knees. If a ghost had suddenly descended from the
coach he could not have been more dismayed. Here he had just put twenty-five
good dollars into Nathaniel's discomfiture, only to have him appear in his own
town smiling and serene as if nothing had been about to happen. It made Hiram
just sick. He watched him and the other young man who had been his fellow
passenger, as they walked down the street toward the Bristol house. He had sat
down when the coach stopped, feeling inadequate to the work of holding himself
upright in the midst of his unusual emotions. Now he got slowly up and went
away toward his home, walking heavily, as if he had been stricken. With head
bent down he studied the ground as he walked. He forgot the mail, forgot
everything, save that he had put twenty-five dollars into a fruitless enterprise.

Midway between the post-office and his home he stopped and wheeled
around with an exclamation of dismay:

"Gosh Ninety!"

Then after a pause he let forth a series of oaths. It was plain Hiram was
stirred to the depths of his evil nature. He had just remembered that Phoebe
was down in the village at the Spaffords and would be likely to see Nathaniel.
His ugly face contracted in a spasm of anger, that gradually died into a settled
expression of vengeance. The time had come, and he would wait no longer. If
he had been more impulsive and less of a coward he would have shot his victim
then and there, but such was not Hiram's way. Stealthily, with deadly surety he
laid his plans; with the patience and the fatality that could only come from the
father of liars himself.

Three whole days did Nathaniel stay in the village, and much of that time
he spent at the Spafford house, walking and talking, and reading with Phoebe.
Three whole days did Hiram spy upon him at every turn, with evil countenance
and indifferent mien, lounging by the house, or happening in the way. He had
written an angry letter to the man in New York, who later excused himself for

not having performed his mission on account of Nathaniel's absence, but promising it should yet be done, and demanding more money.

Janet and Martin Van Rensselaer came down to the Spafford house the last evening, and made a merry party. Hiram hid himself among the lilac bushes at the side of the house, like the serpent of old, and watched the affair all the evening, his heart filled with all the evil that his nature could conceive.

Phoebe, in her simple white frock, with her lovely head crowned with the short curling hair, and her exquisite face agleam with the light and mirth that belong to youth, and which she was tasting for almost the first time, made a beautiful picture. So Miranda thought as she brought in the sugary seed-cakes, and great frosted pitcher of cool drink, made from raspberry and currant jelly, mixed with water from the spring. If Miranda could have known of the watcher outside, the evening might have ended in comedy, for she would certainly have emptied a panful of dishwater from the upper window straight into the lilac bushes. But Miranda's time had not yet come, and neither had Hiram's.

So Nathaniel and Phoebe sat by the open window and said a few last pleasant words, and looked a good-by into one another's eyes, the depth and meaning of which neither had as yet fathomed. They did not know that not two feet away was the evil face of the man who hated them both. He was so near that his viperous breath could almost have touched their cheeks, and his wicked heart, burning with the passionate fires of jealousy and hatred, gathered and devoured their glances as a raging fire will devour fuel. He watched them, and he gloated over them, as a monster will gloat over the victims he intends to destroy.

...ight of health ... face. It was hard to go back, but Phoebe ... the thought that these friends were ture, who would continue even in the midst of daily trials.

Everybody had urged her to stay longer, but Phoebe felt that she had already stayed longer than she should have done, and insisted that she must begin life again, that it was not right to lie idle.

The truth was, Phoebe had in mind a little plan which she wanted to think about and talk over with Albert. This stay with the Spaffords had brought to a climax a great longing she had had in her heart to go to school somewhere for a little while. She had a great thirst for knowledge, and she began to think that perhaps it might be possible to gratify it, for there was that money of hers lying idle in the bank. She might take some of it and go away for a year to a good school if Albert thought so, and she almost believed he would if only he could be persuaded before Emmeline heard of it.

Phoebe had felt her own deficiencies more and more by reason of her delightful correspondence with Nathaniel Graham. She wished to make herself more his equal, that she might really be able to write letters worthy of his perusal. She little dreamed of the trouble that was swiftly descending.

In modern war we sow our harbors and coasts thick with hidden mines ready to explode should the enemy venture within our borders. In much the same fashion that morning Hiram Green started out to lay his mines in readiness for the sweet young life that was unwarily drifting his way.

He had dressed himself soberly, as befitted the part he was to play. He harnessed his horse and chaise, and taking a wide berth of country in his circuit for the day, he drove first to the home of an old aunt of his to whom he had never been bound by many loving ties, yet who served his purpose, for she had a tongue that wagged well, and reached far.

After the greetings had been exchanged Hiram sat down with a funereal air in the big chair his relative had brought out of the parlor in honor of his coming, and prepared to bring forth his errand.

"Aunt Keziah," he began, in a voice which indicated momentous things to come. "I'm in deep trouble!"

"You don't say, Hiram! What's up now? Any of the children dead or sick?"

"No I ain't afflicted in that manner this time," said Hiram. "It's somethin' deeper than that, deeper than sickness er death. It's fear o' disgrace."

"What! Hiram! You ain't ben stealin' er forgin' anybody's name, surely?" The old lady sat up as if she had been shot and fixed her eyes—little eyes like Hiram's with the glitter of steel beads—on her downcast nephew's face.

"No, Aunt, I'm thankful to say I've been kep' from pussonel disgrace," murmured Hiram, piously, with a roll of his eyes indicating that his trust was in a power beyond his own.

"Well, what is it, then? Speak up quick. I'm too old to be kep' in hot water." The aunt spoke snappishly. Hiram perceived that he had made his impression.

"Well, you see it's this way, Aunt. You must uv heard I was takin' notice again."

"That was to be expected, Hiram, you so young an' with children to look after. I hope you picked out a good worker."

"Yes," admitted Hiram, with satisfaction, "she's a right smart worker, an' I thought she was 'bout as near perfect all through as you could find 'em, an' I kinder got my heart sot on her. I've done everythin' she wanted that I knowed, even to buildin' a new house down on the knoll fer her, which wan't necessary ' all, bein' as the old house is much better'n the one she's ben brung up in. Yet I done it fer her, an' I ben courtin' her fer quite a spell back now; ben to see her every night reg'lar, an' home from meetin' an' singin'-school whenver she took notion she wanted to go."

Hiram drew a long sigh, got out a big red and white cotton handkerchief and blew his nose resoundingly. The old lady eyed him suspiciously to gauge his emotion with exactness.

"Long 'but six or eight weeks ago"—Hiram's voice grew husky now—"she took sick. 'Twas this 'ere way. We was comin' home from a barn raisin' over to Woodbury's, an' it was gettin' near dark, an' she took a notion she wanted to pick some vi'lets long the roads. I seen a storm was comin' up, an' I argued with her agin it, but she would hev her way, an' so I let her out an' tole her to hurry up. She got out an' run back o' the kerridge a piece an' begun pickin' an' in a minute all on a suddent somethin' hit the horse's hind leg. I can't tell what it was, mebbe a stone er it might 'a' ben a stick, but I never took no thought at the time. I grabbed fer them reins, an' jest as the horse started to run there come a big clap o' thunder that scared the horse worse'n ever. I hung on to them reins, an' lookin back I seen her standin' kind o' scared like an' white in the road a lookin' after me, an' I hollered back, 'You go to the Widder Duzenberry's till I come back fer yeh. It's goin' to rain.' Then I hed to tend to that horse, fer he was runnin' like the very old scratch. Well, 'course I got him stopped and turned him round an' went back, but there wasn't a sign of her anywhere to be seen. The Widder Duzenberry said she hedn't seen her sence we druv by fust. I went back fer her brother, an' we searched everywhere, but we couldn't find her no

place, an' will you 'blieve it, we couldn't find a sign of h...
next mornin' she come sailin'...

... where
... that big tree taller than the rest, a big
... oak, 't is, that has a squirrel harbour in it? Well, that's the one. They used to meet there. And once she started off on some errand fer her sister-in-law in the coach, an' he es bold es life went 'long. Nobody knows whar they went, some sez Albany, some sez Schenectady, but anyhow she never come back till late the next day, an' no countin' fer where she'd been.

"Her sister-in-law is a nice respectable woman, and they all come of a good family. They'll feel turrible 'bout this, fer they've never 'spicioned her any more'n I done. She's got a sweet purty face like she was a saint—"

"Them is always the very kind that goes to the dogs," quoth Aunt Keziah, shaking her head and laying down her knitting.

"Well, Aunt Keziah," said Hiram, getting out his handkerchief again, "I come to ask your advice in this matter. What be I to do?"

"Do?" snapped Aunt Keziah. "Do, Hiram Green? Why be thankful you found out 'fore you got married. It's hard on you, 'course, but 'tain't near so hard es 'twould 'a' ben ef you'd 'a' found out after you was tied to 'er. An' you just havin' had such a hard time an' all with a sickly wife dyin'. I declare, Hiram Green, you suttin'ly hev been preserved!"

"But don't you think, mebbe, Aunt Keziah, I ought to stick to her? She's such a purty little thing, an' everybody's down on her now, an' she's begged me so hard not to give her up when she's in disgrace. She's promised she'll never hev nothin' more to do with these other fellers—"

There were actually some hypocritical tears being squeezed out of Hiram's little pig-eyes and rolling down in stinted quantities upon the ample kerchief. It would not do to wipe them away when they were so hard to manufacture, so Hiram waited till they were almost evaporated and then mopped his eyes vigorously.

"Well, Hiram Green, are you that soft-hearted! I declare to goodness, but you do need advice! Don't you trust in no sech promises. They ain't wuth the breath they're spoken in. Jest you hev nothin' more to do with the hussy. Thank goodness there's plenty more good workers in the world—healthy ones, too that won't up 'n die on ye jest in harves!"

"Well, Aunt Keziah!"—Hiram arose and cleared his throat as if a funeral ceremony had just been concluded—"I thank yeh fer yer good advice. I may see my way clear to foller it. Jest now I'm in doubt. I wanted to know what you thought, an' then I'll consider the matter. It ain't as though I hedn't been goin' with her pretty steady fer a year back. Yeh see what I'll do'll likely tell on how it goes with her from now on."

"Well, don't you go to be sentimental like, Hiram. That wouldn't set on you at your time o' life. Jest you stand by your rights an' be rid of her. It's what your ma would 'a' said ef she was alive. Now you remember what I say. Don't you be soft-hearted."

"I'll remember, Aunt," said Hiram, dutifully, and went out to his chaise.

He took his slow and doleful way winding up the road, and as soon as he was out of sight beyond the turn the alert old lady put on her sunbonnet and slipped up to her cousin's house half a mile away. She was out of breath with the tremendous news she had to tell, and marvelling all the way that Hiram had forgotten to tell her not to speak of it. Of course he intended to do so, but then of course he wouldn't object to having Lucy Drake know. Lucy was his own cousin once removed, and it was a family affair in a way.

Hiram's next visit was at the Widow Duzenberry's.

Now the Widow Duxenberry had often thought that her good daughter would made a wise choice for Hiram Green, and could rule well over the wild little Greens and be an ornament to the house and farm of Green. Therefore it seemed a special dispensation of Providence that Susanna had that afternoon donned her best sprigged chintz and done her hair up with her grandmother's high-backed comb. She looked proudly over at her daughter as Hiram sat down in the chair that Susanna had primly placed for him near her mother.

When the few preliminary remarks were concluded, and the atmosphere had become somewhat breathless with the excitement of wondering what he had come for, Hiram cleared his throat ominously and began:

"Mrs. Duzenberry," he said, and his countenance took on a deep sadness, "I called today on a very sad errand." The audience was attentive in the extreme. "I want to ask, did you take notice of me an' Phoebe Deane a ridin' by, the day of Woodbury's barn raisin'?"

"Wal, yes," admitted old Mrs. Duzenberry, reluctantly. "Now 't you mention it, I b'lieve I did see you drivin' by, fer there was black clouds comin' up an' I says to Susanna, says I, 'Susanna, we mebbe ought to bring in that web o' cloth that's out to bleach. It mebbe might blow away.' '

"Well, I thought p'raps you did, Mis' Duzenberry, an' I want to ask, did you take notice of how we was sittin' clost to one 'nother, she with her head restin' on my shoulder like? I hate to speak of it, but Mis' Duzenberry, wouldn't you 'a' thought Phoebe Deane was real fond o' me!"

Mother Duzenberry's face darkened. What had the man come for?

"I certain should," she answered, severely. "I d[illegible] in open road."

[illegible] and her eyes [illegible] who was modestly looking out the window.

"Anything else?" Hiram's voice had the husky note now as if he were deeply affected.

"Wal, I might think of somethin' else, gimme time."

"What ef he found out she wan't all he thought she was?"

Mother Duzenberry's face brightened.

"'Course that might 'fect him some," she admitted.

"I see you don't understand me," sighed Hiram. "I take it you ain't heard the bad news 'bout Phoebe Deane."

"She ain't dead, is she? I heard she was better," said Susanna, turning her sharp thin profile toward Hiram.

"No, my good friend," sighed Hiram, "it's worse'n death. It certainly is fer that poor girl. She's to be greatly pitied, however much she may have aired."

The two women were leaning froward now, eager for the news.

"I came to you in my trouble," said Hiram, mopping his face vigorously, "hopin' you would sympathize with me in my extremity, an' help me to jedge what to do. I wouldn't like to do the girl no wrong, but still, considerin' all that's come out the last two days—Say, Mis' Duzenberry, you didn't see no man hangin' round here that day little before we druv by, did you? No stranger, ner nuthin'."

"Why, yes, ma," said Susanna, excitedly. "There was a wagon come by a goin' toward the village, and there was two men, an' one of 'em jumped out an' took somethin' from the other, looked like a bundle er sumthin', an' he walked off towards the woods. He had butternut-colored trousers."

"That's him," said Hiram, frowning, "they say he always wore them trousers when anybody's seen him with her. You know the day they went off in the stage to Albany he was dressed that 'a' way!"

"Did they go off in the stage together in broad daylight? That's scandalous!" exclaimed the mother.

"You know most o' their goin's on happened over near Fundy Road. Aunt Keziah knows all 'bout it. Poor ole lady. She's all broke up. She always set a good store by me, her only livin' nephew. She'll be wantin' me to give up havin' anythin' more to do with Phoebe now, since all this is come out 'bout her goin's on, but I can't rightly make up my mind whether it's right fer me to desert her er not in her time o'trouble."

"I should think you was fully justified," said Mrs. Duzenberry, heartily. "There's other deservin' girls, an' it's puttin' a premium on badness to 'ncourage it that way."

"Good afternoon, Mis' Duzenberry." Hiram rose sadly. "I'm much 'bliged to yeh fer yer advice. I ain't sure yet what I shall do. 'Course I'll be 'bliged to yeh ef you'll jest keep people from talkin' much as yeh ken. I knowed you knowed the fac's an' I thought 'twould be best to come straight to you. Good afternoon, Miss Susanna. Perhaps we may meet again under pleasanter circumstances."

"Land alive!" exclaimed Susanna, as they watched him drive sadly away. "Don't he look broke up! Poor feller!"

"Serves him right fer makin' up to a little pink-cheeked critter like that," said the mother. "Say, Susanna, I ain't sure but you better put on yer bonnet an' run up to Keziah Dart's house an' find out 'bout this. We've got to be real keerful not to get mixed up in it, nohow, but I should like to know jest what she's done. Ef Keziah ain't home run on to Page's. They'll mebbe know. He said they'd ben seen round there. But speak real cautious. It won't do to tell everything you know. I'll mebbe jest step over to the toll-gate. They'll be wantin' to know what Hiram Green was here for. It won't be no harm to mention he was callin' on you. It might take their 'tention off'n him, so's they wouldn't speak 'bout him goin' so much with Phoebe. My! Ain't it a pity! But that's what comes o' havin' good looks. You know I allus told you so, Susanna."

Susanna tossed her head, drew her sunbonnet down over her plain face and went off, while her mother fastened the door and went up to the toll-gate.

Hiram's method as he pursued his course the rest of the afternoon was to call ostensibly on some other business, and then speak of the gossip as a matter of which every one knew, and refer to those on whom he had called before as being able to give more information concerning the facts than he could. He did not ask any more advice, but in one case where he was asked what he was going to do about it he shook his head dubiously and went away without replying.

Most of his calls were in the country, but before he went home he stopped at the home of the village dressmaker. His excuse for going there was that his oldest girl needed a frock for Sunday, and he thought the old woman who kept house for him had enough to do without making it. He asked when she could come, and said he would let her know if that day would be convenient. Just as he was leaving he told her that as she was going everywhere to other people's houses he supposed she would soon hear the terrible stories that were going round about Phoebe Deane, but he wished that if she heard anything about his breaking off with Phoebe she would just say that he intended not to do anything rashly, but would think it over and do what was right.

The keen-eyed newsmonger asked enough questions
in hand, and looked

kitchen chamber
prepared to write a letter to Nathaniel Graham, as she
had promised him she would do that very night, and in it she told him her plans
of going away to school.

Chapter 25

The tongues which Hiram had set wagging were all experts and before many days had passed the fields of gossip were green with springing slander and disgrace for the fair name of Phoebe Deane. All unconsciously she moved above it, making happy plans, and singing her sweet song of hope. She did not mind work, for it was pleasant to feel strong again. She even hummed a sweet tune that she heard Marcia play. Emmeline was puzzled to understand it all.

But the thing that puzzled Emmeline most of all was that Hiram Green had not been near the house since the day he had the talk with her about the village lot, and had boasted that he was going to marry Phoebe before another year.

Steadily every day Hiram's new house was growing. Emmeline could see it from her window, and she wondered if perhaps he was preparing to break his promise and court another girl instead of Phoebe, or was this a part of his plan to stay away until the house was done? It troubled Emmeline every day. Neither could she understand how Phoebe could be happy and settle down so cheerfully, having driven her one suitable lover away.

Phoebe had ventured to discuss the plan of her going away with Albert, who seemed rather disappointed to have her go, but was nevertheless willing, and said that he thought such a plan would have pleased her mother. He broached the subject to Emmeline, and thereupon brought down upon the family a storm of rage. Emmeline scoffed at the idea. She said that Phoebe was already spoiled for anything in life, and that if she used up her money getting more spoiling she couldn't see how in the world she expected to support herself; for she wouldn't be a party to Phoebe's living any longer on them if she spent her money on more schooling. Then Emmeline put on her bonnet and ran across the field to Hiram's farm, where she found him at the knoll superintending the putting up of a great stone chimney.

"Say, look-a-here, Hiram Green," she began, excitedly, getting him off a little way from the workmen, "what do you mean by sech actions? Hev you give up Phoebe Deane, er haven't yeh? 'Cause ef yeh ain't yeh better be tendin' to business. She's got it int' her fool head now to go off to school, an' she'll do it, too. I ken see Albert's jest soft enough to let 'er."

Hiram smiled a peculiar smile.

"Don't you worry, Emmeline. I know what I'm 'bout, an' you'll git your corner lot yit. Phoebe Deane won't go off to no boardin'-school, not yet awhile, 'er I'll miss my guess. Jest you leave it to me!"

"Oh, very well!" said Emmeline, ...

...ept Phoebe herself and ... family and friends. Somehow no one had quite dared to mention it before any of them yet, it was too new and startling.

Sunday morning the Deanes went to church, and there were strange turnings away from them, and much whispering, nodding, and nudging as they passed. It had not been expected that Phoebe would appear in church. It was considered brazen in her to do so. It was evidently all and more true.

Hiram Green came to church but he did not look toward the Deanes' pew. He sat at the back with pious manner and drooping countenance, and after church made his melancholy way out without stopping to talk, or attempting to get near Phoebe. This was observed significantly; also the fact that Mrs. Spafford walked down the aisle in friendly converse with Phoebe Deane as if nothing had happened. Evidently she had not heard yet. Somebody ought to tell her. They discussed the matter in groups on the way home.

Old Mrs. Baldwin and her daughter Belinda were much worried about it. They went so far as to call to the doctor and his wife who were passing their house that afternoon on the way to see a sick patient.

"Doctor," said Mrs. Baldwin, coming out to the sidewalk as the doctor drew up to speak with her, "I ain't a going to bother you a minute but I just wanted to ask if you knew much about this tory that's been going round about Phoebe Deane. It seems as though someone ought to tell Mrs. Spafford. She's been real kind to the girl, and she don't seem to have heard it. I don't know her so well, or I would, but somebody ought to do it. I didn't know but you or your wife would undertake to do it. They walked down the aisle together after church this morning and it seemed too bad. David Spafford wouldn't like to have his wife so conspicuous, I know. Belinda says he was out of town yesterday, so I s'pose he hasn't heard about it yet, but I think something ought to be done."

"Yes, it's a very sad story," chirped the doctor's wife. "I just heard it myself this morning. The doctor didn't want to believe it, but I tell him it comes very straight."

"Oh, yes, it's straight," said Mrs. Baldwin, with an ominous shake of her head and a righteous roll of her eyes. "It's all too straight. I had it from a friend who had it from Hiram Green's aunt's cousin. She said Hiram was just bowed with grief over it, and they were going to have a real hard time to keep him from marrying her in spite of it."

The doctor frowned. He was fond of Phoebe. He felt that they all had better mind their own business and let Phoebe alone.

"I would be quite willing to speak to Miss Hortense or Miss Amelia Spafford," said the doctor's wife. "I'm intimate with them, you know, and they could do as they thought best about telling their niece."

"That's a good idea," said Mrs. Baldwin. "That quite relieves my mind. I was real worried over that sweet little Mrs. Spafford, and she with that pretty little Rose to bring up. They wouldn't of course want a scandal to come anywhere near them. They better look out for that Griscom girl. She comes from poor stock. I said long ago she'd never be any good, and she's been with that Phoebe Deane off an' on a good bit."

"Oh, I think that was all kindness," said the doctor's wife. "Mrs. Spafford was very kind during Phoebe Deane's illness. The doctor knew all about that."

"Yes, I s'spose the doctor knows all 'bout things. That's the reason I called you, and on Sunday too; but I thought it was a work of necessity and mercy. Well, good-afternoon, Doctor, I won't keep you any longer."

"There's that pretty Miss Bristol ought to be told, too, ma," reminded Belinda.

"That's so, Belinda," said the doctor's wife. "I'll take it upon myself to warn her, too. So sad, isn't it? Well, good-bye," and the doctor's chaise drove on. The doctor was inclined to prevent his wife from taking part in the scandal business, but his wife had her own plans which she did not reveal. She shut her thin lips and generally did as she pleased.

The very next day she took her way down the shaded street and called upon the aunts of the house of Spafford, and before she left she had drooped her eyes and told in sepulchral whispers of the disgrace that had befallen the young protegee of their niece, Mrs. David Spafford.

Aunt Amelia and Aunt Hortense lifted their hands in righteous horror and thanked the doctor's wife for the information, saying they were sure Marcia knew nothing of it, and of course they would tell her at once and she would henceforth have nothing further to do with the Deanes.

Then the doctor's wife went on her mission to Janet Bristol.

Janet Bristol was properly scandalized, and charmingly grateful to the doctor's wife. She said of course Phoebe was nothing to her, but she had thought her rather pretty, and interesting. She was obviously bored with the rest of the good woman's call, and when it was over she betook herself to her writing desk where she scribbled off a letter to her cousin Nathaniel concerning a party she wished to give and for which she wanted him and his friend Martin Van Rensselaer to come up. At the close she added a hasty postcript.

"The doctor's wife has just called. She ..."
paragon. Mi.. D

............anda had stayed
... ..∪ wuuiu surely have discovered the state of things,
and revealed it to Marcia. And it happened also that Marcia started off with
David on a long ride early Monday morning, therefore when Aunt Hortense
came down on her direful errand Marcia was not there, and Miranda, seeing
her coming, escaped with Rose through the back door for a walk in the woods.
So another day passed without the scandal reaching either Miranda or Marcia.

It was on Monday morning that the storm broke upon poor Phoebe's
defenseless head.

A neighbor had come over from the next farm a quarter of a mile away
to borrow a cup of hop yeast. It was a queer time to borrow yeast, at an hour
in the week when every well-regulated family was doing its washing, but
that was the neighbor's professed errand. She lingered a moment by the door
with the yeast cup in her hand and talked to Emmeline.

Phoebe was in the yard hanging up clothes, and singing. The little bird
was sitting on the weathervane and calling merrily: "Phoe-bee! Phoe-bee!"

"Are yeh goin' to let her stay here now?" the visitor asked in a whisper
fraught with meaning, and nodded her head toward the girl in the yard.

"Stay?" said Emmeline, looking up aggressively. "Why shouldn't she?
Ain't she been here ever since her mother died? I s'pose she'll stay till she
gets married."

Emmeline was not fond of this neighbor, and therefore did not care to reveal
her family secrets to her. She lived in a red house with windows both ways and
knew all that went on for miles about.

"Guess she won't run much chance of that now," said the neighbor, with
a disagreeable laugh. She was prepared to be sociable if Emmeline opened her
heart, but she knew how to scratch back when she was slapped.

"Well, I sh'd like to know what you mean, Mis' Prinn. I'm sure I don't know
why our Phoebe shouldn't marry es likely es any other girl, an' more so'n some
what ain't got good looks."

(Mrs. Prinn's daughter was not spoken of generally as a beauty.)

"Good looks don't count fer much when they ain't got good morals."

"Indeed! Mis' Prinn. You do talk kind of mysterious. Did you mean to
insinuate that our Phoebe didn't have good morals?"

"I didn't mean to insinuate anything, Mis' Deane. It's all over town the way she's been goin' on, an' I don't see how you can pertend to hide it any longer. Everybody knows it, an' b'lieves it."

"I'd certainly like to know what you mean," demanded Emmeline, facing the woman angrily. "I brung that girl up, an' I guess I know what good morals is. Phoebe may have her weak points, but she's all right morally."

"Fac's is fac's, Mis' Deane," said the neighbor, with a relish.

"I deny that there is any fac's to the contrary," screamed Emmeline, now thoroughly excited into championing the girl whom she hated. The family honor was at stake. The Deanes had never done anything dishonorable or disgraceful.

"I s'pose you don't deny that she spent the night out all night the time o' the storm, do yeh? How d' ye explain that?"

"I should like to know what that hes to do with morals."

The neighbor proceeded to explain with a story so plausible that Emmeline grew livid with rage.

"Well, 'pon my word, you've got a lot to do runnin' round with sech lies as them. Wher'd you get all that, I'd like to know?"

"It all come straight enough, an' everybody knows it, ef you are stone blind. Folks has seen her round in lonely places with a strange feller. They do say he kissed her right in plain sight of the road near the woods one day. An' you know yerself she went off and stayed all night. She was seen in the stage-coach 'long with a strange man. There's witnesses! You can't deny it. What I want to know, is what are you goin' to do 'bout it? 'Cause ef you keep her here after that I can't let my dotter come here anymore. When girls is talked about like that decent girls can't hev nothin' to do with 'em. You think you know a hull lot 'bout that girl out there, singin' songs in this brazen way with the hull town talkin' 'bout her, but she's deceived you, that's what she's done; an' I thought I'd be good enough neighbor to tell you, ef you didn't know a'ready. But es you don't seem to take it as 'twas meant, in kindness, I'd best be goin.'"

"You'd best had," screamed Emmeline, "an' besure you keep your precious dotter to hum. Hum's the place fer delikit little creatures like that. You might find *she* was deceivin' *you* ef you looked sharp enough."

Then Emmeline turned and faced the wondering Phoebe, who had heard the loud voices and slipped in through the wood-shed to escape being drawn into the altercation. She had no idea what it all was about. She had been engaged with her own happy thoughts. "I'd like to know what all this scandal's about, Phoebe Deane. Jest set down there and explain. What kind of goin's on hev you hed, that all the town's talkin' 'bout you? Mis' Prinn comes an' says she can't let her dotter come over here any more ef you stay here. I don't know that it's much loss, fer she never come to 'mount to much, but I can't hev folks talkin' that way. No decent girl ought to have her name kicked around in that style. I may not hev hed a great ejjacation like you think you've got to have, but I knowed enough to keep my name off folks' tongues, ...

...y to answer her, but ...., roused beyond control, would not listen. She stormed and raged at Phoebe, calling her names, and telling her what a trial she had always been, until suddenly Phoebe's new found strength gave away entirely and she dropped back in a faint against the wall, and would have fallen if Albert had not come in just then unperceived, and caught her. He carried her upstairs tenderly and laid her on her bed. In a moment she opened her sad eyes again and looked up at him.

"What's the matter, Phoebe?" he asked, tenderly. "Been working too hard?" But Phoebe could only answer by a rush of tears.

Albert, troubled as a man always is by woman's tears, stumbled downstairs to Emmeline to find out, and was met by an overwhelming story.

"Who says all that 'bout my sister?" he demanded, in a cool voice, and rising with a dignity that sat strangely upon his kindly figure. "She ain't your sister," hissed Emmeline. "She ain't any but a half relation to you, an' it's time you told her so an' turned her out of the house. She'll be a disgrace to you an' your decent wife an' children. I can't have my Alma brought up in a house with a girl that's disgraced herself like that."

"You keep still, Emmeline," said Albert, gravely. "You don't rightly know what you're saying. You've got excited. I'll attend to this matter. What I want to know is, Who said this about my sister? I'll go get Hiram Green to help me, and we'll face the scoundrel, whoever it is, and make him take it back before the whole town."

"What ef it's true!" mocked Emmeline.

"It isn't true. It couldn't be true. You know it couldn't, Emmeline."

"I'm not so sure o' that," raged his wife. "Wait till you hear all," and she proceeded to recount what Mrs. Prinn had told her.

"I am ashamed of you, Emmeline, that you'll think of such a thing for a minute, no matter who told you. Don't say another word about it. I'm going out to find Hiram."

"Ain't you noticed that Hiram ain't ben comin' here lately?" Emmeline's voice was anything but pleasant. Albert looked at her in astonishment.

"Well, what o' that? He's a good man, and he's fond o' Phoebe. He'll be sure to go with me and defend her."

Albert went out and she saw him hurrying down the road toward Hiram's. Hiram, like an old spider, was waiting for him in the barn. He had been expecting him for two days, not thinking it would take so long for the news to spread into the home of the victim. He looked gloomy and non-committal as Albert came up, and greeted him with half-averted eyes.

"I've come to get your help," said Albert, with expectant good will. "Hiram, hev you heard all this fool talk about Phoebe? I can't really believe folks would say that about her, but Emmeline's got it in her head everybody knows it."

"Yes, I heard it," admitted Hiram, reaching out for a straw to chew. "I spent one hull day last week goin' round tryin' to stop it, but 'twant no use. I couldn't even find out who started it. You never ken, them things. But the wust of it is, it's all true."

"What!"

"Yes," said Hiram, dismally, "'tis. I'm sorry to' say it to you, what's ben my friend, 'bout her I hoped to marry some day, but I seen some things myself. I seen thet day they talk 'bout in the edge o' the woods, an' I seen her cut an' run when she heard my wagon comin', an' when she looked up an' see it was me she was deadly pale. That was the fust I knowed she wan't true to me."

Hiram closed his lying lips and looked off sorrowfully at the hills in the distance.

"Hiram, you must be mistaken. There is some explanation."

"All right, Albert, glad you ken think so. Wish't I could. It mos' breaks my heart thinkin' 'bout her. I'm all bound up in havin' her. I'd take her now with all her disgrace an' run the resk o'keepin' her straight ef she'd promise to behave herself. She's might young, an' it does seem too bad. But yeh see, Albert, I seen her myself with my own eyes in the stage-coach along with the same man what kissed her in the woods, an' yeh know yerself she didn't come back till next night."

With a groan Albert sank down on a box near by and covered his face with his hands. He had been well brought up and disgrace like this was something he had never dreamed of. His agony amazed the ice-hearted Hiram, and he almost quailed before the sight of such sorrow in a man, sorrow that he himself had made. It embarrassed him. He turned away to hide his contempt.

"It comes mighty hard on me to see you suffer thet way, Albert, an' not be able to help you," he whined after a minute. "I'll tell you what I'll do. I'll marry her anyway. I'll marry her an' save her reputation. Nobody'll dast say anthing' 'bout my wife, an' ef I marry her that'll be es much es to say all this ain't so, an' mebbe it'll die down."

Albert looked up with manly tears in his eyes.

"That's real good of you, Hiram. I'll take it as mighty kind of you if you think there isn't any other way to stop it. It seems hard on you, though."

"I ain't thinkin' o' myself," ~~~~~~~~~~~~~~~~~~~~~~~~~~~~~~~~~~~~~

~~~~~~ kitchen with a chastened air.
Emmeline eyed him keenly. Phoebe had not come downstairs and his wife had all the work to do again. She was not enjoying the state of things.

Albert sat down and looked at the floor.

"Hiram has been very kind," he said, slowly, "most kind. He has offered to marry Phoebe at once and stop all this talk."

A light of understanding began to dawn in Emmeline's eyes.

"H'm!" she said. Then, after a thoughtful pause. "But I guess Miss Phoebe Deane'll hev a word to say 'bout that. She don't like him a bit."

"Poor child!" moaned Albert. "She'll have to take him, whether she likes him or not. Poor little girl. I blame myself I didn't look after her better. Her mother was a real lady and so good to me when I was home. I promised her I'd keep Phoebe safe. She was such a good woman, it would break her heart to have Phoebe go like this."

"H'm! I don't reckon she was no better than other folks, only she set up to be!" sniffed Emmeline. "Anyhow this is just what might 'a' ben expected from the headstrong way that girl went on. I see now why she was set on goin' off to school. She knowed this was a' comin' an' she wanted to slip an' run 'fore it got out. But she got caught. Sinners generally does." Emmeline wrung out her dishcloth with satisfaction.

"I'll go up now and talk with Phoebe," said Albert, rising sadly as if he had not heard his wife.

"I'm sure I wish you joy of your errand. Ef she ac's to you es she does to me you'll come flyin' down faster'n you went up."

But Albert was tapping at Phoebe's door before Emmeline had finished her sentence.

Chapter 26

"Phoebe," said Albert, gently sitting down beside the bed where she lay wide-eyed, in white-faced misery, trying to comprehend what this new calamity might mean, "I'm mighty sorry for you, little girl. I wish you had come to me with things more. I might 'a' helped you better if I hadn't been so stupid. But I've found a way out of it all for you. I've found a good man that's willing to marry you and give you the protection of his name and home, and we'll just have you married right away quietly here at home, and that'll stop all the talk."

Phoebe turned a look of mingled horror and helplessness on her brother. He did not comprehend it, and thought she was grasping for a thread of hope.

"Yes, Phoebe, Hiram Green is willing to marry you right off in spite of everything, and we've fixed it up to have the wedding right away, tomorrow. That'll give you time to straighten out your things, and Hiram to get the minister—"

But Albert stopped suddenly as Phoebe uttered a piercing scream of fear and started up as if she would fly from the room.

Albert caught her and tried to soothe her.

"What's the matter now, little girl? Don't look like that. It'll all come out right. Is it because you don't like Hiram enough? But child, you'll get to like him more as you know him better. Then you'll be so grateful to think what he saved you from. And besides, Phoebe, there isn't any other way. We couldn't stand the disgrace. What would you mother think? She was always so particular about how you should be brought up. And to have you turn out disgraced would break her heart. Phoebe, don't you see there isn't any other way?"

"Albert, I would rather die than marry that wicked man. He is a bad man. I *know* he is bad. He has been trying to make me marry him for a long time, and now he is just taking advantage of this terrible story. Albert, you know these stories are not ture. You don't believe them, Albert, do you?"

She looked at him with piteous pleading in her beautiful eyes, and he had to turn his own eyes away to hide their wavering. He could not see how this sweet girl could have gone wrong, and yet—there was the evidence!

"You do," said Phoebe. "Albert, you do! You believe all this awful story about me! I never thought you would believe it. But Albert, listen! I will never marry Hiram Green! You may kill me or send me away, or anything you like, but you cannot make me marry him!"

Albert turned his eyes away from the pitiful figure of the pleading girl and set his lips firmly.

"I'm sorry Phoebe, but it's got to be done..."

family, and Alma'll grow up without any friends. I've got to look out for my little girl as well as you, Phoebe, and you must believe me, I'm doing the very best for you I know." Phoebe sat down weakly on the edge of her bed and stared wildly at him. She could not believe that Albert would talk to her so. She could not think of anything to say in answer. She could only stare blankly at him as if he were a terrible apparition.

Albert thought she was quieting down and going to be reasonable, and with a few kind words he backed out of the room. Phoebe dropped back upon her pillow in a frenzy of horror and grief. Wild plans of running away rushed through her brain, which was after all utterly futile, because her limbs seemed suddenly to have grown too feeble to carry her. Her brain refused to think, or to take in any facts except the great horror of scandal that had risen about her and was threatening to overwhelm her.

Emmeline declined to take any dinner up to her. She said if Phoebe wanted anything to eat she might come down and get it, she wasn't going to wait on a girl like that any longer. Albert fixed a nice plate of dinner and carried it up, but Phoebe lay motionless with open eyes turned toward the wall and refused to speak. He put the plate on a chair beside her and went sadly down again. Phoebe wondered how long it would take one to die, and why God had not let her die when she had the fever. What had there been to live for, anyway? One short bright month of happiness!

The memory of it gripped her heart anew with shame and horror. What would they say, all those kind friends? Mrs. Spafford and her husband, Miranda, and Nathaniel Graham? Would they believe it, too? Of course they would, if her own household turned against her. She was defenseless in a desolate world. She would never more have friends and smiles and comfort. She could not go away to school now, for what good would an education be to her with such a disgrace clinging to her name and following her wherever she went? It would be of no use to run away. She might better stay here and die. They could not marry her to Hiram Green if she were dead. Could one die in a week by just lying still?

So the horror in her brain raged over and over, each time bringing some new phase of grief. And now it was a question if her friends would desert her; and now it was the haughty expression on Janet Bristol's face that day she carried the letter to Nathaniel; and now it was the leer on Hiram's face as he put his arm about her on that terrible drive; and now it was the thought that she would have no more of Nathaniel's long, delightful letters.

All day long she lay in this state, and when the darkness fell a half delirious sleep came upon her, which carried the fears and thoughts of the day into its unresting slumber. The morning broke into the sorrow of yesterday, and Phoebe, weak and sick, arose with one thought in her mind; that she must write at once to Nathaniel Graham and tell him all. She must not be a disgrace to him.

With trembling hands, and eyes filled with tears, she wrote:

Dear Mr. Graham:
I am writing to you for the last time. A terrible thing has happened. Someone has been telling awful stories about me and I am in disgrace. I want you to know that these things are not true. I do not even know how they started, for there has never been any foundation for them. But everybody believes them, and I will not disgrace you by writing to you any more. You will probably be told the worst that is said, and perhaps you will believe them as others do. I shall not blame you if you do, for it seems as if even God believed them. I do not know how to prove my innocence, nor what the end of this is to be. I only know that it is not right to keep you in ignorance of my shame, and to let you write any longer to one whose name is held in dishonor. I thank you for all the beautiful times you have put into my life, and I must say good-bye forever.
                                                            Gratefully,
                                                            Phoebe Deane.

The letter was blistered with tears before it was finished. She addressed it and hid it in her frock, for she began to wonder how it would get to the mail. Probably Miranda would never come near her again, and she could not be seen in the village. She dared not ask any one else to mail the letter lest it would never reach its destination.

She spent the rest of the day in quietly putting to rights her little belongings, unpacking and gathering together things she would like to have destroyed if anything should happen to her. She felt weak and dizzy, and the food that Albert continuted to bring to her seemed nauseous. She could not bring herself to taste a mouthful. It was so useless to eat. One only ate to live, and living had been finished for her, it appeared. It was not that she had resolved to make away with herself by starvation. She was too right-minded for that. She was simply stunned by the calamity that had befallen her, and was waiting for the outcome.

Sometimes as she stood at the window looking out across the fields which had been familiar to her since her childhood she had a feeling that she was going away from them all soon. She wondered if her mother felt so before she died.

Then she wondered...

...came out to see her. Emmeline opened the door and her countenance grew black when she recognized the visitor.

"Now, you ken just turn right around and march home," she commanded. "We don't want no folks around. Phoebe Deane's in turrible disgrace, an' you've hed your part in it ef I don't miss my guess. No, you ain't goin' to see her. She's up in her room, and ben shut up there ever since she heard how folks hes found out 'bout her capers. You an' yer Mis' Spafford can keep yer pryin' meddlin' fingers out o' this an' let Phoebe Deane alone from now on. We don't want to see yeh any more. Yer spoilin' an pettin' has only hastened the disgrace."

The door slammed in Miranda's indignant face and Emmeline went back to her work.

"She needs a good shakin'," remarked Miranda, indignantly to herself, "but it might tire me, an' besides I've got other fish to fry."

Undaunted she marched to the back shed and mounted to Phoebe's window, entering as if it had been always the common mode of ingress.

"Wal, fer the land, Phoebe Deane, what's ben a happenin' now?" she asked, mildly, surveying Phoebe, who lay white and weak upon her bed, with her untasted dinner beside her.

"Oh, don't you know all about it, Miranda?" Phoebe began to sob.

"No, I don't know a thing. I ben shut up in the house cookin' for two men Mr. David brung home last night, an they et an' et till I thought there wouldn't be nothin' left fer the family. They was railroad men er somthin'. No, I guess 'twas bankin' men. I fergit what. But they could eat if they did wear their best clothes every day. But say, ef I was you, I wouldn't talk very loud fer the lady downstairs wasn't real glad to see me this time, an' she might invite me to leave rather suddint ef she 'spicioned I was up here."

But Phoebe did not laugh as Miranda had hoped. She only looked at her guest with hungry, hopeless eyes, and it was a long time before Miranda could find out the whole miserable story.

"And Miranda, I've written Mr. Graham a note telling him about it. Of course I couldn't disgrace him by continuing to write any longer, so I've said good-bye to him. Will you do me one last kindness? Will you mail it for me?" Phoebe's whisper was tragic. It brought tears to Miranda's well-fortified eyes.

"'Course I'll mail it fer yeh, child, ef yeh want me to, but 'tain't the last kindness I'll do fer yeh by a long run. Shucks! D'you think I'm goin' to give in this easy an' see you sucked under? Not by a jugful. Now look-a-here, child; ef the hull fool world goes against yeh, I ain't a goin', ner my Mrs. Marcia ain't, neither, I'm plumb sure o' that. Bet *ef* she did I'd stick *anyhow,* so there! Cross my heart ef I don't! *Now.* D'yeh b'lieve me? An' I'll find a way out o' this, somehow. I ain't thought it out yet, but don't you worry. You set up 'n' eat that there piece o' bread an' butter. Never mind ef yeh don't feel like it, you eat it fer me. I can't do nothin' ef yeh don't keep yer strength up. Now you do your part an' we'll get out o' this pickle es good es we did out o' the other one. I ain't goin' to hev all my nursin' wasted. Will yeh be good?"

Phoebe promised meekly. She could not smile. She could only press Miranda's hand, while great tears welled through the long lashes on her cheeks.

"So that old serpent thinks he's got you fast, does he? Well, he'll find hisself mistaken yet, ef I don't miss my guess. The game ain't all played out by a long shot. Marry you next week, will he? Well, we'll see! I may dance at your weddin' yet, but there won't be no Hiram Green as bridegroom. I'd marry him myself 'fore I'd let him hev you, you poor little white dove." And Miranda pressed a great impulsive kiss upon Phoebe's white lips and stole out of the window.

As she hurried along down the road the waving grain in the fields on either side reminded her of whispered gossip. She seemed to see a harvest of scandal ripening all about the poor stricken girl whom she loved, and in her ignorant and original phraseology she murmured to herself the thought of the words of old, "Lo, an enemy hath done this." Miranda felt that she knew pretty well who the enemy was.

"Well," said Marcia, "I think you would enjoy the trip sometime. We might keep a lookout for somebody going who would be company. Or perhaps Mr. Spafford will be going again soon and he would have time to look after you."

"'Fraid I can't wait that long," said Miranda. "I've took a great notion I'd like to have a balzarine frock, an' ef I'm goin' to hev it I'd best get it straight off an' git more good out of it. I look at it this way. I ain't goin' to be young but once, an' time's gettin' on. Ef you don't get balzarine frocks when you're young you most likely won't git 'em 't all, 'cause you'll think 'tain't wuth while. I've got a good bit of money laid by, an' ef you've no 'bjections, an' think you ken spare me fer a couple o' days I think I'd like to go down to New York an' git it. I don't need no lookin' after, so you needn't worry 'bout that. Nobody steals me, an' es long es I got a tongue I ken ast my way 'round New York es well es I can 'round Fundy er any other place."

"Why, of course I can spare you, Miranda, and I suppose you'd be perfectly safe, only I thought you'd enjoy it more if you had good company. When did you think you'd like to go?"

"Well, I've been plannin' it all out comin' up the street. I've baked, an' washed, an' the sweepin' ain't much to do. Ef you don't mind I think I'll go tomorrer mornin'."

"What in the world makes you want to go in such a hurry?"

"Oh, I've just took the notion," said Miranda, smiling. "Mebbe I'll tell yeh when I get back. I shan't be gone more'n a year."

Marcia was a little worried at this sudden turn of affairs. It was not like Miranda to hide things from her. Yet she had such confidence in her that she finally settled down to the thought that it was only a whim and perhaps a good night's sleep would overcome it. But the next morning she found the table fully set for breakfast, and the meal prepared and keeping warm. Beside her plate a scrawled note lay:

Mrs. Marcia, deer. I'll liklie be bak tomorer nite er next, but donte worrie. I got biznes to tend to an I'll tel you bout it wen i get home.

yours til deth, respectfuly,
Miranda Griscom.

P.S. you mite praye ef your a mind. Tak keer uf Feby ef I dont git bak.

Before Marcia could get time to run up and see Phoebe, for she somehow felt that Miranda's sudden departure to New York had to do with her visit to Phoebe the day before, Miss Hortense arrived, with her most commandatory air.

"Marcia, I came on a very special errand," she began, primly. "I was down on Monday, but you were away." There was reproach in the tone.

"Yes, I went with David," responded Marcia, brightly, but Miss Hortense would brook no interruption.

"It's of no consequence now. I would have come yesterday, but we had company all day, the Pattersons from above Schenectady. I couldn't leave very well. But I hurried down this morning. It's about the Deane girl, Marcia. I suppose you haven't heard the dreadful reports that are going around. It really is disgraceful in a decent town. I'm only glad she got out of your house before it became town talk. It all shows what ingratitude there is in human nature, to think she should repay your kindness by allowing herself to be talked about in this shameful way."

Marcia exclaimed in dismay, but Miss Hortense went straight on to the precise and bitter end, giving every detail in the scandal that had come to her ears, details at which even Hiram Green would have opened his eyes wide in surprise, and would never have believed that they grew out of his own story.

Marcia listened in rising indignation.

"I am sorry that any such dreadful story is abroad, Aunt Hortense," she answered, earnestly, "but really, if you knew the girl, you would understand how impossible it is for this to be true. She is as sweet and pure innocent as my little Rose."

"I should be sorry to have David's child compared to that miserable girl, Marcia," said Miss Hortense, severely, rising as she spoke, "and I am sure that after my warning if you do not shut that wretched creature forever out of your acquaintance I shall feel it my duty to appeal to David, and tell him the whole story, though I should dislike to have to mention anything so indelicate before him. David is very particular about the character of women. He was brought up to be; and Amelia and I both agree that he must be told."

"I shall tell him myself, of course, and he will see if anything can be done to stop this ridiculous gossip," said Marcia, indignantly. "David is as fond of Phoebe as I am."

"You will find David will look on it in a very different way, my dear. You are young and a woman. You do not know the evil world. David is a man. Men know. Good-bye, my dear. I have warned you!" And Aunt Hortense went pensively down the street, having done her duty.

Marcia put her bonnet on, took little Rose, and walked straight out to Albert Deane's house, but when she reached there was denied admission. Alma opened the door, but did not ask the caller in. In a moment she came back from

consulting her mother and said: "Ma says Aunt Phoebe~~~~~~~
don't wish to see no one."

~~~~~~~~~~~~~~~~~~~~~~ David.

~~~~~~ Cousin Janet's letter his anger rose to white
~~~~. Every throb of his heart told him that the stories about Phoebe were false.
Like Miranda, he felt at once that an enemy had done this, and he felt like
searching out the enemy at once and throttling him into repentance. He read
the postscript through twice and then sat for a few minutes in deep thought, his
face shaded by his hand. The office work went on about him, but his thoughts
were far away in a sunlit autumn wood. After a little he got up suddenly and
going into the inner office where he could be alone, sat down quickly, and wrote:

My Dear Phoebe: (He had never called her that before, it was always "Miss
Deane.") *I have loved you for a long time, ever since that afternoon that I found
you among the autumn leaves in the woods. I have been trying to wait to tell you
until I could be sure you loved me, but now I can wait no longer. I am lonely
without you. I want you to be here with me. I love you, darling, and will love you
forever, and guard you tenderly, if you will give me the right. Will you forgive this
abrupt letter, and write immediately, giving me the right to come up and tell you all
the rest?*

Yours in faithful love,
Nathaniel Graham.

After he had sent it off enclosed to Miranda, he scribbled another, to Janet.

Dear Janet, it read, *wherever did you get those ridiculous stories about
Phoebe Deane? They are as false as they are foolish. Everybody that knows her
at all knows they could not be true. I insist that you deny them whenever you have
the opportunity, and for my sake that you go and call upon her. I may as well tell
you that I am going to marry her if she will have me, and I want you, Janet, to be
like a sister to her, as you have always been to me. Any breath against her name I
shall consider as against mine also, so please, Janet, stand up for her for my sake.*

Your loving cousin,
Nathaniel.

After these two letters had been dispatched Nathaniel put in the best day's work he had ever done.

Miranda had reached Albany in time to catch the evening boat down the Hudson. She was more tired than she had ever been in all the years of her hard-working life. The bouncing of the stage-coach, the constant change of scenery and fellow passengers, the breathlessness of going into a strange region, had worn upon her nerves. She had not let a single thing pass unnoticed and the result was that even her iron nerves had reached their limit at last. Besides, she was more worried about Phoebe Deane than she had ever been about anything in her life. The ethereal look of the girl as she bade her good-bye the night before had gone to her heart. She half feared Phoebe might fall asleep and never waken while she was gone on her desperate errand of mercy.

"Land sake alive," she murmured to herself, as she crept into her bunk in the tiny stateroom and lay down without putting off any of her garments save her bonnet and cape. "Land sake alive! I feel as ef I'd ben threshin'. No, I feel as ef I'd ben *threshed!*" she corrected. "I didn't know I hed so many bones."

Nevertheless she slept little, having too much to attend to. She wakened at every stop in the night, and she heard all the bells and calls of the crew. Half the time she thought the boat was sinking and wondered if she would be able to swim when she struck the water. Anyhow she meant to try. She had heard it "came natural" to some people.

When morning broke over the heights above the river she watched them grow into splendor and majesty, and long before the city was in sight she was on deck sniffing the air like a veteran war-horse. Her eyes were dilated with excitement, and she made a curious and noticeable figure as she gripped her small bag of modest belongings, and sat strained up and ready for her first experience of city life. She felt a passing regret that she could not pause to take in more of this wonderful trip, but she promised herself to come that way again some day, and hurried over the gang-plank with the others when the boat finally landed. Tucked safely away in her pocket was Phoebe's letter to Nathaniel and safe in her memory was its address. Every passenger with whom she had talked upon the voyage— and she had entered into conversation with all except a man who reminded her of Hiram Green—had given her detailed directions how to get to that address, and the directions had all been different. Some had told her to walk one way and take a cab, some another way. Some had suggested that she take a cab at the wharf. She did none of these things. She gripped her bag firmly and marched past all the officials, through the buildings out into the street. There she stood a moment bewildered by the noise and confusion, a marked figure even in that hurrying throng of busy people. Small boys and drivers immediately beset her. She looked each over carefully and then calmly walked straight ahead. So far New York did not look very promising to her, but she meant to get into a quieter place before she made any inquiries.

At last after she had walked several blocks and was ̶b̶e̶g̶i̶n̶
there was no quiet ̶p̶l̶

̶y̶o̶u̶ ̶w̶e̶r̶e̶ ̶b̶u̶t̶ ̶s̶h̶e̶ says she has come a long distance and ̶m̶u̶s̶t̶ see you at once. Shall I tell her to come again?"

Nathaniel glanced through the door, and there, close behind the careful office boy, stood the wily Miranda. She had run no risks of not seeing Nathaniel. She had followed the boy, strictly against orders.

Her homely face was aglow with the light of her mission, but in spite of freckles and red hair, and the dishevelled state of her appearance, Nathaniel put out an eager hand to welcome her. His first thought was that she had brought an answer to his letter to Phoebe, and his heart leaped up in sudden eagerness. Then at once he knew that it was too soon for that, for he had only sent his own letter in the evening mail.

"Come right in, Miranda," he said, eagerly, "I'm glad to see you. Are you all alone?" Then something in her face caused a twinge of apprehension.

"Is every one all well?"

Miranda sat down and waited until the door was shut. Then she broke forth.

"No, everythin' ain't all well. Everythin' 's all wrong. Phoebe Deane's in turrible trouble, an' she's wrote a letter sayin' good-bye to you, an' ast me to mail it. I said I would, an' I brung it along. I reckon it didn't make no diff'rence whether it travelled in my pocket er in the mailbag, so it got here."

She held out the letter, and Nathaniel's hand shook as he took it. Miranda noticed that he looked pale.

"What has happened, Miranda?" he asked, as he tore open the letter, hardly knowing what he feared.

"Oh, it's that ole snake-in-th'-grass," said Miranda; "I'd be willin' to stake my life on that. No knowin' how he done it, but it's done. There's plenty to help in a business like gossip, when it comes to that. There's ben awful lies told about her, and she's bein' crushed by it. Wal, I hed to come down to New York to get me a new balzarine frock an' I jest thought I'd drop in an' tell yeh the news. Yeh don't know of a good store where I won't get cheated, do yeh?" she asked, making a pretense of rising.

"Sit down, Miranda," commanded Nathaniel. "You're not going away to leave me like this. You must tell me all about it. Miranda, you know, don't you, that Phoebe is my dear friend. You know that I must hear all about it."

"Well, ain't she told you in the letter? I reckon you'll go back on her like her own folks hev done, won't you? An' let that scoundrel git her next week like he's planned."

"What do you mean, Miranda? Tell me at once all about it. You know Phoebe Deane is very dear to me."

Miranda's eyes shone, but she meant to have things in black and white.

"How dear?" she asked, looking up in a business-like way. "Be you goin' to b'lieve what they all say 'bout her, an' let them folks go on talkin', 'til she's all wilted down an' dead? 'Cause ef you be, you don't git a single word out o' me. No, sir!"

"Listen, Miranda. Yesterday I wrote to Phoebe asking her to marry me!"

Satisfaction began to dawn upon the face of the self-appointed envoy extraordinary.

"Well, that ain't no sign you'd do it again today," said Miranda, dryly. "You didn't know nothin' 'bout her bein' in trouble then."

"Yesterday morning, Miranda, I received a letter from my cousin telling me all about it, and I sat down at once and asked Phoebe to marry me."

"You sure you didn't do it out o' pity?" asked Miranda, lifting sharp eyes to search his face. "I shouldn't want to hev nobody marry her out o' pity, the way Hiram Green's going to do, the old nimshi!"

"Miranda, I love her with all my heart, and I will never believe a word against her. I shall make it the object of my life to protect her and make her happy if she will give me the precious treasure of her love in return. Now are you satisfied, you cruel girl, and will you tell me the whole story? For the little I heard from my cousin has only filled me with apprehension."

Then the freckles beamed out and were lost in smiles as Miranda reached a strong hand and grasped Nathaniel's firm white one with a hearty shake.

"You're the right stuff. I knowed you was. That's why I come. I didn't darst tell Mis' Spafford what was up, 'cause she wouldn't 'a' let me come, an' she'd 'a' tried to work it out in some other way. But I hed it all figgered out, an' there wasn't time for any fiddlin' business. It hed to be done t' woncet ef 'twas to be didn't all, so I told her I wanted a pleasure trip an' a new balzarine, an' I come. Now I'm goin' to tell you all 'bout it, an' then ef there's time fer the balzarine 'fore the evenin' boat starts I'll get it, otherwise it'll hev to git the go-by this time, fer I've got to git right back to Phoebe Deane. She looked jest awful 'fore I left, an' there's no tellin' what they'll do to her while I'm gone."

Nathaniel, with loving apprehension in his eyes, listened to the story, told in Miranda's inimitable style, his face darkening with anger over the mention of Hiram's part.

"The scoundrel!" he murmured, clenching his fingers as if he could hardly refrain from going after him and giving him what he deserved.

"He's all that," said Miranda, "an' a heap more. He's ~~~~~~
Albert Deane ~~~~~~

~~~~~~, an' he's told Phoebe she hez to git married in jest a week, er he'll hev to turn her out o' the house. Monday mornin' 's the time set fer the marriage, an' Albert 'lows he won't wait 'nother day. He's promised his wife he'll keep to that."

Nathaniel's face grew stern as he listened, and asked questions. At last he said:

"Miranda, do you think Phoebe Deane cares for me? Will she be willing to marry me?"

"Wal, I sh'd think, ef I know anythin' 't all 'bout Phoebe Deane, she'd give her two eyes to, but she'll be turrible set 'gainst marryin' you with her in disgrace. She'll think it'll bring shame on you."

"Bless her dear heart," murmured Nathaniel, "I suppose she will," and he touched her letter tenderly as if it had been a living thing. Miranda's eyes glistened with jubilation, but she said nothing.

"But we will persuade her out of that," added Nathaniel, with a light of joy in his eyes.

"If you are quite sure it will make her happy," he added, looking at Miranda keenly. "I wouldn't want to have her marry me just to get out of trouble. There might be other ways of helping her, though this way is best."

"Well, I guess you needn't worry 'bout love. She'll love you all right, er my name ain't M'randy!"

"Well, then, we will just have a substitute bridegroom. I wonder if we'll have trouble with Hiram. I suppose very likely we will, but I guess we can manage that. Let me see. This is Thursday. I can arrange my business by tomorrow night so that I can leave it for a few days. If you can stay over till then I will take you to my landlady, who is very kind and will make your stay pleasant. Then we can go back together and plan the arrangements. You'll have to help me, you know, for you are the only medium of communication."

"No, I can't stay a minute longer 'n t'night," said Miranda, rising in a panic and glancing out the window at the sun as if she feared it were already too late to catch the boat; "I've got to get back to Phoebe Deane. She won't eat, an' she's just fadin' away. There might not be any bride by time you got there. 'Sides, she can't git your letter till I get back no how. I'll hev to go home on the boat tonight, an' you come tomorrow. You see, ef there's goin' to be a weddin' I'd like real well to git my balzarine made 'n time to wear to it. That'll give me plenty time, with Mis' Spafford to he'p cut 't out. Do you s'pose there's time fer me to go to the store? It took a long time to git up here from the river."

Nathaniel arose.

"You have plenty of time, and if you'll wait ten minutes I will go with you. We can get some dinner, and go to the store, and we can arrange things on the way."

Miranda settled down in the great office chair and watched Nathaniel's white fingers as they wrote on the legal paper. When it was finished and folded he took another piece of paper and wrote:

My Darling:

I have just received your letter, and I am coming to you as quickly as I can arrange my business to get away. Miranda will bring you this and will tell you all I have said. I will be there in time for the wedding morning, and if you will have me instead of Hiram Green I shall face the whole world by your side, and tell them they are liars. Then I will bring you back with me to stay with me always. My heart is longing to see you and comfort you, but I must not write any more for I have a great deal to do before I go. Only this I must say, if you do not feel you love me, and do not want to marry me, I will help you some other way to get free from this trouble, and to have it all explained before the world. There is just one thing I am resolved upon, and that is that you shall be guarded and loved by me, whether you will marry me or not. You are too precious to suffer.

> *Yours with more love than you can ever fathom,*
> *Nathaniel.*

He sealed, addressed it, and handed it to Miranda, who took it with a gleam of satisfaction in her honest eyes. She was almost willing to run home without her balzarine now that she had that letter. She did not know what he had written, of course, but she knew it was the right thing and would bring the light of hope again to Phoebe's eyes.

Then they went out into the bustling, strange streets of the city.

Miranda was too excited to eat much, though Nathaniel took her to his own boarding-place and tried to make her feel at home. She kept asking if it wasn't almost time for the boat to leave, until he had to explain to her just how much time there was, and how quickly they could get to the wharf.

They went to a store, and Miranda did not take long to pick out her frock. It seemed as if the very one she had always longed for most lay draped upon the counter, and with quick decision she bought it. It had great stripes of soft colors in palm-leaf pattern, blended into harmony in oriental manner, in the exquisite fabric. It seemed to her almost too fine to go with red hair, but she bought it with joyous abandon. The touch of rich blue and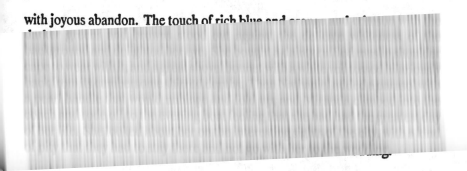

Chapter 28

Miranda reached home on the afternoon coach and bounced into the house with a face full of importance.

"Wal, I'm glad to git back. Did you find the blueberry pies? I put 'em out the pantry winder to cool, an' fergot 'em. I thought of 'em when I was on the boat, but 'twas mos' too late to come back then, so I kep' on.

"Here's my balzarine. Do yeh like it?" and she tossed the bundle into Marcia's lap. "I'm going right at it when I git the work done in the mornin' fer I want to hev it t' wear at Phoebe Deane's weddin'. Did yeh know she was goin' to marry Nathaniel Graham? Say, where's that Rose? I'm most starved for a sight o' her little sweet face. Yer lookin' real good yerself. All's well?"

Marcia listened smilingly to Miranda's torrent of words, and gradually drew the whole story from her handmaid, laughing heartily over the various episodes of Miranda's journey and gravely tender over what Nathaniel had said. Then Miranda heard about Marcia's call on Phoebe, and how she had written Phoebe a letter asking what she could do to help her, and inviting her to come at once to them, but had received no answer.

"An' yeh won't, neither," said Miranda, decidedly. "She'll never git no letter, I'm sure o' that. Ef that old' skunk of a Hiram Green don't git it fust, Mis' Deane'll ferret it out an' keep it from her. She's the meanest thing in the shape of a woman I've seen yit, an' I've hed some experience."

Then Miranda rapidly sketched her plan of procedure, and Marcia added some suggestions. Together they prepared the supper, with the single object of getting Miranda off to Phoebe as soon as the darkness should come.

It was quite dark and Phoebe was lying in a still white heap upon her bed when Miranda stole softly in. By her side lay a long white package she had taken from her little trunk in the closet, and on it was pinned a note. "Dear Miranda, if I die, please take this, from Phoebe."

She had not lighted her candle, and she had not eaten a mouthful all day. The terrible faintness and weakness were becoming constant now. She could only lie on her bed and wait. She could not even think any more. The enemies all about her with their terrible darts had pierced her soul, and her life seemed ebbing away. She felt it going, and did not have the desire to stop it. It was good to be at rest.

Miranda stole in softly, and began to move quietly about the room, finding the candle and softly striking the flint and tinder. Phoebe became gradually conscious of her presence, as out of the midst of a misty dream. Then Miranda came and looked down tenderly into her face.

"Raise yer head up, you poor little thi...

...as asked me to marry him. Wouldn't it be beautiful! But he didn't know when he wrote it—" and the brown head went down as if it were stricken like a lily before a fierce blast.

"Shucks!" said Miranda, dabbing away the mistiness from her eyes. "Yes, he did know, too. His cousin wrote him. Here, you read the other one."

Again Phoebe sat up and read, while Miranda held her candle and tried not to seem to look over her shoulder at the words she could feel in her soul if she could not see with her eyes.

"Oh, it can't be true!" said Phoebe, with face aglow with something that almost seemed the light of another world. "And I mustn't let him, of course. It wouldn't be right for him to have a wife like this—"

"Shucks!" said Miranda again. "Yes, 'tis true, too, and right an' all the rest, an' you've got to set up and get spry, fer there's a sight to do, an' I can't stay much longer. That weddin' 's commin' off on Monday morning—time set fer it. 'Tain't good luck to put off weddin's an' this one 's goin' to go through all right.

"Mr. Nathaniel, he's goin' to bring his cousin an' the Jedge, an' my Mr. David an' Mrs. Marcia's comin' wether they're ast er not, 'cause they knew 'twant no use fer um to wait fer an invite from that sister-in-law of yourn, so they're comin' anyway. Mr. Nathaniel said as how you weren't to worry. He'll git here Saturday night sure, an' ef there was any other 'rangement you'd like to make he was ready, an' you could send your word by me, but he 'greed with me 'twould make less talk ef the weddin' come off at your home where 'twas to be in the fust place, an' then you could go right away from here an' never come back no more. Say, hev ye got anythin' thet's fit to wear? 'Cause ef yeh ain't I'll let yeh have my new balzarine to wear. I'll hev it all done by Sat'day night. Mrs. Marcia's goin' to help me."

Between tears and smiles Phoebe came to herself. Miranda fed her with some strong broth which she had brought along and which she managed to heat after laboriously holding the pail over the candle flame. Then together in the dim candle-light the two girls opened the great white box that lay on the floor beside the bed.

"It's my wedding dress, Miranda. Mother made it for me long ago, before she died, and put it in my trunk to keep for me. It was marked, 'For my little girl when she is going to be married.'

"I opened it and found the letter on the top, for I thought I was going to die, and I wanted to read mother's last letter, but I did not take the frock out because I thought I would never wear it, and it made me feel so bad that I left it in its wrappings. I thought if I died I would like to have you have it, because it is the most precious thing I have and you have done more for me than anybody else ever did, but mother."

Miranda gulped a sudden unexpected sob at this tribute, and it was some time before she could recover her equanimity, though she said "Shucks!" several times.

They took the white bridal garment out of its wrappings and Phoebe tried it on, there in the dimness of the room. It was thin white book-muslin, all daintily embroidered about the neck and sleeves by the dead mother's hand. It fell in soft sheer folds about the white-faced girl, and made her look as if she were just going to take her flight to another world.

In another paper was the veil of fine thread lace, simple and beautiful, and a pair of white gloves which had been the mother's, both yellow with age, and breathing a perfume of lavender. A pair of dainty little white slippers lay in the bottom of the box, wrapped in tissue paper also. Miranda's eyes shone.

"Now you look like the right kind of a bride," she said, standing back and surveying her charge. "That's better 'n all the balzarines in New York."

"You shall wear the balzarine and stand up with me, Miranda," whispered Phoebe, smiling.

"No, sir! We ain't goin't to hev this here weddin' spoiled by no red hair an' freckles, even if 't has got a balzarine. Janet Bristol's got to stan' up. She'll make a picter fer folks to talk 'bout. Mr. Nathaniel said he'd manage his cousin all right, an' 'twould quiet the talk down ef his folks took sides along of you. No, sir, I ain't goin' to do no standin' in this show. I'm goin' to set, an' take it all in. Come now, you get into bed, an' I'll blow out the light an' go home. I reckon I'll be back tomorrer night to take any messages you want took. The'll be plenty o' chance fer you to rest 'fore Monday. Don't say nothin' to yer folks. Let 'em go on with their plans, an' then kinder s'prise 'em."

The next morning Phoebe arose and feeling much refreshed dressed herself carefully and went downstairs. She had a quiet, grave look upon her face, but in her eyes there was a strange light which she could not keep back. Emmeline looked up in surprise when Phoebe came and took hold with the work. She began to say something slighting, but the look in Phoebe's face somehow stopped her. It was a look of joyful exaltation; and Emmeline, firmly believing that the girl was justly talked about, could not understand, and thought it hypocrisy.

Albert came in in a few minutes, ~~and looks~~

Then Phoebe spoke.

"I have done nothing to feel sorry for, Emmeline. I have not sinned. I am only sorry that you have been willing to believe all this against me."

Then she went quietly on with her work, and said no more, though Emmeline's speech was unsealed and she gave Phoebe much good advice during the course of the day.

The next morning near church time Emmeline told Phoebe that Hiram was coming over to see her that morning, and she might open the front parlor to receive him.

"I don't wish to see Hiram, Emmeline," she answered, calmly. "I have nothing whatever to say to him."

"Well, upon my word, Phoebe Deane," said Emmeline, getting red in the face with indignation of the girl. "Goin' to git married tomorrow mornin' an' not wantin' to see Hiram Green! I should think you'd want to talk over 'rangements."

"Yes, I am going to be married tomorrow morning," said Phoebe, with a triumphant ring to her voice, "but I do not want to see Hiram Green. I have no arrangements to talk over with him. My arrangements are all made."

Phoebe went away to her room and remained there the rest of the day.

Nathaniel had arrived. She knew that by special messenger coming and going over the wood-shed roof. There had been sweet messages of cheer, and he had promised to come for her in the morning. Everything was arranged. She could possess her soul in peace and quietness and wait. Her enemies would soon be put to flight. Nathaniel had promised her that, and although she could not see in the least how, she trusted him perfectly.

She had sent her love to him, and the locket with her mother's picture. It was all she had to give her lover, and he understood. It was the one she had worn the first time he ever saw her.

The balzarine frock was finished. The last hook was set in place before supper Saturday night, and Marcia had pronounced it very becoming. It was finished in spite of the fact that Miranda had made several secret excursions into the region of Hiram Green's house and farm. She had made discoveries which she told to no one, but over which she chuckled when quite alone in the kitchen at work. On her first trip she had seen him go out to his milking, and had passed close to the house, where his window was open. She had glanced in, and there on the sill her sharp eyes had discovered the bit of red seal with the lion's head upon it. She had carried too many letters with that seal not to know it at once, and she gleefully seized it and carried it to Nathaniel. She had evidence at last which would give her power over the enemy.

She also discovered that Hiram Green attended to his milking himself, and that he had a habit — if one might judge from two mornings as samples — of going to the spring house himself with the milk and placing the pans on the great stone shelf. This she had seen by judicious hiding behind shrubbery, and trees, and spring-house itself, and spying upon him. Birds and squirrels tell no tales, and the dewey grass soon dried off and left no trace of her footsteps. During one of these excursions she had examined the fastening of the spring-house most carefully, and knew the posibilities of button, hasp, staple, and peg.

The Spaffords and Miranda went to church as usual, and so did the Bristols. The advent of Nathaniel and his friend Mr. Van Rensselaer in the Bristol pew diverted attention from the empty seat behind them, for this morning the Deanes were conspicuous by their absence.

The day passed quietly. Miranda made her usual visit in the early evening. Phoebe had asked her to stay with her, but Miranda said she had some things to do, and departed sooner than usual. The night settled into stillness and Phoebe slept in joyous assurance that it was her last night in the room where she had seen so much sorrow.

In the morning she went down to breakfast as usual. She did not eat much, to be sure, but drank some milk, and then washed the breakfast dishes as calmly as if she expected to keep on washing them all the rest of her life in this same kitchen.

"Hiram'll be over 'bout half past nine, I reckon," said Albert. He had been instructed by Emmeline to say this. "The minister won't come till ten. If you need to talk to Hiram you'll have plenty of time between. You better be all ready."

"I shall not need to talk to Hiram," said Phoebe, as she hung up the dish towels. There was that in her voice as she said it that made Albert look after her wonderingly.

"She's the queerest girl I ever see!" grumbled Emmeline. "One would think by her looks that she expected a chariot of fire to come down an' take her straight up to heaven like 'Lijah. It's kind of dreadful the way she ac's! 'F I was Hiram I'd be 'fraid to marry her."

Miranda arrived over the shed roof soon after Phoebe went upstairs. She wore her old calico, and if one who knew had observed closely, he would have said it was a calico that Miranda never used any more, for it was very old. Her hair was combed with precision and on her head was an elaborate New York bonnet with a white barege veil, but her b̲a̲l̲...

has Hiram Green come yet?" asked Phoebe, anxiously. She was dreading a scene with Hiram.

"Wal, no, not 'zactly," said Miranda. "An what's more, I don't think he will. Fact is I've got him fixed fer a spell, but I ain't goin to say nothin' more 'bout it at present, 'cept that he's detained by bus'ness elsewhar. It's best you shouldn't know nothin' 'bout it ef there's questions ast, but you don't need to worry. 'Less sompin' quite unusual happens he ain't likely to turn up till after the ceremoney. Now, what's to do to you yet? Them hooks all fastened? My, but you do look han'some!"

"Oh, Miranda, you haven't done anything dreadful, have you?"

"No, I ain't," laughed Miranda. "You'd jest split your sides laughin' ef you could see him 'bout now. But there! Don't say 'nother word. I hear voices. The Bristols hev come, an' the minister, too. I reckon your sister-in-law'll hev her hands full slammin' the door in all them faces."

Phoebe, aghast, pulled the curtain aside and peered out.

There in the yard were several carriages, and more driving in the gate. She could hear a great many voices all at once. She saw Mrs. Duzenberry and Susanna getting out of their chaise, and Lemuel Skinner and his wife Hannah, and she thought she heard the village dressmaker's voice high above all, sharp and rasping, the way it always was when she said: "That seam needs pressin'. It does hike up a mite, but it'll be all right when it's pressed."

Phoebe retreated in dismay from the window.

"Oh, Miranda! How did all those people get down there! Emmeline will be so angry. She is in her room dressing yet. It doesn't seem as if I dared go down."

"Fer the land sake, how should I know? I s'pose Providence sent 'em, fer they can't say a single word after the ceremony's over. Their mouths'll be all nicely stopped. Don't you worry."

Miranda answered innocently, but for one instant as she looked at Phoebe's frightened face her guilty heart misgave her. Perhaps she had gone a step too far. For it was Miranda who had slipped here and there after church on Sunday and whispered a brief invitation to those who had gossiped the hardest, wording it in such a way that they all thought it was a personal invitation from Phoebe.

In every case she had added, "Don't say nothin' till after it's over," and each thinking himself especially favored had arrived in conscious pride, and as they passed Hiram Green's new house they had remarked to themselves what a fine man he was for sticking to Phoebe in spite of all the talk.

But Miranda never told her part in this, and Emmeline never got done wondering who invited all those people.

Miranda's momentary confusion was covered by a gentle tap on the door, and Phoebe in a flutter rushed to hide her friend:

"I'm afraid it's Emmeline," she whispered. "She may not let you go down."

"Like to see her keep me up," said Miranda, boldly. "My folks hes come. I ain't 'fraid now," and she boldly swept the trembling bride out of the way and threw the door open.

Janet Bristol in a silken gown of palest pink entered and walked straight up to Phoebe.

"You dear little thing!" she exclaimed. "How sweet you look. That frock is beautiful and the veil makes you perfect. Nathaniel asked me to bring you this and make you wear it. It was his mother's."

She fastened a rope of pearls around Phoebe's neck and kissed her as a sister might have done.

Miranda stood back and gazed with satisfaction on the scene. All was as it should be. She saw nothing further to be desired. Her compunctions were gone.

"Nathaniel is waiting for you at the foot of the stairs," whispered Janet. "He has his mother's ring for you. He wanted me to tell you. Come, they are ready. You must go ahead."

Down the stairs went the trembling bride, followed by her bridesmaid. Miranda grasped her precious parasol and tiptoed on behind.

Nathaniel stood at the foot of the stairs, waiting for her. Emmeline, with a red and angry face, was waiting on her most unexpected guests and had not time to notice what was going on about her. The original wedding guests, consisting of a row of little Greens and the old housekeeper, were submerged in the Sunday gowns of the new arrivals.

"Where's Hiram," whispered Albert, in Emmeline's ear, just as she was giving Hiram's Aunt Keziah Dart a seat at the best end of the room.

"Goodness! Ain't he come yet? I s'posed he was upstairs talkin' to Phoebe. I heard voices."

She wheeled around and there stood the wedding party.

Nathaniel, tall and handsome, with his shy, pale bride upon his arm; Janet, sparkling in her pink gown and enjoying the discomfiture of guests and hostess alike, and smiling over at Martin Van Rensselaer, who stood supporting the bridegroom on the other side; it bewildered Emmeline.

The little assemblage reached out into the front door yard and

had happened? How did all these people get here? Had Phoebe invited them? And why did not somebody stop it?

"Let him speak now, or forever after hold his peace," came the words, and Emmeline gave a great gasp and thought of the corner lot opposite the Seceder church.

It was then that Emmeline became conscious of Miranda in her balzarine and New York bonnet, the very impersonation of mischief, standing in the doorway just behind the bride and watching the scene with a face of triumph. An impulse came to her to charge across the room upon the offending girl and put her out. Here surely was one who had no right in her house and knew it, too. Then all at once she caught the eye of Judge Bristol fixed sternly upon her face, and she became aware of her own countenance and restrained her feelings. For after all it was no mean thing to be allied to the house of Bristol, and to know that the cloud of dishonor which had threatened them was lifted forever. She looked at Judge Bristol's fine face and heavy white hair, and began to swell with conscious pride.

The last "I will" was spoken, the benediction was pronounced, and the hush that followed was broken by Nathaniel's voice.

"I want to say a few words," he said, "about a terrible mistake that has been made by the people of this village regarding my wife's character. I have made a most thorough investigation of the matter during the last two days and I find that the whole thing originated in an infamous lie told with intention to harm one who is entirely innocent. I simply wish to say that whoever has spoken against my wife will have to answer to me for his words in a court of justice, and if any of you who are my friends wish to question any of her past actions be kind enough to come directly to me and they will be fully explained, for there is not a thing in her past that will not bear the searching light of purity and truth."

As soon as he had ceased speaking David and Marcia stepped up with congratulations.

There was a little stir among the guests; the guilty ones melted away faster than they had gathered, each one anxious to get out without being noticed.

The Bristol coach, drawn by two white horses, with coachman and footman in livery, drew up before the door, Nathaniel handed Phoebe in and they were driven away in triumph, the guests that they passed shrinking out of sight into their vehicles as far as possible.

Albert and Emmeline looked into each other's dazed faces; then turned to the old housekeeper, and the row of little Greens, their faces abnormally shining from unusual contact with soap and water, and asked in concert:

"But where is Hiram?"

Miranda, as she rode guilelessly in the carryall with Mrs. Spafford, answered the same question from that lady, with:

"Whar d' you s'pose? I shet him in the spring-house airly this mornin'!"

Then David Spafford laid down upon his knee the reins of the old gray horse, and laughed, loud and long; could not stop laughing; and all day long it kept breaking out, as he remembered Miranda's innocent look and thought of Hiram Green, wrathful and helpless, shut in his own spring-house while his wedding went on without him.

There was a wedding breakfast elaborate and gay at Judge Bristol's, presided over by Janet, who seemed as happy as though she had planned the match herself, and whose smiling wishes were carried out immediately by Martin Van Rensselaer.

There was one more duty for Nathaniel to perform before he took his bride away to a happier home. He must find and face Hiram Green.

So, leaving Phoebe in the care of Mrs. Spafford and his cousin Janet, and himself accompanied by his uncle, Martin Van Rensselaer, and Lemuel Skinner in the capacity of village constable, he got into the family carryall and drove out to Hiram's farm.

Now Nathaniel had not been idle during the Sabbath which intervened between his coming back to the village and his marriage. Aside from the time he spent at the morning church service, he had been doing a Sabbath day's work which he felt would stand well to his account.

He had carefully questioned several of the best known gossips in the village with regard to the story about Phoebe. He had asked keen questions that gave him a plain clue to the whole diabolical plot.

His first act had been to mount his fast horse, and ride out to Ann Jane Bloodgood's, where he had a full account of Phoebe's visit together with a number of missionary items which would have met with more of his attention at another time. Possessed of several valuable facts he had gone pretty straight to most of the houses which Hiram had visited on the first afternoon when he scattered the seed of scandal, and facing the embarrassed scandal-mongers, Nathaniel had made them tell just who had been the first to speak to them of this. In every case after a careful sifting down each owned that Hiram himself had told them the first word. If Nathaniel had not been a lawyer, and keen at his calling, he might not have been able so well and so quickly to have followed

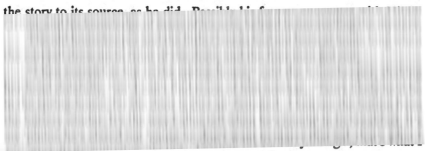

the story to its source, as he did. Possible his f...

think."

"When did you last see Mr. Green?" questioned the Judge, sternly.

"Why, I seen him take the milk pails an' go down towards the barn to milk, an' I aint' seen him sence. I thought 'twar queer he didn't come eat his breakfast, but he's kinder oncertain thet way, so I hurried up an' got off to he'p Mis' Deane."

"Have the cows been milked?" The Judge's voice ignored the old woman's elaborate explanations.

"The hired man, he says so. I ain't ben down to look myself."

"Where are the milk pails?"

"Well, now, I ain't thought to look."

"What does he usually do with the milk? He surely has not taken that with him. Did he bring it in? That ought to give us a clue."

"He most gen'rally takes it straight to the spring-house—" began the old woman.

"Let us go to the spring-house," said Nathaniel.

"I don't see what business 'tis o' yourn," complained the old woman, but they were already on the way, so after a moment's hesitation she threw her apron around her shoulders and went after them. The row of little Greens followed, a curious and perplexed little procession, ready for any scene of interest that might be about to open before them, even though it involved their unloving father.

It was Lemuel Skinner, with his cherry lips pursed importantly, who stepped forward by virtue of his office, turned the wooden button, drew out the peg, pulled off the hasp, and threw the heavy door open.

Out stumbled Hiram Green, half blinded by the light, and rubbing his eyes.

"Mr. Green, we have called to see you on a matter of importance," began Lemuel apologetically, quite as if it were the custom to meet householders on the threshold of their spring house. "Sorry I can't wait to hear it," swaggered Hiram, blinking, and trying to make out who these men were. "I got 'n engagement. Fact is, I'm goin' to be married, an' I'm late a'ready. I'll hev to be excused, Lem!"

"It's quite unnecessary, Mr. Green," said Lemuel, putting out a detaining hand excitedly; "quite unnecessary, I assure you. The wedding is all over. You're not expected any more."

Hiram stood back and surveyed Lemuel with contempt.

"Gosh Ninety!" he sneered. "How could that be when I wan't thar? I guess you didn't know I was goin' to marry Phoebe Deane. I'm right sure there wouldn't no one else marry her."

Nathaniel stepped forward, his face white with indignation.

"You are speaking of my wife, Mr. Green," he said, and his voice was enought to arrest the attention of even the self-complacency of a Hiram Green. "Let me never hear you speak of her in that way again. She did not at any moment in her life intend to marry you. You know that well, though you have tried to weave a web of falsehood about her that would put her in your power. The whole thing is known to me from beginning to end, and I do not intend to let it pass lightly. My wife's good name is everything to me; though it seems you were willing to marry one whom you had yourself defamed.

"I have come here this morning, Mr. Green, to give you your choice between going to jail or going with me at once and taking back all the falsehoods you have told about my wife."

Hiram, in sudden comprehension and fear, glanced around the group, took in the fact of the presence of Judge Bristol; remembered Nathaniel's threat of the year before about bringing him up before his uncle, remembered that Lemuel Skinner was constable; and was filled with consternation.

With the instinct of a coward and a bully he made a sudden lunge forward towards Nathaniel, his fists clenched, and his whole face expressing the fury of a wild animal brought to bay.

"You lie!" he hissed.

But the next instant he lay sprawling at Nathaniel's feet, with Lemuel bustling over him like an excited old hen.

It was Martin Van Rensselaer who had tripped him up just in time.

"Now, gentlemen, gentlemen, don't let's get excited," cackled Lemuel, laying an ineffective hand on the prostrate Hiram.

"Step aside, Mr. Skinner," said Nathaniel, towering over Hiram; "let me settle this matter first. Now, sir you may take you choice. Will you go to jail and await your trial for slander or will you come with us to the people before whom you scattered this outrageous scandal, and take it all back?"

"You've made a big mistake," blustered Hiram. "I never told no stories 'bout Phoebe Deane. It's somebody else 's done it 'ef 'tain't true—I was goin' to marry her to save her reputation."

"How did you think that would save her reputation?" questioned Judge Bristol, and somehow his voice made cold chills creep down Hiram's spine.

"Why, I—I was goin' to deny everythin' after we was married."

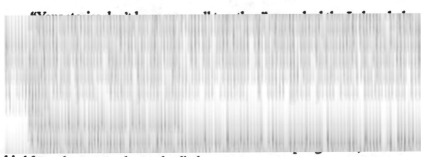

bird from the tree up the road called:

"Phoe-bee! Phoe-be!" insistently, and strange tender light came into Nathaniel's eyes.

"The time is up," said Nathaniel.

"What do you want me to do?" asked the captive, sullenly.

"I want you to go with me to every house that you visited the day you started this mischief and take it all back. Tell them it was untrue, and that you got it up out of whole cloth for your own evil purposes."

"But I can't tell a lie," said Hiram, piously.

"Can't you? Well, it will not be necessary. Come, which will you choose? Do you prefer to go to jail?"

"Gentlemen, I'm in your hands," whined the coward. "Remember I have little children."

"You should have remembered that yourself, and not brought shame upon them and other innocent beings." It was the Judge who spoke these words, like a sentence in court.

"Where hev I got to go?"

Nathaniel named over the places.

Hiram looked black, and swallowed his mortification.

"Well, I s'pose I've got to go. I'm sure I don't want to lose my good name by goin' to jail."

They set him upon his feet, and the little posse moved slowly up the slope to the house and thence to the carryall.

After they were seated in the carryall, Hiram in the back seat with Lemuel and Martin on either side of him, Nathaniel turned to Hiram.

"Now, Mr. Green, we are going first to your aunt's house, and then around to the other places in order. You are to make the following statement and nothing else. You are to say: 'I have come to take back the lies which I told about Miss Phoebe Deane, and to tell you that they are none of them true. I originated them for my own purposes.'"

Hiram's face darkened. He looked as if he would like to kill Nathaniel. He reached out a long arm again as if he would strike him but Lemuel clutched him convulsively, while Martin threw his whole weight upon the other side and he subsided.

"You can have from now until we reach the jail to think about it, Mr. Green. If you prefer to go to jail instead you will not be hindered. Mr. Skinner is here to arrest you on my charge if you will not comply with these conditions."

Sullen and silent sat Hiram. He did not raise his eyes to see the curious passers-by as he rode through town.

They looked at Nathaniel and the Judge, driving with solemn mien as if on some portentous errand; they noted the stranger and the constable on either side of the lowering Hiram; and they drew their own conclusions, for the news of the wedding had spread like wild-fire through the village. Then they stood and watched the carryall out of sight, and even followed it to see if it stopped at the jail.

As they drew near the jail Nathaniel turned around once more to Hiram: "Shall we stop and let you out here, or are you willing to comply with the conditions?"

Hiram raised his eyelashes and gave a sideways glance at the locality, then lowered them quickly as he encountered the impudent gaze of a small boy and muttered:

"Drive on."

Hiram went through the distasteful ordeal sullenly. He repeated the words which Nathaniel insisted upon, after one or two vain attempts to modify them in his own favor, which only made it worse for him in the eyes of his listeners.

"'Pon my word," said Aunt Keziah Dart in a mortified tone. "'F I'd uv told fibs like that I'd 'a' stuck to 'em, an' never giv in, no matter what. I'm 'shamed to own I'm kin to sech a sneak, Hiram Green. Wan't there gals 'nough 'round the country 'thout all that to do?"

At the Duzenberrys' Susanna rendered Hiram the sympathy of silently weeping in the background, while the Widow Duzenberry stood coldly in the foreground acting as if the whole performance were a personal affront. She closed the interview by calling after Hiram from her front door.

"I'm sorry to see yeh in trouble, Mister Green. Remember you'll always find a friend here," and Hiram brightened up some. Nevertheless, there was very little of his old conceit left when he had gone over the whole ground and was finally set free to go his way to his own home.

Then Nathaniel and Phoebe hastened away in the family coach towards Albany to begin their long life journey together.

Late that afternoon Hank Williams coming up from the village brought with him a letter for Hiram Green which he stopped to leave, hoping to find out from Hiram what had happened during the afternoon. The old housekeeper took the letter saying, "Hiram wan't well," and Hank went onward crestfallen.

A few minutes later Hiram tore open his letter. It read:

Mistur Grene,

...household slept Hiram Green went forth from his home to parts unknown, leaving his little children to the tender mercies of Aunt Keziah Dart or whoever might be touched with a feeling of pity for them.

And Miranda, who, without the counsel or knowledge of anyone, had written the remarkable epistle which sent him out, lay down serenely and slept the sleep of the just.

And that same night the moon shone brightly over the Hudson River, like a path of silver for the two who sat long on deck, talking of how they loved Miranda, with laughter that was nigh to tears.

Grace Livingston Hill

Miranda

Book Three in the *Miranda* Trilogy

...right angle, gave a comprehensive glance at the immaculate room, and whisked out on the front stoop with her broom.

Not a cobweb reared in the night remained for any early morning visitor to view with condemning eye, no, not if he arrived before breakfast, for Miranda always descended upon the unsightly gossamer and swept it out of existence the very first thing in the morning.

The steps were swept clean, also the seats on either side of the stoop, even the ceiling and rails, then she descended to the brick pavement and plied her broom like a whirlwind till every fallen leaf and stray bit of dust hurried away before her onslaught. With an air of duty for the moment done, Miranda returned to the stoop, and leaning on her broom gazed diagonally across the street to the great house set back a little from the road, and surrounded by a row of stately stiff gray poplars.

Just so she had stood and gazed every morning, briefly, for the past five years; ever since the owner of that stately mansion had offered her his heart and hand, and the opportunity to bring up his family of seven.

It had been a dark rainy night in the middle of November, that time he first came to see her. All day long it had drizzled, and by evening settled into a steady dismal pour. Miranda had been upstairs, when he knocked, hovering over the baby Rose, tucking the soft blankets with tender brooding hand, stooping low over the cradle to catch the soft music of her rose-leaf breath; and David Spafford had gone to the door to let his neighbor in.

Nathan Whitney, tall, gaunt, gray and embarrassed, stood under his streaming umbrella on the front stoop with a background of rain, and gravely asked if he might see Miss Griscom.

David, surprised but courteous, asked him in, took his dripping umbrella and overcoat from him, and escorted him into the parlor; but his face was a study of mingled emotions when he came softly into the library and shut the door before he told his young wife Marcia that Nathan Whitney was in the parlor and wanted to see Miranda.

Marcia's speaking face went through all the swift changes of surprise and wonder, but without a word save a moment's questioning with her eyes, she went to call Miranda.

"Goodness me!" said that dazed individual, shading the candle from her eyes and looking at her mistress—and friend—with eyes that were almost frightened. "Goodness me! Mrs. Marcia, you don't mean to tell me that Nathan Whitney wants to see *me?*"

"He asked for you, Miranda."

"Why Mrs. Marcia, you must be mistooken. What would he want of me? He must uv ast fer Mr. David."

"No, Mr. David went to the door," said Marcia smiling,"and he distinctly asked for Miss Griscom."

"Griscom! Did he say that name? Didn't he say Mirandy? Then that settles it. It's sompin' 'bout that rascally father uv mine. I've ben expectin' it all along since I was old 'nough to think. But why didn't he go to Grandma? I couldn't do nothin'. Ur—D'you 'spose, Mrs. Marcia, it could be he's a lawin' fer Grandma, tryin' to fix it so's I hev to go back to her? He's a lawyer y'know. But Grandma wouldn't go to do a thing like that 'thout sayin' a thing to Mr. David, would she?"

Miranda's eyes were dilated, and her breath came fast. It seemed strange to Marcia to see the invincible Miranda upset this way.

"Why of course not, Miranda," she said soothingly. "It's likely nothing much. Maybe he's just come to ask you to look after his baby or something. He's seen how well you cared for Rose, and his baby isn't well. I heard today that his sister has to go home next week. Her daughter is going away to teach school this fall."

"Well, I ain't a reg'lar servant, I'll tell him that," said Miranda with a toss of her head, "an' ef I was, I wouldn't work fer him. He's got a pack of the meanest young ones ever walked this earth. They ought to be spanked, every one o' them. I'll just go down an' let him know he's wasting his time comin' after me. Say, Mrs. Marcia, you don't *want* me to go, do you? You ain' *tired* of me, be you? 'Cause I kin go away, back to Gran'ma's ef you be, but I won't be shunted off onto Nathan Whitney."

Marcia assured her that it was the one dread of her life that Miranda would leave her; and comforted, the girl descended to the parlor.

Nathan Whitney, tall, pale, thin, blue-eyed, scant-straw-colored of hair and eyebrow, angular of lip and cheek bone, unemotional of manner, came to his point at once in a tone so cold that it seemed to be a part of the November night sighing round the house.

Miranda, her freckled face gone white with excitement, her piquant, tip-tilted nose alert, her blue eyes under their red lashes keen as steel blades

... with a new dignity as the brief and chilly declaration drew to its close, and her eyes flashed sparks at the calmly confident suitor.

Suddenly, before her gaze, had come the vision of his second wife not dead a year, brown eyes with golden glints and twinkles in them, but filled with sadness as if the life in them were slowly being crushed out; thin cheeks with a dash of crimson in their whiteness that looked as if at one time they might have dimpled in charming curves, lips all drooping that had yet a hint of cupid's bow in their bending. Her oldest boy with all his mischief looked like her, only he was bold and wicked in place of her sadness and submission. Miranda bursting with romance herself, had always felt for the ghost of young Mrs. Whitney's beauty, and wondered how such a girl came to be tied as second wife to a dried-up creature like Nathan Whitney. Therefore, Miranda held him with her eye until his well-prepared speech was done. Then she asked dryly:

"Mr. Whitney, did Mis' Whitney know you wuz cal'clatin' to git married right away agin fer a third time?"

A flush slowly rose from Nathan Whitney's stubbly upper lip and mounted to his high bare forehead, where it mingled into his scant straw-colored locks. His hands, which were thin and bony and showed the big veins like cords to tie the bones together, worked nervously on his knees.

"Just why should you ask that, Miss Griscom?" he demanded, his cold voice a trifle shaken.

"Wal, I thought 't might be," said Miranda nonchalantly, "I couldn't see no other reason why you should come fer me, ner why you should come so soon. 'Tain't skurcely decent, 'nless she 'ranged matters, 'n made you promus. I've heard o' wives doin' thet frum jealousy, bein' so fond o' their lovin' husband thet they couldn't bear to hev him selec' 'nuther. I thought she might a-picked me out ez bein' the onlikeliest she knowed to be fell in love with. Folks don't gen'lly pick out red hair an' freckles when they want to fall in love. I never knowed your fust wife but you showed sech good taste pickin' out the second, Mr. Whitney, I couldn't ever think you didn't know I was homebley, n'less your eyesight's begun failin'."

Nathan Whitney had flushed and paled angrily during this speech, but maintained his cold self-control.

"Miss Griscom, we will not discuss my wife. She was as she was, and she is now departed. Time goes slowly with the bereaved heart, and I have been driven to look around for a mother to my children. If it seems sudden to you, remember that I have a family to consider and must put my own feelings aside. Suffice it to say that I have been looking about for some time and I have noticed your devotion to the child in your care in this household. I felt you would be thoroughly trustworthy to put in charge of my motherless children, and have therefore come to put the matter before you."

"Wal, you kin gather it right up agin and take it home with you," said Miranda with a toss. "I wasn't thinkin' of takin' no famblies to raise. I'm a free an' independent young woman who can earn her own livin', an' when I want to take a fambly to raise I'll go to the poor farm an' selec' one fer myself. At present I'm perfickly confort'ble a livin' with people 'at wants me fer *myself*. I don't hev to git married to some one thet would allus be thinkin' uv my red hair an' freckles, and my father that ran away—"

"Miss Griscom," said Nathan Whitney severely, "I thoroughly respect you, else I should not have made you the offer of my hand in marriage. You are certainly not responsible for the sins your father has committed, and as for your personal appearance, a meek and quiet spirit is often a better adorning—"

But Miranda's spirit could bear no more.

"Well, I guess you needn't go on any farther, Mr. Whitney. I ain't considerin' any sech offers at present, so I guess that ends it. Do you want I should git your ombrell? It's a rainy evenin', ain't it? That your coat? Want I should hep you on with it? Good even'n', Mr. Whitney. Mind thet bottom step, it gits slipp'ry now an' agin."

Miranda closed and bolted the front door hard, and stood with her back leaning against it in a relaxation of relief. Then suddenly she broke into clear merry laughter, and laughed so hard that Marcia came to the library door to see what was the matter.

"Golly! Mrs. Marcia, wha' d'ye think? I got a per*po*sal. Me, with my red hair'n all, I got a perposal! I never 'spected it in the world, but I got it. Golly, ain't it funny?"

"Miranda!" said Marcia coming out into the hall and standing in dismayed amazement to watch her serving maid. "Miranda, what in the world do you mean?"

"Jest what I say," said Miranda. "He wanted to marry me so's I could look after his childern," and she bent double in another convulsion of

...upsairs all alone. Not while I got my senses, Mrs. Marcia. You jest go back in there to your readin' with Mr. David, an' I'll go set the buckwheats fer breakfast. But, Golly! Ain't it funny? Nathan Whitney perposin' to *me!* I'll be *swithered!*" and she vanished into the kitchen laughing.

It was the next morning, when she opened the shutters to the new fresh day with its bright cold air and business-like attitude of having begun the winter, that Miranda began those brief matinal surveys of the house across the way, taking it all in, from the gable ends with their little oriole windows, to the dreary flags that paved the way to the steps with the lofty pillared porch suggestive of aristocracy. It was an immense satisfaction to Miranda's red-haired, freckled-faced soul, to reflect that she might have been mistress of that mansion. It was not like thinking all her life that nobody wanted her, nobody would have her, and she could never be married because she would never be asked. She *had* been asked. She had had her chance and refused, and her bosom swelled with pride. She was here because she wanted to be here on this side of the street, but she might have been there in that other house if she had chosen. She might have been stepmother to that little horde of scared straw-colored girls, and naughty handsome boys who scuttled out of the gate now and then with fearful backward glances toward the house as if they were afraid of their lives, and never by any chance meant to do what they ought to if they could help it. The girls all looked like their drab-and-straw-colored father, but the boys were handsome little fellows with eyes like their mother and a hunted look about their faces. Miranda in her reflections always called them brats!

"The idea uv him thinkin' I'd swap my little Rose fer his spunky little brats!" That was always her ejaculation before she went in and shut the door.

Five separate times during the five years that had intervened, had Nathan Whitney taken his precise way across the street and preferred his request. In varied forms, and with ever increasing fervor he had pressed his suit, until Miranda had come to believe in his sincere desire for her as a housekeeper, if not as a companion, and she held her head higher with pride, as the proposals increased and the years passed by. Day after day she swept the front stoop, and day after day looked over toward the big house across the way with the question to her soul, "You might uv. Ain't you sorry you didn't?" And always her soul responded, "No, I ain't!"

The last time he came Miranda had her final triumph, for he professed that he had conceived a sort of affection for her, in spite of her red hair and questionable parentage, and the girl had sense enough to see that the highest this man had to give he had laid at her feet. She was gracious, in her quaint way, but she sent him on his way with so decided a refusal that no man in his senses would ever attempt to ask her to marry him again; and after the deed had been done she surveyed her wholesome features in the mirror with entire satisfaction. Not a heartstring of her well packed outfit had been stirred during the five years' courting, only her pride had been rippled pleasantly. But now she knew that it was over; no more could she look at the neglected home across the way and feel that any day she might step in and take possession. She had cut the cold man to his heart, what little chilly heart he had, and he would look her way no more, for she had dared to humble him to confessing affection, and then refused him after all. He would keep his well-trained affections in their place hereafter; and would look about in genuine earnest now to get a housekeeper and a mother for his wild flock which had been making rapid strides on the downward course while he was meandering through the toilsome ways of courtship.

Nathan Whitney looked about to such purpose that he was soon able to have his banns published in the church, and everybody at once began to say how altogether suitable and proper it was for Nathan Whitney to take another wife after all these five long years of waiting and mourning his sweet Eliza; and who in all that country round so fit as Maria Bent to deal with the seven wild unruly Whitneys, young and old. Had she not been mistress of the district school for well nigh twelve years gone, and had she not dealt with the Whitneys time and time again to her own glory and the undoing of their best-laid schemes? Maria Bent was just the one, and Nathan Whitney had been a fool not to ask her before. Maybe she might have saved the oldest boy Allan from disgrace.

Strange to say, as soon as Miranda felt herself safe from becoming related to them, her heart softened toward the little Whitneys. Day after day as she swept the front stoop, after the banns had been published, and looked toward the great house which might have been hers, but by her own act had been put out of her life forever, she sighed and thought of the little Whitneys, and questioned her soul: "Could I? Ought I to uv?" but always her soul responded loyally, "No, you couldn't uv. No, you oughtn't uv. Think o' him! You never could uv stood him. Bah!"

... ... Yet, Miranda, on her rival's wedding day, looked across at the great house, and sang, *sang* her joy of freedom.

"I might uv endured them brats, poor little hanted lookin' creatoors, but I never could a-stood that slab-sided, washed-out, fish-eyed man around, nohow you fixed it. My goody! Think o' them all 'long side o' my little Rose!"

And Miranda went into the house, slamming the door joyfully and singing. David upstairs shaving remarked to Marcia:

"Well, Miranda doesn't seem to regret her single blessedness as yet, dear."

Marcia, trying a bright ribbon on little Rose's curls, answered happily:

"And it's a good thing for us she doesn't. I wonder if she'll go to the wedding."

Miranda, later, after the breakfast was cleared away, announced her intention.

"Yes, I'm goin' jest to show I ain't got no feelin's about it. 'Course she don't know. I don't s'pose he'd ever tell her, 'tain't like him. He's one o' them close, sly men thet think it's cost him something ef he tells a woman ennythin', but I'm goin' jest fer my own satisfaction. Then 'course I'll own I'd kinder like to watch her an' think thet might o' ben me ef I ben willin' to leave little Rose, an' you an'—well, ef I'd a ben *will*in'—which I never was. Yes, course I'm goin'."

CHAPTER 2

THE ceremony was held in the schoolhouse in the afternoon. Maria Bent lived with her old mother in two small rooms back of the post-office, not a suitable place for the wedding of Nathan Whitney's bride; so Maria, by reason of her years of service as teacher, was granted permission to use the school-house.

The joyful scholars, radiant at the thought of a new teacher,—any teacher so it be not Maria Bent,—and excited beyond measure over a holiday and a festivity all their own, joyously trimmed the schoolhouse with roses, hollyhocks and long trailing vines from the woods, and for once the smoky walls and much hacked desks blossomed as the rose smothered in the wealth of nature.

The only children who did not participate in the noisy decorations were the young Whitneys. Like scared yellow leaves in a hurricane they scurried away from the path of the storm and hid from the scene of action, peering with jealous eyes and swelling hearts from safe coverts at the enemy who was scouring the woods and gardens in behalf of her who was about to invade the sacredness of their homes. Not that they had hitherto cared much about that home; but it was all they had and the world looked blank and unlivable to them now with the terror of their school days installed for incessant duty.

The little girls with down-drooped yellow lashes, and peaked, sallow faces strangely like their father's, hurried home to hide away their treasures in secret places in the attic, known only to themselves, and to whisper awesomely about how it would be when "she" came.

"She smiled at me in school yesterday," whispered Helena, the sharp fourteen year old. "It was like a gnarled spot on a sour apple that falls before it's ripe."

"Oh, be careful," hushed Prudence, lifting her thin little hands in dismay. "What if Aunt Jane should hear you and tell her. You know she's going to be our mother, and she can do what she likes then."

"Mother nothing!" flouted Helena grandly, "she'll not mother me, I can tell you that. If she lets me alone I'll stay, but if she tries to boss me I'll run away."

Nevertheless Helena took the precaution to tiptoe lightly to the head of the stairs, to be sure the attic door was closed so that no one could hear

worse'n she did us. Besides—"

"Aw, well you needn't cry. We've got enough to do now to keep quiet, and keep out of the way. Where's Nate?"

"I saw him going down toward the saw mill after school—"

"Nate won't stay here long," stated Helena sagely. "He just despises Maria Bent."

"Where would he go?" said Prudence, drying her tears as her little world broke up bit by bit. "Helena Whitney, he's only ten years old!"

"He's a man!" snapped Helena. "Men are diffrunt. Come on, let's go hide in the bushes and see what they get. The idea of Julia Fargo and Harriet Wells making all that fuss getting flowers for her wedding when they've talked about her so; and only last week she took that lovely book away from Harriet Wells just because she took it out in geography class and began to read."

Hand in hand, with swelling throats and smarting eyes filled with tears they would not shed, the motherless children hurried away to the woods to watch in bitterness of spirit the preparations for the wedding, which was almost like watching the building of their own funeral pyres.

Nevertheless the time of hiding could not be for always and the little brood of Whitneys were still under stern discipline. Aunt Jane held them with no easy hand. Promptly at half-past two they issued forth from the big white house clothed in wedding garments, their respective heads neatly dressed in plait or net or glossy ringlet, or firmly plastered down. Young Nathan's rebellious brown curls were smooth as satin the water from their late anointing trickling down his clammy back as with dogged tread and downcast, insurgent look he marched beside his frightened, meek little sisters to the ceremony which was to them all like a death knell.

The familiar old red school-house appeared in the distance down the familiar old street, yet the choking sensation in their throats, and the strange beating and blurring of their eyes gave it an odd appearance of disaster. That surely could not be the old hickory tree that Nate had climbed so often and hidden behind its ample friendly trunk to watch

Maria Bent as she came forth from the school-house door in search of him. How often had he encircled its shielding trunk to keep out of sight when he saw her looking for him! Now, alas, there would be no sheltering hickory for sanctuary from her strong hand, for Maria Bent would be no longer the school marm merely; she would be at close range in their only home; she would be mother! The name had suddenly taken on a gruesome sound, for they had been told that morning by Aunt Jane as she combed and scrubbed and arrayed them, that such address would be required of them henceforth. Call Maria Bent mother! Never!

Nate as he trudged, thought over all the long list of disrespectful appellations that it had been their custom among themselves to call their teacher, beginning with "Bent Maria" and ending with "M'wry-faced-straighten-er-out"; and inwardly resolved to call her nothing at all, or anything he pleased, all the time knowing that he would never dare.

Miranda, on the other side of the street, watched the disconsolate little procession, with their Aunt Jane bringing up the rear, and thanked her stars that she was not going forth to bind herself to their upbringing.

She had purposely lingered behind the Spaffords as they started to the wedding, saying she would follow with little Rose; and she came out of the front door and locked it carefully, just as the Whitneys issued forth from Aunt Jane's grooming. Rose jumped daintily down the steps, one at a time, watching the toes of her little new pink slippers, and tilting the ruffed pink silk parasol her father had brought her from New York. She looked like a sweet pink human rose, and the little prim Whitneys, sleek and scared though they were, turned envious eyes to watch her, almost forgetting for the moment the lump in their throats and the hot, angry feeling in their hearts, while they took in the beauty of the parasol, the grace of the small light feet, and the bobbing floss of golden curls as Rose skipped along by Miranda's side.

Miranda herself was wearing a new green and brown plaid silk, the pride and glory of her heart, bought with her own money and selected by her beloved Mrs. Marcia on her last trip to New York. Her bonnet was green shirred silk with a tiny green feather, and her red hair looked like burnished copper glinting out beneath. Miranda did not know it, never would, but she was growing to be a most attractive woman, and the twinkle of mischief in her eyes made one always look a second time at her cheerful freckled face.

Proudly she looked down at the dainty Rose, and compared her with the unhappy Whitneys doing the funeral march to their father's wedding. Not for any money would she be today in Maria Bent's place, but she walked the prouder and the more contented that she had had the chance.

There was a pleasant bustle about the school-house door when they all arrived. But the little Whitneys, their feuds laid aside at this time of their

own desk, and the result was unique and startling.

"How touching of them to want to please teacher!" exclaimed Ann Bloodgood, who lived in the next township and therefore did not know the current feeling.

But, however touching, the decorations only served to remind the three older Whitneys of their own mother's funeral. Nate hung his head and frowned hard behind the goldenrod-embowered stove, trying not to see or think of that other day five years ago when odors of flowers filled the air and he had had that same lump in his throat and gasp in his chest. That had been bad enough, but this day was worse. He had half a mind even now to bolt through that school-house door and never come back. But when he looked out to calculate how likely he was to get off without being seen, his father came walking up the school-house path. Maria Bent was hanging on his arm, in bright blue silk with a white lace bonnet, white kid gloves and a lace parasol. She was smirking and smiling to this side and that, and bestowing unwontedly loving greetings on the festive row of school girls lined up on either side of the path, stiff and straight all in their best dresses. "Walking pride," Miranda called it, and secretly exulted that she might have been there if she would; yet did not regret her choice.

Miranda had taken up her position where she could stand Rose on a desk to get a good view of the ceremony, and from her point of vantage she also got a vision of handsome little Nathan Whitney, his well-brushed Sunday suit squeezed between the stove and the wall, his soapy curls rumpled by the goldenrod, his stiff collar holding up a very trembling chin surmounted by hard little lips and an angry frown. It was plain that young Nathan was by no means happy at his father's wedding. Something in the whole slouch of his sturdy little figure touched Miranda and she watched him with a hitherto unsuspected sympathy. It was not to be expected of course that a bad boy like Nate Whitney would like to have a stern schoolteacher for his new mother. A gleam of something like pity shone in her eyes as she reflected how often Maria Bent would probably get her "comeuppance" for marrying Nathan Whitney; and how often little Nate Whitney would probably get his "comeuppance" for his pranks. Of the two Miranda was just the least bit inclined to side with the boy for the sake of his half-brother Allan with whom she had gone to school.

Miranda looked up to find him again after the prayer was over, but though her eyes searched quite carefully behind the stove, and under the bowers of goldenrod, he was gone. High in the branches of the friendly hickory, his Sunday clothes bearing a jagged tear in the seat of the trousers, his collar awry, and the shine of his Sunday shoes hopelessly marred and scratched, Nathan Whitney the second surveyed the scene. The prayer had been long enough for him to reach his old shelter in safety, and only the Whitney twins, Julia and Julius, and the five-year-old brother Samuel had seen his escape; and they were too frightened to tell. Miranda's searching gaze finally caught the uplifted look of the twins and Sammy, and following it presently saw the tremble of old hickory. She quickly lowered her eyes, knowing instinctively what had happened, but before she lowered them she caught the gleam of a pair of sorrowful brown eyes so like another pair of brown eyes she knew, looking between the leaves, and they haunted her all through the day.

The ceremony was long over and all the guests had gone home to discuss at length how "he looked," and how "she looked," and the prospect of happiness for the two who had been united in marriage.

Miranda had changed her green and brown plaid silk for a brown calico and a white apron, and was stirring up muffins for tea when she thought she saw a stealthy little figure stealing through the yard close by the hedge, but the early dusk was coming down and it was quite easy to fancy it had been only the shadows on the grass. Miranda was just about to light a candle and begin to set the table, but it was early yet for Mr. David would be late coming home from the office today on account of the time he had taken off for the wedding; and instead she took a bowl and went out to see if she could find some late yellow raspberries on the vines, though she knew quite well there were not likely to be any.

Humming a lively little tune she approached the berry vines, her sharp eyes studying the while the great leaves of pieplant growing next the hedge. They were moving now, stirring gently, almost imperceptibly, one minute, the next bobbing vigorously back and forth as if they had suddenly become animate. Miranda watched them stealthily, the while walking deliberately past them and humming her tune. The leaves became absolutely still as she passed them, though she did not turn her eyes down to them noticeably, but went on a little further and knelt down by the berry bushes voicing her tune in words now:

"Thur wuz a man in our town,
An' he wuz wondrus wise,

.... uark. Here's three whole ras'berries right clost together an' I come real nigh missin' 'em."

She cast an eye toward the pieplant leaves, but they remained motionless. Perhaps she had made a mistake after all. Perhaps there had been no dark little figure stealing along by the hedge. Perhaps her imagination had played her false.

She kept on feeling after berries that were not there, and finally after having secured not more than a handful, she crept softly back by the pieplant bed, for she thought she had heard a soft gasp like the catching of breath, and something stirred within her. She must find out what was moving the leaves.

Suddenly she set her bowl down on the grass and made a soft dive with her hands, lifting up two or three broad leaves and peering under.

It was almost dark now and the forlorn little figure close under the hedge could scarcely be seen, but Miranda's eyes were keen and kind, and she made out the outline of Nate Whitney's curly head, so sleek in the morning, now tousled and rough. He shrank back with his face in the grass, as she lifted the leaves, hoping to escape her notice, but she reached out her two strong hands and drew him forth resisting furiously.

"Lemme alone. I ain't doin' you any harm!" he declared sulkily as she drew his head and shoulders out from the entangling stalks.

There was light enough in the garden to see his face, tear-stained and smeared with mud streaks. His collar was crushed and twisted awry, and his jacket had a great jagged tear in one elbow.

"You poor little motherless sinner!" ejaculated Miranda in a tone she had never used in her life before except for little Rose.

Suddenly she sat down plump on the garden walk and took the forlorn little fellow into her arms, at least as much as she could get hold of, for he was still wriggling and twisting away from her strong hand with all his discomfited young might.

She stooped over his dirty fierce young face and laid her lips on his forehead.

"You poor little soul, I know how you feel and I don't blame you one mite," she whispered, her strong young arms enwrapping him gently.

Then quite suddenly the struggling ceased, the fierce wiry body relaxed, the dirty face and curly head buried themselves quite childishly in her arms, the boy sobbed as if his heart would break, and clung to her as if his life depended on it.

Something wonderfully sweet and new sprang up in Miranda's breast, motherhood stirring in her soul. The clinging hands, the warm wet face, the pitiful sight of this sorrowful child in place of the saucy, impudent, self-possessed boy who dared any mischief that his bright restless mind suggested, touched her heart in a new way. A fierce desire seized her to protect and love him, this boy who needed someone sorely, and for the first time a regret stole into her heart that she was not his new mother. What a thing it would be to have those clinging arms belong to her! Then a wicked exultant thrill passed through her. She had not "walked pride" with Nathan Whitney, but his son had turned to her for comfort, and she loved the boy for it with all her heart. Maria Bent might hold her head high and reign severely in his home, but *she*, Miranda Griscom, would love the little son and help him out of his scrapes from this time forth.

"There, there," she soothed, passing her rough, work-worn hand over the tumbled curls and exulting in their tendency to wrap about her fingers. How soft they were, like a baby's, and yet they belonged to that hard, bad little boy she had always called a "brat!"

"There, there! Just cry it out," she murmured. "I know. I jest guess I know all how you feel. You needn't to mind me. I've been fixed myself, so I didn't like things pretty much, an' I kin see you ain't overly pleased at the change over to your house. You jest cry good an' hard oncet, an' it'll make you feel better. Ef you can't do it hard 'nough by yerself I'll hep you—" and Miranda laid her freckled face on the little muddy cheek of the boy and let her tears mingle with his.

Perhaps it was those hot tears falling on his face, tears that were not his own, that called him back to his boy senses and brought to an end the first crying spell he remembered since he was six years old when Aunt Jane sneered at him and called him a cry-baby, that time he had cut his foot on a scythe. He had been a self-contained, hard, bad, little man ever since till now, when all the foundations of his being seemed shaken with this unexpected sympathy from one whom he had hitherto ranked among his enemies.

His sobs stopped as suddenly as they had begun and for some time he lay still in her arms, his head pressed against her shoulder where she had drawn it, his breath coming hot and quick against her face.

"Can't you tell me what's the matter? Is't anythin' special?" asked the girl gently. One would scarcely have known Miranda's voice. All the hard-

and I guess they wouldn't enny of 'em do much better in your place. I never did admire her much myself, so I ken see how you look at it."

"I hate her!" reiterated the boy again, but this time not so fiercely. "I hate her and I won't let her be my mother, ever! Say, why didn't *you* be it?"

The question was balm and pride to the heart of Miranda. She put her arms the closer around the lonely boy and rocked him gently back and forth, and then smoothed his hair back from his hot dirty forehead. The marvel was he let her do it and did not squirm away.

"Why didn't I? Bless him! Well, I didn't think I'd like it enny better'n you do her. B'sides, ef I had, you'd a hated *me* then."

The boy looked at her steadily through the twilight as though he were turning it over in his mind and then suddenly broke into a shy smile.

"Mebbe I would," he said with honest eyes searching her face, and then half shamefaced, he added shyly: "But anyhow I like you now."

A wild sweet rush of emotion flooded Miranda's soul. Not since she left her unloved, unloving grandmother Heath who lived next door, and came to live with David and Marcia Spafford receiving wages, doing honest work in return, and finding a real home, had such sweet surprise and joy come to her. Sweeter even than the little cherished Rose's kisses was this shy, veiled admiration of the man-child whose lonely life she seemed somehow strangely to understand. All at once she seemed to know how and why he had got the name of being a bad boy, and her heart went out to him as to a kindred spirit. She had seen the soul of him looking out of his beautiful brown eyes in the dusk at her, and she knew he was not all bad, and that it had mostly been the fault of other people when he had really done wrong.

Miranda's arms in their warm pressure answered the boy's words, and she stooped again and laid her lips on his forehead lingeringly, albeit as shyly as a boy might have done it. Miranda was not one to show deep emotion and she was more stirred than ever before.

"Well, I guess we sort o' b'long to each other somehow. Ennyhow we'll be friends. Say, didn't you tear your cloes when you went up that hick'ry?" The child in her arms suddenly straightened up and became the boy with mischief in his eyes and a knowing tilt to his handsome head.

"Say, did you see me go up that tree?"

"No, but I saw you gone; and I saw Sammy's eyes lookin' up, an' I saw the hick'ry movin' some, so I calc'lated you was up there, all right."

"An' you won"t tell?" doubtfully.

"Course I won't tell. It's none o' my business, an' b'sides I could see you wasn't enjoyin' yerse'f to the weddin'. What's more, I'll mend them cloes. There ain't no reason fer M'ria Bent as was, to come inspectin' you yet a whiles. You kin shin up the kitchen roof, can't yeh, to my winder, an' you take off them rips an' tears an' hop into my bed? I'll come up an' mend yeh so's she won't know. Then you ken shin up a tree to yer own winder t' hum an' go to bed, an' like's not she'll never notice them cloes till yer Aunt Jane's gone, an' she'll think they been tore an' mended sometime back, an' she ain't got no call to throw 'em up to yeh. Hed yer supper?"

"Naw. Don't want any."

"That's all right. I'll bring you up some caraway cookies. You like 'em don't yeh? Er hev yeh et too much weddin' cake?"

"Didn't touch their old wedding cake," said the boy sulkily.

"Boy, didn't you go home 'tall since you was in the hick'ry? Wall, I swan! To think you'd miss the reception with all them good things to eat! You must a felt pretty bad. Never mind you, honey. You do's I tell yeh. Just shin right up that roof. Here, eat them raspberries first, they ain't many but they'll stay yeh. I got some fried chicken left over. Don't you worry. Now, let's see you get up there."

Miranda helped Nate from the back kitchen window to mount to the roof and saw him climb lightly and gleefully in at her window, then she bustled in to put supper on the table. Mr. David was not home yet when everything was ready, so with a glass of milk, a plate of bread, jelly, and chicken, and another of cookies she slipped up the back stairs to her small boy, and found him quite contentedly awaiting her coming, his eyes shining a welcome to her through the gathering darkness of the room, as he might have done to any pal in a youthful conspiracy.

"I've got a boarder," she explained grimly a few minutes afterward to the astonished Mrs. Marcia, coming downstairs with her lighted candle, a small pair of trousers and a jacket over her arm.

"A boarder!" Mrs. Marcia had learned to expect the unusual from Miranda, but this was out of the ordinary even for Miranda, at least without permission.

"Yes, you ken take it off my wages. I don't guess he'll remain more'n an hour or so, leastways I'll try to get him off soon fer his own sake. It's that the first day all tore up. She'd get him at a disadvantage. Ain't you got a patch would do to put under this tear, Mrs. Marcia? I took him up some supper. I knowed you wouldn't care, an' I want you should take it off my wages. Yes, that's right. I'll feel better about it ef you do, then I could do it agin ef the notion should take me. I owe a little sumpin' to that boy fer my present state of freedom an' independence, an' I kinda take a likin' to him when he's cryin' you know. After all, I do' no's'e was ever so awful bad."

Mrs. Marcia laid a tender understanding touch on her handmaiden's arm, and with a smile in the dimple by the off-corner of her mouth, and a tear in the eye that Miranda could not see, went to get the patch.

Young Nathan inside of two hours departed by the way of the roof, washed and combed, mended and pressed, as well as Aunt Jane could have done it; but with more than he had had for years, a heart that was almost comforted. He felt that now he had at least one friend in the world who understood him, and meditated as he slid down the kitchen-shed roof, whether it might not be practicable for him to grow up fast and marry Miranda so no one else would carry her off. By the time he had scaled his own kitchen roof and cautiously removed his clothing, hung it up and crept to his own little bed, he had, it is true, quite forgotten this vague idea; but the comfort in his heart remained, and made it possible for him to waken cheerfully the next morning to his new world without that sinking feeling that had been in his heart and stomach ever since he knew that Maria Bent was to be his father's wife.

So that was how it all came about that Miranda Griscom became mother-confessor and chief-comforter to Nathan Whitney's second son, and Nathan became the slave and adorer of little Rose Schuyler Spafford when she was five-years-old-going-on-to-six; and it all began in the year 1838.

CHAPTER 3

THERE was a chapter in Miranda's life that she had never told to a living soul, and which only on rare occasions did she herself take out of her heart and look over. It was only when the wellsprings of her very being were deeply touched in some way as in the quiet and dark of her starlit window; or when she was on her knees at her queer devotions, that she let her mind dwell upon it.

Miranda was twenty-two years old, and entirely heart whole, yet there had been and still was a romance in her life as sweet and precious as any that more favored girls had experienced. That it had been sad and brief, and the hope of its ever coming to anything had long since departed from her heart, made it no less precious to her. It was on account of her strength and sweetness of character, her bubbling good nature and interest in others, and her keen sense of humor that her experience had not hardened or sharpened her one mite. She was one of those strong souls who through not having has learned to forget self, and be content in the joy of others. There was not a fibre of selfishness in the whole of her quaint, intense, delightful make-up. She lived her somewhat lonely life and picked up what crumbs of pleasure she could find; fought her merry, sometimes questionable, warfare for those she loved; served them worshipfully; would give her life for theirs any day; yet kept in her heart one strong secret shrine for the love of her young heart furnished royally with all the hopes and yearnings that any girl knows.

Years ago, it seemed centuries now, before David had brought his girl bride to the old house next door to Grandmother Heath's, where Miranda had been a schoolgirl, eleven—twelve—thirteen years old, there had been a hero in her life. No one had known it, not even the hero. But no knight of old ever was beloved or watched or exalted by fair lady more than was Allan Whitney, half brother of young Nathan—for Maria Bent was of course old Nathan Whitney's third wife.

Allan Whitney was tall and strong, with straight dark hair that fell over his forehead till he had continually to toss it back; a mouth that drooped pathetically above a strong purposeful chin; eyes that held depths of fierceness and sadness that only a passionate temperament knows how to combine; and a reputation altogether worse than any boy that had ever been brought up in the town.

Allan Whitney had been quick and bright, but he would not study at school, and he would not go to work. He had been very much in his time as young Nathan was not, only more so, Miranda thought as she placed the facts honestly before her in the starlight, while she watched to see if there would be a light in the boy's window across the way.

Allan had been in continual rebellion against the universe. In school he was whipped whenever the teacher felt out of sorts with anybody, and he took it with the careless jocular air of one who knows he could "lick the teacher into the middle of next week" if he undertook the job. As it was he generally allowed the chastisement for the sake of the relief from monotony for the rest of the scholars. He would wink slyly at Miranda who sat down in a front seat demurely studying her spelling, as he lounged forward and held out his hand. By a sort of freemasonry he knew her to be of the same temper as himself, and that she both understood and sympathized with him. Five desks back Rowena Higginson was in tears on account of his sufferings, and gentle Annetta Bloodgood turned pale with the sound of each blow from the ferrule, half shuddering in time to the chastisement; but Allan Whitney hugely enjoyed their sentimental sufferings. He knew that every boy in the room admired him for the way he took his whippings, and sought provocations for like martyrdom, that they might emulate his easy air of indifference. When his punishment was over Allan would seek his seat, lazily, a happy grimace on his face, another wink for Miranda, with sometimes a lollipop or some barley sugar laid surreptitiously on her desk as he passed by, and a knowing tweak of her red pigtails, which endearments were waited for on her part with a trembling eagerness that he never suspected. She was only a smart child who knew almost as much as a boy about a boy's code of life, and took his good-natured tormentings as well as a boy could have done; therefore he enjoyed tormenting her.

Nevertheless, though Miranda witnessed his punishments with outward serenity and gloried in his indifference to them, her young soul was filled with bitterness against the teachers for their treatment of her hero, and many a hard knock of discipline did she lay up in store for those same teachers in the future if ever it came her way to give it; and she generally managed sometime, somehow to give it.

"Miss Menchant, is this your hankercher?" she asked sweetly one day after Allan had retired indifferently from a whipping which Miranda knew must have hurt, given merely because Miss Menchant found a large drawing of herself in lifelike lines on the blackboard near Allan's desk, and couldn't locate the artist.

Miss Menchant said severely that it was—as if Miranda were in some way to blame for it's having been on the floor—as indeed she was, having filched it from her teacher's pocket in the coat-room and brought it into the schoolroom ready bated for her prey.

A moment later Miss Menchant picked up the handkerchief from where Miranda had laid it on the desk at her hand, and wiped her face, immediately thereafter dropping it in haste with aloud exclamations and putting her hand with pain to her nose, while a fine large honeybee flew away through the open door of the schoolhouse.

"Miranda!" called the suffering teacher. "Miranda Griscom!" But Miranda, like a good child, had taken her dinner pail and gone home. Her bright brown eye might have been seen taking observations through a knothole at the end of the schoolhouse, but Miss Menchant didn't happen to be looking that way, and when the next morning the teacher asked the little girl if she noticed anything on the handkerchief when she picked it up, Miranda's eyes were sweetly unconscious of the large red knob on the teacher's nose as she answered serenely:

"I didn't take notice to nothin'."

The next time that Allan Whitney was called up for discipline the ruler which usually played a prominent part in the affair was strangely missing, and might have been found in Miranda Griscom's desk if anyone had known where to look for it. It met a watery grave that night in the old mill stream down behind the mill wheel, in company with several of its successors of later years.

Time cures all things, and they usually had women teachers in that school. Allan presently grew so large that few women teachers could whip him and it then became a vital question, when engaging a new teacher, as to whether or not she would be able to "lick" Allan Whitney. One winter they tried a man, a little, knotty shrimp of a man he was, with a high reputation as to intellect, but no more appreciation of a boy than if he had been a boiled owl. Those were days that delighted the souls of the scholars of that school, for it was soon noised abroad that every day was a delight because every day a new drama of contest was flung on the stage for their delectation.

Now, there was behind the platform, where the teacher's desk and chair
were placed, a long, dark room where coats and dinner pails were kept. It

a wide shelf or ledge behind the teacher's desk. This was frequently
adorned with a row of dinner pails. A door to the right of the platform
opened into the teacher's closet, and was usually kept closed, while that to
the left opened into the girls' cloak room and was usually standing open.
Miranda's desk was directly in front of this door, the teacher having found
it handy to have Miranda where he could keep a weather eye out for plots
under a serene and innocent exterior.

When the man teacher, Mr. Applethorn by name, had been in the school
about three weeks and had tried every conceivable plan for the conquering
of Allan Whitney save the time-worn one of "licking" him, it became
apparent that the issue was to be brought to a climax. Miranda had heard
low words from Allan to his friend Bud Hendrake concerning what he
meant to do if "old Appleseed tried it," and while the little girl had great
faith in Allan's strength of body and quickness of mind over against the
little flabby body and quickly aroused temper of the teacher, she
nevertheless reflected that behind him were all the selectmen, and
authority was always at war with poor Allan. It would go hard with him
this time, she knew, if the matter were put in the hands of the selectmen.
She had heard Grandfather Heath talking about it. "One more outrage and
we're done with him." That sentence sent terror to the heart of Miranda,
for the long stretches of school days unenlivened by the careless smile and
merry sayings of Allan Whitney were to her unbearable to think about.
Something must be done to save Allan, and she must do it, for there was
no one else to care. So Miranda had lain awake for a long time trying to
devise a plan by which the injustice done by the teacher to Allan could not
only be avenged, but the immediate danger of a fight between Allan and
the teacher averted, at least for a time. If Allan fought with the teacher and
"licked" him everybody would be sorry for the teacher, for nobody liked
Allan; that is, nobody that had any authority. There it was, always
authority against Allan! Poor little Miranda tossed on her small bed and
thought, and finally fell asleep with her problem unsolved; but she started

for school the next morning with firmly set lips and a determined frown. She would do something, see if she wouldn't!

And then Grandmother Heath called her back to carry a pail of sour cream to Granny MacVane's on her way to school.

Now ordinarily Miranda would not have welcomed the errand away around by Granny MacVane's *before school*—and grandmother was very particular that she should go before school—she liked to get to school early and play hide and seek in the yard, and Grandmother Heath knew it and disapproved. School was not established for amusement, but for education, she frequently remarked when remonstrating with Miranda for starting so early; but this particular morning the girl's face brightened and she took the shining tin pail with alacrity and demurely responded, "Yes ma'am," when her grandmother repeated the command to be sure and go *before* school. She was so nice and obedient about it that the old lady looked after her suspiciously, having learned that the ways of Miranda were devious, and when her exterior was calm, then was the time to be on the alert.

For Miranda had suddenly seen light in the darkness with the advent on the scene of this pail of sour cream. Sour cream would keep. That is it would only grow sourer, which was desirable in a thing like sour cream. There was no reason in the world why that cream had to go to Granny MacVane's before school, especially when it might come in handy for something else besides making gingerbread for Granny MacVane. Besides, Granny MacVane lived beyond the school-house and Grandmother Heath would never know whether she went before or after. Sour cream was a delicacy frequently sent to old Mrs. MacVane, and if she brought the message, "Granny says she's much obliged Gran'ma," there would be no question, and likely nothing further ever thought about it.

Besides, Miranda was willing to take a chance if the stakes were high enough, so she hurried happily off to school with her head held high and the sour cream pail clattering against her dinner pail with reckless hilarity; while Miranda laid her neat little plans.

Arrived at the school-house, she deposited the pail of sour cream together with its mate the dinner pail inconspicuously on the inner ledge of the window over the teacher's desk-chair. The ledge was wide and the pails almost out of sight from the schoolroom. At noon, however, Miranda, after eating her lunch, replaced her empty dinner pail and made a careful rearrangement of all the pails on the ledge, her own and others, so that they were grouped quite innocently nearer to the front edge. Miranda herself was early seated at her desk studying demurely when the others came in.

The very atmosphere that afternoon seemed electric. Even the very little
scholars seemed to understand that something was going to happen before

CHAPTER 4

MIRANDA had played her cards well. She sat studiously in her seat until everybody was out of the schoolroom but Mr. Applethorn, Allan and herself, and then she raised her hand demurely for permission to speak:

"Teacher, please may I go's soon 'z I finish my 'gzamples? Grandma wants me to go to Granny MacVane's on a errand, an' she don't want me to stay out after dark."

The teacher gave a curt permission. He had no time just then to fathom Miranda Griscom's deeps, and had always felt that she belonged to the enemy. She was as well out of the room when he gave Allan Whitney his dues.

Miranda worked away vigorously. The examples were already finished, but she had no mind to leave until the right moment. Such studious ways in Miranda were astonishing, and if Mr. Applethorn had not been otherwise occupied he would certainly have suspected something, seeing Miranda, the usually alert one, bending over her slate, a stubby pencil in her hand, her brows wrinkled hard over a supposedly perplexing question, her two red plaits sticking out at each side, and no eyes nor ears for what was going on in the playground.

Allan Whitney sat serenely whittling a small stick into a very tiny sword, and half whistling under his breath until the master, in a voice that was meant to be stentorian, uttered a solemn: "Silence, sir! I say, *Silence!*"

Allan looked up pleasantly.

"All right sir, just as you say sir."

The master was growing angry. Miranda saw it out of the tail of her eye. He glowered at the boy a minute.

"I said *silence*," he roared. "You've no need to answer further. Just keep silence!"

"Very well, sir, I heard you sir, and I said all right sir, just as you say sir," answered Allan sunnily again, with the most aggravating smile on his face, but not a shade of impudence in his voice. Allan knew how to be impudent in a perfectly respectful way.

"Hold your tongue, sir!" fairly howled the master.

"Oh, thank you, I will sir," said Allan, but it was the teacher who, red and angry, found he had to hold his, while Allan had the last word, for just then the boy who had been appointed to ring the bell appeared in the door

...to his desk, drew forth the ferrule, and threw it with skilful twirl straight into the face of the boy. Then Allan, accepting the challenge, arose and came forward to the platform, but he did not stoop to pick up the ruler and bring it with him according to custom. Instead he came as a man might have come who had just been insulted, his head held high, his eyes glowing darkly in his white set face, for the ruler had struck him across the mouth, and its sting had sunk into his soul. In that blow seemed concentrated all the injustices of all the years when he had been misjudged by his teachers and fellow-townsmen. Not but that he had not been a mischievous, bad boy often and often, but not always; and he resented the fact that when he did try to do right nobody would give him credit for it.

It was just at this crucial moment that Miranda arose with her completed arithmetic paper and fluttered conspicuously up to the desk.

"May I go now, teacher?" she asked sweetly, "I've got 'em all done, every one."

The master waved her away without ceremony. She was to him like a gadfly annoying when he needed all his senses to master the trouble in hand.

Miranda slipped joyously into the cloak room apparently as unconscious of Allan Whitney standing close beside her, as if he had been miles away; and a moment thereafter those who sat in the extreme back of the room might have seen the dim flutter of a brown calico sunbonnet landing on top of the dinner pails just over the master's head, if they had not been too occupied with the changing visage of the master, and the quiet form of Allan standing in defiant attitude before him. Mr. Applethorn was a great believer in deliberation, and was never afraid of a pause. He thought it impressive. At this moment, while he gathered all his courage for the encounter that he knew was before him, he paused and expected to quell Allan Whitney by the glance of his two angry eyes.

The schoolmaster was still seated, though drawn up to his full height with folded arms, looking dignified as he knew how to look, and far more impressive than if he had been standing in front of his tall pupil. Suddenly, before a word had been spoken, and very quietly for a thing of metal, the tin pail on the ledge over his chair began to move forward, as if pushed by a phalanx of its fellows from behind. It came to the edge,—it toppled,—and a broad avalanche of thick white substance gushed forth, preceded by a giddy tin cover, which reeled and pirouetted for a moment on the master's astonished head, took a step down his nose, and waltzed off to the platform and under the stove. This was followed by a concluding white deluge as the pail descended and settled down over the noble brows of Mr. Applethorn, who arose in haste and horror, dripping sour cream, spluttering and snorting like a porpoise, amid a howling, screaming, shouting mob of irreverent scholars who were laughing until the tears streamed down their cheeks.

Miranda, appearing penitently at the door of the cloak room, her brown sunbonnet in her hand, ready tears prepared to be shed if need be, at the loss of her precious sour cream,—accidentally knocked over when she went to get her sunbonnet which some malicious girl must have put up high out of her reach,—found no need for any further efforts on her part. Obviously the fight was over. The schoolmaster was in no condition to administer either justice or injustice to anybody.

Allan Whitney at this crisis arose magnificently to the occasion. With admirable solicitude he relieved the schoolmaster of his unwelcome helmet, and with his own soiled and crumpled handkerchief wiped the lumps of sour cream from his erstwhile adversary's features.

For one blessed hilarious moment the schoolmaster had stood helpless and enraged, blinded and speechless, choking and gasping and dripping sour cream from every point of his hair, nose, collar, chin, and the tips of his very fingers; and the wild mob of hysterical pupils stood on the desks and viewed him, bending double with their mirth, or jumping up and down in their ecstasy. The next moment Allan Whitney had taken command, and with one raised hand had silenced the hilarity, with a second motion had cleared the room, and a low word to one of his devoted slaves brought a pail of water to his side. Then in the seclusion of the empty schoolroom he applied himself to the rescue of Mr. Applethorn.

Miranda, in the shelter of the cloak room door, secure for the moment from the cream-filled eyes of the teacher, watched her hero in awe as he mopped away at his enemy, as tenderly and kindly as if he had been a little child in trouble. She was too filled with mixed emotions to care to play the guileless, saucy part she had prepared for herself in this comedy. She was filled with dread lest after all Allan did not approve of what she had done, and did not like it. That he would be in the least deceived by her sunbonnet trick she never for a moment expected. That he would be angry because she had stopped the fight had ...

...ping out the victim's ... gave the cringing Miranda a large, kind, appreciative wink. Suddenly her sun rose high once more, and her heart sprang lightly up again. She responded with her tongue in her cheek, and a knowing grimace, departing, warmed and satisfied, taking the precaution to make her exit through the window of the cloak room. Down behind the alders by the creek, however, her natural man asserted itself, and she sat down to laugh till she cried over the spectacle of her teacher in a tin pail enveloped in sour cream. Next morning she found a large piece of spruce gum in her desk with a bit of paper wrapped around it on which was written in Allan's familiar scrawl:

"You are a little brick."

The strange thing about it all was that Allan and Mr. Applethorn became excellent friends after that; but the selectmen, though they offered every inducement in their power, could not prevail upon the teacher to remain longer than the end of the month. Poor little Mr. Applethorn could not get over his humiliation before his scholars, and he never quite understood how that sour cream got located over his head, though Allan gave a very plausible explanation and kept him in some mysterious way from making too close an investigation.

After that Allan Whitney always had a glance and a wink, and on rare occasions, a smile, for Miranda, but the boy did not come back to school again after Mr. Applethorn left, and the little girl seldom saw him except on the street. However, her worship of him relaxed no whit and her young heart resented the things that were said about him. Always she was on the watch to do him a good turn, but not for a long time did it come and then it came with a vengeance, a short, sharp trial of her loyalty.

CHAPTER 5

IT was a bitter cold night in November and Miranda had crept up close to the fireplace with her spelling book—not that she cared in the least for her spelling lesson, though there was to be a spelling-down contest the next day in school, but her spelling book was always a good excuse to Grandma Heath for not knitting or spinning of an evening.

Grandpa Heath came in presently, stamping away the snow, and shutting the outside door noisily. One could see he was excited. He strode across the room and hung up the big key that locked the old smokehouse door. Mr. Heath was constable and the old smokehouse was being used for a lockup. It was plain that something had happened.

Miranda looked up alertly, but cast down her eyes at once to her book and was apparently a diligent scholar, even conning her words half aloud. She knew by experience that if she appeared to be listening, all the news would be saved till she was sent off to bed, and then she would have to lie on the floor in the cold with her ear to the pipe hole that was supposed to warm her room in order to get necessary information. If she kept still and was absorbed in her work the chances were her grandfather would forget she was there.

He hung up his coat, muffler and cap, and sat down heavily in his chair across the table from his wife, who was diligently knitting a long gray stocking. The light of the one candle that was frugally burning high on the shelf over the fireplace, flickered fitfully over the whole room and made the old man's face look ashen gray with shadows as he began to talk, nervously fingering his scraggly gray beard:

"Well, I guess we've had a murder!" he spoke shakily, as if he could not himself quite comprehend the fact he was imparting.

"You *guess!*" said his wife sharply, "Don't you *know?* There ain't any halfway about a murder usually."

"Well, he ain't dead yet, but there ain't much chance fer his life. I guess he'll pass away 'fore the mornin'."

"Who? Why don't you ever tell the whole story?" snapped Grandmother Heath excitedly.

"Why, it's old Enoch Taylor. Didn't I say in the first place?"

"No, you didn't. Who done it?"

"Allan Whitney,—leastways he was comin' away with a gun when we

...point. Miranda's spelling book fell clattering to the hearth, where it knocked off the cover from the bowl of yeast set to rise by the warmth, but when her startled grandparents turned to look at her she was apparently sound asleep, sitting on her little cushion on the hearth with her head against the fire jamb.

Her grandmother arose and gave her a vigorous shaking.

"M'randy, git right up off'n that hearth and go to bed. It beats all how a great girl like you can't keep awake to get her lessons. You might a fell in the fire. Wake up, I tell you, an' go to bed this minute!"

Miranda awoke with studied leisure, yawning and dazed, and admirably unconscious of her surroundings. Slowly she picked up her book, rubbing her drowsy eyes, lighted her candle and dragged herself yawning up the stairs to her room, but when she arrived there she did not prepare for bed. Instead she wrapped herself in a quilt and lay down with her ear to the stovepipe hole, her whole body tense and quivering with agony.

The old couple waited until the stair door was latched and the girl's footsteps unmistakably toward the top of the stair, then the Grandmother spoke:

"I'm real glad he's got caught now 'fore he growed up any bigger. I always was afraid M'randy'd take a notion to him an' run off like her mother did. He's good lookin',—the kind like her father was, and such things run in the blood. She was real fond of him a couple of years back— used to fly up like a scratch cat every time any body mentioned his cuttin's up, but she ain't mentioned him lately."

"Aw—you didn't need to worry 'bout that I guess," said her husband meditatively, "he wouldn't ever have took to her. Red hair and a little turned up nose like hers don't go down with these young fellers. Besides, she ain't nothin' but a child, an' he's most a grown man."

"She ain't so bad looking," bristled her grandmother with asperity, and it is a pity that poor, plain Miranda, who fancied herself a blot on the face of the earth for homeliness, could not have overheard her, for it would have softened her heart toward her hard, unloving grandmother to an astonishing degree. Miranda knew that she was a trial to her relatives, and never fancied that they cared for her in the least.

But though Miranda lay on the floor until her grandparents came upstairs for the night, she heard no more about the murder or Allan. Wrapped in her quilt she crept to the window and looked out through the snowy night. There was no wind, and the snow came down like fine powder, small and still, but invincible and steady. Out through the white veil she could dimly see the dark walls of the old smokehouse, white-capped and still.

Out there in the cold and dark and snow was Allan,—her fine, strong, merry Allan! It seemed incredible! He was there charged with murder! and awaiting the morrow! As had happened before, she, Miranda, was the only one in the whole wide world who seemed to have a mind to save him.

When she had first heard her grandfather's words downstairs her heart had almost frozen within her, and for once her natural cunning had almost deserted her. When her book fell it was with difficulty that she kept herself from crying out; but she had sense enough left to put her head against the fireplace and pretend to be asleep. As she closed her eyes the vision of the great black key hanging on the wall beside the clock seemed burned into her brain. It was the symbol of Allan's imprisonment, and it seemed to mock her from its nail, and challenge her to save her hero now if she could.

She had known from the first instant that she would save him, or at least that she would do all in her power to do so. The key had flung her the challenge, and her plan had been forming even as she listened to the story. Now she went over it carefully in every detail.

Out there in the smokehouse Allan was stiff and cold. She knew the smooth, chilly floor of hard clay, the rough, unfriendly feel of the brick walls with the mortar hanging in great blotches over their surface. On the dim raftered ceiling still hung a ham or two, because it was nearer to the house than the new smokehouse, where most of the winter stores were kept—for the lockup was seldom used, in fact had only been called into requisition twice in the three years that Mr. Heath had been constable— and it was handy to run to the old smokehouse door when they needed a slice of ham. Ah, that was an idea. Allan would need food. He could take one of those hams. Her busy brain thought it all out as an older girl might have done, and as soon as she heard the distant rumble of her grandfather's comfortable snore, she crept softly about her preparations. It was too early to make any very decided moves, for her grandmother, though quite deaf, was not always a ready sleeper, and had a way of "sensing" things that she could not hear. It would not be well to arouse grandmother's suspicions and spoil the whole scheme, so she moved cautiously.

Under the eaves, opening through her tiny closet, there stood a trunk containing some of the clothes that used to be her mother's, and she

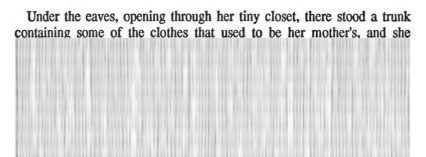

in the middle of her night's sleep. There was no use at all in attempting that, even if it were safe for Allan to delay to drink it, which it was not. But the overcoat he could wear away and no one be any the wiser. Grandmother would not overhaul that trunk for any vagrant moths until next spring now, and what mattered it then what she thought about its absence? As like as not she would be glad to have it gone because it belonged to the hated man who had run away from their daughter, and left her and her little red-haired child to be a burden.

She hesitated about lighting a candle, finally deciding not to risk it, and crept softly into the eaves closet on her hands and knees in the dark, going by her sense of feeling straight to the little hair trunk, and finding the overcoat at the very bottom. She put the other things carefully away, and got back quietly to her room again with the coat, hugging it like a treasure. She laid her cheek for an instant against the worn collar and had a fleeting thrill of affection for the wanderer who had deserted his family, just because the coat was his and was helping her to help Allan.

People were "early to bed and early to rise" in those days. Mr. and Mrs. Heath had retired to their slumber at nine o'clock that night. It was ten before Miranda left her window to stir about the room. The old clock in the kitchen had struck eleven before she found the overcoat and had put everything back in the trunk.

She waited until she had counted out the slow strokes of twelve from the clock before she dared steal down-stairs and softly take the key from its nail by the clock. The cold iron of the key bit into her trembling fingers as if it had been alive, and she almost dropped it. She stood shaking with cold and fright, for it seemed as if every board in the floor that she stepped upon creaked. Once she fell over her grandmother's rocking chair and the rockers dug into her ankles as if they had a grudge against her. Her nerves were so keyed up that the hurt brought tears to her Spartan eyes, and she had to sit down for a minute to bear the pain.

She had carefully canvassed the idea of going out of the door downstairs and had given it up. There was too much risk. First the door opened noisily, and the bar that was put across it at night fitted tightly. It was liable to make a loud grating sound when it was moved. Also, the snow was deep enough that footprints by the door would be noticeable in the morning unless it snowed harder than it was doing now and the wind blew to cover them up. Besides, it would be terrible if any one should see her coming out the door and it should come to her Grandfather's ears that she had done this thing. He would never forgive her and she would have to run away. But worst of all, she dreaded being seen and stopped before she had accomplished her purpose, for the downstairs door was just under her grandmother's window. Therefore, the key secure, she slipped softly into the pantry, found half a loaf of bread, two turnovers and some cookies, and with her booty crept back upstairs again.

When she was at last safely back in her room she drew a long sigh of relief and sat down for a moment to listen and be sure that she had not disturbed the sleepers, then she tied the key on a strong string and hung it around her neck. Next, she wrapped the bread, turnovers and cookies in some clean pieces of white cloth that were given her for the quilt she was piecing, stuffed them carefully into the pockets of the old overcoat, and put on the coat.

It was entirely dark in her room, and she dared not light her candle lest some neighbor should see the light in the window and ask her grandmother next morning who was sick.

Cautiously, with one of her strange upliftings of soul that she called prayer, Miranda opened her window and crept out upon the sill. The roof below her was covered with snow, three or four inches deep, but the window and roof were at the back of the house and no one could see her from there. It was not going to be an easy job getting back with all that snow on the roof, but Miranda wasn't thinking about getting back.

Clinging close to the house she stepped slowly along the shed roof to the edge, trying not to disturb the snow any more than she could help. She had taken the precaution to slip on a pair of stockings over her shoes so that their dampness in the morning might not call forth any comments from her grandmother. At last she reached the cherry tree that grew close to the woodshed roof, and could take hold of its branches and swing herself into it. Then she breathed more freely. The rest was comparatively easy.

Carefully she balanced in the tree, making her way nimbly down, her strong young body swinging lithely from limb to limb unmindful of the snow, and dropped to the snowy ground beneath. She took a few cautious steps as far apart as she could spring, but once out from under the tree she saw that if it continued to snow thick and fast and fine as it was doing now there would be little danger that her footsteps would be discovered in the morning. However, she took the precaution to reach the smokehouse by a detour through the corn patch where tracks in the snow would not be so noticeable. Then, suddenly, she faced a new difficulty. The great old rusty padlock was reinforced

reach it and turn the key, but at last the big door swung open, creaking noisily as it swung, and giving her another fright.

With her hand on her heart, and her eyes straining through the darkness, Miranda stepped inside, her pulses throbbing wildly now, and her breath coming short and quick. There was something awfully gruesome about this dark silent place; it was like a tomb.

CHAPTER 6

THERE was no sound nor movement inside, and at first the girl began to think her quest had been in vain; or perhaps the prisoner had already escaped. If there was a way of escape she made sure Allan would find it; but after a second her senses cleared and she heard soft breathing over in the corner. She crept toward it, and made out a dark form lying in the shadow. She knelt beside it, put her hand out and touched his hair, his heavy beautiful hair that she had admired so many times in school when his head was bent over his book and the light from the window showed purple shadows in its dark depths. It thrilled her now strangely with a sense of privilege and almost of awe to feel how soft it was. Then her hand touched the smoothness of his boy face, and she bent her head quite close, so that she felt his breath on her cheek.

"Allan!" she whispered, "Allan!"

But it was some minutes before she could get him awake with her quiet efforts, for she dared not make a noise, and he was dead with fatigue and anxiety, besides being almost numb with the cold. His head was pillowed on his arm and he had wrapped around him some old sacking that had been given him for his bed. Grandfather Heath as constable did not believe in making the way of the transgressor easy, and he had gone contented to his warm comfortable bed leaving only a few yards of old sacking and a hard clay floor for the supposed criminal to lie upon. This was not cruelty in Grandfather Heath. He called it Justice.

At last Miranda's whispered cries in his ear, and her gentle shakings aroused the boy to a sense of his surroundings. Her arms were about his neck, trying tenderly to bring him to a sitting posture, and her cheek was against his as though her soul could reach his attention by drawing nearer. Her little freckled saucy face, all grave and sorrowful now in the darkness, brought to him a conviction of sympathy he had not known in all his lonely boyhood days, and with his first waking sense the comfort of her presence touched him warmly. He held himself utterly quiet just to be sure that she was there touching him and it was not a dream, somebody caring and calling to him with almost a sob in her breath. For an instant a wild thought of his own mother whom he had never known came to him and then almost immediately he knew that it was Miranda. All the hideous truth of his situation came back to him, as life tragedies will on sudden

she might find out I had my door buttoned and get Grandpa roused up. Or somebody might a heard the door creak. It made a turrible noise. Ain't you most froze? Your hands is like ice—" she touched them softly and then drew them both up to her face and blew on them to warm them with her breath. There's some old mittens of mine in the pocket here, they ain't your size, but mebbe you ken git into 'em, and anyhow they're better'n nothin'. Hurry, cause it would be all no use ef Grandpa woke up—"

Allan sprang up suddenly.

"Where is your grandfather?" he asked anxiously, "Does he know you're here?"

"He's abed and asleep this three hours," said the girl holding up the coat and catching one of his hands to put it in the sleeve. "I heard him tell about you bein' out here, and I jest kep' still and let 'em think I was asleep, so Grandma sent me up to bed and I waited till they went upstairs and got quiet, then I slipped down an' got the key and some vittles, and went back and clumb out my window to the cherry tree so's I wouldn't make a noise with the door. You better walk the rails of the fence till you get out the back pasture and up by the sugar maples. Then you could go through the woods and they couldn't track you even ef it did stop snowin' soon and leave any kind of tracks. But I don't guess it'll stop yet awhile. It's awful fine and still like it was goin' on to snow fer hours. Hev you got any money with you? I put three shillin's in the inside coat pocket. It was all I hed. I thought you might need it. Reach up and git that half a ham over your head. You'll need it. Is there anythin' else you want?"

While she talked she had hurried him into the coat, buttoning it around him as if he had been a child and she his mother; and the tall fellow stooped and let her fasten him in, tucking the collar around his neck.

He shook his head, and softly whispered a hoarse "No" to her question, but it caught in his throat with something like a sob. It was the memory of that sound that had sent the sobs of his young brother Nathan piercing to the soul of her, years later, down beside the pieplant bed.

"Don't you let 'em catch you, Allan," she said anxiously, her hand lingering on his arm, her eyes searching in the dark for his beloved face.

"No, I won't let 'em catch me," he murmured menacingly, "I'll get away all right, but Randa"—he had always called her Randa though no one else in the village ever called her that—"Randa, I want you to know I didn't do it. I didn't kill Enoch Taylor, indeed I didn't. I wasn't even there. I didn't have a thing to do with it."

"O' course you didn't!" said Miranda indignantly, her whole slender body stiffening in the dark. He could feel it as he reached out to put a hand on either of her shoulders.

"Did you 'spose I'd think you could? But ef you told 'em, couldn't you make 'em prove it? Ain't there any way? Do you hev to go away?" Her voice was wistful, pleading, and revealed her heart.

"Nobody would believe me, Randa. You know how folks are here about me."

"I know," she said sorrowfully, her voice trailing almost into tears. "And anyhow" he added, "I couldn't because—well Randa—*I know who did it and I wouldn't tell!*" His voice was deep and earnest. She understood. It was the rules of the game. He had known she would understand. "Oh!" she said in a breath of surrender. "Oh! of course you *couldn't tell!*" then suddenly rousing—"But you mustn't wait," she added anxiously, "somebody might come by, and you ain't got a minute to lose. You'll take care o' yourself, Allan, won't you?"

"Course," he answered almost roughly, "course, Randa. And say, Randa, you're just a great little woman to help me out this way. I don't know's I ought to let you. It'll mebbe get you into trouble."

"Don't you worry 'bout me," said Miranda. "They ain't going to know anything about me helpin' you, and ef they did they can't do nothin' to a girl. I'd just like to see 'em tryin' to take it out o' me. Ef they dare I'll tell 'em how everybody has treated you all these years. You ain't had it fair Allan. Now go quick—"

But the boy turned suddenly and took her in his arms, holding her close in his great rough overcoated clasp, and putting his face down to hers as they stood in the deepest shadow of the old smokehouse.

"There wasn't ever anybody but you understood, Randa," he whispered, "and I ain't going to forget what you've done this time—" The boy's lips searched for hers and met them in a shy embarrassed kiss that sought to pay homage of his soul to her. "Goodbye, Randa, I ain't going to forget, and mebbe—mebbe, some day I can come back and get you—that is ef you're still here waiting."

He kissed her again impetuously, and then as if half ashamed of what he had done he left her standing there in the darkness and slipped out through

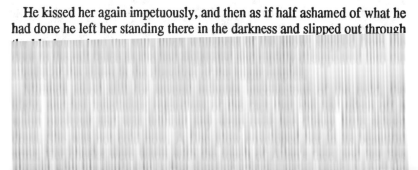

her with joy. He had kissed her and told her he would come back and get her some day if she were still there waiting. What wonder! What joy!

It was the memory of those words that hovered about her like some bright defending angel when Allan's father came six years later to ask her to marry him, and taught her that fine scorn of him. It was what had kept her in her place waiting all the years, and what had drawn her to the younger brother, who was like and yet so unlike Allan.

When Miranda realized where she was standing, and that she must finish her work and get back to her room before she was discovered, she raised both hands to her face and laid them gently on her lips, one over the other, crossed, as if she would touch and hold the sacred kiss that had lain there but the moment before. Then she lifted her face slightly and with her eyes open looking up at the dark rafters, and her fingers still laid lightly on her lips, she murmured solemnly:

"Thanks be!" Gravely she came forth to the business of the night. She reached and fastened the padlock, her warm fingers melting the snow that already again lay thick upon it, and made sure the key was safe about her neck and dropped inside her dress against her warm, palpitating breast to keep it from getting wet and telling tales. She struggled back the beam into place, forcing it into its fastening with all her fierce young might until it rested evenly against the door as before. With her hands and feet she smoothed and kicked the snow into levelness in front of the door. She mounted the fence rail for just an instant and glanced off toward the sugar maples, but there was no sign of a dark figure creeping in the blanketed air of the storm, no sound but the steady falling, falling, of the snow, grain by grain, the little, mighty snow! In a few minutes all possible marks of the escape would be utterly obliterated. With a sigh of relief Miranda stole quickly back to the cherry tree. She had intended to smooth her tracks in retreat one at a time so that the snow would have less to do, but it was not necessary except just about the door of the smoke-house. The snow was doing it all and well. Ten minutes would cover everything; half an hour would make it one white level plain.

The climbing of the cherry tree was a difficult task with chilled body and numb hands, but she accomplished it swiftly, and crept back over the roof and into her own window. Fortunately the snow was dry and brushed off easily. Her dress was not wet so there was no need to invent an excuse for that. With deep thanksgiving she dropped on her knees beside her bed and sobbed her weary heart out into her pillow. Miranda was not one who often cried. In a crisis she was all there and ready for action. She could bear hardships with a jolly twinkle and meet snubbing with a merry grimace, but that kiss had broken her down and she cried as she had never cried before in her life; and prayed her queer heartfelt prayers:

"Oh, God, I didn't never expect no such thing as his being good to me. It was turrible good of you to let him. An' I'm so glad he's safe. So glad! You won't let him get caught will you? He didn't do it you know—say, did you know that I wonder?—'thout his tellin' you? I 'spose you did but I like to think you would a' let me save him anyway, even ef he had. But he didn't do it. He *said* he didn't, and you know he *never* told what wasn't so—he never minded even when it made out against him. But who did do it? God—are you going to let Enoch Taylor die? Allan can't never come back ef you do, he said mebbe—but then I don't suppose there could ever be anythin' like that fer me. But please, I thank you fer makin' him so kind. I can't never remember anybody to huv kissed me before. Of course it was dark an' he couldn't see my red hair,—but then he knowed it was there—he couldn't forget a thing like that—an' it was most as if I was real folks like any other girl. An' please, you'll take good care of him, won't you? Not let him get lost er froze, er hungry, an' find him a nice place with a warm bed an' work to do so's he can earn money, 'cause it ain't in conscience people'll find out how folks felt about him here. He ain't bad, you know, and anyhow you made him, and you must 'uv had some intrust in him. I guess you like him pretty well, don't you, or you wouldn't uv let me get him away 'thout bein' found out. So please, I thank you, and ef you've got anythin' coming to me any time that's real good, jest give it to him instead. Amen."

The prayer ended, she crept into her head, her heart warm and happy, but though the hour was well on to morning she could not sleep, for continually she was going over the wonderful experience in the smokehouse. Allan's tired, regular breathing, the soft feel of his hair when she touched it, and his cheek against hers; his lips when they kissed her, and his whispered words. What it had meant to her to have him take her in his arms and thank her that way and be so kind and glad for what she had done, nobody but a lonely, loveless girl like herself could understand. Over and over her heart thrilled at the wonder of it all—that she had been

same stars, and she prayed he might not be in want or trouble—so she waited. Somehow she found it hard to believe that Allan could easily die, he was so young and strong and vivid—so adequate to all situations. It was easy to find excuse for his not coming back. The world was large and far apart in those days of few railroads, expensive travel, and no telegraph. Even letters were expensive, and not unduly indulged in. There would still be danger for him in return, for old Enoch Taylor's sudden and tragic death, shot in the back near the edge of the town just at the time of early candlelight, was still remembered; and the shadow of young Allan's supposed crime and mysterious disappearance had fallen over his younger brother's reputation and made it what it was. Even his father spoke of him only to warn his younger sons now and then that they follow not in his footsteps. Only in Miranda's heart he really lived, and that was why his younger brother, slender and dark and in many ways much like him, had found a warm place in her heart and love, for he seemed somehow like Allan come back to her again.

Love wasn't in just getting it back again to yourself. It was great just to love; just to know that a beloved one existed.

Not that Miranda ever reasoned things out in so many words. She was keen and practical in daily life, but in her dreams strange fancies floated half formed amid her practicalities, and great truths loomed large upon her otherwise limited horizon. It was so she often caught the meaning of life where wiser souls have failed.

The world is not so large and disconnected after all. One evening just after Miranda had gone next door to live with David and Marcia she heard David reading the *New York Tribune* aloud to his wife while she sewed; little scraps of news and items of interest; what the politicians were doing, and how work was progressing on the canal locks.

"Listen to this," he said half amusedly:

"A boy has travelled through England, Ireland and Wales with only fifty-five dollars in his pocket when he started, and has returned safely. He says he is only five dollars in debt, and gives as his reason for going that he *wished to see the country!"*

Miranda did not understand at all the sympathetic glance of amusement that passed between husband and wife. Her attention had been caught by the facts. A boy! Travelled through all those countries! How very like Allan to do that, and to go on just a little money! It was like him, too, to want to go to see things. It was one of the things in him that had always made good practical people misunderstand him—that wanting to do things just because it was pleasant to do them, and not for any gain or necessity. Miranda smiled to herself as she set the heel of the stocking she was knitting; but she never saw how strange it was that she, the most practical of human beings, should heartily understand and sympathize with the boy who was an idealist. Perhaps she had the same thing in her own nature only she never knew it.

Nevertheless, it became a pleasant pastime for Miranda to look up at the stars at night and share with them her belief that it was Allan who had journeyed all that way, and her pleasure in feeling that he was back in his own land again, nearer to her. All these years she had dreamed out things he might have done, until as the years passed and he did not come, her dreaming became a thing almost without a foundation, a foolish amusement of which she was fond, but ashamed, and only to be indulged in when all the world was asleep and no one could possibly know.

It was so Miranda watched for the light in the gable window across the way, and when it did not come she knew Nathan had crept to his bed without a candle. She went by and by to her bed, and dreamed that Allan came and kissed her just as he had done so long ago when she was but a little girl.

more despised and hunted by every one in authority because he was bright enough to be better; the other in the company of Miranda and little Rose, out in the woods and fields, down by the trout brook fishing, or roaming through the hills watching birds and creeping things; and sometimes sitting at the feet of little Mother Marcia as she told beautiful stories to Nate and Rose, while she held in her arms the sleeping baby brother of little Rose. Here he was a different being. Every hard handsome feature of his face softened into gentleness and set with purpose. All the stubbornness and native error melted away, and his great brown eyes seemed to be seeing things too high for an ordinary boy to comprehend. One could be sure he almost worshipped Mother Marcia, the girl-wife of David Spafford, and looked into her madonna face as she talked or sang softly to her baby, with a foreshadowing of the look that the man he was to be would have some day for the mother of his children.

As for little Rose she was his comrade and pet. With her, always accompanied by Miranda carrying a generous lunch basket, he roamed all the region round about on pleasant holidays. He taught her to fish in the brook, to jump and climb like any boy and to race over the hills with him. Miranda, well pleased, would stray behind and catch up with them now and then, or sit and wait till they chose to race back to her. Rose thought Nathan the strongest and the best boy in all the town, or the wide world for that matter. He was her devoted slave when she demanded flowers or a high branch of red leaves from the tall maple. It was for her sake he applied himself to his lessons as he had never done in his life before, because the first day of her advent in school he had found her with red eyes and nose weeping her heart out at the reprimand he had received for not knowing his spelling lesson. Spelling was his weakest point, but after that he scarcely ever missed a word. His school life became decidedly better so far as knowing his lessons was concerned; though his pranks still kept up. Rose, in truly feminine fashion, rather admired his pranks, and he knew it; though he had always tried to keep them under control since the day when the teacher started to whip him and Rose walked up the aisle with flashing eyes and cheeks like two flames, and said in a brave little voice:

"Teacher, Nate didn't throw that apple core at all. It was Wallie Eggleston. I saw him myself!" And then her lip trembled and she broke down in tears. Nate's face turned crimson and he hung his head, ashamed. It was true that he had not thrown the apple core, but he had done enough to deserve the whipping and he knew it. From that day he refrained from over-torment of the teacher and kept his daring feats for out of school. Also he taught Rose by that unspoken art of a boy, never to "tell on" another boy again.

Mother Marcia watched the intimacy of the little girl and big boy with favor. She felt it was good for Rose, and good for the boy also. Always Miranda or herself was at hand, and never had either of them had reason to doubt the wisdom of the comradeship that had grown between the two children.

But matters were not likely to continue long in this way without the interference of some one. Nathan Whitney got into too many scrapes and slid out of their consequences with a too exasperating skill to have many friends in town. His impudence was unrivalled and his daring was equalled only by his indifference to public opinion. Such a state of things naturally did not tend to make him liked or understood. No one but the three, Rose, her mother and Miranda, ever saw the gentle look of holy reverence on his handsome face, or heard the occasional brief utterances which showed his thoughts were tending toward higher ambitions and finer principles. No others saw the rare smile which glorified his face by a gleam of the real soul of the boy. In after years Marcia often recalled the beautiful youth seated on a low stool holding her baby boy carefully, his face filled with deep pleasure at the privilege, his whole spirit sitting in his eyes in wonder, awe and gentleness as he looked at the little living creature in his arms, or handled it shyly, with rarely tender touch, while Rose sat close beside him well content. At such times the boy seemed almost transfigured. Neither Marcia nor Miranda knew the Nathan who broke windows, threw stones, tied old Mr. Smiles' office door shut while he was dozing over his desk one afternoon; and who filed a bolt, letting out a young scapegrace from the village lockup and helping him to escape from justice and an unappreciative neighborhood into the wide world. They saw only the angelic side to Nathan, the side that nobody else in the wide world dreamed that he possessed.

Nathan spent little time in his home. Shelter during his sleeping hours, and food enough to keep him alive was all he required of it, and more and

more the home and the presiding genius there learned to require less of
him; knowing that she did not possess the power to make him do what she
required. Nathan would n......

[illegible]

............, .,. ......, was let
alone, for what could she do? When she attempted to discipline him he
was not there, neither would he return for hours, sometimes even days
afterward, until she would become alarmed lest he had run away like his
older brother and she might be blamed for it. She found that her husband
was not as easily ruled as she had supposed, and that her famous discipline
of schoolday times must be limited to the little girls and baby Samuel.
Nathan seemed to know by instinct just when it was safe to return and
drop into family life as if nothing had happened, and be let alone. One
word or look and he was off again, staying in the woods for days, and
knowing wild things, trees and brooks as some men know books. He could
always earn a few pennies doing odd jobs for men in the village, for he
was smart and handy, and with what he earned kept himself comfortably
during his temporary absences from the family board. As for sleeping, he
well knew and loved the luxury of a couch on the pine needles under the
singing, sighing boughs, or tucked under the sheltering ledge of a rock on
a stormy night. His brooding young soul watched storm and lightning with
wide eyes that held strange fancies, and thought much about the world and
its ways. Now and again the result of these thoughts would come out in a
single wise sentence to Miranda or little Rose; rarely, but sometimes, to
Mrs. Marcia, always with shyness and as if he had been surprised out of
his natural reserve.

Nathan made no display of his intimacy at the Spaffords. When he went
there it was usually just at dusk, unobtrusively slipping around to Miranda
at the back door. When they went a-roaming on the hills, or fishing, he
never started out with them. He always appeared in the woods just as they
were beginning to think he had forgotten. He usually dropped off their
path on the way home by going across lots before they reached the village,
having a fine instinct that it might bring criticism upon them if they were
seen with him. And thus, because of his carefulness, the beautiful
friendship of Rose and the boy went on for some years and no one thought
anything about it. Nathan never attempted to walk home from school with

Rose as other boys did with the girls they admired. Once or twice when an unexpected rain came on before school closed he slid out of his last class and whirled away through the rain to get her cloak and umbrella, returning just as school "let out," drenched and shamefaced; but he let the little girl think her father had brought them and asked him to give them to her.

One unlucky day, toward evening, Nathan slipped in at the side gate and brought a great bag of chestnuts for Rose, while Mr. David's two prim maiden aunts, Miss Amelia and Miss Hortense Spafford, were tying on their bonnets preparatory to going home after an afternoon call. When Nathan perceived the guests his face grew dark and he backed away toward the door, holding out the bag of nuts toward Rose, and murmuring that he must go at once. By some slip the bag fell between the two and the nuts rolled out in a brown rustling shower over the floor. The boy and girl stooped in quick unison to pick them up, their golden and brown curly heads striking together in a sounding crack, making both forget the presence of their elders and break forth into merry laughter, as they ruefully rubbed their heads and began to gather up the nuts. Nathan was his gentle best self for three or four whole minutes while he picked up nuts and made comical remarks in a low tone to Rose, unconscious of the grim visages of the two aunts in the background, who paused with horrified astonishment in their tying of bonnet strings, to observe the evident intimacy between their grandniece and a dreadful boy whom they recognized as that scapegrace son of Nathan Whitney's.

Marcia did not notice their expressions at first. She was standing close by with her eyes on the graceful girl and alert boy as they struggled playfully for the nuts; she liked to see the two together in the entire unconsciousness of youth playing like children.

But Nathan, sensitive almost to a fault, was quick to feel the antagonistic atmosphere, and suddenly looked up to meet those two keen old pairs of eyes focussed on him in disapproval. He colored all over his handsome face, then grew white and sullen as he rose suddenly to his feet and flashed his defiant habitual attitude, never before worn in the Spafford house.

Standing there for an instant, white with anger, his brows drawn low over his fine dark eyes, his chin raised slightly in defiance (or was it only haughtiness and pride?) his shoulders thrown back, his hands unconsciously clenched down at his sides, and looking straight back into those two pairs of condemning, disapproving eyes, he seemed the very embodiment of the modern poem Invictus, and if he had been a picture it should have borne the inscription, "Every man's hand is against me."

There was utter silence in the room, while four eyes condemned and two eyes defied—offending anew by their defiance. The atmosphere of the

room seemed charged with lightning, and oppression sat sudden upon the
hearts of the mother and daughter who stood by, oppression and growing
indignation. What right had the aunts to judge

. That was what the
boy's eyes said; and the two narrow-minded little old ladies, red with
indignation, cold with pride and prejudice, declined to look honestly at the
question, but let their eyes continue to condemn merely for the joy of
having a chance to condemn him whom they had always condemned.

The boy's haughty undaunted look held them at bay for several seconds,
before he turned coolly away and with a bow of real grace to Marcia and
Rose he went out of the room and closed the door quietly behind him.

There was silence in the room. The tenseness in all faces remained until
they heard him walk across the kitchen entry and close the outside door,
heard his quick, clean step on the flagstones that led around the house; and
then heard the side gate click. He was gone out of hearing and Rose drew
a quick involuntary sigh. He was safe, and the storm had not broken in
time for him to hear. But it broke now in low oncoming threats of look and
tone. Rose was shriveled to misery by the contemptuous glances of her
aunts, coming as they did in unison, and meaning but one thing, that she
was to blamed in some way for this terrible disgrace to the family. Having
disposed of Rose to their satisfaction they turned to her mother.

"Well, I must say I'm surprised, Marcia." It was Aunt Amelia as usual
who opened up the first gun, "In fact, to be plain, I'm deeply shocked!
Living as you have in this town for thirteen and a half years now—[Aunt
Amelia always aimed to be exact]—you cannot fail to have known what a
reputation that boy has. There is no worse in the county, I believe. And
you, the mother of a sweet daughter just budding into womanhood [Rose
was at that time nearly eleven], should be so unwise, nay even wicked and
thoughtless, as to allow a person of the character of Nathan Whitney to
enter your house intimately. I observed that he entered the back door
unannounced—and to present your daughter with a gift! I am shocked
beyond words to express—" and Aunt Amelia paused impressively and
stood looking steadily at the indignant Marcia, shaking her head slightly as
if the offense were too great to be quite comprehended in a breath.

Then Aunt Hortense took up the condemnation.

"Yes, Marcia, I am deeply grieved," she spoke weepily, "to think that our beloved nephew's wife, who has become one of our own family, should so forget herself and her position, and the rights of her family, as to allow that scoundrel to enter her doors, and to speak to her child. It is beyond belief! You cannot be ignorant of his character, my dear! You must know that all the outrages that have been committed in this town have been either perpetrated by him, or he has been their instigator, which in my mind is even worse, because it shows cowardice in not being willing to bear the penalty himself—"

At this point Rose, with flashing blue eyes and cheeks as red as the flowers she was named after, stepped indignantly forward.

"Aunt Amelia, Nathan *isn't* a coward! He isn't afraid of *any*thing in the whole world! He's brave and splendid!"

Miss Amelia turned shocked eyes upon her grandniece; and Miss Hortense, chin up, fairly snuffed the air:

"In my day little girls did not speak until they were spoken to, and never were allowed to put in when their elders were speaking!" "Yes, Marcia," put in Miss Hortense getting out her handkerchief and wiping her eyes offendedly, "you see what your headstrong ideas have brought upon you already. You cannot expect to have a well-behaved child if you allow her to associate with rough boys, and especially when you pick out the lowest in the village, the vilest of the vile!"

Miss Hortense had the fire of eloquence in her eyes, and it was plain there was more to follow. The bad boys of the village were her especial hobby, and since ten years back she had held a grudge against Nathan on account of her pet cat.

Marcia, cool, controlled, tried to interrupt. She was feeling very angry both on her own account and for the boy's sake, but she knew she could do nothing to pour oil on the troubled waters if she lost her temper.

"I think you have made a mistake, Aunt Hortense," she said gently, "Nathan isn't a bad boy. I've known him a good many years and he has some beautiful qualities. He has been over here playing with Rose a great deal and I have never seen him do a mean or selfish thing. I am, in fact, very fond of him, and he has made a good playmate for Rose. He is a little mischievous of course, most boys are, but there is no real badness in him I am sure."

Rose looked at her mother with shining gratitude, but the two old ladies stiffened visibly in their wrath.

"I am mistaken. Am I?" sniffed Miss Hortense. "Yes, I suppose young folks always think they know more than their experienced elders. I have to expect that, but I must do my duty. I shall feel obliged to report this to my nephew and he must deal with it as he sees fit. But whether you think I am mistaken or not, I *know* that you are, and you will sadly rue the day when

perhaps remember him as being still with us when you came to live here, he died about five years ago you know—who was as inoffensive and kind an animal as one could have about a house, was put to terrible torture before our very eyes by this same paragon of a boy whom you are attempting to uphold. My dear, [here she lowered her voice sepulchrally and hissed out the words vindictively with her thin lips] that dreadful boy tied a tin can filled with pebbles to our poor dear Matthew's tail: think of it! His tail! that he always kept so beautifully clean and tucked around him so tidily! We always had a silk patchwork cushion for him to lie on by the fire and he never presumed upon his privileges; and then for him to be so outraged! My dear, it was more than human nature could bear. Poor Matthew was frantic with fear and mortification. He was a dignified cat and had always been treated with consideration, and of course he did not know what to make of it. He attempted to break away from his tormentors but could not; and the tin can came after him, hitting his poor little heels. Oh, I cannot describe to you the awful scene! Poor Hortense and I stood on the stoop and fairly implored that little imp to release poor Matthew, but he went after him all the harder—the vile little wretch—and poor Matthew did not return to the house until after dark. For days he sat licking his poor disfigured tail from which the beautiful fur had all been rubbed, and looking reproachfully at us,—his best friends. He lived for four years after that, but he never was the same cat! Poor Matthew! And I always thought that was the cause of his death! Now do you understand, Marcia?"

"But Aunt Amelia," broke in Marcia gently, trying not to smile, "that was nine years ago, and Nathan has grown up now. He was only five or six years old then, and had run wild since his mother's death. He is almost sixteen now, and very much changed in a great many ways—"

The two old ladies brought severity to bear upon her at once in frowns of differing magnitudes.

"If they do these things in a green tree, what shall be done in the dry?" quoted Aunt Amelia solemnly. "No, Marcia, you are mistaken. The boy was bad from his birth. We are not the only ones who have suffered. He has tied strings across the sidewalk many a dark night to trip people. I have heard of hundreds of his pranks, and now that he is older he doubtless carries his accomplishments into deeper crime. I have heard that he does nothing but hang around the stores and post office. He is a loafer, nothing short of it, and as for honesty, there isn't an orchard in the neighborhood that is safe. If he'll steal apples, he'll do worse when he gets the chance— and he'll make the chance, you may depend upon it. Boys like that always do. You have taken a great risk in letting him into your house. You have fine old silver that has been in the family for years, and many other valuable things. He may take advantage of his knowledge of the place to rob you some dark night. And as for your child, you cannot tell what awful things he may have taught her. I have often watched his face in church and thought how utterly bad and without moral principle he looks. I should not be in the least surprised if he turned out one day to be a murderer!"

Miss Amelia's tones had been gradually rising as she came to this climax, and as she spoke the word *murderer* she threw the whole fervor of her intense and narrow nature into her speech, coming to an eloquent and dramatic pause which was well calculated to impress her audience. But suddenly, like a flash of a glittering sword in air, a piercing scream arose. As she might have screamed if some one had struck her, Rose uttered her furious young protest against injustice. Her beautiful little face, flushed with outraged innocence and glorious in its righteous wrath, shone through the gathering dusk in the room and fairly blazing at her startled aunts, who jumped as if she had been some wild animal suddenly let loose upon them. The scream cut through the space of the little room seeming to pierce every one in it, and quickly upon it came another.

"Stop! Stop!" she cried as if they were still going on, "you shall not say those things! You are bad, wicked women! You shall not say my Nathan is a murderer. You are a murderer yourself if you say so. The Bible says he that hateth his brother is a murderer and you hate him or you would not say such wicked things that are not true. You shall not speak them any more. My Nathan is a good boy and I love him. Don't you *dare* talk like that again." Another scream pointed the sentence and Rose burst into a furious fit of tears and flew across the room, fairly flinging herself into her mother's arms, and sobbing as if her heart would break.

Into this scene of tumult came a calm, strong voice:

"Why, what does all this mean?"

...David, ...king an answer in his wife's face; in the doorway of the pantry stood Miranda, arms akimbo, nostrils spread, eyes blazing like a very war horse that she was, snuffing the bale from afar, and only waiting to be sure how the land lay.

For a moment nobody could say anything for Rose's sobs drowned all else. Marcia had all she could do to soothe and quiet the excited child who had been so strained up for a few minutes that she was now like a runaway team going down hill and unable stop.

David had sense enough to keep still until the air cleared, and meantime he studied the faces of each one in the room, not forgetting Miranda, and was able to get a pretty clear idea of how matters stood before anybody explained.

Presently, however, Rose subsided into low convulsive sobs smothered in her mother's arms, as Marcia drew the little girl down into her lap in the big arm chair, and laying her lips against the hot wet cheek said softly;

"There, there, mother's dear child, get calm, little girl, get calm. Get control of yourself."

The sudden lull gave opportunity for speech, and Miss Amelia, much shaken in body if not in mind, hastened to avail herself of it.

"You may well ask what this means, David," she began, gathering her forces for the combat, and reaching out to steady her trembling hand on the back of a chair.

"Sit down, Aunt Amelia," said David hastening to bring forward two chairs, one for each of the old ladies. "Sit down and don't excite yourself. There's plenty of time to explain."

"I thank you," said Miss Amelia drawing herself up to her full height, "I prefer to stand until I have explained my part in this disgraceful scene. I want you to understand that what I have said has been wholly disinterested. I have been merely trying to protect you and your child from the thoughtless folly of one whose youth must excuse her for her conduct.

Your wife, David, has been admitting to the company of your innocent daughter a person wholly unfit to mingle in respectable society. He came in tonight while we were here, a rough, ill-bred, lubberly fellow, whose familiarity was an insult to your home. I was merely informing Marcia what kind of a boy he was when Rose broke out into the most shocking screams and cries, and used the most disrespectful language toward me, showing plainly the result of her companionship with evil; and not only that but she expressed herself in terms that were unmaidenly and unseemly for a girl, almost a woman, to use. Your mother would never have allowed herself to so far forget herself as to say that she *loved*—actually loved, David,—that was the word she used,—a *boy*. And that too a boy who only needs a few more years to become a hardened criminal. I refer to that scapegrace of a son of Nathan Whitney. And she dared to call him *hers*—*my* Nathan, she said, and was most impudent in her address to me. I think that she should be punished severely and never be allowed to see that young wretch again. I am sure you will bear me out in feeling that I have been outraged—"

But now Rose's sobs dominated everything again, heartbroken and indignant, and Marcia had much ado to keep the child from breaking away from her and rushing from the room. David looked from one to another of his excited relatives and prepared to pour oil on the troubled waters.

"Just a minute, Aunt Amelia," he said coolly as soon as he could be heard. "I think there has been a little misunderstanding here—"

"No misunderstanding at all, David," said the old lady severely drawing herself up with dignity again. "I assure you there is no possible chance for misunderstanding. Your wife actually professes fondness for this young scapegrace, calls his wickedness mischief; and tries to condone his faults, when everybody knows he has been the worst boy in the town for years. I told her that I should inform you of all this and demand for the sake of the family honor that you never allow that fellow! that loafer! that low-down scoundrel!! to enter this house again or speak to our grandniece in the street."

Miss Amelia was trembling with rage and insulted pride, and purple in the face. At this juncture Miranda beat a hasty retreat to the pantry window.

"Golly!" she ejaculated softly to herself. "Golly! wouldn't that old lady make a master hand at cussin' ef she jest didn't hev so much fambly pride! Golly! she couldn't think of words 'nough to call 'im."

Miranda stood for a full minute chuckling and thinking and staring at the sky that was just beginning to redden with the sunset. Words from the other room hastened her thinking. Then with cool deliberation she approached the door again to reconnoitre and take a hand in the battle.

David was just speaking:

"Aunt Ameli...

...words glanced ...her bony old hands grasped the back of the chair shakily, and her whole body trembled.

Her thin lips shook nervously, and caught dryly on her teeth in an agitated way as she tried to enunciate her words with extreme dignity and care.

"No, David, we will not lay the subject aside," she said, "and I shall never feel confidence in Marcia's judgment after what she has said to me about that young villain. I must insist on telling you the whole story. I cannot compromise with sin!"

And then, Miranda discreetly approached with a smile of honeyed sweetness on her freckled face.

"Miss 'Meelia, 'scuse me fer interruptin', but it wasn't your spare-bedroom winders I see open when I went by this afternoon was it? You don't happen t' r'member ef you left 'em open when you come away, do yeh? Cause I thought I sensed a thunder-storm in the air, an' I thought mebbe you'd like me to run down the street an' close 'em fer you, ef you did. Miss Clarrissa's all alone, ain't she?"

"A thunder storm!" said Miss Amelia stiffening into attention at once, alarm bristling from every loop of ribbon on her best black bonnet. "We must go home at once! I never like to be away from home in a thunderstorm; one can never tell what may happen. Come, let us make haste."

"A thunder storm!" said David incredulously, and then catching the innocent look on Miranda's face stopped suddenly. The sky was as clear as an evening bell and a single star glinted out at that moment as the two old ladies issued hastily forth from their nephew's door, but they saw it not; and David, reflecting that there was more than one kind of a thunder storm said nothing. It might be as well to let the atmosphere clear before he took a hand in affairs.

"Shall I walk down with you, Aunt Amelia?" he asked half doubtfully, glancing back toward the stairs up which Marcia had just taken the sobbing Rose.

"No indeed, David," said Miss Amelia decidedly. "Your duty is to your family at such a time as this. One never can tell what may happen, as I said before, and my sister and myself can look out for ourselves."

They closed the door and hurried away down the walk.

Miranda stood at the side gate with bland benevolence on her features.

"You got plenty o' time," she said smilingly. "You ain't got any call to hurry. It'll be quite a spell 'fore the storm gets here. I'm a pretty good weather profit."

"It is not best to take chances," said Aunt Hortense looking up nervously at the rosy sky, "appearances are often deceitful, and there are a great many windows to close for the night."

They swept on down the street and Miranda watched them a moment with satisfaction. Then she looked over at the white-pillared house across the way and frowned. The mother in her trembled at the injustice done the boy she had grown to love.

"There's some folks has a good comeuppance comin' to 'em somewheres or I miss my guess," she murmured as she turned slowly toward the kitchen door, and began to wonder what Mr. David would think of her. Mr. David was too sharp to be deceived long about a thunder storm, and she would not like to incur his disfavor for she worshipped him afar.

Miranda went into the house and made herself scarce for a little while, moving conspicuously among her pots and pans, and voicing her hilarity in a hymn the church choir had sung the day before. But David was for the present quite occupied upstairs. The trembling Rose now fully subdued and quite horrified at what she had dared to say to her aunts, toward whom she had always been taught the utmost respect, lay on her little bed with white and tear-stained face, her body now and then convulsed with a shivering sob. She had confessed her sins quite freely after her aunts had departed, and had agreed that the only thing possible was an abject apology on the morrow, but her sweet drooping mouth and long fluttering lashes betokened that her trouble was not all gone and at last she brought it out in a soft sobbing breath.

"Nathan won't come here any more. I know he won't. I saw it in his face. He'll think you don't want him, and he'll never come round again. He's always that way. He thinks people don't like him—" and she began to cry softly again.

David went and sat down beside his little girl and began to question her. Sometimes Marcia would put in a gentle word, and the eyes of the father and mother met over the child in sweet confidence, with utmost sympathy for her in her childish grief, although they had not condoned one whit the words she had spoken in her quick wrath to her aunts.

"Well, little daughter, close up the tears now," said the father. "Tomorrow you will go down to see your aunts and make it all right with them by telling them how sorry and asham[illegible]

[illegible] conference in the hall for a moment with Marcia sent David downstairs as eagerly as a boy might have gone, and Miranda's heart was in her mouth for a full minute when she looked up from the Johnnycake she was making for supper and saw him standing in the kitchen door. She thought a reprimand must surely be forthcoming.

"Miranda, have you got a good supper cooking, and do you think there would be enough for a guest if I brought one in?"

"Loads!" said Miranda alertly drawing a deep breath of relief and beating her eggs with vigor. "How many of 'em?"

"Only one, and I'm not sure of him yet, but you might put another plate on the table," said David, and taking his hat from the hall table went out the front door.

Miranda put her dish of eggs down on the kitchen table and tiptoed softly into the dining room where the window commanded a view of the street. The candles were not yet lighted so she could not be seen from without, and curiosity was too much for her. She saw David walk across the street to the big pillared Whitney house, and just as he reached the gate she saw a dark figure that walked very much like young Nate, come swinging down the street and meet him. They stood at the gate a minute or two talking, those two shadowy figures, and then David turned and walked back to the house, and the boy scurried around to his own back door. Miranda scuttled back to her eggs with happy heart and was beating away serenely when David opened the kitchen door to say:

"Well, he'll be here in half an hour. Be sure to have plenty of jam and cake." Then David went into the library, took out the New York evening paper, and was soon deeply engrossed in the last reports of Professor Morse's new Electro-Magnetic Telegraph, in the interest of which there was a bill before Congress appropriating thirty thousand dollars for its testing. It was one of the absorbing topics of the day, and David forthwith forgot not only his guest but the unpleasant happenings that had caused him to give the invitation, and Miranda in the kitchen hurrying about to stir some tea cakes and get out a varied assortment of preserves and jams such as boys are supposed to like, need have feared no reference to thunder storms, as she sang her hymns loud and clear:

> "My willing soul would stay
> In such a frame as this,
> And wait to hail the brighter day
> Of everlasting bliss."

Rose presently came down to the kitchen, chastened and sweet, her eyes like forget-me-nots after the rain, her cheeks rosy. Miranda gave her a little hotcake just out of the pan and patted the soft cheek tenderly. She dared not openly speak against the prim aunts who had brought all this trouble on her darling, but her looks pitied and petted Rose and assured her that she did not blame her darling for anything hateful she might have said to those old spitfires. Rose took the sympathy, but did not presume upon it, and her lashes down drooped humbly over the rose in her cheeks. She knew now that she had been very sinful to speak so to poor Aunt Amelia no matter how excited she had been. Aunt Amelia of course did not know Nathan as she did and therefore could not get the right point of view. Aunt Amelia had done it all for what she thought was her good. That was what Mother Marcia had tried to make her little girl feel.

Rose, her cake eaten, walked around the pleasant dining table and noted the festive air of jams and preserves, the sprigged china, and the extra place opposite her own.

"Oh, is there going to be company?" questioned Rose half dismayed.

"Your pa said there might be," said Miranda unconcernedly, trying not to show how glad she was.

"Who?"

"Your pa didn't say who," answered Miranda, just as if she had not seen those two shadowy figures conversing outside the Whitney gate.

Rose slid into the library and sat down on the arm of her father's chair, putting a soft arm around his neck and laying her cheek against his.

"Father, Miranda says there is to be company tonight?" She laid the matter before him seriously.

"Yes," said David rousing out of his perusal of the various methods of insulating wires. "Yes, Rosy posy, Nathan Whitney is coming to supper. I though I'd like to begin to get acquainted with him at once."

"Oh, father dear! You dear, dear father!" cried Rose, hugging him with all her might.

Mother Marcia came smiling downstairs, and just as Miranda was taking up the golden brown loaves of Johnnycake Nathan presented himself, shy and awkward but with eyes that fairly danced with pleasure and anticipation. He had done his best to put himself in festive array and was good to look upon as he stood waiting

...together over the hush of the room; the little girl who had been his pet and playmate in her pretty frock of blue and white with her gold curls bowed—he could just see the sheen of gold in her hair as he raised his eyes in one swift comprehensive glance; Miranda standing at the kitchen door with a steaming dish in her hand and her head bowed decorously, its waves of shining hair like burnished copper; and the gracious sweet lady mother whom he adored, there by his side. Strange thrills of hot and cold crept over his body, and his breath came slowly lest it sound too loud. This was actually the first time in his life that Nathan Whitney had ever taken a meal at any other home than his own!

Meals a-many he had eaten out of a tin pail on his old scarred desk in school, or down by the brook in summer; more meals he had gone without, or taken on the road, of cold pieces hastily purloined in absence of his aunt or stepmother, but never before had he been invited to supper and sat at a beautiful table with snowy linen, silver and china and all the good things people give to company. All this in his honor! He was almost frightened at himself. Not that he was unaccustomed to nice things, for there was plenty of fine linen, rare china, and silver in the great house across the way, but it had not been used familiarly since his mother's death; and was mostly brought out for company occasions, on which occasions it had been young Nathan's habit to absent himself, because the company always seemed to look at him as if he had no right in his father's house.

CHAPTER 9

As HE looked about the cheery table after grace was concluded, Nathan Whitney could hardly believe his own senses that he was really here and by invitation. He rubbed his eyes and almost thought he must be dreaming. For this cause he answered but briefly the opening remarks directed to him, and mainly by "Yes, ma'am," and "No, ma'am," "Yes, sir," and "No, sir."

But David with rare tact began to tell a story with a point so humorous that Nathan forgot his new surroundings and laughed. After that the ice was broken and he talked more freely, and gradually his awe melted so that he was able to do a boy's full justice to the good things that Miranda had with joy prepared.

The talk drifted to the telegraph, for David felt a deep and vital interest in the great invention, and could not keep away long from the subject. Marcia too was just as interested and ready with keen and intelligent questions to which the boy listened appreciatively. He had a boy's natural keenness for mechanical appliances, but no one had ever taken the trouble to explain the telegraph to him. David saw the boy's bright eyes watching him fascinated as he attempted to describe to Marcia the principle on which the wonderful new instrument was supposed to work, and went into detail more than he would have needed to do for Marcia, who had been following each account in the papers as eagerly as if she were a man; and who, understanding, helped along by asking questions, until the boy himself ventured one or two.

David was pleased to see in his questions a high degree of understanding and insight, and his heart warmed quickly toward the young fellow. He forgot entirely that he was putting the guest through an examination at the instigation of his maiden aunts and for the sake of protecting his young daughter. Perhaps he had never had any such idea in "getting acquainted" with Nathan, but certain it is that he did not expect the process of getting acquainted to be so altogether interesting and gratifying. He understood at once why Marcia had said he was "unusual if you could only get at his real soul." As they talked the boy's face had brightened until it fairly glowed

with the pleasure of his surroundings and forgetfulness of his usual feeling
that he was in some measure considered an outlaw.

bill of appropriation for testing it that was before Congress at the time.
The boy's eyes shone.

"It'll be great if Congress lets him have all that money to try it, I think,
don't you? It'll be sure to succeed, won't it?"

"I think so," said David with conviction. "I am firmly convinced that the
telegraph has come to stay. But it is not strange that people doubt it. It is
even a more wonderful invention than the railroad. Why, it is only about
fifteen years since people were hooting and crying out against the idea of
the steam railway and now look how many we have, and how
indispensable to travel it has become."

The boy looked at the man admiringly.

"Say, you go on the railroad a lot, don't you?"

"Why, yes," said David. "My business makes it necessary for me to run
up to New York very frequently. You've been on it, of course?"

The boy's face took on a look of great amusement.

"Me? Oh, no! I've never been, and never expect to have the chance, but
it must be a great experience I've tried to think how it would feel going
along like that without anything really pulling you. I've dreamed lots of
times about taking a ride on the railroad, but I guess that's as near as I'll
ever get to it."

"Well, I don't see why," said David reflectively. "Suppose you go up
with me the next time I go. I'd like to have company and I can explain to
you all about it. I know the engineer well and he'll show us all about the
workings of the engine. Come, will you go?"

"Will I go?" exclaimed Nathan too much excited to choose his words.
"Well I guess I will if I get the chance. Do you mean it, Mr. Spafford?"

"Certainly," said David smiling. "I shall be delighted to have your
company. I shall probably go a week from today. Can you get away from
school?"

Nathan's face darkened.

"I guess there isn't any school going to keep me out of that chance," he said threateningly.

"Would you like me to speak to your father about it?"

"Father won't care," said the boy looking up in surprise. "He never knows where I am, just so I don't bother him."

A fleeting wave of pity swept over Marcia's face as she took in what this must mean to the boy, but David, seeing this was a sore point, said pleasantly:

"I'll make that all right for you," and passed on to discuss the difference the steam railway had made in the length of time it took to go from one city to another, and the consequent ease with which business could be transacted between places at a distance from one another; and from that they went on to speculating about the changes that might come with the telegraph.

"Wouldn't it be wonderful to be able to get a message from Washington in half an hour, for instance?" said David. "Professor Morse claims it is possible. Many doubt it, but I am inclined to believe he knows what he is about and to think that it is only a question of time before we have telegraphs all over the United States, at least in the larger cities and towns."

Nathan's eyes were large.

"Say, it's a big time to be living in, isn't it?"

"It is indeed," said David, his eyes sparkling appreciatively, "but after all, have you ever thought that almost any time is a big time to be living in for a boy or a man who has a work to do in the world?"

It was beautiful to see the waves of feeling go over the boy's face in rich coloring, and deep sparkling of his eyes, and David could but admire him as he watched. What could people mean that they had let this boy remain with the mark of evil upon his reputation? Why had no one tried to pull him out of his lawless ways before? Why had he never tried? What was Mr. Whitney thinking of to let a boy like this go to ruin as everybody said he was going? David resolved that he should never go if effort of his could help save him.

While they talked the Johnnycake, biscuits, cold ham, fried potatoes, tea-cakes, jam, preserves and cake had been disappearing in large quantities, and the time seemed at last to have arrived when the boy could eat no more. Marcia made a little motion to rise.

"We'll go in the other room for worship," she said, and led the way to the parlor where Miranda had quietly preceded them and lit the candles. There was an open fire in the fireplace here too, and the room was bright and cheery with stately reflections in polished mahogany furniture and long mirrors. Nathan hung back at the door and looked about almost in awe. He had not been in this room when he came to the house at other times and it seemed like entering a new world, but almost instantly his attention was held by the pianoforte that stood

. . . . .ug's program; though if he had stopped to think he might have known, for David was an elder in the church, and it was a strange thing for any respectable family of the church to be without family worship in that day. It was a mark of respectability if nothing else.

Miranda was sitting primly in her chair by the door with her hands folded in her lap and her most seraphic look on her merry face. One might almost say she seemed glorified tonight, her satisfaction beamed so effulgently from every golden freckle and every gleaming copper wave of her hair.

Nathan dropped suddenly into the chair on the other side of the door, feeling awkward and out of place for the first time since his host had welcomed him and made him feel at home. Here in this stately "company" room, with a religious service before him, he was again keenly aware of his own shortcomings in the community. He did not belong here and he was a fool to have come. The sullen scowl involuntarily darkened his brow as Rose slipped about the room giving each one a hymn book,—for all the world like church. Nathan took the book reluctantly because she gave it, but his self-consciousness was so great that he dropped it awkwardly, and stooping to pick it up his face grew red with embarrassment.

Marcia, noticing, tried to put him at his ease.

"What hymn do you like best, Nathan?" she asked, but the boy only turned the redder and mumbled that he didn't know.

"Then we'll sing the shepherd psalm. Rose is fond of that," she said, seating herself at the pianoforte.

Nathan fumbled the leaves until he found the place, and then was suddenly entranced with the first notes of the tune as Marcia began to play it over.

Now it happened that the shepherd psalm was the one young Nathan could remember hearing his mother sing to him when he was little. She had sung it, too, to the twins and Samuel when they were babies, and it was associated in his mind with her gentle voice, her smiling eyes and the feel of her arms about him as she tucked him in at night, so when the song burst forth from the lips of the family the young guest had much ado to keep back a great lump that arose in his throat, and to control a strange moisture that stole in his eyes.

> "The Lord's my shepherd, I'll not want;
>   He makes me down to lie
> In pastures green, He leadeth me
>   The quiet waters by—"

Miranda's voice was high and clear while little Rose, sitting in the shelter of her father's arm, joined her bird-like treble to his bass, and Marcia sang alto blending the whole most exquisitely. Nathan stole a covert glance about, saw they were not noticing him at all, and presently he forgot his own strange situation and began to grumble out the air:

> "My table thou hast furnished
> In presence of my foes;—"

(How he wished those Spafford aunts were there to see him sitting thus!—)

> "My head thou dost with oil anoint
> And my cup overflows."

He had a faint idea that it was overflowing now.

> "Goodness and mercy all my life
>   Shall surely follow me;
> And in God's house forevermore
>   My dwelling place shall be."

Would it? Wouldn't that be strange? Would his enemies be surprised some day if they should find him dwelling in heaven?

They were only fleeting thoughts passing through his mind, but the psalm that David read when the hymn was done kept up the thought, "Who shall ascend into the hill of the Lord? or who shall stand in his holy place? He that hath clean hands and a pure heart; who hath not lifted up his soul unto vanity, nor sworn deceitfully. He shall receive the blessing from the Lord and righteousness from the God of his salvation."

Nathan looked down at his rough boy hands, scrubbed till they showed the lines of walnut stain from his afternoon's climbing after nuts. Clean hands and a pure heart? The hands could be got cleaner by continued washings,—but the heart?

The boy was still thinking ~~about it~~

~~...~~ ...g of a tear in his ...

He rose from his knees with an uplifted expression on his face and looked about on the room and these dear people as if he had suddenly found himself companying with angels.

Miranda bustled out to clear off the table. Marcia called Nathan and Rose to the piano, and they all sang a few minutes, then she played one or two gay melodies for them. After that they all went into the library and gathering around the big carved table played jackstraws until it was Rose's bedtime. When Miranda finished the dishes she too came and took a hand in the game, and kept them all laughing with her quaint remarks, talking about the jackstraws as if they were people.

When the big hall clock struck the half hour after eight Rose looked regretfully at her mother and meeting her nod and smile arose obediently, and said good night. Nathan, taking her hand awkwardly for good night, arose also to make his adieus, but David told him to sit down for a few minutes, he wanted to talk to him. So while Marcia and Rose slipped away up stairs, and Miranda went to set the buckwheat cake for breakfast, Nathan settled back half scared and faced the pleasant smile of his host, wondering if he was to be called to account for some of his numerous pranks and if, after all, the happy time had only been a ruse to get him in a corner.

But David did not leave him in uncertainty long.

"What are you going to do with your life, Nathan?" he asked kindly.

"Do with it?" asked the surprised Nathan. "*Do* with it?" Then his brow darkened. "Nothing, I s'pose."

"Oh, no, you don't mean that I'm sure. You're too bright a boy for that, and this is a great age in which to be living, you know. You've got a big man's work to do somewhere in the world. Are you getting ready for it or are you just drifting yet?"

"Just drifting, I guess," said Nathan softly after considering.

"Don't see any chance for anything else," he added apologetically. "Nobody cares what I do anyway" [fiercely].

"Oh, that's nonsense. Why—Nathan—*I* care. I like you, and I want to see you succeed."

A warm red wave of delight flowed over the boy's face and neck, and his eyes flashed one wondering, grateful glance at David. He wanted to say something but couldn't. Words would choke him.

"You're going to college, of course? " said David as a matter of course.

Nathan shook his head.

"How could I?" he asked. "Father'd never send me. He says any money spent on me is thrown away. He was going to send my halfbrother Allan to college but he ran away, and he says he'll never send any of the rest of us—"

"Well, send yourself," said David as if it were quite the expected thing to have a loving parent talk like that. "It will really be the best thing for you in the end anyway. A boy that has to pay his own way makes twice as much of college as the fellow who has everything made easy for him, and I guess you've got grit enough to do it. Get a job right away and begin to lay up money."

"Get a job! *Me* get a job!" laughed Nathan. "Why, nobody'd give me a regular job that I could earn anything much with. They don't like me well enough. They wouldn't trust me. I can get errands and little things to do, but nobody would give me anything worth while."

"Why is that?" David looked keenly but kindly at him.

The boy blushed, and dropped his eyes. At last he answered:

"My own fault, I guess," and smiled as if he were sorry.

"Oh, well, you can soon make that right by showing them you are trustworthy now, you know."

"No," said the boy decidedly, "it's too late. Nobody in this town will give me the chance."

"I will," said David. "I'll give you a job in the printing office if you would like it."

"Wouldn't I though!" said the boy springing to his feet in his excitement. "You just try me. Do you really mean it?"

"Yes, I mean it," said David smiling. "But how about the school?"

"Hang the school," said Nathan frowning. "I want to go to work."

"No, it won't do to hang the school, because then you'll never be able to hold your own working, nor reach up to the bigger things when you have learned the smaller ones. How far have you got in school? What are you studying?"

Nathan told him gloomily, and it was plain there was little interest in the boy's mind for his school.

"I been through it all before anyway," he ~~~~

~~~~~~

~~~ any Latin? David thought it better to ignore a discussion of teachers. He did not think much of the present incumbent himself.

"No."

"Are you in the highest class?"

"Yes."

"What would you think of leaving school and working in the printing office daytimes, and studying Latin and mathematics with me evenings?"

The boy was dumb. He looked at David for a moment, and then dropped his eyes and swallowed hard several times. When he finally raised his eyes again they were full of tears, and this time the boy was not ashamed of them.

"What would you do it for?" he asked when he could speak, his voice utterly broken down with feeling.

"Well, just because I like you and I want to see you get on; and besides, I think I would enjoy it. I'm glad you like the idea. We'll see what can be done. I think in two years at most you might be ready for college if you put in your time well, and by that time you ought to have saved enough to at least start you. There'll be ways to earn your board when you get to college. Lots of fellows do it. Shall I see your father about it, or would you rather do it yourself?"

"Father?" said Nathan wondering again. "Why you don't need to see father. I never ask him about anything. He'd rather not be bothered."

Subsequent experience led David to believe that Nathan was right, for when he went to see Mr. Whitney that grim and unnatural parent strongly advised David to have nothing whatever to do with his scapegrace son, and declared himself unwilling to be responsible for any failure that might ensue if he went contrary to this advice. He said that Nathan was like his mother, not practical in any way, and that he had been nothing but a source of anxiety since he was born, and he had only kept him at school because he did not know what else to do with him. He never expected him to amount to a row of pins. With this encouragement David Spafford undertook the higher education of young Nathan Whitney, strongly suspecting that the father's lack of interest in the son's welfare had its source in an inherent miserliness. Mr. Whitney, however, gave a reluctant permission for his son to leave school and learn the printing business in the office of the *Clarion Call;* but vowed that he would not assist him to fool his time away and spend money pretending he was getting a college education, and if he left school now he needn't do it with any expectation of getting a penny from him for any such nonsense, for he wouldn't give it.

However, David was wise enough that night to say nothing further to the boy about consulting his father, merely telling him, as he said goodnight, that he would expect him to be ready to go to New York with him a week from that day on the early morning train, and that they then would look after purchasing some Latin books, and perhaps get time to run over to the University and find out about entrance requirements so that their work might be intelligent. In the meantime it would be well for Nathan to finish out the week at school, as it was now Wednesday. That would give time to arrange matters at the office, and with his father; then if all was satisfactory he might come to the office Monday morning. There were things he could do both in preparation for the journey and while they were away to help with business, and his salary would begin Monday morning. It wouldn't be much at first, but he might consider that his work began Monday, and that the trip to New York was all in the way of business.

With a heart almost bursting with wonder and joy, and eyes that shone as bright as any of the stars over his head, Nathan walked across the street to his home, ascended a tree to his bedroom window, for he could not bear the sight of anyone just yet, and crept to his bed, where, kneeling with his face in the pillow, he tried to express in a queer little lonely prayer his praise for the great thing that had come to him, mingled with a wistful desire for the "pure heart and clean hands" of those who had a right to the blessing of the Lord. With all his heart he meant to do his part toward making good.

Across the street, high in the side gable, there twinkled the candle of Miranda for a few minutes, and then went out while the owner sat at the window, looking out on the field of stars above her, and thinking deep, wide thoughts.

Now Miranda was the soul of honor on most occasions, but if there came a time when it was to the advantage of those she loved for her to do a little quiet eavesdropping, or to stretch the truth so it would fit a particularly trying circumstance, she generally was able to get a reprieve from her conscience long enough to do it. Therefore, while David had been talking with Nathan in the library, Miranda had had a sudden call to hunt for something in the hall closet, which was located so close to the library door that one standing in the crack of one door might easily hear whole sentences of what

[text obscured]

was at the bottom of the whole scheme, and joy for Nathan of whom she was grown greatly fond, and for whose reputation and uplifting she was intensely jealous.

So it was with a light heart and feet that almost danced that she took her candle-lit way to her little gable room, and after a few simple preparations for the night, put out the light and sat down under the stars to think.

CHAPTER 10

NATHAN was on hand bright and early Monday morning at the office, a look of suppressed excitement in his dark eyes, and a dawning dignity and self-respect in his whole manner.

It was new to him to be expected anywhere and greeted as if he had a right to a business-like welcome. Even in school he had felt the covert protest of the teacher against him always, and had maintained an attitude of having to fight for his rights.

"You are to use this desk for the present," said Morton Howe, the factotum of the office, "and Mr. Spafford wants you to copy those names on that list into that ledger. He'll be down in about an hour. You'll find enough to keep you busy till then, I guess," and the kindly old man pointed to a stool by a high desk, and showed Nathan where to hang his cap.

"It's a real pleasant morning," he added by way of showing the new assistant a little courtesy. "I guess you'll like it here. We all do."

Nathan's face beamed unexpectedly.

"I should say I would," he surprised himself into saying.

"Mr. Spafford's a real kind man to work for." Morton Howe was in his employer's confidence, moreover he worshipped David devotedly.

"I should say he was!" responded Nathan with more fervor than originality.

Then began a new life for Nathan. The two days that proceeded the journey to New York were one long dream of wonder and delight to the boy. There was hard work to be sure, but Nathan hadn't a lazy streak in him, and every word he copied, every errand he ran, every duty he performed was so much intense pleasure to him. To be needed, and to be able to please were so new to him that he looked on each moment of his day with awe lest it might yet prove a dream and slip away from him.

Never had worker of David's been more attentive, more punctilious in performing a task, more respectful or more worshipful—and all his employees loved him.

"I see you got that young nimshi, Nate Whitney, in your office, Dave," said old Mr. Heath the second day of Nathan's service. "You better look out fer yer money. Keep yer safe well locked. He belongs to a bad lot. He's no good himself. I don't see what you took him for."

"I've never had a better office b...

...surprise us all, will he? Wal, his brother did that a number of years ago when he made out to murder Enoch Taylor, an' then git out o' the smokehouse 'ithout unlockin' the door, an' a beam acrost it too; an' me with the key all safe in its usual place and no way of explainin' it, 'cept thet he must a carried some kind o' tools 'long with him, and then fixed the lock all right so's we wouldn't suspect very early in the mornin'. Oh, he surprised us all right, an' your fine little man'll likely turn out to s'prise you in jest some sech way."

"By the way, Mr. Heath," said David more for the sake of changing the subject than because he had much interest in the matter, "how was it that they suspected Allan Whitney of that murder? He never owned up to it, did he?"

"Oh, no, he lied about it o' course."

"But just how did you ever get an idea that Allan Whitney had anything to do with it? He didn't bring the news, did he? I've forgotten how it was, it happened so long ago."

"Not he, he didn't bring no news. He hed too much sense to bring news. No, it was Lawrence Billings brought word about findin' Enoch Taylor a moanin' by the roadside."

"Lawrence Billings!" said David. "Then where did Whitney come in? Billings didn't charge him with it, did he?"

"No, we caught Allan Whitney with a gun not a quarter of a mile away from the spot, tryin' to sneak around to git home 'thout bein' seen."

"But that wasn't exactly proof positive," said David, who had now reached his own gate and was in a hurry to get in the house.

"It was to anybody that knowed Allan," said the hard, positive old man, "an' ef it wa'n't, what more'd you want thun his runnin' away?"

"That told against him of course," said David quietly. "Well, Mr. Heath, I'm going to New York in the morning, anything I can do for you?"

"No, I gen'ally make out to do with what I ken get in our hum stores. You take a big resk when you travel on railroads. I saw in the New York paper the other day where a train of cars was runnin' west from Bawstun last Sat'day, and come in contact with a yoke of oxen near Worcester, throwing the engine off the track and renderin' it completely unfit fer use; *and killin' the oxen!* It seems turrible to encourage a thing that means such a resk to life and property. And here just a few days back there was another accident down below Wilmington. They was runnin' the train *twenty miles an hour!* an they run down a hand car and overturned their engine and *jest ruined it!* A thing like that ain't safe ner reasonable. Too much resk fer me!"

"Yes, there has to be risk in all progress, I suppose; well, goodnight, Mr. Heath," said David, and went smiling into the house to tell Marcia how far behind the times their neighbor was.

Miranda was hovering songfully back and forth between the kitchen and dining room, mindful of any items of news that she could catch, very happy over the pleasure that was to come to Nathan on the morrow and she heard the whole account of David's talk with Mr. Heath, though David thought she was engrossed with her preparations for supper. Miranda had a way like that, leaving an ear and an eye flung out on watch behind her while she did duty somewhere else and nobody suspected. It was always, however, a kindly ear and eye for those she loved.

The reference to Allan Whitney and the murder brought a serious look to her face, and she managed to get behind the door and hear the whole of it. But when mention was made of Lawrence Billings her fact blazed with sudden illumination. Lawrence Billings! It was Lawrence Billings who had committed the crime, of course! Strange that she had never thought of him before! Strange she had never overheard that he had been the one to bring the news!

Lawrence Billings, as a little boy, had followed Allan Whitney like a devoted dog. His sleek, light head, his pale, pasty countenance and faded, furtive blue eyes were always just behind wherever Allan went. No one ever understood why Allan protected him and tolerated him, for he was not of Allan's type, and his native cowardliness was a byword among the other boys. It may be his devotion touched the older boy, or else he was sorry for his widowed mother, whose graying goldish hair, frightened, tired eyes, and wistful, drooping mouth looked pitifully like her son's. However it was, it was well understood from the first day little Lawrence Billings, carrying his slate under his arm, and clinging fearfully to his mother's hand, was brought to the schoolhouse that Allan Whitney had constituted himself a defender. Miranda knew, for she had stood by the school gate when they entered, and seen the appeal of the widow's eyes toward the tall boy in the school yard as the rabble of hoodlums around

her son set up a yell: "Here comes mother's pet!" Something manly in
Allan's eyes had flashed forth and answered that appeal of that mother in

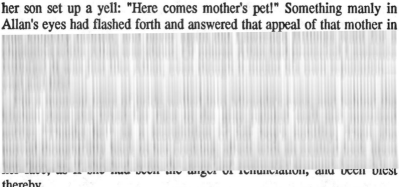

... ., ...g... ... ., ...
thereby.

However, when she thought of Lawrence Billings, her face darkened.
What of the fellow who would allow such sacrifice of one he professed to
love? Did Lawrence know that he was exiling Allan from his home all
these years? Did he realize what it had meant? Had he consented that
Allan should take his crime, or was he in anywise a party to the arrest?

Lawrence Billings still lived in the little old rundown house on the edge
of the village belonging to his mother, and still allowed his mother to take
in sewing for a living, her living and part of his, for his inefficiency had
made it hard for to get or keep any kind of a position. But Lawrence
always managed to keep neatly dressed and to go out with the girls
whenever they would have him. His unlimited leisure and habit of tagging
made him a frequent sight at all gatherings of a social nature whether of
church or town; but weak mouth and expressionless eyes had always been
despised by the thorough-going Miranda, though she had tolerated him
because of Allan. Now, however her mind began to stir fiercely against
him. Could something be done to clear the name of Allan Whitney even if
he never came back to take advantage of it? It was terrible to have a man
like Lawrence Billings walking around smirking when Allan was exiled
and despised.

Of course, Miranda grudgingly admitted to herself she might be
mistaken about Lawrence Billings being the criminal—but she knew she
was not. Now that she had thought of it every word of Allan's, every
circumstance of his behavior toward Lawrence in the past even the
meaningful tone of his voice when he said *"But I know who did it!"*
pointed to the weaker man. Miranda felt she had a clue, yet saw as yet
nothing she could do with it. The conditions were just the same as when
Allan went away. Mrs. Billings, just as faded and wistful, a trifle more
withered, was sewing away and coughing her little hacking apologetic
cough of a Sunday; a trifle more hollow perhaps, but just as sad and

unobtrusive. Who could do anything against such a puny adversary? The girl had an instant's revelation of why Allan had gone away instead of defending himself. It brooded with her through the night and while she was preparing the early breakfast which Nathan had been invited to share with David.

Fried mush and sausage and potatoes, topped off with doughnuts and coffee and applesauce! How good it all tasted to Nathan, eaten in the early candle-lighted room, with the pink dawn just flushing the sky; and Rose, shy and sweet, her eyes still cloudy with sleep, sitting opposite smiling. The boy felt as if he were transformed into another being and entering a new life where all was heaven.

Afterward there was a brief sweet worship; then Miranda stuffed his pockets with seed cakes. Rose walked beside her father, holding his hand silently, as she stole glances across at Nathan, who proudly carried the valise wherein his own insignificant bundle reposed along with David's things. The early morning light was over everything and summer had glanced back and waved a fleeting hand at the day with soft airs and lingering warmth of sunshine. The boy's heart was fairly bursting with happiness.

Oh, the glories and the wonders of that journey! At Schenectady there was a stop of several minutes and David took Nathan forward and introduced him to the engineer, who kindly showed him the engine, taking apparent pride and pleasure in explaining every detail of its working. The engineer had come to be a hero to the boys and knew his admirers when he saw them. He invited Nathan to ride to Albany in the engine with him, and the boy with shining eyes allowed David to accept the invitation for him, and climbed on board feeling as if he were about to mount up on wings and fly to the moon. David went back to his coach and his discussion of Whig versus Loco-Foco.

At Albany a new engineer came on duty and Nathan went back to his place beside David in the carriage. But there was a world of new delight to watch, with David ready to explain everything; and there were two men to whom David introduced him. One, a Mr. Burleigh, was going down to New York to lecture "In Opposition to the Punishment of Death," as the notices in the *Tribune* stated. Nathan listened with tense interest to the discussion for and against capital punishment; the more because the subject had come so near to the elder brother who had been his youthful paragon and idol. David, turning once, caught the look in the boy's eyes and wondered again at the intellectual appreciation he seemed to have, no matter what the subject.

The other gentleman was a Mr. Vail, an intimate friend of and closely associated with Professor Samuel Morse, the inventor of the Electro-Magnetic Telegraph. He had recently ~~~~~~~~~~~~~~~~~~~~~~

~~~~~~ glowed over the fairy tale of science.

Then as they neared the great city of New York about which he had dreamed so many dreams, the boy's heart beat high with excitement. His face went pale with suppressed emotion. He was a boy of few words, and not used to letting anyone know how he felt, but the three men in the coach could not help seeing that he was greatly stirred.

"A fine fellow that," murmured Mr. Vail to Mr. Burleigh as the train drew in at the station, and Nathan seemed engrossed in the various things which David was pointing out to him.

"Yes," assented Mr. Burleigh. "He asked some bright questions. He'll do something in the world himself one day or I'm mistaken. Has a good face."

"Yes, a very good face. I've been thinking as I watched him this morning if more boys were like that we needn't be afraid for the future of our country."

Nathan just then turned, lifting un-self-conscious eyes to the two men opposite, and perceived in a flash; by their close regarding, that the words he had just overheard were spoken concerning himself. A look of wonder, and then of deep shame crossed his face

He dropped his gaze and his long dark lashes swept like a gloomy veil over the bright eager eyes that had just glowed so finely, while a deep wave of crimson spread over his face.

They had thought that of him just seeing him once, these gentlemen! But if they knew how people regarded him at home! Ah, if they knew! He could hear even now the echo of old Squire Heath's ejaculations concerning himself: "That young Whitney's a rascal an' a scoundrel. He'll never amount to a row of pins. He ought to have his hide tanned."

Nathan's confusion was so great that it was unmistakable, and David turning toward him suddenly saw that something was wrong.

"I've just got caught in expressing my opinion of your young friend here," smilingly acknowledged Mr. Vail. "I hope he will pardon my being so personal, but I have taken a great liking to him. I hope he will find it possible to come to Philadelphia some time soon and visit me. I can then show him my instrument. If you should come down next month perhaps you will bring him with you."

The flood of color in the boy's face was illumined by a holy wonder as he looked from one gentleman to the other. Truly he had been lifted out entirely from his old life and set in a sphere where no one knew he was a worthless scoundrel not to be trusted. He heard David promising to bring him with him if possible the next time he went to Philadelphia and he managed to stumble out a few broken words of thanks to both gentlemen, feeling all the time how inadequate they were. but had he known it, words were unnecessary, for his eloquent eyes spoke volumes of gratitude.

The train came to a standstill then and there were pleasant leave-takings with their fellow travellers, after which David and Nathan took their way through the city to the hotel where David usually stopped, Nathan feeling suddenly shy and young and quite countrified.

...ng, busy, happy dream for Nathan. He was with David all day long, save when that busy man was closeted with some great men talking over business matters which were private and confidential. Even then David often took Nathan with him as his secretary, asking him to take notes of things that were said, or occasionally to copy papers. The boy was acquiring great skill in such matters and could write a neat and creditable letter quite satisfactory to his employer. He had a good, natural handwriting as well as a keen mind and willing heart, which are a great outfit in any work.

Everywhere they went David explained who and what people, places and things were. Their trip was liberal education for the boy. He met great men, and saw the sights of the whole city. Every evening when business would allow, they went to some gathering or place of entertainment. He heard a lecture of Phrenology and Magnetism which interested him, and he resolved to try some of the experiments with the boys when he got home. He went to the New York Opera House to attend the Thirty-eighth Anniversary of the Peithologian Society of Columbia College, of which David Spafford was a member, and met Mr. J. Babcock Arden, the Secretary, whose name was signed to the notice of the meeting in the *Tribune*. It seemed wonderful to meet a man whose name was printed out like that in a New York paper. Mr. Arden greeted him as if he were already a man and told him he hoped he would be one of their number some day when he came to college, and Nathan's heart swelled with the determination to fulfil that hope.

They went to several concerts, and Nathan discovered that he enjoyed music immensely. The Philharmonic Society gave its first concert during their stay in the city and it was the boy's first experience in hearing fine singing. He sat as one entranced. Another night they heard Rainer and Dempster, two popular singers who were making a great impression, especially with their rendering of "The Lament of the Irish Emigrant,"

"Locked in the Cradle of the Deep," and "The Free Country." The melodies caught in the boy's brain and kept singing themselves over and over. He also came to know "Auld Robin Gray," a new and popular ballad, "The Death of Warren," "Saw ye Johnnie Coming" and "The Blind Boy." When he was alone he sang them over bit by bit until he felt they were his own. It was thus, coming upon him unaware one day, that David discovered the boy was possessed of a wonderfully clear, flute-like voice, and resolved that he must go to singing school during the winter and must certainly sing in the choir, for such a voice would be an acquisition to the church. He decided to talk with the minister about it as soon as he got home.

Two days after their arrival in New York there came the celebration of the completion of the Croton Water Works. Heralded for days beforehand both by friends and enemies, the day dawned bright and clear and Nathan awoke as excited as if he were a little boy on General Training Day.

There was a six-mile pageant formed on Broadway and Bowling Green, marching through Broadway to Union Square, and down Bowery to Grand Street. There were twenty thousand in the procession and so great was the enthusiasm, according to the papers, that "there might have been two hundred thousand if there had been room for them."

First came the New York firemen, whose interest in the new water system was most natural, and following them in full uniform the Philadelphia firemen, their helmets and bright buttons gleaming in the sun. Then came the Irish, then the Germans, then the Masons, banners and streamers flying, a brilliant display. There was a float bearing the identical printing press on which Franklin worked, and Colonel Stone sat in Franklin's chair printing leaflets all about the Croton Water Works, which were distributed along the way as the procession moved. There was another float bearing two miniature steamboats, and next followed the gold and silver artisans. After them came the cars with models of the pipes and pieces of the machinery used in the water works and maps of the construction; then the artisans whose labor had brought into being the great system. After them came the College, Mechanical and Mercantile Library Society, and last of all the Temperance Societies, whose beautiful banners bearing noble sentiments were greeted with loud acclamation by the people.

There were speeches and singing, and Samuel Stevens gave the history of New York water, telling about the old Tea-Water Pump which gave the only drinkable water until 1825. After that there were cisterns in front of the churches, and later the city appropriated fifteen hundred dollars to a tank on Thirteenth Street.

It was a great day, with bells ringing from morning to night, and the Croton Water Works sending out beautiful jets of water from the hydrants

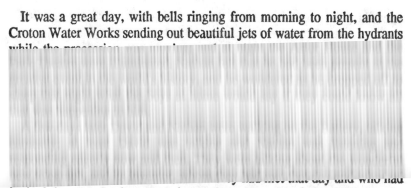

invited them to watch an experiment that was to be tried publicly on the morrow. It was a beautiful moonlight night, and presently as they walked and talked, looking out across the way they saw a little boat proceeding slowly along, one man at the oars and one at the stern. Other idlers on the battery that night might have wondered what kind of fishing the two men were engaged in that took so long a line, but David and Nathan watched with deep interest for they were in the secret of the little boat. In its stern sat Professor Morse with two miles of copper wire wound on a reel, paying it out slowly. It took two hours to lay that first cable between Castle Garden and Governor's Island, and the two who watched did not remain until it was done for they had been invited to be present very early the next morning when the first test was to be made, and so they hurried back to the Astor House to get some sleep before the wonderful event should take place. Nathan was almost too much excited to sleep.

The *New York Herald* came out next morning with this statement:

MORSE'S ELECTRO-MAGNETIC TELEGRAPH.

"This important invention is to be exhibited in operation at Castle Garden between the hours of twelve and one o'clock today. One telegraph will be erected on Governor's Island, and one at the Castle, and messages will be interchanged and others transmitted during the day. Many have been incredulous as to the power this wonderful triumph of science and art. All such may now have an opportunity of fairly testing it. *It is destined to work a complete revolution in the mode of transmitting intelligence throughout the civilized world.*"

At daybreak Professor Morse was on the Battery, and was joined almost immediately by David and Nathan and two or three other friends deeply interested, and the work of preparing for the great test began. At last everything was in readiness, and the eager watchers actually witnessed the transmission of three or four characters between the termini of the line, when suddenly the communication was interrupted and it was found impossible to send any more messages through the conductor. Great was the excitement and anxiety for a few minutes, while the Professor worked with his instrument. Then looking up he pointed out on the water and a light broke into his face, for there lying along the line of the submerged cable were no less than seven vessels! A few minutes' investigation and it was found that one of these vessels in getting under way had raised the line on its anchor. The sailors, unable to understand what it meant, had hauled in about two hundred feet of the line on deck, and finding no end, cut off what they had and carried it away with them. Thus ignominiously ended the first attempt at submarine telegraphing.

A crowd had assembled on the Battery, but when they found there was to be no exhibition they began to disperse with jeers, most of them believing that they had been the victims of a hoax; and Nathan, watching the strong patient lines of the fine face of the inventor, found angry, pitying tears crowding to his own eyes as he felt the disappointment for the man who seemed to him so great a hero. How he wished in his heart that he were a man, and a rich one, that he might furnish the wherewithal for a thorough public test immediately; but he turned away with his heart full of admiration for the man who was bearing so patiently this new disappointment in his great work for the world. Nathan believed in him and in his invention with all his heart. Had he not heard the little click, click of the instrument and seen with his own eyes the strange characters produced? Others might disbelieve and jeer, but he knew, for he had seen and heard.

There were other great men to meet and hear talk, men whom in after years Nathan was to know more about and feel pride at having met, and because David knew a great many Nathan came in the way of seeing them also. There was Ralph Waldo Emerson, who wrote for the *New York Tribune*. That was all Nathan knew about him at the time, and thought that was enough because being with a journalist, he thought journalism the very highest thing in literature. In after years he learned of course to know better and to be exceedingly proud of his brief meeting with so great a man in the world of letters. Then there were Honorable Millard Fillmore and a kindly faced man named Henry Clay, and William Lloyd Garrison, all especial friends of David's and honored accordingly by the boy, who worshipped them from afar.

He heard much talk of things in general: The Indian Treaty; a man named Dickens from England who had travelled in America awhile and written some bitter criticisms of American journalists (how Nathan hated him!); a wonderful flying machine that was in process of being invented by a man named McDermott, which

his neat hand and he entertained secret hopes of making one for himself some day when he had the time. There was another one talked about, made by a man in New Orleans, a hollow machine like the body of a bird, and wings like a bird's with a man inside and light machinery to work the wings, but this seemed not so easy to carry out and Nathan inclined to the first one. Then there was great talk about postage, and the failure to have the rates cut down. Many thought it ought to be cut to five and ten cents with fifteen for long distances, and Nathan found much to think about.

But most of all he heard talk of politics, Whigs and Loco-Focos, and he began to take a deep interest in it all. When almost at the close of their stay David announced that he meant to take in the Whig Convention on the way home the heart of the boy rose to great heights. The Convention was to be held in Goshen, Orange County, 22 miles by steamboat and 44 miles by railroad, and the journey would take five hours. There were a hundred passengers in the party; notable men, and the experience meant much to the boy in after years.

CHAPTER 12

NATHAN came home from New York a new creature. He walked the old familiar streets, and met the neighbors he had known since ever he could remember, as in a dream. It was as if years had passed and given him a new point of view. Behold the former things had passed away and all things had become new. He knew that he was new. He knew that the aspirations and desires of his life had changed, and he bore himself accordingly.

The neighbors looked at him with a puzzled, troubled expression; paused and turned again to look as he passed, and then said reflectively:

"Well, I'll be gormed! Ain't that that young Whitney?"

At least that was what Squire Heath said, as he braced himself against his own gatepost and chewed a straw while Nathan walked erectly down the street away from him. It reminded one of those people long ago who asked:

"Is not this he that sat and begged?"

In former times nobody had been wont even to look at Nathan as he passed.

The boys, his companions in wicked pranks, fell upon him uproariously on his return, inclined to treat his vacation as a joke, and then fell back from him in puzzled bewilderment. He was as if not one of them. Already he gave them the impression that he looked down upon them, although he had no such notion in his mind, and was heartily glad to see them; but his mind was in a confusion and he hardly knew how to reconcile all the new emotions that strove for precedence in his breast. These foolish, loud-voiced children once a part and parcel of himself, did not somehow appeal to him in his new mood. In his heart of hearts he was loyal to them still, and glad to see them, but he wondered just a little why they seemed so trifling to him. It was not altogether the more grownup suit of clothes that David had encouraged him to buy in New York with his advance wages. This of course made him look older; but he had seen a great deal in his short stay and carried responsibilities not a few, besides having come in contact with the great questions and some of the great people of the day. He had had a vision of what it meant to be a man, and his ideals were reaching forth to higher things. He came and went among them gravely with a new and upright bearing and gradually they left him to himself.

for his friends the Spaffords. It was an inevitable circumstance of the new order of things, of course, but it puzzled and gloomed the boy's outlook on life. Yet he would not, could not, go back.

It is true that the attitude of the town toward him had slightly, even imperceptibly, changed. Instead of ignoring him altogether, or being actually combative toward him, they assumed a righteous tolerance of his existence which to the proud young nature was perhaps just as hard to bear. There was a certain sinister quality of grimness in their eyes, too, as they watched him, which he could not help but feel, for he was sensitive as a flower in spite of his courage and strength of character. They were actually disappointed, some of them, that he was seeming to turn out so differently from their prophecies. Had they really wanted him to be bad so they could gloat over him?

Nevertheless, there were great new joys opening up to the boy that fully outbalanced these other things. His work was an intense satisfaction to him. He took pleasure in doing everything just as well as it could be done, and often stayed beyond hours to finish up some bit of writing that could just as well have waited until next day, just to see the pleased surprise in David's eyes when he found out. Also he was actually getting interested in Latin. Not that he was a great student by nature. He had always acquired knowledge too easily to have made him work very hard for it until now and he had also always had too much mischief to give him time to study. But now he desired above all this to please his teacher and stand well in his eyes.

A man could not do as much for Nathan as David had done and not win everlasting gratitude and adoration from him. So Nathan studied.

David was a good teacher, enjoying his task, great progress was made; and the winter sped by on fleet wings.

Miranda, hovering in the background with opportune cookies and hot gingerbread when the evening tasks were over, enjoyed her part in the education and transformation of the boy. He was going to college and she was going to have at least a cookie's worth credit in the matter.

Miranda, as she cooked and swept and made comfort generally for all those with whom she had to do was turning over and over in her mind a plan, and biding her time. There was something she longed do, but did not yet see her way clear to it. The more she thought the more impossible it seemed, yet more determined she became to do it one day.

repair, one cow, several neglected chickens, and an income of sixty dollars per year from some property his father had left. Lawrence could not sew as his mother had done, to work at anything he could do he was ashamed, and he could not get anything he would do; obviously the only thing he could do for himself was to marry a girl with a tidy income and a thrifty hand. This Lawrence Billings set about doing with a will.

He was good looking in a washed-out sort of way, and could drape himself elegantly about a chair in a best parlor. The girls rather liked him around, he was handy. But when it came to marrying, that was another thing! He tried several hearty farmer's daughters in vain. They flouted him openly. But just after Christmas there came to town a young cousin of the postmistress, an orphan, who, rumor said, had a fine house and farm all in her own right. The farm was rented out and she was living on the income. She was pretty and liked to go about, so she accepted Lawrence Billings's attentions with avidity. They were seen together everywhere, and it began to be commonly spoken of as "quite a match after all for poor Lawrence! What a pity his poor mother couldn't have known!"

Miranda, alert and attentive, bristled like a fine red thistle. Lawrence Billings marry a pink-cheeked girl and live on her farm comfortably, when all the time Allan Whitney was, goodness knew where, exiled from home to keep Lawrence comfortable! Not if she could help it.

She came home from church in high dudgeon with a bright spot on either cheek and her eyes snapping. She had sat behind Lawrence Billings and the pink-cheeked Julia Thatcher and had seen their soft looks. Between their heads,—his sleek one and her bonneted one,—had seemed to look down the shadowy face of young Allan, fine and stern and exalted, his sacrifice upon him as he went forth into the whiteness of the storm those long, long years ago. Miranda felt that the time had come for action.

It was late winter, the winter of 1843. The heavy snows were yet on the ground and had no notion thawing. Miranda went up to her room, carefully laid aside her heavy pelisse, her muff and silk-corded bonnet, and changed her dress. Then she went quietly down to the kitchen to place the Sunday dinner, already cooked the day before, on the table. It was a delicious dinner, with one of the best mince pies that ever was eaten, for a climax, but Miranda forgot for once to watch for David's praise and Marcia's quiet satisfaction in the fruit of her labors. She was absorbed beyond any mere immediate interests to rouse her.

"Don't you feel well, Miranda?" questioned Marcia solicitously.

"Well'z ever!" she responded briefly and slammed off to the kitchen where she could have quiet. Never since the time of Phoebe Deane's trouble, when Miranda had put more than one finger in the pie before Phoebe was free from a tyrannical sister-in-law, an undesired lover, a weak brother, and happily married to the man of her choice, had Marcia seen Miranda so abstracted. There must be something the matter. But Miranda was much like a boy. If you wanted to find out what was the matter you would better keep still and not let on that you thought anything, and then perhaps you had a chance. Never, if you kindly inquired. So Marcia, wise in her day and generation, held her peace and made things as easy for her handmaiden as possible.

All that day, the next and the next Miranda gloomed, rushed and absented herself from the family as much as was consistent with her duties. Her lips were pursed till their merry red fairly disappeared. Even to Rose she was almost short. Nathan was the only one who brought a fleeting smile, and that was followed by a look of pain. Miranda was at all times intense, and during this time she was painfully more so.

The third day David came into the dining room with the evening papers, just as Miranda was putting on the supper. He was tired and cold and the firelight looked good to him, so instead of going to the library as usual until Miranda called him for supper, he settled down in his place at the table and began to read.

When his wife came into the room he looked up exultantly:

"Hurrah for Hon. John P. Kennedy! Listen to this, Marcia! 'The Hon. John P. Kennedy submitted a resolution that the bill appropriating thirty thousand dollars, to be expended under the direction of the Secretary of the Treasury, in a series of experiments to test the expediency of the Telegraph projected by Professor Morse, should be passed.' Isn't that great? Sit down, dear, and I'll read it to you while Miranda is putting on the supper."

Marcia settled herself in her little sewing chair and took up the ever-ready knitting that always lay to hand on the small stand between the dining-room windows; while Miranda, her ears alert, tiptoed about not to interrupt the reading nor lose a single word. It was thus that Miranda, through the years in this household, had acquired a really creditable education. David, realizing fully her eagerness to hear, raised his voice

present had done much to encourage science, he did not wish to see the science of mesmerism neglected and overlooked. He therefore proposed that one-half of the appropriation be given to Mr. Fisk, to enable him to carry on experiments, as well as Professor Morse.

"Mr. Houston thought that Millerism should also be included in the benefits of the appropriation—"

A snort from the kitchen door brought the reading to a sudden stop and David looked up to see Miranda, hands on her hips, arms akimbo, standing indignant in the doorway. When it came to a matter of understanding Miranda was "all there."

"Who be they?" she asked, her eyes snapping blue fire.

David loved to see her in this mood, and often wished some of the people who incited her to it could meet her at such a time. He beamed at her now and asked interestedly:

"Who are who, Miranda?"

"Why them two, Mr. Millerism, and the other feller. Who be they and what rights hev they got to butt in to thet there money thet was meant fer the telegraphy?"

Marcia suppressed a hasty smile and David looked down quickly at his paper.

"They're not men, Miranda, they're 'isms.' Millerism is a belief, and mesmerism is a power."

Miranda looked puzzled.

David tried to explain.

"Millerism is the belief that a religious sect called the Millerites hold. They are followers of a man named William Miller. They believe that the end of the world is near; that the day in fact is already set. They have a paper called *The Signs of the Times*. Do you know, Marcia, I read in the *New York Tribune* the other day that they have now set May 23rd of this coming year as the time of the second coming of Christ. They make it a point to be all ready dressed in white robes awaiting the end when it comes."

"Gumps!" interpolated Miranda with scorn. " 'Z if them things made any diffrunce! When it comes to a matter o' robes I'd prefer a heavenly one, and I calc'late on it's being furnished me free o' charge. What's the other ism? Messyism? Ain't it got no more sense to 't than Millerism?"

"Mesmerism? Well, yes, it has. There is perhaps some science back of it, though it is at present very little understood. A man named Franz Mesmer started the idea. He has a theory that one person can produce in another an abnormal condition resembling sleep, during which the mind of the person sleeping is subject to the will of the operator. Mesmer says it is due to animal magnetism. There have been a good many experiments made on this theory, but to my mind it is a dangerous thing, for evil-minded people could use it for great harm to others. It is also claimed that under this power the one who is mesmerized can talk with departed spirits."

"Humph!" commented Miranda. "More gumps! Say, what'r they thinking about to put sech fool men into the governm'nt t' Washin'ton? Can't they see the diffrunce atween things like thet and the telegraphy?"

Miranda, proud in her scientific knowledge, sailed back to her kitchen and took up the muffins for tea, but she had also food for thought and the rest of the evening was silent beyond her wont. It would have been interesting if she had but been in the habit of keeping a diary and setting down her quaint philosophies, but the greater number of them were buried in her own heart, and only the fortunate intimate friend was favored with them now and then.

About a week later Marcia came in from the monthly missionary meeting, which Miranda resolutely refused to attend, declaring that she had missionary work enough in her own kitchen without wasting time hearing a lot of fairy stories about people that lived in the geography and likely weren't much worse than most folks if the real truth were told.

"Miranda," said Marcia coming into the wide pleasant kitchen to untie her bonnet, "you're going to have opportunity to find out what mesmerism is. Your cousin Hannah is going to have a man to visit at her house who understands it and he is going to mesmerize some of the young people. It is Thursday evening and we are invited. Your cousin wanted me to ask you if you would be willing to help serve and clean up afterward. She is going to have coffee and doughnuts."

Miranda tossed her chin high and sniffed, albeit there was a glitter of interest in her eyes. She was not fond of her Cousin Hannah, blonde and proud and selfish, she that had been Hannah Heath, before she married Lemuel Skinner, and had been wont to look down upon her Cousin

Miranda. Ordinarily Miranda could have sent a curt refusal to such a request and Marcia knew it, but the mesmerist was too great a bait.

borrow a cup of molasses for a belated gingerbread, and when she went to her grandmother Heath's on an errand for Marcia; and the more she heard the more thoughtful she became.

"Who's Hannah going to hev to her tea party, Grandma?" she had asked the old lady. Mrs. Heath paused in her knitting, looked over her spectacles and enumerated them:

"The Spaffords, the Waites, Aaron Petrie's folks, the Van Storms, Lawrence Billings, o' course, and Julia Thatcher'n her aunt, Abe Fonda, Lyman Brown, and Elkanah Wilworth's nieces up from New York—"

But Miranda had heard no more after Lawrence Billings, and her mind was off in a tumult of plans. She could hardly wait until David came home that evening to question him.

"Say, Mr. David, wisht you'd tell me more 'bout that mesmerism thing you was readin' 'bout. D'ye say they put 'em to sleep, an' they walked around an' didn't know what they was doin' an' did what the man told 'em to?"

"Well, about that, Miranda, I think you've got the idea."

"Say, d'yu reely b'leeve it, Mr. David? 'Cause I don't b'leeve nobody could make me do all them fool things 'thout I would let 'em."

"No, of course not without your consent, Miranda. I believe they make that point. You've got to surrender your will to theirs before they can do anything. If you resist they have no power. It's a good deal like a temptation. If you stand right up to it and say no, it has no chance with you, but if you let yourself play with it, why it soon gets control."

"But d'you reely b'leeve ther is such a thin' anyway? Could anybody make you do things you didn't think out fer yerself?"

"Why, yes, Miranda, it's this way. There is in us all a power called animal magnetism which if exercised has a very strong influence over other people. You know yourself how some people can persuade others to do almost anything. The power of the eye in looking does a great deal, the touch of the hand in persuasion does more sometimes. Some people too have stronger wills and minds than others, and there is no question but that there is something to it. I have myself seen exhibitions in a small way of the power of mesmerism,—the power of one mind over another. They make people go and find some article that has been hidden, just by laying the hand on the subject and thinking of the place where the article is hidden. Such experiments as that are easy and common now. But as for talking with those who have left this world, that's another thing."

"But some folks reely b'leeve that?"

"They say they do."

"Humph! Gumps!" declared Miranda turning back to the kitchen with a satisfied sniff. Thereafter she went about her work singing at the top of her lungs and not another word did she say about mesmerism or the Skinner tea party, although she walked softly and listened intently whenever anyone else spoke of it.

Miranda went to her Cousin Hannah's early in the afternoon and meekly helped to get things ready. It was not Miranda's way to be meek and Hannah was surprised and touched.

"You can come in and watch them when the professor gets to mesmerizing, M'randy," said Hannah indulgently, noticing with satisfaction the gleam of the green and brown plaid silk beneath Miranda's ample white apron, as she stooped to dust the legs of the whatnot in the corner, and then rose rustlingly to straighten a large knit antimacassar on the back of the mahogany rocking chair.

"I might look in, but I don't take much stock in such goin's on," conceded Miranda loftily. "Did you say you was going to pass cheese with the doughnuts and coffee? I might a brang some along ef I'd knowed. I made more'n we'd reely eat afore it gets stale to our house."

Miranda kept herself well in the background during the early part of the evening, though she made one of the company at the beginning and greeted everybody with a self-respecting manner. That much she demanded as recognition of her family and her good clothes. For the rest it suited her plans to keep out of sight, and she made an excuse to slip into the kitchen, where she found a vantage point behind a door that gave her a view of the whole room and a chance to hear what was being said without being particularly observed. Once, within her range and quite near, Lawrence Billings and Julia Thatcher sat for five full minutes, and Miranda's blood boiled angrily as she saw the evident progress the young man was making in his wooing. Studying the girl's pink cheeks and laughing blue eyes she decided that she was much too good for him, and above the weak-faced young man seemed to rise in vision the strong fine face of Allan Whitney, too noble even to scorn the weak man who had let him go all these years under a crime he had not committed.

Not even Hannah Heath knew when it was that Miranda slipped back into the room and became a part of the company. The fine aroma of coffee came at the same time, however, and whetted everybody's appetite. The

messages to people in the room from their departed friends. The messages were all of a general nature of greeting, and somewhat characteristic of the departed, nothing to make any undesirable cloud on the spirits of the gay company. Everybody was laughing and chattering gaily between times, telling the professor how perfectly wonderful it all was, and how queer he or she felt under his mesmeric influence.

Miranda had watched it all from her covert, and observed keenly every detail of the affair, also the gullibility of the audience. At just the right moment she entered with her great platter of doughnuts and followed it by steaming cups of coffee.

Oh, Miranda! child of loneliness and loyalty! In what school did you learn your cunning?

Just how she contrived to get around the long-haired flabby professor perhaps nobody in the room could have explained, unless it might have been Marcia, who was watching her curiously and wondering what Miranda was up to now. Miranda always had some surprise to spring on people when she went around for days like that with bright red cheeks and her eyes flashing with suppressed excitement. Marcia had warned David to be on the lookout for something interesting. But David was sitting in the corner discussing politics, the various vices and virtues of the Whigs versus the Loco-Focos. He took his coffee and doughnuts entirely unaware of what was going on in the room.

Marcia was watching with delight the arts of Miranda as she laughed and chatted with the guest of the evening, travelling back and forth to the kitchen to bring him more cream and sugar, and the largest, fattest doughnuts. Suddenly Cornelia Van Storm leaned over and began to ask about the last missionary meeting, and Marcia was forced to give attention to the Sandwich Islands for a time.

"They do say that some of those heathens that didn't used to have a thing to wear are getting so fond of clothes that they come to church in real gaudy attire so that the pastors have had to reprove and admonish them," said Cornelia, with a zest in her words as if she were retailing a rare bit of gossip. "If that's so I don't think I'll give any more money to the missionary society. I'm sure I don't see the use of our sacrificing things here at home for them to flaunt the money around there, do you?"

"Why, our money wouldn't go for their dress anyway," said Marcia smiling. "I suppose the poor things dress in what they can get and like. But anyway if we sent money to the Sandwich Islands it would likely go to pay the missionary. You know the work there is perfectly wonderful. Nearly all the children over eight can read the New Testament and they have just dedicated their new church. The King of the Islands gave the land it is built on and most of the money to build it. It is 137 feet long and 72 feet wide and cost quite a good deal."

"Well, I must say if that's so they are quite able to look after themselves, and I for one don't approve of sending any more money there. I never did approve of foreign missions anyway, and this makes me feel more so. I say charity begins at home."

But just at that moment Marcia lifted her eyes and beheld what made her forget the heathen, home and foreign, and give her attention to the other end of the room; for there was Miranda, rosy and bridling like any of the younger girls, allowing the long-haired professor to tie the bandage around her eyes. There was a smile of satisfaction on her pleasant mouth, and a set of determination on her firm shoulders. Marcia was sure the stage was set and the curtain about to rise at last.

_____ ____, and I have long been searching for a suitable medium on which to try an experiment of my own."

David, in the middle of a convincing sentence about Henry Clay, suddenly ceased speaking and wheeled around with a sharp glance across the room, darted first suspiciously at the professor, and then with dismay at his subject. It seemed impossible to connect Miranda with anything as occult as mesmerism. David drew his brows together in a frown. Somehow he didn't quite like the idea of Miranda lending her strong common sense to what seemed to him a foolish business. Still, Miranda generally knew what she was about, and finding a thimble of course was harmless, if that were all.

"We will first give a simple experiment to see if all goes well," went on the professor, "and then, if the lady proves herself an apt subject I will proceed to make an experiment of a deeper nature. Will some one kindly hide the thimble? Mrs. Skinner, you have it, I believe. Yes, thank you, that will do very well."

It is doubtful if anyone in the room save David, whose eyes were upon Miranda, saw the deft quick motion with which she slid the bandage up from one eye and down again in a trice as if she were merely making it easier on her head; but during that instant Miranda's one blue eye took in a good deal, as David observed, and she must have seen the thimble being hidden away in Melissa Hartshorn's luxuriant waving hair which was mounted elaborately on the top of her head. A queer little smile hovered about David Spafford's lips. Miranda was up to her tricks again, and evidently had no belief whatever in the professor's ability. She meant to carry out her part as well as the rest had done and not be thought an impossible subject. She was perhaps intending to try an experiment herself on the professor.

"Now, you must yield your will to mine absolutely," explained the professor as he had done to the others.

"How do you make out to do that?" asked the subject, standing alert and capable, her hands on her hips, her chin assertive as usual.

Marcia caught a look of annoyance on Hannah Skinner's face. She had not expected Miranda to make herself so prominent, and she meant to give her a piece of her mind after it was over, Marcia could easily see that.

"Why, you just relax your mind and your will. Be pliable, as it were, in my hands. Make your mind a blank. Try not to think your own thoughts, but open your mind to obey my slightest thought. Be quiescent. Be pliable, my dear young lady."

Miranda dropped one arm limply at her side and then the other, and managed to make her whole tidy vivid figure slump gradually into an inertness that was fairly comical in one as self-sufficient as Miranda.

"I'm pliable!" she announced in anything but a limp tone.

"Very good, very good, my dear young lady," said the oily professor laying a large moist hand on her brow, and taking one of her hands in his other one. "Now, yield yourself fully!"

Miranda stood limply for a moment and then began to sway gently as she had seen the others do, and to step timidly forth toward Melissa Hartshorn.

The professor cast a triumphant look about the circle of eagerly attentive watchers.

"Very susceptible, very susceptible indeed!" he murmured. "Just as I supposed, unusually susceptible subject!"

David stood watching amusedly, an incredulous twinkle in his eyes. Miranda with studied hesitation was going directly toward the thimble, and when she reached Melissa she stopped as if she had run up against a wall, and groped uncertainly for her hair. In a moment more she had the thimble in her hand.

"You see!" said the professor exultantly. "It is just as I said, the young lady is peculiarly susceptible, and now we will proceed to a most interesting experiment. We will ask some one in the room to step forward and think of something, anything in the room will do, and the subject will tell what he is thinking about. It will be necessary of course to inform me what the object is. Will this gentleman kindly favor us? I will remove the bandage from the subject's eyes. It is unnecessary in this experiment."

Aaron Petrie, rotund and rosy from embarrassment, stepped forward, and Miranda, relieved of her bandage, stared unseeingly straight at him with the look of a sleep walker and did not move.

"You will perceive that the subject is still under powerful influence," murmured the professor, noticing Miranda's dreamy, vacant stare. "That is well. She will be far more susceptible."

He bent his head...

...with intense interest, the professor said in a commanding tone: "Now tell the company what this gentleman is thinking about."

Miranda, her eyes still fixed on space, slowly opened her mouth and spoke, but her voice was drawling and slow with an unnatural monotony: "He—is—wishin'—he—hed—'nuther—doughnut!" she chanted.

The little assembly broke into astonished, half-awed laughter. The receptivity of Aaron Petrie toward all edibles was a matter of common joke. Even in the face of weird scientific experiments one had to laugh about Aaron Petrie's taste for doughnuts.

"Doughnuts! Doughnuts! Very good," said the professor, nervously rubbing his hands together. "The gentleman was thinking of the bit of doughnut on yonder plate, and the subject being so susceptible has doubtless reached a finer shade of thought than the young gentleman realized when he made his general statement to me."

The laugh subsided and trailed off into an exclamation of wonder as the cunning professor made Miranda's original answer a further demonstration of the mysteries of science.

"Now, will this young gentleman give us something?" The professor was still a trifle nervous. Miranda's fixed attitude puzzled him. She was not altogether like his other subjects, and he had an uneasy feeling that she might fail him at some critical point. Nevertheless, he was bound to keep on.

Abe Fonda came boldly forward with a swagger, his eyes fixed on the younger of Elkanah Wilworth's two pretty nieces. Miranda's faraway look did not change. She was having the time of her life, but the best was yet to come.

Abe whispered eagerly in the professor's ear and his eyes sought the pretty girl's again with a smile.

The professor bowed and turned to his subject as before, and Miranda, without waiting for a request, chanted out again:

"Abe's a-thinking—how—purty—Ruth-Ann—Wilworth's curl—in—the back—o'—her—neck—is."

A shout of laughter greeted this, and Abe turned red, while the professor grew still more uneasy. He saw that he was growing in favor with his audience, but the subject was most uncertain, and not at all like other subjects with whom he had experimented. He had a growing suspicion that she was doing some of the work on her own hook and not putting herself absolutely under his influence. It would be as well if he were to go further with her, that he confine his investigations to safe subjects. The dead were safer than the living.

"Well, yes, the young gentleman did mention the younger Miss Wilworth," he said apologetically. "I hope no offense is taken at the exceedingly—that is to say—direct way the subject has of stating the case."

"Oh, no offense whatever," said the sheepish Abe. "It was all quite true I assure you, Miss Wilworth," and he made a low bow toward the blushing, simpering girl.

Now the professor had one stunt which he loved to pull off in any company where he dared. He would call up the spirit of George Washington and question him concerning the coming election, which not only thrilled the audience but often had great weight with them in changing or strengthening their opinions. He knew that the ordinary subject would easily respond yes or no according to his will, and this remarkable young woman, no matter how original her replies, could scarcely make much trouble in politics, and would not be likely to interpolate her own personality with such a subject of conversation. He decided to try it at once, and all the more because the young woman herself had expressed a desire to see an exhibition of his power to communicate with the other world.

"This young woman," began the professor in his most suave tones, "has proved herself so apt a subject that I am going to try something that I seldom dare attempt in public without first having experimented for days with the subject. It may work and it may not, I can scarcely be sure without knowing her better; but as she herself has expressed a desire to yield herself for the experiment I will endeavor to call up some one from the other world—"

David at this sat up suddenly, his eyes searching the blank ones of Miranda. It troubled him to have a member of his household put herself even for a short time under this slippery looking man's influence, and this tampering with the mysterious he did not like. There was no telling what effect it might have upon Miranda, though he had always heretofore thought her the most practical and sensible person he knew. He could not quite understand her willingness to submit to this nonsense. Ought he to interfere? He was to blame himself for having talked to her so much about the subject. He cleared his throat and almost spoke, his eyes still upon the

. . . . saw she looked troubled. He tried to signal to her by a smile and was surprised to receive an answering reassurance as if Marcia too had discovered something.

The professor now stood forth making some slow rhythmical motions with his hands on the girl's forehead and in front of her face. He was just about to speak his directions to her when she rose slowly as though impelled by some unseen force, and stood staring straight ahead of her at the open kitchen door, her eyes strained and wild, her face impressive with a weird solemnity.

"I—see—a—dead—man!" she exclaimed sepulchrally, and the professor rubbed his hands and wafted a few more thought-waves toward this remarkably apt subject.

Had Miranda arranged it with the draft of the kitchen window that just at this stage of the game the kitchen door should come slowly, noisily shut? A distinct shudder went around the company, but the girl continued to gaze raptly toward the door.

"Ask him what are his politics, please," commanded the professor, endeavoring to cast a little cheer upon the occasion.

"He—says—he—was—shot—down—by—Taylor's—woods."

An audible murmur of horror went around the room and everybody sat up and took double notice.

"Twelve—years—ago—" went on the monotonous voice in a high strident key.

"Enoch Taylor, I'll be gormed!" ejaculated old Mr. Heath, resting his horny hands on his knees and leaning forward with bulging eyes.

David could not help but notice that Lawrence Billings, who was sitting opposite to him, started nervously and looked furtively around the company.

"He— says— to— tell— you— his— murderer— is— in— this— room"— chanted Miranda as though she had no personal interest in the matter whatever.

In this room! The thought flashed like lightning from face to face—
"Who is it?" David found his eyes riveted on the pale face of the young
man opposite who seemed unable to take his eyes from Miranda's but sat
white and horrified with a fascinated stare like a bird under the gaze of a
cat.

"He— must— confess— tonight— before— the— clock— strikes—
the— hour— of— midnight"— went on the voice— "or— a— curse—
will— come on— him— and— he— will— die!"

There was a tense stillness in the room that filled everybody with horror,
as if the dead man had suddenly stepped into sight and charged them all
with his murder. They looked from one to another with sudden suspicion
in their eyes. The oily professor stood aghast at the work he had wrought
unaware.

"Oh, now, see here," he began with an attempt to break the tensity of the
moment, "don't let this thing break up the good cheer. We'll just bring this
lady back to herself again and dismiss the deceased for tonight. He
doubtless died with some such thing on his mind, or else he was insane
and keeps the same notions he had when he left this mortal frame. Now
don't let this worry you in the least. There isn't anybody in this room could
commit a murder if he tried, of course; why, you're all ladies and
gentlemen."

All the time the oily anxious man was making wild passes in front of
Miranda's face and trying to press her forehead with his hands, and wake
her up, but Miranda just marched slowly, solemnly, staringly ahead toward
the kitchen door, and everybody in the room but the professor watched
her, fascinated.

She turned when she reached the kitchen door, faced the room once
more, and staring back upon them all uttered once more her curse.

"Enoch— Taylor— say— ef— you— don't— confess— tonight—
before— midnight— you'll— die— and— he ain't goin'— to— leave—
you— till— you— confess."

She jabbed her finger straight forward blindly and it went through the
roached hair on Lawrence Billings's shrinking head and pointed straight at
nothing, but Lawrence Billings jumped and shrieked. In the confusion
Miranda dropped apparently senseless in the kitchen doorway; but just
before she dropped she gave David another slow, solemn wink with one
eye.

_____ with cold water and other stimulants, David had time to discover the absence of Lawrence Billings, though nobody else seemed to notice.

They all tiptoed away from the kitchen at Dr. Budlong's suggestion, and left Miranda to lie quiet and recover. He said he didn't believe in these new fangled things, they were bad for the system, and got people's nerves all stirred up, especially women. He wouldn't allow a woman to be put under mesmeric influence if he had anything to say about it. All women were hysterical, and that was doubtless the matter with Miranda.

The company looked at one another astonished. Who had ever suspected Miranda of having nerves, and going into hysterics? and yet she had proclaimed a murderer in their midst!

They turned to one another and began to converse in low mysterious tones while Miranda lay on the couch in the kitchen with closed eyelids and inward mirth. Presently, as Dr. Budlong counted her pulse and gave her another spoonful of stimulant, she drew a long sigh and turned her face to the wall; he, thinking she was dropping to sleep, tiptoed into the sitting room and closed the kitchen door gently behind him.

Miranda was on the alert at once, turning her head quickly to measure the width of the crack of the door. She held herself quiet for a full minute, and then slipped softly from her couch across the kitchen with the step of a sylph, snatched a mussed tablecloth from the shelf in the pantry where she had put it when she helped Hannah clear off the dinner table, and wrapping it quickly around her and over her head she went out of the back door.

Every movement was light and quick. She paused a second on the back stoop to get her bearings, then sped with swift light steps toward the barn door, which was open. A young moon was riding high in the heavens making weird battle with the clouds, and the light of a lantern shone from the open barn door. Miranda could see the long shadow of a man hitching up a horse with quick, nervous fingers. Lawrence Billings was preparing to take Julia Thatcher home.

Miranda approached the barn, and suddenly emerged into the light in full view of the startled horse just as Lawrence Billings stepped behind him to fasten the traces. The horse, having been roused from a peaceful slumber and not being yet fully awake, beheld the apparition with a snort, and without regard to the man or the unfastened traces reared on his hind legs and attempted to climb backwards into the carryall. There they stood, side by side, the man and the horse, open mouthed, wide nostriled, with protruding eyes; the smoky lantern by the barn door shedding a flickering light over the whole and casting grotesque shadows on the dusty floor.

Miranda, fully realizing her advantage, stood in the half-light of the moon in her fantastic drapery and waved her tableclothed arms, one forefinger wrapped tightly in the linen pointing straight at the frightened man, while she intoned in hollow sounds the words:

"Confess—tonight—or—you—will—die!"

Lawrence Billings's yellow hair rose straight on end and cold creeps went down his back. He snorted like the horse in his fright.

The white apparition moved slowly nearer, nearer to the patch of light in the barn door, and its voice wailed and rose like the wind in November, but the words it spoke were clear and distinct.

"Confess—at—once—or—misfortune—will—overtake—you! Moon—smite—you!—Dogs—bite—you!—Enoch Taylor's speerit—hant you! Yer mother's ghost pass before—you—!"

The white arms waved dismally, and the apparition took another step toward him. Then with a yell that might have been heard all the country round, Lawrence Billings made a wild dash past her to the back door.

"Food pizen you!—Sleep—fright—you!—Earth swaller—you!" screamed the merciless apparition flying after him, and the horse, having reached the limit of his self-control, clattered out into the open and cavorted around the garden until his nerves were somewhat relieved.

Lawrence Billings burst in upon the assembled company in the best parlor with wild eyes and dishevelled hair, and was suddenly confronted with the fact that these people did not believe in ghosts and apparitions. In the warm, bright room with plenty of companions about, he felt the foolishness of telling what he had just seen. His nerve deserted him. He could not face them all and suggest that he had seen a ghost, and so he blurted out an incoherent sentence about his horse. It was frightened at something white in the yard and had run away.

Instantly all hands hurried out to help catch the horse, Lawrence Billings taking care to keep close to the others, and joking fearsomely about the shadowy yard as he stepped forth again from shelter.

Miranda, meantime, had slipped into the kitchen and taken to her couch most decorously, the tablecloth folded neatly close at hand in case she needed it again, and was apparently resting quietly when Hannah tiptoed in to see if she needed

... ...s. it's perfect nonsense; Julia could have walked with him. Mother wanted to ride with Dr. Budlong, and now she'll have to stay all night and I just got the spare bed sheets done up clean and put away. I don't see what you had to go and get into things for tonight, anyhow, Mirandy. You might have known it wasn't a thing for you to meddle with. All this fuss just because you got people worked up about that murder. Why didn't you keep your mouth shut about it? It couldn't do any good now anyway. Say, Mirandy, did you really see any one or hear them say all that stuff?"

"What stuff, Hannah? " said Miranda sleepily. "I disremember what's ben happenin'. My head feels queer. Do you s'pose 'twould hurt me to go home to my own bed?"

"No," said Hannah crossly, "it's the best place you could be. I wish I hadn't asked you to come. I might have known you'd cut up some shine,— you always did,—but I thought you were grown up enough to act like other folks out to a tea party," and with this kind and cousinly remark she slammed into her sitting room again to make what she could of her excited guests.

Miranda, meanwhile, lay still and listened, and when she made out from the sounds that Julia Thatcher and her aunt had driven off in Dr. Budlong's carryall with his family, and that all the ladies who had not already departed were in the spare room putting on their wraps and bonnets, she stole forth softly, the tablecloth hidden under her cloak,—for she had taken the precaution early in the evening to hang her own wraps behind the kitchen door,—and took her way down the street, hovering in the shadows until she saw that Lawrence Billings was coming on behind her.

He was quite near to David and Marcia when he passed where she hid behind a lilac bush on the edge of Judge Waitstill's yard.

"Moon smite yeh,—stars blight yeh," murmured Miranda under her breath, but almost in his ear, and flicked the tablecloth a time or two in the moonlight as he looked back fearfully.

Lawrence hastened his steps until he was close behind another group of homeward-bound guests. Miranda slipped from bush to bush, keeping in the shadows of the trees, until she made sure that he was about to turn off down the road to his own isolated house. Then she slid under a fence and sped across a cornfield. The night was damp and a fine mist like smoke arose from the ground in wreaths of fog and hid her as she ran, but when the young man opened his gate he saw in the changing lights and shadows of the cloud- and moon-lit night a white figure with waving arms standing on his doorstep and moving slowly, steadily down to meet him.

With a gasp of terror he turned and fled back to the main street of the village, the ghost following a short distance behind, with light, uncanny tread and waving arms like wreaths of mist. It was too much for poor Lawrence Billings. Just in front of David Spafford's house he stumbled and fell flat—and here was the ghost all but upon him! With a cry of despair he scrambled to his feet and took refuge on the Spafford stoop, clacking the door knocker loudly in his fright. This was better than Miranda could have hoped. She held her ghostly part by the gate post till David opened the door, then slipped around to a loose pantry shutter and soon made good her entrance into the house. Stepping lightly she took her station near to a crack of a door where she could hear all that went on between David and his late caller. She heard with exultation the reluctant confession, the abject humility of voice, and cringing plea for mercy. Whatever happened now somebody besides herself knew that Allan Whitney was not a murderer. Her heart swelled with triumph as she listened to the frightened voice telling how a shot had struck the old man instead of the rabbit it was intended for, and how he had run to him and done everything he knew how to resuscitate his victim but without avail. In terrible fright he had started for the road, and there met Allan Whitney, who had come back with him and worked over the old man a while, and then told him to go home and say nothing about it, that he would take the gun and if anybody made a fuss he would take the blame; that it didn't matter about him anyway, nobody cared what became of him, but Lawrence had his mother to look out for. The man declared that he hadn't wanted to do it, putting Allan in a position like that, but when he thought of his mother, of course he had to; and anyhow he had hoped Allan would get away all right, and he did. It hadn't seemed so bad for Allan. He was likely as well off somewhere else as here, and he, Lawrence, had his mother to look after.

There was no spectre in this room, and Lawrence Billings was getting back his self-confidence. All the excuses with which he had bolstered himself during the years came flocking back to comfort him as he tried to justify himself before this clear-eyed man for his cowardly hiding behind another.

Something of the contempt that Miranda felt for the weak fellow was manifest in David S...

...g ... ... to go straight to Mr. Whitney. He ought not to be allowed to think another hour that his son has committed a crime. Then we will go to Mr. Heath—"

Lawrence Billings uttered something between a whine and a groan. His face grew whiter and his eyes seemed to fairly stand out.

"What'll we have to go to them for?" he demanded angrily. "Ain't I confessed? Ain't that enough? They can't hang me after all these years, can they? I ain't going to anybody else. I'll leave town if you say so, but I ain't going to do any more confessing."

"No, you will not leave town," said David quietly, laying a strong hand on the trembling shoulder, "and you most certainly will go and confess to those two men. It is the only possible way to make what amends you can for the past. You have put this matter in my hands by coming to me with it, and I cannot let you go until it is handed over to the proper authorities."

"I came to you because I thought you'd be just and merciful," whined the wretch.

"And so I will as far as in me lies. Justice demands that you confess this matter fully and that the whole thing be investigated. Come—!"

CHAPTER 16

MIRANDA watched through a rain of thankful tears as David escorted his guest out of the front door, and then she flew into the parlor and watched as they went arm in arm up the street and knocked at her grandfather's door. She waited with bated breath until a candle-light appeared at her grandfather's bedroom window, and slowly descended the stairs; waited again while the two went in, and another light appeared above, showing that a hasty toilet was being made; stood cold and patient by the window during an interminable time, imagining the conference that must be going on in the Heath kitchen; and finally was rewarded by seeing three men come out of the Heath door and walk slowly down the street to the big house across the way. She noted that Lawrence Billings walked between the other two. She could tell him by his slight build, and cringing attitude as he walked, and once they stopped and seemed to parley, both the other men putting strong hands upon his shoulders.

There was another delay, and she could hear the Whitney knocker sounding hollowly down the silent street. Then a head was thrust out of the upper window and a voice called loudly: "Who's there!" Miranda had opened the parlor window just a crack, and her heart beat wildly as she knelt and laid her ear beside the crack. In a few minutes a light appeared in the fan-shaped window over the front door and then the door itself was opened and the visitors let in.

Miranda waited then only to see the light appear in the front windows and the shadows of the four men against the curtain. Then she dropped on her knees by the window and let her tears have their way. "Thanks be!" she murmured softly again and again. "Thanks be!"

Whatever came now, Allan was cleared. At least three men in the town knew, and they would do the right thing. She was almost dubious about their having told Mr. Whitney. She thought he deserved to feel all the trouble that could come to him through his children for the way he had treated them; but after all it was good to have Allan cleared in the eyes of his father, too.

The conference in the Whitney house was long and Miranda did not wait until it was over. She climbed the stairs softly to her room, answered

Marcia's gentle, "Is that you, Miranda?" with a gruff, "Yes, I ben down in the kitchen quite a spell," and closing her door went straight to the starlit window and gazed out. There was only a star or two on duty that night fully visible

... you at last the thing she set her heart upon. Will the stars take the message, and will you ever come back?

She crept to her bed too excited to sleep, and lay there listening for sounds across the street. The solemn silent night paced on, and still that candle beam shone straight across the road. But at last there were voices, and the opening of a door; grave voices full of weighty matters and an awed goodnight. She went to her window to watch again. David came straight across to his own door, but Lawrence Billings went arm in arm with her grandfather to his home. Not to the smokehouse, cold and damp, where Allan had been put, but into the comfortable quiet house, with at least the carpet-covered sofa to lie upon, and the banked-up fire, and the cat for company. Grandfather Heath would never put Lawrence Billings into the smokehouse, he was too respectable. Miranda, with a lingering thought of Allan and his protection of the weakling, was almost glad that it was so. There was after all something pitifully ridiculous in the thought of Lawrence Billings huddled in the dark of the smokehouse with his fear of ghosts and spectres haunting him on every side. The fine strong Allan in all his youthful courage could not be daunted by it, but Lawrence Billings would crumple all up with the terror of it. Then Miranda went back to her bed, pulled the covers up over her head and laughed till she cried at the remembrance of Lawrence Billings frightened by a tablecloth.

The days that followed were grave and startling. After the revelation on the following morning there came a stream of visitors to the Spafford house to see Miranda. On one pretext or another they asked for her; to the back door for a cup of molasses, or to the front door to know if she would run over and stay with an ailing member of the family that evening while the others went out; anything so they could see Miranda. And always before the interview was ended they managed to bring in the mesmerizing at Hannah Skinner's.

"Say, Mirandy, did you reely see a speret? An' how did you know what to say? Did they tell you words to speak?" one would ask. And Miranda would reply:

"Well, now, Sa'r' Ann! I don' know's I ken' rightly say. You see I disremember seein' any sperets 'tall, 'r hearin' any; an' as fer what I said, I can't 'count fer it. They tell me I talked a lot o' fool nonsense, but it seems t'v all passed from my mind. It's queer how that mesmerizin' works ennyhow. I didn't b'leeve much in it when I went into it, an' I can't say 'z I think much of it now. I 'member seein' a white mist rise off'n the ground when I come home, but I don't much b'leeve sperets walks the' airth, d' you? It don't seem commonsensy, now do y' think? No, I can't rightly say 'z I remember hearin' 'r seein' anythin'. I guess ef I did it all passed off when my head stopped feelin' queer. Funny 'bout Lawrence Billings takin' it to heart that-a-way, wa'n't it? You wouldn't never uv picked him out t' commit a crime, now would you? My Mr. David says it's a c'wince'dence. Quite a c'wince'dence! them's the words he used t' the breakfast table, talkin' to Mrs. Marcia. He says: 'Thet was quite a c'wince'dence, M'randy, but don't you go to meddlin' with that there mesmerism again, f'y was you,' sez he. An' I guess he's 'bout right. Did you hear they was goin' to start up the singin' school again next week?"

And that's about all the information anybody got out of Miranda.

The next few days were marked by the sudden and hasty departure of Julia Thatcher for her home, and the resurrecting of past events in preparation for the trial of Lawrence Billings, which was set for the next week, the interval being given for Enoch Taylor's grandson and only heir to arrive from his distant home.

During this interval Miranda was twice moved to make dainty dishes and take them to Lawrence Billings, who was still in solitary confinement in her grandfather's house. Her grandmother received the dishes grudgingly, told her she was a fool, and slammed the door, but Miranda somehow felt as if she had made it even with her conscience for having put the poor creature into his present position. She knew Allan would like her to show him some little attention, and while she strongly suspected that the dainty dishes never reached the prisoner's tray, still it did her good to make them and take them. Miranda was always a queer mixture of vindictiveness and kindness. She had driven Lawrence Billings to his doom for the sake of Allan and now she felt sorry for him.

It was weeks afterward that Miranda managed to return Hannah Skinner's tablecloth, for Hannah was bitter against her cousin by reason of the notoriety that had been brought upon her. She had made that evening gathering with a mesmerist as entertainer for the sake of popularity, but to be mixed up in a murder case was much too popular even for Hannah.

The way Miranda managed the tablecloth was a simple one after all. She went to see Hannah when she knew Hannah was over at her mother's house. Slipping unobtrusively out of the Spafford house from the ~~~~ the side away from the Heath's ~~~~

~~~~ behind it, and Miranda was out ~~~~ house with the door locked behind her and the key in its place under the mat in a trice. There was no neighbor near enough to have noticed her entrance. The next week, just as Miranda had planned she would do pretty soon, Hannah came across the aisle to the Spafford pew and whispered:

"M'randy, whatever could you have done with my second best tablecloth the night of my party?"

And Miranda glibly responded:

"I put it on the top o' the chest in the dinin' room, Hannah; better look behind it. It might a'fell down, there was so much goin' on thet night."

"It couldn't," said Hannah, "I always move that out when I sweep." But she looked, and to her astonishment found her tablecloth.

"It seems as if there must be some magic about this house," she remarked to Lemuel that night at supper.

"Better not to meddle with such things, my dear," said Lemuel, with his little mouth pursed up like a cherry. "You know I didn't want that man to come here, but you would have him."

"Nonsense!" said Hannah sharply. "It was all Mirandy's doings. If I hadn't invited her there wouldn't have been a bit of this fuss. I thought she would know enough to keep in the kitchen and mind the coffee. I never expected her to want to be mesmerized. Such a fool! I believe she was smitten with the man!"

"Mebbe so! Mebbe so!" chirped Lemuel affably, taking a big bite of Hannah's hot biscuit and honey, and thinking of the days when he was smitten with Hannah.

When this surmise of Hannah's reached Miranda, by way of her grandmother, Miranda chuckled.

"Wal, now, I hadn't thought o' that, gran'ma, but p'raps that was what's the matter. He didn't look to me like much of a man to be smit with; but then when one's gitten' on to be a ole maid like me it ain't seemly to be too pertic'ler. Howsomenever, ef I was smit it didn't go more'n skin deep, so you needn't to worry. I ain't lookin' to disgrace this fam'bly with no greasy-lookin', long-haired jackanapes of a mesmer-man yit awhiles, not s' long 's I kin earn my keep. Want I should stir thet fire up fer yeh 'fore I go back home?"

And Miranda went singing on her way back home chuckling to herself as she went.

"Smit with him! Now ain't that real r'dic'lous? Smit with a thing like thet!"

Then her face went grave and sweet and she paused at the door stone ere she entered and stretched her hands longingly toward the thread of a young moon that was rising back of the barn.

"Oh, Allan!" she murmured softly, and "Oh Allan!" again; and the soul of the little girl that Allan had kissed stood tenderly in her eyes for an instant.

Then she was herself again and went cheerfully in to get supper for the people she loved; and nobody ever dreamed, as they looked at the strong wholesome girl going springily, joyously about her kitchen, of the exquisite youth and depth of feeling hidden away in the depths of her great loving heart. Only Marcia sometimes caught in wonder a passing reminder in Miranda's eyes of the light that glowed in the eyes of little Rose.

...creature wending secret
...trees stood stark and black against the whiteness, like
lonely, solemn sentinels that even in the starlight were picked out in detail
against the night. On such a night it seemed the wise men must have
started on their star-led way, so lonely, so longing, so crying out to be
satisfied, seemed the earth.

A single trapper clad in furs walked silently like one of the creatures he
trapped. He had been out all day and over his shoulder were slung several
fine pelts. He had done well, and the furs he was carrying now would
bring a fancy price. He had but two more traps to visit, then his day's work
would be done and he could go home. He trod the aisles of the night as
surely as one might walk in a familiar park of magnificent distance and
note no object because all were so accustomed.

He did not whistle as he walked. He had formed the stealthy habit of the
creatures of the wild, and his going was like a part of the night, a far cloud
passing would have made as much stir. There was almost a majesty and
rhythm in his movements.

A mile or two further on he knelt beside a deadfall trap and found a fine
lynx as his reward. As easily and deftly as a lady might have stooped in
her garden and plucked a rose he drew forth his knife and took the
beautiful skin to add to those he already carried; made his trap ready for
another victim, and passed on to the last trap.

Several times on the way he paused, alertly, listening; and then stalked
on again. There were sounds enough to the uninitiated,—coyotes howling,
wolves baying, the call of the wild being answered from all directions,—
enough to make a stranger pause and tremble every step of the way. But it
was a sound far more delicate that came to the trained ear of the trapper,
and a perception of a sort of sixth sense that made him pause and gaze
keenly now and again; a faint distant metallic ring, the crackle of a broken

twig, the fall of a branch—they all might have been accounted for in natural ways, yet they were worth marking for what they might mean.

There was nothing in the last trap and it had the appearance of having been tampered with. The trapper was still kneeling beside it, when there came a sound like the tone of a distant organ playing an old church hymn, just a note or two. It might have been the sighing of the wind in the tall trees if there had been wind that night. The man on the ground rose suddenly to his feet and lifted his eyes to the purple-dark of the distance. Faint and far the echo repeated itself—or was it imagination?

The trapper knelt again and quickly adjusted the trap, then swung his pelts to his shoulder once more and strode forward with purpose in his whole bearing. Thrice he paused and listened, but could not be sure he still heard the sound. Just ahead was his cabin of logs. He stopped at the door again, intently listening. Then suddenly the music came again, this time sweet and clear, but far off still, and only in echoing fragments—a bit of an old tune—or was it fancy?—that used to be sung in the church at home in the East. There was only a haunting memory of familiar days in the broken strains—foolishness perhaps—a weakness that seemed to be growing on him in this loneliness.

A moment more he lingered by the door to make sure some one was riding down the trail, then he went in, swung his burden in the corner, made haste to strike a light and make a fire. If the voice he thought he had heard singing was really someone coming down the trail, he might have company to supper that night.

The strong face of the trapper was lighted with new interest as he went about his simple preparations for a guest. Double portions of venison and corn bread were put to cook before the fire, and an extra candle lighted and put in the window toward the mountain trail. When all was ready he went to the door once more and listened and now the voice came full and strong:

"Yes, my native land, I love thee."

High up and far away still, and only now and then a line or phrase distinct, but growing nearer all the time.

The trapper, standing big and strong in his cabin door that barely let his height through without stooping, listened, and his eyes glowed warmly in the starlight. There was something good in the sound of the song. It warmed his heart where it had not been warmed for many a day. He listened an instant, calculated well the distance of his approaching guest, then drew the door to and swung himself away a few paces in the dark. When he returned his arms were filled with fragrant piney boughs which he tossed down in an unoccupied corner of his cabin, not far from the fire, and spread over with a great furry skin. After placing the coffee pot in the fire he went back to the door.

There were distinct and connected words to the song now, and a tune that used to be sung in the

... man, now close at hand. The ring of his horse's footsteps on the crisp snow could be heard, and the singing suddenly stopped. He had seen the light in the window. In a moment more he came into the clearing, greetings were exchanged, and he dismounted.

The newcomer was a man of more than medium height, but he had to look up at the trapper, who towered above him in the starlight.

"I am fortunate to find you at home," he said pleasantly, "I have passed this way several times before but always there was no one here."

He was dressed in buckskin trousers, a waistcoat, and a blue English duffle coat, a material firm, closely woven and thicker than a Mackinaw blanket. Over this was a buffalo overcoat a few inches shorter than the duffle, making a fantastic dress withal. From under his fur cap keen blue eyes looked forth and one could see at a glance from his wide, firm mouth, that he was a man of strong purpose, great powers of fearless execution, reticent, and absolutely self-contained. For a moment the two stood looking quietly, steadily into each other's eyes, gathering, as it were, confidence in one another. What each saw must have been satisfactory, for their handclasp was filled with warm welcome and a degree of liking.

"I am the fortunate one," said the trapper.

"My name's Whitman, Marcus Whitman, missionary from Waiilatpu," went on the newcomer in explanation. "May I camp with you tonight? I've come a long way since daybreak and a sound sleep would be pleasant."

"You're welcome," said the host. "Supper's all ready. I heard you coming down the trail. So you are Dr. Whitman? I've heard of you of course. I'm just a trapper." He waved his hand significantly toward the heap of furs in the corner and the fine pelts hanging about the walls—"My name's Whitney. Take off your coat."

He led the stranger inside and offered him water for washing.

"Whitney is it,—and Whitman,—not much difference is there? Easy to remember. Supper sounds good. That coffee smells like nectar. So you heard singing, did you? I'm not much of a singer I own, but my wife took a lot of pleasure teaching me. She taught me on the way out here, and I try to practice now and then when I'm out in the open where I won't annoy anyone."

"It sounded good," said the trapper. "Made me think of home. Mother used to sing that when I was a little chap,—that one about the spacious firmament on high—"

There was a wistfulness in the trapper's tone to made his guest look at him keenly once again.

"Your mother is gone, then? " he ventured.

"Years ago."

"She's not at home waiting for you to come back then."

"No, she's not at home—"

It was after they were seated at the table and the meal was well under way that the conversation began again.

"You belong to the Hudson Bay Fur people?" The stranger asked the question half anxiously, as though it had been on the tip of his tongue from the first.

"I trade with them—" responded the younger man quickly, "that's all. I was with them for a while,—but there were things I didn't like. A man doesn't care to be angered too often. I'm not much of an American, perhaps you might say, but I don't like to hear my own country sneered at—"

There was deep significance in young Whitney's tone.

"How's that?" The stranger's keen eyes were searching the other's understandingly, a light of sympathy flashing into his own.

"They do not want us Americans," he said, and his voice conveyed a deeper meaning even than his words. "They want this country for England. They want undisputed sway in Oregon!"

"You have felt that, have you?" the guest's eyes were steady and his voice calm. It was impossible to tell just what he himself believed.

"Haven't you seen it? It's to your interest you should understand, if you don't. Why, sir, they don't want you and your mission! They want the Indians to remain ignorant. They don't want them to become civilized. They can make more money out of 'em ignorant!"

The doctor's eyes flashed fire now and his whole speaking face responded:

"I have seen it, yes, I have seen it. But what are the prospects? Do you think they can carry out their wishes?"

"I'm afraid they can," said the trapper half sullenly. "They have done all they can to make their hold secure. They are retiring their servants on farms and making voters of them. Every year more settlers are coming from the Red River country, and they are spreading reports among

Americans that passage over the mountains is impossible. They are alive and awake to the facts. Our government down there at Washington is asleep yet. They haven't an idea what a glorious country this is. Why, I've heard that they are talking of calling l...

[text obscured]

...pring there'll be a way to ...... word. I've thought of writing a letter to the President—Why don't you write a letter, Dr. Whitman? It would have weight coming from you."

"Next Spring will be too late! A letter will be too late, young man. Do you know the peril is at our door? I do not know but it is even now too late. Listen! I have just come from Fort Walla Walla, where I have heard what has stirred my soul. There was a dinner a few days ago at which were present some officers from the fort, employees of the company, and a few Jesuit priests. During the feasting a messenger came saying that immigrants from Red River had crossed the mountains, and had reached Fort Colville on the Columbia. Nearly everybody present received the news enthusiastically, and one priest stood up and shouted: 'Hurrah for Oregon! America is too late! We have got the country!' "

The log in the fireplace fell apart with a thud, and the trapper sprang forward to mend the fire, his fine, strong face showing set and indignant in the glow that blazed up.

"It is not too late yet if only we could get word to headquarters," he said as he came back to his seat, "but the snow fall has already begun. This will clear away and we'll have some good weather yet, but treacherous. No man could get across the mountains alive at this time of year."

"And yet, with so much at stake, a man who loved his country might try—" said Dr. Whitman musingly, and the other man, watching the heavy, thoughtful brow, the determined chin, the very bristling of the iron gray hair, thought that if any man could do it here was the one who would try. There was a long silence and then the trapper spoke:

"I would go in a minute. My life is not worth anything! But what would I be when I got there? No one would listen to me against the words of great men—not even if I brought messages from men who know—And— besides—there are reasons why I cannot go back East!" And he drew a long sigh that came from the depths of bitterness, hard to hear from one so young and strong and full of life.

Mr. Whitman looked at him quickly, keenly, appreciatively, but asked no question. He knew men well, and would not force a confidence.

They presently threw themselves down upon their couches of boughs and fur, with only the firelight to send weird shadows over the cabin room, but they talked on for a long time; of the country, its needs, its possibilities, its prospects; then before they slept the Doctor arose, knelt beside his couch and prayed. And such a prayer! The very gates of heaven neared and seemed opening to let the petition in. The country, the wonderful country! the people, the poor, blinded, ignorant people! That was the burden of his cry. He brought the matter of their conversation home to God in such a way that now it scarcely seemed necessary any longer to get word to Washington about the peril of Oregon, since appeal had been made to a higher authority. Then, in just a word or two the trapper felt himself acknowledged and introduced before the Most High, and he seemed to stand barefaced, looking into the eyes of God, knowing that he was known and cared for.

Overhead the silent age-old stars kept vigil, wise in their far seeing, and marvelling perhaps that the affairs of a mere nation should so stir the soul of a mortal whose life on earth was but a breath at best, since God was in high heaven and all peoples of the earth were His.

Next morning at daybreak the missionary went upon his way to Waiilatpu, and the trapper went his rounds again, yet neither was quite the same as before that long night conference.

One sentence had passed between them as they parted that had told volumes, and that neither would forget. As they looked together at the glory of the dawn, Dr. Whitman turned and gazed deeply into the trapper s eyes.

"Almost—I could ask you to go with me," he said and waited.

A light leapt forth in the other man's eyes.

"And but for one thing—I would go," was the quick reply with a sudden shadowing of his brows.

That was all. They clasped hands warmly with a quick, meaningful pressure and parted, but each was possessed of at least a portion of the other's secret.

...they had come out to ......, away from home and friends, for no selfish motive, and their hearts were in their work. They were met now, as they supposed, to consider the necessities of their work and to consult on ways and means. Each one had built his home with his own hands, tilled his land, planted fields of corn, wheat, potatoes, and melons; taught his Indian neighbors to do the same; and was maintaining, with his wife, a school for Indian children in his neighborhood, in addition to preaching and ministering to the sick for miles around. Two of them came from one hundred and fifty miles away. They were men accustomed to the difficult trail, and to the camp under the stars or stormy skies. They were expected each to bring his family expenses within three hundred dollars a year. They sometimes managed it within one hundred, for they knew the Home Board was poor.

They had known, these missionaries, that there were matters of grave import with relation to the Mission to consider; matters of which they had written to the American Board for advice; and they supposed it was for this they were brought together. But when Dr. Whitman began to talk, instead, of political matters, their faces were grave and unsympathetic.

Dr. Whitman began by laying before his colleagues a very clear statement of the way matters stood with regard to the Hudson Bay Company. He showed how they were scheming to get Oregon for England and made plain what a disastrous thing this would be for the mission, as British sovereignty would mean rule by the Hudson Bay Company, whose chief desire it was to keep away men who would teach the Indians, that they might retain the fur trade, all to the Company's advantage. He told them of the fault that had been found with the Company's agent, Dr. John McLoughlin, of Vancouver, because he had fed some starving American settlers. He made the whole thing plain, though each man already knew the main facts; and then he revealed to them that he proposed to go to Washington, tell these facts to the Government, and try to get them to do something to save Oregon, and with Oregon, the mission, of course. He had called them together to get their sanction and approval of his journey.

There was solemn silence in the great log room when he had done speaking, and the faces of the men were turned away from him. It was plain they were not deeply in sympathy with their enthusiastic colleague. At last one spoke timidly, as though feeling his way, and with his eyes down.

"It seems very commendable that Brother Whitman should be willing to undertake this great journey to save the country and the mission. I make a motion brethren, that we give him our full approval and commendation."

As if the storm of disapproval had burst with the words of good brother Spalding, the others broke forth with dissuasion, argument, condemnation and reproof.

They told him how impossible the journey was at that time of year. He would be throwing away his life, and for what? They bade him think of his mission deserted, and what might happen to his wife and his work if he left them alone for the winter. They clamored of public opinion and how it would be said he had deserted the Lord's work for earthly things. They refused absolutely to give their consent to his crazy scheme; and when he would not be turned from his purpose by all this, they told him in substance they thought he was meddling in matters that were not his concern; that he would better attend to his missionary duties and let politics alone.

Then arose Dr. Whitman from his place, faced his brethren with determined mien, and spoke:

"I was a man first before I became a missionary," he said, "and when I became a missionary I did not expatriate myself. I shall go to the States if I have to sever my connection with the mission!" He brought up his strong, firm hands that had built saw mills, planted gardens, tenderly cared for the sick, been the stay and comfort of many a despairing weary one, and dropped them forcibly again in a fine gesture that showed his mind was made up and nothing could turn it.

Dismay suddenly filled the room and sat on every face. The idea of the mission without Dr. Whitman was appalling. His withdrawal could not be entertained for a moment. At once the whole question was changed, and in a panic those who had been most opposed to his going on the perilous journey, hastened to move that his endeavor be heartily approved.

They besought him, however, to wait until the worst of the winter was over, but he would not listen to them.

The thing he had undertaken to do seemed well nigh an impossibility, a madness to attempt, yet they could not stop him. It was a ride of nearly three thousand miles that he proposed to take, and would occupy three or four months at the shortest, beginning with the first snows of the Autumn and extending through the worst of the Winter months. He would have to carry supplies to last through the whole journey, as well as provender for his horses, and blankets to sleep in

...... in his decision, though it ...... months of long, weary separation and anxiety for her.

Thus, after the two days of conference, consenting unanimously at last to what they could not prevent, the missionaries went back to their stations.

Immediately upon their going Dr. Whitman set about his preparations for the journey. Two days later he took the hurried trip to Walla Walla to visit a patient in that region and also to make some quiet inquiries of Mr. McKinley of the Hudson Bay Company concerning a northern boundary treaty which he had heard was about to be made. What he learned there sent him hurrying on his way back without stopping to rest, until he came to the trapper's cabin in the clearing and found another man whose heart thrilled to the same patriotic tune as his own; and who, but for some secret shadow, would have been ready to risk his life also in this great endeavor to save Oregon.

As he rode on his faithful "cayuse" back toward the mission he did not spend his time in wondering what it could be that could prevent a fine, clear-eyed fellow like that from going back to his home again. He had been too long in that land without a past and known men too well to judge a man by one act, as they have to be judged in the heart of civilization. He knew the man he had just met was in sympathy with his deepest desires, and he trusted him fully and respected his confidence. It was a pity that he could not have gone. The way would have been better for his company. There was nothing further to be said or thought. It is a great thing to trust a man so much that you can be loyal to him even in your thoughts.

It was high noon before he came within sight of the mission: situated on a beautiful level peninsula formed by the branches of the Walla Walla River, nearly three hundred acres of land fenced in, and two hundred under cultivation, all now lying under its first Fall blanket of whiteness.

There at the left was the little adobe house, the first in which his wife and himself had lived when they came out to that country over the long toilsome trail; and off at the right was the new log house, sixty feet long and eighteen feet wide with an extension at the back, making a great T cross. Back of that was the blacksmith shop, and down by the river side the flour mill; all the work of this wonderful man's hands, and the pride and love of his heart. As he looked at it now in its setting of white with the blue ribbon of river twining it about, and the dark of the woods beyond, his heart suddenly failed him at the thought of leaving and the tears dimmed his kind, tender, far-seeing eyes. Down there in the whiteness was the tiny grave of their one little child who had been drowned in the river when scarcely more than a baby; and in the house was his wife, strong, courageous, loving, and ready to speed him on his way in whatever enterprise he undertook. He would have to leave it all and who knew whether he would ever see it again?

But Dr. Whitman was not the man to spend time in thoughts like these. Just one instant he let the pang of his going tear through his heart; the next he spurred his horse forward, knowing there was no time to be lost.

His preparations were few and simple and had been going steadily forward during his absence; yet the news he had learned made it seem necessary to cut down even the two or three days more he had hoped to spend at home and go at once, on the morrow if possible.

The people of Dr. Whitman's household were not of the sort that demurred when he spoke the word "I must." One instant his wife stood aghast at the thought of his going so soon; the next she had set her face to do everything in her power to make it possible and easy for him.

A message was sent at once to General Lovejoy, a young man who had come West that same summer and who had some time ago expressed the belief that it was entirely possible to go through the mountains at that time of year and promised to accompany Dr. Whitman.

The mission was astir far into the night.

It was a bright, clear morning, when they started. The mules stood ready with the supplies well strapped to their backs, the horses saddled, and Lovejoy and the guide already in their saddles when Dr. Whitman came out of the house.

All the Indians who lived near by had come to see the party off and a few of the most devoted proposed to ride the first day's journey with them.

In the doorway stood Mrs. Whitman with thirty or forty little Indian children of the school grouped about her.

Their goodbyes had been said in the quiet of their own room, these two who had left the whole world behind and come out West to do God's work together. They understood one another perfectly, and no selfish wishes were put in the way of the great purposes of their united lives. Each knew what a trial the succeeding months were to be to the other, and each had accepted it; and now as the missionary stood forth to take his leave his wife wore a bright, courageous smile. It was harder perhaps to stay behind than to go and fight storm, peril, wild beast and wilder man, and the man

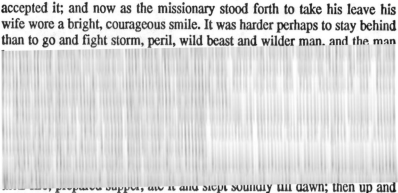

_____, prepared supper, ate it and slept soundly till dawn; then up and off again.

Eleven days they rode, resting on the Sabbath, and reached Fort Hall, four hundred miles from their starting place, at the rate of forty miles a day. Their Indian friends had of course turned back and there were only Whitman, Lovejoy and the guide, with the pack mules. But all along the way they had met Indians who forbade them to proceed. Dr. Whitman well knew by whose instructions they so acted, but in his wise way he held parley with each band and succeeded in going on his way.

At Fort Hall Captain Grant informed him that the Pawnees and Sioux were at war, and it would be death to go through their country, even if he succeeded in getting through the snow in the mountains, which was very deep. He was advised to either turn back or wait until Spring, but he was not the man to do either. Calmly as a mother might have picked up another toy dropped by a peevish child he adjusted his plans and added a thousand miles to his journey. Turning from the direct route he had intended to travel he took the old Spanish trail for Santa Fe. Taking a new guide from Fort Hall he pushed on across the northeast corner of Utah to Fort Uintah in the Uintah Mountains, and now the way grew white with storm, and the weather severe. The snows were deep and blinding, and greatly impeded their progress. A weaker man would have seen the folly (?) of his ways and turned back, but Dr. Whitman kept steadily on as if these things had all been a part of his plans.

They changed guides at Fort Uintah, continuing their journey across Green River over to the Valley of the Grand into what is now the State of Colorado. At Fort Uncompahgre they stopped for a brief rest, made a few purchases, changed guides, then off again.

The trail led over the highlands among the irregular spurs of the Rocky Mountains, and for four or five days more all went well. Steadily, surely, they were making their way toward the goal. It was still a long way off, but the start had been good, and the missionary gave thanks.

Then suddenly one day without warning the air grew white with storm about them. The blinding snow fell with such rapidity, and the wind blew with such violence that in a few minutes they were almost bewildered. They were forced to seek shelter at once, but though a ravine was not far away, and they turned toward it instantly when the storm surrounded them they found great difficulty in reaching it, and had to struggle through high drifts before they found it. In shelter at last with hearts profoundly thankful, they cut cottonwood trees for the animals, made themselves as comfortable in camp as was possible under the circumstances, and sat down to wait while the terrific storm raged about them three or four days.

Still whiteness all about, thick whiteness in the air, shut in from the world, they sat and waited. The strong, patient face of Whitman showed no sign of what might be going on within that eager, impatient soul of his. Off there in one direction through that whiteness was Oregon, beloved Oregon, his wife, his home, his mission, all in peril. Off there through the whiteness in the other direction, miles and miles more away, was a government unawares, toying with a possibility of possession, and knowing not the treasure they were so lightly considering. Here was he, willing and eager with the message, sitting, storm-stayed in the whiteness held by ropes of feather in this mountain fastness, while the nation perchance sold its rich birthright for a mess of pottage. What did it all mean? No hand of man had been able to stay him thus. But it was the hand of God that was holding him now; the soft, white, strong hand of God. He sat patient, submissive, not understanding, but waiting and looking up for the reason.

At last the storm subsided and the weather cleared off intensely cold. Cheerily, though with difficulty, the brave little party made its way again to the highlands, but the snow was so deep and the wind so piercing that after a brief attempt they were forced back to camp to wait for several more days till a change of weather made it safe for them to venture forth again.

At last the weather moderated, and thankfully they made their way up, but after they had wandered about for days hunting the trail the guide at last came to a halt, a sullen look upon his dark countenance and confessed he did not know where he was. He said the snow had so changed the whole look of the country that he could not get his bearings, and was completely lost. He could take them no farther.

This was of course a terrible blow to Dr. Whitman's hope, which had been rising steadily since the storm ceased; but invincible as ever he did not become downcast. Some men would have said that surely now they had done all that was possible, and would have felt thoroughly justified in turning back, and trying to find comfort and safety, at least until Spring;

not so this man. After thinking it over carefully and consulting with Lovejoy they agreed that Whitman should take the guide and try to get back to the Fort for a new guide, while Lovejoy should remain in camp with the pack mules

[illegible text] to go back and return, for the snow was very deep and going slow and uncertain; but Whitman braced his shoulder to the added burden, kept his good cheer, and at last the watcher in the mountains saw his companion returning.

Then slowly, like a train of snails, the little party crept its difficult way through the snow again, on and on, over the mountains, until one fair morning they could sight the winding shore of the Grand River.

Joyfully they hastened forward, as fast as possible, counting every difficulty small now that they saw the river ahead. But when they reached the shore at last despair descended upon them.

The river was from one hundred and fifty to two hundred yards wide, and frozen a third of the way across on either side. The current was so very rapid in the center that even in that bitter weather it had been kept from freezing, and what were they to do? The guide said it would be most perilous to attempt to cross. It looked as if another impossible barrier lay across their way. But Dr. Whitman was not stopping till he had to. He led the little party out upon the ice as far as it was safe, then mounted his brave cayuse and directed Lovejoy and the guide to push him off the ice into the boiling, foaming current; which, after much vain protest, they finally did.

It seemed like casting Whitman into a terrible grave; and at first man and horse completely disappeared under water; but soon came up unbaffled, master and beast appearing to be of one and the same spirit, and buffeted the waves magnificently, making their way gradually, although a long distance down stream, to the opposite shore, where the rider leaped from his horse upon the ice, and soon had the faithful animal safely by his side.

It was no easy task for Lovejoy and the guide to follow the example set, force the mules into the stream, and then to take the perilous trip themselves, but they did so. People couldn't help doing big things when they were around Dr. Whitman. His presence in their midst required it. For very shame they had in some measure to live up to the pattern set.

By the time they were all safely landed Whitman had a good fire burning, and soon they were cheerfully sitting around the blaze drying their frozen clothing, one more peril passed, and one less river between them and the goal.

It was by this time the middle of January, and all over the country the cold was so bitter that many people even in protected towns were frozen to death. Out in the open the cold seemed to be like an iron grip that enfolded one, and slowly, relentlessly grew tighter and tighter. A black stillness seemed to settle upon everything, a vast and universal cold and fear that penetrated into the very soul.

On one of these terrible mornings as the Doctor began his usual preparations for going on, the guide shook his head and protested vigorously. A blinding storm had come on through the night and the wind had made up for what moderation there was in the atmosphere. Travelling was sheer suicide that day but Dr. Whitman had already lost too much time. He laughed off fears, and cheered the others with his hearty voice, and so they set forth well muffled. They were in a deep gorge of the mountains of New Mexico and toiled on for a while in the blinding snow, but when they reached the divide and the wind rushed up from a new direction the biting snow and cold almost drove the horses mad. Whitman saw his terrible mistake, and turned at once to retrace his steps to camp, convinced that to go farther would be folly. This, however, was found to be impossible, for the driving snow had obliterated all trace of the way, and the whole country was deep and white and awful. The sky grew darker until it was almost as black as night, and the snow was falling so heavily that every step became more and more difficult.

Then suddenly hope seemed to vanish, too, and leave the world in absolute darkness. The staunch missionary saw that apparently the end had come. They could not live for more than a few minutes longer in this fearful cold and to go on was as useless as it was impossible, for they could not find their way anywhere.

With the feeling of utter failure he slipped from his saddle and stood beside his horse. Then bending his head he commended himself and his distant wife to the God in whom they both trusted; and with the bitter thought that through his own folly the cause he was serving must be lost, he gave himself up to wait for the white grave which was fast closing in about them.

Suddenly the guide noticed the ears of one of the pack mules, and said, "That mule will find the camp if he can live to get to it."

In great excitement they mounted once more and followed the mule.

He kept on down the divide for a little way, then made a square turn and plunged straight down the steep mountain side, over what seemed fearful precipices, down, down; no one to urge him or guide him; on he went just as if he knew ~~~~~~~~~~~~~~

~~~~~~ he wore.

When the weather moderated once more and they were able to make their way out from camp, Dr. Whitman moved ahead cautiously, not willing to let his own eagerness risk the safety of his whole enterprise again.

One other narrow escape was theirs when they came to the headwaters of the Arkansas after a day in a terrible storm, and found the ice upon the river too thin to bear a man erect, and every stick of wood in the vicinity over on the other side. Dr. Whitman, taking his axe in one hand, a short willow stick in the other, spread himself upon the ice, arms and legs as far apart as possible, and thus crept across, cut the wood, shoved it over, then returned, creeping as before. That night a wolf stole the hatchet for a leather thong that had been bound around the split helve, and the rest of the journey the small comfort of an axe was denied them.

The way to Fort Taos was slow and painful, for the snows were very deep and their provisions were growing less and less, so that they were finally forced to kill and eat the mules. When they reached the Fort at last they had to stay a couple of weeks to rest.

Bent's Fort on the Arkansas River was the next destination and their route led them through Santa Fé, over a well-travelled trail, which, had the season been summer, would have made it easier for them. On the way, however, they met people who gave them word of a party about to leave Bent's Fort for St. Louis. Though there was very little likelihood of his being able to reach them before they left, Dr. Whitman, on his best horse, with a few provisions, started on ahead of his party; but was lost on the way so that Lovejoy with the guide arrived at the Fort ahead of him. Having sent a message to the St. Louis party camped forty miles ahead to wait until the Doctor joined them, Lovejoy went himself a hundred miles back to search for the lost missionary. Failing to find him he returned to the fort and waited anxiously until the doctor came at last, worn and weary, and feeling that his bewilderment and loss of time were a just punishment for his travelling on Sunday in order to make time,—the only time in all the long, toilsome, hurried journey that the good man had travelled on the Sabbath.

Lovejoy was worn out with the hardships and it was decided that he should remain at Fort Bent until Whitman should return in the Summer with a party of emigrants on his way back to Oregon. Dr. Whitman, invincible as ever, taking only one night's rest, pressed on alone to overtake the party of mountain men and go to St. Louis with them.

Four hundred miles and more the trail led him, along the banks of the Arkansas to Great Bend, across the country to Smoky Hill River, down the Kansas River till it joined the Missouri; and about the end of January he reached the little town of Westport, Missouri.

His going was like that of a sower going forth to sow good seed; for as he went, wherever he met anyone he told them of Oregon; how the way thither was open for wagons and women and children; how he had come over that long trail in the Winter snows just to tell them that it was possible, and that they were being deceived by the reports spread by the Hudson Bay Company, who wished to keep the Americans out of Oregon. Everywhere he found people who had intended going West but had been stopped by these very false reports that the way was impassable. He told them to get ready to go with him when he should return. Everywhere he went the reports of his story about Oregon went forth to all the country round about and people were stirred to take their families and go out to claim land in this rich, fertile country. The enthusiasm spread like wild fire. Lovejoy in his resting place was not idle either, but continued to tell the good story, urging all whom he met to go to Oregon and save it for themselves and for their country. It meant a great deal to them that the wonderful missionary who had so successfully crossed the mountains to tell them the story had promised to return and guide them to the promised land.

And so in his fantastic garb of "buffalo coat with a blue border," as he mockingly described his garments, Dr. Whitman went on his way to St. Louis.

In those days it was seldom that one came across the mountains in Winter from Santa Fé or the Columbia, and they gathered around him and plied him with questions. There were fur traders, trappers, adventurers, and contractors for the military posts, all eager to hear the news. They wanted to know the prospects for furs and buffalo hides the next season, but Dr. Whitman had no time for such things. He was in haste to get to Washington. He wanted to know if the Ashburton treaty was concluded, and when he found it had been signed by Webster and Ashburton the Summer before he demanded to know if it covered the Northwest, and how it affected Oregon. He asked if Oregon had been under discussion in Congress and what was being urged about it in the Senate and House. The great question with him was, could he reach Washington before C...

...said, so, alone, the courageous spirit hurried to Washington. Suffering still from his frost-bitten fingers, feet, nose and ears, lacking the sympathy and enthusiasm of even his dearest friends, worn and weary, yet undaunted, he pressed on to complete his task. Arriving in Washington on the third of March, he went at once to interview Daniel Webster, the Secretary of State, to endeavor to convince him that Oregon was worth saving for America.

CHAPTER 19

DAVID SPAFFORD had been in Washington for a week on matters connected with the political situation, in which he was deeply interested, when he happened to call on Hon. Joshua Giddings, who was boarding on Capitol Hill, in what was known as "Duff Green's Row." He was deep in converse with the Honorable gentleman, when another man entered the room, a man whom he did not know but whose strong, fine face instantly attracted him. He was gaunt, almost haggard in appearance, and browned with the weather, but behind his keen blue eyes there burned a fire of earnest purpose that made David instantly feel that he was a man worth knowing. Instinctively he arose as the stranger entered the room, and he noticed that his host did also, and that he went toward the newcomer with an outstretched hand that meant a hearty sympathy with him in whatever cause for which he stood.

"Mr. Spafford, allow me the pleasure of introducing to you Dr. Whitman of Oregon!"

"Oregon!" exclaimed David, grasping the stranger's hand with a thrill of instant interest, "Oregon? Really? How long since?"

"Today," said Marcus Whitman briskly, as if it were only over in the next county, "I just arrived this morning. Left home last October and been travelling ever since."

"You don't say so!" There was wonder, amazement, delight and deep admiration in David's voice. "And how is Oregon?"

"About to be lost to us if something isn't done quickly," said the grave, earnest voice, "That's what I'm here about. I've spent all the eloquence I have on Daniel Webster this morning, but they've got him so filled with the idea that Oregon is of no use to our country because the mountains are impassable that nothing else seems to have any effect. Lord Ashburton, Sir George Simpson and their friends have done their work well."

"How is that?" asked David, keen to understand the situation.

"Why, you see they have been quietly working to impress our statesmen with the idea that the Rocky Mountains are so impassable to wagons that it cannot be peopled from the States, and therefore is of very little value to this country. They want it for themselves,—that is the Hudson Bay

Company wish to retain their control, and keep the Indians in their present state of ignorance, so they can make more advantageous deals with them."

"Sit down and tell me about Oregon," said David, "I have been ~~~~

[illegible faded text]

~~~~ of false representations about the character of the region; and told him I intended to take a train of emigrants over to Oregon this summer, but it made no impression. He thinks I am a dreamer, or a foolish enthusiast, I suppose."

"A man is not fit to be Secretary of State who has not clear vision for the future," said David rising in his excitement and striding across the room restlessly. "He ought to make sure of his facts. Your words may at least set him thinking. Perhaps he will investigate. It is the same thing they are doing to my friend, Professor Morse, and his wonderful invention of the electric telegraph. They will not pass the bill for an appropriation to try the thing out and see if it is a success. See, this session of Congress is all but over and it has only passed the House. There is little hope left for this time. Yet it has been practically proven already in a small way. Think what that will be to the country when the whole United States is able to communicate by electricity and messages can be received within a few minutes of their sending, even from great distances. Who knows, perhaps the whole earth might be girdled some day by an electric telegraph. You have heard of it?"

The tired blue eyes lighted with interest.

"Just a hint or two," said Whitman, "I heard that a man over in England had invented something that would carry messages over a few miles; but very little of the details have reached me. I heard too that some American was working at the same thing, but did not dream it had become a practical thing. It seemed to be a sort of plaything. You say it is really a success? You have seen it? What a miracle! Ah! If it had but been invented a few years sooner, and perfected, and put in working order! If there were only a telegraph over the Rockies I might have been spared this journey and all this time away from my work. I would have kept the wires hot with warnings until they had to heed me."

"Have you seen President Tyler?" asked David, suddenly wheeling and looking keenly at the missionary.

"Not yet," answered the doctor. "My friend, Senator Linn, of Missouri, is trying to arrange an interview for me. I hope to see him this afternoon or tomorrow sometime. Senator Linn is a staunch friend of Oregon. He will do all he can."

And even while they were talking there came a messenger from the Senator saying that the interview was granted.

"I shall be anxious to know how this comes out," said David, watching the kindling fires in the strong, worn face of Whitman.

"You are to be in Washington for several days yet?"

"I am not sure," said David, "I shall stay until Congress adjourns— anyway. I am interested in Professor Morse's bill and don't want to leave as long as there is a chance of doing anything for it."

"And I shall want to know how that comes out also. I shall see you again before you go. You are a man after my own heart," said Dr. Whitman with a hearty grasp of David's hand, and with that he was gone to the interview which meant so much for Oregon, and for the man who had assumed its cause.

All day long that same day, another of God's heroes, with the patience of the ages in his heart, and the perseverance of a genius, sat in the gallery of the Senate and waited; waited for other men to recognize their opportunity and set their seal upon his effort, making it possible to come to something; and all those small-great men sat and bickered about this and that and let the matters that were of world-wide moment slip unnoticed.

Ten long fruitless years had Samuel Morse labored and waited,—hoped and waited in vain for the world to do its part for his Electric Telegraph, since first he caught his vision of what it might be and knew his work in the world. And now, if this day passed without the bill coming before the Senate he would go home to New York with only the fraction of a dollar in his pocket to stand between him and starvation. As he sat and waited while petty business of a nation droned on its way his mind went back over his life; the enviable reputation as a painter he had dropped and left to die for the sake of this new love, this wary elusive maiden of electric charm and uncertainty. If this day failed to bring his finished invention to a place before the world where it could win recognition he was ruined. There was little wish in his mind to go on any farther trying to make a blind world see what he had done for its benefit. Let it go. Let the wonderful invention drop back into the obscurity it had occupied before it was born in his own struggling soul.

As the day dragged on and his friends and acquaintances came and went they spoke to him about his bill. They were sorry for him sitting there so hopelessly, so patiently. Few hoped with him, few bothered even to pity him. All told him there was little hope now that his bill would come to the front at all, with all the business there was yet on the docket, and Congress to adjourn at midnight. Some stopped to say it was a shame, and to [illegible]

Half an hour later, just a few minutes before midnight, his bill was reached, and wonder of wonders! passed; but the man on whose heart it had lain for the long years, whose very life had been given for it day by day, was lying asleep and did not know till morning.

They told him while he sat at breakfast the next morning, and he could scarcely believe his senses that the weary years were over and his chance to put his invention before the world had really come at last.

It was three days later that David, still in Washington but just about to go home, met Dr. Whitman on Pennsylvania Avenue, and extended his hand in greeting:

"So you are here yet!" he exclaimed eagerly, "And how did you come out with Oregon? Did you find Tyler had any better idea about things than Webster did?"

"Not a bit, not a bit," said Whitman grasping the extended hand as if he had found an old friend, "but I think—I believe he understands the situation better now. When I first began to talk I felt almost as if it were useless to try. He was firmly entrenched behind the same views that Webster held, that Oregon was useless to the United States. But I began to tell him all about it. I told that I had gone over the mountains four times, once in the dead of Winter, and that seven years ago I took a wagon over. I informed him that I intend to carry a large party back with me in the Spring, and that we, being American citizens, would claim protection from the national government. I showed him my frozen limbs and he looked in my face and believed me! Then I told him all about the climate and soil and the importance of Oregon to the nation, and he began to be convinced. At last he gave me a conditional promise of protection if my emigration plan succeeds. My last word to him was that the emigrants *would go over and would look to him for protection* when they reached their destination, and would expect the moral support of the government and the necessary legislation by Congress. In parting he wished me success in the undertaking. And now,—" and the missionary's face lit up with eager determination, "now, God giving me life and strength, I will connect the Missouri and Columbia with a wagon track so deep and plain that neither national envy nor sectional fanaticism will ever blot it out."

"God bless you in your wonderful undertaking," said David reverently. "And who knows but some day your wagon track may be a railroad."

The far-seeing eyes of the missionary rested on the other man's face in growing wonder and the light of the miracle believer shone in them as he said in a tone of awe:

"Who knows."

And then he briskly changed his tone.

"Your telegraph came out all right. I'm glad. Oh, God is in all these things. They must come out right sooner or later even though the people through whom they come are slow and hard of heart, and filled with their own devices. I wish you were going to Oregon with me."

"I wish I were," said David heartily, "Nothing would delight me more, but I guess my work is here for the present."

"You are right. We need such men as you in the East to keep things straight; level-headed, far-seeing men are scarce. I shall feel safer out in Oregon for knowing you are here at work, thinking and acting and voting, and writing,—for they tell me you have great power in that direction. Give Oregon a good word now and then."

"I will indeed," said David smiling, "You have made me an ardent supporter of the cause. I could wish that more of my party understood the matter fully. There is a general feeling among Whigs that we should stick to Abolition and not bother with Annexation. I think they are wrong in that. I shall do my little best to make a few men see. I wish I might have the pleasure of another talk with you. How soon are you leaving this part of the world? Couldn't you spend a few days with me at my home up in New York State?"

"I haven't much time," said the missionary, "But New York State,— where in New York State? Any where near Ithaca? I must go to Boston to attend a meeting of the Prudential Committee of the American Board. There are important matters connected with the Mission for me to attend to; I must have a day with my old friend Parker in Ithaca, and then I must go home for a brief visit with father and mother. If I could work it in I'd be delighted to see you in your home. It would be a memory to carry back— but you see how it is, my time is short."

"But our home is right on your way. You might at least stop over night with us. Why not go on with me tomorrow? Or do you have to stay in Washington longer?"

"No, I guess I have done about all I can here now," said the missionary, "and I ought to be on the move. I have one or two more people to see, but I hope to see them today. I'll try to do it. What time do you leave?"

"I was expecting to take the morning train, but can wait until afternoon

CHAPTER 20

MIRANDA tied on a clean apron, put a finishing touch to the tea table and went to the window to watch. The afternoon train was in and it would be time for the people to be coming from it. Rose had taken her little brother and gone down the street to stand at the corner and watch for her father, for a letter had come that morning saying he hoped to get home that day.

Miranda had made rusk for supper and there was chicken with gravy and applesauce and a custard pie. Mrs. Marcia was sitting by the dining room window where she could see a long distance down the street. Her knitting was in her hands, but her eyes were down the street with a light of welcome in them and the pink flush of her soft cheek told the keen-eyed Miranda how eagerly she watched for her husband's coming. Miranda at the pantry window where she could see the street as well without obstructing Marcia's view, exulted in the joy of the household whom she served, and watched as eagerly for the home coming of the master as if he had been her own. Having none of her own she loved these dear people whole heartedly and devotedly.

"Well, he's comin'," she said bustling into the dining room, "an' he's got a queer lookin' pusson with him. 'Spose he's bringin' him to supper? It beats all how Mr. David does pick up queer lookin' pussons that has a his'try to 'em. This one looks like he'd killed a bear and put on his skin. Well, there's plenty o' chicken an' rusks, an' there's three pumpkin pies an' a mince down cellar ef the custard ain't 'nuff. Do you 'spose he's bringin' him in?"

Miranda patted the fresh napkins and slipped up behind Marcia for another view of the street.

"It looks like it," said Mrs. Marcia. "Yes, they're turning in at the gate. Better put another plate on and fill the spare room pitcher. He'll likely want to wash."

"Spare room pitcher's full," said Miranda triumphantly, " 'spose I wouldn't keep that ready when Mr. David was a comin' an' might bring comp'ney? Guess I'll put on a dish o' plum jam too—" and Miranda hastened happily and importantly away. There was nothing she delighted in more than to be ready for the unexpected; and company was her joy and opportunity.

In a moment more Rose and her little brother came dancing into the

"Come right in my boy and have supper with us," said David heartily. "Miranda, have you another plate handy? Nathan, I want you to know this great man and hear him talk. This is Dr. Whitman of Oregon and he has ridden three thousand miles across the Rocky Mountains to save Oregon for the United States. Mr. Whitman, this is my right hand man, Nathan Whitney. Some day when he gets through his college education he'll be coming out to be a Senator or Governor or something."

Dr. Whitman, with the human, eager look in his face that made him interested at once in all mankind, rose from his seat and stretched out a hand to the shy boy, looking searchingly in his face.

"Whitney! Whitney! Where have I heard that name recently? Ah, yes, I remember, out in Oregon just the night before I left. He was a young trapper, and I noticed the name because it was so like my own. We had supper together in his cabin and I stayed all night with him. I took a great liking to him. He was in thorough sympathy with me in my undertaking. I would have liked to bring him with me, but he said there were reasons why he could not come East, so I did not urge him. But he certainly was a fine fellow, and I am looking forward to seeing him again when I go home. Who knows but he is a relative of yours? I'll have to tell him about the boy I saw of his name, when I get back, and how you are coming out to us when you are through with your education."

Nathan's eyes shone over this hearty greeting, and he managed to stammer out a few words in answer, and drop into the seat Miranda had prepared for him, his eyes fixed on the keen, worn face of the visitor.

They all settled back into their seats once more going on with their supper, and no one noticed Miranda, who during the introduction had stood stock still in the kitchen doorway, her face as white as a ghost, and the tea towel which she had held in her hand lying unheeded on the spotless floor at her feet, while she grasped the door frame with one hand and involuntarily pressed the other hand to her fluttering heart.

"You must have a good many fine young fellows out there," said David, as he helped Nathan generously to chicken and mashed potato.

"Well, not so many,—not so many! A good many are pretty rough specimens. They almost have to be, you know, for it's a hard life,—a rough, hard, lonely life out there. But this man was unusual. I knew it the minute I laid eyes on him. I was riding down the mountain trail singing hymns to while away the time. I sing occasionally when I'm out where no one can hear me; my wife likes me to do it for practice you know—" he smiled his rare whimsical smile—"and when I reached the clearing and the little cabin that stood there, I saw a light in the window, and at the door stood a great, tall giant of a fellow waiting to welcome me. He said he had heard me singing and the song was one his mother used to sing when he was a little shaver. Well, I went in and found he had supper all ready for me, and a good supper, too. Perhaps you don't know how good corn bread and venison can taste after a long day on the trail. He had a nice little cabin with a cheery fire going, and the table spread for two. All around the walls pelts were hung, and there were fresh pine branches in the corner for a bed, with a great buffalo hide spread over, the finest bed you ever lay upon. We talked way into the night, and he told me a lot of things about the Hudson Bay Company. He was an unusually fine fellow—"

Miranda stood spellbound still in the doorway, and the coffee obviously boiled over on the fire. Marcia had to speak to her twice before she turned with a jump and a bright wave of color over her face and went to her neglected task. When she brought the coffee pot to the table her hand was trembling so that she could scarcely set it down.

The table talk was very interesting. Stories of the trail, anecdotes of the mission, descriptions of the Indians and their way of life; incidents of the long, long pilgrimage East, and details of the stay in Washington and Whitman's work there. Nathan sat with red cheeks and shining eyes, forgetting to eat; Rose, round-eyed and eager, watched him and listened too; Marcia, noting Miranda, absorbed in the doorway gathered little David into her arms and let his sleepy head fall on her shoulder, rather than disturb the conversation by slipping away to put him to bed, or send Miranda away to do it.

At last Nathan mustered courage to ask a question.

"How did you come to go out there in the first place?"

Whitman turned his keen blue eyes on the boy and smiled.

"I think it was reading the pathetic story of the Indians who came East in search of the Book of Heaven. Did you ever happen to hear it?"

Nathan shook his head, and David seeing his eager look urged: "Tell it to us, won't you, Doctor?"

"A few years ago," began the missionary, "a white man was present at some of the Indian religious ceremonies and he told them that that was not the way to worship the Great Spirit, that the white men had a Book of Heaven that would [illegible] to teach them.

"These four Indians arrived at St. Louis after a long, hard journey on foot over the mountains and finally presented themselves before General Clark and told him what they had come for. General Clark was puzzled and perhaps not a little troubled at this responsibility thrust upon him, but he received the Indians courteously and tried to explain to them about the Book of Heaven. He said there was such a book and he told them the story of man from the creation as well as the story of the Saviour, and tried to explain to them all the moral precepts and commandments laid down in the Bible. Then, feeling perhaps that he had done his duty, he tried to make the visit of these four men a pleasant time to them. He took them all over the city and showed them everything; and they of course were greatly pleased and delighted with much that they saw, especially with riding around in a carriage on wheels, which pleased them more than anything else they saw.

"But the hard journey and the change of food was too much for two of the men and they died while in St. Louis. The other two, dismayed and sorrowing, and not feeling very well themselves, prepared to go back to their homes. Before they left the city, however, General Clark gave them a banquet, at the close of which one of the Indian chiefs made a farewell speech, through an interpreter of course, and one of the men present wrote it down. It got into the papers and it was the reading of this speech, perhaps, more than anything else, that determined me to go if possible to preach the gospel to the Indians. He said:

" 'I came to you over a trail of many moons from the setting sun. You were the friend of my fathers, who have all gone the long way. I came with one eye partly opened, for more light for my people who sit in darkness. I go back with both eyes closed. How can I go back blind to my blind people? I made my way to you with strong arms, through many enemies and strange lands, that I might carry back much to them. I go back with both arms broken and empty. The two fathers who came with me—the braves of many winters and wars—we leave asleep here by your great water. They were tired in many moons and their moccasins wore out. My people sent me to get the white man's Book from Heaven. You took me where you allow your women to dance as we do not ours, and the Book was not there. You took me where they worship the Great Spirit with candles, and the Book was not there. You showed me the images of good spirits and pictures of the good land beyond, but the Book was not among them. I am going back the long, sad trail, to my people of the dark land. You make my feet heavy with burdens of gifts, and my moccasins will grow old in carrying them, but the Book is not among them. When I tell my poor, blind people, after one more snow, in the big council, that I did not bring the Book, no word will be spoken by our old men or by our young braves. One by one they will rise up and go out in silence. My people will die in darkness, and they will go on the long path to the other hunting grounds. No white man will go with them, and no white man's Book to make the way plain. I have no more words.'

"It is among the people of that tribe that sent those chiefs after the Book of Heaven, that I am now working."

It was late when they arose from the supper table and went into the parlor for worship. Miranda roused from her absorption finally, and tiptoed around softly removing dishes from the table and putting everything in order in the kitchen for morning, but she kept the kitchen door open wide and handled each dish gently that she might hear every word the great man spoke; and all the while her heart throbbed loudly under her ruffled white bib apron, and her thoughts were busy as her fingers, while on her lips there grew and grew that steady look of determination.

Nathan did not go home until after ten o'clock, a most unearthly hour for people to sit up in those days, and when he took his leave the missionary grasped his hand again and looked steadily into his clear, brown eyes:

"Boy, don't forget that you are coming out to Oregon some day to help us make a great country of it. We need such men as you are going to be. Get good ready and then come, but don't be too long about it. It is strange—" and he turned to David smiling—"but this boy has taken a great hold on me. His eyes are like the eyes of that young trapper I told you about, young Whitney. Perhaps you'll find a distant relative in him when you get there, lad. I must tell him about you. Goodnight."

The front door closed and Nathan went home under the stars feeling as though in some subtle way a great honor had been bestowed upon him. Miranda, in the back hall, turned and fled up the stairs with her candle, but she had heard every word, and her heart was beating so hard she could scarcely get her breath when she reached her room.

She put down her candle on the bureau and went and sat down on the edge of her bed with her eyes shining and her hand on her heart. After a minute she went softly over to her mirror and stood looking into it.

disremember where I left mine the las' time I wrote a letter."

David, rather surprised, found her a pen, ink and paper, and Miranda went happily back to her room, taking the precaution to stop in the kitchen and procure a couple of extra candles.

Through the long night watches Miranda sat oblivious of cold or weariness, and wrote; and then laboriously rewrote.

"Now what do you suppose Miranda is up to this time," said David to his wife upstairs. "She's just borrowed writing materials. Is she inspired to literature do you suppose? Or does she want to set down some of the wonderful tales she heard this evening?"

"There's no telling," said Marcia smiling, "she's just the oddest, dearest thing that ever was made. What ever we should do without her I don't know. She would make a wonderful wife for some man, if one could be found who was good enough for her, which I very much doubt—that is one who knew enough to appreciate her—but it's lucky for us that she doesn't seem inclined that way. Oh—David! It's so good to have you back again. The time has been so long!"

And straightway these two married lovers forgot Miranda and her concerns in their own deep joy of each other.

CHAPTER 21

IN the early dawn of the morning, when the candle flickered with a sickly light against the rosy gleam that came from the East, Miranda finished, signed and sealed her letter. On her bureau lay a goodly pile of little bits of paper, torn very fine, the debris of her night's work.

Fine feelings had Miranda, and very conscious was she of the Allan who had left her with the promise of return some day. As if his kiss were still fresh upon her lips, she shrank from any hint that he was bound to come back to her. Not for worlds would she have him think she held him responsible for that kiss, or that it meant anything else but the only gratitude he could then show for the release she gave him to go from his prison and trial into the world of freedom. He must not think this letter had any personal interest for her at all. The years had gone by and she was no fool. The kiss and his last words had been precious experiences that she had treasured through all this while, but to which of course she really had no right in any sense such as kisses usually meant. The possibility that Allan was still alive and might some day get her letter brought her face to face with the practical side of life, and she felt that after sending that letter she could not cheat herself into believing that he belonged to her any longer. She would have to surrender what had come to be the sweetest thing in her soul; but it was right of course, and she was odd enough to give up such foolishness. This one night she would exult in speaking to him once more, feeling that he was hers and that his fate hung yet in her hands. Then after she had done her best to give him the truth, his fate would be in his own hands and she could do nothing more for him. And so she wrote and smiled, and tore up her letters, though they were all of them matter of fact and none of them foolish; and at last with a sigh and a glance at the advancing morning she finished and sealed one; knowing that her time of delight was over, and she must return to the plain sordid world, the jolly old-maid life that was ahead of her.

The letter when it was finished read:

"Mr. Allan Whitney, Esq.

"Dear sir:—I now take my pen in hand to let you know that I am well
and hope you are the same—"

beginning she searched in vain for further sentences that would be
applicable to the occasion, and at last in desperation plunged into her own
original language.

"And if you are really Allan Whitney I guess you'll know who you are
an why I'm writin. Ef you ain't the right one no harm's done. But I felt like
if 'twas really you I'd ought to let you know. I wouldn't uv thought it was
you, only this misshunery man said your name was Whitney, an said you
was tall with brown eyes an couldn't come East, so I sensed it might be
you. And I'd uv left you know sooner ef I'd knowed where to write, only it
only happened a couple o' weeks past ennyhow, and maybe the man won't
ever get back with this ennyhow cause he says its a powerful long way, an
he most died comin, an it seems to me you run a turrible resk with Injuns
out there, only I spose you didn't want to come back till you knowed. And
I hope I ain't speakin too plain ef this should fall into the hands of any
Injuns who could read, but ennyhow its all over now. And so I perseed to
give you the noos.

"Bout three weeks ago come last Wednesday Lawrence Billings got
scared at a mezmerizin that Hannah Heath got up, with a long haired man
to do the mezmerizin who said he could call the dead. So on the way home
Lawrence Billings got scarder and scarder an he stopped at Mr. David
Spaffords and owned up to what he'd done, an they hed a trial an found
him guilty, but they let him off cause he said he didn't go to do it, an
Enoch Taylor's grandson didn't hev time to come to the trial, but
everybody knows he done it now, an so I thought you would feel better to
know too, and Mr. David Spafford he says there hed been injustice done
an so they put a advertisement in the New York papers ennybody knowin
the whereabouts of the one they'd thought done it—you know who I
mean—I wont write out names count o' the Injuns might get this—they
would get a reward, an the town passed a lot of resolutions about how

sorry they was them doin an injustice. So I thought you'd ought to know. So I wont write enny more as it's late an I hev to get breakfast fer that misshunery. He's visitin my Mr. David and Mrs. Marcia where I live now an he told us stories about the Injuns.

"And you might like to know that your brother Nathan is growed tall an fine an he's goin to colledge in the Fall. Mr. David's' ben teachin him. He's real smart an looks a lot like you.

"The misshunery man says you don't hev bedclothes fer your beds, only wild animals skins. I could send you a quilt I pieced all myself, risin sun pattern, real bright an pretty, red an yellow an green, ef you'd like it. If you'll jest let me know it's really you I'll send it the first chancet I get. So no more at present. Your humble servant,

                                                      Randa Griscom."

The reverting to the childish name by which he had called her, and her mention of the bed quilt were her only concessions to sentiment, and she sealed the letter liberally and quickly, that her conscience should not rebuke her for those; then freshening up her toilet she crept down to the kitchen to get a breakfast fit for a king for the "misshunery man."

Fortune favored her. Dr. Whitman came down to breakfast five whole minutes before the rest of the family appeared and sat down in the pleasant bay window of the dining room to read a paper that lay there. After brightly peering at his kindly face through the crack of the kitchen door Miranda ventured forth, her letter in her hand carefully hidden in the folds of her ample kitchen apron.

"Pleasant mornin'," she addressed him briskly. "Real springy. Guess the snow'll soon be gone."

Dr. Whitman laid down the paper and smiled his good morning pleasantly.

"Them was real enterestin' stories you was tellin' us last night," she went on; and he perceived she had an object in her conversation and waited for her to lead up to it.

"I was takin' notice of what you said 'bout that trapper," she glided on easily, "and wonderin' ef it might be a Whitney I used to know in school. He went off West somewheres—" Miranda was never hampered for lack of facts when she needed them. If they were not there at hand she invented them. "I couldn't say 'g'zactly where, n'whiles he was gone his mother died; an' there ain't much of ennybody left that cares; an' there was some things 'twould be to his 'dvantage to know. I'd a wrote an' told him long ago only I didn't know where to send it, an' I jest was wonderin' ef you'd mind takin' a letter to him. 'Course it mightn't be the same man, an' then agin it might. It can't do no harm to try. You didn't happen to know what his fust name was, did you? Cause that might help a lot."

"Why no, I'm afraid I don't," said Dr. Whitman interestedly. "I have

[illegible faded text]

, [illegible] said Miranda with a nonchalant toss of her ruddy head, "I jest was intres'ted when you spoke about him 'cause I thought he might like to know a few things 'bout his home I ben hearin lately. I jest writ him a short letter, an' ef he turned out to be Allan Whitney you might give it to him ef you'll be so kind. 'Taint likely he'll remember me, it's ben some years sence I seen him. I'm jest M'randy Griscom, an' he's likely hed lots o' friends sence me."

"Not out there, Miss Griscom, I can vouch for that. You know there are very few ladies out in that region, that is, *white* ladies of course. My wife was the first white woman the Indians around our mission had ever seen, and they couldn't do enough for her when she first came. A man out there gets lonely, Miss Griscom, and doesn't easily forget his lady friends."

The way he said "lady" made Miranda feel as though she had on her best plaid silk, and her china crepe shawl and was going to a wedding at Judge Waitstill's. She grew rosy with pleasure, dimpling and smiling consciously. The missionary's eyes were upon her and he was thinking what a wholesome, handsome young woman this was, and what a fine thing it would be for a man like that handsome young trapper to have a wife like her coming out to keep him company. He was conscious of a half wish that he might be the bearer of some pleasant message to the young man who had impressed him so deeply.

"A man might be proud to call you his friend," added the kindly doctor with a frank smile.

Miranda ducked a sudden little courtesy in acknowledgment of the compliment, when she heard footsteps coming down the stairs, and in a panic produced her letter and held it out.

"Thank you," she said breathlessly, and "Here's the letter. You won't tell anybody I spoke about it, will you? Cause nobody knows anythin' about it."

"Of course not, of course not," said the missionary, putting the letter in his inside pocket, you may rely on me to keep your secrets safely, and I'm sure I hope the young man appreciates what a fine girl is waiting at home for him. I'd like to see you out there brightening his lonely cabin for him. The West needs such women as you are—"

But Miranda, blushing to the roots of her copper gold hair had fled to the kitchen shed where she fanned her burning cheeks with her kitchen apron and struggled with some astonishing tears that had come upon the scene.

She never remembered how she got that breakfast on the table, nor whether the buckwheats were right or not that morning. Her thoughts were in a flutter and her heart was wildly pounding in her breast, the words the kindly missionary had spoken had stirred up all the latent hopes and desires of her whole well-controlled nature, and put her in a state of perturbation which bordered on hysteria.

"Golly!" she said to herself once when she fled to the harbor of the kitchen shed for the fifth time that morning. "My golly! To think he'd say those things to me—me! A real old maid, that's what I be. And he talkin' like that. He ought to get hisself some spectacles. He can't see straight. My golly! I hope he won't say nothin' like that to Allan ef it's reely him I'd die of shame. Now you wouldn't think a sensible misshunery man like him with a fur coat an' all would talk like that to a hombley red-haired thing like me. Golly! You wouldn't!"

Late that afternoon Whitman went on his way, with many a "thank you" for the pleasant visit he had enjoyed, and many a last word about Oregon, but before he left the house he stepped into the kitchen and shook hands with Miranda.

"I shall carry your letter safely, and I hope my man is the right one. Keep a soft spot in your heart for Oregon, my dear young lady, and if ever you get a chance to come out and brighten the home of some good man out there, don't fail to come." And Miranda, giggling and blushing, took her moist hands out of the dish water, wiped them on her apron, and shook hands heartily with him. She went to the pantry window and watched him through a furtive tear as he went down the street, carrying her letter under that buffalo coat, and walking away so sturdily into the great world where perhaps Allan was waiting for him. Then she murmured half under her breath:

"Golly! What ef I should!"

famous Whig speaker in town and I thought it might interest you to get a
few minutes of his speech. It's just a stump speech, and the gathering will
be held in front of the tavern. It's on our way to the train, and if you get
tired of it we can stop in the office until train time."

The guest's eyes sparkled.

"Good! I'm glad to get a touch of modern home politics. You don't know
how hard it seems sometimes not to get word who has been elected for a
whole year after election. What chance do you think there is for the
election of Clay?"

"It's hard to say yet," answered David. "There is a great deal of
speculating and betting going on, of course. One man, a Loco-Foco, has
made a great parade of betting $10,000 on the choice of president. But
how does he do it? He picks out the twenty States that he thinks least
likely to go for Clay and offers to bet five hundred on each, leaving the six
strongest Whig States out of the question."

"Just what are Clay's cards for the presidency? I really haven't been
paying much attention to the matter since I came. You know my mind has
been full of other matters."

"Well, the Abolitionists of course, first, then the Liberty Men and
Manufacturers of the North, the Native Americans, and those who are for
Bank and Internal Improvements—"

"Just how do the Whigs stand with regard to annexation?"

"The opposite party is trying to force the Whigs into standing *against*
annexation but their leaders do not come out openly on the subject. There
is a great divergence of opinion on the subject. Of course one of the great
hobbies of the Whigs is tariff. We believe in home production."

At that moment they came in sight of the tavern, and saw the crowd
gathered and the speaker already in the midst of his speech. The farmers
had come in from all the country round, and their teams were hitched at
the side of the road up the street as far as one could see, while the men

themselves were listening eagerly to the words of the orator who stood in their midst on a temporary platform in front of the tavern. It was an interesting spectacle.

The speaker's voice was big and clear and almost as soon as they turned the corner they could catch the drift of his words.

"Suppose," he was saying, "that New Jersey should be able to produce bread more cheaply than to buy it elsewhere. Then of course you would say they ought not to import it. But suppose also that hemp grew in New Jersey in such abundance that people could make a dollar a day more from hemp than bread, by giving all their time to the production of hemp and buying their bread. Should they not then buy their bread?

"Now it is easy to suppose that bread, well-baked, should grow in spontaneous profusion in a country, while hemp, ready rotted and cleaned, should insist on obscuring the entire surface of another country, but Nature has ordered differently—"

An audible smile rippled over the surface of the audience, who were visibly moved by the argument, although their faces had a grim, set look as if they had taken counsel before they came with their inner consciousness not to be too easily led.

"It's a strange and curious thing to watch a crowd like that swayed by one man's eloquence, isn't it? What a great power one human being has over another! And what tremendous responsibilities a man takes when he undertakes to decide these great questions for his neighbors!" said Whitman in a low tone as they turned off the sidewalk and went to stand under a great tree nearer to the speaker.

"They do indeed!" said David seriously. "A man ought not to speak like that until he knows absolutely what he is talking about. I sometimes think more harm is done by careless eloquence than in any other way. I wish you were going to stay longer. We would have a meeting like this for you to tell people about Oregon. Everybody ought to hear from the lips of one who really knows—"

But the sentence was suddenly arrested by the loud tones of the speaker who had reached another point in his address:

"Next, as to Oregon—" he was saying. "It is more than twenty years since we made a compact that the people of each nation should occupy that wild and distant region, being governed by their respective laws and magistrates. Not a whisper of dissatisfaction was heard during our opponents' administration, but now when election time draws near they desire to cover up important issues with this foolish and rash talk of forcing the country into war, and with Great Britain—"

David drew his watch softly from his pocket and glanced at it, then started in surprise.

"I'm afraid, Dr. Whitman," he whispered, "that we ought to be going if you wish to get a comfortable seat in the train. I must have looked at my watch wrong before, for it is ten minutes later than I thought."

I have met you and had this good talk with you. Perhaps when you get the wagon route established, or at least when the railroad is running out your way, my wife and I will visit you. Wouldn't that be great? And we may be able to send you a telegram before that comes. Think of that? Ah! There is Nathan with your bag looking for us. I fancy he has secured you a seat already. I might have thought of that and let you stay five minutes longer at the meeting."

"It's just as well," said the missionary smiling, "for if I had stayed much longer I might have had to speak. I couldn't hold in many more minutes, and then my train would have gone and left me. That's a fine boy you have. I'll be proud and glad to see him coming out West some day. Well, I suppose the time has come to part—I am so glad I have had this delightful visit at your home, and shall think of you often when I get back, and tell my wife about you. Don't forget Oregon!"

The good man climbed into the seat Nathan had reserved for him and gave the boy's hand a hearty grasp and a few kind words of encouragement, then amid a big noise of shouting trainmen the train moved out of the station.

Nathan, as he walked slowly beside David toward the office, suddenly looked up and said:

"I'd like to go out there some day and help make that country. Do you think I could?"

"I surely do," said David, "if we can spare you from the East. Get your education and then we'll see what your work in the world is to be. You are doing good work now, and I look to see you come through your examinations this Spring with flying colors and enter college in the Fall."

"I shall do my best," was all Nathan said in reply, but his eyes shone with gratitude and wonder over the way life was opening up for him.

It was the next week that Miranda went to her first missionary meeting. It came about in this way.

Mrs. Marcia had twisted her ankle slipping down the last three steps of the cellar stairs, and she had a paper to read in the meeting.

"I suppose I could manage to get there in the carryall," she said looking troubled, when David came home at noon and bent over her couch in great distress, while Miranda prepared a tempting tray and brought it to her side.

"No indeed!" said David emphatically. "We'll not take any risks with a thing like that. You'll stay right here on the couch till Dr. Budlong says you're able to go out."

"But my paper! They were depending on me to tell about the North American Indians. I promised to take the whole time."

"Well, you have your paper all clearly written out. Let Rose carry it over to Mrs. Judge Waitstill's. She's the president, and she's a good reader. Run over right away with it, Rose, so she can look it over beforehand. Is this it, here on the desk?"

Marcia subsided, content to be taken care of, and Rose started down the street on her errand. But in a few minutes she returned, the paper still in her hand.

"Mrs. Waitstill's gone out in the country to her cousin's for dinner and won't be back till she goes straight to the church for missionary meeting. Sarah Ann said she wasn't going herself today because she had to fry doughnuts, so she couldn't take it."

"Now, you see I must go, David," said Marcia half rising from her couch.

"Now, Marcia, surely there is some one else. Why I can take it over to the meeting myself if necessary, or couldn't Rose run down to the church—"

"I'll take it, Mr. David," said Miranda grimly, "and read it too ef thur ain't no one else by to do it better."

"Would you really, Miranda?" said Marcia, wondering what kind of fate her paper would meet in Miranda's original handling, "I didn't ask you because you're so set against missionary meetings."

"Well, I don't know's I've changed my 'pinion of missionary meetin's, but ef they've got to be why they sha'n't go wantin' your paper, not ef I hev to lay all my 'pinions on the floor an' walk on 'em. I use 'ter be a tol'ble good reader. Gimme a try at it. Ef I don't hit it right on all them Injun names I heerd you reelin' off to Mr. David th' other evenin' there's one thing, no one'll know the diffrunce."

"Oh, I can tell you how to pronounce them. There's only one that's important and that's Waiilatpu. It's pronounced Wy-ee-lat-poo. I think you can get through all right. It's good of you to go, Miranda, and I presume Mrs. Waitstill will be willing to read the paper."

So Miranda, attired in her best plaid silk and her handsome pelisse and bonnet, sallied forth to her first missionary meeting; serene with confidence in her own ability as a reader, she breezily entered the sacred

into common vernacular, but she had a dramatic quality of naturalness about her reading which made you presently forget her rare English; and before she had finished reading the first page of Mrs. Marcia's fine clear handwriting she had the attention of her audience to a woman. Even her Grandmother Heath leaned over with one hand up to her deaf ear, and her sharp eye suspiciously fixed on her granddaughter whom from her cradle she had learned to regard with suspicion. Miranda had always been up to some prank, and it was impossible for Mrs. Heath to think that her sudden appearance at the missionary meeting bode any good.

But the reading went steadily on, Miranda sailing glibly over the two or three Indian names as though she had lived in Oregon all her life; and the reader like any public performer under like circumstances became aware that her audience was spellbound. The knowledge went to her head, and she threw in comments as she went along, facts that Dr. Whitman had told in her hearing, which made the story all the more dramatic. Marcia would have been much amused if she could have heard how her paper had grown. Miranda, among other things, dilated somewhat freely upon the fact that the missionaries were obliged often to live mainly upon horse meat. At which her grandmother gasped and adjusted her spectacles, trying to look over the girl's shoulder to see if such revolting things were really in the original text. Miranda went volubly on however, and when the paper had drawn to a close she folded it reluctantly and looked calmly around upon her audience.

"They say they ain't got any bedcloes," she announced spicily, "jest hev to use furs, an' I shouldn't think that would be a bit healthy. Don't you think 'twould be a good idea ef we was to make a few bed quilts an' send to 'em? They might hev good scriptur patterns an' be real elevatin'. I was thinkin' o' beginin' one all red and white an' black hearts. I ain't got any black caliker, but I got some chocolate brown with sprigs onto it. I don't 'spose the Injuns would know the diffrunce."

Miranda's suggestion did not meet with marked enthusiasm from the ladies, who sat with folded hands and disapproving expressions. After an impressive silence, Mrs. Waitstill spoke:

"It was real good of you, M'randy, to come and read Mrs. Spafford's paper for us, and I'm sure we all appreciate hearing these strange and wonderful things about the savages. We might consult the Board about sending a quilt if that seems advisable to the ladies. I should think one quilt would be enough for our society to send in case it seems advisable. Of course there are a great many other societies to help the cause along. I am sure we all ought to be thankful that we are born in a civilized land. Mrs. Budlong, will you lead us in a closing prayer?"

During the long, quavering, inaudible prayer which followed, Miranda sat in her importance with decorously bowed head, and heart that beat high with excitement; and when she caught a sentence of petition for "the nation that sits in darkness," there swept over her a sudden wild desire to pray, too. But her prayer was not for the heathen in his ignorance and sin. "Oh, God, take care o' Allan! Oh, God, keep him safe from the Injuns, and make it be him, make it be reely him out there, please!" This was her silent prayer over and over.

"M'randy Griscom! Lemme see that paper," demanded her irate Grandmother the minute the closing hymn was sung, "I don't b'leeve Mis' Spafford ever wrote that stuff about their eatin' horse flesh. Why 'taint decent! Why,—they'd be cannibals! Where is that place, M'randy? I don't b'leeve there's any sech writin' there!"

Miranda pointed in triumph to the sentence: "During the first years the principal meat of the missionaries was horse flesh."

"Wal, I swan!" said Grandmother Heath quite forgetting herself, "Jest look here, Mis' Waitstill, it's really here."

Miranda with a look of injured innocence and a glitter of the conqueror in her eye received the manuscript back and rolled it up ostentatiously. She took her lofty way home feeling quite a pioneer in the cause of missions, and hugging a secret delight that she had been permitted to be even so close to Allan as to have read about the place where he might possibly be living.

That night at the supper tables of the village there was grave discussion concerning the morality of missionaries who for their own carnal pleasure would kill and eat a horse.

"And it wasn't as if they didn't have corn and potatoes and parsnips and beans and things," declared Mrs. Eliphalet Scripture, "the paper said they had taken seed there and planted good gardens. Seems 'zif they might 'a gone without meat, or taken a good supply o' ham with 'em. Think of killing and eating our Dobbin!"

"Well, Patience, I don't know's that's any worse than killing and eating our cow Sukey, and we don't think anything of eating cows," responded Eliphalet while taking a comfortable mouthful of his excellent pork chop.

headed now she thinks she can even tell Mis Wantsun what to do. I declare 'twas r'dic'lous. I was 'shamed o' her b'longin' to me this afternoon."

"Wal, I told you 'twould be jest so ef you let her go over thar to live. I 'spose it's too late to undo it now, but I allus did think David Spafford was an unpractical man. He 'ncourages all sorts o' new fangled things. You know he was hot an' heavy fer the railroad, an' now they've got it, what hev they got? Why, I read in the paper tonight how a farmer lost his barn an' all his winter crop he hed stored in it through a spark from the engine lightin' on the roof, an' burnin' it up root an' branch. An' now he's all took up with this telegraphy they wasted thirty thousand dollars on in Congress. Fool nonsense I call it! Allus' gettin' up som'thin' new, as ef the good ole things our fathers hed wasn't good nuf fer enny of us. As fur as this missionary business goes it don't strike me. I take it ef th' Almighty hedn't a wanted them Injuns off there by themsel's He wouldn't 'a put 'em thar, an' it's meddlin' with Providence to interfere. Tryin' to Christianize 'em! If Providence hed a wanted 'em Christianized do you guess He'd a put 'em off thousands o' miles in an' outlandish place where they git so demoralized that they eat horse meat? No, I say ef they choose to live way off there let 'em stay savages an' kill 'emselves off. I heard the other day how some big Senator 'r other said that every country needed a place where they could send all their scallawags to, and this here Oregon was just the very thing fer that, 'twas the mos' God fersaken land you ever see, nothin' growin' there, and no way to git to it, an' the mountains so high you couldn't git a wagon ner a woman acrost 'em. An' here comes David Spafford spoutin' a lot o' nonsense 'bout Oregon, how it's a garding of roses an' potatoes, an' a great place to live, an' the comin' country, an' all that sort of stuff; an' citin' that thar queer lookin' missionary Whitman he hed t'other day visitin' him. In my 'pinion thet man was a liar an' a hypocrite. Why, M'lissy, what 'd'e want to come rigged out like that ef he wa'n't? He might a put on cloes like any Christian. He was just a pertendin' he was a missionary so's to git Dave Spafford to write one of his nice, pretty pieces 'bout Oregon so he could git rid of the land he hez out thar at a big price. Take my word fer it, M'lissy, that man was jest a wolf in sheep's clothin'—an' that thar buffalo hide he wore was jest stuck on fer effect. Oh, Dave Spafford's turrible easy took in. You jest better tell M'randy ef she 'spects to stay round thar hob-nobbin' with those Spaffords she needn't to expect to lean back on us when they git sick o' her."

The old lady, nodding her agreement, took a long satisfying draught from her tea saucer, and Grandfather Heath having delivered himself as the head of the house cut a large, thick slice of bread from the loaf, spread it liberally with apple butter, and took a huge bite.

"An' I ain't goin' to waste no bed quilts on the Injuns," reiterated Mrs. Heath.

"Wal, I suttenly shouldn't," agreed her husband." I don't hold much with these missions anyhow. Let them as does support 'em, I say. Eatin' good horse flesh! Hump! They might better stay to hum an' do some *real work*, I say!"

place called Independence, a few miles beyond the Missouri. There were nearly a thousand in the company and this would tell greatly for the occupation of Oregon. He said that a great many cattle were going but no sheep. The next year would tell for sheep.

"You will be the best judge of what can be done, how far you can exert yourself in these matters and whether the secret service fund can be obtained—" he wrote. "As now decided in my mind, this Oregon will be occupied by American citizens. Those who go will only open the way for more another year. Wagons will go all the way, I have no doubt, this year. But remember that sheep and cattle are indispensable for Oregon. I mean to try to impress on the Secretary of War that sheep are more important to Oregon interest than soldiers. We want to get sheep and stock from the Government for Indians, instead of money for their lands. I have written him on the main interests of the Indian country, but I mean to write him again.

"I shall not be surprised to see some of you on our side of the mountains in the near future—"

David was reading the letter, and Miranda, according to her usual custom when anything of interest was going on in the other room, was hovering near the door working as silently as possible. When he had read this sentence a sudden queer choking noise, half giggle, half cough, from the kitchen door caused him to look up; but Miranda had disappeared and was clattering some pans in the closet noisily, so David, thinking nothing more of it, read on to the end.

Miranda thumped her pots and pans that night as usual, but she went around with a dreamy expression, and every now and again it seemed to her a sheep's head peered pathetically at her from a corner, or blinked across the room from space, and the gentle insistent "ba-a-a" of some little woolly creature from the meadow behind her grandfather's barn would make her heart strings tighten and the smile grow in her eyes. The days went by, and the slow caravan wound its two hundred wagons, cattle and horses, and at their head the man whose untiring energy, strong spirit, and undaunted courage had brought him thousands of perilous miles to gather them together for this great endeavor. Safely in his keeping went the letter, and with it travelled Miranda's spirit.

Well had she listened to the missionary's story of his experiences, and stored them in her heart. There were wide rivers to cross where quicksand and strong currents vied with one another for their destruction. There were fearful heights to climb and sudden perilous precipices to avoid. There were hostile tribes, hunger, heartache, cold and sickness to be met, and the days would be long and hard before they came to the promised land. Miranda knew it all and followed them day by day.

Night after night she crept to her window, gazed up at the stars and prayed: "Oh, God, make it really him and let him get the letter!" Then she went to her bed and dreamed of a strange place of wonderful beauty and wildness, inhabited by a savage folk, and infested with shadowy forms of skulking furry creatures; who were always preventing her as she searched, searched for Allan—just to tell him there was a letter coming.

Miranda's interest in missionary meetings increased and she took great pride in putting her mite into the collection which was taken at each meeting.

During these days there grew a sweetness in Miranda's life. She had always been bright, cheery, and ready to lend a hand to anybody in need; but there had been about some of her remarks a hardness, almost bitterness, that sometimes gave a sharp edge to her tongue, and a gleam of relish to her eyes. Now these faults seemed to fade, and though she still made her quaint sarcastic remarks about the people she disliked, it was as though something had softened and gentled all her outlook on life, and she had found out how to look with leniency on slack, shiftless people, and even on those who were "hard as nails," which was one of her favorite phrases.

She seemed to grow prettier, too, as the Spring came on and deepened into Summer. Naturally of a slender build, she had taken on a plumpness that enhanced her beauty without giving her an appearance of stoutness. She glowed with health, and her color came and went with the freshness and coloring of a child. Her years sat lightly upon her, so that most people looked upon her as still a young girl in spite of the fact that they had known her since she was a baby and could count the time, upon occasion, shaking their heads and saying:

"Mirandy's gettin' on in years, it's high time she was gettin' settled if she's ever goin' to be. She'll soon be an old maid."

Miranda's contemporaries grew up, married, brought their babies to be baptized in the church, and took on matronly ways; the next younger set grew up and did the same; and still Miranda kept the bloom of youth. Her twenty-seven years might have been ~~~~ ~~~~

...ny girl she had always been. They hadn't expected her to marry, somehow, but they did think she should grow into a silent background and begin to recede into maturity as other girls did. Grandmother Heath and Hannah felt it most, and bewailed it openly in Miranda's hearing, which only served to make her delight the more in shocking them by some of her youthful pranks.

But that summer a quiet, unconscious difference grew in her, that made even those who disapproved of her doings turn and look after her curiously when she passed, as at a vision. It seemed almost as if she were growing beautiful, and those who had known her long and classified her as red haired, freckled and homely, couldn't understand why there was now something unfamiliar in her face. In truth, she seemed like some late lovely bud unfolding slowly into a most unexpected bloom of startling sweetness. Grandmother Heath looked at her sometimes with a pang of conscience and thought she saw resemblance to the girl's dead mother, whose beauty had been more ethereal than was common in the Heath family. Hannah looked at her in church and resented the change without in the least realizing or recognizing it.

There was a kind of expectancy growing in Miranda's eyes, and a quick trick of the color in her cheek that added piquancy to her ways. One evening after watching the girl's changing countenance during a glowing recital of one of her own escapades in which as usual she had worsted some grumpy old sinner and set some poor innocent struggling one free from a petty thraldom, Marcia said to her husband:

"I declare, David, I can't understand why it is that Miranda has been left to give us comfort all these years. She seems to me far more attractive than most of the younger girls in town. Isn't it strange some man doesn't find it out?"

"Miranda has prickles on the outside," said David laughing, "she doesn't let any but her friends see her real worth. I fancy her sharp tongue keeps

many away who might come after her, and so they never learn what they
are losing. I doubt if there are very many men in town who would know
enough to appreciate her. There are not very many good enough for her."

"That's true," Marcia heartily agreed, "but sometimes, although I should
miss her very much, I can't bear to think she will never have a home of her
own and some one to love her and take care of her, as I have—"

"Dear little unselfish woman," and David stooping touched her forehead
with his lips, "there is no other like you in the whole world."

Meantime the caravan with the letter wound its long, slow way over the
hundreds of miles, crossing rivers which hindered them for days, making
skin boats of buffalo hides to carry their goods; and again, with the
wagons chained together and driving at a tremendous rate over a ford to
escape being mired in the quicksands; discouraged, disheartened and
weary; out of provisions, many of them sick and worn out, they kept on.
Always at their head, in their midst, everywhere he was needed, that
sturdy indomitable figure of Whitman, swimming a river on his horse
again and again, back and forth, to find the best ford and encourage those
who were crossing, planning for their comfort, finding out ways to get the
wagons through when everyone said there was no passage; quietly
adopting three daughters of a family whose father and mother died on the
journey; and finally late in August, bringing the company safely to Fort
Hall.

Here they were met with the information given them by the trading
people of the Hudson Bay Company that it was foolish and impossible for
them to attempt to take their wagons through to Columbia—they could
never accomplish it.

Dr. Whitman had been absent from the company for a few hours and
when he returned he found them in a state of terrible distress.

But when he discovered the cause of their anxiety he came cheerfully
forward and said: "My countrymen, you have trusted me thus far. Believe
me now and I will take your wagons to the Columbia River."

The pilot who had brought them so far left them and went back to
Missouri, and Whitman took charge of the company. So, with many
misgivings, and amid the repeated warnings and coldly given advice of the
Hudson Bay people, they started on once more.

It was late in August and the new trail over the Blue Mountains was
rocky and steep, often obstructed by a thick growth of sage two or three
feet high. The only wagon that had ever before gone farther than Fort Hall
was Dr. Whitman's, but with strong faith in their leader and a firm
determination to overcome all obstacles they pressed on their way. They
forded more rivers, passed through narrow, difficult valleys filled with
timber, and again through fertile valleys lying between snowclad

mountains; encountered severe snow storms in the mountains, losing their cattle in the timber and finding the road terribly rough and almost impassable at times, yet pressing on, ever on, until at last on the tenth of October they reached Whitman's Mission

[text obscured]

vegetables. For a few days they rested and feasted after the hard fare of the journey, and then went on to the Williamette Valley south of the Columbia, where most of them intended to remain.

It was some time before Dr. Whitman had matters at the mission in such shape that he could go out himself to deliver Miranda's letter, but as soon as possible he took a trip to Fort Walla Walla and timed his coming to the cabin in the clearing so that he might hope to find his friend. But no cheerful light shone out across the darkness and no friendly form was waiting at the door to greet him this time. The cabin was closed and dark, and when he succeeded in opening the door he found no sign of the owner's recent occupancy.

With a feeling of deep regret he lighted a candle that stood on the table and looked the place over carefully. There were clothes hanging on the wall, and a few pelts, but there were few eatables and the fire had been dead for days. Well, at least the owner had not moved away. But what terrible fate might have been his in this land of wide wastes, fierce hates, evil beasts, great silences, who could know? Time only could tell, and even time might not choose to reveal.

With a sigh the faithful messenger sat down at the rough table and wrote a note:

"Friend Whitney: I have just returned from the East with a large emigration. I have a letter which I think is for you from an old friend, and which I think has good news. I am much disappointed not to find you at home. Come over and see me as soon as you return and get the letter. It is important.

Yours truly,
MARCUS WHITMAN,
Waiilatpu."

With another regretful look around he put the note where it would be safe and attract attention at once when the owner came back, then fastening up the door he mounted his horse and rode away, the letter still in his pocket.

Inquiry by the way and when he reached home brought no information concerning the absent trapper. There was nothing to do but keep the letter safely, and hope and wonder.

There were matters enough to keep the mind of the missionary busy at the mission. During his absence there had been a quiet influence of enemies at work poisoning the minds of the Indians. One of the results of this had been the burning of the gristmill, together with a large portion of his store of grain. There was much to be done to get things in running order again, for the passing of the emigrants had depleted his stores greatly. Then there had been a good deal of sickness among the missionaries and he had several trips to make in his capacity as physician. Most of all he was anxious about his beloved wife, who had been ill during his absence and who had been away part of the time with friends at another mission. As soon as things were made comfortable at Waiilatpu he hurried after her, rejoicing to find her much better.

While Whitman had been East a provisional government had been organized, an Executive Committee being elected and a body of laws adopted, but the number of Americans and English were so equally divided that little else had been done, each side moving cautiously because of the other, until more settlers should arrive. Now, however, all was changed, for the majority of voters were Americans! There were matters about the government which demanded his attention.

In addition to all this the growing alienation of the Indians was a matter for constant anxiety. There was one comfort, however, in the fact that his own Indians about him were never kinder nor more docile, and those whom he had left in charge of his crops had done their work well, cultivating the land almost as well as if he had been there himself.

The Winter drew on and the Indians came back from their wanderings to the station as usual. Dr. Whitman's Sabbath services in February had an attendance of two or three hundred, and his work grew heavier all the time.

Some of the emigrants wintered at the mission, expecting to be able to get work breaking land for the Indians, taking their pay in horses, or planting some land for themselves; but the Indians were most of them in such a state of mind that they would not pay for breaking land because it was *their own*, and they would not plant it for themselves because they had been told that the Americans were going to overrun the country and would benefit by it. They also annoyed Whitman and attempted to prevent him and his men from breaking a new field lest he should sell his crops to the emigrants and make money out of *their lands*. Constant daily

cultivated, yet unwilling to do anything much toward that end, or to pay for having it done. They complained that they had taught their language to the white men but the white men had not taught them theirs. They wished to have everything the white man had, and to be civilized, yet wished to have it without trouble to themselves.

Through all the Winter, though many others came and went, the young trapper Whitney, from the cabin in the clearing on the way to the Fort, came not, nor was he heard from by any, though Dr. Whitman inquired often and several times took journeys that way to see if he had returned. So still the letter waited.

Back in the East as Spring came on, one evening David Spafford was reading the paper aloud as usual, with Marcia knitting by his side, while Miranda cleared off the supper table.

He read a brief item down at the bottom of the column:

"Another expedition is said to be about to start to go to the Rocky Mountains. This will rendezvous at Independence. There are ten women in the company."

A strange sense of quiet in the room made both David and Marcia look up suddenly, and they beheld Miranda, standing wistful in the doorway unconscious of their gaze, with a strange, far away look in her eyes, the hungry appeal of a woman's soul for all that life was meant to be to her. One would never think of the word "fragile" in describing Miranda, yet Marcia thinking it over afterward, almost thought she had seen a hint of fragility about her, but decided that it was instead a growing refinement of the spirit. They both looked away at once and David went on reading, so Miranda never knew they had seen that glimpse of her secret soul, understanding and sympathizing because they themselves knew love. They never connected her look with the item in the paper, not even for an instant, and they could not have understood of course why that should have brought the heart hunger into her eyes; but they grew more careful and tender of her from day to day, if that could be possible, because of that they had seen.

The great excitement that Spring was the going of Nathan down to New York to take his examinations, and great was the rejoicing and the feast prepared by Miranda the day word came that he had passed in everything and might enter college in the Autumn.

Politics in the East were at high pressure all that Summer. Stump speeches and mass meetings were the order of the day and night. Banners were flying everywhere, some with pictures of the presidential candidates, others with talismanic inscriptions that set the people's imagination on fire as they passed. Everywhere were bulletin boards setting forth reasons why men should vote for this candidate or that. The name of Clay was on the lips of some, with praise and loud acclaim, while others told of all that Polk stood for, and were just as enthusiastic in his praise. Those who thought and wrought and *cared* spent anxious days and nights; then talked and wrought the harder.

Now the time began to draw near when messengers from the far country might be expected. Dr. Whitman had said that he hoped there might be a chance of sending back word of his safe arrival before the Winter had set in, and Miranda naturally had hoped, a little, that her letter might have reached its destination and perhaps have brought some recognition then, yet no word had come from Dr. Whitman; but now the Winter was passed and it was time to hope again.

Miranda began to peruse the *Tribune* every night, and no word of Oregon or Indians escaped her, but neither did she find anything to make her hope that travellers had arrived from over the Rockies. She had heard them tell how the missionaries were often a year and a half getting a letter from Massachusetts, and she had set her faith and her patience for a long wait, so her courage did not fail; but as the warm weather came on, that spirit look came oftener in her eyes, as if patience were trying her soul almost too far; and Marcia, noticing it, suggested a trip to New York and a few days at the sea. She even hinted that she and Rose and little David would go along, but to her surprise Miranda seemed almost panic-stricken and declared she didn't care for journeyings.

"You and Mr. David go, honey," she said indulgently, "an' I'll stay home an' clean house. It's jest the chance I ben watchin' fer to get all slicked up 'thout nobody knowin' it. I don't keer fer the big cities much, an' oncet in a lifetime's nuf fer me. As fer the o'shn, I kinda think 'twould give me the creeps, so much water all goin' to waste, jest settin' thar ar gettin' in the

way when folks wants to go acrost. Guess I'll jest stay t' hum an' clean
house, Mrs. Marcia ef it's all the same t' you."

And stay she did, as cheery and sturdy as ever except now and again

afternoons. But no letter had come for her, nor indeed did she really much
expect one. She had told herself again and again that there was no
obligation on his part to write, and men didn't write letters unless they had
to. He might perhaps sometime write and say he thanked her for letting
him know, that was all her hope; for that the color came and went in her
cheeks; her eyes grew bright and her breath grew short whenever she went
to the post office.

The summer waned, the far-away look grew in Miranda's eyes, the
wrangling about politics went on to its climax and at last the morning of
election day came.

CHAPTER 24

THE morning train came in bringing a few wanderers from home who had come back to vote. They hurried down the street which seemed to have a cleared-up, holiday look, almost like Sunday, save that groups of men were standing about laughing, gesticulating, talking, with anything but their Sunday attitude.

None of them had time to notice a stranger who got off the train with them and stood a moment looking about him as if to get his bearings.

He was a tall, broad-shouldered fellow, well dressed and well groomed. His handsome face was bronzed as if he had been out in all weathers, but he was clean shaven and his hair cut in the way they were wearing it in New York. All his garments were new and fine, and the carpet bag he carried was of the best. There was about him, moreover, an air of being entirely superior to his clothes which gave him a commanding presence. The station agent turned to look curiously after him as he stepped off the platform, starting down the street. He half ran after the stranger, begrudging someone else the right to direct him, and wondering why the man had not stopped to inquire the way of him, for a stranger he certainly must be.

But the stranger did not appear to see him so the agent stood and watched till he turned the corner by the court house into the main street. Then he went reluctantly back to his work. It was hard luck on a day like this to have to stay around the station all day instead of being about the polls with the other men.

Passing the courthouse the stranger crossed over in front of the Presbyterian Church, walked down the street slowly and surveyed each well-known place as he came to it. There was the bank with its great white pillars and its stone steps where he had played marbles twenty years or more ago. Next stood the old house where Elkanah Wilworth lived and from whose small attic windows he and young Elkanah of the third generation had fired peas on the heads of the unsuspecting passers below.

Eleazer Peck lived next door. They had tied a cat to his front door and left her scratching and howling one evening while they enjoyed the view of Eleazer, candle in hand, come to see what it was all about. There was the store kept by Cornelius Van Storm and John Doubleday, with its delightful collection of calico, coffee, nails, eggs, plows, etc., in exciting confusion. How he had loved that store! The hours he had spent in a nail

the stranger curiously; never knowing him for the bad little boy who used to tickle the horse's hind legs while he was setting a fore shoe, in the days of his apprenticeship.

Across the street was the post office; next, the two taverns, one on either side of the street, and here the groups were assembled and the interest was centred, for the voting place was close by.

The stranger paused and looked about him.

Just at the edge of the road stood David Spafford, a trifle older, with a touch of gray in his hair, but the same kindly, hearty expression he remembered when he was a little boy. David was evidently waiting for the return of a slender young fellow with dark hair and an oddly familiar back who had run out to speak to some men in a wagon. Two excited fellows were arguing loudly in the road. Could one of them be Silas Waite? He wasn't sure. And that must be Lyman Rutherford with his hat off pushing his hair back. He couldn't quite see his face, but was sure it was his attitude. He was talking with Eliphalet Scripture. Tough old Eliphalet Scripture alive yet and not a day older to all appearances! That man behind him with the gray beaver hat couldn't be anybody else but old Mr. Heath, and he was talking with Lemuel Skinner. H'm! Lemuel Skinner used to go with Hannah Heath! Did he win her finally, the stranger wondered?

Ah! There went old Caleb Budlong across the street as hale and chipper as ever, and his doctor's carryall was hitched near at hand in front of the opposite tavern.

How unchanged and natural it all looked, and only he was strange—a stranger in his own home. No one knew him.

He looked about with a great loneliness upon him, and his eyes fell upon a single figure standing in front of a billboard on which "HENRY CLAY" stood out in large letters under a poising eagle. It was his own father, grave, silent, severe-looking as ever—among men, yet not of them! Not ten feet away, yet with no thought that his own son was so close at hand!

For an instant the young man started as if to go to him, then drew back in the shadow of the tavern again, and after a moment more passed on down the street. No, he would not speak to him, would not let anybody know yet who he was. There was just one human being in all his home village who had the right to recognize him first and greet him, and to her he was going.

His passing had been so quiet that few had seemed to notice him, though a stranger of such fine presence could scarcely walk through town and not turn many curious eyes his way; but no one knew who he might be.

A group of small boys playing at marbles on the side walk looked impudently up at him and warned him not to spoil their game. He stepped obligingly round it, and almost felt as if one of them might be his former self.

On down the pleasant street he passed till he came to his own old home, standing white pillared and stately behind its high hedges, and holding out no more friendly welcome now than it had done to him in childhood. He hesitated and looked toward it a moment, a rush of old loneliness and sorrows coming over him, then deliberately turned toward David Spafford's house, walked into the front gate, and knocked at the door.

Now Miranda had the house to herself for the day, for Marcia and the children had gone to the aunts for dinner, and David was to go there at noon. Miranda had taken the day to bake pumpkin pies and fry doughnuts. When the knocker sounded through the house she was deep in the business with her sleeves rolled above her plump elbows and a dust of flour on her cheek and chin. She waited to cut the round hole in another doughnut before answering the knock.

The morning sunshine was bright, but the hall was slightly dark, and when she opened the door her eyes were blinded for a moment. She could see only a figure standing on the stoop, the tall fine figure of a stranger with a travelling bag in his hand.

In haste to get back to her doughnuts she did not wait for him to speak but curtly told him:

"Mr. Spafford is out. He won't be in till evening."

But the stranger stepped calmly in as he replied:

"I didn't want to see Mr. Spafford, I came to see you."

Miranda caught her breath and stepped back surveying him aghast. In all the years she had guarded Mr. Spafford's front door, and back door, never had she met such effrontery as this, actually getting in the door in spite of her! Who could this be who dared to say he had come to see her? He did not look like a person who would be rude, and yet rude he certainly was. She drew the door wider open that the light might fall on his face, and turned to look at him, but he put out one hand and pushed it gently shut.

"Randa, don't you know me?" he said softly, and somehow in an instant she was carried back to the old smoke-house and the dark snowy night when the one love of her heart went from her.

For a full minute joy and confusion rolled over her, and then she struggled to her senses.

"But, oh!" she gasped again, drawing away from him. "Come in, won't you?"

She led him into the parlor where it was bright with Autumn sunshine and the reflection of yellow leaves from the trees outside. But when she turned to look upon him she beheld a stranger, tall, handsome, with the garments of a fashionable gentleman, and a lot of fineness and nobleness which seemed to set him miles above her. She drew back abashed.

"Oh, Allan! Is it really you?" she cried half fearfully. "You look so grown up an' diffrunt!"

A great light was shining in Allan's eyes as he looked at her.

"It's really me, Randa, only it's been a good many years, and maybe I'm a little taller. And it's really you! I'd have known you anywhere—those eyes,—and that hair—" he passed his hand softly over Miranda's copper locks that were ruffled into little rings and sprangles all over her head, though they had been neatly piled in place early in the morning. "Why, Randa, I knew you the minute my eyes lit on you—only, Randa, I didn't expect you'd be so—so *beautiful!*" A frightened look came into Miranda's eyes.

"Beautiful! *Me?*" she cried aghast. "Oh, what makes you talk like that?" She turned her head away and great tears welled into her eyes. He had come, the Allan she had waited for so long, and he was making fun of her! It was more than she could bear!

"Randa!" His arms were about her again, and he lifted her face. "Look up, Randa! Look into my eyes, I mean it. You *are* beautiful! How could you help knowing it? You're the most beautiful woman I ever saw! Look into my eyes and see I mean it."

Miranda looked, and what she saw there filled her with wonder and joy, satisfying all the hunger and longing which had for years filled her eyes with that yearning look.

"Why, Randa, don't you know I've dreamed about you? I've always meant to come back when I could and when your letter came saying it was all right I hurried off as soon as possible. I've dreamed you all out as you used to be, and then tried to think how you looked grown up. Those eyes all full of sparkle like sunshine on the water where it sifted through the chestnut leaves into the depths of the pool down by the old swimming hole, do you remember? That dimple in the corner of your mouth when you laughed, and the other one in your other cheek that played at hide and seek with it, and made you look so wicked and so innocent both at the same time. That sweet mouth that used to look like crying whenever I got whipped at school. The white, soft, roundness under your chin. How often I've wished I could hold it in my hand this way! And the little curl in the back of your neck where your hair was parted! Why, Randa, I've spent hours dreaming it all out; and it's just as I thought, only better—much, *much* more *beautiful!*"

But all this was too much for Miranda. The strong-minded, the courageous-hearted, the irrepressible, the indomitable! She who had borne loneliness and lovelessness and hardness unflinchingly, melted as wax under this loving admiration, buried her face in the strong arms around her and wept.

"Why, Randa, little Randa! Have I hurt you?" he whispered softly. "Have I perhaps made a mistake and spoken too soon? Maybe there is some one else ahead of me and I had no right—!"

But here Miranda's face like a Summer thundercloud lifted fiercely:

" 'Z if thur c'd *ever* be anybody else!" she sobbed.

"Then what you crying about, child?"

" 'Cause—you—come-n-n-n—look so fine—an' say all them po'try things just like I was one o' the Waitstill girls, an' I'm only me—jest plain, hombly, turn-up-nose, freckle-faced, red-haired M'randy Griscom! An' you ain't looked at me real good yet ur you'd know. You ben dreamin' an' you got things all halo'd up like them ugly saints in pictures they paint a ring o' light over thur heads an' call 'em a saint,—but it don't make 'em no prettier 'z I c'n see. Mrs. Marcia's got one she says is painted by a great man, but thur ain't no ring o' light round my head, an' when you look at me good you'll see thur ain't. An' then you won't think that way any more. Only I ain't ever hed nobody talk thet way to me afore, an' it real kinda hurt thet it don't b'long t' me. Guess I'm gettin' nervous though I ain't sensed it afore. You see I never knowed what I'd missed till you spoke thet way, an' 'tain't so easy to think o' givin' it up 'cause it don't b'long to me." Miranda struggled to wipe away the tears with her kitchen apron, but Allan put it from her hand, wiping them on his own fine clean handkerchief; taking her

"Maybe you don't love me, Randa, but I sort of thought—you see when you were just a little girl you always took my part, and slipped me apples and gingerbread out of your dinner pail—I was a great hog to eat them away from you, but boys are selfish beasts when they're young and I guess they take it for granted the world was made for 'em till they get a little sense in their heads, and some of 'em never get it;—and then you fixed that cream so it'd pour over the teacher and stop his whipping me; and you saved my life—Miranda, you know you saved my life at great risk to yourself. You needn't tell me. I know your hard old grandfather and what he might have done to you if he'd found out. Miranda, I've loved you ever since. I didn't know it just at first, when I stole out of the smokehouse that night in the snow and got away into the world. I was all excited and glad to go, and you were only a little part of it that I was grateful for. Something made me want to kiss you when I left, but I didn't think much about it then.

"I got through the woods to the river by the next night, and found a haystack to sleep under till the snow let up. I was so tired I fell asleep, but after I'd slept a little while I woke up and thought they were after me, your grandfather and the officers; and I put my hand outside the haystack into the snow and remembered where I was, and knew I must keep still till morning. I lay very still and thought it all over, how you'd done—how you'd always done for me all my life, and what a sweet little thing you'd always been to me, so quiet and out-of-sight except when you were needed. So smart and saucy to other folks, so keen to find ways to help me when I was in trouble; and I thought of the curl in your neck, too, and the way you turned your head on the side when you used to sit in front of me in school, and the shine on the waves in your hair. Then I thought of the kiss, how warm and soft your lips felt when they touched mine out there in the falling snow, and all of a sudden I knew I loved you and that I should come back some day and get you if it was thousands of miles I had to go.

But somehow, it never came to me to think that some other fellow might have got you before I came. You always seemed so to belong to me. You see, I didn't realize how beautiful you would have grown, and how you might have forgotten me—me off working in a wilderness and growing like a wild creature—"

"You!" cried Miranda, drawing back and looking at him. "You, Allan Whitney, *wild!* Why, you're a—why, you're a—why, you're a *real gentleman!* an' me? I'm jest—M'randy!"

"You're just what I want!" said Allan stooping to kiss her again. And just at that inopportune moment a smell loud and virulent made itself felt in the house.

"Oh, *my golly!* That's my fat burnin'!" said Miranda, struggling from the arms of her lover and fleeing to the kitchen. "Jest to think I'd git so overcome thet I'd fergit them doughnuts!"

But Allan Whitney had not come three thousand miles to be left in the parlor while his lady fried doughnuts, and he followed her precipitately to the kitchen and proceeded to hinder her at every turn of her hand.

elbow.

"You didn't!"

Miranda stopped operations to look at him in wonder.

"Now, ain't that great! All that time! Why, the misshunery man said he 'spected to git home afore the Summer was over."

"He did get home," said Allan watching the sunshine on her hair as it shone through the window and thinking how dear and good her quaint speech sounded to him. "He got home in October and came right up to my cabin, but I wasn't there, I'd gone to Vancouver. I had a good chance to make a lot of money—I'll tell you all about it later when we have more time—so I went, and thought I'd probably get back in a week or so, but things went slick and I stayed till I'd got the thing through that I went for, and that wasn't till February. Then I had things in shape so I could work 'em from anywhere and I went back to my cabin; and there I found a note from Whitman saying he had a letter for me, at least he thought it was for me, from a friend in the East, and it was important.

"Well, I knew he must be mistaken, because there wasn't any way any of my friends could know where I was. But I took a great notion to Whitman one night when he stayed with me, and I wanted to see him again and hear all about his trip East in the Winter time. I knew he was back for the settlers in the Williamette had brought the news, but I wanted to see him and hear all about it from his own lips. So as soon as I could get my cabin straightened up a bit I went down to Waiilatpu to see him.

"He gave me a hearty welcome and hurried me right into the house. Then he left me for a minute, going into another room, but came back at once with your letter which he laid in my hand.

" 'Is that your letter?' he asked, and looked me through with his kind eyes. You know how sharp and pleasant they are, Randa. I looked at the letter and then I looked up into his face.

"It was a long time since I'd been afraid of anybody finding me away out there. At first, after I went away from home I used to start awake at night thinking old Mr. Heath was after me, and many's the time I've dodged around corners in New York to get away from people I thought looked at me suspiciously. But after I went out to Oregon and got used to the bigness of it all, and the farawayness of everything else, I sort of forgot that anybody could think they had a right to arrest me and shut me up away from the sky and the trees and the living creatures. I forgot there was such a thing as hanging, and I got strong and able to defend myself. Somehow when you've neighbored alongside of the wild things and the fierce beasts you don't get afraid of just men any more.

"But that morning, for a minute, when Whitman asked me if my name was Allan, and looked at me that way, it kind of came to me all suddenly, that he'd been East and maybe mentioned me, or heard some one say I'd killed a man. Then I looked up into his eyes and I knew I could trust him. I knew whatever he believed he'd not go back on me; and I determined to make a clean breast of it if I had to—not mentioning any names of course, for I hadn't protected poor Larry all these years just to go back on him now. And anyhow, I didn't seem much to care. I'd made some money, enough to be comfortable on, and yet life didn't look very interesting to me; just living on and making more money and hoarding it up with nobody to enjoy it with me. If I'd had a real home and a family it would have been different. I'd have cared then. But I couldn't ask any girl to marry me and have her find out some day that folks thought I was a murderer. And anyhow I hadn't seen any girl I wanted to marry. There weren't many out there and what there were I didn't train with. It just always seemed to me I'd kind of been left out of life somehow, and what was the use of living? At least, that's the way it seemed after I'd begun to succeed and didn't have to work so-dog-weary hard just to get food to keep me alive.

"So when I looked in Whitman's eyes I never turned away, nor flinched. I just owned up I was Allan Whitney all right, no matter what he knew. Then I waited to see how he would take it, but there didn't any severe look come in his face. Instead he just kind of smiled all through his eyes as if he were real glad, but he'd known it was so all along.

" 'Well, I just felt it in my bones you were,' he said, gripping hold of my hand real hard. 'And I'm mighty glad of it. You're good enough for her I guess, and she's one of the salt of the earth or I miss my guess. You're to be congratulated that you have a woman like that somewhere in the world that cares enough to hunt you up and write to you. She's a fine friend for anybody to have. Now read your letter!' And with that he went off and left me alone.

"You'd better believe I opened that letter pretty quick then for something told me there must be something wonderful in it, and when I looked at the name, 'Randa Griscom,' signed at the bottom just as you used

smile of pride, but she said nothing.

"I had to go back to Vancouver to see to some things, and when I finally got on my way I found one of the fellows in my train was sick and wasn't fit to travel fast. He hadn't let me know because he was afraid I wouldn't take him along, knowing I was in a hurry, and he was anxious to get home to his mother. Of course I couldn't leave him to come along alone behind—he wasn't fit to travel at all, really, and some days we just had to stay in camp if the weather wasn't good,—just on his account. At last when we got about a third of the way he broke down completely and was real downright sick, and we had to camp out and take care of him. Then the guide got ugly and went back on us; said he wouldn't go with us unless we went off and left the fellow with an Indian for his nurse and a few provisions but of course I couldn't do a thing like that—"

"Of course not!" snapped Miranda sympathetically.

"Well, it was some six weeks before we got under way again with the fellow on a sort of swinging bed between two horses, and then it was most two weeks before we could do more than crawl three or four miles a day. But he got a little strength after a bit, and we finally made out to reach the next fort.

"The rest of the party hurried on from there, but the poor fellow who'd been sick begged so hard for me not to leave him that I couldn't see my way clear to do it, so I put by for a couple of weeks more till he got real rested and we got together a guide, some more outfit, and a wagon, and started on again. The wagon was one some emigrants had left behind when they'd gone West, having been told they couldn't possibly get it over the mountains—fool nonsense by the way, plenty of wagons have been over now—but this one did us a good turn. It was hard going sometimes though, but we jogged on slowly, and at last got to St. Louis, where I left my man with his mother, the happiest soul I ever hope to see on this earth. I felt impatient a good many times at the long delay when I was in such a hurry to get back and see if you were really here yet, but I can't say I regretted getting that fellow to his mother alive. I tell you she was real glad to see him!"

Miranda, her eyes like two stars, her rolling pin in one hand and a velvety circle of dough in the other, came and stood before him.

"Oh, Allan, that was jest like you! Why, I couldn't no more think o' your goin' off on your own pleasurin' leavin' a poor dyin' weaklin' alone, then I c'd think o' God not lightin' the stars nights, an' lettin' His airth go dark. Why, it was jest that in you made me —"

Miranda stopped in confusion, and regardless of rolling pin and dough Allan wrapped her in his arms again, stooping and whispering in her ear: "Made you what, Randa?"

But Miranda would not tell, and presently the doughnuts in the frying fat cried out to be attended to, and Miranda flew back to her duty.

It was a long beautiful day. Sometime before late afternoon these two who took no note of time sat down to a delicious lunch together, cold biscuits, ham, apple pie, fresh doughnuts and milk; but they might as well have feasted on sawdust for all they knew how it tasted, they were so absorbed in one another.

They talked of all the years that were passed, and the experiences they had been through. Allan had actually gone abroad for a year and worked his way here and there seeing the sights in the old world. Miranda told him of the item she had heard read from the *Tribune*, and they smiled together over the littleness of the world after all. It appeared, too, that there were stars in Oregon whose friendly faithfulness had often cheered the exile from his home. Stars were queer things, knowing the secrets of the ages, looking down from a height so great that petty details were sublimated by the vastness of the comprehension, yet shining with such calm assurance that it would all be right in the end. These two had both felt it, only they didn't quite express it that way.

"I mostly waited till I got a glimpse of the stars when I got discombobulated," declared Miranda naively. "They, bein' up so high, an' so sot an' shiny, kinda seemed to steady me. They musta kinda seemt t' say, 'M'randy, M'randy! You jest never you mind. We ben up here hunderds an' hunderds o' years jest doin' our duty shinin' where we was put, an' we hed to shine jest th' same when 'twas stormin' an' no folks down thar c'd see us 'n appreciate us, an' when 'twas the darkest night we did our best shinin' 'cause folks could see us better then; an' M'randy, the things what makes you feel bad down thar ain't much more'n little thin storm clouds passin' over yer head, and pourin' down a few drops o' rain an' a stab er two o' lightnin' jest to kinda give yeh somepin' to think 'bout, so M'randy, don't you mind, you jest keep a shinin' an' they'll all pass by, an' some these days thur won't be no more storms 'tall. An' M'randy, you jest look out when thet time comes t' it finds you shinin'!' So, I get kinda set un agin, an' come downstairs next mornin' tryin' to shine my very

"Strange," said Allan, musing and putting out a hand tenderly to touch the edge of the girl's rolled up sleeve. "The stars meant a lot to me too. Nights when I'd be out alone with my traps they seemed to kind of travel with me from place to place and somehow I fancied sometimes there were voices whispering around them, friendly voices—I used almost to think I was getting daffy. The voices seemed to speak about me as if they cared!"

"I reckon them was the prayers," said Miranda with a strangely softened look on her face, pausing in her wiping of a dish to look meditatively at him. "I prayed a lot. I do' kno's it done much good. I s'pose most of 'em didn't get much higher'n the stars ef they got that fur, an' there they stuck, but it done me good ennyhow, even ef God wouldn't care fer prayers sech ez mine. Landsakes!"

Miranda broke off suddenly and dropping her dishtowel began to roll down her sleeves. "Ef thar ain't my Mrs. Marcia an' Mr. David coming down the street an' you in the kitchen! Not a stroke done fer supper neither! What'll they think? Come, you'd best go in the parlor. They'll say I hedn't any manners to bring a gentleman like you into the kitchen."

But the guest arose in a panic.

"No, Randa, jest let me get my bag before they come in and I'll slip out the back door now. I don't want to see anybody yet. I'll come over right after supper and make a formal call. I must go home and see father and the children—now. Do you guess they'll be glad or sorry to see me?"

He strode through to the hall, seized his bag and made good his escape out the back door just as the front door was being opened by the householders, but Miranda slipped out after him into the evening dusk.

"Allan!" she called softly, and Allan stepped back to the door stone. "Allan, I forgot to tell yeh, did you know yer pa was married again?"

"Gosh! Is he? Who did he marry, Randa, anybody I know?"

"M'ria Bent," said Miranda, "she taught school after you left fer 'bout five years an' then she married him. Don't you r'member her?"

"Yes, Randa, I remember her," said Allan, making a wry face, "but I shan't trouble her if she doesn't trouble me. Good-bye, I'll be back this evening," and he caught her hand and pressed it tenderly.

Miranda hustled back into the kitchen and began a tremendous clatter among the pans, her cheeks as red as roses, just as Marcia came into the kitchen.

"So you got back a'ready!" she exclaimed in well feigned surprise. "Well, I got some belated, but I'll hev supper in three jerks of a lamb's tail now. I thought you wouldn't be hungry early, hevin' a big comp'ney dinner, like you always do up to Mis' Spaffordzes. Did you hev a good time?"

"Very pleasant," said Marcia gently, "and you,—were you lonely, Miranda?"

"Not pertick'ilarly," was Miranda's indifferent reply, with her head in the pantry. "I hed callers. Say, did you know Mis' Frisbee's goin' to give up tailorin' an' go'n live with her dotter over to Fundy? S'r' Ann says she told her so herself."

The inference was that Sarah Ann had been the caller.

"Why, no, I hadn't heard it," said Marcia carefully rolling her bonnet strings. "She'll be greatly missed by the people she's always sewed for. Did Sarah Ann say how Mrs. Waitstill was today?"

"No, she didn't say," answered Miranda after a moment's pause while she cut the cake. It did go against the grain for Miranda to deceive Mrs. Marcia, but this was an emergency and couldn't be helped.

Allan Whitney, the town scapegrace, stealing from the
house prison in the thick of a winter's snow storm with the stigma of
murderer upon him, and his own father's anathema added to that of the
village fathers, was one person; this fine bronzed handsome gentleman
attired in New York's latest fashion, walking with the free swing of one
who had ranged the western vastnesses, haloed with the romance of the
wild and unknown distance where heroes are bred, reconciled to his
family, acquitted from all his past crimes, and spending money like a
prince, was entirely another. The village fathers welcomed him, the
village mothers feasted him, the village daughters courted him, and the
village sons were jealous of him.

The young man had not been in the town twenty-four hours before the
invitations began to pour in, and Maria Whitney held her head a full inch
higher and prepared to take on reflected glory. There was only one bitter
pill about it all. She had discovered that the house in which they lived was
Allan's, willed to him by his own mother in case his father died before he
did. If Maria survived her husband she could not hope to live in the stately
old mansion and rule it as she chose. However, Allan's father was not dead
yet, and it was worth while making friends with Allan. There was no
telling what might happen to him out there in the wilds where he lived and
seemed to intend to live.

The Waitstills were the first to make a tea party, as was becoming that
they should, and they were closely followed by the Van Storms, the
Rutherfords and all the other notables of the town.

For a couple of weeks Allan accepted these civilities amiably, taking
them as a sign that the town was repenting for all its past misjudgment of
himself. He went agreeably to all the tea parties, calmly unaware of the
marked attention paid him by the ladies, and devoted himself to earnest
conversation about Oregon with the men. But strange to say his
indifference only made the ladies more assiduous in their attentions, and

one evening after supper Allan suddenly awoke to the fact that he was surrounded by a circle of them and the one woman in all the world for him was not present. He turned his attention from Lyman Rutllerford's last remarks about the annexation of Texas and looked from one woman to another keenly, questioningly. Why was Miranda not among them? Now that he thought of it she had not been present at any gathering since his return. What was the meaning of it? Did they not know that she was his friend? But of course not. He must attend to letting them know at once. He would speak to Miranda about it the very next day.

In the morning early Allan was going, down the street to the post office as he had done every morning since his return home, for he had sent a very important letter to Washington and was daily expecting an answer. As he passed the Van Storm's, Cornelia Van Storm came radiantly out of the house door and joined him, gushing over the beauty of the morning and the happy chance (?) that made him her companion down the street. She professed to have deep interest in Oregon and to desire above all things to have more information concerning it. She asked numerous questions and Allan answered them briefly. He had keen memories of Cornelia Van Storm's snicker in the schoolroom years ago when he was called up for a whipping. Up to that time he had thought her pretty, but that snicker he had never forgiven, and not all her blandishments could cover her mistake of the past. In truth his mind was a little distraught, for he was sure he saw a slim, alert figure coming toward him up the street, and his whole attention was riveted upon it.

Miranda was returning in haste from an errand for Mrs. Marcia, for it was high time the bread was put in the pans, and if she delayed it would get too light. Miranda hated bread with big holes in it.

Allan watched her light footsteps, with their long, easy swing, and the spring of the whole little figure, his heart filling with pride that she loved him. The woman beside him had pink cheeks and blue eyes that languished on occasion—they were languishing now, but in vain—she wore handsome garments and cast ravishing glances at him, but it was as if a wall of iron rose between them, and he could only see Miranda.

A moment more and Miranda was passing them. Cornelia Van Storm looked up to get her reward for the compliment she had been giving, and saw her companion's eyes were not upon her. With vexation she looked to see who might be distracting his attention, and to her amazement saw only Miranda Griscom. She stiffened haughtily and flung an angry stare at Miranda, then turning back to Allan beheld him bowing most deferentially to her, "exactly as if she were a real lady," Cornelia declared to her mother on returning, "the impudent thing!"

Miranda was never one to be cowed by a situation. She smiled her merriest, and called out:

"Mornin'!"

Her voice was loud and clear, intended for Miranda's ear.

"I'm afraid not, Miss Van Storm," said Allan curtly. "I—ah—shall be very busy this evening. Good morning, I must step in here and see Mr. Spafford," and Allan abruptly left her, pausing, however on the steps of the newspaper office to look down the street after Miranda, an act which was not lost on the observing Cornelia.

"The idea!" she said indignantly to her mother afterwards. "The very idea of his looking after *her*. It was odious!"

But Allan was getting his eyes open. He remained in the office only a moment, not even waiting to find out if David was there, and then forgetting his important letter, he went back down the street after Miranda.

She was not in sight any more. Wings had taken her feet, and she was in the kitchen thumping away at her batch of dough, kneading it as if she had all the Van Storms and Rutherfords and Waitstills and the rest of the female population of the town done up in the mass and was having her way with them, while down her cheeks rolled tears of bitterness and humiliation, so that she had to turn her face away from her work, and wipe it on her sleeve to keep them from dropping on her work. Then the overwhelming hurt came upon her so forcefully, that, secure in the fact that Marcia was upstairs sewing and the children were off at school, she turned and hid her face in her crossed arms and sobbed.

Allan was wise enough not to go to the front door and rouse the house. He went straight to the kitchen, and lifting the latch half dubiously, peered in; then strode across the threshold and folded the sobbing woman in his arms.

"Randa," he said. "Randa, tell me why she did that and why you haven't been asked to any of the parties? I've looked for you every time and you neve came." But Miranda only sobbed the harder.

"Randa," he kept on tenderly, "dear little girl, don't cry Randa! Why are you crying?"

"I ain't," sobbed Miranda trying to draw away from him, her head still hidden in her arms, her voice all trembly and unlike her, "I guess what broke me up was jest seein' the truth all sudden like when I be havin' sech a lovely dream. Don't Allan, you mustn't put yer arms round me, it ain't the right thin'. You'd oughta go court one o' them other girls what'd give their eye teeth to git yeh. You kin git anybody in town now, an' I see it. I ain't fit fer yeh. I'm jes M'randy Griscom, an' nobody thinks I'm any 'count. You'r a fine gentleman, an' you ought to hev somebody thet is like yeh. You ben real kind an' good teh me, but you hedn't seen them others when you fust come home, an' it stan's to reason you'd like 'em better'n me. It's all right, an' I want you to know I don't grudge yeh, only it come on me kinda suddent, me not ever havin' hed anythin' lovin' in my life afore. I'd oughta hed better sense n't 'a let yeh think I was any 'count, I—"

But a big gentle hand softly covered her trembling lips that were bravely trying to send him away; and Allan's face came down close to her wet burning cheeks.

"Little girl—Randa—darling, don't you know I *love you*?" he said. "What'd you think I came three thousand miles for? Just to be invited to Waitstill's to supper, and walk simpering down the street with that smirking Cornelia Van Storm? Why, Randa, she can't hold a candle to you,—they can't any of them. You're just the only woman in all the world for me. If I can't have you I'll go back to Oregon and live in my log cabin all alone. I'll sit by my fire nights and think about how you wouldn't have me, and what it would have been if you would. But there's nobody else for me, for Randa, you're all the world to me! As for the rest of this hanged old town, if they can't appreciate you I've no use for them, and I'll not go to another one of their stiff old parties unless they invite you. Why, Randa, I love you, and I'm going to have our banns published next Sunday! We'll just be married right away and show 'em where we stand."

But at that Miranda rose up in her might and protested, the tears and smiles chasing each other down her cheeks. Indeed she couldn't be married yet, she hadn't her things ready, and she couldn't and wouldn't be married without being ready. Neither would she have him tell the community yet. If he felt that way she was content. Let them keep their secret a little longer, and not have the whole town staring and gossiping.

He held her in his arms and kissed the tears away, bringing out the dimples; then he made her sit down and tell him just what she would do. He must go back in the spring at the latest, for he had promised Dr. Whitman he would come with answers from the government at Washington, and also to accompany and advise some more emigrants who were going to Oregon. Would she go with him?

This question happily settled, they came to their senses after a time, and Miranda went on with her kneading, while Allan hurried after his belated mail.

rumored through the town that he and David Spafford were working together for some mysterious political affairs pertaining to annexation. The girls admired Allan all the more because of his abstracted manner and distant ways, and strove the harder to gain his attention; but none of them, not even the keen-eyed Cornelia, suspected that the main part of his visit was not in the Spafford library with David, but in the dining room with Miranda; whose strong sense of the fitness of things would not permit her to take possession of any higher room in the house than the dining room.

In those days Miranda sang about her work like a bird and day by day grew younger and more beautiful. Her eyes shone like the stars that had taught her so many years; her cheeks were pink and white like the little blush roses that grew around the front stoop trellis. She set fine stitches in her garments, finished a wonderful quilt she was piecing, and dreamed her beautiful dreams. Whenever she went about the village and met any of the girls who were interested in Allan, she looked at them half pityingly. No more did their haughty ways and silly airs about him hurt her. She knew in her heart that he was hers, by all the rights of God and man. He had loved her long as she had loved him, and he wanted no other. She could afford to pity and be kind.

So she answered their questions about him, they little thinking that they were talking to his future wife.

"Yes, Mr. Whitney's goin' back t' Oregon," she told a group of them at the apple paring, when they gathered around her to ply her with questions, while they let her do the most of the work. "I herd 'im say he couldn't stay away from thar very long. He misses th' animals an' Injuns a lot. Gettin' use t'em thet way makes it hard yeh know. It's real good of you all to be so kinda nice to him now when he went away from here in disgrace. I was thinkin' thet over t' myse'f th' other night, an' I sez to myse'f, 'M'randy, jest see what a diffrunce!' Why, I kin remember when Allan Whitney wasn't thought much of in this town. He was shut up in my gran'pa's smoke-house fer murder, an' everybody couldn't say too much agin 'im, an' now here he comes back, hevin' travelled, an' made a lot o' money, and fit ba'rs an' coyotties, an' wil' cats an' things, an' ev'ybody's ez nice ez pie an' ready to fergive 'im. It does beat all what a diffrunce a bit o' money makes, an' a han'some face. He's the same Allan Whitney, why didn't you make a fuss over him afore?"

"Mirandy Griscom, I think you're perfectly dreadful, mentioning things like that about a respectable young man; bringing up things he did when he was a child, and horribly exaggerating them anyway. They didn't shut him up for murder at all, they only arrested him because he had a gun and they wanted to find out where he got it and trace the murderer."

"Well, now, *is thet* so?" said Miranda innocently. "Why ain't it real strange I ain't never heard thet afore? Me livin' in Gran'pa's house all thet time too. Well, now, I'm pleased to know it. H'm! Well, beats all what time will do. There might be some more things come out some day, who knows. C'r'neelyah, ain't yeh cuttin' them apples pretty thick?"

"Cut them yourself then," said Cornelia vexedly, throwing down her knife. "I'm sure such work never was very agreeable to me anyway. I suppose you've had more experience."

"P'raps I hev," said Miranda cheerfully.

"But I advise you," snapped Cornelia as she turned away, "not to talk about things you don't know anything about, or you'll get into trouble. It's never wise to talk about things you're not acquainted with."

"No," said Miranda, "thet's a fact, it ain't! I wouldn't ef I was you."

"What do you mean?"

"Oh, nothin'," said Miranda. "don't git riled. P'raps you'll onderstand one o' these days."

The matter that detained Allan Whitney in Washington had to do with the passage of a bill in behalf of Oregon, and his quiet vigilance and convincing words did much to further the interests of Oregon.

It did him good to be in touch with things at their fountain-head. His heart thrilled when he met great men, recognizing the things they stood for, and the questions that were going to stir the country in the coming years. He felt also deep hope for his own adopted territory in the far West, and his young, strong enthusiasm moved many great minds to look into matters and to put the weight of their influence on his side.

Letters passed between him and Miranda, many and often, but by reason of the precaution the lovers took to send all their letters enclosed to or from David Spafford, no word of the correspondence leaked out, though the postmistress knew the affairs of the neighborhood. Miranda had a shrinking from having her sweet secret bandied about the town, which had given both herself and Allan such rough handling and unkind judgment; and Allan understood and agreed with her.

. . . not always long letters, for the two writers were more than

deep interest. This event was the flashing of the first message sent by Professor Morse's electric telegraph on the new test line that had just been completed from Baltimore to Washington. Allan always counted himself most fortunate to have been among those who witnessed the sending of that first message, "What hath God wrought," over the wires, and when he returned he had a great story to tell to those who gathered that night around David Spafford's supper table.

Nathan was there, home from college for a few days, and sitting at the feet of his elder brother with worshipful eyes, listening to the wonders of his experiences. Miranda, bringing in hot muffins as fast as the plate was emptied, listened too, and her heart swelled with pride that Allan had been present at that great event, taking his place in the world of great men, higher than her highest dreams for him.

Grandfather Heath dropped in to bring David a town report that had to be published in the paper, and listened to the account. He set his ugly, stubborn lip that had objected to every new thing under heaven ever since he was born, and fixed his cold eye on Allan while he talked. When Allan at last looked up he faced the same glitter of two steely orbs that had met him that night so many years ago when he had shouldered the gun of a murderer to save him for his mother's sake. It was all there just the same, Phariseeism, blindness, unreasonableness and stolid stubbornness. Grandfather Heath had not changed an iota through the years and would not on this side the grave. He had fought every improvement since he was old enough to fight and would with his dying breath.

"H'm!" he said to Allan's final sentence. "How did yeh *know* they *wa'n't* foolin' yeh? As fur as I'm consarned I *don't believe* no sech fool nonsense, an' ef *'twas* true it would be mighty dangerous an' a mighty *blasphemous* undertakin' to persume to use the lightnin' fer writin' messages. You don't ketch me hevin' anythin' to do with sech goin's on. I say let well 'nough alone, thet's what I say. Writin' letters is good enough fer me. Better take

my 'dvice an' not fool with the lightnin'; besides, you'll find out ther ain't
nothin' in it. It's all a big swindle to git money out of folks, an' you'll find
it out some day to yer sorrow. I never git took in by them things. Wal,
goodnight."

Allan had much to say to David that night, of all that had befallen him
in Washington and all he had been able to do for Oregon; and when
Miranda had finished the dishes she brought her sewing, and sat shyly
down at Marcia's request in the library.

But presently Rose went upstairs to bed, and Marcia went to see if
young David's hoarseness was better, and in a few minutes David the
father made an excuse to go out so that Allan and Miranda were left alone
Then Allan turned to Miranda with a smile and said:

"Well, Randa, my work is done, and now how soon will you be ready to
take the trail with me?"

Nobody thought much of it when they all filed into the pew, though it would have been more according to common custom if Allan had sat in his father's seat. Everybody knew of Allan's friendship and somewhat mysterious business relations with David. No one thought anything at all of Miranda, except, perhaps, Cornelia Van Storm.

It was David who managed that Allan should go into the seat next to Miranda, and Marcia should sit next to himself.

The service went on as usual, until toward the close, when the minister stood up and published the banns of Miss Miranda Griscom and Mr. Allan Whitney.

A stillness and astonishment that could be felt swept over the congregation in its decorous closing stir. The women who had been fastening their fur collars around their necks paused in the act; the small children whose hoods and coats had been quietly applied were suddenly left to their own devices, while all eyes were fixed upon the minister, and then furtively turned toward the Spafford pew where sat Miranda inwardly trembling but outwardly calm. Her face was as sweet and demure with its long down-drooped lashes as any bride-to-be could desire. Her white, soft neck showed beneath the cape of her green silk bonnet, and one small ruddy curl just glimpsed below willfully. Her hands were folded over her handkerchief, and her cheeks were very pink.

Allan sat tall and proud beside her. Just when the strain of the silence in the church was at its tensest he looked down at Miranda and smiled tenderly, and she by some occult power was drawn to look up with starry eyes and smile back the most lovely smile that woman's face could wear, full of adoring trust, and selflessness but with a kind of power of self-reliance, and strength to suffer too, if need be, yet be glad.

As their eyes met a kind of glory came into their faces, and all the congregation looking on saw and were profoundly moved, even in the midst of the astonishment and disapproval.

It was only a flash, passed in an instant of time, and neither of the actors in the little scene was aware that they had plighted their troth in the eyes of the world and given a sacred vision of their love that had stirred hearts to their depths. Such brief fleeting visions of what life and love may be, are little glimpsings into what heaven is and earth might become, if only hearts were pure and purged from selfishness.

Grandmother Heath saw, and remembered her own wooing, with a strange forgotten thrill; recalled the look on the face of Miranda's mother when she married "that scallawag of a Griscom," and felt a sudden pang for her own harshness toward her suffering child. For the first time since the baby Miranda was placed in her unloving arms she saw a beauty and a nobleness in her, for gratified pride had done for her what natural affection had never done. Grandmother Heath was unmitigatedly pleased. She had never thought Miranda would marry at all, and here she had surprised them all and taken a prize. The Whitney family was an old and wealthy one, and this Allan had wiped out old scores and made himself not only respected but highly approved and quite run after by the whole village. Grandmother Heath drew a long breath and swelled up satisfiedly in her pew.

Hannah Heath dropped her pretty lower lip in almost childish amazement for a moment, then preened herself and tried to look as if she had known of the engagement for years, and was enjoying the surprise of everybody now.

Cornelia Van Storm, her admiring eyes glued to Allan's handsome shoulders during the whole service, had the full benefit of the smile that passed between the lovers, and cast angry, jealous eyes at Miranda, biting her lips to keep back the mortified tears. Yet she knew in her heart that the love between those two was unusual, and that there was little likelihood that any man would ever look at her like that. It was a revelation to poor spoiled Cornelia, both of her own selfish heart, incapable of loving anybody as Miranda did; and of the fact that there was such love in the world.

Nathan Whitney, senior, at the end of his pew across the aisle, beside his sharp, unpleasant wife, lifted his expressionless countenance like a metal mask that had no power to show the inner man, and with his cold eyes saw the delicate face of Miranda gloried with that smile. No one could have told what he was thinking as he dropped his gaze emotionlessly, and meditated on the irony of a fate that gave the prize he so much coveted to his own son.

But to Maria, his wife, no kindly mask was given to veil her chagrin from prying eyes. Maria had always been jealous and scornful of Miranda, for she had learned of her husband's attentions before his marriage to herself, and had been mortified that she had been a second choice with such a rival as Miranda Griscom. She despised Miranda for her father's ~~come, since she occupied the~~ position of helper in David Spafford's

around to congratulate the two, expressing their astonishment in hushed Sabbath tones.

It was almost pitiful to see the pride with which Grandmother Heath and Hannah pressed complacently up to share in the glory of the occasion. Miranda took her grandmother's newly developed affection gently, as if love were too precious a thing to be scorned, even when it came too late; but her old mischievousness returned upon her when she saw Hannah, and she could not forbear calling out clearly, so that those around could hear:

"Mornin', Hannah, kinda took you by s'prise, didn't I?"

Then with a smile at the discomfited Hannah, and a sly wink at Nathan, who stood grinning appreciatively by with Rose, she took Allan's arm and walked proudly-humble down the street, her time of recognition come at last. Yet it had not brought the triumphant elation she had expected, only deep, deep joy.

Grandmother Heath did not stop at anything when she got started, and during the next two weeks Marcia thought she understood where Miranda got her tendency to stretch the truth upon occasion. For somehow Grandmother Heath gave out the impression that her "beloved Granddaughter Miranda" was going as a missionary, and she actually set the missionary society to sewing on that quilt that Miranda had suggested for the Indians, only the quilt was now destined for Miranda instead of the Indians.

There were many extra sessions of the missionary society in the houses of the different members, and the interest in the North American Indians grew visibly. An actual missionary in their midst was a wonderful incentive.

When Marcia heard that Miranda was supposed to be going as a missionary she tried pleasantly to make plain that this was a mistake, but was met with such indignant replies on every hand that she refrained from further enlightenment. After all, what was the harm in their thinking so, when old Mrs. Heath seemed so set on it? Miranda would undoubtedly be a missionary wherever she went, though not perhaps the kind the American Board usually sent out.

When Miranda heard of it she sat down weakly in the big rocking chair and laughed till she cried.

"Oh, Mrs. Marcia! Now ain't that the very funniest you ever heard tell 'bout! Me teachin' the Injuns! Golly! I never thought they'd think I was even good enough to be scalped by a Injun. *Ain't* that the very funniest you ever heard? And *Gran'ma!* did you ever see the beat of her? She'll be havin' horse flesh on the dinner table next, jest to kinda get uset to bein' related to a misshunery! Golly! I never thought I'd git thar! A misshunery! Wal, I *am* beat!"

Both Miranda and Allan wished to have the wedding a very quiet affair, for they had planned to take the stage coach immediately, as soon as the ceremony was over, and cut across the country to join the emigration party. Allan had already arranged for their outfit and had everything in readiness for their comfort on the way.

But when the missionary idea took hold of the town there was no having things quiet. The people had determined to make as much of the occasion as possible. So there was a large wedding and by reason of the interest the missionary society took in the affair, the suggestion was made that the ceremony be in the church.

When this idea was first suggested to Miranda she looked startled and then a sudden softened glory grew in her eyes. Wasn't it just like the God of the stars to lend her His house to be married in when she hadn't any earthly father's house of her own? And then, it sort of seemed to set the seal of respectability and forgiveness on her and Allan, and sanctify their union,—they two who had been so long left outside the pale as it were. And so it was arranged.

Maria Bent did not like it, it took all the glory away from her, whose school-house wedding was still talked of in the annals of the village gossip.

Some of the girls who had been ignored by Allan Whitney did not like it. They said they did not see what right Miranda Griscom had to be married in the church just because she was going to be a missionary; and Cornelia Van Storm tossed her head and put in with:

"You know she isn't really a missionary. That's all poppycock! Allan Whitney is nothing but a common fur trader after all."

It was a beautiful, solemn, simple wedding. The wedding breakfast was prepared by the bride herself and eaten by the relatives and intimate friends of both families at high noon. They went away early so that the bride might have plenty of time to get ready for the journey. Then, late in the afternoon, when the Spring shadows were beginning to lengthen on the new grass, and the fresh young leaves on the trees to wave their yellow .... as if they were tired of the day, they heard the silvery

Marcia was kissing her and whispering in her ear:

"Oh, Miranda, Miranda! My dear, dear sister! How ever am I going to do without you!"

Then indeed did Miranda give way and cry on Marcia's shoulder for the space of half a second.

"I guess it's me'll be askin' thet about you, many times," she sniffed, trying to straighten up and smile as Allan came hurrying down the steps with David, and the children rushing behind, their hands full of violets they had picked for her to take along.

Then they all said goodbye again, the horn sounded, and they were seated in the old stage, Miranda and Allan, riding off together out into the great world of life.

Everywhere along the way were friendly faces, waving handkerchiefs, and cheery words of well wishing. There was Grandmother Heath at her gate, actually a smile on her wrinkled old face, and Grandfather Heath at the door behind her waving a stiff old hand.

"Seems like't was jest some fool dream I was dreamin' an' I'd wake up purty soon an' find 'twasn't me 'tall," whispered Miranda through the happy tears.

"No, it's a blessed reality," reassured Allan in a low tone so that their fellow travellers could not hear.

Then they went around the curve and down the hill on the old corduroy road and were lost to the sight of the village.

CHAPTER 28

A FEW days later, out on the trail they started; quite a company of them, men, women, and children, with Allan as captain of the party, and Miranda,—her new role of missionary already begun,—as comforter-in-chief to all of them.

The tears were all forgotten now in the joy that had dawned upon her. To love and to be loved, to be with her beloved all the time, to be able to plan and look ahead to their home together, that was happiness enough for Miranda. The journey, hard and laborious to some, was one grand, continuous picnic to her. Not much of play had come to her childhood, save as she stole it by the way and suffered for it afterwards in hard words, cold looks and deprivations. The fun she had wrenched from life had been of her own manufacture. The flowers, the birds, the trees she loved had often been too far away from duty for her to enjoy, and the adventures she had experienced had all been in rescuing those she loved from unhappiness.

But now all this was changed.

Here was sky wide and limitless. Here were trees in profusion and birds in the poetry of their existence setting up new homes on every hand, lofty branch or humble bushes. Here were carpets of bloom in their passing. Here were rivers deep and wide and difficult to be forded with all the excitement and delight that any child could wish.

Miranda did not shrink from the crossings, no matter what the peril. She rode her horse like a man, on occasion, and scorned the wagons if she might ride by her husband's side. To ride and swim her horse across a river became one of her great ambitions. For Miranda had returned to her childhood and was sipping all the innocent delights and excitements her untamed nature craved. And Allan was proud of her.

Like two children they rode together, taking the perils and the hardships. Never once did Miranda's heart turn back with longing to the East. She was a true pioneer and looked forward with joy to the cabin in the clearing. What need had she to be homesick? She had her beloved with her, and the same stars were overhead. She carried her home where she went. Behind her in the wagon and on the pack mules were her treasures—

gifts of the dear ones at home; and not the least among them was a bundle
of quilts wrought in many colors and curious designs; one highly prized
f.... *ha m:..:......... ....:atv was curiously fashioned in flaming red and

weakness. Buffaloes were not found as soon as hoped and the p.....
grew short; so that hunger stalked beside them in the way. Rivers were
swollen and disputed their passing; untimely snow storms overtook them
in the mountains; wagons broke down and had to be mended or
abandoned; Indians with hostile men appeared and shadowed them for a
distance; death even entered their ranks and took a little child and its
mother; discouragements were flung at them by unfriendly ones along the
way; yet never in all the long weeks did Miranda lose courage or grow
faint-hearted. She was riding upon the high places of the earth and she
knew it and was glad.

She was writing a letter to send home to Marcia, a long diary letter such
as Marcia had suggested. It would not be finished till she reached her
destination, and it might not get back home for a year or two, there was no
telling, but it gave Miranda a cheery, happy feeling around her heart to
write it, as if she were looking in upon the dear ones at home for a little
while.

That letter was worth reading. It reached Marcia almost a year and a
half from the day of the wedding, and brought tears and smiles and much
delight to all who read it. It was so absolutely Mirandaish.

"Dear Mrs. Marcia in pertickiler, an' Mr. David ef he cares, an' o' course
Rose, an' little Davy; an' then anybody else you want.

"Wal, we're started, an' you'd laugh to kill ef you could see us. A long
line o' wagguns with white piller cases over 'em, looks fer all the world
like a big washday hung out to dry. I wouldn't ride inside one of 'em fer
anythin', but I s'pose they're all right fer them as likes 'em. I don't think
much of the women in this set. They don't hev much manners ur else they
got too much, an' ain't got no strength. You gotta hev a pretty good
mixture of manners an' strength ef you want to git on in this world. There's
one real pretty little thin' she's mos' cried her eyes out a'ready. I donno
what she come fer, n' else she hed to, her husband's so sot on goin'. An' a

lot of 'em jerk they're chil'ren roun' like they was a bag o' meal. Poor little souls! I'm doin' what I kin to make up fer it. I'm dretful glad you put in all them sugar plums. They come in handy now. I don't guess the Injun's'll hev many lef' when I git thar.

"We passed a river this mornin', great shinin' thin' like a silver ribbon windin' round amongst the green valley. God musta hed a good time makin' thin's. I sensed it some today when I was lookin' at thet river, an' thet valley all laying there so pretty. Seemed he must a felt most like I do when I'd git a hull row o' pies an' cakes an' thin's made fer the minister's donation party, plum, an' mince, an' punkin', an' apple, an' custard, an' fruit, real black, an' a big fine marble cake! D'you s'pose it cud seem thet' way t' Him? . . . We crossed a river with quicksands yesterday, an' hed to lock the wagguns together with chains. Dr. Whitman taught 'em how to do it, they say. He's a great man. You'd oughta see us, it's real enterestin'. I'll tell you how it is. Every night there's five men on guard and five more 'n th' day time. At night the wagguns is ranged in a round circle, an' the mules an' horses tied inside. Early mornin' they let 'em outside awhile to feed. Then they hev to be cotched an' saddled. It takes a while. Every man hes so many things to do, an' knows his work. They hev to put on a powder flask, an' knife in their belt an' their gun afore 'em when they start each day. Oncet we rode nine hours without stoppin'. We gen'aly take two hours noonin', turn out the animals, get dinner, wash dishes an' thet like. At night we pitch tents, spread buffalo skins on the ground, then oilcloth fer a floor, an' fix yur thin's around out o' the hay, leavin' a place in the middle to eat. Thur was some Injuns came around and most o' the wimmen got scared. I didn't see much to 'em to be scared 'bout. They look dirty to me, an' don't hev nouf cloes to their backs...."

The letter went on to tell the daily occurrences of the way, noting the places, and the incidents, and one notable extract touched Marcia's heart more than all the rest:

"Wal, we come to a mounting this mornin', a real live mounting! It's thar yet right in front o' me. I got my dishes all washed an' I'm restin' an' lookin' at it by spells. You don't never need to go eny further to wonder, ef you oncet see a mounting. It's the biggest, comfortablest, settledest thin' you ever could a 'thought of. It jest sets right thar, never stirs, never seems to mind what happens round it, ur what goes over it; can't disturb him, he's a mounting! Might cut down all his forests, he wouldn't care, he'd grow some more. Might walk over him all day'n annoy him a lot, he jest sets thar an' looks up, an' by an' by all them thet annoys passes on an' *thars the mounting yit* jes' same, and he knew 'twould be so, 'cause he's a mounting. He can't die. They can't nobody move him, he's too big. 'Cept mebbe God ~~might. But God made him, so he don't~~ care 'bout thet, 'cause ef God could

with a wreath o' haze round his feet at night. He's a mounting. An' God musta been real pleased when He got him done. He musta been most best pleased of all when He made a mounting. I'm real glad He made 'em, and glad I lived to see one. When you come you must come this way, an' see my mounting. They say thur's goin' to be some more 'fore we git through, but I don't b'leeve none of 'em'll be so pretty as this."

The rest of the letter told of the further experiences and the homecoming, first to Waiilatpu, where they were welcomed with open arms by the missionaries, and kept and rested a while; and then to the cabin where they had a beautiful time beginning to keep house, and here Miranda's descriptions of the house and her attempts to fix it up to her mind were laughable.

Marcia, after they had enjoyed the letter thoroughly at home, took it with her in her pocket wherever she went, and let Miranda's many friends enjoy it also. She carried it first with her when David took them out on a drive, Marcia on the back seat with her daughter Rose, who was grown suddenly into young womanhood and young David with his father in the front of the carryall.

They drove straight to the house of Hannah Skinner, where Grandma Heath had come to live, after the sudden death of old Mr. Heath, which occurred a few weeks after Miranda left home.

Hannah and the old lady, both pleased at the sight of the Spafford carriage at their door, came out to welcome their guests, the cat following amiably behind.

"I've got a letter from Miranda and I thought you'd like to read it," said Marcia, leaning out of the carriage and smiling.

The old lady's face brightened.

"A letter from M'randy! Now you don't say. Well, ain't thet real interestin'? How does she git on missunaryin'? Seems sorta like gettin' word from another world, don't it? Do get out and come in."

And so the letter was read to the two women who listened in great wonder, and boasted around for many a day with "M'randy says this" an' "My Cousin M'randy says so and so," until the village smiled and wondered, and Miranda's record of discreditable scrapes was all forgotten under the halo of a missionary.

In due time the letter travelled to Nathan at college firing him with a deep desire to go out West, and when he came home in the Spring he was full of it, till finally David said:

"Well, my boy, go try it. Allan said it would do you good and you could earn something out there. We'll see if there are some people going, and you go out for a year or two and then come back and finish your college course. A rest and a little touch of nature will do you good."

As suddenly as that it came, and a few weeks later, Nathan bade them all an excited, happy farewell, and started out into the great far country also.

Rose, like a sweet, frightened flower, looked after the coach that bore him away, and fled to the window in Miranda's room, to stay alone until night fell and the stars came out to comfort her and help her understand.

Poor little Rose with your astonished feet taking the first steps into the path of sorrow and loss! How long the way lies before you beaten hard by many feet, yet you, too, will one day reach the higher ground and see your mountain!

blood.

Slowly, stealthily, out of the West there arose a menacing cloud. Shadowy it was at first, like a mote that one tries to brush away from a tired eye, still floating and insisting upon being seen.

Low stirrings in the grass, and sounds like the hiss of some moving, poisonous serpent; forms phantom-like and vanishing when search is made—gone, always gone, when you look—yet there, convincingly there, but elusive; stealthy footsteps in the night; prying, peering, breathless; these things were in the very atmosphere.

There had been a growing uneasiness among the Indians ever since Dr. Whitman's return with the emigrants. An enemy was at work, that was plain to be seen. Strange rumors were abroad; silent, subtle impressions, averted glances, muttered gutturals.

Still, Whitman and his workers went steadily on, omitting no one of their arduous tasks, not hesitating to visit the sick among known enemies, withholding no kindness even from the stolid and ungrateful.

Several times contagious diseases raged among the Indians with fearful fatality. The missionaries were faithful and indefatigable, giving themselves night and day with medicine and nursing to save as many as possible.

Finally an epidemic of measles broke out among them, sweeping away large numbers.

Frantic and fearful they sent for the missionary doctor, though they often omitted to follow directions afterward, or sent for their own medicine man with his incantations and weird ceremonies. Death stalked among them and the story went forth, from what source who could quite be sure?—that the missionary was poisoning them to clear the country of Indians and take their lands for the white people.

The faint cloud on the horizon now grew large and dark with portent. Ominous thunders threatened in the distance, drawing nearer and more certain. The mission knew its peril. Dr. Whitman was thoroughly convinced that a plot to murder the missionaries was nearly completed, yet he kept steadily on with his work. Day after day he told his wife and friends all that he saw and what the appearances led him to fear. Carefully and prayerfully he walked, with the light of another world on his face, knowing not at what moment he would be called away from this.

He visited the Indian camp, on the Umatilla River; called on the Bishop and the vicar general who had just arrived at the place, and had brief interviews; then rode out to where a fellow missionary was encamped, reaching there about sunset. They talked the situation over calmly, discussing the possibilities and probabilities.

"My death may do as much good to Oregon as my life can do," said the man who had crossed the Rockies and a continent in midwinter to save Oregon.

Though weary and worn, he did not stay to rest, for there was severe sickness at his home, and he started late that night on his lonely ride of forty miles back to the mission, reaching there at dawn. Then a hurried interview with his wife, a few words and tears of tenderness, cut short by calls to attend the sick.

"Greater love hath no man than this, that a man lay down his life!"

Ever had this man taken the lead in all the hard things; sacrificing, never thinking of himself; plunging into the icy river first; not asking others to go where he was unwilling to lead;—like his Master whom he served.

It was as if God would not take from him the eternal right of leadership, for which he had formed him and called him; and so arranged that even in death he should still lead.

While the sun was shining high in the heavens, stealthily, like evil shadows, the Indians gathered around the mission that once had been a happy home, and where the work was still going steadily on as if no menace in the air were felt.

Suddenly the shadows sprang from covert hiding on every side! Evil faces, stealthy steppings, flashing knives, and the deed was done! Dr. Whitman was the first to fall, a tomahawk plunged twice into his head; then the carnage began, and continued for eight days.

The first news was brought to Miranda as she stood at her cabin door watching for Allan.

He did not come with his usual cheery whistle, but striding into the clearing with deep sorrow in his eyes, and an ominous look of threatening about his mouth. His wife knew at once that something terrible had happened.

"Is it them pesky Injuns?" she asked in a voice she had taught to be low and guarded. "Drat 'em! They's ben two of 'em round the house this very mornin', an' they looked like they was up to som'pin'. What hev they ben doin'?"

"T'... have killed Dr. Whitman!"

misshunery. Kill Dr. Whitman! 'Z it they could kill him... Tony... couldn't do thet! *Men* couldn't do thet! Why, a man like thet'll live ferever, yeh *can't stop him*! He ain't ben jest a livin' body, he's a livin' soul. He'll go on livin' long 'z the world stan's, 'n longer! He'll live ferever! He's like a mounting! Can't tech him! Kill *him*? Wal, I guess not!"

Miranda whirled her back abruptly round and let the tears course down her cheeks. But in an instant she had herself in hand and turned back, her face wet, her eyes snapping fire.

"Wal, what we goin' to do 'bout it?"

"Do about it?" asked Allan half astonished, then a grim look settling about his mouth, he said decidedly:

"We're going to get you out of this horrible country and safe somewhere as soon as we can go."

"Wal, thet's jest what we *ain't* goin' to do," said Miranda decidedly, "I ain't no wax doll whose nose'll melt off in the sun, an' thur ain't no tomyhawk goin' to tech me. We're goin' to git to work right here'n now an' teach them pesky Injuns some manners. You don't mean to tell me, Allan Whitney, thet you would sneak off an' take yer wife away to hide her in pink cotton while them dear misshuneries is settin' thar sorrerin' fer him"—she choked but went bravely on—"an' in danger, mebbe, needin' pertection. Allan Whitney, thet ain't you! I know you better'n thet! An' ef hevin' a wife hes made you sech a fool, baby'n, coward she'd better git hers'f tomyhawked right here an' now an' git out o' yer way. I wouldn't be worth my salt ef I couldn't stand by yeh an' he'p yeh do yer duty like the brave man yeh air. How long sence it happened?"

"Randa, dear, you don't understand. It's been going on several days. There's been a massacre. You know there are over seventy people in and around the mission and they've killed fourteen of them already. Dr. Whitman and his wife first, and some of the sick people; and over fifty of them have been taken prisoners. One man got away up to the fort and they wouldn't take him in. What do you think of that? I tell you this is a horrible country and I want to get you out of it."

"Name o' sense! Why didn't you tell me afore? Ain't you done nothin' 'bout it yet? You ain't goin' to give up an' let this go on? *Prisoners!* Them poor women an' children! You gotta git up a regiment 'mongst the settlers an' git out after 'em. How 'bout them es is killed? Hev they ben buried yet? Somebody oughtta go right down to the mission an' tend to thin's. Where's Nathan? Ain't he comin' back purty soon? He'n I c'n go down to the mission. Mebbe ther ain't nobody thar, an' 'tain't safe, so many wild animals as thur is round. You go git the settlers t'gether an' fight them Injuns! It's time they was taught a good sound lesson."

Allan stood staring at his wife in amazement and admiration.

"Randa, I can't. I can't have you go down to that horrible place, and I can't leave you here alone. I don't know where Nathan is. You're a woman, and you're my wife. I must protect you."

"Stuff an' nonsense!" said Miranda, hurrying around the cabin picking up things to take with her. "This is a time o' war an' you can't sit aroun' an' act soft then. Ain't I as good a right to act like a man in a time like this as you hev, I'd like to know? Ef I get tomyhawked I will, an' thet's the whole on it. It's got to come sometime I guess, an' my time ain't comin' till it's ready, an' you can't stop it ef it's really here. Sides, thet don't matter a hull lot. Thet ain't the way that misshunery man talked ennyhow, an' now he's gone I reckon we've got to do our best to take his place. Ef I git prisonered I bet I give 'em a lively time of it afore they git done with me ennyhow. Come on, Allan, don't you try to stop me doin' my duty, fer yeh can't ennyhow, an' it ain't reasonable at a time like this. Them pris'ners gotta be set free. We gotta be c'rageous an' not think o' oursel'es. Ef ennythin' happens to us this ain't the hull o' livin',—down here ain't. You go git the horses ready, an' I'll put up a couple o' bundles, an' I'll ride 'long o' you till I find somebody to go to Waiilatpu with me. Hurry up now, it ain't no use argyin'! I'm willin' 'nouf to go back East when I've done what thur is to do, but—not till then!"

Allan stooped and kissed his wife, a look almost of awe upon his face.

"Randa, you are wonderful!" he said softly. "I have no right to stop you!" and without another word he went out and saddled the horses.

quietly, unobtrusively as he had lived, his face changed or softened by death. What secret emotions he had had died with him, and men read nothing from his silent face.

His wife Maria, not relishing the care of the younger children who were just grown to the annoying age, packed them off to their Aunt Jane in Albany and betook herself on an indefinite trip to New York. By the ordering of the will she had received enough money to make her comfortable during her lifetime, and the house did not belong to her, so she was free to go. She had few friends in the village where she had lived so many years, and preferred to leave it behind her forever.

The old house was closed. The grass grew tall in the yard, the hedges rough and scraggly, and cobwebs wrought their riotous lacery across doors and window casements, a lonely deserted sight for those who looked across from the windows of the Spafford house. Rose had often cast a wistful glance toward the vine-covered gateway as she threw open her windows in the morning, wishing she might see the familiar figure of Nathan and hear his cheery whistle as he came down the walk. He had been gone a long while and only one letter had come from him, in St. Louis on his way out.

But one morning in late glowing Summer the cobwebby shutters were thrown wide, and Miranda rested her plump, bare arms on the window sill and leaned out, drawing in deep breaths of her native air and smiling in broad satisfaction.

The years had passed, long in their waiting, changes had been fulfilled, and at last Miranda had come into her own. She was mistress of the great white house and she was happy.

Miranda, Allan and Nathan had been home for nearly a week, and they had been welcomed with open arms and glad smiles. They had told their tales of terror, bloodshed, peril and deliverance. They had visited their friends, heard the news, social, religious, political, and now they had come home. The house had been cleaned and polished to the last degree. The cobwebs were no more. Nathan was even now out in the yard with a big scythe mowing down the tall grass. The Whitney children, Samuel and the twins, were coming on the afternoon stage. Allan was going into the newspaper office with David. Miranda was content.

"Golly!" she said as she sniffed the cinnamon roses under the window, "Golly! I'm glad thur ain't no pesky Injuns 'round here. They may be all well 'nouf fer them 'at likes 'em, but not fer me. The misshunery business ain't what it's cracked up to be. I've hed my try at it an' I don't want no more. I don't grudge 'em all the things they stole out o' the cabin when we was off chasin' 'em, seein' they left me my rose quilt thet my little Rose made with her baby fingers fer me, an' I've only one regret an' thet's the risin' sun quilt they got, fer I don't 'xpect ever t' git anuther misshunery quilt agin; but then 'twas meant fer 'em in the beginnin' an' mebbe it'll do some good to 'em, an' convert 'em from the error of thur ways. They suttenly need it. Anyhow I ain't goin' to fret. I've got all I want, an' I'm real glad I've seen a mounting. It's som'pin' to go 'ith the stars."

Her eyes grew wide and serious, and a sweet look came around her mouth.

Across the street Rose stepped out on the front stoop with a broom wafting the cobwebs dreamily from the railing, and waving a graceful hand to Miranda. Nathan dropped his scythe and went over to her. Miranda watched them, a gentle look glorifying her face, and remembered how she used to come out on that stoop over there and look across thinking she might have been the mistress of this house but wasn't. How queer it all was! She was here with Allan, having the life of all the others she would have chosen if she had had the choice. Would it be that way when you got to heaven? Would you look back and see where you used to be, and look at your old self and wonder? How little the trials and crosses looked, now that they all were passed! You did get things on this earth, too,—stars, and mountains, and heroes—and happiness!

Miranda, in the gladness of her heart lifted her sweet, brown eyes, the merry twinkles all sparkling with earnestness, to the blue of the deep Summer sky above the waving tree tops, and murmured softly under her breath:

"Thanks be! Thanks be!" Then she took her broom and went to work.